LITERATURE
An Introduction to Fiction, Poetry, and Drama

Second Edition

X. J. KENNEDY
Tufts University

LITTLE, BROWN AND COMPANY

Boston · Toronto

Library of Congress Catalog Card No. 78-61737

THIRD PRINTING

Published simultaneously in Canada
by Little, Brown & Company (Canada) Limited

Printed in the United States of America

Acknowledgments

Cover photo courtesy of Maitland Edey.

FICTION

Sherwood Anderson. "The Egg." Reprinted by permission of Harold Ober Associates Incorporated. Copyright 1920 by Eleanor Copenhaver Anderson.
Ray Bradbury. "The Pedestrian." © 1951 by Ray Bradbury. Reprinted by permission of Harold Matson Co., Inc.
Richard Brautigan. "The Kool-Aid Wino" by Richard Brautigan from *Trout Fishing in America*. Copyright © 1967 by Richard Brautigan. Reprinted by permission of Delacorte Press/Seymour Lawrence.
Truman Capote. "Miriam." Copyright 1945 and renewed 1973 by Conde Nast Publications, Inc. Reprinted from *Selected Writings of Truman Capote* by permission of Random House, Inc.
Raymond Chandler. "I'll Be Waiting" from *The Simple Art of Murder* by Raymond Chandler. Copyright 1950 by Raymond Chandler. Reprinted by permission of Houghton Mifflin Company.
Anton Chekhov. "In Exile" from *Anton Chekhov: Selected Stories*, translated by Ann Dunnigan. Copyright © 1960 by Ann Dunnigan. Reprinted by arrangement with The New American Library, New York, N. Y.
John Collier. "The Chaser." © 1940, renewal © 1968 by John Collier. Reprinted by permission of Harold Matson Co., Inc.
Joseph Conrad. "The Secret Sharer." Copyright 1910 by Harper Bros., from *Twixt Land and Sea* by Joseph Conrad. Reprinted by permission of Doubleday & Company, Inc.
William Faulkner. "A Rose for Emily" from *Collected Stories of William Faulkner*. Copyright 1930 and renewed 1958 by William Faulkner. "Barn Burning" from *Collected Stories of William Faulkner*. Copyright 1939 and renewed 1967 by Estelle Faulkner and Jill Faulkner Summers. Both reprinted by permission of Random House, Inc.
Gustave Flaubert. Excerpt from *Madame Bovary* by Gustave Flaubert, translated by Francis Steegmuller. Copyright © 1957 by Francis Steegmuller. Reprinted by permission of Random House, Inc.
E. M. Forster. Excerpt from *Aspects of the Novel*. Copyright 1927 by Harcourt Brace Jovanovich, Inc.; copyright 1955 by E. M. Forster. Reprinted by permission of the publishers, Harcourt Brace Jovanovich, Inc., and Edward Arnold, London.
Jakob and Wilhelm Grimm. "Godfather Death" from *The Juniper Tree and Other Tales from Grimm*, selected by Lore Segal and Randall Jarrell. Pictures by Maurice Sendak. Translation copyright © 1973 by Lore Segal. Pictures copyright © 1973 by Maurice Sendak. Selection and arrangement copyright © 1973 by Lore Segal and Maurice Sendak. Reprinted with the permission of Farrar, Straus & Giroux, Inc.
Dashiell Hammett. Excerpt from *The Maltese Falcon*. Copyright 1929, 1930 by Alfred A. Knopf, Inc. and renewed 1957, 1958 by Dashiell Hammett. Reprinted by permission of the publisher.

(Continued on page 1389)

iv   Acknowledgments

Thurs Dec. 9 8-11

Caldwell
306

771

Peabody
Auditorium

- Footnote -
1. William Faulkner, "Barn Burning,"
Literature: An Introduction to Fiction,
Poetry, and Drama, X. J. Kennedy, ed.
(Boston: Little Brown and Company, 1976)
p. 64.

3 Haikus 5, 7, 5
12 my Duchess

7 15

pg. 453
17a

p. 413 Louliest of trees
p. 422 Locomotive
p. 423
p. 425 Sick
p. 438 Chimney

pg. 447 - 448 - 450
allusion - 449 - top - 450

Closed form
pg. 567 - 575

Figures of Speech
487 - middle pg. 492
2 poems p 418

Shall I compare thee - 478
" when in Disgrace pg. 802

p. 1446

LITERATURE

~~Ho o man~~

Why does it take Oedipus
so long to admit that he is
the killer of Laos.

How essential to the play is
the fact that Othello is a
black man, a Moor & not a
native of Venice

Does the downfall of Othello
proceed from any flow in his nature,
Or is his downfall entirely the
work of Iago.

p. 470
p. 416

Other books by X. J. Kennedy

Nude Descending a Staircase, poems
Mark Twain's Frontier (with JAMES CAMP), text-anthology
Growing into Love, poems
Bulsh, a poem
Breaking and Entering, new and selected poems
Pegasus Descending, A Book of the Best Bad Verse
    (with JAMES CAMP and KEITH WALDROP), anthology
Messages, A Thematic Anthology of Poetry
Emily Dickinson in Southern California, poems
An Introduction to Poetry, Fourth Edition
Celebrations after the Death of John Brennan, a poem
One Winter Night in August, poems for children
The Phantom Ice Cream Man, poems for children
Three Tenors, One Vehicle
    (with JAMES CAMP and KEITH WALDROP), song lyrics
An Introduction to Fiction, Second Edition

PREFACE

Literature, in the widest sense, is just about anything written. It is even what you receive in the mail if you send for free literature about a weight-reducing plan or a motorcycle. In the sense that concerns us in this book, literature is a kind of art, usually written, that offers pleasure and illumination. (We say it is *usually* written, for there is oral literature, too. Few would deny the name of literature to "Bonny Barbara Allan" and certain other immortal folk ballads, though they were not set down in writing until centuries after they were originated.)

Literature — the book in your hands — is really three books between two covers. Its opening third contains the whole of the text-anthology *An Introduction to Fiction, Second Edition;* its middle third, the whole of *An Introduction to Poetry, Fourth Edition;* and its closing third is a text-anthology of drama that includes twelve plays. All together, the book attempts to provide the college student with a reasonably compact introduction to the study and appreciation of stories, poems, and plays. I assume that appreciation begins in loving attention to words on a page. Speed reading has its uses; but in entering the world of a story, poem, or play, there are times when, as Robert Frost remarked, the reader who reads for speed "misses the best part of what a good writer puts into it." Close reading, then, is essential. Still, I do not believe that close reading tells us everything, that it is wrong to read a literary work by any light except that of the work itself. At times this book will suggest different approaches: referring to facts of an author's life; comparing an early draft with a finished version; looking for myth; seeing the conventions (or usual elements) of a kind of writing — seeing, for instance, that an old mansion, cobwebbed and creaking, is the setting for a Gothic horror story.

A Word about Careers

Students tend to agree that to read writers such as Sophocles, Shakespeare, and Tolstoi is probably good for the spirit, and most even take some pleasure in the experience. But many, if they are not planning to teach English and are impatient to begin some other career, often wonder whether the study of literature, however enjoyable, is not a waste of time—or at least, an annoying obstacle.

This objection may seem reasonable, but it rests on a shaky assumption. It can be argued that, on the contrary, success in a career is *not* mostly a matter of learning certain information and skills that belong exclusively to a certain profession. In most careers, according to a business executive, people often fail not because they don't understand their jobs, but because they don't understand the people they work with, or their clients or customers; and so they can't imagine another person's point of view. To leap outside the walls of your self, to see through another person's eyes—this is an experience that literature abundantly offers. Although, if you are lucky, you may never meet (or have to do business with) anyone *exactly* like Mrs. Turpin in the story "Revelation," you probably will learn much about the kind of person she is from Flannery O'Connor's fictional portrait of her. Reading Tolstoi's short novel *The Death of Ivan Ilych,* you enter the mind of a petty bureaucrat, a judge. Though he is a Russian of the last century, in his habits of thought you may find him amazingly similar to many people now living in America. What is it like to be black, a white may wonder? Possibly Shakespeare, Langston Hughes, and James Alan McPherson have something to tell. What is it like to be a woman? A man who would learn can read, for a start, Emily Dickinson, Sylvia Plath, Anne Sexton, Adrienne Rich, Katherine Mansfield, Joyce Carol Oates, Grace Paley, and Eudora Welty.

Racing single-mindedly toward careers, some students move like horses wearing blinders. For many, the goals seem fixed and sure: competent nurses, accountants, and dental technicians seem always needed. Still, many who confine their attention to a single kind of learning eventually come to feel a sense of dissatisfaction. Recently, a highly trained and highly paid tool and die maker, asked by his instructor at a college why he had enrolled in an evening literature course, replied, "I just decided there has to be more to life than work, a few beers, and the bowling alley." Other students find that in our society some careers, like waves in the sea, may rise or fall with a speed quite unexpected. Think how many professions we now take for granted didn't even exist a few years ago—for instance, jobs in computer programming, energy conservation, and disco management. Others that had once seemed a person's security for life have been cut back and nearly ruined: cobblery, commercial fishing, railroading. In a society always in change, perhaps the most risky course is to lock oneself into a certain career, unwilling to consider any other. In point of fact, the U.S. Department of Labor has shown that the average person changes careers three times in a working life. When for some unforeseen reason such a change has to be made, basic skills may be one's most valuable credentials, together with some knowledge (in depth) of the human heart.

Literature, as they know who teach it, has basic skills to provide. Being an art of words, it can help you become more sensitive to language—your own and other people's. Poetry especially helps you to see the difference between a word that is exactly right and a word that is merely good enough—what Mark Twain calls "the difference between the lightning and the lightning-bug." Read a fine writer alertly, with enjoyment, and some of the writer's ways with words may grow on you. Most jobs today (and even the task of making out a long-form tax return) still call for some close reading and comprehensible writing. Indeed, habits of language can even determine one's place in a society—as Bernard Shaw, though dealing with a different society, demonstrates with humor in *Pygmalion*. (By the way, if a career you have in mind has anything to do with advertising—whether writing it or using it or resisting it—be sure to read Chapter Sixteen, on suggestions inherent in words.)

That is why most colleges, however thorough the specialized career training they provide, see a need for generalized training as well, and insist on basic courses in the humanities. No one can promise, of course, that your study of literature will result in cash profit; but at least the kind of wealth that literature provides is immune to fluctuations of the Dow Jones average. Besides, should you discover in yourself a fondness for great reading, then it is likely that in no season of your life will you become incurably bored or feel totally alone—even after you make good in your career, even when there is nothing on television.

Changes in This Edition

Instructors familiar with the first edition will notice much that is familiar, much that is newly added. Half the stories, about one quarter of the poems, and seven of the twelve plays are new to this edition. For the most part these changes reflect the experience of at least 125 instructors who taught from the book (or from its component books); and in accord with their suggestions, I have tried to replace everything that most found only slightly useful, or not useful.

In general, the effect of this revision should be to increase the proportion of material that students are likely to find engaging and absorbing but not discouragingly difficult. Some selections, relatively problem-free, now lead to others that offer greater challenges. In the chapter on character in fiction, for instance, Brautigan's "The Kool-Aid Wino" now directly precedes Singer's richer and more complicated "Gimpel the Fool." The first short story that students will meet if the plan of the book is followed (which it need not be) is John Updike's readable and contemporary "A & P," replacing Chekhov's more difficult "In Exile"—retained but now one of the "Stories for Further

Study," where at the instructor's discretion it may be added to the course or left out.

Another revolution has taken place in the chapters "Writing about Fiction," "Writing about Poetry," and "Writing about Drama." I have tried (with what success the instructor can judge) to make them more specific and more practical. Although these chapters still contain brief illustrations from the work of professional critics, student writing is now their prime concern, with student papers their examples. There is a new appendix, "Writing about Literature," designed to supply some introductory notes on literary theory, and then to accompany the student step by step through the planning, organization, and writing of a paper.

In the fiction section, the largest innovation is the addition of the detective story in Chapter Seven, along with more ample displays of science fiction and the Gothic story. In the poetry section, "What a Poem Says First," a new part of Chapter Fourteen, lays fresh emphasis on reading for denotation. Besides, the book continues to devote a chapter to reading for the suggestions in words. In drama, "The Theater in the Twentieth Century" has been brought up to the present; and for the longest plays, questions are now arranged act by act, followed by general questions. Instructors who wish information on other changes in the book will find it in the preface to the Instructor's Manual to Accompany *Literature, Second Edition.*

A Note on Texts and Dates

Effort has been made to provide the best available texts and (when necessary) sound translations. Rolf Fjelde's 1978 version of *A Doll House* seems to light a few corners of Ibsen's play that most of us have not seen before; and so it is the version now included.

In this edition, a date appears to the right of each title. This is the date of a story or a poem's first publication in book form; or, in the case of a play, the date of its first performance. Parentheses around a date indicate a date of composition — given when a work, such as a poem of Emily Dickinson, was written much earlier than it first appeared. No attempt has been made to guess dates for medieval popular ballads.

Acknowledgments

Besides debts contracted in the past, this book now owes much to many who made fresh contributions. Michael Fixler gave of his wisdom about poetry and how to teach it. Kevin Hayter suggested teachable poems. Sylvan Barnet continued to read my manuscript and to tell me of anything that bothered him. James Leonard and members of his Language Arts faculty at Cuyahoga Community College, Western Campus, had me take part in a grueling seminar and shared their minds and their problems. I stand in debt to them all, especially to Richard Charnigo, David M. Cratty, Dennis Gabriel, Katherine P. Honesty, George Kemp, Richard Matthews, Jan Pae, Ed Raimer, James Webster, and Andy Yaronczyk. Other users of the last edition (or of one or more of its component books) who made specific suggestions include Nathan Albert, Dana K. Anderson, David Anderson, Angela Ashton, John Barrett, R. M. Barrett, Glynn Baugher, James F. Bellman, Dennis Berthiaume, Robert Blanchard, Michael D. Bliss, Alan K. Buckford, Peter V. Cenci, Hale Chatfield, Dolores J. Clark, Americus J. Cleffi, Theodore R. Cogswell, Lura L. Cook, Del Corey, Betty C. Craig, Fara Darland, Mary Ann Dazey, Brian J. Delaney, William L. Edgerton, Gerard L. Evans, Charles Fanning, Linda Farrell, Mike Finnegan, Margaret W. Freeman, Ruth L. Friedman, Albert Furtwangler, Robert E. Garlitz, Natalie M. Gatlin, George Gleason, Ernest Gleckman, Frederick Goldberg, Larry B. Gorse, Paul D. Green, Philip M. Griffith, Madeleine Hamermesh, Neva N. Harden, Terry Heller, E. R. Hutchison, Sr., Iris Jennings, Lucille Johnsen, Arnold Johnson, Quentin G. Johnson, Kenneth G. Johnston, Carol Juliusburger, C. W. Kaltenbach, Robert A. Kelly, Mark Kelso, F. D. Kievitt, Juliet W. Kincaid, John Kinch, Blossom Kirschenbaum, Tom Knetzo, Joseph Knight, Stanley J. Kozikowski, Ralph Latham, Elsie Leach, Patrick Lesley, Marilyn Levin, David H. Lindstrom, J. M. Linebarger, Gary Litt, Ed Luter, James Lynch, William M. Lytell, Nancy Malone, Silvine Marbury, Enid Marlink, James Martin, Robert L. McBroom, Glenn Meeter, Philip R. Micks, Charles Miller, Thomas A. Mozola, Sister Miriam J. Murphy, M. A. Nelson, James W. Newcomb, Jean M. O'Meara, Richard F. Patteson, Terri Paul, Jim Perkins, Fred Pfeil, Thom Pigaga, G. E. Pittenger, M. Evelyn Poe, Joseph Raboy, Robert Reiter, Kraft H. Rompf, Martin J. Rosenblum, Kathy Rosengren, George W. Sackman, Marilyn R. Satlof, Mary Savage, Mariette T. Sawchuk, Ted Schaefer, G. J. Schiffhorst, Margaret Schoenberg, William D. Shanebeck, John L. Simons, Keith Slocum, Frank Steele, Donald H. Stevenson, Muriel H. Tyssen, Robert L. Vales, Stanley M. Vogel, Steve A. Ward, Randall E. Wells, Celine Marie Werner, Michelle Werner (while a student at Kenyon College), Clyde V. Williams, Clemewell Young, and Elena Zimmerman. On the publisher's staff, Dale Anderson, Jan Beatty, Charles H. Christensen, Elizabeth Schaaf, Elizabeth Philipps, and Andrea Pozgay were just some of those who made the book a mutual cause, not just a mutual product. I remain grateful to students at Tufts, Michigan, North Carolina (Greensboro), Wellesley, California (Irvine), and Leeds, for reading literature with me. Dorothy M. Kennedy gave faith and hope, and contributed some of the book's more pointed questions.

TOPICAL CONTENTS

CONTENTS

11 Stories for Further Study 271

POETRY 407

12 Entrances 411

13 Listening to a Voice 419

TONE 419

THE PERSON IN THE POEM 423

15 Imagery   464

MORE ABOUT HAIKU   470

FOR REVIEW AND FURTHER STUDY   471

16 Saying and Suggesting   476

22   Poems for the Eye   597

23   Symbol   607

30 Poems for Further Study

LITERATURE

FICTION

Here is a story, perhaps one of the shortest ever written, and one of the most difficult to forget:

> A woman is sitting in her old, shuttered house. She knows that she is alone in the whole world; every other thing is dead.
>
> The doorbell rings.

This small tale of terror, credited to Thomas Bailey Aldrich, has much to be said for it despite its brevity. It sets a scene, it places a character in a situation that awakens our interest. Although we don't really have time to come to know the character well, for a moment we enter her thoughts and begin to share her feelings. Then something happens. The story ends with impact, and leaves us with cause to wonder — who or what rang the doorbell? Like a good many richer, longer, and more complicated stories, this one — in just a few words — engages our imaginations.

Evidently, what a story contains (and suggests) doesn't depend on its size. Our discussion of fiction will begin with some other stories that happen to be brief. We will be looking first at two ancient kinds of story — the fable and the tale — and then at a modern short story. (Because not all stories are short, later on you will find a chapter giving a terse history of the novel and some advice on reading novels and studying them.) Chapter by chapter, the elements of fiction will be considered in the hope that by being able to break up a story into its parts, you will come to have a keener appreciation of how a story is put together. Three types of fiction probably familiar to you — the Gothic story (the creaking old mansion kind of thing), science fiction, and the detective story — will be dealt with. You will find pointers, too, on telling good stories from bad, and for writing your own critical papers. Besides the chapter "Writing about Fiction," an appendix at the back of this book contains general suggestions for reading literature and for writing papers not only about stories but about poetry and plays as well.

In class discussion, you may be called on to communicate your responses to fiction (or to any other literature you read). In order to help you express yourself easily and accurately, this book will offer a few critical terms that may be of use to you. These words and phrases will appear in **bold face** when they are first defined. If anywhere in this book you meet a critical term you don't know or don't recall, just look it up in the Index of Terms (on the inside back cover).

All in all, there are five fables and tales, two short novels, and thirty-two short stories. I hope you will encounter among them at least a few stories you will immediately enjoy and possibly care to remember.

1 What Is Fiction?

After the shipwreck that marooned him on his desert island, Robinson Crusoe, in the story by Daniel Defoe, stood gazing over the water where pieces of cargo from his ship were floating by. Along came "two shoes, not mates." It is the qualification *not mates* that makes the detail memorable. We could well believe that a thing so striking and odd must have been seen, and not invented. But in truth Defoe, like other masters of the art of fiction, had the power to make us believe his imaginings. Borne along by the art of the storyteller, we trust what we are told, even though the story may be sheer fantasy.

Fiction (from the Latin *fictio*, "a shaping, a counterfeiting") is a name for stories not entirely factual, but at least partially shaped, made up, imagined. It is true that in some fiction, such as a historical novel, a writer draws upon factual information in presenting scenes, events, and characters. But the factual information in a historical novel, unlike that in a history book, is of secondary importance. Many firsthand accounts of the American Civil War were written by men who had fought in it, but few eyewitnesses give us so keen a sense of actual life on the battlefront as the author of *The Red Badge of Courage*, Stephen Crane, a young man born after the war was over. In fiction, the "facts" may or may not be true, and a story is none the worse for their being entirely imaginary. What we expect from fiction is a sense of how people act, not an authentic chronicle of how, at some past time, a few people acted.

As children, we used to read (if we were lucky and formed the habit) to steep ourselves in romance, mystery, and adventure. As adults, we still do: at an airport, perhaps, while waiting for a flight, we pass the time with some newsstand paperback full of fast action and brisk dialogue. Certain fiction, of course, calls for closer attention. To read a novel by the Russian master Dostoevsky instead of a thriller about secret agent James Bond is somewhat like playing chess instead of a game of tic-tac-toe. This is not to say that a great novel does not provide entertainment. In fact, it may offer more deeply satisfying entertainment than a novel of violence and soft-core pornography, in which stick figures connive, go to bed, and kill one another in accord with some market-tested formula. Reading **literary fiction** (as distinguished from fiction as a commercial product — the formula kind of spy, detective, Western, love, jungle, or other adventure story), we are not necessarily led on by the promise of thrills; we do not keep reading mainly to find out what happens next. Indeed, a literary story might even disclose in its opening lines everything that happened, then spend the rest of its length revealing what that happening meant. Reading literary fiction is no merely passive activity, but one that demands both attention and insight-lending participation. In return, it offers rewards. In some works of literary fiction, in Joseph Conrad's *The Secret Sharer* and Leo Tolstoi's *The Death of Ivan Ilych,* we see more deeply into the minds and hearts of the characters than we ever see into those of our family, our close friends, our lovers — or even ourselves.

FABLE AND TALE

Modern literary fiction in English has been dominated by two forms: the novel and the short story. The two have many elements in common (and in this book a further discussion of the novel as a special form will be given in Chapter Ten). Perhaps we will be able to define the short story more meaningfully — for it has other traits more essential than just a particular length — if first, for comparison, we consider some other, related varieties of fiction: the fable and the tale. Ancient forms whose origins date back to the time of word-of-mouth storytelling, the fable and the tale are relatively simpler in structure; in them we can plainly see elements also found in the short story (and in the novel). To begin, here is a classic **fable:** a brief story that sets forth some pointed comment on human life. Along with many other fables credited to the Greek slave Aesop (whether he actually lived or not), it belongs to our common heritage. Whenever we speak of "sour grapes," "the lion's share," "to cry, 'Wolf!'," or "to kill the goose that laid the golden eggs," we refer to Aesop, often unconsciously.

Aesop (fifth and sixth centuries B.C.)
THE FROGS WHO WANTED A KING

Some frogs who lived in a pond were bored with freedom, so they sent a petition to Zeus and asked to be given a king. Although the god thought the frogs better off as they were, to oblige them he hurled a log into their pond. Hearing the splash, the frogs were terrified, and scurried to the pond's far corners. But by and by, seeing that the log lay motionless, they approached, and growing bolder said to one another, "What, is this our powerful king?" Soon they were jumping out of the water and squatting on the log, croaking in contempt.

After a while they tired of this sport. Again some of them went to Zeus and asked him to get rid of such a lazy, do-nothing king and send them a more forceful one. Annoyed, Zeus caused a great stork to descend to the pond. Frogs were his favorite food.

This story contains little decoration; it seems practically all skin and bones. For in a fable, everything leads directly to the moral, or message, which is sometimes stated at the end ("Moral: haste makes waste"), sometimes implied. In this particular fable, the moral is implied. How would you state it? The characters in a fable may be people, or even inanimate objects; but generally, as in this example, they are talking animals who exhibit human behavior. Evidently it would not have helped to put across the moral if Aesop had portrayed his characters in greater detail, nor if he had taken us deeper into their thought processes. Clear as it is, the moral would not have been better demonstrated by the inclusion of more elaborate descriptions of the pond or the court of Zeus. Probably such descriptions would have seemed unnecessary and distracting. The main thing we need to know about the frogs is that they are the sort who, like some people, are never satisfied. By its very bareness and simplicity, a fable fixes its lesson in memory. (One theory is that Aesop made up this story in order to persuade the Athenians that the rule of King Peisistratus, a do-nothing, ought to be tolerated.)

Fables may be teaching devices, but it is doubtful that a fable such as "The Frogs Who Wanted a King" would have enjoyed so long a life unless it gave pleasure as well as instruction. From its very first words, this brief story promises to entertain us by posing some problem faced by the main characters. Absurd as this problem is, we are engaged by it, and we enjoy following the gradual working out of its solution. The solution is unhappy; still, we appreciate its rightness and conclude that the frogs' punishment was richly deserved.

The name *tale* (from the Old English *talu*, "speech") is sometimes applied to any story, whether short or long, true or fictitious. *Tale* being a more evocative name than *story*, writers sometimes call their stories "tales" as if to imply something handed down from the past (as Nathaniel Hawthorne did in naming his *Twice-Told Tales*). But defined in a more limited sense, a **tale** is a story, usually short, that sets forth strange and wonderful events in more or less bare summary, without detailed character-drawing. "Tale" is pretty much synonymous with "yarn," for it implies a story in which the main concern is revelation of the marvelous rather than revelation of character. In the tale of Aladdin in *The Arabian Nights*, for instance, we take away a more vivid impression of the summoning of the genie than of Aladdin's mind or personality. Because ancient stories such as *The Arabian Nights* and *Grimm's Fairy Tales* were told aloud before someone captured them in writing, the storytellers had to limit themselves to brief descriptions. Probably spoken around a fire or hearth, such a tale tends to be less complicated and less closely detailed than a story written for the printed page, whose reader can linger over it. Still, such tales *can* be complicated. It is not merely greater length that makes a short story different from a tale or a fable: a mark of a short story is a fully delineated character.

Even modern tales favor supernatural or fantastic events: for instance, the **tall tale,** that variety of folk story that recounts the deeds of a superhero (Paul Bunyan, John Henry, Mike Fink) or of the story teller. If the story teller is telling about his own imaginary experience, his bragging yarn is usually told with a straight face to listeners who take pleasure in scoffing at it. Although the **fairy tale,** set in a world of magic and enchantment, is sometimes the work of a modern author (notably Hans Christian Andersen), well-known examples are those German folktales probably originated in the Middle Ages, collected by the brothers Grimm and first printed in 1812–1815. The label *fairy tale* is something of an English misnomer because in the Grimm stories fairies as opposed to witches and goblins are in a minority. (The Grimms called their collection *Kinder- und Hausmärchen,* "Children's Stories and Household Stories.") Enjoyed by adults as well as by children, many of the tales collected by the scholarly brothers embody the dreams and fears of uneducated storytellers and their audiences. Less familiar than "Hansel and Gretel," "Rapunzel," or "Snow White and the Seven Dwarfs," a memorable example follows.

Jakob and Wilhelm Grimm (1785–1863, 1786–1859)

GODFATHER DEATH   1822 (from oral tradition)

Translated by Lore Segal

A poor man had twelve children and worked night and day just to get enough bread for them to eat. Now when the thirteenth came into the world, he did not know what to do and in his misery ran out onto the great highway to ask the first person he met to be godfather. The first to come along was God, and he already knew what it was that weighed on the man's mind and said, "Poor man, I pity you. I will hold your child at the font and I will look after it and make it happy upon earth." "Who are you?" asked the man. "I am God." "Then I don't want you for a godfather," the man said. "You give to the rich and let the poor go hungry." That was how the man talked because he did not understand how wisely God shares out wealth and poverty, and thus he turned from the Lord and walked on. Next came the Devil and said, "What is it you want? If you let me be godfather to your child, I will give him gold as much as he can use, and all the pleasures of the world besides." "Who are you?" asked the man. "I am the Devil." "Then I don't want you for a godfather," said the man. "You deceive and mislead mankind." He walked on and along came spindle-legged Death striding toward him and said, "Take me as godfather." The man asked,

"Who are you?" "I am Death who makes all men equal." Said the man, "Then you're the one for me; you take rich and poor without distinction. You shall be godfather." Answered Death, "I will make your child rich and famous, because the one who has me for a friend shall want for nothing." The man said, "Next Sunday is the baptism. Be there in good time." Death appeared as he had promised and made a perfectly fine godfather.

When the boy was of age, the godfather walked in one day, told him to come along, and led him out into the woods. He showed him an herb which grew there and said, "This is your christening gift. I shall make you into a famous doctor. When you are called to a patient's bedside I will appear and if I stand at the sick man's head you can boldly say that you will cure him and if you give him some of this herb he will recover. But if I stand at the sick man's feet, then he is mine, and you must say there is no help for him and no doctor on this earth could save him. But take care not to use the herb against my will or it could be the worse for you."

It wasn't long before the young man had become the most famous doctor in the whole world. "He looks at a patient and right away he knows how things stand, whether he will get better or if he's going to die." That is what they said about him, and from near and far the people came, took him to see the sick, and gave him so much money he became a rich man. Now it happened that the king fell ill. The doctor was summoned to say if he was going to get well. When he came to the bed, there stood Death at the feet of the sick man, so that no herb on earth could have done him any good. If I could only just this once out-wit Death! thought the doctor. He'll be annoyed, I know, but I am his godchild and he's sure to turn a blind eye. I'll take my chance. And so he lifted the sick man and laid him the other way around so that Death was standing at his head. Then he gave him some of the herb and the king began to feel better and was soon in perfect health. But Death came toward the doctor, his face dark and angry, threatened him with raised forefinger, and said, "You have tricked me. This time I will let it pass because you are my godchild, but if you ever dare do such a thing again, you put your own head in the noose and it is you I shall carry away with me."

Soon after that, the king's daughter lapsed into a deep illness. She was his only child, he wept day and night until his eyes failed him and he let it be known that whoever saved the princess from death should become her husband and inherit the crown. When the doctor came to the sick girl's bed, he saw Death at her feet. He ought to have remembered his godfather's warning, but the great beauty of the princess and the happiness of becoming her husband so bedazzled him that he threw caution to the winds, nor did he see Death's angry glances and how he lifted his hand in the air and threatened him with his bony fist. He picked the sick girl up and laid her head where her feet had lain, then he gave her some of the herb and at once her cheeks reddened and life stirred anew.

When Death saw himself cheated of his property the second time, he strode toward the doctor on his long legs and said, "It is all up with you, and now it is your turn," grasped him harshly with his ice-cold hand so that the doctor could not resist, and led him to an underground cave, and here he saw thousands upon thousands of lights burning in rows without end, some big, some middle-sized, others small. Every moment some went out and others lit up so that the little flames seemed to be jumping here and there in perpetual exchange. "Look," said Death, "these are the life lights of mankind. The big ones belong to children, the middle-sized ones to married couples in their best years, the little ones belong to very old people. Yet children and the young often have only little lights." "Show me my life light," said the doctor, imagining that it must be one of the big ones. Death pointed to a little stub threatening to go out and said, "Here it is." "Ah, dear godfather," said the terrified doctor, "light me a new one, do it, for my sake, so that I may enjoy my life and become king and marry the beautiful princess." "I cannot," answered Death. "A light must go out before a new one lights up." "Then set the old on top of a new one so it can go on burning when the first is finished," begged the doctor. Death made as if to grant his wish, reached for a tall new taper, but because he wanted revenge he purposely fumbled and the little stub fell over and went out. Thereupon the doctor sank to the ground and had himself fallen into the hands of death.

PLOT

Unlike Aesop's fable of the frogs, "Godfather Death" does not seem designed to impart much practical, worldly advice. To be sure, it conveys a lesson: *You can't cheat Death* — but that is hardly a lesson of much use to us. Like a fable, the Grimm brothers' tale seems stark in its lack of detail and in the swiftness of its telling. Compared with the fully portrayed characters of many modern stories, the characters of father, son, king, princess, and even Death himself seem hardly more than stick figures. It may have been that to draw ample characters would not have contributed to the storytellers' design; that, indeed, to have done so would have been inartistic. Yet "Godfather Death" is a compelling story. By what methods does it arouse and sustain our interest?

From the opening sentence of the tale, we watch the unfolding of a **dramatic situation:** a person is involved in some conflict. First, this character is a poor man with children to feed, in conflict with the world; very soon, we find him in conflict with God and with the Devil besides. Drama in fiction occurs in any clash of wills, desires, or powers — whether it be a conflict of character against character, character against society, character against some natural force, or, as in "Godfather Death," character against some supernatural entity.

Like any shapely tale, "Godfather Death" has a beginning, a middle, and an end. In fact, it is unusual to find a story that so clearly displays the elements of structure which critics have found in many classic works of fiction and drama. The tale begins with an **exposition:** the opening portion that sets the scene (if any), introduces the main characters, tells us what happened before the story opened, and provides any other background information that we need in order to understand and care about the events to follow. In "Godfather Death" the exposition is brief: all in the opening paragraph. The middle section of the story begins with Death's giving the herb to the boy, and his warning not to defy him. This moment introduces a new conflict (a **complication**), and by this time it is clear that the son and not the father is to be the central human character of the story. Death's godson is the principal person who strives: the **protagonist** (a better term than **hero,** since it may apply equally well to a central character who is not especially brave or virtuous).

The **suspense,** the pleasurable anxiety we feel that heightens our attention to the story, inheres in our wondering how it will all turn out. Will the doctor triumph over Death? Even though we suspect, early in the story, that the doctor stands no chance against such a superhuman **antagonist,** we want to see for ourselves the outcome of his defiance. A storyteller can try to incite our anticipation by giving us some **fore-shadowing** or indication of events to come. In "Godfather Death" the foreshadowings are apparent in Death's warnings ("but if you ever dare do such a thing again, you put your own head in the noose"). When the doctor defies his godfather for the first time — when he saves the king — we have a **crisis,** a moment of high tension. The tension is momentarily resolved when Death lets him off. Then an even greater crisis — the turning point in the action — occurs with the doctor's second defiance in restoring the princess to life. In the last section of the story, with the doctor in the underworld, events come to a **climax,** the moment of greatest tension, at which the outcome is to be decided, when the terrified doctor begs for a new candle. Will Death grant him one? Will he live, become king, and marry the princess? The outcome or **conclusion** — also called the **resolution** or **denouement** ("the untying of the knot") — quickly follows as Death allows the little candle to go out.

Such a structure of events arising out of a conflict may be called the plot of the story. Like many terms used in literary discussion, *plot* is blessed with several meanings. Sometimes it refers simply to the events in a story. In this book, **plot** will mean the artistic arrangement of those events. Different arrangements of the same material are possible. A writer might decide to tell of the events in chronological order, beginning with the earliest; or he might open his story with the last event, then tell what led up to it. Sometimes a writer chooses to skip rapidly over the exposition and begin **in medias res** (Latin, "in the midst of things"), first presenting some exciting or significant moment, then filling in what happened earlier. This method is by no means a modern invention: Homer begins the *Odyssey* with his hero mysteriously late in returning from war and his son searching for him; John Milton's *Paradise Lost* opens with Satan already defeated in his revolt against the Lord. A device useful to writers for filling in what happened earlier is the **flashback** (or **retrospect**), a scene relived in a character's memory.

To have a plot, a story does not need an intense, sustained conflict such as we find in "Godfather Death," a tale especially economical in its structure of crisis, climax, and conclusion. Although a highly dramatic story may tend to assume such a clearly recognizable structure, many contemporary writers avoid it, considering it too contrived and arbitrary. In commercial fiction, in which exciting conflict is everything and in which the writer has to manufacture all possible suspense, such a structure is often obvious. In popular detective, Western, and adventure novels; in juvenile fiction (the perennial Hardy Boys and Nancy Drew books); and in popular series on television (soap operas, police and hospital thrillers, mysteries, and cowboy stories) it is often easy to recognize crisis, climax, and conclusion. The presence of these elements does not necessarily indicate inferior literature (as "Godfather Death" shows); yet when reduced to parts of a formula, the result may seem stale and contrived.[1] Such plots may be (as the contemporary French novelist Alain Robbe-Grillet has put it) mere anecdotes, providing trumped-up surprises for "the panting reader."[2]

THE SHORT STORY

The teller of a tale relies heavily upon the method of **summary:** terse, general narration as in "Godfather Death" ("It wasn't long before the young man had become the most famous doctor in the whole world"). But in a **short story,** a form more realistic than the tale and of modern origin, the writer usually presents the main events in greater fullness. Fine writers of short stories, while they may use summary at times (often to give some portion of a story less emphasis), are skilled in rendering a **scene:** a vivid or dramatic moment described in enough detail to create the illusion that the reader is practically there. Avoiding long summary, they try to *show* rather than simply to *tell;* as if following Mark Twain's advice to authors: "Don't say, 'The old lady screamed.' Bring her on and let her scream."

A short story is more than just a sequence of happenings. Its **setting,** or environment,[3] may be no less important than the events themselves. A finely wrought short story has the richness and concision of an excellent lyric poem. Spontaneous and natural as the finished story may seem, the writer has written it so artfully that there is meaning in

[1] In the heyday of the **pulp magazines** (so called for their cheap paper), some professional writers even relied on a mechanical device called Plotto: a tin arrow-spinner pointed to numbers and the writer looked them up in a book that listed necessary ingredients — type of hero, type of villain, sort of conflict, crisis, climax, conclusion.

[2] "On Several Obsolete Notions," *For a New Novel* (New York: Grove Press, 1966).

[3] The term *setting* is generally taken to include not only the geographical place in which the events in a story happen, but also the historical era, the daily lives or customs of the characters, and perhaps the season of the year. Where the story takes place is its **locale.**

even seemingly casual speeches and apparently trivial details. If we skim it hastily, skipping the descriptive passages, we miss significant parts. Some literary short stories, unlike commercial fiction in which the main interest centers in physical action or conflict, tell of an **epiphany:** some moment of insight, discovery, or revelation by which a character's life, or view of life, is greatly altered.[4] (For such moments in fiction, see the stories in this book by James Joyce, Leo Tolstoi, John Steinbeck, Bernard Malamud, and Joyce Carol Oates.) Other short stories tell of the initiation of a character into experience or maturity: one such **story of initiation** is William Faulkner's "Barn Burning" (Chapter Four), in which a boy finds it necessary to defy his father and suddenly to grow into manhood. Less obviously dramatic, perhaps, than "Godfather Death,"such a story may be no less powerful.

The fable and the tale are ancient forms; the short story is of more recent origin. In the nineteenth century, writers of fiction were encouraged by a large, literate audience of middle-class readers who wanted to see their lives reflected in faithful mirrors. Skillfully representing ordinary life, many writers perfected the art of the short story: in Russia, Anton Chekhov; in France, Honoré de Balzac, Gustave Flaubert, and Guy de Maupassant; and in America, Nathaniel Hawthorne and Edgar Allan Poe (although the Americans seem less fond of everyday life than of dream and fantasy). It would be false to claim that, in passing from the fable and the tale to the short story, fiction has made a triumphant progress; or to claim that, because short stories are modern, they are superior to fables and tales. Fable, tale, and short story are distinct forms, each able to achieve its own effects. (Incidentally, fable and tale are far from being extinct today: you can find many recent examples.) Lately, in the hands of Donald Barthelme, Joyce Carol Oates, John Barth, and other innovative writers, the conventions of the short story have been changing; and at the moment, stories of epiphany and initiation have become more scarce.

But let us begin with a contemporary short story whose protagonist *does* undergo an initiation into maturity. To notice the difference between a short story and a tale, you may find it helpful to compare John Updike's "A & P" with "Godfather Death." Although Updike's short story is centuries distant from the Grimm tale in its method of telling and in its setting, you may be reminded of "Godfather Death" in the main character's dramatic situation. In order to defend a young woman, a young man has to defy his mentor — here, the boss of a supermarket! So doing, he places himself in jeopardy. Updike has the protagonist tell his own story, amply and with humor. How does it differ from a tale?

[4] From the Greek *epiphainein*, "to show forth." In Christian tradition, the Feast of the Epiphany commemorates the revelation to the Magi of the birth of Christ.

John Updike (b. 1932)

A & P

1961

In walks these three girls in nothing but bathing suits. I'm in the third check-out slot, with my back to the door, so I don't see them until they're over by the bread. The one that caught my eye first was the one in the plaid green two-piece. She was a chunky kid, with a good tan and a sweet broad soft-looking can with those two crescents of white just under it, where the sun never seems to hit, at the top of the backs of her legs. I stood there with my hand on a box of HiHo crackers trying to remember if I rang it up or not. I ring it up again and the customer starts giving me hell. She's one of these cash-register-watchers, a witch about fifty with rouge on her cheekbones and no eyebrows, and I know it made her day to trip me up. She'd been watching cash registers for fifty years and probably never seen a mistake before.

By the time I got her feathers smoothed and her goodies into a bag — she gives me a little snort in passing, if she'd been born at the right time they would have burned her over in Salem — by the time I get her on her way the girls had circled around the bread and were coming back, without a pushcart, back my way along the counters, in the aisle between the check-outs and the Special bins. They didn't even have shoes on. There was this chunky one, with the two-piece — it was bright green and the seams on the bra were still sharp and her belly was still pretty pale so I guessed she just got it (the suit) — there was this one, with one of those chubby berry-faces, the lips all bunched to-gether under her nose, this one, and a tall one, with black hair that hadn't quite frizzed right, and one of these sunburns right across under the eyes, and a chin that was too long — you know, the kind of girl other girls think is very "strik-ing" and "attractive" but never quite makes it, as they very well know, which is why they like her so much — and then the third one, that wasn't quite so tall. She was the queen. She kind of led them, the other two peeking around and mak-ing their shoulders round. She didn't look around, not this queen, she just walked straight on slowly, on these long white prima-donna legs. She came down a little hard on her heels, as if she didn't walk in her bare feet that much, putting down her heels and then letting the weight move along to her toes as if she was testing the floor with every step, putting a little deliberate extra action into it. You never know for sure how girls' minds work (do you really think it's a mind in there or just a little buzz like a bee in a glass jar?) but you got the idea she had talked the other two into coming in here with her, and now she was showing them how to do it, walk slow and hold yourself straight.

She had on a kind of dirty-pink — beige maybe, I don't know — bathing suit with a little nubble all over it and, what got me, the straps were down. They were off her shoulders looped loose around the cool tops of her arms, and I guess as a result the suit had slipped a little on her, so all around the top of the cloth there was this shining rim. If it hadn't been there you wouldn't have known there could have been anything whiter than those shoulders. With the straps pushed off, there was nothing between the top of the suit and the top of her head except just *her*, this clean bare plane of the top of her chest down from the shoulder bones like a dented sheet of metal tilted in the light. I mean, it was more than pretty.

She had sort of oaky hair that the sun and salt had bleached, done up in a bun that was unravelling, and a kind of prim face. Walking into the A & P with your straps down, I suppose it's the only kind of face you *can* have. She held her head so high her neck, coming up out of those white shoulders, looked kind of stretched, but I didn't mind. The longer her neck was, the more of her there was.

She must have felt in the corner of her eye me and over my shoulder Stokesie in the second slot watching, but she didn't tip. Not this queen. She kept her eyes moving across the racks, and stopped, and turned so slow it made my stomach rub the inside of my apron, and buzzed to the other two, who kind of huddled against her for relief, and they all three of them went up the cat-and-dog-food-breakfast-cereal-macaroni-rice-raisins-seasonings-spreads-spaghetti-soft-drinks-crackers-and-cookies aisle. From the third slot I look straight up this aisle to the meat counter, and I watched them all the way. The fat one with the tan sort of fumbled with the cookies, but on second thought she put the packages back. The sheep pushing their carts down the aisle — the girls were walking against the usual traffic (not that we have one-way signs or anything) — were pretty hilarious. You could see them, when Queenie's white shoulders dawned on them, kind of jerk, or hop, or hiccup, but their eyes snapped back to their own baskets and on they pushed. I bet you could set off dynamite in an A & P and the people would by and large keep reaching and checking oatmeal off their lists and muttering "Let me see, there was a third thing, began with A, asparagus, no, ah, yes, applesauce!" or whatever it is they do mutter. But there was no doubt, this jiggled them. A few houseslaves in pin curlers even looked around after pushing their carts past to make sure what they had seen was correct.

You know, it's one thing to have a girl in a bathing suit down on the beach, where what with the glare nobody can look at each other much anyway, and another thing in the cool of the A & P, under the fluorescent lights, against all those stacked packages, with her feet paddling along naked over our checkerboard green-and-cream rubber-tile floor.

"Oh Daddy," Stokesie said beside me. "I feel so faint."

"Darling," I said. "Hold me tight." Stokesie's married, with two babies chalked up on his fuselage already, but as far as I can tell that's the only difference. He's twenty-two, and I was nineteen this April.

"Is it done?" he asks, the responsible married man finding his voice. I forgot to say he thinks he's going to be manager some sunny day, maybe in 1990 when it's called the Great Alexandrov and Petrooshki Tea Company or something.

What he meant was, our town is five miles from a beach, with a big summer colony out on the Point, but we're right in the middle of town, and the women generally put on a shirt or shorts or something before they get out of the car into the street. And anyway these are usually women with six children and varicose veins mapping their legs and nobody, including them, could care less. As I say, we're right in the middle of town, and if you stand at our front doors you can see two banks and the Congregational church and the newspaper store and three real-estate offices and about twenty-seven old freeloaders tearing up Central Street because the sewer broke again. It's not as if we're on the Cape; we're north of Boston and there's people in this town haven't seen the ocean for twenty years.

The girls had reached the meat counter and were asking McMahon something. He pointed, they pointed, and they shuffled out of sight behind a pyramid of Diet Delight peaches. All that was left for us to see was old McMahon patting his mouth and looking after them sizing up their joints. Poor kids, I began to feel sorry for them, they couldn't help it.

Now here comes the sad part of the story, at least my family says it's sad but I don't think it's sad myself. The store's pretty empty, it being Thursday afternoon, so there was nothing much to do except lean on the register and wait for the girls to show up again. The whole store was like a pinball machine and I didn't know which tunnel they'd come out of. After a while they come around out of the far aisle, around the light bulbs, records at discount of the Caribbean Six or Tony Martin Sings or some such gunk you wonder they waste the wax on, sixpacks of candy bars, and plastic toys done up in cellophane that fall apart when a kid looks at them anyway. Around they come, Queenie still leading the way, and holding a little gray jar in her hand. Slots Three through Seven are unmanned and I could see her wondering between Stokes and me, but Stokesie with his usual luck draws an old party in baggy gray pants who stumbles up with four giant cans of pineapple juice (what do these bums *do* with all that pineapple juice? I've often asked myself) so the girls come to me. Queenie puts down the jar and I take it into my fingers icy cold. Kingfish Fancy Herring Snacks in Pure Sour Cream: 49¢. Now her hands are empty, not a ring or a bracelet, bare as God made them, and I wonder where the money's coming from. Still with that prim look she lifts a folded dollar bill out of the hollow at the center of her nubbled pink top. The jar went heavy in my hand. Really, I thought that was so cute.

Then everybody's luck begins to run out. Lengel comes in from haggling with a truck full of cabbages on the lot and is about to scuttle into that door marked MANAGER behind which he hides all day when the girls touch his eye. Lengel's pretty dreary, teaches Sunday school and the rest, but he doesn't miss that much. He comes over and says, "Girls, this isn't the beach."

Queenie blushes, though maybe it's just a brush of sunburn I was noticing for the first time, now that she was so close. "My mother asked me to pick up a jar of herring snacks." Her voice kind of startled me, the way voices do when you see the people first, coming out so flat and dumb yet kind of tony, too, the way it ticked over "pick up" and "snacks." All of a sudden I slid right down her voice into her living room. Her father and the other men were standing around in ice-cream coats and bow ties and the women were in sandals picking up herring snacks on toothpicks off a big plate and they were all holding drinks the color of water with olives and sprigs of mint in them. When my parents have somebody over they get lemonade and if it's a real racy affair Schlitz in tall glasses with "They'll Do It Every Time" cartoons stenciled on.

"That's all right," Lengel said. "But this isn't the beach." His repeating this struck me as funny, as if it had just occurred to him, and he had been thinking all these years the A & P was a great big dune and he was the head lifeguard. He didn't like my smiling — as I say he doesn't miss much — but he concentrates on giving the girls that sad Sunday-school-superintendent stare.

Queenie's blush is no sunburn now, and the plump one in plaid, that I liked better from the back — a really sweet can — pipes up, "We weren't doing any shopping. We just came in for the one thing."

"That makes no difference," Lengel tells her, and I could see from the way his eyes went that he hadn't noticed she was wearing a two-piece before. "We want you decently dressed when you come in here."

"We *are* decent," Queenie says suddenly, her lower lip pushing, getting sore now that she remembers her place, a place from which the crowd that runs the A & P must look pretty crummy. Fancy Herring Snacks flashed in her very blue eyes.

"Girls, I don't want to argue with you. After this come in here with your shoulders covered. It's our policy." He turns his back. That's policy for you. Policy is what the kingpins want. What the others want is juvenile delinquency.

All this while, the customers had been showing up with their carts but, you know, sheep, seeing a scene, they had all bunched up on Stokesie, who shook open a paper bag as gently as peeling a peach, not wanting to miss a word. I could feel in the silence everybody getting nervous, most of all Lengel, who asks me, "Sammy, have you rung up this purchase?"

I thought and said "No" but it wasn't about that I was thinking. I go through the punches, 4, 9, GROC, TOT — it's more complicated than you think, and after you do it often enough, it begins to make a little song, that you hear words to, in my case "Hello (*bing*) there, you (*gung*) hap-py *pee*-pul (*splat*)!" — the *splat* being the drawer flying out. I uncrease the bill, tenderly as you may imagine, it just having come from between the two smoothest scoops of vanilla I had ever known were there, and pass a half and a penny into her narrow pink palm, and nestle the herrings in a bag and twist its neck and hand it over, all the time thinking.

The girls, and who'd blame them, are in a hurry to get out, so I say "I quit" to Lengel quick enough for them to hear, hoping they'll stop and watch me, their unsuspected hero. They keep right on going, into the electric eye; the door flies open and they flicker across the lot to their car, Queenie and Plaid and Big Tall Goony-Goony (not that as raw material she was so bad), leaving me with Lengel and a kink in his eyebrow.

"Did you say something, Sammy?"

"I said I quit."

"I thought you did."

"You didn't have to embarrass them."

"It was they who were embarrassing us."

I started to say something that came out "Fiddle-de-doo." It's a saying of my grandmother's, and I know she would have been pleased.

"I don't think you know what you're saying," Lengel said.

"I know you don't," I said. "But I do." I pull the bow at the back of my apron and start shrugging it off my shoulders. A couple customers that had been heading for my slot begin to knock against each other, like scared pigs in a chute.

Lengel sighs and begins to look very patient and old and gray. He's been a friend of my parents for years. "Sammy, you don't want to do this to your Mom and Dad," he tells me. It's true, I don't. But it seems to me that once you begin a gesture it's fatal not to go through with it. I fold the apron, "Sammy" stitched in red on the pocket, and put it on the counter, and drop the bow tie on top of it. The bow tie is theirs, if you've ever wondered. "You'll feel this for the rest of your life," Lengel says, and I know that's true, too, but remembering how he made that pretty girl blush makes me so scrunchy inside I punch the No Sale tab and the machine whirs "pee-pul" and the drawer splats out. One advantage to this scene taking place in summer, I can follow this up with a clean exit, there's no fumbling around getting your coat and galoshes, I just saunter into the electric eye in my white shirt that my mother ironed the night before, and the door heaves itself open, and outside the sunshine is skating around on the asphalt.

I look around for my girls, but they're gone, of course. There wasn't anybody but some young married screaming with her children about some candy they didn't get by the door of a powder-blue Falcon station wagon. Looking back in the big windows, over the bags of peat moss and aluminum lawn furniture stacked on the pavement, I could see Lengel in my place in the slot, checking the sheep through. His face was dark gray and his back stiff, as if he'd just had an injection of iron, and my stomach kind of fell as I felt how hard the world was going to be to me hereafter.

QUESTIONS

1. Notice how artfully Updike arranges details to set the story in a perfectly ordinary supermarket. What details stand out for you as particularly true to life? What does this close attention to detail contribute to the story?
2. How fully does Updike draw the character of Sammy? What traits (admirable or otherwise) does Sammy show? Is he any less a hero for wanting the girls to notice his heroism? To what extent is he more thoroughly and fully portrayed than the doctor in "Godfather Death"?
3. What part of the story seems exposition? (See the definition of *exposition* on page 8.) Of what value to the story is the carefully detailed portrait of Queenie, the leader of the three girls?
4. As the story develops, do you detect any change in Sammy's feelings toward the girls? Do you agree with a reader who called Sammy "a sexist pig who suddenly sees the light"?
5. At what point in "A & P" does the dramatic conflict become apparent? What moment in the story brings the crisis? What is the climax of the story?
6. Why, exactly, does Sammy quit his job?
7. Does anything lead you to *expect* Sammy to make some gesture of sympathy for the three girls? What incident earlier in the story (before Sammy quits) seems a foreshadowing?
8. What do you understand from the conclusion of the story? What does Sammy mean when he acknowledges "how hard the world was going to be . . . hereafter"?
9. What comment does Updike — through Sammy — make on supermarket society?

2 Point of View

In the opening lines of *The Adventures of Huckleberry Finn*, Mark Twain takes care to separate himself from the central character, who is to tell his own story:

> You don't know about me, without you have read a book by the name of *The Adventures of Tom Sawyer*, but that ain't no matter. That book was made by Mr. Mark Twain, and he told the truth, mainly.

Twain wrote the novel, but the **narrator** or speaker is Huck Finn, the one from whose perspective the story is told. Obviously in the case of *Huckleberry Finn*, the narrator of a story is not the same person as the "real life" author, the one given the by-line. In employing Huck as his narrator, Twain selects a special angle of vision: not his own, exactly, but that of a resourceful boy moving through the thick of events, with a mind at times shrewd, at other times innocent. Through Huck's eyes, Twain takes in certain scenes, actions, and characters and — as only Huck's angle of vision could have enabled Twain so well to do — records them memorably.

Not every narrator in fiction is, like Huck Finn, a central character, one in the thick of events. Some narrators play only minor parts in the stories they tell; others take no active part at all. In the tale of "Godfather Death," we have a narrator who does not participate in the events he recounts. He is not a character in the story but is someone not even named, who stands at some distance from the action recording what the main characters say and do; recording also, at times, what they think, feel, or desire. He seems to have unlimited knowledge: he even knows the mind of Death, who "because he wanted revenge" let the doctor's candle go out. More humanly restricted in their knowledge, other narrators can see into the mind of only a single character. They may be less willing to express opinions than the narrator of "Godfather Death" ("He ought to have remembered his godfather's warning"). A story may even be told by a narrator who seems so impartial and aloof that he limits himself to reporting only overheard conversation and to describing, without comment or opinion, the appearances of things. Evidently, narrators greatly differ in kind; however, since stories usually are told by someone, virtually every story has some kind of narrator.[1] It is rare in modern fiction for the "real life" author to try to step out from behind his typewriter and tell the story. Real persons can tell stories, but when such a story is *written*, the result is usually *non*fiction: a memoir, an account of travels, an autobiography.[2]

To identify the narrator of a story, describing any part he plays in the events and any limits placed upon his knowledge, is to identify the story's **point of view.** In a short story, it is usual for the writer to maintain one point of view from beginning to end, but there is nothing to stop him from introducing other points of view as well. In his long, panoramic novel *War and Peace*, Leo Tolstoi, encompassing the vast drama of Napoleon's invasion of Russia, freely shifts the point of view in and out of the minds of many characters, among them Napoleon himself.

Theoretically, a great many points of view are possible. A narrator who says "I" might conceivably be involved in events to a much greater or a much lesser degree: as the protagonist, as some other major character, as some minor character, as a mere passive spectator, or even as a character who arrives late upon the scene and then tries to piece together what happened. Evidently, too, a narrator's knowledge might vary in gradations from total omniscience to almost total ignorance. But in reading fiction, again and again we encounter certain familiar and recognizable points of view. Here is a list of them — admittedly just a rough abstraction — that may provide a few terms with which to discuss the stories that you read and to describe their points of view:

Narrator a participant (writing in the first person):
1. a major character
2. a minor character

Narrator a nonparticipant (writing in the third person):
3. all-knowing (seeing into any of the characters)
4. seeing into one major character
5. seeing into one minor character
6. objective (not seeing into any characters)

[1] Some theorists reserve the term *narrator* for a character who tells a story in the first person. We use it in a wider sense: to mean a recording consciousness that an author creates, who may or may not be a participant in the events of the story. In the view of Wayne C. Booth, the term *narrator* can be dispensed with in dealing with a rigorously impersonal "fly on the wall" story, containing no editorializing and confined to the presentation of surfaces: "In Hemingway's 'The Killers,' for example, there is no narrator other than the implicit second self that Hemingway creates as he writes" (*The Rhetoric of Fiction* [Chicago: University of Chicago Press, 1961], p. 151).

[2] Another relationship between the author and the story will be discussed in Chapter Four, "Tone and Style."

When the narrator is cast as a **participant** in the events of the story, he or she is a dramatized character who says "I." Such a narrator may be the protagonist (Huck Finn) or may be an **observer,** a minor character standing a little to one side, watching a story unfold that mainly concerns someone else.

A narrator who remains a **nonparticipant** does not appear in the story as a character. Viewing the characters, perhaps seeing into the minds of one or more of them, such a narrator refers to them as "he," "she," or "they." When **all-knowing** (or **omniscient**), the narrator sees into the minds of all (or some) characters, moving when necessary from one to another. This is the point of view in "Godfather Death," whose narrator knows the feelings and motives of the father, of the doctor, and even of Death himself. In that he adds an occasional comment or opinion, this narrator may be said also to show **editorial omniscience** (as we can tell from his disapproving remark that the doctor "ought to have remembered" and his observation that the father did not understand "how wisely God shares out wealth and poverty"). A narrator who shows **impartial omniscience** presents the thoughts and actions of the characters, but does not judge them or comment on them.

When a nonparticipating narrator sees events through the eyes of a single character, whether a major character or a minor one, the resulting point of view is sometimes called **limited omniscience** or **selective omniscience.** The author, of course, selects which character to see through; the omniscience is his and not the narrator's. In William Faulkner's "Barn Burning" (Chapter Four), the narrator is almost entirely confined to knowing the thoughts and perceptions of a boy, the central character. Here is another example. Early in his novel *Madame Bovary*, Gustave Flaubert tells of the first time a young country doctor, Charles Bovary, meets Emma, the woman later to become his wife. The doctor has been summoned late at night to set the broken leg of a farmer, Emma's father.

> A young woman wearing a blue merino dress with three flounces came to the door of the house to greet Monsieur Bovary, and she ushered him into the kitchen, where a big open fire was blazing. Around its edges the farm hands' breakfast was bubbling in small pots of assorted sizes. Damp clothes were drying inside the vast chimney-opening. The fire shovel, the tongs, and the nose of the bellows, all of colossal proportions, shone like polished steel; and along the walls hung a lavish array of kitchen utensils, glimmering in the bright light of the fire and in the first rays of the sun that were now beginning to come in through the window-panes.
>
> Charles went upstairs to see the patient. He found him in bed, sweating under blankets, his nightcap lying where he had flung it. He was a stocky little man of fifty, fair-skinned, blue-eyed, bald in front and wearing earrings. On a chair beside him was a big decanter of brandy:

he had been pouring himself drinks to keep up his courage. But as soon as he saw the doctor he dropped his bluster, and instead of cursing as he had been doing for the past twelve hours he began to groan weakly.

The fracture was a simple one, without complications of any kind. Charles couldn't have wished for anything easier. Then he recalled his teachers' bedside manner in accident cases, and proceeded to cheer up his patient with all kinds of facetious remarks — a truly surgical attention, like the oiling of a scalpel. For splints, they sent someone to bring a bundle of laths from the carriage shed. Charles selected one, cut it into lengths and smoothed it down with a piece of broken window glass, while the maidservant tore sheets for bandages and Mademoiselle Emma tried to sew some pads. She was a long time finding her workbox, and her father showed his impatience. She made no reply; but as she sewed she kept pricking her fingers and raising them to her mouth to suck.

Charles was surprised by the whiteness of her fingernails. They were almond-shaped, tapering, as polished and shining as Dieppe ivories. Her hands, however, were not pretty — not pale enough, perhaps, a little rough at the knuckles; and they were too long, without softness of line. The finest thing about her was her eyes. They were brown, but seemed black under the long eyelashes; and she had an open gaze that met yours with fearless candor.[3]

In this famous scene, Charles Bovary is beholding people and objects in a natural sequence. On first meeting Emma, he notices only her dress, as though less interested in the woman who opens the door than in passing through to the warm fire. Concerned with pads for his patient's splint, the doctor observes just the hands of the woman sewing them. Obliged to wait for the splints, he then has the leisure to notice her face, her remarkable eyes. (By the way, note the effect of the word *yours* in the last sentence of the passage. It is as if the reader, seeing through the doctor's eyes, suddenly became one with him.) Who is the narrator? Not Charles Bovary, nor Gustave Flaubert, but someone able to enter the minds of others — here limited to knowing the thoughts and perceptions of a single character.

In the **objective** point of view, the narrator does not enter the mind of any character but describes events from the outside. Telling us what people say and how their faces look, he leaves us to infer their thoughts and feelings. So inconspicuous is the narrator that this point of view has been called "the fly on the wall." This assumes the existence of a fly with a highly discriminating gaze, who knows which details to look for to communicate the deepest meaning. Some critics would say that in the objective point of view, the narrator disappears altogether. Consider this passage by a writer famous for remaining objective, Dashiell Hammett, in his mystery novel *The Maltese Falcon*, describing his private detective Sam Spade:

[3] *Madame Bovary,* translated by Francis Steegmuller (New York: Random House, 1957). Modern Library edition, pp. 16–17.

Spade's thick fingers made a cigarette with deliberate care, sifting a measured quantity of tan flakes down into curved paper, spreading the flakes so that they lay equal at the ends with a slight depression in the middle, thumbs rolling the paper's inner edge down and up under the outer edge as forefingers pressed it over, thumb and fingers sliding to the paper cylinder's ends to hold it even while tongue licked the flap, left forefinger and thumb pinching their ends while right forefinger and thumb smoothed the damp seam, right forefinger and thumb twisting their end and lifting the other to Spade's mouth.[4]

In Hammett's novel, this sentence comes at a moment of crisis: just after Spade has been roused from bed in the middle of the night by a phone call telling him that his partner has been murdered. Even in time of stress (we infer), Spade is deliberate, cool, efficient, and painstaking. Hammett refrains from applying all those adjectives to Spade; to do so would be to exercise editorial omniscience and to destroy the objective point of view.

Besides the common points of view just listed, uncommon points of view are possible. In *Flush*, a fictional biography of Elizabeth Barrett Browning, Virginia Woolf employs an unusual observer as narrator: the poet's pet cocker spaniel. In "The Circular Valley," a short story by Paul Bowles, a man and a woman are watched by a sinister spirit trying to take possession of them, and we see the human characters through the spirit's vague consciousness. The narrator, however, is human, and a nonparticipant.[5] Possible also, but seldom attempted, is a story written in the *second* person.[6]

The attitudes and opinions of the narrator are not necessarily those of the author; in fact, there may be a clear conflict between what we are told and what, apparently, we are supposed to believe. A story may be told by an **innocent narrator** or a **naive narrator,** a character who fails to understand all the implications of the story. One such innocent narrator (despite his sometimes shrewd perceptions) is Huckleberry Finn. Because Huck accepts without question the morality and lawfulness of slavery, he feels guilty about helping Jim, a runaway slave. But, far from condemning Huck for his defiance of the law — "All right, then, I'll *go* to hell," Huck tells himself, deciding against returning Jim to captivity — the author, and the reader along with him, silently applaud. Naive in the extreme is the narrator of one part of William Faulk-

---

[4] Chapter Two, "Death in the Fog," *The Maltese Falcon* (New York: Knopf, 1929).

[5] *The Delicate Prey and Other Stories*, second edition (New York: Ecco Press, 1972).

[6] "On a summer night as you were strolling down to your corner cigar store, a long black limousine purred up and stopped beside you, and a harsh, evil voice ordered, 'Get in.'" (From the beginning of a pulp magazine short story, "The House of Ecstasy," by Ralph Milne Farley.) But as Phil Stong remarked of the story, included in his anthology *The Other Worlds* (New York: W. Funk, 1941), the whole thing suffers from the very start if you lack a corner cigar store.

ner's novel *The Sound and the Fury*, the idiot Benjy, a grown man with the intellect of a child. In a story told by an **unreliable narrator,** the point of view is that of a person who, we perceive, is deceptive, self-deceptive, deluded, or deranged. As though seeking ways to be faithful to uncertainty, contemporary writers have been particularly fond of unreliable narrators.

Virginia Woolf compared life to "a luminous halo, a semi-transparent envelope surrounding us from the beginning of consciousness to the end."[7] To capture such a reality, modern writers of fiction have employed many strategies. One is the method of writing called **stream of consciousness,** from a phrase coined by psychologist William James to describe the procession of thoughts passing through the mind. In fiction, stream of consciousness is a kind of selective omniscience: the presentation of thoughts and sense impressions in a lifelike fashion — not in a sequence arranged by logic, but mingled randomly. When in his novel *Ulysses* James Joyce takes us into the mind of Leopold Bloom, an ordinary Dublin mind well-stocked with trivia and fragments of odd learning, the reader may have an impression not of a smoothly flowing stream but of an ocean of miscellaneous things, all crowded and jostling.

> As he set foot on O'Connell bridge a puffball of smoke plumed up from the parapet. Brewery barge with export stout. England. Sea air sours it, I heard. Be interesting some day to get a pass through Hancock to see the brewery. Regular world in itself. Vats of porter, wonderful. Rats get in too. Drink themselves bloated as big as a collie floating.[8]

Perceptions — such as the smoke from the brewery barge — trigger Bloom's reflections. A moment later, as he casts a crumpled paper ball off the bridge, he recalls a bit of science he learned in school, the rate of speed of a falling body: "thirty-two feet per sec."

Stream of consciousness writing usually occurs in relatively short passages, but in *Ulysses* Joyce employs it extensively. Similar in method, an **interior monologue** is an extended presentation of a character's thoughts, not in the seemingly helter-skelter order of a stream of consciousness, but in an arrangement as if the character were speaking out loud to himself, for us to overhear. A famous interior monologue comes at the end of *Ulysses* when Joyce gives us the rambling memories and reflections of earth-mother Molly Bloom.

Every point of view has limitations. Even **total omniscience,** a knowledge of the minds of all of the characters, has its disadvantages. Such a point of view requires high skill to manage, without the story-teller's losing his way in a multitude of different perspectives. In fact, there are evident advantages in having a narrator not know everything.

[7] "Modern Fiction," in *Collected Essays* (New York: Harcourt Brace Jovanovich, 1967).
[8] *Ulysses* (New York: Random House, 1934). Modern Library edition, p. 150.

We are accustomed to seeing the world through one pair of eyes, to having truths only gradually occur to us. Henry James, whose theory and practice of fiction have been influential, held that an excellent way to tell a story was through the fine but bewildered mind of an observer. "It seems probable," James wrote, "that if we were never bewildered there would never be a story to tell about us; we should partake of the superior nature of the all-knowing immortals whose annals are dreadfully dull so long as flurried humans are not, for the positive relief of bored Olympians, mixed up with them."[9]

By using a particular point of view, an author may artfully withhold information, if need be, rather than immediately present it to us. If, for instance, the suspense in a story depends upon our not knowing until the end that the protagonist is a secret agent, the author would be ill advised to tell the story from the protagonist's point of view. If a character acts as the narrator, the author must make sure that the character possesses (or can obtain) enough information to tell the story adequately. Clearly, the author makes a fundamental decision in selecting, from many possibilities, a story's point of view. What we readers admire, if the story is effective, is not only skill in execution, but also powers of choice.

Here is a short story memorable for many reasons, among them for its point of view. The locale, by the way, is Dublin, Ireland, and the time is late in the nineteenth century. "Araby" is one story from a collection entitled *Dubliners*, James Joyce's searching examination of lives in his native city.

James Joyce (1882–1941)

ARABY   (1905)

North Richmond Street, being blind°, was a quiet street except at the hour when the Christian Brothers' School set the boys free. An uninhabited house of two stories stood at the blind end, detached from its neighbors in a square ground. The other houses of the street, conscious of decent lives within them, gazed at one another with brown imperturbable faces.

The former tenant of our house, a priest, had died in the back drawing-room. Air, musty from having long been enclosed, hung in all the rooms, and the waste room behind the kitchen was littered with old useless papers. Among these I found a few paper-covered books, the pages of which were curled and damp: *The Abbot,* by Walter Scott, *The Devout Communicant* and *The Memoirs of*

---

[9] Preface to *The Princess Casamassima*, reprinted in *The Art of the Novel*, edited by R. P. Blackmur (New York: Scribner's, 1934).
being blind: being a dead-end street.

Vidocq°. I liked the last best because its leaves were yellow. The wild garden behind the house contained a central apple-tree and a few straggling bushes under one of which I found the late tenant's rusty bicycle-pump. He had been a very charitable priest; in his will he had left all his money to institutions and the furniture of his house to his sister.

When the short days of winter came dusk fell before we had well eaten our dinners. When we met in the street the houses had grown sombre. The space of sky above us was the color of ever-changing violet and towards it the lamps of the street lifted their feeble lanterns. The cold air stung us and we played till our bodies glowed. Our shouts echoed in the silent street. The career of our play brought us through the dark muddy lanes behind the houses where we ran the gantlet of the rough tribes from the cottages, to the back doors of the dark dripping gardens where odors arose from the ashpits, to the dark odorous stables where a coachman smoothed and combed the horse or shook music from the buckled harness. When we returned to the street light from the kitchen windows had filled the areas. If my uncle was seen turning the corner we hid in the shadow until we had seen him safely housed. Or if Mangan's sister° came out on the doorstep to call her brother in to his tea we watched her from our shadow peer up and down the street. We waited to see whether she would remain or go in and, if she remained, we left our shadow and walked up to Mangan's steps resignedly. She was waiting for us, her figure defined by the light from the half-opened door. Her brother always teased her before he obeyed and I stood by the railings looking at her. Her dress swung as she moved her body and the soft rope of her hair tossed from side to side.

Every morning I lay on the floor in the front parlor watching her door. The blind was pulled down within an inch of the sash so that I could not be seen. When she came out on the doorstep my heart leaped. I ran to the hall, seized my books and followed her. I kept her brown figure always in my eye and, when we came near the point at which our ways diverged, I quickened my pace and passed her. This happened morning after morning. I had never spoken to her, except for a few casual words, and yet her name was like a summons to all my foolish blood.

Her image accompanied me even in places the most hostile to romance. On Saturday evenings when my aunt went marketing I had to go to carry some of the parcels. We walked through the flaring streets, jostled by drunken men and bargaining women, amid the curses of laborers, the shrill litanies of shopboys who stood on guard by the barrels of pigs' cheeks, the nasal chanting of street singers, who sang a *come-all-you* about O'Donovan Rossa°, or a ballad about the troubles in our native land. These noises converged in a single sensa-

The Abbot . . . Vidocq: a popular historical romance (1820); a book of pious meditations by an eighteenth-century English Franciscan, Pacificus Baker; and the autobiography of François-Jules Vidocq (1775–1857), a criminal who later turned detective.

Mangan's sister: an actual young woman in this story, but the phrase recalls Irish poet James Clarence Mangan (1803–1849) and his best-known poem, "Dark Rosaleen," which personifies Ireland as a beautiful woman for whom the poet yearns.

come-all-you about O'Donovan Rossa: The street singers earned their living by singing timely songs that usually began, "Come all you gallant Irishmen / And listen to my song." Their subject, also called Dynamite Rossa, was a popular hero jailed by the British for advocating violent rebellion.

tion of life for me: I imagined that I bore my chalice safely through the throng of foes. Her name sprang to my lips at moments in strange prayers and praises which I myself did not understand. My eyes were often full of tears (I could not tell why) and at times a flood from my heart seemed to pour itself out into my bosom. I thought little of the future. I did not know whether I would ever speak to her or not or, if I spoke to her, how I could tell her of my confused adoration. But my body was like a harp and her words and gestures were like fingers running upon the wires.

One evening I went into the back drawing-room in which the priest had died. It was a dark rainy evening and there was no sound in the house. Through one of the broken panes I heard the rain impinge upon the earth, the fine incessant needles of water playing in the sodden beds. Some distant lamp or lighted window gleamed below me. I was thankful that I could see so little. All my senses seemed to desire to veil themselves and, feeling that I was about to slip from them, I pressed the palms of my hands together until they trembled, murmuring: *O love! O love!* many times.

— At last she spoke to me. When she addressed the first words to me I was so confused that I did not know what to answer. She asked me was I going to *Araby*. I forget whether I answered yes or no. It would be a splendid bazaar, she said; she would love to go.

— And why can't you? I asked.

While she spoke she turned a silver bracelet round and round her wrist. She could not go, she said, because there would be a retreat that week in her convent°. Her brother and two other boys were fighting for their caps and I was alone at the railings. She held one of the spikes, bowing her head towards me. The light from the lamp opposite our door caught the white curve of her neck, lit up her hair that rested there and, falling, lit up the hand upon the railing. It fell over one side of her dress and caught the white border of a petticoat, just visible as she stood at ease.

— It's well for you, she said.

— If I go, I said, I will bring you something.

What innumerable follies laid waste my waking and sleeping thoughts after that evening! I wished to annihilate the tedious intervening days. I chafed against the work of school. At night in my bedroom and by day in the classroom her image came between me and the page I strove to read. The syllables of the word *Araby* were called to me through the silence in which my soul luxuriated and cast an Eastern enchantment over me. I asked for leave to go to the bazaar on Saturday night. My aunt was surprised and hoped it was not some Freemason° affair. I answered few questions in class. I watched my master's face pass from amiability to sternness; he hoped I was not beginning to idle. I could not call my wandering thoughts together. I had hardly any patience with the serious work of life which, now that it stood between me and my desire, seemed to me child's play, ugly monotonous child's play.

a retreat . . . in her convent: a week devoted to religious observances more intense than usual, at the convent school Miss Mangan attends; probably she will have to listen to a series of Hellfire sermons.

Freemason: Catholics in Ireland viewed the Masonic order as a Protestant conspiracy against them.

On Saturday morning I reminded my uncle that I wished to go to the bazaar in the evening. He was fussing at the hall-stand, looking for the hat-brush, and answered me curtly:

— Yes, boy, I know.

As he was in the hall I could not go into the front parlor and lie at the window. I left the house in bad humor and walked slowly towards the school. The air was pitilessly raw and already my heart misgave me.

When I came home to dinner my uncle had not yet been home. Still it was early. I sat staring at the clock for some time and, when its ticking began to irritate me, I left the room. I mounted the staircase and gained the upper part of the house. The high cold empty gloomy rooms liberated me and I went from room to room singing. From the front window I saw my companions playing below in the street. Their cries reached me weakened and indistinct and, leaning my forehead against the cool glass, I looked over at the dark house where she lived. I may have stood there for an hour, seeing nothing but the brown-clad figure cast by my imagination, touched discreetly by the lamplight at the curved neck, at the hand upon the railings and at the border below the dress.

When I came downstairs again I found Mrs. Mercer sitting at the fire. She was an old garrulous woman, a pawnbroker's widow, who collected used stamps for some pious purpose. I had to endure the gossip of the tea-table. The meal was prolonged beyond an hour and still my uncle did not come. Mrs. Mercer stood up to go: she was sorry she couldn't wait any longer, but it was after eight o'clock and she did not like to be out late, as the night air was bad for her. When she had gone I began to walk up and down the room, clenching my fists. My aunt said:

— I'm afraid you may put off your bazaar for this night of Our Lord.

At nine o'clock I heard my uncle's latchkey in the halldoor. I heard him talking to himself and heard the hall-stand rocking when it had received the weight of his overcoat. I could interpret these signs. When he was midway through his dinner I asked him to give me the money to go to the bazaar. He had forgotten.

— The people are in bed and after their first sleep now, he said.

I did not smile. My aunt said to him energetically:

— Can't you give him the money and let him go? You've kept him late enough as it is.

My uncle said he was very sorry he had forgotten. He said he believed in the old saying: *All work and no play makes Jack a dull boy.* He asked me where I was going and, when I had told him a second time he asked me did I know *The Arab's Farewell to his Steed*°. When I left the kitchen he was about to recite the opening lines of the piece to my aunt.

I held a florin tightly in my hand as I strode down Buckingham Street towards the station. The sight of the streets thronged with buyers and glaring with gas recalled to me the purpose of my journey. I took my seat in a third-class carriage of a deserted train. After an intolerable delay the train moved out of the station slowly. It crept onward among ruinous houses and over the twin-

---

The Arab's Farewell to His Steed: The uncle garbles the title of Victorian poet Caroline Norton's "The Arab to His Favorite Steed," a sentimental ballad about an Arab who sells his beloved horse, then regrets the loss and flings away the gold he has received. Note the echo of "Araby" in the song title.

kling river. At Westland Row Station a crowd of people pressed to the carriage doors; but the porters moved them back, saying that it was a special train for the bazaar. I remained alone in the bare carriage. In a few minutes the train drew up beside an improvised wooden platform. I passed out on to the road and saw by the lighted dial of a clock that it was ten minutes to ten. In front of me was a large building which displayed the magical name.

I could not find any sixpenny entrance and, fearing that the bazaar would be closed, I passed in quickly through a turnstile, handing a shilling to a weary-looking man. I found myself in a big hall girdled at half its height by a gallery. Nearly all the stalls were closed and the greater part of the hall was in darkness. I recognized a silence like that which pervades a church after a service. I walked into the center of the bazaar timidly. A few people were gathered about the stalls which were still open. Before a curtain, over which the words *Café Chantant°* were written in colored lamps, two men were counting money on a salver°. I listened to the fall of the coins.

Remembering with difficulty why I had come I went over to one of the stalls and examined porcelain vases and flowered tea-sets. At the door of the stall a young lady was talking and laughing with two young gentlemen. I remarked their English accents and listened vaguely to their conversation.

— O, I never said such a thing!

— O, but you did!

— O, but I didn't!

— Didn't she say that?

— Yes. I heard her.

— O, there's a . . . fib!

Observing me the young lady came over and asked me did I wish to buy anything. The tone of her voice was not encouraging; she seemed to have spoken to me out of a sense of duty. I looked humbly at the great jars that stood like eastern guards at either side of the dark entrance to the stall and murmured:

— No, thank you.

The young lady changed the position of one of the vases and went back to the two young men. They began to talk of the same subject. Once or twice the young lady glanced at me over her shoulder.

I lingered before her stall, though I knew my stay was useless, to make my interest in her wares seem the more real. Then I turned away slowly and walked down the middle of the bazaar. I allowed the two pennies to fall against the sixpence in my pocket. I heard a voice call from one end of the gallery that the light was out. The upper part of the hall was now completely dark.

Gazing up into the darkness I saw myself as a creature driven and derided by vanity; and my eyes burned with anguish and anger.

QUESTIONS

1. From what point of view does James Joyce tell this story? Does the narrator of "Araby" seem a boy — a naive or innocent narrator — or a mature man looking back through a boy's eyes?
2. Besides the boy, who is the other major character in the story? How do we

Café Chantant: name for a Paris nightspot featuring topical songs.
salver: a tray like that used in serving Holy Communion.

know that the boy's view of this character is not exactly identical with the author's view? (It may help to look closely at some of the narrator's descriptions of the other major character, and of his own feelings.)

3. At what other moments in the story does the boy romanticize, or project an air of enchantment upon the commonplace?

4. At what moments in the story — and in what particular details — does the boy confront reality? Exactly what, in his visit to the bazaar, does he find so bitterly disillusioning? (Does his confrontation with reality take place only at the end?)

5. Why does the story seem best told by a major character who participates in its events? Imagine "Araby" told from some other point of view. Why would the story probably become less moving and less effective?

William Faulkner (1897–1962)

A Rose for Emily   1931

I

When Miss Emily Grierson died, our whole town went to her funeral: the men through a sort of respectful affection for a fallen monument, the women mostly out of curiosity to see the inside of her house, which no one save an old man-servant — a combined gardener and cook — had seen in at least ten years.

It was a big, squarish frame house that had once been white, decorated with cupolas and spires and scrolled balconies in the heavily lightsome style of the seventies, set on what had once been our most select street. But garages and cotton gins had encroached and obliterated even the august names of that neighborhood; only Miss Emily's house was left, lifting its stubborn and coquettish decay above the cotton wagons and the gasoline pumps — an eyesore among eyesores. And now Miss Emily had gone to join the representatives of those august names where they lay in the cedar-bemused cemetery among the ranked and anonymous graves of Union and Confederate soldiers who fell at the battle of Jefferson.

Alive, Miss Emily had been a tradition, a duty, and a care; a sort of hereditary obligation upon the town, dating from that day in 1894 when Colonel Sartoris, the mayor — he who fathered the edict that no Negro woman should appear on the streets without an apron — remitted her taxes, the dispensation dating from the death of her father on into perpetuity. Not that Miss Emily would have accepted charity. Colonel Sartoris invented an involved tale to the effect that Miss Emily's father had loaned money to the town, which the town, as a matter of business, preferred this way of repaying. Only a man of Colonel Sartoris' generation and thought could have invented it, and only a woman could have believed it.

When the next generation, with its more modern ideas, became mayors and aldermen, this arrangement created some little dissatisfaction. On the first of the year they mailed her a tax notice. February came, and there was no reply. They wrote her a formal letter, asking her to call at the sheriff's office at her convenience. A week later the mayor wrote her himself, offering to call or to send his car for her, and received in reply a note on paper of an archaic shape, in a thin, flowing calligraphy in faded ink, to the effect that she no longer went out at all. The tax notice was also enclosed, without comment.

They called a special meeting of the Board of Aldermen. A deputation waited upon her, knocked at the door through which no visitor had passed since she ceased giving china-painting lessons eight or ten years earlier. They were admitted by the old Negro into a dim hall from which a stairway mounted into still more shadow. It smelled of dust and disuse — a close, dank smell. The Negro led them into the parlor. It was furnished in heavy, leather-covered furniture. When the Negro opened the blinds of one window, they could see that the leather was cracked; and when they sat down, a faint dust rose sluggishly about their thighs, spinning with slow motes in the single sun-ray. On a tarnished gilt easel before the fireplace stood a crayon portrait of Miss Emily's father.

They rose when she entered — a small, fat woman in black, with a thin gold chain descending to her waist and vanishing into her belt, leaning on an ebony cane with a tarnished gold head. Her skeleton was small and spare; perhaps that was why what would have been merely plumpness in another was obesity in her. She looked bloated, like a body long submerged in motionless water, and of that pallid hue. Her eyes, lost in the fatty ridges of her face, looked like two small pieces of coal pressed into a lump of dough as they moved from one face to another while the visitors stated their errand.

She did not ask them to sit. She just stood in the door and listened quietly until the spokesman came to a stumbling halt. Then they could hear the invisible watch ticking at the end of the gold chain.

Her voice was dry and cold. "I have no taxes in Jefferson. Colonel Sartoris explained it to me. Perhaps one of you can gain access to the city records and satisfy yourselves."

"But we have. We are the city authorities, Miss Emily. Didn't you get a notice from the sheriff, signed by him?"

"I received a paper, yes," Miss Emily said. "Perhaps he considers himself the sheriff . . . I have no taxes in Jefferson."

"But there is nothing on the books to show that, you see. We must go by the — "

"See Colonel Sartoris. I have no taxes in Jefferson."

"But, Miss Emily — "

"See Colonel Sartoris." (Colonel Sartoris had been dead almost ten years.) "I have no taxes in Jefferson. Tobe!" The Negro appeared. "Show these gentlemen out."

II

So she vanquished them, horse and foot, just as she had vanquished their fathers thirty years before about the smell. That was two years after her father's death and a short time after her sweetheart — the one we believed would marry her — had deserted her. After her father's death she went out very little; after her sweetheart went away, people hardly saw her at all. A few of the ladies had the temerity to call, but were not received, and the only sign of life about the place was the Negro man — a young man then — going in and out with a market basket.

"Just as if a man — any man — could keep a kitchen properly," the ladies said; so they were not surprised when the smell developed. It was another link between the gross, teeming world and the high and mighty Griersons.

A neighbor, a woman, complained to the mayor, Judge Stevens, eighty years old.

"But what will you have me do about it, madam?" he said.

"Why, send her word to stop it," the woman said. "Isn't there a law?"

"I'm sure that won't be necessary," Judge Stevens said. "It's probably just a snake or a rat that nigger of hers killed in the yard. I'll speak to him about it."

The next day he received two more complaints, one from a man who came in diffident deprecation. "We really must do something about it, Judge. I'd be the last one in the world to bother Miss Emily, but we've got to do something." That night the Board of Aldermen met — three graybeards and one younger man, a member of the rising generation.

"It's simple enough," he said. "Send her word to have her place cleaned up. Give her a certain time to do it in, and if she don't . . ."

"Dammit, sir," Judge Stevens said, "will you accuse a lady to her face of smelling bad?"

So the next night, after midnight, four men crossed Miss Emily's lawn and slunk about the house like burglars, sniffing along the base of the brickwork and at the cellar openings while one of them performed a regular sowing motion with his hand out of a sack slung from his shoulder. They broke open the cellar door and sprinkled lime there, and in all the outbuildings. As they recrossed the lawn, a window that had been dark was lighted and Miss Emily sat in it, the light behind her, and her upright torso motionless as that of an idol. They crept quietly across the lawn and into the shadow of the locusts that lined the street. After a week or two the smell went away.

That was when people had begun to feel really sorry for her. People in our town, remembering how old lady Wyatt, her great-aunt, had gone completely crazy at last, believed that the Griersons held themselves a little too high for what they really were. None of the young men were quite good enough for Miss Emily and such. We had long thought of them as a tableau, Miss Emily a slender figure in white in the background, her father a spraddled silhouette in the foreground, his back to her and clutching a horsewhip, the two of them framed by the back-flung front door. So when she got to be thirty and was still single, we were not pleased exactly, but vindicated; even with insanity in the family she wouldn't have turned down all of her chances if they had really materialized.

When her father died, it got about that the house was all that was left to her; and in a way, people were glad. At last they could pity Miss Emily. Being left alone, and a pauper, she had become humanized. Now she too would know the old thrill and the old despair of a penny more or less.

The day after his death all the ladies prepared to call at the house and offer condolence and aid, as is our custom. Miss Emily met them at the door, dressed as usual and with no trace of grief on her face. She told them that her father was not dead. She did that for three days, with the ministers calling on her, and the doctors, trying to persuade her to let them dispose of the body. Just as they were about to resort to law and force, she broke down, and they buried her father quickly.

We did not say she was crazy then. We believed she had to do that. We remembered all the young men her father had driven away, and we knew that with nothing left, she would have to cling to that which had robbed her, as people will.

III

She was sick for a long time. When we saw her again, her hair was cut short, making her look like a girl, with a vague resemblance to those angels in colored church windows — sort of tragic and serene.

The town had just let the contracts for paving the sidewalks, and in the summer after her father's death they began the work. The construction company came with niggers and mules and machinery, and a foreman named Homer Barron, a Yankee — a big, dark, ready man, with a big voice and eyes lighter than his face. The little boys would follow in groups to hear him cuss the niggers, and the niggers singing in time to the rise and fall of picks. Pretty soon he knew everybody in town. Whenever you heard a lot of laughing anywhere about the square, Homer Barron would be in the center of the group. Presently we began to see him and Miss Emily on Sunday afternoons driving in the yellow-wheeled buggy and the matched team of bays from the livery stable.

At first we were glad that Miss Emily would have an interest, because the ladies all said, "Of course a Grierson would not think seriously of a Northerner, a day laborer." But there were still others, older people, who said that even grief could not cause a real lady to forget *noblesse oblige*° — without calling it *noblesse oblige*. They just said, "Poor Emily. Her kinsfolk should come to her." She had some kin in Alabama; but years ago her father had fallen out with them over the estate of old lady Wyatt, the crazy woman, and there was no communication between the two families. They had not even been represented at the funeral.

And as soon as the old people said, "Poor Emily," the whispering began. "Do you suppose it's really so?" they said to one another. "Of course it is. What else could . . ." This behind their hands; rustling of craned silk and satin behind jalousies closed upon the sun of Sunday afternoon as the thin, swift clop-clop-clop of the matched team passed: "Poor Emily."

She carried her head high enough — even when we believed that she was fallen. It was as if she demanded more than ever the recognition of her dignity as the last Grierson; as if it had wanted that touch of earthiness to reaffirm her imperviousness. Like when she bought the rat poison, the arsenic. That was over a year after they had begun to say "Poor Emily," and while the two female cousins were visiting her.

"I want some poison," she said to the druggist. She was over thirty then, still a slight woman, though thinner than usual, with cold, haughty black eyes in a face the flesh of which was strained across the temples and about the eye-sockets as you imagine a lighthouse-keeper's face ought to look. "I want some poison," she said.

"Yes, Miss Emily. What kind? For rats and such? I'd recom — "

"I want the best you have. I don't care what kind."

noblesse oblige: the obligation of a member of the nobility to behave with honor and dignity.

The druggist named several. "They'll kill anything up to an elephant. But what you want is — "

"Arsenic," Miss Emily said. "Is that a good one?"

"Is . . . arsenic? Yes, ma'am. But what you want — "

"I want arsenic."

The druggist looked down at her. She looked back at him, erect, her face like a strained flag. "Why, of course," the druggist said. "If that's what you want. But the law requires you to tell what you are going to use it for."

Miss Emily just stared at him, her head tilted back in order to look him eye for eye, until he looked away and went and got the arsenic and wrapped it up. The Negro delivery boy brought her the package; the druggist didn't come back. When she opened the package at home there was written on the box, under the skull and bones: "For rats."

IV

So the next day we all said, "She will kill herself"; and we said it would be the best thing. When she had first begun to be seen with Homer Barron, we had said, "She will marry him." Then we said, "She will persuade him yet," because Homer himself had remarked — he liked men, and it was known that he drank with the younger men in the Elks' Club — that he was not a marrying man. Later we said, "Poor Emily" behind the jalousies as they passed on Sunday afternoon in the glittering buggy, Miss Emily with her head high and Homer Barron with his hat cocked and a cigar in his teeth, reins and whip in a yellow glove.

Then some of the ladies began to say that it was a disgrace to the town and a bad example to the young people. The men did not want to interfere, but at last the ladies forced the Baptist minister — Miss Emily's people were Episcopal — to call upon her. He would never divulge what happened during that interview, but he refused to go back again. The next Sunday they again drove about the streets, and the following day the minister's wife wrote to Miss Emily's relations in Alabama.

So she had blood-kin under her roof again and we sat back to watch developments. At first nothing happened. Then we were sure that they were to be married. We learned that Miss Emily had been to the jeweler's and ordered a man's toilet set in silver, with the letters H. B. on each piece. Two days later we learned that she had bought a complete outfit of men's clothing, including a nightshirt, and we said, "They are married." We were really glad. We were glad because the two female cousins were even more Grierson than Miss Emily had ever been.

So we were not surprised when Homer Barron — the streets had been finished some time since — was gone. We were a little disappointed that there was not a public blowing-off, but we believed that he had gone on to prepare for Miss Emily's coming, or to give her a chance to get rid of the cousins. (By that time it was a cabal, and we were all Miss Emily's allies to help circumvent the cousins.) Sure enough, after another week they departed. And, as we had expected all along, within three days Homer Barron was back in town. A neighbor saw the Negro man admit him at the kitchen door at dusk one evening.

And that was the last we saw of Homer Barron. And of Miss Emily for some time. The Negro man went in and out with the market basket, but the front door remained closed. Now and then we would see her at a window for a moment, as the men did that night when they sprinkled the lime, but for almost six months she did not appear on the streets. Then we knew that this was to be expected too; as if that quality of her father which had thwarted her woman's life so many times had been too virulent and too furious to die.

When we next saw Miss Emily, she had grown fat and her hair was turning gray. During the next few years it grew grayer and grayer until it attained an even pepper-and-salt iron-gray, when it ceased turning. Up to the day of her death at seventy-four it was still that vigorous iron-gray, like the hair of an active man.

From that time on her front door remained closed, save for a period of six or seven years, when she was about forty, during which she gave lessons in china-painting. She fitted up a studio in one of the downstairs rooms, where the daughters and granddaughters of Colonel Sartoris' contemporaries were sent to her with the same regularity and in the same spirit that they were sent to church on Sundays with a twenty-five-cent piece for the collection plate. Meanwhile her taxes had been remitted.

Then the newer generation became the backbone and the spirit of the town, and the painting pupils grew up and fell away and did not send their children to her with boxes of color and tedious brushes and pictures cut from the ladies' magazines. The front door closed upon the last one and remained closed for good. When the town got free postal delivery, Miss Emily alone refused to let them fasten the metal numbers above her door and attach a mailbox to it. She would not listen to them.

Daily, monthly, yearly we watched the Negro grow grayer and more stooped, going in and out with the market basket. Each December we sent her a tax notice, which would be returned by the post office a week later, unclaimed. Now and then we would see her in one of the downstairs windows — she had evidently shut up the top floor of the house — like the carven torso of an idol in a niche, looking or not looking at us, we could never tell which. Thus she passed from generation to generation — dear, inescapable, impervious, tranquil, and perverse.

And so she died. Fell ill in the house filled with dust and shadows, with only a doddering Negro man to wait on her. We did not even know she was sick; we had long since given up trying to get any information from the Negro. He talked to no one, probably not even to her, for his voice had grown harsh and rusty, as if from disuse.

She died in one of the downstairs rooms, in a heavy walnut bed with a curtain, her gray head propped on a pillow yellow and moldy with age and lack of sunlight.

V

The Negro met the first of the ladies at the front door and let them in, with their hushed, sibilant voices and their quick, curious glances, and then he disappeared. He walked right through the house and out the back and was not seen again.

The two female cousins came at once. They held the funeral on the second day, with the town coming to look at Miss Emily beneath a mass of bought flowers, with the crayon face of her father musing profoundly above the bier and the ladies sibilant and macabre; and the very old men — some in their brushed Confederate uniforms — on the porch and the lawn, talking of Miss Emily as if she had been a contemporary of theirs, believing that they had danced with her and courted her perhaps, confusing time with its mathematical progression, as the old do, to whom all the past is not a diminishing road but, instead, a huge meadow which no winter ever quite touches, divided from them now by the narrow bottle-neck of the most recent decade of years.

Already we knew that there was one room in that region above stairs which no one had seen in forty years, and which would have to be forced. They waited until Miss Emily was decently in the ground before they opened it.

The violence of breaking down the door seemed to fill this room with pervading dust. A thin, acrid pall as of the tomb seemed to lie everywhere upon this room decked and furnished as for a bridal: upon the valance curtains of faded rose color, upon the rose-shaded lights, upon the dressing table, upon the delicate array of crystal and the man's toilet things backed with tarnished silver, silver so tarnished that the monogram was obscured. Among them lay collar and tie, as if they had just been removed, which, lifted, left upon the surface a pale crescent in the dust. Upon a chair hung the suit, carefully folded; beneath it the two mute shoes and the discarded socks.

The man himself lay in the bed.

For a long while we just stood there, looking down at the profound and fleshless grin. The body had apparently once lain in the attitude of an embrace, but now the long sleep that outlasts love, that conquers even the grimace of love, had cuckolded him. What was left of him, rotted beneath what was left of the nightshirt, had become inextricable from the bed in which he lay; and upon him and upon the pillow beside him lay that even coating of the patient and biding dust.

Then we noticed that in the second pillow was the identation of a head. One of us lifted something from it, and leaning forward, that faint and invisible dust dry and acrid in the nostrils, we saw a long strand of iron-gray hair.

QUESTIONS

1. What is meaningful in the final detail that the strand of hair on the second pillow is *iron-gray?*
2. Who is the unnamed narrator? For whom does he profess to be speaking?
3. Why does "A Rose for Emily" seem better told from his point of view than if it were told (like James Joyce's "Araby") from the point of view of the main character?
4. What foreshadowings of the discovery of the body of Homer Barron are we given earlier in the story? Share your experience in reading "A Rose for Emily": did the foreshadowings give away the ending for you? Did they heighten your interest?
5. What contrasts does the narrator draw between changing reality and Emily's refusal or inability to recognize change?
6. How do the character and background of Emily Grierson differ from those of Homer Barron? What general observations about the society that Faulkner depicts can be made from his portraits of these two characters and from his account of life in this one Mississippi town?

7. Does the story seem to you totally grim, or do you find any humor in it?
8. What do you infer to be the author's attitude toward Emily Grierson? Is she simply a murderous madwoman? Why do you suppose Faulkner calls his story "A Rose . . ."?

Doris Lessing (b. 1919)

A Woman on a Roof

point of view — 3rd person (voice)

Tom is major character

chronological order

1963

It was during the week of hot sun, that June.

Three men were at work on the roof, where the leads got so hot they had the idea of throwing water on to cool them. But the water steamed, then sizzled; and they made jokes about getting an egg from some woman in the flats under them, to poach it for their dinner. By two it was not possible to touch the guttering they were replacing, and they speculated about what workmen did in regularly hot countries. Perhaps they should borrow kitchen gloves with the egg? They were all a bit dizzy, not used to the heat; and they shed their coats and stood side by side squeezing themselves into a foot-wide patch of shade against a chimney, careful to keep their feet in the thick socks and boots out of the sun. There was a fine view across several acres of roofs. Not far off a man sat in a deck chair reading the newspapers. Then they saw her, between chimneys, about fifty yards away. She lay face down on a brown blanket. They could see the top part of her: black hair, a flushed solid back, arms spread out.

"She's stark naked," said Stanley, sounding annoyed.

Harry, the oldest, a man of about forty-five, said: "Looks like it."

Young Tom, seventeen, said nothing, but he was excited and grinning.

Stanley said: "Someone'll report her if she doesn't watch out."

"She thinks no one can see," said Tom, craning his head all ways to see more.

At this point the woman, still lying prone, brought her two hands up behind her shoulders with the ends of a scarf in them, tied it behind her back, and sat up. She wore a red scarf tied around her breasts and brief red bikini pants. This being the first day of the sun she was white, flushing red. She sat smoking, and did not look up when Stanley let out a wolf whistle. Harry said: "Small things amuse small minds," leading the way back to their part of the roof, but it was scorching. Harry said: "Wait, I'm going to rig up some shade," and disappeared down the skylight into the building. Now that he'd gone, Stanley and Tom went to the farthest point they could to peer at the woman. She had moved, and all they could see were two pink legs stretched on the blanket. They whistled and shouted but the legs did not move. Harry came back with a blanket and shouted: "Come on, then." He sounded irritated with them. They clambered back to him and he said to Stanley: "What about your missus?" Stanley was newly married, about three months. Stanley said, jeering: "What about my missus?" — preserving his independence. Tom said nothing, but his mind was full of the nearly naked woman. Harry slung the blanket, which he had borrowed from a friendly woman downstairs, from the stem of a television aerial to a row of chimney-pots. This shade fell across the piece of gutter they had to replace. But the shade kept moving, they had to adjust the blanket, and not much progress was made. At last some of the heat left the roof, and they worked fast, making up for lost time. First Stanley, then Tom, made a trip to the end of the roof to see the woman. "She's on her back," Stanley said, adding a jest which made Tom snicker, and the older man smile tolerantly. Tom's report was that she hadn't moved, but it was a lie. He wanted to keep what he had seen to himself: he had caught her in the act of rolling down the little red pants over her hips, till they were no more than a small triangle. She was on her back, fully visible, glistening with oil.

Next morning, as soon as they came up, they went to look. She was already there, face down, arms spread out, naked except for the little red pants. She had turned brown in the night. Yesterday she was a scarlet-and-white woman, today she was a brown woman. Stanley let out a whistle. She lifted her head, startled, as if she'd been asleep, and looked straight over at them. The sun was in her eyes, she blinked and stared, then she dropped her head again. At this gesture of indifference, they all three, Stanley, Tom and old Harry, let out whistles and yells. Harry was doing it in parody of the younger men, making fun of them, but he was also angry. They were all angry because of her utter indifference to the three men watching her.

"Bitch," said Stanley.

"She should ask us over," said Tom, snickering.

Harry recovered himself and reminded Stanley: "If she's married, her old man wouldn't like that."

"Christ," said Stanley virtuously, "if my wife lay about like that, for everyone to see, I'd soon stop her."

Harry said, smiling: "How do you know, perhaps she's sunning herself at this very moment?"

"Not a chance, not on our roof." The safety of his wife put Stanley into a good humor, and they went to work. But today it was hotter than yesterday; and several times one or the other suggested they should tell Matthew, the foreman, and ask to leave the roof until the heat wave was over. But they didn't. There was work to be done in the basement of the big block of flats, but up here they felt free, on a different level from ordinary humanity shut in the streets or the buildings. A lot more people came out on to the roofs that day, for an hour at midday. Some married couples sat side by side in deck chairs, the women's legs stockingless and scarlet, the men in vests with reddening shoulders.

The woman stayed on her blanket, turning herself over and over. She ignored them, no matter what they did. When Harry went off to fetch more screws, Stanley said: "Come on." Her roof belonged to a different system of roofs, separated from theirs at one point by about twenty feet. It meant a scrambling climb from one level to another, edging along parapets, clinging to chimneys, while their big boots slipped and slithered, but at last they stood on a small square projecting roof looking straight down at her, close. She sat smoking, reading a book. Tom thought she looked like a poster, or a magazine cover, with the blue sky behind her and her legs stretched out. Behind her a great crane at work on a new building in Oxford Street° swung its black arm across roofs in a great arc. Tom imagined himself at work on the crane, adjusting the arm to swing over and pick her up and swing her back across the sky to drop her near him.

Oxford Street: busy shopping street in central London.

They whistled. She looked up at them, cool and remote, then went on reading. Again, they were furious. Or, rather, Stanley was. His sun-heated face was screwed into a rage as he whistled again and again, trying to make her look up. Young Tom stopped whistling. He stood beside Stanley, excited, grinning; but he felt as if he were saying to the woman: Don't associate me with *him*, for his grin was apologetic. Last night he had thought of the unknown woman before he slept, and she had been tender with him. This tenderness he was remembering as he shifted his feet by the jeering, whistling Stanley, and watched the indifferent, healthy brown woman a few feet off, with the gap that plunged to the street between them. Tom thought it was romantic, it was like being high on two hilltops. But there was a shout from Harry, and they clambered back. Stanley's face was hard, really angry. The boy kept looking at him and wondered why he hated the woman so much, for by now he loved her.

They played their little games with the blanket, trying to trap shade to work under; but again it was not until nearly four that they could work seriously, and they were exhausted, all three of them. They were grumbling about the weather by now. Stanley was in a thoroughly bad humor. When they made their routine trip to see the woman before they packed up for the day, she was apparently asleep, face down, her back all naked save for the scarlet triangle on her buttocks. "I've got a good mind to report her to the police," said Stanley, and Harry said: "What's eating you? What harm's she doing?"

"I tell you, if she was my wife!"

"But she isn't, is she?" Tom knew that Harry, like himself, was uneasy at Stanley's reaction. He was normally a sharp young man, quick at his work, making a lot of jokes, good company.

"Perhaps it will be cooler tomorrow," said Harry.

But it wasn't; it was hotter, if anything, and the weather forecast said the good weather would last. As soon as they were on the roof, Harry went over to see if the woman was there, and Tom knew it was to prevent Stanley going, to put off his bad humor. Harry had grownup children, a boy the same age as Tom, and the youth trusted and looked up to him.

Harry came back and said: "She's not there."

"I bet her old man has put his foot down," said Stanley, and Harry and Tom caught each other's eyes and smiled behind the young married man's back.

Harry suggested they should get permission to work in the basement, and they did, that day. But before packing up Stanley said: "Let's have a breath of fresh air." Again Harry and Tom smiled at each other as they followed Stanley up to the roof, Tom in the devout conviction that he was there to protect the woman from Stanley. It was about five-thirty, and a calm, full sunlight lay over the roofs. The great crane still swung its black arm from Oxford Street to above their heads. She was not there. Then there was a flutter of white from behind a parapet, and she stood up, in a belted, white dressing-gown. She had been there all day, probably, but on a different patch of roof, to hide from them. Stanley did not whistle; he said nothing, but watched the woman bend to collect papers, books, cigarettes, then fold the blanket over her arm. Tom was thinking: If they weren't here, I'd go over and say . . . what? But he knew from his nightly dreams of her that she was kind and friendly. Perhaps she would ask him down to her flat? Perhaps . . . He stood watching her disappear down the skylight. As she went, Stanley let out a shrill derisive yell; she started, and it seemed as if she nearly fell. She clutched to save herself, they could hear things falling. She looked straight at them, angry. Harry said, facetiously: "Better be careful on those slippery ladders, love." Tom knew he said it to save her from Stanley, but she could not know it. She vanished, frowning. Tom was full of a secret delight, because he knew her anger was for the others, not for him.

"Roll on some rain," said Stanley, bitter, looking at the blue evening sky.

Next day was cloudless, and they decided to finish the work in the basement. They felt excluded, shut in the grey cement basement fitting pipes, from the holiday atmosphere of London in a heat wave. At lunchtime they came up for some air, but while the married couples, and the men in shirt-sleeves or vests, were there, she was not there, either on her usual patch of roof or where she had been yesterday. They all, even Harry, clambered about, between chimney-pots, over parapets, the hot leads stinging their fingers. There was not a sign of her. They took off their shirts and vests and exposed their chests, feeling their feet sweaty and hot. They did not mention the woman. But Tom felt alone again. Last night she had him into her flat: it was big and had fitted white carpets and a bed with a padded white leather head-board. She wore a black filmy negligée and her kindness to Tom thickened his throat as he remembered it. He felt she had betrayed him by not being there.

And again after work they climbed up, but still there was nothing to be seen of her. Stanley kept repeating that if it was as hot as this tomorrow he wasn't going to work and that's all there was to it. But they were all there next day. By ten the temperature was in the middle seventies, and it was eighty long before noon. Harry went to the foreman to say it was impossible to work on the leads in that heat; but the foreman said there was nothing else he could put them on, and they'd have to. At midday they stood, silent, watching the skylight on her roof open, and then she slowly emerged in her white gown, holding a bundle of blanket. She looked at them, gravely, then went to the part of the roof where she was hidden from them. Tom was pleased. He felt she was more his when the other men couldn't see her. They had taken off their shirts and vests, but now they put them back again, for they felt the sun bruising their flesh. "She must have the hide of a rhino," said Stanley, tugging at guttering and swearing. They stopped work, and sat in the shade, moving around behind chimney stacks. A woman came to water a yellow window box opposite them. She was middleaged, wearing a flowered summer dress. Stanley said to her: "We need a drink more than them." She smiled and said: "Better drop down to the pub quick, it'll be closing in a minute." They exchanged pleasantries, and she left them with a smile and a wave.

"Not like Lady Godiva°," said Stanley. "She can give us a bit of a chat and a smile."

"You didn't whistle at *her*," said Tom, reproving.

"Listen to him," said Stanley, "you didn't whistle, then?"

But the boy felt as if he hadn't whistled, as if only Harry and Stanley had.

Lady Godiva: Stanley compares the woman on the roof to the heroine of a medieval English legend. On a bet with her husband, to make him abolish a heavy tax on the people of Coventry, Godiva rode naked through the streets. No one was supposed to look at her. (Peeping Tom looked, and was struck blind.)

He was making plans, when it was time to knock off work, to get left behind and somehow make his way over to the woman. The weather report said the hot spell was due to break, so he had to move quickly. But there was no chance of being left. The other two decided to knock off work at four, because they were exhausted. As they went down, Tom quickly climbed a parapet and hoisted himself higher by pulling his weight up a chimney. He caught a glimpse of her lying on her back, her knees up, eyes closed, a brown woman lolling in the sun. He slipped and clattered down, as Stanley looked for information: "She's gone down," he said. He felt as if he had protected her from Stanley, and that she must be grateful to him. He could feel the bond between the woman and himself.

Next day, they stood around on the landing below the roof, reluctant to climb up into the heat. The woman who had lent Harry the blanket came out and offered them a cup of tea. They accepted gratefully, and sat around Mrs. Pritchett's kitchen an hour or so, chatting. She was married to an airline pilot. A smart blonde, of about thirty, she had an eye for the handsome sharp-faced Stanley; and the two teased each other while Harry sat in a corner, watching, indulgent, though his expression reminded Stanley that he was married. And young Tom felt envious of Stanley's ease in badinage°; felt, too, that Stanley's getting off with Mrs. Pritchett left his romance with the woman on the roof safe and intact.

"I thought they said the heat wave'd break," said Stanley, sullen, as the time approached when they really would have to climb up into the sunlight.

"You don't like it, then?" asked Mrs. Pritchett.

"All right for some," said Stanley. "Nothing to do but lie about as if it was a beach up there. Do you ever go up?"

"Went up once," said Mrs. Pritchett. "But it's a dirty place up there, and it's too hot."

"Quite right too," said Stanley.

Then they went up, leaving the cool neat little flat and the friendly Mrs. Pritchett.

As soon as they were up they saw her. The three men looked at her, resentful at her ease in this punishing sun. Then Harry said, because of the expression on Stanley's face: "Come on, we've got to pretend to work, at least."

They had to wrench another length of guttering that ran beside a parapet out of its bed, so that they could replace it. Stanley took it in his two hands, tugged, swore, stood up. "Fuck it," he said, and sat down under a chimney. He lit a cigarette. "Fuck them," he said. "What do they think we are, lizards? I've got blisters all over my hands." Then he jumped up and climbed over the roofs and stood with his back to them. He put his fingers either side of his mouth and let out a shrill whistle. Tom and Harry squatted, not looking at each other, watching him. They could just see the woman's head, the beginnings of her brown shoulders. Stanley whistled again. Then he began stamping with his feet, and whistled and yelled and screamed at the woman, his face getting scarlet. He seemed quite mad, as he stamped and whistled, while the woman did not move, she did not move a muscle.

"Barmy," said Tom.

badinage: (French), teasing, playful conversation.

"Yes," said Harry, disapproving.

Suddenly the older man came to a decision. It was, Tom knew, to save some sort of scandal or real trouble over the woman. Harry stood up and began packing tools into a length of oily cloth. "Stanley," he said, commanding. At first Stanley took no notice, but Harry said: "Stanley, we're packing it in, I'll tell Matthew."

Stanley came back, cheeks mottled, eyes glaring.

"Can't go on like this," said Harry. "It'll break in a day or so. I'm going to tell Matthew we've got sunstroke, and if he doesn't like it, it's too bad." Even Harry sounded aggrieved, Tom noted. The small, competent man, the family man with his grey hair, who was never at a loss, sounded really off balance. "Come on," he said, angry. He fitted himself into the open square in the roof, and went down, watching his feet on the ladder. Then Stanley went, with not a glance at the woman. Then Tom, who, his throat beating with excitement, silently promised her on a backward glance: Wait for me, wait, I'm coming.

On the pavement Stanley said: "I'm going home." He looked white now, so perhaps he really did have sunstroke. Harry went off to find the foreman, who was at work on the plumbing of some flats down the street. Tom slipped back, not into the building they had been working on, but the building on whose roof the woman lay. He went straight up, no one stopping him. The skylight stood open, with an iron ladder leading up. He emerged on to the roof a couple of yards from her. She sat up, pushing back her black hair with both hands. The scarf across her breasts bound them tight, and brown flesh bulged around it. Her legs were brown and smooth. She stared at him in silence. The boy stood grinning, foolish, claiming the tenderness he expected from her.

"What do you want?" she asked.

"I . . . I came to . . . make your acquaintance," he stammered, grinning, pleading with her.

They looked at each other, the slight, scarlet-faced excited boy, and the serious, nearly naked woman. Then, without a word, she lay down on her brown blanket, ignoring him.

"You like the sun, do you?" he enquired of her glistening back.

Not a word. He felt panic, thinking of how she had held him in her arms, stroked his hair, brought him where he sat, lordly, in her bed, a glass of some exhilarating liquor he had never tasted in life. He felt that if he knelt down, stroked her shoulders, her hair, she would turn and clasp him in her arms.

He said: "The sun's all right for you, isn't it?"

She raised her head, set her chin on two small fists. "Go away," she said. He did not move. "Listen," she said, in a slow reasonable voice, where anger was kept in check, though with difficulty; looking at him, her face weary with anger, "if you get a kick out of seeing women in bikinis, why don't you take a sixpenny bus ride to the Lido°? You'd see dozens of them, without all this mountaineering."

She hadn't understood him. He felt her unfairness pale him. He stammered: "But I like you, I've been watching you and . . ."

"Thanks," she said, and dropped her face again, turned away from him.

Lido: a section of London's Hyde Park.

She lay there. He stood there. She said nothing. She had simply shut him out. He stood, saying nothing at all, for some minutes. He thought: She'll have to say something if I stay. But the minutes went past, with no sign of them in her, except in the tension of her back, her thighs, her arms — the tension of waiting for him to go.

He looked up at the sky, where the sun seemed to spin in heat; and over the roofs where he and his mates had been earlier. He could see the heat quivering where they had worked. And they expect us to work in these conditions! he thought, filled with righteous indignation. The woman hadn't moved. A bit of hot wind blew her black hair softly; it shone, and was iridescent. He remembered how he had stroked it last night.

Resentment of her at last moved him off and away down the ladder, through the building, into the street. He got drunk then, in hatred of her.

⌐ Next day when he woke the sky was grey. He looked at the wet grey and thought, vicious: Well, that's fixed you, hasn't it now? That's fixed you good and proper.

The three men were at work early on the cool leads, surrounded by damp drizzling roofs where no one came to sun themselves, black roofs, slimy with rain. Because it was cool now, they would finish the job that day, if they hurried.

QUESTIONS

1. What do you understand from the story's last line?
2. What is a *protagonist?* (See the definition on page 9, if necessary.) Who is the protagonist in this story?
3. Who tells the story? Does this narrator take us into the mind of each character? Of certain characters? Of a single one?
4. Suppose "A Woman on a Roof" were told in the first person from the point of view of the sunbather herself. What do you think the story would lose, or gain?
5. Pay special notice to the setting in this story. How does weather help account for the behavior of the characters? Comment on the effectiveness of the descriptions of the heat wave; of the final rain.
6. Are there any similarities between what happens in this story and what happens in James Joyce's "Araby"? How do the two stories differ in point of view?
7. Recall Stanley's calling the sunbather Lady Godiva. What is meaningful in Tom's name? How accurate is a critic's remark that this is "a recent rooftop version of the Godiva story"?
8. What do you think Doris Lessing is saying? Do you find her story a comment on any familiar attitudes of men toward women? Does she show any sympathy for the three men?

3 Character

Theophrastus (372?–287? B.C.)
THE MAN WITHOUT TACT (about 300 B.C.)

Tactlessness is a painful inability to act at the right time. The Man Without Tact is one who comes up to a desperately busy friend and asks his opinion. He brings musicians to serenade his girl on a day when she lies sick in bed. He approaches someone who has just put up bail for another and lost it, and asks, "Can you stand bail for me too?" He shows up to testify at a trial after it is all over. Invite him to a wedding and he harangues on women's fickleness. Come back from a long weary journey and he asks you to go for a walk. No sooner strike a bargain to sell someone something than he happens by, bringing someone else who would have paid you more for it. He delights to take the floor and tell some long involved story to people who already know it by heart. He is quick to volunteer to do some business you do not wish done but cannot refuse. Whenever you are low on funds from sending sacrifices to the temple, he never fails to show up and demand the money you owe him. When your servant has to be whipped for some misdemeanor, he looks on and describes how, after just such a whipping, a boy of his went out and hanged himself. When two people are having a dispute arbitrated, even though both wish it over with, he manages to set them at each other's throats again. Whenever he wants to dance, he seizes the hand of someone who is still cold sober.

"The Man Without Tact," one of thirty sketches in the *Characters* of Theophrastus, may recall someone we have met before. Evidently the ancient Greek writer is portraying no one individual but a familiar and long-lasting human type. From popular fiction and drama, both classic and contemporary, we are acquainted with many such stereotyped characters. Called **stock characters,** they are often known by some outstanding trait or traits: the *bragging* soldier of Greek and Roman comedy, the prince *charming* of fairy tales, the *mad* scientist of horror movies, the *loyal* sidekick of Westerns, the *greedy* explorer of Tarzan films, the *beautiful but dumb* blonde of 1920-vintage musical comedies, the *brilliant but alcoholic* brain surgeon of medical thrillers on television. Stock characters are especially convenient for writers of commercial fiction: they require little detailed portraiture, since we already know them well. However, most writers of the literary story attempt to create characters who strike us, not as stereotypes, but as unique individuals. While stock characters tend to have single dominant virtues and vices, characters in the finest contemporary short stories tend to have many facets, like people we meet.

A **character,** then, is presumably an imagined person who inhabits a story — although that simple definition may admit to a few exceptions. (In George Stewart's novel *Storm,* the protagonist is the wind; in Richard Adams's *Watership Down*, the central characters are rabbits.) But usually we recognize, in the main characters of a story, human personalities that become familiar to us. If the story seems "true to life," we generally find that its characters act in a reasonably consistent manner, and that the author has provided them with **motivation:** sufficient reason to behave as they do. Should a character behave in a sudden and unexpected way, seeming to deny what we have been told about his nature or personality, we trust that he had a reason, and that sooner or later we will discover it. This is not to claim that *all* authors insist that their characters behave with absolute consistency, for (as we shall see later in this chapter) certain contemporary stories feature characters who sometimes act without any apparent reason. Nor can we say that, in good fiction, characters never change or develop. In "A Christmas Carol," Charles Dickens tells how Ebeneezer Scrooge, a tightfisted miser, reforms overnight, suddenly gives to the poor, and endeavors to assist his clerk's struggling family. But Dickens amply demonstrates why Scrooge had such a change of heart: four ghostly visitors, stirring kind memories the old miser had forgotten and also warning him of the probable consequences of his habits, provide the character (and hence the story) with adequate motivation.

To borrow the useful terms of the English novelist E. M. Forster, characters may seem **flat** or **round,** depending on whether a writer sketches or sculptures them. A flat character usually has only one outstanding trait or feature, or at most a few distinguishing marks: for example, the familiar stock character of the mad scientist, with his lust for absolute power and his crazily gleaming eyes. Flat characters, however, need not be stock characters: in all of literature there is probably only one Tiny Tim, though his functions in "A Christmas Carol" are mainly to invoke blessings and to remind others of their Christian duties. Some writers, notably Balzac, who peopled his many novels with hosts of characters, try to distinguish the flat ones by giving each a single odd physical feature or mannerism — a nervous twitch, a piercing gaze, an obsessive fondness for oysters. Round characters, however, present us with more facets — that is, their authors portray them in greater depth and in more generous detail. Such a round character may appear to us only as he appears to the other characters in the story. If their views of him differ, we will see him from more than one side. In Chekhov's "In Exile" (page 320), we are given two sharply different views of the gentleman with the consumptive daughter. To cynical old Semyon, he is a fool; to the sympathetic Tartar, he is admirable. To us, perhaps, he is neither simply foolish nor wholly admirable. In other stories, we enter a character's mind and come to know him through his own thoughts, feelings, and perceptions. By the time we finish reading James Joyce's "Araby" (Chapter Two), we are well acquainted with the boy who tells his story and probably find him amply three-dimensional.

Flat characters tend to stay the same throughout a story, but round characters often change — learn or become enlightened, grow or deteriorate. In William Faulkner's "Barn Burning" (Chapter Four), the boy Sarty Snopes, driven to defy his proud and violent father, becomes at the story's end more knowing and more mature. (Some critics call a fixed character static; a changing one, dynamic.) This is not to damn a flat character as an inferior work of art. In most fiction — even the greatest — minor characters tend to be flat instead of round. Why? Rounding them would cost time and space; and so enlarged, they might only distract us from the central characters.

"A character, first of all, is the noise of his name," according to the novelist William Gass.[1] Names, chosen artfully, can indicate natures. A simple illustration is the completely virtuous Squire Allworthy, the foster father in *Tom Jones* by Henry Fielding. Subtler, perhaps, is the custom of giving a character a name that makes an allusion: a reference to some famous person, place, or thing in history, in other fiction, or in actuality. For his central characters in *Moby Dick,* Herman Melville chose names from the Old Testament, calling his tragic and domineering Ahab after a biblical tyrant who came to a bad end, and his wandering narrator Ishmael after a biblical outcast. Whether or not it includes an allusion, a good name often reveals the character of the character. Charles Dickens, a vigorous and richly suggestive christener, named a charming confidence man Mr. Jingle (suggesting something jingly, light, and superficially pleasant), named a couple of shyster lawyers Dodgson and Fogg (suggesting dodging evasiveness and foglike obscuration), and named two heartless educators, who grimly drill their schoolchildren in "hard facts," Gradgrind and M'Choakumchild. Henry James, who so loved names that he kept lists of them for characters he might someday conceive, chose for a sensitive, cultured gentleman the name of Lambert Strether; for a down-to-earth, benevolent individual, the name of Mrs. Bread. (But James may have wished to indicate that names cannot be identified with people absolutely, in giving the frag-

[1] "The Concept of Character in Fiction," in *Fiction and the Figures of Life* (New York: Knopf, 1970).

ile, considerate heroine of the *The Spoils of Poynton* the harsh-sounding name of Fleda Vetch.)

Instead of a hero, many a recent novel has featured an **antihero:** an ordinary, unglorious twentieth-century citizen, usually drawn (according to Sean O'Faolain) as a man "groping, puzzled, cross, mocking, frustrated, and isolated.[2] If epic poets once portrayed their heroes as decisive leaders of their people, embodying their people's highest ideals, antiheroes tend to be loners, without perfections, just barely able to survive. Antiheroes lack "character," as defined by psychologist Anthony Quinton to mean a person's conduct or "persistence and consistency in seeking to realize his long-term aims."[3] A gulf separates Leopold Bloom, antihero of James Joyce's novel *Ulysses,* from the hero of the Greek *Odyssey.* In Homer's epic, Ulysses wanders the Mediterranean, battling monsters and overcoming enchantments. In Joyce's novel, Bloom wanders the littered streets of Dublin, peddling advertising space.

Evidently, not only fashions in heroes but also attitudes toward human nature have undergone change. In the eighteenth century, the Scottish philosopher David Hume argued that the nature of an individual is relatively fixed and unalterable. Hume noted, however, a few exceptions: "A person of an obliging disposition gives a peevish answer; but he has the toothache or has not dined. A stupid fellow discovers an obvious alacrity in his carriage; but he has met with a sudden piece of good fortune." For a long time after Hume, novelists and short-story writers seem to have assumed that characters behave nearly always in a predictable fashion and that their actions ought to be consistent with their personalities. Now and again, a writer differed: Jane Austen in *Pride and Prejudice* has her protagonist Elizabeth Bennet remark to the citified Mr. Darcy, who fears that life in the country cannot be amusing, "But people themselves alter so much, that there is something to be observed in them for ever."

Many contemporary writers of fiction would deny even that people have definite selves to alter. Following Sigmund Freud and other modern psychologists, they assume that a large part of human behavior is shaped in the unconscious — that, for instance, a person might fear horses not because of a basically timid nature, but because of unconscious memories of having been nearly trampled by a horse when a child. To some writers it now appears that what Hume called a "disposition" (now called a "personality") is more vulnerable to change from such causes as age, disease, neurosis, psychic shock, or brainwashing than was once believed. Hence, some characters in twentieth-

---

[2] *The Vanishing Hero* (Boston: Little, Brown, 1957).
[3] "The Continuity of Persons," *Times Literary Supplement* issue on "The Nature of Character," 27 July 1973.

century fiction appear to be shifting bundles of impulses. "You musn't look in my novel for the old stable ego of character," wrote D. H. Lawrence to a friend about *The Rainbow;* and in that novel and other novels Lawrence demonstrated his view of individuals as bits of one vast Life Force, spurred to act by incomprehensible passions and urges — the "dark gods" in them. The idea of the **gratuitous act,** a deed without cause or motive, is explored in André Gide's novel *Lafcadio's Adventures,* in which an ordinary young man without homicidal tendencies abruptly and for no reason pushes a stranger from a speeding train. The usual limits of character are playfully violated by Virginia Woolf in *Orlando,* a novel whose protagonist, defying time, lives right on from Elizabethan days into the present, changing in midstory from a man into a woman. Characterization, as practiced by nineteenth-century novelists, almost entirely disappears in Franz Kafka's *The Castle,* whose protagonist has no home, no family, no definite appearance — not even a name, just the initial *K.* Characters are things of the past, insists the contemporary French novelist Alain Robbe-Grillet. Still, many writers of fiction go on portraying them.

James Thurber (1894–1961)

THE CATBIRD SEAT   1945

Mr. Martin bought the pack of Camels on Monday night in the most crowded cigar store on Broadway. It was theater time and seven or eight men were buying cigarettes. The clerk didn't even glance at Mr. Martin, who put the pack in his overcoat pocket and went out. If any of the staff at F & S had seen him buy the cigarettes, they would have been astonished, for it was generally known that Mr. Martin did not smoke, and never had. No one saw him.

It was just a week to the day since Mr. Martin had decided to rub out Mrs. Ulgine Barrows. The term "rub out" pleased him because it suggested nothing more than the correction of an error — in this case an error of Mr. Fitweiler. Mr. Martin had spent each night of the past week working out his plan and examining it. As he walked home now he went over it again. For the hundredth time he resented the element of imprecision, the margin of guesswork that entered into the business. The project as he had worked it out was casual and bold, the risks were considerable. Something might go wrong anywhere along the line. And therein lay the cunning of his scheme. No one would ever see in it the cautious, painstaking hand of Erwin Martin, head of the filing department at F & S, of whom Mr. Fitweiler had once said, "Man is fallible but Martin isn't." No one would see his hand, that is, unless it were caught in the act.

Sitting in his apartment, drinking a glass of milk, Mr. Martin reviewed his case against Mrs. Ulgine Barrows, as he had every night for seven nights. He began at the beginning. Her quacking voice and braying laugh had first profaned the halls of F & S on March 7, 1941 (Mr. Martin had a head for dates). Old Roberts, the personnel chief, had introduced her as the newly appointed special adviser to the president of the firm, Mr. Fitweiler. The woman had appalled Mr. Martin instantly, but he hadn't shown it. He had given her his dry hand, a look of studious concentration, and a faint smile. "Well," she had said, looking at the papers on his desk, "are you lifting the oxcart out of the ditch?" As Mr. Martin recalled that moment, over his milk, he squirmed slightly. He must keep his mind on her crimes as a special adviser, not on her peccadillos as a personality. This he found difficult to do, in spite of entering an objection and sustaining it. The faults of the woman as a woman kept chattering on in his mind like an unruly witness. She had, for almost two years now, baited him. In the halls, in the elevator, even in his own office, into which she romped now and then like a circus horse, she was constantly shouting these silly questions at him. "Are you lifting the oxcart out of the ditch? Are you tearing up the pea patch? Are you hollering down the rain barrel? Are you scraping around the bottom of the pickle barrel? Are you sitting in the catbird seat?"

It was Joey Hart, one of Mr. Martin's two assistants, who had explained what the gibberish meant. "She must be a Dodger fan°," he had said. "Red Barber announces the Dodger games over the radio and he uses those expressions — picked 'em up down South." Joey had gone on to explain one or two. "Tearing up the pea patch" meant going on a rampage; "sitting in the catbird seat" meant sitting pretty, like a batter with three balls and no strikes on him. Mr. Martin dismissed all this with an effort. It had been annoying, it had driven him near to distraction, but he was too solid a man to be moved to murder by anything so childish. It was fortunate, he reflected as he passed on to the important charges against Mrs. Barrows, that he had stood up under it so well. He had maintained always an outward appearance of polite tolerance. "Why, I even believe you like the woman," Miss Paird, his other assistant, had once said to him. He had simply smiled.

A gavel rapped in Mr. Martin's mind and the case proper was resumed. Mrs. Ulgine Barrows stood charged with willful, blatant, and persistent attempts to destroy the efficiency and system of F & S. It was competent, material, and relevant to review her advent and rise to power. Mr. Martin had got the story from Miss Paird, who seemed always able to find things out. According to her, Mrs. Barrows had met Mr. Fitweiler at a party, where she had rescued him from the embraces of a powerfully built drunken man who had mistaken the president of F & S for a famous retired Middle Western football coach. She had led him to a sofa and somehow worked upon him a monstrous magic. The aging gentleman had jumped to the conclusion there and then that this was a woman of singular attainments, equipped to bring out the best in him and in the firm. A week later he had introduced her into F & S as his special adviser. On that day confusion got its foot in the door. After Miss Tyson, Mr. Brundage, and Mr. Bartlett had been fired and Mr. Munson had taken his hat and stalked out, mailing in his resignation later, old Roberts had been emboldened to speak to Mr. Fitweiler. He mentioned that Mr. Munson's department had been "a little disrupted" and hadn't they perhaps better resume the old system there? Mr. Fitweiler had said certainly not. He had the greatest faith in Mrs. Barrows' ideas. "They require a little seasoning, a little seasoning, is all," he had added.

Dodger fan: At the time of this story, the Dodgers were the Brooklyn Dodgers.

Mr. Roberts had given it up. Mr. Martin reviewed in detail all the changes wrought by Mrs. Barrows. She had begun chipping at the cornices of the firm's edifice and now she was swinging at the foundation stones with a pickaxe.

Mr. Martin came now, in his summing up, to the afternoon of Monday, November 2, 1942 — just one week ago. On that day, at 3 P.M., Mrs. Barrows had bounced into his office. "Boo!" she had yelled. "Are you scraping around the bottom of the pickle barrel?" Mr. Martin had looked at her from under his green eyeshade, saying nothing. She had begun to wander about the office, taking it in with her great, popping eyes. "Do you really need *all* these filing cabinets?" she had demanded suddenly. Mr. Martin's heart had jumped. "Each of these files," he had said, keeping his voice even, "plays an indispensable part in the system of F & S." She had brayed at him, "Well, don't tear up the pea patch!" and gone to the door. From there she had bawled, "But you sure have got a lot of fine scrap in here!" Mr. Martin could no longer doubt that the finger was on his beloved department. Her pickaxe was on the upswing, poised for the first blow. It had not come yet; he had received no blue memo from the enchanted Mr. Fitweiler bearing nonsensical instructions deriving from the obscene woman. But there was no doubt in Mr. Martin's mind that one would be forthcoming. He must act quickly. Already a precious week had gone by. Mr. Martin stood up in his living room, still holding his milk glass. "Gentlemen of the jury," he said to himself, "I demand the death penalty for this horrible person."

The next day Mr. Martin followed his routine, as usual. He polished his glasses more often and once sharpened an already sharp pencil, but not even Miss Paird noticed. Only once did he catch sight of his victim; she swept past him in the hall with a patronizing "Hi!" At five-thirty he walked home, as usual, and had a glass of milk, as usual. He had never drunk anything stronger in his life — unless you could count ginger ale. The late Sam Schlosser, the S of F & S, had praised Mr. Martin at a staff meeting several years before for his temperate habits. "Our most efficient worker neither drinks nor smokes," he had said. "The results speak for themselves." Mr. Fitweiler had sat by, nodding approval.

Mr. Martin was still thinking about that red-letter day as he walked over to the Schrafft's on Fifth Avenue near Forty-sixth Street. He got there, as he always did, at eight o'clock. He finished his dinner and the financial page of the *Sun* at a quarter to nine, as he always did. It was his custom after dinner to take a walk. This time he walked down Fifth Avenue at a casual pace. His gloved hands felt moist and warm, his forehead cold. He transferred the Camels from his overcoat to a jacket pocket. He wondered, as he did so, if they did not represent an unnecessary note of strain. Mrs. Barrows smoked only Luckies. It was his idea to puff a few puffs on a Camel (after the rubbing-out), stub it out in the ashtray holding her lipstick-stained Luckies, and thus drag a small red herring across the trail. Perhaps it was not a good idea. It would take time. He might even choke, too loudly.

Mr. Martin had never seen the house on West Twelfth Street where Mrs. Barrows lived, but he had a clear enough picture of it. Fortunately, she had bragged to everybody about her ducky first-floor apartment in the perfectly darling three-story redbrick. There would be no doorman or other attendants;

just the tenants of the second and third floors. As he walked along, Mr. Martin realized that he would get there before nine-thirty. He had considered walking north on Fifth Avenue from Schrafft's to a point from which it would take him until ten o'clock to reach the house. At that hour people were less likely to be coming in or going out. But the procedure would have made an awkward loop in the straight thread of his casualness, and he had abandoned it. It was impossible to figure when people would be entering or leaving the house, anyway. There was a great risk at any hour. If he ran into anybody, he would simply have to place the rubbing-out of Ulgine Barrows in the inactive file forever. The same thing would hold true if there were someone in her apartment. In that case he would just say that he had been passing by, recognized her charming house and thought to drop in.

It was eighteen minutes after nine when Mr. Martin turned into Twelfth Street. A man passed him, and a man and a woman talking. There was no one within fifty paces when he came to the house, halfway down the block. He was up the steps and in the small vestibule in no time, pressing the bell under the card that said "Mrs. Ulgine Barrows." When the clicking in the lock started, he jumped forward against the door. He got inside fast, closing the door behind him. A bulb in a lantern hung from the hall ceiling on a chain seemed to give a monstrously bright light. There was nobody on the stair, which went up ahead of him along the left wall. A door opened down the hall in the wall on the right. He went toward it swiftly, on tiptoe.

"Well, for God's sake, look who's here!" bawled Mrs. Barrows, and her braying laugh rang out like the report of a shotgun. He rushed past her like a football tackle, bumping her. "Hey, quit shoving!" she said, closing the door behind them. They were in her living room, which seemed to Mr. Martin to be lighted by a hundred lamps. "What's after you?" she said. "You're as jumpy as a goat." He found he was unable to speak. His heart was wheezing in his throat. "I — yes," he finally brought out. She was jabbering and laughing as she started to help him off with his coat. "No, no," he said. "I'll put it here." He took it off and put it on a chair near the door. "Your hat and gloves, too," she said. "You're in a lady's house." He put his hat on top of the coat. Mrs. Barrows seemed larger than he had thought. He kept his gloves on. "I was passing by," he said. "I recognized — is there anyone here?" She laughed louder than ever. "No," she said, "we're all alone. You're as white as a sheet, you funny man. Whatever *has* come over you? I'll mix you a toddy." She started toward a door across the room. "Scotch-and-soda be all right? But say, you don't drink, do you?" She turned and gave him her amused look. Mr. Martin pulled himself together. "Scotch-and-soda will be all right," he heard himself say. He could hear her laughing in the kitchen.

Mr. Martin looked quickly around the living room for the weapon. He had counted on finding one there. There were andirons and a poker and something in a corner that looked like an Indian club. None of them would do. It couldn't be that way. He began to pace around. He came to a desk. On it lay a metal paper knife with an ornate handle. Would it be sharp enough? He reached for it and knocked over a small brass jar. Stamps spilled out of it and it fell to the floor with a clatter. "Hey," Mrs. Barrows yelled from the kitchen, "are you tearing up the pea patch?" Mr. Martin gave a strange laugh. Picking up the knife, he tried its point against his left wrist. It was blunt. It wouldn't do.

When Mrs. Barrows reappeared, carrying two highballs, Mr. Martin, standing there with his gloves on, became acutely conscious of the fantasy he had wrought. Cigarettes in his pocket, a drink prepared for him — it was all too grossly improbable. It was more than that; it was impossible. Somewhere in the back of his mind a vague idea stirred, sprouted. "For heaven's sake, take off those gloves," said Mrs. Barrows. "I always wear them in the house," said Mr. Martin. The idea began to bloom, strange and wonderful. She put the glasses on a coffee table in front of a sofa and sat on the sofa. "Come over here, you odd little man," she said. Mr. Martin went over and sat beside her. It was difficult getting a cigarette out of the pack of Camels, but he managed it. She held a match for him, laughing. "Well," she said, handing him his drink, "this is perfectly marvelous. You with a drink and a cigarette."

Mr. Martin puffed, not too awkwardly, and took a gulp of the highball. "I drink and smoke all the time," he said. He clinked his glass against hers. "Here's nuts to that old windbag, Fitweiler," he said, and gulped again. The stuff tasted awful, but he made no grimace. "Really, Mr. Martin," she said, her voice and posture changing, "you are insulting our employer." Mrs. Barrows was now all special adviser to the president. "I am preparing a bomb," said Mr. Martin, "which will blow the old goat higher than hell." He had only had a little of the drink, which was not strong. It couldn't be that. "Do you take dope or something?" Mrs. Barrows asked coldly. "Heroin," said Mr. Martin. "I'll be coked to the gills when I bump that old buzzard off." "Mr. Martin!" she shouted, getting to her feet. "That will be all of that. You must go at once." Mr. Martin took another swallow of his drink. He tapped his cigarette out in the ashtray and put the pack of Camels on the coffee table. Then he got up. She stood glaring at him. He walked over and put on his hat and coat. "Not a word about this," he said, and laid an index finger against his lips. All Mrs. Barrows could bring out was "Really!" Mr. Martin put his hand on the doorknob. "I'm sitting in the catbird seat," he said. He stuck his tongue out at her and left. Nobody saw him go.

Mr. Martin got to his apartment, walking, well before eleven. No one saw him go in. He had two glasses of milk after brushing his teeth, and he felt elated. It wasn't tipsiness, because he hadn't been tipsy. Anyway, the walk had worn off all effects of the whisky. He got in bed and read a magazine for a while. He was asleep before midnight.

Mr. Martin got to the office at eight-thirty the next morning, as usual. At a quarter to nine, Ulgine Barrows, who had never before arrived at work before ten, swept into his office. "I'm reporting to Mr. Fitweiler now!" she shouted. "If he turns you over to the police, it's no more than you deserve!" Mr. Martin gave her a look of shocked surprise. "I beg your pardon?" he said. Mrs. Barrows snorted and bounced out of the room, leaving Miss Paird and Joey Hart staring after her. "What's the matter with that old devil now?" asked Miss Paird. "I have no idea," said Mr. Martin, resuming his work. The other two looked at him and then at each other. Miss Paird got up and went out. She walked slowly past the closed door of Mr. Fitweiler's office. Mrs. Barrows was yelling inside, but she was not braying. Miss Paird could not hear what the woman was saying. She went back to her desk.

Forty-five minutes later, Mrs. Barrows left the president's office and went into her own, shutting the door. It wasn't until half an hour later that Mr. Fitweiler sent for Mr. Martin. The head of the filing department, neat, quiet, attentive, stood in front of the old man's desk. Mr. Fitweiler was pale and nervous. He took his glasses off and twiddled them. He made a small, bruffing sound in his throat. "Martin," he said, "you have been with us more than twenty years." "Twenty-two, sir," said Mr. Martin. "In that time," pursued the president, "your work and your — uh — manner have been exemplary." "I trust so, sir," said Mr. Martin. "I have understood, Martin," said Mr. Fitweiler, "that you have never taken a drink or smoked." "That is correct, sir," said Mr. Martin. "Ah, yes." Mr. Fitweiler polished his glasses. "You may describe what you did after leaving the office yesterday, Martin," he said. Mr. Martin allowed less than a second for his bewildered pause. "Certainly, sir," he said. "I walked home. Then I went to Schrafft's for dinner. Afterward I walked home again. I went to bed early, sir, and read a magazine for a while. I was asleep before eleven." "Ah, yes," said Mr. Fitweiler again. He was silent for a moment, searching for the proper words to say to the head of the filing department. "Mrs. Barrows," he said finally, "Mrs. Barrows has worked hard, Martin, very hard. It grieves me to report that she has suffered a severe breakdown. It has taken the form of a persecution complex accompanied by distressing hallucinations." "I am very sorry, sir," said Mr. Martin. "Mrs. Barrows is under the delusion," continued Mr. Fitweiler, "that you visited her last evening and behaved yourself in an — uh — unseemly manner." He raised his hand to silence Mr. Martin's little pained outcry. "It is the nature of these psychological diseases," Mr. Fitweiler said, "to fix upon the least likely and most innocent party as the — uh — source of persecution. These matters are not for the lay mind to grasp, Martin. I've just had my psychiatrist, Dr. Fitch, on the phone. He would not, of course, commit himself, but he made enough generalizations to substantiate my suspicions. I suggested to Mrs. Barrows when she had completed her — uh — story to me this morning, that she visit Dr. Fitch, for I suspected a condition at once. She flew, I regret to say, into a rage, and demanded — uh — requested that I call you on the carpet. You may not know, Martin, but Mrs. Barrows had planned a reorganization of your department — subject to my approval, of course, subject to my approval. This brought you, rather than anyone else, to her mind — but again that is a phenomenon for Dr. Fitch and not for us. So, Martin, I am afraid Mrs. Barrows' usefulness here is at an end." "I am dreadfully sorry, sir," said Mr. Martin.

It was at this point that the door to the office blew open with the suddenness of a gas-main explosion and Mrs. Barrows catapulted through it. "Is the little rat denying it?" she screamed. "He can't get away with that!" Mr. Martin got up and moved discreetly to a point beside Mr. Fitweiler's chair. "You drank and smoked at my apartment," she bawled at Mr. Martin, "and you know it! You called Mr. Fitweiler an old windbag and said you were going to blow him up when you got coked to the gills on your heroin!" She stopped yelling to catch her breath and a new glint came into her popping eyes. "If you weren't such a drab, ordinary little man," she said, "I'd think you'd planned it all. Sticking your tongue out, saying you were sitting in the catbird seat, because you thought no one would believe me when I told it! My God, it's really too perfect!" She brayed loudly and hysterically, and the fury was on her again. She glared at Mr. Fitweiler. "Can't you see how he has tricked us, you old fool? Can't you see his little game?" But Mr. Fitweiler had been surreptitiously pressing all the buttons under the top of his desk and employees of F & S began pouring into the room. "Stockton," said Mr. Fitweiler, "you and Fishbein will take Mrs. Barrows to her home. Mrs. Powell, you will go with them." Stockton, who had played a little football in high school, blocked Mrs. Barrows as she made for Mr. Martin. It took him and Fishbein together to force her out of the door into the hall, crowded with stenographers and office boys. She was still screaming imprecations at Mr. Martin, tangled and contradictory imprecations. The hub-bub finally died out down the corridor.

"I regret that this has happened," said Mr. Fitweiler. "I shall ask you to dismiss it from your mind, Martin." "Yes, sir," said Mr. Martin, anticipating his chief's "That will be all" by moving to the door. "I will dismiss it." He went out and shut the door, and his step was light and quick in the hall. When he entered his department he had slowed down to his customary gait, and he walked quietly across the room to the W20 file, wearing a look of studious concentration.

QUESTIONS

1. What are the outstanding traits of Mr. Martin's character, as others in the story see him? What false impressions of himself does he leave with Mrs. Barrows after he visits her apartment?
2. What do we know about Mr. Martin's inner self that is unknown to the other characters in the story? Why *isn't* he a stock character — merely the fussy, colorless, mild-mannered little man familiar from comic strips and television comedy?
3. Sum up your impressions of Mrs. Ulgine Barrows. What peculiarities does Thurber give her? What elements of her character lead her into conflict with Mr. Martin?
4. How convincing is the motivation that the author gives Mr. Martin? For what reasons does Martin go to Mrs. Barrows's apartment with the notion of killing her? Why does he then pretend to vices he doesn't have, insult his employer, and stick out his tongue at Mrs. Barrows?
5. What is the point of view, and how is it appropriate to this story? Why could not the story be told equally well from the point of view of Mrs. Barrows, or from that of a totally objective narrator, who could not see into the mind of any character?
6. Recall the definition of an *antihero* (page 45). Would you call Mr. Martin an antihero? What do you take to be James Thurber's attitude toward him? How can you tell?

Richard Brautigan (b. 1935)

THE KOOL-AID WINO   1967

When I was a child I had a friend who became a Kool-Aid wino as the result of a rupture. He was a member of a very large and poor German family. All the older children in the family had to work in the fields during the summer, picking beans for two-and-one-half cents a pound to keep the family going. Everyone worked except my friend who couldn't because he was ruptured.

There was no money for an operation. There wasn't even money to buy him a truss. So he stayed home and became a Kool-Aid wino.

One morning in August I went over to his house. He was still in bed. He looked up at me from underneath a tattered revolution of old blankets. He had never slept under a sheet in his life.

"Did you bring the nickel you promised?" he asked.

"Yeah," I said. "It's here in my pocket."

"Good."

He hopped out of bed and he was already dressed. He had told me once that he never took off his clothes when he went to bed.

"Why bother?" he had said. "You're only going to get up, anyway. Be prepared for it. You're not fooling anyone by taking your clothes off when you go to bed."

He went into the kitchen, stepping around the littlest children, whose wet diapers were in various stages of anarchy. He made his breakfast: a slice of homemade bread covered with Karo syrup and peanut butter.

"Let's go," he said.

We left the house with him still eating the sandwich. The store was three blocks away, on the other side of a field covered with heavy yellow grass. There were many pheasants in the field. Fat with summer they barely flew away when we came up to them.

"Hello," said the grocer. He was bald with a red birthmark on his head. The birthmark looked just like an old car parked on his head. He automatically reached for a package of grape Kool-Aid and put it on the counter.

"Five cents."

"He's got it," my friend said.

I reached into my pocket and gave the nickel to the grocer. He nodded and the old red car wobbled back and forth on the road as if the driver were having an epileptic seizure.

We left.

My friend led the way across the field. One of the pheasants didn't even bother to fly. He ran across the field in front of us like a feathered pig.

When we got back to my friend's house the ceremony began. To him the making of Kool-Aid was a romance and a ceremony. It had to be performed in an exact manner and with dignity.

First he got a gallon jar and we went around to the side of the house where the water spigot thrust itself out of the ground like the finger of a saint, surrounded by a mud puddle.

He opened the Kool-Aid and dumped it into the jar. Putting the jar under the spigot, he turned the water on. The water spit, splashed and guzzled out of the spigot.

He was careful to see that the jar did not overflow and the precious Kool-Aid spill out onto the ground. When the jar was full he turned the water off with a sudden but delicate motion like a famous brain surgeon removing a disordered portion of the imagination. Then he screwed the lid tightly onto the top of the jar and gave it a good shake.

The first part of the ceremony was over.

Like the inspired priest of an exotic cult, he had performed the first part of the ceremony well.

His mother came around the side of the house and said in a voice filled with sand and string, "When are you going to do the dishes? . . . Huh?"

"Soon," he said.

"Well, you better," she said.

When she left, it was as if she had never been there at all. The second part of the ceremony began with him carrying the jar very carefully to an abandoned chicken house in the back. "The dishes can wait," he said to me. Bertrand Russell could not have stated it better.

He opened the chicken house door and we went in. The place was littered with half-rotten comic books. They were like fruit under a tree. In the corner was an old mattress and beside the mattress were four quart jars. He took the gallon jar over to them, and filled them carefully not spilling a drop. He screwed their caps on tightly and was now ready for a day's drinking.

You're supposed to make only two quarts of Kool-Aid from a package, but he always made a gallon, so his Kool-Aid was a mere shadow of its desired potency. And you're supposed to add a cup of sugar to every package of Kool-Aid, but he never put any sugar in his Kool-Aid because there wasn't any sugar to put in it.

He created his own Kool-Aid reality and was able to illuminate himself by it.

Questions

1. Does Brautigan give his antihero any motivation? Why does the Kool-Aid wino withdraw into his private world? Sum up the effect of these details of his *real* world: "a tattered revolution of old blankets," "wet diapers . . . in various stages of anarchy," the pheasant "like a feathered pig," the mother who asks him to do the dishes.
2. "When the jar was full he turned the water off with a sudden but delicate motion like a famous brain surgeon removing a disordered portion of the imagination." In this statement about the wino, and in the portrait of him that emerges from the whole story, how would you sum up the narrator's attitude?
3. As a character, is the grocer "round" or "flat"? What is his most outstanding feature?
4. Compare the Kool-Aid wino with the boy who tells his story in James Joyce's "Araby" (Chapter Two) and with the boy Sarty Snopes in William Faulkner's "Barn Burning" (Chapter Four). Which are the static characters, which the dynamic?
5. Make up a new story in which the Kool-Aid wino is the main character, and tell it (or write it) in brief summary. What kinds of situations and events would seem to follow from the nature of this character?

Isaac Bashevis Singer (b. 1904)

Gimpel the Fool   1953

Translated by Saul Bellow

I am Gimpel the fool. I don't think myself a fool. On the contrary. But that's what folks call me. They gave me the name while I was still in school. I had seven names in all: imbecile, donkey, flax-head, dope, glump, ninny, and fool.

The last name stuck. What did my foolishness consist of? I was easy to take in. They said, "Gimpel, you know the rabbi's wife has been brought to childbed?" So I skipped school. Well, it turned out to be a lie. How was I supposed to know? She hadn't had a big belly. But I never looked at her belly. Was that really so foolish? The gang laughed and hee-hawed, stomped and danced and chanted a good-night prayer. And instead of the raisins they give when a woman's lying in, they stuffed my hand full of goat turds. I was no weakling. If I slapped someone he'd see all the way to Cracow. But I'm really not a slugger by nature. I think to myself, Let it pass. So they take advantage of me.

I was coming home from school and heard a dog barking. I'm not afraid of dogs, but of course I never want to start up with them. One of them may be mad, and if he bites there's not a Tartar in the world who can help you. So I made tracks. Then I looked around and saw the whole market place wild with laughter. It was no dog at all but Wolf-Leib the thief. How was I supposed to know it was he? It sounded like a howling bitch.

When the pranksters and leg-pullers found that I was easy to fool, every one of them tried his luck with me. "Gimpel, the Czar is coming to Frampol; Gimpel, the moon fell down in Turbeen; Gimpel, little Hodel Furpiece found a treasure behind the bathhouse." And I like a *golem*° believed everyone. In the first place, everything is possible, as it is written in the Wisdom of the Fathers, I've forgotten just how. Second, I had to believe when the whole town came down on me! If I ever dared to say, "Ah, you're kidding!" there was trouble. People got angry. "What do you mean! You want to call everyone a liar?" What was I to do? I believed them, and I hope at least that did them some good.

I was an orphan. My grandfather who brought me up was already bent toward the grave. So they turned me over to a baker, and what a time they gave me there! Every woman or girl who came to bake a pan of cookies or dry a batch of noodles had to fool me at least once. "Gimpel, there's a fair in heaven; Gimpel, the rabbi gave birth to a calf in the seventh month; Gimpel, a cow flew over the roof and laid brass eggs." A student from the yeshiva° came once to buy a roll, and he said, "You, Gimpel, while you stand here scraping with your baker's shovel the Messiah has come. The dead have arisen." "What do you mean?" I said. "I heard no one blowing the ram's horn!" He said, "Are you deaf?" And all began to cry, "We heard it, we heard!" Then in came Reitze the candle-dipper and called out in her hoarse voice, "Gimpel, your father and mother have stood up from the grave. They're looking for you."

To tell the truth, I knew very well that nothing of the sort had happened, but all the same, as folks were talking, I threw on my wool vest and went out. Maybe something had happened. What did I stand to lose by looking? Well, what a cat music went up! And then I took a vow to believe nothing more. But that was no go either. They confused me so that I didn't know the big end from the small.

I went to the rabbi to get some advice. He said, "It is written, better to be a fool all your days than for one hour to be evil. You are not a fool. They are the fools. For he who causes his neighbor to feel shame loses Paradise himself."

golem: simpleton. From the Hebrew: "a yet-unformed thing" (*Psalms* 139:16); a mere robot, a shapeless mass.
yeshiva: school of theology.

Nevertheless the rabbi's daughter took me in. As I left the rabbinical court she said, "Have you kissed the wall yet?" I said, "No; what for?" She answered, "It's a law; you've got to do it after every visit." Well, there didn't seem to be any harm in it. And she burst out laughing. It was a fine trick. She put one over on me, all right.

I wanted to go off to another town, but then everyone got busy matchmaking, and they were after me so they nearly tore my coat tails off. They talked at me and talked until I got water on the ear. She was no chaste maiden, but they told me she was virgin pure. She had a limp, and they said it was deliberate, from coyness. She had a bastard, and they told me the child was her little brother. I cried, "You're wasting your time. I'll never marry that whore." But they said indignantly, "What a way to talk! Aren't you ashamed of yourself? We can take you to the rabbi and have you fined for giving her a bad name." I saw then that I wouldn't escape them so easily and I thought, They're set on making me their butt. But when you're married the husband's the master, and if that's all right with her it's agreeable to me too. Besides, you can't pass through life unscathed, nor expect to.

I went to her clay house, which was built on the sand, and the whole gang, hollering and chorusing, came after me. They acted like bearbaiters. When we came to the well they stopped all the same. They were afraid to start anything with Elka. Her mouth would open as if it were on a hinge, and she had a fierce tongue. I entered the house. Lines were strung from wall to wall and clothes were drying. Barefoot she stood by the tub, doing the wash. She was dressed in a worn hand-me-down gown of plush. She had her hair put up in braids and pinned across her head. It took my breath away, almost, the reek of it all.

Evidently she knew who I was. She took a look at me and said, "Look who's here! He's come, the drip. Grab a seat."

I told her all; I denied nothing. "Tell me the truth," I said, "are you really a virgin, and is that mischievous Yechiel actually your little brother? Don't be deceitful with me, for I'm an orphan."

"I'm an orphan myself," she answered, "and whoever tries to twist you up, may the end of his nose take a twist. But don't let them think they can take advantage of me. I want a dowry of fifty guilders, and let them take up a collection besides. Otherwise they can kiss my you-know-what." She was very plain-spoken. I said, "It's the bride and not the groom who gives a dowry." Then she said, "Don't bargain with me. Either a flat 'yes' or a flat 'no' — go back where you came from."

I thought, No bread will ever be baked from *this* dough. But ours is not a poor town. They consented to everything and proceeded with the wedding. It so happened that there was a dysentery epidemic at the time. The ceremony was held at the cemetery gates, near the little corpse-washing hut. The fellows got drunk. While the marriage contract was being drawn up I heard the most pious high rabbi ask, "Is the bride a widow or a divorced woman?" And the sexton's wife answered for her, "Both a widow and divorced." It was a black moment for me. But what was I to do, run away from under the marriage canopy?

There was singing and dancing. An old granny danced opposite me, hugging a braided white *chalah°*. The master of revels made a "God 'a mercy" in memory of the bride's parents. The schoolboys threw burrs, as on *Tishe b' Av* fast day°. There were a lot of gifts after the sermon: a noodle board, a kneading trough, a bucket, brooms, ladles, household articles galore. Then I took a look and saw two strapping young men carrying a crib. "What do we need this for?" I asked. So they said, "Don't rack your brains about it. It's all right, it'll come in handy." I realized I was going to be rooked. Take it another way though, what did I stand to lose? I reflected, I'll see what comes of it. A whole town can't go altogether crazy.

2

At night I came where my wife lay, but she wouldn't let me in. "Say, look here, is this what they married us for?" I said. And she said, "My monthly has come." "But yesterday they took you to the ritual bath, and that's afterward, isn't it supposed to be?" "Today isn't yesterday," said she, "and yesterday's not today. You can beat it if you don't like it." In short, I waited.

Not four months later she was in childbed. The townsfolk hid their laughter with their knuckles. But what could I do? She suffered intolerable pains and clawed at the walls. "Gimpel," she cried, "I'm going. Forgive me!" The house filled with women. They were boiling pans of water. The screams rose to the welkin.

The thing to do was to go to the House of Prayer to repeat Psalms, and that was what I did.

The townsfolk liked that, all right. I stood in a corner saying Psalms and prayers, and they shook their heads at me. "Pray, pray!" they told me. "Prayer never made any woman pregnant." One of the congregation put a straw to my mouth and said, "Hay for the cows." There was something to that too, by God!

She gave birth to a boy. Friday at the synagogue the sexton stood up before the Ark, pounded on the reading table, and announced, "The wealthy Reb Gimpel invites the congregation to a feast in honor of the birth of a son." The whole House of Prayer rang with laughter. My face was flaming. But there was nothing I could do. After all, I *was* the one responsible for the circumcision honors and rituals.

Half the town came running. You couldn't wedge another soul in. Women brought peppered chick-peas, and there was a keg of beer from the tavern. I ate and drank as much as anyone, and they all congratulated me. Then there was a circumcision, and I named the boy after my father, may he rest in peace. When all were gone and I was left with my wife alone, she thrust her head through the bed-curtain and called me to her.

"Gimpel," said she, "why are you silent? Has your ship gone and sunk?"

"What shall I say?" I answered. "A fine thing you've done to me! If my mother had known of it she'd have died a second time."

She said, "Are you crazy, or what?"

---

chalah: loaf of bread glazed with egg white, a Sabbath and holiday delicacy.
Tishe b'Av: day of mourning that commemorates disasters and persecutions.

"How can you make such a fool," I said, "of one who should be the lord and master?"

"What's the matter with you?" she said. "What have you taken it into your head to imagine?"

I saw that I must speak bluntly and openly. "Do you think this is the way to use an orphan?" I said. "You have borne a bastard."

She answered, "Drive this foolishness out of your head. The child is yours."

"How can he be mine?" I argued. "He was born seventeen weeks after the wedding."

She told me then that he was premature. I said, "Isn't he a little too premature?" She said she had had a grandmother who carried just as short a time and she resembled this grandmother of hers as one drop of water does another. She swore to it with such oaths that you would have believed a peasant at the fair if he had used them. To tell the plain truth, I didn't believe her; but when I talked it over next day with the schoolmaster he told me that the very same thing had happened to Adam and Eve. Two they went up to bed, and four they descended.

"There isn't a woman in the world who is not the granddaughter of Eve," he said.

That was how it was — they argued me dumb. But then, who really knows how such things are?

I began to forget my sorrow. I loved the child madly, and he loved me too. As soon as he saw me he'd wave his little hands and want me to pick him up, and when he was colicky I was the only one who could pacify him. I bought him a little bone teething ring and a little gilded cap. He was forever catching the evil eye from someone, and then I had to run to get one of those abracadabras for him that would get him out of it. I worked like an ox. You know how expenses go up when there's an infant in the house. I don't want to lie about it; I didn't dislike Elka either, for that matter. She swore at me and cursed, and I couldn't get enough of her. What strength she had! One of her looks could rob you of the power of speech. And her orations! Pitch and sulphur, that's what they were full of, and yet somehow also full of charm. I adored her every word. She gave me bloody wounds though.

In the evening I brought her a white loaf as well as a dark one, and also poppyseed rolls I baked myself. I thieved because of her and swiped everything I could lay hands on, macaroons, raisins, almonds, cakes. I hope I may be forgiven for stealing from the Saturday pots the women left to warm in the baker's oven. I would take out scraps of meat, a chunk of pudding, a chicken leg or head, a piece of tripe, whatever I could nip quickly. She ate and became fat and handsome.

I had to sleep away from home all during the week, at the bakery. On Friday nights when I got home she always made an excuse of some sort. Either she had heartburn, or a stitch in the side, or hiccups, or headaches. You know what women's excuses are. I had a bitter time of it. It was rough. To add to it, this little brother of hers, the bastard, was growing bigger. He'd put lumps on me, and when I wanted to hit back she'd open her mouth and curse so powerfully I saw a green haze floating before my eyes. Ten times a day she threatened to divorce me. Another man in my place would have taken French leave and disappeared. But I'm the type that bears it and says nothing. What's one to do? Shoulders are from God, and burdens too.

One night there was a calamity in the bakery; the oven burst, and we almost had a fire. There was nothing to do but go home, so I went home. Let me, I thought, also taste the joy of sleeping in bed in midweek. I didn't want to wake the sleeping mite and tiptoed into the house. Coming in, it seemed to me that I heard not the snoring of one but, as it were, a double snore, one a thin enough snore and the other like the snoring of a slaughtered ox. Oh, I didn't like that! I didn't like it at all. I went up to the bed, and things suddenly turned black. Next to Elka lay a man's form. Another in my place would have made an uproar, and enough noise to rouse the whole town, but the thought occurred to me that I might wake the child. A little thing like that — why frighten a little swallow like that, I thought. All right then, I went back to the bakery and stretched out on a sack of flour, and till morning I never shut an eye. I shivered as if I had had malaria. "Enough of being a donkey," I said to myself. "Gimpel isn't going to be a sucker all his life. There's a limit even to the foolishness of a fool like Gimpel."

In the morning I went to the rabbi to get advice, and it made a great commotion in the town. They sent the beadle for Elka right away. She came, carrying the child. And what do you think she did? She denied it, denied everything, bone and stone! "He's out of his head," she said. "I know nothing of dreams or divinations." They yelled at her, warned her, hammered on the table, but she stuck to her guns: it was a false accusation, she said.

The butchers and the horse-traders took her part. One of the lads from the slaughterhouse came by and said to me, "We've got our eye on you, you're a marked man." Meanwhile the child started to bear down and soiled itself. In the rabbinical court there was an Ark of the Covenant, and they couldn't allow that, so they sent Elka away.

I said to the rabbi, "What shall I do?"

"You must divorce her at once," said he.

"And what if she refuses?" I asked.

He said, "You must serve the divorce, that's all you'll have to do."

I said, "Well, all right, Rabbi. Let me think about it."

"There's nothing to think about," said he. "You mustn't remain under the same roof with her."

"And if I want to see the child?" I asked.

"Let her go, the harlot," said he, "and her brood of bastards with her."

The verdict he gave was that I mustn't even cross her threshold — never again, as long as I should live.

During the day it didn't bother me so much. I thought, It was bound to happen, the abscess had to burst. But at night when I stretched out upon the sacks I felt it all very bitterly. A longing took me, for her and for the child. I wanted to be angry, but that's my misfortune exactly, I don't have it in me to be really angry. In the first place — this was how my thoughts went — there's bound to be a slip sometimes. You can't live without errors. Probably that lad who was with her led her on and gave her presents and what not, and women are often long on hair and short on sense, and so he got around her. And then since she denies it so, maybe I was only seeing things? Hallucinations do happen. You see a figure or a mannikin or something, but when you come up closer it's nothing, there's not a thing there. And if that's so, I'm doing her an injustice. And when I got so far in my thoughts I started to weep. I sobbed so that I wet the flour where I lay. In the morning I went to the rabbi and told him that I had made a mistake. The rabbi wrote on with his quill, and he said that if that were so he would have to reconsider the whole case. Until he had finished I wasn't to go near my wife, but I might send her bread and money by messenger.

3

Nine months passed before all the rabbis could come to an agreement. Letters went back and forth. I hadn't realized that there could be so much erudition about a matter like this.

Meantime Elka gave birth to still another child, a girl this time. On the Sabbath I went to the synagogue and invoked a blessing on her. They called me up to the Torah, and I named the child for my mother-in-law, may she rest in peace. The louts and loudmouths of the town who came into the bakery gave me a going over. All Frampol refreshed its spirits because of my trouble and grief. However, I resolved that I would always believe what I was told. What's the good of *not* believing? Today it's your wife you don't believe; tomorrow it's God Himself you won't take stock in.

By an apprentice who was her neighbor I sent her daily a corn or a wheat loaf, or a piece of pastry, rolls or bagels, or, when I got the chance, a slab of pudding, a slice of honeycake, or wedding strudel — whatever came my way. The apprentice was a goodhearted lad, and more than once he added something on his own. He had formerly annoyed me a lot, plucking my nose and digging me in the ribs, but when he started to be a visitor to my house he became kind and friendly. "Hey, you, Gimpel," he said to me, "you have a very decent little wife and two fine kids. You don't deserve them."

"But the things people say about her," I said.

"Well, they have long tongues," he said, "and nothing to do with them but babble. Ignore it as you ignore the cold of last winter."

One day the rabbi sent for me and said, "Are you certain, Gimpel, that you were wrong about your wife?"

I said, "I'm certain."

"Why, but look here! You yourself saw it."

"It must have been a shadow," I said.

"The shadow of what?"

"Just of one of the beams, I think."

"You can go home then. You owe thanks to the Yanover rabbi. He found an obscure reference in Maimonides that favored you."

I seized the rabbi's hand and kissed it.

I wanted to run home immediately. It's no small thing to be separated for so long a time from wife and child. Then I reflected, I'd better go back to work now, and go home in the evening. I said nothing to anyone, although as far as my heart was concerned it was like one of the Holy Days. The women teased and twitted me as they did every day, but my thought was, Go on, with your loose talk. The truth is out, like the oil upon the water. Maimonides says it's right, and therefore it is right!

At night, when I had covered the dough to let it rise, I took my share of bread and a little sack of flour and started homeward. The moon was full and the stars were glistening, something to terrify the soul. I hurried onward, and before me darted a long shadow. It was winter, and a fresh snow had fallen. I had a mind to sing, but it was growing late and I didn't want to wake the householders. Then I felt like whistling, but remembered that you don't whistle at night because it brings the demons out. So I was silent and walked as fast as I could.

Dogs in the Christian yards barked at me when I passed, but I thought, Bark your teeth out! What are you but mere dogs? Whereas I am a man, the husband of a fine wife, the father of promising children.

As I approached the house my heart started to pound as though it were the heart of a criminal. I felt no fear, but my heart went thump! thump! Well, no drawing back. I quietly lifted the latch and went in. Elka was asleep. I looked at the infant's cradle. The shutter was closed, but the moon forced its way through the cracks. I saw the newborn child's face and loved it as soon as I saw it — immediately — each tiny bone.

Then I came nearer to the bed. And what did I see but the apprentice lying there beside Elka. The moon went out all at once. It was utterly black, and I trembled. My teeth chattered. The bread fell from my hands and my wife waked and said, "Who is that, ah?"

I muttered, "It's me."

"Gimpel?" she asked. "How come you're here? I thought it was forbidden."

"The rabbi said," I answered and shook as with a fever.

"Listen to me, Gimpel," she said, "go out to the shed and see if the goat's all right. It seems she's been sick." I have forgotten to say that we had a goat. When I heard she was unwell I went into the yard. The nannygoat was a good little creature. I had a nearly human feeling for her.

With hesitant steps I went up to the shed and opened the door. The goat stood there on her four feet. I felt her everywhere, drew her by the horns, examined her udders, and found nothing wrong. She had probably eaten too much bark. "Good night, little goat," I said. "Keep well." And the little beast answered with a "Maa" as though to thank me for the good will.

I went back. The apprentice had vanished.

"Where," I asked, "is the lad?"

"What lad?" my wife answered.

"What do you mean?" I said. "The apprentice. You were sleeping with him."

"The things I have dreamed this night and the night before," she said, "may they come true and lay you low, body and soul! An evil spirit has taken root in you and dazzles your sight." She screamed out, "You hateful creature! You moon calf! You spook! You uncouth man! Get out, or I'll scream all Frampol out of bed!"

Before I could move, her brother sprang out from behind the oven and struck me a blow on the back of the head. I thought he had broken my neck. I felt that something about me was deeply wrong, and I said, "Don't make a scandal. All that's needed now is that people should accuse me of raising spooks and *dybbuks*°." For that was what she had meant. "No one will touch bread of my baking."

In short, I somehow calmed her.

"Well," she said, "that's enough. Lie down, and be shattered by wheels."

Next morning I called the apprentice aside. "Listen here, brother!" I said. And so on and so forth. "What do you say?" He stared at me as though I had dropped from the roof or something.

"I swear," he said, "you'd better go to an herb doctor or some healer. I'm afraid you have a screw loose, but I'll hush it up for you." And that's how the thing stood.

To make a long story short, I lived twenty years with my wife. She bore me six children, four daughters and two sons. All kinds of things happened, but I neither saw nor heard. I believed, and that's all. The rabbi recently said to me, "Belief in itself is beneficial. It is written that a good man lives by his faith."

Suddenly my wife took sick. It began with a trifle, a little growth upon the breast. But she evidently was not destined to live long; she had no years. I spent a fortune on her. I have forgotten to say that by this time I had a bakery of my own and in Frampol was considered to be something of a rich man. Daily the healer came, and every witch doctor in the neighborhood was brought. They decided to use leeches, and after that to try cupping. They even called a doctor from Lublin, but it was too late. Before she died she called me to her bed and said, "Forgive me, Gimpel."

I said, "What is there to forgive? You have been a good and faithful wife."

"Woe, Gimpel!" she said. "It was ugly how I deceived you all these years. I want to go clean to my Maker, and so I have to tell you that the children are not yours."

If I had been clouted on the head with a piece of wood it couldn't have bewildered me more.

"Whose are they?" I asked.

"I don't know," she said, "there were a lot. . . . But they're not yours." And as she spoke she tossed her head to the side, her eyes turned glassy, and it was all up with Elka. On her whitened lips there remained a smile.

I imagined that, dead as she was, she was saying, "I deceived Gimpel. That was the meaning of my brief life."

4

One night, when the period of mourning was done, as I lay dreaming on the flour sacks, there came the Spirit of Evil himself and said to me, "Gimpel, why do you sleep?"

I said, "What should I be doing? Eating *kreplach*°?"

"The whole world deceives you," he said, "and you ought to deceive the world in your turn."

"How can I deceive all the world?" I asked him.

dybbuks: demons, or souls of the dead, who take possession of people.
kreplach: a kind of dumpling containing meat, cheese, or other filling.

He answered, "You might accumulate a bucket of urine every day and at night pour it into the dough. Let the sages of Frampol eat filth."

"What about judgment in the world to come?" I said.

"There is no world to come," he said. "They've sold you a bill of goods and talked you into believing you carried a cat in your belly. What nonsense!"

"Well then," I said, "and is there a God?"

He answered, "There is no God either."

"What," I said, "*is* there, then?"

"A thick mire."

He stood before my eyes with a goatish beard and horns, longtoothed, and with a tail. Hearing such words, I wanted to snatch him by the tail, but I tumbled from the flour sacks and nearly broke a rib. Then it happened that I had to answer the call of nature, and, passing, I saw the risen dough, which seemed to say to me, "Do it!" In brief, I let myself be persuaded.

At dawn the apprentice came. We kneaded the bread, scattered caraway seeds on it, and set it to bake. Then the apprentice went away, and I was left sitting in the little trench by the oven, on a pile of rags. Well, Gimpel, I thought, you've revenged yourself on them for all the shame they've put on you. Outside the frost glittered, but it was warm beside the oven. The flames heated my face. I bent my head and fell into a doze.

I saw in a dream, at once, Elka in her shroud. She called to me, "What have you done, Gimpel?"

I said to her, "It's all your fault," and started to cry.

"You fool!" she said. "You fool! Because I was false is everything false too? I never deceived anyone but myself. I'm paying for it all, Gimpel. They spare you nothing here."

I looked at her face. It was black. I was startled and waked, and remained sitting dumb. I sensed that everything hung in the balance. A false step now and I'd lose Eternal Life. But God gave me His help. I seized the long shovel and took out the loaves, carried them into the yard, and started to dig a hole in the frozen earth.

My apprentice came back as I was doing it. "What are you doing, boss?" he said, and grew pale as a corpse.

"I know what I'm doing," I said, and I buried it all before his very eyes.

Then I went home, took my hoard from its hiding place, and divided it among the children. "I saw your mother tonight," I said. "She's turning black, poor thing."

They were so astounded they couldn't speak a word.

"Be well," I said, "and forget that such a one as Gimpel ever existed." I put on my short coat, a pair of boots, took the bag that held my prayer shawl in one hand, my stick in the other, and kissed the *mezzuzah*°. When people saw me in the street they were greatly surprised.

"Where are you going?" they said.

I answered, "Into the world." And so I departed from Frampol.

I wandered over the land, and good people did not neglect me. After many years I became old and white; I heard a great deal, many lies and false-

mezzuzah: a small oblong container, affixed near the front door of the house, which holds copies of Biblical verses (including a reminder to obey God's laws when traveling away from home).

hoods, but the longer I lived the more I understood that there were really no lies. Whatever doesn't really happen is dreamed at night. It happens to one if it doesn't happen to another, tomorrow if not today, or a century hence if not next year. What difference can it make? Often I heard tales of which I said, "Now this is a thing that cannot happen." But before a year had elapsed I heard that it actually had come to pass somewhere.

Going from place to place, eating at strange tables, it often happens that I spin yarns — improbable things that could never have happened — about devils, magicians, windmills, and the like. The children run after me, calling, "Grandfather, tell us a story." Sometimes they ask for particular stories, and I try to please them. A fat young boy once said to me, "Grandfather, it's the same story you told us before." The little rogue, he was right.

So it is with dreams too. It is many years since I left Frampol, but as soon as I shut my eyes I am there again. And whom do you think I see? Elka. She is standing by the washtub, as at our first encounter, but her face is shining and her eyes are radiant as the eyes of a saint, and she speaks outlandish words to me, strange things. When I wake I have forgotten it all. But while the dream lasts I am comforted. She answers all my queries, and what comes out is that all is right. I weep and implore, "Let me be with you." And she consoles me and tells me to be patient. The time is nearer than it is far. Sometimes she strokes and kisses me and weeps upon my face. When I awaken I feel her lips and taste the salt of her tears.

No doubt the world is entirely an imaginary world, but it is only once removed from the true world. At the door of the hovel where I lie, there stands the plank on which the dead are taken away. The gravedigger Jew has his spade ready. The grave waits and the worms are hungry; the shrouds are prepared — I carry them in my beggar's sack. Another *shnorrer*° is waiting to inherit my bed of straw. When the time comes I will go joyfully. Whatever may be there, it will be real, without complication, without ridicule, without deception. God be praised: there even Gimpel cannot be deceived.

Questions

1. In what ways does Gimpel appear to deserve his nickname *the fool?* In what other ways is Gimpel not foolish at all?
2. What does Gimpel find to love in the character of Elka? Consider in particular the scene of her deathbed confession and her later appearance in Gimpel's dreams.
3. Why does Gimpel momentarily listen to the Devil? How is he delivered from temptation? For what reasons does he finally divide his wealth and become a poor wanderer? Would you call him a dynamic character, or a static character — one who grows and develops in the course of the story, or one who remains unchanged?
4. "No doubt the world is entirely an imaginary world, but it is only once removed from the true world." Comment on this statement in the closing paragraph. What do you think it means?
5. What elements of the supernatural do you find in "Gimpel the Fool"? What details of down-to-earth realism?
6. In what respects does the story resemble a fable? Is it possible to draw any moral from it?

shnorrer: a beggar, a traveling panhandler.

4 Tone and Style

In many Victorian novels it was customary for some commentator, presumably the author, to interrupt the story from time to time, remarking upon the action, offering philosophic asides, or explaining the procedures to be followed in telling the story.

> Two hours later, Dorothea was seated in an inner room or boudoir of a handsome apartment in the Via Sistina. I am sorry to add that she was sobbing bitterly. . . .
> — George Eliot in *Middlemarch* (1873)

> But let the gentle-hearted reader be under no apprehension whatsoever. It is not destined that Eleanor shall marry Mr. Slope or Bertie Stanhope.
> — Anthony Trollope in *Barchester Towers* (1857)

> And, as we bring our characters forward, I will ask leave, as a man and a brother, not only to introduce, but occasionally to step down from the platform, and talk about them: if they are good and kindly, to love them and shake them by the hand; if they are silly, to laugh at them confidentially in the reader's sleeve; if they are wicked and heartless, to abuse them in the strongest terms which politeness admits of.
> — William Makepeace Thackeray in *Vanity Fair* (1847–1848)

Of course, the voice of this commentator was not identical with that of the "real life" author — the one toiling over an inkpot, worrying about publication deadlines and whether the rent would be paid. At times the living author might have been far different in personality from that usually wise and cheerful intruder who kept addressing the reader of the book. Much of the time, to be sure, the author probably agreed with whatever attitudes his alter ego expressed. But, in effect, the author created the character of a commentator to speak for him and throughout the novel artfully sustained that character's voice.

Such intrusions, although sometimes useful to the "real" author and enjoyable to the reader, are today rare. Modern storytellers, carefully keeping out of sight, seldom comment on their plots and characters. Apparently they agree with Anton Chekhov that a writer should not judge his characters but should serve as their "impartial witness."

And yet, no less definitely than Victorian novelists who introduced commentators, every writer of an effective story no doubt has feelings toward his characters and events. The author presumably cares about these imaginary people and, in order for the story to grasp and sustain our interest, has to make us see these people in such a way that we, too, will care about them. When at the beginning of "In Exile" Chekhov introduces us to the Tartar, he does so with a description that arouses sympathy:

> The Tartar was worn out and ill, and, wrapping himself in his rags, he talked about how good it was in the province of Simbirsk, and what a beautiful and clever wife he had left at home. He was not more than twenty-five, and in the firelight his pale, sickly face and woebegone expression made him seem like a boy.

Other than the comparison of the Tartar to a child, the details in this passage seem mostly factual: the young man's illness, ragged clothes, facial expression, and topics of conversation. But these details form a portrait that stirs pity. By his selection of these imaginary details out of countless others that he might have included, Chekhov firmly directs our feelings about the Tartar, so miserable and pathetic in his sickness and his homesickness. We cannot know, of course, exactly what the living Chekhov felt; but at least we can be sure that we are supposed to share the compassion and tenderness of the narrator — Chekhov's impartial (but human) witness.

Not only the author's choice of details may lead us to infer his attitude, but also his choice of characters, events, and situations, and his choice of words. When the narrator of Joseph Conrad's *Heart of Darkness* comes upon an African outpost littered with abandoned machines and notices "a boiler wallowing in the grass," the exact word *wallowing* conveys an attitude: that there is something swinish about this scene of careless waste. Whatever leads us to infer the author's attitude is commonly called **tone**. Like a tone of voice, the tone of a story may communicate amusement, anger, affection, sorrow, contempt. It implies the feelings of the author, so far as we can sense them. Those feelings may be similar to feelings expressed by the narrator of the story (or by any character), but sometimes they may be dissimilar, even sharply opposed. The characters in a story may regard an event as sad, but we sense that the author regards it as funny. To understand the tone of a story, then, is to understand some attitude more fundamental to the story than whatever attitude the characters explicitly declare.

The tone of a story, like a tone of voice, may convey not simply one attitude, but a medley. Reading "Gimpel the Fool" (Chapter Three), we have mingled feelings toward Gimpel and his "foolishness": amusement that Gimpel is so easily deceived; sympathy, perhaps, for his excessive innocence; admiration for his unwavering faith in God and fellow man. Often the tone of a literary story will be too rich and complicated to sum up in one or two words. But to try to describe the tone of such a story may be a useful way to penetrate to its center and to grasp the whole of it.

One of the clearest indications of the tone of a story is the **style** in which it is written. In general, style refers to the individual traits or characteristics of a piece of writing; to a writer's particular ways of managing words that we come to recognize as habitual or customary. A distinctive style clearly marks the work of a fine writer: we can tell his work from that of anyone else. From one story to another, however, the writer may fittingly modify his style, and in some stories, style may be altered meaningfully as the story goes along. In his novel *As I Lay Dying,* William Faulkner changes narrators with every chapter, and he distinguishes the narrators one from another by giving each an individual style or manner of speaking. Though each narrator has his own style, the book as a whole demonstrates Faulkner's style as well. For instance, one chapter is written from the point of view of a small boy, Vardaman Bundren, member of a family of poor Mississippi tenant farmers, whose view of a horse in a barn reads like this:

> It is as though the dark were resolving him out of his integrity, into an unrelated scattering of components — snuffings and stampings; smells of cooling flesh and ammoniac hair; an illusion of a coordinated whole of splotched hide and strong bones within which, detached and secret and familiar, an *is* different from my *is*.[1]

How can a small boy unaccustomed to libraries use words like *integrity, components, illusion,* and *coordinated*? Elsewhere in the story, Vardaman says aloud, with no trace of literacy, "Hit was a-laying right there on the ground." Apparently, in the passage it is not the voice of the boy that we are hearing, but something resembling the voice of William Faulkner, elevated and passionate, expressing the boy's thoughts in a style that admits Faulknerian words.

Usually, *style* indicates a mode of expression: the language a writer uses. In this sense, the notion of style includes such traits as the length and complexity of sentences, and **diction,** or choice of words: abstract or concrete, bookish ("unrelated scattering of components") or close to speech ("Hit was a-laying right there on the ground"). Involved in the idea of style, too, is any habitual use of imagery, patterns of sound, figures of speech, or other devices.

To see what style means, compare the stories at the end of this chapter by William Faulkner ("Barn Burning") and by Ernest Hemingway ("A Clean, Well-Lighted Place"). Faulkner frequently falls into a style in which a statement, as soon as uttered, is followed by another

[1] Modern Library edition (New York: Random House, 1930), p. 379.

statement expressing the idea in a more emphatic way. Sentences are interrupted with parenthetical elements (asides, like this) thrust into them unexpectedly. At times, Faulkner writes of seemingly ordinary matters as if giving a speech in a towering passion. Here, from "Barn Burning," is a description of how a boy's father delivers a rug:

> "Don't you want me to help?" he whispered. His father did not answer and now he heard again that stiff foot striking the hollow portico with that wooden and clocklike deliberation, that outrageous overstatement of the weight it carried. The rug, hunched, not flung (the boy could tell that even in the darkness) from his father's shoulder struck the angle of wall and floor with a sound unbelievably loud, thunderous, then the foot again, unhurried and enormous; a light came on in the house and the boy sat, tense, breathing steadily and quietly and just a little fast, though the foot itself did not increase its beat at all, descending the steps now; now the boy could see him.

Although this passage may seem a needlessly elaborate description of a man's footsteps and of his manner of setting down a rug, Faulkner is not merely indulging in language for its own sake. As you will find when you read the whole story, this rug-delivery is central to the story, and so is the father's profound defiance — indicated by his walk. By devices of style — by *metaphor* and *simile* ("wooden and clocklike"), by exact qualification ("not flung"), by emphatic adjectives ("loud, thunderous") — Faulkner is carefully placing his emphases. By the words he selects to describe the father's stride, Faulkner directs how we feel toward the man and perhaps also indicates his own wondering but skeptical attitude toward a character whose very footfall is "outrageous" and "enormous." (Fond of long sentences like the last one in the quoted passage, Faulkner once remarked that there are sentences that need to be written the way a circus acrobat pedals a bicycle on a high wire: rapidly, so as not to fall off.)

Hemingway's famous style includes both short sentences and long, but when the sentences are long they tend to be relatively simple in construction. Hemingway likes long compound sentences (clause plus clause plus clause), sometimes joined with "and's." He interrupts such a sentence with a dependent clause or a parenthetical element much less frequently than Faulkner does. The effect is like listening to speech:

> In the day time the street was dusty, but at night the dew settled the dust and the old man liked to sit late because he was deaf and now at night it was quiet and he felt the difference.

Hemingway is a master of swift, terse dialogue, and often casts whole scenes in the form of conversation. As if he were a closemouthed speaker unwilling to let his feelings loose, the narrator of a Hemingway story often addresses us in understatement, implying greater depths of feeling than he puts into words. Read the following story and you will see that its style and tone cannot be separated.

Ernest Hemingway (1899–1961)
A CLEAN, WELL-LIGHTED PLACE   1933

It was late and every one had left the café except an old man who sat in the shadow the leaves of the tree made against the electric light. In the day time the street was dusty, but at night the dew settled the dust and the old man liked to sit late because he was deaf and now at night it was quiet and he felt the difference. The two waiters inside the café knew that the old man was a little drunk, and while he was a good client they knew that if he became too drunk he would leave without paying, so they kept watch on him.

"Last week he tried to commit suicide," one waiter said.

"Why?"

"He was in despair."

"What about?"

"Nothing."

"How do you know it was nothing?"

"He has plenty of money."

They sat together at a table that was close against the wall near the door of the café and looked at the terrace where the tables were all empty except where the old man sat in the shadow of the leaves of the tree that moved slightly in the wind. A girl and a soldier went by in the street. The street light shone on the brass number on his collar. The girl wore no head covering and hurried beside him.

"The guard will pick him up," one waiter said.

"What does it matter if he gets what he's after?"

"He had better get off the street now. The guard will get him. They went by five minutes ago."

The old man sitting in the shadow rapped on his saucer with his glass. The younger waiter went over to him.

"What do you want?"

The old man looked at him. "Another brandy," he said.

"You'll be drunk," the waiter said. The old man looked at him. The waiter went away.

"He'll stay all night," he said to his colleague. "I'm sleepy now. I never get into bed before three o'clock. He should have killed himself last week."

The waiter took the brandy bottle and another saucer from the counter inside the café and marched out to the old man's table. He put down the saucer and poured the glass full of brandy.

"You should have killed yourself last week," he said to the deaf man. The old man motioned with his finger. "A little more," he said. The waiter poured on into the glass so that the brandy slopped over and ran down the stem into the top saucer of the pile. "Thank you," the old man said. The waiter took the bottle back inside the café. He sat down at the table with his colleague again.

"He's drunk now," he said.

"He's drunk every night."

"What did he want to kill himself for?"

"How should I know."

"How did he do it?"

"He hung himself with a rope."

"Who cut him down?"

"His niece."

"Why did they do it?"

"Fear for his soul."

"How much money has he got?"

"He's got plenty."

"He must be eighty years old."

"Anyway I should say he was eighty."

"I wish he would go home. I never get to bed before three o'clock. What kind of hour is that to go to bed?"

"He stays up because he likes it."

"He's lonely. I'm not lonely. I have a wife waiting in bed for me."

"He had a wife once too."

"A wife would be no good to him now."

"You can't tell. He might be better with a wife."

"His niece looks after him. You said she cut him down."

"I know."

"I wouldn't want to be that old. An old man is a nasty thing."

"Not always. This old man is clean. He drinks without spilling. Even now, drunk. Look at him."

"I don't want to look at him. I wish he would go home. He has no regard for those who must work."

The old man looked from his glass across the square, then over at the waiters.

"Another brandy," he said, pointing to his glass. The waiter who was in a hurry came over.

"Finished," he said, speaking with that omission of syntax stupid people employ when talking to drunken people or foreigners. "No more tonight. Close now."

"Another," said the old man.

"No. Finished." The waiter wiped the edge of the table with a towel and shook his head.

The old man stood up, slowly counted the saucers, took a leather coin purse from his pocket and paid for the drinks, leaving half a peseta tip.

The waiter watched him go down the street, a very old man walking unsteadily but with dignity.

"Why didn't you let him stay and drink?" the unhurried waiter asked. They were putting up the shutters. "It is not half-past two."

"I want to go home to bed."

"What is an hour?"

"More to me than to him."

"An hour is the same."

"You talk like an old man yourself. He can buy a bottle and drink at home."

"It's not the same."

"No, it is not," agreed the waiter with a wife. He did not wish to be unjust. He was only in a hurry.

"And you? You have no fear of going home before your usual hour?"

"Are you trying to insult me?"

"No, hombre, only to make a joke."

"No," the waiter who was in a hurry said, rising from pulling down the metal shutters. "I have confidence. I am all confidence."

"You have youth, confidence, and a job," the older waiter said. "You have everything."

"And what do you lack?"

"Everything but work."

"You have everything I have."

"No. I have never had confidence and I am not young."

"Come on. Stop talking nonsense and lock up."

"I am of those who like to stay late at the café," the older waiter said. "With all those who do not want to go to bed. With all those who need a light for the night."

"I want to go home and into bed."

"We are of two different kinds," the older waiter said. He was now dressed to go home. "It is not only a question of youth and confidence although those things are very beautiful. Each night I am reluctant to close up because there may be some one who needs the café."

"Hombre, there are bodegas° open all night long."

"You do not understand. This is a clean and pleasant café. It is well lighted. The light is very good and also, now, there are shadows of the leaves."

"Good night," said the younger waiter.

"Good night," the other said. Turning off the electric light he continued the conversation with himself. It is the light of course but it is necessary that the place be clean and pleasant. You do not want music. Certainly you do not want music. Nor can you stand before a bar with dignity although that is all that is provided for these hours. What did he fear? It was not fear or dread. It was a nothing that he knew too well. It was all a nothing and a man was nothing too. It was only that and light was all it needed and a certain cleanness and order. Some lived in it and never felt it but he knew it all was nada y pues nada y nada y pues nada°. Our nada who art in nada, nada be thy name thy kingdom nada thy will be nada in nada as it is in nada. Give us this nada our daily nada and nada us our nada as we nada our nadas and nada us not into nada but deliver us from nada; pues nada. Hail nothing full of nothing, nothing is with thee. He smiled and stood before a bar with a shining steam pressure coffee machine.

"What's yours?" asked the barman.

"Nada."

"Otro loco mas°," said the barman and turned away.

"A little cup," said the waiter.

The barman poured it for him.

bodegas: wine cellars.

nada y pues . . . nada: nothingness and then nothingness and nothingness and then nothingness.

Otro loco mas: another lunatic.

"The light is very bright and pleasant but the bar is unpolished," the waiter said.

The barman looked at him but did not answer. It was too late at night for conversation.

"You want another copita?" the barman asked.

"No, thank you," said the waiter and went out. He disliked bars and bodegas. A clean, well-lighted café was a very different thing. Now, without thinking further, he would go home to his room. He would lie in the bed and finally, with daylight, he would go to sleep. After all, he said to himself, it is probably only insomnia. Many must have it.

QUESTIONS

1. What besides insomnia makes the older waiter reluctant to go to bed? Comment especially on his meditation with its *nada* refrain. Why does he so well understand the old man's need for a café? What does the café represent for the two of them?
2. Compare the younger waiter and the older waiter in their attitudes toward the old man. Whose attitude do you take to be closer to that of the author? Even though Hemingway does not editorially state his own feelings, how does he make them clear to us?
3. Point to sentences that establish the style of the story. What is distinctive in them? What repetitions of words or phrases seem particularly effective? Does Hemingway seem to favor a simple or an erudite vocabulary?
4. What is the story's point of view? Discuss its appropriateness.

William Faulkner (1897–1962)
BARN BURNING
1939

The store in which the Justice of the Peace's court was sitting smelled of cheese. The boy, crouched on his nail keg at the back of the crowded room, knew he smelled cheese, and more: from where he sat he could see the ranked shelves close-packed with the solid, squat, dynamic shapes of tin cans whose labels his stomach read, not from the lettering which meant nothing to his mind but from the scarlet devils and the silver curve of fish — this, the cheese which he knew he smelled and the hermetic meat which his intestines believed he smelled coming in intermittent gusts momentary and brief between the other constant one, the smell and sense just a little of fear because mostly of despair and grief, the old fierce pull of blood. He could not see the table where the Justice sat and before which his father and his father's enemy (*our enemy* he thought in that despair; *ourn! mine and hisn both! He's my father!*) stood, but he could hear them, the two of them that is, because his father had said no word yet:

"But what proof have you, Mr. Harris?"

"I told you. The hog got into my corn. I caught it up and sent it back to him. He had no fence that would hold it. I told him so, warned him. The next time I put the hog in my pen. When he came to get it I gave him enough wire to patch up his pen. The next time I put the hog up and kept it. I rode down to his house and saw the wire I gave him still rolled on to the spool in his yard.

I told him he could have the hog when he paid me a dollar pound fee. That evening a nigger came with the dollar and got the hog. He was a strange nigger. He said, 'He say to tell you wood and hay kin burn.' I said, 'What?' 'That whut he say to tell you,' the nigger said. 'Wood and hay kin burn.' That night my barn burned. I got the stock out but I lost the barn."

"Where is the nigger? Have you got him?"

"He was a strange nigger, I tell you. I don't know what became of him."

"But that's not proof. Don't you see that's not proof?"

"Get that boy up here. He knows." For a moment the boy thought too that the man meant his older brother until Harris said, "Not him. The little one. The boy," and, crouching, small for his age, small and wiry like his father, in patched and faded jeans even too small for him, with straight, uncombed, brown hair and eyes gray and wild as storm scud, he saw the men between himself and the table part and become a lane of grim faces, at the end of which he saw the Justice, a shabby, collarless, graying man in spectacles, beckoning him. He felt no floor under his bare feet; he seemed to walk beneath the palpable weight of the grim turning faces. His father, stiff in his black Sunday coat donned not for the trial but for the moving, did not even look at him. *He aims for me to lie,* he thought, again with that frantic grief and despair. *And I will have to do hit.*

"What's your name, boy?" the Justice said.

"Colonel Sartoris Snopes," the boy whispered.

"Hey?" the Justice said. "Talk louder. Colonel Sartoris? I reckon anybody named for Colonel Sartoris in this country can't help but tell the truth, can they?" The boy said nothing. *Enemy! Enemy!* he thought; for a moment he could not even see, could not see that the Justice's face was kindly nor discern that his voice was troubled when he spoke to the man named Harris: "Do you want me to question this boy?" But he could hear, and during those subsequent long seconds while there was absolutely no sound in the crowded little room save that of quiet and intent breathing it was as if he had swung outward at the end of a grape vine, over a ravine, and at the top of the swing had been caught in a prolonged instant of mesmerized gravity, weightless in time.

"No!" Harris said violently, explosively. "Damnation! Send him out of here!" Now time, the fluid world, rushed beneath him again, the voices coming to him again through the smell of cheese and sealed meat, the fear and despair and the old grief of blood:

"This case is closed. I can't find against you, Snopes, but I can give you advice. Leave this country and don't come back to it."

His father spoke for the first time, his voice cold and harsh, level, without emphasis: "I aim to. I don't figure to stay in a country among people who . . ." he said something unprintable and vile, addressed to no one.

"That'll do," the Justice said. "Take your wagon and get out of this country before dark. Case dismissed."

His father turned, and he followed the stiff black coat, the wiry figure walking a little stiffly from where a Confederate provost's man's musket ball had taken him in the heel on a stolen horse thirty years ago, followed the two backs now, since his older brother had appeared from somewhere in the crowd, no taller than the father but thicker, chewing tobacco steadily, between the two lines of grim-faced men and out of the store and across the worn gallery and down the sagging steps and among the dogs and half-grown boys in the mild May dust, where as he passed a voice hissed:

"Barn burner!"

Again he could not see, whirling; there was a face in a red haze, moonlike, bigger than the full moon, the owner of it half again his size, he leaping in the red haze toward the face, feeling no blow, feeling no shock when his head struck the earth, scrabbling up and leaping again, feeling no blow this time either and tasting no blood, scrabbling up to see the other boy in full flight and himself already leaping into pursuit as his father's hand jerked him back, the harsh, cold voice speaking above him: "Go get in the wagon."

It stood in a grove of locusts and mulberries across the road. His two hulking sisters in their Sunday dresses and his mother and her sister in calico and sunbonnets were already in it, sitting on and among the sorry residue of the dozen and more movings which even the boy could remember — the battered stove, the broken beds and chairs, the clock inlaid with mother-of-pearl, which would not run, stopped at some fourteen minutes past two o'clock of a dead and forgotten day and time, which had been his mother's dowry. She was crying, though when she saw him she drew her sleeve across her face and began to descend from the wagon. "Get back," the father said.

"He's hurt. I got to get some water and wash his . . ."

"Get back in the wagon," his father said. He got in too, over the tail-gate. His father mounted to the seat where the older brother already sat and struck the gaunt mules two savage blows with the peeled willow, but without heat. It was not even sadistic; it was exactly that same quality which in later years would cause his descendants to over-run the engine before putting a motor car into motion, striking and reining back in the same movement. The wagon went on, the store with its quiet crowd of grimly watching men dropped behind; a curve in the road hid it. *Forever* he thought. *Maybe he's done satisfied now, now that he has . . .* stopping himself, not to say it aloud even to himself. His mother's hand touched his shoulder.

"Does hit hurt?" she said.

"Naw," he said. "Hit don't hurt. Lemme be."

"Can't you wipe some of the blood off before hit dries?"

"I'll wash to-night," he said. "Lemme be, I tell you."

The wagon went on. He did not know where they were going. None of them ever did or ever asked, because it was always somewhere, always a house of sorts waiting for them a day or two days or even three days away. Likely his father had already arranged to make a crop on another farm before he . . . Again he had to stop himself. He (the father) always did. There was something about his wolflike independence and even courage when the advantage was at least neutral which impressed strangers, as if they got from his latent ravening ferocity not so much a sense of dependability as a feeling that his ferocious conviction in the rightness of his own actions would be of advantage to all whose interest lay with his.

That night they camped, in a grove of oaks and beeches where a spring ran. The nights were still cool and they had a fire against it, of a rail lifted from a nearby fence and cut into lengths — a small fire, neat, niggard almost, a shrewd fire; such fires were his father's habit and custom always, even in freezing weather. Older, the boy might have remarked this and wondered why not a big one; why should not a man who had not only seen the waste and extravagance of war, but who had in his blood an inherent voracious prodigality with material not his own, have burned everything in sight? Then he might have gone a step farther and thought that that was the reason: that niggard blaze was the living fruit of nights passed during those four years in the woods hiding from all men, blue or gray, with his strings of horses (captured horses, he called them). And older still, he might have divined the true reason: that the element of fire spoke to some deep mainspring of his father's being, as the element of steel or of powder spoke to other men, as the one weapon for the preservation of integrity, else breath were not worth the breathing, and hence to be regarded with respect and used with discretion.

But he did not think this now and he had seen those same niggard blazes all his life. He merely ate his supper beside it and was already half asleep over his iron plate when his father called him, and once more he followed the stiff back, the stiff and ruthless limp, up the slope and on to the starlit road where, turning, he could see his father against the stars but without face or depth — a shape black, flat, and bloodless as though cut from tin in the iron folds of the frockcoat which had not been made for him, the voice harsh like tin and without heat like tin:

"You were fixing to tell them. You would have told him."

He didn't answer. His father struck him with the flat of his hand on the side of the head, hard but without heat, exactly as he had struck the two mules at the store, exactly as he would strike either of them with any stick in order to kill a horse fly, his voice still without heat or anger: "You're getting to be a man. You got to learn. You got to learn to stick to your own blood or you ain't going to have any blood to stick to you. Do you think either of them, any man there this morning, would? Don't you know all they wanted was a chance to get at me because they knew I had them beat? Eh?" Later, twenty years later, he was to tell himself, "If I had said they wanted only truth, justice, he would have hit me again." But now he said nothing. He was not crying. He just stood there. "Answer me," his father said.

"Yes," he whispered. His father turned.

"Get on to bed. We'll be there tomorrow."

Tomorrow they were there. In the early afternoon the wagon stopped before a paintless two-room house identical almost with the dozen others it had stopped before even in the boy's ten years, and again, as on the other dozen occasions, his mother and aunt got down and began to unload the wagon, although his two sisters and his father and brother had not moved.

"Likely hit ain't fitten for hawgs," one of the sisters said.

"Nevertheless, fit it will and you'll hog it and like it," his father said. "Get out of them chairs and help your Ma unload."

The two sisters got down, big, bovine, in a flutter of cheap ribbons; one of them drew from the jumbled wagon bed a battered lantern, the other a worn broom. His father handed the reins to the older son and began to climb stiffly over the wheel. "When they get unloaded, take the team to the barn and feed them." Then he said, and at first the boy thought he was still speaking to his brother: "Come with me."

"Me?" he said.

"Yes," his father said. "You."

"Abner," his mother said. His father paused and looked back — the harsh level stare beneath the shaggy, graying, irascible brows.

"I reckon I'll have a word with the man that aims to begin tomorrow owning me body and soul for the next eight months."

They went back up the road. A week ago — or before last night, that is — he would have asked where they were going, but not now. His father had struck him before last night but never before had he paused afterward to explain why; it was as if the blow and the following calm, outrageous voice still rang, repercussed, divulging nothing to him save the terrible handicap of being young, the light weight of his few years, just heavy enough to prevent his soaring free of the world as it seemed to be ordered but not heavy enough to keep him footed solid in it, to resist it and try to change the course of its events.

Presently he could see the grove of oaks and cedars and the other flowering trees and shrubs where the house would be, though not the house yet. They walked beside a fence massed with honeysuckle and Cherokee roses and came to a gate swinging open between two brick pillars, and now, beyond a sweep of drive, he saw the house for the first time and at that instant he forgot his father and the terror and despair both, and even when he remembered his father again (who had not stopped) the terror and despair did not return. Because, for all the twelve movings, they had sojourned until now in a poor country, a land of small farms and fields and houses, and he had never seen a house like this before. *Hit's big as a courthouse* he thought quietly, with a surge of peace and joy whose reason he could not have thought into words, being too young for that: *They are safe from him. People whose lives are a part of this peace and dignity are beyond his touch, he no more to them than a buzzing wasp: capable of stinging for a little moment but that's all; the spell of this peace and dignity rendering even the barns and stable and cribs which belong to it impervious to the puny flames he might contrive* . . . this, the peace and joy, ebbing for an instant as he looked again at the stiff black back, the stiff and implacable limp of the figure which was not dwarfed by the house, for the reason that it had never looked big anywhere and which now, against the serene columned backdrop, had more than ever that impervious quality of something cut ruthlessly from tin, depthless, as though, sidewise to the sun, it would cast no shadow. Watching him, the boy remarked the absolutely undeviating course which his father held and saw the stiff foot come squarely down in a pile of fresh droppings where a horse had stood in the drive and which his father could have avoided by a simple change of stride. But it ebbed only for a moment, though he could not have thought this into words either, walking on in the spell of the house, which he could even want but without envy, without sorrow, certainly never with that ravening and jealous rage which unknown to him walked in the ironlike black coat before him: *Maybe he will feel it too. Maybe it will even change him now from what maybe he couldn't help but be.*

They crossed the portico. Now he could hear his father's stiff foot as it came down on the boards with clocklike finality, a sound out of all proportion to the displacement of the body it bore and which was not dwarfed either by the white door before it, as though it had attained to a sort of vicious and ravening minimum not to be dwarfed by anything — the flat, wide, black hat, the formal coat of broadcloth which had once been black but which had now that friction-glazed greenish cast of the bodies of old house flies, the lifted sleeve which was too large, the lifted hand like a curled claw. The door opened so promptly that the boy knew the Negro must have been watching them all the time, an old man with neat grizzled hair, in a linen jacket, who stood barring the door with his body, saying, "Wipe yo foots, white man, fo you come in here. Major ain't home nohow."

"Get out of my way, nigger," his father said, without heat too, flinging the door back and the Negro also and entering, his hat still on his head. And now the boy saw the prints of the stiff foot on the doorjamb and saw them appear on the pale rug behind the machinelike deliberation of the foot which seemed to bear (or transmit) twice the weight which the body compassed. The Negro was shouting "Miss Lula! Miss Lula!" somewhere behind them, then the boy, deluged as though by a warm wave by a suave turn of the carpeted stair and a pendant glitter of chandeliers and a mute gleam of gold frames, heard the swift feet and saw her too, a lady — perhaps he had never seen her like before either — in a gray, smooth gown with lace at the throat and an apron tied at the waist and the sleeves turned back, wiping cake or biscuit dough from her hands with a towel as she came up the hall, looking not at his father at all but at the tracks on the blond rug with an expression of incredulous amazement.

"I tried," the Negro cried. "I tole him to . . ."

"Will you please go away?" she said in a shaking voice. "Major de Spain is not at home. Will you please go away?"

His father had not spoken again. He did not speak again. He did not even look at her. He just stood stiff in the center of the rug, in his hat, the shaggy iron-gray brows twitching slightly above the pebble-colored eyes as he appeared to examine the house with brief deliberation. Then with the same deliberation he turned; the boy watched him pivot on the good leg and saw the stiff foot drag round the arc of the turning, leaving a final long and fading smear. His father never looked at it, he never once looked down at the rug. The Negro held the door. It closed behind them, upon the hysteric and indistinguishable woman-wail. His father stopped at the top of the steps and scraped his boot clean on the edge of it. At the gate he stopped again. He stood for a moment, planted stiffly on the stiff foot, looking back at the house. "Pretty and white, ain't it?" he said. "That's sweat. Nigger sweat. Maybe it ain't white enough yet to suit him. Maybe he wants to mix some white sweat with it."

Two hours later the boy was chopping wood behind the house within which his mother and aunt and the two sisters (the mother and aunt, not the two girls, he knew that; even at this distance and muffled by walls the flat loud voices of the two girls emanated an incorrigible idle inertia) were setting up the stove to prepare a meal, when he heard the hooves and saw the linen-clad man on a fine sorrel mare, whom he recognized even before he saw the rolled rug in front of the Negro youth following on a fat bay carriage horse — a suffused, angry face vanishing, still at full gallop, beyond the corner of the house where his father and brother were sitting in the two tilted chairs; and a moment later, almost before he could have put the axe down, he heard the hooves again and watched the sorrel mare go back out of the yard, already galloping again. Then his father began to shout one of the sisters' names, who presently emerged backward from the kitchen door dragging the rolled rug along the ground by one end while the other sister walked behind it.

"If you ain't going to tote, go on and set up the wash pot," the first said.

"You, Sarty!" the second shouted. "Set up the wash pot!" His father appeared at the door, framed against that shabbiness, as he had been against that other bland perfection, impervious to either, the mother's anxious face at his shoulder.

"Go on," the father said. "Pick it up." The two sisters stooped, broad, lethargic; stooping, they presented an incredible expanse of pale cloth and a flutter of tawdry ribbons.

"If I thought enough of a rug to have to git hit all the way from France I wouldn't keep hit where folks coming in would have to tromp on hit," the first said. They raised the rug.

"Abner," the mother said. "Let me do it."

"You go back and git dinner," his father said. "I'll tend to this."

From the woodpile through the rest of the afternoon the boy watched them, the rug spread flat in the dust beside the bubbling wash pot, the two sisters stooping over it with that profound and lethargic reluctance, while the father stood over them in turn, implacable and grim, driving them though never raising his voice again. He could smell the harsh homemade lye they were using; he saw his mother come to the door once and look toward them with an expression not anxious now but very like despair; he saw his father turn, and he fell to with the axe and saw from the corner of his eye his father raise from the ground a flattish fragment of field stone and examine it and return io the pot, and this time his mother actually spoke: "Abner. Abner. Please don't. Please, Abner."

Then he was done too. It was dusk; the whippoorwills had already begun. He could smell coffee from the room where they would presently eat the cold food remaining from the mid-afternoon meal, though when he entered the house he realized they were having coffee again probably because there was a fire on the hearth, before which the rug now lay spread over the backs of the two chairs. The tracks of his father's foot were gone. Where they had been were now long, water-cloudy scoriations resembling the sporadic course of a lilliputian mowing machine.

It still hung there while they ate the cold food and then went to bed, scattered without order or claim up and down the two rooms, his mother in one bed, where his father would later lie, the older brother in the other, himself, the aunt, and the two sisters on pallets on the floor. But his father was not in bed yet. The last thing the boy remembered was the depthless, harsh silhouette of the hat and coat bending over the rug and it seemed to him that he had not even closed his eyes when the silhouette was standing over him, the fire almost dead behind it, the stiff foot prodding him awake. "Catch up the mule," his father said.

When he returned with the mule his father was standing in the black door, the rolled rug over his shoulder. "Ain't you going to ride?" he said.

"No. Give me your foot."

He bent his knee into his father's hand, the wiry, surprising power flowed smoothly, rising, he rising with it, on to the mule's bare back (they had owned a saddle once; the boy could remember it though not when or where) and with the same effortlessness his father swung the rug up in front of him. Now in the starlight they retraced the afternoon's path, up the dusty road rife with honeysuckle, through the gate and up the black tunnel of the drive to the lightless house, where he sat on the mule and felt the rough warp of the rug drag across his thighs and vanish.

"Don't you want me to help?" he whispered. His father did not answer and now he heard again that stiff foot striking the hollow portico with that wooden and clocklike deliberation, that outrageous overstatement of the weight it carried. The rug, hunched, not flung (the boy could tell that even in the darkness) from his father's shoulder struck the angle of wall and floor with a sound unbelievably loud, thunderous, then the foot again, unhurried and enormous; a light came on in the house and the boy sat, tense, breathing steadily and quietly and just a little fast, though the foot itself did not increase its beat at all, descending the steps now; now the boy could see him.

"Don't you want to ride now?" he whispered. "We kin both ride now," the light within the house altering now, flaring up and sinking. *He's coming down the stairs now*, he thought. He had already ridden the mule up beside the horse block; presently his father was up behind him and he doubled the reins over and slashed the mule across the neck, but before the animal could begin to trot the hard, thin arm came around him, the hard, knotted hand jerking the mule back to a walk.

In the first red rays of the sun they were in the lot, putting plow gear on the mules. This time the sorrel mare was in the lot before he heard it at all, the rider collarless and even bareheaded, trembling, speaking in a shaking voice as the woman in the house had done, his father merely looking up once before stooping again to the hame he was buckling, so that the man on the mare spoke to his stooping back:

"You must realize you have ruined that rug. Wasn't there anybody here, any of your women . . ." he ceased, shaking, the boy watching him, the older brother leaning now in the stable door, chewing, blinking slowly and steadily at nothing apparently. "It cost a hundred dollars. But you never had a hundred dollars. You never will. So I'm going to charge you twenty bushels of corn against your crop. I'll add it in your contract and when you come to the commissary you can sign it. That won't keep Mrs. de Spain quiet but maybe it will teach you to wipe your feet off before you enter her house again."

Then he was gone. The boy looked at his father, who still had not spoken or even looked up again, who was now adjusting the logger-head in the hame.

"Pap," he said. His father looked at him — the inscrutable face, the shaggy brows beneath which the gray eyes glinted coldly. Suddenly the boy went toward him, fast, stopping as suddenly. "You done the best you could!" he cried. "If he wanted hit done different why didn't he wait and tell you how? He won't git no twenty bushels! He won't git none! We'll gether hit and hide hit! I kin watch . . ."

"Did you put the cutter back in that straight stock like I told you?"

"No, sir," he said.

"Then go do it."

That was Wednesday. During the rest of that week he worked steadily, at what was within his scope and some which was beyond it, with an industry that did not need to be driven nor even commanded twice; he had this from his mother, with the difference that some at least of what he did he liked to do, such as splitting wood with the half-size axe which his mother and aunt had earned, or saved money somehow, to present him with at Christmas. In company with the two older women (and on one afternoon, even one of the sisters), he built pens for the shoat and the cow which were a part of his father's contract with the landlord, and one afternoon, his father being absent, gone somewhere on one of the mules, he went to the field.

They were running a middle buster now, his brother holding the plow straight while he handled the reins, and walking beside the straining mule, the rich black soil shearing cool and damp against his bare ankles, he thought *Maybe this is the end of it. Maybe even that twenty bushels that seems hard to have to pay for just a rug will be a cheap price for him to stop forever and always from being what he used to be;* thinking, dreaming now, so that his brother had to speak sharply to him to mind the mule: *Maybe he even won't collect the twenty bushels. Maybe it will all add up and balance and vanish — corn, rug, fire; the terror and grief; the being pulled two ways like between two teams of horses — gone, done with for ever and ever.*

Then it was Saturday; he looked up from beneath the mule he was harnessing and saw his father in the black coat and hat. "Not that," his father said. "The wagon gear." And then, two hours later, sitting in the wagon bed behind his father and brother on the seat, the wagon accomplished a final curve, and he saw the weathered paintless store with its tattered tobacco- and patent-medicine posters and the tethered wagons and saddle animals below the gallery. He mounted the gnawed steps behind his father and brother, and there again was the lane of quiet, watching faces for the three of them to walk through. He saw the man in spectacles sitting at the plank table and he did not need to be told this was a Justice of the Peace; he sent one glare of fierce, exultant, partisan defiance at the man in collar and cravat now, whom he had seen but twice before in his life, and that on a galloping horse, who now wore on his face an expression not of rage but of amazed unbelief which the boy could not have known was at the incredible circumstance of being sued by one of his own tenants, and came and stood against his father and cried at the Justice: "He ain't done it! He ain't burnt . . ."

"Go back to the wagon," his father said.

"Burnt?" the Justice said. "Do I understand this rug was burned too?"

"Does anybody here claim it was?" his father said. "Go back to the wagon." But he did not, he merely retreated to the rear of the room, crowded as that other had been, but not to sit down this time, instead, to stand pressing among the motionless bodies, listening to the voices:

"And you claim twenty bushels of corn is too high for the damage you did to the rug?"

"He brought the rug to me and said he wanted the tracks washed out of it. I washed the tracks out and took the rug back to him."

"But you didn't carry the rug back to him in the same condition it was in before you made the tracks on it."

His father did not answer, and now for perhaps half a minute there was no sound at all save that of breathing, the faint, steady suspiration of complete and intent listening.

"You decline to answer that, Mr. Snopes?" Again his father did not answer. "I'm going to find against you, Mr. Snopes. I'm going to find that you were responsible for the injury to Major de Spain's rug and hold you liable for it. But twenty bushels of corn seems a little high for a man in your circumstances to have to pay. Major de Spain claims it cost a hundred dollars. October corn will be worth about fifty cents. I figure that if Major de Spain can stand a ninety-five dollar loss on something he paid cash for, you can stand a five-dollar loss you haven't earned yet. I hold you in damages to Major de Spain to the amount of ten bushels of corn over and above your contract with him, to be paid to him out of your crop at gathering time. Court adjourned."

It had taken no time hardly, the morning was but half begun. He thought they would return home and perhaps back to the field, since they were late, far behind all other farmers. But instead his father passed on behind the wagon, merely indicating with his hand for the older brother to follow with it, and crossed the road toward the blacksmith shop opposite, pressing on after his father, overtaking him, speaking, whispering up at the harsh, calm face beneath the weathered hat: "He won't git no ten bushels neither. He won't git one. We'll . . ." until his father glanced for an instant down at him, the face absolutely calm, the grizzled eyebrows tangled above the cold eyes, the voice almost pleasant, almost gentle:

"You think so? Well, we'll wait till October anyway."

The matter of the wagon — the setting of a spoke or two and the tightening of the tires — did not take long either, the business of the tires accomplished by driving the wagon into the spring branch behind the shop and letting it stand there, the mules nuzzling into the water from time to time, and the boy on the seat with the idle reins, looking up the slope and through the sooty tunnel of the shed where the slow hammer rang and where his father sat on an upended cypress bolt, easily, either talking or listening, still sitting there when the boy brought the dripping wagon up out of the branch and halted it before the door.

"Take them on to the shade and hitch," his father said. He did so and returned. His father and the smith and a third man squatting on his heels inside the door were talking, about crops and animals; the boy, squatting too in the ammoniac dust and hoof-parings and scales of rust, heard his father tell a long and unhurried story out of the time before the birth of the older brother even when he had been a professional horsetrader. And then his father came up beside him where he stood before a tattered last year's circus poster on the other side of the store, gazing rapt and quiet at the scarlet horses, the incredible poisings and convolutions of tulle and tights and the painted leers of comedians, and said, "It's time to eat."

But not at home. Squatting beside his brother against the front wall, he watched his father emerge from the store and produce from a paper sack a segment of cheese and divide it carefully and deliberately into three with his pocket knife and produce crackers from the same sack. They all three squatted on the gallery and ate, slowly, without talking; then in the store again, they drank from a tin dipper tepid water smelling of the cedar bucket and of living beech trees. And still they did not go home. It was a horse lot this time, a tall rail fence upon and along which men stood and sat and out of which one by one horses were led, to be walked and trotted and then cantered back and forth along the road while the slow swapping and buying went on and the sun began to slant westward, they — the three of them — watching and listening, the older brother with his muddy eyes and his steady, inevitable tobacco, the father commenting now and then on certain of the animals, to no one in particular.

It was after sundown when they reached home. They ate supper by lamplight, then, sitting on the doorstep, the boy watched the night fully accomplish, listening to the whippoorwills and the frogs, when he heard his mother's voice: "Abner! No! No! Oh, God. Oh, God. Abner!" and he rose, whirled, and saw the altered light through the door where a candle stub now burned in a bottle neck on the table and his father, still in the hat and coat, at once formal and burlesque as though dressed carefully for some shabby and ceremonial violence, emptying the reservoir of the lamp back into the five-gallon kerosene can from which it had been filled, while the mother tugged at his arm until he shifted the lamp to the other hand and flung her back, not savagely or viciously, just hard, into the wall, her hands flung out against the wall for balance, her mouth open and in her face the same quality of hopeless despair as had been in her voice. Then his father saw him standing in the door.

"Go to the barn and get that can of oil we were oiling the wagon with," he said. The boy did not move. Then he could speak.

"What . . ." he cried. "What are you . . ."

"Go get that oil," his father said. "Go."

Then he was moving, running, outside the house, toward the stable: this the old habit, the old blood which he had not been permitted to choose for himself, which had been bequeathed him willy nilly and which had run for so long (and who knew where, battening on what of outrage and savagery and lust) before it came to him. *I could keep on*, he thought. *I could run on and on and never look back, never need to see his face again. Only I can't. I can't*, the rusted can in his hand now, the liquid sploshing in it as he ran back to the house and into it, into the sound of his mother's weeping in the next room, and handed the can to his father.

"Ain't you going to even send a nigger?" he cried. "At least you sent a nigger before!"

This time his father didn't strike him. The hand came even faster than the blow had, the same hand which had set the can on the table with almost excruciating care flashing from the can toward him too quick for him to follow it, gripping him by the back of his shirt and on to tiptoe before he had seen it quit the can, the face stooping at him in breathless and frozen ferocity, the cold, dead voice speaking over him to the older brother who leaned against the table, chewing with that steady, curious, sidewise motion of cows:

"Empty the can into the big one and go on. I'll catch up with you."

"Better tie him up to the bedpost," the brother said.

"Do like I told you," the father said. Then the boy was moving, his bunched shirt and the hard, bony hand between his shoulder-blades, his toes just touching the floor, across the room and into the other one, past the sisters siting with spread heavy thighs in the two chairs over the cold hearth, and to where his mother and aunt sat side by side on the bed, the aunt's arms about his mother's shoulders.

"Hold him," the father said. The aunt made a startled movement. "Not you," the father said. "Lennie. Take hold of him. I want to see you do it." His mother took him by the wrist. "You'll hold him better than that. If he gets loose don't you know what he is going to do? He will go up yonder." He jerked his head toward the road. "Maybe I'd better tie him."

"I'll hold him," his mother whispered.

"See you do then." Then his father was gone, the stiff foot heavy and measured upon the boards, ceasing at last.

Then he began to struggle. His mother caught him in both arms, he jerking and wrenching at them. He would be stronger in the end, he knew that. But he had no time to wait for it. "Lemme go!" he cried. "I don't want to have to hit you!"

"Let him go!" the aunt said. "If he don't go, before God, I am going up there myself!"

"Don't you see I can't?" his mother cried. "Sarty! Sarty! No! No! Help me, Lizzie!"

Then he was free. His aunt grasped at him but it was too late. He whirled, running, his mother stumbled forward on to her knees behind him, crying to the nearer sister: "Catch him, Net! Catch him!" But that was too late too, the sister (the sisters were twins, born at the same time, yet either of them now gave the impression of being, encompassing as much living meat and volume and weight as any other two of the family) not yet having begun to rise from the chair, her head, face, alone merely turned, presenting to him in the flying instant an astonishing expanse of young female features untroubled by any surprise even, wearing only an expression of bovine interest. Then he was out of the room, out of the house, in the mild dust of the starlit road and the heavy rifeness of honeysuckle, the pale ribbon unspooling with terrific slowness under his running feet, reaching the gate at last and turning in, running, his heart and lungs drumming, on up the drive toward the lighted house, the lighted door. He did not knock, he burst in, sobbing for breath, incapable for the moment of speech; he saw the astonished face of the Negro in the linen jacket without knowing when the Negro had appeared.

"De Spain!" he cried, panted. "Where's . . ." then he saw the white man too emerging from a white door down the hall. "Barn!" he cried. "Barn!"

"What?" the white man said. "Barn?"

"Yes!" the boy cried. "Barn!"

"Catch him!" the white man shouted.

But it was too late this time too. The Negro grasped his shirt, but the entire sleeve, rotten with washing, carried away, and he was out that door too and in the drive again, and had actually never ceased to run even while he was screaming into the white man's face.

Behind him the white man was shouting, "My horse! Fetch my horse!" and he thought for an instant of cutting across the park and climbing the fence into the road, but he did not know the park nor how high the vine-massed fence might be and he dared not risk it. So he ran on down the drive, blood and breath roaring; presently he was in the road again though he could not see it. He could not hear either: the galloping mare was almost upon him before he heard her, and even then he held his course, as if the very urgency of his wild grief and need must in a moment more find him wings, waiting until the ultimate instant to hurl himself aside and into the weed-choked roadside ditch as the horse thundered past and on, for an instant in furious silhouette against the stars, the tranquil early summer night sky which, even before the shape of the horse and rider vanished, stained abruptly and violently upward: a long, swirling roar incredible and soundless, blotting the stars, and he springing up and into the road again, running again, knowing it was too late yet still running even after he heard the shot and an instant later, two shots, pausing now without knowing he had ceased to run, crying "Pap! Pap!", running again before he knew he had begun to run, stumbling, tripping over something and scrabbling up again without ceasing to run, looking backward over his shoulder at the glare as he got up, running on among the invisible trees, panting, sobbing, "Father! Father!"

At midnight he was sitting on the crest of a hill. He did not know it was midnight and he did not know how far he had come. But there was no glare behind him now and he sat now, his back toward what he had called home for four days anyhow, his face toward the dark woods which he would enter when breath was strong again, small, shaking steadily in the chill darkness, hugging himself into the remainder of his thin, rotten shirt, the grief and despair now no longer terror and fear but just grief and despair. *Father. My father*, he thought. "He was brave!" he cried suddenly, aloud but not loud, no more than a whisper: "He was! He was in the war! He was in Colonel Sartoris' cav'ry!" not knowing that his father had gone to that war a private in the fine old European sense, wearing no uniform, admitting the authority of and giving fidelity to no man or army or flag, going to war as Malbrouck himself did: for booty — it meant nothing and less than nothing to him if it were enemy booty or his own.

The slow constellations wheeled on. It would be dawn and then sun-up after a while and he would be hungry. But that would be tomorrow and now he was only cold, and walking would cure that. His breathing was easier now and he decided to get up and go on, and then he found that he had been asleep because he knew it was almost dawn, the night almost over. He could tell that from the whippoorwills. They were everywhere now among the dark trees below him, constant and inflectioned and ceaseless, so that, as the instant for giving over to the day birds drew nearer and nearer, there was no interval at all between them. He got up. He was a little stiff, but walking would cure that too as it would the cold, and soon there would be the sun. He went on down the hill, toward the dark woods within which the liquid silver voices of the birds called unceasing — the rapid and urgent beating of the urgent and quiring heart of the late spring night. He did not look back.

QUESTIONS

1. After delivering his warning to Major de Spain, the boy Snopes does not actually witness what happens to his father and brother, nor what happens to the Major's barn. But what do you assume does happen? What evidence is given in the story?
2. What do you understand to be Faulkner's opinion of Abner Snopes? Make a guess, indicating details in the story that convey attitudes.
3. Which adjectives best describe the general tone of the story: calm, amused, disinterested, scornful, marveling, excited, impassioned? Point out passages that may be so described. What do you notice about the style in which these passages are written?

4. In tone and style, how does "Barn Burning" compare with Faulkner's story "A Rose for Emily" (Chapter Two)? To what do you attribute any differences?
5. Suppose that, instead of "Barn Burning," Faulkner had written another story told by Abner Snopes in the first person. Why would such a story need a style different from that of "Barn Burning"? (Suggestion: notice Faulkner's descriptions of Abner Snopes's voice.)
6. Although "Barn Burning" takes place some thirty years after the Civil War, how does the war significantly figure in it?

A NOTE ON IRONY

If a student declares, "Oh, sure, I just *love* to have four papers fall due on the same day," the statement contains **irony.** This is **verbal irony,** the most familiar kind, in which we understand the speaker's meaning to be far from the usual meaning of his words — in this case, quite the opposite. (When the irony is, as here, a somewhat sour statement tinged with mockery, it is usually called **sarcasm.**)

Irony, of course, occurs in writing as well as in conversation. When in a comic moment in Isaac Bashevis Singer's "Gimpel the Fool" (Chapter Three) the sexton announces, "The wealthy Reb Gimpel invites the congregation to a feast in honor of the birth of a son," the people at the synagogue burst into laughter. They know that Gimpel, in contrast to the sexton's words, is not a wealthy man but a humble baker; that the son is not his own but his wife's lover's; and that the birth brings no honor to anybody. Verbal irony, then, is marked by a contrast or discrepancy between what is *said* and what is *meant.* But stories often contain other kinds of irony besides such verbal irony. A situation, for example, can be ironic if it contains some wry contrast or incongruity. In James Thurber's "The Catbird Seat" (Chapter Three), it is an **ironic situation** that the mildest, most apparently harmless man in an office should plot murder, claim to be a heroin addict, and cause the firing of the office tyrant. Another ironic situation, one that also produces a comic effect, occurs in "A Keelboatman's Ghost Story" by Mark Twain (page 311). After two big brawling riverboatmen brag of their superhuman strength, and claim that they can split rocks with a mere glance and can blot out the sun itself, "a little black-whiskered chap" gets up and thrashes the two of them.

An entire story may be told from an **ironic point of view.** Whenever we sense a sharp distinction between the narrator of a story and the author, irony is likely to occur — especially when the narrator is telling us something that we are clearly expected to doubt or to interpret very differently. In "Gimpel the Fool," for instance, Gimpel (who tells his own story) keeps insisting on trusting people; but the author, a shrewder observer, makes it clear to us that the people Gimpel trusts are only tricking him. (This irony, by the way, does not prevent Gimpel from expressing a few things that Isaac Bashevis Singer believes, and perhaps expects us to believe.) And when we read Hemingway's "A Clean, Well-Lighted Place," surely we feel that most of the time the older waiter speaks for the author. Though the waiter gives us a respectful, compassionate view of a lonely old man, and we don't doubt that the view is Hemingway's, still, in the closing lines of the story we are reminded that author and waiter are not identical. Musing on the sleepless night ahead of him, the waiter tries to shrug off his problem — "After all, it is probably only insomnia" — but the reader, who recalls the waiter's bleak view of *nada,* nothingness, knows that it certainly isn't mere insomnia that keeps him awake, but a dread of solitude and death. At that crucial moment, Hemingway and the older waiter part company, and we perceive an ironic point of view (and also a verbal irony — "After all, it is probably only insomnia").

Storytellers are sometimes fond of ironic twists of fate — developments that reveal a terrible distance between what people deserve and what they get, between what is and what ought to be. In the novels of Thomas Hardy, some hostile fate keeps playing tricks to thwart the central characters. For instance, in *Tess of the D'Urbervilles,* an all-important letter, thrust under a door, by chance slides beneath a carpet and is not received. An obvious prank of fate occurs in O. Henry's short story "The Gift of the Magi," in which a young wife sells her beautiful hair to buy her poor young husband a watch chain for Christmas, not knowing that, to buy combs for her hair, he has sold his watch. Such an irony is sometimes called an **irony of fate** or a **cosmic irony,** for it suggests that some malicious fate (or other spirit in the universe) is deliberately frustrating human efforts. (In O. Henry's story, however, the twist of fate leads to a happy ending; for the author suggests that, by their futile sacrifices, the lovers are drawn closer together.)

To notice an irony gives pleasure. It may move us to laughter, make us feel wonder, or arouse our sympathy. By so involving us, irony — whether in a statement, a situation, an unexpected event, or a point of view — can render a story more likely to strike us, to affect us, and to be remembered.

John Collier (b. 1901)

THE CHASER   1940

Alan Austen, as nervous as a kitten, went up certain dark and creaky stairs in the neighborhood of Pell Street, and peered about for a long time on the dim landing before he found the name he wanted written obscurely on one of the doors.

He pushed open this door, as he had been told to do, and found himself in a tiny room, which contained no furniture but a plain kitchen table, rocking chair, and an ordinary chair. On one of the dirty buff-colored walls were a couple of shelves, containing in all perhaps a dozen bottles and jars.

An old man sat in the rocking chair, reading a newspaper. Alan, without a word, handed him the card he had been given. "Sit down, Mr. Austen," said the old man very politely. "I am glad to make your acquaintance."

"Is it true," asked Alan, "that you have a certain mixture that has — er — quite extraordinary effects?"

"My dear sir," replied the old man, "my stock in trade is not very large — I don't deal in laxatives and teething mixtures — but such as it is, it is varied. I think nothing I sell has effects which could be precisely described as ordinary."

"Well, the fact is —" began Alan.

"Here, for example," interrupted the old man, reaching for a bottle from the shelf. "Here is a liquid as colorless as water, almost tasteless, quite imperceptible in coffee, milk, wine, or any other beverage. It is also quite imperceptible to any known method of autopsy."

"Do you mean it is a poison?" cried Alan, very much horrified.

"Call it cleaning fluid if you like," said the old man indifferently. "Lives need cleaning. Call it a spot-remover. 'Out, damned spot!' Eh? 'Out, brief candle!' "°

"I want nothing of that sort," said Alan.

"Probably it is just as well," said the old man. "Do you know the price of this? For one teaspoonful, which is sufficient, I ask five thousand dollars. Never less. Not a penny less."

"I hope all your mixtures are not as expensive," said Alan apprehensively.

"Oh, dear, no," said the old man. "It would be no good charging that sort of price for a love potion, for example. Young people who need a love potion very seldom have five thousand dollars. Otherwise they would not need a love potion."

"I'm glad to hear you say so," said Alan.

"I look at it like this," said the old man. "Please a customer with one article, and he will come back when he needs another. Even if it *is* more costly. He will save up for it, if necessary."

"So," said Alan, "you really do sell love potions?"

"If I did not sell love potions," said the old man, reaching for another bottle, "I should not have mentioned the other matter to you. It is only when one is in a position to oblige that one can afford to be so confidential."

"And these potions," said Alan. "They are not just — just — er —"

"Oh, no," said the old man. "Their effects are permanent, and extend far beyond the mere casual impulse. But they include it. Oh, yes, they include it. Bountifully. Insistently. Everlastingly."

"*Out, damned spot! . . . Out, brief candle!*": The old man quotes from Shakespeare's *Macbeth*. "Out, damned spot!" is from the speech of the guilt-ridden Lady Macbeth, who while sleepwalking keeps trying to cleanse blood from her hands (*Macbeth* V, i, 37). "Out, brief candle!" is from Macbeth's famous soliloquy on being told of the death of his queen: "Tomorrow, and tomorrow, and tomorrow / Creep in this petty pace from day to day / To the last syllable of recorded time; / And all our yesterdays have lighted fools / The way to dusty death. Out, out, brief candle! / Life's but a walking shadow . . ." (V, v, 19–24).

"Dear me!" said Alan, attempting a look of scientific detachment. "How very interesting!"

"But consider the spiritual side," said the old man.

"I do, indeed," said Alan.

"For indifference," said the old man, "they substitute devotion. For scorn, adoration. Give one tiny measure of this to the young lady — its flavor is imperceptible in orange juice, soup, or cocktails — and however gay and giddy she is, she will change altogether. She'll want nothing but solitude, and you."

"I can hardly believe it," said Alan. "She is so fond of parties."

"She will not like them any more," said the old man. "She'll be afraid of the pretty girls you may meet."

"She'll actually be jealous?" cried Alan in a rapture. "Of me?"

"Yes, she will want to be everything to you."

"She is, already. Only she doesn't care about it."

"She will, when she has taken this. She will care intensely. You'll be her sole interest in life."

"Wonderful!" cried Alan.

"She'll want to know all you do," said the old man. "All that has happened to you during the day. Every word of it. She'll want to know what you are thinking about, why you smile suddenly, why you are looking sad."

"That is love!" cried Alan.

"Yes," said the old man. "How carefully she'll look after you! She'll never allow you to be tired, to sit in a draft, to neglect your food. If you are an hour late, she'll be terrified. She'll think you are killed, or that some siren has caught you."

"I can hardly imagine Diana like that!" cried Alan.

"You will not have to use your imagination," said the old man. "And by the way, since there are always sirens, if by any chance you *should,* later on, slip a little, you need not worry. She will forgive you, in the end. She'll be terribly hurt, of course, but she'll forgive you — in the end."

"That will not happen," said Alan fervently.

"Of course not," said the old man. "But, if it does, you need not worry. She'll never divorce you. Oh, no! And, of course, she herself will never give you the least grounds for — not divorce, of course — but even uneasiness."

"And how much," said Alan, "how much is this wonderful mixture?"

"It is not so dear," said the old man, "as the spot remover, as I think we agreed to call it. No. That is five thousand dollars; never a penny less. One has to be older than you are, to indulge in that sort of thing. One has to save up for it."

"But the love potion?" said Alan.

"Oh, that," said the old man, opening the drawer in the kitchen table, and taking out a tiny, rather dirty-looking phial. "That is just a dollar."

"I can't tell you how grateful I am," said Alan, watching him fill it.

"I like to oblige," said the old man. "Then customers come back, later in life, when they are rather better off, and want more expensive things. Here you are. You will find it very effective."

"Thank you again," said Alan. "Goodbye."

"*Au revoir,*" said the old man.

QUESTIONS

1. What do we understand from the last two lines of the story?
2. Explain how this ending can be called an irony.
3. At what other moments in the story does Alan apparently fail to perceive grim events in his future (while we do perceive them)? Which statements made by the old man contain ironies?
4. What does Alan expect from the woman he will marry? Are we supposed to sympathize with his expectations?
5. How much do we know about the old man and about Alan Austen? How closely does the author describe their appearances (features, clothing, manners, individual traits) and personalities? Are they unique persons or stock characters?
6. Does "The Chaser" most nearly fit the definition of a fable, a tale, or a short story?

5 Theme

The **theme** of a story is whatever general idea or insight the entire story reveals. In some stories the theme is unmistakable. At the end of Aesop's fable of the council of the mice that can't decide who will bell the cat, the theme is stated in the moral: *It is easier to propose a thing than to carry it out.* In a work of commercial fiction, too, the theme (if there is any) tends to be obvious. Consider a typical detective thriller in which, say, a rookie policeman trained in scientific methods of crime detection sets out to solve a mystery sooner than his rival, a veteran sleuth whose only laboratory is carried under his hat. Perhaps the veteran solves the case, leading to the conclusion (and the theme), "The old ways are the best ways after all." Another story by the same writer might dramatize the same rivalry but reverse the outcome, having the rookie win, thereby reversing the theme: "The times are changing! Let's shake loose from old-fashioned ways." In such commercial entertainments, a theme is like a length of rope with which the writer, patently and mechanically, trusses the story neatly (usually too neatly) into meaningful shape.

In literary fiction, a theme is seldom so obvious. That is, a theme need not be a moral or a message; it may be what the happenings add up to, what the story is about. When we come to the end of a finely wrought short story such as Ernest Hemingway's "A Clean, Well-Lighted Place" (Chapter Four), it may be easy to sum up the plot — to say what happens — but it may be difficult to sum up in a sentence the story's main idea. Evidently, Hemingway relates events — how a younger waiter gets rid of an old man and how an older waiter then goes to a coffee bar — but in themselves these events seem relatively slight, while the story as a whole seems large (for its size) and full of meaning. For the meaning, we must look to other elements in the story, besides what happens in it. And it is clear that Hemingway is most deeply concerned with the thoughts and feelings of the older waiter, the character who has more and more to say as the story progresses, until at the end the story is entirely confined to his thoughts and perceptions. What is meaningful in these thoughts and perceptions? The older waiter understands the old man and sympathizes with his need for a clean, well-lighted place. If we say that, we are still talking about what happens in the story, though we have gone beyond merely recording its external events. But a theme is usually stated in *general* terms. Another try: "Solitary people who cannot sleep need a cheerful, orderly place where they can drink with dignity." That's a little better. We have indicated, at least, that Hemingway's story is about more than just an old man and a couple of waiters. But what about the older waiter's meditation on *nada*, nothingness? Coming near the end of the story, it takes great emphasis; and probably no good statement of Hemingway's theme can leave it out. Still another try at a statement: "Solitary people need a place of refuge from their terrible awareness that their lives (or perhaps, human lives) are essentially meaningless." Neither this nor any other statement of the story's theme is unarguably right, but at least the sentence helps the reader to bring into focus one central idea that Hemingway seems to be driving at. When we finish reading "A Clean, Well-Lighted Place," we feel that there *is* such a theme, a unifying vision, even though we cannot reduce it absolutely to a tag. Like some freshwater lake alive with creatures, Hemingway's story is a broad expanse, reflecting in many directions. No wonder that many different readers will view it differently.

Unlike Aesop's fable of the frogs who wanted a king, Hemingway's story does not set forth a moral. Moral inferences may be drawn from the story, no doubt — for Hemingway is indirectly giving us advice for properly regarding and sympathizing with the lonely, the uncertain, and the old. But the story doesn't set forth a lesson that we are supposed to put into practice. One could argue that "A Clean, Well-Lighted Place" contains *several* themes — and other statements could be made to take in Hemingway's views of love, of communication between people, of dignity. Great short stories, like great symphonies, frequently have more than one theme.

Stories also can have themes so slight and tenuous that there seems little point in looking for them. After reading Richard Brautigan's gentle character sketch, "The Kool-Aid Wino" (Chapter Three), an extremely serious reader might declare that the behavior of the title character demonstrates the theme that, say, "Solitude, poverty, and introspection breed strange rituals," but to charge so unassuming a story with so heavy a theme would be like asking a butterfly to serve as a carrier pigeon. As a rule of thumb, however, we can assume that if a story leaves us with much still to think about, it probably has a theme worth trying to state.

In many a fine short story, theme is the center, the moving force, the principle of unity. Clearly, such a theme is something other than the characters and events of its story. To say of James Joyce's "Araby" (Chapter Two) that it is about a boy who goes to a bazaar to buy a gift for a young woman, only to arrive too late, is to summarize plot, not theme. (The theme *might* be put, "The illusions of a romantic child are vulnerable," or it might be put in any of a few hundred other ways.) Although the title of Isaac Bashevis Singer's "Gimpel the Fool" (Chapter Three) indicates the central character and suggests the subject (his "foolishness"), the theme — the larger realization that the story leaves us with — has to do not with foolishness, but with how to be wise.

In trying to state the theme of a story as accurately and inclusively as possible, you may find it useful to consider these points:

1. Look back once more at the title of the story. In the light of what you have read, what does it indicate?
2. Does the main character in any way change in the course of the story? Does this character arrive at any eventual realization or understanding? Are you left with any realization or understanding you did not have before?
3. Does the author make any general observations about life or human nature? Do the characters make any? (Caution: characters now and again will utter opinions with which the reader is not necessarily supposed to agree.)
4. Does the story contain any especially curious objects, mysterious flat characters, significant animals, repeated names, song titles, or whatever, that hint toward meanings larger than such things ordinarily have? In literary stories, such symbols may point to central themes. (For a short discussion of symbolism and a few illustrations, see Chapter Six.)
5. When you have worded your statement of theme, have you cast your statement into general terms, not just given a plot summary?
6. Does your statement hold true for the story as a whole, not for just part of it?

In distilling a statement of theme from a rich and complicated story, we have, of course, no more encompassed the whole story than a paleontologist taking a plaster mold of a petrified footprint has captured a living brontosaurus. A writer (other than a fabulist) does not usually set out with theme in hand, determined to make every detail in the story work to demonstrate it. Well then, the skeptical reader may ask, if only *some* stories have themes, if those themes may be hard to sum up, and if readers will probably disagree in their summations, why bother to state themes? Isn't it too much trouble? Surely it is, unless the effort to state a theme ends in pleasure and profit. Trying to sum up the point of a story in our own words is merely one way to make ourselves better aware of whatever we may have understood only vaguely and tentatively. Attempted with loving care, such statements may bring into focus our scattered impressions of a rewarding story, may help to clarify and hold fast whatever wisdom the storyteller has offered us.

Flannery O'Connor (1925–1964)

REVELATION

The doctor's waiting room, which was very small, was almost full when the Turpins entered and Mrs. Turpin, who was very large, made it look even smaller by her presence. She stood looming at the head of the magazine table set in the center of it, a living demonstration that the room was inadequate and ridiculous. Her little bright black eyes took in all the patients as she sized up the seating situation. There was one vacant chair and a place on the sofa occupied by a blond child in a dirty blue romper who should have been told to move over and make room for the lady. He was five or six, but Mrs. Turpin saw at once that no one was going to tell him to move over. He was slumped down in the seat, his arms idle at his sides and his eyes idle in his head; his nose ran unchecked.

Mrs. Turpin put a firm hand on Claud's shoulder and said in a voice that included anyone who wanted to listen, "Claud, you sit in that chair there," and gave him a push down into the vacant one. Claud was florid and bald and sturdy, somewhat shorter than Mrs. Turpin, but he sat down as if he were accustomed to doing what she told him to.

Mrs. Turpin remained standing. The only man in the room besides Claud was a lean stringy old fellow with a rusty hand spread out on each knee, whose eyes were closed as if he were asleep or dead or pretending to be so as not to get up and offer her his seat. Her gaze settled agreeably on a well-dressed grey-haired lady whose eyes met hers and whose expression said: if that child belonged to me, he would have some manners and move over — there's plenty of room there for you and him too.

Claud looked up with a sigh and made as if to rise.

"Sit down," Mrs. Turpin said. "You know you're not supposed to stand on that leg. He has an ulcer on his leg," she explained.

Claud lifted his foot onto the magazine table and rolled his trouser leg up to reveal a purple swelling on a plump marble-white calf.

"My!" the pleasant lady said. "How did you do that?"

"A cow kicked him," Mrs. Turpin said.

"Goodness!" said the lady.

Claud rolled his trouser leg down.

"Maybe the little boy would move over," the lady suggested, but the child did not stir.

"Somebody will be leaving in a minute," Mrs. Turpin said. She could not understand why a doctor — with as much money as they made charging five dollars a day to just stick their head in the hospital door and look at you — couldn't afford a decent-sized waiting room. This one was hardly bigger than a garage. The table was cluttered with limp-looking magazines and at one end of it there was a big green glass ash tray full of cigaret butts and cotton wads with little blood spots on them. If she had had anything to do with the running of the place, that would have been emptied every so often. There were no chairs against the wall at the head of the room. It had a rectangular-shaped panel in it that permitted a view of the office where the nurse came and went and the secretary listened to the radio. A plastic fern in a gold pot sat in the opening and trailed its fronds down almost to the floor. The radio was softly playing gospel music.

Just then the inner door opened and a nurse with the highest stack of yellow hair Mrs. Turpin had ever seen put her face in the crack and called for the next patient. The woman sitting beside Claud grasped the two arms of her chair and hoisted herself up; she pulled her dress free from her legs and lumbered through the door where the nurse had disappeared.

Mrs. Turpin eased into the vacant chair, which held her tight as a corset. "I wish I could reduce," she said, and rolled her eyes and gave a comic sigh.

"Oh, *you* aren't fat," the stylish lady said.

"Ooooo I am too," Mrs. Turpin said. "Claud he eats all he wants to and never weighs over one hundred and seventy-five pounds, but me I just look at something good to eat and I gain some weight," and her stomach and shoulders shook with laughter. "You can eat all you want to, can't you, Claud?" she asked, turning to him.

Claud only grinned.

"Well, as long as you have such a good disposition," the stylish lady said, "I don't think it makes a bit of difference what size you are. You just can't beat a good disposition."

Next to her was a fat girl of eighteen or nineteen, scowling into a thick blue book which Mrs. Turpin saw was entitled *Human Development*. The girl raised her head and directed her scowl at Mrs. Turpin as if she did not like her looks. She appeared annoyed that anyone should speak while she tried to read. The poor girl's face was blue with acne and Mrs. Turpin thought how pitiful it was to have a face like that at that age. She gave the girl a friendly smile but the girl only scowled the harder. Mrs. Turpin herself was fat but she had always had good skin, and, though she was forty-seven years old, there was not a wrinkle in her face except around her eyes from laughing too much.

Next to the ugly girl was the child, still in exactly the same position, and next to him was a thin leathery old woman in a cotton print dress. She and Claud had three sacks of chicken feed in their pump house that was in the same print. She had seen from the first that the child belonged with the old woman. She could tell by the way they sat — kind of vacant and white-trashy, as if they would sit there until Doomsday if nobody called and told them to get up. And at right angles but next to the well-dressed pleasant lady was a lank-faced woman who was certainly the child's mother. She had on a yellow sweat shirt and wine-colored slacks, both gritty-looking, and the rims of her lips were stained with snuff. Her dirty yellow hair was tied behind with a little piece of red paper ribbon. Worse than niggers any day, Mrs. Turpin thought.

The gospel hymn playing was, "When I looked up and He looked down," and Mrs. Turpin, who knew it, supplied the last line mentally, "And wona these days I know I'll we-eara crown."

Without appearing to, Mrs. Turpin always noticed people's feet. The well-dressed lady had on red and grey suede shoes to match her dress. Mrs. Turpin had on her good black patent leather pumps. The ugly girl had on Girl Scout shoes and heavy socks. The old woman had on tennis shoes and the white-trashy mother had on what appeared to be bedroom slippers, black straw with gold braid threaded through them — exactly what you would have expected her to have on.

Sometimes at night when she couldn't go to sleep, Mrs. Turpin would occupy herself with the question of who she would have chosen to be if she couldn't have been herself. If Jesus had said to her before he made her, "There's only two places available for you. You can either be a nigger or white-trash," what would she have said? "Please, Jesus, please," she would have said, "just let me wait until there's another place available," and he would have said, "No, you have to go right now and I have only those two places so make up your mind." She would have wiggled and squirmed and begged and pleaded but it would have been no use and finally she would have said, "All right, make me a nigger then — but that don't mean a trashy one." And he would have made her a neat clean respectable Negro-woman, herself but black.

Next to the child's mother was a red-headed youngish woman, reading one of the magazines and working a piece of chewing gum, hell for leather, as Claud would say. Mrs. Turpin could not see the woman's feet. She was not white-trash, just common. Sometimes Mrs. Turpin occupied herself at night naming the classes of people. On the bottom of the heap were most colored people, not the kind she would have been if she had been one, but most of them; then next to them — not above, just away from — were the white-trash; then above them were the home-owners, and above them the home-and-land owners, to which she and Claud belonged. Above she and Claud were people with a lot of money and much bigger houses and much more land. But here the complexity of it would begin to bear in on her, for some of the people with a lot of money were common and ought to be below she and Claud and some of the people who had good blood had lost their money and had to rent and then there were colored people who owned their homes and land as well. There was a colored dentist in town who had two red Lincolns and a swimming pool and a farm with registered white-face cattle on it. Usually by the time she had fallen asleep all the classes of people were moiling and roiling around in her head, and she would dream they were all crammed in together in a box car, being ridden off to be put in a gas oven.

"That's a beautiful clock," she said and nodded to her right. It was a big wall clock, the face encased in a brass sunburst.

"Yes, it's very pretty," the stylish lady said agreeably. "And right on the dot too," she added, glancing at her watch.

The ugly girl beside her cast an eye upward at the clock, smirked, then looked directly at Mrs. Turpin and smirked again. Then she returned her eyes to her book. She was obviously the lady's daughter because, although they didn't look anything alike as to disposition, they both had the same shape of face and the same blue eyes. On the lady they sparkled pleasantly but in the girl's seared face they appeared alternately to smolder and to blaze.

What if Jesus had said, "All right, you can be white-trash or a nigger or ugly"!

Mrs. Turpin felt an awful pity for the girl, though she thought it was one thing to be ugly and another to act ugly.

The woman with the snuff-stained lips turned around in her chair and looked up at the clock. Then she turned back and appeared to look a little to the side of Mrs. Turpin. There was a cast in one of her eyes. "You want to know wher you can get you one of themther clocks?" she asked in a loud voice.

"No, I already have a nice clock," Mrs. Turpin said. Once somebody like her got a leg in the conversation, she would be all over it.

"You can get you one with green stamps," the woman said. "That's most likely wher he got hisn. Save you up enough, you can get you most anythang. I got me some joo'ry."

Ought to have got you a wash rag and some soap, Mrs. Turpin thought.

"I get contour sheets with mine," the pleasant lady said.

The daughter slammed her book shut. She looked straight in front of her, directly through Mrs. Turpin and on through the yellow curtain and the plate glass window which made the wall behind her. The girl's eyes seemed lit all of a sudden with a peculiar light, an unnatural light like night road signs give. Mrs. Turpin turned her head to see if there was anything going on outside that she should see, but she could not see anything. Figures passing cast only a pale shadow through the curtain. There was no reason the girl should single her out for her ugly looks.

"Miss Finley," the nurse said, cracking the door. The gum-chewing woman got up and passed in front of her and Claud and went into the office. She had on red high-heeled shoes.

Directly across the table, the ugly girl's eyes were fixed on Mrs. Turpin as if she had some very special reason for disliking her.

"This is wonderful weather, isn't it?" the girl's mother said.

"It's good weather for cotton if you can get the niggers to pick it," Mrs. Turpin said, "but niggers don't want to pick cotton any more. You can't get the white folks to pick it and now you can't get the niggers — because they got to be right up there with the white folks."

"They gonna *try* anyways," the white-trash woman said, leaning forward.

"Do you have one of those cotton-picking machines?" the pleasant lady asked.

"No," Mrs. Turpin said, "they leave half the cotton in the field. We don't have much cotton anyway. If you want to make it farming now, you have to have a little of everything. We got a couple of acres of cotton and a few hogs and chickens and just enough white-face that Claud can look after them himself."

"One thang I don't want," the white-trash woman said, wiping her mouth with the back of her hands. "Hogs. Nasty stinking things, a-gruntin and a-rootin all over the place."

Mrs. Turpin gave her the merest edge of her attention. "Our hogs are not dirty and they don't stink," she said. "They're cleaner than some children I've seen. Their feet never touch the ground. We have a pig-parlor — that's where you raise them on concrete," she explained to the pleasant lady, "and Claud scoots them down with the hose every afternoon and washes off the floor." Cleaner by far than that child right there, she thought. Poor nasty little thing. He had not moved except to put the thumb of his dirty hand into his mouth.

The woman turned her face away from Mrs. Turpin. "I know I wouldn't scoot down no hog with no hose," she said to the wall.

You wouldn't have no hog to scoot down, Mrs. Turpin said to herself.

"A-gruntin and a-rootin and a-groanin," the woman muttered.

"We got a little of everything," Mrs. Turpin said to the pleasant lady. "It's no use in having more than you can handle yourself with help like it is. We found enough niggers to pick our cotton this year but Claud he has to go after them and take them home again in the evening. They can't walk that half a mile. No they can't. I tell you," she said and laughed merrily, "I sure am tired of buttering up niggers, but you got to love em if you want em to work for you. When they come in the morning, I run out and I say, 'Hi yawl this morning?' and when Claud drives them off to the field I just wave to beat the band and they just wave back." And she waved her hand rapidly to illustrate.

"Like you read out of the same book," the lady said, showing she understood perfectly.

"Child, yes," Mrs. Turpin said. "And when they come in from the field, I run out with a bucket of icewater. That's the way it's going to be from now on," she said. "You may as well face it."

"One thang I know," the white-trash woman said. "Two thangs I ain't going to do: love no niggers or scoot down no hog with no hose." And she let out a bark of contempt.

The look that Mrs. Turpin and the pleasant lady exchanged indicated they both understood that you had to *have* certain things before you could *know* certain things. But every time Mrs. Turpin exchanged a look with the lady, she was aware that the ugly girl's peculiar eyes were still on her, and she had trouble bringing her attention back to the conversation.

"When you got something," she said, "you got to look after it." And when you ain't got a thing but breath and britches, she added to herself, you can afford to come to town every morning and just sit on the Court House coping and spit.

A grotesque revolving shadow passed across the curtain behind her and was thrown palely on the opposite wall. Then a bicycle clattered down against the outside of the building. The door opened and a colored boy glided in with a tray from the drug store. It had two large red and white paper cups on it with tops on them. He was a tall, very black boy in discolored white pants and a green nylon shirt. He was chewing gum slowly, as if to music. He set the tray down in the office opening next to the fern and stuck his head through to look for the secretary. She was not in there. He rested his arms on the ledge and waited, his narrow bottom stuck out, swaying slowly to the left and right. He raised a hand over his head and scratched the base of his skull.

"You see that button there, boy?" Mrs. Turpin said. "You can punch that and she'll come. She's probably in the back somewhere."

"Is thas right?" the boy said agreeably, as if he had never seen the button before. He leaned to the right and put his finger on it. "She sometime out," he said and twisted around to face his audience, his elbows behind him on the counter. The nurse appeared and he twisted back again. She handed him a dollar and he rooted in his pocket and made the change and counted it out to her. She gave him fifteen cents for a tip and he went out with the empty tray. The heavy door swung to slowly and closed at length with the sound of suction. For a moment no one spoke.

"They ought to send all them niggers back to Africa," the white-trash woman said. "That's wher they come from in the first place."

"Oh, I couldn't do without my good colored friends," the pleasant lady said.

"There's a heap of things worse than a nigger," Mrs. Turpin agreed. "It's all kinds of them just like it's all kinds of us."

"Yes, and it takes all kinds to make the world go round," the lady said in her musical voice.

As she said it, the raw-complexioned girl snapped her teeth together. Her lower lip turned downwards and inside out, revealing the pale pink inside of her mouth. After a second it rolled back up. It was the ugliest face Mrs. Turpin had ever seen anyone make and for a moment she was certain that the girl had made it at her. She was looking at her as if she had known and disliked her all her life — all of Mrs. Turpin's life, it seemed too, not just all the girl's life. Why, girl, I don't even know you, Mrs. Turpin said silently.

She forced her attention back to the discussion. "It wouldn't be practical to send them back to Africa," she said. "They wouldn't want to go. They got it too good here."

"Wouldn't be what they wanted — if I had anythang to do with it," the woman said.

"It wouldn't be a way in the world you could get all the niggers back over there," Mrs. Turpin said. "They'd be hiding out and lying down and turning sick on you and wailing and hollering and raring and pitching. It wouldn't be a way in the world to get them over there."

"They got over here," the trashy woman said. "Get back like they got over."

"It wasn't so many of them then," Mrs. Turpin explained.

The woman looked at Mrs. Turpin as if here was an idiot indeed but Mrs. Turpin was not bothered by the look, considering where it came from.

"Nooo," she said, "they're going to stay here where they can go to New York and marry white folks and improve their color. That's what they all want to do, every one of them, improve their color."

"You know what comes of that, don't you?" Claud asked.

"No, Claud, what?" Mrs. Turpin said.

Claud's eyes twinkled. "White-faced niggers," he said with never a smile.

Everybody in the office laughed except the white-trash and the ugly girl. The girl gripped the book in her lap with white fingers. The trashy woman looked around her from face to face as if she thought they were all idiots. The old woman in the feed sack dress continued to gaze expressionless across the floor at the high-top shoes of the man opposite her, the one who had been pretending to be asleep when the Turpins came in. He was laughing heartily, his hands still spread out on his knees. The child had fallen to the side and was lying now almost face down in the old woman's lap.

While they recovered from their laughter, the nasal chorus on the radio kept the room from silence.

> *"You go to blank blank*
> *And I'll go to mine*
> *But we'll all blank along*
> *To-geth-ther,*
> *And all along the blank*
> *We'll hep each other out*
> *Smile-ling in any kind of*
> *Weath-ther!"*

Mrs. Turpin didn't catch every word but she caught enough to agree with the spirit of the song and it turned her thoughts sober. To help anybody out that needed it was her philosophy of life. She never spared herself when she found somebody in need, whether they were white or black, trash or decent. And of all she had to be thankful for, she was most thankful that this was so. If Jesus had said, "You can be high society and have all the money you want and be thin and svelte-like, but you can't be a good woman with it," she would have had to say, "Well don't make me that then. Make me a good woman and it don't matter what else, how fat or how ugly or how poor!" Her heart rose. He had not made her a nigger or white-trash or ugly! He had made her herself and given her a little of everything. Jesus, thank you! she said. Thank you thank you thank you! Whenever she counted her blessings she felt as buoyant as if she weighed one hundred and twenty-five pounds instead of one hundred and eighty.

"What's wrong with your little boy?" the pleasant lady asked the white-trashy woman.

"He has a ulcer," the woman said proudly. "He ain't give me a minute's peace since he was born. Him and her are just alike," she said, nodding at the old woman, who was running her leathery fingers through the child's pale hair. "Look like I can't get nothing down them two but Co' Cola and candy."

That's all you try to get down em, Mrs. Turpin said to herself. Too lazy to light the fire. There was nothing you could tell her about people like them that she didn't know already. And it was not just that they didn't have anything. Because if you gave them everything, in two weeks it would all be broken or filthy or they would have chopped it up for lightwood. She knew all this from her own experience. Help them you must, but help them you couldn't.

All at once the ugly girl turned her lips inside out again. Her eyes were fixed like two drills on Mrs. Turpin. This time there was no mistaking that there was something urgent behind them.

Girl, Mrs. Turpin exclaimed silently, I haven't done a thing to you! The girl might be confusing her with somebody else. There was no need to sit by and let herself be intimidated. "You must be in college," she said boldly, looking directly at the girl. "I see you reading a book there."

The girl continued to stare and pointedly did not answer.

Her mother blushed at this rudeness. "The lady asked you a question, Mary Grace," she said under her breath.

"I have ears," Mary Grace said.

The poor mother blushed again. "Mary Grace goes to Wellesley College," she explained. She twisted one of the buttons on her dress. "In Massachusetts," she added with a grimace. "And in the summer she just keeps right on studying. Just reads all the time, a real book worm. She's done real well at Wellesley; she's taking English and Math and History and Psychology and Social Studies," she rattled on, "and I think it's too much. I think she ought to get out and have fun."

The girl looked as if she would like to hurl them all through the plate glass window.

"Way up north," Mrs. Turpin murmured and thought, well, it hasn't done much for her manners.

"I'd almost rather to have him sick," the white-trash woman said, wrenching the attention back to herself. "He's so mean when he ain't. Look like some children just take natural to meanness. It's some gets bad when they get sick but he was the opposite. Took sick and turned good. He don't give me no trouble now. It's me waitin to see the doctor," she said.

If I was going to send anybody back to Africa, Mrs. Turpin thought, it would be your kind, woman. "Yes, indeed," she said aloud, but looking up at the ceiling, "it's a heap of things worse than a nigger." And dirtier than a hog, she added to herself.

"I think people with bad dispositions are more to be pitied than anyone on earth," the pleasant lady said in a voice that was decidedly thin.

"I thank the Lord he has blessed me with a good one," Mrs. Turpin said. "The day has never dawned that I couldn't find something to laugh at."

"Not since she married me anyways," Claud said with a comical straight face.

Everybody laughed except the girl and the white-trash.

Mrs. Turpin's stomach shook. "He's such a caution," she said, "that I can't help but laugh at him."

The girl made a loud ugly noise through her teeth.

Her mother's mouth grew thin and tight. "I think the worst thing in the world," she said, "is an ungrateful person. To have everything and not appreciate it. I know a girl," she said, "who has parents who would give her anything, a little brother who loves her dearly, who is getting a good education, who wears the best clothes, but who can never say a kind word to anyone, who never smiles, who just criticizes and complains all day long."

"Is she too old to paddle?" Claud asked.

The girl's face was almost purple.

"Yes," the lady said, "I'm afraid there's nothing to do but leave her to her folly. Some day she'll wake up and it'll be too late."

"It never hurt anyone to smile," Mrs. Turpin said. "It just makes you feel better all over."

"Of course," the lady said sadly, "but there are just some people you can't tell anything to. They can't take criticism."

"If it's one thing I am," Mrs. Turpin said with feeling, "it's grateful. When I think who all I could have been besides myself and what all I got, a little of everything, and a good disposition besides, I just feel like shouting, 'Thank you, Jesus, for making everything the way it is!' It could have been different!" For one thing, somebody else could have got Claud. At the thought of this, she was flooded with gratitude and a terrible pang of joy ran through her. "Oh thank you, Jesus, Jesus, thank you!" she cried aloud.

The book struck her directly over her left eye. It struck almost at the same instant that she realized the girl was about to hurl it. Before she could utter a sound, the raw face came crashing across the table toward her, howling. The girl's fingers sank like clamps into the soft flesh of her neck. She heard the mother cry out and Claud shout, "Whoa!" There was an instant when she was certain that she was about to be in an earthquake.

All at once her vision narrowed and she saw everything as if it were happening in a small room far away, or as if she were looking at it through the wrong end of a telescope. Claud's face crumpled and fell out of sight. The nurse ran in, then out, then in again. Then the gangling figure of the doctor rushed out of the inner door. Magazines flew this way and that as the table turned over. The girl fell with a thud and Mrs. Turpin's vision suddenly reversed itself and she saw everything large instead of small. The eyes of the white-trashy woman were staring hugely at the floor. There the girl, held down on one side by the nurse and on the other by her mother, was wrenching and turning in their grasp. The doctor was kneeling astride her, trying to hold her arm down. He managed after a second to sink a long needle into it.

Mrs. Turpin felt entirely hollow except for her heart which swung from side to side as if it were agitated in a great empty drum of flesh.

"Somebody that's not busy call for the ambulance," the doctor said in the off-hand voice young doctors adopt for terrible occasions.

Mrs. Turpin could not have moved a finger. The old man who had been sitting next to her skipped nimbly into the office and made the call, for the secretary still seemed to be gone.

"Claud!" Mrs. Turpin called.

He was not in his chair. She knew she must jump up and find him but she felt like some one trying to catch a train in a dream, when everything moves in slow motion and the faster you try to run the slower you go.

"Here I am," a suffocated voice, very unlike Claud's, said.

He was doubled up in the corner on the floor, pale as paper, holding his leg. She wanted to get up and go to him but she could not move. Instead, her gaze was drawn slowly downward to the churning face on the floor, which she could see over the doctor's shoulder.

The girl's eyes stopped rolling and focused on her. They seemed a much lighter blue than before, as if a door that had been tightly closed behind them was now open to admit light and air.

Mrs. Turpin's head cleared and her power of motion returned. She leaned forward until she was looking directly into the fierce brilliant eyes. There was no doubt in her mind that the girl did know her, knew her in some intense and personal way, beyond time and place and condition. "What you got to say to me?" she asked hoarsely and held her breath, waiting, as for a revelation.

The girl raised her head. Her gaze locked with Mrs. Turpin's. "Go back to hell where you came from, you old wart hog," she whispered. Her voice was low but clear. Her eyes burned for a moment as if she saw with pleasure that her message had struck its target.

Mrs. Turpin sank back in her chair.

After a moment the girl's eyes closed and she turned her head wearily to the side.

The doctor rose and handed the nurse the empty syringe. He leaned over and put both hands for a moment on the mother's shoulders, which were shaking. She was sitting on the floor, her lips pressed together, holding Mary Grace's hand in her lap. The girl's fingers were gripped like a baby's around her thumb. "Go on to the hospital," he said. "I'll call and make the arrangements."

"Now let's see that neck," he said in a jovial voice to Mrs. Turpin. He began to inspect her neck with his first two fingers. Two little moon-shaped lines like pink fish bones were indented over her windpipe. There was the beginning of an angry red swelling above her eye. His fingers passed over this also.

"Lea' me be," she said thickly and shook him off. "See about Claud. She kicked him."

"I'll see about him in a minute," he said and felt her pulse. He was a thin grey-haired man, given to pleasantries. "Go home and have yourself a vacation the rest of the day," he said and patted her on the shoulder.

Quit your pattin me, Mrs. Turpin growled to herself.

"And put an ice pack over that eye," he said. Then he went and squatted down beside Claud and looked at his leg. After a moment he pulled him up and Claud limped after him into the office.

Until the ambulance came, the only sounds in the room were the tremulous moans of the girl's mother, who continued to sit on the floor. The white-trash woman did not take her eyes off the girl. Mrs. Turpin looked straight ahead at nothing. Presently the ambulance drew up, a long dark shadow, behind the curtain. The attendants came in and set the stretcher down beside the girl and lifted her expertly onto it and carried her out. The nurse helped the mother gather up her things. The shadow of the ambulance moved silently away and the nurse came back in the office.

"That ther girl is going to be a lunatic, ain't she?" the white-trash woman asked the nurse, but the nurse kept on to the back and never answered her.

"Yes, she's going to be a lunatic," the white-trash woman said to the rest of them.

"Po' critter," the old woman murmured. The child's face was still in her lap. His eyes looked idly out over her knees. He had not moved during the disturbance except to draw one leg up under him.

"I thank Gawd," the white-trash woman said fervently, "I ain't a lunatic."

Claud came limping out and the Turpins went home.

As their pick-up truck turned into their own dirt road and made the crest of the hill, Mrs. Turpin gripped the window ledge and looked out suspiciously. The land sloped gracefully down through a field dotted with lavender weeds and at the start of the rise their small yellow frame house, with its little flower beds spread out around it like a fancy apron, sat primly in its accustomed place between two giant hickory trees. She would not have been startled to see a burnt wound between two blackened chimneys.

Neither of them felt like eating so they put on their house clothes and lowered the shade in the bedroom and lay down, Claud with his leg on a pillow and herself with a damp washcloth over her eye. The instant she was flat on her back, the image of a razor-backed hog with warts on its face and horns coming out behind its ears snorted into her head. She moaned, a low quiet moan.

"I am not," she said tearfully, "a wart hog. From hell." But the denial had no force. The girl's eyes and her words, even the tone of her voice, low but clear, directed only to her, brooked no repudiation. She had been singled out for the message, though there was trash in the room to whom it might justly have been applied. The full force of this fact struck her only now. There was a woman there who was neglecting her own child but she had been overlooked. The message had been given to Ruby Turpin, a respectable, hard-working, church-going woman. The tears dried. Her eyes began to burn instead with wrath.

She rose on her elbow and the washcloth fell into her hand. Claud was lying on his back, snoring. She wanted to tell him what the girl had said. At the same time, she did not wish to put the image of herself as a wart hog from hell into his mind.

"Hey, Claud," she muttered and pushed his shoulder.

Claud opened one pale baby blue eye.

She looked into it warily. He did not think about anything. He just went his way.

"Wha, whasit?" he said and closed the eye again.

"Nothing," she said. "Does your leg pain you?"

"Hurts like hell," Claud said.

"It'll quit terreckly," she said and lay back down. In a moment Claud was snoring again. For the rest of the afternoon they lay there. Claud slept. She scowled at the ceiling. Occasionally she raised her fist and made a small stabbing motion over her chest as if she was defending her innocence to invisible guests who were like the comforters of Job, reasonable-seeming but wrong.

About five-thirty Claud stirred. "Got to go after those niggers," he sighed, not moving.

She was looking straight up as if there were unintelligible handwriting on the ceiling. The protuberance over her eye had turned a greenish-blue. "Listen here," she said.

"What?"

"Kiss me."

Claud leaned over and kissed her loudly on the mouth. He pinched her side and their hands interlocked. Her expression of ferocious concentration did not change. Claud got up, groaning and growling, and limped off. She continued to study the ceiling.

She did not get up until she heard the pick-up truck coming back with the Negroes. Then she rose and thrust her feet in her brown oxfords, which she did not bother to lace, and stumped out onto the back porch and got her red plastic bucket. She emptied a tray of ice cubes into it and filled it half full of water and went out into the back yard. Every afternoon after Claud brought the hands in, one of the boys helped him put out hay and the rest waited in the back of the truck until he was ready to take them home. The truck was parked in the shade under one of the hickory trees.

"Hi yawl this evening?" Mrs. Turpin asked grimly, appearing with the bucket and the dipper. There were three women and a boy in the truck.

"Us doin nicely," the oldest woman said. "Hi you doin?" and her gaze stuck immediately on the dark lump on Mrs. Turpin's forehead. "You done fell down, ain't you?" she asked in a solicitous voice. The old woman was dark and almost toothless. She had on an old felt hat of Claud's set back on her head. The other two women were younger and lighter and they both had new bright green sun hats. One of them had hers on her head; the other had taken hers off and the boy was grinning beneath it.

Mrs. Turpin set the bucket down on the floor of the truck. "Yawl hep yourselves," she said. She looked around to make sure Claud had gone. "No. I didn't fall down," she said, folding her arms. "It was something worse than that."

"Ain't nothing bad happen to you!" the old woman said. She said it as if they all knew that Mrs. Turpin was protected in some special way by Divine Providence. "You just had you a little fall."

"We were in town at the doctor's office for where the cow kicked Mr. Turpin," Mrs. Turpin said in a flat tone that indicated they could leave off their foolishness. "And there was this girl there. A big fat girl with her face all broke out. I could look at that girl and tell she was peculiar but I couldn't tell how. And me and her mama were just talking and going along and all of a sudden WHAM! She throws this big book she was reading at me and . . ."

"Naw!" the old woman cried out.

"And then she jumps over the table and commences to choke me."

"Naw!" they all exclaimed, "naw!"

"Hi come she do that?" the old woman asked. "What ail her?"

Mrs. Turpin only glared in front of her.

"Somethin ail her," the old woman said.

"They carried her off in an ambulance," Mrs. Turpin continued, "but before she went she was rolling on the floor and they were trying to hold her down to give her a shot and she said something to me." She paused. "You know what she said to me?"

"What she say?" they asked.

"She said," Mrs. Turpin began, and stopped, her face very dark and heavy. The sun was getting whiter and whiter, blanching the sky overhead so that the leaves of the hickory tree were black in the face of it. She could not bring forth the words. "Something real ugly," she muttered.

"She sho shouldn't said nothin ugly to you," the old woman said. "You so sweet. You the sweetest lady I know."

"She pretty too," the one with the hat on said.

"And stout," the other one said. "I never knowed no sweeter white lady."

"That's the truth befo' Jesus," the old woman said. "Amen! You des as sweet and pretty as you can be."

Mrs. Turpin knew just exactly how much Negro flattery was worth and it added to her rage. "She said," she began again and finished this time with a fierce rush of breath, "that I was an old wart hog from hell."

There was an astounded silence.

"Where she at?" the youngest woman cried in a piercing voice.

"Lemme see her. I'll kill her!"

"I'll kill her with you!" the other one cried.

"She b'long in the sylum," the old woman said emphatically. "You the sweetest white lady I know."

"She pretty too," the other two said. "Stout as she can be and sweet. Jesus satisfied with her!"

"Deed he is," the old woman declared.

Idiots! Mrs. Turpin growled to herself. You could never say anything intelligent to a nigger. You could talk at them but not with them. "Yawl ain't drunk your water," she said shortly. "Leave the bucket in the truck when you're finished with it. I got more to do than just stand around and pass the time of day," and she moved off and into the house.

She stood for a moment in the middle of the kitchen. The dark protuberance over her eye looked like a miniature tornado cloud which might any moment sweep across the horizon of her brow. Her lower lip protruded dangerously. She squared her massive shoulders. Then she marched into the front of the house and out the side door and started down the road to the pig parlor. She had the look of a woman going single-handed, weaponless, into battle.

The sun was a deep yellow now like a harvest moon and was riding westward very fast over the far tree line as if it meant to reach the hogs before she did. The road was rutted and she kicked several good-sized stones out of her path as she strode along. The pig parlor was on a little knoll at the end of a lane that ran off from the side of the barn. It was a square of concrete as large as a small room, with a board fence about four feet high around it. The concrete floor sloped slightly so that the hog wash could drain off into a trench where it was carried to the field for fertilizer. Claud was standing on the outside, on the edge of the concrete, hanging onto the top board, hosing down the floor inside. The hose was connected to the faucet of a water trough nearby.

Mrs. Turpin climbed up beside him and glowered down at the hogs inside. There were seven long-snouted bristly shoats in it — tan with liver-colored spots — and an old sow a few weeks off from farrowing. She was lying on her side grunting. The shoats were running about shaking themselves like idiot children, their little slit pig eyes searching the floor for anything left. She had read that pigs were the most intelligent animal. She doubted it. They were supposed to be smarter than dogs. There had even been a pig astronaut. He had performed his assignment perfectly but died of a heart attack afterwards because they left him in his electric suit, sitting upright throughout his examination when naturally a hog should be on all fours.

A-gruntin and a-rootin and a-groanin.

"Gimme that hose," she said, yanking it away from Claud. "Go on and carry them niggers home and then get off that leg."

"You look like you might have swallowed a mad dog," Claud observed, but he got down and limped off. He paid no attention to her humors.

Until he was out of earshot, Mrs. Turpin stood on the side of the pen, holding the hose and pointing the stream of water at the hind quarters of any shoat that looked as if it might try to lie down. When he had had time to get over the hill, she turned her head slightly and her wrathful eyes scanned the path. He was nowhere in sight. She turned back again and seemed to gather herself up. Her shoulders rose and she drew in her breath.

"What do you send me a message like that for?" she said in a low fierce voice, barely above a whisper but with the force of a shout in its concentrated fury. "How am I a hog and me both? How am I saved and from hell too?" Her free fist was knotted and with the other she gripped the hose, blindly pointing the stream of water in and out of the eye of the old sow whose outraged squeal she did not hear.

The pig parlor commanded a view of the back pasture where their twenty beef cows were gathered around the hay-bales Claud and the boy had put out. The freshly cut pasture sloped down to the highway. Across it was their cotton field and beyond that a dark green dusty wood which they owned as well. The sun was behind the wood, very red, looking over the paling of trees like a farmer inspecting his own hogs.

"Why me?" she rumbled. "It's no trash around here, black or white, that I haven't given to. And break my back to the bone every day working. And do for the church."

She appeared to be the right size woman to command the arena before her. "How am I a hog?" she demanded. "Exactly how am I like them?" and she jabbed the stream of water at the shoats. "There was plenty of trash there. It didn't have to be me.

"If you like trash better, go get yourself some trash then," she railed. "You could have made me trash. Or a nigger. If trash is what you wanted why didn't you make me trash?" She shook her fist with the hose in it and a watery snake appeared momentarily in the air. "I could quit working and take it easy and be filthy," she growled. "Lounge about the sidewalks all day drinking root beer. Dip snuff and spit in every puddle and have it all over my face. I could be nasty.

"Or you could have made me a nigger. It's too late for me to be a nigger," she said with deep sarcasm, "but I could act like one. Lay down in the middle of the road and stop traffic. Roll on the ground."

In the deepening light everything was taking on a mysterious hue. The pasture was growing a peculiar glassy green and the streak of highway had turned lavender. She braced herself for a final assault and this time her voice rolled out over the pasture. "Go on," she yelled, "call me a hog! Call me a hog again. From hell. Call me a wart hog from hell. Put that bottom rail on top. There'll still be a top and bottom!"

A garbled echo returned to her.

A final surge of fury shook her and she roared, "Who do you think you are?"

The color of everything, field and crimson sky, burned for a moment with a transparent intensity. The question carried over the pasture and across the highway and the cotton field and returned to her clearly like an answer from beyond the wood.

She opened her mouth but no sound came out of it.

A tiny truck, Claud's, appeared on the highway, heading rapidly out of sight. Its gears scraped thinly. It looked like a child's toy. At any moment a bigger truck might smash into it and scatter Claud's and the niggers' brains all over the road.

Mrs. Turpin stood there, her gaze fixed on the highway, all her muscles rigid, until in five or six minutes the truck reappeared, returning. She waited until it had had time to turn into their own road. Then like a monumental statue coming to life, she bent her head slowly and gazed, as if through the very heart of mystery, down into the pig parlor at the hogs. They had settled all in one corner around the old sow who was grunting softly. A red glow suffused them. They appeared to pant with a secret life.

Until the sun slipped finally behind the tree line, Mrs. Turpin remained there with her gaze bent to them as if she were absorbing some abysmal life-giving knowledge. At last she lifted her head. There was only a purple streak in the sky, cutting through a field of crimson and leading, like an extension of the highway, into the descending dusk. She raised her hands from the side of the pen in a gesture hieratic and profound. A visionary light settled in her eyes. She saw the streak as a vast swinging bridge extending upward from the earth through a field of living fire. Upon it a vast horde of souls were rumbling toward heaven. There were whole companies of white-trash, clean for the first time in their lives, and bands of black niggers in white robes, and battalions of freaks and lunatics shouting and clapping and leaping like frogs. And bringing up the end of the procession was a tribe of people whom she recognized at once as those who, like herself and Claud, had always had a little of everything and the God-given wit to use it right. She leaned forward to observe them closer. They were marching behind the others with great dignity, accountable as they had always been for good order and common sense and respectable behavior. They alone were on key. Yet she could see by their shocked and altered faces that even their virtues were being burned away. She lowered her hands and gripped the rail of the hog pen, her eyes small but fixed unblinkingly on what lay ahead. In a moment the vision faded but she remained where she was, immobile.

At length she got down and turned off the faucet and made her slow way on the darkening path to the house. In the woods around her the invisible cricket choruses had struck up, but what she heard were the voices of the souls climbing upward into the starry field and shouting hallelujah.

QUESTIONS

1. How does Mrs. Turpin see herself before Mary Grace calls her a wart hog?
2. What is the narrator's attitude toward Mrs. Turpin in the beginning of the story? How can you tell? Does this attitude change, or stay the same, at the end?
3. Describe the relationship between Mary Grace and her mother. What annoying platitudes does the mother mouth? Which of Mrs. Turpin's opinions seem especially to anger Mary Grace?
4. Sketch the plot of the story. What moment or event do you take to be the crisis, or turning point? What is the climax? What is the conclusion?
5. What do you infer from Mrs. Turpin's conversation with the black farm workers? Is she their friend? Why does she now find their flattery unacceptable ("Jesus satisfied with her")?
6. When, near the end of the story, Mrs. Turpin roars, "Who do you think you are?", an echo "returned to her clearly like an answer from beyond the wood" (page 106). Explain.
7. What is the final revelation given to Mrs. Turpin? (To state it is to state the theme of the story.) What new attitude does the revelation impart? (How is Mrs. Turpin left with a new vision of humanity?)
8. Other stories in this book contain revelations: "Gimpel the Fool," "Angel Levine," "The Death of Ivan Ilych." If you have read them, try to sum up the supernatural revelation made to the central character in each story. In each, is the revelation the same as a statement of the story's central theme?

Grace Paley (b. 1922)

THE LOUDEST VOICE

There is a certain place where dumb-waiters boom, doors slam, dishes crash; every window is a mother's mouth bidding the street shut up, go skate somewhere else, come home. My voice is the loudest.

There, my own mother is still as full of breathing as me and the grocer stands up to speak to her. "Mrs. Abramowitz," he says, "people should not be afraid of their children."

"Ah, Mr. Bialik," my mother replies, "if you say to her or her father 'Ssh,' they say, 'In the grave it will be quiet.'"

"From Coney Island to the cemetery," says my papa. "It's the same subway; it's the same fare."

I am right next to the pickle barrel. My pinky is making tiny whirlpools in the brine. I stop a moment to announce: "Campbell's Tomato Soup. Campbell's Vegetable Beef Soup. Campbell's S-c-otch Broth . . ."

"Be quiet," the grocer says, "the labels are coming off."

"Please, Shirley, be a little quiet," my mother begs me.

In that place the whole street groans: Be quiet! Be quiet! but steals from the happy chorus of my inside self not a tittle or a jot.

There, too, but just around the corner, is a red brick building that has been old for many years. Every morning the children stand before it in double lines which must be straight. They are not insulted. They are waiting anyway.

I am usually among them. I am, in fact, the first, since I begin with "A."

One cold morning the monitor tapped me on the shoulder. "Go to Room 409, Shirley Abramowitz," he said. I did as I was told. I went in a hurry up a down staircase to Room 409, which contained sixth-graders. I had to wait at the desk without wiggling until Mr. Hilton, their teacher, had time to speak.

After five minutes he said, "Shirley?"

"What?" I whispered.

He said, "My! My! Shirley Abramowitz! They told me you had a particularly loud, clear voice and read with lots of expression. Could that be true?"

"Oh yes," I whispered.

"In that case, don't be silly; I might very well be your teacher someday. Speak up, speak up."

"Yes," I shouted.

"More like it," he said. "Now, Shirley, can you put a ribbon in your hair or a bobby pin? It's too messy."

"Yes!" I bawled.

"Now, now, calm down." He turned to the class. "Children, not a sound. Open at page 39. Read till 52. When you finish, start again." He looked me over once more. "Now, Shirley, you know, I suppose, that Christmas is coming. We are preparing a beautiful play. Most of the parts have been given out. But I still need a child with a strong voice, lots of stamina. Do you know what stamina is? You do? Smart kid. You know, I heard you read 'The Lord is my shepherd' in Assembly yesterday. I was very impressed. Wonderful delivery. Mrs. Jordan, your teacher, speaks highly of you. Now listen to me,

Shirley Abramowitz, if you want to take the part and be in the play repeat after me, 'I swear to work harder than I ever did before.'"

I looked to heaven and said at once, "Oh, I swear." I kissed my pinky and looked at God.

"That is an actor's life, my dear," he explained. "Like a soldier's, never tardy or disobedient to his general, the director. Everything," he said, "absolutely everything will depend on you."

That afternoon, all over the building, children scraped and scrubbed the turkeys and the sheaves of corn off the schoolroom windows. Goodbye Thanksgiving. The next morning a monitor brought red paper and green paper from the office. We made new shapes and hung them on the walls and glued them to the doors.

The teachers became happier and happier. Their heads were ringing like the bells of childhood. My best friend Evie was prone to evil, but she did not get a single demerit for whispering. We learned "Holy Night" without an error. "How wonderful!" said Miss Glacé, the student teacher. "To think that some of you don't even speak the language!" We learned "Deck the Halls" and "Hark! The Herald Angels". . . . They weren't ashamed and we weren't embarrassed.

Oh, but when my mother heard about it all, she said to my father: "Misha, you don't know what's going on there. Cramer is the head of the Tickets Committee."

"Who?" asked my father. "Cramer? Oh yes, an active woman."

"Active? Active has to have a reason. Listen," she said sadly, "I'm surprised to see my neighbors making tra-la-la for Christmas."

My father couldn't think of what to say to that. Then he decided: "You're in America! Clara, you wanted to come here. In Palestine the Arabs would be eating you alive. Europe you had pogroms°. Argentina is full of Indians. Here you got Christmas. . . . Some joke, ha?"

"Very funny, Misha. What is becoming of you? If we came to a new country a long time ago to run away from tyrants, and instead we fall into a creeping pogrom, that our children learn a lot of lies, so what's the joke? Ach, Misha, your idealism is going away."

"So is your sense of humor."

"That I never had, but idealism you had a lot of."

"I'm the same Misha Abramovitch, I didn't change an iota. Ask anyone."

"Only ask me," says my mama, may she rest in peace. "I got the answer."

Meanwhile the neighbors had to think of what to say too.

Marty's father said: "You know, he has a very important part, my boy."

"Mine also," said Mr. Sauerfeld.

"Not my boy!" said Mrs. Klieg. "I said to him no. The answer is no. When I say no! I mean no!"

The rabbi's wife said, "It's disgusting!" But no one listened to her. Under the narrow sky of God's great wisdom she wore a strawberry-blond wig.

Every day was noisy and full of experience. I was Right-hand Man. Mr. Hilton said: "How could I get along without you, Shirley?"

pogroms: Russian for "devastations"; organized massacres.

He said: "Your mother and father ought to get down on their knees every night and thank God for giving them a child like you."

He also said: "You're absolutely a pleasure to work with, my dear, dear child."

Sometimes he said: "For God's sakes, what did I do with the script? Shirley! Shirley! Find it."

Then I answered quietly: "Here it is, Mr. Hilton."

Once in a while, when he was very tired, he would cry out: "Shirley, I'm just tired of screaming at those kids. Will you tell Ira Pushkov not to come in till Lester points to that star the second time?"

Then I roared: "Ira Pushkov, what's the matter with you? Dope! Mr. Hilton told you five times already, don't come in till Lester points to that star the second time."

"Ach, Clara," my father asked, "what does she do there till six o'clock she can't even put the plates on the table?"

"Christmas," said my mother coldly.

"Ho! Ho!" my father said. "Christmas. What's the harm? After all, history teaches everyone. We learn from reading this is a holiday from pagan times also, candles, lights, even Chanukah. So we learn it's not altogether Christian. So if they think it's a private holiday, they're only ignorant, not patriotic. What belongs to history, belongs to all men. You want to go back to the Middle Ages? Is it better to shave your head with a secondhand razor? Does it hurt Shirley to learn to speak up? It does not. So maybe someday she won't live between the kitchen and the shop. She's not a fool."

I thank you, Papa, for your kindness. It is true about me to this day. I am foolish but I am not a fool.

That night my father kissed me and said with great interest in my career, "Shirley, tomorrow's your big day. Congrats."

"Save it," my mother said. Then she shut all the windows in order to prevent tonsillitis.

In the morning it snowed. On the street corner a tree had been decorated for us by a kind city administration. In order to miss its chilly shadow our neighbors walked three blocks east to buy a loaf of bread. The butcher pulled down black window shades to keep the colored lights from shining on his chickens. Oh, not me. On the way to school, with both my hands I tossed it a kiss of tolerance. Poor thing, it was a stranger in Egypt.

I walked straight into the auditorium past the staring children. "Go ahead, Shirley!" said the monitors. Four boys, big for their age, had already started work as propmen and stagehands.

Mr. Hilton was very nervous. He was not even happy. Whatever he started to say ended in a sideward look of sadness. He sat slumped in the middle of the first row and asked me to help Miss Glacé. I did this, although she thought my voice too resonant and said, "Show-off!"

Parents began to arrive long before we were ready. They wanted to make a good impression. From among the yards of drapes I peeked out at the audience. I saw my embarrassed mother.

Ira, Lester, and Meyer were pasted to their beards by Miss Glacé. She almost forgot to thread the star on its wire, but I reminded her. I coughed a few times to clear my throat. Miss Glacé looked around and saw that everyone was in costume and on line waiting to play his part. She whispered, "All right . . ." Then:

Jackie Sauerfeld, the prettiest boy in first grade, parted the curtains with his skinny elbow and in a high voice sang out:

"Parents dear
We are here
To make a Christmas play in time.
It we give
In narrative
And illustrate with pantomime."

He disappeared.

My voice burst immediately from the wings to the great shock of Ira, Lester, and Meyer, who were waiting for it but were surprised all the same. "I remember, I remember, the house where I was born . . ."

Miss Glacé yanked the curtain open and there it was, the house — an old hayloft, where Celia Kornbluh lay in the straw with Cindy Lou, her favorite doll. Ira, Lester, and Meyer moved slowly from the wings toward her, sometimes pointing to a moving star and sometimes ahead to Cindy Lou.

It was a long story and it was a sad story. I carefully pronounced all the words about my lonesome childhood, while little Eddie Braunstein wandered upstage and down with his shepherd's stick, looking for sheep. I brought up lonesomeness again, and not being understood at all except by some women everybody hated. Eddie was too small for that and Marty Groff took his place, wearing his father's prayer shawl. I announced twelve friends, and half the boys in the fourth grade gathered round Marty, who stood on an orange crate while my voice harangued. Sorrowful and loud, I declaimed about love and God and Man, but because of the terrible deceit of Abie Stock we came suddenly to a famous moment. Marty, whose remembering tongue I was, waited at the foot of the cross. He stared desperately at the audience. I groaned, "My God, my God why hast thou forsaken me?" The soldiers who were sheiks grabbed poor Marty to pin him up to die, but he wrenched free, turned again to the audience, and spread his arms aloft to show despair and the end. I murmured at the top of my voice, "The rest is silence, but as everyone in this room, in this city — in this world — now knows, I shall have life eternal."

That night Mrs. Kornbluh visited our kitchen for a glass of tea.

"How's the virgin?" asked my father with a look of concern.

"For a man with a daughter, you got a fresh mouth, Abramovitch."

"Here," said my father kindly, "have some lemon, it'll sweeten your disposition."

They debated a little in Yiddish, then fell in a puddle of Russian and Polish. What I understood next was my father, who said, "Still and all, it was certainly a beautiful affair, you have to admit, introducing us to the beliefs of a different culture."

"Well, yes," said Mrs. Kornbluh. "The only thing . . . you know Charlie Turner — that cute boy in Celia's class — a couple others? They got very small parts or no part at all. In very bad taste, it seemed to me. After all, it's their religion."

"Ach," explained my mother, "what could Mr. Hilton do? They got very small voices; after all, why should they holler? The English language they know from the beginning by heart. They're blond like angels. You think it's so important they should get in the play? Christmas . . . the whole piece of goods . . . they own it."

I listened and listened until I couldn't listen any more. Too sleepy, I climbed out of bed and kneeled. I made a little church of my hands and said, "Hear, O Israel . . . " Then I called out in Yiddish, "Please, good night, good night. Ssh." My father said, "Ssh yourself," and slammed the kitchen door.

I was happy. I fell asleep at once. I had prayed for everybody: my talking family, cousins far away, passersby, and all the lonesome Christians. I expected to be heard. My voice was certainly the loudest.

QUESTIONS

1. What does Shirley's mother mean in her final remark about the Christian children? ("They got very small voices; after all, why should they holler?")
2. Why does Shirley's father approve of her learning "to speak up"?
3. Sum up the main theme of Grace Paley's story. What does the title of the story have to do with it?

6 Symbol

In F. Scott Fitzgerald's novel *The Great Gatsby*, a huge pair of bespectacled eyes stares across a wilderness of ash heaps, from a billboard advertising the services of an oculist. Repeatedly entering into the story, the advertisement comes to mean more than simply the availability of eye examinations. Fitzgerald has a character liken it to the eyes of God; he hints that some sad, compassionate spirit is brooding as it watches the passing procession of mankind. Such an object is a **symbol:** in literature, a thing that suggests more than its literal meaning. Symbols generally do not "stand for" any one meaning, nor for anything absolutely definite; they point, they hint, or, as Henry James put it, they cast long shadows. To take a large example: in Herman Melville's *Moby Dick,* the great white whale of the book's title apparently means more than the literal dictionary-definition meaning of an aquatic mammal. He also suggests more than the devil, to whom some of the characters liken him. The great whale, as the story unfolds, comes to imply an amplitude of meanings: among them the forces of nature and the whole created universe. This indefinite multiplicity of meanings is characteristic of a symbolic story and distinguishes it from an **allegory,** a story in which persons, places, and things form a system of clearly labeled equivalents.

In a simple allegory, characters and other ingredients tend to stand for definite other meanings, which are often abstractions. Supreme allegories are found in some biblical parables ("The kingdom of Heaven is like a man who sowed good seed in his field. . . ," Matthew 13:24–30). A classic allegory is the medieval play *Everyman,* whose hero represents us all, and who, deserted by false friends called Kindred and Goods, faces the judgment of God accompanied only by a faithful friend called Good Deeds. In John Bunyan's seventeenth-century *Pilgrim's Progress,* the protagonist, Christian, struggles along the difficult road toward salvation, meeting along the way persons such as Mr. Worldly Wiseman, who directs him into a more comfortable path (a wrong turn), and the residents of a town called Fair Speech, among them a hypocrite named Mr. Facing-both-ways. Not all allegories are simple: Dante's *Divine Comedy,* written in the Middle Ages, continues to reveal new meanings to careful readers. Allegory was much beloved in the Middle Ages, but in contemporary fiction it is rare. One modern instance is George Orwell's long fable *Animal Farm*, in which (among its double meanings) barnyard animals stand for human victims and totalitarian oppressors.

Symbols in fiction tend not to be abstract terms like *love* or *truth*, but to be perceptible objects (or worded descriptions that cause us to imagine them). In William Faulkner's "A Rose for Emily" (Chapter Two), Miss Emily's invisible watch ticking at the end of a golden chain indicates not only the passage of time, but suggests that time passes without even being noticed by the watch's owner, and the golden chain carries suggestions of wealth and authority. Often the symbols we meet in fiction are inanimate objects, but other things also may function symbolically. In James Joyce's "Araby" (Chapter Two), the very name of the bazaar — the poetic name for Arabia — suggests magic, romance, and *The Arabian Nights;* its syllables (the narrator tells us) "cast an Eastern enchantment over me." Even a locale, or a feature of physical topography, can provide rich suggestions: the icy Siberian river in Anton Chekhov's "In Exile" (p. 320), beside whose frozen banks we find Semyon locking up and suppressing his human feelings. Recall Ernest Hemingway's "A Clean, Well-Lighted Place" (Chapter Four), in which the café is not merely a café, but an island of refuge from night, chaos, loneliness, old age, and impending death.

In some novels and stories, symbolic characters make brief cameo appearances. Such characters tend not to be well-rounded and fully known, but to be seen fleetingly and to remain slightly mysterious. In *Heart of Darkness,* a short novel by Joseph Conrad, a steamship company that hires men to work in the Congo maintains in its waiting room two women who knit black wool — like the classical Fates. Usually such a symbolic character is more a portrait than a person — or somewhat portrait-like, as Faulkner's Miss Emily, who twice appears at a window of her house "like the carven torso of an idol in a niche." Though Faulkner invests Miss Emily with life and vigor, he also invests her with symbolic hints: she seems almost to personify the vanishing aristocracy of the antebellum South, still maintaining a black servant and being ruthlessly betrayed by a moneymaking Yankee. Sometimes a part of a character's body or a single attribute may convey symbolic meaning: a baleful eye, as in Edgar Allan Poe's "The Tell-Tale Heart" (Chapter Seven); or as in Grace Paley's "The Loudest Voice" (Chapter Five), a distinctive voice that suggests that its owner, unlike the Christian children with their small voices, feels proudly and triumphantly different.

Much as a symbolic whale contains more meaning than an ordinary whale, a **symbolic act** is a gesture with larger significance than usual. For the boy's father in Faulkner's "Barn Burning" (Chapter Four), the act of destroying a barn is no mere act of spite, but an expression of his profound hatred for anything not belonging to him. Faulkner adds that burning a barn reflects the father's memories of the "waste and extravagance of war"; and further adds that "the element of fire spoke to some deep mainspring" in his being. However, a symbolic act doesn't have to be a gesture as large as starting a conflagration. Before setting out in pursuit of the great white whale, Melville's Captain Ahab in *Moby Dick* deliberately snaps his tobacco pipe and throws it away, as if to suggest (among other things) that he will let no pleasure or pastime distract him from his vengeance.

Why do writers have to symbolize — why don't they tell us outright? One advantage of a symbol is that it is so compact, and yet so fully laden. Both starkly concrete and slightly mysterious, like Miss Emily's invisibly ticking watch, it may impress us with all the force of something beheld in a dream or in a nightmare. When Joyce, in describing the Dublin boy arrived at last in Araby only to find it shoddy and expensive and about to close for the night, the symbol of that exotically named bazaar (and its clash with its actual counterpart) tells us more about growing into maturity and watching cherished illusions disappear, than if Joyce had written a long treatise on the subject.

To some extent (it may be claimed), all stories are symbolic. Merely by holding up for our inspection certain characters and their actions, the writer lends them *some* special significance. But this is to think of *symbol* in an extremely broad and inclusive way. For the usual purposes of reading a story and understanding it, there is probably little point in looking for symbolism in every word, in every stick or stone, in every striking of a match, in every minor character. Still, to be on the alert for symbols when reading fiction is perhaps wiser than to ignore them. Not to admit that symbolic meanings may be present, or to refuse to think about them, would be another way to misread a story — or to read no farther than its outer edges.

How, then, do you recognize a symbol in fiction when you meet it? Fortunately, the storyteller often gives the symbol particular emphasis. It may be mentioned repeatedly throughout the story; it may even supply the story with a title ("Araby," "Barn Burning," "A Clean, Well-Lighted Place"). At times, a crucial symbol will open a story or end it. Unless an object, act, or character is given some such special emphasis and importance, we may generally feel safe in taking it at face value. Probably it isn't a symbol if it points clearly and unmistakably toward some single meaning, like a whistle in a factory, whose blast at noon means lunch. But an object, an act, or a character is surely symbolic (and almost as surely displays high literary art) if, when we finish the story, we realize that it was that particular item — those gigantic eyes; that clean, well-lighted café; that burning of a barn — which led us to the author's theme, the essential meaning.

Nathaniel Hawthorne (1804–1864)

THE MINISTER'S BLACK VEIL 1836

A Parable[1]

The sexton stood in the porch of Milford meeting-house, pulling busily at the bell-rope. The old people of the village came stooping along the street. Children, with bright faces, tripped merrily beside their parents, or mimicked a graver gait, in the conscious dignity of their Sunday clothes. Spruce bachelors looked sidelong at the pretty maidens, and fancied that the Sabbath sunshine made them prettier than on week days. When the throng had mostly streamed into the porch, the sexton began to toll the bell, keeping his eye on the Reverend Mr. Hooper's door. The first glimpse of the clergyman's figure was the signal for the bell to cease its summons.

"But what has good Parson Hooper got upon his face?" cried the sexton in astonishment.

All within hearing immediately turned about, and beheld the semblance of Mr. Hooper, pacing slowly his meditative way towards the meeting-house. With one accord they started, expressing more wonder than if some strange minister were coming to dust the cushions of Mr. Hooper's pulpit.

"Are you sure it is our parson?" inquired Goodman Gray of the sexton.

"Of a certainty it is good Mr. Hooper," replied the sexton. "He was to have exchanged pulpits with Parson Shute, of Westbury; but Parson Shute sent to excuse himself yesterday, being to preach a funeral sermon."

The cause of so much amazement may appear sufficiently slight. Mr. Hooper, a gentlemanly person, of about thirty, though still a bachelor, was dressed with due clerical neatness, as if a careful wife had starched his band, and brushed the weekly dust from his Sunday's garb. There was but one thing remarkable in his appearance. Swathed about his forehead, and hanging down over his face, so low as to be shaken by his breath, Mr. Hooper had on a black veil. On a nearer view it seemed to consist of two folds of crape, which entirely concealed his features, except the mouth and chin, but probably did not intercept his sight, further than to give a darkened aspect to all living and inanimate things. With this gloomy shade before him, good Mr. Hooper walked onward, at a slow and quiet pace, stooping somewhat, and looking on the ground, as is customary with abstracted men, yet nodding kindly to those of his parishioners who still waited on the meeting-house steps. But so wonder-struck were they that his greeting hardly met with a return.

"I can't really feel as if good Mr. Hooper's face was behind that piece of crape," said the sexton.

"I don't like it," muttered an old woman, as she hobbled into the meeting-house. "He has changed himself into something awful, only by hiding his face."

[1] Another clergyman in New England, Mr. Joseph Moody, of York, Maine, who died about eighty years since, made himself remarkable by the same eccentricity that is here related of the Reverend Mr. Hooper. In his case, however, the symbol had a different import. In early life he had accidentally killed a beloved friend; and from that day till the hour of his own death, he hid his face from men.

"Our parson has gone mad!" cried Goodman Gray, following him across the threshold.

A rumor of some unaccountable phenomenon had preceded Mr. Hooper into the meeting-house, and set all the congregation astir. Few could refrain from twisting their heads towards the door; many stood upright, and turned directly about; while several little boys clambered upon the seats, and came down again with a terrible racket. There was a general bustle, a rustling of the women's gowns and shuffling of the men's feet, greatly at variance with that hushed repose which should attend the entrance of the minister. But Mr. Hooper appeared not to notice the perturbation of his people. He entered with an almost noiseless step, bent his head mildly to the pews on each side, and bowed as he passed his oldest parishioner, a white-haired great grandsire, who occupied an arm-chair in the centre of the aisle. It was strange to observe how slowly this venerable man became conscious of something singular in the appearance of his pastor. He seemed not fully to partake of the prevailing wonder, till Mr. Hooper had ascended the stairs, and showed himself in the pulpit, face to face with his congregation, except for the black veil. That mysterious emblem was never once withdrawn. It shook with his measured breath, as he gave out the psalm; it threw its obscurity between him and the holy page, as he read the Scriptures; and while he prayed, the veil lay heavily on his uplifted countenance. Did he seek to hide it from the dread Being whom he was addressing?

Such was the effect of this simple piece of crape, that more than one woman of delicate nerves was forced to leave the meeting-house. Yet perhaps the pale-faced congregation was almost as fearful a sight to the minister, as his black veil to them.

Mr. Hooper had the reputation of a good preacher, but not an energetic one: he strove to win his people heavenward by mild, persuasive influences, rather than to drive them thither by the thunders of the Word. The sermon which he now delivered was marked by the same characteristics of style and manner as the general series of his pulpit oratory. But there was something, either in the sentiment of the discourse itself, or in the imagination of the auditors, which made it greatly the most powerful effort that they had ever heard from their pastor's lips. It was tinged, rather more darkly than usual, with the gentle gloom of Mr. Hooper's temperament. The subject had reference to secret sin, and those sad mysteries which we hide from our nearest and dearest, and would fain conceal from our own consciousness, even forgetting that the Omniscient can detect them. A subtle power was breathed into his words. Each member of the congregation, the most innocent girl, and the man of hardened breast, felt as if the preacher had crept upon them, behind his awful veil, and discovered their hoarded iniquity of deed or thought. Many spread their clasped hands on their bosoms. There was nothing terrible in what Mr. Hooper said, at least, no violence; and yet, with every tremor of his melancholy voice, the hearers quaked. An unsought pathos came hand in hand with awe. So sensible were the audience of some unwonted attribute in their minister, that they longed for a breath of wind to blow aside the veil, almost believing that a stranger's visage would be discovered, though the form, gesture, and voice were those of Mr. Hooper.

At the close of the services, the people hurried out with indecorous confusion, eager to communicate their pent-up amazement, and conscious of lighter spirits the moment they lost sight of the black veil. Some gathered in little circles, huddled closely together, with their mouths all whispering in the center; some went homeward alone, wrapt in silent meditation; some talked loudly, and profaned the Sabbath day with ostentatious laughter. A few shook their sagacious heads, intimating that they could penetrate the mystery; while one or two affirmed that there was no mystery at all, but only that Mr. Hooper's eyes were so weakened by the midnight lamp, as to require a shade. After a brief interval, forth came good Mr. Hooper also, in the rear of his flock. Turning his veiled face from one group to another, he paid due reverence to the hoary heads, saluted the middle aged with kind dignity as their friend and spiritual guide, greeted the young with mingled authority and love, and laid his hands on the little children's heads to bless them. Such was always his custom on the Sabbath day. Strange and bewildered looks repaid him for his courtesy. None, as on former occasions, aspired to the honor of walking by their pastor's side. Old Squire Saunders, doubtless by an accidental lapse of memory, neglected to invite Mr. Hooper to his table, where the good clergyman had been wont to bless the food, almost every Sunday since his settlement. He returned, therefore, to the parsonage, and, at the moment of closing the door, was observed to look back upon the people, all of whom had their eyes fixed upon the minister. A sad smile gleamed faintly from beneath the black veil, and flickered about his mouth, glimmering as he disappeared.

"How strange," said a lady, "that a simple black veil, such as any woman might wear on her bonnet, should become such a terrible thing on Mr. Hooper's face!"

"Something must surely be amiss with Mr. Hooper's intellects," observed her husband, the physician of the village. "But the strangest part of the affair is the effect of this vagary, even on a sober-minded man like myself. The black veil, though it covers only our pastor's face, throws its influence over his whole person, and makes him ghostlike from head to foot. Do you not feel it so?"

"Truly do I," replied the lady; "and I would not be alone with him for the world. I wonder he is not afraid to be alone with himself!"

"Men sometimes are so," said her husband.

The afternoon service was attended with similar circumstances. At its conclusion, the bell tolled for the funeral of a young lady. The relatives and friends were assembled in the house, and the more distant acquaintances stood about the door, speaking of the good qualities of the deceased, when their talk was interrupted by the appearance of Mr. Hooper, still covered with his black veil. It was now an appropriate emblem. The clergyman stepped into the room where the corpse was laid, and bent over the coffin, to take a last farewell of his deceased parishioner. As he stooped, the veil hung straight down from his forehead, so that, if her eyelids had not been closed forever, the dead maiden might have seen his face. Could Mr. Hooper be fearful of her glance, that he so hastily caught back the black veil? A person who watched the interview between the dead and living, scrupled not to affirm, that, at the instant when the clergyman's features were disclosed, the corpse had slightly shuddered, rustling the shroud and muslin cap, though the countenance retained the composure of death. A superstitious old woman was the only witness of this prodigy. From the coffin Mr. Hooper passed into the chamber of the mourners, and thence to the head of the staircase, to make the funeral prayer. It was a tender and heart-dissolving prayer, full of sorrow, yet so imbued with celestial hopes, that the music of a heavenly harp, swept by the fingers of the dead, seemed faintly to be heard among the saddest accents of the minister. The people trembled, though they but darkly understood him when he prayed that they, and himself, and all of mortal race, might be ready, as he trusted this young maiden had been, for the dreadful hour that should snatch the veil from their faces. The bearers went heavily forth, and the mourners followed, saddening all the street, with the dead before them, and Mr. Hooper in his black veil behind.

"Why do you look back?" said one in the procession to his partner.

"I had a fancy," replied she, "that the minister and the maiden's spirit were walking hand in hand."

"And so had I, at the same moment," said the other.

That night, the handsomest couple in Milford village were to be joined in wedlock. Though reckoned a melancholy man, Mr. Hooper had a placid cheerfulness for such occasions, which often excited a sympathetic smile where livelier merriment would have been thrown away. There was no quality of his disposition which made him more beloved than this. The company at the wedding awaited his arrival with impatience, trusting that the strange awe, which had gathered over him throughout the day, would now be dispelled. But such was not the result. When Mr. Hooper came, the first thing that their eyes rested on was the same horrible black veil, which had added deeper gloom to the funeral, and could portend nothing but evil to the wedding. Such was its immediate effect on the guests that a cloud seemed to have rolled duskily from beneath the black crape, and dimmed the light of the candles. The bridal pair stood up before the minister. But the bride's cold fingers quivered in the tremulous hand of the bridegroom, and her deathlike paleness caused a whisper that the maiden who had been buried a few hours before was come from her grave to be married. If ever another wedding were so dismal, it was that famous one where they tolled the wedding knell. After performing the ceremony, Mr. Hooper raised a glass of wine to his lips, wishing happiness to the new-married couple in a strain of mild pleasantry that ought to have brightened the features of the guests, like a cheerful gleam from the hearth. At that instant, catching a glimpse of his figure in the looking-glass, the black veil involved his own spirit in the horror with which it overwhelmed all others. His frame shuddered, his lips grew white, he spilt the untasted wine upon the carpet, and rushed forth into the darkness. For the Earth, too, had on her Black Veil.

The next day, the whole village of Milford talked of little else than Parson Hooper's black veil. That, and the mystery concealed behind it, supplied a topic for discussion between acquaintances meeting in the street, and good women gossiping at their open windows. It was the first item of news that the tavern-keeper told to his guests. The children babbled of it on their way to school. One imitative little imp covered his face with an old black handkerchief, thereby so affrighting his playmates that the panic seized himself, and he well-nigh lost his wits by his own waggery.

It was remarkable that of all the busybodies and impertinent people in the parish, not one ventured to put the plain question to Mr. Hooper, where-fore° he did this thing. Hitherto, whenever there appeared the slightest call for such interference, he had never lacked advisers, nor shown himself averse to be guided by their judgment. If he erred at all, it was by so painful a degree of self-distrust, that even the mildest censure would lead him to consider an in-different action as a crime. Yet, though so well acquainted with this amiable weakness, no individual among his parishioners chose to make the black veil a subject of friendly remonstrance. There was a feeling of dread, neither plainly confessed nor carefully concealed, which caused each to shift the responsibility upon another, till at length it was found expedient to send a deputation of the church, in order to deal with Mr. Hooper about the mystery, before it should grow into a scandal. Never did an embassy so ill discharge its duties. The minis-ter received them with friendly courtesy, but became silent, after they were seated, leaving to his visitors the whole burden of introducing their important business. The topic, it might be supposed, was obvious enough. There was the black veil swathed round Mr. Hooper's forehead, and concealing every feature above his placid mouth, on which, at times, they could perceive the glimmering of a melancholy smile. But that piece of crape, to their imagination, seemed to hang down before his heart, the symbol of a fearful secret between him and them. Were the veil but cast aside, they might speak freely of it, but not till then. Thus they sat a considerable time, speechless, confused, and shrinking uneasily from Mr. Hooper's eye, which they felt to be fixed upon them with an invisible glance. Finally, the deputies returned abashed to their constituents, pronouncing the matter too weighty to be handled, except by a council of the churches, if, indeed, it might not require a general synod.

But there was one person in the village unappalled by the awe with which the black veil had impressed all beside herself. When the deputies returned without an explanation, or even venturing to demand one, she, with the calm energy of her character, determined to chase away the strange cloud that ap-peared to be settling round Mr. Hooper, every moment more darkly than be-fore. As his plighted wife, it should be her privilege to know what the black veil concealed. At the minister's first visit, therefore, she entered upon the sub-ject with a direct simplicity, which made the task easier both for him and her. After he had seated himself, she fixed her eyes steadfastly upon the veil, but could discern nothing of the dreadful gloom that had so overawed the multi-tude: it was but a double fold of crape, hanging down from his forehead to his mouth, and slightly stirring with his breath.

"No," said she aloud, and smiling, "there is nothing terrible in this piece of crape, except that it hides a face which I am always glad to look upon. Come, good sir, let the sun shine from behind the cloud. First lay aside your black veil: then tell me why you put it on."

Mr. Hooper's smile glimmered faintly.

"There is an hour to come," said he, "when all of us shall cast aside our veils. Take it not amiss, beloved friend, if I wear this piece of crape till then."

"Your words are a mystery, too," returned the young lady. "Take away the veil from them, at least."

"Elizabeth, I will," said he, "so far as my vow may suffer me. Know, then,

wherefore: why.

this veil is a type and a symbol, and I am bound to wear it ever, both in light and darkness, in solitude and before the gaze of multitudes, and as with strangers, so with my familiar friends. No mortal eye will see it withdrawn. This dismal shade must separate me from the world: even you, Elizabeth, can never come behind it!"

"What grievous affliction hath befallen you," she earnestly inquired, "that you should thus darken your eyes forever?"

"If it be a sign of mourning," replied Mr. Hooper, "I, perhaps, like most other mortals, have sorrows dark enough to be typified by a black veil."

"But what if the world will not believe that it is the type of an innocent sorrow?" urged Elizabeth. "Beloved and respected as you are, there may be whispers that you hide your face under the consciousness of secret sin. For the sake of your holy office, do away this scandal!"

The color rose into her cheeks as she intimated the nature of the rumors that were already abroad in the village. But Mr. Hooper's mildness did not forsake him. He even smiled again — that same sad smile, which always appeared like a faint glimmering of light, proceeding from the obscurity beneath the veil.

"If I hide my face for sorrow, there is cause enough," he merely replied; "and if I cover it for secret sin, what mortal might not do the same?"

And with this gentle, but unconquerable obstinacy did he resist all her entreaties. At length Elizabeth sat silent. For a few moments she appeared lost in thought, considering, probably, what new methods might be tried to withdraw her lover from so dark a fantasy, which, if it had no other meaning, was perhaps a symptom of mental disease. Though of a firmer character than his own, the tears rolled down her cheeks. But, in an instant, as it were, a new feeling took the place of sorrow: her eyes were fixed insensibly on the black veil, when, like a sudden twilight in the air, its terrors fell around her. She arose, and stood trembling before him.

"And do you feel it then, at last?" said he mournfully.

She made no reply, but covered her eyes with her hand, and turned to leave the room. He rushed forward and caught her arm.

"Have patience with me, Elizabeth!" cried he, passionately. "Do not desert me, though this veil must be between us here on earth. Be mine, and hereafter there shall be no veil over my face, no darkness between our souls! It is but a mortal veil — it is not for eternity! O! you know not how lonely I am, and how frightened, to be alone behind my black veil. Do not leave me in this miserable obscurity forever!"

"Lift the veil but once, and look me in the face," said she.

"Never! It cannot be!" replied Mr. Hooper.

"Then farewell!" said Elizabeth.

She withdrew her arm from his grasp, and slowly departed, pausing at the door, to give one long shuddering gaze, that seemed almost to penetrate the mystery of the black veil. But, even amid his grief, Mr. Hooper smiled to think that only a material emblem had separated him from happiness, though the horrors, which it shadowed forth, must be drawn darkly between the fondest of lovers.

From that time no attempts were made to remove Mr. Hooper's black veil, or, by a direct appeal, to discover the secret which it was supposed to hide. By persons who claimed a superiority to popular prejudice, it was reckoned merely an eccentric whim, such as often mingles with the sober actions of men otherwise rational, and tinges them all with its own semblance of insanity. But with the multitude, good Mr. Hooper was irreparably a bugbear. He could not walk the street with any peace of mind, so conscious was he that the gentle and timid would turn aside to avoid him, and that others would make it a point of hardihood to throw themselves in his way. The impertinence of the latter class compelled him to give up his customary walk at sunset to the burial ground; for when he leaned pensively over the gate, there would always be faces behind the gravestones, peeping at his black veil. A fable went the rounds that the stare of the dead people drove him thence. It grieved him, to the very depth of his kind heart, to observe how the children fled from his approach, breaking up their merriest sports, while his melancholy figure was yet afar off. Their instinctive dread caused him to feel more strongly than aught else, that a preternatural horror was interwoven with the threads of the black crape. In truth, his own antipathy to the veil was known to be so great, that he never willingly passed before a mirror, nor stooped to drink at a still fountain, lest, in its peaceful bosom, he should be affrighted by himself. This was what gave plausibility to the whispers, that Mr. Hooper's conscience tortured him for some great crime too horrible to be entirely concealed, or otherwise than so obscurely intimated. Thus, from beneath the black veil, there rolled a cloud into the sunshine, an ambiguity of sin or sorrow, which enveloped the poor minister, so that love or sympathy could never reach him. It was said that ghost and fiend consorted with him there. With self-shudderings and outward terrors, he walked continually in its shadow, groping darkly within his own soul, or gazing through a medium that saddened the whole world. Even the lawless wind, it was believed, respected his dreadful secret, and never blew aside the veil. But still good Mr. Hooper sadly smiled at the pale visages of the worldly throng as he passed by.

Among all its bad influences, the black veil had the one desirable effect, of making its wearer a very efficient clergyman. By the aid of his mysterious emblem — for there was no other apparent cause — he became a man of awful power over souls that were in agony for sin. His converts always regarded him with a dread peculiar to themselves, affirming, though but figuratively, that, before he brought them to celestial light, they had been with him behind the black veil. Its gloom, indeed, enabled him to sympathize with all dark affections. Dying sinners cried aloud for Mr. Hooper, and would not yield their breath till he appeared; though ever, as he stooped to whisper consolation, they shuddered at the veiled face so near their own. Such were the terrors of the black veil, even when Death had bared his visage! Strangers came long distances to attend service at his church, with the mere idle purpose of gazing at his figure, because it was forbidden them to behold his face. But many were made to quake ere they departed! Once, during Governor Belcher's administration, Mr. Hooper was appointed to preach the election sermon. Covered with his black veil, he stood before the chief magistrate, the council, and the representatives, and wrought so deep an impression, that the legislative measures of that year were characterized by all the gloom and piety of our earliest ancestral sway.

In this manner Mr. Hooper spent a long life, irreproachable in outward act, yet shrouded in dismal suspicions; kind and loving, though unloved, and dimly feared; a man apart from men, shunned in their health and joy, but ever summoned to their aid in mortal anguish. As years wore on, shedding their snows above his sable veil, he acquired a name throughout the New England churches, and they called him Father Hooper. Nearly all his parishioners, who were of mature age when he was settled, had been borne away by many a funeral: he had one congregation in the church, and a more crowded one in the churchyard; and having wrought so late into the evening, and done his work so well, it was now good Father Hooper's turn to rest.

Several persons were visible by the shaded candlelight, in the death chamber of the old clergyman. Natural connections he had none. But there was the decorously grave, though unmoved physician, seeking only to mitigate the last pangs of the patient whom he could not save. There were the deacons, and other eminently pious members of his church. There, also, was the Reverend Mr. Clark, of Westbury, a young and zealous divine, who had ridden in haste to pray by the bedside of the expiring minister. There was the nurse, no hired handmaiden of death, but one whose calm affection had endured thus long in secrecy, in solitude, amid the chill of age, and would not perish, even at the dying hour. Who, but Elizabeth! And there lay the hoary head of good Father Hooper upon the death pillow, with the black veil still swathed about his brow, and reaching down over his face, so that each more difficult gasp of his faint breath caused it to stir. All through life that piece of crape had hung between him and the world: it had separated him from cheerful brotherhood and woman's love, and kept him in that saddest of all prisons, his own heart; and still it lay upon his face, as if to deepen the gloom of his darksome chamber, and shade him from the sunshine of eternity.

For some time previous, his mind had been confused, wavering doubtfully between the past and the present, and hovering forward, as it were, at intervals, into the indistinctness of the world to come. There had been feverish turns, which tossed him from side to side, and wore away what little strength he had. But in his most convulsive struggles, and in the wildest vagaries of his intellect, when no other thought retained its sober influence, he still showed an awful solicitude lest the black veil should slip aside. Even if his bewildered soul could have forgotten, there was a faithful woman at this pillow, who, with averted eyes, would have covered that aged face, which she had last beheld in the comeliness of manhood. At length the death-stricken old man lay quietly in the torpor of mental and bodily exhaustion, with an imperceptible pulse, and breath that grew fainter and fainter, except when a long, deep, and irregular inspiration seemed to prelude the flight of his spirit.

The minister of Westbury approached the bedside.

"Venerable Father Hooper," said he, "the moment of your release is at hand. Are you ready for the lifting of the veil that shuts in time from eternity?"

Father Hooper at first replied merely by a feeble motion of his head; then, apprehensive, perhaps, that his meaning might be doubted, he exerted himself to speak.

"Yea," said he, in faint accents, "my soul hath a patient weariness until that veil be lifted."

"And is it fitting," resumed the Reverend Mr. Clark, "that a man so given to prayer, of such a blameless example, holy in deed and thought, so far as mortal judgment may pronounce; is it fitting that a father in the church should leave a shadow on his memory, that may seem to blacken a life so pure? I pray you, my venerable brother, let not this thing be! Suffer us to be gladdened by your triumphant aspect as you go to your reward. Before the veil of eternity be lifted, let me cast aside this black veil from your face!"

And thus speaking, the Reverend Mr. Clark bent forward to reveal the mystery of so many years. But, exerting a sudden energy, that made all the beholders stand aghast, Father Hooper snatched both his hands from beneath the bedclothes, and pressed them strongly on the black veil, resolute to struggle, if the minister of Westbury would contend with a dying man.

"Never!" cried the veiled clergyman. "On earth, never!"

"Dark old man!" exclaimed the affrighted minister, "with what horrible crime upon your soul are you now passing to the judgment?"

Father Hooper's breath heaved; it rattled in his throat; but, with a mighty effort, grasping forward with his hands, he caught hold of life, and held it back till he should speak. He even raised himself in bed; and there he sat, shivering with the arms of death around him, while the black veil hung down, awful, at that last moment, in the gathered terrors of a lifetime. And yet the faint, sad smile, so often there, now seemed to glimmer from its obscurity, and linger on Father Hooper's lips.

"Why do you tremble at me alone?" cried he, turning his veiled face round the circle of pale spectators. "Tremble also at each other! Have men avoided me, and women shown no pity, and children screamed and fled, only for my black veil? What, but the mystery which it obscurely typifies, has made this piece of crape so awful? When the friend shows his inmost heart to his friend; the lover to his best beloved; when man does not vainly shrink from the eye of his Creator, loathsomely treasuring up the secret of his sin; then deem me a monster, for the symbol beneath which I have lived, and die! I look around me, and, lo! on every visage a Black Veil!"

While his auditors shrank from one another, in mutual affright, Father Hooper fell back upon his pillow, a veiled corpse, with a faint smile lingering on the lips. Still veiled, they laid him in his coffin, and a veiled corpse they bore him to the grave. The grass of many years has sprung up and withered on that grave, the burial stone is moss-grown, and good Mr. Hooper's face is dust; but awful is still the thought that it mouldered beneath the Black Veil!

Questions

1. Do you feel sympathy for Mr. Hooper, or do you see him as a crank who likes to make himself miserable? Can you infer Hawthorne's attitude toward him?
2. Recalling early American history, explain the author's observation that, after Mr. Hooper preached to the state legislature, the rest of the year's lawmaking was characterized by "all the gloom and piety of our earliest ancestral sway."
3. How is the veil a positive advantage to Mr. Hooper as a minister? How does it cause him suffering and loss?
4. In the minister's dying words, we are told that all men try to conceal themselves from friend, from best beloved, and from God. Earlier in the story, in what way or ways has the veil suggested each of these three attempts at disguise?
5. In his discussion of this story in his review of Hawthorne's *Twice-Told Tales*, Edgar Allan Poe suggests an original interpretation: "The *moral* put into the

mouth of the dying minister will be supposed to convey the *true* import of the narrative; and that a crime of dark dye (having reference to the "young lady") has been committed, is a point which only minds congenial with that of the author will perceive." Can you find any evidence in the story to support or refute this interpretation?

6. Suppose Hawthorne had indicated in the story that, like the Mr. Joseph Moody whom he mentions in his footnote, Mr. Hooper had veiled his face to atone for having accidentally killed a friend. What would have been lost?

7. Hawthorne subtitles his story "A Parable," but a **parable** usually is a brief allegorical story designed to teach a certain lesson. (For instance, recall the parable of the Prodigal Son in Luke 15, in which Jesus implies that the elder son's return to his father's house is like a sinner's return to the ways of the Lord.) Does Hawthorne's story actually seem to you such a clear-cut parable? Does it leave you with an evident moral or does it leave you still thinking and wondering?

Katherine Mansfield (1888–1923)

A Dill Pickle   1920

And then, after six years, she saw him again. He was seated at one of those little bamboo tables decorated with a Japanese vase of paper daffodils. There was a tall plate of fruit in front of him, and very carefully, in a way she recognized immediately as his "special" way, he was peeling an orange.

He must have felt that shock of recognition in her for he looked up and met her eyes. Incredible! He didn't know her! She smiled; he frowned. She came towards him. He closed his eyes an instant, but opening them his face lit up as though he had struck a match in a dark room. He laid down the orange and pushed back his chair, and she took her little warm hand out of her muff and gave it to him.

"Vera!" he exclaimed. "How strange. Really, for a moment I didn't know you. Won't you sit down? You've had lunch? Won't you have some coffee?"

She hesitated, but of course she meant to.

"Yes, I'd like some coffee." And she sat down opposite him.

"You've changed. You've changed very much," he said, staring at her with that eager, lighted look. "You look so well. I've never seen you look so well before."

"Really?" She raised her veil and unbuttoned her high fur collar. "I don't feel very well. I can't bear this weather, you know."

"Ah, no. You hate the cold. . . ."

"Loathe it." She shuddered. "And the worst of it is that the older one grows . . ."

He interrupted her. "Excuse me," and tapped on the table for the waitress. "Please bring some coffee and cream." To her: "You are sure you won't eat anything? Some fruit, perhaps. The fruit here is very good."

"No, thanks. Nothing."

"Then that's settled." And smiling just a hint too broadly he took up the orange again. "You were saying — the older one grows —"

"The colder," she laughed. But she was thinking how well she remembered that trick of his — the trick of interrupting her — and of how it used to exasperate her six years ago. She used to feel then as though he, quite suddenly, in the middle of what she was saying, put his hand over her lips, turned from her, attended to something different, and then took his hand away, and with just the same slightly too broad smile, gave her his attention again. . . . Now we are ready. That is settled.

"The colder!" He echoed her words, laughing too. "Ah, ah. You still say the same things. And there is another thing about you that is not changed at all — your beautiful voice — your beautiful way of speaking." Now he was very grave; he leaned towards her, and she smelled the warm, stinging scent of the orange peel. "You have only to say one word and I would know your voice among all other voices. I don't know what it is — I've often wondered — that makes your voice such a — haunting memory. . . . Do you remember that first afternoon we spent together at Kew Gardens? You were so surprised because I did not know the names of any flowers. I am still just as ignorant for all your telling me. But whenever it is very fine and warm, and I see some bright colors — it's awfully strange — I hear your voice saying: 'Geranium, marigold and verbena.' And I feel those three words are all I recall of some forgotten, heavenly language. . . . You remember that afternoon?"

"Oh, yes, very well." She drew a long, soft breath, as though the paper daffodils between them were almost too sweet to bear. Yet, what had remained in her mind of that particular afternoon was an absurd scene over the tea table. A great many people taking tea in a Chinese pagoda, and he behaving like a maniac about the wasps — waving them away, flapping at them with his straw hat, serious and infuriated out of all proportion to the occasion. How delighted the sniggering tea drinkers had been. And how she had suffered.

But now, as he spoke, that memory faded. His was the truer. Yes, it had been a wonderful afternoon, full of geranium and marigold and verbena, and — warm sunshine. Her thoughts lingered over the last two words as though she sang them.

In the warmth, as it were, another memory unfolded. She saw herself sitting on a lawn. He lay beside her, and suddenly, after a long silence, he rolled over and put his head in her lap.

"I wish," he said, in a low, troubled voice, "I wish that I had taken poison and were about to die — here now!"

At that moment a little girl in a white dress, holding a long, dripping water lily, dodged from behind a bush, stared at them, and dodged back again. But he did not see. She leaned over him.

"Ah, why do you say that? I could not say that."

But he gave a kind of soft moan, and taking her hand he held it to his cheek.

"Because I know I am going to love you too much — far too much. And I shall suffer so terribly, Vera, because you never, never will love me."

He was certainly far better looking now than he had been then. He had lost all that dreamy vagueness and indecision. Now he had the air of a man who has found his place in life, and fills it with a confidence and an assurance which was, to say the least, impressive. He must have made money, too. His clothes were admirable, and at that moment he pulled a Russian cigarette case out of his pocket.

"Won't you smoke?"

"Yes, I will." She hovered over them. "They look very good."

"I think they are. I get them made for me by a little man in St. James's Street. I don't smoke very much. I'm not like you — but when I do, they must be delicious, very fresh cigarettes. Smoking isn't a habit with me; it's a luxury — like perfume. Are you still so fond of perfumes? Ah, when I was in Russia . . ."

She broke in: "You've really been to Russia?"

"Oh, yes. I was there for over a year. Have you forgotten how we used to talk of going there?"

"No, I've not forgotten."

He gave a strange half laugh and leaned back in his chair. "Isn't it curious. I have really carried out all those journeys that we planned. Yes, I have been to all those places that we talked of, and stayed in them long enough to — as you used to say, 'air oneself' in them. In fact, I have spent the last three years of my life travelling all the time. Spain, Corsica, Siberia, Russia, Egypt. The only country left is China, and I mean to go there, too, when the war is over."

As he spoke, so lightly, tapping the end of his cigarette against the ash-tray, she felt the strange beast that had slumbered so long within her bosom stir, stretch itself, yawn, prick up its ears, and suddenly bound to its feet, and fix its longing, hungry stare upon those far away places. But all she said was, smiling gently: "How I envy you."

He accepted that. "It has been," he said, "very wonderful — especially Russia. Russia was all that we had imagined, and far, far more. I even spent some days on a river boat on the Volga. Do you remember that boatman's song that you used to play?"

"Yes." It began to play in her mind as she spoke.

"Do you ever play it now?"

"No, I've no piano."

He was amazed at that. "But what has become of your beautiful piano?"

She made a little grimace. "Sold. Ages ago."

"But you were so fond of music," he wondered.

"I've no time for it now," said she.

He let it go at that. "That river life," he went on, "is something quite special. After a day or two you cannot realize that you have ever known another. And it is not necessary to know the language — the life of the boat creates a bond between you and the people that's more than sufficient. You eat with them, pass the day with them, and in the evening there is that endless singing."

She shivered, hearing the boatman's song break out again loud and tragic, and seeing the boat floating on the darkening river with melancholy trees on either side. . . . "Yes, I should like that," said she, stroking her muff.

"You'd like almost everything about Russian life," he said warmly. "It's so informal, so impulsive, so free without question. And then the peasants are so splendid. They are such human beings — yes, that is it. Even the man who drives your carriage has — has some real part in what is happening. I remember the evening a party of us, two friends of mine and the wife of one of them, went for a picnic by the Black Sea. We took supper and champagne and ate and drank on the grass. And while we were eating the coachman came up. 'Have a dill pickle,' he said. He wanted to share with us. That seemed to me so right, so — you know what I mean?"

And she seemed at that moment to be sitting on the grass beside the mysteriously Black Sea, black as velvet, and rippling against the banks in silent, velvet waves. She saw the carriage drawn up to one side of the road, and the little group on the grass, their faces and hands white in the moonlight. She saw the pale dress of the woman outspread and her folded parasol, lying on the grass like a huge pearl crochet hook. Apart from them, with his supper in a cloth on his knees, sat the coachman. "Have a dill pickle," said he, and although she was not certain what a dill pickle was, she saw the greenish glass jar with a red chili like a parrot's beak glimmering through. She sucked in her cheeks; the dill pickle was terribly sour. . . .

"Yes, I know perfectly what you mean," she said.

In the pause that followed they looked at each other. In the past when they had looked at each other like that they had felt such a boundless understanding between them that their souls had, as it were, put their arms round each other and dropped into the same sea, content to be drowned, like mournful lovers. But now, the surprising thing was that it was he who held back. He who said:

"What a marvellous listener you are. When you look at me with those wild eyes I feel that I could tell you things that I would never breathe to another human being."

Was there just a hint of mockery in his voice or was it her fancy? She could not be sure.

"Before I met you," he said, "I had never spoken of myself to anybody. How well I remember one night, the night that I brought you the little Christmas tree, telling you all about my childhood. And of how I was so miserable that I ran away and lived under a cart in our yard for two days without being discovered. And you listened, and your eyes shone, and I felt that you had even made the little Christmas tree listen too, as in a fairy story."

But of that evening she had remembered a little pot of caviar. It had cost seven and sixpence. He could not get over it. Think of it — a tiny jar like that costing seven and sixpence. While she ate it he watched her, delighted and shocked.

"No, really, that is eating money. You could not get seven shillings into a little pot that size. Only think of the profit they must make. . . ." And he had begun some immensely complicated calculations. . . . But now good-bye to the caviar. The Christmas tree was on the table, and the little boy lay under the cart with his head pillowed on the yard dog.

"The dog was called Bosun," she cried delightedly.

But he did not follow. "Which dog? Had you a dog? I don't remember a dog at all."

"No, no. I mean the yard dog when you were a little boy." He laughed and snapped the cigarette case to.

"Was he? Do you know I had forgotten that. It seems such ages ago. I cannot believe that it is only six years. After I had recognized you to-day — I had to take such a leap — I had to take a leap over my whole life to get back to that time. I was such a kid then." He drummed on the table. "I've often thought how I must have bored you. And now I understand so perfectly why you wrote to me as you did — although at the time that letter nearly finished my life. I found it again the other day, and I couldn't help laughing as I read it. It was so clever — such a true picture of me." He glanced up. "You're not going?"

She had buttoned her collar again and drawn down her veil.

"Yes, I am afraid I must," she said, and managed a smile. Now she knew that he had been mocking.

"Ah, no, please," he pleaded. "Don't go just for a moment," and he caught up one of her gloves from the table and clutched at it as if that would hold her. "I see so few people to talk to nowadays, that I have turned into a sort of barbarian," he said. "Have I said something to hurt you?"

"Not a bit," she lied. But as she watched him draw her glove through his fingers, gently, gently, her anger really did die down, and besides, at the moment he looked more like himself of six years ago. . . .

"What I really wanted then," he said softly, "was to be a sort of carpet — to make myself into a sort of carpet for you to walk on so that you need not be hurt by the sharp stones and the mud that you hated so. It was nothing more positive than that — nothing more selfish. Only I did desire, eventually, to turn into a magic carpet and carry you away to all those lands you longed to see."

As he spoke she lifted her head as though she drank something; the strange beast in her bosom began to purr. . . .

"I felt that you were more lonely than anybody else in the world," he went on, "and yet, perhaps, that you were the only person in the world who was really, truly alive. Born out of your time," he murmured, stroking the glove, "fated."

Ah, God! What had she done! How had she dared to throw away her happiness like this. This was the only man who had ever understood her. Was it too late? Could it be too late? *She* was that glove that he held in his fingers. . . .

"And then the fact that you had no friends and never had made friends with people. How I understood that, for neither had I. Is it just the same now?"

"Yes," she breathed. "Just the same. I am as alone as ever."

"So am I," he laughed gently, "just the same."

Suddenly with a quick gesture he handed her back the glove and scraped his chair on the floor. "But what seemed to me so mysterious then is perfectly plain to me now. And to you, too, of course. . . . It simply was that we were such egoists, so self-engrossed, so wrapped up in ourselves that we hadn't a corner in our hearts for anybody else. Do you know," he cried, naive and hearty, and dreadfully like another side of that old self again, "I began studying a Mind System when I was in Russia, and I found that we were not peculiar at all. It's quite a well known form of . . ."

She had gone. He sat there, thunder-struck, astounded beyond words. . . . And then he asked the waitress for his bill.

"But the cream has not been touched," he said. "Please do not charge me for it."

QUESTIONS

1. Why do you suppose the story is called "A Dill Pickle"? What suggestions do we derive from the pickle (both as it appears in the anecdote of the Russian coachman and as Vera imagines it) that lend it central importance to the story?
2. What impressions do you have of the character of Vera and of that of her for-

mer friend? Do you think it likely that they ever could have been happy together?

3. What meaningful hints do you find in certain other particulars, besides the dill pickle? Try to state what is suggested by the fruit that the gentleman is enjoying (and that Vera declines), the "paper daffodils between them" (contrasted with memories of real flowers), the cigarettes, the names of faraway places, the little pot of caviar, Vera's sold piano, her act of drawing down her veil when about to leave, the glove.

7 Three Currents in Fiction

THE GOTHIC STORY

When in movies or on television we watch a terrifying yarn of a sinister old mansion full of secret panels and corridors, in which suits of armor walk by night and ghosts peer from the windows, we recognize the trappings of that long-lived species of fiction, the **Gothic story.** *The Castle of Otranto, A Gothic Story* (1764), by the English author Horace Walpole, began the genre, provided its name, and established its favorite conventions. In Walpole's horrific short novel, Otranto is a cobwebbed ruin full of underground passages and massive doors that slam unexpectedly. Beautiful young virgins find themselves terrorized. There are awful objects: a statue that bleeds, a portrait that steps from its frame, a giant helmet that crashes down on a young man and leaves him "dashed to pieces." Atmosphere is essential to a Gothic story: dusty halls, shadowy landscapes, moonlit woods with whispering servants "seen at a distance imperfectly through the dusk" (to quote from Anne Radcliffe's novel *The Mysteries of Udolpho,* 1794). Ghostly happenings often have natural explanations; in Charlotte Brontë's classic *Jane Eyre* (1847), bloodcurdling screams and a mysterious fire in a bed turn out to have been produced by a madwoman. In *Jane Eyre,* by the way, we find the model for a whole legion of heroines in contemporary fiction. In the best-selling Gothic romances of Victoria Holt, Phyllis A. Whitney, and others, young women similarly find love while working as governesses in ominous mansions. Like Charlotte Brontë's durable heroine, the central character of much recent Gothic fiction (both literary and commercial) tends to be a sensitive woman enclosed in a world that resembles a terrifying dream.

Lacking any local castles, American authors of Gothic stories have had to make do with dark old houses — like the ones in Nathaniel Hawthorne's novel *The House of the Seven Gables* and in Edgar Allan Poe's short story in this chapter. Earlier than Hawthorne and Poe, the novelist Charles Brockden Brown had transplanted Gothic horror to America. In Brown's *Wieland* (1798), for example, after erecting a strange pagan temple in darkest Pennsylvania, a man bursts into flame as though torched by an invisible hand. More recently popular, the stories of H. P. Lovecraft (1890–1937) create their own mythology. A race of demonic beings, long ago banished from the earth, keeps trying to return. Decaying New England villages, their favorite ports of entry, provide suitable atmosphere. William Faulkner, who brought the Gothic tradition to Mississippi, gives his story "A Rose for Emily" (Chapter Two) some of its conventional elements: a run-down mansion, a mysterious servant, a madwoman, a hideous secret. But Faulkner's story, in its larger theme of an aristocrat who refuses to admit that her world has vanished, goes far beyond its Gothic conventions. Faulkner's tremendous impact on younger writers has given rise to an entire loosely knit school of **Southern Gothic fiction,** including many novels and stories of Shirley Ann Grau, Carson McCullers, Fred Chappell, Flannery O'Connor, and Truman Capote (see "Miriam" in this chapter). In the hands of skillful writers, past and present, the Gothic story does not merely display spooky props and moody settings, but mirrors dark and disturbing recesses of human consciousness.

Edgar Allan Poe (1809–1849)

THE TELL-TALE HEART   1850

True! — nervous — very, very dreadfully nervous I had been and am; but why *will* you say that I am mad? The disease had sharpened my senses — not destroyed — not dulled them. Above all was the sense of hearing acute. I heard all things in the heaven and in the earth. I heard many things in hell. How, then, am I mad? Hearken! and observe how healthily — how calmly I can tell you the whole story.

It is impossible to say how first the idea entered my brain; but once conceived, it haunted me day and night. Object there was none. Passion there was none. I loved the old man. He had never wronged me. He had never given me insult. For his gold I had no desire. I think it was his eye! yes, it was this! One of his eyes resembled that of a vulture — a pale blue eye, with a film over it. Whenever it fell upon me, my blood ran cold; and so by degrees — very gradually — I made up my mind to take the life of the old man, and thus rid myself of the eye for ever.

Now this is the point. You fancy me mad. Madmen know nothing. But you should have seen *me*. You should have seen how wisely I proceeded — with what caution — with what foresight — with what dissimulation I went to work! I was never kinder to the old man than during the whole week before I killed him. And every night, about midnight, I turned the latch of his door and opened it — oh, so gently! And then, when I had made an opening sufficient for my head, I put in a dark lantern, all closed, closed, so that no light shone out, and then I thrust in my head. Oh, you would have laughed to see how cunningly I thrust it in! I moved it slowly — very, very slowly, so that I might not disturb the old man's sleep. It took me an hour to place my whole head within the opening so far that I could see him as he lay upon his bed. Ha! — would a madman have been so wise as this? And then, when my head was well in the room, I undid the lantern cautiously — oh, so cautiously — cautiously (for the hinges creaked) — I undid it just so much that a single thin ray fell upon the vulture eye. And this I did for seven long nights — every night just at midnight — but I found the eye always closed; and so it was impossible to do the work; for it was not the old man who vexed me, but his Evil Eye. And every morning, when the day broke, I went boldly into the chamber, and spoke courageously to him, calling him by name in a hearty tone, and inquiring how he had passed the night. So you see he would have been a very profound old man, indeed, to suspect that every night, just at twelve, I looked in upon him while he slept.

Upon the eighth night I was more than usually cautious in opening the door. A watch's minute hand moves more quickly than did mine. Never before that night had I *felt* the extent of my own powers — of my sagacity. I could scarcely contain my feelings of triumph. To think that there I was, opening the door, little by little, and he not even to dream of my secret deeds or thoughts. I fairly chuckled at the idea; and perhaps he heard me; for he moved on the bed suddenly, as if startled. Now you may think that I drew back — but no. His room was as black as pitch with the thick darkness (for the shutters were close fastened, through fear of robbers), and so I knew that he could not see the opening of the door, and I kept pushing it on steadily, steadily.

I had my head in, and was about to open the lantern, when my thumb slipped upon the tin fastening, and the old man sprang up in the bed, crying out — "Who's there?"

I kept quite still and said nothing. For a whole hour I did not move a muscle, and in the meantime I did not hear him lie down. He was still sitting up in the bed listening; — just as I have done, night after night, hearkening to the death watches° in the wall.

Presently I heard a slight groan, and I knew it was the groan of mortal terror. It was not a groan of pain or of grief — oh, no! — it was the low stifled sound that arises from the bottom of the soul when overcharged with awe. I knew the sound well. Many a night, just at midnight, when all the world slept, it has welled up from my own bosom, deepening, with its dreadful echo, the terrors that distracted me. I say I knew it well. I knew what the old man felt, and pitied him, although I chuckled at heart. I knew that he had been lying awake ever since the first slight noise, when he had turned in the bed. His fears had been ever since growing upon him. He had been trying to fancy them causeless, but could not. He had been saying to himself — "It is nothing but the wind in the chimney — it is only a mouse crossing the floor," or "it is merely a cricket which has made a single chirp." Yes, he had been trying to comfort himself with these suppositions; but he had found all in vain. *All in vain;* because Death, in approaching him, had stalked with his black shadow before him, and enveloped the victim. And it was the mournful influence of the unperceived shadow that caused him to feel — although he neither saw nor heard — to *feel* the presence of my head within the room.

When I had waited a long time, very patiently, without hearing him lie

---

death watches: beetles that infest timbers. Their clicking sound was thought to be an omen of death.

down, I resolved to open a little — a very, very little crevice in the lantern. So I opened it — you cannot imagine how stealthily, stealthily — until, at length, a single dim ray, like the thread of the spider, shot from out the crevice and full upon the vulture eye.

It was open — wide, wide open — and I grew furious as I gazed upon it. I saw it with perfect distinctness — all a dull blue, with a hideous veil over it that chilled the very marrow in my bones; but I could see nothing else of the old man's face or person: for I had directed the ray as if by instinct, precisely upon the damned spot.

And now have I not told you that what you mistake for madness is but over-acuteness of the senses? — now, I say, there came to my ears a low, dull, quick sound, such as a watch makes when enveloped in cotton. I knew *that* sound well too. It was the beating of the old man's heart. It increased my fury, as the beating of a drum stimulates the soldier into courage.

But even yet I refrained and kept still. I scarcely breathed. I held the lantern motionless. I tried how steadily I could maintain the ray upon the eye. Meantime the hellish tattoo of the heart increased. It grew quicker and quicker, and louder and louder every instant. The old man's terror *must* have been extreme! It grew louder, I say, louder every moment! — do you mark me well? I have told you that I am nervous: so I am. And now at the dead hour of the night, amid the dreadful silence of that old house, so strange a noise as this excited me to uncontrollable terror. Yet, for some minutes longer I refrained and stood still. But the beating grew louder, louder! I thought the heart must burst. And now a new anxiety seized me — the sound would be heard by a neighbor! The old man's hour had come! With a loud yell, I threw open the lantern and leaped into the room. He shrieked once — once only. In an instant I dragged him to the floor, and pulled the heavy bed over him. I then smiled gaily, to find the deed so far done. But, for many minutes, the heart beat on with a muffled sound. This, however, did not vex me; it would not be heard through the wall. At length it ceased. The old man was dead. I removed the bed and examined the corpse. Yes, he was stone, stone dead. I placed my hand upon the heart and held it there many minutes. There was no pulsation. He was stone dead. His eye would trouble me no more.

If still you think me mad, you will think so no longer when I describe the wise precautions I took for the concealment of the body. The night waned, and I worked hastily, but in silence. First of all I dismembered the corpse. I cut off the head and the arms and the legs.

I then took up three planks from the flooring of the chamber, and deposited all between the scantlings. I then replaced the boards so cleverly, so cunningly, that no human eye — not even *his* — could have detected any thing wrong. There was nothing to wash out — no stain of any kind — no blood-spot whatever. I had been too wary for that. A tub had caught all — ha! ha!

When I had made an end of these labors, it was four o'clock — still dark as midnight. As the bell sounded the hour, there came a knocking at the street door. I went down to open it with a light heart, — for what had I *now* to fear? There entered three men, who introduced themselves, with perfect suavity, as officers of the police. A shriek had been heard by a neighbor during the night;

suspicion of foul play had been aroused; information had been lodged at the police office, and they (the officers) had been deputed to search the premises.

I smiled, — for *what* had I to fear? I bade the gentlemen welcome. The shriek, I said, was my own in a dream. The old man, I mentioned, was absent in the country. I took my visitors all over the house. I bade them search — search *well*. I led them, at length, to *his* chamber. I showed them his treasures, secure, undisturbed. In the enthusiasm of my confidence, I brought chairs into the room, and desired them *here* to rest from their fatigues, while I myself, in the wild audacity of my perfect triumph, placed my own seat upon the very spot beneath which reposed the corpse of the victim.

The officers were satisfied. My *manner* had convinced them. I was singularly at ease. They sat, and while I answered cheerily, they chatted familiar things. But, ere long, I felt myself getting pale and wished them gone. My head ached, and I fancied a ringing in my ears: but still they sat and still chatted. The ringing became more distinct: — it continued and became more distinct: I talked more freely to get rid of the feeling: but it continued and gained definitiveness — until, at length, I found that the noise was *not* within my ears.

No doubt I now grew *very* pale: — but I talked more fluently, and with a heightened voice. Yet the sound increased — and what could I do? It was *a low, dull, quick sound — much such a sound as a watch makes when enveloped in cotton.* I gasped for breath — and yet the officers heard it not. I talked more quickly — more vehemently; but the noise steadily increased. I arose and argued about trifles, in a high key and with violent gesticulations, but the noise steadily increased. Why *would* they not be gone? I paced the floor to and fro with heavy strides, as if excited to fury by the observation of the men — but the noise steadily increased. Oh God! what *could* I do? I foamed — I raved — I swore! I swung the chair upon which I had been sitting, and grated it upon the boards, but the noise arose over all and continually increased. It grew louder — louder — *louder!* And still the men chatted pleasantly, and smiled. Was it possible they heard not? Almighty God! — no, no! They heard! — they suspected! — they *knew!* — they were making a mockery of my horror! — this I thought, and this I think. But any thing was better than this agony! Any thing was more tolerable than this derison! I could bear those hypocritical smiles no longer! I felt that I must scream or die! — and now — again! — hark! louder! louder! louder! *louder!* —

"Villains!" I shrieked, "dissemble no more! I admit the deed! — tear up the planks! — here, here! — it is the beating of his hideous heart!"

QUESTIONS

1. Is "The Tell-Tale Heart" a story of the supernatural or does the beating of the dead man's heart have any probable *natural* explanation?
2. From the opening paragraph, what are your impressions of the narrator? Is his testimony going to be reliable or unreliable? By what later statements does he confirm your first impressions of him?
3. Explain the superstition of the Evil Eye. What part does it play in the story?
4. What is unusual about the style in which Poe's story is written? Why is its style appropriate to it? (Suggestion: read aloud some passage or passages of

the story that especially characterize the narrator. Try paragraph three, or the final two paragraphs.)

5. What elements in the story seem typical of Gothic fiction?
6. Read the discussion of this story by Patrick F. Quinn on pages 223–224, and consider the suggestion that, in trying to kill the old man, the madman is trying to kill himself. How much sense (if any) does Quinn's argument make to you?

Truman Capote (b. 1924)

Miriam
1949

For several years, Mrs. H. T. Miller had lived alone in a pleasant apartment (two rooms with kitchenette) in a remodeled brownstone near the East River. She was a widow: Mr. H. T. Miller had left a reasonable amount of insurance. Her interests were narrow, she had no friends to speak of, and she rarely journeyed farther than the corner grocery. The other people in the house never seemed to notice her: her clothes were matter-of-fact, her hair iron-gray, clipped and casually waved; she did not use cosmetics, her features were plain and inconspicuous, and on her last birthday she was sixty-one. Her activities were seldom spontaneous: she kept the two rooms immaculate, smoked an occasional cigarette, prepared her own meals and tended a canary.

Then she met Miriam. It was snowing that night. Mrs. Miller had finished drying the supper dishes and was thumbing through an afternoon paper when she saw an advertisement of a picture playing at a neighborhood theater. The title sounded good, so she struggled into her beaver coat, laced her galoshes and left the apartment, leaving one light burning in the foyer: she found nothing more disturbing than a sensation of darkness.

The snow was fine, falling gently, not yet making an impression on the pavement. The wind from the river cut only at street crossings. Mrs. Miller hurried, her head bowed, oblivious as a mole burrowing a blind path. She stopped at a drugstore and bought a package of peppermints.

A long line stretched in front of the box office; she took her place at the end. There would be (a tired voice groaned) a short wait for all seats. Mrs. Miller rummaged in her leather handbag till she collected exactly the correct change for admission. The line seemed to be taking its own time and, looking around for some distraction, she suddenly became conscious of a little girl standing under the edge of the marquee.

Her hair was the longest and strangest Mrs. Miller had ever seen: absolutely silver-white, like an albino's. It flowed waist-length in smooth, loose lines. She was thin and fragilely constructed. There was a simple, special elegance in the way she stood with her thumbs in the pockets of a tailored plum-velvet coat.

Mrs. Miller felt oddly excited, and when the little girl glanced toward her, she smiled warmly. The little girl walked over and said, "Would you care to do me a favor?"

"I'd be glad to, if I can," said Mrs. Miller.

"Oh, it's quite easy. I merely want you to buy a ticket for me; they won't let me in otherwise. Here, I have the money." And gracefully she handed Mrs. Miller two dimes and a nickel.

They went into the theater together. An usherette directed them to a lounge; in twenty minutes the picture would be over.

"I feel just like a genuine criminal," said Mrs. Miller gaily, as she sat down. "I mean that sort of thing's against the law, isn't it? I do hope I haven't done the wrong thing. Your mother knows where you are, dear? I mean she does, doesn't she?"

The little girl said nothing. She unbuttoned her coat and folded it across her lap. Her dress underneath was prim and dark blue. A gold chain dangled about her neck, and her fingers, sensitive and musical-looking, toyed with it. Examining her more attentively, Mrs. Miller decided the truly distinctive feature was not her hair, but her eyes; they were hazel, steady, lacking any child-like quality whatsoever and, because of their size, seemed to consume her small face.

Mrs. Miller offered a peppermint. "What's your name, dear?"

"Miriam," she said, as though, in some curious way, it were information already familiar.

"Why, isn't that funny — my name's Miriam, too. And it's not a terribly common name either. Now, don't tell me your last name's Miller!"

"Just Miriam."

"But isn't that funny?"

"Moderately," said Miriam, and rolled the peppermint on her tongue.

Mrs. Miller flushed and shifted uncomfortably. "You have such a large vocabulary for such a little girl."

"Do I?"

"Well, yes," said Mrs. Miller, hastily changing the topic to: "Do you like the movies?"

"I really wouldn't know," said Miriam. "I've never been before."

Women began filling the lounge; the rumble of the newsreel bombs exploded in the distance. Mrs. Miller rose, tucking her purse under her arm. "I guess I'd better be running now if I want to get a seat," she said. "It was nice to have met you."

Miriam nodded ever so slightly.

It snowed all week. Wheels and footsteps moved soundlessly on the street, as if the business of living continued secretly behind a pale but impenetrable curtain. In the falling quiet there was no sky or earth, only snow lifting in the wind, frosting the window glass, chilling the rooms, deadening and hushing the city. At all hours it was necessary to keep a lamp lighted, and Mrs. Miller lost track of the days: Friday was no different from Saturday and on Sunday she went to the grocery: closed, of course.

That evening she scrambled eggs and fixed a bowl of tomato soup. Then, after putting on a flannel robe and cold-creaming her face, she propped herself up in bed with a hot-water bottle under her feet. She was reading the *Times* when the doorbell rang. At first she thought it must be a mistake and whoever it was would go away. But it rang and rang and settled to a persistent buzz. She looked at the clock: a little after eleven; it did not seem possible, she was always asleep by ten.

Climbing out of bed, she trotted barefoot across the living room. "I'm coming, please be patient." The latch was caught; she turned it this way and that way and the bell never paused an instant. "Stop it," she cried. The bolt gave way and she opened the door an inch. "What in heaven's name?"

"Hello," said Miriam.

"Oh . . . why, hello," said Mrs. Miller, stepping hesitantly into the hall. "You're that little girl."

"I thought you'd never answer, but I kept my finger on the button; I knew you were home. Aren't you glad to see me?"

Mrs. Miller did not know what to say. Miriam, she saw, wore the same plum-velvet coat and now she had also a beret to match; her white hair was braided in two shining plaits and looped at the ends with enormous white ribbons.

"Since I've waited so long, you could at least let me in," she said.

"It's awfully late. . . ."

Miriam regarded her blankly. "What difference does that make? Let me in. It's cold out here and I have on a silk dress." Then, with a gentle gesture, she urged Mrs. Miller aside and passed into the apartment.

She dropped her coat and beret on a chair. She was indeed wearing a silk dress. White silk. White silk in February. The skirt was beautifully pleated and the sleeves long; it made a faint rustle as she strolled about the room. "I like your place," she said. "I like the rug, blue's my favorite color." She touched a paper rose in a vase on the coffee table. "Imitation," she commented wanly. "How sad. Aren't imitations sad?" She seated herself on the sofa, daintily spreading her skirt.

"What do you want?" asked Mrs. Miller.

"Sit down," said Miriam. "It makes me nervous to see people stand."

Mrs. Miller sank to a hassock. "What do you want?" she repeated.

"You know, I don't think you're glad I came."

For a second time Mrs. Miller was without an answer; her hand motioned vaguely. Miriam giggled and pressed back on a mound of chintz pillows. Mrs. Miller observed that the girl was less pale than she remembered; her cheeks were flushed.

"How did you know where I lived?"

Miriam frowned. "That's no question at all. What's your name? What's mine?"

"But I'm not listed in the phone book."

"Oh, let's talk about something else."

Mrs. Miller said, "Your mother must be insane to let a child like you wander around at all hours of the night — and in such ridiculous clothes. She must be out of her mind."

Miriam got up and moved to a corner where a covered bird cage hung from a ceiling chain. She peeked beneath the cover. "It's a canary," she said. "Would you mind if I woke him? I'd like to hear him sing."

"Leave Tommy alone," said Mrs. Miller, anxiously. "Don't you dare wake him."

"Certainly," said Miriam. "But I don't see why I can't hear him sing." And then, "Have you anything to eat? I'm starving! Even milk and a jam sandwich would be fine."

"Look," said Mrs. Miller, arising from the hassock, "look — if I make some nice sandwiches will you be a good child and run along home? It's past midnight, I'm sure."

"It's snowing," reproached Miriam. "And cold and dark."

"Well, you shouldn't have come here to begin with," said Mrs. Miller, struggling to control her voice. "I can't help the weather. If you want anything to eat you'll have to promise to leave."

Miriam brushed a braid against her cheek. Her eyes were thoughtful, as if weighing the proposition. She turned toward the bird cage. "Very well," she said, "I promise."

How old is she? Ten? Eleven? Mrs. Miller, in the kitchen, unsealed a jar of strawberry preserves and cut four slices of bread. She poured a glass of milk and paused to light a cigarette. *And why has she come?* Her hand shook as she held the match, fascinated, till it burned her finger. The canary was singing; singing as he did in the morning and at no other time. "Miriam," she called, "Miriam, I told you not to disturb Tommy." There was no answer. She called again; all she heard was the canary. She inhaled the cigarette and discovered she had lighted the cork-tip end and — oh, really, she mustn't lose her temper.

She carried the food in on a tray and set it on the coffee table. She saw first that the bird cage still wore its night cover. And Tommy was singing. It gave her a queer sensation. And no one was in the room. Mrs. Miller went through an alcove leading to her bedroom; at the door she caught her breath.

"What are you doing?" she asked.

Miriam glanced up and in her eyes there was a look that was not ordinary. She was standing by the bureau, a jewel case opened before her. For a minute she studied Mrs. Miller, forcing their eyes to meet, and she smiled. "There's nothing good here," she said. "But I like this." Her hand held a cameo brooch. "It's charming."

"Suppose — perhaps you'd better put it back," said Mrs. Miller, feeling suddenly the need of some support. She leaned against the door frame; her head was unbearably heavy; a pressure weighted the rhythm of her heartbeat. The light seemed to flutter defectively. "Please, child — a gift from my husband . . ."

"But it's beautiful and I want it," said Miriam. *"Give it to me."*

As she stood, striving to shape a sentence which would somehow save the brooch, it came to Mrs. Miller there was no one to whom she might turn; she was alone; a fact that had not been among her thoughts for a long time. Its sheer emphasis was stunning. But here in her own room in the hushed snow-city were evidences she could not ignore or, she knew with startling clarity, resist.

Miriam ate ravenously, and when the sandwiches and milk were gone, her fingers made cobweb movements over the plate, gathering crumbs. The cameo gleamed on her blouse, the blonde profile like a trick reflection of its wearer. "That was very nice," she sighed, "though now an almond cake or a cherry would be ideal. Sweets are lovely, don't you think?"

Mrs. Miller was perched precariously on the hassock, smoking a cigarette. Her hair net had slipped lopsided and loose strands straggled down her face.

Her eyes were stupidly concentrated on nothing and her cheeks were mottled in red patches, as though a fierce slap had left permanent marks.

"Is there a candy — a cake?"

Mrs. Miller tapped ash on the rug. Her head swayed slightly as she tried to focus her eyes. "You promised to leave if I made the sandwiches," she said.

"Dear me, did I?"

"It was a promise and I'm tired and I don't feel well at all."

"Mustn't fret," said Miriam. "I'm only teasing."

She picked up her coat, slung it over her arm, and arranged her beret in front of a mirror. Presently she bent close to Mrs. Miller and whispered, "Kiss me good night."

"Please — I'd rather not," said Mrs. Miller.

Miriam lifted a shoulder, arched an eyebrow. "As you like," she said, and went directly to the coffee table, seized the vase containing the paper roses, carried it to where the hard surface of the floor lay bare, and hurled it downward. Glass sprayed in all directions and she stamped her foot on the bouquet.

Then slowly she walked to the door, but before closing it she looked back at Mrs. Miller with a slyly innocent curiosity.

Mrs. Miller spent the next day in bed, rising once to feed the canary and drink a cup of tea; she took her temperature and had none, yet her dreams were feverishly agitated; their unbalanced mood lingered even as she lay staring wide-eyed at the ceiling. One dream threaded through the others like an elusively mysterious theme in a complicated symphony, and the scenes it depicted were sharply outlined, as though sketched by a hand of gifted intensity: a small girl, wearing a bridal gown and a wreath of leaves, led a gray procession down a mountain path, and among them there was unusual silence till a woman at the rear asked, "Where is she taking us?" "No one knows," said an old man marching in front. "But isn't she pretty?" volunteered a third voice. "Isn't she like a frost flower . . . so shining and white?"

Tuesday morning she woke up feeling better; harsh slats of sunlight, slanting through Venetian blinds, shed a disrupting light on her unwholesome fancies. She opened the window to discover a thawed, mild-as-spring day; a sweep of clean new clouds crumpled against a vastly blue, out-of-season sky; and across the low line of rooftops she could see the river and smoke curving from tugboat stacks in a warm wind. A great silver truck plowed the snow-banked street, its machine sound humming in the air.

After straightening the apartment, she went to the grocer's, cashed a check and continued to Schrafft's where she ate breakfast and chatted happily with the waitress. Oh, it was a wonderful day — more like a holiday — and it would be so foolish to go home.

She boarded a Lexington Avenue bus and rode up to Eighty-sixth Street; it was here that she had decided to do a little shopping.

She had no idea what she wanted or needed, but she idled along, intent only upon the passers-by, brisk and preoccupied, who gave her a disturbing sense of separateness.

It was while waiting at the corner of Third Avenue that she saw the man: an old man, bowlegged and stooped under an armload of bulging packages; he wore a shabby brown coat and a checkered cap. Suddenly she realized they were exchanging a smile: there was nothing friendly about this smile, it was merely two cold flickers of recognition. But she was certain she had never seen him before.

He was standing next to an El pillar, and as she crossed the street he turned and followed. He kept quite close; from the corner of her eye she watched his reflection wavering on the shopwindows.

Then in the middle of the block she stopped and faced him. He stopped also and cocked his head, grinning. But what could she say? Do? Here, in broad daylight, on Eighty-sixth Street? It was useless and, despising her own helplessness, she quickened her steps.

Now Second Avenue is a dismal street, made from scraps and ends; part cobblestone, part asphalt, part cement; and its atmosphere of desertion is permanent. Mrs. Miller walked five blocks without meeting anyone, and all the while the steady crunch of his footfalls in the snow stayed near. And when she came to a florist's shop, the sound was still with her. She hurried inside and watched through the glass door as the old man passed; he kept his eyes straight ahead and didn't slow his pace, but he did one strange, telling thing: he tipped his cap.

"Six white ones, did you say?" asked the florist. "Yes," she told him, "white roses." From there she went to a glassware store and selected a vase, presumably a replacement for the one Miriam had broken, though the price was intolerable and the vase itself (she thought) grotesquely vulgar. But a series of unaccountable purchases had begun, as if by prearranged plan: a plan of which she had not the least knowledge or control.

She bought a bag of glazed cherries, and at a place called the Knickerbocker Bakery she paid forty cents for six almond cakes.

Within the last hour the weather had turned cold again; like blurred lenses, winter clouds cast a shade over the sun, and the skeleton of an early dusk colored the sky; a damp mist mixed with the wind and the voices of a few children who romped high on mountains of gutter snow seemed lonely and cheerless. Soon the first flake fell, and when Mrs. Miller reached the brownstone house, snow was falling in a swift screen and foot tracks vanished as they were printed.

The white roses were arranged decoratively in the vase. The glazed cherries shone on a ceramic plate. The almond cakes, dusted with sugar, awaited a hand. The canary fluttered on its swing and picked at a bar of seed.

At precisely five the doorbell rang. Mrs. Miller *knew* who it was. The hem of her housecoat trailed as she crossed the floor. "Is that you?" she called.

"Naturally," said Miriam, the word resounding shrilly from the hall. "Open this door."

"Go away," said Mrs. Miller.

"Please hurry . . . I have a heavy package."

"Go away," said Mrs. Miller. She returned to the living room, lighted a cigarette, sat down and calmly listened to the buzzer; on and on and on. "You might as well leave. I have no intention of letting you in."

Shortly the bell stopped. For possibly ten minutes Mrs. Miller did not move. Then, hearing no sound, she concluded Miriam had gone. She tiptoed to the door and opened it a sliver; Miriam was half-reclining atop a cardboard box with a beautiful French doll cradled in her arms.

"Really, I thought you were never coming," she said peevishly. "Here, help me get this in, it's awfully heavy."

It was not spell-like compulsion that Mrs. Miller felt, but rather a curious passivity; she brought in the box, Miriam the doll. Miriam curled up on the sofa, not troubling to remove her coat or beret, and watched disinterestedly as Mrs. Miller dropped the box and stood trembling, trying to catch her breath.

"Thank you," she said. In the daylight she looked pinched and drawn, her hair less luminous. The French doll she was loving wore an exquisite powdered wig and its idiot glass eyes sought solace in Miriam's. "I have a surprise," she continued. "Look into my box."

Kneeling, Mrs. Miller parted the flaps and lifted out another doll; then a blue dress which she recalled as the one Miriam had worn that first night at the theater; and of the remainder she said, "It's all clothes. Why?"

"Because I've come to live with you," said Miriam, twisting a cherry stem. "Wasn't it nice of you to buy me the cherries . . . ?"

"But you can't! For God's sake go away — go away and leave me alone!"

". . . and the roses and the almond cakes? How really wonderfully generous. You know, these cherries are delicious. The last place I lived was with an old man; he was terribly poor and we never had good things to eat. But I think I'll be happy here." She paused to snuggle her doll closer. "Now, if you'll just show me where to put my things . . ."

Mrs. Miller's face dissolved into a mask of ugly red lines; she began to cry, and it was an unnatural, tearless sort of weeping, as though, not having wept for a long time, she had forgotten how. Carefully she edged backward till she touched the door.

She fumbled through the hall and down the stairs to a landing below. She pounded frantically on the door of the first apartment she came to; a short, red-headed man answered and she pushed past him. "Say, what the hell is this?" he said. "Anything wrong, lover?" asked a young woman who appeared from the kitchen, drying her hands. And it was to her that Mrs. Miller turned.

"Listen," she cried, "I'm ashamed behaving this way but — well, I'm Mrs. H. T. Miller and I live upstairs and . . ." She pressed her hands over her face. "It sounds so absurd. . . ."

The woman guided her to a chair, while the man excitedly rattled pocket change. "Yeah?"

"I live upstairs and there's a little girl visiting me, and I suppose that I'm afraid of her. She won't leave and I can't make her and — she's going to do something terrible. She's already stolen my cameo, but she's about to do something worse — something terrible!"

The man asked, "Is she a relative, huh?"

Mrs. Miller shook her head. "I don't know who she is. Her name's Miriam, but I don't know for certain who she is."

"You gotta calm down, honey," said the woman, stroking Mrs. Miller's arm. "Harry here'll tend to this kid. Go on, lover." And Mrs. Miller said, "The door's open — 5A."

After the man left, the woman brought a towel and bathed Mrs. Miller's face. "You're very kind," Mrs. Miller said. "I'm sorry to act like such a fool, only this wicked child. . . ."

"Sure, honey," consoled the woman. "Now, you better take it easy."

Mrs. Miller rested her head in the crook of her arm; she was quiet enough to be asleep. The woman turned a radio dial; a piano and a husky voice filled the silence and the woman, tapping her foot, kept excellent time. "Maybe we oughta go up too," she said.

"I don't want to see her again. I don't want to be anywhere near her."

"Uh huh, but what you shoulda done, you shoulda called a cop."

Presently they heard the man on the stairs. He strode into the room frowning and scratching the back of his neck, "Nobody there," he said, honestly embarrassed. "She musta beat it."

"Harry, you're a jerk," announced the woman. "We been sitting here the whole time and we woulda seen . . ." she stopped abruptly, for the man's glance was sharp.

"I looked all over," he said, "and there just ain't nobody there. Nobody, understand?"

"Tell me," said Mrs. Miller, rising, "tell me, did you see a large box? Or a doll?"

"No, ma'am, I didn't."

And the woman, as if delivering a verdict, said, "Well, for cryinout-loud. . . ."

Mrs. Miller entered her apartment softly; she walked to the center of the room and stood quite still. No, in a sense it had not changed: the roses, the cakes, and the cherries were in place. But this was an empty room, emptier than if the furnishings and familiars were not present, lifeless and petrified as a funeral parlor. The sofa loomed before her with a new strangeness: its vacancy had a meaning that would have been less penetrating and terrible had Miriam been curled on it. She gazed fixedly at the space where she remembered setting the box and, for a moment, the hassock spun desperately. And she looked through the window; surely the river was real, surely snow was falling — but then, one could not be certain witness to anything: Miriam, so vividly *there* — and yet, where was she? Where, where?

As though moving in a dream, she sank to a chair. The room was losing shape; it was dark and getting darker and there was nothing to be done about it; she could not lift her hand to light a lamp.

Suddenly, closing her eyes, she felt an upward surge, like a diver emerging from some deeper, greener depth. In times of terror or immense distress, there are moments when the mind waits, as though for a revelation, while a skein of calm is woven over thought; it is like a sleep, or a supernatural trance; and during this lull one is aware of a force of quiet reasoning: well, what if she had never known a girl named Miriam? that she had been foolishly frightened on the street? In the end, like everything else, it was of no importance. For the only thing she had lost to Miriam was her identity, but now she knew she had found again the person who lived in this room, who cooked her own meals, who owned a canary, who was someone she could trust and believe in: Mrs. H. T. Miller.

Listening in contentment, she became aware of a double sound: a bureau drawer opening and closing; she seemed to hear it long after completion — opening and closing. Then gradually, the harshness of it was replaced by the murmur of a silk dress and this, delicately faint, was moving nearer and swelling in intensity till the walls trembled with the vibration and the room was caving under a wave of whispers. Mrs. Miller stiffened and opened her eyes to a dull, direct stare.

"Hello," said Miriam.

QUESTIONS

1. "Miriam" takes place not in a haunted mansion, but in an ordinary apartment block in New York City — how then can it be called a Gothic story?
2. By what descriptive details does the author make the little girl appear strange and unearthly? In what ways is she childlike, even ordinary?
3. What supernatural powers does Miriam apparently possess?
4. What do you make of the sinister old man who pursues Mrs. Miller? Why is he carrying "an armload of bulging packages"?
5. What meaning (if any) do you attach to Mrs. Miller's being named Miriam too?
6. Do you take Mrs. Miller to be mentally unstable, like the narrator of "The Tell-Tale Heart," and the girl Miriam to be all in her mind? How does Capote encourage us to trust — or distrust — Mrs. Miller's view of things?
7. In "Miriam" and in "The Tell-Tale Heart," do you find any moral or message? If not, do you consider the lack to be a deficiency in these two Gothic stories?

SCIENCE FICTION

The writer of **science fiction** imagines further limits to what the human race can fashion, or find out. Science fiction stories may take place in the present or in the past, but most often they are set in the immediate or distant future. Although tales of extraterrestrial voyages are as ancient as the second-century Greek writer Lucian's *True History*, in which a ship is borne to the moon by a whirlwind, science fiction as we know it developed in the nineteenth century when technology began making seven-league strides and people awoke to undreamed-of possibilities — both hopeful and frightening. In this view, science fiction, according to its recent historian Brian Aldiss, is "a lively sub-genre of Gothic," taking in "fears generated by change and the technological advances which are the chief agents of change."[1] Clearly a Gothic novel in

[1] *Billion Year Spree: The History of Science Fiction* (New York: Doubleday, 1973); Chapter One. This distinction has the virtue of separating science fiction from *The Divine Comedy*, tales of imaginary voyages, and **utopian fiction** (a kind of prophetic writing setting forth the writer's conception of an ideal society named for Thomas More's *Utopia*, 1516). Definitely science fiction, however, in its fear of engineered change, is much **anti-utopian fiction**: George Orwell's *1984* (1949), a grim view of a totalitarian state in which Big Brother observes all citizens from television sets placed in their rooms; and Aldous Huxley's *Brave New World* (1932), in which technology serves the purposes of thought-control and the mindless pursuit of pleasure (movies have been replaced by "feelies," whose audiences enjoy the tactile sensations of love scenes on bearskin rugs).

trappings and atmosphere, Mary Wollstonecraft Godwin Shelley's *Frankenstein: or, The Modern Prometheus* (1818) thus appears to be the first modern science fiction classic. Today, in Aldiss's opinion, science fiction still holds an element of fearful wonder: where is science heading and what will the future hold? Taking a different view, another theorist, Mark Rose, finds contemporary science fiction satisfying a "healthy love of wonder," satisfied in past centuries by tales of giants and dragons.[2]

In the nineteenth century, wonderful inventions were the stocks-in-trade of much early science fiction. French writer Jules Verne enjoyed a great vogue with his novels of fabulous voyages, such as *A Journey to the Center of the Earth* (1864) and *From the Earth to the Moon* (1865). Verne, who liked to spin a rousing adventure yarn and who prided himself on his scientific accuracy, now seems antiquated (his astronauts were fired into space from a cannon, which feat would have flattened them). Much less dated appear the early novels of English author and historian H. G. Wells, even though fact has overtaken them. (In *The First Men in the Moon,* 1897, Wells wafts men to the moon by a substance that defines gravity.) Wells, who suggested plots to hundreds of later science fiction writers, was less interested in gadgets than in the impact of science upon society. In *The Time Machine* (1895), he imagines a future world in which workers toil underground while only a leisure class enjoys the sunlight. Like much science fiction today, Wells's pioneering works seem animated by a kind of social criticism. Clearly science fiction is a variety of **fantasy,** an imaginative story that freely departs from fact, or even from probability.[3] But in science fiction, an imagined world often mirrors our own.

For the most part, twentieth-century science fiction in English has developed in the pulp magazines, beginning in 1926 with *Amazing Stories.* Contemporary science fiction owes much to John W. Campbell, who from 1938 until 1971 edited the magazine *Analog* (which was first called *Astounding Stories,* then *Astounding Science-Fiction*). Campbell's innovation was to advise his authors to write as if for some popular magazine in the far future. Whereas earlier science fiction had told

[2] Introduction to *Science Fiction, A Collection of Critical Essays* (Englewood Cliffs, N.J.: Prentice-Hall, 1976).
[3] Distinctions between *science fiction, science fantasy,* and *fantasy* are sometimes merely arbitrary. But some science fiction fans reserve the term *fantasy* for a kind of fiction based not on science but on traditional mythology (stories of magic, ghosts, witches, or vampires, for instance), or on some personal myth (one invented by a writer, such as J. R. R. Tolkien's magic ring that confers infinite power in his trilogy *The Lord of the Rings*). A noble attempt at a distinction has been offered by science fiction writer Miriam Allen de Ford (quoted by Aldiss): "Science fiction deals with improbable possibilities, fantasy with plausible impossibilities." Darko Suvin, in another attempt, finds science fiction different from myth, fairy tale, and fantasy in that it postulates a world other than that of its author: an empirical world, one whose laws can be known. ("On the Poetics of the Science Fiction Genre," *College English* 34 [December, 1972], pp. 372–383.)

of trips to Mars by means of marvelous devices, in a tone of innocent wonder, Campbell's more sophisticated writers began their stories with Mars already colonized and the marvelous devices everyday facts of life.

The recent growth of serious interest in science fiction has been phenomenal (and the recent popular success of films such as *Star Wars,* 1977, more phenomenal still). No longer confined to pulp magazines with covers showing Flash Gordons saving damsels from bug-eyed monsters, much science fiction today is esteemed by critics, by general readers, and by thoughtful writers attracted by its open defiance of nineteenth-century realism and by its apparently endless possibilities.

Kurt Vonnegut, Jr. (b. 1922)

HARRISON BERGERON   1961

The year was 2081, and everybody was finally equal. They weren't only equal before God and the law. They were equal every which way. Nobody was smarter than anybody else. Nobody was better looking than anybody else. Nobody was stronger or quicker than anybody else. All this equality was due to the 211th, 212th, and 213th Amendments to the Constitution, and to the unceasing vigilance of agents of the United States Handicapper General.

Some things about living still weren't quite right, though. April, for instance, still drove people crazy by not being springtime. And it was in that clammy month that the H-G men took George and Hazel Bergeron's fourteen-year-old son, Harrison, away.

It was tragic, all right, but George and Hazel couldn't think about it very hard. Hazel had a perfectly average intelligence, which meant she couldn't think about anything except in short bursts. And George, while his intelligence was way above normal, had a little mental handicap radio in his ear. He was required by law to wear it at all times. It was tuned to a government transmitter. Every twenty seconds or so, the transmitter would send out some sharp noise to keep people like George from taking unfair advantage of their brains.

George and Hazel were watching television. There were tears on Hazel's cheeks, but she'd forgotten for the moment what they were about.

On the television screen were ballerinas.

A buzzer sounded in George's head. His thoughts fled in panic, like bandits from a burglar alarm.

"That was a real pretty dance, that dance they just did," said Hazel.

"Huh?" said George.

"That dance — it was nice," said Hazel.

"Yup," said George. He tried to think a little about the ballerinas. They weren't really very good — no better than anybody else would have been, anyway. They were burdened with sashweights and bags of birdshot, and their faces were masked, so that no one, seeing a free and graceful gesture or a pretty face, would feel like something the cat drug in. George was toying with the vague notion that maybe dancers shouldn't be handicapped. But he didn't get very far with it before another noise in his ear radio scattered his thoughts.

George winced. So did two out of the eight ballerinas.

Hazel saw him wince. Having no mental handicap herself, she had to ask George what the latest sound had been.

"Sounded like somebody hitting a milk bottle with a ball peen hammer," said George.

"I'd think it would be real interesting, hearing all the different sounds," said Hazel, a little envious. "All the things they think up."

"Um," said George.

"Only, if I was Handicapper General, you know what I would do?" said Hazel. Hazel, as a matter of fact, bore a strong resemblance to the Handicapper General, a woman named Diana Moon Glampers. "If I was Diana Moon Glampers," said Hazel, "I'd have chimes on Sunday — just chimes. Kind of in honor of religion."

"I could think, if it was just chimes," said George.

"Well — maybe make 'em real loud," said Hazel. "I think I'd make a good Handicapper General."

"Good as anybody else," said George.

"Who knows better'n I do what normal is?" said Hazel.

"Right," said George. He began to think glimmeringly about his abnormal son who was now in jail, about Harrison, but a twenty-one-gun salute in his head stopped that.

"Boy!" said Hazel, "that was a doozy, wasn't it?"

It was such a doozy that George was white and trembling, and tears stood on the rims of his red eyes. Two of the eight ballerinas had collapsed to the studio floor, were holding their temples.

"All of a sudden you look so tired," said Hazel. "Why don't you stretch out on the sofa, so's you can rest your handicap bag on the pillows, honeybunch." She was referring to the forty-seven pounds of birdshot in a canvas bag, which was padlocked around George's neck. "Go on and rest the bag for a little while," she said. "I don't care if you're not equal to me for a while."

George weighed the bag with his hands. "I don't mind it," he said. "I don't notice it any more. It's just a part of me."

"You been so tired lately — kind of wore out," said Hazel. "If there was just some way we could make a little hole in the bottom of the bag, and just take out a few of them lead balls. Just a few."

"Two years in prison and two thousand dollars fine for every ball I took out," said George. "I don't call that a bargain."

"If you could just take a few out when you came home from work," said Hazel. "I mean — you don't compete with anybody around here. You just set around."

"If I tried to get away with it," said George, "then other people'd get away with it — and pretty soon we'd be right back to the dark ages again, with everybody competing against everybody else. You wouldn't like that, would you?"

"I'd hate it," said Hazel.

"There you are," said George. "The minute people start cheating on laws, what do you think happens to society?"

If Hazel hadn't been able to come up with an answer to this question, George couldn't have supplied one. A siren was going off in his head.

"Reckon it'd fall all apart," said Hazel.

"What would?" said George blankly.

"Society," said Hazel uncertainly. "Wasn't that what you just said?"

"Who knows?" said George.

The television program was suddenly interrupted for a news bulletin. It wasn't clear at first as to what the bulletin was about, since the announcer, like all announcers, had a serious speech impediment. For about half a minute, and in a state of high excitement, the announcer tried to say, "Ladies and gentlemen —"

He finally gave up, handed the bulletin to a ballerina to read.

"That's all right —" Hazel said of the announcer, "he tried. That's the big thing. He tried to do the best he could with what God gave him. He should get a nice raise for trying so hard."

"Ladies and gentlemen —" said the ballerina, reading the bulletin. She must have been extraordinarily beautiful, because the mask she wore was hideous. And it was easy to see that she was the strongest and most graceful of all the dancers, for her handicap bags were as big as those worn by two-hundred-pound men.

And she had to apologize at once for her voice, which was a very unfair voice for a woman to use. Her voice was a warm, luminous, timeless melody. "Excuse me —" she said, and she began again, making her voice absolutely uncompetitive.

"Harrison Bergeron, age fourteen," she said in a grackle squawk, "has just escaped from jail, where he was held on suspicion of plotting to overthrow the government. He is a genius and an athlete, is under-handicapped, and should be regarded as extremely dangerous."

A police photograph of Harrison Bergeron was flashed on the screen upside down, then sideways, upside down again, then right side up. The picture showed the full length of Harrison against a background calibrated in feet and inches. He was exactly seven feet tall.

The rest of Harrison's appearance was Halloween and hardware. Nobody had ever borne heavier handicaps. He had outgrown hindrances faster than the H-G men could think them up. Instead of a little ear radio for a mental handicap, he wore a tremendous pair of earphones, and spectacles with thick wavy lenses. The spectacles were intended to make him not only half blind, but to give him whanging headaches besides.

Scrap metal was hung all over him. Ordinarily, there was a certain symmetry, a military neatness to the handicaps issued to strong people, but Harrison looked like a walking junkyard. In the race of life, Harrison carried three hundred pounds.

And to offset his good looks, the H-G men required that he wear at all times a red rubber ball for a nose, keep his eyebrows shaved off, and cover his even white teeth with black caps at snaggle-tooth random.

"If you see this boy," said the ballerina, "do not — I repeat, do not — try to reason with him."

There was the shriek of a door being torn from its hinges.

Screams and barking cries of consternation came from the television set. The photograph of Harrison Bergeron on the screen jumped again and again, as though dancing to the tune of an earthquake.

George Bergeron correctly identified the earthquake, and well he might have — for many was the time his own home had danced to the same crashing tune. "My God —" said George, "that must be Harrison!"

The realization was blasted from his mind instantly by the sound of an automobile collision in his head.

When George could open his eyes again, the photograph of Harrison was gone. A living, breathing Harrison filled the screen.

Clanking, clownish, and huge, Harrison stood in the center of the studio. The knob of the uprooted studio door was still in his hand. Ballerinas, technicians, musicians, and announcers cowered on their knees before him, expecting to die.

"I am the Emperor!" cried Harrison. "Do you hear? I am the Emperor! Everybody must do what I say at once!" He stamped his foot and the studio shook.

"Even as I stand here —" he bellowed, "crippled, hobbled, sickened — I am a greater ruler than any man who ever lived! Now watch me become what I *can* become!"

Harrison tore the straps of his handicap harness like wet tissue paper, tore straps guaranteed to support five thousand pounds.

Harrison's scrap-iron handicaps crashed to the floor.

Harrison thrust his thumbs under the bar of the padlock that secured his head harness. The bar snapped like celery. Harrison smashed his headphones and spectacles against the wall.

He flung away his rubber-ball nose, revealed a man that would have awed Thor, the god of thunder.

"I shall now select my Empress!" he said, looking down on the cowering people. "Let the first woman who dares rise to her feet claim her mate and her throne!"

A moment passed, and then a ballerina arose, swaying like a willow.

Harrison plucked the mental handicap from her ear, snapped off her physical handicaps with marvelous delicacy. Last of all, he removed her mask.

She was blindingly beautiful.

"Now —" said Harrison, taking her hand, "shall we show the people the meaning of the word dance? Music!" he commanded.

The musicians scrambled back into their chairs, and Harrison stripped them of their handicaps, too. "Play your best," he told them, "and I'll make you barons and dukes and earls."

The music began. It was normal at first — cheap, silly, false. But Harrison snatched two musicians from their chairs, waved them like batons as he sang the music as he wanted it played. He slammed them back into their chairs.

The music began again and was much improved.

Harrison and his Empress merely listened to the music for a while — listened gravely, as though synchronizing their heartbeats with it.

They shifted their weights to their toes.

Harrison placed his big hands on the girl's tiny waist, letting her sense the weightlessness that would soon be hers.

And then, in an explosion of joy and grace, into the air they sprang!

Not only were the laws of the land abandoned, but the law of gravity and the laws of motion as well.

They reeled, whirled, swiveled, flounced, capered, gamboled, and spun.

They leaped like deer on the moon.

The studio ceiling was thirty feet high, but each leap brought the dancers nearer to it.

It became their obvious intention to kiss the ceiling.

They kissed it.

And then, neutralizing gravity with love and pure will, they remained suspended in air inches below the ceiling, and they kissed each other for a long, long time.

It was then that Diana Moon Glampers, the Handicapper General, came into the studio with a double-barreled ten-gauge shotgun. She fired twice, and the Emperor and the Empress were dead before they hit the floor.

Diana Moon Glampers loaded the gun again. She aimed it at the musicians and told them they had ten seconds to get their handicaps back on.

It was then that the Bergerons' television tube burned out.

Hazel turned to comment about the blackout to George. But George had gone out into the kitchen for a can of beer.

George came back in with the beer, paused while a handicap signal shook him up. And then he sat down again. "You been crying?" he said to Hazel.

"Yup," she said.

"What about?" he said.

"I forget," she said. "Something real sad on television."

"What was it?" he said.

"It's all kind of mixed up in my mind," said Hazel.

"Forget sad things," said George.

"I always do," said Hazel.

"That's my girl," said George. He winced. There was the sound of a rivetting gun in his head.

"Gee — I could tell that one was a doozy," said Hazel.

"You can say that again," said George.

"Gee —" said Hazel, "I could tell that one was a doozy."

QUESTIONS

1. What tendencies in present-day American society is Vonnegut satirizing? Does the story argue *for* anything? How would you sum up its theme?

2. Is Diana Moon Glampers a "flat" or a "round" character? (If you need to review these terms, see page 43.) Would you call Vonnegut's characterization of her "realistic"? (If not, why doesn't it need to be?)

3. From what point of view is the story told? Why is it more effective than if Harrison Bergeron had told his own story in the first person?

4. Two sympathetic critics of Vonnegut's work, Karen and Charles Wood, have said of his stories: "Vonnegut proves repeatedly . . . that men and women remain fundamentally the same, no matter what technology surrounds them." Try applying this comment to "Harrison Bergeron." Do you agree?

Ray Bradbury (b. 1920)

THE PEDESTRIAN

1953

To enter out into that silence that was the city at eight o'clock of a misty evening in November, to put your feet upon that buckling concrete walk, to step over grassy seams and make your way, hands in pockets, through the silences, that was what Mr. Leonard Mead most dearly loved to do. He would stand upon the corner of an intersection and peer down long moonlit avenues of sidewalk in four directions, deciding which way to go, but it really made no difference; he was alone in this world of 2053 A.D., or as good as alone, and with a final decision made, a path selected, he would stride off, sending patterns of frosty air before him like the smoke of a cigar.

Sometimes he would walk for hours and miles and return only at midnight to his house. And on his way he would see the cottages and homes with their dark windows, and it was not unequal to walking through a graveyard where only the faintest glimmers of firefly light appeared in flickers behind the windows. Sudden gray phantoms seemed to manifest upon inner room walls where a curtain was still undrawn against the night, or there were whisperings and murmurs where a window in a tomb-like building was still open.

Mr. Leonard Mead would pause, cock his head, listen, look, and march on, his feet making no noise on the lumpy walk. For long ago he had wisely changed to sneakers when strolling at night, because the dogs in intermittent squads would parallel his journey with barkings if he wore hard heels, and lights might click on and faces appear and an entire street be startled by the passing of a lone figure, himself, in the early November evening.

On this particular evening he began his journey in a westerly direction, toward the hidden sea. There was a good crystal frost in the air; it cut the nose and made the lungs blaze like a Christmas tree inside; you could feel the cold light going on and off, all the branches filled with invisible snow. He listened to the faint push of his soft shoes through autumn leaves with satisfaction, and whistled a cold quiet whistle between his teeth, occasionally picking up a leaf as he passed, examining its skeletal pattern in the infrequent lamplights as he went on, smelling its rusty smell.

"Hello, in there," he whispered to every house on every side as he moved. "What's up tonight on Channel 4, Channel 7, Channel 9? Where are the cowboys rushing, and do I see the United States Cavalry over the next hill to the rescue?"

The street was silent and long and empty, with only his shadow moving like the shadow of a hawk in mid-country. If he closed his eyes and stood very still, frozen, he could imagine himself upon the center of a plain, a wintry, windless Arizona desert with no house in a thousand miles, and only dry river beds, the streets, for company.

"What is it now?" he asked the houses, noticing his wrist watch. "Eight-thirty P.M.? Time for a dozen assorted murders? A quiz? A revue? A comedian falling off the stage?"

Was that a murmur of laughter from within a moon-white house? He hesitated, but went on when nothing more happened. He stumbled over a particularly uneven section of sidewalk. The cement was vanishing under flowers and grass. In ten years of walking by night or day, for thousands of miles, he had never met another person walking, not one in all that time.

He came to a cloverleaf intersection which stood silent where two main highways crossed the town. During the day it was a thunderous surge of cars, the gas stations open, a great insect rustling and a ceaseless jockeying for position as the scarab-beetles, a faint incense puttering from their exhausts, skimmed homeward to the far directions. But now these highways, too, were like streams in a dry season, all stone and bed and moon radiance.

He turned back on a side street, circling around toward his home. He was within a block of his destination when the lone car turned a corner quite suddenly and flashed a fierce white cone of light upon him. He stood entranced, not unlike a night moth, stunned by the illumination, and then drawn toward it.

A metallic voice called to him:

"Stand still. Stay where you are! Don't move!"

He halted.

"Put up your hands!"

"But ——" he said.

"Your hands up! Or we'll shoot!"

The police, of course, but what a rare, incredible thing; in a city of three million, there was only *one* police car left, wasn't that correct? Ever since a year ago, 2052, the election year, the force had been cut down from three cars to one. Crime was ebbing; there was no need now for the police, save for this one lone car wandering and wandering the empty streets.

"Your name?" said the police car in a metallic whisper. He couldn't see the men in it for the bright light in his eyes.

"Leonard Mead," he said.

"Speak up!"

"Leonard Mead!"

"Business or profession?"

"I guess you'd call me a writer."

"No profession," said the police car, as if talking to itself. The light held him fixed, like a museum specimen, needle thrust through chest.

"You might say that," said Mr. Mead. He hadn't written in years. Magazines and books didn't sell any more. Everything went on in the tomb-like houses at night now, he thought, continuing his fancy. The tombs, ill-lit by television light, where the people sat like the dead, the gray or multi-colored lights touching their faces, but never really touching them.

"No profession," said the phonograph voice, hissing. "What are you doing out?"

"Walking," said Leonard Mead.

"Walking!"

"Just walking," he said simply, but his face felt cold.

"Walking, just walking, walking?"

"Yes, sir."

"Walking where? For what?"

"Walking for air. Walking to *see*."

"Your address!"

"Eleven South Saint James Street."

"And there is air *in* your house, you have an air *conditioner*, Mr. Mead?"

"Yes."

"And you have a viewing screen in your house to see with?"

"No."

"No?" There was a crackling quiet that in itself was an accusation.

"Are you married, Mr. Mead?"

"No."

"Not married," said the police voice behind the fiery beam. The moon was high and clear among the stars and the houses were gray and silent.

"Nobody wanted me," said Leonard Mead with a smile.

"Don't speak unless you're spoken to!"

Leonard Mead waited in the cold night.

"Just *walking*, Mr. Mead?"

"Yes."

"But you haven't explained for what purpose."

"I explained; for air, and to see, and just to walk."

"Have you done this often?"

"Every night for years."

The police car sat in the center of the street with its radio throat faintly humming.

"Well, Mr. Mead," it said.

"Is that all?" he asked politely.

"Yes," said the voice. "Here." There was a sigh, a pop. The back door of the police car sprang wide. "Get in."

"Wait a minute, I haven't done anything!"

"Get in."

"I protest!"

"Mr. Mead."

He walked like a man suddenly drunk. As he passed the front window of the car he looked in. As he had expected, there was no one in the front seat, no one in the car at all.

"Get in."

He put his hand to the door and peered into the back seat, which was a little cell, a little black jail with bars. It smelled of riveted steel. It smelled of harsh antiseptic; it smelled too clean and hard and metallic. There was nothing soft there.

"Now if you had a wife to give you an alibi," said the iron voice. "But ——"

"Where are you taking me?"

The car hesitated, or rather gave a faint whirring click, as if information, somewhere, was dropping card by punch-slotted card under electric eyes. "To the Psychiatric Center for Research on Regressive Tendencies."

He got in. The door shut with a soft thud. The police car rolled through the night avenues, flashing its dim lights ahead.

They passed one house on one street a moment later, one house in an entire city of houses that were dark, but this one particular house had all of its electric lights brightly lit, every window a loud yellow illumination, square and warm in the cool darkness.

"That's *my* house," said Leonard Mead.

No one answered him.

The car moved down the empty river-bed streets and off away, leaving the empty streets with the empty sidewalks, and no sound and no motion all the rest of the chill November night.

QUESTIONS

1. By what details does the author indicate that Leonard Mead, unlike his neighbors, enjoys his body and his senses?
2. As far as you can infer it, what is the author's attitude toward television?
3. Of what value to the story is its style of writing? Point to some of Bradbury's colorful comparisons.
4. Sum up the theme. How similar is it to the theme of "Harrison Bergeron"?
5. Stanislaw Lem, Polish author of *Solaris* (1961) and other novels, once made this thoughtful criticism of Ray Bradbury (and some other science fiction writers):

> The revolt against the machine and against civilization, the praise of the "aesthetic" nature of catastrophe, the dead-end course of human civilization — these are their foremost problems, the intellectual content of their works. Such SF is as it were *a priori* vitiated by pessimism, in the sense that anything that may happen will be for the worse. ("The Time-Travel Story and Related Matters of SF Structuring," *Science Fiction Studies 1* [1974], pp. 143–154.)

How might Lem's objection be raised against both "The Pedestrian" and "Harrison Bergeron"? Do you agree with it?

Ursula K. Le Guin (b. 1929)
THE ONES WHO WALK AWAY FROM OMELAS   1973

(Variations on a theme by William James)°

With a clamor of bells that set the swallows soaring, the Festival of Summer came to the city Omelas, bright-towered by the sea. The rigging of the boats in harbor sparkled with flags. In the streets between houses with red roofs and

(Variations on a theme by William James): The author has recalled finding the germ for her story in an essay by William James (1842–1910), an American philosopher and pioneer experimental psychologist:

> Or if the hypothesis were offered us of a world in which . . . utopias should all be outdone, and millions kept permanently happy on the one simple condition that a certain lost soul on the far-off edge of things should lead a life of lonely torment, what except a specifical and independent sort of emotion can it be which would make us immediately feel, even though an impulse arose within us to clutch at the happiness so offered, how hideous a thing would be its enjoyment when deliberately accepted as the fruit of such a bargain? ("The Moral Philosopher and the Moral Life," in *Collected Essays and Reviews.* London: Longmans, Green, 1920.)

painted walls, between old moss-grown gardens and under avenues of trees, past great parks and public buildings, processions moved. Some were decorous: old people in long stiff robes of mauve and grey, grave master workmen, quiet, merry women carrying their babies and chatting as they walked. In other streets the music beat faster, a shimmering of gong and tambourine, and the people went dancing, the procession was a dance. Children dodged in and out, their high calls rising like the swallows' crossing flights over the music and the singing. All the processions wound towards the north side of the city, where on the great water-meadow called the Green Fields boys and girls, naked in the bright air, with mud-stained feet and ankles and long, lithe arms, exercised their restive horses before the race. The horses wore no gear at all but a halter without bit. Their manes were braided with streamers of silver, gold, and green. They flared their nostrils and pranced and boasted to one another; they were vastly excited, the horse being the only animal who has adopted our ceremonies as his own. Far off to the north and west the mountains stood up half encircling Omelas on her bay. The air of morning was so clear that the snow still crowning the Eighteen Peaks burned with white-gold fire across the miles of sunlit air, under the dark blue of the sky. There was just enough wind to make the banners that marked the racecourse snap and flutter now and then. In the silence of the broad green meadows one could hear the music winding through the city streets, farther and nearer and ever approaching, a cheerful faint sweetness of the air that from time to time trembled and gathered together and broke out into the great joyous clanging of the bells.

Joyous! How is one to tell about joy? How describe the citizens of Omelas?

They were not simple folk, you see, though they were happy. But we do not say the words of cheer much any more. All smiles have become archaic. Given a description such as this one tends to make certain assumptions. Given a description such as this one tends to look next for the King, mounted on a splendid stallion and surrounded by his noble knights, or perhaps in a golden litter borne by great-muscled slaves. But there was no king. They did not use swords, or keep slaves. They were not barbarians. I do not know the rules and laws of their society, but I suspect that they were singularly few. As they did without monarchy and slavery, so they also got on without the stock exchange, the advertisement, the secret police, and the bomb. Yet I repeat that these were not simple folk, not dulcet shepherds, noble savages, bland utopians. They were not less complex than us. The trouble is that we have a bad habit, encouraged by pedants and sophisticates, of considering happiness as something rather stupid. Only pain is intellectual, only evil interesting. This is the treason of the artist: a refusal to admit the banality of evil and the terrible boredom of pain. If you can't lick 'em, join 'em. If it hurts, repeat it. But to praise despair is to condemn delight, to embrace violence is to lose hold of everything else. We have almost lost hold; we can no longer describe a happy man, nor make any celebration of joy. How can I tell you about the people of Omelas? They were not naïve and happy children — though their children were, in fact, happy. They were mature, intelligent, passionate adults whose lives were not wretched. O miracle! but I wish I could describe it better. I wish I could convince you. Omelas sounds in my words like a city in a fairy tale, long ago and far away, once upon a time. Perhaps it would be best if you imagined it as your own fancy bids, assuming it will rise to the occasion, for certainly I cannot suit you all. For instance, how about technology? I think that there would be no cars or helicopters in and above the streets; this follows from the fact that the people of Omelas are happy people. Happiness is based on a just discrimination of what is necessary, what is neither necessary nor destructive, and what is destructive. In the middle category, however — that of the unnecessary but undestructive, that of comfort, luxury, exuberance, etc. — they could perfectly well have central heating, subway trains, washing machines, and all kinds of marvelous devices not yet invented here, floating light-sources, fuelless power, a cure for the common cold. Or they could have none of that: it doesn't matter. As you like it. I incline to think that people from towns up and down the coast have been coming in to Omelas during the last days before the Festival on very fast little trains and double-decked trams, and that the train station of Omelas is actually the handsomest building in town, though plainer than the magnificent Farmers' Market. But even granted trains, I fear that Omelas so far strikes some of you as goody-goody. Smiles, bells, parades, horses, bleh. If so, please add an orgy. If an orgy would help, don't hesitate. Let us not, however, have temples from which issue beautiful nude priests and priestesses already half in ecstasy and ready to copulate with any man or woman, lover or stranger, who desires union with the deep godhead of the blood, although that was my first idea. But really it would be better not to have any temples in Omelas — at least, not manned temples. Religion yes, clergy no. Surely the beautiful nudes can just wander about, offering themselves like divine soufflés to the hunger of the needy and the rapture of the flesh. Let them join the processions. Let tambourines be struck above the copulations, and the glory of desire be proclaimed upon the gongs, and (a not unimportant point) let the offspring of these delightful rituals be beloved and looked after by all. One thing I know there is none of in Omelas is guilt. But what else should there be? I thought at first there were no drugs, but that is puritanical. For those who like it, the faint insistent sweetness of *drooz* may perfume the ways of the city, *drooz* which first brings a great lightness and brilliance to the mind and limbs, and then after some hours a dreamy languor, and wonderful visions at last of the very arcana and inmost secrets of the Universe, as well as exciting the pleasure of sex beyond all belief; and it is not habit-forming. For more modest tastes I think there ought to be beer. What else, what else belongs in the joyous city? The sense of victory, surely, the celebration of courage. But as we did without clergy, let us do without soldiers. The joy built upon successful slaughter is not the right kind of joy; it will not do; it is fearful and it is trivial. A boundless and generous contentment, a magnanimous triumph felt not against some outer enemy but in communion with the finest and fairest in the souls of all men everywhere and the splendor of the world's summer: this is what swells the hearts of the people of Omelas, and the victory they celebrate is that of life. I really don't think many of them need to take *drooz*.

Most of the processions have reached the Green Fields by now. A marvelous smell of cooking goes forth from the red and blue tents of the provisioners. The faces of small children are amiably sticky; in the benign grey beard of a man a couple of crumbs of rich pastry are entangled. The youths and girls have mounted their horses and are beginning to group around the starting line of the course. An old woman, small, fat, and laughing, is passing out flowers from a basket, and tall young men wear her flowers in their shining hair. A child of nine or ten sits at the edge of the crowd, alone, playing on a wooden flute. People pause to listen, and they smile, but they do not speak to him, for he never ceases playing and never sees them, his dark eyes wholly rapt in the sweet, thin magic of the tune.

He finishes, and slowly lowers his hands holding the wooden flute.

As if that little private silence were the signal, all at once a trumpet sounds from the pavilion near the starting line: imperious, melancholy, piercing. The horses rear on their slender legs, and some of them neigh in answer. Sober-faced, the young riders stroke the horses' necks and soothe them, whispering, "Quiet, quiet, there my beauty, my hope. . . ." They begin to form in rank along the starting line. The crowds along the racecourse are like a field of grass and flowers in the wind. The Festival of Summer has begun.

Do you believe? Do you accept the festival, the city, the joy? No? Then let me describe one more thing.

In a basement under one of the beautiful public buildings of Omelas, or perhaps in the cellar of one of its spacious private homes, there is a room. It has one locked door, and no window. A little light seeps in dustily between cracks in the boards, secondhand from a cobwebbed window somewhere across the cellar. In one corner of the little room a couple of mops, with stiff, clotted, foul-smelling heads, stand near a rusty bucket. The floor is dirt, a little damp to the touch, as cellar dirt usually is. The room is about three paces long and two wide: a mere broom closet or disused tool room. In the room a child is sitting. It could be a boy or a girl. It looks about six, but actually is nearly ten. It is feeble-minded. Perhaps it was born defective, or perhaps it has become imbecile through fear, malnutrition, and neglect. It picks its nose and occasionally fumbles vaguely with its toes or genitals, as it sits hunched in the corner farthest from the bucket and the two mops. It is afraid of the mops. It finds them horrible. It shuts its eyes, but it knows the mops are still standing there; and the door is locked; and nobody will come. The door is always locked; and nobody ever comes, except that sometimes — the child has no understanding of time or interval — sometimes the door rattles terribly and opens, and a person, or several people, are there. One of them may come in and kick the child to make it stand up. The others never come close, but peer in at it with frightened, disgusted eyes. The food bowl and the water jug are hastily filled, the door is locked, the eyes disappear. The people at the door never say anything, but the child, who has not always lived in the tool room, and can remember sunlight and its mother's voice, sometimes speaks. "I will be good," it says. "Please let me out. I will be good!" They never answer. The child used to scream for help at night, and cry a good deal, but now it only makes a kind of whining, "eh-haa, eh-haa," and it speaks less and less often. It is so thin there are no calves to its legs; its belly protrudes; it lives on a half-bowl of corn meal and grease a day. It is naked. Its buttocks and thighs are a mass of festered sores, as it sits in its own excrement continually.

They all know it is there, all the people of Omelas. Some of them have come to see it, others are content merely to know it is there. They all know that it has to be there. Some of them understand why, and some do not, but they all understand that their happiness, the beauty of their city, the tenderness of their friendships, the health of their children, the wisdom of their scholars, the skill of their makers, even the abundance of their harvest and the kindly weathers of their skies, depend wholly on this child's abominable misery.

This is usually explained to children when they are between eight and twelve, whenever they seem capable of understanding; and most of those who come to see the child are young people, though often enough an adult comes, or comes back, to see the child. No matter how well the matter has been explained to them, these young spectators are always shocked and sickened at the sight. They feel disgust, which they had thought themselves superior to. They feel anger, outrage, impotence, despite all the explanations. They would like to do something for the child. But there is nothing they can do. If the child were brought up into the sunlight out of the vile place, if it were cleaned and fed and comforted, that would be a good thing, indeed; but if it were done, in that day and hour all the prosperity and beauty and delight of Omelas would wither and be destroyed. Those are the terms. To exchange all the goodness and grace of every life in Omelas for that single, small improvement: to throw away the happiness of thousands for the chance of the happiness of one: that would be to let guilt within the walls indeed.

The terms are strict and absolute; there may not even be a kind word spoken to the child.

Often the young people go home in tears, or in a tearless rage, when they have seen the child and faced this terrible paradox. They may brood over it for weeks or years. But as time goes on they begin to realize that even if the child could be released, it would not get much good of its freedom: a little vague pleasure of warmth and food, no doubt, but little more. It is too degraded and imbecile to know any real joy. It has been afraid too long ever to be free of fear. Its habits are too uncouth for it to respond to humane treatment. Indeed, after so long it would probably be wretched without walls about it to protect it, and darkness for its eyes, and its own excrement to sit in. Their tears at the bitter injustice dry when they begin to perceive the terrible justice of reality, and to accept it. Yet it is their tears and anger, the trying of their generosity and the acceptance of their helplessness, which are perhaps the true source of the splendor of their lives. Theirs is no vapid, irresponsible happiness. They know that they, like the child, are not free. They know compassion. It is the existence of the child, and their knowledge of its existence, that makes possible the nobility of their architecture, the poignancy of their music, the profundity of their science. It is because of the child that they are so gentle with children. They know that if the wretched one were not there snivelling in the dark, the other one, the flute-player, could make no joyful music as the young riders line up in their beauty for the race in the sunlight of the first morning of summer.

Now do you believe in them? Are they not more credible? But there is one more thing to tell, and this is quite incredible.

At times one of the adolescent girls or boys who go to see the child does not go home to weep or rage, does not, in fact, go home at all. Sometimes also a man or woman much older falls silent for a day or two, and then leaves home. These people go out into the street, and walk down the street alone. They keep walking, and walk straight out of the city of Omelas, through the beautiful gates. They keep walking across the farmlands of Omelas. Each one goes alone, youth or girl, man or woman. Night falls; the traveler must pass down village streets, between the houses with yellow-lit windows, and on out into the darkness of the fields. Each alone, they go west or north, towards the mountains. They go on. They leave Omelas, they walk ahead into the darkness, and they do not come back. The place they go towards is a place even less imaginable to most of us than the city of happiness. I cannot describe it at all. It is possible that it does not exist. But they seem to know where they are going, the ones who walk away from Omelas.

QUESTIONS

1. Does the author share the narrator's opinion of Omelas? What are we supposed to think of those who walk away? (How can you tell? Which comments seem ironic?)
2. What do we learn about the narrator's own society? How does it compare with Omelas?
3. Do you find in the story any implied criticism of our own society?
4. How do you account for the narrator's willingness to let us readers add to the story anything we like? — "If an orgy would help, don't hesitate" (page 156). Doesn't Ursula Le Guin care what her story includes?
5. Do you agree that this story is science fiction, or would you argue that it isn't?
6. Is "The Ones Who Walk Away from Omelas" a fable, a tale, or a short story?

THE DETECTIVE STORY

For about a century, the **detective story,** or fictional account of the unraveling of a crime (usually murder), has enjoyed tremendous popularity. Although theorists do not agree on why so many millions have enjoyed reading about the violent deaths of their fellow citizens, most literary historians agree that the form was originated by Edgar Allan Poe practically single-handedly. In his tales of the Parisian sleuth C. Auguste Dupin, beginning in 1841 with "The Murders in the Rue Morgue," Poe established both a story-pattern and a typical private investigator. Dupin, a brilliant logician who solves crimes by sheer mental power, is an eccentric who prefers night to day, shuns fresh air, and burns perfumed candles. His exploits are observed and narrated by a friend less brilliant than he. In "Rue Morgue," Poe even invented a favorite variety of modern detective story, the locked-room mystery. Two mutilated bodies are discovered in a room that no human being could have entered. In his solution, however, Poe violates a cardinal rule of later mystery writers: the murderer is not a human being but an ape. Still, in this story and others, Poe fixes a conventional detective story plot: a crime is discovered, an innocent person is suspected, clues are scouted out. In the climax, the detective reveals the identity of the true criminal and explains the process of his own reasoning.

Apparently, Poe's Dupin greatly influenced the British writer Arthur Conan Doyle in his conception of the most celebrated fictional detective of all time. When Doyle introduced Sherlock Holmes in 1887 in his novel *A Study in Scarlet,* the character, with his amazing feats of deduction, won immediate popularity. And this popularity has not diminished: to this day, throngs of visitors to London go looking for the Baker Street lodgings of Holmes and his friend Dr. Watson, as though expecting the rooms to be real and open to the public.

Under the spell of Doyle, scores of later writers were further to develop the **whodunit,** or novel of find-the-culprit, and to invite readers to match wits with a detective in working out the solution to the crime. (Sherlock Holmes had often sped far ahead of the reader in following a trail of clues, for Doyle had sometimes withheld from all but Holmes some essential shred of evidence.) A genuinely original sleuth appears in G. K. Chesterton's stories of Father Brown, a priest who tracks down criminals not in order to turn them over to the law, but in order to help them redeem their souls. Agatha Christie, in her stories of Miss Marple, was to create another unusual detective, an aging gentlewoman who lives in a singularly violent country village.

Back in America, a different, more harshly realistic kind of detective story was to emerge in the 1920s — when organized crime began to hit its stride and provided writers with plenty of fresh material. The editor of *Black Mask* magazine, Joseph T. Shaw, decided to shun what he called "the crossword puzzle" sort of story in favor of violence, action, and high tension. "To constitute a murder," Shaw declared, "the victim must be a real human being of flesh and blood" — a convincing corpse, not a number in a code to be deciphered.[4] Seeking writers able to produce what he wanted, Shaw encouraged and published the early work of Dashiell Hammett, Raymond Chandler, and many more. While in the British-made traditional detective story, murder had tended to occur at a weekend lawn party on a country estate, with an array of well-dressed suspects holding sherry glasses while a detective questioned them, Hammett and Chandler took urban landscapes for their settings — often run-down neighborhoods in Los Angeles — and peopled them with gamblers, sneak-thieves, and racketeers. "Hammett," said Chandler, "took murder out of the Venetian vase and dropped it into the alley." Both writers cultivated a spare, fast-paced style, implying emotion rather than stating it. Often, they selected an objective point of view, relating events as if witnessed by a fly on the wall. (For an illustration, see the passage from Hammett's *The Maltese Falcon* given on page 19.) Their novels, written not for *Black Mask* but for a wider audience, could thus be transferred readily to the movie screen, where frequently Humphrey Bogart personified their private detectives. The hero of the fiction of Hammett, Chandler, and (later) Ross Macdonald is a different brand of detective from C. Auguste Dupin or Sherlock Holmes. A

[4] Introduction to *The Hard-boiled Omnibus: Early Stories from* Black Mask (New York: Simon and Schuster, 1946).

tough-nosed loner quicker to act than to think, he is a man doing a difficult job with great integrity: a common man (as Chandler once explained) who moves down mean streets but "who is not himself mean, who is neither tarnished nor afraid."[5]

A. Conan Doyle (1859–1930)
THE ADVENTURE OF THE SPECKLED BAND   1892

In glancing over my notes of the seventy-odd cases in which I have, during the last eight years, studied the methods of my friend, Sherlock Holmes, I find many tragic, some comic, a large number merely strange, but none commonplace; for, working as he did rather for the love of his art than for the acquirement of wealth, he refused to associate himself with any investigation which did not tend toward the unusual, and even the fantastic. Of all these varied cases, however, I cannot recall any which presented more singular features than that which was associated wth the well-known Surrey family of the Roylott of Stoke Moran. The events in question occurred in the early days of my association with Holmes, when we were sharing rooms as bachelors in Baker Street. It is possible that I might have placed them upon record before, but a promise of secrecy was made at the time, from which I have only been freed during the last month by the untimely death of the lady to whom the pledge was given. It is perhaps as well that the facts should now come to light, for I have reasons to know that there are wide-spread rumors as to the death of Dr. Grimesby Roylott which tend to make the matter even more terrible than the truth.

It was early in April in the year '83 that I woke one morning to find Sherlock Holmes standing, fully dressed, by the side of my bed. He was a late riser as a rule, and as the clock on the mantel-piece showed me that it was only a quarter past seven, I blinked up at him in some surprise, and perhaps just a little resentment, for I was myself regular in my habits.

"Very sorry to knock you up, Watson," said he, "but it's the common lot this morning. Mrs. Hudson has been knocked up; she retorted upon me; and I on you."

"What is it, then — a fire?"

"No; a client. It seems that a young lady has arrived in a considerable state of excitement, who insists upon seeing me. She is waiting now in the sitting-room. Now, when young ladies wander about the metropolis at this hour of the morning, and knock sleepy people up out of their beds, I presume that it is something very pressing which they have to communicate. Should it prove to be an interesting case, you would, I am sure, wish to follow it from the outset. I thought, at any rate, that I should call you and give you the chance."

"My dear fellow, I would not miss it for anything."

I had no keener pleasure than in following Holmes in his professional investigations, and in admiring the rapid deductions, as swift as intuitions, and yet always founded on a logical basis, with which he unraveled the problems

---

[5] From an essay, "The Simple Art of Murder," introducing a collection of stories by the same title (Boston: Houghton Mifflin, 1950).

which were submitted to him. I rapidly threw on my clothes, and was ready in a few minutes to accompany my friend down to the sitting-room. A lady dressed in black and heavily veiled, who had been sitting in the window, rose as we entered.

"Good-morning, madam," said Holmes, cheerily. "My name is Sherlock Holmes. This is my intimate friend and associate, Dr. Watson, before whom you can speak as freely as before myself. Ha! — I am glad to see that Mrs. Hudson has had the good sense to light the fire. Pray draw up to it, and I shall order you a cup of hot coffee, for I observe that you are shivering."

"It is not cold which makes me shiver," said the woman, in a low voice, changing her seat as requested.

"What then?"

"It is fear, Mr. Holmes. It is terror." She raised her veil as she spoke, and we could see that she was indeed in a pitiable state of agitation, her face all drawn and gray, with restless, frightened eyes, like those of some hunted animal. Her features and figure were those of a woman of thirty, but her hair was shot with premature gray, and her expression was weary and haggard. Sherlock Holmes ran her over with one of his quick, all-comprehensive glances.

"You must not fear," said he, soothingly, bending forward and patting her forearm. "We shall soon set matters right, I have no doubt. You have come in by train this morning, I see."

"You know me, then?"

"No, but I observe the second half of a return ticket in the palm of your left glove. You must have started early, and yet you had a good drive in a dog-cart, along heavy roads, before you reached the station."

The lady gave a violent start, and stared in bewilderment at my companion.

"There is no mystery, my dear madam," said he, smiling. "The left arm of your jacket is spattered with mud in no less than seven places. The marks are perfectly fresh. There is no vehicle save a dog-cart which throws up mud in that way, and then only when you sit on the left-hand side of the driver."

"Whatever your reasons may be, you are perfectly correct," said she. "I started from home before six, reached Leatherhead at twenty past, and came in by the first train to Waterloo°. Sir, I can stand this strain no longer; I shall go mad if it continues. I have no one to turn to — none, save only one, who cares for me, and he, poor fellow, can be of little aid. I have heard of you, Mr. Holmes; I have heard of you from Mrs. Farintosh, whom you helped in the hour of her sore need. It was from her that I had your address. Oh, sir, do you not think that you could help me, too, and at least throw a little light through the dense darkness which surrounds me? At present it is out of my power to reward you for your services, but in a month or six weeks I shall be married, with the control of my own income, and then at least you shall not find me ungrateful."

Holmes turned to his desk, and unlocking it, drew out a small casebook, which he consulted.

"Farintosh," said he. "Ah, yes, I recall the case; it was concerned with an opal tiara. I think it was before your time, Watson. I can only say, madam, that I shall be happy to devote the same care to your case as I did to that of your

Waterloo: London railroad station.

friend. As to reward, my profession is its own reward; but you are at liberty to defray whatever expenses I may be put to, at the time which suits you best. And now I beg that you will lay before us everything that may help us in forming an opinion upon the matter."

"Alas!" replied our visitor, "the very horror of my situation lies in the fact that my fears are so vague, and my suspicions depend so entirely upon small points, which might seem trivial to another, that even he to whom of all others I have a right to look for help and advice, looks upon all that I tell him about it as the fancies of a nervous woman. He does not say so, but I can read it from his soothing answers and averted eyes. But I have heard, Mr. Holmes, that you can see deeply into the manifold wickedness of the human heart. You may advise me how to walk amid the dangers which encompass me."

"I am all attention, madam."

"My name is Helen Stoner, and I am living with my step-father, who is the last survivor of one of the oldest Saxon families in England, the Roylotts of Stoke Moran, on the western border of Surrey."

Holmes nodded his head. "The name is familiar to me," said he.

"The family was at one time among the richest in England, and the estates extended over the borders into Berkshire in the north, and Hampshire in the west. In the last century, however, four successive heirs were of a dissolute and wasteful disposition, and the family ruin was eventually completed by a gambler in the days of the Regency°. Nothing was left save a few acres of ground, and the two-hundred-year-old house, which is itself crushed under a heavy mortgage. The last squire dragged out his existence there, living the horrible life of an aristocratic pauper; but his only son, my step-father, seeing that he must adapt himself to the new conditions, obtained an advance from a relative, which enabled him to take a medical degree, and went out to Calcutta, where, by his professional skill and his force of character, he established a large practice. In a fit of anger, however, caused by some robberies which had been perpetrated in the house, he beat his native butler to death, and narrowly escaped a capital sentence. As it was, he suffered a long term of imprisonment, and afterward returned to England a morose and disappointed man.

"When Dr. Roylott was in India he married my mother, Mrs. Stoner, the young widow of Major-General Stoner, of the Bengal Artillery. My sister Julia and I were twins, and we were only two years old at the time of my mother's remarriage. She had a considerable sum of money — not less than 1,000 pounds a year — and this she bequeathed to Dr. Roylott entirely while we resided with him, with a provision that a certain annual sum should be allowed to each of us in the event of our marriage. Shortly after our return to England my mother died — she was killed eight years ago in a railway accident near Crewe. Dr. Roylott then abandoned his attempts to establish himself in practice in London, and took us to live with him in the old ancestral house at Stoke Moran. The money which my mother had left was enough for all our wants, and there seemed to be no obstacle to our happiness.

"But a terrible change came over our step-father about this time. Instead of making friends and exchanging visits with our neighbors, who had at first

Regency: period of British history from 1811 to 1820 when George (later George IV) ruled in place of the incapacitated George III.

been overjoyed to see a Roylott of Stoke Moran back in the old family seat, he shut himself up in his house, and seldom came out save to indulge in ferocious quarrels with whoever might cross his path. Violence of temper approaching to mania has been hereditary in the men of the family, and in my step-father's case it had, I believe, been increased by his long residence in the tropics. A series of disgraceful brawls took place, two of which ended in the police-court, until at last he became the terror of the village, and the folks would fly at his approach, for he is a man of immense strength, and absolutely uncontrollable in his anger.

"Last week he hurled the local blacksmith over a parapet into a stream; and it was only by paying over all the money which I could gather together that I was able to avert another public exposure. He had no friends at all save the wandering gypsies, and he would give these vagabonds leave to encamp upon the few acres of bramble-covered land which represent the family estate, and would accept in return the hospitality of their tents, wandering away with them sometimes for weeks on end. He has a passion also for Indian animals, which are sent over to him by a correspondent, and he has at this moment a cheetah and a baboon, which wander freely over his grounds, and are feared by the villagers almost as much as their master.

"You can imagine from what I say that my poor sister Julia and I had no great pleasure in our lives. No servant would stay with us, and for a long time we did all the work of the house. She was but thirty at the time of her death, and yet her hair had already begun to whiten, even as mine has."

"Your sister is dead, then?"

"She died just two years ago, and it is of her death that I wish to speak to you. You can understand that, living the life which I have described, we were little likely to see anyone of our own age and position. We had, however, an aunt, my mother's maiden sister, Miss Honoria Westphail, who lives near Harrow, and we were occasionally allowed to pay short visits at this lady's house. Julia went there at Christmas two years ago, and met there a half-pay major of marines, to whom she became engaged. My step-father learned of the engagement when my sister returned, and offered no objection to the marriage; but within a fortnight of the day which had been fixed for the wedding, the terrible event occurred which has deprived me of my only companion."

Sherlock Holmes had been leaning back in his chair with his eyes closed and his head sunk in a cushion, but he half opened his lids now and glanced at his visitor.

"Pray be precise as to details," said he.

"It is easy for me to be so, for every event of that dreadful time is seared into my memory. The manorhouse is, as I have already said, very old, and only one wing is now inhabited. The bedrooms in this wing are on the ground floor, the sitting-rooms being in the central block of the buildings. Of these bedrooms the first is Dr. Roylott's, the second my sister's, and the third my own. There is no communication between them, but they all open out into the same corridor. Do I make myself plain?"

"Perfectly so."

"The windows of the three rooms open out upon the lawn. That fatal night Dr. Roylott had gone to his room early, though we knew that he had not retired to rest, for my sister was troubled by the smell of the strong Indian cigars which it was his custom to smoke. She left her room, therefore, and came into mine, where she sat for some time, chatting about her approaching wedding. At eleven o'clock she rose to leave me, but she paused at the door and looked back.

" 'Tell me, Helen,' said she, 'have you ever heard any one whistle in the dead of the night?'

" 'Never,' said I.

" 'I suppose that you could not possibly whistle, yourself, in your sleep?'

" 'Certainly not. But why?'

" 'Because during the last few nights I have always, about three in the morning, heard a low, clear whistle. I am a light sleeper, and it has awakened me. I cannot tell where it came from — perhaps from the next room, perhaps from the lawn. I thought that I would just ask you whether you had heard it.'

" 'No, I have not. It must be those wretched gypsies in the plantation.'

" 'Very likely. And yet if it were on the lawn, I wonder that you did not hear it also.'

" 'Ah, but I sleep more heavily than you.'

" 'Well, it is of no great consequence, at any rate.' She smiled back at me, closed my door, and a few moments later I heard her key turn in the lock.''

"Indeed," said Holmes. "Was it your custom always to lock yourselves in at night?"

"Always."

"And why?"

"I think that I mentioned to you that the doctor kept a cheetah and a baboon. We had no feeling of security unless our doors were locked."

"Quite so. Pray proceed with your statement."

"I could not sleep that night. A vague feeling of impending misfortune impressed me. My sister and I, you will recollect, were twins, and you know how subtle are the links which bind two souls which are so closely allied. It was a wild night. The wind was howling outside, and the rain was beating and splashing against the windows. Suddenly, amid all the hubbub of the gale, there burst forth the wild scream of a terrified woman. I knew that it was my sister's voice. I sprang from my bed, wrapped a shawl round me, and rushed into the corridor. As I opened my door I seemed to hear a low whistle, such as my sister described, and a few moments later a clanging sound, as if a mass of metal had fallen. As I ran down the passage my sister's door was unlocked, and revolved slowly upon its hinges. I stared at it horror-stricken, not knowing what was about to issue from it. By the light of the corridor-lamp I saw my sister appear at the opening, her face blanched with terror, her hands groping for help, her whole figure swaying to and fro like that of a drunkard. I ran to her and threw my arms round her, but at that moment her knees seemed to give way and she fell to the ground. She writhed as one who is in terrible pain, and her limbs were dreadfully convulsed. At first I thought that she had not recognized me, but as I bent over her, she suddenly shrieked out, in a voice which I shall never forget: 'Oh, my God! Helen! It was the band! The speckled band!' There was something else which she would fain have said, and she stabbed with her finger into the air in the direction of the doctor's room, but a fresh convulsion seized her and choked her words. I rushed out, calling loudly for my step-father, and I met him hastening from his room in his dressing-gown. When he reached my sister's side she was unconscious, and though he poured brandy down her throat and sent for medical aid from the village, all efforts were in vain, for she slowly sank and died without having recovered her consciousness. Such was the dreadful end of my beloved sister."

"One moment," said Holmes; "are you sure about this whistle and metallic sound? Could you swear to it?"

"That was what the county coroner asked me at the inquiry. It is my strong impression that I heard it, and yet, among the crash of the gale and the creaking of an old house, I may possibly have been deceived."

"Was your sister dressed?"

"No, she was in her night-dress. In her right hand was found the charred stump of a match, and in her left a match-box."

"Showing that she had struck a light and looked about her when the alarm took place. That is important. And what conclusions did the coroner come to?"

"He investigated the case with great care, for Dr. Roylott's conduct had long been notorious in the county, but he was unable to find any satisfactory cause of death. My evidence showed that the door had been fastened upon the inner side, and the windows were blocked by old-fashioned shutters with broad iron bars, which were secured every night. The walls were carefully sounded, and were shown to be quite solid all round, and the flooring was also thoroughly examined, with the same result. The chimney is wide, but is barred up by four large staples. It is certain, therefore, that my sister was quite alone when she met her end. Besides, there were no marks of any violence upon her."

"How about poison?"

"The doctors examined her for it, but without success."

"What do you think that this unfortunate lady died of, then?"

"It is my belief that she died of pure fear and nervous shock, though what it was that frightened her I cannot imagine."

"Were there gypsies in the plantation at the time?"

"Yes, there are nearly always some there."

"Ah, and what did you gather from this allusion to a band — a speckled band?"

"Sometimes I have thought that it was merely the wild talk of delirium, sometimes that it may have referred to some band of people, perhaps to these very gypsies in the plantation. I do not know whether the spotted handkerchiefs which so many of them wear over their heads might have suggested the strange adjective which she used."

Holmes shook his head like a man who is far from being satisfied.

"These are very deep waters," said he; "pray go on with your narrative."

"Two years have passed since then, and my life had been until lately lonelier than ever. A month ago, however, a dear friend, whom I have known for many years, has done me the honor to ask my hand in marriage. His name is Armitage — Percy Armitage — the second son of Mr. Armitage, of Crane Water, near Reading. My step-father has offered no opposition to the match, and we are to be married in the course of the spring. Two days ago some repairs were started in the west wing of the building, and my bedroom wall has been pierced, so that I have had to move into the chamber in which my sister died, and to sleep in the very bed in which she slept.

"Imagine, then, my thrill of terror when last night, as I lay awake, thinking over her terrible fate, I suddenly heard in the silence of the night the low whistle which had been the herald of her own death. I sprang up and lit the lamp, but nothing was to be seen in the room. I was too shaken to go to bed again, however; so I dressed, and as soon as it was daylight I slipped down, got a dog-cart at the 'Crown Inn,' which is opposite, and drove to Leatherhead, from whence I have come on this morning with the one object of seeing you and asking your advice."

"You have done wisely," said my friend. "But have you told me all?"

"Yes, all."

"Miss Roylott, you have not. You are screening your step-father."

"Why, what do you mean?"

For answer Holmes pushed back the frill of black lace which fringed the hand that lay upon our visitor's knee. Five little livid spots, the marks of four fingers and a thumb, were printed upon the white wrist.

"You have been cruelly used," said Holmes.

The lady colored deeply and covered over her injured wrist. "He is a hard man," she said, "and perhaps he hardly knows his own strength."

There was a long silence, during which Holmes leaned his chin upon his hands and stared into the crackling fire.

"This is a very deep business," he said, at last. "There are a thousand details which I should desire to know before I decide upon our course of action. Yet we have not a moment to lose. If we were to come to Stoke Moran today, would it be possible for us to see over these rooms without the knowledge of your step-father?"

"As it happens, he spoke of coming into town today upon some most important business. It is probable that he will be away all day, and that there would be nothing to disturb you. We have a housekeeper now, but she is old and foolish, and I could easily get her out of the way."

"Excellent. You are not averse to this trip, Watson?"

"By no means."

"Then we shall both come. What are you going to do yourself?"

"I have one or two things which I would wish to do now that I am in town. But I shall return by the twelve o'clock train, so as to be there in time for your coming."

"And you may expect us early in the afternoon. I have myself some small business matters to attend to. Will you not wait and breakfast?"

"No, I must go. My heart is lightened already since I have confided my trouble to you. I shall look forward to seeing you again this afternoon." She dropped her thick black veil over her face and glided from the room.

"And what do you think of it all, Watson?" asked Sherlock Holmes, leaning back in his chair.

"It seems to me to be a most dark and sinister business."

"Dark enough and sinister enough."

"Yet if the lady is correct in saying that the flooring and walls are sound, and that the door, window, and chimney are impassable, then her sister must have been undoubtedly alone when she met her mysterious end."

"What becomes, then, of these nocturnal whistles, and what of the very peculiar words of the dying woman?"

"I cannot think."

"When you combine the ideas of whistles at night, the presence of a band of gypsies who are on intimate terms with this old doctor, the fact that we have every reason to believe the doctor has an interest in preventing his step-daughter's marriage, the dying allusion to a band, and, finally, the fact that Miss Helen Stoner heard a metallic clang, which might have been caused by one of those metal bars which secured the shutters falling back into its place, I think that there is good ground to think that the mystery may be cleared along those lines."

"But what, then, did the gypsies do?"

"I cannot imagine."

"I see many objections to any such theory."

"And so do I. It is precisely for that reason that we are going to Stoke Moran this day. I want to see whether the objections are fatal, or if they may be explained away. But what, in the name of the devil!"

The ejaculation had been drawn from my companion by the fact that our door had been suddenly dashed open, and that a huge man had framed himself in the aperture. His costume was a peculiar mixture of the professional and of the agricultural, having a black top-hat, a long frock-coat, and a pair of high gaiters, with a hunting-crop swinging in his hand. So tall was he that his hat actually brushed the cross-bar of the doorway, and his breadth seemed to span it across from side to side. A large face, seared with a thousand wrinkles, burned yellow with the sun, and marked with every evil passion, was turned from one to the other of us, while his deep-set, bile-shot eyes, and his high, thin, fleshless nose, gave him somewhat the resemblance to a fierce old bird of prey.

"Which of you is Holmes?" asked this apparition.

"My name, sir; but you have the advantage of me," said my companion, quietly.

"I am Dr. Grimesby Roylott, of Stoke Moran."

"Indeed, doctor," said Holmes, blandly. "Pray take a seat."

"I will do nothing of the kind. My step-daughter has been here. I have traced her. What has she been saying to you?"

"It is a little cold for the time of the year," said Holmes.

"What has she been saying to you?" screamed the old man, furiously.

"But I have heard that the crocuses promise well," continued my companion, imperturbably.

"Ha! You put me off, do you?" said our new visitor, taking a step forward and shaking his hunting-crop. "I know you, you scoundrel! I have heard of you before. You are Holmes, the meddler."

My friend smiled.

"Holmes, the busybody!"

His smile broadened.

"Holmes, the Scotland-yard Jack-in-office!"

Holmes chuckled heartily. "Your conversation is most entertaining," said he. "When you go out, close the door, for there is a decided draught."

"I will go when I have said my say. Don't you dare to meddle with my affairs. I know that Miss Stoner has been here. I traced her! I am a dangerous man to fall foul of! See here." He stepped swiftly forward, seized the poker, and bent it into a curve with his huge brown hands.

"See that you keep yourself out of my grip," he snarled; and hurling the twisted poker into the fireplace, he strode out of the room.

"He seems a very amiable person," said Holmes, laughing. "I am not quite so bulky, but if he had remained I might have shown him that my grip was not much more feeble than his own." As he spoke he picked up the steel poker, and with a sudden effort straightened it out again.

"Fancy his having the insolence to confound me with the official detective force! This incident gives zest to our investigation, however, and I only trust that our little friend will not suffer from her imprudence in allowing this brute to trace her. And now, Watson, we shall order breakfast, and afterward I shall walk down to Doctors' Commons, where I hope to get some data which may help us in this matter."

It was nearly one o'clock when Sherlock Holmes returned from his excursion. He held in his hand a sheet of blue paper, scrawled over with notes and figures.

"I have seen the will of the deceased wife," said he. "To determine its exact meaning I have been obliged to work out the present prices of the investments with which it is concerned. The total income, which at the time of the wife's death was little short of 1,100 pounds, is now, through the fall in agricultural prices, not more than 750 pounds. Each daughter can claim an income of 250 pounds, in case of marriage. It is evident, therefore, that if both girls had married, this beauty would have had a mere pittance, while even one of them would cripple him to a very serious extent. My morning's work has not been wasted, since it has proved that he had the very strongest motives for standing in the way of anything of the sort. And now, Watson, this is too serious for dawdling, especially as the old man is aware that we are interesting ourselves in his affairs; so if you are ready, we shall call a cab and drive to Waterloo. I should be very much obliged if you would slip your revolver into your pocket. An Eley's No. 2 is an excellent argument with gentlemen who can twist steel pokers into knots. That and a toothbrush are, I think, all that we need."

At Waterloo, we were fortunate in catching a train for Leatherhead, where we hired a trap at the station inn, and drove for four or five miles through the lovely Surrey lanes. It was a perfect day, with a bright sun and a few fleecy clouds in the heavens. The trees and wayside hedges were just throwing out their first green shoots, and the air was full of the pleasant smell of the moist earth. To me at least there was a strange contrast between the sweet promise of the spring and the sinister quest upon which we were engaged. My companion sat in front of the trap, his arms folded, his hat pulled down over his eyes, and his chin sunk upon his breast, buried in the deepest thought. Suddenly, however, he started, tapped me on the shoulder, and pointed over the meadows.

"Look there!" said he.

A heavily timbered park stretched up in a gentle slope, thickening into a grove at the highest point. From amid the branches there jutted out the gray gables and high roof-tree of a very old mansion.

"Stoke Moran?" said he.

"Yes, sir, that be the house of Dr. Grimesby Roylott," remarked the driver.

"There is some building going on there," said Holmes; "that is where we are going."

"There's the village," said the driver, pointing to a cluster of roofs some distance to the left; "but if you want to get to the house, you'll find it shorter to get over this stile, and so by the foot-path over the fields. There it is, where the lady is walking."

"And the lady, I fancy, is Miss Stoner," observed Holmes, shading his eyes. "Yes, I think we had better do as you suggest."

We got off, paid our fare, and the trap rattled back on its way to Leatherhead.

"I thought it as well," said Holmes, as we climbed the stile, "that this fellow should think we had come here as architects or on some definite business. It may stop his gossip. Good-afternoon, Miss Stoner. You see that we have been as good as our word."

Our client of the morning had hurried forward to meet us with a face which spoke her joy. "I have been waiting so eagerly for you!" she cried, shaking hands with us warmly. "All has turned out splendidly. Dr. Roylott has gone to town, and it is unlikely that he will be back before evening."

"We have had the pleasure of making the doctor's acquaintance," said Holmes, and in a few words he sketched out what had occurred. Miss Stoner turned white to the lips as she listened.

"Good heavens!" she cried, "he has followed me, then."

"So it appears."

"He is so cunning that I never know when I am safe from him. What will he say when he returns?"

"He must guard himself, for he may find that there is some one more cunning than himself upon his track. You must lock yourself up from him tonight. If he is violent, we shall take you away to your aunt's at Harrow. Now, we must make the best use of our time, so kindly take us at once to the rooms which we are to examine."

The building was of gray, lichen-blotched stone, with a high central portion, and two curving wings, like the claws of a crab, thrown out on each side. In one of these wings the windows were broken, and blocked with wooden boards, while the roof was partly caved in, a picture of ruin. The central portion was in little better repair, but the right-hand block was comparatively modern, and the blinds in the windows, with the blue smoke curling up from the chimneys, showed that this was where the family resided. Some scaffolding had been erected against the end wall, and the stone-work had been broken into, but there were no signs of any workmen at the moment of our visit. Holmes walked slowly up and down the ill-trimmed lawn, and examined with deep attention the outsides of the windows.

"This, I take it, belongs to the room in which you used to sleep, the center one to your sister's, and the one next to the main building to Dr. Roylott's chamber?"

"Exactly so. But I am now sleeping in the middle one."

"Pending the alterations, as I understand. By-the-way, there does not seem to be any very pressing need for repairs at that end wall."

"There were none. I believe that it was an excuse to move me from my room."

"Ah! that is suggestive. Now, on the other side of this narrow wing runs the corridor from which these three rooms open. There are windows in it, of course?"

"Yes, but very small ones. Too narrow for any one to pass through."

"As you both locked your doors at night, your rooms were unapproachable from that side. Now, would you have the kindness to go into your room and bar your shutters."

Miss Stoner did so, and Holmes, after a careful examination through the open window, endeavored in every way to force the shutter open, but without success. There was no slit through which a knife could be passed to raise the bar. Then with his lens he tested the hinges, but they were of solid iron, built firmly into the massive masonry. "Hum!" said he, scratching his chin in some perplexity; "my theory certainly presents some difficulties. No one could pass these shutters if they were bolted. Well, we shall see if the inside throws any light upon the matter."

A small side door led into the whitewashed corridor from which the three bedrooms opened. Holmes refused to examine the third chamber, so we passed at once to the second, that in which Miss Stoner was now sleeping, and in which her sister had met with her fate. It was a homely little room, with a low ceiling and a gaping fireplace, after the fashion of old country-houses. A brown chest of drawers stood in one corner, a narrow white-counterpaned bed in another, and a dressing-table on the left-hand side of the window. These articles, with two small wicker-work chairs, made up all the furniture in the room, save for a square of Wilton carpet in the center. The boards round and the paneling of the walls were of brown, worm-eaten oak, so old and discolored that it may have dated from the original building of the house. Holmes drew one of the chairs into a corner and sat silent, while his eyes traveled round and round and up and down, taking in every detail of the apartment.

"Where does that bell communicate with?" he asked, at last, pointing to a thick bell-rope which hung down beside the bed, the tassel actually lying upon the pillow.

"It goes to the housekeeper's room."

"It looks newer than the other things?"

"Yes, it was only put there a couple of years ago."

"Your sister asked for it, I suppose?"

"No, I never heard of her using it. We used always to get what we wanted for ourselves."

"Indeed, it seemed unnecessary to put so nice a bell-pull there. You will excuse me for a few minutes while I satisfy myself as to this floor." He threw himself down upon his face with his lens in hand, and crawled swiftly backward, examining minutely the cracks between the boards. Then he did the same with the wood-work with which the chamber was paneled. Finally he walked over to the bed, and spent some time in staring at it, and in running his eye up and down the wall. Finally he took the bell-rope in his hand and gave it a brisk tug.

"Why, it's a dummy," said he.

"Won't it ring?"

"No, it is not even attached to a wire. This is very interesting. You can see now that it is fastened to a hook just above where the little opening for the ventilator is."

"How very absurd! I never noticed that before."

"Very strange!" muttered Holmes, pulling at the rope. "There are one or two very singular points about this room. For example, what a fool a builder must be to open a ventilator into another room, when, with the same trouble, he might have communicated with the outside air!"

"That is also quite modern," said the lady.

"Done about the same time as the bell-rope?" remarked Holmes.

"Yes, there were several little changes carried out about that time."

"They seem to have been of a most interesting character — dummy bell-ropes, and ventilators which do not ventilate. With your permission, Miss Stoner, we shall now carry our researches into the inner apartment."

Dr. Grimesby Roylott's chamber was larger than that of his stepdaughter, but was as plainly furnished. A camp-bed, a small wooden shelf full of books, mostly of a technical character, an arm-chair beside the bed, a plain wooden chair against the wall, a round table, and a large iron safe were the principal things which met the eye.

Holmes walked slowly round and examined each and all of them with the keenest interest.

"What's in here?" he asked, tapping the safe.

"My step-father's business papers."

"Oh, you have seen inside, then?"

"Only once, some years ago. I remember that it was full of papers."

"There isn't a cat in it, for example?"

"No. What a strange idea!"

"Well, look at this!" He took up a small saucer of milk which stood on the top of it.

"No; we don't keep a cat. But there is a cheetah and a baboon."

"Ah, yes, of course! Well, a cheetah is just a big cat, and yet a saucer of milk does not go very far in satisfying its wants, I dare say. There is one point which I should wish to determine." He squatted down in front of the wooden chair, and examined the seat of it with the greatest attention.

"Thank you. That is quite settled," said he, rising and putting his lens in his pocket. "Hello! — Here is something interesting!"

The object which had caught his eye was a small doglash hung on one corner of the bed. The lash, however, was curled upon itself, and tied so as to make a loop of whip-cord.

"What do you make of that, Watson?"

"It's a common enough lash. But I don't know why it should be tied."

"That is not quite so common, is it? Ah, me! it's a wicked world, and when a clever man turns his brains to crime it is the worst of all. I think that I have seen enough now, Miss Stoner, and with your permission we shall walk out upon the lawn."

I had never seen my friend's face so grim or his brow so dark as it was when we turned from the scene of this investigation. We had walked several times up and down the lawn, neither Miss Stoner nor myself liking to break in upon his thoughts before he roused himself from his reverie.

"It is very essential, Miss Stoner," said he, "that you should absolutely follow my advice in every respect."

"I shall most certainly do so."

"The matter is too serious for any hesitation. Your life may depend upon your compliance."

"I assure you that I am in your hands."

"In the first place, both my friend and I must spend the night in your room."

Both Miss Stoner and I gazed at him in astonishment.

"Yes, it must be so. Let me explain. I believe that that is the village inn over there?"

"Yes, that is the 'Crown.'"

"Very good. Your windows would be visible from there?"

"Certainly."

"You must confine yourself to your room, on pretense of a headache, when your step-father comes back. Then when you hear him retire for the night, you must open the shutters of your window, undo the hasp, put your lamp there as a signal to us, and then withdraw quietly with everything which you are likely to want into the room which you used to occupy. I have no doubt that, in spite of the repairs, you could manage there for one night."

"Oh, yes, easily."

"The rest you will leave in our hands."

"But what will you do?"

"We shall spend the night in your room, and we shall investigate the cause of this noise which has disturbed you."

"I believe, Mr. Holmes, that you have already made up your mind," said Miss Stoner, laying her hand upon my companion's sleeve.

"Perhaps I have."

"Then, for pity's sake, tell me what was the cause of my sister's death."

"I should prefer to have clearer proofs before I speak."

"You can at least tell me whether my own thought is correct, and if she died from some sudden fright."

"No, I do not think so. I think that there was probably some more tangible cause. And now, Miss Stoner, we must leave you, for if Dr. Roylott returned and saw us, our journey would be in vain. Goodbye, and be brave, for if you will do what I have told you, you may rest assured that we shall soon drive away the dangers that threaten you."

Sherlock Holmes and I had no difficulty in engaging a bedroom and sitting-room at the "Crown Inn." They were on the upper floor, and from our window we could command a view of the avenue gate, and of the inhabited wing of Stoke Moran Manor-House. At dusk we saw Dr. Grimesby Roylott drive past, his huge form looming up beside the little figure of the lad who drove him. The boy had some slight difficulty in undoing the heavy iron gates, and we heard the hoarse roar of the doctor's voice, and saw the fury with which he shook his clenched fists at him. The trap drove on, and a few minutes later we saw a sudden light spring up among the trees as the lamp was lit in one of the sitting-rooms.

"Do you know, Watson," said Holmes, as we sat together in the gathering darkness, "I have really some scruples as to taking you tonight. There is a distinct element of danger."

"Can I be of assistance?"

"Your presence might be invaluable."

"Then I shall certainly come."

"It is very kind of you."

"You speak of danger. You have evidently seen more in these rooms than was visible to me."

"No, but I fancy that I may have deduced a little more. I imagine that you saw all that I did."

"I saw nothing remarkable save the bell-rope, and what purpose that could answer I confess is more than I can imagine."

"You saw the ventilator, too?"

"Yes, but I do not think that it is such a very unusual thing to have a small opening between two rooms. It was so small that a rat could hardly pass through."

"I knew that we should find a ventilator before ever we came to Stoke Moran."

"My dear Holmes!"

"Oh, yes, I did. You remember in her statement she said that her sister could smell Dr. Roylott's cigar. Now, of course, that suggested at once that there must be a communication between the two rooms. It could only be a small one, or it would have been remarked upon at the coroner's inquiry. I deduced a ventilator."

"But what harm can there be in that?"

"Well, there is at least a curious coincidence of dates. A ventilator is made, a cord is hung, and a lady who sleeps in the bed dies. Does not that strike you?"

"I cannot as yet see any connection."

"Did you observe anything very peculiar about that bed?"

"No."

"It was clamped to the floor. Did you ever see a bed fastened like that before?"

"I cannot say that I have."

"The lady could not move her bed. It must always be in the same relative position to the ventilator and to the rope — for so we may call it, since it was clearly never meant for a bell-pull."

"Holmes," I cried, "I seem to see dimly what you are hinting at! We are only just in time to prevent some subtle and horrible crime."

"Subtle enough and horrible enough. When a doctor does go wrong, he is the first of criminals. He has nerve, and he has knowledge. Palmer and Pritchard were among the heads of their profession. This man strikes even deeper; but I think, Watson, that we shall be able to strike deeper still. But we shall have horrors enough before the night is over; for goodness' sake let us have a quiet pipe, and turn our minds for a few hours to something more cheerful."

About nine o'clock the light among the trees was extinguished, and all was dark in the direction of the Manor-House. Two hours passed slowly away, and then, suddenly, just at the stroke of eleven, a single bright light shone out in front of us.

"That is our signal," said Holmes, springing to his feet; "it comes from the middle window."

As we passed out he exchanged a few words with the landlord, explaining that we were going on a late visit to an acquaintance, and that it was possible that we might spend the night there. A moment later we were out on the dark road, a chill wind blowing in our faces, and one yellow light twinkling in front of us through the gloom to guide us on our somber errand.

There was little difficulty in entering the grounds, for unrepaired breaches gaped in the park wall. Making our way among the trees, we reached the lawn, crossed it, and were about to enter through the window, when out from a clump of laurel-bushes there darted what seemed to be a hideous and dis-torted child, who threw itself upon the grass with writhing limbs, and then ran swiftly across the lawn into the darkness.

"My God!" I whispered; "did you see it?"

Holmes was for the moment as startled as I. His hand closed like a vise upon my wrist in his agitation. Then he broke into a low laugh, and put his lips to my ear.

"It is a nice household," he murmured. "That is the baboon."

I had forgotten the strange pets which the doctor affected. There was a cheetah, too; perhaps we might find it upon our shoulders at any moment. I confess that I felt easier in my mind when, after following Holmes' example and slipping off my shoes, I found myself inside the bedroom. My companion noiselessly closed the shutters, moved the lamp onto the table, and cast his eyes round the room. All was as we had seen it in the daytime. Then creeping up to me and making a trumpet of his hand, he whispered into my ear again so gently that it was all that I could do to distinguish the words:

"The least sound would be fatal to our plans."

I nodded to show that I had heard.

"We must sit without light. He would see it through the ventilator."

I nodded again.

"Do not go asleep; your very life may depend upon it. Have your pistol ready in case we should need it. I will sit on the side of the bed, and you in that chair."

I took out my revolver and laid it on the corner of the table.

Holmes had brought up a long, thin cane, and this he placed upon the bed beside him. By it he laid the box of matches and the stump of a candle. Then he turned down the lamp, and we were left in darkness.

How shall I ever forget that dreadful vigil? I could not hear a sound, not even the drawing of a breath, and yet I knew that my companion sat open-eyed, within a few feet of me, in the same state of nervous tension in which I was myself. The shutters cut off the least ray of light, and we waited in ab-solute darkness. From outside came the occasional cry of a night-bird, and once at our very window a long-drawn, cat-like whine, which told us that the cheetah was indeed at liberty. Far away we could hear the deep tones of the parish clock, which boomed out every quarter of an hour. How long they seemed, those quarters! Twelve struck, and one and two and three, and still we sat waiting silently for whatever might befall.

Suddenly there was the momentary gleam of a light up in the direction of the ventilator, which vanished immediately, but was succeeded by a strong smell of burning oil and heated metal. Someone in the next room had lit a dark-lantern. I heard a gentle sound of movement, and then all was silent once more, though the smell grew stronger. For half an hour I sat with straining ears. Then suddenly another sound became audible — a very gentle, soothing sound, like that of a small jet of steam escaping continually from a kettle. The instant that we heard it, Holmes sprang from the bed, stuck a match, and lashed furiously with his cane at the bell-pull.

"You see it, Watson?" he yelled. "You see it?"

But I saw nothing. At the moment when Holmes struck the light I heard a low, clear whistle, but the sudden glare flashing into my weary eyes made it impossible for me to tell what it was at which my friend lashed so savagely. I could, however, see that his face was deadly pale, and filled with horror and loathing.

He had ceased to strike, and was gazing up at the ventilator, when suddenly there broke from the silence of the night the most horrible cry to which I have ever listened. It swelled up louder and louder, a hoarse yell of pain and fear and anger all mingled in the one dreadful shriek. They say that away down in the village, and even in the distant parsonage, that cry raised the sleepers from their beds. It struck cold to our hearts, and I stood gazing at Holmes, and he at me, until the last echoes of it had died away into the silence from which it rose.

"What can it mean?" I gasped.

"It means that it is all over," Holmes answered. "And perhaps, after all, it is for the best. Take your pistol, and we will enter Dr. Roylott's room."

With a grave face he lit the lamp and led the way down the corridor. Twice he struck at the chamber door without any reply from within. Then he turned the handle and entered, I at his heels, with the cocked pistol in my hand.

It was a singular sight which met our eyes. On the table stood a dark-lantern with the shutter half open, throwing a brilliant beam of light upon the iron safe, the door of which was ajar. Beside this table, on the wooden chair, sat Dr. Grimesby Roylott, clad in a long gray dressing gown, his bare ankles protruding beneath, and his feet thrust into red heelless Turkish slippers. Across his lap lay the short stock with the long lash which we had noticed during the day. His chin was cocked upward and his eyes were fixed in a dreadful, rigid stare at the corner of the ceiling. Round his brow he had a peculiar yellow band, with brownish speckles, which seemed to be bound tightly round his head. As we entered he made neither sound nor motion.

"The band! the speckled band!" whispered Holmes.

I took a step forward. In an instant his strange headgear began to move, and there reared itself from among his hair the squat diamond-shaped head and puffed neck of a loathsome serpent.

"It is a swamp adder!" cried Holmes; "the deadliest snake in India. He has died within ten seconds of being bitten. Violence does, in truth, recoil upon the violent, and the schemer falls into the pit which he digs for another. Let us thrust this creature back into its den, and we can then remove Miss Stoner to some place of shelter, and let the county police know what has happened."

As he spoke he drew the dog-whip swiftly from the dead man's lap, and throwing the noose round the reptile's neck, he drew it from its horrid perch, and carrying it at arm's-length, threw it into the iron safe, which he closed upon it.

Such are the true facts of the death of Dr. Grimesby Roylott, of Stoke Moran. It is not necessary that I should prolong a narrative which has already run to too great a length, by telling how we broke the sad news to the terrified girl, how we conveyed her by the morning train to the care of her good aunt at Harrow, of how the slow process of official inquiry came to the conclusion that the doctor met his fate while indiscreetly playing with a dangerous pet. The little which I had yet to learn of the case was told me by Sherlock Holmes as we traveled back next day.

"I had," said he, "come to an entirely erroneous conclusion, which shows, my dear Watson, how dangerous it always is to reason from insufficient data. The presence of the gypsies, and the use of the word 'band,' which was used by the poor girl, no doubt to explain the appearance which she had caught a hurried glimpse of by the light of her match, were sufficient to put me upon an entirely wrong scent. I can only claim the merit that I instantly reconsidered my position when, however, it became clear to me that whatever danger threatened an occupant of the room could not come either from the window or the door. My attention was speedily drawn, as I have already remarked to you, to this ventilator, and to the bell-rope which hung down to the bed. The discovery that this was a dummy, and that the bed was clamped to the floor, instantly gave rise to the suspicion that the rope was there as bridge for something passing through the hole and coming to the bed. The idea of a snake instantly occurred to me, and when I coupled it with my knowledge that the doctor was furnished with a supply of creatures from India, I felt that I was probably on the right track. The idea of using a form of poison which could not possibly be discovered by any chemical test was just such a one as would occur to a clever and ruthless man who had had an Eastern training. The rapidity with which such a poison would take effect would also, from his point of view, be an advantage. It would be a sharp-eyed coroner, indeed, who could distinguish the two little dark punctures which would show where the poison fangs had done their work. Then I thought of the whistle. Of course he must recall the snake before the morning light revealed it to the victim. He had trained it, probably by the use of the milk which we saw, to return to him when summoned. He would put it through this ventilator at the hour that he thought best, with the certainty that it would crawl down the rope and land on the bed. It might not bite the occupant, perhaps she might escape every night for a week, but sooner or later she must fall a victim.

"I had come to these conclusions before ever I had entered his room. An inspection of his chair showed me that he had been in the habit of standing on it, which of course would be necessary in order that he should reach the ventilator. The sight of the safe, the saucer of milk, and the loop of whip-cord were enough to finally dispel any doubts which may have remained. The metallic clang heard by Miss Stoner was obviously caused by her step-father hastily closing the door of his safe upon its terrible occupant. Having once made up my mind, you know the steps which I took in order to put the matter to the proof. I heard the creature hiss, as I have no doubt that you did also, and I instantly lit the light and attacked it."

"With the result of driving it through the ventilator."

"And also with the result of causing it to turn upon its master at the other side. Some of the blows of my cane came home, and roused its snakish temper, so that it flew upon the first person it saw. In this way I am no doubt indirectly responsible for Dr. Grimesby Roylott's death, and I cannot say that it is likely to weigh very heavily upon my conscience."

QUESTIONS

1. Willing to get out of bed at the beginning of the story, Watson observes, "I had no keener pleasure than in following Holmes in his professional investigations, and in admiring the rapid deductions, as swift as intuitions, and yet always founded on a logical basis, with which he unraveled the problems which were submitted to him." What wonderful deductions does Holmes make as the story unfolds?
2. What traits render Sherlock Holmes a unique character besides his powers of intellect?
3. What is there to be said for the author's choice of Watson as the narrator for the story, instead of Sherlock Holmes? Imagine the story told by Holmes himself in the first person. What would be lost?
4. What is striking or memorable about Dr. Grimesby Roylott when we first meet him? How early in the story do you suspect him to be a murderer?
5. Do the murder of Julia Stoner and the attempted murder of her sister Helen seem to you too ingeniously contrived? Discuss: are the criminal's methods plausible?
6. What do Dr. Roylott's strange pets add to the story — the baboon, glimpsed once, and the cheetah, that does not appear at all?
7. In what ways does "The Adventure of the Speckled Band" resemble a Gothic story?

Raymond Chandler (1888–1959)

I'LL BE WAITING   1950

At one o'clock in the morning, Carl, the night porter, turned down the last of three table lamps in the main lobby of the Windermere Hotel. The blue carpet darkened a shade or two and the walls drew back into remoteness. The chairs filled with shadowy loungers. In the corners were memories like cobwebs.

Tony Reseck yawned. He put his head on one side and listened to the frail, twittery music from the radio room beyond a dim arch at the far side of the lobby. He frowned. That should be his radio room after one A.M. Nobody should be in it. That red-haired girl was spoiling his nights.

The frown passed and a miniature of a smile quirked at the corners of his lips. He sat relaxed, a short, pale, paunchy, middle-aged man with long, delicate fingers clasped on the elk's tooth on his watch chain; the long delicate fingers of a sleight-of-hand artist, fingers with shiny, molded nails and tapering first joints, fingers a little spatulate at the ends. Handsome fingers. Tony

Reseck rubbed them gently together and there was peace in his quiet, sea-gray eyes.

The frown came back on his face. The music annoyed him. He got up with a curious litheness, all in one piece, without moving his clasped hands from the watch chain. At one moment he was leaning back relaxed, and the next he was standing balanced on his feet, perfectly still, so that the movement of rising seemed to be a thing imperfectly perceived, an error of vision.

He walked with small, polished shoes delicately across the blue carpet and under the arch. The music was louder. It contained the hot, acid blare, the frenetic, jittering runs of a jam session. It was too loud. The red-haired girl sat there and stared silently at the fretted part of the big radio cabinet as though she could see the band with its fixed professional grin and the sweat running down its back. She was curled up with her feet under her on a davenport which seemed to contain most of the cushions in the room. She was tucked among them carefully, like a corsage in the florist's tissue paper.

She didn't turn her head. She leaned there, one hand in a small fist on her peach-colored knee. She was wearing lounging pajamas of heavy ribbed silk embroidered with black lotus buds.

"You like Goodman, Miss Cressy?" Tony Reseck asked.

The girl moved her eyes slowly. The light in there was dim, but the violet of her eyes almost hurt. They were large, deep eyes without a trace of thought in them. Her face was classical and without expression.

She said nothing.

Tony smiled and moved his fingers at his sides, one by one, feeling them move. "You like Goodman, Miss Cressy?" he repeated gently.

"Not to cry over," the girl said tonelessly.

Tony rocked back on his heels and looked at her eyes. Large, deep, empty eyes. Or were they? He reached down and muted the radio.

"Don't get me wrong," the girl said. "Goodman makes money, and a lad that makes legitimate money these days is a lad you have to respect. But this jitterbug music gives me the backdrop of a beer flat. I like something with roses in it."

"Maybe you like Mozart," Tony said.

"Go on, kid me," the girl said.

"I wasn't kidding you, Miss Cressy. I think Mozart was the greatest man that ever lived — and Toscanini is his prophet."

"I thought you were the house dick." She put her head back on a pillow and stared at him through her lashes. "Make me some of that Mozart," she added.

"It's too late," Tony sighed. "You can't get it now."

She gave him another long lucid glance. "Got the eye on me, haven't you, flatfoot?" She laughed a little, almost under her breath. "What did I do wrong?"

Tony smiled his toy smile. "Nothing, Miss Cressy. Nothing at all. But you need some fresh air. You've been five days in this hotel and you haven't been outdoors. And you have a tower room."

She laughed again. "Make me a story about it. I'm bored."

"There was a girl here once had your suite. She stayed in the hotel a whole week, like you. Without going out at all, I mean. She didn't speak to anybody hardly. What do you think she did then?"

The girl eyed him gravely. "She jumped her bill."

He put his long delicate hand out and turned it slowly, fluttering the fingers, with an effect almost like a lazy wave breaking. "Unh-uh. She sent down for her bill and paid it. Then she told the hop to be back in half an hour for her suitcases. Then she went out on her balcony."

The girl leaned forward a little, her eyes still grave, one hand capping her peach-colored knee. "What did you say your name was?"

"Tony Reseck."

"Sounds like a hunky."

"Yeah," Tony said. "Polish."

"Go on, Tony."

"All the tower suites have private balconies, Miss Cressy. The walls of them are too low, for fourteen stories above the street. It was a dark night, that night, high clouds." He dropped his hand with a final gesture, a farewell gesture. "Nobody saw her jump. But when she hit, it was like a big gun going off."

"You're making it up, Tony." Her voice was a clean dry whisper of sound.

He smiled his toy smile. His quiet sea-gray eyes seemed almost to be smoothing the long waves of her hair. "Eve Cressy," he said musingly. "A name waiting for lights to be in."

"Waiting for a tall dark guy that's no good, Tony. You wouldn't care why. I was married to him once. I might be married to him again. You can make a lot of mistakes in just one lifetime." The hand on her knee opened slowly until the fingers were strained back as far as they would go. Then they closed quickly and tightly, and even in that dim light the knuckles shone like little polished bones. "I played him a low trick once. I put him in a bad place — without meaning to. You wouldn't care about that either. It's just that I owe him something."

He leaned over softly and turned the knob on the radio. A waltz formed itself dimly on the warm air. A tinsel waltz, but a waltz. He turned the volume up. The music gushed from the loud-speaker in a swirl of shadowed melody. Since Vienna died, all waltzes are shadowed.

The girl put her head on one side and hummed three or four bars and stopped with a sudden tightening of her mouth.

"Eve Cressy," she said. "It was in lights once. At a bum night club. A dive. They raided it and the lights went out."

He smiled at her almost mockingly. "It was no dive while you were there, Miss Cressy. That's the waltz the orchestra always played when the old porter walked up and down in front of the hotel entrance, all swelled up with his medals on his chest. *The Last Laugh.* Emil Jannings°. You wouldn't remember that one, Miss Cressy."

"Spring, Beautiful Spring," she said. "No, I never saw it."

He walked three steps away from her and turned. "I have to go upstairs and palm doorknobs. I hope I didn't bother you. You ought to go to bed now. It's pretty late."

The tinsel waltz stopped and a voice began to talk. The girl spoke through the voice, "You really thought something like that — about the balcony?"

He nodded. "I might have," he said softly. "I don't any more."

The Last Laugh. Emil Jannings: Reseck is recalling a classic German silent film of 1925, in which Jannings starred.

"No chance, Tony." Her smile was a dim lost leaf. "Come and talk to me some more. Redheads don't jump, Tony. They hang on — and wither."

He looked at her gravely for a moment and then moved away over the carpet. The porter was standing in the archway that led to the main lobby. Tony hadn't looked that way yet, but he knew somebody was there. He always knew if anybody was close to him. He could hear the grass grow, like the donkey in *The Blue Bird*°.

The porter jerked his chin at him urgently. His broad face above the uniform collar looked sweaty and excited. Tony stepped up close to him and they went together through the arch and out to the middle of the dim lobby.

"Trouble?" Tony asked wearily.

"There's a guy outside to see you, Tony. He won't come in. I'm doing a wipe-off on the plate glass of the doors and he comes up beside me, a tall guy. 'Get Tony,' he says, out of the side of his mouth."

Tony said, "Uh-huh," and looked at the porter's pale blue eyes. "Who was it?"

"Al, he said to say he was."

Tony's face became as expressionless as dough. "Okay." He started to move off.

The porter caught his sleeve. "Listen, Tony. You got any enemies?"

Tony laughed politely, his face still like dough.

"Listen, Tony." The porter held his sleeve tightly. "There's a big black car down the block, the other way from the hacks. There's a guy standing beside it with his foot on the running board. This guy that spoke to me, he wears a dark-colored, wrap-around overcoat with a high collar turned up against his ears. His hat's way low. You can't hardly see his face. He says, 'Get Tony,' out of the side of his mouth. You ain't got any enemies, have you, Tony?"

"Only the finance company," Tony said. "Beat it."

He walked slowly and a little stiffly across the blue carpet, up the three shallow steps to the entrance lobby with the three elevators on one side and the desk on the other. Only one elevator was working. Beside the open doors, his arms folded, the night operator stood silent in a neat blue uniform with silver facings. A lean, dark Mexican named Gomez. A new boy, breaking in on the night shift.

The other side was the desk, rose marble, with the night clerk leaning on it delicately. A small neat man with a wispy reddish mustache and cheeks so rosy they looked rouged. He stared at Tony and poked a nail at his mustache.

Tony pointed a stiff index finger at him, folded the other three fingers tight to his palm, and flicked his thumb up and down on the stiff finger. The clerk touched the other side of his mustache and looked bored.

Tony went on past the closed and darkened newsstand and the side entrance to the drugstore, out to the brassbound plate-glass doors. He stopped just inside them and took a deep, hard breath. He squared his shoulders, pushed the doors open and stepped out into the cold, damp, night air.

The street was dark, silent. The rumble of traffic on Wilshire, two blocks

donkey in The Blue Bird: This sensitive talking animal was a character in the once-popular 1909 play by the Belgian dramatist Maurice Maeterlinck, about a child's search for ideal happiness.

away, had no body, no meaning. To the left were two taxis. Their drivers leaned against a fender, side by side, smoking. Tony walked the other way. The big dark car was a third of a block from the hotel entrance. Its lights were dimmed and it was only when he was almost up to it that he heard the gentle sound of its engine turning over.

A tall figure detached itself from the body of the car and strolled toward him, both hands in the pockets of the dark overcoat with the high collar. From the man's mouth a cigarette tip glowed faintly, a rusty pearl.

They stopped two feet from each other.

The tall man said, "Hi, Tony. Long time no see."

"Hello, Al. How's it going?"

"Can't complain." The tall man started to take his right hand out of his overcoat pocket, then stopped and laughed quietly. "I forgot. Guess you don't want to shake hands."

"That don't mean anything," Tony said. "Shaking hands. Monkeys can shake hands. What's on your mind, Al?"

"Still the funny little fat guy, eh, Tony?"

"I guess." Tony winked his eyes tight. His throat felt tight.

"You like your job back there?"

"It's a job."

Al laughed his quiet laugh again. "You take it slow, Tony. I'll take it fast. So it's a job and you want to hold it. Oke. There's a girl named Eve Cressy flopping in your quiet hotel. Get her out. Fast and right now."

"What's the trouble?"

The tall man looked up and down the street. A man behind in the car coughed lightly. "She's hooked with a wrong number. Nothing against her personal, but she'll lead trouble to you. Get her out, Tony. You got maybe an hour."

"Sure," Tony said aimlessly, without meaning.

Al took his hand out of his pocket and stretched it against Tony's chest. He gave him a light lazy push. "I wouldn't be telling you just for the hell of it, little fat brother. Get her out of there."

"Okay," Tony said, without any tone in his voice.

The tall man took back his hand and reached for the car door. He opened it and started to slip in like a lean black shadow.

Then he stopped and said something to the men in the car and got out again. He came back to where Tony stood silent, his pale eyes catching a little dim light from the street.

"Listen, Tony. You always kept your nose clean. You're a good brother, Tony."

Tony didn't speak.

Al leaned toward him, a long urgent shadow, the high collar almost touching his ears. "It's trouble business, Tony. The boys won't like it, but I'm telling you just the same. This Cressy was married to a lad named Johnny Ralls. Ralls is out of Quentin two, three days, or a week. He did a three-spot for manslaughter. The girl put him there. He ran down an old man one night when he was drunk, and she was with him. He wouldn't stop. She told him to go in and tell it, or else. He didn't go in. So the Johns come for him."

Tony said, "That's too bad."

"It's kosher, kid. It's my business to know. This Ralls flapped his mouth in stir about how the girl would be waiting for him when he got out, all set to forgive and forget, and he was going straight to her."

Tony said, "What's he to you?" His voice had a dry, stiff crackle, like thick paper.

Al laughed. "The trouble boys want to see him. He ran a table at a spot on the Strip and figured out a scheme. He and another guy took the house for fifty grand. The other lad coughed up, but we still need Johnny's twenty-five. The trouble boys don't get paid to forget."

Tony looked up and down the dark street. One of the taxi drivers flicked a cigarette stub in a long arc over the top of one of the cabs. Tony watched it fall and spark on the pavement. He listened to the quiet sound of the big car's motor.

"I don't want any part of it," he said. "I'll get her out."

Al backed away from him, nodding. "Wise kid. How's mom these days?"

"Okay," Tony said.

"Tell her I was asking for her."

"Asking for her isn't anything," Tony said.

Al turned quickly and got into the car. The car curved lazily in the middle of the block and drifted back toward the corner. Its lights went up and sprayed on a wall. It turned a corner and was gone. The lingering smell of its exhaust drifted past Tony's nose. He turned and walked back into the hotel. He went along to the radio room.

The radio still muttered, but the girl was gone from the davenport in front of it. The pressed cushions were hollowed out by her body. Tony reached down and touched them. He thought they were still warm. He turned the radio off and stood there, turning a thumb slowly in front of his body, his hand flat against his stomach. Then he went back through the lobby toward the elevator bank and stood beside a majolica° jar of white sand. The clerk fussed behind a pebbled-glass screen at one end of the desk. The air was dead.

The elevator bank was dark. Tony looked at the indicator of the middle car and saw that it was at 14.

"Gone to bed," he said under his breath.

The door of the porter's room beside the elevators opened and the little Mexican night operator came out in street clothes. He looked at Tony with a quiet sidewise look out of eyes the color of dried-out chestnuts.

"Good night, boss."

"Yeah," Tony said absently.

He took a thin dappled cigar out of his vest pocket and smelled it. He examined it slowly, turning it around in his neat fingers. There was a small tear along the side. He frowned at that and put the cigar away.

There was a distant sound and the hand on the indicator began to steal around the bronze dial. Light glittered up in the shaft and the straight line of the car floor dissolved the darkness below. The car stopped and the doors opened, and Carl came out of it.

majolica: enameled pottery.

His eyes caught Tony's with a kind of jump and he walked over to him, his head on one side, a thin shine along his pink upper lip.

"Listen, Tony."

Tony took his arm in a hard swift hand and turned him. He pushed him quickly, yet somehow casually, down the steps to the dim main lobby and steered him into a corner. He let go of the arm. His throat tightened again, for no reason he could think of.

"Well?" he said darkly. "Listen to what?"

The porter reached into a pocket and hauled out a dollar bill. "He gimme this," he said loosely. His glittering eyes looked past Tony's shoulder at nothing. They winked rapidly. "Ice and ginger ale."

"Don't stall," Tony growled.

"Guy in 14B," the porter said.

"Lemme smell your breath."

The porter leaned toward him obediently.

"Liquor," Tony said harshly.

"He gimme a drink."

Tony looked down at the dollar bill. "Nobody's in 14B. Not on my list," he said.

"Yeah. There is." The porter licked his lips and his eyes opened and shut several times. "Tall dark guy."

"All right," Tony said crossly. "All right. There's a tall dark guy in 14B and he gave you a buck and a drink. Then what?"

"Gat under his arm," Carl said, and blinked.

Tony smiled, but his eyes had taken on the lifeless glitter of thick ice. "You take Miss Cressy up to her room?"

Carl shook his head. "Gomez. I saw her go up."

"Get away from me," Tony said between his teeth. "And don't accept any more drinks from the guests."

He didn't move until Carl had gone back into his cubbyhole by the elevators and shut the door. Then he moved silently up the three steps and stood in front of the desk, looking at the veined rose marble, the onyx pen set, the fresh registration card in its leather frame. He lifted a hand and smacked it down hard on the marble. The clerk popped out from behind the glass screen like a chipmunk coming out of its hole.

Tony took a flimsy out of his breast pocket and spread it on the desk. "No 14B on this," he said in a bitter voice.

The clerk wiped politely at his mustache. "So sorry. You must have been out to supper when he checked in."

"Who?"

"Registered as James Watterson, San Diego." The clerk yawned.

"Ask for anybody?"

The clerk stopped in the middle of the yawn and looked at the top of Tony's head. "Why, yes. He asked for a swing band. Why?"

"Smart, fast and funny," Tony said. "If you like 'em that way." He wrote on his flimsy and stuffed it back into his pocket. "I'm going upstairs and palm doorknobs. There's four tower rooms you ain't rented yet. Get up on your toes, son. You're slipping."

"I make out," the clerk drawled, and completed his yawn. "Hurry back, pop. I don't know how I'll get through the time."

"You could shave that pink fuzz off your lip," Tony said, and went across to the elevators.

He opened up a dark one and lit the dome light and shot the car up to fourteen. He darkened it again, stepped out and closed the doors. This lobby was smaller than any other, except the one immediately below it. It had a single blue-paneled door in each of the walls other than the elevator wall. On each door was a gold number and letter with a gold wreath around it. Tony walked over to 14A and put his ear to the panel. He heard nothing. Eve Cressy might be in bed asleep, or in the bathroom, or out on the balcony. Or she might be sitting there in the room, a few feet from the door, looking at the wall. Well, he wouldn't expect to be able to hear her sit and look at the wall. He went over to 14B and put his ear to that panel. This was different. There was a sound in there. A man coughed. It sounded somehow like a solitary cough. There were no voices. Tony pressed the small nacre° button beside the door.

Steps came without hurry. A thickened voice spoke through the panel. Tony made no answer, no sound. The thickened voice repeated the question. Lightly, maliciously, Tony pressed the bell again.

Mr. James Watterson, of San Diego, should now open the door and give forth noise. He didn't. A silence fell beyond that door that was like the silence of a glacier. Once more Tony put his ear to the wood. Silence utterly.

He got out a master key on a chain and pushed it delicately into the lock of the door. He turned it, pushed the door inward three inches and withdrew the key. Then he waited.

"All right," the voice said harshly. "Come in and get it."

Tony pushed the door wide and stood there, framed against the light from the lobby. The man was tall, black-haired, angular and white-faced. He held a gun. He held it as though he knew about guns.

"Step right in," he drawled.

Tony went in through the door and pushed it shut with his shoulder. He kept his hands a little out from his sides, the clever fingers curled and slack. He smiled his quiet little smile.

"Mr. Watterson?"

"And after that what?"

"I'm the house detective here."

"It slays me."

The tall, white-faced, somehow handsome and somehow not handsome man backed slowly into the room. It was a large room with a low balcony around two sides of it. French doors opened out on the little, private, open-air balcony that each of the tower rooms had. There was a grate set for a log fire behind a paneled screen in front of a cheerful davenport. A tall misted glass stood on a hotel tray beside a deep, cozy chair. The man backed toward this and stood in front of it. The large, glistening gun dropped and pointed at the floor.

"It slays me," he said. "I'm in the dump an hour and the house copper

---

nacre: mother-of-pearl; white substance from the inner lining of an oyster shell.

gives me the buzz. Okay, sweetheart, look in the closet and bathroom. But she just left."

"You didn't see her yet," Tony said.

The man's bleached face filled with unexpected lines. His thickened voice edged toward a snarl. "Yeah? Who didn't I see yet?"

"A girl named Eve Cressy."

The man swallowed. He put his gun down on the table beside the tray. He let himself down into the chair backwards, stiffly, like a man with a touch of lumbago. Then he leaned forward and put his hands on his kneecaps and smiled brightly between his teeth. "So she got here, huh? I didn't ask about her yet. I'm a careful guy. I didn't ask yet."

"She's been here five days," Tony said. "Waiting for you. She hasn't left the hotel a minute."

The man's mouth worked a little. His smile had a knowing tilt to it. "I got delayed a little up north," he said smoothly. "You know how it is. Visiting old friends. You seem to know a lot about my business, copper."

"That's right, Mr. Ralls."

The man lunged to his feet and his hand snapped at the gun. He stood leaning over, holding it on the table, staring. "Dames talk too much," he said with a muffled sound in his voice, as though he held something soft between his teeth and talked through it.

"Not dames, Mr. Ralls."

"Huh?" The gun slithered on the hard wood of the table. "Talk it up, copper. My mind reader just quit."

"Not dames. Guys. Guys with guns."

The glacier silence fell between them again. The man straightened his body slowly. His face was washed clean of expression, but his eyes were haunted. Tony leaned in front of him, a shortish plump man with a quiet, pale, friendly face and eyes as simple as forest water.

"They never run out of gas — those boys," Johnny Ralls said, and licked at his lip. "Early and late, they work. The old firm never sleeps."

"You know who they are?" Tony said softly.

"I could maybe give nine guesses. And twelve of them would be right."

"The trouble boys," Tony said, and smiled a brittle smile.

"Where is she?" Johnny Ralls asked harshly.

"Right next door to you."

The man walked to the wall and left his gun lying on the table. He stood in front of the wall, studying it. He reached up and gripped the grill-work of the balcony railing. When he dropped his hand and turned, his face had lost some of its lines. His eyes had a quieter glint. He moved back to Tony and stood over him.

"I've got a stake," he said. "Eve sent me some dough and I built it up with a touch I made up north. Case dough, what I mean. The trouble boys talk about twenty-five grand." He smiled crookedly. "Five C's° I can count. I'd have a lot of fun making them believe that, I would."

"What did you do with it?" Tony asked indifferently.

Five C's: five hundred dollars (a C is a "century note").

"I never had it, copper. Leave that lay. I'm the only guy in the world that believes it. It was a little deal I got suckered on."

"I'll believe it," Tony said.

"They don't kill often. But they can be awful tough."

"Mugs," Tony said with a sudden bitter contempt. "Guys with guns. Just mugs."

Johnny Ralls reached for his glass and drained it empty. The ice cubes tinkled softly as he put it down. He picked his gun up, danced it on his palm, then tucked it, nose down, into an inner breast pocket. He stared at the carpet.

"How come you're telling me this, copper?"

"I thought maybe you'd give her a break."

"And if I wouldn't?"

"I kind of think you will," Tony said.

Johnny Ralls nodded quietly. "Can I get out of here?"

"You could take the service elevator to the garage. You could rent a car. I can give you a card to the garageman."

"You're a funny little guy," Johnny Ralls said.

Tony took out a worn ostrich-skin billfold and scribbled on a printed card. Johnny Ralls read it, and stood holding it, tapping it against a thumbnail.

"I could take her with me," he said, his eyes narrow.

"You could take a ride in a basket too," Tony said. "She's been here five days, I told you. She's been spotted. A guy I know called me up and told me to get her out of here. Told me what it was all about. So I'm getting you out instead."

"They'll love that," Johnny Ralls said. "They'll send you violets."

"I'll weep about it on my day off."

Johnny Ralls turned his hand over and stared at the palm. "I could see her, anyway. Before I blow. Next door to here, you said?"

Tony turned on his heel and started for the door. He said over his shoulder, "Don't waste a lot of time, handsome. I might change my mind."

The man said, almost gently, "You might be spotting me right now, for all I know."

Tony didn't turn his head. "That's a chance you have to take."

He went on to the door and passed out of the room. He shut it carefully, silently, looked once at the door of 14A and got into his dark elevator. He rode it down to the linen-room floor and got out to remove the basket that held the service elevator open at that floor. The door slid quietly shut. He held it so that it made no noise. Down the corridor, light came from the open door of the housekeeper's office. Tony got back into his elevator and went on down to the lobby.

The little clerk was out of sight behind his pebbled-glass screen, auditing accounts. Tony went through the main lobby and turned into the radio room. The radio was on again, soft. She was there, curled on the davenport again. The speaker hummed to her, a vague sound so low that what it said was as wordless as the murmur of trees. She turned her head slowly and smiled at him.

"Finished palming doorknobs? I couldn't sleep worth a nickel. So I came down again. Okay?"

He smiled and nodded. He sat down in a green chair and patted the plump brocade arms of it. "Sure, Miss Cressy."

"Waiting is the hardest kind of work, isn't it? I wish you'd talk to that radio. It sounds like a pretzel being bent."

Tony fiddled with it, got nothing he liked, set it back where it had been.

"Beer-parlor drunks are all the customers now."

She smiled at him again.

"I don't bother you being here, Miss Cressy?"

"I like it. You're a sweet little guy, Tony."

He looked stiffly at the floor and a ripple touched his spine. He waited for it to go away. It went slowly. Then he sat back, relaxed again, his neat fingers clasped on his elk's tooth. He listened. Not to the radio — to far-off, uncertain things, menacing things. And perhaps to just the safe whir of wheels going away into a strange night.

"Nobody's all bad," he said out loud.

The girl looked at him lazily. "I've met two or three I was wrong on, then."

He nodded. "Yeah," he admitted judiciously. "I guess there's some that are."

The girl yawned and her deep violet eyes half closed. She nestled back into the cushions. "Sit there a while, Tony. Maybe I could nap."

"Sure. Not a thing for me to do. Don't know why they pay me."

She slept quickly and with complete stillness, like a child. Tony hardly breathed for ten minutes. He just watched her, his mouth a little open. There was a quiet fascination in his limpid eyes, as if he was looking at an altar.

Then he stood up with infinite care and padded away under the arch to the entrance lobby and the desk. He stood at the desk listening for a little while. He heard a pen rustling out of sight. He went around the corner to the row of house phones in little glass cubbyholes. He lifted one and asked the night operator for the garage.

It rang three or four times and then a boyish voice answered, "Windermere Hotel. Garage speaking."

"This is Tony Reseck. That guy Watterson I gave a card to. He leave?"

"Sure, Tony. Half an hour almost. Is it your charge?"

"Yeah," Tony said. "My party. Thanks. Be seein' you."

He hung up and scratched his neck. He went back to the desk and slapped a hand on it. The clerk wafted himself around the screen with his greeter's smile in place. It dropped when he saw Tony.

"Can't a guy catch up on his work?" he grumbled.

"What's the professional rate on 14B?"

The clerk stared morosely. "There's no professional rate in the tower."

"Make one. The fellow left already. Was there only an hour."

"Well, well," the clerk said airily. "So the personality didn't click tonight. We get a skip-out."

"Will five bucks satisfy you?"

"Friend of yours?"

"No. Just a drunk with delusions of grandeur and no dough."

"Guess we'll have to let it ride, Tony. How did he get out?"

"I took him down the service elevator. You was asleep. Will five bucks satisfy you?"

"Why?"

The worn ostrich-skin wallet came out and a weedy five slipped across the marble. "All I could shake him for," Tony said loosely.

The clerk took the five and looked puzzled. "You're the boss," he said, and shrugged. The phone shrilled on the desk and he reached for it. He listened and then pushed it toward Tony. "For you."

Tony took the phone and cuddled it close to his chest. He put his mouth close to the transmitter. The voice was strange to him. It had a metallic sound. Its syllables were meticulously anonymous.

"Tony? Tony Reseck?"

"Talking."

"A message from Al. Shoot?"

Tony looked at the clerk. "Be a pal," he said over the mouthpiece. The clerk flicked a narrow smile at him and went away. "Shoot," Tony said into the phone.

"We had a little business with a guy in your place. Picked him up scramming. Al had a hunch you'd run him out. Tailed him and took him to the curb. Not so good. Backfire."

Tony held the phone very tight and his temples chilled with the evaporation of moisture. "Go on," he said. "I guess there's more."

"A little. The guy stopped the big one. Cold. Al — Al said to tell you good-by."

Tony leaned hard against the desk. His mouth made a sound that was not speech.

"Get it?" The metallic voice sounded impatient, a little bored. "This guy had him a rod. He used it. Al won't be phoning anybody any more."

Tony lurched at the phone, and the base of it shook on the rose marble. His mouth was a hard dry knot.

The voice said, "That's as far as we go, bud. G'night." The phone clicked dryly, like a pebble hitting a wall.

Tony put the phone down in its cradle very carefully, so as not to make any sound. He looked at the clenched palm of his left hand. He took a handkerchief out and rubbed the palm softly and straightened the fingers out with his other hand. Then he wiped his forehead. The clerk came around the screen again and looked at him with glinting eyes.

"I'm off Friday. How about lending me that phone number?"

Tony nodded at the clerk and smiled a minute frail smile. He put his handkerchief away and patted the pocket he had put it in. He turned and walked away from the desk, across the entrance lobby, down the three shallow steps, along the shadowy reaches of the main lobby, and so in through the arch to the radio room once more. He walked softly, like a man moving in a room where somebody is very sick. He reached the chair he had sat in before and lowered himself into it inch by inch.

The girl slept on, motionless, in that curled-up looseness achieved by some women and all cats. Her breath made no sound against the vague murmur of the radio.

Tony Reseck leaned back in the chair and clasped his hands on his elk's tooth and quietly closed his eyes.

QUESTIONS

1. What meanings do you find in the title "I'll Be Waiting"?
2. Is Tony Reseck a stock character — the hard-boiled detective — or is he an individual? As Chandler portrays him, is Tony just "the funny little fat guy" (in his brother's description)?
3. In his meeting with Al outside the hotel, how does Tony apparently feel toward his brother? For what reasons? How are his feelings made clear to us?
4. What is Tony's attitude toward Eve Cressy? Consider this interpretation: Tony is in love with her. Deliberately, he sends Johnny Ralls into a trap, hoping that Ralls will be killed, so that Tony will then have no rival for Eve's affections. Does this theory seem to you plausible?
5. What are the responsibilities of a house detective, as they emerge in this story? Discuss the following suggestion by a critic: "The hotel of Raymond Chandler is an island of civilization and light, surrounded by darkness, chaos, and violence. The house dick's job is to defend the island and its legitimate guests, to keep its enemies at bay."
6. What are some distinguishing features of Raymond Chandler's style of writing? Point to details that Chandler, by his way of putting them, makes memorable.

8 Evaluating Fiction

When we **evaluate** a story, we consider it and place a value on it. Perhaps we decide that it is a masterpiece, or a bit of trash, or (like most fiction we read) a work of some value in between. No cut-and-dried method of judgment will work on every story, and so this chapter has none to propose. Still, there are certain things we can look for in a story — usually clear indications of the degree of its author's competence.

In judging the quality of a certain baseball glove, we first have to be aware that a catcher's mitt differs — for good reasons — from a first baseman's glove. It is no less true that, before evaluating a story, we need to recognize its nature. To see, for instance, that a story is a fable (or perhaps a tale) may save us from condemning it as a failed short story. Or is it a piece of Gothic fiction? If so, we expect it to rely on certain conventions — a spooky mansion or castle, maybe, or a persecuted heroine, or blood-curdling noises in the night. Knowing it for what it is, we won't find fault with it for lacking "realism." Besides, to recognize a Gothic story might help us see how fresh and original an author manages to be, though using some handed-down conventions. Is the story a piece of commercial fiction, tailored to a formula, or a literary story unique in its design? Apparently, we can't demand of a writer of hard-boiled detective stories the subtlety of James Joyce, nor can we discard Joyce's "Araby" for lacking slam-bang action. Some stories, especially those in popular magazines, are just light and entertaining bits of fluff. No point in damning them, unless we dislike fluff, or find them written badly. Of course, we are within our rights if we prefer solidity to fluff, or prefer the kind of story Joyce writes to a typical detective story by Raymond Chandler. Aesop's fable of "The Frogs Who Wanted a King," while simpler and briefer than Joseph Conrad's short novel *The Secret Sharer,* is no less a complete and satisfactory work of art. And yet, considered in a different light, Conrad's story may appear a greater work than Aesop's in that it reveals greater meaning and enfolds more life.

Masterpieces may contain flaws; and so, whenever we can, we

need to consider a story in its entirety. Some novels by Thomas Hardy and by Theodore Dreiser impress (on the whole), despite passages of stilted dialogue and other clumsy writing. If a story totally fails to enlist our sympathies, probably it suffers from some basic ineptitude: choice of an inappropriate point of view, a style ill suited to its theme, or possibly an insufficient knowledge of human beings. In some ineffectual stories, things important to the writer (and to the story) remain private and unmentioned. In other stories, the writer's interests may be perfectly clear but they may not interest the reader, for they are not presented with sufficient art.

Some stories fail from **sentimentality,** a defect in a work whose writer seems to feel tremendous emotion and implies that we too should feel it, but does not provide us with enough reason to share such feelings. Sentimentality is rampant in televised weekday afternoon soap operas, whose characters usually palpitate with passion for reasons not quite known, and who speak in melodramatic tones as if heralding the end of the world. In some fiction, conventional objects (locks of baby hair, posthumously awarded medals, pressed roses) frequently signal, "Let's have a good cry!" Revisiting home after her marriage, the character Amelia in William Makepeace Thackeray's *Vanity Fair* effuses about the bed she slept in when a virgin: "Dear little bed! how many a long night had she wept on its pillow."[1] Teary sentimentality is more common in nineteenth-century fiction than in ours. We have gone to the other extreme, some critics think, into a sentimentality of the violent and the hard-boiled. But in a grossly sentimental work of any kind, failure inheres in our refusal to go along with the author's implied attitudes. We laugh when we are expected to cry, feel delight when we are supposed to be horrified.

In evaluating a story, we may usefully ask a few questions:

1. What is the tone of the story? By what means and how effectively is it communicated?
2. What is the point of view? Does it seem appropriate and effective in this particular story? Imagine the story told from a different point of view; would such a change be for the worse or for the better? If the narrator comments editorially on the characters and events, are his opinions pointed and revealing, or are they platitudes?
3. Does the story show us unique and individual scenes, events, and characters — or weary stereotypes?

---

[1]Sentimentality in fiction is older than the Victorians. Popular in eighteenth-century England, the **sentimental novel** (or **novel of sensibility**) specialized in characters whose ability to shed quick and copious tears signified their virtuous hearts. Oliver Goldsmith's *The Vicar of Wakefield* (1766) and Henry Mackenzie's *The Man of Feeling* (1771) are classics of the genre. An abundance of tears does not prevent such novels from having merit.

4. Are there any evident symbols? If so, do they direct us to the story's central theme, or do they distract us from it?
5. How appropriate to the theme of the story, and to its subject matter, are its tone and style? Is it ever difficult or impossible to sympathize with the attitudes of the author (insofar as we can tell what they are)?
6. Does our interest in the story mainly depend on following its plot, on finding out what will happen next? Or does the author go beyond the events to show us what they mean? Are the events (however fantastic) credible, or are they incredibly melodramatic? Does the plot greatly depend upon farfetched coincidence?
7. Has the writer caused his characters, events, and settings to come alive? Has he presented them full of breath and motion, or simply told us about them in the abstract ("She was a lovable girl whose life had been highly exciting")? Unless the story is a fable or a tale, in which there is no point in detailed description or in deep portrayal of character, or unless the writer is summarizing certain less essential parts of the story to make other parts stand out — then we may well expect the story to contain enough vividly imagined detail to make us believe in it.

EXERCISE: *Evaluation by Comparison*

Here are two pieces of fiction dealing with similar experiences, both first printed in the nineteenth century. After reading the two, compare them and try them by asking some of the questions above. Be ready to offer your own evaluations of them, either in writing or in class discussion.

The first story, although a chapter taken from a novel, is separate from the novel's main action. The preceding twenty-five chapters concern a poor boy in a small factory town, the son of a captain believed lost at sea. In this chapter the author gives us a flashback to show what happened to the captain, changes the scene to the South Seas, and presents characters whom we meet for the first time.

Horatio Alger, Jr. (1834–1899)

Out on the Ocean   1874

We must now go back nearly two years. Five men were floating about in a boat in the Southern ocean. They looked gaunt and famished. For a week they had lived on short allowance, and now for two days they had been entirely without food. There was in their faces that look, well-nigh hopeless, which their wretched situation naturally produced. For one day, also, they had been without water, and the torments of thirst were worse than the cravings of hunger. These men were Captain Rushton and four sailors of the ship *Norman*, whose burning has already been described.

One of the sailors, Bunsby, was better educated and more intelligent than the rest, and the captain spoke to him as a friend and an equal, for all the distinctions of rank were broken down by the immediate prospect of a terrible death.

"How is all this going to end, Bunsby?" said the captain, in a low voice, turning from a vain search for some sail in sight, and addressing his subordinate.

"I am afraid there is only one way," answered Bunsby. "There is not much prospect of our meeting a ship."

"And, if we do, it is doubtful if we can attract their attention."

"I should like the chance to try."

"I never knew before how much worse thirst is than hunger."

"Do you know, captain, if this lasts much longer, I shall be tempted to swallow some of this sea water."

"It will only make matters worse."

"I know it, but, at least, it will moisten my throat."

The other sailors sat stupid and silent, apparently incapable of motion.

"I wish I had a plug of tobacco," said one, at last.

"If there were any use in wishing, I'd wish myself on shore," said the second.

"We'll never see land again," said the third, gloomily. "We're bound for Davy Jones' locker."

"I'd like to see my old mother before I go down," said the first.

"I've got a mother, too," said the third. "If I could only have a drop of the warm tea such as she used to make! She's sitting down to dinner now, most likely, little thinking that her Jack is dying of hunger out here."

There was a pause, and the captain spoke again.

"I wish I knew whether that bottle will ever reach shore. When was it we launched it?"

"Four days since."

"I've got something here I wish I could get to my wife." He drew from his pocketbook a small, folded paper.

"What is that, captain?" asked Bunsby.

"It is my wife's fortune."

"How is that, captain?"

"That paper is good for five thousand dollars."

"Five thousand dollars wouldn't do us much good here. It wouldn't buy a pound of bread, or a pint of water."

"No; but it would — I hope it will — save my wife and son from suffering. Just before I sailed on this voyage I took five thousand dollars — nearly all my savings — to a man in our village to keep till I returned, or, if I did not return, to keep in trust for my wife and child. This is the paper he gave me in acknowledgment."

"Is he a man you can trust, captain?"

"I think so. It is the superintendent of the factory in our village — a man rich, or, at any rate, well-to-do. He has a good reputation for integrity."

"Your wife knew you had left the money in his hands?"

"No; I meant it as a surprise to her."

"It is a pity you did not leave that paper in her hands."

"What do you mean, Bunsby?" asked the captain, nervously. "You don't think this man will betray his trust?"

"I can't say, captain, for I don't know the man; but I don't like to trust any man too far."

Captain Rushton was silent for a moment. There was a look of trouble on his face.

"You make me feel anxious, Bunsby. It is hard enough to feel that I shall probably never again see my wife and child — on earth, I mean — but to think that they may possibly suffer want makes it more bitter."

"The man may be honest, captain. Don't trouble yourself too much."

"I see that I made a mistake. I should have left this paper with my wife. Davis can keep this money, and no one will be the wiser. It is a terrible temptation."

"Particularly if the man is pressed for money."

"I don't think that. He is considered a rich man. He ought to be one, and my money would be only a trifle to him."

"Let us hope it is so, captain," said Bunsby, who felt that further discussion would do no good, and only embitter the last moments of his commander. But anxiety did not so readily leave the captain. Added to the pangs of hunger and the cravings of thirst was the haunting fear that by his imprudence his wife and child would suffer.

"Do you think it would do any good, Bunsby," he said, after a pause, "to put this receipt in a bottle, as I did the letter?"

"No, captain, it is too great a risk. There is not more than one chance in a hundred of its reaching its destination. Besides, suppose you should be picked up, and go home without the receipt; he might refuse to pay you."

"He would do so at the peril of his life, then," said the captain, fiercely. "Do you think, if I were alive, I would let any man rob me of the savings of my life?"

"Other men have done so."

"It would not be safe to try it on me, Bunsby."

"Well, captain?"

"It is possible that I may perish, but you may be saved."

"Not much chance of it."

"Yet it is possible. Now, if that happens, I have a favor to ask of you."

"Name it, captain."

"I want you, if I die first, to take this paper, and guard it carefully; and, if you live to get back, to take it to Millville, and see that justice is done to my wife and child."

"I promise that, captain; but I think we shall die together."

Twenty-four hours passed. The little boat still rocked hither and thither on the ocean billows. The five faces looked more haggard, and there was a wild, eager look upon them, as they scanned the horizon, hoping to see a ship. Their lips and throats were dry and parched.

"I can't stand it no longer," said one — it was the sailor I have called Jack — "I shall drink some of the sea water."

"Don't do it, Jack," said Bunsby. "You'll suffer more than ever."

"I can't," said Jack, desperately; and, scooping up some water in the hollow of his hand, he drank it eagerly. Again and again he drank with feverish eagerness.

"How is it?" said the second sailor.

"I feel better," said Jack; "my throat was so dry."

"Then I'll take some, too."

The other two sailors, unheeding the remonstrances of Bunsby and the captain, followed the example of Jack. They felt relief for the moment, but soon their torments became unendurable. With parched throats, gasping for breath, they lay back in agony. Suffering themselves, Captain Rushton and Bunsby regarded with pity the greater sufferings of their wretched companions.

"This is horrible," said the captain.

"Yes," said Bunsby, sadly. "It can't last much longer now."

His words were truer than he thought. Unable to endure his suffering, the sailor named Jack suddenly staggered to his feet.

"I can't stand it any longer," he said, wildly; "good-by, boys," and before his companions well knew what he intended to do, he had leaped over the side of the boat, and sunk in the ocean waves.

There was a thrilling silence, as the waters closed over his body.

Then the second sailor also rose to his feet.

"I'm going after Jack," he said, and he, too, plunged into the waves.

The captain rose as if to hinder him, but Bunsby placed his hand upon his arm.

"It's just as well, captain. We must all come to that, and the sooner, the more suffering is saved."

"That's so," said the other sailor, tormented like the other two by thirst, aggravated by his draughts of seawater. "Good-by, Bunsby! Good-by, captain! I'm going!"

He, too, plunged into the sea, and Bunsby and the captain were left alone.

"You won't desert me, Bunsby?" said the captain.

"No, captain. I haven't swallowed seawater like those poor fellows. I can stand it better."

"There is no hope of life," said the captain, quietly; "but I don't like to go unbidden into my Maker's presence."

"Nor I. I'll stand by you, captain."

"This is a fearful thing, Bunsby. If it would only rain."

"That would be some relief."

As if in answer to his wish, the drops began to fall — slowly at first, then more copiously, till at last their clothing was saturated, and the boat partly filled with water. Eagerly they squeezed out the welcome drops from their clothing, and felt a blessed relief. They filled two bottles they had remaining with the precious fluid.

"If those poor fellows had only waited," said the captain.

"They are out of suffering now," said Bunsby.

The relief was only temporary, and they felt it to be so. They were without food, and the two bottles of water would not last them long. Still, there was a slight return of hope, which survives under the most discouraging circumstances.

Stephen Crane (1871–1900)

THE OPEN BOAT

A Tale Intended to be after the Fact:
Being the Experience of Four Men from the Sunk Steamer **Commodore°**

I

None of them knew the color of the sky. Their eyes glanced level, and were fastened upon the waves that swept toward them. These waves were of the hue of slate, save for the tops, which were of foaming white, and all of the men knew the colors of the sea. The horizon narrowed and widened, and dipped and rose, and at all times its edge was jagged with waves that seemed thrust up in points like rocks.

Many a man ought to have a bathtub larger than the boat which here rode upon the sea. These waves were most wrongfully and barbarously abrupt and tall, and each frothtop was a problem in small-boat navigation.

The cook squatted in the bottom, and looked with both eyes at the six inches of gunwale which separated him from the ocean. His sleeves were rolled over his fat forearms, and the two flaps of his unbuttoned vest dangled as he bent to bail out the boat. Often he said, "Gawd! that was a narrow clip." As he remarked it he invariably gazed eastward over the broken sea.

The oiler, steering with one of the two oars in the boat, sometimes raised himself suddenly to keep clear of water that swirled in over the stern. It was a thin little oar, and it seemed often ready to snap.

The correspondent°, pulling at the other oar, watched the waves and wondered why he was there.

The injured captain, lying in the bow, was at this time buried in that profound dejection and indifference which comes, temporarily at least, to even the bravest and most enduring when, willy-nilly, the firm fails, the army loses, the ship goes down. The mind of the master of a vessel is rooted deep in the timbers of her, though he command for a day or a decade; and this captain had on him the stern impression of a scene in the grays of dawn of seven turned faces, and later a stump of a topmast with a white ball on it, that slashed to and fro at the waves, went low and lower, and down. Thereafter there was something strange in his voice. Although steady, it was deep with mourning, and of a quality beyond oration or tears.

"Keep 'er a little more south, Billie," said he.

"A little more south, sir," said the oiler in the stern.

A seat in this boat was not unlike a seat upon a bucking broncho, and by the same token a broncho is not much smaller. The craft pranced and reared and plunged like an animal. As each wave came, and she rose for it, she seemed like a horse making at a fence outrageously high. The manner of her scramble over these walls of water is a mystic thing, and, moreover, at the top of them were ordinarily these problems in white water, the foam racing down from the summit of each wave requiring a new leap, and a leap from

---

Steamer Commodore: an actual vessel, wrecked off the coast of Florida in 1897.

the correspondent: foreign correspondent, newspaper reporter.

the air. Then, after scornfully bumping a crest, she would slide and race and splash down a long incline, and arrive bobbing and nodding in front of the next menace.

A singular disadvantage of the sea lies in the fact that after successfully surmounting one wave you discover that there is another behind it just as important and just as nervously anxious to do something effective in the way of swamping boats. In a ten-foot dinghy one can get an idea of the resources of the sea in the line of waves that is not probable to the average experience which is never at sea in a dinghy. As each slaty wall of water approached, it shut all else from the view of the men in the boat, and it was not difficult to imagine that this particular wave was the final outburst of the ocean, the last effort of the grim water. There was a terrible grace in the move of the waves, and they came in silence, save for the snarling of the crests.

In the wan light the faces of the men must have been gray. Their eyes must have glinted in strange ways as they gazed steadily astern. Viewed from a balcony, the whole thing would doubtless have been weirdly pictur- esque. But the men in the boat had no time to see it, and if they had had leisure, there were other things to occupy their minds. The sun swung steadily up the sky, and they knew it was broad day because the color of the sea changed from slate to emerald green streaked with amber lights, and the foam was like tumbling snow. The process of the breaking day was unknown to them. They were aware only of this effect upon the color of the waves that rolled toward them.

In disjointed sentences the cook and the correspondent argued as to the difference between a life-saving station and a house of refuge. The cook had said: "There's a house of refuge just north of the Mosquito Inlet Light, and as soon as they see us they'll come off in their boat and pick us up."

"As soon as who see us?" said the correspondent.

"The crew," said the cook.

"Houses of refuge don't have crews," said the correspondent. "As I understand them, they are only places where clothes and grub are stored for the benefit of shipwrecked people. They don't carry crews."

"Oh, yes, they do," said the cook.

"No, they don't," said the correspondent.

"Well, we're not there yet, anyhow," said the oiler, in the stern.

"Well," said the cook, "perhaps it's not a house of refuge that I'm think- ing of as being near Mosquito Inlet Light; perhaps it's a life-saving station."

"We're not there yet," said the oiler in the stern.

II

As the boat bounced from the top of each wave the wind tore through the hair of the hatless men, and as the craft plopped her stern down again the spray slashed past them. The crest of each of these waves was a hill, from the top of which the men surveyed for a moment a broad tumultuous expanse, shining and wind-riven. It was probably splendid, it was probably glorious, this play of the free sea, wild with lights of emerald and white and amber.

"Bully good thing it's an on-shore wind," said the cook. "If not, where would we be? Wouldn't have a show."

"That's right," said the correspondent.

The busy oiler nodded his assent.

Then the captain, in the bow, chuckled in a way that expressed humor, contempt, tragedy, all in one. "Do you think we've got much of a show now, boys?" said he.

Whereupon the three were silent, save for a trifle of hemming and hawing. To express any particular optimism at this time they felt to be childish and stupid, but they all doubtless possessed this sense of the situation in their minds. A young man thinks doggedly at such times. On the other hand, the ethics of their condition was decidedly against any open suggestion of hopelessness. So they were silent.

"Oh, well," said the captain, soothing his children, "we'll get ashore all right."

But there was that in his tone which made them think; so the oiler quoth, "Yes! if this wind holds."

The cook was bailing. "Yes! if we don't catch hell in the surf."

Canton-flannel gulls flew near and far. Sometimes they sat down on the sea, near patches of brown seaweed that rolled over the waves with a movement like carpets on a line in a gale. The birds sat comfortably in groups, and they were envied by some in the dinghy, for the wrath of the sea was no more to them than it was to a covey of prairie chickens a thousand miles inland. Often they came very close and stared at the men with black bead-like eyes. At these times they were uncanny and sinister in their unblinking scrutiny, and the men hooted angrily at them, telling them to be gone. One came, and evidently decided to alight on the top of the captain's head. The bird flew parallel to the boat and did not circle, but made short sidelong jumps in the air in chicken-fashion. His black eyes were wistfully fixed upon the captain's head. "Ugly brute," said the oiler to the bird. "You look as if you were made with a jackknife." The cook and the correspondent swore darkly at the creature. The captain naturally wished to knock it away with the end of the heavy painter, but he did not dare do it, because anything resembling an emphatic gesture would have capsized this freighted boat; and so, with his open hand, the captain gently and carefully waved the gull away. After it had been discouraged from the pursuit the captain breathed easier on account of his hair, and others breathed easier because the bird struck their minds at this time as being somehow gruesome and ominous.

In the meantime the oiler and the correspondent rowed. And also they rowed. They sat together in the same seat, and each rowed an oar. Then the oiler took both oars; then the correspondent took both oars; then the oiler; then the correspondent. They rowed and they rowed. The very ticklish part of the business was when the time came for the reclining one in the stern to take his turn at the oars. By the very last star of truth, it is easier to steal eggs from under a hen than it was to change seats in the dinghy. First the man in the stern slid his hand along the thwart and moved with care, as if he were of Sèvres°. Then the man in the rowing-seat slid his hand along the other thwart. It was all done with the most extraordinary care. As the two sidled past each other, the whole party kept watchful eyes on the coming wave, and the captain cried: "Look out, now! Steady, there!"

Sèvres: chinaware made in this French town.

The brown mats of seaweed that appeared from time to time were like islands, bits of earth. They were travelling, apparently, neither one way nor the other. They were, to all intents, stationary. They informed the men in the boat that it was making progress slowly toward the land.

The captain, rearing cautiously in the bow after the dinghy soared on a great swell, said that he had seen the lighthouse at Mosquito Inlet. Presently the cook remarked that he had seen it. The correspondent was at the oars then, and for some reason he too wished to look at the lighthouse; but his back was toward the far shore, and the waves were important, and for some time he could not seize an opportunity to turn his head. But at last there came a wave more gentle than the others, and when at the crest of it he swiftly scoured the western horizon.

"See it?" said the captain.

"No," said the correspondent, slowly; "I didn't see anything."

"Look again," said the captain. He pointed. "It's exactly in that direction."

At the top of another wave the correspondent did as he was bid, and this time his eyes chanced on a small, still thing on the edge of the swaying horizon. It was precisely like the point of a pin. It took an anxious eye to find a lighthouse so tiny.

"Think we'll make it, Captain?"

"If this wind holds and the boat don't swamp, we can't do much else," said the captain.

The little boat, lifted by each towering sea and splashed viciously by the crests, made progress that in the absence of seaweed was not apparent to those in her. She seemed just a wee thing wallowing, miraculously top up, at the mercy of five oceans. Occasionally a great spread of water, like white flames, swarmed into her.

"Bail her, cook," said the captain, serenely.

"All right, Captain," said the cheerful cook.

III

It would be difficult to describe the subtle brotherhood of men that was here established on the seas. No one said that it was so. No one mentioned it. But it dwelt in the boat, and each man felt it warm him. They were a captain, an oiler, a cook, and a correspondent, and they were friends — friends in a more curiously iron-bound degree than may be common. The hurt captain, lying against the water-jar in the bow, spoke always in a low voice and calmly; but he could never command a more ready and swiftly obedient crew than the motley three of the dinghy. It was more than a mere recognition of what was best for the common safety. There was surely in it a quality that was personal and heart-felt. And after this devotion to the commander of the boat, there was this comradeship, that the correspondent, for instance, who had been taught to be cynical of men, knew even at the time was the best experience of his life. But no one said that it was so. No one mentioned it.

"I wish we had a sail," remarked the captain. "We might try my overcoat on the end of an oar, and give you two boys a chance to rest." So the cook and the correspondent held the mast and spread wide the overcoat; the oiler steered; and the little boat made good way with her new rig. Sometimes the oiler had to scull sharply to keep a sea from breaking into the boat, but otherwise sailing was a success.

Meanwhile the lighthouse had been growing slowly larger. It had now almost assumed color, and appeared like a little gray shadow on the sky. The man at the oars could not be prevented from turning his head rather often to try for a glimpse of this little gray shadow.

At last, from the top of each wave, the men in the tossing boat could see land. Even as the lighthouse was an upright shadow on the sky, this land seemed but a long black shadow on the sea. It certainly was thinner than paper. "We must be about opposite New Smyrna," said the cook, who had coasted this shore often in schooners. "Captain, by the way, I believe they abandoned that life-saving station there about a year ago."

"Did they?" said the captain.

The wind slowly died away. The cook and the correspondent were not now obliged to slave in order to hold high the oar. But the waves continued their old impetuous swooping at the dinghy, and the little craft, no longer under way, struggled woundily over them. The oiler or the correspondent took the oars again.

Shipwrecks are apropos of nothing. If men could only train for them and have them occur when the men had reached pink condition, there would be less drowning at sea. Of the four in the dinghy none had slept any time worth mentioning for two days and two nights previous to embarking in the dinghy, and in the excitement of clambering about the deck of a foundering ship they had also forgotten to eat heartily.

For these reasons, and for others, neither the oiler nor the correspondent was fond of rowing at this time. The correspondent wondered ingenuously how in the name of all that was sane could there be people who thought it amusing to row a boat. It was not an amusement; it was a diabolical punishment, and even a genius of mental aberrations could never conclude that it was anything but a horror to the muscles and a crime against the back. He mentioned to the boat in general how the amusement of rowing struck him, and the weary-faced oiler smiled in full sympathy. Previously to the foundering, by the way, the oiler had worked double watch in the engine-room of the ship.

"Take her easy now, boys," said the captain. "Don't spend yourselves. If we have to run a surf you'll need all your strength, because we'll sure have to swim for it. Take your time."

Slowly the land arose from the sea. From a black line it became a line of black and a line of white — trees and sand. Finally the captain said that he could make out a house on the shore. "That's the house of refuge, sure," said the cook. "They'll see us before long, and come out after us."

The distant lighthouse reared high. "The keeper ought to be able to make us out now, if he's looking through a glass," said the captain. "He'll notify the life-saving people."

"None of those other boats could have got ashore to give word of the wreck," said the oiler, in a low voice, "else the life-boat would be out hunting us."

Slowly and beautifully the land loomed out of the sea. The wind came again. It had veered from the north-east to the south-east. Finally a new sound struck the ears of the men in the boat. It was the low thunder of the surf on the shore. "We'll never be able to make the lighthouse now," said the captain. "Swing her head a little more north, Billie."

"A little more north, sir," said the oiler.

Whereupon the little boat turned her nose once more down the wind, and all but the oarsman watched the shore grow. Under the influence of this expansion doubt and direful apprehension were leaving the minds of the men. The management of the boat was still most absorbing, but it could not prevent a quiet cheerfulness. In an hour, perhaps, they would be ashore.

Their backbones had become thoroughly used to balancing in the boat, and they now rode this wild colt of a dinghy like circus men. The correspondent thought that he had been drenched to the skin, but happening to feel in the top pocket of his coat, he found therein eight cigars. Four of them were soaked with sea-water; four were perfectly scatheless. After a search, somebody produced three dry matches; and thereupon the four waifs rode impudently in their little boat and, with an assurance of an impending rescue shining in their eyes, puffed at the big cigars, and judged well and ill of all men. Everybody took a drink of water.

IV

"Cook," remarked the captain, "there don't seem to be any signs of life about your house of refuge."

"No," replied the cook. "Funny they don't see us!"

A broad stretch of lowly coast lay before the eyes of the men. It was of low dunes topped with dark vegetation. The roar of the surf was plain, and sometimes they could see the white lip of a wave as it spun up the beach. A tiny house was blocked out black upon the sky. Southward, the slim lighthouse lifted its little gray length.

Tide, wind, and waves were swinging the dinghy northward. "Funny they don't see us," said the men.

The surf's roar was here dulled, but its tone was nevertheless thunderous and mighty. As the boat swam over the great rollers the men sat listening to this roar. "We'll swamp sure," said everybody.

It is fair to say here that there was not a life-saving station within twenty miles in either direction; but the men did not know this fact, and in consequence they made dark and opprobrious remarks concerning the eyesight of the nation's life-savers. Four scowling men sat in the dinghy and surpassed records in the invention of epithets.

"Funny they don't see us."

The light-heartedness of a former time had completely faded. To their sharpened minds it was easy to conjure pictures of all kinds of incompetency and blindness and, indeed, cowardice. There was the shore of the populous land, and it was bitter and bitter to them that from it came no sign.

"Well," said the captain, ultimately, "I suppose we'll have to make a try for ourselves. If we stay out here too long, we'll none of us have strength left to swim after the boat swamps."

And so the oiler, who was at the oars, turned the boat straight for the shore. There was a sudden tightening of muscles. There was some thinking.

"If we don't all get ashore," said the captain — "if we don't all get ashore, I suppose you fellows know where to send news of my finish?"

They then briefly exchanged some addresses and admonitions. As for the reflections of the men, there was a great deal of rage in them. Perchance they might be formulated thus: "If I am going to be drowned — if I am going to be drowned — if I am going to be drowned, why, in the name of the seven mad gods who rule the sea, was I allowed to come thus far and contemplate sand and trees? Was I brought here merely to have my nose dragged away as I was about to nibble the sacred cheese of life? It is preposterous. If this old ninny-woman, Fate, cannot do better than this, she should be deprived of the management of men's fortunes. She is an old hen who knows not her intention. If she has decided to drown me, why did she not do it in the beginning and save me all this trouble? The whole affair is absurd. — But no; she cannot mean to drown me. She dare not drown me. She cannot drown me. Not after all this work." Afterward the man might have had an impulse to shake his fist at the clouds. "Just you drown me, now, and then hear what I call you!"

The billows that came at this time were more formidable. They seemed always just about to break and roll over the little boat in a turmoil of foam. There was a preparatory and long growl in the speech of them. No mind unused to the sea would have concluded that the dinghy could ascend these sheer heights in time. The shore was still afar. The oiler was a wily surfman. "Boys," he said swiftly, "she won't live three minutes more, and we're too far out to swim. Shall I take her to sea again, Captain?"

"Yes; go ahead!" said the captain.

This oiler, by a series of quick miracles and fast and steady oarsmanship, turned the boat in the middle of the surf and took her safely to sea again.

There was a considerable silence as the boat bumped over the furrowed sea to deeper water. Then somebody in gloom spoke: "Well, anyhow, they must have seen us from the shore by now."

The gulls went in slanting flight up the wind toward the gray, desolate east. A squall, marked by dingy clouds and clouds brick-red like smoke from a burning building, appeared from the south-east.

"What do you think of those life-saving people? Ain't they peaches?"

"Funny they haven't seen us."

"Maybe they think we're out here for sport! Maybe they think we're fishin'. Maybe they think we're damned fools."

It was a long afternoon. A changed tide tried to force them southward, but wind and wave said northward. Far ahead, where coast-line, sea, and sky formed their mighty angle, there were little dots which seemed to indicate a city on the shore.

"St. Augustine?"

The captain shook his head. "Too near Mosquito Inlet."

And the oiler rowed, and then the correspondent rowed; then the oiler rowed. It was a weary business. The human back can become the seat of more aches and pains than are registered in books for the composite anatomy of a regiment. It is a limited area, but it can become the theatre of innumerable muscular conflicts, tangles, wrenches, knots, and other comforts.

"Did you ever like to row, Billie?" asked the correspondent.

"No," said the oiler; "hang it!"

When one exchanged the rowing-seat for a place in the bottom of the boat, he suffered a bodily depression that caused him to be careless of everything save an obligation to wiggle one finger. There was cold sea-water swashing to and fro in the boat, and he lay in it. His head, pillowed on a thwart, was within an inch of the swirl of a wave-crest, and sometimes a particularly obstreperous sea came inboard and drenched him once more. But these matters did not annoy him. It is almost certain that if the boat had capsized he would have tumbled comfortably upon the ocean as if he felt sure that it was a great soft mattress.

"Look! There's a man on the shore!"

"Where?"

"There! See 'im?"

"Yes, sure! He's walking along."

"Now he's stopped. Look! He's facing us!"

"He's waving at us!"

"So he is! By thunder!"

"Ah, now we're all right! Now we're all right! There'll be a boat out here for us in half an hour."

"He's going on. He's running. He's going up to that house there."

The remote beach seemed lower than the sea, and it required a searching glance to discern the little black figure. The captain saw a floating stick, and they rowed to it. A bath towel was by some weird chance in the boat, and, tying this on the stick, the captain waved it. The oarsman did not dare turn his head, so he was obliged to ask questions.

"What's he doing now?"

"He's standing still again. He's looking, I think. — There he goes again — toward the house. — Now he's stopped again."

"Is he waving at us?"

"No, not now; he was, though."

"Look! There comes another man!"

"He's running."

"Look at him go, would you!"

"Why, he's on a bicycle. Now he's met the other man. They're both waving at us. Look!"

"There comes something up the beach."

"What the devil is that thing?"

"Why, it looks like a boat."

"Why, certainly, it's a boat."

"No; it's on wheels."

"Yes, so it is. Well, that must be the life-boat. They drag them along shore on a wagon."

"That's the life-boat, sure."

"No, by God, it's — it's an omnibus."

"I tell you it's a life-boat."

"It is not! It's an omnibus. I can see it plain. See? One of these big hotel omnibuses."

"By thunder, you're right. It's an omnibus, sure as fate. What do you suppose they are doing with an omnibus? Maybe they are going around collecting the life-crew, hey?"

"That's it, likely. Look! There's a fellow waving a little black flag. He's standing on the steps of the omnibus. There come those other two fellows. Now they're all talking together. Look at the fellow with the flag. Maybe he ain't waving it!"

"That ain't a flag, is it? That's his coat. Why, certainly, that's his coat."

"So it is; it's his coat. He's taken it off and is waving it around his head. But would you look at him swing it!"

"Oh, say, there isn't any life-saving station there. That's just a winter-resort hotel omnibus that has brought over some of the boarders to see us drown."

"What's that idiot with the coat mean? What's he signalling, anyhow?"

"It looks as if he were trying to tell us to go north. There must be a life-saving station up there."

"No; he thinks we're fishing. Just giving us a merry hand. See? Ah, there, Willie!"

"Well, I wish I could make something out of those signals. What do you suppose he means?"

"He don't mean anything; he's just playing."

"Well, if he'd just signal us to try the surf again, or to go to sea and wait, or go north, or go south, or go to hell, there would be some reason in it. But look at him! He just stands there and keeps his coat revolving like a wheel. The ass!"

"There come more people."

"Now there's quite a mob. Look! Isn't that a boat?"

"Where? Oh, I see where you mean. No, that's no boat."

"That fellow is still waving his coat."

"He must think we like to see him do that. Why don't he quit it? It don't mean anything."

"I don't know. I think he is trying to make us go north. It must be that there's a life-saving station there somewhere."

"Say, he ain't tired yet. Look at 'im wave!"

"Wonder how long he can keep that up. He's been revolving his coat ever since he caught sight of us. He's an idiot. Why aren't they getting men to bring a boat out? A fishingboat — one of those big yawls — could come out here all right. Why don't he do something?"

"Oh, it's all right now."

"They'll have a boat out here for us in less than no time, now that they've seen us."

A faint yellow tone came into the sky over the low land. The shadows on the sea slowly deepened. The wind bore coldness with it, and the men began to shiver.

"Holy smoke!" said one, allowing his voice to express his impious mood, "if we keep on monkeying out here! If we've got to flounder out here all night!"

"Oh, we'll never have to stay here all night! Don't you worry. They've seen us now, and it won't be long before they'll come chasing out after us."

The shore grew dusky. The man waving a coat blended gradually into this gloom, and it swallowed in the same manner the omnibus and the group of people. The spray, when it dashed uproariously over the side, made the voyagers shrink and swear like men who were being branded.

"I'd like to catch the chump who waved the coat. I feel like socking him one, just for luck."

"Why? What did he do?"

"Oh, nothing, but then he seemed so damned cheerful."

In the meantime the oiler rowed, and then the correspondent rowed, and then the oiler rowed. Gray-faced and bowed forward, they mechanically, turn by turn, plied the leaden oars. The form of the lighthouse had vanished from the southern horizon, but finally a pale star appeared, just lifting from the sea. The streaked saffron in the west passed before the all-merging darkness, and the sea to the east was black. The land had vanished, and was expressed only by the low and drear thunder of the surf.

"If I am going to be drowned — if I am going to be drowned — if I am going to be drowned, why, in the name of the seven gods who rule the sea, was I allowed to come thus far and contemplate sand and trees? Was I brought here merely to have my nose dragged away as I was about to nibble the sacred cheese of life?"

The patient captain, drooped over the water-jar, was sometimes obliged to speak to the oarsman.

"Keep her head up! Keep her head up!"

"Keep her head up, sir." The voices were weary and low.

This was surely a quiet evening. All save the oarsman lay heavily and listlessly in the boat's bottom. As for him, his eyes were just capable of noting the tall black waves that swept forward in a most sinister silence, save for an occasional subdued growl of a crest.

The cook's head was on a thwart, and he looked without interest at the water under his nose. He was deep in other scenes. Finally he spoke. "Billie," he murmured, dreamfully, "what kind of pie do you like best?"

V

"Pie!" said the oiler and the correspondent, agitatedly. "Don't talk about those things, blast you!"

"Well," said the cook, "I was just thinking about ham sandwiches, and — "

A night on the sea in an open boat is a long night. As darkness settled finally, the shine of the light, lifting from the sea in the south, changed to full gold. On the northern horizon a new light appeared, a small bluish gleam on the edge of the waters. These two lights were the furniture of the world. Otherwise there was nothing but waves.

Two men huddled in the stern, and distances were so magnificent in the dinghy that the rower was enabled to keep his feet partly warm by thrusting them under his companions. Their legs indeed extended far under the rowing-seat until they touched the feet of the captain forward. Sometimes, despite the efforts of the tired oarsman, a wave came piling into the boat, an icy wave of the night, and the chilling water soaked them anew. They would twist their bodies for a moment and groan, and sleep the dead sleep once more, while the water in the boat gurgled about them as the craft rocked.

The plan of the oiler and the correspondent was for one to row until he lost the ability, and then arouse the other from his sea-water couch in the bottom of the boat.

The oiler plied the oars until his head drooped forward and the over-powering sleep blinded him; and he rowed yet afterward. Then he touched a man in the bottom of the boat, and called his name. "Will you spell me for a little while?" he said meekly.

"Sure, Billie," said the correspondent, awaking and dragging himself to a sitting position. They exchanged places carefully, and the oiler, cuddling down in the sea-water at the cook's side, seemed to go to sleep instantly.

The particular violence of the sea had ceased. The waves came without snarling. The obligation of the man at the oars was to keep the boat headed so that the tilt of the rollers would not capsize her, and to preserve her from filling when the crests rushed past. The black waves were silent and hard to be seen in the darkness. Often one was almost upon the boat before the oarsman was aware.

In a low voice the correspondent addressed the captain. He was not sure that the captain was awake, although this iron man seemed to be always awake. "Captain, shall I keep her making for that light north, sir?"

The same steady voice answered him. "Yes. Keep it about two points off the port bow."

The cook had tied a life-belt around himself in order to get even the warmth which this clumsy cork contrivance could donate, and he seemed almost stove-like when a rower, whose teeth invariably chattered wildly as soon as he ceased his labor, dropped down to sleep.

The correspondent, as he rowed, looked down at the two men sleeping underfoot. The cook's arm was around the oiler's shoulders, and, with their fragmentary clothing and haggard faces, they were the babes of the sea — a grotesque rendering of the old babes in the wood.

Later he must have grown stupid at his work, for suddenly there was a growling of water, and a crest came with a roar and a swash into the boat, and it was a wonder that it did not set the cook afloat in his life-belt. The cook continued to sleep, but the oiler sat up, blinking his eyes and shaking with the new cold.

"Oh, I'm awful sorry, Billie," said the correspondent, contritely.

"That's all right, old boy," said the oiler, and lay down again and was asleep.

Presently it seemed that even the captain dozed, and the correspondent thought that he was the one man afloat on all the oceans. The wind had a voice as it came over the waves, and it was sadder than the end.

There was a long, loud swishing astern of the boat, and a gleaming trail of phosphorescence, like blue flame, was furrowed on the black waters. It might have been made by a monstrous knife.

Then there came a stillness, while the correspondent breathed with open mouth and looked at the sea.

Suddenly there was another swish and another long flash of bluish light, and this time it was alongside the boat, and might almost have been reached with an oar. The correspondent saw an enormous fin speed like a shadow through the water, hurling the crystalline spray and leaving the long glowing trail.

The correspondent looked over his shoulder at the captain. His face was hidden, and he seemed to be asleep. He looked at the babes of the sea. They certainly were asleep. So, being bereft of sympathy, he leaned a little way to one side and swore softly into the sea.

But the thing did not then leave the vicinity of the boat. Ahead or astern, on one side or the other, at intervals long or short, fled the long sparkling streak, and there was to be heard the *whirroo* of the dark fin. The speed and power of the thing was greatly to be admired. It cut the water like a gigantic and keen projectile.

The presence of this biding thing did not affect the man with the same horror that it would if he had been a picnicker. He simply looked at the sea dully and swore in an undertone.

Nevertheless, it is true that he did not wish to be alone with the thing. He wished one of his companions to awake by chance and keep him company with it. But the captain hung motionless over the water-jar, and the oiler and the cook in the bottom of the boat were plunged in slumber.

VI

"If I am going to be drowned — if I am going to be drowned — if I am going to be drowned, why, in the name of the seven mad gods who rule the sea, was I allowed to come thus far and contemplate sand and trees?"

During this dismal night, it may be remarked that a man would conclude that it was really the intention of the seven mad gods to drown him, despite the abominable injustice of it. For it was certainly an abominable injustice to drown a man who had worked so hard, so hard. The man felt it would be a crime most unnatural. Other people had drowned at sea since galleys swarmed with painted sails, but still ——

When it occurs to a man that nature does not regard him as important, and that she feels she would not maim the universe by disposing of him, he at first wishes to throw bricks at the temple, and he hates deeply the fact that there are no bricks and no temples. Any visible expression of nature would surely be pelleted with his jeers.

Then, if there be no tangible thing to hoot, he feels, perhaps, the desire to confront a personification and indulge in pleas, bowed to one knee, and with hands supplicant, saying, "Yes, but I love myself."

A high cold star on a winter's night is the word he feels that she says to him. Thereafter he knows the pathos of his situation.

The men in the dinghy had not discussed these matters, but each had, no doubt, reflected upon them in silence and according to his mind. There was seldom any expression upon their faces save the general one of complete weariness. Speech was devoted to the business of the boat.

To chime the notes of his emotion, a verse mysteriously entered the correspondent's head. He had even forgotten that he had forgotten this verse, but it suddenly was in his mind.

A soldier of the Legion lay dying in Algiers;
There was lack of woman's nursing, there was dearth of woman's tears;

But a comrade stood beside him, and he took that comrade's hand,
And he said, "I never more shall see my own, my native land°."

In his childhood the correspondent had been made acquainted with the fact that a soldier of the Legion lay dying in Algiers, but he had never regarded the fact as important. Myriads of his school-fellows had informed him of the soldier's plight, but the dinning had naturally ended by making him perfectly indifferent. He had never considered it his affair that a soldier of the Legion lay dying in Algiers, nor had it appeared to him as a matter for sorrow. It was less to him than the breaking of a pencil's point.

Now, however, it quaintly came to him as a human, living thing. It was no longer merely a picture of a few throes in the breast of a poet, meanwhile drinking tea and warming his feet at the grate; it was an actuality — stern, mournful, and fine.

The correspondent plainly saw the soldier. He lay on the sand with his feet out straight and still. While his pale left hand was upon his chest in an attempt to thwart the going of his life, the blood came between his fingers. In the far Algerian distance, a city of low square forms was set against a sky that was faint with the last sunset hues. The correspondent, plying the oars and dreaming of the slow and slower movements of the lips of the soldier, was moved by a profound and perfectly impersonal comprehension. He was sorry for the soldier of the Legion who lay dying in Algiers.

The thing which had followed the boat and waited had evidently grown bored at the delay. There was no longer to be heard the slash of the cutwater, and there was no longer the flame of the long trail. The light in the north still glimmered, but it was apparently no nearer to the boat. Sometimes the boom of the surf rang in the correspondent's ears, and he turned the craft seaward then and rowed harder. Southward, some one had evidently built a watch-fire on the beach. It was too low and too far to be seen, but it made a shimmering, roseate reflection upon the bluff in back of it, and this could be discerned from the boat. The wind came stronger, and sometimes a wave suddenly raged out like a mountain cat, and there was to be seen the sheen and sparkle of a broken crest.

The captain, in the bow, moved on his water-jar and sat erect. "Pretty long night," he observed to the correspondent. He looked at the shore. "Those life-saving people take their time."

"Did you see that shark playing around?"

"Yes, I saw him. He was a big fellow, all right."

"Wish I had known you were awake."

Later the correspondent spoke into the bottom of the boat.

"Billie!" There was a slow and gradual disentanglement.

"Billie, will you spell me?"

"Sure," said the oiler.

As soon as the correspondent touched the cold, comfortable sea-water in the bottom of the boat and had huddled close to the cook's life-belt he was deep in sleep, despite the fact that his teeth played all the popular airs. This

---

A soldier of the Legion . . . native land: The correspondent remembers a Victorian ballad about a German dying in the French Foreign Legion, "Bingen on the Rhine" by Carolyn Norton.

sleep was so good to him that it was but a moment before he heard a voice call his name in a tone that demonstrated the last stages of exhaustion. "Will you spell me?"

"Sure, Billie."

The light in the north had mysteriously vanished, but the correspondent took his course from the wide-awake captain.

Later in the night they took the boat farther out to sea, and the captain directed the cook to take one oar at the stern and keep the boat facing the seas. He was to call out if he should hear the thunder of the surf. This plan enabled the oiler and the correspondent to get respite together. "We'll give those boys a chance to get into shape again," said the captain. They curled down and, after a few preliminary chatterings and trembles, slept once more the dead sleep. Neither knew they had bequeathed to the cook the company of another shark, or perhaps the same shark.

As the boat caroused on the waves, spray occasionally bumped over the side and gave them a fresh soaking, but this had no power to break their repose. The ominous slash of the wind and the water affected them as it would have affected mummies.

"Boys," said the cook, with the notes of every reluctance in his voice, "she's drifted in pretty close. I guess one of you had better take her to sea again." The correspondent, aroused, heard the crash of the toppled crests.

As he was rowing, the captain gave him some whisky-and-water, and this steadied the chills out of him. "If I ever get ashore and anybody shows me even a photograph of an oar ——"

At last there was a short conversation.

"Billie! — Billie, will you spell me?"

"Sure," said the oiler.

VII

When the correspondent again opened his eyes, the sea and the sky were each of the gray hue of the dawning. Later, carmine and gold was painted upon the waters. The morning appeared finally, in its splendor, with a sky of pure blue, and the sunlight flamed on the tips of the waves.

On the distant dunes were set many little black cottages, and a tall white windmill reared above them. No man, nor dog, nor bicycle appeared on the beach. The cottages might have formed a deserted village.

The voyagers scanned the shore. A conference was held in the boat. "Well," said the captain, "if no help is coming, we might better try a run through the surf right away. If we stay out here much longer we will be too weak to do anything for ourselves at all." The others silently acquiesced in this reasoning. The boat was headed for the beach. The correspondent wondered if none ever ascended the tall wind-tower, and if then they never looked seaward. This tower was a giant, standing with its back to the plight of the ants. It represented in a degree, to the correspondent, the serenity of nature amid the struggles of the individual — nature in the wind, and nature in the vision of men. She did not seem cruel to him then, nor beneficent, nor treacherous, nor wise. But she was indifferent, flatly indifferent. It is, perhaps, plausible that a man in this situation, impressed with the unconcern of the universe, should see the innumerable flaws of his life, and have them taste wickedly in his mind, and wish for another chance. A distinction between right and wrong seems absurdly clear to him, then, in this new ignorance of the grave-edge, and he understands that if he were given another opportunity he would mend his conduct and his words, and be better and brighter during an introduction or at a tea.

"Now, boys," said the captain, "she is going to swamp sure. All we can do is to work her in as far as possible, and then when she swamps, pile out and scramble for the beach. Keep cool now, and don't jump until she swamps sure."

The oiler took the oars. Over his shoulders he scanned the surf. "Captain," he said, "I think I'd better bring her about and keep her head-on to the seas and back her in."

"All right, Billie," said the captain. "Back her in." The oiler swung the boat then, and, seated in the stern, the cook and the correspondent were obliged to look over their shoulders to contemplate the lonely and indifferent shore.

The monstrous inshore rollers heaved the boat high until the men were again enabled to see the white sheets of water scudding up the slanted beach. "We won't get in very close," said the captain. Each time a man could wrest his attention from the rollers, he turned his glance toward the shore, and in the expression of the eyes during this contemplation there was a singular quality. The correspondent, observing the others, knew that they were not afraid, but the full meaning of their glances was shrouded.

As for himself, he was too tired to grapple fundamentally with the fact. He tried to coerce his mind into thinking of it, but the mind was dominated at this time by the muscles, and the muscles said they did not care. It merely occurred to him that if he should drown it would be a shame.

There were no hurried words, no pallor, no plain agitation. The men simply looked at the shore. "Now, remember to get well clear of the boat when you jump," said the captain.

Seaward the crest of a roller suddenly fell with a thunderous crash, and the long white comber came roaring down upon the boat.

"Steady now," said the captain. The men were silent. They turned their eyes from the shore to the comber and waited. The boat slid up the incline, leaped at the furious top, bounced over it, and swung down the long back of the wave. Some water had been shipped, and the cook bailed it out.

But the next crest crashed also. The tumbling, boiling flood of white water caught the boat and whirled it almost perpendicular. Water swarmed in from all sides. The correspondent had his hands on the gunwale at this time, and when the water entered at that place he swiftly withdrew his fingers, as if he objected to wetting them.

The little boat, drunken with this weight of water, reeled and snuggled deeper into the sea.

"Bail her out, cook! Bail her out!" said the captain.

"All right, Captain," said the cook.

"Now, boys, the next one will do for us sure," said the oiler. "Mind to jump clear of the boat."

The third wave moved forward, huge, furious, implacable. It fairly swallowed the dinghy, and almost simultaneously the men tumbled into the sea. A piece of life-belt had lain in the bottom of the boat, and as the correspondent went overboard he held this to his chest with his left hand.

The January water was icy, and he reflected immediately that it was colder than he had expected to find it off the coast of Florida. This appeared to his dazed mind as a fact important enough to be noted at the time. The coldness of the water was sad; it was tragic. This fact was somehow mixed and confused with his opinion of his own situation, so that it seemed almost a proper reason for tears. The water was cold.

When he came to the surface he was conscious of little but the noisy water. Afterward he saw his companions in the sea. The oiler was ahead in the race. He was swimming strongly and rapidly. Off to the correspondent's left, the cook's great white and corked back bulged out of the water; and in the rear the captain was hanging with his one good hand to the keel of the overturned dinghy.

There is a certain immovable quality to a shore, and the correspondent wondered at it amid the confusion of the sea.

It seemed also very attractive; but the correspondent knew that it was a long journey, and he paddled leisurely. The piece of life-preserver lay under him, and sometimes he whirled down the incline of a wave as if he were on a hand-sled.

But finally he arrived at a place in the sea where travel was beset with difficulty. He did not pause swimming to inquire what manner of current had caught him, but there his progress ceased. The shore was set before him like a bit of scenery on a stage, and he looked at it and understood with his eyes each detail of it.

As the cook passed, much farther to the left, the captain was calling to him, "Turn over on your back, cook! Turn over on your back and use the oar."

"All right, sir." The cook turned on his back, and, paddling with an oar, went ahead as if he were a canoe.

Presently the boat also passed to the left of the correspondent, with the captain clinging with one hand to the keel. He would have appeared like a man raising himself to look over a board fence if it were not for the extraordinary gymnastics of the boat. The correspondent marvelled that the captain could still hold to it.

They passed on nearer to shore — the oiler, the cook, the captain — and following them went the water-jar, bouncing gaily over the seas.

The correspondent remained in the grip of this strange new enemy — a current. The shore, with its white slope of sand and its green bluff topped with little silent cottages, was spread like a picture before him. It was very near to him then, but he was impressed as one who, in a gallery, looks at a scene from Brittany or Algiers.

He thought: "I am going to drown? Can it be possible? Can it be possible? Can it be possible?" Perhaps an individual must consider his own death to be the final phenomenon of nature.

But later a wave perhaps whirled him out of this small deadly current, for he found suddenly that he could again make progress toward the shore. Later still he was aware that the captain, clinging with one hand to the keel of the dinghy, had his face turned away from the shore and toward him, and was calling his name. "Come to the boat! Come to the boat!"

In his struggle to reach the captain and the boat, he reflected that when one gets properly wearied drowning must really be a comfortable arrangement — a cessation of hostilities accompanied by a large degree of relief; and he was glad of it, for the main thing in his mind for some moments had been horror of the temporary agony. He did not wish to be hurt.

Presently he saw a man running along the shore. He was undressing with most remarkable speed. Coat, trousers, shirt, everything flew magically off him.

"Come to the boat!" called the captain.

"All right, Captain." As the correspondent paddled, he saw the captain let himself down to bottom and leave the boat. Then the correspondent performed his one little marvel of the voyage. A large wave caught him and flung him with ease and supreme speed completely over the boat and far beyond it. It struck him even then as an event in gymnastics and a true miracle of the sea. An overturned boat in the surf is not a plaything to a swimming man.

The correspondent arrived in water that reached only to his waist, but his condition did not enable him to stand for more than a moment. Each wave knocked him into a heap, and the undertow pulled at him.

Then he saw the man who had been running and undressing, and undressing and running, come bounding into the water. He dragged ashore the cook, and then waded toward the captain; but the captain waved him away and sent him to the correspondent. He was naked — naked as a tree in winter; but a halo was about his head, and he shone like a saint. He gave a strong pull, and a long drag, and a bully heave at the correspondent's hand. The correspondent, schooled in the minor formulae, said, "Thanks, old man." But suddenly the man cried, "What's that?" He pointed a swift finger. The correspondent said, "Go."

In the shallows, face downward, lay the oiler. His forehead touched sand that was periodically, between each wave, clear of the sea.

The correspondent did not know all that transpired afterward. When he achieved safe ground he fell, striking the sand with each particular part of his body. It was as if he had dropped from a roof, but the thud was grateful to him.

It seems that instantly the beach was populated with men with blankets, clothes, and flasks, and women with coffee-pots and all the remedies sacred to their minds. The welcome of the land to the men from the sea was warm and generous; but a still and dripping shape was carried slowly up the beach, and the land's welcome for it could only be the different and sinister hospitality of the grave.

When it came night, the white waves paced to and fro in the moonlight, and the wind brought the sound of the great sea's voice to the men on the shore, and they felt that they could then be interpreters.

QUESTIONS

1. Both "Out on the Ocean" and "The Open Boat" are sea stories. In each, how vividly is the sea presented? (True, "The Open Boat" is longer, and evidently has the advantage in such a comparison; but carefully consider any descriptions of the sea given in "Out on the Ocean" and decide how memorable they seem to you.)

2. In the two stories, what characters are "round"? What characters are "flat"? Mere roundness is no virtue in itself, so try to assess how well each writer succeeds in making you feel thoroughly familiar with the *central* characters. (You might compare, in particular, the two captains, or Bunsby and the correspondent.)

3. Both stories give us the thoughts of men who face death. In which story do these thoughts seem more interesting?

4. In "Out on the Ocean," why does Bunsby urge the captain not to prevent the men from jumping overboard? How well do subsequent events bear out the wisdom of his advice?

5. In "The Open Boat," consider the passage in Part IV about "the old ninny-woman, Fate." What does it contribute to the story?

6. Having answered the last two questions, you will have noticed that both stories describe events in nature (the behavior of the sea or the weather) that might seem ironic mockery of the shipwrecked men. Which writer seems more keenly aware of this irony?

7. In "Out on the Ocean," what passages of description seem memorable not only for what they say but for their style of writing? What passages in "The Open Boat" are written memorably?

8. What symbols appear in either story? What do they suggest?

9. What is the main theme of each story, if there is any? How clearly and fully does the story illustrate it?

10. What secondary themes enrich each story? See, for instance, the paragraph on comradeship at the beginning of Part III of "The Open Boat." Compare it with the second paragraph of "Out on the Ocean." In which story are the sentiments expressed in these passages more fully illustrated by the story in its entirety?

11. Compare the editorial comments on hope and dejection: in "Out on the Ocean," the closing lines of the story; in "The Open Boat," Part I, the sixth paragraph. In each story, how clearly do events seem to illustrate the narrator's suggestion that despair, in men, tends to be temporary?

12. All in all, which is the deeper, richer, more memorable, and more satisfying story?

9 Writing about Fiction

Unlike a brief poem, or a painting you can take in with one long glance, a work of fiction — even a short story — may be too complicated to hold all at once in the mind's eye. Before you can write about it, you may need to give it two or more careful readings, and even then, as you begin to think further about it, you will probably have to thumb through it to reread certain passages. The first time through, perhaps it is best just to read attentively, open to whatever pleasure and wisdom the story may afford. On second look, you may find it useful to read with pencil in hand, either to mark your personal copy or to take notes to jog your memory. To see the design and meaning of a story need not be a boring chore — any more than it is to land a fighting fish and to study it with admiration.

Like any coherent, forceful essay, a good discussion of fiction doesn't just toss forth a random lot of impressions. It makes some point about which the writer feels strongly. In order to write a meaningful paper, then, you need something you *want* to say — a meaningful topic. For suggestions on finding such a topic (also some pointers on organizing, writing, revising, and finishing your paper), please see the appendix, "Writing about Literature," which begins on page 1377. Its advice may be applied to papers on fiction, poetry, and drama. The present chapter will set forth some common methods particularly useful for your writing about stories.

EXPLICATION

Explication is the patient unfolding of meanings in a work of literature. An explication — that is, an essay that follows this method — proceeds carefully through a story, poem, or play, usually interpreting it line by line — perhaps even word by word. A good explication dwells on details, as well as on larger things. It brings them to the attention of a reader who might have missed them (since the reader probably hasn't read so closely as the writer of the explication). Alert and willing to take pains, the writer of such an essay notices anything meaningful that isn't obvious, whether it is a colossal theme suggested by a symbol, or a little hint contained in a single word.

To write an honest explication of a story takes time and space, probably too much time and space to devote to a long and complex story unless you are writing a huge term paper, an honors thesis, or a dissertation. A thorough explication of Joseph Conrad's *The Secret Sharer* would be likely to run much longer than the rich and intriguing short novel itself. Even the very shortest of short stories, of course, may offer plenty to unfold. Ordinarily, the method of explication is best suited to a paper that deals only with a short passage or section of a story: a key scene, a crucial conversation, a statement of theme, an opening or closing paragraph. Certain storytellers, those especially fond of language, invite closer attention to their words than others do. Edgar Allan Poe, for one, is a poet sensitive to the rhythms of his sentences, and a symbolist whose stories abound in suggestions. Here is an explication, by a student, of a short but essential passage in Poe's "The Tell-Tale Heart" (page 132), in which the narrator, a madman, tells how he spied each night upon his victim, an old man. The passage occurs in the third paragraph of the story, and (to help us follow the explication) the student quotes it in full at the beginning of her paper. (Poe's story, by the way, is brief. If you haven't yet read it, you can do so in only a few minutes, so that this paper — and all the others to be included in this chapter — will make more sense to you.)

By Lantern Light: An Explication of a Passage
in "The Tell-Tale Heart"

And every night, about midnight, I turned the latch of his
door and opened it---oh, so gently! And then, when I had
made an opening sufficient for my head, I put in a dark
lantern, all closed, closed, so that no light shone out,
and then I thrust in my head. Oh, you would have laughed
to see how cunningly I thrust it in! I moved it slowly---
very, very slowly, so that I might not disturb the old
man's sleep. It took me an hour to place my whole head
within the opening so far that I could see·him as he lay
upon his bed. Ha!---would a madman have been so wise as
this? And then, when my head was well in the room, I
undid the lantern cautiously---oh, so cautiously---
cautiously (for the hinges creaked)---I undid it just so
much that a single thin ray fell upon the vulture eye.
And this I did for seven long nights---every night just at
midnight---but I found the eye always closed; and so it was
impossible to do the work; for it was not the old man who
vexed me, but his Evil Eye.

Although Poe has indicated in the first lines of his story that the

person who addresses us is insane, it is only when we come to the speaker's account of his preparations for murdering the old man that we imagine him in action, and so find his madness fully revealed. Even more convincingly than his earlier words (for we might possibly think that someone who claims to hear things in heaven and hell is a religious mystic), these preparations reveal him to be mad. What strikes us is that they are so elaborate and meticulous. A significant detail is the exactness of his schedule for spying: "every night just at midnight." The words with which he describes his motions also convey the most extreme care (and I will indicate them with italics): "how wisely I proceeded -- with what caution," "I turned the latch of his door and opened it -- oh, so gently!", "how cunningly I thrust [my head] in! I moved it slowly, very slowly," "I undid the lantern cautiously -- oh, so cautiously -- cautiously." Taking a whole hour to intrude his head into the room, he asks, "Ha! would a madman be as wise as this?" But of course the word wise is unconsciously ironic, for clearly it is not wisdom the speaker displays, but an absurd degree of care, an almost fiendish ingenuity. Such behavior, I understand, is typical of certain mental illnesses. All his careful preparations that he thinks prove him sane only convince us instead that he is mad.

Obviously his behavior is self-defeating. He wants to catch the "vulture eye" open, and yet he takes all these pains not to disturb the old man's sleep. If he behaved logically, he might go barging into the bedroom with his lantern ablaze, shouting at the top of his voice. And yet, if we can see things his way, there is a strange logic to his reasoning. He regards the eye as a creature in itself, quite apart from its possessor. "It was not," he says, "the old man who vexed me, but his Evil Eye." Apparently, to be inspired to do his deed, the madman needs to behold the eye -- at least, this is my understanding of his remark, "I found the eye always closed; and so it was impossible to do the work." Poe's choice of the word work, by the way, is also revealing. Murder is made to seem a duty or a job; and anyone who so regards murder is either extremely cold-blooded, like a hired killer for a gangland assassination, or else deranged. Besides, the word suggests again the curious sense of detachment that the speaker feels toward the owner of the eye.

In still another of his assumptions, the speaker shows that he is madly logical, or operating on the logic of a dream. There seems a dream-like relationship between his dark lantern "all closed, closed, so that no light shone out," and the sleeping victim. When the madman opens his lantern so that it emits a single ray, he is hoping that the eye in the old man's head will be open too, letting out its corresponding gleam. The latch that he turns so gently, too, seems like the eye, whose lid needs to be opened in order for the murderer to go ahead. It is as though the speaker is <u>trying</u> to get the eyelid to lift. By taking such great pains and by going through all this nightly ritual, he is practicing some kind of magic, whose rules are laid down not by our logic, but by the logic of dreams.

An unusually well-written paper, "By Lantern Light" cost the student two or three careful revisions. Rather than attempting to say something about *everything* in the passage from Poe, she selects only those details that strike her as most meaningful. In her very first sentence, she briefly shows us how the passage functions in the context of Poe's story: how it clinches our suspicions that the narrator is mad. In writing her paper, the student went by the following rough, simple outline — nothing more than a list of the points she wanted to express:

1. Speaker's extreme care and exactness -- typical of some mental illnesses.

2. Speaker doesn't act by usual logic but by a crazy logic.

3. Dream-like connection between latch & lantern and old man's eye.

As she wrote, she followed her brief list, setting forth her ideas one at a time, one idea to a paragraph. There is a different (and still easier) way to organize an explication: just work through the original passage line by line or sentence by sentence. The danger of this procedure is that you may find yourself falling into a boring singsong: "In the first sentence I noticed . . . ," "In the next sentence . . . ," "Now in the third sentence . . . ," "Finally, in the last paragraph. . . ." (If you choose to organize an explication in such a way, then boldly vary your transitions.) Notice that the student who wrote "By Lantern Light" doesn't inch through the passage sentence by sentence, but freely takes up its details in whatever order she likes. Less fussy than Poe's madman, she neatly writes in three corrections, saving herself retyping. And why, in her first paragraph, does she change Poe's word *it* to *my head*? Coming upon a piece of a sentence quoted out of context, the reader might forget what *it* refers to — and so the writer places the alteration in brackets, to indicate that the changed words are her own.

In a long critical essay that doesn't adhere to a single method all the way through, the method of explication may appear from time to time — as when the critic, in discussing a story, stops to unravel a particularly knotty passage. But useful as it may be to know how to write an explication of fiction, it is probably still more useful (in most literature courses) to know how to write an analysis.

ANALYSIS

Assignment: "Write an **analysis** of a story or novel." So what do you do? Following the method of analysis (from the Greek: "breaking up"), you separate a story or novel into its component parts, then (usually) select a single part for close study. One likely topic for an analysis might be "The Character of James Thurber's Mr. Martin" (referring to "The Catbird Seat"), in which the writer would concentrate on showing us Martin's highly individual features and traits of personality. Other typical analyses might be written about, say, "Folk Humor in Mark Twain's *Huckleberry Finn*," or "Gothic Elements in a Story by Joyce Carol Oates" (referring to "Where Are You Going, Where Have You Been?"), or "The Unidentified Narrator in 'A Rose for Emily.'" To be sure, no element of a story dwells in isolation from the story's other elements. In "The Tell-Tale Heart," the madness of the central character apparently makes it necessary to tell the story from a certain point of view and probably helps determine the author's choice of theme, setting, symbolism, tone, style, and ironies. But it would be mind-boggling to try to study all those elements simultaneously. For this reason, the writer of an analysis generally studies just one element, though he may suggest — probably at the start of the essay — its relation to the whole story. Indeed, analysis is the method of this book, in which, chapter by chapter, we have separated fiction into its components of plot, point of view, character, tone and style, and so on. If you have read the discussion of the plot of "Godfather Death" (pages 6–8), or the attempt to state the theme of Hemingway's "A Clean, Well-Lighted Place" (pages 90–91), then you have already read some brief essays in analysis. Here is a student-written analysis of "The Tell-Tale Heart," dealing with a single element — the story's point of view.

The Hearer of the Tell-Tale Heart

Although there are many things we do not know about the narrator of Edgar Allan Poe's story "The Tell-Tale Heart" -- is he a son? a servant? a companion? -- there is one thing we are sure of from the start. He is mad. In the opening paragraph, Poe makes the narrator's condition un-mistakeable, not only from his excited and worked-up speech (full of dashes and exclamation points), but also from his wild claims. He says it is merely some disease which has sharpened his senses that has made people call him crazy. However, who but a madman would say, "I heard all things in the heaven and in the earth," and brag how his ear is a kind of CB radio, listening in on Hell? Such a statement leaves no doubt that the point of view in the story is an ironic one.

Because the participating narrator is telling his story in the first person, certain details in the story stand out more than others. When the narrator goes on to tell how he watches the old man sleeping, he rivets his attention on the old man's "vulture eye." When a ray from his lantern finds the Evil Eye open, he says, "I could see nothing else of the old man's face or person." Actually, the reader can see almost nothing else about the old man anywhere in the rest of the story. All we are told is that the old man treated the younger man well, and we gather that the old man was rich, because his house is full of treasures. We do not have any clear idea of what the old man looks like, though, nor do we know how he talks, since we are not given any of his words. Our knowledge of him is mainly confined to his eye and its effect on the narrator. This confinement gives that symbolic eye a lot of importance in the story. The narrator tells us all we know and directs our atten-tion to certain parts of it.

This point of view raises an interesting question. Since we are dependent on the narrator for all our information, how do we know the whole story isn't just a nightmare of his demented mind? There is really no way we can be sure it isn't, as far as I can see. I assume, however, that there really is a dark shuttered house and an old man and real policemen who start snooping around when screams are heard in the neighborhood, because it is a more memorable story if it is a crazy man's view of reality than if it is all just a terrible dream. What we can't take stock in is the madman's interpretation of what happens. Poe keeps putting distances between what the narrator says and what we are supposed to think, apparently. For instance: the narrator has boasted that he is calm and clear in the head, but as soon as he starts (in the second paragraph) trying to explain why he killed the old man, we gather that he is confused, to say the least. "I think it was his eye!" the narrator exclaims, as if not quite sure. As he goes on to explain how he conducted the murder, we realize that he is a man with a fixed idea working with a patience that is certainly mad, almost diabolical.

Some readers might wonder if "The Tell-Tale Heart" is a story of the supernatural. Is the heartbeat that the narrator hears a ghost come back to haunt him? Here, I think, the point of view is our best guide to what to believe. There is a simple explanation for the heartbeat: it is all in the madman's mind. Perhaps he feels such guilt that he starts hearing things. Still another explanation is possible, one suggested by Daniel Hoffman, a critic who has discussed the story: the killer hears the sound of his own heart.[1] Hoffman's explanation (which I don't like as well as mine) also is a natural one, and it fits the story as a whole. Back when the narrator first entered the old man's bedroom to kill him, the heartbeat sounded so loud to him that he was afraid the neighbors would hear it too. Evidently they didn't, so Hoffman may be right in thinking that the sound was only that of his own heart pounding in his ears. Whichever explanation you take, it is a more down-to-earth and reasonable explanation than that (as the narrator

---

[1] Poe Poe Poe Poe Poe Poe Poe (New York: Anchor, 1973), p. 227.

believes) the heart is still alive, even though its owner has been cut
to pieces. Then, too, the police keep chatting. If they heard the
heartbeat too, wouldn't they leap to their feet, draw their guns, and
look all around the room? As the rest of the story has kept showing us,
the narrator's view of things is ~~always~~ untrustworthy. You don't kill
someone just because you dislike the look in his eye. You don't think
that such a murder is funny. For all its Gothic atmosphere of the old
dark house with a secret hidden inside, "The Tell-Tale Heart" is not a
ghost story. We have only to see its point of view to know that it is a
study in abnormal psychology.

A temptation in writing an analysis is to want to include all sorts
of insights that the writer proudly wishes to display even though they
aren't related to the main idea. In the preceding essay, the student resists this temptation admirably. In fairly plump and ample paragraphs,
he works out his ideas, and he supports his contentions with specific
references to Poe's story. While his paper is not brilliantly written and
while it contains no insight so fresh as the suggestion (by the writer of
the first paper) that the madman's lantern is like the old man's head,
still, it is a good brief analysis. By sticking faithfully to his purpose and
by confronting the problems he raises ("how do we know the whole
story isn't just a nightmare?"), the writer persuades us that he understands, not only the story's point of view, but the story in its entirety.

Just to illustrate, now, the method of analysis in the hands of a
professional, here is a discussion of "The Tell-Tale Heart" by Patrick
F. Quinn, a scholar and teacher of literature. Quinn's analysis occurs in
a book-length study of Poe's work and reputation.[1] In a chapter dealing
with several of Poe's stories, Quinn discovers in all of them a similar
theme — that a man may have a living ghost, a spiritual double or
twin. Poe's most famous expression of this theme occurs in another of
his tales, "William Wilson," in which a hard-drinking gambler is annoyed by the continual appearance of his rival, a virtuous double of
himself who, oddly, bears the same name. Unable to stand his double
any longer, he finally stabs the man. Dying, the double takes on the
killer's own face. (The notion of such a double is an ancient one; and,
by the way, you will meet it again in Joseph Conrad's short novel, *The
Secret Sharer*.) Such a theme certainly isn't obvious in "The Tell-Tale
Heart," and many readers find in the story no theme at all. But Quinn
believes the theme to be implied and, in his analysis, persuasively

[1] *The French Face of Edgar Poe* (Carbondale, Ill.: Southern Illinois University Press, 1957),
pp. 234–237.

sorts out details in the story which, in his opinion, convey it. Quinn, a skilled quoter, gives in full a passage from Poe that greatly strengthens his argument. Just before he begins his analysis, Quinn points out that the madman of "The Tell-Tale Heart" shows by his actions that he is mad, despite his claims to sanity.

But the engrossing interest this story has depends less on the general fact that the hero is mad than on the particular kind of madness that his case involves. What was the nature of his crime? He had no hatred for his victim. Quite the reverse: "I loved the old man." And so he casts about for a reason, a convincing motive: "I think it was his eye! yes, it was this! He had the eye of a vulture — a pale blue eye, with a film over it. Whenever it fell upon me, my blood ran cold; and so by degrees — very gradually — I made up my mind to take the life of the old man, and thus rid myself of the eye forever." A simpler solution, but one which the criminal apparently did not consider, would have been to leave the house, a house of which we are told that only the two men lived there. That this solution did not occur to the murderer is one more indication of his mental derangement; but, more than this, it carries a suggestion of the strange relationship in which the two characters were involved. Thus the feelings of the old man when he awoke to discover his executioner at the door were feelings that the executioner could identify himself with:

He was still sitting up in the bed listening; — just as I have done night after night, hearkening to the death watches in the wall. Presently I heard a slight groan, and I knew it was the groan of mortal terror. It was not a groan of pain or of grief — oh no! — it was the low stifled sound that arises from the bottom of the soul when overcharged with awe. I knew the sound well. Many a night just at midnight, when all the world slept, it has welled up from my own bosom, deepening, with its dreadful echo, the terrors that distracted me.

He carried a lantern but had no need of it. Without its aid he was able to see the old man as he lay on his bed, although the time was midnight and the room was "black as pitch with the thick darkness." He could see him well enough with the mind's eye, Poe is implying here; for the act of murder in this story took place on a psychological as well as a physical level, and the nature and meaning of the crime must be sought in the psychology of the hero rather than in the immediately visible external details of his actions.

The murderer identified himself with his victim: "I knew what the old man felt, and pitied him, although I chuckled at heart." But what he did not know was that through this crime he was unconsciously seeking his own death. The shuttered lantern in his hand chanced to symbolize the thing he hated, the pale blue eye of the old man, the eye with a film over it. Whenever that eye fell on him, his blood ran cold. Thus he used the lantern to project a beam of light that filled the old man with terror, and in this way executioner and victim exchanged experiences. But so closely had the madman identified himself with his adversary that the murder he committed also brought on his own death. With unwitting irony he later tells the police that the scream heard during the night was his own, "in a dream." Objectively, this is false, for the scream was uttered by the old man. But subjectively, in the unconscious merging of himself and his victim, that cry was his own. And then at the end of the story another sound is to be identified, the beating of the telltale heart. By an amazing stroke, Poe brings in a detail that makes the story, if taken on a literal, realistic plane, patently absurd; but which, if interpreted for its psychological significance, becomes a brilliant climax to the hidden drama that has been unfolding. The ever-louder heartbeats heard by the criminal, are they, as he says, the sound of the beating of the old man's heart, that old man whose corpse has been dismembered and concealed under the planking in the room? Certainly not — on the plane of realistic and objective fact. It is the "hideous heart" of the criminal himself which he hears. But if we remember that the criminal sought his own death in that of his victim, and that he had in effect become the man who now lies dead, then what he tells the police is true. His conscious purpose was to lie to them about the earlier scream, but then, unconsciously, he told the truth. Now, consciously, he attempts to tell the truth, and this time he is unconsciously in error. And inevitably so. For his consciousness, his very being, had become intrinsicate with that of the man he killed, and with the extinction of his victim the power to separate illusion from reality became extinct in him and his madness was complete. How appropriate to this case, therefore, are the words of Wilson's murdered double: *"In me didst thou exist — and, in my death, see by this image, which is thine own, how utterly thou hast murdered thyself."*

Each analysis has dealt with a single element of Poe's story — the student's with point of view and Quinn's with theme. Still another familiar writing assignment, the **card report,** asks one to analyze a story into its *several* elements. Usually confined to the front and back of one 5 by 8-inch index card, such a report is just as challenging to write as an essay, if not more so. To do the job well, you have to see the story in its elements, then specify them succinctly and accurately. Here (on the following pages) is a typical card report listing and detailing the essentials of "The Tell-Tale Heart." In this assignment, the student was asked to include:

1. The title of the story and the date of its original publication.
2. The author's name and dates.
3. A terse summary of the main events of the story, given in chronological order.
4. The name (if any) of the central character, together with a description of that character's main traits or features.
5. Other characters in the story, dealt with in the same fashion.
6. A short description of the setting.
7. The narrator of the story. (To identify him or her is, of course, to define the point of view from which the story is told.)
8. A description of the general tone of the story, as well as it can be sensed: the author's apparent feelings toward the central character or the main events.

9. Some comments on the style in which the story is written. (Brief illustrative quotations are helpful, insofar as space permits.)

10. Whatever kinds of irony the story contains, and what they contribute to the story.

11. In a sentence, the story's main theme.

12. Leading symbols (if the story has any), with an educated guess at whatever each symbol suggests.

13. Finally, an evaluation of the story as a whole, concisely setting forth the student's opinion of it. (Some instructors regard this as the most important part of the report, and most students find that, by the time they have so painstakingly separated the ingredients of the story, they have arrived at a definite opinion of it.)

To fit so much into the space of a single card is, admittedly, somewhat like trying to engrave the Declaration of Independence on the head of a pin. The student who wrote this succinct report had to spoil a few trial cards before he was able to do it. Every word has to count, and making them count is a discipline worthwhile in almost any sort of expository writing. Some students enjoy the challenge. In doing such a report, while you may feel severely limited, you'll probably be surprised at how thoroughly you come to understand a story. Besides, if

```
(Student's name)                    (Course and section)

Story: "The Tell-Tale Heart," 1850
Author: Edgar Allan Poe (1809-1849)

Events in summary: (1) Dreading one vulturelike eye of the old man he
shares a house with, a madman determines to kill its owner.  (2) Each
night he spies upon the sleeping old man, but finding the eye shut,
he stays his hand.  (3) On the eighth night, finding the eye open, he
suffocates its owner beneath the mattress and conceals the dismem-
bered body under the floor of the bedchamber.  (4) Entertaining some
inquiring police officers in the very room where the body lies hidden,
the killer again hears (or thinks he hears) the beat of his victim's
heart.  (5) Terrified, convinced that the policemen also hear  the
heartbeat growing louder, the killer confesses his crime.
     Central character: An unnamed younger man whom people call mad,
who claims that a nervous disease has greatly sharpened his sense
perceptions.  He is proud of his own cleverness.  Other characters:
The old man, whose leading feature is one pale blue, filmed eye; said
to be rich, kind, and lovable.  (Also three policemen, not individ-
ually described.)
     Setting: A shuttered house full of wind, mice, and treasures;
pitch dark even in the afternoon.
     Narrator: The madman himself.
     Tone: Horror at the events described, skepticism toward the
narrator's claims to be sane, revulsion (or at least detachment) from
his gaiety and laughter.
```

Style: Written as if told aloud by a deranged man eager to be believed, the story is punctuated by laughter, interjections
("Hearken!"), nervous halts, and fresh beginnings--indicated by
dashes that grow more frequent as the story goes on and the narrator
becomes more excited. Poe often relies on general adjectives ("mournful," "hideous," "hellish") to convey atmosphere; also on exact details: the lantern that emits "a single dim ray, like the thread of
a spider."
    Irony: The whole story is ironic in its point of view. Presum-
ably the author is not mad, nor does he share the madman's self-
admiration, nor join in his glee ("I then smiled gaily, to find the
deed so far done"). Many of the narrator's statements therefore seem
verbal ironies: his account of taking an hour to move his head
through the bedroom door--"Oh, you would have laughed to see how
cunningly I thrust it in!" Probably we would have shuddered.
    Theme: Possibly "Murder will out," but I really don't find any
theme either stated or clearly implied.

Symbols: The vulture eye, called an Evil Eye (in superstition, one
that can implant a curse), perhaps suggesting too the all-seeing eye
of God the Father, from whom no guilt can be concealed. The ghostly
heartbeat, sound of the victim coming back to be avenged (or the God
who cannot be slain?). Death watches: beetles said to be death omens,
whose ticking sound foreshadows the sound of the tell-tale heart "as
a watch makes when enveloped in cotton."

Evaluation: Despite the overwrought style (to me slightly comic-
bookish), a powerful story, admirable for its concision and for its
memorable portrait of a deranged killer. Poe knows how it is to be
mad.

you care to keep the card for future reference, it won't take much storage
room. A longer story, even a novel, may be analyzed in the same way;
but insist on taking a second card if you are asked to analyze some
especially hefty and complicated novel — say, Leo Tolstoi's panoramic,
thousand-page *War and Peace.*

COMPARISON AND CONTRAST

If you were to write on the topic, "Attitudes toward Television in
'Harrison Bergeron' and 'The Pedestrian'" (to take the Kurt Vonnegut
and Ray Bradbury stories in Chapter Seven), you would probably find
yourself employing at least one other method. It might be **comparison,**
in which you would place the two stories side by side and point out
their similarities; or it might be **contrast,** in which you would point out
their differences.

    Most of the time, in dealing with a pair of stories, you will find
them similar in certain respects and different in others; and so you will
be using both methods in writing your paper. No law requires you to
devote equal space to each method. You might have to do more contrasting than comparing, or the other way around. If, for example, the
stories are obviously similar but subtly different, you will probably
briefly compare them, listing the similarities, and then, at greater

length, contrast them by calling attention to their important differences. If, however, the stories at first glance seem as different as peas from polecats, and yet they are in fact closely related, you'll probably spend most of your time comparing them rather than contrasting them. (Your paper might not just compare and contrast, but also analyze, in that you might select one particular element of the stories for your investigation.) Other topics for papers involving two stories might be "The Lifeboat as Locale in Horatio Alger's 'Out on the Ocean' and Stephen Crane's 'The Open Boat'" (a topic that might invite more contrast than comparison, since Alger's lifeboat is a hunk of wood while Crane's is a miniature universe); "The Theme of Coming of Age in James Joyce's 'Araby' and William Faulkner's 'Barn Burning'"; and "The Fascinated Prey: A Comparison of the Situations of Connie in Joyce Carol Oates's 'Where Are You Going, Where Have You Been?' and Mrs. Miller in Truman Capote's 'Miriam.'"

Evidently, it is easier (and more meaningful) to compare and contrast two stories that seem to have much in common than two that seem (and in fact are) unrelated. An essay that likened Aesop's fable of the frogs who wanted a king and Richard Brautigan's comic study in character, "The Kool-Aid Wino," just might reveal startling and unexpected similarities; but more likely, it would seem as far-fetched, strained, and pointless as trying to yoke together a flea and a mule.

You can, of course, write an essay in comparison and contrast that treats not a pair of stories but a single story. You might compare and contrast, say, the personalities of the two ships' captains in Conrad's *The Secret Sharer;* or you might contrast Mrs. Turpin's view of herself with the girl Mary Grace's view of her in Flannery O'Connor's "Revelation."

If your topic calls for both comparison and contrast, and you are dealing with two stories, don't write the first half of your paper all about one story, then pivot and write the second half about the other, never permitting the two to mingle. The result probably would not be a unified essay in contrast and comparison, but two separate commentaries yoked together. One workable way to organize such a paper is (before you begin) to make a brief list of points to look for in each story, then, as you write, to consider each point — first in one story and then in the other. For instance, here is a simple outline for an essay bringing together William Faulkner's "A Rose for Emily" and Flannery O'Connor's "Revelation." The topic is "Two Would-be Aristocrats: The Characters of Emily Grierson and Mrs. Turpin."

1. Character's view of her own innate superiority

    a. Emily

    b. Mrs. Turpin

2. Author's evaluation of character's moral worth

   a. Emily

   b. Mrs. Turpin

3. Character's ability to change

   a. Emily

   b. Mrs. Turpin

It is best, however, not to follow such an outline in plodding, mechanical fashion ("Well, now it's time to whip over to Mrs. Turpin again"), lest your readers feel they are watching a back-and-forth tennis match. Some points are bound to interest you more than others, and, when they do, you will want to give them greater emphasis.

TOPICS FOR WRITING

What kinds of topics are likely to result in papers that will reveal something about works of fiction? Here is a list of typical topics, suitable to papers of various lengths, offered in the hope of stimulating your own ideas. For specific advice on finding a topic of your own, see the Appendix: Writing about Literature.

TOPICS FOR BRIEF PAPERS (250–500 WORDS)

1. Consider a short story in which the central character has to make a decision or must take some decisive step that will alter the rest of his or her life. Faulkner's "Barn Burning" is one such story, another is Updike's "A & P." As concisely but thoroughly as you can, explain the nature of the character's decision, the reasons for it, and its probable consequences (as suggested by what the author tells us).

2. Write an informal (rather than a complete) explication of the opening paragraph or first few lines of a story. Show us how it prepares us for what will happen. (An alternate topic: take instead a *closing* paragraph and sum up whatever insight it leaves us with.) Don't feel obliged to deal with everything in the passage, as you would do in writing a more nearly complete explication. Within this suggested word length, limit your discussion to whatever strikes you as most essential.

3. Choosing a story other than "Revelation" or "The Loudest Voice" (included in the chapter on Theme), state in your own words its central theme, and indicate whatever you find in the story that makes this theme apparent. Among stories in this book that have especially prominent themes are "Barn Burning," "Gimpel the Fool," "The Minister's Black Veil," "The Pedestrian," and "The Ones Who Walk Away from Omelas."

4. Make a card report (see pages 225–226) on a short story in the Stories for Further Study, or one suggested by your instructor. Include all the elements in the report illustrated in this chapter (unless your instructor wishes you to emphasize some particular element or offers other advice).

5. Write a brief fable of your own invention, perhaps illustrating some familiar proverb ("Too many cooks spoil the broth," "A rolling stone gathers no

moss"). It can be an imitation of Aesop's "The Frogs Who Wanted a King" or of other traditional fables you know; or it can be a fable in a modern manner. (For an example of the latter, see Le Guin's "The Ones Who Walk Away from Omelas.") You may state a moral at the end, or you may try to leave the moral unstated but obvious.

6. After you have written such a fable, write a short account of the problems you met in thinking it up and in writing it, and how you surmounted them.

7. Take a short story not included in this book — one by a writer of high reputation and a distinctive style, such as William Faulkner, Ernest Hemingway, Flannery O'Connor, Edgar Allan Poe, Mark Twain, or some other suggested by your instructor. Insert at some point in the story a passage of your own composition, in which you try to imitate the writer's style as closely as possible. Type out two or three pages of part of the story including your forgery, give copies to the other members of the class, and see if anyone can detect the point at which the writer's prose stops and yours begins.

TOPICS FOR MORE EXTENDED PAPERS (600–1,000 WORDS)

1. Choose a short passage (one of, say, three or four sentences) in a story, a passage that interests you. Perhaps it will contain a decisive moment in a plot, a revealing comment on a character, or a statement of the story's central theme. Then write a reasonably thorough explication. Like the writer of the paper "By Lantern Light" (page 216), go through the passage in some detail, noticing particular words that especially convey the author's meanings.

2. Write an analysis of a short story, singling out an element such as the author's voice (tone, style, irony), point of view, character theme, symbolism, or Gothic elements (if the story has any). Try to show how this element functions in the story as a whole. For a typical paper in response to this assignment, see "The Hearer of 'The Tell-Tale Heart'" (page 220).

3. Write an essay comparing and contrasting two stories similar in theme. Some possibilities might be stories that concern the experience of minorities in America ("The Loudest Voice," "Angel Levine") or that examine some conflict between illusion and reality ("Araby," "A Dill Pickle," "Gimpel the Fool," "A Blind Man").

4. Write an essay taking the measure of two stories that, although both may be good, differ markedly in quality. Evaluate them and give reasons for your judgments. Stories similar enough to be meaningfully compared might include two character studies of women who come to understand themselves ("Revelation" and "The Chrysanthemums") or perhaps two science fiction stories ("The Pedestrian" and "The Ones Who Walk Away from Omelas").

5. Analyze a story in which a character experiences some tremendous realization or revelation. How does the writer prepare us for the moment of enlightenment? What is the nature of each realization or revelation? How does it affect the character? Stories to consider might include "In Exile," "Araby," "Gimpel the Fool," "Revelation," "The Death of Ivan Ilych," "The Chrysanthemums," and "Angel Levine."

6. Explore how humor functions in a story. What is funny? How is humor implied by the story's tone or style? Does humor help set forth a theme, or reveal character? Any of the following stories deserve exploration: "The Catbird Seat," "The Kool-Aid Wino," "Gimpel the Fool," "Revelation," "The Loudest Voice," "Harrison Bergeron," "A Keelboatman's Ghost Story," "A Hunger Artist," "First Confession," "The Egg," "Petrified Man," "Angel Levine," "A & P," "Why I Like Country Music."

7. Write a debunking essay blasting a story in this book that you dislike intensely. Be careful to stick to the text of the story in offering criticisms, and support your charges with plenty of evidence.
8. For anyone interested in a career in teaching: explain how you would teach a certain story, either to some imaginary class, or to the class you belong to now.

Topics for Long Papers (1,500 words or more)

1. Selecting a short story from the anthology at the back of this book, or taking one suggested by your instructor, write an informal essay setting forth (as thoroughly as you can) your understanding of it. Point out any difficulties you encountered in first reading the story, for the benefit of other students who might meet the same difficulties. If there are any particularly complicated passages, briefly explicate them. An ample statement of the meaning of the story probably will not deal only with plot or only with theme, but will also consider how the story is written and structured.
2. Dealing with a single element of fiction, write an analysis of Conrad's *The Secret Sharer* or Tolstoi's *The Death of Ivan Ilych*, or of some other short novel that your instructor suggests to you.
3. Take a short story in which most of the events take place in the physical world (rather than inside some character's mind), and translate it into a one-act play, complete with stage directions. After you have done so, you might present a reading of it with the aid of other members of the class and then perhaps discuss what you had to do to the story to make a play of it.
4. Taking an author in this book whose work appeals to you, read at least three or four of his or her other stories. Then write an analysis of them, concentrating on an element of fiction that you find present in all.
5. Again going beyond this book to read other stories, compare and contrast two writers' handling of a similar theme. Let your essay build to a conclusion in which you state your opinion: which author's expression of theme is deeper, or more memorable?

10 Reading the Novel

Among the forms of imaginative literature in our language, the novel has long been the favorite of both writers and readers. For more than two hundred years, only the lyric poem has rivaled the novel in attracting outstanding practitioners. As far as we can tell from sales figures, the novel has far outdistanced the popularity of other literary forms. Broadly defined, a **novel** is a book-length story in prose, whose author tries to create the sense that, while we read, we experience actual life.

This sense of actuality, which is also found in artful short stories, may be the quality that sets the novel apart from other long prose narratives. Why do we not apply the name *novel* to (for instance) *Gulliver's Travels*? In his marvel-filled account of Lemuel Gulliver's voyages among pygmies, giants, civilized horses, and noxious humanoid swine, Jonathan Swift does not seem primarily concerned that we find his story credible. Though he arrays the adventures of Gulliver in painstaking detail (and, ironically, has Gulliver swear to the truth of them), Swift neither attempts nor achieves a convincing illusion of life. For *Gulliver's Travels* is a satire, pointing out resemblances between noble horses and man's reasoning faculties, between debased apes and man's kinship with the beasts.

Unlike other major literary forms — drama, lyric, ballad, and epic — the novel is a relative newcomer. Originally, the drama in ancient Greece came alive only when actors performed it; the epic or heroic poem (from the classic *Iliad* through the Old English *Beowulf*), only when a bard sang or chanted it. But the English novel came to maturity in literate times, in the eighteenth century, and by its nature was something different: a story to be communicated silently, at whatever moment and at whatever pace (whether quickly or slowly and meditatively) that the reader desired.

Exactly when did the novel begin? Depending on what each considers a novel, literary historians disagree. It is sure that prose narratives, of some kind, are of early origin. From the second century B.C., there were prose stories written in Greek, probably to be consumed by people of wealth and leisure, who could read them or have them read aloud. Later, in Elizabethan England, the growing numbers of literate people and the development of cheap printing encouraged the long prose story. One such narrative that still seems lively is Thomas Nashe's *The Unfortunate Traveller, or, The Life of Jack Wilton* (1594), a racy account of a courtier's intrigues in far-off Italy and Germany. Widely known in the late Middle Ages was the long story in verse or prose, usually about knights and their adventures, called the **romance** because originally written in French or another Romance language. An English example is the *Morte d'Arthur* (1485), Thomas Mallory's retelling of the King Arthur legend. Later, after the decline of knights and chivalry, a type of prose fiction still called *romance* continued to thrive: an idealized love story of noble heroes and heroines. Such was *Clelia* by Mademoiselle de Scudéry, a work that Joseph Addison (in a *Spectator* paper of 1711) reported finding in a rather moony-minded lady's library: a copy "which opened of itself in the place that describes two lovers in a bower."

And yet these earlier works lack certain essential qualities we expect in the modern novel: credible characters, some of them drawn in the round; psychological depth; some attention to the larger fabric of the society in which the events take place; and descriptive detail, at least enough to make us feel that we are witnessing the actual. Authors of medieval romances (unlike most modern novelists) felt free to include fantastic or improbable characters, events, and situations. Such a romance as *Tristan and Isolte,* with its plot based upon the effects of a magical love potion, seems about as far from a modern realistic novel (say, a psychologically probing account of a love affair) as a medieval tale (such as "Godfather Death," Chapter One) is different from a realistic short story. (See the discussion of *tale* and *short story* in Chapter One.) Closer to today's novel than a romance are the surviving fragments of *The Satyricon* by the first-century Roman writer Petronius, a cynical, bawdy narrative of life and manners in Nero's empire; and the two-part *Don Quixote* of Miguel de Cervantes (1605 and 1615), with its profound portraits of the idealizing Don and his skeptical, down-to-earth squire Sancho Panza — another work that takes in a wide portion of its society.

Some say the English novel begins with Samuel Richardson's *Pamela: or, Virtue Rewarded* (1740). (And some say it begins two decades earlier with the fiction of Daniel Defoe, but most agree that with *Pamela* the English novel had emerged.) Like romances such as *Clelia,* Richardson's novel revolves around a prolonged courtship, but love (as Richardson sees it) is closer to earth. He tells the history of a virtuous servant girl defending her honor against the advances of her employer, "Mr. B.," who pursues her until trapped into legal marriage. Partially because of its method of narration — *Pamela* is an **epistolary**

novel, [1] one told in a series of letters — Richardson's story seems immediate and believable. Like Petronius and Cervantes, Richardson explores manners and morals. In a society that barred women from employment (except in menial jobs such as domestic service and prostitution), virginity was a poor girl's only wealth; and, as Richardson shows, the art of her life was to preserve it till she married, thus assuring herself of respect and economic security.

The popularity of *Pamela* gave rise to many imitations. Among the most notable is Henry Fielding's *Joseph Andrews* (1742), in which Fielding, reversing the sexual roles, purports to tell the story of Pamela's equally virtuous brother Joseph, who defends his virginity against the onslaughts of his employer, one Lady Booby. But as he wrote his novel, Fielding found himself drawn to do more than just burlesque Richardson; and at least one of the book's characters turned out to be one of the great rounded figures in all English fiction: the bumbling, good-hearted Parson Adams.

In his preface Fielding announces *Joseph Andrews* as a "comic epic in prose," and in branding his book an epic he suggests that his hero, like the heroes of *The Iliad* and *The Odyssey*, embodies the customs and ideals of his people — however English, urban, and middle-class. Fielding and other eighteenth-century writers were fond of comparing their works to the Greek and Roman classics, but it is evident that, between classical epic and English novel, the main similarity is that both are long. Being the outgrowth of a more physically daring society than that of mercantile England, the epic naturally boasted heroes of a taller, more superhuman order. It admitted magic (Circe's transformation of men into swine in *The Odyssey*), the intervention of goddesses, and journeys to the world of the dead and to remote lands. Reading *Pamela* and *Joseph Andrews*, readers met no Achilles or Ulysses, no supernatural Sirens; they met ordinary bourgeois people whose concerns resembled their own. In the English novel, a hero is a mere mortal — but perhaps, as in Daniel Defoe's *Robinson Crusoe*, a brilliantly endowed mortal, worthy of the novelist's attention. Reading of Crusoe puttering about his island, taming wild goats, and learning to manufacture crockery, Defoe's readers must have felt flattered. Never before had practical, everyday concerns seemed so important — and who would have thought that an ordinary English subject could be so self-sufficient?

Some definitions of the novel would more strictly limit its province. "The Novel is a picture of real life and manners, and of the time

---

[1] Other celebrated epistolary novels include Richardson's later *Clarissa Harlowe* (1748) and Tobias Smollett's *Humphrey Clinker* (1771). In recent times the form is rare, but Mark Harris's *Wake Up, Stupid* (New York: Knopf, 1959) is one contemporary example.

in which it was written," declared Clara Reeve in 1785, thus distinguishing the novel from the romance, which "describes what never happened nor is likely to happen." By so specifying that the novel depicts life in the present day, the critic was probably observing the derivation of the word *novel*. Akin to the French word for "news" (*nouvelles*), it comes from the Italian *novella* ("something new and small"), a term applied to a newly made story taking place in recent times, and not a traditional story taking place long ago.

Also drawing a line between novel and romance, Nathaniel Hawthorne, in his preface to *The House of the Seven Gables* (1851), restricted the novel "not merely to the possible, but to the probable and ordinary course of man's experience." A romance had no such limitations.[2] Such a definition would deny the name of *novel* to any fantastic or speculative story — to, say, the gothic novel and the science fiction novel (two kinds of fiction discussed more fully in Chapter Seven). Carefully bestowed, the labels *novel* and *romance* may be useful to distinguish between the true-to-life story of usual people in the novel's own times (such as George Eliot's *Silas Marner* or John Updike's *Couples*) and the larger-than-life story of daring deeds and high adventure, set in the past or future or in some timeless land (such as Walter Scott's *Ivanhoe* or J. R. R. Tolkien's *Lord of the Rings*). But the labels are difficult to apply to much of recent fiction, in which ordinary life is sometimes mingled with outlandishness. Who can say that, for instance, James Joyce's *Ulysses* is not a novel, though it contains a bizarre account of the hero's night-time wanderings, rendered strange by moments of dream and of drunken hallucination? (At one moment, a cake of soap rises where the moon ought to be. And yet the total effect, as in any successful novel, is a sense of the actual.)

This sense of the actual is, perhaps, the hallmark of a novel, whether or not the events it relates are literally possible. To achieve this sense, novelists have employed many devices, and frequently have tried to pass off their storytelling as reporting. Hawthorne, in his introduction to *The Scarlet Letter,* gives a minute account of his finding certain documents, on which he claims to base his novel, tied with a faded red ribbon and gathering dust in a customshouse. More recently, Vladimir Nabokov's *Pale Fire* (1962) tells its story in the form of a scholarly edition of a 999-line poem, complete with a biographical commentary by a friend of the late poet. Samuel Richardson's device of casting *Pamela* into the form of personal letters helped lend the story an appearance of being not invented, but discovered. Another method favored by early novelists was to write as though setting down a memoir or an autobiography. Daniel Defoe, whose

---

[2] For a more recent provocative critical book that also separates novel from romance, see Richard Chase, *The American Novel and Its Tradition* (New York: Anchor, 1957).

skill in feigning such memoirs was phenomenal, even succeeded in writing the supposedly true confessions of a woman retired from a life of crime, *Moll Flanders* (1722), and in maintaining a vivid truthfulness:

> Going through Aldersgate Street, there was a pretty little child who had been at a dancing-school, and was going home all alone; and my prompter, like a true devil, set me upon this innocent creature. I talked to it, and it prattled to me again, and I took it by the hand and led it along till I came to a paved alley that goes into Bartholomew Close, and I led it in there. The child said that was not its way home. I said, "Yes, my dear, it is; I'll show you the way home." The child had a little necklace on of gold beads, and I had my eye upon that, and in the dark of the alley I stooped, pretending to mend the child's clog that was loose, and took off her necklace, and the child never felt it, and so led the child on again. Here, I say, the devil put me upon killing the child in the dark alley, that it might not cry, but the very thought frighted me so that I was ready to drop down; but I turned the child about and bade it go back again. . . . The last affair left no great concern upon me, for as I did the poor child no harm, I only said to myself, I had given the parents a just reproof for their negligence in leaving the poor little lamb to come home by itself, and it would teach them to take more care of it another time.

What could sound more like the voice of an experienced child-robber than this manner of excusing her crime, and even justifying it?

The more incredible the story, the harder a novelist may work to make it appear factual, and the more he may rely upon devices that will give it the look of a document. Mary Shelley's *Frankenstein; or, The Modern Prometheus* opens with a series of letters from a sea captain whose vessel has rescued the scientist Victor Frankenstein from an ice floe (where he had been looking for his monster). Similarly, Bram Stoker's improbable *Dracula* is told entirely in fictitious documents: diaries, journals, memoranda, a ship's log, a newspaper clipping.

To some, it would appear that the task of the novelist is just to toss together such a heap of documents. Informed that a student had given up the study of mathematics to become a novelist, the logician David Hilbert drily remarked, "It was just as well: he did not have enough imagination to become a first-rate mathematician."[3] It is true that some novelists place great emphasis on research and notetaking. Arthur Halley, author of best-sellers such as *Wheels* (about the Detroit car industry) and *Airport* (about an airport), reportedly starts work on a novel by interviewing people in whatever glamorous profession he plans to expose, gathering stacks of note-cards to make sure that his slightest detail is accurate. Clearly, however, any novel can grow to completion only through a process of creation, selection, and arrange-

[3] Quoted by William H. Gass, *Fiction and the Figures of Life* (New York: Knopf, 1970).

ment. Raw facts cannot leap into a novel by themselves — whether the novel is a paperback shocker about a famous crime, or whether it is Theodore Dreiser's impressive study of a murder case, inspired by newspaper accounts, *An American Tragedy.*

Much more than reportage, novels grounded in fact have helped to reform the worlds in which they were written. More effectively than editorials, the novels of Charles Dickens helped rouse Victorian readers to protest injustices in orphan asylums, boarding schools, and debtors' prisons. In America, sympathetic cries of outrage greeted Harriet Beecher Stowe's antislavery novel *Uncle Tom's Cabin* and Herman Melville's *White Jacket,* with its candid views of flogging and other mistreatment of sailors in the Navy. Not until Upton Sinclair published *The Jungle* in 1906, with its grim picture of unappetizing conditions in the stockyards, was Congress persuaded to enact the first pure food laws. The point is not that the novel is mere propaganda, but that the novel can be a powerful instrument for social action, and that many novelists of varied persuasions have wielded it. Since World War II, Jean-Paul Sartre in France has argued that, for any novelist, some kind of political commitment is necessary — a view disputed by French novelist Alain Robbe-Grillet, who declares that the writer best serves society by commitment to art.

Lately much discussed has been the **nonfiction novel:** Truman Capote's term for his account of crime and punishment in Kansas, *In Cold Blood* (1966). Based on interviews with the accused and with other principals in the case, Capote's book attempts social history in novel form, complete with dialogue, interior monologue, and symbol. Recently, Norman Mailer's *The Armies of the Night* (1968) has also been called a nonfiction novel: an account (in which the author is a character) of the 1967 march in Washington, D.C., to protest the war in Vietnam. Perhaps the name "nonfiction novel" is newer than the form. In the past, writers of autobiography have frequently cast their memoirs into what looks like novel form: Richard Wright in *Black Boy* (1945), William Burroughs in *Junkie* (1953). Derived not from the author's memory but from his reporting, John Hersey's *Hiroshima* (1946) reconstructs the lives of six survivors of the atom bomb as if they were fictional. In reading such works we may nearly forget we are reading literal truth, so well do the techniques of the novel lend remembered facts an air of immediacy and renewed life.

VARIETIES OF THE NOVEL

A familiar kind of fiction that claims a basis in fact is the **historical novel,** a detailed reconstruction of life in another time, perhaps in another place. In some historical novels the author attempts a faithful picture of daily life in another era, as does Robert Graves in *I, Claudius*

(1934), a novel of patrician Rome. More often, history is a backdrop for an exciting story of love and heroic adventure. This latter is a kind of literary entertainment made popular by Sir Walter Scott in his series of novels beginning with *Waverley* (1814). In America, history, more or less freely adapted, has been the province of novelists from Gore Vidal's recent *Burr* as far back as James Fenimore Cooper's *The Spy* (whose masquerading hero is revealed in the end to be George Washington). Wholly or partly realistic in approach, Nathaniel Hawthorne's *The Scarlet Letter* (set in Puritan Boston), Herman Melville's *Moby Dick* (set in the heyday of Yankee whalers), and Stephen Crane's *The Red Badge of Courage* (set in the battlefields of the Civil War) are historical novels in that their authors lived considerably later than the scenes and events that they depicted — and strove for truthfulness, by imaginative means.

Certain other varieties of novel will be familiar to anyone who scans the racks of paperback books in any drugstore: the mystery or detective novel, the Western novel, the science fiction novel, and other enduring types. Classified according to less well-known species, novels are sometimes said to belong to a certain category if they contain some recognizable kind of structure or theme. Such a category is the **bildungsroman** (German for a "novel of growth or development"), sometimes called the **apprenticeship novel** after its classic example, *Wilhelm Meister's Apprenticeship* (1796) by Johann Wolfgang von Goethe. This is the kind of novel in which a youth struggles toward maturity, seeking, perhaps, some consistent world view or philosophy of life. Sometimes the apprenticeship novel is evidently the author's recollection of his own early life: James Joyce's *Portrait of the Artist as a Young Man* (1914) and Thomas Wolfe's *Look Homeward, Angel* (1929). Like these two examples, such a novel may dwell on the fact that the self-portrayed hero is an artist in conflict with his society. Other apprenticeship novels include Mark Twain's *Huckleberry Finn*, J. D. Salinger's *The Catcher in the Rye*, and John Knowles's *A Separate Peace*. These categories are not mutually exclusive: a novel can be both a *bildungsroman* and a historical novel.

In a **picaresque novel** (to mention another famous category), a likable scoundrel wanders through a series of adventures, living by his wits and duping the straight citizenry. The name comes from Spanish: *pícaro*, "rascal" or "rogue." The classic picaresque novel is the anonymous Spanish *Life of Lazarillo de Tormes* (1554), imitated by many English writers, among them Henry Fielding in his story of a London thief and racketeer, *Jonathan Wild* (1743). Mark Twain's *Huckleberry Finn* owes something to the tradition; like early picaresque novels, it is told in a series of episodes rather than in one all-unifying plot and is narrated in the first person by a hero at odds with respectable society ("dismal regular and decent," Huck Finn calls it). In Twain's novel, however, the traveling swindlers who claim to be a duke and a dauphin are much more typical rogues of picaresque fiction than Huck himself, an honest innocent. Modern novels worthy of the name include Thomas Mann's *Confessions of Felix Krull, Confidence Man* (1955); J. P. Donleavy's *The Ginger Man* (1965); and Saul Bellow's *The Adventures of Augie March* (1953).

To be thoroughly told, a complex story with many scenes and many characters sometimes extends beyond the covers of a single novel. Marcel Proust's two-million-word *Remembrance of Things Past* is one continuous novel, though in seven volumes. Also taking French society for his canvas, Émile Zola wrote twenty separate but related novels to unfold the elaborate chronicles of the family Rougon-Macquart. Tracing the fortunes of another family in Edwardian England, John Galsworthy wrote a **trilogy** (a group of three novels in a sequence), *The Forsyte Saga*, then continued in a second trilogy, *A Modern Comedy*, to trace the lives of Soames Forsyte's later descendants. Other considerable trilogies include Arnold Bennett's *The Clayhanger Family*, John Dos Passos's *U.S.A.*, James T. Farrell's *Studs Lonigan*, and Theodore Dreiser's three novels about businessman Frank Cowperwood (*The Financier, The Titan,* and *The Stoic*). A sequence of *four* novels is usually called a **tetralogy,** such as Ford Maddox Ford's novels about a hero named Tietjens (*Some Do Not, No More Parades, A Man Could Stand Up,* and *The Last Post*), although Lawrence Durrell preferred to call his series of four novels *The Alexandria Quartet*.

Mainly (but not merely) a description of size, the term **short novel** refers to a narrative midway in length between a short story and a novel (which latter, according to E. M. Forster, has to have at least 50,000 words). Generally a short novel, like a short story, centers on just one or two characters but, unlike a short story, has room to reveal them in greater fullness and depth, sometimes taking in a longer span of time. Two short novels are included in this book: Leo Tolstoi's *The Death of Ivan Ilych* and Joseph Conrad's *The Secret Sharer*.[4] Sometimes a short novel is also called a **novelette** (a term formerly much used by magazines that featured long fiction), or a **nouvelle,** or a **novella;** but these names are out of fashion. "Please do not call my short novels *novelettes,* or even worse, *novellas,*" insists Katherine Anne Porter in the preface to her *Collected Stories.* "*Novelette* is classical usage for a trivial dime-novel sort of thing; *novella* is a slack, boneless, affected word that we do not need to describe anything."[5]

---

[4] For an anthology of short novels containing some provocative discussion of the form, see *Nine Modern Classics*, ed. Sylvan Barnet, Morton Berman, and William Burto (Boston: Little, Brown, 1973).

[5] A *novella* in the late Middle Ages indicated (as we have mentioned) a short story of recent origin and contemporary setting. Often it dealt playfully with the hoodwinking of husbands and the seduction of wives, as in many of the novellas that make up *The Decameron* of Giovanni Boccaccio (mid-fourteenth century).

HOW TO READ A NOVEL

A novel can entertain us richly, and yet the finest novels do more than help us pass the time. As the critic and novelist Lionel Trilling has said, the greatness and value of the novel of the last two centuries has resided in its "involving the reader himself in the moral life, inviting him to put his own motives under examination, suggesting that reality is not as his conventional education has led him to see it."[6] Fine novels, as if by turning on lights and opening windows, help us behold aspects of other people (and of ourselves) that we had not observed before.

This view of the novel as a serious and enlightening work of art is relatively modern. For a long while, through much of the nineteenth century, the reader of novels had to combat the prejudice that novel-reading was at best a harmless and trivial diversion, and at worst, a demoralizing vice. In 1820 young Thomas Babington Macaulay felt it necessary to write to his father and defend himself against the charge that he was a novel-reader — hence, an idler frittering away his father's money. Only in 1884, in his essay "The Art of Fiction," did Henry James notice signs of change in the public attitude that "a novel is a novel, as a pudding is a pudding, and that our only business with it could be to swallow it."

If, as readers of novels, we care to be more than pudding-swallowers, we expect to pay some attention to the novelist's insights and wisdom, and to the methods by which he practices his art. Unlike the short story, the novel, being long and inclusive, cannot leave us with a single intense impression when we finish reading it. Requiring of us a longer span of attention, it is a more difficult work to perceive in its entirety — especially if we have had to read it in many sittings, hours or days apart.

Trying to perceive a novel as a whole, we may find it helpful to look for the same elements that we have noticed in reading short stories. By asking ourselves leading questions, we may be drawn more deeply into the novel's world, and may come to recognize and appreciate the techniques of the novelist. Does the novel have themes, or an overall theme? Who is its central character? What is the author's kind of narrative voice? What do we know about his tone, style, and use of irony? Why is this novel written from a particular point of view, rather than from another? If the novel in question is large and thickly populated, it may help to read it with a pencil, taking brief notes. Forced to put the novel aside and later return to it, the reader may find that the notes refresh the memory. Note-taking habits differ, but perhaps these might be no more than, say, "Theme introduced, p. 27," or, "Old clothes

---

[6] "Manners, Morals, and the Novel" in *The Liberal Imagination* (New York: Viking, 1949).

dealer, p. 109 — walking symbol?" Some readers find it useful to note briefly whatever each chapter accomplishes. Others make lists of a novel's characters, especially when reading classic Russian novels in which the reader has to recall that Alexey Karamazov is also identified by his pet name Aloysha, or that, in Leo Tolstoi's *Anna Karenina,* Princess Catherine Alexándrovna Shcherbátskaya and "Kitty" are one and the same.

Once our reading of a novel is finished and we prepare to discuss it or write about it, it may be a good idea to browse through it again, rereading brief portions. This method of overall browsing may also help when first approaching a bulky and difficult novel. Just as an explorer mapping an unfamiliar territory may find it best to begin by taking an aerial view of it, so the reader approaching an exceptionally thick and demanding novel may wish, at the start, to look for its general shape. This is the method of certain professional book-reviewers, who size up a novel (even an easy-to-read spy story, since they are not reading for pleasure) by skimming the first chapter, a middle chapter or two, and the last chapter; then going back and browsing at top speed through the rest. Reading a novel in this grim fashion, of course, the reviewer does not really know it thoroughly, any more than a tourist knows the mind and heart of a foreign people after just strolling in a capital city and riding a tour bus to a few monuments. However, the reviewer's method will provide a general notion of what the author is doing, and at the very least will tell something of his tone, style, point of view, and competence. We suggest this method only as a way to *approach* a book that, otherwise, the reader might not want to approach at all. It may be a comfort in studying some obdurate-looking or highly experimental novel, such as James Joyce's *Ulysses* or Henry James's *The Sacred Fount.* But the reader will find it necessary to return to the book, in order to know it, and to read it honestly, in detail.

There is, of course, no short cut to novel-reading, and probably the best method is to settle in comfort and read the book through: with your own eyes, not with the borrowed glasses of literary criticism, reading for whatever you find yourself coming to expect, balancing your alertness to the novel's possible flaws and shortcomings against your sympathetic willingness to enter its offered world. With patience, you may end with an understanding of both what the novelist attempted to do and how well he did it, with a rich array of your own responses, and possibly with a deepened awareness of other people, and of yourself and your life.

The death of the novel is continually being predicted. The competition of television drama is too much for it, some believe; indeed, there is hard evidence that such competition exists. In Brittany, France, when antigovernment protesters blew up the only television transmitter in the province, booksellers the very next day reported their business increased by as much as twenty percent.[7] But recently in England and North America, television dramas have been sending people in vast numbers back to the books dramatized: Tolstoi's *War and Peace*, Galsworthy's *The Forsyte Saga*. Storytelling in some form will continue until the end of the human race, predicts the critic Leslie Fiedler, who says he would not mourn the death of the novel, "that fat, solid commodity invented by the bourgeoisie for the ends of commerce and culture-climbing."[8] Meanwhile, each year new novels by the hundreds continue to appear and wistfully look for a public. A chosen few reach tens of thousands of readers through book clubs, and, through paperback reprint editions, occasionally millions more. To forecast the end of the novel seems risky. For the novel exercises the imagination of the beholder. At any hour, at a touch of the hand, it opens and (with no warm-up) begins to speak. Once printed, it consumes no further energy. Often so small it may be carried in a pocket, it may yet survive by its ability to contain multitudes (a "capacious vessel," Henry James called it): a thing both a work of art and an amazingly compact system for the storage and retrieval of imagined life.

A SHORT NOVEL FOR READING AND STUDY

Here is a short novel, *The Secret Sharer*, by the Polish-born English author Joseph Conrad. On one level, it is a suspenseful story of a young captain newly in command of his first vessel, determined to prove himself, who finds himself face to face with a surprising challenge — one so strange that it makes him question his own sanity. On other levels, Conrad's story is packed with suggestion; and many readers find that it has something very personal to say to them. Read it and you will discover how a short novel — even one so unusually concise — can explore its themes in greater depth than a short story usually can.

Although, like many of Conrad's most famous works, *The Secret Sharer* is a sea story, it isn't just a yarn of sudden death and threatened mutiny, of storm-tossed waves and mysterious islands. Actually, as you will see, all these matters do indeed appear in it vividly; and yet the young captain's experience is (in its way) more unnerving than what happens in a conventional, swashbuckling sea tale. For in Conrad's view the ship is a narrow arena of conflict — a conflict no less intense for the fact that it takes place within a single human spirit.

Notice how the story begins: slowly and quietly, almost as though the captain were telling us his dream, with the sailing ship at anchor in the Gulf of Siam, awaiting a wind to continue its interrupted voyage home. Dreamlike, too, is the appearance of a mysterious naked swim-

[7] Reported in *The New York Times*, March 5, 1974.
[8] "The End of the Novel" in *Waiting for the End* (New York: Stein and Day, 1964).

mer, who lends the story a curious power. For *The Secret Sharer* contains a **motif,** or situation familiar in myth and literature — that of the living ghost.[9] In folklore and in primitive belief, there is a widespread idea that each living creature has a spiritual twin or double. In some legends, its appearance foretells the death of its original. In German folk tales, such an apparition is called a *doppelgänger* ("double-goer," or walking double). This motif has been prominent in other fiction: in Fyodor Dostoyevsky's novel *The Double,* a poor clerk finds that in everything he attempts a double successfully rivals him; and in Edgar Allan Poe's tale "William Wilson," a dissipated man finds his footsteps hounded by a double, a figure of virtue. The critic Patrick F. Quinn had even discovered this motif in Poe's "The Tell-Tale Heart" (in Chapter Seven; see Quinn's analysis of the story on page 223). Will Conrad's story prove similarly fantastic and incredible? On the contrary, a wealth of realistic detail makes it seem perfectly true. Conrad did not invent (or crib from books) his knowledge of shipboard life and of the Eastern seas. During his sixteen years in the British merchant fleet, the writer-to-be worked his way from deckhand to captain, making voyages in the Indian Ocean and the Malay Archipelago. In a Conrad story, an exotic locale is neither daymare nor dream.

Ever since *The Secret Sharer* first appeared in 1913, readers and critics have been fascinated by it. The unfolding of its meanings continues even today. The reader who meets it for the first time, then, need feel no guilt at being unable to state all that it means. Here's fair warning: Conrad is a deliberate symbolist, who loves to drop hints. Who (or what) is suggested by the captain's double? But let Conrad's narrator tell his story, and perhaps the question will come alive for you. At least, you will see why *The Secret Sharer* tends to grip us and make us wonder, why it fixes itself in memory, and possibly even lures us to return to it — as readers caught in its spell have been lured again and again for the past seven decades.

Joseph Conrad (1857–1924)
THE SECRET SHARER   1913

I

On my right hand there were lines of fishing stakes resembling a mysterious system of half-submerged bamboo fences, incomprehensible in its division of the domain of tropical fishes, and crazy of aspect as if abandoned forever by

[9] Other illustrations of such situations include the Romeo and Juliet motif (lovers whose families are enemies) and the Cinderella motif (poor girl becomes princess thanks to fairy godmother). Sometimes also called a motif, after a repeated phrase in music, is anything repeated over and over, that lends a story unity and thematic meaning — a phrase or saying, a line from a song, the name of a street or a distant country (as the name *Araby* in James Joyce's short story of that title).

some nomad tribe of fishermen now gone to the other end of the ocean; for there was no sign of human habitation as far as the eye could reach. To the left a group of barren islets, suggesting ruins of stone walls, towers, and blockhouses, had its foundations set in a blue sea that itself looked solid, so still and stable did it lie below my feet; even the track of light from the westering sun shone smoothly, without that animated glitter which tells of an imperceptible ripple. And when I turned my head to take a parting glance at the tug which had just left us anchored outside the bar, I saw the straight line of the flat shore joined to the stable sea, edge to edge, with a perfect and unmarked closeness, in one leveled floor half brown, half blue under the enormous dome of the sky. Corresponding in their insignificance to the islets of the sea, two small clumps of trees, one on each side of the only fault in the impeccable joint, marked the mouth of the river Meinam we had just left on the first preparatory stage of our homeward journey; and, far back on the inland level, a larger and loftier mass, the grove surrounding the great Paknam pagoda, was the only thing on which the eye could rest from the vain task of exploring the monotonous sweep of the horizon. Here and there gleams as of a few scattered pieces of silver marked the windings of the great river; and on the nearest of them, just within the bar, the tug steaming right into the land became lost to my sight, hull and funnel and masts, as though the impassive earth had swallowed her up without an effort, without a tremor. My eye followed the light cloud of her smoke, now here, now there, above the plain, according to the devious curves of the stream, but always fainter and farther away, till I lost it at last behind the miter-shaped hill of the great pagoda. And then I was left alone with my ship, anchored at the head of the Gulf of Siam.

She floated at the starting point of a long journey, very still in an immense stillness, the shadows of her spars flung far to the eastward by the setting sun. At that moment I was alone on her decks. There was not a sound in her — and around us nothing moved, nothing lived, not a canoe on the water, not a bird in the air, not a cloud in the sky. In this breathless pause at the threshold of a long passage we seemed to be measuring our fitness for a long and arduous enterprise, the appointed task of both our existences to be carried out, far from all human eyes, with only sky and sea for spectators and for judges.

There must have been some glare in the air to interfere with one's sight, because it was only just before the sun left us that my roaming eyes made out beyond the highest ridges of the principal islet of the group something which did away with the solemnity of perfect solitude. The tide of darkness flowed on swiftly; and with tropical suddenness a swarm of stars came out above the shadowy earth, while I lingered yet, my hand resting lightly on my ship's rail as if on the shoulder of a trusted friend. But, with all that multitude of celestial bodies staring down at one, the comfort of quiet communion with her was gone for good. And there were also disturbing sounds by this time — voices, footsteps forward; the steward flitted along the main-deck, a busily ministering spirit; a hand bell tinkled urgently under the poop deck. . . .

I found my two officers waiting for me near the supper table, in the lighted cuddy°. We sat down at once, and as I helped the chief mate, I said:

cuddy: ship's officers' living space, usually below the bridge, used for lounge and dining room.

"Are you aware that there is a ship anchored inside the islands? I saw her mastheads above the ridge as the sun went down."

He raised sharply his simple face, overcharged by a terrible growth of whisker, and emitted his usual ejaculations: "Bless my soul, sir! You don't say so!"

My second mate was a round-cheeked, silent young man, grave beyond his years, I thought; but as our eyes happened to meet I detected a slight quiver on his lips. I looked down at once. It was not my part to encourage sneering on board my ship. It must be said, too, that I knew very little of my officers. In consequence of certain events of no particular significance, except to myself, I had been appointed to the command only a fortnight before. Neither did I know much of the hands forward. All these people had been together for eighteen months or so, and my position was that of the only stranger on board. I mention this because it has some bearing on what is to follow. But what I felt most was my being a stranger to the ship; and if all the truth must be told, I was somewhat of a stranger to myself. The youngest man on board (barring the second mate), and untried as yet by a position of the fullest responsibility, I was willing to take the adequacy of the others for granted. They had simply to be equal to their tasks; but I wondered how far I should turn out faithful to that ideal conception of one's own personality every man sets up for himself secretly.

Meantime the chief mate, with an almost visible effect of collaboration on the part of his round eyes and frightful whiskers, was trying to evolve a theory of the anchored ship. His dominant trait was to take all things into earnest consideration. He was of a painstaking turn of mind. As he used to say, he "liked to account to himself" for practically everything that came in his way, down to a miserable scorpion he had found in his cabin a week before. The why and the wherefore of that scorpion — how it got on board and came to select his room rather than the pantry (which was a dark place and more what a scorpion would be partial to), and how on earth it managed to drown itself in the inkwell of his writing desk — had exercised him infinitely. The ship within the islands was much more easily accounted for; and just as we were about to rise from table he made his pronouncement. She was, he doubted not, a ship from home lately arrived. Probably she drew too much water to cross the bar except at the top of spring tides. Therefore she went into that natural harbor to wait for a few days in preference to remaining in an open roadstead.

"That's so," confirmed the second mate, suddenly, in his slightly hoarse voice. "She draws over twenty feet. She's the Liverpool ship *Sephora* with a cargo of coal. Hundred and twenty-three days from Cardiff."

We looked at him in surprise.

"The tugboat skipper told me when he came on board for your letters, sir," explained the young man. "He expects to take her up the river the day after tomorrow."

After thus overwhelming us with the extent of his information he slipped out of the cabin. The mate observed regretfully that he "could not account for that young fellow's whims." What prevented him telling us all about it at once, he wanted to know.

I detained him as he was making a move. For the last two days the crew had had plenty of hard work, and the night before they had very little sleep. I felt painfully that I — a stranger — was doing something unusual when I directed him to let all hands turn in without setting an anchor watch. I proposed to keep on deck myself till one o'clock or thereabouts. I would get the second mate to relieve me at that hour.

"He will turn out the cook and the steward at four," I concluded, "and then give you a call. Of course at the slightest sign of any sort of wind we'll have the hands up and make a start at once."

He concealed his astonishment. "Very well, sir." Outside the cuddy he put his head in the second mate's door to inform him of my unheard-of caprice to take a five hours' anchor watch on myself. I heard the other raise his voice incredulously — "What? The Captain himself?" Then a few more murmurs, a door closed, then another. A few moments later I went on deck.

My strangeness, which had made me sleepless, had prompted that unconventional arrangement, as if I had expected in those solitary hours of the night to get on terms with the ship of which I knew nothing, manned by men of whom I knew very little more. Fast alongside a wharf, littered like any ship in port with a tangle of unrelated things, invaded by unrelated shore people, I had hardly seen her yet properly. Now, as she lay cleared for sea, the stretch of her main-deck seemed to me very fine under the stars. Very fine, very roomy for her size, and very inviting. I descended the poop and paced the waist, my mind picturing to myself the coming passage through the Malay Archipelago, down the Indian Ocean, and up the Atlantic. All its phases were familiar enough to me, very characteristic, all the alternatives which were likely to face me on the high seas — everything! . . . except the novel responsibility of command. But I took heart from the reasonable thought that the ship was like other ships, the men like other men, and that the sea was not likely to keep any special surprises expressly for my discomfiture.

Arrived at that comforting conclusion, I bethought myself of a cigar and went below to get it. All was still down there. Everybody at the after end of the ship was sleeping profoundly. I came out again on the quarterdeck, agreeably at ease in my sleeping suit on that warm breathless night, barefooted, a glowing cigar in my teeth, and, going forward, I was met by the profound silence of the fore end of the ship. Only as I passed the door of the forecastle I heard a deep, quiet, trustful sigh of some sleeper inside. And suddenly I rejoiced in the great security of the sea as compared with the unrest of the land, in my choice of that untempted life presenting no disquieting problems, invested with an elementary moral beauty by the absolute straightforwardness of its appeal and by the singleness of its purpose.

The riding light in the forerigging burned with a clear, untroubled, as if symbolic, flame, confident and bright in the mysterious shades of the night. Passing on my way aft along the other side of the ship, I observed that the rope side ladder, put over, no doubt, for the master of the tug when he came to fetch away our letters, had not been hauled in as it should have been. I became annoyed at this, for exactitude in some small matters is the very soul of discipline. Then I reflected that I had myself peremptorily dismissed my officers from duty, and by my own act had prevented the anchor watch being formally set and things properly attended to. I asked myself whether it was wise ever to interfere with the established routine of duties even from the kindest of motives. My action might have made me appear eccentric. Goodness only knew how that absurdly whiskered mate would "account" for my conduct, and what the whole ship thought of that informality of their new captain. I was vexed with myself.

Not from compunction certainly, but, as it were mechanically, I proceeded to get the ladder in myself. Now a side ladder of that sort is a light affair and comes in easily, yet my vigorous tug, which should have brought it flying on board, merely recoiled upon my body in a totally unexpected jerk. What the devil! . . . I was so astounded by the immovableness of the ladder that I remained stockstill, trying to account for it to myself like that imbecile mate of mine. In the end, of course, I put my head over the rail.

The side of the ship made an opaque belt of shadow on the darkling glassy shimmer of the sea. But I saw at once something elongated and pale floating very close to the ladder. Before I could form a guess a faint flash of phosphorescent light, which seemed to issue suddenly from the naked body of a man, flickered in the sleeping water with the elusive, silent play of summer lightning in a night sky. With a gasp I saw revealed to my stare a pair of feet, the long legs, a broad livid back immersed right up to the neck in a greenish cadaverous glow. One hand, awash, clutched the bottom rung of the ladder. He was complete but for the head. A headless corpse! The cigar dropped out of my gaping mouth wth a tiny plop and a short hiss quite audible in the absolute stillness of all things under heaven. At that I suppose he raised up his face, dimly pale oval in the shadow of the ship's side. But even then I could only barely make out down there the shape of his black-haired head. However, it was enough for the horrid, frost-bound sensation which had gripped me about the chest to pass off. The moment of vain exclamations was past, too. I only climbed on the spare spar and leaned over the rail as far as I could, to bring my eyes nearer to that mystery floating alongside.

As he hung by the ladder, like a resting swimmer, the sea lightning played about his limbs at every stir; and he appeared in it ghastly, silvery, fishlike. He remained as mute as a fish, too. He made no motion to get out of the water, either. It was inconceivable that he should not attempt to come on board, and strangely troubling to suspect that perhaps he did not want to. And my first words were prompted by just that troubled incertitude.

"What's the matter?" I asked in my ordinary tone, speaking down to the face upturned exactly under mine.

"Cramp," it answered, no louder. Then slightly anxious, "I say, no need to call anyone."

"I was not going to," I said.

"Are you alone on deck?"

"Yes."

I had somehow the impression that he was on the point of letting go the ladder to swim away beyond my ken — mysterious as he came. But, for the moment, this being appearing as if he had risen from the bottom of the sea (it was certainly the nearest land to the ship) wanted only to know the time. I told him. And he, down there, tentatively:

"I suppose your captain's turned in?"

"I am sure he isn't," I said.

He seemed to struggle with himself, for I heard something like the low, bitter murmur of doubt. "What's the good?" His next words came out with a hesitating effort.

"Look here, my man. Could you call him out quietly?"

I thought the time had come to declare myself.

"I am the captain."

I heard a "By Jove!" whispered at the level of the water. The phosphorescence flashed in the swirl of the water all about his limbs, his other hand seized the ladder.

"My name's Leggatt."

The voice was calm and resolute. A good voice. The self-possession of that man had somehow induced a corresponding state in myself. It was very quietly that I remarked:

"You must be a good swimmer."

"Yes. I've been in the water practically since nine o'clock. The question for me now is whether I am to let go this ladder and go on swimming till I sink from exhaustion, or— to come on board here."

I felt this was no mere formula of desperate speech, but a real alternative in the view of a strong soul. I should have gathered from this that he was young; indeed, it is only the young who are ever confronted by such clear issues. But at the time it was pure intuition on my part. A mysterious communication was established already between us two — in the face of that silent, darkened tropical sea. I was young, too; young enough to make no comment. The man in the water began suddenly to climb up the ladder, and I hastened away from the rail to fetch some clothes. Before entering the cabin I stood still, listening in the lobby at the foot of the stairs. A faint snore came through the closed door of the chief mate's room. The second mate's door was on the hook, but the darkness in there was absolutely soundless. He, too, was young and could sleep like a stone. Remained the steward, but he was not likely to wake up before he was called. I got a sleeping suit out of my room and, coming back on deck, saw the naked man from the sea sitting on the main hatch, glimmering white in the darkness, his elbows on his knees and his head in his hands. In a moment he had concealed his damp body in a sleeping suit of the same gray-stripe pattern as the one I was wearing and followed me like my double on the poop. Together we moved right aft, barefooted, silent.

"What is it?" I asked in a deadened voice, taking the lighted lamp out of the binnacle, and raising it to his face.

"An ugly business."

He had rather regular features; a good mouth; light eyes under somewhat heavy, dark eyebrows; a smooth, square forehead; no growth on his cheeks; a small, brown mustache, and a well-shaped, round chin. His expression was concentrated, meditative, under the inspecting light of the lamp I held up to his face; such as a man thinking hard in solitude might wear. My sleeping suit was just right for his size. A well-knit young fellow of twenty-five at most. He caught his lower lip with the edge of white, even teeth.

"Yes," I said, replacing the lamp in the binnacle. The warm, heavy tropical night closed upon his head again.

"There's a ship over there," he murmured.

"Yes, I know. The *Sephora*. Did you know of us?"

"Hadn't the slightest idea. I am the mate of her —" He paused and corrected himself. "I should say I *was*."

"Aha! Something wrong?"

"Yes. Very wrong indeed. I've killed a man."

"What do you mean? Just now?"

"No, on the passage. Weeks ago. Thirty-nine south. When I say a man —"

"Fit of temper," I suggested, confidently.

The shadowy, dark head, like mine, seemed to nod imperceptibly above the ghostly gray of my sleeping suit. It was, in the night, as though I had been faced by my own reflection in the depths of a somber and immense mirror.

"A pretty thing to have to own up to for a Conway boy," murmured my double, distinctly.

"You're a Conway boy?"

"I am," he said, as if startled. Then, slowly . . . "Perhaps you too —"

It was so; but being a couple of years older I had left before he joined. After a quick interchange of dates a silence fell; and I thought suddenly of my absurd mate with his terrific whiskers and the "Bless my soul — you don't say so" type of intellect. My double gave me an inkling of his thoughts by saying: "My father's a parson in Norfolk. Do you see me before a judge and jury on that charge? For myself I can't see the necessity. There are fellows that an angel from heaven — And I am not that. He was one of those creatures that are just simmering all the time with a silly sort of wickedness. Miserable devils that have no business to live at all. He wouldn't do his duty and wouldn't let anybody else do theirs. But what's the good of talking! You know well enough the sort of ill-conditioned snarling cur —"

He appealed to me as if our experiences had been as identical as our clothes. And I knew well enough the pestiferous danger of such a character where there are no means of legal repression. And I knew well enough also that my double there was no homicidal ruffian. I did not think of asking him for details, and he told me the story roughly in brusque, disconnected sentences. I needed no more. I saw it all going on as though I were myself inside that other sleeping suit.

"It happened while we were setting a reefed foresail, at dusk. Reefed foresail! You understand the sort of weather. The only sail we had left to keep the ship running; so you may guess what it had been like for days. Anxious sort of job, that. He gave me some of his cursed insolence at the sheet. I tell you I was overdone with this terrific weather that seemed to have no end to it. Terrific, I tell you — and a deep ship. I believe the fellow himself was half crazed with funk. It was no time for gentlemanly reproof, so I turned round and felled him like an ox. He up and at me. We closed just as an awful sea made for the ship. All hands saw it coming and took to the rigging, but I had him by the throat, and went on shaking him like a rat, the men above us yelling, 'Look out! look out!' Then a crash as if the sky had fallen on my head. They say that for over ten minutes hardly anything was to be seen of the ship — just the three masts and a bit of the forecastle head and of the poop all awash driving along in a smother of foam. It was a miracle that they found us, jammed together behind the forebitts°. It's clear that I meant business, because I was holding him by the throat still when they picked us up. He was black in the face. It was too much for them. It seems they rushed us aft together, gripped as we were, screaming 'Murder!' like a lot of lunatics, and broke into the cuddy. And the ship running for her life, touch and go all the time, any minute her last in a sea fit to turn your hair gray only a-looking at it. I understand that the skipper, too, started raving like the rest of them. The man had been deprived of sleep for more than a week, and to have this sprung on him at the height of a furious gale nearly drove him out of his mind. I wonder they didn't fling me overboard after getting the carcass of their precious shipmate out of my fingers. They had rather a job to separate us, I've been told. A sufficiently fierce story to make an old judge and a respectable jury sit up a bit. The first thing I heard when I came to myself was the maddening howling of that endless gale, and on that the voice of the old man. He was hanging on to my bunk, staring into my face out of his sou'wester.

" 'Mr. Leggatt, you have killed a man. You can act no longer as chief mate of this ship.' "

His care to subdue his voice made it sound monotonous. He rested a hand on the end of the skylight to steady himself with, and all that time did not stir a limb, so far as I could see. "Nice little tale for a quiet tea party," he concluded in the same tone.

One of my hands, too, rested on the end of the skylight; neither did I stir a limb, so far as I knew. We stood less than a foot from each other. It occurred to me that if old "Bless my soul — you don't say so" were to put his head up the companion and catch sight of us, he would think he was seeing double, or imagine himself come upon a scene of weird witchcraft; the strange captain having a quiet confabulation by the wheel with his own gray ghost. I became very much concerned to prevent anything of the sort. I heard the other's soothing undertone.

"My father's a parson in Norfolk," it said. Evidently he had forgotten he had told me this important fact before. Truly a nice little tale.

"You had better slip down into my stateroom now," I said, moving off stealthily. My double followed my movements; our bare feet made no sound; I let him in, closed the door with care, and, after giving a call to the second mate, returned on deck for my relief.

"Not much sign of any wind yet," I remarked when he approached.

"No sir. Not much," he assented, sleepily, in his hoarse voice, with just enough deference, no more, and barely suppressing a yawn.

"Well, that's all you have to look out for. You have got your orders."

"Yes, sir."

I paced a turn or two on the poop and saw him take up his position face forward with his elbow in the ratlines of the mizzen rigging before I went below. The mate's faint snoring was still going on peacefully. The cuddy lamp was burning over the table on which stood a vase with flowers, a polite attention from the ship's provision merchant — the last flowers we should see for the next three months at the very least. Two bunches of bananas hung from the beam symmetrically, one on each side of the rudder casing. Everything was as

---

forebitts: a pair of posts on the forward part of the deck, used for fastening cables or lines.

before in the ship — except that two of her captain's sleeping suits were simultaneously in use, one motionless in the cuddy, the other keeping very still in the captain's stateroom.

It must be explained here that my cabin had the form of the capital letter L, the door being within the angle and opening into the short part of the letter. A couch was to the left, the bed place to the right; my writing desk and the chronometers' table faced the door. But anyone opening it, unless he stepped right inside, had no view of what I call the long (or vertical) part of the letter. It contained some lockers surmounted by a bookcase; and a few clothes, a thick jacket or two, caps, oilskin coat, and such like, hung on hooks. There was at the bottom of that part a door opening into my bathroom, which could be entered also directly from the saloon. But that way was never used.

The mysterious arrival had discovered the advantage of this particular shape. Entering my room, lighted strongly by a big bulkhead lamp swung on gimbals above my writing desk, I did not see him anywhere till he stepped out quietly from behind the coats hung in the recessed part.

"I heard somebody moving about, and went in there at once," he whispered.

I, too, spoke under my breath.

"Nobody is likely to come in here without knocking and getting permission."

He nodded. His face was thin and the sunburn faded, as though he had been ill. And no wonder. He had been, I heard presently, kept under arrest in his cabin for nearly seven weeks. But there was nothing sickly in his eyes or in his expression. He was not a bit like me, really; yet, as we stood leaning over my bed place, whispering side by side, with our dark heads together and our backs to the door, anybody bold enough to open it stealthily would have been treated to the uncanny sight of a double captain busy talking in whispers with his other self.

"But all this doesn't tell me how you came to hang on to our side ladder," I inquired, in the hardly audible murmurs we used, after he had told me something more of the proceedings on board the *Sephora* once the bad weather was over.

"When we sighted Java Head I had had time to think all those matters out several times over. I had six weeks of doing nothing else, and with only an hour or so every evening for a tramp on the quarter-deck."

He whispered, his arms folded on the side of my bed place, staring through the open port. And I could imagine perfectly the manner of this thinking out — a stubborn if not a steadfast operation; something of which I should have been perfectly incapable.

"I reckoned it would be dark before we closed with the land," he continued, so low that I had to strain my hearing near as we were to each other, shoulder touching shoulder almost. "So I asked to speak to the old man. He always seemed very sick when he came to see me— as if he could not look me in the face. You know, that foresail saved the ship. She was too deep to have run long under bare poles. And it was I that managed to set it for him. Anyway, he came. When I had him in my cabin — he stood by the door looking at me as if I had the halter around my neck already — I asked him right away to leave my cabin door unlocked at night while the ship was going through Sunda

Straits. There would be the Java coast within two or three miles, off Angier Point. I wanted nothing more. I've had a prize for swimming my second year in the Conway."

"I can believe it," I breathed out.

"God only knows why they locked me in every night. To see some of their faces you'd have thought they were afraid I'd go about at night strangling people. Am I a murdering brute? Do I look it? By Jove! If I had been he wouldn't have trusted himself like that into my room. You'll say I might have chucked him aside and bolted out, there and then — it was dark already. Well, no. And for the same reason I wouldn't think of trying to smash the door. There would have been a rush to stop me at the noise, and I did not mean to get into a confounded scrimmage. Somebody else might have got killed — for I would not have broken out only to get chucked back, and I did not want any more of that work. He refused, looking more sick than ever. He was afraid of the men, and also of that old second mate of his who had been sailing with him for years — a gray-headed old humbug; and his steward, too, had been with him devil knows how long — seventeen years or more — a dogmatic sort of loafer who hated me like poison, just because I was the chief mate. No chief mate ever made more than one voyage in the *Sephora*, you know. Those two old chaps ran the ship. Devil only knows what the skipper wasn't afraid of (all his nerve went to pieces altogether in that hellish spell of bad weather we had) — of what the law would do to him — of his wife, perhaps. Oh, yes! she's on board. Though I don't think she would have meddled. She would have been only too glad to have me out of the ship in any way. The 'brand of Cain' business, don't you see. That's all right. I was ready enough to go off wandering on the face of the earth — and that was price enough to pay for an Abel of that sort°. Anyhow, he wouldn't listen to me. 'This thing must take its course. I represent the law here." He was shaking like a leaf. 'So you won't?' 'No!' 'Then I hope you will be able to sleep on that,' I said, and turned my back on him. 'I wonder that *you* can,' cries he, and locks the door.

"Well after that, I couldn't. Not very well. That was three weeks ago. We have had a slow passage through the Java Sea; drifted about Carimata for ten days. When we anchored here they thought, I suppose, it was all right. The nearest land (and that's five miles) is the ship's destination; the consul would soon set about catching me; and there would have been no object in bolting to these islets there. I don't suppose there's a drop of water on them. I don't know how it was, but tonight that steward, after bringing me my supper, went out to let me eat it, and left the door unlocked. And I ate it — all there was, too. After I had finished I strolled out on the quarter-deck. I don't know that I meant to do anything. A breath of fresh air was all I wanted, I believe. Then a sudden temptation came over me. I kicked off my slippers and was in the water before I had made up my mind fairly. Somebody heard the splash and they raised an awful hullabaloo. 'He's gone! Lower the boats! He's committed suicide! No, he's swimming.' Certainly I was swimming. It's not so easy for a swimmer like me to commit suicide by drowning. I landed on the nearest islet before the boat left the ship's side. I heard them pulling about in the dark, hailing, and so on, but

---

The 'brand of Cain' . . . of that sort: After slaying his brother Abel, Cain became a wanderer, bearing a distinctive brand or mark. (See Genesis 4.)

after a bit they gave up. Everything quieted down and the anchorage became as still as death. I sat down on a stone and began to think. I felt certain they would start searching for me at daylight. There was no place to hide on those stony things — and if there had been, what would have been the good? But now I was clear of that ship, I was not going back. So after a while I took off all my clothes, tied them up in a bundle with a stone inside, and dropped them in the deep water on the outer side of that islet. That was suicide enough for me. Let them think what they liked, but I didn't mean to drown myself. I meant to swim till I sank — but that's not the same thing. I struck out for another of these little islands, and it was from that one that I first saw your riding light. Something to swim for. I went on easily, and on the way I came upon a flat rock a foot or two above water. In the daytime, I dare say, you might make it out with a glass from your poop. I scrambled up on it and rested myself for a bit. Then I made another start. That last spell must have been over a mile."

His whisper was getting fainter and fainter, and all the time he stared straight out through the porthole, in which there was not even a star to be seen. I had not interrupted him. There was something that made comment impossible in his narrative, or perhaps in himself; a sort of feeling, a quality, which I can't find a name for. And when he ceased, all I found was a futile whisper: "So you swam for our light?"

"Yes — straight for it. It was something to swim for. I couldn't see any stars low down because the coast was in the way, and I couldn't see the land, either. The water was like glass. One might have been swimming in a confounded thousand-feet deep cistern with no place for scrambling out anywhere; but what I didn't like was the notion of swimming round and round like a crazed bullock before I gave out; and as I didn't mean to go back . . . No. Do you see me being hauled back, stark naked, off one of these little islands by the scruff of the neck and fighting like a wild beast? Somebody would have got killed for certain, and I did not want any of that. So I went on. Then your ladder —"

"Why didn't you hail the ship?" I asked, a little louder.

He touched my shoulder lightly. Lazy footsteps came right over our heads and stopped. The second mate had crossed from the other side of the poop and might have been hanging over the rail for all we knew.

"He couldn't hear us talking — could he?" My double breathed into my very ear, anxiously.

His anxiety was an answer, a sufficient answer, to the question I had put to him. An answer containing all the difficulty of that situation. I closed the porthole quietly, to make sure. A louder word might have been overheard.

"Who's that?" he whispered then.

"My second mate. But I don't know much more of the fellow than you do."

And I told him a little about myself. I had been appointed to take charge while I least expected anything of the sort, not quite a fortnight ago. I didn't know either the ship or the people. Hadn't had the time in port to look about me or size anybody up. And as to the crew, all they knew was that I was appointed to take the ship home. For the rest, I was almost as much of a stranger on board as himself, I said. And at the moment I felt it most acutely. I felt that it would take very little to make me a suspect person in the eyes of the ship's company.

He had turned about meantime; and we, the two strangers in the ship, faced each other in identical attitudes.

"Your ladder —" he murmured, after a silence. "Who'd have thought of finding a ladder hanging over at night in a ship anchored out here! I felt just then a very unpleasant faintness. After the life I've been leading for nine weeks, anybody would have got out of condition. I wasn't capable of swimming round as far as your rudder chains. And, lo and behold! there was a ladder to get hold of. After I gripped it I said to myself, 'What's the good?' When I saw a man's head looking over I thought I would swim away presently and leave him shouting — in whatever language it was. I didn't mind being looked at. I — I liked it. And then you speaking to me so quietly — as if you had expected me — made me hold on a little longer. It had been a confounded lonely time — I don't mean while swimming. I was glad to talk a little to somebody that didn't belong to the *Sephora*. As to asking for the captain, that was a mere impulse. It could have been no use, with all the ship knowing about me and the other people pretty certain to be round here in the morning. I don't know — I wanted to be seen, to talk with somebody, before I went on. I don't know what I would have said. . . . 'Fine night, isn't it?' or something of the sort."

"Do you think they will be round here presently?" I asked with some incredulity.

"Quite likely," he said, faintly.

He looked extremely haggard all of a sudden. His head rolled on his shoulders.

"H'm. We shall see then. Meantime get into that bed," I whispered. "Want help? There."

It was a rather high bed place with a set of drawers underneath. This amazing swimmer really needed the lift I gave him by seizing his leg. He tumbled in, rolled over on his back, and flung one arm across his eyes. And then, with his face nearly hidden, he must have looked exactly as I used to look in that bed. I gazed upon my other self for a while before drawing across carefully the two green serge curtains which ran on a brass rod. I thought for a moment of pinning them together for greater safety, but I sat down on the couch, and once there I felt unwilling to rise and hunt for a pin. I would do it in a moment. I was extremely tired, in a peculiarly intimate way, by the strain of stealthiness, by the effort of whispering and the general secrecy of this excitement. It was three o'clock by now and I had been on my feet since nine, but I was not sleepy; I could not have gone to sleep. I sat there, fagged out, looking at the curtains, trying to clear my mind of the confused sensation of being in two places at once, and greatly bothered by an exasperating knocking in my head. It was a relief to discover suddenly that it was not in my head at all, but on the outside of the door. Before I could collect myself the words "Come in" were out of my mouth, and the steward entered with a tray, bringing in my morning coffee. I had slept, after all, and I was so frightened that I shouted, "This way! I am here, steward," as though he had been miles away. He put down the tray on the table next to the couch and only then said, very quietly, "I can see you are here, sir." I felt him give me a keen look, but I dared not meet his eyes just then. He must have wondered why I had drawn the curtains of my bed before going to sleep on the couch. He went out, hooking the door open as usual.

I heard the crew washing decks above me. I knew I would have been told at once if there had been any wind. Calm, I thought, and I was doubly vexed. Indeed, I felt dual more than ever. The steward reappeared suddenly in the doorway. I jumped up from the couch so quickly that he gave a start.

"What do you want here?"

"Close your port, sir — they are washing decks."

"It is closed," I said, reddening.

"Very well, sir." But he did not move from the doorway and returned my stare in an extraordinary, equivocal manner for a time. Then his eyes wavered, all his expression changed, and in a voice unusually gentle, almost coaxingly:

"May I come in to take the empty cup away, sir?"

"Of course!" I turned my back on him while he popped in and out. Then I unhooked and closed the door and even pushed the bolt. This sort of thing could not go on very long. The cabin was as hot as an oven, too. I took a peep at my double, and discovered that he had not moved, his arm was still over his eyes; but his chest heaved; his hair was wet; his chin glistened with perspiration. I reached over him and opened the port.

"I must show myself on deck," I reflected.

Of course, theoretically, I could do what I liked, with no one to say nay to me within the whole circle of the horizon; but to lock my cabin door and take the key away I did not dare. Directly I put my head out of the companion I saw the group of my two officers, the second mate barefooted, the chief mate in long India-rubber boots, near the break of the poop, and the steward halfway down the poop ladder talking to them eagerly. He happened to catch sight of me and dived, the second ran down on the maindeck shouting some order or other, and the chief mate came to meet me, touching his cap.

There was a sort of curiosity in his eye that I did not like. I don't know whether the steward had told them that I was "queer" only, or downright drunk, but I know the man meant to have a good look at me. I watched him coming with a smile which, as he got into point-blank range, took effect and froze his very whiskers. I did not give him time to open his lips.

"Square the yards by lifts and braces before the hands go to breakfast."

It was the first particular order I had given on board that ship; and I stayed on deck to see it executed, too. I had felt the need of asserting myself without loss of time. That sneering young cub got taken down a peg or two on that occasion, and I also seized the opportunity of having a good look at the face of every foremast man as they filed past me to go to the after braces. At breakfast time, eating nothing myself, I presided with such frigid dignity that the two mates were only too glad to escape from the cabin as soon as decency permitted; and all the time the dual working of my mind distracted me almost to the point of insanity. I was constantly watching myself, my secret self, as dependent on my actions as my own personality, sleeping in that bed, behind that door which faced me as I sat at the head of the table. It was very much like being mad, only it was worse because one was aware of it.

I had to shake him for a solid minute, but when at last he opened his eyes it was in the full possession of his senses, with an inquiring look.

"All's well so far," I whispered. "Now you must vanish into the bathroom."

He did so, as noiseless as a ghost, and then I rang for the steward, and facing him boldly, directed him to tidy up my stateroom while I was having my bath — "and be quick about it." As my tone admitted of no excuses, he said, "Yes, sir," and ran off to fetch his dustpan and brushes. I took a bath and did most of my dressing, splashing, and whistling softly for the steward's edification, while the secret sharer of my life stood drawn up bolt upright in that little space, his face looking very sunken in daylight, his eyelids lowered under the stern, dark line of his eyebrows drawn together by a slight frown.

When I left him there to go back to my room the steward was finishing dusting. I sent for the mate and engaged him in some insignificant conversation. It was, as it were, trifling with the terrific character of his whiskers; but my object was to give him an opportunity for a good look at my cabin. And then I could at last shut, with a clear conscience, the door of my stateroom and get my double back into the recessed part. There was nothing else for it. He had to sit still on a small folding stool, half smothered by the heavy coats hanging there. We listened to the steward going into the bathroom out of the saloon, filling the water bottles there, scrubbing the bath, setting things to rights, whisk, bang, clatter — out again into the saloon — turn the key — click. Such was my scheme for keeping my second self invisible. Nothing better could be contrived under the circumstances. And there we sat; I at my writing desk ready to appear busy with some papers, he behind me out of sight of the door. It would not have been prudent to talk in daytime; and I could not have stood the excitement of that queer sense of whispering to myself. Now and then, glancing over my shoulder, I saw him far back there, sitting rigidly on the low stool, his bare feet close together, his arms folded, his head hanging on his breast — and perfectly still. Anybody would have taken him for me.

I was fascinated by it myself. Every moment I had to glance over my shoulder. I was looking at him when a voice outside the door said:

"Beg pardon, sir."

"Well!" . . . I kept my eyes on him, and so when the voice outside the door announced, "There's a ship's boat coming our way, sir." I saw him give a start — the first movement he had made for hours. But he did not raise his bowed head.

"All right. Get the ladder over."

I hesitated. Should I whisper something to him? But what? His immobility seemed to have been never disturbed. What could I tell him he did not know already? . . . Finally I went on deck.

II

The skipper of the *Sephora* had a thin red whisker all round his face, and the sort of complexion that goes with hair of that color; also the particular, rather smeary shade of blue in the eyes. He was not exactly a showy figure; his shoulders were high, his stature but middling — one leg slightly more bandy than the other. He shook hands, looking vaguely around. A spiritless tenacity was his main characteristic, I judged. I behaved with politeness which seemed to disconcert him. Perhaps he was shy. He mumbled to me as if he were ashamed of what he was saying; gave his name (it was something like Archbold — but at this distance of years I hardly am sure), his ship's name, and a few other particulars of that sort, in the manner of a criminal making a reluctant and doleful confession. He had had terrible weather on the passage out — terrible — terrible — wife aboard, too.

By this time we were seated in the cabin and the steward brought in a tray with a bottle and glasses. "Thanks! No." Never took liquor. Would have some water, though. He drank two tumblerfuls. Terrific thirsty work. Ever since daylight had been exploring the islands round his ship.

"What was that for — fun?" I asked, with an appearance of polite interest.

"No!" He sighed. "Painful duty."

As he persisted in his mumbling and I wanted my double to hear every word, I hit upon the the notion of informing him that I regretted to say I was hard of hearing.

"Such a young man, too!" he nodded, keeping his smeary blue, unintelligent eyes fastened upon me. "What was the cause of it — some disease?" he inquired, without the least sympathy and as if he thought that, if so, I'd got no more than I deserved.

"Yes; disease," I admitted in a cheerful tone which seemed to shock him. But my point was gained, because he had to raise his voice to give me his tale. It is not worth while to record that version. It was just over two months since all this had happened, and he had thought so much about it that he seemed completely muddled as to its bearings, but still immensely impressed.

"What would you think of such a thing happening on board your own ship? I've had the *Sephora* for these fifteen years. I am a well-known shipmaster."

He was densely distressed — and perhaps I should have sympathized with him if I had been able to detach my mental vision from the unsuspected sharer of my cabin as though he were my second self. There he was on the other side of the bulkhead, four or five feet from us, no more, as we sat in the saloon. I looked politely at Captain Archbold (if that was his name), but it was the other I saw, in a gray sleeping suit, seated on a low stool, his bare feet close together, his arms folded, and every word said between us falling into the ears of his dark head bowed on his chest.

"I have been at sea now, man and boy, for seven-and-thirty years, and I've never heard of such a thing happening in an English ship. And that it should be my ship. Wife on board, too."

I was hardly listening to him.

"Don't you think," I said, "that the heavy sea which, you told me, came aboard just then might have killed the man? I have seen the sheer weight of a sea kill a man very neatly, by simply breaking his neck."

"Good God!" he uttered, impressively, fixing his smeary blue eyes on me. "The sea! No man killed by the sea ever looked like that." He seemed positively scandalized at my suggestion. And as I gazed at him certainly not prepared for anything original on his part, he advanced his head close to mine and thrust his tongue out at me so suddenly that I couldn't help starting back.

After scoring over my calmness in this graphic way he nodded wisely. If I had seen the sight, he assured me, I would never forget it as long as I lived. The weather was too bad to give the corpse a proper sea burial. So next day at dawn they took it up on the poop, covering its face with a bit of bunting; he read a short prayer, and then, just as it was, in its oilskins and long boots, they launched it amongst those mountainous seas that seemed ready every moment to swallow up the ship herself and the terrified lives on board of her.

"That reefed foresail saved you," I threw in.

"Under God — it did," he exclaimed fervently. "It was by a special mercy, I firmly believe, that it stood some of those hurricane squalls."

"It was the setting of that sail which —" I began.

"God's own hand in it," he interrupted me. "Nothing less could have done it. I don't mind telling you that I hardly dared give the order. It seemed impossible that we could touch anything without losing it, and then our last hope would have been gone."

The terror of that gale was on him yet. I let him go on for a bit, then said, casually — as if returning to a minor subject:

"You were very anxious to give up your mate to the shore people, I believe?"

He was. To the law. His obscure tenacity on that point had in it something incomprehensible and a little awful; something, as it were, mystical, quite apart from his anxiety that he should not be suspected of "countenancing any doings of that sort." Seven-and-thirty virtuous years at sea, of which over twenty of immaculate command, and the last fifteen in the *Sephora*, seemed to have laid him under some pitiless obligation.

"And you know," he went on, groping shame-facedly amongst his feelings, "I did not engage that young fellow. His people had some interest with my owners. I was in a way forced to take him on. He looked very smart, very gentlemanly, and all that. But do you know — I never liked him, somehow. I am a plain man. You see, he wasn't exactly the sort for the chief mate of a ship like the *Sephora*."

I had become so connected in thoughts and impressions with the secret sharer of my cabin that I felt as if I, personally, were being given to understand that I, too, was not the sort that would have done for the chief mate of a ship like the *Sephora*. I had no doubt of it in my mind.

"Not at all the style of man. You understand," he insisted, superfluously, looking hard at me.

I smiled urbanely. He seemed at a loss for a while.

"I suppose I must report a suicide."

"Beg pardon?"

"Sui-cide! That's what I'll have to write to my owners directly I get in."

"Unless you manage to recover him before tomorrow," I assented, dispassionately. . . . "I mean, alive."

He mumbled something which I really did not catch, and I turned my ear to him in a puzzled manner. He fairly bawled:

"The land — I say, the mainland is at least seven miles off my anchorage."

"About that."

My lack of excitement, of curiosity, of surprise, of any sort of pronounced interest, began to arouse his distrust. But except for the felicitous pretense of deafness I had not tried to pretend anything. I had felt utterly incapable of playing the part of ignorance properly, and therefore was afraid to try. It is also certain that he had brought some ready-made suspicions with him, and that he viewed my politeness as a strange and unnatural phenomenon. And yet how else could I have received him? Not heartily! That was impossible for psychological reasons, which I need not state here. My only object was to keep off his inquiries. Surlily? Yes, but surliness might have provoked a point-blank question. From its novelty to him and from its nature, punctilious courtesy was the manner best calculated to restrain the man. But there was the danger of his breaking through my defense bluntly. I could not, I think, have met him by a direct lie, also for psychological (not moral) reasons. If he had only known how afraid I was of his putting my feeling of identity with the other to the test! But, strangely enough — (I thought of it only afterwards) — I believe that he was not a little disconcerted by the reverse side of that weird situation, by something in me that reminded him of the man he was seeking — suggested a mysterious similitude to the young fellow he had distrusted and disliked from the first.

However that might have been, the silence was not very prolonged. He took another oblique step.

"I reckon I had no more than a two-mile pull to your ship. Not a bit more."

"And quite enough, too, in this awful heat," I said.

Another pause full of mistrust followed. Necessity, they say, is mother of invention, but fear, too, is not barren of ingenious suggestions. And I was afraid he would ask me point-blank for news of my other self.

"Nice little saloon, isn't it?" I remarked, as if noticing for the first time the way his eyes roamed from one closed door to the other. "And very well fitted out, too. Here, for instance," I continued, reaching over the back of my seat negligently and flinging the door open, "is my bathroom."

He made an eager movement, but hardly gave it a glance. I got up, shut the door of the bathroom, and invited him to have a look round, as if I were very proud of my accommodation. He had to rise and be shown round, but he went through the business without any raptures whatever.

"And now we'll have a look at my stateroom," I declared, in a voice as loud as I dared to make it, crossing the cabin to the starboard side with purposely heavy steps.

He followed me in and gazed around. My intelligent double had vanished. I played my part.

"Very convenient — isn't it?"

"Very nice. Very comf. . . ." He didn't finish and went out brusquely as if to escape from some unrighteous wiles of mine. But it was not to be. I had been too frightened not to feel vengeful; I felt I had him on the run, and I meant to keep him on the run. My polite insistence must have had something menacing in it, because he gave in suddenly. And I did not let him off a single item; mate's room, pantry, storerooms, the very sail locker which was also under the poop — he had to look into them all. When at last I showed him out on the quarter-deck he drew a long, spiritless sigh, and mumbled dismally that he must really be going back to his ship now. I desired my mate, who had joined us, to see to the captain's boat.

The man of whiskers gave a blast on the whistle which he used to wear hanging round his neck, and yelled, "Sephora's away!" My double down here in my cabin must have heard, and certainly could not feel more relieved than I. Four fellows came running out from somewhere forward and went over the side, while my own men, appearing on deck too, lined the rail. I escorted my visitor to the gangway ceremoniously, and nearly overdid it. He was a tenacious beast. On the very ladder he lingered, and in that unique, guiltily conscientious manner of sticking to the point:

"I say . . . you . . . you don't think that —"

I covered his voice loudly:

"Certainly not. . . . I am delighted. Good-by."

I had an idea of what he meant to say, and just saved myself by the privilege of defective hearing. He was too shaken generally to insist, but my mate, close witness of that parting, looked mystified and his face took on a thoughtful cast. As I did not want to appear as if I wished to avoid all communication with my officers, he had the opportunity to address me.

"Seems a very nice man. His boat's crew told our chaps a very extraordinary story, if what I am told by the steward is true. I suppose you had it from the captain, sir?"

"Yes. I had a story from the captain."

"A very horrible affair — isn't it, sir?"

"It is."

"Beats all these tales we hear about murders in Yankee ships."

"I don't think it beats them. I don't think it resembles them in the least."

"Bless my soul — you don't say so! But of course I've no acquaintance whatever with American ships, not I, so I couldn't go against your knowledge. It's horrible enough for me. . . . But the queerest part is that those fellows seemed to have some idea the man was hidden aboard here. They had really. Did you ever hear of such a thing?"

"Preposterous — isn't it?"

We were walking to and fro athwart the quarter-deck. No one of the crew forward could be seen (the day was Sunday), and the mate pursued:

"There was some little dispute about it. Our chaps took offense. 'As if we would harbor a thing like that,' they said. 'Wouldn't you like to look for him in our coalhole?' Quite a tiff. But they made it up in the end. I suppose he did drown himself. Don't you, sir?"

"I don't suppose anything."

"You have no doubt in the matter, sir?"

"None whatever."

I left him suddenly. I felt I was producing a bad impression, but with my double down there it was most trying to be on deck. And it was almost as trying to be below. Altogether a nerve-trying situation. But on the whole I felt less torn in two when I was with him. There was no one in the whole ship whom I dared take into my confidence. Since the hands had got to know his story, it would have been impossible to pass him off for anyone else, and an accidental discovery was to be dreaded now more than ever. . . .

The steward being engaged in laying the table for dinner, we could talk only with our eyes when I first went down. Later in the afternoon we had a cautious try at whispering. The Sunday quietness of the ship was against us; the stillness of air and water around her was against us; the elements, the men were against us — everything was against us in our secret partnership; time itself — for this could not go on forever. The very trust in Providence was, I suppose, denied to his guilt. Shall I confess that this thought cast me down very much? And as to the chapter of accidents which counts for so much in the book of success, I could only hope that it was closed. For what favorable accident could be expected?

"Did you hear everything?" were my first words as soon as we took up our position side by side, leaning over my bed place.

He had. And the proof of it was his earnest whisper, "The man told you he hardly dared to give the order."

I understood the reference to be to that saving foresail.

"Yes. He was afraid of its being lost in the setting."

"I assure you he never gave the order. He may think he did, but he never gave it. He stood there with me on the break of the poop after the main topsail blew away, and whimpered about our last hope — positively whimpered about it and nothing else — and the night coming on! To hear one's skipper go on like that in such weather was enough to drive any fellow out of his mind. It worked me up into a sort of desperation. I just took it into my own hands and went away from him, boiling, and — But what's the use telling you? *You* know! . . . Do you think that if I had not been pretty fierce with them I should have got the men to do anything? Not I! The bo's'n perhaps? Perhaps! It wasn't a heavy sea — it was a sea gone mad! I suppose the end of the world will be something like that; and a man may have the heart to see it coming once and be done with it — but to have to face it day after day — I don't blame anybody. I was precious little better than the rest. Only — I was an officer of that old coal wagon, anyhow —"

"I quite understand," I conveyed that sincere assurance into his ear. He was out of breath with whispering; I could hear him pant slightly. It was all very simple. The same strung-up force which had given twenty-four men a chance, at least, for their lives, had, in a sort of recoil, crushed an unworthy mutinous existence.

But I had no leisure to weigh the merits of the matter — footsteps in the saloon, a heavy knock. "There's enough wind to get under way with, sir." Here was the call of a new claim upon my thoughts and even upon my feelings.

"Turn the hands up," I cried through the door. "I'll be on deck directly."

I was going out to make the acquaintance of my ship. Before I left the cabin our eyes met — the eyes of the only two strangers on board. I pointed to the recessed part where the little campstool awaited him and laid my finger on my lips. He made a gesture — somewhat vague — a little mysterious, accompanied by a faint smile, as if of regret.

This is not the place to enlarge upon the sensations of a man who feels for the first time a ship move under his feet to his own independent word. In my case they were not unalloyed. I was not wholly alone with my command; for there was that stranger in my cabin. Or rather, I was not completely and wholly with her. Part of me was absent. That mental feeling of being in two places at once affected me physically as if the mood of secrecy had penetrated my very soul. Before an hour had elapsed since the ship had begun to move, having occasion to ask the mate (he stood by my side) to take a compass bearing of the pagoda, I caught myself reaching up to his ear in whispers. I say I caught myself, but enough had escaped to startle the man. I can't describe it otherwise than by saying that he shied. A grave, preoccupied manner, as though he were in possession of some perplexing intelligence, did not leave him henceforth. A little later I moved away from the rail to look at the compass with such a stealthy gait that the helmsman noticed it — and I could not help noticing the unusual roundness of his eyes. These are trifling instances, though it's to no commander's advantage to be suspected of ludicrous eccentricities. But I was also more seriously affected. There are to a seaman certain words, gestures, that should in given conditions come as naturally, as instinctively, as the winking of a menaced eye. A certain order should spring on to his lips without thinking; a certain sign should get itself made, so to speak, without reflection. But all unconscious alertness had abandoned me. I had to make an effort of will to recall myself back (from the cabin) to the conditions of the moment. I felt that I was appearing an irresolute commander to those people who were watching me more or less critically.

And, besides, there were the scares. On the second day out, for instance, coming off deck in the afternoon (I had straw slippers on my bare feet) I stopped at the open pantry door and spoke to the steward. He was doing something there with his back to me. At the sound of my voice he nearly jumped out of his skin, as the saying is, and incidentally broke a cup.

"What on earth's the matter with you?" I asked, astonished.

He was extremely confused. "Beg your pardon, sir. I made sure you were in your cabin."

"You see I wasn't."

"No, sir. I could have sworn I had heard you moving in there not a moment ago. It's most extraordinary . . . very sorry, sir."

I passed on with an inward shudder. I was so identified with my secret double that I did not even mention the fact in those scanty, fearful whispers we exchanged. I suppose he had made some slight noise of some kind or other. And yet, haggard as he appeared, he looked always perfectly self-controlled, more than calm — almost invulnerable. On my suggestion he remained almost entirely in the bathroom, which, upon the whole, was the safest place. There could be really no shadow of an excuse for anyone ever wanting to go in there, once the steward had done with it. It was a very tiny place. Sometimes he reclined on the floor, his legs bent, his head sustained on one elbow. At others I would find him on the campstool, sitting in his gray sleeping suit and with his cropped hair like a patient, unmoved convict. At night I would smuggle him into my bed place, and we would whisper together, with the regular footfalls of the officer of the watch passing and repassing over our heads. It was an infinitely miserable time. It was lucky that some tins of fine preserves were stowed in a locker in my stateroom; hard bread I could always get hold of; and so he lived on stewed chicken, *pâté de foie gras*, asparagus, cooked oysters, sardines — on all sorts of abominable sham delicacies out of tins. My early-morning coffee he always drank; and it was all I dared do for him in that respect.

Every day there was the horrible maneuvering to go through so that my room and then the bathroom should be done in the usual way. I came to hate the sight of the steward, to abhor the voice of that harmless man. I felt that it was he who would bring the disaster of discovery. It hung like a sword over our heads.

The fourth day out, I think (we were then working down the east side of the Gulf of Siam, tack for tack, in light winds and smooth water) — the fourth day, I say, of this miserable juggling with the unavoidable, as we sat at our evening meal, that man, whose slightest movement I dreaded, after putting down the dishes ran up on deck busily. This could not be dangerous. Presently he came down again; and then it appeared that he had remembered a coat of mine which I had thrown over a rail to dry after having been wetted in a shower which had passed over the ship in the afternoon. Sitting stolidly at the head of the table I became terrified at the sight of the garment on his arm. Of course he made for my door. There was no time to lose.

"Steward," I thundered. My nerves were so shaken that I could not govern my voice and conceal my agitation. This was the sort of thing that made my terrifically whiskered mate tap his forehead with his forefinger. I had detected him using that gesture while talking on deck with a confidential air to the carpenter. It was too far to hear a word, but I had no doubt that this pantomime could only refer to the strange new captain.

"Yes, sir," the pale-faced steward turned resignedly to me. It was this maddening course of being shouted at, checked without rhyme or reason, arbitrarily chased out of my cabin, suddenly called into it, sent flying out of his pantry on incomprehensible errands, that accounted for the growing wretchedness of his expression.

"Where are you going with that coat?"

"To your room, sir."

"Is there another shower coming?"

"I'm sure I don't know, sir. Shall I go up again and see, sir?"

"No! never mind."

My object was attained, as of course my other self in there would have heard everything that passed. During this interlude my two officers never raised their eyes off their respective plates; but the lip of that confounded cub, the second mate, quivered visibly.

I expected the steward to hook my coat on and come out at once. He was very slow about it; but I dominated my nervousness sufficiently not to shout after him. Suddenly I became aware (it could be heard plainly enough) that the fellow for some reason or other was opening the door of the bathroom. It was the end. The place was literally not big enough to swing a cat in. My voice died in my throat and I went stony all over. I expected to hear a yell of surprise and terror, and made a movement, but had not the strength to get on my legs. Everything remained still. Had my second self taken the poor wretch by the throat? I don't know what I could have done next moment if I had not seen the steward come out of my room, close the door, and then stand quietly by the sideboard.

"Saved," I thought. "But, no! Lost! Gone! He was gone!"

I laid my knife and fork down and leaned back in my chair. My head swam. After a while, when sufficiently recovered to speak in a steady voice, I instructed my mate to put the ship round at eight o'clock himself.

"I won't come on deck," I went on. "I think I'll turn in, and unless the wind shifts I don't want to be disturbed before midnight. I feel a bit seedy."

"You did look middling bad a little while ago," the chief mate remarked without showing any great concern.

They both went out, and I stared at the steward clearning the table. There was nothing to be read on that wretched man's face. But why did he avoid my eyes, I asked myself. Then I thought I should like to hear the sound of his voice.

"Steward!"

"Sir!" Startled as usual.

"Where did you hang up that coat?"

"In the bathroom, sir." The usual anxious tone. "It's not quite dry yet, sir."

For some time longer I sat in the cuddy. Had my double vanished as he had come? But of his coming there was an explanation, whereas his disappearance would be inexplicable. . . . I went slowly into my dark room, shut the door, lighted the lamp, and for a time, dared not turn round. When at last I did I saw him standing bolt-upright in the narrow recessed part. It would not be true to say I had a shock, but an irresistible doubt of his bodily existence flitted through my mind. Can it be, I asked myself, that he is not visible to eyes other than mine? It was like being haunted. Motionless, with a grave face, he raised his hands slightly at me in a gesture which meant clearly, "Heavens! what a narrow escape!" Narrow indeed. I think I had come creeping quietly as near insanity as any man who has not actually gone over the border. The gesture restrained me, so to speak.

The mate with the terrific whiskers was now putting the ship on the other tack. In the moment of profound silence which follows upon the hands going to their stations I heard on the poop his raised voice: "Hard alee!" and the distant shout of the order repeated on the main-deck. The sails, in that light breeze, made but a faint fluttering noise. It ceased. The ship was coming round slowly: I held my breath in the renewed stillness of expectation; one wouldn't have thought that there was a single living soul on her decks. A sudden brisk shout, "Mainsail haul!" broke the spell, and in the noisy cries and rush overhead of the men running away with the main brace we two, down in my cabin, came together in our usual position by the bed place.

He did not wait for my question. "I heard him fumbling here and just managed to squat myself down in the bath," he whispered to me. "The fellow only opened the door and put his arm in to hang the coat up. All the same —"

"I never thought of that," I whispered back, even more appalled than before at the closeness of the shave, and marveling at that something unyielding in his character which was carrying him through so finely. There was no agitation in his whisper. Whoever was being driven distracted, it was not he. He was sane. And the proof of his sanity was continued when he took up the whispering again.

"It would never do for me to come to life again."

It was something that a ghost might have said. But what he was alluding to was his old captain's reluctant admission of the theory of suicide. It would obviously serve his turn — if I had understood at all the view which seemed to govern the unalterable purpose of his action.

"You must maroon me as soon as ever you can get amongst these islands off the Cambodge shore," he went on.

"Maroon you! We are not living in a boy's adventure tale," I protested. His scornful whispering took me up.

"We aren't indeed! There's nothing of a boy's tale in this. But there's nothing else for it. I want no more. You don't suppose I am afraid of what can be done to me? Prison or gallows or whatever they may please. But you don't see me coming back to explain such things to an old fellow in a wig and twelve respectable tradesmen, do you? What can they know whether I am guilty or not — or of *what* I am guilty, either? That's my affair. What does the Bible say? 'Driven off the face of the earth°.' Very well, I am off the face of the earth now. As I came at night so I shall go."

"Impossible!" I murmured. "You can't."

"Can't? . . . Not naked like a soul on the Day of Judgment. I shall freeze on to this sleeping suit. The Last Day is not yet — and . . . you have understood thoroughly. Didn't you?"

I felt suddenly ashamed of myself. I may say truly that I understood — and my hesitation in letting that man swim away from my ship's side had been a mere sham sentiment, a sort of cowardice.

"It can't be done now till next night," I breathed out. "The ship is on the off-shore track and the wind may fail us."

"As long as I know that you understand," he whispered. "But of course you do. It's a great satisfaction to have got somebody to understand. You seem to have been there on purpose." And in the same whisper, as if we two whenever we talked had to say things to each other which were not fit for the world to hear, he added, "It's very wonderful."

We remained side by side talking in our secret way — but sometimes silent or just exchanging a whispered word or two at long intervals. And as usual he stared through the port. A breath of wind came now and again into our faces. The ship might have been moored in dock, so gently and on an even keel she slipped through the water, that did not murmur even at our passage, shadowy and silent like a phantom sea.

At midnight I went on deck, and to my mate's great surprise put the ship round on the other tack. His terrible whiskers flitted round me in silent criticism. I certainly should not have done it if it had been only a question of getting out of that sleepy gulf as quickly as possible. I believe he told the second mate, who relieved him, that it was a great want of judgment. The other only yawned. That intolerable cub shuffled about so sleepily and lolled against the rails in such a slack, improper fashion that I came down on him sharply.

"Aren't you properly awake yet?"

"Yes, sir! I am awake."

"Well, then, be good enough to hold yourself as if you were. And keep a lookout. If there's any current we'll be closing with some islands before daylight."

The east side of the gulf is fringed with islands, some solitary, others in groups. On the blue background of the high coast they seem to float on silvery patches of calm water, arid and gray, or dark green and rounded like clumps of evergreen bushes, with the larger ones, a mile or two long, showing the outlines of ridges, ribs of gray rock under the dank mantle of matted leafage. Unknown to trade, to travel, almost to geography, the manner of life they harbor is an unsolved secret. There must be villages — settlements of fishermen at

'Driven off the face of the earth': The sharer again thinks of himself as Cain. In Genesis 4:14 Cain addresses the Lord: "Behold, thou hast driven me out this day from the face of the earth."

least — on the largest of them, and some communication with the world is probably kept up by native craft. But all that forenoon, as we headed for them, fanned along by the faintest of breezes, I saw no sign of man or canoe in the field of the telescope I kept pointing at the scattered group.

At noon I gave no orders for a change of course, and the mate's whiskers became much concerned and seemed to be offering themselves unduly to my notice. At last I said:

"I am going to stand right in. Quite in — as far as I can take her."

The stare of extreme surprise imparted an air of ferocity also to his eyes, and he looked truly terrific for a moment.

"We're not doing well in the middle of the gulf," I continued, casually. "I am going to look for the land breezes tonight."

"Bless my soul! Do you mean, sir, in the dark amongst the lot of all them islands and reefs and shoals?"

"Well — if there are any regular land breezes at all on this coast one must get close inshore to find them, mustn't one?"

"Bless my soul!" he exclaimed again under his breath. All that afternoon he wore a dreamy, contemplative appearance which in him was a mark of perplexity. After dinner I went into my stateroom as if I meant to take some rest. There we two bent our dark heads over a half-unrolled chart lying on my bed.

"There," I said. "It's got to be Koh-ring. I've been looking at it ever since sunrise. It has got two hills and a low point. It must be inhabited. And on the coast opposite there is what looks like the mouth of a biggish river — with some towns, no doubt, not far up. It's the best chance for you that I can see."

"Anything. Koh-ring let it be."

He looked thoughtfully at the chart as if surveying chances and distances from a lofty height — and following with his eyes his own figure wandering on the blank land of Cochin-China, and then passing off that piece of paper clean out of sight into uncharted regions. And it was as if the ship had two captains to plan her course for her. I had been so worried and restless running up and down that I had not had the patience to dress that day. I had remained in my sleeping suit, with straw slippers and a soft floppy hat. The closeness of the heat in the gulf had been most oppressive, and the crew were used to seeing me wandering in that airy attire.

"She will clear the south point as she heads now," I whispered into his ear. "Goodness only knows when, though, but certainly after dark. I'll edge her in to half a mile, as far as I may be able to judge in the dark —"

"Be careful," he murmured, warningly — and I realized suddenly that all my future, the only future for which I was fit, would perhaps go irretrievably to pieces in any mishap to my first command.

I could not stop a moment longer in the room. I motioned him to get out of sight and made my way on the poop. That unplayful cub had the watch. I walked up and down for a while thinking things out, then beckoned him over.

"Send a couple of hands to open the two quarterdeck ports," I said, mildly.

He actually had the impudence, or else so forgot himself in his wonder at such an incomprehensible order, as to repeat:

"Open the quarter-deck ports! What for, sir?"

"The only reason you need concern yourself about is because I tell you to do so. Have them open wide and fastened properly."

He reddened and went off, but I believe made some jeering remark to the carpenter as to the sensible practice of ventilating a ship's quarter-deck. I know he popped into the mate's cabin to impart the fact to him because the whiskers came on deck, as it were by chance, and stole glances at me from below — for signs of lunacy or drunkenness, I suppose.

A little before supper, feeling more restless than ever, I rejoined, for a moment, my second self. And to find him sitting so quietly was surprising, like something against nature, inhuman.

I developed my plan in a hurried whisper.

"I shall stand in as close as I dare and then put her round. I will presently find means to smuggle you out of here into the sail locker, which communicates with the lobby. But there is an opening, a sort of square for hauling the sails out, which gives straight on the quarterdeck and which is never closed in fine weather, so as to give air to the sails. When the ship's way is deadened in stays and all the hands are aft at the main braces you will have a clear road to slip out and get overboard through the open quarter-deck port. I've had them both fastened up. Use a rope's end to lower yourself into the water so as to avoid a splash — you know. It could be heard and cause some beastly complication."

He kept silent for a while, then whispered, "I understand."

"I won't be there to see you go," I began with an effort. "The rest . . . I only hope I have understood, too."

"You have. From first to last" — and for the first time there seemed to be a faltering, something strained in his whisper. He caught hold of my arm, but the ringing of the supper bell made me start. He didn't though; he only released his grip.

After supper I didn't come below again till well past eight o'clock. The faint, steady breeze was loaded with dew; and the wet, darkened sails held all there was of propelling power in it. The night, clear and starry, sparkled darkly, and the opaque, lightless patches shifting slowly against the low stars were the drifting islets. On the port bow there was a big one more distant and shadowily imposing by the great space of sky it eclipsed.

On opening the door I had a back view of my very own self looking at a chart. He had come out of the recess and was standing near the table.

"Quite dark enough," I whispered.

He stepped back and leaned against my bed with a level, quiet glance. I sat on the couch. We had nothing to say to each other. Over our heads the officer of the watch moved here and there. Then I heard him move quickly. I knew what that meant. He was making for the companion; and presently his voice was outside my door.

"We are drawing in pretty fast, sir. Land looks rather close."

"Very well," I answered. "I am coming on deck directly."

I waited till he was gone out of the cuddy, then rose. My double moved too. The time had come to exchange our last whispers, for neither of us was ever to hear each other's natural voice.

"Look here!" I opened a drawer and took out three sovereigns. "Take this anyhow. I've got six and I'd give you the lot, only I must keep a little money to buy some fruit and vegetables for the crew from native boats as we go through Sunda Straits."

He shook his head.

"Take it," I urged him, whispering desperately. "No one can tell what —"

He smiled and slapped meaningly the only pocket of the sleeping jacket. It was not safe, certainly. But I produced a large old silk handkerchief of mine, and tying the three pieces of gold in a corner, pressed it on him. He was touched, I supposed, because he took it at last and tied it quickly round his waist under the jacket, on his bare skin.

Our eyes met; several seconds elapsed, till, our glances still mingled, I extended my hand and turned the lamp out. Then I passed through the cuddy, leaving the door of my room wide open. . . . "Steward!"

He was still lingering in the pantry in the greatness of his zeal, giving a rub-up to a plated cruet stand the last thing before going to bed. Being careful not to wake up the mate, whose room was opposite, I spoke in an undertone.

He looked round anxiously. "Sir!"

"Can you get me a little hot water from the galley?"

"I am afraid, sir, the galley fire's been out for some time now."

"Go and see."

He flew up the stairs.

"Now," I whispered, loudly, into the saloon — too loudly, perhaps, but I was afraid I couldn't make a sound. He was by my side in an instant — the double captain slipped past the stairs — through a tiny dark passage . . . a sliding door. We were in the sail locker, scrambling on our knees over the sails. A sudden thought struck me. I saw myself wandering barefooted, bareheaded, the sun beating on my dark poll. I snatched off my floppy hat and tried hurriedly in the dark to ram it on my other self. He dodged and fended off silently. I wonder what he thought had come to me before he understood and suddenly desisted. Our hands met gropingly, lingered united in a steady, motionless clasp for a second. . . . No word was breathed by either of us when they separated.

I was standing quietly by the pantry door when the steward returned.

"Sorry, sir. Kettle barely warm. Shall I light the spirit lamp?"

"Never mind."

I came out on deck slowly. It was now a matter of conscience to shave the land as close as possible — for now he must go overboard whenever the ship was put in stays. Must! There could be no going back for him. After a moment I walked over the leeward and my heart flew into my mouth at the nearness of the land on the bow. Under any other circumstances I would not have held on a minute longer. The second mate had followed me anxiously.

I looked on till I felt I could command my voice.

"She will weather," I said then in a quiet tone.

"Are you going to try that, sir?" he stammered out incredulously.

I took no notice of him and raised my tone just enough to be heard by the helmsman.

"Keep her good full."

"Good full, sir."

The wind fanned my cheek, the sails slept, the world was silent. The strain of watching the dark loom of the land grow bigger and denser was too much for me. I had shut my eyes — because the ship must go closer. She must! The stillness was intolerable. Were we standing still?

When I opened my eyes the second view started my heart with a thump. The black southern hill of Koh-ring seemed to hang right over the ship like a towering fragment of the ever-lasting night. On that enormous mass of blackness there was not a gleam to be seen, not a sound to be heard. It was gliding irresistibly towards us and yet seemed already within reach of the hand. I saw the vague figures of the watch grouped in the waist, gazing in awed silence.

"Are you going on, sir?" inquired an unsteady voice at my elbow.

I ignored it. I had to go on.

"Keep her full. Don't check her way. That won't do now," I said, warningly.

"I can't see the sails very well," the helmsman answered me, in strange, quavering tones.

Was she close enough? Already she was, I won't say in the shadow of the land, but in the very blackness of it, already swallowed up as it were, gone too close to be recalled, gone from me altogether.

"Give the mate a call," I said to the young man who stood at my elbow as still as death. "And turn all hands up."

My tone had a borrowed loudness reverberated from the height of the land. Several voices cried out together; "We are all on deck, sir."

Then stillness again, with the great shadow gliding closer, towering higher, without a light, without a sound. Such a hush had fallen on the ship that she might have been a bark of the dead floating in slowly under the very gate of Erebus.

"My God! Where are we?"

It was the mate moaning at my elbow. He was thunderstruck, and as it were deprived of the moral support of his whiskers. He clapped his hands and absolutely cried out, "Lost!"

"Be quiet," I said, sternly.

He lowered his tone, but I saw the shadowy gesture of his despair. "What are we doing here?"

"Looking for the land wind."

He made as if to tear his hair, and addressed me recklessly.

"She will never get out. You have done it, sir. I knew it'd end in something like this. She will never weather, and you are too close now to stay. She'll drift ashore before she's round. O my God!"

I caught his arm as he was raising it to batter his poor devoted head, and shook it violently.

"She's ashore already," he wailed, trying to tear himself away.

"Is she? . . . Keep good full there!"

"Good full, sir," cried the helmsman in a frightened, thin, childlike voice.

I hadn't let go the mate's arm and went on shaking it. "Ready about, do you hear? You go forward" — shake — "and stop there" — shake — "and hold your noise" — shake — "and see these head-sheets properly overhauled" — shake, shake — shake.

And all the time I dared not look towards the land lest my heart should fail me. I released my grip at last and he ran forward as if fleeing for dear life.

I wondered what my double there in the sail locker thought of this commotion. He was able to hear everything — and perhaps he was able to understand why, on my conscience, it had to be thus close — no less. My first order "Hard alee!" re-echoed ominously under the towering shadow of Koh-ring as if I had shouted in a mountain gorge. And then I watched the land intently. In that smooth water and light wind it was impossible to feel the ship coming-to. No! I could not feel her. And my second self was making now ready to ship out and lower himself overboard. Perhaps he was gone already . . . ?

The great black mass brooding over our very mastheads began to pivot away from the ship's side silently. And now I forgot the secret stranger ready to depart, and remembered only that I was a total stranger to the ship. I did not know her. Would she do it? How was she to be handled?

I swung the mainyard and waited helplessly. She was perhaps stopped, and her very fate hung in the balance, with the black mass of Koh-ring like the gate of the everlasting night towering over her taffrail. What would she do now? Had she way on her yet? I stepped to the side swiftly, and on the shadowy water I could see nothing except a faint phosphorescent flash revealing the glassy smoothness of the sleeping surface. It was impossible to tell — and I had not learned yet the feel of my ship. Was she moving? What I needed was something easily seen, a piece of paper, which I could throw overboard and watch. I had nothing on me. To run down for it I didn't dare. There was no time. All at once my strained, yearning stare distinguished a white object floating within a yard of the ship's side. White on the black water. A phosphorescent flash passed under it. What was that thing? . . . I recognized my own floppy hat. It must have fallen off his head . . . and he didn't bother. Now I had what I wanted — the saving mark for my eyes. But I hardly thought of my other self, now gone from the ship, to be hidden forever from all friendly faces, to be a fugitive and a vagabond on the earth, with no brand of the curse on his sane forehead to stay a slaying hand° . . . too proud to explain.

And I watched the hat — the expression of my sudden pity for his mere flesh. It had been meant to save his homeless head from the dangers of the sun. And now — behold — it was saving the ship, by serving me for a mark to help out the ignorance of my strangeness. Ha! It was drifting forward, warning me just in time that the ship had gathered sternway.

"Shift the helm," I said in a low voice to the seaman standing still like a statue.

The man's eyes glistened wildly in the binnacle light as he jumped round to the other side and spun round the wheel.

I walked to the break of the poop. On the overshadowed deck all hands stood by the forebraces waiting for my order. The stars ahead seemed to be gliding from right to left. And all was so still in the world that I heard the quiet remark, "She's round," passed in a tone of intense relief between two seamen.

---

to be a fugitive . . . slaying hand: Conrad alludes again to the Biblical story of Cain, one of whose punishments was to become "a fugitive and a vagabond" on the earth. "And the Lord set a mark upon Cain, lest any finding him should kill him" (Genesis 4:15).

"Let go and haul."

The foreyards ran round with a great noise, amidst cheery cries. And now the frightful whiskers made themselves heard giving various orders. Already the ship was drawing ahead. And I was alone with her. Nothing! no one in the world should stand now between us, throwing a shadow on the way of silent knowledge and mute affection, the perfect communion of a seaman with his first command.

Walking to the taffrail, I was in time to make out, on the very edge of a darkness thrown by a towering black mass like the very gateway of Erebus — yes, I was in time to catch an evanescent glimpse of my white hat left behind to mark the spot where the secret sharer of my cabin and of my thoughts, as though he were my second self, had lowered himself into the water to take his punishment: a free man, a proud swimmer striking out for a new destiny.

QUESTIONS

1. How does Conrad heighten our sense of the dreamlike strangeness of the captain's first encounter with Leggatt? Consider in particular the opening paragraphs of the story, the captain's preparations to stand watch, his description of the swimmer in the water.

2. In Chapter One, with what details does Conrad enforce the captain's impression that Leggatt is his double?

3. Why does the captain almost immediately feel such a strong common bond between himself and Leggatt? As the story proceeds, what is it that the captain and the secret sharer share?

4. The man he killed, Leggatt tells the captain, was "one of those creatures . . . Miserable devils that have no business to live at all" (page 248). Apparently, the captain doesn't quarrel with this assertion. How do you account for the captain's seemingly indulgent attitude toward manslaughter?

5. Imagine yourself a member of the ship's crew in the days after the secret sharer comes aboard. What impressions of your commanding officer and his behavior would you be likely to voice?

6. Recall the captain's remark, on having installed Leggatt in his cabin, "the dual working of my mind distracted me almost to the point of insanity" (page 254). Is it possible to read the story as being told by an unreliable narrator? Consider the suggestion that the captain is a deluded, even psychotic storyteller, like the narrator of Edgar Allan Poe's "The Tell-Tale Heart"; and that the secret sharer is the fantasy of his troubled imagination, who finally disappears when the captain regains his sanity. What evidence can you find in the story to support or refute this interpretation?

7. A student's comment and question: "Leggatt's life and the tale he tells are much more challenging and exciting than the captain's problems. Why didn't Conrad center the story on Leggatt, and tell the whole thing from his point of view?"

8. What meanings do you find in Leggatt's lost sun hat, floating in the water?

9. At the end, with the departure of the secret sharer, what changes have taken place in the captain's own character and situation? What resemblance do you find between the future we expect for the captain and Leggatt's "new destiny"?

10. How would you sum up the central theme of this short novel? (More than one summation may be possible.)

11 Stories for Further Study

For human intercourse, as soon as we look at it for its own sake and not as a social adjunct, is seen to be haunted by a specter. We cannot understand each other, except in a rough-and-ready way; we cannot reveal ourselves, even when we want to; what we call intimacy is only a makeshift; perfect knowledge is an illusion. But in the novel we can know perfectly, and, apart from the general pleasure of reading, we can find here a compensation for their dimness in life. In this direction fiction is truer than history, because it goes beyond the evidence, and each of us knows from his own experience that there is something beyond the evidence, and even if the novelist has not got it correctly, well — he has tried.

— E. M. Forster, *Aspects of the Novel*

Leo Tolstoi (1828–1910)

The Death of Ivan Ilych   1886

Translated by Louise and Aylmer Maude

I

During an interval in the Melvinski trial in the large building of the Law Courts, the members and public prosecutor met in Ivan Egorovich Shebek's private room, where the conversation turned on the celebrated Krasovski case. Fëdor Vasilievich warmly maintained that it was not subject to their jurisdiction, Ivan Egorovich maintained the contrary, while Peter Ivanovich, not having entered into the discussion at the start, took no part in it but looked through the *Gazette* which had just been handed in.

"Gentlemen," he said, "Ivan Ilych has died!"

"You don't say so!"

"Here, read it yourself," replied Peter Ivanovich, handing Fëdor Vasilievich the paper still damp from the press. Surrounded by a black border were the words: "Praskovya Fëdorovna Golovina, with profound sorrow, informs relatives and friends of the demise of her beloved husband Ivan Ilych Golovin, Member of the Court of Justice, which occurred on February the 4th of this year 1882. The funeral will take place on Friday at one o'clock in the afternoon."

Ivan Ilych had been a colleague of the gentlemen present and was liked by them all. He had been ill for some weeks with an illness said to be incurable. His post had been kept open for him, but there had been conjectures that in case of his death Alexeev might receive his appointment, and that either Vinnikov or Shtabel would succeed Alexeev. So on receiving the news of Ivan Ilych's death the first thought of each of the gentlemen in that private room was of the changes and promotions it might occasion among themselves or their acquaintances.

"I shall be sure to get Shtabel's place or Vinnikov's," thought Fëdor Vasilievich. "I was promised that long ago, and the promotion means an extra eight hundred rubles a year for me besides the allowance."

"Now I must apply for my brother-in-law's transfer from Kaluga," thought Peter Ivanovich. "My wife will be very glad, and then she won't be able to say that I never do anything for her relations."

"I thought he would never leave his bed again," said Peter Ivanovich aloud. "It's very sad."

"But what really was the matter with him?"

"The doctors couldn't say — at least they could, but each of them said something different. When last I saw him I thought he was getting better."

"And I haven't been to see him since the holidays. I always meant to go."

"Had he any property?"

"I think his wife had a little — but something quite trifling."

"We shall have to go to see her, but they live so terribly far away."

"Far away from you, you mean. Everything's far away from your place."

"You see, he never can forgive my living on the other side of the river," said Peter Ivanovich, smiling at Shebek. Then, still talking of the distances between different parts of the city, they returned to the Court.

Besides considerations as to the possible transfers and promotions likely to result from Ivan Ilych's death, the mere fact of the death of a near acquaintance aroused, as usual, in all who heard of it the complacent feeling that "it is he who is dead and not I."

Each one thought or felt, "Well, he's dead but I'm alive!" But the more intimate of Ivan Ilych's acquaintances, his so-called friends, could not help thinking also that they would now have to fulfil the very tiresome demands of propriety by attending the funeral service and paying a visit of condolence to the widow.

Fëdor Vasilievich and Peter Ivanovich had been his nearest acquaintances. Peter Ivanovich had studied law with Ivan Ilych and had considered himself to be under obligations to him.

Having told his wife at dinner-time of Ivan Ilych's death and of his conjecture that it might be possible to get her brother transferred to their circuit, Peter Ivanovich sacrificed his usual nap, put on his evening clothes, and drove to Ivan Ilych's house.

At the entrance stood a carriage and two cabs. Leaning against the wall in the hall downstairs near the cloak-stand was a coffin-lid covered with cloth of gold, ornamented with gold cord and tassels, that had been polished up with metal powder. Two ladies in black were taking off their fur cloaks. Peter Ivanovich recognized one of them as Ivan Ilych's sister, but the other was a stranger to him. His colleague Schwartz was just coming downstairs, but on seeing Peter Ivanovich enter he stopped and winked at him, as if to say: "Ivan Ilych has made a mess of things — not like you and me."

Schwartz's face with his Piccadilly whiskers and his slim figure in evening dress had as usual an air of elegant solemnity which contrasted with the playfulness of his character and had a special piquancy here, or so it seemed to Peter Ivanovich.

Peter Ivanovich allowed the ladies to precede him and slowly followed them upstairs. Schwartz did not come down but remained where he was, and Peter Ivanovich understood that he wanted to arrange where they should play bridge that evening. The ladies went upstairs to the widow's room, and Schwartz with seriously compressed lips but a playful look in his eyes, indicated by a twist of his eyebrows the room to the right where the body lay.

Peter Ivanovich, like everyone else on such occasions, entered feeling uncertain what he would have to do. All he knew was that at such times it is always safe to cross oneself. But he was not quite sure whether one should make obeisances while doing so. He therefore adopted a middle course. On entering the room he began crossing himself and made a slight movement resembling a bow. At the same time, as far as the motion of his head and arm allowed, he surveyed the room. Two young men — apparently nephews, one of whom was a high-school pupil — were leaving the room, crossing themselves as they did so. An old woman was standing motionless, and a lady with strangely arched eyebrows was saying something to her in a whisper. A vigorous, resolute Church Reader, in a frock-coat, was reading something in a loud voice with an expression that precluded any contradiction. The butler's assistant, Gerasim, stepping lightly in front of Peter Ivanovich, was strewing something on the floor. Noticing this, Peter Ivanovich was immediately aware of a faint odor of a decomposing body.

The last time he had called on Ivan Ilych, Peter Ivanovich had seen Gerasim in the study. Ivan Ilych had been particularly fond of him and he was performing the duty of a sick nurse.

Peter Ivanovich continued to make the sign of the cross, slightly inclining his head in an intermediate direction between the coffin, the Reader, and the icons on the table in a corner of the room. Afterwards, when it seemed to him that this movement of his arm in crossing himself had gone on too long, he stopped and began to look at the corpse.

The dead man lay, as dead men always lie, in a specially heavy way, his rigid limbs sunk in the soft cushions of the coffin, with the head forever bowed on the pillow. His yellow waxen brow with bald patches over his sunken temples was thrust up in the way peculiar to the dead, the protruding nose seeming to press on the upper lip. He was much changed and had grown even thinner since Peter Ivanovich had last seen him, but, as is always the case with the dead, his face was handsomer and above all more dignified than when he was alive. The expression on the face said that what was necessary had been accomplished, and accomplished rightly. Besides this there was in that expression a reproach and a warning to the living. This warning seemed to Peter Ivanovich out of place, or at least not applicable to him. He felt a certain discomfort and so he hurriedly crossed himself once more and turned and went out of the door — too hurriedly and too regardless of propriety, as he himself was aware.

Schwartz was waiting for him in the adjoining room with legs spread wide apart and both hands toying with his top-hat behind his back. The mere sight of that playful, well-groomed, and elegant figure refreshed Peter Ivanovich. He felt that Schwartz was above all these happenings and would not surrender to any depressing influences. His very look said that this incident of a church service for Ivan Ilych could not be a sufficient reason for infringing the order of the session — in other words, that it would certainly not prevent his unwrapping a new pack of cards and shuffling them that evening while a footman placed four fresh candles on the table: in fact, that there was no reason for supposing that this incident would hinder their spending the evening agreeably. Indeed he said this in a whisper as Peter Ivanovich passed him, proposing that they should meet for a game at Fëdor Vasilievich's. But apparently Peter Ivanovich was not destined to play bridge that evening. Praskovya Fëdorovna (a short, fat woman who despite all efforts to the contrary had continued to broaden steadily from her shoulders downwards and who had the same extraordinarily arched eyebrows as the lady who had been standing by the coffin), dressed all in black, her head covered with lace, came out of her own room with some other ladies, conducted them to the room where the dead body lay, and said: "The service will begin immediately. Please go in."

Schwartz, making an indefinite bow, stood still, evidently neither accepting nor declining this invitation. Praskovya Fëdorovna, recognizing Peter Ivanovich, sighed, went close up to him, took his hand, and said: "I know you were a true friend of Ivan Ilych . . ." and looked at him awaiting some suitable response. And Peter Ivanovich knew that, just as it had been the right thing to cross himself in that room, so what he had to do here was to press her hand, sigh, and say, "Believe me. . . ." So he did all this and as he did it felt that the desired result had been achieved: that both he and she were touched.

"Come with me. I want to speak to you before it begins," said the widow. "Give me your arm."

Peter Ivanovich gave her his arm and they went to the inner rooms, passing Schwartz, who winked at Peter Ivanovich compassionately.

"That does for our bridge! Don't object if we find another player. Perhaps you can cut in when you do escape," said his playful look.

Peter Ivanovich sighed still more deeply and despondently, and Praskovya Fëdorovna pressed his arm gratefully. When they reached the drawing-room, upholstered in pink cretonne and lighted by a dim lamp, they sat down at the table — she on a sofa and Peter Ivanovich on a low pouffe, the springs of which yielded spasmodically under his weight. Praskovya Fëdorovna had been on the point of warning him to take another seat, but felt that such a warning was out of keeping with her present condition and so changed her mind. As he sat down on the pouffe Peter Ivanovich recalled how Ivan Ilych had arranged this room and had consulted him regarding this pink cretonne with green leaves. The whole room was full of furniture and knick-knacks, and on her way to the sofa the lace of the widow's black shawl caught on the carved edge of the table. Peter Ivanovich rose to detach it, and the springs of the pouffe, relieved of his weight, rose also and gave him a push. The widow began detaching her shawl herself, and Peter Ivanovich again sat down, suppressing the rebellious springs of the pouffe under him. But the widow had not quite freed herself and Peter Ivanovich got up again, and again the pouffe rebelled and even creaked. When this was all over she took out a clean cambric handkerchief and began to weep. The episode with the shawl and the struggle with the pouffe had cooled Peter Ivanovich's emotions and he sat there with a sullen look on his face. This awkward situation was interrupted by Sokolov, Ivan Ilych's butler, who came to report that the plot in the cemetery that Praskovya Fëdorovna had chosen would cost two hundred rubles. She stopped weeping and, looking at Peter Ivanovich with the air of a victim, remarked in French that it was very hard for her. Peter Ivanovich made a silent gesture signifying his full conviction that it must indeed be so.

"Please smoke," she said in a magnanimous yet crushed voice, and turned to discuss with Sokolov the price of the plot for the grave.

Peter Ivanovich while lighting his cigarette heard her inquiring very circumstantially into the prices of different plots in the cemetery and finally decide which she would take. When that was done she gave instructions about engaging the choir. Sokolov then left the room.

"I look after everything myself," she told Peter Ivanovich, shifting the albums that lay on the table; and noticing that the table was endangered by his cigarette-ash, she immediately passed him an ashtray, saying as she did so: "I consider it an affectation to say that my grief prevents my attending to practical affairs. On the contrary, if anything can — I won't say console me, but — distract me, it is seeing to everything concerning him." She again took out her handkerchief as if preparing to cry, but suddenly, as if mastering her feeling, she shook herself and began to speak calmly. "But there is something I want to talk to you about."

Peter Ivanovich bowed, keeping control of the springs of the pouffe, which immediately began quivering under him.

"He suffered terribly the last few days."

"Did he?" said Peter Ivanovich.

"Oh, terribly! He screamed unceasingly, not for minutes but for hours. For the last three days he screamed incessantly. It was unendurable. I cannot understand how I bore it; you could hear him three rooms off. Oh, what I have suffered!"

"Is it possible that he was conscious all that time?" asked Peter Ivanovich.

"Yes," she whispered. "To the last moment. He took leave of us a quarter of an hour before he died, and asked us to take Volodya away."

The thought of the sufferings of this man he had known so intimately, first as a merry little boy, then as a school-mate, and later as a grown-up colleague, suddenly struck Peter Ivanovich with horror, despite an unpleasant consciousness of his own and this woman's dissimulation. He again saw that brow, and that nose pressing down on the lip, and felt afraid for himself.

"Three days of frightful suffering and then death! Why, that might suddenly, at any time, happen to me," he thought, and for a moment felt terrified. But — he did not himself know how — the customary reflection at once occurred to him that this had happened to Ivan Ilych and not to him, and that it should not and could not happen to him, and that to think that it could would be yielding to depression which he ought not to do, as Schwartz's expression plainly showed. After which reflection Peter Ivanovich felt reassured, and began to ask with interest about the details of Ivan Ilych's death, as though death was an accident natural to Ivan Ilych but certainly not to himself.

After many details of the really dreadful physical sufferings Ivan Ilych had endured (which details he learnt only from the effect those sufferings had produced on Praskovya Fëdorovna's nerves) the widow apparently found it necessary to get to business.

"Oh, Peter Ivanovich, how hard it is! How terribly, terribly hard!" and she again began to weep.

Peter Ivanovich sighed and waited for her to finish blowing her nose. When she had done so he said, "Believe me . . ." and she again began talking and brought out what was evidently her chief concern with him — namely, to question him as to how she could obtain a grant of money from the government on the occasion of her husband's death. She made it appear that she was asking Peter Ivanovich's advice about her pension, but he soon saw that she already knew about that to the minutest detail, more even than he did himself. She knew how much could be got out of the government in consequence of her husband's death, but wanted to find out whether she could not possibly extract something more. Peter Ivanovich tried to think of some means of doing so, but after reflecting for a while and, out of propriety, condemning the government for its niggardliness, he said he thought that nothing more could be got. Then she sighed and evidently began to devise means of getting rid of her visitor. Noticing this, he put out his cigarette, rose, pressed her hand, and went out into the anteroom.

In the dining-room where the clock stood that Ivan Ilych had liked so much and had bought at an antique shop, Peter Ivanovich met a priest and a few acquaintances who had come to attend the service, and he recognized Ivan Ilych's daughter, a handsome young woman. She was in black and her slim figure appeared slimmer than ever. She had a gloomy, determined, almost angry expression, and bowed to Peter Ivanovich as though he were in some way to blame. Behind her, with the same offended look, stood a wealthy young man, an examining magistrate, whom Peter Ivanovich also knew and who was her fiancé, as he had heard. He bowed mournfully to them and was about to pass into the death-chamber, when from under the stairs appeared the figure of Ivan Ilych's schoolboy son, who was extremely like his father. He seemed a little Ivan Ilych, such as Peter Ivanovich remembered when they studied law together. His tear-stained eyes had in them the look that is seen in the eyes of boys of thirteen or fourteen who are not pure-minded. When he saw Peter Ivanovich he scowled morosely and shamefacedly. Peter Ivanovich nodded to him and entered the death-chamber. The service began: candles, groans, incense, tears, and sobs. Peter Ivanovich stood looking gloomily down at his feet. He did not look once at the dead man, did not yield to any depressing influence, and was one of the first to leave the room. There was no one in the anteroom, but Gerasim darted out of the dead man's room, rummaged with his strong hands among the fur coats to find Peter Ivanovich's, and helped him on with it.

"Well, friend Gerasim," said Peter Ivanovich, so as to say something. "It's a sad affair, isn't it?"

"It's God's will. We shall all come to it some day," said Gerasim, displaying his teeth — the even, white teeth of a healthy peasant — and, like a man in the thick of urgent work, he briskly opened the front door, called the coachman, helped Peter Ivanovich into the sledge, and sprang back to the porch as if in readiness for what he had to do next.

Peter Ivanovich found the fresh air particularly pleasant after the smell of incense, the dead body, and carbolic acid.

"Where to, sir?" asked the coachman.

"It's not too late even now. . . . I'll call round on Fëdor Vasilievich."

He accordingly drove there and found them just finishing the first rubber, so that it was quite convenient for him to cut in.

II

Ivan Ilych's life had been most simple and most ordinary and therefore most terrible.

He had been a member of the Court of Justice, and died at the age of forty-five. His father had been an official who after serving in various ministries and departments in Petersburg had made the sort of career which brings men to positions from which by reason of their long service they cannot be dismissed, though they are obviously unfit to hold any responsible position, and for whom therefore posts are specially created, which though fictitious carry salaries of from six to ten thousand rubles that are not fictitious, and in receipt of which they live on to a great age.

Such was the Privy Councillor and superfluous member of various superfluous institutions, Ilya Epimovich Golovin.

He had three sons, of whom Ivan Ilych was the second. The eldest son was following in his father's footsteps only in another department, and was already approaching that stage in the service at which a similar sinecure would be reached. The third son was a failure. He had ruined his prospects in a number of positions and was now serving in the railway department. His father and brothers, and still more their wives, not merely disliked meeting him, but avoided remembering his existence unless compelled to do so. His sister had married Baron Greff, a Petersburg official of her father's type. Ivan Ilych was *le phénix de la famille°* as people said. He was neither as cold and formal as his elder brother nor as wild as the younger, but was a happy mean between them — an intelligent, polished, lively, and agreeable man. He had studied with his younger brother at the School of Law, but the latter had failed to complete the course and was expelled when he was in the fifth class. Ivan Ilych finished the course well. Even when he was at the School of Law he was just what he remained for the rest of his life: a capable, cheerful, good-natured, and sociable man, though strict in the fulfilment of what he considered to be his duty: and he considered his duty to be what was so considered by those in authority. Neither as a boy nor as a man was he a toady, but from early youth was by nature attracted to people of high station as a fly is drawn to the light, assimilating their ways and views of life and establishing friendly relations with them. All the enthusiasms of childhood and youth passed without leaving much trace on him; he succumbed to sensuality, to vanity, and latterly among the highest classes to liberalism, but always within limits which his instinct unfailingly indicated to him as correct.

At school he had done things which had formerly seemed to him very horrid and made him feel disgusted with himself when he did them; but when later on he saw that such actions were done by people of good position and that they did not regard them as wrong, he was able not exactly to regard them as right, but to forget about them entirely or not be at all troubled at remembering them.

Having graduated from the School of Law and qualified for the tenth rank of the civil service, and having received money from his father for his equipment, Ivan Ilych ordered himself clothes at Scharmer's, the fashionable tailor, hung a medallion inscribed *respice finem°* on his watch-chain, took leave of his professor and the prince who was patron of the school, had a farewell dinner with his comrades at Donon's first-class restaurant, and with his new and fashionable portmanteau, linen, clothes, shaving and other toilet appliances, and a travelling rug all purchased at the best shops, he set off for one of the provinces where, through his father's influence, he had been attached to the Governor as an official for special service.

In the province Ivan Ilych soon arranged as easy and agreeable a position for himself as he had had at the School of Law. He performed his official tasks, made his career, and at the same time amused himself pleasantly and decorously. Occasionally he paid official visits to country districts, where he behaved with dignity both to his superiors and inferiors, and performed the duties entrusted to him, which related chiefly to the sectarians°, with an exactness and incorruptible honesty of which he could not but feel proud.

In official matters, despite his youth and taste for frivolous gaiety, he was exceedingly reserved, punctilious, and even severe; but in society he was often amusing and witty, and always good-natured, correct in his manner, and *bon*

le phénix de la famille: "the prize of the family."
respice finem: "Think of the end (of your life)."
sectarians: dissenters from the Orthodox Church.

enfant°, as the Governor and his wife — with whom he was like one of the family — used to say of him.

In the province he had an affair with a lady who made advances to the elegant young lawyer, and there was also a milliner; and there were carousals with aides-de-camp who visited the district, and after-supper visits to a certain outlying street of doubtful reputation; and there was too some obsequiousness to his chief and even to his chief's wife, but all this was done with such a tone of good breeding that no hard names could be applied to it. It all came under the heading of the French saying: *"Il faut que jeunesse se passe."°* It was all done with clean hands, in clean linen, with French phrases, and above all among people of the best society and consequently with the approval of people of rank.

So Ivan Ilych served for five years and then came a change in his official life. The new and reformed judicial institutions were introduced, and new men were needed. Ivan Ilych became such a new man. He was offered the post of examining magistrate, and he accepted it though the post was in another province and obliged him to give up the connections he had formed and to make new ones. His friends met to give him a send-off; they had a group-photograph taken and presented him with a silver cigarette-case, and he set off to his new post.

As examining magistrate Ivan Ilych was just as *comme il faut°* and decorous a man, inspiring general respect and capable of separating his official duties from his private life, as he had been when acting as an official on special service. His duties now as examining magistrate were far more interesting and attractive than before. In his former position it had been pleasant to wear an undress uniform made by Scharmer, and to pass through the crowd of petitioners and officials who were timorously awaiting an audience with the Governor, and who envied him as with free and easy gait he went straight into his chief's private room to have a cup of tea and a cigarette with him. But not many people had been directly dependent on him — only police officials and the sectarians when he went on special missions — and he liked to treat them politely, almost as comrades, as if he were letting them feel that he who had the power to crush them was treating them in this simple, friendly way. There were then but few such people. But now, as an examining magistrate, Ivan Ilych felt that everyone without exception, even the most important and self-satisfied, was in his power, and that he need only write a few words on a sheet of paper with a certain heading, and this or that important, self-satisfied person would be brought before him in the role of an accused person or a witness, and if he did not choose to allow him to sit down, would have to stand before him and answer his questions. Ivan Ilych never abused his power; he tried on the contrary to soften its expression, but the consciousness of it and of the possibility of softening its effect, supplied the chief interest and attraction of his office. In his work itself, especially in his examinations, he very soon acquired a method of eliminating all considerations irrelevant to the legal aspect of the case, and reducing even the most complicated case to a form in which it would be presented on paper only in its externals, completely excluding his personal

bon enfant: like a well-behaved child.
"Il faut que jeunesse se passe": "Youth doesn't last."
comme il faut: "as required," rule-abiding.

opinion of the matter, while above all observing every prescribed formality. The work was new and Ivan Ilych was one of the first men to apply the new Code of 1864°.

On taking up the post of examining magistrate in a new town, he made new acquaintances and connections, placed himself on a new footing, and assumed a somewhat different tone. He took up an attitude of rather dignified aloofness towards the provincial authorities, but picked out the best circle of legal gentlemen and wealthy gentry living in the town and assumed a tone of slight dissatisfaction with the government, of moderate liberalism, and of enlightened citizenship. At the same time, without at all altering the elegance of his toilet, he ceased shaving his chin and allowed his beard to grow as it pleased.

Ivan Ilych settled down very pleasantly in this new town. The society there, which inclined towards opposition to the Governor, was friendly, his salary was larger, and he began to play *vint*°, which he found added not a little to the pleasure of life, for he had a capacity for cards, played good-humoredly, and calculated rapidly and astutely, so that he usually won.

After living there for two years he met his future wife, Praskovya Fëdorovna Mikhel, who was the most attractive, clever, and brilliant girl of the set in which he moved, and among other amusements and relaxations from his labors as examining magistrate, Ivan Ilych established light and playful relations with her.

While he had been an official on special service he had been accustomed to dance, but now as an examining magistrate it was exceptional for him to do so. If he danced now, he did it as if to show that though he served under the reformed order of things, and had reached the fifth official rank, yet when it came to dancing he could do it better than most people. So at the end of an evening he sometimes danced with Praskovya Fëdorovna, and it was chiefly during these dances that he captivated her. She fell in love with him. Ivan Ilych had at first no definite intention of marrying, but when the girl fell in love with him he said to himself: "Really, why shouldn't I marry?"

Praskovya Fëdorovna came of a good family, was not bad-looking, and had some little property. Ivan Ilych might have aspired to a more brilliant match, but even this was good. He had his salary, and she, he hoped, would have an equal income. She was well connected, and was a sweet, pretty, and thoroughly correct young woman. To say that Ivan Ilych married because he fell in love with Praskovya Fëdorovna and found that she sympathized with his views of life would be as incorrect as to say that he married because his social circle approved of the match. He was swayed by both these considerations: the marriage gave him personal satisfaction, and at the same time it was considered the right thing by the most highly placed of his associates.

So Ivan Ilych got married.

The preparations for marriage and the beginning of married life, with its conjugal caresses, the new furniture, new crockery, and new linen, were very pleasant until his wife became pregnant — so that Ivan Ilych had begun to

Code of 1864: The emancipation of the serfs in 1861 was followed by a thorough all-round reform of judicial proceedings. [Translators' note.]
vint: a form of bridge. [Translators' note.]

think that marriage would not impair the easy, agreeable, gay, and always decorous character of his life, approved of by society and regarded by himself as natural, but would even improve it. But from the first months of his wife's pregnancy, something new, unpleasant, depressing, and unseemly, and from which there was no way of escape, unexpectedly showed itself.

His wife, without any reason — *de gaieté de cœur*° as Ivan Ilych expressed it to himself — began to disturb the pleasure and propriety of their life. She began to be jealous without any cause, expected him to devote his whole attention to her, found fault with everything, and made coarse and ill-mannered scenes.

At first Ivan Ilych hoped to escape from the unpleasantness of this state of affairs by the same easy and decorous relation to life that had served him heretofore: he tried to ignore his wife's disagreeable moods, continued to live in his usual easy and pleasant way, invited friends to his house for a game of cards, and also tried going out to his club or spending his evenings with friends. But one day his wife began upbraiding him so vigorously, using such coarse words, and continued to abuse him every time he did not fulfil her demands, so resolutely and with such evident determination not to give way till he submitted — that is, till he stayed at home and was bored just as she was — that he became alarmed. He now realized that matrimony — at any rate with Praskovya Fëdorovna — was not always conducive to the pleasures and amenities of life, but on the contrary often infringed both comfort and propriety, and that he must therefore entrench himself against such infringement. And Ivan Ilych began to seek for means of doing so. His official duties were the one thing that imposed upon Praskovya Fëdorovna, and by means of his official work and the duties attached to it he began struggling with his wife to secure his own independence.

With the birth of their child, the attempts to feed it and the various failures in doing so, and with the real and imaginary illnesses of mother and child, in which Ivan Ilych's sympathy was demanded but about which he understood nothing, the need of securing for himself an existence outside his family life became still more imperative.

As his wife grew more irritable and exacting and Ivan Ilych transferred the center of gravity of his life more and more to his official work, so did he grow to like his work better and become more ambitious than before.

Very soon, within a year of his wedding, Ivan Ilych had realized that marriage, though it may add some comforts to life, is in fact a very intricate and difficult affair towards which in order to perform one's duty, that is, to lead a decorous life approved of by society, one must adopt a definite attitude just as towards one's official duties.

And Ivan Ilych evolved such an attitude towards married life. He only required of it those conveniences — dinner at home, housewife, and bed — which it could give him, and above all that propriety of external forms required by public opinion. For the rest he looked for light-hearted pleasure and propriety, and was very thankful when he found them, but if he met with antagonism and querulousness he at once retired into his separate fenced-off world of official duties, where he found satisfaction.

Ivan Ilych was esteemed a good official, and after three years was made

de gaieté de cœur: "from pure whim."

Assistant Public Prosecutor. His new duties, their importance, the possibility of indicting and imprisoning anyone he chose, the publicity his speeches received, and the success he had in all these things, made his work still more attractive.

More children came. His wife became more and more querulous and ill-tempered, but the attitude Ivan Ilych had adopted towards his home life rendered him almost impervious to her grumbling.

After seven years' service in that town he was transferred to another province as Public Prosecutor. They moved, but were short of money and his wife did not like the place they moved to. Though the salary was higher the cost of living was greater, besides which two of their children died and family life became still more unpleasant for him.

Praskovya Fëdorovna blamed her husband for every inconvenience they encountered in their new home. Most of the conversations between husband and wife, especially as to the children's education, led to topics which recalled former disputes, and those disputes were apt to flare up again at any moment. There remained only those rare periods of amorousness which still came to them at times but did not last long. These were islets at which they anchored for a while and then again set out upon that ocean of veiled hostility which showed itself in their aloofness from one another. This aloofness might have grieved Ivan Ilych had he considered that it ought not to exist, but he now regarded the position as normal, and even made it the goal at which he aimed in family life. His aim was to free himself more and more from those unpleasantnesses and to give them a semblance of harmlessness and propriety. He attained this by spending less and less time with his family, and when obliged to be at home he tried to safeguard his position by the presence of outsiders. The chief thing however was that he had his official duties. The whole interest of his life now centered in the official world and that interest absorbed him. The consciousness of his power, being able to ruin anybody he wished to ruin, the importance, even the external dignity of his entry into court, or meetings with his subordinates, his success with superiors and inferiors, and above all his masterly handling of cases, of which he was conscious — all this gave him pleasure and filled his life, together with chats with his colleagues, dinners, and bridge. So that on the whole Ivan Ilych's life continued to flow as he considered it should do — pleasantly and properly.

So things continued for another seven years. His eldest daughter was already sixteen, another child had died, and only one son was left, a schoolboy and a subject of dissension. Ivan Ilych wanted to put him in the School of Law, but to spite him Praskovya Fëdorovna entered him at the High School. The daughter had been educated at home and had turned out well: the boy did not learn badly either.

III

So Ivan Ilych lived for seventeen years after his marriage. He was already a Public Prosecutor of long standing, and had declined several proposed transfers while awaiting a more desirable post, when an unanticipated and unpleasant occurrence quite upset the peaceful course of his life. He was expecting to be offered the post of presiding judge in a University town, but Happe somehow came to the front and obtained the appointment instead. Ivan Ilych became irritable, reproached Happe, and quarrelled both with him and with his immediate superiors — who became colder to him and again passed him over when other appointments were made.

This was in 1880, the hardest year of Ivan Ilych's life. It was then that it became evident on the one hand that his salary was insufficient for them to live on, and on the other that he had been forgotten, and not only this, but that what was for him the greatest and most cruel injustice appeared to others a quite ordinary occurrence. Even his father did not consider it his duty to help him. Ivan Ilych felt himself abandoned by everyone, and that they regarded his position with a salary of 3,500 rubles as quite normal and even fortunate. He alone knew that with the consciousness of the injustices done him, with his wife's incessant nagging, and with the debts he had contracted by living beyond his means, his position was far from normal.

In order to save money that summer he obtained leave of absence and went with his wife to live in the country at her brother's place.

In the country, without his work, he experienced *ennui* for the first time in his life, and not only *ennui* but intolerable depression, and he decided that it was impossible to go on living like that, and that it was necessary to take energetic measures.

Having passed a sleepless night pacing up and down the veranda, he decided to go to Petersburg and bestir himself, in order to punish those who had failed to appreciate him and to get transferred to another ministry.

Next day, despite many protests from his wife and her brother, he started for Petersburg with the sole object of obtaining a post with a salary of five thousand rubles a year. He was no longer bent on any particular department, or tendency, or kind of activity. All he now wanted was an appointment to another post with a salary of five thousand rubles, either in the administration, in the banks, with the railways, in one of the Empress Marya's Institutions°, or even in the customs — but it had to carry with it a salary of five thousand rubles and be in a ministry other than that in which they had failed to appreciate him.

And this quest of Ivan Ilych's was crowned with remarkable and unexpected success. At Kursk an acquaintance of his, F. I. Ilyin, got into the first-class carriage, sat down beside Ivan Ilych, and told him of a telegram just received by the Governor of Kursk announcing that a change was about to take place in the ministry: Peter Ivanovich was to be superseded by Ivan Semënovich.

The proposed change, apart from its significance for Russia, had a special significance for Ivan Ilych, because by bringing forward a new man, Peter Petrovich, and consequently his friend Zachar Ivanovich, it was highly favorable for Ivan Ilych, since Zachar Ivanovich was a friend and colleague of his.

In Moscow this news was confirmed, and on reaching Petersburg Ivan Ilych found Zachar Ivanovich and received a definite promise of an appointment in his former department of Justice.

A week later he telegraphed to his wife: "Zachar in Miller's place. I shall receive appointment on presentation of report."

Empress Marya's Institutions: orphanages.

Thanks to this change of personnel, Ivan Ilych had unexpectedly obtained an appointment in his former ministry which placed him two stages above his former colleagues besides giving him five thousand rubles salary and three thousand five hundred rubles for expenses connected with his removal. All his ill humor towards his former enemies and the whole department vanished, and Ivan Ilych was completely happy.

He returned to the country more cheerful and contented than he had been for a long time. Praskovya Fëdorovna also cheered up and a truce was arranged between them. Ivan Ilych told of how he had been fêted by everybody in Petersburg, how all those who had been his enemies were put to shame and now fawned on him, how envious they were of his appointment, and how much everybody in Petersburg had liked him.

Praskovya Fëdorovna listened to all this and appeared to believe it. She did not contradict anything, but only made plans for their life in the town to which they were going. Ivan Ilych saw with delight that these plans were his plans, that he and his wife agreed, and that, after a stumble, his life was regaining its due and natural character of pleasant lightheartedness and decorum.

Ivan Ilych had come back for a short time only, for he had to take up his new duties on the 10th of September. Moreover, he needed time to settle into the new place, to move all his belongings from the province, and to buy and order many additional things: in a word, to make such arrangements as he had resolved on, which were almost exactly what Praskovya Fëdorovna too had decided on.

Now that everything had happened so fortunately, and that he and his wife were at one in their aims and moreover saw so little of one another, they got on together better than they had done since the first years of marriage. Ivan Ilych had thought of taking his family away with him at once, but the insistence of his wife's brother and her sister-in-law, who had suddenly become particularly amiable and friendly to him and his family, induced him to depart alone.

So he departed, and the cheerful state of mind induced by his success and by the harmony between his wife and himself, the one intensifying the other, did not leave him. He found a delightful house, just the thing both he and his wife had dreamt of. Spacious, lofty reception rooms in the old style, a convenient and dignified study, rooms for his wife and daughter, a study for his son — it might have been specially built for them. Ivan Ilych himself superintended the arrangements, chose the wallpapers, supplemented the furniture (preferably with antiques which he considered particularly *comme il faut*), and supervised the upholstering. Everything progressed and progressed and approached the ideal he had set himself: even when things were only half completed they exceeded his expectations. He saw what a refined and elegant character, free from vulgarity, it would all have when it was ready. On falling asleep he pictured to himself how the reception-room would look. Looking at the yet unfinished drawing-room he could see the fireplace, the screen, the what-not, the little chairs dotted here and there, the dishes and plates on the walls, and the bronzes, as they would be when everything was in place. He was pleased by the thought of how his wife and daughter, who shared his taste in this matter, would be impressed by it. They were certainly not expecting as much. He had been particularly successful in finding, and buying cheaply, antiques which gave a particularly aristocratic character to the whole place. But in his letters he intentionally understated everything in order to be able to surprise them. All this so absorbed him that his new duties — though he liked his official work — interested him less than he had expected. Sometimes he even had moments of absentmindedness during the Court Sessions, and would consider whether he should have straight or curved cornices for his curtains. He was so interested in it all that he often did things himself, rearranging the furniture, or rehanging the curtains. Once when mounting a stepladder to show the upholsterer, who did not understand, how he wanted the hangings draped, he made a false step and slipped, but being a strong and agile man he clung on and only knocked his side against the knob of the window frame. The bruised place was painful but the pain soon passed, and he felt particularly bright and well just then. He wrote: "I feel fifteen years younger." He thought he would have everything ready by September, but it dragged on till mid-October. But the result was charming not only in his eyes but to everyone who saw it.

In reality it was just what is usually seen in the houses of people of moderate means who want to appear rich, and therefore succeed only in resembling others like themselves: there were damasks, dark wood, plants, rugs, and dull and polished bronzes — all the things people of a certain class have in order to resemble other people of that class. His house was so like the others that it would never have been noticed, but to him it all seemed to be quite exceptional. He was very happy when he met his family at the station and brought them to the newly furnished house all lit up, where a footman in a white tie opened the door into the hall decorated with plants, and when they went on into the drawing-room and the study uttering exclamations of delight. He conducted them everywhere, drank in their praises eagerly, and beamed with pleasure. At tea that evening, when Praskovya Fëdorovna among other things asked him about his fall, he laughed and showed them how he had gone flying and had frightened the upholsterer.

"It's a good thing I'm a bit of an athlete. Another man might have been killed, but I merely knocked myself, just here; it hurts when it's touched, but it's passing off already — it's only a bruise."

So they began living in their new home — in which, as always happens, when they got thoroughly settled in they found they were just one room short — and with the increased income, which as always was just a little (some five hundred rubles) too little, but it was all very nice.

Things went particularly well at first, before everything was finally arranged and while something had still to be done: this thing bought, that thing ordered, another thing moved, and something else adjusted. Though there were some disputes between husband and wife, they were both so well satisfied and had so much to do that it all passed off without any serious quarrels. When nothing was left to arrange it became rather dull and something seemed to be lacking, but they were then making acquaintances, forming habits, and life was growing fuller.

Ivan Ilych spent his mornings at the law courts and came home to dinner, and at first he was generally in a good humor, though he occasionally became irritable just on account of his house. (Every spot on the tablecloth or the upholstery, and every broken window-blind string, irritated him. He had devoted so much trouble to arranging it all that every disturbance of it distressed him.)

But on the whole his life ran its course as he believed life should do: easily, pleasantly, and decorously.

He got up at nine, drank his coffee, read the paper, and then put on his undress uniform and went to the law courts. There the harness in which he worked had already been stretched to fit him and he donned it without a hitch: petitioners, inquiries at the chancery, the chancery itself, and the sittings public and administrative. In all this the thing was to exclude everything fresh and vital, which always disturbs the regular course of official business, and to admit only official relations with people, and then only on official grounds. A man would come, for instance, wanting some information. Ivan Ilych, as one in whose sphere the matter did not lie, would have nothing to do with him: but if the man had some business with him in his official capacity, something that could be expressed on officially stamped paper, he would do everything, positively everything he could within the limits of such relations, and in doing so would maintain the semblance of friendly human relations, that is, would observe the courtesies of life. As soon as the official relations ended, so did everything else. Ivan Ilych possessed this capacity to separate his real life from the official side of affairs and not mix the two, in the highest degree, and by long practice and natural aptitude had brought it to such a pitch that sometimes, in the manner of a virtuoso, he would even allow himself to let the human and official relations mingle. He let himself do this just because he felt that he could at any time he chose resume the strictly official attitude again and drop the human relation. And he did it all easily, pleasantly, correctly, and even artistically. In the intervals between the sessions he smoked, drank tea, chatted a little about politics, a little about general topics, a little about cards, but most of all about official appointments. Tired, but with the feelings of a virtuoso — one of the first violins who has played his part in an orchestra with precision — he would return home to find that his wife and daughter had been out paying calls, or had a visitor, and that his son had been to school, had done his homework with his tutor, and was duly learning what is taught at High Schools. Everything was as it should be. After dinner, if they had no visitors, Ivan Ilych sometimes read a book that was being much discussed at the time, and in the evening settled down to work, that is, read official papers, compared the depositions of witnesses, and noted paragraphs of the Code applying to them. This was neither dull nor amusing. It was dull when he might have been playing bridge, but if no bridge was available it was at any rate better than doing nothing or sitting with his wife. Ivan Ilych's chief pleasure was giving little dinners to which he invited men and women of good social position, and just as his drawing-room resembled all other drawing-rooms so did his enjoyable little parties resemble all other such parties.

Once they even gave a dance. Ivan Ilych enjoyed it and everything went off well, except that it led to a violent quarrel with his wife about the cakes and sweets. Praskovya Fëdorovna had made her own plans, but Ivan Ilych insisted on getting everything from an expensive confectioner and ordered too many cakes, and the quarrel occurred because some of those cakes were left over and the confectioner's bill came to forty-five rubles. It was a great and disagreeable quarrel. Praskovya Fëdorovna called him "a fool and an imbecile," and he clutched at his head and made angry allusions to divorce.

But the dance itself had been enjoyable. The best people were there, and Ivan Ilych had danced with Princess Trufonova, a sister of the distinguished founder of the Society "Bear my Burden."

The pleasures connected with his work were pleasures of ambition; his social pleasures were those of vanity; but Ivan Ilych's greatest pleasure was playing bridge. He acknowledged that whatever disagreeable incident happened in his life, the pleasure that beamed like a ray of light above everything else was to sit down to bridge with good players, not noisy partners, and of course to four-handed bridge (with five players it was annoying to have to stand out, though one pretended not to mind), to play a clever and serious game (when the cards allowed it), and then to have supper and drink a glass of wine. After a game of bridge, especially if he had won a little (to win a large sum was unpleasant), Ivan Ilych went to bed in specially good humor.

So they lived. They formed a circle of acquaintances among the best people and were visited by people of importance and by young folk. In their views as to their acquaintances, husband, wife, and daughter were entirely agreed, and tacitly and unanimously kept at arm's length and shook off the various shabby friends and relations who, with much show of affection, gushed into the drawing-room with its Japanese plates on the walls. Soon these shabby friends ceased to obtrude themselves and only the best people remained in the Golovins' set.

Young men made up to Lisa, and Petrishchev, an examining magistrate and Dmitri Ivanovich Petrishchev's son and sole heir, began to be so attentive to her that Ivan Ilych had already spoken to Praskovya Fëdorovna about it, and considered whether they should not arrange a party for them, or get up some private theatricals.

So they lived, and all went well, without change, and life flowed pleasantly.

IV

They were all in good health. It could not be called ill health if Ivan Ilych sometimes said that he had a queer taste in his mouth and felt some discomfort in his left side.

But this discomfort increased and, though not exactly painful, grew into a sense of pressure in his side accompanied by ill humor. And his irritability became worse and worse and began to mar the agreeable, easy, and correct life that had established itself in the Golovin family. Quarrels between husband and wife became more and more frequent, and soon the ease and amenity disappeared and even the decorum was barely maintained. Scenes again became frequent, and very few of those islets remained on which husband and wife could meet without an explosion. Praskovya Fëdorovna now had good reason to say that her husband's temper was trying. With characteristic exaggeration she said he had always had a dreadful temper, and that it had needed all her good nature to put up with it for twenty years. It was true that now the quarrels were started by him. His bursts of temper always came just before dinner, often just as he began to eat his soup. Sometimes he noticed that a plate or dish was chipped, or the food was not right, or his son put his elbow on the table, or his daughter's hair was not done as he liked it, and for all this he blamed Praskovya Fëdorovna. At first she retorted and said disagreeable things to him, but once or twice he fell into such a rage at the beginning of dinner that she realized it was due to some physical derangement brought on by taking food, and so she restrained herself and did not answer, but only hurried to get the dinner over. She regarded this self-restraint as highly praiseworthy. Having come to the conclusion that her husband had a dreadful temper and made her life miserable, she began to feel sorry for herself, and the more she pitied herself the more she hated her husband. She began to wish he would die; yet she did not want him to die because then his salary would cease. And this irritated her against him still more. She considered herself dreadfully unhappy just because not even his death could save her, and though she concealed her exasperation, that hidden exasperation of hers increased his irritation also.

After one scene in which Ivan Ilych had been particularly unfair and after which he had said in explanation that he certainly was irritable but that it was due to his not being well, she said that if he was ill it should be attended to, and insisted on his going to see a celebrated doctor.

He went. Everything took place as he had expected and as it always does. There was the usual waiting and the important air assumed by the doctor, with which he was so familiar (resembling that which he himself assumed in court), and the sounding and listening, and the questions which called for answers that were foregone conclusions and were evidently unnecessary, and the look of importance which implied that "if only you put yourself in our hands we will arrange everything — we know indubitably how it has to be done, always in the same way for everybody alike." It was all just as it was in the law courts. The doctor put on just the same air towards him as he himself put on towards an accused person.

The doctor said that so-and-so indicated that there was so-and-so inside the patient, but if the investigation of so-and-so did not confirm this, then he must assume that and that. If he assumed that and that, then . . . and so on. To Ivan Ilych only one question was important: was his case serious or not? But the doctor ignored that inappropriate question. From his point of view it was not the one under consideration, the real question was to decide between a floating kidney, chronic catarrh, or appendicitis. It was not a question of Ivan Ilych's life or death, but one between a floating kidney and appendicitis. And that question the doctor solved brilliantly, as it seemed to Ivan Ilych, in favor of the appendix, with the reservation that should an examination of the urine give fresh indications the matter would be reconsidered. All this was just what Ivan Ilych had himself brilliantly accomplished a thousand times in dealing with men on trial. The doctor summed up just as brilliantly, looking over his spectacles triumphantly and even gaily at the accused. From the doctor's summing up Ivan Ilych concluded that things were bad, but that for the doctor, and perhaps for everybody else, it was a matter of indifference, though for him it was bad. And this conclusion struck him painfully, arousing in him a great feeling of pity for himself and of bitterness towards the doctor's indifference to a matter of such importance.

He said nothing of this, but rose, placed the doctor's fee on the table, and remarked with a sigh: "We sick people probably often put inappropriate questions. But tell me, in general, is this complaint dangerous, or not? . . ."

The doctor looked at him sternly over his spectacles with one eye, as if to say: "Prisoner, if you will not keep to the questions put to you, I shall be obliged to have you removed from the court."

"I have already told you what I consider necessary and proper. The analysis may show something more." And the doctor bowed.

Ivan Ilych went out slowly, seated himself disconsolately in his sledge, and drove home. All the way home he was going over what the doctor had said, trying to translate those complicated, obscure, scientific phrases into plain language and find in them an answer to the question: "Is my condition bad? Is it very bad? Or is there as yet nothing much wrong?" And it seemed to him that the meaning of what the doctor had said was that it was very bad. Everything in the streets seemed depressing. The cabmen, the houses, the passers-by, and the shops, were dismal. His ache, this dull gnawing ache that never ceased for a moment, seemed to have acquired a new and more serious significance from the doctor's dubious remarks. Ivan Ilych now watched it with a new and oppressive feeling.

He reached home and began to tell his wife about it. She listened, but in the middle of his account his daughter came in with her hat on, ready to go out with her mother. She sat down reluctantly to listen to this tedious story, but could not stand it long, and her mother too did not hear him to the end.

"Well, I am very glad," she said. "Mind now to take your medicine regularly. Give me the prescription and I'll send Gerasim to the chemist's." And she went to get ready to go out.

While she was in the room Ivan Ilych had hardly taken time to breathe, but he sighed deeply when she left it.

"Well," he thought, "perhaps it isn't so bad after all."

He began taking his medicine and following the doctor's directions, which had been altered after the examination of the urine. But then it happened that there was a contradiction between the indications drawn from the examination of the urine and the symptoms that showed themselves. It turned out that what was happening differed from what the doctor had told him, and that he had either forgotten, or blundered, or hidden something from him. He could not, however, be blamed for that, and Ivan Ilych still obeyed his orders implicitly and at first derived some comfort from doing so.

From the time of his visit to the doctor, Ivan Ilych's chief occupation was the exact fulfilment of the doctor's instructions regarding hygiene and the taking of medicine, and the observation of his pain and his excretions. His chief interests came to be people's ailments and people's health. When sickness, deaths, or recoveries were mentioned in his presence, especially when the illness resembled his own, he listened with agitation which he tried to hide, asked questions, and applied what he heard to his own case.

The pain did not grow less, but Ivan Ilych made efforts to force himself to think that he was better. And he could do this so long as nothing agitated him. But as soon as he had any unpleasantness with his wife, any lack of success in his official work, or held bad cards at bridge, he was at once acutely sensible of his disease. He had formerly borne such mischances, hoping soon to adjust what was wrong, to master it and attain success, or make a grand slam. But now every mischance upset him and plunged him into despair. He would say to himself: "There now, just as I was beginning to get better and the medicine had begun to take effect, comes this accursed misfortune, or unpleasantness. . . ." And he was furious with the mishap, or with the people who were causing the unpleasantness and killing him, for he felt that this fury was killing him but could not restrain it. One would have thought that it should have been clear to him that this exasperation with circumstances and people aggravated his illness, and that he ought therefore to ignore unpleasant occurrences. But he drew the very opposite conclusion: he said that he needed peace, and he watched for everything that might disturb it and became irritable at the slightest infringement of it. His condition was rendered worse by the fact that he read medical books and consulted doctors. The progress of his disease was so gradual that he could deceive himself when comparing one day with another — the difference was so slight. But when he consulted the doctors it seemed to him that he was getting worse, and even very rapidly. Yet despite this he was continually consulting them.

That month he went to see another celebrity, who told him almost the same as the first had done but put his questions rather differently, and the interview with this celebrity only increased Ivan Ilych's doubts and fears. A friend of a friend of his, a very good doctor, diagnosed his illness again quite differently from the others, and though he predicted recovery, his questions and suppositions bewildered Ivan Ilych still more and increased his doubts. A homœopathist diagnosed the disease in yet another way, and prescribed medicine which Ivan Ilych took secretly for a week. But after a week, not feeling any improvement and having lost confidence both in the former doctor's treatment and in this one's, he became still more despondent. One day a lady acquaintance mentioned a cure effected by a wonder-working icon. Ivan Ilych caught himself listening attentively and beginning to believe that it had occurred. This incident alarmed him. 'Has my mind really weakened to such an extent?" he asked himself. "Nonsense! It's all rubbish. I mustn't give way to nervous fears but having chosen a doctor must keep strictly to his treatment. That is what I will do. Now it's all settled. I won't think about it, but will follow the treatment seriously till summer, and then we shall see. From now there must be no more of this wavering!" This was easy to say but impossible to carry out. The pain in his side oppressed him and seemed to grow worse and more incessant, while the taste in his mouth grew stranger and stranger. It seemed to him that his breath had a disgusting smell, and he was conscious of a loss of appetite and strength. There was no deceiving himself: something terrible, new, and more important than anything before in his life, was taking place within him of which he alone was aware. Those about him did not understand or would not understand it, but thought everything in the world was going on as usual. That tormented Ivan Ilych more than anything. He saw that his household, especially his wife and daughter who were in a perfect whirl of visiting, did not understand anything of it and were annoyed that he was so depressed and so exacting, as if he were to blame for it. Though they tried to disguise it he saw that he was an obstacle in their path, and that his wife had adopted a definite line in regard to his illness and kept to it regardless of anything he said or did. Her attitude was this: "You know," she would say to her friends, "Ivan Ilych can't do as other people do, and keep to the treatment prescribed for him. One day he'll take his drops and keep strictly to his diet and go to bed in good time, but the next day unless I watch him he'll suddenly forget his medicine, eat sturgeon — which is forbidden — and sit up playing cards till one o'clock in the morning."

"Oh, come, when was that?" Ivan Ilych would ask in vexation. "Only once at Peter Ivanovich's."

"And yesterday with Shebek."

"Well, even if I hadn't stayed up, this pain would have kept me awake."

"Be that as it may you'll never get well like that, but will always make us wretched."

Praskovya Fëdorovna's attitude to Ivan Ilych's illness, as she expressed it both to others and to him, was that it was his own fault and was another of the annoyances he caused her. Ivan Ilych felt that this opinion escaped her involuntarily — but that did not make it easier for him.

At the law courts too, Ivan Ilych noticed, or thought he noticed, a strange attitude towards himself. It sometimes seemed to him that people were watching him inquisitively as a man whose place might soon be vacant. Then again, his friends would suddenly begin to chaff him in a friendly way about his low spirits, as if the awful, horrible, and unheard-of thing that was going on within him, incessantly gnawing at him and irresistibly drawing him away, was a very agreeable subject for jests. Schwartz in particular irritated him by his jocularity, vivacity, and *savoir-faire*, which reminded him of what he himself had been ten years ago.

Friends came to make up a set and they sat down to cards. They dealt, bending the new cards to soften them, and he sorted the diamonds in his hand and found he had seven. His partner said "No trumps" and supported him with two diamonds. What more could be wished for? It ought to be jolly and lively. They would make a grand slam. But suddenly Ivan Ilych was conscious of that gnawing pain, that taste in his mouth, and it seemed ridiculous that in such circumstances he should be pleased to make a grand slam.

He looked at his partner Mikhail Mikhaylovich, who rapped the table with his strong hand and instead of snatching up the tricks pushed the cards courteously and indulgently towards Ivan Ilych that he might have the pleasure of gathering them up without the trouble of stretching out his hand for them. "Does he think I am too weak to stretch out my arm?" thought Ivan Ilych, and forgetting what he was doing he over-trumped his partner, missing the grand slam by three tricks. And what was most awful of all was that he saw how upset Mikhail Mikhaylovich was about it but did not himself care. And it was dreadful to realize why he did not care.

They all saw that he was suffering, and said: "We can stop if you are tired. Take a rest." Lie down? No, he was not at all tired, and he finished the rubber. All were gloomy and silent. Ivan Ilych felt that he had diffused this gloom over them and could not dispel it. They had supper and went away, and Ivan Ilych was left alone with the consciousness that his life was poisoned and was poisoning the lives of others, and that this poison did not weaken but penetrated more and more deeply into his whole being.

With this consciousness, and with physical pain besides the terror, he must go to bed, often to lie awake the greater part of the night. Next morning he had to get up again, dress, go to the law courts, speak, and write; or if he did not go out, spend at home those twenty-four hours a day each of which was a torture. And he had to live thus all alone on the brink of an abyss, with no one who understood or pitied him.

V

So one month passed and then another. Just before the New Year his brother-in-law came to town and stayed at their house. Ivan Ilych was at the law courts and Praskovya Fëdorovna had gone shopping. When Ivan Ilych came home and entered his study he found his brother-in-law there — a healthy, florid man — unpacking his portmanteau himself. He raised his head on hearing Ivan Ilych's footsteps and looked up at him for a moment without a word. That stare told Ivan Ilych everything. His brother-in-law opened his mouth to utter an exclamation of surprise but checked himself, and that action confirmed it all.

"I have changed, eh?"

"Yes, there is a change."

And after that, try as he would to get his brother-in-law to return to the subject of his looks, the latter would say nothing about it. Praskovya Fëdorovna came home and her brother went out to her. Ivan Ilych locked the door and began to examine himself in the glass, first full face, then in profile. He took up a portrait of himself taken with his wife, and compared it with what he saw in the glass. The change in him was immense. Then he bared his arms to the elbow, looked at them, drew the sleeves down again, sat down on an ottoman, and grew blacker than night.

"No, no, this won't do!" he said to himself, and jumped up, went to the table, took up some law papers, and began to read them, but could not continue. He unlocked the door and went into the reception-room. The door leading to the drawing-room was shut. He approached it on tiptoe and listened.

"No, you are exaggerating!" Praskovya Fëdorovna was saying.

"Exaggerating! Don't you see it? Why, he's a dead man! Look at his eyes — there's no light in them. But what is it that is wrong with him?"

"No one knows. Nikolaevich said something, but I don't know what. And Leshchetitsky° said quite the contrary. . . ."

Ivan Ilych walked away, went to his own room, lay down, and began musing: "The kidney, a floating kidney." He recalled all the doctors had told him of how it detached itself and swayed about. And by an effort of imagination he tried to catch that kidney and arrest it and support it. So little was needed for this, it seemed to him. "No, I'll go to see Peter Ivanovich° again." He rang, ordered the carriage, and got ready to go.

"Where are you going, Jean?" asked his wife, with a specially sad and exceptionally kind look.

This exceptionally kind look irritated him. He looked morosely at her. "I must go to see Peter Ivanovich."

He went to see Peter Ivanovich, and together they went to see his friend, the doctor. He was in, and Ivan Ilych had a long talk with him.

Reviewing the anatomical and physiological details of what in the doctor's opinion was going on inside him, he understood it all.

Nikolaevich, Leshchetitsky: two doctors, the latter a celebrated specialist. [Translators' note.]
Peter Ivanovich: That was the friend whose friend was a doctor. [Translators' note.]

There was something, a small thing, in the vermiform appendix. It might all come right. Only stimulate the energy of one organ and check the activity of another, then absorption would take place and everything would come right. He got home rather late for dinner, ate his dinner, and conversed cheerfully, but could not for a long time bring himself to go back to work in his room. At last, however, he went to his study and did what was necessary, but the consciousness that he had put something aside — an important, intimate matter which he would revert to when his work was done — never left him. When he had finished his work he remembered that this intimate matter was the thought of his vermiform appendix. But he did not give himself up to it, and went to the drawing-room for tea. There were callers there, including the examining magistrate who was a desirable match for his daughter, and they were conversing, playing the piano, and singing. Ivan Ilych, as Praskovya Fëdorovna remarked, spent that evening more cheerfully than usual, but he never for a moment forgot that he had postponed the important matter of the appendix. At eleven o'clock he said good-night and went to his bedroom. Since his illness he had slept alone in a small room next to his study. He undressed and took up a novel by Zola, but instead of reading it he fell into thought, and in his imagination that desired improvement in the vermiform appendix occurred. There was the absorption and evacuation and the re-establishment of normal activity. "Yes, that's it!" he said to himself. "One need only assist nature, that's all." He remembered his medicine, rose, took it, and lay down on his back watching for the beneficent action of the medicine and for it to lessen the pain. "I need only take it regularly and avoid all injurious influences. I am already feeling better, much better." He began touching his side: it was not painful to the touch. "There, I really don't feel it. It's much better already." He put out the light and turned on his side. . . . "The appendix is getting better, absorption is occurring." Suddenly he felt the old, familiar, dull, gnawing pain, stubborn and serious. There was the same familiar loathsome taste in his mouth. His heart sank and he felt dazed. "My God! My God!" he muttered. "Again, again! and it will never cease." And suddenly the matter presented itself in a quite different aspect. "Vermiform appendix! Kidney!" he said to himself. "It's not a question of appendix or kidney, but of life and . . . death. Yes, life was there and now it is going, going and I cannot stop it. Yes. Why deceive myself? Isn't it obvious to everyone but me that I'm dying, and that it's only a question of weeks, days . . . it may happen this moment. There was light and now there is darkness. I was here and now I'm going there! Where?" A chill came over him, his breathing ceased, and he felt only the throbbing of his heart.

"When I am not, what will there be? There will be nothing. Then where shall I be when I am no more? Can this be dying? No, I don't want to!" He jumped up and tried to light the candle, felt for it with trembling hands, dropped candle and candlestick on the floor, and fell back on his pillow.

"What's the use? It makes no difference," he said to himself, staring with wide-open eyes into the darkness. "Death. Yes, death. And none of them know or wish to know it, and they have no pity for me. Now they are playing." (He heard through the door the distant sound of a song and its accompaniment.) "It's all the same to them, but they will die too! Fools! I first, and they later, but it will be the same for them. And now they are merry . . . the beasts!"

Anger choked him and he was agonizingly, unbearably miserable. "It is impossible that all men have been doomed to suffer this awful horror!" He raised himself.

"Something must be wrong. I must calm myself — must think it all over from the beginning." And he again began thinking. "Yes, the beginning of my illness: I knocked my side, but I was still quite well that day and the next. It hurt a little, then rather more. I saw the doctors, then followed despondency and anguish, more doctors, and I drew nearer to the abyss. My strength grew less and I kept coming nearer and nearer, and now I have wasted away and there is no light in my eyes. I think of the appendix — but this is death! I think of mending the appendix, and all the while here is death! Can it really be death?" Again terror seized him and he gasped for breath. He leant down and began feeling for the matches, pressing with his elbow on the stand beside the bed. It was in his way and hurt him, he grew furious with it, pressed on it still harder, and upset it. Breathless and in despair he fell on his back, expecting death to come immediately.

Meanwhile the visitors were leaving. Praskovya Fëdorovna was seeing them off. She heard something fall and came in.

"What has happened?"

"Nothing. I knocked it over accidentally."

She went out and returned with a candle. He lay there panting heavily, like a man who has run a thousand yards, and stared upwards at her with a fixed look.

"What is it, Jean?"

"No . . . o . . . thing. I upset it." ("Why speak of it? She won't understand," he thought.)

And in truth she did not understand. She picked up the stand, lit his candle, and hurried away to see another visitor off. When she came back he still lay on his back, looking upwards.

"What is it? Do you feel worse?"

"Yes."

She shook her head and sat down.

"Do you know, Jean, I think we must ask Leshchetitsky to come and see you here."

This meant calling in the famous specialist, regardless of expense. He smiled malignantly and said "No." She remained a little longer and then went up to him and kissed his forehead.

While she was kissing him he hated her from the bottom of his soul and with difficulty refrained from pushing her away.

"Good-night. Please God you'll sleep."

"Yes."

VI

Ivan Ilych saw that he was dying, and he was in continual despair.

In the depth of his heart he knew he was dying, but not only was he not accustomed to the thought, he simply did not and could not grasp it.

The syllogism he had learnt from Kiezewetter's Logic: "Caius is a man, men are mortal, therefore Caius is mortal," had always seemed to him correct as applied to Caius, but certainly not as applied to himself. That Caius — man in the abstract — was mortal, was perfectly correct, but he was not Caius, not an abstract man, but a creature quite, quite separate from all others. He had been little Vanya, with a mamma and a papa, with Mitya and Volodya, with the toys, a coachman and a nurse, afterwards with Katenka and with all the joys, griefs, and delights of childhood, boyhood, and youth. What did Caius know of the smell of that striped leather ball Vanya had been so fond of? Had Caius kissed his mother's hand like that, and did the silk of her dress rustle so for Caius? Had he rioted like that at school when the pastry was bad? Had Caius been in love like that? Could Caius preside at a session as he did? "Caius really was mortal, and it was right for him to die; but for me, little Vanya, Ivan Ilych, with all my thoughts and emotions, it's altogether a different matter. It cannot be that I ought to die. That would be too terrible."

Such was his feeling.

"If I had to die like Caius I should have known it was so. An inner voice would have told me so, but there was nothing of the sort in me and I and all my friends felt that our case was quite different from that of Caius. And now here it is!" he said to himself. "It can't be. It's impossible! But here it is. How is this? How is one to understand it?"

He could not understand it, and tried to drive this false, incorrect, morbid thought away and to replace it by other proper and healthy thoughts. But that thought, and not the thought only but the reality itself, seemed to come and confront him.

And to replace that thought he called up a succession of others, hoping to find in them some support. He tried to get back into the former current of thoughts that had once screened the thought of death from him. But strange to say, all that had formerly shut off, hidden, and destroyed his consciousness of death, no longer had that effect. Ivan Ilych now spent most of his time in attempting to re-establish that old current. He would say to himself: "I will take up my duties again — after all I used to live by them." And banishing all doubts he would go to the law courts, enter into conversation with his colleagues, and sit carelessly as was his wont, scanning the crowd with a thoughtful look and leaning both his emaciated arms on the arms of his oak chair; bending over as usual to a colleague and drawing his papers nearer he would interchange whispers with him, and then suddenly raising his eyes and sitting erect would pronounce certain words and open the proceedings. But suddenly in the midst of those proceedings the pain in his side, regardless of the stage the proceedings had reached, would begin its own gnawing work. Ivan Ilych would turn his attention to it and try to drive the thought of it away, but without success. *It* would come and stand before him and look at him, and he would be petrified and the light would die out of his eyes, and he would again begin asking himself whether *It* alone was true. And his colleagues and subordinates would see with surprise and distress that he, the brilliant and subtle judge, was becoming confused and making mistakes. He would shake himself, try to pull himself together, manage somehow to bring the sitting to a close, and return home with the sorrowful consciousness that his judicial labors could not as formerly hide from him what he wanted them to hide, and could not deliver him from *It*. And what was worst of all was that *It* drew his attention to itself not in order to make him take some action but only that he should look at *It*, look it straight in the face: look at it and, without doing anything, suffer inexpressibly.

And to save himself from this condition Ivan Ilych looked for consolations — new screens — and new screens were found and for a while seemed to save him, but then they immediately fell to pieces or rather became transparent, as if *It* penetrated them and nothing could veil *It*.

In these latter days he would go into the drawing-room he had arranged — that drawing-room where he had fallen and for the sake of which (how bitterly ridiculous it seemed) he had sacrificed his life — for he knew that his illness originated with that knock. He would enter and see that something had scratched the polished table. He would look for the cause of this and find that it was the bronze ornamentation of an album, that had got bent. He would take up the expensive album which he had lovingly arranged, and feel vexed with his daughter and her friends for their untidiness — for the album was torn here and there and some of the photographs turned upside down. He would put it carefully in order and bend the ornamentation back into position. Then it would occur to him to place all those things in another corner of the room, near the plants. He could call the footman, but his daughter or wife would come to help him. They would not agree, and his wife would contradict him, and he would dispute and grow angry. But that was all right, for then he did not think about *It*. *It* was invisible.

But then, when he was moving something himself, his wife would say: "Let the servants do it. You will hurt yourself again." And suddenly *It* would flash through the screen and he would see it. It was just a flash, and he hoped it would disappear, but he would involuntarily pay attention to his side. "It sits there as before, gnawing just the same!" And he could no longer forget *It*, but could distinctly see it looking at him from behind the flowers. "What is it all for?"

"It really is so! I lost my life over that curtain as I might have done when storming a fort. Is that possible? How terrible and how stupid. It can't be true! It can't, but it is."

He would go to his study, lie down, and again be alone with *It*: face to face with *It*. And nothing could be done with *It* except to look at it and shudder.

VII

How it happened it is impossible to say because it came about step by step, unnoticed, but in the third month of Ivan Ilych's illness, his wife, his daughter, his son, his acquaintances, the doctors, the servants, and above all he himself, were aware that the whole interest he had for other people was whether he would soon vacate his place, and at last release the living from the discomfort caused by his presence and be himself released from his sufferings.

He slept less and less. He was given opium and hypodermic injections of morphine, but this did not relieve him. The dull depression he experienced in a somnolent condition at first gave him a little relief, but only as something new, afterwards it became as distressing as the pain itself or even more so.

Special foods were prepared for him by the doctors' orders, but all those foods became increasingly distasteful and disgusting to him.

For his excretions also special arrangements had to be made, and this was a torment to him every time — a torment from the uncleanliness, the unseemliness, and the smell, and from knowing that another person had to take part in it.

But just through this most unpleasant matter, Ivan Ilych obtained comfort. Gerasim, the butler's young assistant, always came in to carry the things out. Gerasim was a clean, fresh peasant lad, grown stout on town food and always cheerful and bright. At first the sight of him, in his clean Russian peasant costume, engaged on that disgusting task embarrassed Ivan Ilych.

Once when he got up from the commode too weak to draw up his trousers, he dropped into a soft armchair and looked with horror at his bare, enfeebled thighs with the muscles so sharply marked on them.

Gerasim with a firm light tread, his heavy boots emitting a pleasant smell of tar and fresh winter air, came in wearing a clean Hessian apron, the sleeves of his print shirt tucked up over his strong, bare young arms; and refraining from looking at his sick master out of consideration for his feelings, and restraining the joy of life that beamed from his face, he went up to the commode.

"Gerasim!" said Ivan Ilych in a weak voice.

Gerasim started, evidently afraid he might have committed some blunder, and with a rapid movement turned his fresh, kind, simple young face which just showed the first downy signs of a beard.

"Yes, sir?"

"That must be very unpleasant for you. You must forgive me. I am helpless."

"Oh, why, sir," and Gerasim's eyes beamed and he showed his glistening white teeth, "what's a little trouble? It's a case of illness with you, sir."

And his deft strong hands did their accustomed task, and he went out of the room stepping lightly. Five minutes later he as lightly returned.

Ivan Ilych was still sitting in the same position in the armchair.

"Gerasim," he said when the latter had replaced the freshly-washed utensil. "Please come here and help me." Gerasim went up to him. "Lift me up. It is hard for me to get up, and I have sent Dmitri away."

Gerasim went up to him, grasped his master with his strong arms deftly but gently, in the same way that he stepped — lifted him, supported him with one hand, and with the other drew up his trousers and would have set him down again, but Ivan Ilych asked to be led to the sofa. Gerasim, without an effort and without apparent pressure, led him, almost lifting him, to the sofa and placed him on it.

"Thank you. How easily and well you do it all!"

Gerasim smiled again and turned to leave the room. But Ivan Ilych felt his presence such a comfort that he did not want to let him go.

"One thing more, please move up that chair. No, the other one — under my feet. It is easier for me when my feet are raised."

Gerasim brought the chair, set it down gently in place, and raised Ivan Ilych's legs on to it. It seemed to Ivan Ilych that he felt better while Gerasim was holding up his legs.

"It's better when my legs are higher," he said. "Place that cushion under them."

Gerasim did so. He again lifted the legs and placed them, and again Ivan

Ilych felt better while Gerasim held his legs. When he set them down Ivan Ilych fancied he felt worse.

"Gerasim," he said. "Are you busy now?"

"Not at all, sir," said Gerasim, who had learnt from the townsfolk how to speak to gentlefolk.

"What have you still to do?"

"What have I to do? I've done everything except chopping the logs for tomorrow."

"Then hold my legs up a bit higher, can you?"

"Of course I can. Why not?" And Gerasim raised his master's legs higher and Ivan Ilych thought that in that position he did not feel any pain at all.

"And how about the logs?"

"Don't trouble about that, sir. There's plenty of time."

Ivan Ilych told Gerasim to sit down and hold his legs, and began to talk to him. And strange to say it seemed to him that he felt better while Gerasim held his legs up.

After that Ivan Ilych would sometimes call Gerasim and get him to hold his legs on his shoulders, and he liked talking to him. Gerasim did it all easily, willingly, simply, and with a good nature that touched Ivan Ilych. Health, strength, and vitality in other people were offensive to him, but Gerasim's strength and vitality did not mortify but soothed him.

What tormented Ivan Ilych most was the deception, the lie, which for some reason they all accepted, that he was not dying but was simply ill, and that he only need keep quiet and undergo a treatment and then something very good would result. He however knew that do what they would nothing would come of it, only still more agonizing suffering and death. This deception tortured him — their not wishing to admit what they all knew and what he knew, but wanting to lie to him concerning his terrible condition, and wishing and forcing him to participate in that lie. Those lies — lies enacted over him on the eve of his death and destined to degrade this awful, solemn act to the level of their visitings, their curtains, their sturgeon for dinner — were a terrible agony for Ivan Ilych. And strangely enough, many times when they were going through their antics over him he had been within a hairbreadth of calling out to them: "Stop lying! You know and I know that I am dying. Then at least stop lying about it!" But he had never had the spirit to do it. The awful, terrible act of his dying was, he could see, reduced by those about him to the level of a casual, unpleasant, and almost indecorous incident (as if someone entered a drawing-room diffusing an unpleasant odor) and this was done by that very decorum which he had served all his life long. He saw that no one felt for him, because no one even wished to grasp his position. Only Gerasim recognized it and pitied him. And so Ivan Ilych felt at ease only with him. He felt comforted when Gerasim supported his legs (sometimes all night long) and refused to go to bed, saying: "Don't you worry, Ivan Ilych. I'll get sleep enough later on," or when he suddenly became familiar and exclaimed: "If you weren't sick it would be another matter, but as it is, why should I grudge a little trouble?" Gerasim alone did not lie; everything showed that he alone understood the facts of the case and did not consider it necessary to disguise them, but simply felt sorry for his emaciated and enfeebled master. Once when Ivan Ilych was sending him away he even said straight out: "We shall all of us die, so why should I grudge a little trouble?" — expressing the fact that he did not think his work burdensome, because he was doing it for a dying man and hoped someone would do the same for him when his time came.

Apart from this lying, or because of it, what most tormented Ivan Ilych was that no one pitied him as he wished to be pitied. At certain moments after prolonged suffering he wished most of all (though he would have been ashamed to confess it) for someone to pity him as a sick child is pitied. He longed to be petted and comforted. He knew he was an important functionary, that he had a beard turning grey, and that therefore what he longed for was impossible, but still he longed for it. And in Gerasim's attitude towards him there was something akin to what he wished for, and so that attitude comforted him. Ivan Ilych wanted to weep, wanted to be petted and cried over, and then his colleague Shebek would come, and instead of weeping and being petted, Ivan Ilych would assume a serious, severe, and profound air, and by force of habit would express his opinion on a decision of the Court of Cassation and would stubbornly insist on that view. This falsity around him and within him did more than anything else to poison his last days.

VIII

It was morning. He knew it was morning because Gerasim had gone, and Peter the footman had come and put out the candles, drawn back one of the curtains, and begun quietly to tidy up. Whether it was morning or evening, Friday or Sunday, made no difference, it was all just the same: the gnawing, unmitigated, agonizing pain, never ceasing for an instant, the consciousness of life inexorably waning but not yet extinguished, the approach of that ever dreaded and hateful Death which was the only reality, and always the same falsity. What were days, weeks, hours, in such a case?

"Will you have some tea, sir?"

"He wants things to be regular, and wishes the gentlefolk to drink tea in the morning," thought Ivan Ilych, and only said "No."

"Wouldn't you like to move onto the sofa, sir?"

"He wants to tidy up the room, and I'm in the way. I am uncleanliness and disorder," he thought, and said only:

"No, leave me alone."

The man went on bustling about. Ivan Ilych stretched out his hand. Peter came up, ready to help.

"What is it, sir?"

"My watch."

Peter took the watch which was close at hand and gave it to his master.

"Half-past eight. Are they up?"

"No, sir, except Vladimir Ivanovich" (the son) "who has gone to school. Praskovya Fëdorovna ordered me to wake her if you asked for her. Shall I do so?"

"No, there's no need to." "Perhaps I'd better have some tea," he thought, and added aloud: "Yes, bring me some tea."

Peter went to the door, but Ivan Ilych dreaded being left alone. "How can I keep him here? Oh yes, my medicine." "Peter, give me my medicine." "Why not? Perhaps it may still do me some good." He took a spoonful and swallowed it. "No, it won't help. It's all tomfoolery, all deception," he decided as soon as he became aware of the familiar, sickly, hopeless taste. "No, I can't believe in it any longer. But the pain, why this pain? If it would only cease just for a moment!" And he moaned. Peter turned towards him. "It's all right. Go and fetch me some tea."

Peter went out. Left alone Ivan Ilych groaned not so much with pain, terrible though that was, as from mental anguish. Always and forever the same, always these endless days and nights. If only it would come quicker! If only *what* would come quicker? Death, darkness? . . . No, no! Anything rather than death!

When Peter returned with the tea on a tray, Ivan Ilych stared at him for a time in perplexity, not realizing who and what he was. Peter was disconcerted by that look and his embarrassment brought Ivan Ilych to himself.

"Oh, tea! All right, put it down. Only help me to wash and put on a clean shirt."

And Ivan Ilych began to wash. With pauses for rest, he washed his hands and then his face, cleaned his teeth, brushed his hair, and looked in the glass. He was terrified by what he saw, especially by the limp way in which his hair clung to his pallid forehead.

While his shirt was being changed he knew that he would be still more frightened at the sight of his body, so he avoided looking at it. Finally he was ready. He drew on a dressing-gown, wrapped himself in a plaid, and sat down in the armchair to take his tea. For a moment he felt refreshed, but soon as he began to drink the tea he was again aware of the same taste, and the pain also returned. He finished it with an effort, and then lay down stretching out his legs, and dismissed Peter.

Always the same. Now a spark of hope flashes up, then a sea of despair rages, and always pain; always pain, always despair, and always the same. When alone he had a dreadful and distressing desire to call someone, but he knew beforehand that with others present it would be still worse. "Another dose of morphine — to lose consciousness. I will tell him, the doctor, that he must think of something else. It's impossible, impossible, to go on like this."

An hour and another pass like that. But now there is a ring at the door bell. Perhaps it's the doctor? It is. He comes in fresh, hearty, plump, and cheerful, with that look on his face that seems to say: "There now, you're in a panic about something, but we'll arrange it all for you directly!" The doctor knows this expression is out of place here, but he has put it on once for all and can't take it off — like a man who has put on a frock-coat in the morning to pay a round of calls.

The doctor rubs his hands vigorously and reassuringly.

"Brr! How cold it is! There's such a sharp frost; just let me warm myself!" he says, as if it were only a matter of waiting till he was warm, and then he would put everything right.

"Well now, how are you?"

Ivan Ilych feels that the doctor would like to say: "Well, how are our affairs?" but that even he feels that this would not do, and says instead: "What sort of a night have you had?"

Ivan Ilych looks at him as much as to say: "Are you really never ashamed of lying?" But the doctor does not wish to understand this question, and Ivan

Ilych says: "Just as terrible as ever. The pain never leaves me and never subsides. If only something. . . ."

"Yes, you sick people are always like that. . . . There, now I think I am warm enough. Even Praskovya Fëdorovna, who is so particular, could find no fault with my temperature. Well, now I can say good-morning," and the doctor presses his patient's hand.

Then, dropping his former playfulness, he begins with a most serious face to examine the patient, feeling his pulse and taking his temperature, and then begins the sounding and auscultation.

Ivan Ilych knows quite well and definitely that all this is nonsense and pure deception, but when the doctor, getting down on his knee, leans over him, putting his ear first higher then lower, and performs various gymnastic movements over him with a significant expression on his face, Ivan Ilych submits to it all as he used to submit to the speeches of the lawyers, though he knew very well that they were all lying and why they were lying.

The doctor, kneeling on the sofa, is still sounding him when Praskovya Fëdorovna's silk dress rustles at the door and she is heard scolding Peter for not having let her know of the doctor's arrival.

She comes in, kisses her husband, and at once proceeds to prove that she has been up a long time already, and only owing to a misunderstanding failed to be there when the doctor arrived.

Ivan Ilych looks at her, scans her all over, sets against her the whiteness and plumpness and cleanness of her hands and neck, the gloss of her hair, and the sparkle of her vivacious eyes. He hates her with his whole soul. And the thrill of hatred he feels for her makes him suffer from her touch.

Her attitude towards him and his disease is still the same. Just as the doctor had adopted a certain relation to his patient which he could not abandon, so had she formed one towards him — that he was not doing something he ought to do and was himself to blame, and that she reproached him lovingly for this — and she could not now change that attitude.

"You see he doesn't listen to me and doesn't take his medicine at the proper time. And above all he lies in a position that is no doubt bad for him — with his legs up."

She described how he made Gerasim hold his legs up.

The doctor smiled with a contemptuous affability that said: "What's to be done? These sick people do have foolish fancies of that kind, but we must forgive them."

When the examination was over the doctor looked at his watch, and then Praskovya Fëdorovna announced to Ivan Ilych that it was of course as he pleased, but she had sent today for a celebrated specialist who would examine him and have a consultation with Michael Danilovich (their regular doctor).

"Please don't raise any objections. I am doing this for my own sake," she said ironically, letting it be felt that she was doing it all for his sake and only said this to leave him no right to refuse. He remained silent, knitting his brows. He felt that he was so surrounded and involved in a mesh of falsity that it was hard to unravel anything.

Everything she did for him was entirely for her own sake, and she told him she was doing for herself what she actually was doing for herself, as if that was so incredible that he must understand the opposite.

At half-past eleven the celebrated specialist arrived. Again the sounding began and the significant conversations in his presence and in another room, about the kidneys and the appendix, and the questions and answers, with such an air of importance that again, instead of the real question of life and death which now alone confronted him, the question arose of the kidney and appendix which were not behaving as they ought to and would now be attacked by Michael Danilovich and the specialist and forced to amend their ways.

The celebrated specialist took leave of him with a serious though not hopeless look, and in reply to the timid question Ivan Ilych, with eyes glistening with fear and hope, put to him as to whether there was a chance of recovery, said that he could not vouch for it but there was a possibility. The look of hope with which Ivan Ilych watched the doctor out was so pathetic that Praskovya Fëdorovna, seeing it, even wept as she left the room to hand the doctor his fee.

The gleam of hope kindled by the doctor's encouragement did not last long. The same room, the same pictures, curtains, wallpaper, medicine bottles, were all there, and the same aching suffering body, and Ivan Ilych began to moan. They gave him a subcutaneous injection and he sank into oblivion.

It was twilight when he came to. They brought him his dinner and he swallowed some beef tea with difficulty, and then everything was the same again and night was coming on.

After dinner, at seven o'clock, Praskovya Fëdorovna came into the room in evening dress, her full bosom pushed up by her corset, and with traces of powder on her face. She had reminded him in the morning that they were going to the theatre. Sarah Bernhardt was visiting the town and they had a box, which he had insisted on their taking. Now he had forgotten about it and her toilet offended him, but he concealed his vexation when he remembered that he had himself insisted on their securing a box and going because it would be an instructive and aesthetic pleasure for the children.

Praskovya Fëdorovna came in, self-satisfied but yet with a rather guilty air. She sat down and asked how he was, but, as he saw, only for the sake of asking and not in order to learn about it, knowing that there was nothing to learn — and then went on to what she really wanted to say: that she would not on any account have gone but that the box had been taken and Helen and their daughter were going, as well as Petrishchev (the examining magistrate, their daughter's fiancé), and that it was out of the question to let them go alone; but that she would have much preferred to sit with him for a while; and he must be sure to follow the doctor's orders while she was away.

"Oh, and Fëdor Petrovich" (the fiancé) "would like to come in. May he? And Lisa?"

"All right."

Their daughter came in in full evening dress, her fresh young flesh exposed (making a show of that very flesh which in his own case caused so much suffering), strong, healthy, evidently in love, and impatient with illness, suffering, and death, because they interfered with her happiness.

Fëdor Petrovich came in too, in evening dress, his hair curled *à la Capoul*°, a tight stiff collar round his long sinewy neck, an enormous white shirt-

---

à la Capoul: imitating the hair-do of Victor Capoul, a contemporary French singer.

front, and narrow black trousers tightly stretched over his strong thighs. He had one white glove tightly drawn on, and was holding his opera hat in his hand.

Following him the schoolboy crept in unnoticed, in a uniform, poor little fellow, and wearing gloves. Terribly dark shadows showed under his eyes, the meaning of which Ivan Ilych knew well.

His son had always seemed pathetic to him, and now it was dreadful to see the boy's frightened look of pity. It seemed to Ivan Ilych that Vasya was the only one besides Gerasim who understood and pitied him.

They all sat down and again asked how he was. A silence followed. Lisa asked her mother about the opera-glasses, and there was an altercation between mother and daughter as to who had taken them and where they had been put. This occasioned some unpleasantness.

Fëdor Petrovich inquired of Ivan Ilych whether he had ever seen Sarah Bernhardt. Ivan Ilych did not at first catch the question, but then replied: "No, have you seen her before?"

"Yes, in *Adrienne Lecouvreur.*"

Praskovya Fëdorovna mentioned some rôles in which Sarah Bernhardt was particularly good. Her daughter disagreed. Conversation sprang up as to the elegance and realism of her acting — the sort of conversation that is always repeated and is always the same.

In the midst of the conversation Fëdor Petrovich glanced at Ivan Ilych and became silent. The others also looked at him and grew silent. Ivan Ilych was staring with glittering eyes straight before him, evidently indignant with them. This had to be rectified, but it was impossible to do so. The silence had to be broken, but for a time no one dared to break it and they all became afraid that the conventional deception would suddenly become obvious and the truth become plain to all. Lisa was the first to pluck up courage and break that silence, but by trying to hide what everybody was feeling, she betrayed it.

"Well, if we are going it's time to start," she said, looking at her watch, a present from her father, and with a faint and significant smile at Fëdor Petrovich relating to something known only to them. She got up with a rustle of her dress.

They all rose, said good-night, and went away.

When they had gone it seemed to Ivan Ilych that he felt better; the falsity had gone with them. But the pain remained — that same pain and that same fear that made everything monotonously alike, nothing harder and nothing easier. Everything was worse.

Again minute followed minute and hour followed hour. Everything remained the same and there was no cessation. And the inevitable end of it all became more and more terrible.

"Yes, send Gerasim here," he replied to a question Peter asked.

IX

His wife returned late at night. She came in on tiptoe, but he heard her, opened his eyes, and made haste to close them again. She wished to send Gerasim away and to sit with him herself, but he opened his eyes and said: "No, go away."

"Are you in great pain?"

"Always the same."

"Take some opium."

He agreed and took some. She went away.

Till about three in the morning he was in a state of stupefied misery. It seemed to him that he and his pain were being thrust into a narrow, deep black sack, but though they were pushed further and further in they could not be pushed to the bottom. And this, terrible enough in itself, was accompanied by suffering. He was frightened yet wanted to fall through the sack, he struggled but yet cooperated. And suddenly he broke through, fell, and regained consciousness. Gerasim was sitting at the foot of the bed dozing quietly and patiently, while he himself lay with his emaciated stockinged legs resting on Gerasim's shoulders; the same shaded candle was there and the same unceasing pain.

"Go away, Gerasim," he whispered.

"It's all right, sir. I'll stay a while."

"No. Go away."

He removed his legs from Gerasim's shoulders, turned sideways onto his arm, and felt sorry for himself. He only waited till Gerasim had gone into the next room and then restrained himself no longer but wept like a child. He wept on account of his helplessness, his terrible loneliness, the cruelty of man, the cruelty of God, and the absence of God.

"Why hast Thou done all this? Why hast Thou brought me here? Why, why dost Thou torment me so terribly?"

He did not expect an answer and yet wept because there was no answer and could be none. The pain again grew more acute, but he did not stir and did not call. He said to himself: "Go on! Strike me! But what is it for? What have I done to Thee? What is it for?"

Then he grew quiet and not only ceased weeping but even held his breath and became all attention. It was as though he were listening not to an audible voice but to the voice of his soul, to the current of thoughts arising within him.

"What is it you want?" was the first clear conception capable of expression in words, that he heard.

"What do you want? What do you want?" he repeated to himself.

"What do I want? To live and not to suffer," he answered.

And again he listened with such concentrated attention that even his pain did not distract him.

"To live? How?" asked his inner voice.

"Why, to live as I used to — well and pleasantly."

"As you lived before, well and pleasantly?" the voice repeated.

And in imagination he began to recall the best moments of his pleasant life. But strange to say none of those best moments of his pleasant life now seemed at all what they had then seemed — none of them except the first recollections of childhood. There, in childhood, there had been something really pleasant with which it would be possible to live if it could return. But the child who had experienced that happiness existed no longer, it was like a reminiscence of somebody else.

As soon as the period began which had produced the present Ivan Ilych, all that had then seemed joys now melted before his sight and turned into something trivial and often nasty.

And the further he departed from childhood and the nearer he came to the present the more worthless and doubtful were the joys. This began with the School of Law. A little that was really good was still found there — there was lightheartedness, friendship, and hope. But in the upper classes there had already been fewer of such good moments. Then during the first years of his official career, when he was in the service of the Governor, some pleasant moments again occurred; they were the memories of love for a woman. Then all became confused and there was still less of what was good; later on again there was still less that was good, and the further he went the less there was. His marriage, a mere accident, then the disenchantment that followed it, his wife's bad breath and the sensuality and hypocrisy: then that deadly official life and those preoccupations about money, a year of it, and two, and ten, and twenty, and always the same thing. And the longer it lasted the more deadly it became. "It is as if I had been going downhill while I imagined I was going up. And that is really what it was. I was going up in public opinion, but to the same extent life was ebbing away from me. And now it is all done and there is only death."

"Then what does it mean? Why? It can't be that life is so senseless and horrible. But if it really has been so horrible and senseless, why must I die and die in agony? There is something wrong!"

"Maybe I did not live as I ought to have done," it suddenly occurred to him. "But how could that be, when I did everything properly?" he replied, and immediately dismissed from his mind this, the sole solution of all the riddles of life and death, as something quite impossible.

"Then what do you want now? To live? Live how? Live as you lived in the law courts when the usher proclaimed 'The judge is coming!' The judge is coming, the judge!" he repeated to himself. "Here he is, the judge. But I am not guilty!" he exclaimed angrily. "What is it for?" And he ceased crying, but turning his face to the wall continued to ponder on the same question: Why, and for what purpose, is there all this horror? But however much he pondered he found no answer. And whenever the thought occurred to him, as it often did, that it all resulted from his not having lived as he ought to have done, he at once recalled the correctness of his whole life and dismissed so strange an idea.

X

Another fortnight passed. Ivan Ilych now no longer left his sofa. He would not lie in bed but lay on the sofa, facing the wall nearly all the time. He suffered ever the same unceasing agonies and in his loneliness pondered always on the same insoluble question: "What is this? Can it be that it is Death?" And the inner voice answered: "Yes, it is Death."

"Why these sufferings?" And the voice answered, "For no reason — they just are so." Beyond and besides this there was nothing.

From the very beginning of his illness, ever since he had first been to see the doctor, Ivan Ilych's life had been divided between two contrary and alternating moods: now it was despair and the expectation of this uncomprehended and terrible death, and now hope and an intently interested observation of the functioning of his organs. Now before his eyes there was only a kidney or an intestine that temporarily evaded its duty, and now only that incomprehensible and dreadful death from which it was impossible to escape.

These two states of mind had alternated from the very beginning of his illness, but the further it progressed the more doubtful and fantastic became the conception of the kidney, and the more real the sense of impending death.

He had but to call to mind what he had been three months before and what he was now, to call to mind with what regularity he had been going downhill, for every possibility of hope to be shattered.

Latterly during that loneliness in which he found himself as he lay facing the back of the sofa, a loneliness in the midst of a populous town and surrounded by numerous acquaintances and relations but that yet could not have been more complete anywhere — either at the bottom of the sea or under the earth — during that terrible loneliness Ivan Ilych had lived only in memories of the past. Pictures of his past rose before him one after another. They always began with what was nearest in time and then went back to what was most remote — to his childhood — and rested there. If he thought of the stewed prunes that had been offered him that day, his mind went back to the raw shrivelled French plums of his childhood, their peculiar flavor and the flow of saliva when he sucked their stones, and along with the memory of that taste came a whole series of memories of those days: his nurse, his brother, and their toys. "No, I mustn't think of that. . . . It is too painful," Ivan Ilych said to himself, and brought himself back to the present — to the button on the back of the sofa and the creases in its morocco. "Morocco is expensive, but it does not wear well: there had been a quarrel about it. It was a different kind of quarrel and a different kind of morocco that time when we tore father's portfolio and were punished, and mamma brought us some tarts. . . ." And again his thoughts dwelt on his childhood, and again it was painful and he tried to banish them and fix his mind on something else.

Then again together with that chain of memories another series passed through his mind — of how his illness had progressed and grown worse. There also the further back he looked the more life there had been. There had been more of what was good in life and more of life itself. The two merged together. "Just as the pain went on getting worse and worse, so my life grew worse and worse," he thought. "There is one bright spot there at the back, at the beginning of life, and afterwards all becomes blacker and blacker and proceeds more and more rapidly — in inverse ratio to the square of the distance from death," thought Ivan Ilych. And the example of a stone falling downwards with increasing velocity entered his mind. Life, a series of increasing sufferings, flies further and further towards its end — the most terrible suffering. "I am flying. . . ." He shuddered, shifted himself, and tried to resist, but was already aware that resistance was impossible, and again, with eyes weary of gazing but unable to cease seeing what was before them, he stared at the back of the sofa and waited — awaiting that dreadful fall and shock and destruction.

"Resistance is impossible!" he said to himself. "If I could only understand what it is all for! But that too is impossible. An explanation would be possible if it could be said that I have not lived as I ought to. But it is impossible to say that," and he remembered all the legality, correctitude, and propriety of his life. "That at any rate can certainly not be admitted," he thought, and his lips smiled ironically as if someone could see that smile and be taken in by it. "There is no explanation! Agony, death. . . . What for?"

Another two weeks went by in this way and during that fortnight an event occurred that Ivan Ilych and his wife had desired. Petrishchev formally proposed. It happened in the evening. The next day Praskovya Fëdorovna came into her husband's room considering how best to inform him of it, but that very night there had been a fresh change for the worse in his condition. She found him still lying on the sofa but in a different position. He lay on his back, groaning and staring fixedly straight in front of him.

She began to remind him of his medicines, but he turned his eyes towards her with such a look that she did not finish what she was saying; so great an animosity, to her in particular, did that look express.

"For Christ's sake let me die in peace!" he said.

She would have gone away, but just then their daughter came in and went up to say good morning. He looked at her as he had done at his wife, and in reply to her inquiry about his health said dryly that he would soon free them all of himself. They were both silent and after sitting with him for a while went away.

"Is it our fault?" Lisa said to her mother. "It's as if we were to blame! I am sorry for papa, but why should we be tortured?"

The doctor came at his usual time. Ivan Ilych answered "Yes" and "No," never taking his angry eyes from him, and at last said: "You know you can do nothing for me, so leave me alone."

"We can ease your sufferings."

"You can't even do that. Let me be."

The doctor went into the drawing-room and told Praskovya Fëdorovna that the case was very serious and that the only resource left was opium to allay her husband's sufferings, which must be terrible.

It was true, as the doctor said, that Ivan Ilych's physical sufferings were terrible, but worse than the physical sufferings were his mental sufferings, which were his chief torture.

His mental sufferings were due to the fact that that night, as he looked at Gerasim's sleepy, good-natured face with its prominent cheekbones, the question suddenly occurred to him: "What if my whole life has really been wrong?"

It occurred to him that what had appeared perfectly impossible before, namely that he had not spent his life as he should have done, might after all be true. It occurred to him that his scarcely perceptible attempts to struggle against what was considered good by the most highly placed people, those scarcely noticeable impulses which he had immediately suppressed, might have been the real thing, and all the rest false. And his professional duties and the whole arrangement of his life and of his family, and all his social and official interests, might all have been false. He tried to defend all those things to himself and suddenly felt the weakness of what he was defending. There was nothing to defend.

"But if that is so," he said to himself, "and I am leaving this life with the consciousness that I have lost all that was given me and it is impossible to rectify it — what then?"

He lay on his back and began to pass his life in review in quite a new way. In the morning when he saw first his footman, then his wife, then his daughter, and then the doctor, their every word and movement confirmed to him the awful truth that had been revealed to him during the night. In them he saw himself — all that for which he had lived — and saw clearly that it was not real at all, but a terrible and huge deception which had hidden both life and death. This consciousness intensified his physical suffering tenfold. He groaned and tossed about, and pulled at his clothing which choked and stifled him. And he hated them on that account.

He was given a large dose of opium and became unconscious, but at noon his sufferings began again. He drove everybody away and tossed from side to side.

His wife came to him and said:

"Jean, my dear, do this for me. It can't do any harm and often helps. Healthy people often do it."

He opened his eyes wide.

"What? Take communion? Why? It's unnecessary! However. . . ."

She began to cry.

"Yes, do, my dear. I'll send for our priest. He is such a nice man."

"All right. Very well," he muttered.

When the priest came and heard his confession, Ivan Ilych was softened and seemed to feel a relief from his doubts and consequently from his sufferings, and for a moment there came a ray of hope. He again began to think of the vermiform appendix and the possibility of correcting it. He received the sacrament with tears in his eyes.

When they laid him down again afterwards he felt a moment's ease, and the hope that he might live awoke in him again. He began to think of the operation that had been suggested to him. "To live! I want to live!" he said to himself.

His wife came in to congratulate him after his communion, and when uttering the usual conventional words she added:

"You feel better, don't you?"

Without looking at her he said "Yes."

Her dress, her figure, the expression of her face, the tone of her voice, all revealed the same thing. "This is wrong, it is not as it should be. All you have lived for and still live for is falsehood and deception, hiding life and death from you." And as soon as he admitted that thought, his hatred and his agonizing physical suffering again sprang up, and with that suffering a consciousness of the unavoidable, approaching end. And to this was added a new sensation of grinding shooting pain and a feeling of suffocation.

The expression of his face when he uttered that "yes" was dreadful. Having uttered it, he looked her straight in the eyes, turned on his face with a rapidity extraordinary in his weak state and shouted:

"Go away! Go away and leave me alone!"

XII

From that moment the screaming began that continued for three days, and was so terrible that one could not hear it through two closed doors without horror. At the moment he answered his wife he realized that he was lost, that there was no return, that the end had come, the very end, and his doubts were still unsolved and remained doubts.

"Oh! Oh! Oh!" he cried in various intonations. He had begun by screaming "I won't!" and continued screaming on the letter O.

For three whole days, during which time did not exist for him, he struggled in that black sack into which he was being thrust by an invisible, resistless force. He struggled as a man condemned to death struggles in the hands of the executioner, knowing that he cannot save himself. And every moment he felt that despite all his efforts he was drawing nearer and nearer to what terrified him. He felt that his agony was due to his being thrust into that black hole and still more to his not being able to get right into it. He was hindered from getting into it by his conviction that his life had been a good one. That very justification of his life held him fast and prevented his moving forward, and it caused him most torment of all.

Suddenly some force struck him in the chest and side, making it still harder to breathe, and he fell through the hole and there at the bottom was a light. What had happened to him was like the sensation one sometimes experiences in a railway carriage when one thinks one is going backwards while one is really going forwards and suddenly becomes aware of the real direction.

"Yes, it was all not the right thing," he said to himself, "but that's no matter. It can be done. But what *is* the right thing?" he asked himself, and suddenly grew quiet.

This occurred at the end of the third day, two hours before his death. Just then his schoolboy son had crept softly in and gone up to the bedside. The dying man was still screaming desperately and waving his arms. His hand fell on the boy's head, and the boy caught it, pressed it to his lips, and began to cry.

At that very moment Ivan Ilych fell through and caught sight of the light, and it was revealed to him that though his life had not been what it should have been, this could still be rectified. He asked himself, "What *is* the right thing?" and grew still, listening. Then he felt that someone was kissing his hand. He opened his eyes, looked at his son, and felt sorry for him. His wife came up to him and he glanced at her. She was gazing at him open-mouthed, with undried tears on her nose and cheek and a despairing look on her face. He felt sorry for her too.

"Yes, I am making them wretched," he thought. "They are sorry, but it will be better for them when I die." He wished to say this but had not the strength to utter it. "Besides, why speak? I must act," he thought. With a look at his wife he indicated his son and said: "Take him away . . . sorry for him . . . sorry for you too. . . ." He tried to add, "Forgive me," but said "forgo" and waved his hand, knowing that He whose understanding mattered would understand.

And suddenly it grew clear to him that what had been oppressing him and would not leave him was all dropping away at once from two sides, from ten sides, and from all sides. He was sorry for them, he must act so as not to hurt them: release them and free himself from these sufferings. "How good and how simple!" he thought. "And the pain?" he asked himself. "What has become of it? Where are you, pain?"

He turned his attention to it.

"Yes, here it is. Well, what of it? Let the pain be."

"And death . . . where is it?"

He sought his former accustomed fear of death and did not find it. "Where is it? What death?" There was no fear because there was no death.

In place of death there was light.

"So that's what it is!" he suddenly exclaimed aloud. "What joy!"

To him all this happened in a single instant, and the meaning of that instant did not change. For those present his agony continued for another two hours. Something rattled in his throat, his emaciated body twitched, then the gasping and rattle became less and less frequent.

"It is finished!" said someone near him.

He heard these words and repeated them in his soul.

"Death is finished," he said to himself. "It is no more!"

He drew in a breath, stopped in the midst of a sigh, stretched out, and died.

Mark Twain
[Samuel Langhorne Clemens] (1835–1910)
A Keelboatman's Ghost Story[1]   1883

In the heyday of the steamboating prosperity, the river from end to end was flaked with coal-fleets and timber-rafts, all managed by hand, and employing hosts of the rough characters whom I have been trying to describe. I remember the annual processions of mighty rafts that used to glide by Hannibal when I was a boy — an acre or so of white, sweet-smelling boards in each raft, a crew of two dozen men or more, three or four wigwams scattered about the raft's vast level space for storm-quarters — and I remember the rude ways and the tremendous talk of their big crews, the ex-keelboatmen and their admiringly patterning successors; for we used to swim out a quarter or a third of a mile and get on these rafts and have a ride.

By way of illustrating keelboat talk and manners, and that now departed and hardly remembered raft life, I will throw in, in this place, a chapter from a book which I have been working at°, by fits and starts, during the past five or six years, and may possibly finish in the course of five or six more. The book is a story which details some passages in the life of an ignorant village boy, Huck Finn, son of the town drunkard of my time out West, there. He has run away from his persecuting father, and from a persecuting good widow who wishes to make a nice, truth-telling, respectable boy of him; and with him a slave of the widow's has also escaped. They have found a fragment of a lumber-raft (it is high water and dead summer-time), and are floating down the river by night, and hiding in the willows by day — bound for Cairo, whence the negro will seek freedom in the heart of the free states. But, in a fog, they pass Cairo without knowing it. By and by they begin to suspect the truth, and Huck Finn is per-

[1] This story is contained in Chapter III of Mark Twain's memoir *Life on the Mississippi* (1883). The title has been supplied by the editor.

a book which I have been working at: The Adventures of Huckleberry Finn, begun in 1876 but not published until 1885. The chapter that Twain decided to "throw in" here did not find its way into the finished novel.

suaded to end the dismal suspense by swimming down to a huge raft which they have seen in the distance ahead of them, creeping aboard under cover of the darkness, and gathering the needed information by eavesdropping:

But you know a young person can't wait very well when he is impatient to find a thing out. We talked it over, and by and by Jim said it was such a black night, now, that it wouldn't be no risk to swim down to the big raft and crawl aboard and listen — they would talk about Cairo, because they would be calculating to go ashore there for a spree, maybe; or anyway they would send boats ashore to buy whisky or fresh meat or something. Jim had a wonderful level head, for a nigger: he could most always start a good plan when you wanted one.

I stood up and shook my rags off and jumped into the river, and struck out for the raft's light. By and by, when I got down nearly to her, I eased up and went slow and cautious. But everything was all right — nobody at the sweeps. So I swum down along the raft till I was most abreast the camp-fire in the middle, then I crawled aboard and inched along and got in among some bundles of shingles on the weather side of the fire. There was thirteen men there — they was the watch on deck of course. And a mighty rough-looking lot, too. They had a jug, and tin cups, and they kept the jug moving. One man was singing — roaring, you may say; and it wasn't a nice song — for a parlor, anyway. He roared through his nose, and strung out the last word of every line very long. When he was done they all fetched a kind of Injun war-whoop, and then another was sung. It begun:

"There was a woman in our towdn,
    In our towdn did dwed'l [dwell],
She loved her husband dear-i-lee,
    But another man twyste as wed'l.

"Singing too, riloo, riloo, riloo,
    Ri-too, riloo, rilay---e,
She loved her husband dear-i-lee,
    But another man twyste as wed'l."

And so on — fourteen verses. It was kind of poor, and when he was going to start on the next verse one of them said it was the tune the old cow died on; and another one said: "Oh, give us a rest!" And another one told him to take a walk. They made fun of him till he got mad and jumped up and begun to cuss the crowd, and said he could lam any thief in the lot.

They was all about to make a break for him, but the biggest man there jumped up and says:

"Set whar you are, gentlemen. Leave him to me; he's my meat."

Then he jumped up in the air three times, and cracked his heels together every time. He flung off a buckskin coat that was all hung with fringes, and says, "You lay thar tell the chawin-up's done"; and flung his hat down, which was all over ribbons, and says, "You lay thar tell his sufferin's is over."

Then he jumped up in the air and cracked his heels together again, and shouted out:

"Whoo-oop! I'm the old original iron-jawed, brass-mounted, copper-bellied corpse-maker from the wilds of Arkansaw! Look at me! I'm the man they call Sudden Death and General Desolation! Sired by a hurricane, dam'd by an earthquake, half-brother to the cholera, nearly related to the smallpox on the mother's side! Look at me! I take nineteen alligators and a bar'l of whisky for breakfast when I'm in robust health, and a bushel of rattlesnakes and a dead body when I'm ailing. I split the everlasting rocks with my glance, and I squench the thunder when I speak! Whoo-oop! Stand back and give me room according to my strength! Blood's my natural drink, and the wails of the dying is music to my ear. Cast your eye on me, gentlemen! and lay low and hold your breath, for I'm 'bout to turn myself loose!"

All the time he was getting this off, he was shaking his head and looking fierce, and kind of swelling around in a little circle, tucking up his wristbands, and now and then straightening up and beating his breast with his fist, saying, "Look at me, gentlemen!" When he got through, he jumped up and cracked his heels together three times, and let off a roaring "Whoo-oop! I'm the bloodiest son of a wildcat that lives!"

Then the man that had started the row tilted his old slouch hat down over his right eye; then he bent stooping forward, with his back sagged and his south end sticking out far, and his fists a-shoving out and drawing in in front of him, and so went around in a little circle about three times, swelling himself up and breathing hard. Then he straightened, and jumped up and cracked his heels together three times before he lit again (that made them cheer), and he began to shout like this:

"Whoo-oop! bow your neck and spread, for the kingdom of sorrow's a-coming! Hold me down to the earth, for I feel my powers a-working! whoo-oop! I'm a child of sin, *don't* let me get a start! Smoked glass, here, for all! Don't attempt to look at me with the naked eye, gentlemen! When I'm playful I use the meridians of longitude and parallels of latitude for a seine, and drag the Atlantic Ocean for whales! I scratch my head with the lightning and purr myself to sleep with the thunder! When I'm cold, I bile the Gulf of Mexico and bathe in it; when I'm hot I fan myself with an equinoctial storm; when I'm thirsty I reach up and suck a cloud dry like a sponge; when I range the earth hungry, famine follows in my tracks! Whoo-oop! Bow your neck and spread! I put my hand on the sun's face and make it night in the earth; I bite a piece out of the moon and hurry the seasons; I shake myself and crumble the mountains! Contemplate me through leather — *don't* use the naked eye! I'm the man with a petrified heart and biler-iron bowels! The massacre of isolated communities is the pastime of my idle moments, the destruction of nationalities the serious business of my life! The boundless vastness of the great American desert is my inclosed property, and I bury my dead on my own premises!" He jumped up and cracked his heels together three times before he lit (they cheered him again), and as he come down he shouted out: "Whoo-oop! bow your neck and spread, for the Pet Child of Calamity's a-coming!"

Then the other one went to swelling around and blowing again — the first one — the one they called Bob; next, the Child of Calamity chipped in again, bigger than ever; then they both got at it at the same time, swelling round and round each other and punching their fists most into each other's faces, and whooping and jawing like Injuns; then Bob called the Child names, and the Child called him names back again; next, Bob called him a heap rougher names, and the Child come back at him with the very worst kind of language; next, Bob knocked the Child's hat off, and the Child picked it up and kicked Bob's ribbony hat about six foot; Bob went and got it and said never mind, this warn't going to be the last of this thing, because he was a man that never forgot and never forgive, and so the Child better look out, for there was a time a-coming, just as sure as he was a living man, that he would have to answer to him with the best blood in his body. The Child said no man was willinger than he for that time to come, and he would give Bob fair warning, *now*, never to cross his path again, for he could never rest till he had waded in his blood, for such was his nature, though he was sparing him now on account of his family, if he had one.

Both of them was edging away in different directions, growling and shaking their heads and going on about what they was going to do; but a little black-whiskered chap skipped up and says:

"Come back here, you couple of chicken-livered cowards, and I'll thrash the two of ye!"

And he done it, too. He snatched them, he jerked them this way and that, he booted them around, he knocked them sprawling faster than they could get up. Why, it warn't two minutes till they begged like dogs — and how the other lot did yell and laugh and clap their hands all the way through, and shout, "Sail in, Corpse-Maker!" "Hi! at him again, Child of Calamity!" "Bully for you, little Davy!" Well, it was a perfect pow-wow for a while. Bob and the Child had red noses and black eyes when they got through. Little Davy made them own up that they was sneaks and cowards and not fit to eat with a dog or drink with a nigger; then Bob and the Child shook hands with each other, very solemn, and said they had always respected each other and was willing to let bygones be bygones. So then they washed their faces in the river; and just then there was a loud order to stand by for a crossing, and some of them went forward to man the sweeps there, and the rest went aft to handle the after sweeps.

I lay still and waited for fifteen minutes, and had a smoke out of a pipe that one of them left in reach; then the crossing was finished, and they stumped back and had a drink around and went to talking and singing again. Next they got out an old fiddle, and one played, and another patted juba, and the rest turned themselves loose on a regular old-fashioned keelboat breakdown. They couldn't keep that up very long without getting winded, so by and by they settled around the jug again.

They sung "Jolly, Jolly Raftsman's the Life for Me," with a rousing chorus, and then they got to talking about differences betwixt hogs, and their different kind of habits; and next about women and their different ways; and next about the best ways to put out houses that was afire; and next about what ought to be done with the Injuns; and next about what a king had to do, and how much he got; and next about how to make cats fight; and next about what to do when a man has fits; and next about differences betwixt clear-water rivers and muddy-water ones. The man they called Ed said the muddy Mississippi water was wholesomer to drink than the clear water of the Ohio; he said if you let a pint of this yaller Mississippi water settle, you would have about a half to three-quarters of an inch of mud in the bottom, according to the stage of the river, and then it warn't no better than Ohio water — what you wanted to do was to keep it stirred up — and when the river was low, keep mud on hand to put in and thicken the water up the way it ought to be.

The Child of Calamity said that waṣ so; he said there was nutritiousness in the mud, and a man that drunk Mississippi water could grow corn in his stomach if he wanted to. He says:

"You look at the graveyards; that tells the tale. Trees won't grow worth shucks in a Cincinnati graveyard, but in a Sent Louis graveyard they grow upwards of eight hundred foot high. It's all on account of the water the people drunk before they laid up. A Cincinnati corpse don't richen a soil any."

And they talked about how Ohio water didn't like to mix with Mississippi water. Ed said if you take the Mississippi on a rise when the Ohio is low, you'll find a wide band of clear water all the way down the east side of the Mississippi for a hundred mile or more, and the minute you get out a quarter of a mile from shore and pass the line, it is all thick and yaller the rest of the way across. Then they talked about how to keep tobacco from getting moldy, and from that they went into ghosts and told about a lot that other folks had seen; but Ed says:

"Why don't you tell something that you've seen yourselves? Now let me have a say. Five years ago I was on a raft as big as this, and right along here it was a bright moonshiny night, and I was on watch and boss of the stabboard oar forrard, and one of my pards was a man named Dick Allbright, and he come along to where I was sitting, forrard — gaping and stretching, he was — and stooped down on the edge of the raft and washed his face in the river, and come and set down by me and got out his pipe, and had just got it filled, when he looks up and says:

" 'Why looky-here,' he says, 'ain't that Buck Miller's place, over yander in the bend?'

" 'Yes,' says I, 'it is — why?' He laid his pipe down and leaned his head on his hand, and says:

" 'I thought we'd be furder down.' I says:

" 'I thought it, too, when I went off watch' — we was standing six hours on and six off — 'but the boys told me,' I says, 'that the raft didn't seem to hardly move, for the last hour,' says I, 'though she's a-slipping along all right now,' says I. He give a kind of a groan, and says:

" 'I've seed a raft act so before, along here,' he says, ' 'pears to me the current has most quit above the head of this bend durin' the last two years,' he says.

"Well, he raised up two or three times, and looked away off and around on the water. That started me at it, too. A body is always doing what he sees somebody else doing, though there mayn't be no sense in it. Pretty soon I see a black something floating on the water away off to stabboard and quartering behind us. I see he was looking at it, too. I says:

" 'What's that?' He says, sort of pettish:

" ' 'Tain't nothing but an old empty bar'l.'

" 'An empty bar'l!' says I, 'why,' says I, 'a spy-glass is a fool to *your* eyes. How can you tell it's an empty bar'l?' He says:

" 'I don't know; I reckon it ain't a bar'l, but I thought it might be,' says he.

" 'Yes,' I says, 'so it might be, and it might be anything else, too; a body can't tell nothing about it, such a distance as that,' I says.

"We hadn't nothing else to do, so we kept on watching it. By and by I says:

"'Why, looky-here, Dick Allbright, that thing's a-gaining on us, I believe.'

"He never said nothing. The thing gained and gained, and I judged it must be a dog that was about tired out. Well, we swung down into the crossing, and the thing floated across the bright streak of the moonshine, and by George, it *was* a bar'l. Says I:

"'Dick Allbright, what made you think that thing was a bar'l, when it was half a mile off?' says I. Says he:

"'I don't know.' Says I:

"'You tell me, Dick Allbright.' Says he:

"'Well, I knowed it was a bar'l; I've seen it before; lots has seen it; they says it's a ha'nted bar'l.'

"I called the rest of the watch, and they come and stood there, and I told them what Dick said. It floated right along abreast, now, and didn't gain any more. It was about twenty foot off. Some was for having it aboard, but the rest didn't want to. Dick Allbright said rafts that had fooled with it had got bad luck by it. The captain of the watch said he didn't believe in it. He said he reckoned the bar'l gained on us because it was in a little better current than what we was. He said it would leave by and by.

"So then we went to talking about other things, and we had a song, and then a breakdown; and after that the captain of the watch called for another song; but it was clouding up now, and the bar'l stuck right thar in the same place, and the song didn't seem to have much warm-up to it, somehow, and so they didn't finish it, and there warn't any cheers, but it sort of dropped flat, and nobody said anything for a minute. Then everybody tried to talk at once, and one chap got off a joke, but it warn't no use, they didn't laugh, and even the chap that made the joke didn't laugh at it, which ain't usual. We all just settled down glum, and watched the bar'l, and was oneasy and oncomfortable. Well, sir, it shut down black and still, and then the wind began to moan around, and next the lightning began to play and the thunder to grumble. And pretty soon there was a regular storm, and in the middle of it a man that was running aft stumbled and fell and sprained his ankle so that he had to lay up. This made the boys shake their heads. And every time the lightning come, there was that bar'l, with the blue lights winking around it. We was always on the lookout for it. But by and by, toward dawn, she was gone. When the day come we couldn't see her anywhere, and we warn't sorry, either.

"But next night about half past nine, when there was songs and high jinks going on, here she comes again, and took her old roost on the stabboard side. There warn't no more high jinks. Everybody got solemn; nobody talked; you couldn't get anybody to do anything but set around moody and look at the bar'l. It begun to cloud up again. When the watch changed, the off watch stayed up, 'stead of turning in. The storm ripped and roared around all night, and in the middle of it another man tripped and sprained his ankle, and had to knock off. The bar'l left toward day, and nobody see it go.

"Everybody was sober and down in the mouth all day. I don't mean the kind of sober that comes of leaving liquor alone — not that. They was quiet, but they all drunk more than usual — not together, but each man sidled off and took it private, by himself.

"After dark the off watch didn't turn in; nobody sung, nobody talked; the boys didn't scatter around, neither; they sort of huddled together, forrard; and for two hours they set there, perfectly still, looking steady in the one direction, and heaving a sigh once in a while. And then, here comes the bar'l again. She took up her old place. She stayed there all night; nobody turned in. The storm come on again, after midnight. It got awful dark; the rain poured down; hail, too; the thunder boomed and roared and bellowed; the wind blowed a hurricane; and the lightning spread over everything in big sheets of glare, and showed the whole raft as plain as day; and the river lashed up white as milk as far as you could see for miles, and there was the bar'l jiggering along, same as ever. The captain ordered the watch to man the after sweeps for a crossing, and nobody would go — no more sprained ankles for them, they said. They wouldn't even *walk* aft. Well, then, just then the sky split wide open, with a crash, and the lightning killed two men of the after watch, and crippled two more. Crippled them how, say you? Why, *sprained their ankles!*

"The bar'l left in the dark betwixt lightnings, toward dawn. Well, not a body eat a bite at breakfast that morning. After that the men loafed around, in twos and threes, and talked low together. But none of them herded with Dick Allbright. They all give him the cold shake. If he come around where any of the men was, they split up and sidled away. They wouldn't man the sweeps with him. The captain had all the skiffs hauled up on the raft, alongside of his wigwam, and wouldn't let the dead men be took ashore to be planted; he didn't believe a man that got ashore would come back; and he was right.

"After night come, you could see pretty plain that there was going to be trouble if that bar'l come again; there was such a muttering going on. A good many wanted to kill Dick Allbright, because he'd seen the bar'l on other trips, and that had an ugly look. Some wanted to put him ashore. Some said: 'Let's all go ashore in a pile, if the bar'l comes again.'

"This kind of whispers was still going on, the men being bunched together forrard watching for the bar'l, when lo and behold you! here she comes again. Down she comes, slow and steady, and settles into her old tracks. You could 'a' heard a pin drop. Then up comes the captain, and says:

" 'Boys, don't be a pack of children and fools; I don't want this bar'l to be dogging us all the way to Orleans, and *you* don't. Well, then, how's the best way to stop it? Burn it up — that's the way. I'm going to fetch it aboard,' he says. And before anybody could say a word, in he went.

"He swum to it, and as he come pushing it to the raft, the men spread to one side. But the old man got it aboard and busted in the head, and there was a baby in it! Yes, sir; a stark-naked baby. It was Dick Allbright's baby; he owned up and said so.

" 'Yes,' he says, a-leaning over it, 'yes, it is my own lamented darling, my poor lost Charles William Allbright deceased,' says he — for he could curl his tongue around the bulliest words in the language when he was a mind to, and lay them before you without a jint started anywheres. Yes, he said, he used to live up at the head of this bend, and one night he choked his child, which was crying, not intending to kill it — which was prob'ly a lie — and then he was scared, and buried it in a bar'l, before his wife got home, and off he went, and struck the northern trail and went to rafting; and this was the third year that the bar'l had chased him. He said the bad luck always begun light, and lasted till four men was killed, and then the bar'l didn't come any more after that. He said if the men would stand it one more night — and was a-going on like that — but the men had got enough. They started to get out a boat to take him ashore and lynch him, but he grabbed the little child all of a sudden and jumped overboard with it, hugged up to his breast and shedding tears, and we never see him again in this life, poor old suffering soul, nor Charles William neither."

"*Who* was shedding tears?" says Bob; "was it Allbright or the baby?"

"Why, Allbright, of course; didn't I tell you the baby was dead? Been dead three years — how could it cry?"

"Well, never mind how it could cry — how could it *keep* all that time?" says Davy. "You answer me that."

"I don't know how it done it," says Ed. "It done it, though — that's all I know about it."

"Say — what did they do with the bar'l?" says the Child of Calamity.

"Why, they hove it overboard, and it sunk like a chunk of lead."

"Edward, did the child look like it was choked?" says one.

"Did it have its hair parted?" says another.

"What was the brand on that bar'l, Eddy?" says a fellow they called Bill.

"Have you got the papers for them statistics, Edmund?" says Jimmy.

"Say, Edwin, was you one of the men that was killed by the lightning?" says Davy.

"Him? Oh, no! he was both of 'em," says Bob. Then they all haw-hawed.

"Say, Edward, don't you reckon you'd better take a pill? You look bad — don't you feel pale?" says the Child of Calamity.

"Oh, come, now, Eddy," says Jimmy, "show up; you must 'a' kept part of that bar'l to prove the thing by. Show us the bung-hole — *do* — and we'll all believe you."

"Say, boys," says Bill, "less divide it up. Thar's thirteen of us. I can swaller a thirteenth of the yarn, if you can worry down the rest."

Ed got up mad and said they could all go to some place which he ripped out pretty savage, and then walked off aft, cussing to himself, and they yelling and jeering at him, and roaring and laughing so you could hear them a mile.

"Boys, we'll split a watermelon on that," says the Child of Calamity; and he came rummaging around in the dark amongst the shingle bundles where I was, and put his hand on me. I was warm and soft and naked; so he says "Ouch!" and jumped back.

"Fetch a lantern or a chunk of fire here, boys — there's a snake here as big as a cow!"

So they run there with a lantern, and crowded up and looked in on me.

"Come out of that, you beggar!" says one.

"Who are you?" says another.

"What are you after here? Speak up prompt, or overboard you go."

"Snake him out, boys. Snatch him out by the heels."

I began to beg, and crept out amongst them trembling. They looked me over, wondering, and the Child of Calamity says:

"A cussed thief! Lend a hand and less heave him overboard!"

"No," says Big Bob, "less get out the paint-pot and paint him a sky-blue all over from head to heel, and *then* heave him over."

"Good! that's it. Go for the paint, Jimmy."

When the paint come, and Bob took the brush and was just going to begin, the others laughing and rubbing their hands, I begun to cry, and that sort of worked on Davy, and he says:

" 'Vast there. He's nothing but a cub. I'll paint the man that teches him!"

So I looked around on them, and some of them grumbled and growled, and Bob put down the paint, and the others didn't take it up.

"Come here to the fire, and less see what you're up to here," says Davy. "Now set down there and give an account of yourself. How long have you been aboard here?"

"Not over a quarter of a minute, sir," says I.

"How did you get dry so quick?"

"I don't know, sir. I'm always that way, mostly."

"Oh, you are, are you? What's your name?"

I warn't going to tell my name. I didn't know what to say, so I just says: "Charles William Allbright, sir."

Then they roared — the whole crowd; and I was mighty glad I said that, because, maybe, laughing would get them in a better humor.

When they got done laughing, Davy says:

"It won't hardly do, Charles William. You couldn't have growed this much in five year, and you was a baby when you come out of the bar'l, you know, and dead at that. Come, now, tell a straight story, and nobody 'll hurt you, if you ain't up to anything wrong. What *is* your name?"

"Aleck Hopkins, sir. Aleck James Hopkins."

"Well, Aleck, where did you come from, here?"

"From a trading-scow. She lays up the bend yonder. I was born on her. Pap has traded up and down here all his life; and he told me to swim off here, because when you went by he said he would like to get some of you to speak to a Mr. Jonas Turner, in Cairo, and tell him —"

"Oh, come!"

"Yes, sir, it's as true as the world. Pap he says —"

"Oh, your grandmother!"

They all laughed, and I tried again to talk, but they broke in on me and stopped me.

"Now, looky-here," says Davy; "you're scared, and so you talk wild. Honest, now, do you live in a scow, or is it a lie?"

"Yes, sir, in a trading-scow. She lays up at the head of the bend. But I warn't born in her. It's our first trip."

"Now you're talking! What did you come aboard here for? To steal?"

"No, sir, I didn't. It was only to get a ride on the raft. All boys does that."

"Well, I know that. But what did you hide for?"

"Sometimes they drive the boys off."

"So they do. They might steal. Looky-here; if we let you off this time, will you keep out of these kind of scrapes hereafter?"

" 'Deed I will, boss. You try me."

"All right, then. You ain't but little ways from shore. Overboard with you, and don't you make a fool of yourself another time this way. Blast it, boy, some raftsmen would rawhide you till you were black and blue!"

I didn't wait to kiss good-by, but went overboard and broke for shore. When Jim come along by and by, the big raft was away out of sight around the point. I swum out and got aboard, and was mighty glad to see home again.

The boy did not get the information he was after, but his adventure has furnished the glimpse of the departed raftsman and keelboatman which I desire to offer in this place.

Anton Chekhov (1860–1904)

IN EXILE   1892

Translated by Ann Dunnigan

Old Semyon, whose nickname was Preacher, and a young Tartar, whose name no one knew, were sitting by a campfire on the bank of the river; the other three ferrymen were inside the hut. Semyon, a gaunt, toothless old man of sixty, broad-shouldered and still healthy-looking, was drunk; he would have gone to bed long ago, but he had a bottle in his pocket and was afraid his comrades in the hut would ask him for a drink of vodka. The Tartar was worn out and ill, and, wrapping himself in his rags, he talked about how good it was in the province of Simbirsk, and what a beautiful and clever wife he had left at home. He was not more than twenty-five, and in the firelight his pale, sickly face and woebegone expression made him seem like a boy.

"Well, this is no paradise, of course," said Preacher. "You can see for yourself: water, bare banks, nothing but clay wherever you look. . . . It's long past Easter and there's still ice on the river . . . and this morning there was snow."

"Bad! Bad!" said the Tartar, surveying the landscape with dismay.

A few yards away the dark, cold river flowed, growling and sluicing against the pitted clay banks as it sped on to the distant sea. At the edge of the bank loomed a capacious barge, which ferrymen call a *karbas*. Far away on the opposite bank crawling snakes of fire were dying down then reappearing — last year's grass being burned. Beyond the snakes there was darkness again. Little blocks of ice could be heard knocking against the barge. It was cold and damp. . . .

The Tartar glanced at the sky. There were as many stars as there were at home, the same blackness, but something was lacking. At home, in the province of Simbirsk, the stars and the sky seemed altogether different.

"Bad! Bad!" he repeated.

"You'll get used to it!" said Preacher with a laugh. "You're still young and foolish — the milk's hardly dry on your lips — and in your foolishness you think there's no one more unfortunate than you, but the time will come when you'll say to yourself: may God give everyone such a life. Just look at me. In a week's time the floods will be over and we'll launch the ferry; you'll all go gadding about Siberia, while I stay here, going back and forth, from one bank to the other. For twenty-two years now that's what I've been doing. Day and night. The pike and the salmon under the water and me on it. That's all I want. God give everyone such a life."

The Tartar threw some brushwood onto the fire, lay down closer to it, and said, "My father is sick man. When he dies, my mother, my wife, will come here. Have promised."

"And what do you want a mother and a wife for?" asked Preacher. "Just foolishness, brother. It's the devil stirring you up, blast his soul! Don't listen to him, the Evil One! Don't give in to him. When he goes on about women, spite him: I don't want them! When he talks to you about freedom, you stand up to him: I don't want it! I want nothing! No father, no mother, no wife, no freedom, no house nor home! I want nothing, damn their souls!"

Preacher took a swig at the bottle and went on, "I'm no simple peasant, brother; I don't come from the servile class; I'm a deacon's son, and when I was free I lived in Kursk, and used to go around in a frock coat; but now I've brought myself to such a point that I can sleep naked on the ground and eat grass. And God give everyone such a life. I don't want anything, I'm not afraid of anyone, and the way I see it, there's no man richer or freer than I am. When they sent me here from Russia, from the very first day I jibbed: I want nothing! The devil was at me about my wife, about my kin, about freedom, but I told him: I want nothing! And I stuck to it; and here, you see, I live well, I don't complain. But if anyone humors the devil and listens to him even once, he's lost, no salvation for him. He'll be stuck fast in the bog, up to his ears, and he'll never get out.

"It's not only the likes of you, foolish peasants, that are lost, but even the well-born and educated. Fifteen years ago they sent a gentleman here from Russia. He forged a will or something — wouldn't share with his brothers. It was said he was a prince or a baron, but maybe he was only an official, who knows? Well, the gentleman came here, and the first thing, he bought himself a house and land in Mukhortinskoe. 'I want to live by my own labor,' says he, 'in the sweat of my brow, because I'm no longer a gentleman, but an exile.' . . . 'Well,' says I, 'may God help you, that's the right thing.' He was a young man then, a hustler, always on the move; he used to do the mowing himself, catch fish, ride sixty versts° on horseback. But here was the trouble: from the very first year he began riding to Gyrino to the post office. He used to stand on my ferry and sigh, 'Ah, Semyon, for a long time now they haven't sent me any money from home.' . . . 'You don't need money, Vasily Sergeich. What good is it? Throw off the past, forget it as if it had never happened, as if it was only a dream, and start life afresh. Don't listen to the devil,' I tell him, 'he'll bring you to no good; he'll tighten the noose. Now you want money,' says I, 'and in a little while, before you know it, you'll want something else, and then more and more. But,' says I; 'if you want to be happy, the very first thing is not to want anything.' Yes. . . . 'And if fate has cruelly wronged you and me,' says I, 'it's no good going down on your knees to her and asking her favor; you have to spurn her and laugh at her, otherwise she'll laugh at you.' That's what I said to him. . . .

"Two years later I ferried him over to this side, and he was rubbing his hands together and laughing. 'I'm going to Gyrino,' says he, 'to meet my wife.

sixty versts: about forty miles.

She has taken pity on me and come here.° She's so kind and good!' He was panting with joy. Next day he comes with his wife. A young, beautiful lady in a hat, carrying a baby girl in her arms. And plenty of baggage of all sorts. My Vasily Sergeich was spinning around her; couldn't take his eyes off her; couldn't praise her enough. 'Yes, brother Semyon, even in Siberia people can live!' . . . 'Well,' thinks I, 'just you wait; better not rejoice too soon.' . . . And from that time on, almost every week he went to Gyrino to find out if money had been sent from Russia. As for money — it took plenty! 'It's for my sake that her youth and beauty are going to ruin here in Siberia,' he says, 'sharing with me my bitter fate, and for this,' he says, 'I ought to provide her with every diversion.' To make it more cheerful for his lady he took up with the officials and with all sorts of riffraff. And there had to be food and drink for this crowd, of course, and they must have a piano, and a fuzzy little lap dog on the sofa — may it croak! . . . Luxury, in short, indulgence. The lady did not stay with him long. How could she? Clay, water, cold, no vegetables for you, no fruit; un-educated and drunken people all around, no manners at all, and she a pampered lady from the capital. . . . Naturally, she grew tired of it. Besides, her husband, say what you like, was no longer a gentleman, but an exile — not exactly an honor.

"Three years later, I remember, on the eve of the Assumption, someone shouted from the other side. I went over in the ferry, and what do I see but the lady — all muffled up, and with her a young gentleman, an official. There was a troika. . . . And after I ferried them across, they got in it and vanished into thin air! That was the last that was seen of them. Toward morning Vasily Sergeich galloped up to the ferry. 'Didn't my wife pass this way, Semyon, with a gentle-man in spectacles?' . . . 'She did,' says I. 'Seek the wind in the fields!' He galloped off in pursuit of them, and didn't stop for five days and five nights. Afterwards, when I took him over to the other side, he threw himself down on the ferry, beat his head against the planks, and howled. 'So that's how it is,' says I. . . . I laughed and recalled to him: 'Even in Siberia people can live!' And he beat his head all the more.

"After that he began to long for freedom. His wife had slipped away to Russia, so, naturally, he was drawn there, both to see her and to rescue her from her lover. And, my friend, he took to galloping off every day, either to the post office or the authorities; he kept sending in petitions, and presenting them personally, asking to be pardoned so he could go back home; and he used to tell how he had spent some two hundred rubles on telegrams alone. He sold his land, and mortgaged his house to the Jews. He grew gray, stooped, and yellow in the face, as if he was consumptive. He'd talk to you and go: khe-khe-khe . . . and there would be tears in his eyes. He struggled with those petitions for eight years, but now he has recovered his spirits and is more cheerful: he's thought up a new indulgence. His daughter, you see, has grown up. He keeps an eye on her, dotes on her. And, to tell the truth, she's all right, a pretty little thing, black-browed, and with a lively disposition. Every Sunday he goes to church with her in Gyrino. Side by side they stand on the ferry, she laughing

She has taken pity on me and come here: In Russia at the time it was customary for the czar, in banishing criminals and political dissenters to Siberia, to permit their wives and fam-ilies to accompany them into exile provided they could pay their own transportation and support.

and he not taking his eyes off her. 'Yes, Semyon,' says he, 'even in Siberia people can live. Even in Siberia there is happiness. Look,' says he, 'see what a daughter I've got! I suppose you wouldn't find another like her if you went a thousand versts.' . . . 'Your daughter,' says I, 'is a fine young lady, that's true, certainly. . . .' But I think to myself: Wait a while. . . . The girl is young, her blood is dancing, she wants to live, and what life is there here? And, my friend, she did begin to fret. . . . She withered and withered, wasted away, fell ill; and now she's completely worn out. Consumption.

"That's your Siberian happiness for you, the pestilence take it! That's how people can live in Siberia! . . . He's taken to running after doctors and taking them home with him. As soon as he hears that there's a doctor or quack two or three hundred versts away, he goes to fetch him. A terrible lot of money has been spent on doctors; to my way of thinking, it would have been better to spend it on drink. . . . She'll die anyway. She's certain to die, and then he'll be completely lost. He'll hang himself from grief, or run away to Russia — that's sure. He'll run away, they'll catch him, there'll be a trial, and then hard labor; they'll give him a taste of the lash. . . ."

"Good, good," muttered the Tartar, shivering with cold.

"What's good?" asked Preacher.

"Wife and daughter. . . . Let hard labor, let suffer; he saw his wife and daughter. . . . You say: want nothing. But nothing is bad! Wife was with him three years — God gave him that. Nothing is bad; three years is good. How you not understand?"

Shivering and stuttering, straining to pick out the Russian words, of which he knew so few, the Tartar said God forbid one should fall sick and die in a strange land, and be buried in the cold, sodden earth; that if his wife came to him even for one day, even for one hour, he would be willing to accept any torture whatsoever, and thank God for it. Better one day of happiness than nothing.

After that he again described the beautiful and clever wife he had left at home; then, clutching his head with both hands, he began crying and assuring Semyon that he was innocent and had been falsely accused. His two brothers and his uncle stole some horses from a peasant, and beat the old man till he was half dead, and the commune had not judged fairly, but had contrived a sentence by which all three brothers were sent to Siberia, while the uncle, a rich man, remained at home.

"You'll get u-u-used to it!" said Semyon.

The Tartar relapsed into silence and fixed his tearful eyes on the fire; his face expressed bewilderment and fright, as though he still did not understand why he was here in the dark, in the damp, among strangers, instead of in the province of Simbirsk. Preacher lay down near the fire, chuckled at something, and began singing in an undertone.

"What joy has she with her father?" he said a little later. "He loves her, she's a consolation to him, it's true; but you have to mind your p's and q's with him, brother: he's a strict old man, a severe old man. And strictness is not what young girls want. . . . They want petting and ha-ha-ha and ho-ho-ho, scents and pomades! Yes. . . . Ekh, life, life!" sighed Semyon, getting up with difficulty. "The vodka's all gone, so it's time to sleep. Eh? I'm going, my boy."

Left alone, the Tartar put more brushwood onto the fire, lay down, and, looking into the blaze, began thinking of his native village, and of his wife: if she would come only for a month, even for a day, then, if she liked, she might go back again. Better a month or even a day than nothing. But if she kept her promise and came, how could he provide for her? Where could she live?

"If not something to eat, how you live?" the Tartar asked aloud.

He was paid only ten kopecks for working at the oars a day and a night; the passengers gave him tips, it was true, but the ferrymen shared everything among themselves, giving nothing to the Tartar, but only making fun of him. And he was hungry, cold, and frightened from want. . . . Now, when his whole body was shivering and aching, he ought to go into the hut and lie down to sleep, but he had nothing there to cover himself with, and it was colder there than on the river bank; here, too, he had nothing to put over him, but at least he could make a fire. . . .

In another week, when the floods had subsided and the ferry could sail, none of the ferrymen except Semyon would be needed, and the Tartar would begin going from village to village, looking for work and begging alms. His wife was only seventeen years old; beautiful, pampered, shy — could she possibly go from village to village, her face unveiled, begging? No, even to think of it was dreadful. . . .

It was already growing light; the barge, the bushes of rose-willow, and the ripples on the water were clearly distinguishable, and looking back there was the steep clay precipice, below it the little hut thatched with brown straw, and above clung the huts of the villagers. The cocks were already crowing in the village.

The red clay precipice, the barge, the river, the strange, unkind people, hunger, cold, illness — perhaps all this did not exist in reality. Probably it was all a dream, thought the Tartar. He felt that he was asleep, and hearing his own snoring. . . . Of course, he was at home in the province of Simbirsk, and he had only to call his wife by name for her to answer, and in the next room his mother. . . . However, what awful dreams there are! Why? The Tartar smiled and opened his eyes. What river was this? The Volga?

"Bo-o-at!" someone shouted from the other side. "Kar-ba-a-s!"

The Tartar woke up and went to wake his comrades, to row over to the other side. Putting on their torn sheepskins as they came, the ferrymen appeared on the bank, swearing in hoarse, sleepy voices, and shivering from the cold. After their sleep, the river, from which there came a piercing gust of cold air, evidently struck them as revolting and sinister. They were not quick to jump into the barge. The Tartar and the three ferrymen took up the long, broad-bladed oars, which looked like crabs' claws in the darkness. Semyon leaned his belly against the long tiller. The shouting from the other side continued, and two shots were fired from a revolver; the man probably thought that the ferrymen were asleep or had gone off to the village tavern.

"All right, plenty of time!" said Preacher in the tone of a man who is convinced that there is no need to hurry in this world — that it makes no difference, really, and nothing will come of it.

The heavy, clumsy barge drew away from the bank and floated between the rose-willows; and only because the willows slowly receded was it possible to see that the barge was not standing still but moving. The ferrymen plied the oars evenly, in unison; Preacher hung over the tiller on his belly, and, describing an arc in the air, flew from one side of the boat to the other. In the darkness it looked as if the men were sitting on some antideluvian animal with long paws, and sailing to a cold, bleak land, the very one of which we sometimes dream in nightmares.

They passed beyond the willows and floated out into the open. The rhythmic thump and splash of the oars were now audible on the further shore, and someone shouted, "Hurry! Hurry!" Another ten minutes passed and the barge bumped heavily against the landing stage.

"And it keeps coming down, and coming down!" muttered Semyon, wiping the snow from his face. "Where it comes from, God only knows!"

On the other side stood a thin old man of medium height wearing a jacket lined with fox fur and a white lambskin cap. He was standing at a little distance from his horses and not moving; he had a concentrated, morose expression, as if, trying to remember something, he had grown angry with his unyielding memory. When Semyon went up to him with a smile and took off his cap, he said, "I'm hastening to Anastasyevka. My daughter is worse again, and they say there's a new doctor at Anastasyevka."

They dragged the tarantass° onto the barge and rowed back. The man, whom Semyon called Vasily Sergeich, stood motionless all the way back, his thick lips tightly compressed, his eyes fixed on one spot; when the coachman asked permission to smoke in his presence, he made no reply, as if he had not heard. And Semyon, hanging over the tiller on his belly, glanced mockingly at him and said, "Even in Siberia people can live. Li-i-ve!"

There was a triumphant expression on Preacher's face, as if he had proved something and was rejoicing that it had turned out exactly as he had surmised. The helpless, unhappy look of the man in the fox-lined jacket evidently afforded him great satisfaction.

"It's muddy driving now, Vasily Sergeich," he said when the horses were harnessed on the bank. "You'd better have waited a week or two till it gets drier. . . . Or else not have gone at all. . . . If there were any sense in going, but, as you yourself know, people have been driving about for ever and ever, by day and by night, and there's never any sense in it. That's the truth!"

Vasily Sergeich tipped him without a word, got into the tarantass, and drove off.

"See there, he's gone galloping off for a doctor!" said Semyon, shrinking with cold. "Yes, looking for a real doctor is like chasing the wind in the fields, or catching the devil by the tail, damn your soul! What freaks! Lord forgive me, a sinner!"

The Tartar went up to Preacher and, looking at him with hatred and abhorrence, trembling, mixing Tartar words with his broken Russian, said, "He is good — good. You bad! You bad! Gentleman is good soul, excellent, and you beast, you bad! Gentleman alive and you dead. . . . God created man to be live, be joyful, be sad and sorrow, but you want nothing. . . . You not live, you stone, clay! Stone want nothing and you want nothing. . . . You stone — and God not love you, love gentleman!"

tarantass: a heavy horse-drawn carriage with four wheels.

Everyone laughed; the Tartar frowned scornfully and, with a gesture of despair, wrapped himself in his rags and went to the fire. Semyon and the ferrymen trailed off to the hut.

"It's cold," said one of the ferrymen hoarsely as he stretched out on the straw that covered the damp floor.

"Well, it's not warm!" one of the others agreed. "It's a hard life!"

They all lay down. The door was blown open by the wind, and snow drifted into the hut. No one felt like getting up and closing the door; it was cold and they were lazy.

"I'm all right!" said Semyon, falling asleep. "God give everyone such a life."

"You're a hard case, we know that. Even the devils won't take you!"

From outside there came sounds like the howling of a dog.

"What's that? Who's there?"

"It's the Tartar crying."

"He'll get u-u-used to it!" said Semyon, and instantly fell asleep.

Soon the others fell asleep too. And the door remained unclosed.

Sherwood Anderson (1876–1941)

The Egg

1920

My father was, I am sure, intended by nature to be a cheerful, kindly man. Until he was thirty-four years old he worked as a farmhand for a man named Thomas Butterworth whose place lay near the town of Bidwell, Ohio. He had then a horse of his own, and on Saturday evenings drove into town to spend a few hours in social intercourse with other farmhands. In town he drank several glasses of beer and stood about in Ben Head's saloon — crowded on Saturday evenings with visiting farmhands. Songs were sung and glasses thumped on the bar. At ten o'clock father drove home along a lonely country road, made his horse comfortable for the night, and himself went to bed, quite happy in his position in life. He had at that time no notion of trying to rise in the world.

It was in the spring of his thirty-fifth year that father married my mother, then a country school-teacher, and in the following spring I came wriggling and crying into the world. Something happened to the two people. They became ambitious. The American passion for getting up in the world took possession of them.

It may have been that mother was responsible. Being a school-teacher she had no doubt read books and magazines. She had, I presume, read of how Garfield, Lincoln, and other Americans rose from poverty to fame and greatness, and as I lay beside her — in the days of her lying-in — she may have dreamed that I would some day rule men and cities. At any rate she induced father to give up his place as a farmhand, sell his horse, and embark on an independent enterprise of his own. She was a tall silent woman with a long nose and troubled gray eyes. For herself she wanted nothing. For father and myself she was incurably ambitious.

The first venture into which the two people went turned out badly. They rented ten acres of poor stony land on Grigg's Road, eight miles from Bidwell, and launched into chicken-raising. I grew into boyhood on the place and got my first impressions of life there. From the beginning they were impressions of disaster, and if, in my turn, I am a gloomy man inclined to see the darker side of life, I attribute it to the fact that what should have been for me the happy joyous days of childhood were spent on a chicken farm.

One unversed in such matters can have no notion of the many and tragic things that can happen to a chicken. It is born out of an egg, lives for a few weeks as a tiny fluffy thing such as you will see pictured on Easter cards, then becomes hideously naked, eats quantities of corn and meal bought by the sweat of your father's brow, gets diseases called pip, cholera, and other names, stands looking with stupid eyes at the sun, becomes sick and dies. A few hens and now and then a rooster, intended to serve God's mysterious ends, struggle through to maturity. The hens lay eggs out of which come other chickens and the dreadful cycle is thus made complete. It is all unbelievably complex. Most philosophers must have been raised on chicken farms. One hopes for so much from a chicken and is so dreadfully disillusioned. Small chickens, just setting out on the journey of life, look so bright and alert and they are in fact so dreadfully stupid. They are so much like people they mix one up in one's judgments of life. If disease does not kill them, they wait until your expectations are thoroughly aroused and then walk under the wheels of a wagon — to go squashed and dead back to their maker. Vermin infest their youth, and fortunes must be spent for curative powders. In later life I have seen how a literature has been built up on the subject of fortunes to be made out of the raising of chickens. It is intended to be read by the gods who have just eaten of the tree of the knowledge of good and evil. It is a hopeful literature and declares that much may be done by simple ambitious people who own a few hens. Do not be led astray by it. It was not written for you. Go hunt for gold on the frozen hills of Alaska, put your faith in the honesty of a politician, believe if you will that the world is daily growing better and that good will triumph over evil, but do not read and believe the literature that is written concerning the hen. It was not written for you.

I, however, digress. My tale does not primarily concern itself with the hen. If correctly told it will center on the egg. For ten years my father and mother struggled to make our chicken farm pay and then they gave up their struggle and began another. They moved into the town of Bidwell, Ohio, and embarked in the restaurant business. After ten years of worry with incubators that did not hatch, and with tiny — and in their own way lovely — balls of fluff that passed on into semi-naked pullethood and from that into dead henhood, we threw all aside and, packing our belongings on a wagon, drove down Grigg's Road toward Bidwell, a tiny caravan of hope looking for a new place from which to start on our upward journey through life.

We must have been a sad-looking lot, not, I fancy, unlike refugees fleeing from a battlefield. Mother and I walked in the road. The wagon that contained our goods had been borrowed for the day from Mr. Albert Griggs, a neighbor. Out of its side stuck the legs of cheap chairs, and at the back of the pile of beds, tables, and boxes filled with kitchen utensils was a crate of live chickens, and on top of that the baby carriage in which I had been wheeled about in my infancy. Why we stuck to the baby carriage I don't know. It was unlikely other children would be born and the wheels were broken. People who have few possessions cling tightly to those they have. That is one of the facts that make life so discouraging.

Father rode on top of the wagon. He was then a bald-headed man of forty-five, a little fat, and from long association with mother and the chickens he had become habitually silent and discouraged. All during our ten years on the chicken farm he had worked as a laborer on neighboring farms and most of the money he had earned had been spent for remedies to cure chicken diseases, on Wilmer's White Wonder Cholera Cure or Professor Bidlow's Egg Producer or some other preparations that mother found advertised in the poultry papers. There were two little patches of hair on father's head just above his ears. I remember that as a child I used to sit looking at him when he had gone to sleep in a chair before the stove on Sunday afternoons in the winter. I had at that time already begun to read books and have notions of my own, and the bald path that led over the top of his head was, I fancied, something like a broad road, such a road as Caesar might have made on which to lead his legions out of Rome and into the wonders of an unknown world. The tufts of hair that grew above father's ears were, I thought, like forests. I fell into a half-sleeping, half-waking state and dreamed I was a tiny thing going along the road into a far beautiful place where there were no chicken farms and where life was a happy eggless affair.

One might write a book concerning our flight from the chicken farm into town. Mother and I walked the entire eight miles — she to be sure that nothing fell from the wagon and I to see the wonders of the world. On the seat of the wagon beside father was his greatest treasure. I will tell you of that.

On a chicken farm, where hundreds and even thousands of chickens come out of eggs, surprising things sometimes happen. Grotesques are born out of eggs as out of people. The accident does not often occur — perhaps once in a thousand births. A chicken is, you see, born that has four legs, two pairs of wings, two heads, or what not. The things do not live. They go quickly back to the hand of their maker that has for a moment trembled. The fact that the poor little things could not live was one of the tragedies of life to father. He had some sort of notion that if he could but bring into henhood or roosterhood a five-legged hen or a two-headed rooster his fortune would be made. He dreamed of taking the wonder about the county fairs and of growing rich by exhibiting it to other farmhands.

At any rate, he saved all the little monstrous things that had been born on our chicken farm. They were preserved in alcohol and put each in its own glass bottle. These he had carefully put into a box, and on our journey into town it was carried on the wagon seat beside him. He drove the horses with one hand and with the other clung to the box. When we got to our destination, the box was taken down at once and the bottles removed. All during our days as keepers of a restaurant in the town of Bidwell, Ohio, the grotesques in their little glass bottles sat on a shelf back of the counter. Mother sometimes protested, but father was a rock on the subject of his treasure. The grotesques were, he declared, valuable. People, he said, liked to look at strange and wonderful things.

Did I say that we embarked in the restaurant business in the town of Bidwell, Ohio? I exaggerated a little. The town itself lay at the foot of a low hill and on the shore of a small river. The railroad did not run through the town and the station was a mile away to the north at a place called Pickleville. There had been a cider mill and pickle factory at the station, but before the time of our coming they had both gone out of business. In the morning and in the evening busses came down to the station along a road called Turner's Pike from the hotel on the main street of Bidwell. Our going to the out-of-the-way place to embark in the restaurant business was mother's idea. She talked of it for a year and then one day went off and rented an empty store building opposite the railroad station. It was her idea that the restaurant would be profitable. Traveling men, she said, would be always waiting around to take trains out of town and town people would come to the station to await incoming trains. They would come to the restaurant to buy pieces of pie and drink coffee. Now that I am older I know that she had another motive in going. She was ambitious for me. She wanted me to rise in the world, to get into a town school and become a man of the towns.

At Pickleville father and mother worked hard, as they always had done. At first there was the necessity of putting our place into shape to be a restaurant. That took a month. Father built a shelf on which he put tins of vegetables. He painted a sign on which he put his name in large red letters. Below his name was the sharp command — "EAT HERE" — that was so seldom obeyed. A showcase was bought and filled with cigars and tobacco. Mother scrubbed the floors and the walls of the room. I went to school in the town and was glad to be away from the farm, from the presence of the discouraged, sad-looking chickens. Still I was not very joyous. In the evening I walked home from school along Turner's Pike and remembered the children I had seen playing in the town school yard. A troop of little girls had gone hopping about and singing. I tried that. Down along the frozen road I went hopping solemnly on one leg. "Hippity Hop To The Barber Shop," I sang shrilly. Then I stopped and looked doubtfully about. I was afraid of being seen in my gay mood. It must have seemed to me that I was doing a thing that should not be done by one who, like myself, had been raised on a chicken farm where death was a daily visitor.

Mother decided that our restaurant should remain open at night. At ten in the evening a passenger train went north past our door followed by a local freight. The freight crew had switching to do in Pickleville, and when the work was done they came to our restaurant for hot coffee and food. Sometimes one of them ordered a fried egg. In the morning at four they returned north-bound and again visited us. A little trade began to grow up. Mother slept at night and during the day tended the restaurant and fed our boarders while father slept. He slept in the same bed mother had occupied during the night and I went off to the town of Bidwell and to school. During the long nights, while mother and I slept, father cooked meats that were to go into sandwiches for the lunch baskets of our boarders. Then an idea in regard to getting up in the world came into his head. The American spirit took hold of him. He also became ambitious.

In the long nights when there was little to do, father had time to think. That was his undoing. He decided that he had in the past been an unsuccessful man because he had not been cheerful enough and that in the future he would adopt a cheerful outlook on life. In the early morning he came upstairs and got into bed with mother. She woke and the two talked. From my bed in the corner I listened.

It was father's idea that both he and mother should try to entertain the people who came to eat at our restaurant. I cannot now remember his words, but he gave the impression of one about to become in some obscure way a kind of public entertainer. When people, particularly young people from the town of Bidwell, came into our place, as on very rare occasions they did, bright entertaining conversation was to be made. From father's words I gathered that something of the jolly innkeeper effect was to be sought. Mother must have been doubtful from the first, but she said nothing discouraging. It was father's notion that a passion for the company of himself and mother would spring up in the breasts of the younger people of the town of Bidwell. In the evening bright happy groups would come singing down Turner's Pike. They would troop shouting with joy and laughter into our place. There would be song and festivity. I do not mean to give the impression that father spoke so elaborately of the matter. He was, as I have said, an uncommunicative man. "They want some place to go. I tell you they want some place to go," he said over and over. That was as far as he got. My own imagination has filled in the blanks.

For two or three weeks this notion of father's invaded our house. We did not talk much, but in our daily lives tried earnestly to make smiles take the place of glum looks. Mother smiled at the boarders and I, catching the infection, smiled at our cat. Father became a little feverish in his anxiety to please. There was, no doubt, lurking somewhere in him, a touch of the spirit of the showman. He did not waste much of his ammunition on the railroad men he served at night, but seemed to be waiting for a young man or woman from Bidwell to come in to show what he could do. On the counter in the restaurant there was a wire basket kept always filled with eggs, and it must have been before his eyes when the idea of being entertaining was born in his brain. There was something pre-natal about the way eggs kept themselves connected with the development of his idea. At any rate, an egg ruined his new impulse in life. Late one night I was awakened by a roar of anger coming from father's throat. Both mother and I sat upright in our beds. With trembling hands she lighted a lamp that stood on a table by her head. Downstairs the front door of our restaurant went shut with a bang and in a few minutes father tramped up the stairs. He held an egg in his hand and his hand trembled as though he were having a chill. There was a half-insane light in his eyes. As he stood glaring at us I was sure he intended throwing the egg at either mother or me. Then he laid it gently on the table beside the lamp and dropped on his knees beside mother's bed. He began to cry like a boy, and I, carried away by his grief, cried with him. The two of us filled the little upstairs room with our wailing voices. It is ridiculous, but of the picture we made I can remember only the fact that mother's hand continually stroked the bald path that ran across the top of his head. I have forgotten what mother said to him and how she induced him to tell her of what had happened downstairs. His explanation also has gone out of my mind. I remember only my own grief and fright and the shiny path over father's head glowing in the lamplight as he knelt by the bed.

As to what happened downstairs. For some unexplainable reason I know the story as well as though I had been a witness to my father's discomfiture. One in time gets to know many unexplainable things. On that evening young Joe Kane, son of a merchant of Bidwell, came to Pickleville to meet his father, who was expected on the ten-o'clock evening train from the South. The train was three hours late and Joe came into our place to loaf about and to wait for its arrival. The local freight train came in and the freight crew were fed. Joe was left alone in the restaurant with father.

From the moment he came into our place the Bidwell young man must have been puzzled by my father's actions. It was his notion that father was angry at him for hanging around. He noticed that the restaurant-keeper was apparently disturbed by his presence and he thought of going out. However, it began to rain and he did not fancy the long walk to town and back. He bought a five-cent cigar and ordered a cup of coffee. He had a newspaper in his pocket and took it out and began to read. "I'm waiting for the evening train. It's late," he said apologetically.

For a long time father, whom Joe Kane had never seen before, remained silently gazing at his visitor. He was no doubt suffering from an attack of stage fright. As so often happens in life he had thought so much and so often of the situation that now confronted him that he was somewhat nervous in its presence.

For one thing, he did not know what to do with his hands. He thrust one of them nervously over the counter and shook hands with Joe Kane. "How-de-do," he said. Joe Kane put his newspaper down and stared at him. Father's eyes lighted on the basket of eggs that sat on the counter and he began to talk. "Well," he began hesitatingly, "well, you have heard of Christopher Columbus, eh?" He seemed to be angry. "That Christopher Columbus was a cheat," he declared emphatically. "He talked of making an egg stand on its end. He talked, he did, and then he went and broke the end of the egg°."

My father seemed to his visitor to be beside himself at the duplicity of Christopher Columbus. He muttered and swore. He declared it was wrong to teach children that Christopher Columbus was a great man when, after all, he cheated at the critical moment. He had declared he would make an egg stand on end and then, when his bluff had been called, he had done a trick. Still grumbling at Columbus, father took an egg from the basket on the counter and began to walk up and down. He rolled the egg between the palms of his hands. He smiled genially. He began to mumble words regarding the effect to be produced on an egg by the electricity that comes out of the human body. He declared that, without breaking its shell and by virtue of rolling it back and forth in his hands, he could stand the egg on its end. He explained that the warmth of his hands and the gentle rolling movement he gave the egg created a new center of gravity, and Joe Kane was mildly interested. "I have handled thousands of eggs," father said. "No one knows more about eggs than I do."

He stood the egg on the counter and it fell on its side. He tried the trick again and again, each time rolling the egg between the palms of his hands and saying the words regarding the wonders of electricity and the laws of gravity. When after a half-hour's effort he did succeed in making the egg stand for a moment, he looked up to find that his visitor was no longer watching. By the

---

"That Christopher Columbus was a cheat. . . ." The father is thinking of an anecdote about Columbus, probably invented by a sixteenth-century Italian historian. According to the story, after Columbus had returned to Spain from the New World, he was asked whether there were not many other men who could have made the same voyage. In answer, Columbus challenged his hearers to make an egg stand on end. When all failed, he broke the end of the egg and stood it up, demonstrating that once again he had done what many could have done, but had failed to do.

time he had succeeded in calling Joe Kane's attention to the success of his effort, the egg had again rolled over and lay on its side.

Afire with the showman's passion and at the same time a good deal disconcerted by the failure of his first effort, father now took the bottles containing the poultry monstrosities down from their place on the shelf and began to show them to his visitor. "How would you like to have seven legs and two heads like this fellow?" he asked, exhibiting the most remarkable of his treasures. A cheerful smile played over his face. He reached over the counter and tried to slap Joe Kane on the shoulder as he had seen men do in Ben Head's saloon when he was a young farmhand and drove to town on Saturday evenings. His visitor was made a little ill by the sight of the body of the terribly deformed bird floating in the alcohol in the bottle and got up to go. Coming from behind the counter, father took hold of the young man's arm and led him back to his seat. He grew a little angry and for a moment had to turn his face away and force himself to smile. Then he put the bottles back on the shelf. In an outburst of generosity he fairly compelled Joe Kane to have a fresh cup of coffee and another cigar at his expense. Then he took a pan and filling it with vinegar, taken from a jug that sat beneath the counter, he declared himself about to do a new trick. "I will heat this egg in this pan of vinegar," he said. "Then I will put it through the neck of a bottle without breaking the shell. When the egg is inside the bottle it will resume its normal shape and the shell will become hard again. Then I will give the bottle with the egg in it to you. You can take it about with you wherever you go. People will want to know how you got the egg in the bottle. Don't tell them. Keep them guessing. That is the way to have fun with this trick."

Father grinned and winked at his visitor. Joe Kane decided that the man who confronted him was mildly insane but harmless. He drank the cup of coffee that had been given him and began to read his paper again. When the egg had been heated in vinegar, father carried it on a spoon to the counter and going into a back room got an empty bottle. He was angry because his visitor did not watch him as he began to do his trick, but nevertheless went cheerfully to work. For a long time he struggled, trying to get the egg to go through the neck of the bottle. He put the pan of vinegar back on the stove, intending to reheat the egg, then picked it up and burned his fingers. After a second bath in the hot vinegar, the shell of the egg had been softened a little, but not enough for his purpose. He worked and worked and a spirit of desperate determination took possession of him. When he thought that at last the trick was about to be consummated, the delayed train came in at the station and Joe Kane started to go nonchalantly out at the door. Father made a last desperate effort to conquer the egg and make it do the thing that would establish his reputation as one who knew how to entertain guests who came into his restaurant. He worried the egg. He attempted to be somewhat rough with it. He swore and the sweat stood out on his forehead. The egg broke under his hand. When the contents spurted over his clothes, Joe Kane, who had stopped at the door, turned and laughed.

A roar of anger rose from my father's throat. He danced and shouted a string of inarticulate words. Grabbing another egg from the basket on the counter, he threw it, just missing the head of the young man as he dodged through the door and escaped.

Father came upstairs to mother and me with an egg in his hand. I do not know what he intended to do. I imagine he had some idea of destroying it, of destroying all eggs, and that he intended to let mother and me see him begin. When, however, he got into the presence of mother, something happened to him. He laid the egg gently on the table and dropped on his knees by the bed as I have already explained. He later decided to close the restaurant for the night and to come upstairs and get into bed. When he did so, he blew out the light and after much muttered conversation both he and mother went to sleep. I suppose I went to sleep also, but my sleep was troubled. I awoke at dawn and for a long time looked at the egg that lay on the table. I wondered why eggs had to be and why from the egg came the hen who again laid the egg. The question got into my blood. It has stayed there, I imagine, because I am the son of my father. At any rate, the problem remains unsolved in my mind. And that, I con-clude, is but another evidence of the complete and final triumph of the egg — at least as far as my family is concerned.

Franz Kafka (1883–1924)

A Hunger Artist   1924

Translated by Edwin and Willa Muir

During these last decades the interest in professional fasting has markedly diminished. It used to pay very well to stage such great performances under one's own management, but today that is quite impossible. We live in a differ-ent world now. At one time the whole town took a lively interest in the hunger artist; from day to day of his fast the excitement mounted; everybody wanted to see him at least once a day; there were people who bought season tickets for the last few days and sat from morning till night in front of his small barred cage; even in the nighttime there were visiting hours, when the whole effect was heightened by torch flares; on fine days the cage was set out in the open air, and then it was the children's special treat to see the hunger artist; for their elders he was often just a joke that happened to be in fashion, but the children stood open-mouthed, holding each other's hands for greater security, marveling at him as he sat there pallid in black tights, with his ribs sticking out so promi-nently, not even on a seat but down among straw on the ground, sometimes giving a courteous nod, answering questions with a constrained smile, or per-haps stretching an arm through the bars so that one might feel how thin it was, and then again withdrawing deep into himself, paying no attention to anyone or anything, not even to the all-important striking of the clock that was the only piece of furniture in his cage, but merely staring into vacancy with half-shut eyes, now and then taking a sip from a tiny glass of water to moisten his lips.

Besides casual onlookers there were also relays of permanent watchers selected by the public, usually butchers, strangely enough, and it was their task to watch the hunger artist day and night, three of them at a time, in case he should have some secret recourse to nourishment. This was nothing but a formality, instituted to reassure the masses, for the initiates knew well enough that during his fast the artist would never in any circumstances, not even under forcible compulsion, swallow the smallest morsel of food; the honor of his profession forbade it. Not every watcher, of course, was capable of understanding this, there were often groups of night watchers who were very lax in carrying out their duties and deliberately huddled together in a retired corner to play cards with great absorption, obviously intending to give the hunger artist the chance of a little refreshment, which they supposed he could draw from some private hoard. Nothing annoyed the artist more than such watchers; they made him miserable; they made his fast seem unendurable; sometimes he mastered his feebleness sufficiently to sing during their watch for as long as he could keep going, to show them how unjust their suspicions were. But that was of little use; they only wondered at his cleverness in being able to fill his mouth even while singing. Much more to his taste were the watchers who sat close up to the bars, who were not content with the dim night lighting of the hall but focused him in the full glare of the electric pocket torch given them by the impresario. The harsh light did not trouble him at all. In any case he could never sleep properly, and he could always drowse a little, whatever the light, at any hour, even when the hall was thronged with noisy onlookers. He was quite happy at the prospect of spending a sleepless night with such watchers; he was ready to exchange jokes with them, to tell them stories out of his nomadic life, anything at all to keep them awake and demonstrate to them again that he had no eatables in his cage and that he was fasting as not one of them could fast. But his happiest moment was when the morning came and an enormous breakfast was brought them, at his expense, on which they flung themselves with the keen appetite of healthy men after a weary night of wakefulness. Of course there were people who argued that this breakfast was an unfair attempt to bribe the watchers, but that was going rather too far, and when they were invited to take on a night's vigil without a breakfast, merely for the sake of the cause, they made themselves scarce, although they stuck stubbornly to their suspicions.

Such suspicions, anyhow, were a necessary accompaniment to the profession of fasting. No one could possibly watch the hunger artist continuously, day and night, and so no one could produce first-hand evidence that the fast had really been rigorous and continuous; only the artist himself could know that; he was therefore bound to be the sole completely satisfied spectator of his own fast. Yet for other reasons he was never satisfied; it was not perhaps mere fasting that had brought him to such skeleton thinness that many people had regretfully to keep away from his exhibitions, because the sight of him was too much for them, perhaps it was dissatisfaction with himself that had worn him down. For he alone knew, what no other initiate knew, how easy it was to fast. It was the easiest thing in the world. He made no secret of this, yet people did not believe him; at the best they set him down as modest, most of them, however, thought he was out for publicity or else was some kind of cheat who found it easy to fast because he had discovered a way of making it easy, and then had the impudence to admit the fact, more or less. He had to put up with all that, and in the course of time had got used to it, but his inner dissatisfaction always rankled, and never yet, after any term of fasting — this must be granted to his credit — had he left the cage of his own free will. The longest period of fasting was fixed by his impresario at forty days, beyond that term he was not allowed to go, not even in great cities, and there was good reason for it, too. Experience had proved that for about forty days the interest of the public could be stimulated by a steadily increasing pressure of advertisement, but after that the town began to lose interest, sympathetic support began notably to fall off; there were of course local variations as between one town and another or one country and another, but as a general rule forty days marked the limit. So on the fortieth day the flower-bedecked cage was opened, enthusiastic spectators filled the hall, a military band played, two doctors entered the cage to measure the results of the fast, which were announced through a megaphone, and finally two young ladies appeared, blissful at having been selected for the honor, to help the hunger artist down the few steps leading to a small table on which was spread a carefully chosen invalid repast. And at this very moment the artist always turned stubborn. True, he would entrust his bony arms to the outstretched helping hands of the ladies bending over him, but stand up he would not. Why stop fasting at this particular moment, after forty days of it? He had held out for a long time, an illimitably long time; why stop now, when he was in his best fasting form, or rather, not yet quite in his best fasting form? Why should he be cheated of the fame he would get for fasting longer, for being not only the record hunger artist of all time, which presumably he was already, but for beating his own record by a performance beyond human imagination, since he felt that there were no limits to his capacity for fasting? His public pretended to admire him so much, why should it have so little patience with him; if he could endure fasting longer, why shouldn't the public endure it? Besides, he was tired, he was comfortable sitting in the straw, and now he was supposed to lift himself to his full height and go down to a meal the very thought of which gave him a nausea that only the presence of the ladies kept him from betraying, and even that with an effort. And he looked up into the eyes of the ladies who were apparently so friendly and in reality so cruel, and shook his head, which felt too heavy on its strengthless neck. But then there happened yet again what always happened. The impresario came forward, without a word — for the band made speech impossible — lifted his arms in the air above the artist, as if inviting Heaven to look down upon its creature here in the straw, this suffering martyr, which indeed he was, although in quite another sense; grasped him around the emaciated waist, with exaggerated caution, so that the frail condition he was in might be appreciated; and committed him to the care of the blenching ladies, not without secretly giving him a shaking so that his legs and body tottered and swayed. The artist now submitted completely; his head lolled on his breast as if it had landed there by chance; his body was hollowed out; his legs in a spasm of self-preservation clung close to each other at the knees, yet scraped on the ground as if it were not really solid ground, as if they were only trying to find solid ground; and the whole weight of his body, a featherweight after all, relapsed onto one of the ladies, who, looking round for help and panting a little — this post of honor was not at all what she had expected it to be — first stretched her neck as far as she could to keep her face at least free from contact with the artist, then finding this impossible, and her more fortunate companion not coming to her aid but merely holding extended on her own trembling hand the little bunch of knucklebones that was the artist's, to the great delight of the spectators burst into tears and had to be replaced by an attendant who had long been stationed in readiness. Then came the food, a little of which the impresario managed to get between the artist's lips, while he sat in a kind of half-fainting trance, to the accompaniment of cheerful patter designed to distract the public's attention from the artist's condition; after that, a toast was drunk to the public, supposedly prompted by a whisper from the artist in the impresario's ear; the band confirmed it with a mighty flourish, the spectators melted away, and no one had any cause to be dissatisfied with the proceedings, no one except the hunger artist himself, he only, as always.

So he lived for many years, with small regular intervals of recuperation, in visible glory, honored by the world, yet in spite of that troubled in spirit, and all the more troubled because no one would take his trouble seriously. What comfort could he possibly need? What more could he possibly wish for? And if some good-natured person, feeling sorry for him, tried to console him by pointing out that his melancholy was probably caused by fasting, it could happen, especially when he had been fasting for some time, that he reacted with an outburst of fury and to the general alarm began to shake the bars of his cage like a wild animal. Yet the impresario had a way of punishing these outbreaks which he rather enjoyed putting into operation. He would apologize publicly for the artist's behavior, which was only to be excused, he admitted, because of the irritability caused by fasting; a condition hardly to be understood by well-fed people; then by natural transition he went on to mention the artist's equally incomprehensible boast that he could fast for much longer than he was doing; he praised the high ambition, the good will, the great self-denial undoubtedly implicit in such a statement; and then quite simply countered it by bringing out photographs, which were also on sale to the public, showing the artist on the fortieth day of a fast lying in bed almost dead from exhaustion. This perversion of the truth, familiar to the artist though it was, always unnerved him afresh and proved too much for him. What was a consequence of the premature ending of his fast was here presented as the cause of it! To fight against this lack of understanding, against a whole world of non-understanding, was impossible. Time and again in good faith he stood by the bars listening to the impresario, but as soon as the photographs appeared he always let go and sank with a groan back on to his straw, and the reassured public could once more come close and gaze at him.

A few years later when the witnesses of such scenes called them to mind, they often failed to understand themselves at all. For meanwhile the aforementioned change in public interest had set in; it seemed to happen almost overnight; there may have been profound causes for it, but who was going to bother about that; at any rate the pampered hunger artist suddenly found himself deserted one fine day by the amusement seekers, who went streaming past him to other more favored attractions. For the last time the impresario hurried him over half Europe to discover whether the old interest might still survive here and there; all in vain; everywhere, as if by secret agreement, a positive revulsion from professional fasting was in evidence. Of course it could not really have sprung up so suddenly as all that, and many premonitory symptoms which had not been sufficiently remarked or suppressed during the rush and glitter of success now came retrospectively to mind, but it was now too late to take any countermeasures. Fasting would surely come into fashion again at some future date, yet that was no comfort for those living in the present. What, then, was the hunger artist to do? He had been applauded by thousands in his time and could hardly come down to showing himself in a street booth at village fairs, and as for adopting another profession, he was not only too old for that but too fanatically devoted to fasting. So he took leave of the impresario, his partner in an unparalleled career, and hired himself to a large circus; in order to spare his own feelings he avoided reading the conditions of his contract.

A large circus with its enormous traffic in replacing and recruiting men, animals and apparatus can always find a use for people at any time, even for a hunger artist, provided of course that he does not ask too much, and in this particular case anyhow it was not only the artist who was taken on but his famous and long-known name as well; indeed considering the peculiar nature of his performance, which was not impaired by advancing age, it could not be objected that here was an artist past his prime, no longer at the height of his professional skill, seeking a refuge in some quiet corner of a circus; on the contrary, the hunger artist averred that he could fast as well as ever, which was entirely credible; he even alleged that if he were allowed to fast as he liked, and this was at once promised him without more ado, he could astound the world by establishing a record never yet achieved, a statement which certainly provoked a smile among the other professionals, since it left out of account the change in public opinion, which the hunger artist in his zeal conveniently forgot.

He had not, however, actually lost his sense of the real situation and took it as a matter of course that he and his cage should be stationed, not in the middle of the ring as a main attraction, but outside, near the animal cages, on a site that was after all easily accessible. Large and gaily painted placards made a frame for the cage and announced what was to be seen inside it. When the public came thronging out in the intervals to see the animals, they could hardly avoid passing the hunger artist's cage and stopping there for a moment; perhaps they might even have stayed longer had not those pressing behind them in the narrow gangway, who did not understand why they should be held up on their way towards the excitements of the menagerie, made it impossible for anyone to stand gazing quietly for any length of time. And that was the reason why the hunger artist, who had of course been looking forward to these visiting hours as the main achievement of his life, began instead to shrink from them. At first he could hardly wait for the intervals; it was exhilarating to watch the crowds come streaming his way, until only too soon — not even the most obstinate self-deception, clung to almost consciously, could hold out against the fact — the conviction was borne in upon him that these people, most of them, to judge from their actions, again and again, without exception, were all on their way to the menagerie. And the first sight of them from the distance remained the best. For when they reached his cage he was at once deafened by the storm of shouting and abuse that arose from the two contending factions, which renewed themselves continuously, of those who wanted to stop and stare at him — he soon began to dislike them more than the others — not out of real interest but only out of obstinate self-assertiveness, and those who wanted to go straight on to the animals. When the first great rush was past, the stragglers came along, and these, whom nothing could have prevented from stopping to look at him as long as they had breath, raced past with long strides, hardly even glancing at him, in their haste to get to the menagerie in time. And all too rarely did it happen that he had a stroke of luck, when some father of a family fetched up before him with his children, pointed a finger at the hunger artist and explained at length what the phenomenon meant, telling stories of earlier years when he himself had watched similar but much more thrilling performances, and the children, still rather uncomprehending, since neither inside nor outside school had they been sufficiently prepared for this lesson — what did they care about fasting? — yet showed by the brightness of their intent eyes that new and better times might be coming. Perhaps, said the hunger artist to himself many a time, things would be a little better if his cage were set not quite so near the menagerie. That made it too easy for people to make their choice, to say nothing of what he suffered from the stench of the menagerie, the animals' restlessness by night, the carrying past of raw lumps of flesh for the beasts of prey, the roaring at feeding times, which depressed him continually. But he did not dare to lodge a complaint with the management; after all, he had the animals to thank for the troops of people who passed his cage, among whom there might always be one here and there to take an interest in him, and who could tell where they might seclude him if he called attention to his existence and thereby to the fact that, strictly speaking, he was only an impediment on the way to the menagerie.

A small impediment, to be sure, one that grew steadily less. People grew familiar with the strange idea that they could be expected, in times like these, to take an interest in a hunger artist, and with this familiarity the verdict went out against him. He might fast as much as he could, and he did so; but nothing could save him now, people passed him by. Just try to explain to anyone the art of fasting! Anyone who has no feeling for it cannot be made to understand it. The fine placards grew dirty and illegible, they were torn down; the little notice board telling the number of fast days achieved, which at first was changed carefully every day, had long stayed at the same figure, for after the first few weeks even this small task seemed pointless to the staff; and so the artist simply fasted on and on, as he had once dreamed of doing, and it was no trouble to him, just as he had always foretold, but no one counted the days, no one, not even the artist himself, knew what records he was already breaking, and his heart grew heavy. And when once in a time some leisurely passer-by stopped, made merry over the old figure on the board and spoke of swindling, that was in its way the stupidest lie ever invented by indifference and inborn malice, since it was not the hunger artist who was cheating; he was working honestly, but the world was cheating him of his reward.

Many more days went by, however, and that too came to an end. An overseer's eye fell on the cage one day and he asked the attendants why this perfectly good cage should be left standing there unused with dirty straw inside it; nobody knew, until one man, helped out by the notice board, remembered about the hunger artist. They poked into the straw with sticks and found him in it. "Are you still fasting?" asked the overseer. "When on earth do you mean to stop?" "Forgive me, everybody," whispered the hunger artist; only the overseer, who had his ear to the bars, understood him. "Of course," said the overseer, and tapped his forehead with a finger to let the attendants know what state the man was in, "we forgive you." "I always wanted you to admire my fasting," said the hunger artist. "We do admire it," said the overseer, affably. "But you shouldn't admire it," said the hunger artist. "Well, then we don't admire it," said the overseer, "but why shouldn't we admire it?" "Because I have to fast, I can't help it," said the hunger artist. "What a fellow you are," said the overseer; "and why can't you help it?" "Because," said the hunger artist, lifting his head a little and speaking, with his lips pursed, as if for a kiss, right into the overseer's ear, so that no syllable might be lost, "because I couldn't find the food I liked. If I had found it, believe me, I should have made no fuss and stuffed myself like you or anyone else." These were his last words, but in his dimming eyes remained the firm though no longer proud persuasion that he was still continuing to fast.

"Well, clear this out now!" said the overseer, and they buried the hunger artist, straw and all. Into the cage they put a young panther. Even the most insensitive felt it refreshing to see this wild creature leaping around the cage that had so long been dreary. The panther was all right. The food he liked was brought him without hesitation by the attendants; he seemed not even to miss his freedom; his noble body, furnished almost to the bursting point with all that it needed, seemed to carry freedom around with it too; somewhere in his jaws it seemed to lurk; and the joy of life streamed with such ardent passion from his throat that for the onlookers it was not easy to stand the shock of it. But they braced themselves, crowded round the cage, and did not want ever to move away.

D. H. Lawrence (1885–1930)

The Blind Man   1922

Isabel Pervin was listening for two sounds — for the sound of wheels on the drive outside and for the noise of her husband's footsteps in the hall. Her dearest and oldest friend, a man who seemed almost indispensable to her living, would drive up in the rainy dusk of the closing November day. The trap had gone to fetch him from the station. And her husband, who had been blinded in Flanders°, and who had a disfiguring mark on his brow, would be coming in from the outhouses.

He had been home for a year now. He was totally blind. Yet they had been very happy. The Grange was Maurice's own place. The back was a farmstead, and the Wernhams, who occupied the rear premises, acted as farmers. Isabel lived with her husband in the handsome rooms in front. She and he had been almost entirely alone together since he was wounded. They talked and sang and read together in a wonderful and unspeakable intimacy. Then she reviewed books for a Scottish newspaper, carrying on her old interest, and he occupied himself a good deal with the farm. Sightless, he could still discuss everything with Wernham, and he could also do a good deal of work about the place — menial work, it is true, but it gave him satisfaction. He milked the cows, carried in the pails, turned the separator, attended to the pigs and horses. Life was still very full and strangely serene for the blind man, peaceful with the almost incomprehensible peace of immediate contact in darkness. With his wife he had a whole world, rich and real and invisible.

They were newly and remotely happy. He did not even regret the loss

Flanders: territory along the North Sea in France, Belgium, and the Netherlands; scene of bitter fighting between Allied and German infantrymen in World War I.

of his sight in these times of dark, palpable joy. A certain exultance swelled his soul.

But as time wore on, sometimes the rich glamor would leave them. Sometimes, after months of this intensity, a sense of burden overcame Isabel, a weariness, a terrible *ennui*, in that silent house approached between a colonnade of tall-shafted pines. Then she felt she would go mad, for she could not bear it. And sometimes he had devastating fits of depression, which seemed to lay waste his whole being. It was worse than depression — a black misery, when his own life was a torture to him, and when his presence was unbearable to his wife. The dread went down to the roots of her soul as these black days recurred. In a kind of panic she tried to wrap herself up still further in her husband. She forced the old spontaneous cheerfulness and joy to continue. But the effort it cost her was almost too much. She knew she could not keep it up. She felt she would scream with the strain, and would give anything, anything, to escape. She longed to possess her husband utterly; it gave her inordinate joy to have him entirely to herself. And yet, when again he was gone in a black and massive misery, she could not bear him, she could not bear herself; she wished she could be snatched away off the earth altogether, anything rather than live at this cost.

Dazed, she schemed for a way out. She invited friends, she tried to give him some further connection with the outer world. But it was no good. After all their joy and suffering, after their dark, great year of blindness and solitude and unspeakable nearness, other people seemed to them both shallow, rattling, rather impertinent. Shallow prattle seemed presumptuous. He became impatient and irritated, she was wearied. And so they lapsed into their solitude again. For they preferred it.

But now, in a few weeks' time, her second baby would be born. The first had died, an infant, when her husband first went out to France. She looked with joy and relief to the coming of the second. It would be her salvation. But also she felt some anxiety. She was thirty years old, her husband was a year younger. They both wanted the child very much. Yet she could not help feeling afraid. She had her husband on her hands, a terrible joy to her, and a terrifying burden. The child would occupy her love and attention. And then, what of Maurice? What would he do? If only she could feel that he, too, would be at peace and happy when the child came! She did so want to luxuriate in a rich, physical satisfaction of maternity. But the man, what would he do? How could she provide for him, how avert those shattering black moods of his, which destroyed them both?

She sighed with fear. But at this time Bertie Reid wrote to Isabel. He was her old friend, a second or third cousin, a Scotchman, as she was a Scotchwoman. They had been brought up near to one another, and all her life he had been her friend, like a brother, but better than her own brothers. She loved him — though not in the marrying sense. There was a sort of kinship between them, an affinity. They understood one another instinctively. But Isabel would never have thought of marrying Bertie. It would have seemed like marrying in her own family.

Bertie was a barrister° and a man of letters, a Scotchman of the intellectual

barrister: one "called to the bar"; in British law, one who can plead a case in court.

type, quick, ironical, sentimental, and on his knees before the woman he adored but did not want to marry. Maurice Pervin was different. He came of a good old country family — the Grange was not a very great distance from Oxford. He was passionate, sensitive, perhaps over-sensitive, wincing — a big fellow with heavy limbs and a forehead that flushed painfully. For his mind was slow, as if drugged by the strong provincial blood that beat in his veins. He was very sensitive to his own mental slowness, his feelings being quick and acute. So that he was just the opposite to Bertie, whose mind was much quicker than his emotions, which were not so very fine.

From the first the two men did not like each other. Isabel felt that they *ought* to get on together. But they did not. She felt that if only each could have the clue to the other there would be such a rare understanding between them. It did not come off, however. Bertie adopted a slightly ironical attitude, very offensive to Maurice, who returned the Scotch irony with English resentment, a resentment which deepened sometimes into stupid hatred.

This was a little puzzling to Isabel. However, she accepted it in the course of things. Men were made freakish and unreasonable. Therefore, when Maurice was going out to France for the second time, she felt that, for her husband's sake, she must discontinue her friendship with Bertie. She wrote to the barrister to this effect. Bertram Reid simply replied that in this, as in all other matters, he must obey her wishes, if these were indeed her wishes.

For nearly two years nothing had passed between the two friends. Isabel rather gloried in the fact; she had no compunction. She had one great article of faith, which was, that husband and wife should be so important to one another, that the rest of the world simply did not count. She and Maurice were husband and wife. They loved one another. They would have children. Then let everybody and everything else fade into insignificance outside this connubial felicity. She professed herself quite happy and ready to receive Maurice's friends. She was happy and ready: the happy wife, the ready woman in possession. Without knowing why, the friends retired abashed, and came no more. Maurice, of course, took as much satisfaction in this connubial absorption as Isabel did.

He shared in Isabel's literary activities, she cultivated a real interest in agriculture and cattle-raising. For she, being at heart perhaps an emotional enthusiast, always cultivated the practical side of life and prided herself on her mastery of practical affairs. Thus the husband and wife had spent the five years of their married life. The last had been one of blindness and unspeakable intimacy. And now Isabel felt a great indifference coming over her, a sort of lethargy. She wanted to be allowed to bear her child in peace, to nod by the fire and drift vaguely, physically, from day to day. Maurice was like an ominous thunder-cloud. She had to keep waking up to remember him.

When a little note came from Bertie, asking if he were to put up a tombstone to their dead friendship, and speaking of the real pain he felt on account of her husband's loss of sight, she had a pang, a fluttering agitation of re-awakening. And she read the letter to Maurice.

"Ask him to come down," he said.

"Ask Bertie to come here!" she re-echoed.

"Yes — if he wants to."

Isabel paused for a few moments.

"I know he wants to — he'd only be too glad," she replied. "But what about you, Maurice? How would you like it?"

"I should like it."

"Well — in that case — But I thought you didn't care for him —"

"Oh, I don't know. I might think differently of him now," the blind man replied. It was rather abstruse to Isabel.

"Well, dear," she said, "if you're quite sure —"

"I'm sure enough. Let him come," said Maurice.

So Bertie was coming, coming this evening, in the November rain and darkness. Isabel was agitated, racked with her old restlessness and indecision. She had always suffered from this pain of doubt, just an agonizing sense of uncertainty. It had begun to pass off, in the lethargy of maternity. Now it returned, and she resented it. She struggled as usual to maintain her calm, composed, friendly bearing, a sort of mask she wore over all her body.

A woman had lighted a tall lamp beside the table and spread the cloth. The long dining-room was dim, with its elegant but rather severe pieces of old furniture. Only the round table glowed softly under the light. It had a rich, beautiful effect. The white cloth glistened and dropped its heavy, pointed lace corners almost to the carpet, the china was old and handsome, creamy-yellow, with a blotched pattern of harsh red and deep blue, the cups large and bell-shaped, the teapot gallant. Isabel looked at it with superficial appreciation.

Her nerves were hurting her. She looked automatically again at the high, uncurtained windows. In the last dusk she could just perceive outside a huge fir-tree swaying its boughs: it was as if she thought it rather than saw it. The rain came flying on the window panes. Ah, why had she no peace? These two men, why did they tear at her? Why did they not come — why was there this suspense?

She sat in a lassitude that was really suspense and irritation. Maurice, at least, might come in — there was nothing to keep him out. She rose to her feet. Catching sight of her reflection in a mirror, she glanced at herself with a slight smile of recognition, as if she were an old friend to herself. Her face was oval and calm, her nose a little arched. Her neck made a beautiful line down to her shoulder. With hair knotted loosely behind, she had something of a warm, maternal look. Thinking this of herself, she arched her eyebrows and her rather heavy eyelids, with a little flicker of a smile, and for a moment her grey eyes looked amused and wicked, a little sardonic, out of her transfigured Madonna face.

Then, resuming her air of womanly patience — she was really fatally self-determined — she went with a little jerk towards the door. Her eyes were slightly reddened.

She passed down the wide hall and through a door at the end. Then she was in the farm premises. The scent of dairy, and of farm-kitchen, and of farm-yard and of leather almost overcame her: but particularly the scent of dairy. They had been scalding out the pans. The flagged passage in front of her was dark, puddled, and wet. Light came out from the open kitchen door. She went forward and stood in the doorway. The farm-people were at tea, seated at a little distance from her, round a long, narrow table, in the center of which stood a white lamp. Ruddy faces, ruddy hands holding food, red mouths working, heads bent over the tea-cups: men, land-girls, boys: it was tea-time, feeding-time. Some faces caught sight of her. Mrs. Wernham, going round behind the chairs with a large black teapot, halting slightly in her walk, was not aware of her for a moment. Then she turned suddenly.

"Oh, is it Madam!" she exclaimed. "Come in, then, come in! We're at tea." And she dragged forward a chair.

"No, I won't come in," said Isabel. "I'm afraid I interrupt your meal."

"No — no — not likely, Madam, not likely."

"Hasn't Mr. Pervin come in, do you know?"

"I'm sure I couldn't say! Missed him, have you, Madam?"

"No, I only wanted him to come in," laughed Isabel, as if shyly.

"Wanted him, did ye? Get up, boy — get up, now —"

Mrs. Wernham knocked one of the boys on the shoulder. He began to scrape to his feet, chewing largely.

"I believe he's in top stable," said another face from the table.

"Ah! No, don't get up. I'm going myself," said Isabel.

"Don't you go out of a dirty night like this. Let the lad go. Get along wi' ye, boy," said Mrs. Wernham.

"No, no," said Isabel, with a decision that was always obeyed. "Go on with your tea, Tom. I'd like to go across to the stable, Mrs. Wernham."

"Did ever you hear tell!" exclaimed the woman.

"Isn't the trap late?" asked Isabel.

"Why, no," said Mrs. Wernham, peering into the distance at the tall, dim clock. "No, Madam — we can give it another quarter or twenty minutes yet, good — yes, every bit of a quarter."

"Ah! It seems late when darkness falls so early," said Isabel.

"It do, that it do. Bother the days, that they draw in so," answered Mrs. Wernham. "Proper miserable!"

"They are," said Isabel, withdrawing.

She pulled on her overshoes, wrapped a large tartan shawl around her, put on a man's felt hat, and ventured out along the causeways of the first yard. It was very dark. The wind was roaring in the great elms behind the outhouses. When she came to the second yard the darkness seemed deeper. She was unsure of her footing. She wished she had brought a lantern. Rain blew against her. Half she liked it, half she felt unwilling to battle.

She reached at last the just visible door of the stable. There was no sign of a light anywhere. Opening the upper half, she looked in: into a simple well of darkness. The smell of horses, and ammonia, and of warmth was startling to her, in that full night. She listened with all her ears but could hear nothing save the night, and the stirring of a horse.

"Maurice!" she called, softly and musically, though she was afraid. "Maurice — are you there?"

Nothing came from the darkness. She knew the rain and wind blew in upon the horses, the hot animal life. Feeling it wrong, she entered the stable and drew the lower half of the door shut, holding the upper part close. She did not stir, because she was aware of the presence of the dark hind-quarters of the horses, though she could not see them, and she was afraid. Something wild stirred in her heart.

She listened intensely. Then she heard a small noise in the distance — far away, it seemed — the chink of a pan, and a man's voice speaking a brief word. It would be Maurice, in the other part of the stable. She stood motionless, waiting for him to come through the partition door. The horses were so terrifyingly near to her, in the invisible.

The loud jarring of the inner door-latch made her start; the door was opened. She could hear and feel her husband entering and invisibly passing among the horses near to her, darkness as they were, actively intermingled. The rather low sound of his voice as he spoke to the horses came velvety to her nerves. How near he was, and how invisible! The darkness seemed to be in a strange swirl of violent life, just upon her. She turned giddy.

Her presence of mind made her call, quietly and musically:

"Maurice! Maurice — dea-ar!"

"Yes," he answered. "Isabel?"

She saw nothing, and the sound of his voice seemed to touch her.

"Hello!" she answered cheerfully, straining her eyes to see him. He was still busy, attending to the horses near her, but she saw only darkness. It made her almost desperate.

"Won't you come in, dear?" she said.

"Yes, I'm coming. Just half a minute. *Stand over — now!* Trap's not come, has it?"

"Not yet," said Isabel.

His voice was pleasant and ordinary, but it had a slight suggestion of the stable to her. She wished he would come away. Whilst he was so utterly invisible, she was afraid of him.

"How's the time?" he asked.

"Not yet six," she replied. She disliked to answer into the dark. Presently he came very near to her, and she retreated out of doors.

"The weather blows in here," he said, coming steadily forward, feeling for the doors. She shrank away. At last she could dimly see him.

"Bertie won't have much of a drive," he said, as he closed the doors.

"He won't indeed!" said Isabel calmly, watching the dark shape at the door.

"Give me your arm, dear," she said.

She pressed his arm close to her, as she went. But she longed to see him, to look at him. She was nervous. He walked erect, with face rather lifted, but with a curious tentative movement of his powerful, muscular legs. She could feel the clever, careful, strong contact of his feet with the earth, as she balanced against him. For a moment he was a tower of darkness to her, as if he rose out of the earth.

In the house-passage he wavered and went cautiously, with a curious look of silence about him as he felt for the bench. Then he sat down heavily. He was a man with rather sloping shoulders, but with heavy limbs, powerful legs that seemed to know the earth. His head was small, usually carried high and light. As he bent down to unfasten his gaiters and boots he did not look blind. His hair was brown and crisp, his hands were large, reddish, intelligent, the veins stood out in the wrists; and his thighs and knees seemed massive. When he stood up his face and neck were surcharged with blood, the veins stood out on his temples. She did not look at his blindness.

Isabel was always glad when they had passed through the dividing door into their own regions of repose and beauty. She was a little afraid of him, out there in the animal grossness of the back. His bearing also changed, as he smelt the familiar indefinable odor that pervaded his wife's surroundings, a delicate, refined scent, very faintly spicy. Perhaps it came from the potpourri bowls.

He stood at the foot of the stairs, arrested, listening. She watched him, and her heart sickened. He seemed to be listening to fate.

"He's not here yet," he said. "I'll go up and change."

"Maurice," she said, "you're not wishing he wouldn't come, are you?"

"I couldn't quite say," he answered. "I feel myself rather on the qui vive.°"

"I can see you are," she answered. And she reached up and kissed his cheek. She saw his mouth relax into a slow smile.

"What are you laughing at?" she said roguishly.

"You consoling me," he answered.

"Nay," she answered. "Why should I console you? You know we love each other — you know *how* married we are! What does anything else matter?"

"Nothing at all, my dear."

He felt for her face and touched it, smiling.

"You're all right, aren't you?" he asked anxiously.

"I'm wonderfully all right, love," she answered. "It's you I am a little troubled about, at times."

"Why me?" he said, touching her cheeks delicately with the tips of his fingers. The touch had an almost hypnotizing effect on her.

He went away upstairs. She saw him mount into the darkness, unseeing and unchanging. He did not know that the lamps on the upper corridor were unlighted. He went on into the darkness with unchanging step. She heard him in the bath-room.

Pervin moved about almost unconsciously in his familiar surroundings, dark though everything was. He seemed to know the presence of objects before he touched them. It was a pleasure to him to rock thus through a world of things, carried on the flood in a sort of blood-prescience. He did not think much or trouble much. So long as he kept this sheer immediacy of blood-contact with the substantial world he was happy, he wanted no intervention of visual consciousness. In this state there was a certain rich positivity, bordering sometimes on rapture. Life seemed to move in him like a tide lapping, lapping, and advancing, enveloping all things darkly. It was a pleasure to stretch forth the hand and meet the unseen object, clasp it, and possess it in pure contact. He did not try to remember, to visualize. He did not want to. The new way of consciousness substituted itself in him.

The rich suffusion of this state generally kept him happy, reaching its culmination in the consuming passion for his wife. But at times the flow would seem to be checked and thrown back. Then it would beat inside him like a tangled sea, and he was tortured in the shattered chaos of his own blood. He grew to dread this arrest, this throw-back, this chaos inside himself, when

on the qui vive: on the alert, on guard. (*"Qui vive?"*, French, is a sentry's challenge: "Who goes there?")

he seemed merely at the mercy of his own powerful and conflicting elements. How to get some measure of control or surety, this was the question. And when the question rose maddening in him, he would clench his fists as if he would *compel* the whole universe to submit to him. But it was in vain. He could not even compel himself.

Tonight, however, he was still serene, though little tremors of unreasonable exasperation ran through him. He had to handle the razor very carefully, as he shaved, for it was not at one with him, he was afraid of it. His hearing also was too much sharpened. He heard the woman lighting the lamps on the corridor, and attending to the fire in the visitors' room. And then, as he went to his room, he heard the trap arrive. Then came Isabel's voice, lifted and calling, like a bell ringing:

"Is it you, Bertie? Have you come?"

And a man's voice answered out of the wind:

"Hello, Isabel! There you are."

"Have you had a miserable drive? I'm so sorry we couldn't send a closed carriage. I can't see you at all, you know."

"I'm coming. No, I liked the drive — it was like Perthshire°. Well, how are you? You're looking fit as ever, as far as I can see."

"Oh, yes," said Isabel. "I'm wonderfully well. How are you? Rather thin, I think —"

"Worked to death — everybody's old cry. But I'm all right, Ciss. How's Pervin? — isn't he here?"

"Oh, yes, he's upstairs changing. Yes, he's awfully well. Take off your wet things; I'll send them to be dried."

"And how are you both, in spirits? He doesn't fret?"

"No — no, not at all. No, on the contrary, really. We've been wonderfully happy, incredibly. It's more than I can understand — so wonderful: the nearness, and the peace —"

"Ah! Well, that's awfully good news —"

They moved away. Pervin heard no more. But a childish sense of desolation had come over him, as he heard their brisk voices. He seemed shut out — like a child that is left out. He was aimless and excluded, he did not know what to do with himself. The helpless desolation came over him. He fumbled nervously as he dressed himself, in a state almost of childishness. He disliked the Scotch accent in Bertie's speech, and the slight response it found on Isabel's tongue. He disliked the slight purr of complacency in the Scottish speech. He disliked intensely the glib way in which Isabel spoke of their happiness and nearness. It made him recoil. He was fretful and beside himself like a child, he had almost a childish nostalgia to be included in the life circle. And at the same time he was a man, dark and powerful and infuriated by his own weakness. By some fatal flaw, he could not be by himself, he had to depend on the support of another. And this very dependence enraged him. He hated Bertie Reid, and at the same time he knew the hatred was nonsense, he knew it was the outcome of his own weakness.

He went downstairs. Isabel was alone in the diningroom. She watched him enter, head erect, his feet tentative. He looked so strong-blooded and

Perthshire: scenic district of Bertie's native Scotland.

healthy and, at the same time, cancelled. Cancelled — that was the word that flew across her mind. Perhaps it was his scar suggested it.

"You heard Bertie come, Maurice?" she said.

"Yes — isn't he here?"

"He's in his room. He looks very thin and worn."

"I suppose he works himself to death."

A woman came in with a tray — and after a few minutes Bertie came down. He was a little dark man, with a very big forehead, thin, wispy hair, and sad, large eyes. His expression was inordinately sad — almost funny. He had odd, short legs.

Isabel watched him hesitate under the door, and glance nervously at her husband. Pervin heard him and turned.

"Here you are, now," said Isabel. "Come, let us eat."

Bertie went across to Maurice.

"How are you, Pervin?" he said, as he advanced.

The blind man stuck his hand out into space, and Bertie took it.

"Very fit. Glad you've come," said Maurice.

Isabel glanced at them, and glanced away, as if she could not bear to see them.

"Come," she said. "Come to table. Aren't you both awfully hungry? I am, tremendously."

"I'm afraid you waited for me," said Bertie, as they sat down.

Maurice had a curious monolithic way of sitting in a chair, erect and distant. Isabel's heart always beat when she caught sight of him thus.

"No," she replied to Bertie. "We're very little later than usual. We're having a sort of high tea, not dinner. Do you mind? It gives us such a nice long evening, uninterrupted."

"I like it," said Bertie.

Maurice was feeling, with curious little movements, almost like a cat kneading her bed, for his plate, his knife and fork, his napkin. He was getting the whole geography of his cover into his consciousness. He sat erect and inscrutable, remote-seeming. Bertie watched the static figure of the blind man, the delicate tactile discernment of the large, ruddy hands, and the curious mindless silence of the brow, above the scar. With difficulty he looked away, and without knowing what he did, picked up a little crystal bowl of violets from the table, and held them to his nose.

"They are sweet-scented," he said. "Where do they come from?"

"From the garden — under the windows," said Isabel.

"So late in the year — and so fragrant! Do you remember the violets under Aunt Bell's south wall?"

The two friends looked at each other and exchanged a smile, Isabel's eyes lighting up.

"Don't I?" she replied. "*Wasn't* she queer!"

"A curious old girl," laughed Bertie. "There's a streak of freakishness in the family, Isabel."

"Ah — but not in you and me, Bertie," said Isabel. "Give them to Maurice, will you?" she added, as Bertie was putting down the flowers. "Have you smelled the violets, dear? Do! — they are so scented."

Maurice held out his hand, and Bertie placed the tiny bowl against his large, warm-looking fingers. Maurice's hand closed over the thin white fingers of the barrister. Bertie carefully extricated himself. Then the two watched the blind man smelling the violets. He bent his head and seemed to be thinking. Isabel waited.

"Aren't they sweet, Maurice?" she said at last, anxiously.

"Very," he said. And he held out the bowl. Bertie took it. Both he and Isabel were a little afraid, and deeply disturbed.

The meal continued. Isabel and Bertie chatted spasmodically. The blind man was silent. He touched his food repeatedly, with quick, delicate touches of his knife-point, then cut irregular bits. He could not bear to be helped. Both Isabel and Bertie suffered: Isabel wondered why. She did not suffer when she was alone with Maurice. Bertie made her conscious of a strangeness.

After the meal the three drew their chairs to the fire, and sat down to talk. The decanters were put on a table near at hand. Isabel knocked the logs on the fire, and clouds of brilliant sparks went up the chimney. Bertie noticed a slight weariness in her bearing.

"You will be glad when your child comes now, Isabel?" he said.

She looked up to him with a quick wan smile.

"Yes, I shall be glad," she answered. "It begins to seem long. Yes, I shall be very glad. So will you, Maurice, won't you?" she added.

"Yes, I shall," replied her husband.

"We are both looking forward so much to having it," she said.

"Yes, of course," said Bertie.

He was a bachelor, three or four years older than Isabel. He lived in beautiful rooms overlooking the river, guarded by a faithful Scottish man-servant. And he had his friends among the fair sex — not lovers, friends. So long as he could avoid any danger of courtship or marriage, he adored a few good women with constant and unfailing homage, and he was chivalrously fond of quite a number. But if they seemed to encroach on him, he withdrew and detested them.

Isabel knew him very well, his beautiful constancy, and kindness, also his incurable weakness, which made him unable ever to enter into close contact of any sort. He was ashamed of himself because he could not marry, could not approach women physically. He wanted to do so. But he could not. At the center of him he was afraid, helplessly and even brutally afraid. He had given up hope, had ceased to expect any more that he could escape his own weakness. Hence he was a brilliant and successful barrister, also a *littérateur* of high repute, a rich man, and a great social success. At the center he felt himself neuter, nothing.

Isabel knew him well. She despised him even while she admired him. She looked at his sad face, his little short legs, and felt contempt of him. She looked at his dark grey eyes, with their uncanny, almost chidlike, intuition, and she loved him. He understood amazingly — but she had no fear of his understanding. As a man she patronized him.

And she turned to the impassive, silent figure of her husband. He sat leaning back, with folded arms, and face a little uptilted. His knees were straight and massive. She sighed, picked up the poker, and again began to prod the fire, to rouse the clouds of soft brilliant sparks.

"Isabel tells me," Bertie began suddenly, "that you have not suffered unbearably from the loss of sight."

Maurice straightened himself to attend but kept his arms folded.

"No," he said, "not unbearably. Now and again one struggles against it, you know. But there are compensations."

"They say it is much worse to be stone deaf," said Isabel.

"I believe it is," said Bertie. "Are there compensations?" he added, to Maurice.

"Yes. You cease to bother about a great many things." Again Maurice stretched his figure, stretched the strong muscles of his back, and leaned backwards, with uplifted face.

"And that is a relief," said Bertie. "But what is there in place of the bothering? What replaces the activity?"

There was a pause. At length the blind man replied, as out of a negligent, unattentive thinking:

"Oh, I don't know. There's a good deal when you're not active."

"Is there?" said Bertie. "What, exactly? It always seems to me that when there is no thought and no action, there is nothing."

Again Maurice was slow in replying.

"There is something," he replied. "I couldn't tell you what it is."

And the talk lapsed once more, Isabel and Bertie chatting gossip and reminiscence, the blind man silent.

At length Maurice rose restlessly, a big obtrusive figure. He felt tight and hampered. He wanted to go away.

"Do you mind," he said, "if I go and speak to Wernham?"

"No — go along, dear," said Isabel.

And he went out. A silence came over the two friends. At length Bertie said:

"Nevertheless, it is a great deprivation, Cissie."

"It is, Bertie. I know it is."

"Something lacking all the time," said Bertie.

"Yes, I know. And yet — and yet — Maurice is right. There is something else, something *there,* which you never knew was there, and which you can't express."

"What is there?" asked Bertie.

"I don't know — it's awfully hard to define it — but something strong and immediate. There's something strange in Maurice's presence — indefinable — but I couldn't do without it. I agree that it seems to put one's mind to sleep. But when we're alone I miss nothing; it seems awfully rich, almost splendid, you know."

"I'm afraid I don't follow," said Bertie.

They talked desultorily. The wind blew loudly outside, rain chattered on the window-panes, making a sharp drum-sound because of the closed, mellow-golden shutters inside. The logs burned slowly, with hot, almost invisible small flames. Bertie seemed uneasy, there were dark circles round his eyes. Isabel, rich with her approaching maternity, leaned looking into the fire. Her hair curled in odd, loose strands, very pleasing to the man. But she had a curious feeling of old woe in her heart, old, timeless night-woe.

"I suppose we're all deficient somewhere," said Bertie.

"I suppose so," said Isabel wearily.

"Damned, sooner or later."

"I don't know," she said, rousing herself. "I feel quite all right, you know. The child coming seems to make me indifferent to everything, just placid. I can't feel that there's anything to trouble about, you know."

"A good thing, I should say," he replied slowly.

"Well, there it is. I suppose it's just Nature. If only I felt I needn't trouble about Maurice, I should be perfectly content —"

"But you feel you must trouble about him?"

"Well — I don't know — " She even resented this much effort.

The night passed slowly. Isabel looked at the clock. "I say," she said. "It's nearly ten o'clock. Where can Maurice be? I'm sure they're all in bed at the back. Excuse me a moment."

She went out, returning almost immediately.

"It's all shut up and in darkness," she said. "I wonder where he is. He must have gone out to the farm —"

Bertie looked at her.

"I suppose he'll come in," he said.

"I suppose so," she said. "But it's unusual for him to be out now."

"Would you like me to go out and see?"

"Well — if you wouldn't mind. I'd go, but — " She did not want to make the physical effort.

Bertie put on an old overcoat and took a lantern. He went out from the side door. He shrank from the wet and roaring night. Such weather had a nervous effect on him: too much moisture everywhere made him feel almost imbecile. Unwilling, he went through it all. A dog barked violently at him. He peered in all the buildings. At last, as he opened the upper door of a sort of intermediate barn, he heard a grinding noise, and looking in, holding up his lantern, saw Maurice, in his shirt-sleeves, standing listening, holding the handle of a turnip-pulper. He had been pulping sweet roots, a pile of which lay dimly heaped in a corner behind him.

"That you, Wernham?" said Maurice, listening.

"No, it's me," said Bertie.

A large, half-wild grey cat was rubbing at Maurice's leg. The blind man stooped to rub its sides. Bertie watched the scene, then unconsciously entered and shut the door behind him. He was in a high sort of barnplace, from which, right and left, ran off the corridors in front of the stalled cattle. He watched the slow, stooping motion of the other man, as he caressed the great cat.

Maurice straightened himself.

"You came to look for me?" he said.

"Isabel was a little uneasy," said Bertie.

"I'll come in. I like messing about doing these jobs."

The cat had reared her sinister, feline length against his leg, clawing at his thigh affectionately. He lifted her claws out of his flesh.

"I hope I'm not in your way at all at the Grange here," said Bertie, rather shy and stiff.

"My way? No, not a bit. I'm glad Isabel has somebody to talk to. I'm afraid it's I who am in the way. I know I'm not very lively company. Isabel's all right, don't you think? She's not unhappy, is she?"

"I don't think so."

"What does she say?"

"She says she's very content — only a little troubled about you."

"Why me?"

"Perhaps afraid that you might brood," said Bertie, cautiously.

"She needn't be afraid of that." He continued to caress the flattened grey head of the cat with his fingers. "What I am a bit afraid of," he resumed, "is that she'll find me a dead weight, always alone with me down here."

"I don't think you need think that," said Bertie, though this was what he feared himself.

"I don't know," said Maurice. "Sometimes I feel it isn't fair that she's saddled with me." Then he dropped his voice curiously, "I say," he asked, secretly struggling, "is my face much disfigured? Do you mind telling me?"

"There is the scar," said Bertie, wondering. "Yes, it is a disfigurement. But more pitiable than shocking."

"A pretty bad scar, though," said Maurice.

"Oh, yes."

There was a pause.

"Sometimes I feel I am horrible," said Maurice, in a low voice, talking as if to himself. And Bertie actually felt a quiver of horror.

"That's nonsense," he said.

Maurice again straightened himself, leaving the cat.

"There's no telling," he said. Then again, in an odd tone, he added: "I don't really know you, do I?"

"Probably not," said Bertie.

"Do you mind if I touch you?"

The lawyer shrank away instinctively. And yet, out of very philanthropy, he said, in a small voice: "Not at all."

But he suffered as the blind man stretched out a strong, naked hand to him. Maurice accidentally knocked off Bertie's hat.

"I thought you were taller," he said, starting. Then he laid his hand on Bertie Reid's head, closing the dome of the skull in a soft, firm grasp, gathering it, as it were; then, shifting his grasp and softly closing again, with a fine, close pressure, till he had covered the skull and the face of the smaller man, tracing the brows, and touching the full, closed eyes, touching the small nose and the nostrils, the rough, short moustache, the mouth, the rather strong chin. The hand of the blind man grasped the shoulder, the arm, the hand of the other man. He seemed to take him, in the soft, travelling grasp.

"You seem young," he said quietly, at last.

The lawyer stood almost annihilated, unable to answer.

"Your head seems tender, as if you were young," Maurice repeated. "So do your hands. Touch my eyes, will you? — touch my scar."

Now Bertie quivered with revulsion. Yet he was under the power of the blind man, as if hypnotized. He lifted his hand, and laid the fingers on the scar, on the scarred eyes. Maurice suddenly covered them with his own hand, pressed the fingers of the other man upon his disfigured eye-sockets, trembling in every fibre, and rocking slightly, slowly, from side to side. He remained thus for a minute or more, whilst Bertie stood as if in a swoon, unconscious, imprisoned.

Then suddenly Maurice removed the hand of the other man from his brow, and stood holding it in his own.

"Oh, my God," he said, "we shall know each other now, shan't we? We shall know each other now."

Bertie could not answer. He gazed mute and terror-struck, overcome by his own weakness. He knew he could not answer. He had an unreasonable fear, lest the other man should suddenly destroy him. Whereas Maurice was actually filled with hot, poignant love, the passion of friendship. Perhaps it was this very passion of friendship which Bertie shrank from most.

"We're all right together now, aren't we?" said Maurice. "It's all right now, as long as we live, so far as we're concerned?"

"Yes," said Bertie, trying by any means to escape.

Maurice stood with head lifted, as if listening. The new delicate fulfilment of mortal friendship had come as a revelation and surprise to him, something exquisite and unhoped-for. He seemed to be listening to hear if it were real.

Then he turned for his coat.

"Come," he said, "we'll go to Isabel."

Bertie took the lantern and opened the door. The cat disappeared. The two men went in silence along the causeways. Isabel, as they came, thought their footsteps sounded strange. She looked up pathetically and anxiously for their entrance. There seemed a curious elation about Maurice. Bertie was haggard, with sunken eyes.

"What is it?" she asked.

"We've become friends," said Maurice, standing with his feet apart, like a strange colossus.

"Friends!" re-echoed Isabel. And she looked again at Bertie. He met her eyes with a furtive, haggard look; his eyes were as if glazed with misery.

"I'm so glad," she said, in sheer perplexity.

"Yes," said Maurice.

He was indeed so glad. Isabel took his hand with both hers, and held it fast.

"You'll be happier now, dear," she said.

But she was watching Bertie. She knew that he had one desire — to escape from this intimacy, this friendship, which had been thrust upon him. He could not bear it that he had been touched by the blind man, his insane reserve broken in. He was like a mollusc whose shell is broken.

John Steinbeck (1902–1968)

The Chrysanthemums   1938

The high grey-flannel fog of winter closed off the Salinas Valley° from the sky and from all the rest of the world. On every side it sat like a lid on the mountains and made of the great valley a closed pot. On the broad, level land floor

Salinas Valley: south of San Francisco in the Coast Ranges region of California. Steinbeck, born in Salinas, made the valley the locale of much of his fiction.

the gang plows bit deep and left the black earth shining like metal where the shares had cut. On the foothill ranches across the Salinas River, the yellow stubble fields seemed to be bathed in pale cold sunshine, but there was no sunshine in the valley now in December. The thick willow scrub along the river flamed with sharp and positive yellow leaves.

It was a time of quiet and of waiting. The air was cold and tender. A light wind blew up from the southwest so that the farmers were mildly hopeful of a good rain before long; but fog and rain do not go together.

Across the river, on Henry Allen's foothill ranch there was little work to be done, for the hay was cut and stored and the orchards were plowed up to receive the rain deeply when it should come. The cattle on the higher slopes were becoming shaggy and rough-coated.

Elisa Allen, working in her flower garden, looked down across the yard and saw Henry, her husband, talking to two men in business suits. The three of them stood by the tractor shed, each man with one foot on the side of the little Fordson. They smoked cigarettes and studied the machine as they talked.

Elisa watched them for a moment and then went back to her work. She was thirty-five. Her face was lean and strong and her eyes were as clear as water. Her figure looked blocked and heavy in her gardening costume, a man's black hat pulled low down over her eyes, clod-hopper shoes, a figured print dress almost completely covered by a big corduroy apron with four big pockets to hold the snips, the trowel and scratcher, the seeds and the knife she worked with. She wore heavy leather gloves to protect her hands while she worked.

She was cutting down the old year's chrysanthemum stalks with a pair of short and powerful scissors. She looked down toward the men by the tractor shed now and then. Her face was eager and mature and handsome; even her work with the scissors was over-eager, over-powerful. The chrysanthemum stems seemed too small and easy for her energy.

She brushed a cloud of hair out of her eyes with the back of her glove, and left a smudge of earth on her cheek in doing it. Behind her stood the neat white farm house with red geraniums close-banked around it as high as the windows. It was a hard-swept looking little house with hard-polished windows, and a clean mud-mat on the front steps.

Elisa cast another glance toward the tractor shed. The strangers were getting into their Ford coupe. She took off a glove and put her strong fingers down into the forest of new green chrysanthemum sprouts that were growing around the old roots. She spread the leaves and looked down among the close-growing stems. No aphids were there, no sowbugs or snails or cutworms. Her terrier fingers destroyed such pests before they could get started.

Elisa started at the sound of her husband's voice. He had come near quietly, and he leaned over the wire fence that protected her flower garden from cattle and dogs and chickens.

"At it again," he said. "You've got a strong new crop coming."

Elisa straightened her back and pulled on the gardening glove again. "Yes. They'll be strong this coming year." In her tone and on her face there was a little smugness.

"You've got a gift with things," Henry observed. "Some of those yellow chrysanthemums you had this year were ten inches across. I wish you'd work out in the orchard and raise some apples that big."

Her eyes sharpened. "Maybe I could do it, too. I've a gift with things, all right. My mother had it. She could stick anything in the ground and make it grow. She said it was having planters' hands that knew how to do it."

"Well, it sure works with flowers," he said.

"Henry, who were those men you were talking to?"

"Why, sure, that's what I came to tell you. They were from the Western Meat Company. I sold those thirty head of three-year-old steers. Got nearly my own price, too."

"Good," she said. "Good for you."

"And I thought," he continued, "I thought how it's Saturday afternoon, and we might go into Salinas for dinner at a restaurant, and then to a picture show — to celebrate, you see."

"Good," she repeated. "Oh, yes. That will be good."

Henry put on his joking tone. "There's fights tonight. How'd you like to go to the fights?"

"Oh, no," she said breathlessly. "No, I wouldn't like fights."

"Just fooling, Elisa. We'll go to a movie. Let's see. It's two now. I'm going to take Scotty and bring down those steers from the hill. It'll take us maybe two hours. We'll go in town about five and have dinner at the Cominos Hotel. Like that?"

"Of course I'll like it. It's good to eat away from home."

"All right, then. I'll go get up a couple of horses."

She said, "I'll have plenty of time to transplant some of these sets, I guess."

She heard her·husband calling Scotty down by the barn. And a little later she saw the two men ride up the pale yellow hillside in search of the steers.

There was a little square sandy bed kept for rooting the chrysanthemums. With her trowel she turned the soil over and over, and smoothed it and patted it firm. Then she dug ten parallel trenches to receive the sets. Back at the chrysanthemum bed she pulled out the little crisp shoots, trimmed off the leaves of each one with her scissors and laid it on a small orderly pile.

A squeak of wheels and plod of hoofs came from the road. Elisa looked up. The country road ran along the dense bank of willows and cottonwoods that bordered the river, and up this road came a curious vehicle, curiously drawn. It was an old spring-wagon, with a round canvas top on it like the cover of a prairie schooner. It was drawn by an old bay horse and a little grey-and-white burro. A big stubble-bearded man sat between the cover flaps and drove the crawling team. Underneath the wagon, between the hind wheels, a lean and rangy mongrel dog walked sedately. Words were painted on the canvas, in clumsy, crooked letters. "Pots, pans, knives, sisors, lawn mores, Fixed." Two rows of articles, and the triumphantly definitive "Fixed" below. The black paint had run down in little sharp points beneath each letter.

Elisa, squatting on the ground, watched to see the crazy, loose-jointed wagon pass by. But it didn't pass. It turned into the farm road in front of her house, crooked old wheels skirling and squeaking. The rangy dog darted from between the wheels and ran ahead. Instantly the two ranch shepherds flew out at him. Then all three stopped, and with stiff and quivering tails, with taut straight legs, with ambassadorial dignity, they slowly circled, sniffing daintily.

The caravan pulled up to Elisa's wire fence and stopped. Now the newcomer dog, feeling out-numbered, lowered his tail and retired under the wagon with raised hackles and bared teeth.

The man on the wagon seat called out, "That's a bad dog in a fight when he gets started."

Elisa laughed. "I see he is. How soon does he generally get started?"

The man caught up her laughter and echoed it heartily. "Sometimes not for weeks and weeks," he said. He climbed stiffly down, over the wheel. The horse and the donkey drooped like unwatered flowers.

Elisa saw that he was a very big man. Although his hair and beard were greying, he did not look old. His worn black suit was wrinkled and spotted with grease. The laughter had disappeared from his face and eyes the moment his laughing voice ceased. His eyes were dark, and they were full of the brooding that gets in the eyes of teamsters and of sailors. The calloused hands he rested on the wire fence were cracked, and every crack was a black line. He took off his battered hat.

"I'm off my general road, ma'am," he said. "Does this dirt road cut over across the river to the Los Angeles highway?"

Elisa stood up and shoved the thick scissors in her apron pocket. "Well, yes, it does, but it winds around and then fords the river. I don't think your team could pull through the sand."

He replied with some asperity, "It might surprise you what them beasts can pull through."

"When they get started?" she asked.

He smiled for a second. "Yes. When they get started."

"Well," said Elisa, "I think you'll save time if you go back to the Salinas road and pick up the highway there."

He drew a big finger down the chicken wire and made it sing. "I ain't in any hurry, ma'am. I go from Seattle to San Diego and back every year. Takes all my time. About six months each way. I aim to follow nice weather."

Elisa took off her gloves and stuffed them in the apron pocket with the scissors. She touched the under edge of her man's hat, searching for fugitive hairs. "That sounds like a nice kind of a way to live," she said.

He leaned confidentially over the fence. "Maybe you noticed the writing on my wagon. I mend pots and sharpen knives and scissors. You got any of them things to do?"

"Oh, no," she said quickly. "Nothing like that." Her eyes hardened with resistance.

"Scissors is the worst thing," he explained. "Most people just ruin scissors trying to sharpen 'em, but I know how. I got a special tool. It's a little bobbit kind of thing, and patented. But it sure does the trick."

"No. My scissors are all sharp."

"All right, then. Take a pot," he continued earnestly, "a bent pot, or a pot with a hole. I can make it like new so you don't have to buy no new ones. That's a saving for you."

"No," she said shortly. "I tell you I have nothing like that for you to do."

His face fell to an exaggerated sadness. His voice took on a whining undertone. "I ain't had a thing to do today. Maybe I won't have no supper tonight.

You see I'm off my regular road. I know folks on the highway clear from Seattle to San Diego. They save their things for me to sharpen up because they know I do it so good and save them money."

"I'm sorry," Elisa said irritably. "I haven't anything for you to do."

His eyes left her face and fell to searching the ground. They roamed about until they came to the chrysanthemum bed where she had been working. "What's them plants, ma'am?"

The irritation and resistance melted from Elisa's face. "Oh, those are chrysanthemums, giant whites and yellows. I raise them every year, bigger than anybody around here."

"Kind of a long-stemmed flower? Looks like a quick puff of colored smoke?" he asked.

"That's it. What a nice way to describe them."

"They smell kind of nasty till you get used to them," he said.

"It's a good bitter smell," she retorted, "not nasty at all."

He changed his tone quickly. "I like the smell myself."

"I had ten-inch blooms this year," she said.

The man leaned farther over the fence. "Look. I know a lady down the road a piece, has got the nicest garden you ever seen. Got nearly every kind of flower but no chrysantheums. Last time I was mending a copper-bottom washtub for her (that's a hard job but I do it good), she said to me, 'If you ever run acrost some nice chrysantheums I wish you'd try to get me a few seeds.' That's what she told me."

Elisa's eyes grew alert and eager. "She couldn't have known much about chrysanthemums. You *can* raise them from seed, but it's much easier to root the little sprouts you see there."

"Oh," he said. "I s'pose I can't take none to her, then."

"Why yes you can," Elisa cried. "I can put some in damp sand, and you can carry them right along with you. They'll take root in the pot if you keep them damp. And then she can transplant them."

"She'd sure like to have some, ma'am. You say they're nice ones?"

"Beautiful," she said. "Oh, beautiful." Her eyes shone. She tore off the battered hat and shook out her dark pretty hair. "I'll put them in a flower pot, and you can take them right with you. Come into the yard."

While the man came through the picket gate Elisa ran excitedly along the geranium-bordered path to the back of the house. And she returned carrying a big red flower pot. The gloves were forgotten now. She kneeled on the ground by the starting bed and dug up the sandy soil with her fingers and scooped it into the bright new flower pot. Then she picked up the little pile of shoots she had prepared. With her strong fingers she pressed them into the sand and tamped around them with her knuckles. The man stood over her. "I'll tell you what to do," she said. "You remember so you can tell the lady."

"Yes, I'll try to remember."

"Well, look. These will take root in about a month. Then she must set them out, about a foot apart in good rich earth like this, see?" She lifted a handful of dark soil for him to look at. "They'll grow fast and tall. Now remember this: In July tell her to cut them down, about eight inches from the ground."

"Before they bloom?" he asked.

"Yes, before they bloom." Her face was tight with eagerness. "They'll grow right up again. About the last of September the buds will start."

She stopped and seemed perplexed. "It's the budding that takes the most care," she said hesitantly. "I don't know how to tell you." She looked deep into his eyes, searchingly. Her mouth opened a little, and she seemed to be listening. "I'll try to tell you," she said. "Did you ever hear of planting hands?"

"Can't say I have, ma'am."

"Well, I can only tell you what it feels like. It's when you're picking off the buds you don't want. Everything goes right down into your fingertips. You watch your fingers work. They do it themselves. You can feel how it is. They pick and pick the buds. They never make a mistake. They're with the plant. Do you see? Your fingers and the plant. You can feel that, right up your arm. They know. They never make a mistake. You can feel it. When you're like that you can't do anything wrong. Do you see that? Can you understand that?"

She was kneeling on the ground looking up at him. Her breast swelled passionately.

The man's eyes narrowed. He looked away self-consciously. "Maybe I know," he said. "Sometimes in the night in the wagon there —"

Elisa's voice grew husky. She broke in on him, "I've never lived as you do, but I know what you mean. When the night is dark — why, the stars are sharp-pointed, and there's quiet. Why, you rise up and up! Every pointed star gets driven into your body. It's like that. Hot and sharp and — lovely."

Kneeling there, her hand went out toward his legs in the greasy black trousers. Her hesitant fingers almost touched the cloth. Then her hand dropped to the ground. She crouched low like a fawning dog.

He said, "It's nice, just like you say. Only when you don't have no dinner, it ain't."

She stood up then, very straight, and her face was ashamed. She held the flower pot out to him and placed it gently in his arms. "Here. Put it in your wagon, on the seat, where you can watch it. Maybe I can find something for you to do."

At the back of the house she dug in the can pile and found two old and battered aluminum saucepans. She carried them back and gave them to him. "Here, maybe you can fix these."

His manner changed. He became professional. "Good as new I can fix them." At the back of his wagon he set a little anvil, and out of an oily tool box dug a small machine hammer. Elisa came through the gate to watch him while he pounded out the dents in the kettles. His mouth grew sure and knowing. At a difficult part of the work he sucked his under-lip.

"You sleep right in the wagon?" Elisa asked.

"Right in the wagon, ma'am. Rain or shine I'm dry as a cow in there."

"It must be nice," she said. "It must be very nice. I wish women could do such things."

"It ain't the right kind of a life for a woman."

Her upper lip raised a little, showing her teeth. "How do you know? How can you tell?" she said.

"I don't know, ma'am," he protested. "Of course I don't know. Now here's your kettles, done. You don't have to buy no new ones."

"How much?"

"Oh, fifty cents'll do. I keep my prices down and my work good. That's why I have all them satisfied customers up and down the highway."

Elisa brought him a fifty-cent piece from the house and dropped it in his hand. "You might be surprised to have a rival some time. I can sharpen scissors, too. And I can beat the dents out of little pots. I could show you what a woman might do."

He put his hammer back in the oily box and shoved the little anvil out of sight. "It would be a lonely life for a woman, ma'am, and a scarey life, too, with animals creeping under the wagon all night." He climbed over the singletree, steadying himself with a hand on the burro's white rump. He settled himself in the seat, picked up the lines. "Thank you kindly, ma'am," he said. "I'll do like you told me; I'll go back and catch the Salinas road."

"Mind," she called, "if you're long in getting there, keep the sand damp."

"Sand, ma'am? . . . Sand? Oh, sure. You mean around the chrysantheums. Sure I will." He clucked his tongue. The beasts leaned luxuriously into their collars. The mongrel dog took his place between the back wheels. The wagon turned and crawled out the entrance road and back the way it had come, along the river.

Elisa stood in front of her wire fence watching the slow progress of the caravan. Her shoulders were straight, her head thrown back, her eyes half-closed, so that the scene came vaguely into them. Her lips moved silently, forming the words "Good-bye — good-bye." Then she whispered, "That's a bright direction. There's a glowing there." The sound of her whisper startled her. She shook herself free and looked about to see whether anyone had been listening. Only the dogs had heard. They lifted their heads toward her from their sleeping in the dust, and then stretched out their chins and settled asleep again. Elisa turned and ran hurriedly into the house.

In the kitchen she reached behind the stove and felt the water tank. It was full of hot water from the noonday cooking. In the bathroom she tore off her soiled clothes and flung them into the corner. And then she scrubbed herself with a little block of pumice, legs and thighs, loins and chest and arms, until her skin was scratched and red. When she had dried herself she stood in front of a mirror in her bedroom and looked at her body. She tightened her stomach and threw out her chest. She turned and looked over her shoulder at her back.

After a while she began to dress, slowly. She put on her newest under-clothing and her nicest stockings and the dress which was the symbol of her prettiness. She worked carefully on her hair, penciled her eyebrows and rouged her lips.

Before she was finished she heard the little thunder of hoofs and the shouts of Henry and his helper as they drove the red steers into the corral. She heard the gate bang shut and set herself for Henry's arrival.

His step sounded on the porch. He entered the house calling, "Elisa, where are you?"

"In my room, dressing. I'm not ready. There's hot water for your bath. Hurry up. It's getting late."

When she heard him splashing in the tub, Elisa laid his dark suit on the bed, and shirt and socks and tie beside it. She stood his polished shoes on the floor beside the bed. Then she went to the porch and sat primly and stiffly down. She looked toward the river road where the willow-line was still yellow with frosted leaves so that under the high grey fog they seemed a thin band of sunshine. This was the only color in the grey afternoon. She sat unmoving for a long time. Her eyes blinked rarely.

Henry came banging out of the door, shoving his tie inside his vest as he came. Elisa stiffened and her face grew tight. Henry stopped short and looked at her. "Why — why, Elisa. You look so nice!"

"Nice? You think I look nice? What do you mean by 'nice'?"

Henry blundered on. "I don't know. I mean you look different, strong and happy."

"I am strong? Yes, strong. What do you mean 'strong'?"

He looked bewildered. "You're playing some kind of a game," he said helplessly. "It's a kind of a play. You look strong enough to break a calf over your knee, happy enough to eat it like a watermelon."

For a second she lost her rigidity. "Henry! Don't talk like that. You didn't know what you said." She grew complete again. "I'm strong," she boasted. "I never knew before how strong."

Henry looked down toward the tractor shed, and when he brought his eyes back to her, they were his own again. "I'll get out the car. You can put on your coat while I'm starting."

Elisa went into the house. She heard him drive to the gate and idle down his motor, and then she took a long time to put on her hat. She pulled it here and pressed it there. When Henry turned the motor off she slipped into her coat and went out.

The little roadster bounced along on the dirt road by the river, raising the birds and driving the rabbits into the brush. Two cranes flapped heavily over the willow-line and dropped into the river-bed.

Far ahead on the road Elisa saw a dark speck. She knew.

She tried not to look as they passed it, but her eyes would not obey. She whispered to herself sadly, "He might have thrown them off the road. That wouldn't have been much trouble, not very much. But he kept the pot," she explained. "He had to keep the pot. That's why he couldn't get them off the road."

The roadster turned a bend and she saw the caravan ahead. She swung full around toward her husband so she could not see the little covered wagon and the mismatched team as the car passed them.

In a moment it was over. The thing was done. She did not look back.

She said loudly, to be heard above the motor, "It will be good, tonight, a good dinner."

"Now you're changed again," Henry complained. He took one hand from the wheel and patted her knee. "I ought to take you in to dinner oftener. It would be good for both of us. We get so heavy out on the ranch."

"Henry," she asked, "could we have wine at dinner?"

"Sure we could. Say! That will be fine."

She was silent for a while; then she said, "Henry, at those prize fights, do the men hurt each other very much?"

"Sometimes a little, not often. Why?"

"Well, I've read how they break noses, and blood runs down their chests. I've read how the fighting gloves get heavy and soggy with blood."

He looked around at her. "What's the matter, Elisa? I didn't know you read things like that." He brought the car to a stop, then turned to the right over the Salinas River bridge.

"Do any women ever go to the fights?" she asked.

"Oh, sure, some. What's the matter, Elisa? Do you want to go? I don't think you'd like it, but I'll take you if you really want to go."

She relaxed limply in the seat. "Oh, no. No. I don't want to go. I'm sure I don't." Her face was turned away from him. "It will be enough if we can have wine. It will be plenty." She turned up her coat collar so he could not see that she was crying weakly — like an old woman.

Frank O'Connor (1903–1966)
FIRST CONFESSION   1952

All the trouble began when my grandfather died and my grandmother — my father's mother — came to live with us. Relations in the one house are a strain at the best of times, but, to make matters worse, my grandmother was a real old countrywoman and quite unsuited to the life in town. She had a fat, wrinkled old face, and, to Mother's great indignation, went round the house in bare feet — the boots had her crippled, she said. For dinner she had a jug of porter and a pot of potatoes with — sometimes — a bit of salt fish, and she poured out the potatoes on the table and ate them slowly, with great relish, using her fingers by way of a fork.

Now, girls are supposed to be fastidious, but I was the one who suffered most from this. Nora, my sister, just sucked up to the old woman for the penny she got every Friday out of the old-age pension, a thing I could not do. I was too honest, that was my trouble; and when I was playing with Bill Connell, the sergeant-major's son, and saw my grandmother steering up the path with the jug of porter sticking out from beneath her shawl I was mortified. I made excuses not to let him come into the house, because I could never be sure what she would be up to when we went in.

When Mother was at work and my grandmother made the dinner I wouldn't touch it. Nora once tried to make me, but I hid under the table from her and took the bread-knife with me for protection. Nora let on to be very indignant (she wasn't, of course, but she knew Mother saw through her, so she sided with Gran) and came after me. I lashed out at her with the bread-knife, and after that she left me alone. I stayed there till Mother came in from work and made my dinner, but when Father came in later Nora said in a shocked voice: "Oh, Dadda, do you know what Jackie did at dinnertime?" Then, of course, it all came out; Father gave me a flaking; Mother interfered, and for days after that he didn't speak to me and Mother barely spoke to Nora. And all because of that old woman! God knows, I was heart-scalded.

Then, to crown my misfortunes, I had to make my first confession and communion. It was an old woman called Ryan who prepared us for these. She was about the one age with Gran; she was well-to-do, lived in a big house on Montenotte, wore a black cloak and bonnet, and came every day to school at three o'clock when we should have been going home, and talked to us of hell. She may have mentioned the other place as well, but that could only have been by accident, for hell had the first place in her heart.

She lit a candle, took out a new half-crown, and offered it to the first boy who would hold one finger — only one finger! — in the flame for five minutes by the school clock. Being always very ambitious I was tempted to volunteer, but I thought it might look greedy. Then she asked were we afraid of holding one finger — only one finger! — in a little candle flame for five minutes and not afraid of burning all over in roasting hot furnaces for all eternity. "All eternity! Just think of that! A whole lifetime goes by and it's nothing, not even a drop in the ocean of your sufferings." The woman was really interesting about hell, but my attention was all fixed on the half-crown. At the end of the lesson she put it back in her purse. It was a great disappointment; a religious woman like that, you wouldn't think she'd bother about a thing like a half-crown.

Another day she said she knew a priest who woke one night to find a fellow he didn't recognize leaning over the end of his bed. The priest was a bit frightened — naturally enough — but he asked the fellow what he wanted, and the fellow said in a deep, husky voice that he wanted to go to confession. The priest said it was an awkward time and wouldn't it do in the morning, but the fellow said that last time he went to confession, there was one sin he kept back, being ashamed to mention it, and now it was always on his mind. Then the priest knew it was a bad case, because the fellow was after making a bad confession and committing a mortal sin. He got up to dress, and just then the cock crew in the yard outside, and — lo and behold! — when the priest looked round there was no sign of the fellow, only a smell of burning timber, and when the priest looked at his bed didn't he see the print of two hands burned in it? That was because the fellow had made a bad confession. This story made a shocking impression on me.

But the worst of all was when she showed us how to examine our conscience. Did we take the name of the Lord, our God, in vain? Did we honor our father and our mother? (I asked her did this include grandmothers and she said it did.) Did we love our neighbors as ourselves? Did we covet our neighbor's goods? (I thought of the way I felt about the penny that Nora got every Friday.) I decided that, between one thing and another, I must have broken the whole ten commandments, all on account of that old woman, and so far as I could see, so long as she remained in the house I had no hope of ever doing anything else.

I was scared to death of confession. The day the whole class went I let on to have a toothache, hoping my absence wouldn't be noticed; but at three o'clock, just as I was feeling safe, along comes a chap with a message from Mrs. Ryan that I was to go to confession myself on Saturday and be at the chapel for communion with the rest. To make it worse, Mother couldn't come with me and sent Nora instead.

Now, that girl had ways of tormenting me that Mother never knew of. She held my hand as we went down the hill, smiling sadly and saying how sorry she was for me, as if she were bringing me to the hospital for an operation.

"Oh, God help us!" she moaned. "Isn't it a terrible pity you weren't a good boy? Oh, Jackie, my heart bleeds for you! How will you ever think of all your sins? Don't forget you have to tell him about the time you kicked Gran on the shin."

"Lemme go!" I said, trying to drag myself free of her. "I don't want to go to confession at all."

"But sure, you'll have to go to confession, Jackie," she replied in the same regretful tone. "Sure, if you didn't, the parish priest would be up to the house, looking for you. 'Tisn't, God knows, that I'm not sorry for you. Do you remember the time you tried to kill me with the bread-knife under the table? And the language you used to me? I don't know what he'll do with you at all, Jackie. He might have to send you up to the bishop."

I remember thinking bitterly that she didn't know the half of what I had to tell — if I told it. I knew I couldn't tell it, and understood perfectly why the fellow in Mrs. Ryan's story made a bad confession; it seemed to me a great shame that people wouldn't stop criticizing him. I remember that steep hill down to the church, and the sunlit hillsides beyond the valley of the river, which I saw in the gaps between the houses like Adam's last glimpse of Paradise.

Then, when she had maneuvered me down the long flight of steps to the chapel yard, Nora suddenly changed her tone. She became the raging malicious devil she really was.

"There you are!" she said with a yelp of triumph, hurling me through the church door. "And I hope he'll give you the penitential psalms, you dirty little caffler."

I knew then I was lost, given up to eternal justice. The door with the colored-glass panels swung shut behind me, the sunlight went out and gave place to deep shadow, and the wind whistled outside so that the silence within seemed to crackle like ice under my feet. Nora sat in front of me by the confession box. There were a couple of old women ahead of her, and then a miserable-looking poor devil came and wedged me in at the other side, so that I couldn't escape even if I had the courage. He joined his hands and rolled his eyes in the direction of the roof, muttering aspirations in an anguished tone, and I wondered had he a grandmother too. Only a grandmother could account for a fellow behaving in that heartbroken way, but he was better off than I, for he at least could go and confess his sins; while I would make a bad confession and then die in the night and be continually coming back and burning people's furniture.

Nora's turn came, and I heard the sound of something slamming, and then her voice as if butter wouldn't melt in her mouth, and then another slam, and out she came. God, the hypocrisy of women! Her eyes were lowered, her head was bowed, and her hands were joined very low down on her stomach, and she walked up the aisle to the side altar looking like a saint. You never saw such an exhibition of devotion; and I remembered the devilish malice with which she had tormented me all the way from our door, and wondered were all religious people like that, really. It was my turn now. With the fear of damnation in my soul I went in, and the confessional door closed of itself behind me.

It was pitch-dark and I couldn't see priest or anything else. Then I really began to be frightened. In the darkness it was a matter between God and me, and He had all the odds. He knew what my intentions were before I even started; I had no chance. All I had ever been told about confession got mixed up in my mind, and I knelt to one wall and said: "Bless me, father, for I have sinned; this is my first confession." I waited for a few minutes, but nothing happened, so I tried it on the other wall. Nothing happened there either. He had me spotted all right.

It must have been then that I noticed the shelf at about one height with my head. It was really a place for grown-up people to rest their elbows, but in my distracted state I thought it was probably the place you were supposed to kneel. Of course, it was on the high side and not very deep, but I was always good at climbing and managed to get up all right. Staying up was the trouble. There was room only for my knees, and nothing you could get a grip on but a sort of wooden moulding a bit above it. I held on to the moulding and repeated the words a little louder, and this time something happened all right. A slide was slammed back; a little light entered the box, and a man's voice said: "Who's there?"

" 'Tis me, father," I said for fear he mightn't see me and go away again. I couldn't see him at all. The place the voice came from was under the moulding, about level with my knees, so I took a good grip of the moulding and swung myself down till I saw the astonished face of a young priest looking up at me. He had to put his head on one side to see me, and I had to put mine on one side to see him, so we were more or less talking to one another upside-down. It struck me as a queer way of hearing confessions, but I didn't feel it my place to criticize.

"Bless me, father, for I have sinned; this is my first confession," I rattled off all in one breath, and swung myself down the least shade more to make it easier for him.

"What are you doing up there?" he shouted in an angry voice, and the strain the politeness was putting on my hold of the moulding, and the shock of being addressed in such an uncivil tone, were too much for me. I lost my grip, tumbled, and hit the door an unmerciful wallop before I found myself flat on my back in the middle of the aisle. The people who had been waiting stood up with their mouths open. The priest opened the door of the middle box and came out, pushing his biretta back from his forehead; he looked something terrible. Then Nora came scampering down the aisle.

"Oh, you dirty little caffler!" she said. "I might have known you'd do it. I might have known you'd disgrace me. I can't leave you out of my sight for one minute."

Before I could even get to my feet to defend myself she bent down and gave me a clip across the ear. This reminded me that I was so stunned I had even forgotten to cry, so that people might think I wasn't hurt at all, when in fact I was probably maimed for life. I gave a roar out of me.

"What's all this about?" the priest hissed, getting angrier than ever and pushing Nora off me. "How dare you hit the child like that, you little vixen?"

"But I can't do my penance with him, father," Nora cried, cocking an outraged eye up at him.

"Well, go and do it, or I'll give you some more to do," he said, giving me a hand up. "Was it coming to confession you were, my poor man?" he asked me.

" 'Twas, father," said I with a sob.

"Oh," he said respectfully, "a big hefty fellow like you must have terrible sins. Is this your first?"

" 'Tis, father," said I.

"Worse and worse," he said gloomily. "The crimes of a life-time. I don't know will I get rid of you at all today. You'd better wait now till I'm finished with these old ones. You can see by the looks of them they haven't much to tell."

"I will, father," I said with something approaching joy.

The relief of it was really enormous. Nora stuck out her tongue at me from behind his back, but I couldn't even be bothered retorting. I knew from the very moment that man opened his mouth that he was intelligent above the ordinary. When I had time to think, I saw how right I was. It only stood to reason that a fellow confessing after seven years would have more to tell than people that went every week. The crimes of a lifetime, exactly as he said. It was only what he expected, and the rest was the cackle of old women and girls with their talk of hell, the bishop, and the penitential psalms. That was all they knew. I started to make my examination of conscience, and barring the one bad business of my grandmother it didn't seem so bad.

The next time, the priest steered me into the confession box himself and left the shutter back the way I could see him get in and sit down at the further side of the grille from me.

"Well, now," he said, "what do they call you?"

"Jackie, father," said I.

"And what's a-trouble to you, Jackie?"

"Father," I said, feeling I might as well get it over while I had him in good humor, "I had it all arranged to kill my grandmother."

He seemed a bit shaken by that, all right, because he said nothing for quite a while.

"My goodness," he said at last, "that'd be a shocking thing to do. What put that into your head?"

"Father," I said, feeling very sorry for myself, "she's an awful woman."

"Is she?" he asked. "What way is she awful?"

"She takes porter, father," I said, knowing well from the way Mother talked of it that this was a mortal sin, and hoping it would make the priest take a more favorable view of my case.

"Oh, my!" he said, and I could see he was impressed.

"And snuff, father," said I.

"That's a bad case, sure enough, Jackie," he said.

"And she goes round in her bare feet, father," I went on in a rush of self-pity, "and she knows I don't like her, and she gives pennies to Nora and none to me, and my da sides with her and flakes me, and one night I was so heart-scalded I made up my mind I'd have to kill her."

"And what would you do with the body?" he asked with great interest.

"I was thinking I could chop that up and carry it away in a barrow I have," I said.

"Begor, Jackie," he said, "do you know you're a terrible child?"

"I know, father," I said, for I was just thinking the same thing myself. "I tried to kill Nora too with a bread-knife under the table, only I missed her."

"Is that the little girl that was beating you just now?" he asked.

"'Tis, father."

"Someone will go for her with a bread-knife one day, and he won't miss her," he said rather cryptically. "You must have great courage. Between ourselves, there's a lot of people I'd like to do the same to but I'd never have the nerve. Hanging is an awful death."

"Is it, father?" I asked with the deepest interest — I was always very keen on hanging. "Did you ever see a fellow hanged?"

"Dozens of them," he said solemnly. "And they all died roaring."

"Jay!" I said.

"Oh, a horrible death!" he said with great satisfaction. "Lots of the fellows I saw killed their grandmothers too, but they all said 'twas never worth it."

He had me there for a full ten minutes talking, and then walked out the chapel yard with me. I was genuinely sorry to part with him, because he was the most entertaining character I'd ever met in the religious line. Outside, after the shadow of the church, the sunlight was like the roaring of waves on a beach; it dazzled me; and when the frozen silence melted and I heard the screech of trams on the road my heart soared. I knew now I wouldn't die in the night and come back, leaving marks on my mother's furniture. It would be a great worry to her, and the poor soul had enough.

Nora was sitting on the railing, waiting for me, and she put on a very sour puss when she saw the priest with me. She was mad jealous because a priest had never come out of the church with her.

"Well," she asked coldly, after he left me, "what did he give you?"

"Three Hail Marys," I said.

"Three Hail Marys," she repeated incredulously. "You mustn't have told him anything."

"I told him everything," I said confidently.

"About Gran and all?"

"About Gran and all."

(All she wanted was to be able to go home and say I'd made a bad confession.)

"Did you tell him you went for me with the bread-knife?" she asked with a frown.

"I did to be sure."

"And he only gave you three Hail Marys?"

"That's all."

She slowly got down from the railing with a baffled air. Clearly, this was beyond her. As we mounted the steps back to the main road she looked at me suspiciously.

"What are you sucking?" she asked.

"Bullseyes."

"Was it the priest gave them to you?"

"'Twas."

"Lord God," she wailed bitterly, "some people have all the luck! 'Tis no advantage to anybody trying to be good. I might just as well be a sinner like you."

Eudora Welty (b. 1909)

PETRIFIED MAN   1939

"Reach in my purse and git me a cigarette without no powder in it if you kin, Mrs. Fletcher, honey," said Leota to her ten o'clock shampoo-and-set customer. "I don't like no perfumed cigarettes."

Mrs. Fletcher gladly reached over to the lavender shelf under the lavender-framed mirror, shook a hair net loose from the clasp of the patent-leather bag, and slapped her hand down quickly on a powder puff which burst out when the purse was opened.

"Why, look at the peanuts, Leota!" said Mrs. Fletcher in her marvelling voice.

"Honey, them goobers has been in my purse a week if they's been in it a day. Mrs. Pike bought them peanuts."

"Who's Mrs. Pike?" asked Mrs. Fletcher, settling back. Hidden in this den of curling fluid and henna packs, separated by a lavender swing-door from the other customers, who were being gratified in other booths, she could give her curiosity its freedom. She looked expectantly at the black part in Leota's yellow curls as she bent to light the cigarette.

"Mrs. Pike is this lady from New Orleans," said Leota, puffing, and pressing into Mrs. Fletcher's scalp with strong red-nailed fingers. "A friend, not a customer. You see, like maybe I told you last time, me and Fred and Sal and Joe all had us a fuss, so Sal and Joe up and moved out, so we didn't do a thing but rent out their room. So we rented it to Mrs. Pike. And Mr. Pike." She flicked an ash into the basket of dirty towels. "Mrs. Pike is a very decided blonde. *She* bought me the peanuts."

"She must be cute," said Mrs. Fletcher.

"Honey, 'cute' ain't the word for what she is. I'm tellin' you, Mrs. Pike is attractive. She has her a good time. She's got a sharp eye out, Mrs. Pike has."

She dashed the comb through the air, and paused dramatically as a cloud of Mrs. Fletcher's hennaed hair floated out of the lavender teeth like a small storm-cloud.

"Hair fallin'."

"Aw, Leota."

"Uh-huh, commencin' to fall out," said Leota, combing again, and letting fall another cloud.

"Is it any dandruff in it?" Mrs. Fletcher was frowning, her hair-line eyebrows diving down toward her nose, and her wrinkled, beady-lashed eyelids batting with concentration.

"Nope." She combed again. "Just fallin' out."

"Bet it was that last perm'nent you gave me that did it," Mrs. Fletcher said cruelly. "Remember you cooked me fourteen minutes."

"You had fourteen minutes comin' to you," said Leota with finality.

"Bound to be somethin'," persisted Mrs. Fletcher. "Dandruff, dandruff. I couldn't of caught a thing like that from Mr. Fletcher, could I?"

"Well," Leota answered at last, "you know what I heard in here yestiddy, one of Thelma's ladies was settin' over yonder in Thelma's booth gittin' a machineless, and I don't mean to insist or insinuate or anything, Mrs. Fletcher, but Thelma's lady just happ'med to throw out — I forgotten what she was talkin' about at the time — that you was p-r-e-g., and lots of times that'll make your hair do awful funny, fall out and God knows what all. It just ain't our fault, is the way I look at it."

There was a pause. The women stared at each other in the mirror.

"Who was it?" demanded Mrs. Fletcher.

"Honey, I really couldn't say," said Leota. "Not that you look it."

"Where's Thelma? I'll get it out of her," said Mrs. Fletcher.

"Now, honey, I wouldn't go and git mad over a little thing like that," Leota said, combing hastily, as though to hold Mrs. Fletcher down by the hair. "I'm sure it was somebody didn't mean no harm in the world. How far gone are you?"

"Just wait," said Mrs. Fletcher, and shrieked for Thelma, who came in and took a drag from Leota's cigarette.

"Thelma, honey, throw your mind back to yestiddy if you kin," said Leota, drenching Mrs. Fletcher's hair with a thick fluid and catching the overflow in a cold wet towel at her neck.

"Well, I got my lady half wound for a spiral," said Thelma doubtfully.

"This won't take but a minute," said Leota. "Who is it you got in there, old Horse Face? Just cast your mind back and try to remember who your lady was yestiddy who happ'm to mention that my customer was pregnant, that's all. She's dead to know."

Thelma drooped her blood-red lips and looked over Mrs. Fletcher's head into the mirror. "Why, honey, I ain't got the faintest," she breathed. "I really don't recollect the faintest. But I'm sure she meant no harm. I declare, I forgot my hair finally got combed and thought it was a stranger behind me."

"Was it that Mrs. Hutchinson?" Mrs. Fletcher was tensely polite.

"Mrs. Hutchinson? Oh, Mrs. Hutchinson." Thelma batted her eyes. "Naw, precious, she come on Thursday and didn't ev'm mention your name. I doubt if she ev'm knows you're on the way."

"Thelma!" cried Leota staunchly.

"All I know is, whoever it is 'll be sorry some day. Why, I just barely knew it myself!" cried Mrs. Fletcher. "Just let her wait!"

"Why? What're you gonna do to her?"

It was a child's voice, and the women looked down. A little boy was making tents with aluminum wave pinchers on the floor under the sink.

"Billy Boy, hon, mustn't bother nice ladies," Leota smiled. She slapped him brightly and behind her back waved Thelma out of the booth. "Ain't Billy Boy a sight? Only three years old and already just nuts about the beauty-parlor business."

"I never saw him here before," said Mrs. Fletcher, still unmollified.

"He ain't been here before, that's how come," said Leota. "He belongs to Mrs. Pike. She got her a job but it was Fay's Millinery. He oughtn't to try on those ladies' hats, they come down over his eyes like I don't know what. They just git to look ridiculous, that's what, an' of course he's gonna put 'em on: hats. They tole Mrs. Pike they didn't appreciate him hangin' around there. Here, he couldn't hurt a thing."

"Well! I don't like children that much," said Mrs. Fletcher.

"Well!" said Leota moodily.

"Well! I'm almost tempted not to have this one," said Mrs. Fletcher. "That Mrs. Hutchinson! Just looks straight through you when she sees you on the street and then spits at you behind your back."

"Mr. Fletcher would beat you on the head if you didn't have it now," said Leota reasonably. "After going this far."

Mrs. Fletcher sat up straight. "Mr. Fletcher can't do a thing with me."

"He can't!" Leota winked at herself in the mirror.

"No, siree, he can't. If he so much as raises his voice against me, he knows good and well I'll have one of my sick headaches, and then I'm just not fit to live with. And if I really look that pregnant already —"

"Well, now, honey, I just want you to know — I habm't told any of my ladies and I ain't goin' to tell 'em — even that you're losin' your hair. You just get you one of those Stork-a-Lure dresses and stop worryin'. What people don't know don't hurt nobody, as Mrs. Pike says."

"Did you tell Mrs. Pike?" asked Mrs. Fletcher sulkily.

"Well, Mrs. Fletcher, look, you ain't ever goin' to lay eyes on Mrs. Pike or her lay eyes on you, so what diffunce does it make in the long run?"

"I knew it!" Mrs. Fletcher deliberately nodded her head so as to destroy a ringlet Leota was working on behind her ear. "Mrs. Pike!"

Leota sighed. "I reckon I might as well tell you. It wasn't any more Thelma's lady tole me you was pregnant than a bat."

"Not Mrs. Hutchinson?"

"Naw, Lord! It was Mrs. Pike."

"Mrs. Pike!" Mrs. Fletcher could only sputter and let curling fluid roll into her ear. "How could Mrs. Pike possibly know I was pregnant or otherwise, when she doesn't even know me? The nerve of some people!"

"Well, here's how it was. Remember Sunday?"

"Yes," said Mrs. Fletcher.

"Sunday, Mrs. Pike an' me was all by ourself. Mr. Pike and Fred had gone over to Eagle Lake, sayin' they was goin' to catch 'em some fish, but they didn't a course. So we was settin' in Mrs. Pike's car, it's a 1939 Dodge —"

"1939, eh," said Mrs. Fletcher.

"— An' we was gettin' us a Jax beer apiece — that's the beer that Mrs. Pike says is made right in N.O., so she won't drink no other kind. So I seen you drive up to the drugstore an' run in for just a secont, leavin' I reckon Mr. Fletcher in the car, an' come runnin' out with looked like a perscription. So I says to Mrs. Pike, just to be makin' talk, 'Right yonder's Mrs. Fletcher, and I reckon that's Mr. Fletcher — she's one of my regular customers,' I says."

"I had on a figured print," said Mrs. Fletcher tentatively.

"You sure did," agreed Leota. "So Mrs. Pike, she give you a good look — she's very observant, a good judge of character, cute as a minute, you know — and she says, 'I bet you another Jax that lady's three months on the way.'"

"What gall!" said Mrs. Fletcher. "Mrs. Pike!"

"Mrs. Pike ain't goin' to bite you," said Leota. "Mrs. Pike is a lovely girl, you'd be crazy about her, Mrs. Fletcher. But she can't sit still a minute. We went to the travellin' freak show yestiddy after work. I got through early — nine o'clock. In the vacant store next door. What, you ain't been?"

"No, I despise freaks," declared Mrs. Fletcher.

"Aw. Well, honey, talkin' about bein' pregnant an' all, you ought to see those twins in a bottle, you really owe it to yourself."

"What twins?" asked Mrs. Fletcher out of the side of her mouth.

"Well, honey, they got these two twins in a bottle, see? Born joined plumb together — dead a course." Leota dropped her voice into a soft lyrical hum. "They was about this long — pardon — must of been full time, all right, wouldn't you say? — an' they had these two heads an' two faces an' four arms an' four legs, all kind of joined *here*. See, this face looked this-a-way, and the other face looked that-a-way, over their shoulder, see. Kinda pathetic."

"Glah!" said Mrs. Fletcher disapprovingly.

"Well, ugly? Honey, I mean to tell you — their parents was first cousins and all like that. Billy Boy, git me a fresh towel from off Teeny's stack — this 'n's wringin' wet — an' quit ticklin' my ankles with that curler. I declare! He don't miss nothin'."

"Me and Mr. Fletcher aren't one speck of kin, or he could never of had me," said Mrs. Fletcher placidly.

"Of course not!" protested Leota. "Neither is me an' Fred, not that we know of. Well, honey, what Mrs. Pike liked was the pygmies. They've got these pygmies down there, too, an' Mrs. Pike was just wild about 'em. You know, the teeniest men in the universe? Well, honey, they can just rest back on their little bohunkus an' roll around an' you can't hardly tell if they're sittin' or standin'. That'll give you some idea. They're about forty-two years old. Just suppose it was your husband!"

"Well, Mr. Fletcher is five foot nine and one half," said Mrs. Fletcher quickly.

"Fred's five foot ten," said Leota, "but I tell him he's still a shrimp, account of I'm so tall." She made a deep wave over Mrs. Fletcher's other temple with the comb. "Well, these pygmies are a kind of a dark brown, Mrs. Fletcher. Not bad-lookin' for what they are, you know."

"I wouldn't care for them," said Mrs. Fletcher. "What does that Mrs. Pike see in them?"

"Aw, I don't know," said Leota. "She's just cute, that's all. But they got this man, this petrified man, that ever'thing ever since he was nine years old, when it goes through his digestion, see, somehow Mrs. Pike says it goes to his joints and has been turning to stone."

"How awful!" said Mrs. Fletcher.

"He's forty-two too. That looks like a bad age."

"Who said so, that Mrs. Pike? I bet she's forty-two," said Mrs. Fletcher.

"Naw," said Leota, "Mrs. Pike's thirty-three, born in January, an Aquarian. He could move his head — like this. A course his head and mind ain't a joint, so to speak, and I guess his stomach ain't, either — not yet, anyways. But see — his food, he eats it, and it goes down, see, and then he digests it" — Leota rose on her toes for an instant — "and it goes out to his joints and before you can say 'Jack Robinson,' it's stone — pure stone. He's turning to stone. How'd you like to be married to a guy like that? All he can do, he can move his head just a quarter of an inch. A course he *looks* just *terrible.*"

"I should think he would," said Mrs. Fletcher frostily. "Mr. Fletcher takes bending exercises every night of the world. I make him."

"All Fred does is lay around the house like a rug. I wouldn't be surprised if he woke up some day and couldn't move. The petrified man just sat there moving his quarter of an inch though," said Leota reminiscently.

"Did Mrs. Pike like the petrified man?" asked Mrs. Fletcher.

"Not as much as she did the others," said Leota deprecatingly. "And then she likes a man to be a good dresser, and all that."

"Is Mr. Pike a good dresser?" asked Mrs. Fletcher sceptically.

"Oh, well, yeah," said Leota, "but he's twelve or fourteen years older'n her. She ast Lady Evangeline about him."

"Who's Lady Evangeline?" asked Mrs. Fletcher.

"Well, it's this mind reader they got in the freak show," said Leota. "Was real good. Lady Evangeline is her name, and if I had another dollar I wouldn't do a thing but have my other palm read. She had what Mrs. Pike said was the 'sixth mind' but she had the worst manicure I ever saw on a living person."

"What did she tell Mrs. Pike?" asked Mrs. Fletcher.

"She told her Mr. Pike was as true to her as he could be and besides, would come into some money."

"Humph!" said Mrs. Fletcher. "What does he do?"

"I can't tell," said Leota, "because he don't work. Lady Evangeline didn't tell me enough about my nature or anything. And I would like to go back and find out some more about this boy. Used to go with this boy until he got married to this girl. Oh, shoot, that was about three and a half years ago, when you was still goin' to the Robert E. Lee Beauty Shop in Jackson. He married her for her money. Another fortune-teller tole me that at the time. So I'm not in love with him any more, anyway, besides being married to Fred, but Mrs. Pike thought, just for the hell of it, see, to ask Lady Evangeline was he happy."

"Does Mrs. Pike know everything about you already?" asked Mrs. Fletcher unbelievingly. "Mercy!"

"Oh, yeah, I tole her ever'thing about ever'thing, from now on back to I don't know when — to when I first started goin' out," said Leota. "So I ast Lady Evangeline for one of my questions, was he happily married, and she says, just like she was glad I ask her, 'Honey,' she says, 'naw, he idn't. You write down this day, March 8, 1941,' she says, 'and mock it down: three years from today him and her won't be occupyin' the same bed.' There it is, up on the wall with them other dates — see, Mrs. Fletcher? And she says, 'Child, you ought to be glad you didn't git him, because he's so mercenary.' So I'm glad I married Fred. He sure ain't mercenary, money don't mean a thing to him. But I sure would like to go back and have my other palm read."

"Did Mrs. Pike believe in what the fortuneteller said?" asked Mrs. Fletcher in a superior tone of voice.

"Lord, yes, she's from New Orleans. Ever'body in New Orleans believes ever'thing spooky. One of 'em in New Orleans before it was raided says to Mrs. Pike one summer she was goin' to go from State to State and meet some grey-headed men, and, sure enough, she says she went on a beautician convention up to Chicago. . . ."

"Oh!" said Mrs. Fletcher. "Oh, is Mrs. Pike a beautician too?"

"Sure she is," protested Leota. "She's a beautician. I'm goin' to git her in here if I can. Before she married. But it don't leave you. She says sure enough, there was three men who was a very large part of making her trip what it was, and they all three had grey in their hair and they went in six States. Got Christmas cards from 'em. Billy Boy, go see if Thelma's got any dry cotton. Look how Mrs. Fletcher's a-drippin'."

"Where did Mrs. Pike meet Mr. Pike?" asked Mrs. Fletcher primly.

"On another train," said Leota.

"I met Mr. Fletcher, or rather he met me, in a rental library," said Mrs. Fletcher with dignity, as she watched the net come down over her head.

"Honey, me an' Fred, we met in a rumble seat eight months ago and we was practically on what you might call the way to the altar inside of half an hour," said Leota in a guttural voice, and bit a bobby pin open. "Course it don't last. Mrs. Pike says nothin' like that ever lasts."

"Mr. Fletcher and myself are as much in love as the day we married," said Mrs. Fletcher belligerently as Leota stuffed cotton into her ears.

"Mrs. Pike says it don't last," repeated Leota in a louder voice. "Now go git under the dryer. You can turn yourself on, can't you? I'll be back to comb you out. Durin' lunch I promised to give Mrs. Pike a facial. You know — free. Her bein' in the business, so to speak."

"I bet she needs one," said Mrs. Fletcher, letting the swing-door fly back against Leota. "Oh, pardon me."

A week later, on time for her appointment, Mrs. Fletcher sank heavily into Leota's chair after first removing a drug-store rental book, called *Life Is Like That,* from the seat. She stared in a discouraged way into the mirror.

"You can tell it when I'm sitting down, all right," she said.

Leota seemed preoccupied and stood shaking out a lavender cloth. She began to pin it around Mrs. Fletcher's neck in silence.

"I said you sure can tell it when I'm sitting straight on and coming at you this way," Mrs. Fletcher said.

"Why, honey, naw you can't," said Leota gloomily. "Why, I'd never know. If somebody was to come up to me on the street and say, 'Mrs. Fletcher is pregnant!' I'd say, 'Heck, she don't look it to me.'"

"If a certain party hadn't found it out and spread it around, it wouldn't be too late even now," said Mrs. Fletcher frostily, but Leota was almost choking her with the cloth, pinning it so tight, and she couldn't speak clearly. She paddled her hands in the air until Leota wearily loosened her.

"Listen, honey, you're just a virgin compared to Mrs. Montjoy," Leota was going on, still absent-minded. She bent Mrs. Fletcher back in the chair and, sighing, tossed liquid from a teacup on to her head and dug both hands into her scalp. "You know Mrs. Montjoy — her husband's that premature-grey-headed fella?"

"She's in the Trojan Garden Club, is all I know," said Mrs. Fletcher.

"Well, honey," said Leota, but in a weary voice, "she come in here not the week before and not the day before she had her baby — she come in here the very selfsame day, I mean to tell you. Child, we was all plumb scared to death. There she was! Come for her shampoo an' set. Why, Mrs. Fletcher, in an hour an' twenty minutes she was layin' up there in the Babtist Hospital with a seb'm-pound son. It was that close a shave. I declare, if I hadn't been so tired I would of drank up a bottle of gin that night."

"What gall," said Mrs. Fletcher. "I never knew her at all well."

"See, her husband was waitin' outside in the car, and her bags was all packed an' in the back seat, an' she was all ready, 'cept she wanted her sham-poo an' set. An' havin' one pain right after another. Her husband kep' comin' in here, scared-like, but couldn't do nothin' with her a course. She yelled bloody murder, too, but she always yelled her head off when I give her a perm'nent."

"She must of been crazy," said Mrs. Fletcher. "How did she look?"

"Shoot!" said Leota.

"Well, I can guess," said Mrs. Fletcher. "Awful."

"Just wanted to look pretty while she was havin' her baby, is all," said

Leota airily. "Course, we was glad to give the lady what she was after — that's our motto — but I bet a hour later she wasn't payin' no mind to them little end curls. I bet she wasn't thinkin' about she ought to have on a net. It wouldn't of done her no good if she had."

"No, I don't suppose it would," said Mrs. Fletcher.

"Yeah man! She was a-yellin'. Just like when I give her perm'nent."

"Her husband ought to make her behave. Don't it seem that way to you?" asked Mrs. Fletcher. "He ought to put his foot down."

"Ha," said Leota. "A lot he could do. Maybe some women is soft."

"Oh, you mistake me, I don't mean for her to get soft — far from it! Women have to stand up for themselves, or there's just no telling. But now you take me — I ask Mr. Fletcher's advice now and then, and he appreciates it, especially on something important, like is it time for a permanent — not that I've told him about the baby. He says, 'Why, dear, go ahead!' Just ask their *advice*."

"Huh! If I ever ast Fred's advice we'd be floatin' down the Yazoo River on a houseboat or somethin' by this time," said Leota. "I'm sick of Fred. I told him to go over to Vicksburg."

"Is he going?" demanded Mrs. Fletcher.

"Sure. See, the fortune-teller — I went back and had my other palm read, since we've got to rent the room agin — said my lover was goin' to work in Vicksburg, so I don't know who she could mean, unless she meant Fred. And Fred ain't workin' here — that much is so."

"Is he going to work in Vicksburg?" asked Mrs. Fletcher. "And —"

"Sure. Lady Evangeline said so. Said the future is going to be brighter than the present. He don't want to go, but I ain't gonna put up with nothin' like that. Lays around the house an' bulls — did bull — with that good-for-nothin' Mr. Pike. He says if he goes who'll cook, but I says I never get to eat anyway — not meals. Billy Boy, take Mrs. Grover that *Screen Secrets* and leg it."

Mrs. Fletcher heard stamping feet go out the door.

"Is that that Mrs. Pike's little boy here again?" she asked, sitting up gingerly.

"Yeah, that's still him." Leota stuck out her tongue.

Mrs. Fletcher could hardly believe her eyes. "Well! How's Mrs. Pike, your attractive new friend with the sharp eyes who spreads it around town that perfect strangers are pregnant?" she asked in a sweetened tone.

"Oh, Mizziz Pike." Leota combed Mrs. Fletcher's hair with heavy strokes.

"You act like you're tired," said Mrs. Fletcher.

"Tired? Feel like it's four o'clock in the afternoon already," said Leota. "I ain't told you the awful luck we had, me and Fred? It's the worst thing you ever heard of. Maybe *you* think Mrs. Pike's got sharp eyes. Shoot, there's a limit! Well, you know, we rented out our room to this Mr. and Mrs. Pike from New Orleans when Sal an' Joe Fentress got mad at us 'cause they drank up some home-brew we had in the closet — Sal an' Joe did. So, a week ago Sat'day Mr. and Mrs. Pike moved in. Well, I kinda fixed up the room, you know — put a sofa pillow on the couch and picked some ragged robbins and put in a vase, but they never did say they appreciated it. Anyway, then I put some old magazines on the table."

"I think that was lovely," said Mrs. Fletcher.

"Wait. So, come night 'fore last, Fred and this Mr. Pike, who Fred just took up with, was back from they said they was fishin', bein' as neither one of 'em has got a job to his name, and we was all settin' around in their room. So Mrs. Pike was settin' there readin' a old *Startling G-Man Tales* that was mine, mind you, I'd bought it myself, and all of a sudden she jumps! — into the air — you'd 'a' thought she'd set on a spider — an' says, 'Canfield' — ain't that silly, that's Mr. Pike — 'Canfield, my God A'mighty,' she says, 'honey,' she says, 'we're rich, and you won't have to work.' Not that he turned one hand anyway. Well, me and Fred rushes over to her, and Mr. Pike, too, and there she sets, pointin' her finger at a photo in my copy of *Startling G-Man.* 'See that man?' yells Mrs. Pike. 'Remember him, Canfield?' 'Never forget a face,' says Mr. Pike. 'It's Mr. Petrie, that we stayed with him in the apartment next to ours in Toulouse Street in N.O. for six weeks. Mr. Petrie.' 'Well,' says Mrs. Pike, like she can't hold out one secont longer, 'Mr. Petrie is wanted for five hundred dollars cash, for rapin' four women in California, and I know where he is.'"

"Mercy!" said Mrs. Fletcher. "Where was he?"

At some time Leota had washed her hair and now she yanked her up by the back locks and sat her up.

"Know where he was?"

"I certainly don't," Mrs. Fletcher said. Her scalp hurt all over.

Leota flung a towel around the top of her customer's head. "Nowhere else but in that freak show! I saw him just as plain as Mrs. Pike. *He* was the petrified man!"

"Who would ever have thought that!" cried Mrs. Fletcher sympathetically.

"So Mr. Pike says, 'Well whatta you know about that,' an' he looks real hard at the photo and whistles. And she starts dancin' and singin' about their good luck. She meant our bad luck! I made a point of tellin' that fortune-teller the next time I saw her. I said, 'Listen, that magazine was layin' around the house for a month, and there was the freak show runnin' night an' day, not two steps away from my own beauty parlor, with Mr. Petrie just settin' there waitin'. An' it had to be Mr. and Mrs. Pike, almost perfect strangers.'"

"What gall," said Mrs. Fletcher. She was only sitting there, wrapped in a turban, but she did not mind.

"Fortune-tellers don't care. And Mrs. Pike, she goes around actin' like she thinks she was Mrs. God," said Leota. "So they're goin' to leave tomorrow, Mr. and Mrs. Pike. And in the meantime I got to keep that mean, bad little ole kid here, gettin' under my feet ever' minute of the day an' talkin' back too."

"Have they gotten the five hundred dollars' reward already?" asked Mrs. Fletcher.

"Well," said Leota, "at first Mr. Pike didn't want to do anything about it. Can you feature that? Said he kinda liked that ole bird and said he was real nice to 'em, lent 'em money or somethin'. But Mrs. Pike simply tole him he could just go to hell, and I can see her point. She says, 'You ain't worked a lick in six months, and here I make five hundred dollars in two seconts, and what thanks do I get for it? You go to hell, Canfield,' she says. So," Leota went on in a despondent voice, "they called up the cops and they caught the ole bird, all right, right there in the freak show where I saw him with my own eyes, thinkin' he was petrified. He's the one. Did it under his real name — Mr. Petrie.

Four women in California, all in the month of August. So Mrs. Pike gits five hundred dollars. And my magazine, and right next door to my beauty parlor. I cried all night, but Fred said it wasn't a bit of use and to go to sleep, because the whole thing was just a sort of coincidence—you know: can't do nothin' about it. He says it put him clean out of the notion of goin' to Vicksburg for a few days till we rent out the room again — no tellin' who we'll git this time."

"But can you imagine anybody knowing this old man, that's raped four women?" persisted Mrs. Fletcher, and she shuddered audibly. "Did Mrs. Pike *speak* to him when she met him in the freak show?"

Leota had begun to comb Mrs. Fletcher's hair. "I says to her, I says, 'I didn't notice you fallin' on his neck when he was the petrified man — don't tell me you didn't recognize your fine friend?' And she says, 'I didn't recognize him with that white powder all over his face. He just looked familiar.' Mrs. Pike says, 'and lots of people look familiar.' But she says that ole petrified man did put her in mind of somebody. She wondered who it was! Kep' her awake, which man she'd ever knew it reminded her of. So when she seen the photo, it all come to her. Life a flash. Mr. Petrie. The way he'd turn his head and look at her when she took him in his breakfast."

"Took him in his breakfast!" shrieked Mrs. Fletcher. "Listen — don't tell me. I'd 'a' felt something."

"Four women. I guess those women didn't have the faintest notion at the time they'd be worth a hundred an' twenty-five bucks a piece some day to Mrs. Pike. We ast her how old the fella was then, an' she says he musta had one foot in the grave, at least. Can you beat it?"

"Not really petrified at all, of course," said Mrs. Fletcher meditatively. She drew herself up. "I'd 'a' felt something," she said proudly.

"Shoot! I did feel somethin'," said Leota. "I tole Fred when I got home I felt so funny. I said, 'Fred, that ole petrified man sure did leave me with a funny feelin'.' He says, 'Funny-haha or funny-peculiar?' and I says, 'Funny-peculiar.'" She pointed her comb into the air emphatically.

"I'll bet you did," said Mrs. Fletcher.

They both heard a crackling noise.

Leota screamed, "Billy Boy! What you doin' in my purse?"

"Aw, I'm just eatin' these ole stale peanuts up," said Billy Boy.

"You come here to me!" screamed Leota, recklessly flinging down the comb, which scattered a whole ashtray full of bobby pins and knocked down a row of Coca-Cola bottles. "This is the last straw!"

"I caught him! I caught him!" giggled Mrs. Fletcher. "I'll hold him on my lap. You bad, bad boy, you! I guess I better learn how to spank little old bad boys," she said.

Leota's eleven o'clock customer pushed open the swing-door upon Leota paddling him heartily with the brush, while he gave angry but belittling screams which penetrated beyond the booth and filled the whole curious beauty parlor. From everywhere ladies began to gather round to watch the paddling. Billy Boy kicked both Leota and Mrs. Fletcher as hard as he could, Mrs. Fletcher with her new fixed smile.

Billy Boy stomped through the group of wildhaired ladies and went out the door, but flung back the words, "If you're so smart, why ain't you rich?"

Bernard Malamud (b. 1914)

ANGEL LEVINE   1955

Manischevitz, a tailor, in his fifty-first year suffered many reverses and indignities. Previously a man of comfortable means, he overnight lost all he had, when his establishment caught fire and, after a metal container of cleaning fluid exploded, burned to the ground. Although Manischevitz was insured against fire, damage suits by two customers who had been hurt in the flames deprived him of every penny he had collected. At almost the same time, his son, of much promise, was killed in the war, and his daughter, without so much as a word of warning, married a lout and disappeared with him as off the face of the earth. Thereafter Manischevitz was victimized by excruciating backaches and found himself unable to work even as a presser — the only kind of work available to him — for more than an hour or two daily, because beyond that the pain from standing became maddening. His Fanny, a good wife and mother, who had taken in washing and sewing, began before his eyes to waste away. Suffering shortness of breath, she at last became seriously ill and took to her bed. The doctor, a former customer of Manischevitz, who out of pity treated them, at first had difficulty diagnosing her ailment but later put it down as hardening of the arteries at an advanced stage. He took Manischevitz aside, prescribed complete rest for her, and in whispers gave him to know there was little hope.

Throughout his trials Manischevitz had remained somewhat stoic, almost unbelieving that all this had descended upon his head, as if it were happening, let us say, to an acquaintance or some distant relative; it was in sheer quantity of woe incomprehensible. It was also ridiculous, unjust, and because he had always been a religious man, it was in a way an affront to God. Manischevitz believed this in all his suffering. When his burden had grown too crushingly heavy to be borne he prayed in his chair with shut hollow eyes: "My dear God, sweetheart, did I deserve that this should happen to me?" Then recognizing the worthlessness of it, he put aside the complaint and prayed humbly for assistance: "Give Fanny back her health, and to me for myself that I shouldn't feel pain in every step. Help now or tomorrow is too late. This I don't have to tell you." And Manischevitz wept.

Manischevitz's flat, which he had moved into after the disastrous fire, was a meager one, furnished with a few sticks of chairs, a table, and bed, in one of the poorer sections of the city. There were three rooms: a small, poorly-papered living room; an apology for a kitchen, with a wooden icebox; and the comparatively large bedroom where Fanny lay in a sagging secondhand bed, gasping for breath. The bedroom was the warmest room of the house and it was here, after his outburst to God, that Manischevitz, by the light of two small bulbs overhead, sat reading his Jewish newspaper. He was not truly reading, because his thoughts were everywhere; however the print offered a convenient resting place for his eyes, and a word or two, when he permitted himself to comprehend them, had the momentary effect of helping him forget his troubles. After a short while he discovered, to his surprise, that he was actively scanning the news, searching for an item of great interest to him. Exactly what he thought he would read he couldn't say — until he realized, with some astonishment, that he was expecting to discover something about himself. Manischevitz put his paper down and looked up with the distinct impression that someone had entered the apartment, though he could not remember having heard the sound of the door opening. He looked around: the room was very still, Fanny sleeping, for once, quietly. Half-frightened, he watched her until he was satisfied she wasn't dead; then, still disturbed by the thought of an unannounced visitor, he stumbled into the living room and there had the shock of his life, for at the table sat a Negro reading a newspaper he had folded up to fit into one hand.

"What do you want here?" Manischevitz asked in fright.

The Negro put down the paper and glanced up with a gentle expression. "Good evening." He seemed not to be sure of himself, as if he had got into the wrong house. He was a large man, bonily built, with a heavy head covered by a hard derby, which he made no attempt to remove. His eyes seemed sad, but his lips, above which he wore a slight mustache, sought to smile; he was not otherwise prepossessing. The cuffs of his sleeves, Manischevitz noted, were frayed to the lining and the dark suit was badly fitted. He had very large feet. Recovering from his fright, Manischevitz guessed he had left the door open and was being visited by a case worker from the Welfare Department — some came at night — for he had recently applied for relief. Therefore he lowered himself into a chair opposite the Negro, trying, before the man's uncertain smile, to feel comfortable. The former tailor sat stiffly but patiently at the table, waiting for the investigator to take out his pad and pencil and begin asking questions; but before long he became convinced the man intended to do nothing of the sort.

"Who are you?" Manischevitz at last asked uneasily.

"If I may, insofar as one is able to, identify myself, I bear the name of Alexander Levine."

In spite of all his troubles Manischevitz felt a smile growing on his lips. "You said Levine?" he politely inquired.

The Negro nodded. "That is exactly right."

Carrying the jest farther, Manischevitz asked, "You are maybe Jewish?"

"All my life I was, willingly."

The tailor hesitated. He had heard of black Jews but had never met one. It gave an unusual sensation.

Recognizing in afterthought something odd about the tense of Levine's remark, he said doubtfully, "You ain't Jewish anymore?"

Levine at this point removed his hat, revealing a very white part in his black hair, but quickly replaced it. He replied, "I have recently been disincarnated into an angel. As such, I offer you my humble assistance, if to offer is within my province and ability — in the best sense." He lowered his eyes in apology. "Which calls for added explanation: I am what I am granted to be, and at present the completion is in the future."

"What kind of angel is this?" Manischevitz gravely asked.

"A bona fide angel of God, within prescribed limitations," answered Levine, "not to be confused with the members of any particular sect, order, or organization here on earth operating under a similar name."

Manischevitz was thoroughly disturbed. He had been expecting something but not this. What sort of mockery was it — provided Levine was an angel — of a faithful servant who had from childhood lived in the synagogues, always concerned with the word of God?

To test Levine he asked, "Then where are your wings?"

The Negro blushed as well as he was able. Manischevitz understood this from his changed expression. "Under certain circumstances we lose privileges and prerogatives upon returning to earth, no matter for what purpose, or endeavoring to assist whosoever."

"So tell me," Manischevitz said triumphantly, "how did you get here?"

"I was transmitted."

Still troubled, the tailor said, "If you are a Jew, say the blessing for bread."

Levine recited it in sonorous Hebrew.

Although moved by the familiar words Manischevitz still felt doubt that he was dealing with an angel.

"If you are an angel," he demanded somewhat angrily, "give me the proof."

Levine wet his lips. "Frankly, I cannot perform either miracles or near miracles, due to the fact that I am in a condition of probation. How long that will persist or even consist, I admit, depends on the outcome."

Manischevitz racked his brains for some means of causing Levine positively to reveal his true identity, when the Negro spoke again:

"It was given me to understand that both your wife and you require assistance of a salubrious nature?"

The tailor could not rid himself of the feeling that he was the butt of a jokester. Is this what a Jewish angel looks like? he asked himself. This I am not convinced.

He asked a last question. "So if God sends to me an angel, why a black? Why not a white that there are so many of them?"

"It was my turn to go next," Levine explained.

Manischevitz could not be persuaded. "I think you are a faker."

Levine slowly rose. His eyes showed disappointment and worry. "Mr. Manischevitz," he said tonelessly, "if you should desire me to be of assistance to you any time in the near future, or possibly before, I can be found" — he glanced at his fingernails — "in Harlem."

He was by then gone.

The next day Manischevitz felt some relief from his backache and was able to work four hours at pressing. The day after, he put in six hours; and the third day four again. Fanny sat up a little and asked for some halvah to suck. But on the fourth day the stabbing, breaking ache afflicted his back, and Fanny again lay supine, breathing with blue-lipped difficulty.

Manischevitz was profoundly disappointed at the return of his active pain and suffering. He had hoped for a longer interval of easement, long enough to have some thought other than of himself and his troubles. Day by day, hour by hour, minute after minute, he lived in pain, pain his only memory, questioning the necessity of it, inveighing against it, also, though with affection, against God. Why *so much*, Gottenyu°? If He wanted to teach His servant a lesson for some reason, some cause — the nature of His nature — to teach him, say, for reasons of his weakness, his pride, perhaps, during his years of prosperity, his frequent neglect of God — to give him a little lesson,

Gottenyu: "an exclamation that is uttered with affection, despair, or irony . . . a warm, informal, personal way of enlisting God's attention" (Leo Rosten, *The Joys of Yiddish.* New York: McGraw-Hill, 1968).

why then any of the tragedies that had happened to him, any *one* would have sufficed to chasten him. But *all together* — the loss of both his children, his means of livelihood, Fanny's health and his — that was too much to ask one frail-boned man to endure. Who, after all, was Manischevitz that he had been given so much to suffer? A tailor. Certainly not a man of talent. Upon him suffering was largely wasted. It went nowhere, into nothing: into more suffering. His pain did not earn him bread, nor fill the cracks in the wall, nor lift, in the middle of the night, the kitchen table; only lay upon him, sleepless, so sharply, oppressively, that he could many times have cried out yet not heard himself through this thickness of misery.

In this mood he gave no thought to Mr. Alexander Levine, but at moments when the pain wavered, slightly diminishing, he sometimes wondered if he had been mistaken to dismiss him. A black Jew and angel to boot — very hard to believe, but suppose he *had* been sent to succor him, and he, Manischevitz, was in his blindness too blind to comprehend? It was this thought that put him on the knife-point of agony.

Therefore the tailor, after much self-questioning and continuing doubt, decided he would seek the self-styled angel in Harlem. Of course he had great difficulty, because he had not asked for specific directions, and movement was tedious to him. The subway took him to 116th Street, and from there he wandered in the dark world. It was vast and its lights lit nothing. Everywhere were shadows, often moving. Manischevitz hobbled along with the aid of a cane, and not knowing where to seek in the blackened tenement buildings, looked fruitlessly through store windows. In the stores he saw people and *everybody* was black. It was an amazing thing to observe. When he was too tired, too unhappy to go farther, Manischevitz stopped in front of a tailor's store. Out of familiarity with the appearance of it, with some sadness he entered. The tailor, an old skinny Negro with a mop of woolly gray hair, was sitting cross-legged on his workbench, sewing a pair of full-dress pants that had a razor slit all the way down the seat.

"You'll excuse me, please, gentleman," said Manischevitz, admiring the tailor's deft, thimbled fingerwork, "but you know maybe somebody by the name Alexander Levine?"

The tailor, who Manischevitz thought, seemed a little antagonistic to him, scratched his scalp.

"Cain't say I ever heared dat name."

"Alex-ander Lev-ine," Manischevitz repeated it.

The man shook his head. "Cain't say I heared."

About to depart, Manischevitz remembered to say: "He is an angel, maybe."

"Oh *him*," said the tailor clucking. "He hang out in dat honky tonk down here a ways." He pointed with his skinny finger and returned to the pants.

Manischevitz crossed the street against a red light and was almost run down by a taxi. On the block after the next, the sixth store from the corner was a cabaret, and the name in sparkling lights was Bella's. Ashamed to go in, Manischevitz gazed through the neon-lit window, and when the dancing couples had parted and drifted away, he discovered at a table on the side, towards the rear, Levine.

He was sitting alone, a cigarette butt hanging from the corner of his mouth, playing solitaire with a dirty pack of cards, and Manischevitz felt a touch of pity for him, for Levine had deteriorated in appearance. His derby was dented and had a gray smudge on the side. His ill-fitting suit was shabbier, as if he had been sleeping in it. His shoes and trouser cuffs were muddy, and his face was covered with an impenetrable stubble the color of licorice. Manischevitz, though deeply disappointed, was about to enter, when a big-breasted Negress in a purple evening gown appeared before Levine's table, and with much laughter through many white teeth, broke into a vigorous shimmy. Levine looked straight at Manischevitz with a haunted expression, but the tailor was too paralyzed to move or acknowledge it. As Bella's gyrations continued, Levine rose, his eyes lit in excitement. She embraced him with vigor, both his hands clasped around her big restless buttocks and they tangoed together across the floor, loudly applauded by the noisy customers. She seemed to have lifted Levine off his feet and his large shoes hung limp as they danced. They slid past the windows where Manischevitz, white-faced, stood staring in. Levine winked slyly and the tailor left for home.

.   .   .   .   .

Fanny lay at death's door. Through shrunken lips she muttered concerning her childhood, the sorrows of the marriage bed, the loss of her children, yet wept to live. Manischevitz tried not to listen, but even without ears he would have heard. It was not a gift. The doctor panted up the stairs, a broad but bland, unshaven man (it was Sunday), and soon shook his head. A day at most, or two. He left at once, not without pity, to spare himself Manischevitz's multiplied sorrow; the man who never stopped hurting. He would someday get him into a public home.

Manischevitz visited a synagogue and there spoke to God, but God had absented himself. The tailor searched his heart and found no hope. When she died he would live dead. He considered taking his life although he knew he wouldn't. Yet it was something to consider. Considering, you existed. He railed against God — Can you love a rock, a broom, an emptiness? Baring his chest, he smote the naked bones, cursing himself for having believed.

Asleep in a chair that afternoon, he dreamed of Levine. He was standing before a faded mirror, preening small decaying opalescent wings. "This means," mumbled Manischevitz, as he broke out of sleep, "that it is possible he could be an angel." Begging a neighbor lady to look in on Fanny and occasionally wet her lips with a few drops of water, he drew on his thin coat, gripped his walking stick, exchanged some pennies for a subway token, and rode to Harlem. He knew this act was the last desperate one of his woe: to go without belief, seeking a black magician to restore his wife to invalidism. Yet if there was no choice, he did at least what was chosen.

He hobbled to Bella's but the place had changed hands. It was now, as he breathed, a synagogue in a store. In the front, towards him, were several rows of empty wooden benches. In the rear stood the Ark, its portals of rough wood covered with rainbows of sequins; under it a long table on which lay the sacred scroll unrolled, illuminated by the dim light from a bulb on a chain overhead. Around the table, as if frozen to it and the scroll, which they all touched with their fingers, sat four Negroes wearing skullcaps. Now as they read the Holy Word, Manischevitz could, through the plate glass window, hear the singsong chant of their voices. One of them was old, with a gray beard. One was bubble-eyed. One was humpbacked. The fourth was a boy, no older than thirteen. Their heads moved in rhythmic swaying. Touched by this sight from his childhood and youth, Manischevitz entered and stood silent in the rear.

"Neshoma," said bubble eyes, pointing to the word with a stubby finger. "Now what dat mean?"

"That's the word that means soul," said the boy. He wore glasses.

"Let's git on wid de commentary," said the old man.

"Ain't necessary," said the humpback. "Souls is immaterial substance. That's all. The soul is derived in that manner. The immateriality is derived from the substance, and they both, causally an' otherwise, derived from the soul. There can be no higher."

"That's the highest."

"Over de top."

"Wait a minute," said bubble eyes. "I don't see what is dat immaterial substance. How come de one gits hitched up to de odder?" He addressed the humpback.

"Ask me something hard. Because it is substanceless immateriality. It couldn't be closer together, like all the parts of the body under one skin — closer."

"Hear now," said the old man.

"All you done is switched de words."

"It's the primum mobile, the substanceless substance from which comes all things that were incepted in the idea — you, me and everything and body else."

"Now how did all dat happen? Make it sound simple."

"It de speerit," said the old man. "On de face of de water moved de speerit. An' dat was good. It say so in de Book. From de speerit ariz de man."

"But now listen here. How come it become substance if it all de time a spirit?"

"God alone done dat."

"Holy! Holy! Praise His Name."

"But has dis spirit got some kind of a shade or color?" asked bubble eyes, deadpan.

"Man of course not. A spirit is a spirit."

"Then how come we is colored?" he said with a triumphant glare.

"Ain't got nothing to do wid dat."

"I still like to know."

"God put the spirit in all things," answered the boy. "He put it in the green leaves and the yellow flowers. He put it with the gold in the fishes and the blue in the sky. That's how come it came to us."

"Amen."

"Praise Lawd and utter loud His speechless name."

"Blow de bugle till it bust the sky."

They fell silent, intent upon the next word. Manischevitz approached them.

"You'll excuse me," he said. "I am looking for Alexander Levine. You know him maybe?"

"That's the angel," said the boy.

"Oh, *him*," snuffed bubble eyes.

"You'll find him at Bella's. It's the establishment right across the street," the humpback said.

Manischevitz said he was sorry that he could not stay, thanked them, and limped across the street. It was already night. The city was dark and he could barely find his way.

But Bella's was bursting with the blues. Through the window Manischevitz recognized the dancing crowd and among them sought Levine. He was sitting loose-lipped at Bella's side table. They were tippling from an almost empty whiskey fifth. Levine had shed his old clothes, wore a shiny new checkered suit, pearl-gray derby, cigar, and big, two-tone button shoes. To the tailor's dismay, a drunken look had settled upon his formerly dignified face. He leaned toward Bella, tickled her ear lobe with his pinky, while whispering words that sent her into gales of raucous laughter. She fondled his knee.

Manischevitz, girding himself, pushed open the door and was not welcomed.

"This place reserved."

"Beat it, pale puss."

"Exit, Yankel, Semitic trash."

But he moved towards the table where Levine sat, the crowd breaking before him as he hobbled forward.

"Mr. Levine," he spoke in a trembly voice. "Is here Manischevitz."

Levine glared blearily. "Speak yo' piece, son."

Manischevitz shuddered. His back plagued him. Cold tremors tormented his crooked legs. He looked around, everybody was all ears.

"You'll excuse me. I would like to talk to you in a private place."

"Speak, Ah is a private pusson."

Bella laughed piercingly. "Stop it, boy, you killin' me."

Manischevitz, no end disturbed, considered fleeing but Levine addressed him:

"Kindly state the pu'pose of yo' communication with yo's truly."

The tailor wet cracked lips. "You are Jewish. This I am sure."

Levine rose, nostrils flaring. "Anythin' else yo' got to say?"

Manischevitz's tongue lay like stone.

"Speak now or fo'ever hold off."

Tears blinded the tailor's eyes. Was ever man so tried? Should he say he believed a half-drunken Negro to be an angel?

The silence slowly petrified.

Manischevitz was recalling scenes of his youth as a wheel in his mind whirred: believe, do not, yes, no, yes, no. The pointer pointed to yes, to between yes and no, to no, no it was yes. He sighed. It moved but one had still to make a choice.

"I think you are an angel from God." He said it in a broken voice, thinking, If you said it it was said. If you believed it you must say it. If you believed, you believed.

The hush broke. Everybody talked but the music began and they went on dancing. Bella, grown bored, picked up the cards and dealt herself a hand.

Levine burst into tears. "How you have humiliated me."

Manischevitz apologized.

"Wait'll I freshen up." Levine went to the men's room and returned in his old clothes.

No one said goodbye as they left.

They rode to the flat via subway. As they walked up the stairs Manischevitz pointed with his cane at his door.

"That's all been taken care of," Levine said. "You best go in while I take off."

Disappointed that it was so soon over but torn by curiosity, Manischevitz followed the angel up three flights to the roof. When he got there the door was already padlocked.

Luckily he could see through a small broken window. He heard an odd noise, as though of a whirring of wings, and when he strained for a wider view, could have sworn he saw a dark figure borne aloft on a pair of magnificent black wings.

A feather drifted down. Manischevitz gasped as it turned white, but it was only snowing.

He rushed downstairs. In the flat Fanny wielded a dust mop under the bed and then upon the cobwebs on the wall.

"A wonderful thing, Fanny," Manischevitz said. "Believe me, there are Jews everywhere."

Joyce Carol Oates (b. 1938)

WHERE ARE YOU GOING, WHERE HAVE YOU BEEN? 1970

For Bob Dylan

Her name was Connie. She was fifteen and she had a quick nervous giggling habit of craning her neck to glance into mirrors, or checking other people's faces to make sure her own was all right. Her mother, who noticed everything and knew everything and who hadn't much reason any longer to look at her own face, always scolded Connie about it. "Stop gawking at yourself, who are you? You think you're so pretty?" she would say. Connie would raise her eyebrows at these familiar complaints and look right through her mother, into a shadowy vision of herself as she was right at that moment: she knew she was pretty and that was everything. Her mother had been pretty once too, if you could believe those old snapshots in the album, but now her looks were gone and that was why she was always after Connie.

"Why don't you keep your room clean like your sister? How've you got your hair fixed — what the hell stinks? Hair spray? You don't see your sister using that junk."

Her sister June was twenty-four and still lived at home. She was a secretary in the high school Connie attended, and if that wasn't bad enough —

with her in the same building — she was so plain and chunky and steady that Connie had to hear her praised all the time by her mother and her mother's sisters. June did this, June did that, she saved money and helped clean the house and cooked and Connie couldn't do a thing, her mind was all filled with trashy daydreams. Their father was away at work most of the time and when he came home he wanted supper and he read the newspaper at supper and after supper he went to bed. He didn't bother talking much to them, but around his bent head Connie's mother kept picking at her until Connie wished her mother was dead and she herself was dead and it was all over. "She makes me want to throw up sometimes," she complained to her friends. She had a high, breathless, amused voice which made everything she said sound a little forced, whether it was sincere or not.

There was one good thing: June went places with girl friends of hers, girls who were just as plain and steady as she, and so when Connie wanted to do that her mother had no objections. The father of Connie's best girl friend drove the girls the three miles to town and left them off at a shopping plaza, so that they could walk through the stores or go to a movie, and when he came to pick them up again at eleven he never bothered to ask what they had done.

They must have been familiar sights, walking around that shopping plaza in their shorts and flat ballerina slippers that always scuffed the sidewalk, with charm bracelets jingling on their thin wrists; they would lean together to whisper and laugh secretly if someone passed by who amused or interested them. Connie had long dark blond hair that drew anyone's eye to it, and she wore part of it pulled up on her head and puffed out and the rest of it she let fall down her back. She wore a pull-over jersey blouse that looked one way when she was at home and another way when she was away from home. Everything about her had two sides to it, one for home and one for anywhere that was not home: her walk that could be childlike and bobbing, or languid enough to make anyone think she was hearing music in her head, her mouth which was pale and smirking most of the time, but bright and pink on these evenings out, her laugh which was cynical and drawling at home — "Ha, ha, very funny" — but high-pitched and nervous anywhere else, like the jingling of the charms on her bracelet.

Sometimes they did go shopping or to a movie, but sometimes they went across the highway, ducking fast across the busy road, to a drive-in restaurant where older kids hung out. The restaurant was shaped like a big bottle, though squatter than a real bottle, and on its cap was a revolving figure of a grinning boy who held a hamburger aloft. One night in mid-summer they ran across, breathless with daring, and right away someone leaned out a car window and invited them over, but it was just a boy from high school they didn't like. It made them feel good to be able to ignore him. They went up through the maze of parked and cruising cars to the bright-lit, fly-infested restaurant, their faces pleased and expectant as if they were entering a sacred building that loomed out of the night to give them what haven and what blessing they yearned for. They sat at the counter and crossed their legs at the ankles, their thin shoulders rigid with excitement, and listened to the music that made everything so good: the music was always in the background like music at a church service, it was something to depend upon.

A boy named Eddie came in to talk with them. He sat backwards on his stool, turning himself jerkily around in semi-circles and then stopping and turning again, and after a while he asked Connie if she would like something to eat. She said she did and so she tapped her friend's arm on her way out — her friend pulled her face up into a brave droll look — and Connie said she would meet her at eleven, across the way. "I just hate to leave her like that," Connie said earnestly, but the boy said that she wouldn't be alone for long. So they went out to his car and on the way Connie couldn't help but let her eyes wander over the windshields and faces all around her, her face gleaming with a joy that had nothing to do with Eddie or even this place; it might have been the music. She drew her shoulders up and sucked in her breath with the pure pleasure of being alive, and just at that moment she happened to glance at a face just a few feet from hers. It was a boy with shaggy black hair, in a convertible jalopy painted gold. He stared at her and then his lips widened into a grin. Connie slit her eyes at him and turned away, but she couldn't help glancing back and there he was still watching her. He wagged a finger and laughed and said, "Gonna get you, baby," and Connie turned away again without Eddie noticing anything.

She spent three hours with him, at the restaurant where they ate hamburgers and drank Cokes in wax cups that were always sweating, and then down an alley a mile or so away, and when he left her off at five to eleven only the movie house was still open at the plaza. Her girl friend was there, talking with a boy. When Connie came up the two girls smiled at each other and Connie said, "How was the movie?" and the girl said, "*You* should know." They rode off with the girl's father, sleepy and pleased, and Connie couldn't help but look at the darkened shopping plaza with its big empty parking lot and its signs that were faded and ghostly now, and over at the drive-in restaurant where cars were still circling tirelessly. She couldn't hear the music at this distance.

Next morning June asked her how the movie was and Connie said, "So-so."

She and that girl and occasionally another girl went out several times a week that way, and the rest of the time Connie spent around the house — it was summer vacation — getting in her mother's way and thinking, dreaming, about the boys she met. But all the boys fell back and dissolved into a single face that was not even a face, but an idea, a feeling, mixed up with the urgent insistent pounding of the music and the humid night air of July. Connie's mother kept dragging her back to the daylight by finding things for her to do or saying, suddenly, "What's this about the Pettinger girl?"

And Connie would say nervously, "Oh, her. That dope." She always drew thick clear lines between herself and such girls, and her mother was simple and kindly enough to believe her. Her mother was so simple, Connie thought, that it was maybe cruel to fool her so much. Her mother went scuffling around the house in old bedroom slippers and complained over the telephone to one sister about the other, then the other called up and the two of them complained about the third one. If June's name was mentioned her mother's tone was approving, and if Connie's name was mentioned it was disapproving. This did not really mean she disliked Connie and actually Connie thought that her mother preferred her to June because she was prettier, but the two of them kept up a pretense of exasperation, a sense that they were tugging and struggling over something of little value to either of them. Sometimes, over coffee, they were almost friends, but something would come up — some vexation that was like a fly buzzing suddenly around their heads — and their faces went hard with contempt.

One Sunday Connie got up at eleven — none of them bothered with church — and washed her hair so that it could dry all day long, in the sun. Her parents and sister were going to a barbecue at an aunt's house and Connie said no, she wasn't interested, rolling her eyes to let her mother know just what she thought of it. "Stay home alone then," her mother said sharply. Connie sat out back in a lawn chair and watched them drive away, her father quiet and bald, hunched around so that he could back the car out, her mother with a look that was still angry and not at all softened through the windshield, and in the back seat poor old June all dressed up as if she didn't know what a barbecue was, with all the running yelling kids and the flies. Connie sat with her eyes closed in the sun, dreaming and dazed with the warmth about her as if this were a kind of love, the caresses of love, and her mind slipped over onto thoughts of the boy she had been with the night before and how nice he had been, how sweet it always was, not the way someone like June would suppose but sweet, gentle, the way it was in movies and promised in songs; and when she opened her eyes she hardly knew where she was, the back yard ran off into weeds and a fence-line of trees and behind it the sky was perfectly blue and still. The asbestos "ranch house" that was now three years old startled her — it looked small. She shook her head as if to get awake.

It was too hot. She went inside the house and turned on the radio to drown out the quiet. She sat on the edge of her bed, barefoot, and listened for an hour and a half to a program called XYZ Sunday Jamboree, record after record of hard, fast, shrieking songs she sang along with, interspersed by exclamations from "Bobby King": "An' look here you girls at Napoleon's — Son and Charley want you to pay real close attention to this song coming up!"

And Connie paid close attention herself, bathed in a glow of slow-pulsed joy that seemed to rise mysteriously out of the music itself and lay languidly about the airless little room, breathed in and breathed out with each gentle rise and fall of her chest.

After a while she heard a car coming up the drive. She sat up at once, startled, because it couldn't be her father so soon. The gravel kept crunching all the way in from the road — the driveway was long — and Connie ran to the window. It was a car she didn't know. It was an open jalopy, painted a bright gold that caught the sunlight opaquely. Her heart began to pound and her fingers snatched at her hair, checking it, and she whispered "Christ. Christ," wondering how bad she looked. The car came to a stop at the side door and the horn sounded four short taps as if this were a signal Connie knew.

She went into the kitchen and approached the door slowly, then hung out the screen door, her bare toes curling down off the step. There were two boys in the car and now she recognized the driver: he had shaggy, shabby black hair that looked crazy as a wig and he was grinning at her.

"I ain't late, am I?" he said.

"Who the hell do you think you are?" Connie said.

"Toldja I'd be out, didn't I?"

"I don't even know who you are."

She spoke sullenly, careful to show no interest or pleasure, and he spoke in a fast bright monotone. Connie looked past him to the other boy, taking her time. He had fair brown hair, with a lock that fell onto his forehead. His sideburns gave him a fierce, embarrassed look, but so far he hadn't even bothered to glance at her. Both boys wore sunglasses. The driver's glasses were metallic and mirrored everything in miniature.

"You wanta come for a ride?" he said.

Connie smirked and let her hair fall loose over one shoulder.

"Don'tcha like my car? New paint job," he said. "Hey."

"What?"

"You're cute."

She pretended to fidget, chasing flies away from the door.

"Don'tcha believe me, or what?" he said.

"Look, I don't even know who you are," Connie said in disgust.

"Hey, Ellie's got a radio, see. Mine's broke down." He lifted his friend's arm and showed her the little transistor the boy was holding, and now Connie began to hear the music. It was the same program that was playing inside the house.

"Bobby King?" she said.

"I listen to him all the time. I think he's great."

"He's kind of great," Connie said reluctantly.

"Listen, that guy's *great*. He knows where the action is."

Connie blushed a little, because the glasses made it impossible for her to see just what this boy was looking at. She couldn't decide if she liked him or if he was just a jerk, and so she dawdled in the doorway and wouldn't come down or go back inside. She said, "What's all that stuff painted on your car?"

"Can'tcha read it?" He opened the door very carefully, as if he was afraid it might fall off. He slid out just as carefully, planting his feet firmly on the ground, the tiny metallic world in his glasses slowing down like gelatine hardening and in the midst of it Connie's bright green blouse. "This here is my name, to begin with," he said. ARNOLD FRIEND was written in tar-like black letters on the side, with a drawing of a round grinning face that reminded Connie of a pumpkin, except it wore sunglasses. "I wanta introduce myself, I'm Arnold Friend and that's my real name and I'm gonna be your friend, honey, and inside the car's Ellie Oscar, he's kinda shy." Ellie brought his transistor radio up to his shoulder and balanced it there. "Now these numbers are a secret code, honey," Arnold Friend explained. He read off the numbers 33, 19, 17 and raised his eyebrows at her to see what she thought of that, but she didn't think much of it. The left rear fender had been smashed and around it was written, on the gleaming gold background: DONE BY CRAZY WOMAN DRIVER. Connie had to laugh at that. Arnold Friend was pleased at her laughter and looked up at her. "Around the other side's a lot more — you wanta come and see them?"

"No."

"Why not?"

"Why should I?"

"Don'tcha wanta see what's on the car? Don'tcha wanta go for a ride?"

"I don't know."

"Why not?"

"I got things to do."

"Like what?"

"Things."

He laughed as if she had said something funny. He slapped his thighs. He was standing in a strange way, leaning back against the car as if he were balancing himself. He wasn't tall, only an inch or so taller than she would be if she came down to him. Connie liked the way he was dressed, which was the way all of them dressed: tight faded jeans stuffed into black, scuffed boots, a belt that pulled his waist in and showed how lean he was, and a white pull-over shirt that was a little soiled and showed the hard small muscles of his arms and shoulders. He looked as if he probably did hard work, lifting and carrying things. Even his neck looked muscular. And his face was a familiar face, some-how: the jaw and chin and cheeks slightly darkened, because he hadn't shaved for a day or two, and the nose long and hawk-like, sniffing as if she were a treat he was going to gobble up and it was all a joke.

"Connie, you ain't telling the truth. This is your day set aside for a ride with me and you know it," he said, still laughing. The way he straightened and recovered from his fit of laughing showed that it had been all fake.

"How do you know what my name is?" she said suspiciously.

"It's Connie."

"Maybe and maybe not."

"I know my Connie," he said, wagging his finger. Now she remembered him even better, back at the restaurant, and her cheeks warmed at the thought of how she sucked in her breath just at the moment she passed him — how she must have looked to him. And he had remembered her. "Ellie and I come out here especially for you," he said. "Ellie can sit in back. How about it?"

"Where?"

"Where what?"

"Where're we going?"

He looked at her. He took off the sunglasses and she saw how pale the skin around his eyes was, like holes that were not in shadow but instead in light. His eyes were chips of broken glass that catch the light in an amiable way. He smiled. It was as if the idea of going for a ride somewhere, to some place, was a new idea to him.

"Just for a ride, Connie sweetheart."

"I never said my name was Connie," she said.

"But I know what it is. I know your name and all about you, lots of things," Arnold Friend said. He had not moved yet but stood still leaning back against the side of his jalopy. "I took a special interest in you, such a pretty girl, and found out all about you like I know your parents and sister are gone somewheres and I know where and how long they're going to be gone, and I know who you were with last night, and your best girl friend's name is Betty. Right?"

He spoke in a simple lilting voice, exactly as if he were reciting the words to a song. His smile assured her that everything was fine. In the car Ellie turned up the volume on his radio and did not bother to look around at them.

"Ellie can sit in the back seat," Arnold Friend said. He indicated his friend with a casual jerk of his chin, as if Ellie did not count and she should not bother with him.

"How'd you find out all that stuff?" Connie said.

"Listen: Betty Schultz and Tony Fitch and Jimmy Pettinger and Nancy Pettinger," he said, in a chant. "Raymond Stanley and Bob Hutter —"

"Do you know all those kids?"

"I know everybody."

"Look, you're kidding. You're not from around here."

"Sure."

"But — how come we never saw you before?"

"Sure you saw me before," he said. He looked down at his boots, as if he were a little offended. "You just don't remember."

"I guess I'd remember you," Connie said.

"Yeah?" He looked up at this, beaming. He was pleased. He began to mark time with the music from Ellie's radio, tapping his fists lightly together. Connie looked away from his smile to the car, which was painted so bright it almost hurt her eyes to look at it. She looked at that name, ARNOLD FRIEND. And up at the front fender was an expression that was familiar — MAN THE FLYING SAUCERS. It was an expression kids had used the year before, but didn't use this year. She looked at it for a while as if the words meant something to her that she did not yet know.

"What're you thinking about? Huh?" Arnold Friend demanded. "Not worried about your hair blowing around in the car, are you?"

"No."

"Think I maybe can't drive good?"

"How do I know?"

"You're a hard girl to handle. How come?" he said. "Don't you know I'm your friend? Didn't you see me put my sign in the air when you walked by?"

"What sign?"

"My sign." And he drew an X in the air, leaning out toward her. They were maybe ten feet apart. After his hand fell back to his side the X was still in the air, almost visible. Connie let the screen door close and stood perfectly still inside it, listening to the music from her radio and the boy's blend together. She stared at Arnold Friend. He stood there so stiffly relaxed, pretending to be relaxed, with one hand idly on the door handle as if he were keeping himself up that way and had no intention of ever moving again. She recognized most things about him, the tight jeans that showed his thighs and buttocks and the greasy leather boots and the tight shirt, and even that slippery friendly smile of his, that sleepy dreamy smile that all the boys used to get across ideas they didn't want to put into words. She recognized all this and also the singsong way he talked, slightly mocking, kidding, but serious and a little melancholy, and she recognized the way he tapped one fist against the other in homage to the perpetual music behind him. But all these things did not come together.

She said suddenly, "Hey, how old are you?"

His smile faded. She could see then that he wasn't a kid, he was much older — thirty, maybe more. At this knowledge her heart began to pound faster.

"That's a crazy thing to ask. Can'tcha see I'm your own age?"

"Like hell you are."

"Or maybe a coupla years older, I'm eighteen."

"Eighteen?" she said doubtfully.

He grinned to reassure her and lines appeared at the corners of his mouth. His teeth were big and white. He grinned so broadly his eyes became slits and she saw how thick the lashes were, thick and black as if painted with a black tar-like material. Then he seemed to become embarrassed, abruptly, and looked over his shoulder at Ellie. "*Him,* he's crazy," he said. "Ain't he a riot, he's a nut, a real character." Ellie was still listening to the music. His sunglasses told nothing about what he was thinking. He wore a bright orange shirt unbuttoned halfway to show his chest, which was a pale, bluish chest and not muscular like Arnold Friend's. His shirt collar was turned up all around and the very tips of the collar pointed out past his chin as if they were protecting him. He was pressing the transistor radio up against his ear and sat there in a kind of daze, right in the sun.

"He's kinda strange," Connie said.

"Hey, she says you're kinda strange! Kinda strange!" Arnold Friend cried. He pounded on the car to get Ellie's attention. Ellie turned for the first time and Connie saw with shock that he wasn't a kid either — he had a fair, hairless face, cheeks reddened slightly as if the veins grew too close to the surface of his skin, the face of a forty-year-old baby. Connie felt a wave of dizziness rise in her at this sight and she stared at him as if waiting for something to change the shock of the moment, make it all right again. Ellie's lips kept shaping words, mumbling along with the words blasting in his ear.

"Maybe you two better go away," Connie said faintly.

"What? How come?" Arnold Friend cried. "We come out here to take you for a ride. It's Sunday." He had the voice of the man on the radio now. It was the same voice, Connie thought. "Don'tcha know it's Sunday all day and honey, no matter who you were with last night today you're with Arnold Friend and don't you forget it! — Maybe you better step out here," he said, and this last was in a different voice. It was a little flatter, as if the heat was finally getting to him.

"No. I got things to do."

"Hey."

"You two better leave."

"We ain't leaving until you come with us."

"Like hell I am —"

"Connie, don't fool around with me. I mean, I mean, don't fool *around,*" he said, shaking his head. He laughed incredulously. He placed his sunglasses on top of his head, carefully, as if he were indeed wearing a wig, and brought the stems down behind his ears. Connie stared at him, another wave of dizziness and fear rising in her so that for a moment he wasn't even in focus but was just a blur, standing there against his gold car, and she had the idea that he had driven up the driveway all right but had come from nowhere before that and belonged nowhere and that everything about him and even about the music that was so familiar to her was only half real.

"If my father comes and sees you —"

"He ain't coming. He's at a barbecue."

"How do you know that?"

"Aunt Tillie's. Right now they're — uh — they're drinking. Sitting around," he said vaguely, squinting as if he were staring all the way to town and over to Aunt Tillie's back yard. Then the vision seemed to get clear and he nodded energetically. "Yeah. Sitting around. There's your sister in a blue dress, huh? And high heels, the poor sad bitch — nothing like you, sweetheart! And your mother's helping some fat woman with the corn, they're cleaning the corn — husking the corn —"

"What fat woman?" Connie cried.

"How do I know what fat woman. I don't know every goddam fat woman in the world!" Arnold Friend laughed.

"Oh, that's Mrs. Hornby. . . . Who invited her?" Connie said. She felt a little light-headed. Her breath was coming quickly.

"She's too fat. I don't like them fat. I like them the way you are, honey," he said, smiling sleepily at her. They stared at each other for a while, through the screen door. He said softly, "Now what you're going to do is this: you're going to come out that door. You're going to sit up front with me and Ellie's going to sit in the back, the hell with Ellie, right? This isn't Ellie's date. You're my date. I'm your lover, honey."

"What? You're crazy —"

"Yes, I'm your lover. You don't know what that is but you will," he said. "I know that too. I know all about you. But look: it's real nice and you couldn't ask for nobody better than me, or more polite. I always keep my word. I'll tell you how it is, I'm always nice at first, the first time. I'll hold you so tight you won't think you have to try to get away or pretend anything because you'll know you can't. And I'll come inside you where it's all secret and you'll give in to me and you'll love me —"

"Shut up! You're crazy!" Connie said. She backed away from the door. She put her hands against her ears as if she'd heard something terrible, something not meant for her. "People don't talk like that, you're crazy," she muttered. Her heart was almost too big now for her chest and its pumping made sweat break out all over her. She looked out to see Arnold Friend pause and then take a step toward the porch lurching. He almost fell. But, like a clever drunken man, he managed to catch his balance. He wobbled in his high boots and grabbed hold of one of the porch posts.

"Honey?" he said. "You still listening?"

"Get the hell out of here!"

"Be nice, honey. Listen."

"I'm going to call the police —"

He wobbled again and out of the side of his mouth came a fast spat curse, an aside not meant for her to hear. But even this "Christ!" sounded forced. Then he began to smile again. She watched this smile come, awkward as if he were smiling from inside a mask. His whole face was a mask, she thought wildly, tanned down onto his throat but then running out as if he had plastered make-up on his face but had forgotten about his throat.

"Honey —? Listen, here's how it is. I always tell the truth and I promise you this: I ain't coming in that house after you."

"You better not! I'm going to call the police if you — if you don't —"

"Honey," he said, talking right through her voice, "honey, I'm not coming in there but you are coming out here. You know why?"

She was panting. The kitchen looked like a place she had never seen before, some room she had run inside but which wasn't good enough, wasn't going to help her. The kitchen window had never had a curtain, after three years, and there were dishes in the sink for her to do — probably — and if you ran your hand across the table you'd probably feel something sticky there.

"You listening, honey? Hey?"

"— going to call the police —"

"Soon as you touch the phone I don't need to keep my promise and can come inside. You won't want that."

She rushed forward and tried to lock the door. Her fingers were shaking. "But why lock it," Arnold Friend said gently, talking right into her face. "It's just a screen door. It's just nothing." One of his boots was at a strange angle, as if his foot wasn't in it. It pointed out to the left, bent at the ankle. "I mean, anybody can break through a screen door and glass and wood and iron or anything else if he needs to, anybody at all and specially Arnold Friend. If the place got lit up with a fire honey you'd come running out into my arms, right into my arms and safe at home — like you knew I was your lover and'd stopped fooling around. I don't mind a nice shy girl but I don't like no fooling around." Part of those words were spoken with a slight rhythmic lilt, and Connie somehow recognized them — the echo of a song from last year, about a girl rushing into her boy friend's arms and coming home again —

Connie stood barefoot on the linoleum floor, staring at him. "What do you want?" she whispered.

"I want you," he said.

"What?"

"Seen you that night and thought, that's the one, yes sir. I never needed to look any more."

"But my father's coming back. He's coming to get me. I had to wash my hair first —" She spoke in a dry, rapid voice, hardly raising it for him to hear.

"No, your daddy is not coming and yes, you had to wash your hair and you washed it for me. It's nice and shining and all for me, I thank you, sweetheart," he said, with a mock bow, but again he almost lost his balance. He had to bend and adjust his boots. Evidently his feet did not go all the way down; the boots must have been stuffed with something so that he would seem taller. Connie stared out at him and behind him Ellie in the car, who seemed to be looking off toward Connie's right, into nothing. This Ellie said, pulling the words out of the air one after another as if he were just discovering them, "You want me to pull out the phone?"

"Shut your mouth and keep it shut," Arnold Friend said, his face red from bending over or maybe from embarrassment because Connie had seen his boots. "This ain't none of your business."

"What — what are you doing? What do you want?" Connie said. "If I call the police they'll get you, they'll arrest you —"

"Promise was not to come in unless you touch that phone, and I'll keep that promise," he said. He resumed his erect position and tried to force his shoulders back. He sounded like a hero in a movie, declaring something important. He spoke too loudly and it was as if he were speaking to someone behind Connie. "I ain't made plans for coming in that house where I don't belong but just for you to come out to me, the way you should. Don't you know who I am?"

"You're crazy," she whispered. She backed away from the door but did not want to go into another part of the house, as if this would give him permission to come through the door. "What do you. . . . You're crazy, you . . ."

"Huh? What're you saying, honey?"

Her eyes darted everywhere in the kitchen. She could not remember what it was, this room.

"This is how it is, honey: you come out and we'll drive away, have a nice ride. But if you don't come out we're gonna wait till your people come home and then they're all going to get it."

"You want that telephone pulled out?" Ellie said. He held the radio away from his ear and grimaced, as if without the radio the air was too much for him.

"I toldja shut up, Ellie," Arnold Friend said, "you're deaf, get a hearing aid, right? Fix yourself up. This little girl's no trouble and's gonna be nice to me, so Ellie keep to yourself, this ain't your date — right? Don't hem in on me. Don't hog. Don't crush. Don't bird dog. Don't trail me," he said in a rapid meaningless voice, as if he were running through all the expressions he'd learned but was no longer sure which one of them was in style, then rushing on to new ones, making them up with his eyes closed, "Don't crawl under my fence, don't squeeze in my chipmunk hole, don't sniff my glue, suck my popsicle, keep your own greasy fingers on yourself!" He shaded his eyes and peered in at Connie, who was backed against the kitchen table. "Don't mind him honey he's just a creep. He's a dope. Right? I'm the boy for you and like I said you come out here nice like a lady and give me your hand, and nobody else gets hurt, I mean, your nice old bald-headed daddy and your mummy and your sister in her high heels. Because listen: why bring them in this?"

"Leave me alone," Connie whispered.

"Hey, you know that old woman down the road, the one with the chickens and stuff — you know her?"

"She's dead!"

"Dead? What? You know her?" Arnold Friend said.

"She's dead —"

"Don't you like her?"

"She's dead — she's — she isn't here any more —"

"But don't you like her, I mean, you got something against her? Some grudge or something?" Then his voice dipped as if he were conscious of a rudeness. He touched the sunglasses perched on top of his head as if to make sure they were still there. "Now you be a good girl."

"What are you going to do?"

"Just two things, or maybe three," Arnold Friend said. "But I promise it won't last long and you'll like me that way you get to like people you're close to. You will. It's all over for you here, so come on out. You don't want your people in any trouble, do you?"

She turned and bumped against a chair or something, hurting her leg, but she ran into the back room and picked up the telephone. Something roared in her ear, a tiny roaring, and she was so sick with fear that she could do nothing but listen to it — the telephone was clammy and very heavy and her fingers groped down to the dial but were too weak to touch it. She began to scream into the phone, into the roaring. She cried out, she cried for her mother, she felt her breath start jerking back and forth in her lungs as if it were something Arnold Friend were stabbing her with again and again with no tenderness. A noisy sorrowful wailing rose all about her and she was locked inside it the way she was locked inside the house.

After a while she could hear again. She was sitting on the floor with her wet back against the wall.

Arnold Friend was saying from the door, "That's a good girl. Put the phone back."

She kicked the phone away from her.

"No, honey. Pick it up. Put it back right."

She picked it up and put it back. The dial tone stopped.

"That's a good girl. Now you come outside."

She was hollow with what had been fear, but what was now just an emptiness. All that screaming had blasted it out of her. She sat, one leg cramped under her, and deep inside her brain was something like a pinpoint of light that kept going and would not let her relax. She thought, I'm not going to see my mother again. She thought, I'm not going to sleep in my bed again. Her bright green blouse was all wet.

Arnold Friend said, in a gentle-loud voice that was like a stage voice, "The place where you came from ain't there any more, and where you had in mind to go is cancelled out. This place you are now — inside your daddy's house — is nothing but a cardboard box I can knock down any time. You know that and always did know it. You hear me?"

She thought, I have got to think. I have to know what to do.

"We'll go out to a nice field, out in the country here where it smells so nice and it's sunny," Arnold Friend said. "I'll have my arms around you so you won't need to try to get away and I'll show you what love is like, what it does. The hell with this house! It looks solid all right," he said. He ran a fingernail down the screen and the noise did not make Connie shiver, as it would have the day before. "Now put your hand on your heart, honey. Feel that? That feels solid too but we know better, be nice to me, be sweet like you can because what else is there for a girl like you but to be sweet and pretty and give in? — and get away before her people come back?"

She felt her pounding heart. Her hand seemed to enclose it. She thought for the first time in her life that it was nothing that was hers, that belonged to her, but just a pounding, living thing inside this body that wasn't really hers either.

"You don't want them to get hurt," Arnold Friend went on. "Now get up, honey. Get up all by yourself."

She stood.

"Now turn this way. That's right. Come over here to me — Ellie, put that away, didn't I tell you? You dope. You miserable creepy dope," Arnold Friend said. His words were not angry but only part of an incantation. The incantation was kindly. "Now come out through the kitchen to me honey and let's see a smile, try it, you're a brave sweet little girl and now they're eating corn and hot-dogs cooked to bursting over an outdoor fire, and they don't know one thing about you and never did and honey you're better than them because not a one of them would have done this for you."

Connie felt the linoleum under her feet; it was cool. She brushed her hair back out of her eyes. Arnold Friend let go of the post tentatively and opened his arms for her, his elbows pointing in toward each other and his wrists limp, to show that this was an embarrassed embrace and a little mocking, he didn't want to make her self-conscious.

She put out her hand against the screen. She watched herself push the door slowly open as if she were safe back somewhere in the other doorway, watching this body and this head of long hair moving out into the sunlight where Arnold Friend waited.

"My sweet little blue-eyed girl," he said, in a half-sung sigh that had nothing to do with her brown eyes but was taken up just the same by the vast sunlit reaches of the land behind him and on all sides of him, so much land that Connie had never seen before and did not recognize except to know that she was going to it.

James Alan McPherson (b. 1943)
WHY I LIKE COUNTRY MUSIC   1977

No one will believe that I like country music. Even my wife scoffs when told such a possibility exists. "Go on!" Gloria tells me. "I can see blues, bebop, maybe even a little buckdancing. But not bluegrass." Gloria says, "Hillbilly stuff is not just music. It's like the New York Stock Exchange. The minute you see a sharp rise in it, you better watch out."

I tend to argue the point, but quietly, and mostly to myself. Gloria was born and raised in New York; she has come to believe in the stock exchange as the only index of economic health. My perceptions were shaped in South Carolina; and long ago I learned there, as a waiter in private clubs, to gauge economic flux by the tips people gave. We tend to disagree on other matters too, but the thing that gives me most frustration is trying to make her understand why I like country music. Perhaps it is because she hates the South and has capitulated emotionally to the horror stories told by refugees from down home. Perhaps it is because Gloria is third generation Northern-born. I do not know. What I do know is that, while the two of us are black, the distance between us is sometimes as great as that between Ibo and Yoruba°. And I do know that, despite her protestations, I like country music.

"You are crazy," Gloria tells me.

I tend to argue the point, but quietly, and mostly to myself.

Of course I do not like all country stuff; just pieces that make the right connections. I like banjo because sometimes I hear ancestors in the strumming. I like the fiddlelike refrain in "Dixie" for the very same reason. But most of all I like square dancing — the interplay between fiddle and caller, the stomping, the swishing of dresses, the strutting, the proud turnings, the laughter. Most of all I like the laughter. In recent months I have wondered why I like this music and this dance. I have drawn no general conclusions, but from time to time I suspect it is because the square dance is the only dance form I ever mastered.

"I wouldn't say that in public," Gloria warns me.

I agree with her, but still affirm the truth of it, although quietly, and mostly to myself.

Dear Gloria: This is the truth of how it was:

Ibo and Yoruba: West African peoples, each distinct in language and culture.

In my youth in that distant country, while others learned to strut, I grew stiff as a winter cornstalk. When my playmates harmonized their rhythms, I stood on the sidelines in atonic detachment. While they shimmied, I merely jerked in lackluster imitation. I relate these facts here, not in remorse or self-castigation, but as a true confession of my circumstances. In those days, down in our small corner of South Carolina, proficiency in dance was a form of story-telling. A boy could say, "I traveled here and there, saw this and fought that, conquered him and made love to her, lied to them, told a few others the truth, just so I could come back here and let you know what things out there are really like." He could communicate all this with smooth, graceful jiggles of his round bottom, synchronized with intricately coordinated sweeps of his arms and small, unexcited movements of his legs. Little girls could communicate much more.

But sadly, I could do none of it. Development of these skills depended on the ministrations of family and neighbors. My family did not dance; our closest neighbor was a true-believing Seventh Day Adventist. Moreover, most new dances came from up North, brought to town usually by people returning to riff on the good life said to exist in those far Northern places. They prowled our dirt streets in rented Cadillacs; paraded our brick sidewalks exhibiting styles abstracted from the fullness of life in Harlem, South Philadelphia, Roxbury, Baltimore and the South Side of Chicago. They confronted our provincial clothes merchants with the arrogant reminder, "But people ain't wearin' this in New Yokkk!" Each of their movements, as well as their world-weary smooth-ness, told us locals meaningful tales of what was missing in our lives. Unfortu-nately, those of us under strict parental supervision, or those of us without Northern connections, could only stand at a distance and worship these en-voys of culture. We stood on the sidelines — styleless, gestureless, danceless, doing nothing more than an improvised one-butt shuffle — hoping for one of them to touch our lives. It was my good fortune, during my tenth year on the sidelines, to have one of these Northerners introduce me to the square dance.

My dear, dear Gloria, her name was Gweneth Lawson:

She was a pretty, chocolate brown little girl with dark brown eyes and two long black braids. After all these years, the image of these two braids evokes in me all there is to remember about Gweneth Lawson. They were plaited across the top of her head and hung to a point just above the back of her Peter Pan collar. Sometimes she wore two bows, one red and one blue, and these tended to sway lazily near the place on her neck where the smooth brown of her skin and the white of her collar met the ink-bottle black of her hair. Even when I cannot remember her face, I remember the rainbow of deep, rich colors in which she lived. This is so because I watched them, every weekday, from my desk directly behind her in our fourth-grade class. And she wore the most magical perfume, or lotion, smelling just slightly of fresh-cut lemons, that wafted back to me whenever she made the slightest movement at her desk. Now I must tell you this much more, dear Gloria: whenever I smell fresh lemons, whether in the market or at home, I look around me — not for Gweneth Lawson, but for some quiet corner where I can revive in private certain mem-ories of her. And in pursuing these memories across such lemony bridges, I rediscover that I loved her.

Gweneth was from the South Carolina section of Brooklyn. Her parents had sent her south to live with her uncle, Mr. Richard Lawson, the brick mason, for an unspecified period of time. Just why they did this I do not know, unless it was their plan to have her absorb more of South Carolina folkways than conditions in Brooklyn would allow. She was a gentle, soft-spoken girl; I recall no condescension in her manner. This was all the more admirable because our unrestrained awe of a Northern-born black person usually induced in him some grand sense of his own importance. You must know that in those days older folks would point to someone and say, "He's from the North," and the statement would be sufficient in itself. Mothers made their children behave by advising that, if they led exemplary lives and attended church regularly, when they died they would go to New York. Only someone who understands what London meant to Dick Whittington°, or how California and the suburbs function in the national mind, could appreciate the mythical dimensions of this Northlore.

But Gweneth Lawson was above regional idealization. Though I might have loved her partly because she was a Northerner, I loved her more because of the world of colors that seemed to be suspended about her head. I loved her glowing forehead and I loved her bright, dark brown eyes; I loved the black braids, the red and blue and sometimes yellow and pink ribbons; I loved the way the deep, rich brown of her neck melted into the pink or white cloth of her Peter Pan collar; I loved the lemony vapor on which she floated and from which, on occasion, she seemed to be inviting me to be buoyed up, up, up into her happy world; I loved the way she caused my heart to tumble whenever, during a restless moment, she seemed about to turn her head in my direction; I loved her more, though torturously, on the many occasions when she did not turn. Because I was a shy boy, I loved the way I could love her silently, at least six hours a day, without ever having to disclose my love.

My platonic state of mind might have stretched onward into a blissful infinity had not Mrs. Esther Clay Boswell, our teacher, made it her business to pry into the affair. Although she prided herself on being a strict disciplinarian, Mrs. Boswell was not without a sense of humor. A round, full-breasted woman in her early forties, she liked to amuse herself, and sometimes the class as well, by calling the attention of all eyes to whomever of us violated the structure she imposed on classroom activities. She was particularly hard on people like me who could not contain an impulse to daydream, or those who allowed their eyes to wander too far away from lessons printed on the blackboard. A black and white sign posted under the electric clock next to the door summed up her attitude toward this kind of truancy: NOTICE TO ALL CLOCKWATCHERS, it read, TIME PASSES. WILL YOU? Nor did she abide timidity in her students. Her voice booming, "Speak up, boy!" was more than enough to cause the more emotional among us, including me, to break into convenient flows of warm tears. But by doing this we violated yet another rule, one on which depended our very survival in Mrs. Esther Clay Boswell's class. She would spell out this rule for us as she paced before her desk, slapping a thick, homemade ruler against the flat of her brown palm. "There ain't no *babies* in here," she would recite. *Thaap!* "Anybody thinks he's still a *baby* . . ." *Thaap!* ". . . should crawl back home to his mama's *titty.*" *Thaap!* "You little bunnies shed your *last water* . . ." *Thaap!*

Dick Whittington: English merchant (1358?–1423), whose life gave rise to a popular legend in which churchbells tell the boy Whittington that he will become Lord Mayor of London.

". . . the minute you left home to come in here." *Thaap!* "From now on, you g'on do all your *cryin'* . . ." *Thaap!* ". . . in church!" *Thaap!* Whenever one of us compelled her to make this speech it would seem to me that her eyes paused overlong on my face. She would seem to be daring me, as if suspicious that, in addition to my secret passion for Gweneth Lawson, which she might excuse, I was also in the habit of throwing fits of temper.

She had read me right. I was the product of too much attention from my father. He favored me, paraded me around on his shoulder, inflated my ego constantly with what, among us at least, was a high compliment: "You my nigger if you don't get no bigger." This statement, along with my father's generous attentions, made me selfish and used to having my own way. I *expected* to have my own way in most things, and when I could not, I tended to throw tantrums calculated to break through any barrier raised against me.

Mrs. Boswell was also perceptive in assessing the extent of my infatuation with Gweneth Lawson. Despite my stealth in telegraphing emissions of affection into the back part of Gweneth's brain, I could not help but observe, occasionally, Mrs. Boswell's cool glance pausing on the two of us. But she never said a word. Instead, she would settle her eyes momentarily on Gweneth's face and then pass quickly to mine. But in that instant she seemed to be saying, "Don't look back now, girl, but I *know* that bald-headed boy behind you has you on his mind." She seemed to watch me daily, with a combination of amusement and absolute detachment in her brown eyes. And when she stared, it was not at me but at the normal focus of my attention: the end of Gweneth Lawson's black braids. Whenever I sensed Mrs. Boswell watching I would look away quickly, either down at my brown desk top or across the room to the blackboard. But her eyes could not be eluded this easily. Without looking at anyone in particular, she could make a specific point to one person in a manner so general that only long afterward did the real object of her attention realize it had been intended for him.

"Now you little brown bunnies," she might say, "and you black buck rabbits and you few cottontails mixed in, some of you starting to smell yourselves under the arms without knowing what it's all about." And here, it sometimes seemed to me, she allowed her eyes to pause casually on me before resuming their sweep of the entire room. "Now I know your mamas already made you think life is a bed of roses, but in *my* classroom you got to know the footpaths through the *sticky* parts of the rosebed." It was her custom during this ritual to prod and goad those of us who were developing reputations for meekness and indecision; yet her method was Socratic in that she compelled us, indirectly, to supply our own answers by exploiting one person as the walking symbol of the error she intended to correct. Clarence Buford, for example, an oversized but good-natured boy from a very poor family, served often as the helpmeet in this exercise.

"Buford," she might begin, slapping the ruler against her palm, "how does a tongue-tied country boy like you expect to get a wife?"

"I don't want no wife," Buford might grumble softly.

Of course the class would laugh.

"Oh yes you do," Mrs. Boswell would respond. "All you buck rabbits want wives." *Thaap!* "So how do you let a girl know you not just a bump on a log?"

"I know! I know!" a high voice might call from a seat across from mine. This, of course, would be Leon Pugh. A peanut-brown boy with curly hair, he seemed to know everything. Moreover, he seemed to take pride in being the only one who knew answers to life questions and would wave his arms excitedly whenever our attentions were focused on such matters. It seemed to me his voice would be extra loud and his arms waved more strenuously whenever he was certain that Gweneth Lawson, seated across from him, was interested in an answer to Mrs. Esther Clay Boswell's question. His eager arms, it seemed to me, would be reaching out to grasp Gweneth instead of the question asked.

"Buford, you twisted-tongue, bunion-toed country boy," Mrs. Boswell might say, ignoring Leon Pugh's hysterical arm-waving, "you gonna let a cottontail like Leon get a girlfriend before you?"

"I don't want no girlfriend," Clarence Buford would almost sob. "I don't like no girls."

The class would laugh again while Leon Pugh manipulated his arms like a flight navigator under battle conditions. "I know! I know! I swear to *God* I know!"

When at last Mrs. Boswell would turn in his direction, I might sense that she was tempted momentarily to ask me for an answer. But as in most such exercises, it was the worldly-wise Leon Pugh who supplied this. "What do *you* think, Leon?" she would ask inevitably, but with a rather lifeless slap of the ruler against her palm.

"My daddy told me . . ." Leon would shout, turning slyly to beam at Gweneth, ". . . my daddy and my big brother from the Bronx New York told me that to git *anythin'* in this world you gotta learn how to blow your own horn."

"Why, Leon?" Mrs. Boswell might ask in a bored voice.

"Because," the little boy would recite, puffing out his chest, "because if you don't blow your own horn ain't nobody else g'on blow it for you. That's what my daddy said."

"What do you think about that, Buford?" Mrs. Boswell would ask.

"I don't want no girlfriend anyhow," the puzzled Clarence Buford might say.

And then the cryptic lesson would suddenly be dropped.

This was Mrs. Esther Clay Boswell's method of teaching. More than anything written on the blackboard, her questions were calculated to make us turn around in our chairs and inquire in guarded whispers of each other, and especially of the wise and confident Leon Pugh, "What does she mean?" But none of us, besides Pugh, seemed able to comprehend what it was we ought to know but did not know. And Mrs. Boswell, plump brown fox that she was, never volunteered any more in the way of confirmation than was necessary to keep us interested. Instead, she paraded around us, methodically slapping the homemade ruler against her palm, suggesting by her silence more depth to her question, indeed, more implications in Leon's answer, than we were then able to perceive. And during such moments, whether inspired by selfishness or by the peculiar way Mrs. Boswell looked at me, I felt that finding answers to such questions was a task she had set for me, of all the members of the class.

Of course Leon Pugh, among other lesser lights, was my chief rival for the affections of Gweneth Lawson. All during the school year, from September through the winter rains, he bested me in my attempts to look directly into her eyes and say a simple, heartfelt "hey." This was my ambition, but I never seemed able to get close enough to her attention. At Thanksgiving I helped draw a bounteous yellow cornucopia on the blackboard, with fruits and flowers matching the colors that floated around Gweneth's head; Leon Pugh made one by himself, a masterwork of silver paper and multicolored crepe, which he hung on the door. Its silver tail curled upward to a point just below the face of Mrs. Boswell's clock. At Christmas, when we drew names out of a hat for the exchange of gifts, I drew the name of Queen Rose Phipps, a fairly unattractive squash-yellow girl of absolutely no interest to me. Pugh, whether through collusion with the boy who handled the lottery or through pure luck, pulled forth from the hat the magic name of Gweneth Lawson. He gave her a set of deep purple bows for her braids and a basket of pecans from his father's tree. Uninterested now in the spirit of the occasion, I delivered to Queen Rose Phipps a pair of white socks. Each time Gweneth wore the purple bows she would glance over at Leon and smile. Each time Queen Rose wore my white socks I would turn away in embarrassment, lest I should see them pulling down into her shoes and exposing her skinny ankles.

After class, on wet winter days, I would trail along behind Gweneth to the bus stop, pause near the steps while she entered, and follow her down the aisle until she chose a seat. Usually, however, in clear violation of the code of conduct to which all gentlemen were expected to adhere, Leon Pugh would already be on the bus and shouting to passersby, "Move off! Get away! This here seat by me is reserved for the girl from Brooklyn New York." Discouraged but not defeated, I would swing into the seat next nearest her and cast calf-eyed glances of wounded affection at the back of her head or at the brown, rainbow profile of her face. And at her stop, some eight or nine blocks from mine, I would disembark behind her along with a crowd of other love-struck boys. There would then follow a well-rehearsed scene in which all of us, save Leon Pugh, pretended to have gotten off the bus either too late or too soon to wend our proper paths homeward. And at slight cost to ourselves we enjoyed the advantage of being able to walk close by her as she glided toward her uncle's green-frame house. There, after pausing on the wooden steps and smiling radiantly around the crowd like a spring sun in that cold winter rain, she would sing, "Bye, y'all," and disappear into the structure with the mystery of a goddess. Afterward I would walk away, but slowly, much slower than the other boys, warmed by the music and light in her voice against the sharp, wet winds of the February afternoon.

I loved her, dear Gloria, and I danced with her and smelled the lemony youth of her and told her that I loved her, all this in a way you would never believe:

You would not know or remember, as I do, that in those days, in our area of the country, we enjoyed a pleasingly ironic mixture of Yankee and Confederate folkways. Our meals and manners, our speech, our attitudes toward certain ambiguous areas of history, even our acceptance of tragedy as the normal course of life — these things and more defined us as Southern. Yet the stern morality of our parents, their toughness and penny-pinching and attitudes toward work, their covert allegiance toward certain ideals, even the directions toward which they turned our faces, made us more Yankee than Cavalier.

Moreover, some of our schools were named for Confederate men of distinction, but others were named for the stern-faced believers who had swept down from the North to save a people back, back long ago, in those long forgotten days of once upon a time. Still, our schoolbooks, our required classroom songs, our flags, our very relation to the statues and monuments in public parks, negated the story that these dreamers from the North had ever come. We sang the state song, memorized the verses of homegrown poets, honored in our books the names and dates of historical events both before and after that Historical Event which, in our region, supplanted even the division of the millennia introduced by the followers of Jesus Christ. Given the silent circumstances of our cultural environment, it was ironic, and perhaps just, that we maintained a synthesis of two traditions no longer supportive of each other. Thus it became traditional at our school to celebrate the arrival of spring on May first by both the ritual plaiting of the Maypole and square dancing.

On that day, as on a few others, the Superintendent of Schools and several officials were likely to visit our schoolyard and stand next to the rusty metal swings, watching the fourth, fifth, and sixth graders bob up and down and behind and before each other, around the gaily painted Maypoles. These happy children would pull and twist long runs of billowy crepe paper into wondrous, multicolored plaits. Afterward, on the edges of thunderous applause from teachers, parents and visiting dignitaries, a wave of elaborately costumed children would rush out onto the grounds in groups of eight and proceed with the square dance. "Doggone!" the Superintendent of Schools was heard to exclaim on one occasion. "Y'all do it so good it just makes your *bones* set up and take notice."

Such was the schedule two weeks prior to May first, when Mrs. Boswell announced to our class that as fourth graders we were now eligible to participate in the festivities. The class was divided into two general sections of sixteen each, one group preparing to plait the pole and a second group, containing an equal number of boys and girls, practicing turns for our part in the square dance. I was chosen to square dance; so was Leon Pugh. Gweneth Lawson was placed with the pole plaiters. I was depressed until I remembered, happily, that I could not dance a lick. I reported this fact to Mrs. Boswell just after the drawing, during recess, saying that my lack of skill would only result in our class making a poor showing. I asked to be reassigned to the group of Maypole plaiters. Mrs. B. looked me over with considerable amusement tugging at the corners of her mouth. "Oh, you don't have to *dance* to do the square dance," she said. "That's a dance that was made up to mock folks that couldn't dance." She paused a second before adding thoughtfully: "The worse you are at dancing, the better you can square dance. It's just about the best dance in the world for a stiff little bunny like you."

"I want to plait the Maypole," I said.

"You'll square dance or I'll grease your little butt," Mrs. Esther Clay Boswell said.

"I ain't gonna do *nothin'*!" I muttered. But I said this quietly, and mostly to myself, while walking away from her desk. For the rest of the day she watched me closely, as if she knew what I was thinking.

The next morning I brought a note from my father. "Dear Mrs. Boswell:" I had watched him write earlier that morning, "My boy does not square dance.

Please excuse him as I am afraid he will break down and cry and mess up the show. Yours truly . . ."

Mrs. Boswell said nothing after she had read the note. She merely waved me to my seat. But in the early afternoon, when she read aloud the lists of those assigned to dancing and Maypole plaiting, she paused as my name rolled off her tongue. "You don't have to stay on the square dance team," she called to me. "You go on out in the yard with the Maypole team."

I was ecstatic. I hurried to my place in line some three warm bodies behind Gweneth Lawson. We prepared to march out.

"Wait a minute," Mrs. Boswell called. "Now it looks like we got seventeen bunnies on the Maypole team and fifteen on the square dance. We have to even things up." She made a thorough examination of both lists, scratching her head. Then she looked carefully up and down the line of stomping Maypoleites. "Miss Gweneth Lawson, you cute little cottontail you, it looks like you gonna have to go over to the square dance team. That'll give us eight sets of partners for the square dance . . . but now we have another problem." She made a great display of counting the members of the two squads of square dancers. "Now there's sixteen square dancers all right, but when we pair them off we got a problem of higher mathematics. With nine girls and only seven *boys*, looks like we gotta switch a girl from square dancing to Maypole and a boy from Maypole to square dancing."

I waited hopefully for Gweneth Lawson to volunteer. But just at that moment the clever Leon Pugh grabbed her hand and began jitterbugging as though he could hardly wait for the record player to be turned on and the dancing to begin.

"What a cute couple," Mrs. Boswell observed absently. "Now which one of you other girls wants to join up with the Maypole team?"

Following Pugh's example, the seven remaining boys grabbed the girls they wanted as partners. Only skinny Queen Rose Phipps and shy Beverly Hankins remained unclaimed. Queen Rose giggled nervously.

"Queen Rose," Mrs. B. called, "I know you don't mind plaiting the Maypole." She waved her ruler in a gesture of casual dismissal. Queen Rose raced across the room and squeezed into line.

"*Now*," Mrs. Boswell said, "I need a boy to come across to the square dancers."

I was not unmindful of the free interchange of partners involved in square dancing, even though Leon Pugh had beat me in claiming the partner of my choice. All I really wanted was one moment swinging Gweneth Lawson in my arms. I raised my hand slowly.

"Oh, not *you*, little bunny," Mrs. Boswell said. "You and your daddy claim you don't like to square dance." She slapped her ruler against her palm. *Thaap! Thaap!* Then she said, "Clarence Buford, I *know* a big-footed country boy like you can square dance better than anybody. Come on over here and kiss cute little Miss Beverly Hankins."

"I don't like no girls *noway*," Buford mumbled. But he went over and stood next to the giggling Beverly Hankins.

"Now!" said Mrs. B. "March on out in that yard and give that pole a good plaiting!"

We started to march out. Over my shoulder, as I reached the door, I glimpsed the overjoyed Leon Pugh whirling lightly on his toes. He sang in a confident tone:

"I saw the Lord give Moses a pocketful of roses.
I skid Ezekiel's wheel on a ripe banana peel.
I rowed the Nile, flew over a stile,
Saw Jack Johnson pick his teeth
With toenails from Jim Jeffries'° feets . . ."

"Grab your partners!" Mrs. Esther Clay Boswell was saying as the oak door slammed behind us.

I had been undone. For almost two weeks I was obliged to stand on the sidelines and watch Leon Pugh allemande left and do-si-do my beloved Gweneth. Worse, she seemed to be enjoying it. But I must give Leon proper credit: he was a dancing fool. In a matter of days he had mastered, and then improved on, the various turns and bows and gestures of the square dance. He leaped while the others plodded, whirled each girl through his arms with lightness and finesse, chattered playfully at the other boys when they tumbled over their own feet. Mrs. Boswell stood by the record player calling, "Put some *strut* in it, Buford, you big potato sack. Watch Leon and see how *he* does it." I leaned against the classroom wall and watched the dancers, my own group having already exhausted the limited variations possible in matters of Maypole plaiting.

At home each night I begged my father to send another note to Mrs. Boswell, this time stating that I had no interest in the Maypole. But he resisted my entreaties and even threatened me with a whipping if I did not participate and make him proud of me. The real cause of his irritation was the considerable investment he had already made in purchasing an outfit for me. Mrs. Boswell had required all her students, square dancers and Maypole plaiters alike, to report on May first in outfits suitable for square dancing. My father had bought a new pair of dungarees, a blue shirt, a red and white polka-dot bandanna and a cowboy hat. He was in no mood to bend under the emotional weight of my new demands. As a matter of fact, early in the morning of May first he stood beside my bed with the bandanna in his left hand and his leather belt in his right hand, just in case I developed a sudden fever.

I dragged myself heavily through the warm, blue spring morning toward school, dressed like a carnival cowboy. When I entered the classroom I sulked against the wall, being content to watch the other children. And what happy buzzings and jumping and excitement they made as they compared costumes. Clarence Buford wore a Tom Mix hat° and a brown vest over a green shirt with red six-shooter patterns embossed on its collar. Another boy, Paul Carter, was dressed entirely in black, with a fluffy white handkerchief puffing from his neck. But Leon Pugh caught the attention of all our eyes. He wore a red and white checkered shirt, a loose green bandanna clasped at his throat by a shining silver buffalo head, brown chaps sewed onto his dungarees, and shiny brown cowboy boots with silver spurs that clanked each time he moved.

Jack Johnson . . . Jim Jeffries: In 1910 Johnson, the first black to hold the title of heavyweight champion of the world, knocked out former champion Jeffries in fifteen rounds.
Tom Mix hat: a white cowboy hat. Mix, a star of the silent screen, died in 1940 but survived as a character of comics and of a radio serial.

In his hand he carried a carefully creased brown cowboy hat. He announced his fear that it would lose its shape and planned to put it on only when the dancing started. He would allow no one to touch it. Instead, he stood around clanking his feet and smoothing the crease in his fabulous hat and saying loudly, "My daddy says it pays to look good no matter what you put on."

The girls seemed prettier and much older than their ages. Even Queen Rose Phipps wore rouge on her cheeks that complemented her pale color. Shy Beverly Hankins had come dressed in a blue and white checkered bonnet and a crisp blue apron; she looked like a frontier mother. But Gweneth Lawson, my Gweneth Lawson, dominated the group of girls. She wore a long red dress with sheaves and sheaves of sparkling white crinoline belling it outward so it seemed she was floating. On her honey-brown wrists golden bracelets sparkled. A deep blue bandanna enclosed her head with the wonder of a summer sky. Black patent leather shoes glistened like half-hidden stars beneath the red and white of her hemline. She stood smiling before us and we marveled. At that moment I would have given the world to have been able to lead her about on my arm.

Mrs. Boswell watched us approvingly from behind her desk. Finally, at noon, she called, "Let's go on out!" Thirty-two living rainbows cascaded toward the door. Pole plaiters formed one line. Square dancers formed another. Mrs. Boswell strolled officiously past us in review. It seemed to me she almost paused while passing the spot where I stood on line. But she brushed past me, straightening an apron here, applying spittle and a rub to a rouged cheek there, waving a wary finger at an overanxious boy. Then she whacked her ruler against her palm and led us out into the yard. The fifth and sixth graders had already assembled. On one end of the playground were a dozen or so tall painted poles with long, thin wisps of green and blue and yellow and rust-brown crepe floating lazily on the sweet spring breezes.

"Maypole teams *up!*" called Mr. Henry Lucas, our principal, from his platform by the swings. Beside him stood the white Superintendent of Schools (who said later of the square dance, it was reported to all the classes, "Lord, y'all square dance so *good* it makes me plumb *ashamed* us white folks ain't takin' better care of our art stuff."). "Maypole teams up!" Mr. Henry Lucas shouted again. Some fifty of us, screaming shrilly, rushed to grasp our favorite color crepe. Then, to the music of "Sing Praise for All the Brightness and the Joy of Spring," we pulled and plaited in teams of six or seven until every pole was twisted as tight and as colorfully as the braids on Gweneth Lawson's head. Then, to the applause of proud teachers and parents and the whistles of the Superintendent of Schools, we scattered happily back under the wings of our respective teachers. I stood next to Mrs. Boswell, winded and trembling but confident I had done my best. She glanced down at me and said in a quiet voice, "I do believe you are learning the rhythm of the thing."

I did not respond.

"Let's *go!*" Leon Pugh shouted to the other kids, grabbing Gweneth Lawson's arm and taking a few clanking steps forward.

"Wait a minute, Leon," Mrs. Boswell hissed. "Mr. Lucas has to change the record."

Leon sighed. "But if we don't git out there first, all them other teams will take the best spots."

"Wait!" Mrs. Boswell ordered.

Leon sulked. He inched closer to Gweneth. I watched him swing her hand impatiently. He stamped his feet and his silver spurs jangled.

Mrs. Boswell looked down at his feet. "Why, Leon," she said, "you can't go out there with razors on your shoes."

"These ain't razors," Leon muttered. "These here are spurs my brother in Bronx New York sent me just for this here dance."

"You have to take them off," Mrs. Boswell said.

Leon growled. But he reached down quickly and attempted to jerk the silver spurs from the heels of his boots. They did not come off. "No time!" he called, standing suddenly. "Mr. Lucas done put the record on."

"Leon, you might *cut* somebody with those things," Mrs. Boswell said. "Miss Gweneth Lawson's pretty red dress could get caught in those things and then she'll fall as surely as I'm standin' here."

"I'll just go out with my boots off," Leon replied.

But Mrs. Boswell shook her head firmly. "You just run on to the lunch-room and ask cook for some butter or mayo. That'll help 'em slip off." She paused, looking out over the black dirt playground. "And if you miss this first dance, why there'll be a second and maybe even a third. We'll get a Maypole plaiter to sub for you."

My heart leaped. Leon sensed it and stared at me. His hand tightened on Gweneth's as she stood radiant and smiling in the loving spring sunlight. Leon let her hand drop and bent quickly, pulling at the spurs with the fury of a Samson.

"Square dancers *up!*" Mr. Henry Lucas called.

"Sonofa*bitch!*" Leon grunted.

"Square dancers *up!*" called Mr. Lucas.

The fifth and sixth graders were screaming and rushing toward the center of the yard. Already the record was scratching out the high, slick voice of the caller. "*Sonofabitch!*" Leon moaned.

Mrs. Boswell looked directly at Gweneth, standing alone and abandoned next to Leon. "Miss Gweneth Lawson," Mrs. Boswell said in a cool voice, "it's a cryin' shame there ain't no prince to take you to that ball out there."

I do not remember moving, but I know I stood with Gweneth at the center of the yard. What I did there I do not know, but I remember watching the movements of others and doing what they did just after they had done it. Still, I cannot remember just when I looked into my partner's face or what I saw there. The scratchy voice of the caller bellowed directions and I obeyed:

> "*Allemande left with your left hand*
> *Right to your partner with a right and left grand . . .*"

Although I was told later that I made an allemande right instead of left, I have no memory of the mistake.

> "*When you get to your partner pass her by*
> *And pick up the next girl on the sly . . .*"

Nor can I remember picking up any other girl. I only remember that during many turns and do-si-dos I found myself looking into the warm brown eyes of

Gweneth Lawson. I recall that she smiled at me. I recall that she laughed on another turn. I recall that I laughed with her an eternity later.

> "... *promenade that dear old thing*
> *Throw your head right back and sing* be-*cause, just*
> be-*cause ..."*

I do remember quite well that during the final promenade before the record ended, Gweneth stood beside me and I said to her in a voice much louder than that of the caller, "When I get up to Brooklyn I hope I see you." But I do not remember what she said in response. I want to remember that she smiled.

I know I smiled, dear Gloria. I smiled with the lemonness of her and the loving of her pressed deep into those saving places of my private self. It was my plan to savor these, and I did savor them. But when I reached New York, many years later, I did not think of Brooklyn. I followed the old, beaten, steady paths into uptown Manhattan. By then I had learned to dance to many other kinds of music. And I had forgotten the savory smell of lemon. But I think sometimes of Gweneth now when I hear country music. And although it is difficult to explain to you, I still maintain that I am no mere arithmetician in the art of the square dance. I am into the calculus of it.

"Go on!" you will tell me, backing into your Northern mythology. "I can see the hustle, the hump, maybe even the Ibo highlife. But no hillbilly."

These days I am firm about arguing the point, but, as always, quietly, and mostly to myself.

POETRY

TO THE MUSE ⟋ textbook

Give me leave, Muse, in plain view to array
Your shift and bodice by the light of day.
I would have brought an epic. Be not vexed
Instead to grace a niggling schoolroom text;
Let down your sanction, help me to oblige
Him who would lead fresh devots to your liege,
And at your altar, grant that in a flash
They, he and I know incense from dead ash.
                                        —X.J.K.

What is poetry? Pressed for an answer, Robert Frost made a classic reply: "Poetry is the kind of thing poets write." In all likelihood, Frost was not trying merely to evade the question but to chide his questioner into thinking for himself. A trouble with definitions is that they may stop thought. If Frost had said, "Poetry is a rhythmical composition of words expressing an attitude, designed to surprise and delight, and to arouse an emotional response," the questioner might have settled back in his chair, content to have learned the truth about poetry. He would have learned nothing, or not so much as he might learn by continuing to wonder.

The nature of poetry eludes simple definitions. (In this respect it is rather like jazz Asked after one of his concerts, "What is jazz?" Louis Armstrong replied, "Man, if you gotta ask, you'll never know.") Definitions will be of little help at first, if we are to know poetry and respond to it. We have to go to it willing to see and hear. For this reason, you are asked in reading this book not to be in any hurry to decide what poetry is, but instead to study poems and to let them grow in your mind. At the end of our discussions of poetry, the problem of definition will be taken up again (for those who may wish to pursue it).

Confronted with a formal introduction to poetry, you may be wondering, "Who needs it?" and you may well be right. You hardly can have avoided meeting poetry before; and perhaps you already have a friendship, or at least a fair acquaintance, with some of the great English-speaking poets of all time. What this book provides is an introduction to the *study* of poetry. It tries to help you look at a poem closely, to offer you a wider and more accurate vocabulary with which to express what poems say to you. It will suggest ways to judge for yourself the poems you read. It may set forth some poems new to you.

A frequent objection is that poetry ought not to be studied at all. In this view, a poem is either a series of gorgeous noises to be funneled through one ear and out the other without being allowed to trouble the mind or an experience so holy that to analyze it in a classroom is as cruel and mechanical as dissecting a hummingbird. To the first view, it might be countered that a good poem has something to say that perhaps is worth listening to. To the second view, it might be argued that poems are much less perishable than hummingbirds, and luckily, we can study them in flight. The risk of a poem's dying from observation is not nearly so great as the risk of not really seeing it at all. It is doubtful that any excellent poem has ever vanished from human memory because people have read it too closely. More likely, poems that vanish are poems that no one reads closely, for no one cares.

Good poetry is something to care about. In fact, an ancient persuasion of mankind is that the hearing of a poem, as well as the making of a poem, can be a religious act. Poetry, in speech and song, was part of classic Greek drama, which for playwright, actor, and spectator alike was a holy-day ceremony. The Greeks' belief that a poet writes a poem only by supernatural assistance is clear from the invocations to the Muse that begin the *Iliad* and the *Odyssey* and from the opinion of Socrates (in Plato's *Ion*) that a poet has no powers of invention until divinely inspired. Among the ancient Celts, poets were regarded as magicians and priests, and whoever insulted one of them might expect to receive a curse in rime potent enough to afflict him with boils and to curdle the milk of his cows. Such identifications between the poet and the magician are less common these days, although we know that poetry is involved in the primitive white-magic of children, who bring themselves good luck in a game with the charm "Roll, roll, Tootsie-roll!/ Roll the marble in the hole!" and who warn against a hex while jumping a sidewalk: "Step on a crack, / Break your mother's back." But in this age when men pride themselves that a computer may solve the riddle of all creation as soon as it is programmed, magic seems to some people of small importance and so does poetry. It is dangerous, however, to dismiss what we do not logically understand. To read a poem at all, we have to be willing to offer it responses *besides* a logical understanding. Whether we attribute the effect of a poem to a divine spirit or to the reactions of our glands and cortexes, we have to take the reading of poetry seriously (not solemnly), if only because — as some of the poems in this book may demonstrate — few other efforts can repay us so generously, both in wisdom and in joy.

If, as I hope you will do, you sometimes browse in the book for fun, you may be annoyed to see so many questions following the poems. Should you feel this way, try reading with a slip of paper to cover up the questions. You will then — if the Muse should inspire you — have paper in hand to write a poem.

12 Entrances

How do we read a poem? A literal-minded answer might be, "Just let your eye light on it"; but there is more to poetry than meets the eye. What Shakespeare called "the mind's eye" also plays a part. Many a reader who has no trouble understanding and enjoying prose finds poetry difficult. This is to be expected. At first glance, a poem usually will make some sense and give some pleasure, but it may not yield everything at once. Sometimes it only hints at meaning still to come if we will keep after it. Poetry is not to be galloped over like the daily news: a poem differs from most prose in that it is to be read slowly, carefully, and attentively. Not all poems are difficult, of course, and some can be understood and enjoyed on first seeing. But good poems yield more if read twice; and the best poems—after ten, twenty, or a hundred readings—still go on yielding.

Approaching a thing written in lines and surrounded with white space, we need not expect it to be a poem just because it is **verse.** (Any composition in lines of more or less regular rhythm, usually ending in rimes, is verse.) Here, for instance, is a specimen of verse that few will call poetry:

> Thirty days hath September,
> April, June, and November;
> All the rest have thirty-one
> Excepting February alone,
> To which we twenty-eight assign
> Till leap year makes it twenty-nine.

To a higher degree than that classic memory-tickler, poetry appeals to the mind and arouses feelings. Poetry may state facts, but, more important, it makes imaginative statements that we may value even if its facts are incorrect. Coleridge's error in placing a star within the horns of the crescent moon in "The Rime of the Ancient Mariner" does not stop the passage from being good poetry, though it is faulty astronomy. According to one poet, Gerard Manley Hopkins, poetry is "to be heard for its own sake and interest even over and above its interest of meaning."

There are other elements in a poem besides plain prose sense: sounds, images, rhythms, figures of speech. These may strike us and please us even before we ask, "But what does it all mean?"

This is a truth not readily grasped by anyone who regards a poem as a kind of puzzle written in secret code with a message slyly concealed. The effect of a poem (one's whole mental and emotional response to it) consists in much more than simply a message. By its musical qualities, by its suggestions, it can work on the reader's unconscious. T. S. Eliot put it well when he said in *The Use of Poetry and the Use of Criticism* that the prose sense of a poem is chiefly useful in keeping the reader's mind "diverted and quiet, while the poem does its work upon him." Eliot went on to liken the meaning of a poem to the bit of meat a burglar brings along to throw to the family dog. What is the work of a poem? To touch us, to stir us, to make us glad, and possibly even to tell us something.

How to set about reading a poem? Here are a few suggestions.

To begin with, read the poem once straight through, with no particular expectations; read open-mindedly. Let yourself experience whatever you find, without worrying just yet about the large general and important ideas the poem contains (if indeed it contains any). Don't dwell on a troublesome word or difficult passage—just push on. Some of the difficulties may seem smaller when you read the poem for a second time; at least, they will have become parts of a whole for you.

On second reading, read for the exact sense of all the words; if there are words you don't understand, look them up in a dictionary. Dwell on any difficult parts as long as you need to.

If you read the poem silently to yourself, sound its words in your mind. (This is a technique that will get you nowhere in a speed-reading course, but it may help the poem to do its work on you.) Better still, read the poem aloud, or hear someone else read it. You may discover meanings you didn't perceive in it before. Even if you are no actor, to decide how to speak a poem can be an excellent method of getting to understand it. Some poems, like bells, seem heavy till heard. Listen while reading the following lines from Alexander Pope's *Dunciad*. Attacking the minor poet James Ralph, who had sung the praises of a mistress named Cynthia, Pope makes the goddess of Dullness exclaim:

> "Silence, ye wolves! while Ralph to Cynthia howls,
> And makes night hideous—answer him, ye owls!"

When *ye owls* slide together and become *yowls,* poor Ralph's serenade is turned into the nightly outcry of a cat.

Try to **paraphrase** the poem as a whole, or perhaps just the more difficult lines. In paraphrasing, we put into our own words what we understand the poem to say, restating ideas that seem essential, coming out and stating what the poem may only suggest. This may sound like a heartless thing to do to a poem, but good poems can stand it. In fact, to compare a poem to its paraphrase is an excellent way to see the distance between poetry and prose.

A. E. Housman (1859–1936)

LOVELIEST OF TREES, THE CHERRY NOW   1896

Loveliest of trees, the cherry now
Is hung with bloom along the bough,
And stands about the woodland ride
Wearing white for Eastertide.

Now, of my threescore years and ten, *70*   5
Twenty will not come again,
And take from seventy springs a score,
It only leaves me fifty more.

And since to look at things in bloom
Fifty springs are little room,
About the woodlands I will go   10
To see the cherry hung with snow.

20 yrs old
"running out of time"

Though simple, Housman's poem is far from simple-minded, and it contains at least one possible problem: what, in this instance, is a *ride*? If we guess, we won't be far wrong; but a dictionary helps: "a road or path through the woods, especially for horseback riding." A paraphrase of the poem might say something like this (in language easier to forget than the original): "Now it is Easter time, and the cherry tree in the woods by the path is in blossom. I'm twenty, my life is passing. I expect to live the average life-span of seventy. That means I'm going to see only fifty more springs, so I had better go out into the woods and start looking." And the paraphrase might add, to catch the deeper implication, "Life is brief and fleeting: I must enjoy beauty while I may."

These dull remarks, roughly faithful to what Housman is saying, are clearly as far from being poetry as a cherry pit is far from being a cherry. Still, they can help whoever makes the paraphrase to see the main argument of Housman's poem: its **theme** or central thought. Theme isn't the same thing as **subject,** the central topic. In "Loveliest of trees," the subject is cherry blossoms, or the need to look at them, but the theme is "Time flies: enjoy beauty now!" Not all poems clearly assert a proposition, but many do; some even declare their themes in their very first lines: "Gather ye rose-buds while ye may" — enjoy love before it's too late. The theme stated in that famous opening line (from Robert Herrick's "To the Virgins, to Make Much of Time," page 761) is so familiar that it has a name: **carpe diem** (Latin for "seize the day"), a favorite argument of poets from Horace to Housman.

A paraphrase, of course, never tells *all* that a poem contains; nor will every reader agree that a particular paraphrase is accurate. We all make our own interpretations; and sometimes the total meaning of a poem evades even the poet who wrote it. Asked to explain his difficult *Sordello*, Robert Browning replied that when he had written the poem only God and he knew what it meant; but "Now, only God knows." Still, to analyze a poem *as if* we could be certain of its meaning is, in general, more fruitful than to proceed as if no certainty could ever be had. The latter approach is likely to end in complete subjectivity: the attitude of the reader who says, "Housman's 'Loveliest of trees' is really about a walk in the snow; it is, because I think it is. How can you prove me wrong?"

All of us bring to our readings of poems certain personal associations, as Housman's "Loveliest of trees" might convey a particular pleasure to a reader who had climbed cherry trees when he was small. To some extent, these associations are inevitable, even to be welcomed. But we need to distinguish between irrelevant, tangential responses and those the poem calls for. The reader who can't stand "Loveliest of trees" because cherries remind him of blood, is reading a poem of his own, not Housman's.

Housman's poem is a **lyric:** a short poem expressing the thoughts and feelings of a single speaker. (As its Greek name suggests, a lyric originally was sung to the music of a lyre.) Often a lyric is written in the first person ("About the woodlands *I* will go"), but not always. It may be, for instance, a description of an object or an experience in which the poet isn't even mentioned. Housman's first stanza, printed by itself as a complete poem, would still be a lyric. Though a lyric may relate an incident, we tend to think of it as a reflective poem in which little physical action takes place — unlike a **narrative poem,** one whose main concern is to tell a story.

At the moment, it is a safe bet that, in English and other Western languages, lyrics are more plentiful than other kinds of poetry (novels having virtually replaced the long narrative poems esteemed from the time of Homer's *Odyssey* to the time of Tennyson's *Idylls of the King*). **Didactic poetry,** to mention one other kind, is poetry apparently written to teach or to state a message. In a lyric, the speaker may express sadness; in a didactic poem, he may explain that sadness is inherent in life. Poems that impart a body of knowledge, like Ovid's *Art of Love* and Lucretius's *On the Nature of Things,* are didactic. Such instructive poetry was favored especially by classical Latin poets and by English poets of the eighteenth century. In *The Fleece* (1757), John Dyer celebrated the British woolen industry and included practical advice on raising sheep:

> In cold stiff soils the bleaters oft complain
> Of gouty ails, by shepherds termed the halt:
> Those let the neighboring fold or ready crook
> Detain, and pour into their cloven feet

Corrosive drugs, deep-searching arsenic,
Dry alum, verdegris, or vitriol keen.

One might agree with Dr. Johnson's comment on Dyer's effort: "The subject, Sir, cannot be made poetical." But it may be argued that didactic poetry (to quote a recent view) "is not intrinsically any less poetic because of its subject-matter than lines about a rose fluttering in the breeze are intrinsically more poetic because of their subject-matter."[1] John Milton also described sick sheep in "Lycidas," a poem few readers have thought unpoetic:

The hungry sheep look up, and are not fed,
But, swoll'n with wind and the rank mist they draw,
Rot inwardly, and foul contagion spread . . .

What makes Milton's lines better poetry than Dyer's is, among other things, a difference in attitude. Sick sheep to Dyer mean the loss of a few shillings and pence; to Milton, whose sheep stand for English Christendom, they mean a moral catastrophe.

Now and again we meet a poem—perhaps startling and memorable—into which the method of paraphrase won't take us far. Some portion of any deep poem resists explanation, but certain poems resist it almost entirely. Many poems of religious mystics seem closer to dream than waking. So do poems that record hallucinations or drug experiences, such as Coleridge's "Kubla Khan" (page 730), as well as poems that embody some private system of beliefs, such as Blake's "The Sick Rose" (page 725), or the same poet's lines from *Jerusalem*,

For a Tear is an Intellectual thing,
And a Sigh is the Sword of an Angel King.

So do nonsense poems, translations of primitive folk songs, and surreal poems.[2] Such poetry may move us and give pleasure (although not, perhaps, the pleasure of mental understanding). We do it no harm by trying to paraphrase it, though we may fail. Whether logically clear or strangely opaque, good poems appeal to the intelligence and do not shrink from it.

So far, we have taken it for granted that poetry differs from prose; yet all our strategies for reading poetry—plowing straight on through and then going back, isolating difficulties, trying to paraphrase, reading aloud, using a dictionary—are no different from those we might employ

---

[1] Sylvan Barnet, Morton Berman, and William Burto, *A Dictionary of Literary, Dramatic, and Cinematic Terms*, 2nd ed. (Boston: Little, Brown, 1971).

[2] The French poet André Breton, founder of **surrealism,** a movement in art and writing, declared that a higher reality exists, which to mortal eyes looks absurd. To mirror that reality, surrealist poets are fond of bizarre and dreamlike objects such as soluble fish and white-haired revolvers.

in unraveling a complicated piece of prose. Poetry, after all, is similar to prose in most respects; at the very least, it is written in the same language. And like prose, poetry imparts knowledge. It tells us, for instance, something about the season and habitat of cherry trees and how one can feel toward them. Maybe a poet knows no more of cherry trees than a writer of seed-catalog descriptions, if as much. And yet Housman's perception of cherry blossoms as snow, with the implication that they too will soon melt and disappear, indicates a kind of knowledge that seed catalogs do not ordinarily reveal.

Robert Francis (b. 1901)

CATCH   1950

Two boys uncoached are tossing a poem together,
Overhand, underhand, backhand, sleight of hand, every hand,
Teasing with attitudes, latitudes, interludes, altitudes,
High, make him fly off the ground for it, low, make him stoop,
Make him scoop it up, make him as-almost-as-possible miss it,   5
Fast, let him sting from it, now, now fool him slowly,
Anything, everything tricky, risky, nonchalant,
Anything under the sun to outwit the prosy,
Over the tree and the long sweet cadence down,
Over his head, make him scramble to pick up the meaning,   10
And now, like a posy, a pretty one plump in his hands.

QUESTIONS

1. Who are the two boys in this poem?
2. Point out a few of the most important similarities in this extended comparison.
3. Consider especially line 8: *Anything under the sun to outwit the prosy*. What, in your own words, does Robert Francis mean?

Emily Dickinson (1830–1886)

I TASTE A LIQUOR NEVER BREWED   (about 1860)

I taste a liquor never brewed–
From Tankards scooped in Pearl–
Not all the Frankfort Berries
Yield such an Alcohol!

Inebriate of Air–am I–   5
And Debauchee of Dew–
Reeling–thro endless summer days–
From inns of Molten Blue–

When "Landlords" turn the drunken Bee
Out of the Foxglove's door–
When Butterflies–renounce their "drams"–
I shall but drink the more!

Till Seraphs swing their snowy Hats–
And Saints–to windows run–
To see the little Tippler
From Manzanilla come!

10

15

I TASTE A LIQUOR NEVER BREWED. 3. *Frankfort Berries:* grapes of the many vineyards near Frankfort on the Main, Germany. In another version of this poem, the third line reads, "Not all the Vats upon the Rhine." 16. *Manzanilla:* Perhaps the poet was thinking of Manzanillo, a port city in Cuba from which rum was shipped; there is also a Spanish sherry called Manzanilla. In the poet's other version, the last line reads, "Leaning against the– Sun–."

QUESTIONS

1. Is this lyric, narrative, or didactic poetry?
2. Does Emily Dickinson say anything in particular in this poem, or is she just waxing ecstatic? Try to paraphrase her poem and state its theme.
3. After having made your paraphrase, go back to the poem and see what qualities or elements it has that your paraphrase (naturally) lacks. What does this comparison tell you about the differences between prose and poetry?

Donald Finkel (b. 1929)

HANDS– *poem has hands*

1966

The poem makes truth a little more disturbing,
like a good bra, lifts it and holds it out
in both hands. (In some of the flashier stores
there's a model with the hands stitched on, in red or black.)

Lately the world you wed, for want of such hands,
sags in the bed beside you like a tired wife.
For want of such hands, the face of the moon is bored,
the tree does not stretch and yearn, nor the groin tighten.

5

Devious or frank, in any case,
the poem is calculated to arouse.
Lean back and let its hands play freely on you:
there comes a moment, lifted and aroused,
when the two of you are equally beautiful.

10

QUESTIONS

1. At what moments in "Hands" do you sense that the poet is kidding?
2. Playful as this poem may be, what serious points does Finkel make about the nature of poetry? Explain how, in his view, "real life" relates to poetry (lines

1–3); how the world seems poorer without poetry (lines 5–9); how the reader can be *lifted and aroused* (line 12).

Robinson Jeffers (1887–1962)

To the Stone-Cutters   1925

Stone-cutters fighting time with marble, you foredefeated
Challengers of oblivion
Eat cynical earnings, knowing rock splits, records fall down,
The square-limbed Roman letters
Scale in the thaws, wear in the rain. The poet as well   5
Builds his monument mockingly;
For man will be blotted out, the blithe earth die, the brave sun
Die blind, his heart blackening:
Yet stones have stood for a thousand years, and pained thoughts found
The honey of peace in old poems.   10

William Shakespeare (1564–1616)

Not marble nor the gilded monuments   1609

Not marble nor the gilded monuments
Of princes shall outlive this pow'rful rime;
But you shall shine more bright in these contènts
Than unswept stone, besmeared with sluttish time.
When wasteful war shall statues overturn,   5
And broils° root out the work of masonry,   *brawls, battles*
Nor Mars his sword nor war's quick fire shall burn
The living record of your memory.
'Gainst death and all oblivious enmity
Shall you pace forth; your praise shall still find room   10
Even in the eyes of all posterity
That wear this world out to the ending doom.
   So, till the Judgment that° yourself arise,   *when*
   You live in this, and dwell in lovers' eyes.

Questions

1. What subject do these two poems have in common?
2. State in your own words each poet's theme. How do the two appear to differ in their attitudes toward poetry?
3. Is Shakespeare making a wild boast, or does the statement in lines 1–8 seem at all borne out by events of the past four centuries?

418   Entrances

13 Listening to a Voice

TONE

In late-show Westerns, when one hombre taunts another, it is customary for the second to drawl, "Smile when you say that, pardner" or "Mister, I don't like your tone of voice." Sometimes in reading a poem, although we neither can see a face nor hear a voice, we can infer the poet's attitude from other evidence.

Like tone of voice, **tone** in literature often conveys an attitude toward the person addressed. Like the manner of a person, the manner of a poem may be friendly or belligerent toward its reader, condescending or respectful. Again like tone of voice, the tone of a poem may tell us how the speaker feels about himself or herself: cocksure or humble, for example. But most of the time when we ask, "What is the tone of a poem?" we mean, "What attitude does the poet take toward a theme or a subject?" Is the poet being affectionate, hostile, earnest, playful, sarcastic, or what? We may never be able to know, of course, the poet's personal feelings. All we need know is how to feel when we read a poem.

Strictly speaking, tone isn't an attitude; it is whatever in the poem makes an attitude clear to us: the choice of certain words instead of others, the picking out of certain details. In Housman's "Loveliest of trees," for example, the poet communicates his admiration for a cherry tree's beauty by singling out for attention its white blossoms; had he wanted to show his dislike for the tree, he might have concentrated on its broken branches, birdlime, or snails. Rightly to perceive the tone of a poem, we need to read the poem carefully, paying attention to whatever suggestions we find in it.

Theodore Roethke (1908–1963)

MY PAPA'S WALTZ   1948

The whiskey on your breath
Could make a small boy dizzy;
But I hung on like death:
Such waltzing was not easy.

We romped until the pans
Slid from the kitchen shelf;
My mother's countenance
Could not unfrown itself.

The hand that held my wrist
Was battered on one knuckle;
At every step you missed
My right ear scraped a buckle.

You beat time on my head
With a palm caked hard by dirt,
Then waltzed me off to bed
Still clinging to your shirt.

What is the tone of this poem? Most readers find the speaker's attitude toward his father warmly affectionate, and take this recollection of
childhood to be a happy one. But at least one reader, concentrating on
certain details and ignoring others, once wrote: "Roethke expresses his
resentment for his father, a drunken brute with dirty hands and a
whiskey breath who carelessly hurt the child's ear and manhandled
him." Although this reader accurately noticed some of the events in the
poem, he completely missed the tone of the poem, and so misunderstood it altogether. Among other things, this reader didn't notice the
rollicking rhythms of the poem; the playfulness of a rime like *dizzy* and
easy; the joyful suggestions of the words *waltz, waltzing,* and *romped.*
Probably the reader didn't stop to visualize this scene in all its comedy,
with kitchen pans falling and the father happily using his son's head for
a drum. Nor did he stop to feel the suggestions in the last line, with the
boy *still clinging* with persistent love.

Such a poem, though it includes lifelike details that aren't pretty,
has a tone relatively easy to recognize. So does **satiric poetry,** a kind of
comic poetry that generally conveys a message. Usually its tone is one of
detached amusement, withering contempt, and implied superiority. In
a satiric poem, the poet ridicules some person or persons (or perhaps
some kind of human behavior), examining the victim by the light of
certain principles and implying that the reader, too, ought to feel contempt for the victim.

Countee Cullen (1903–1946)
For a Lady I Know   1925

She even thinks that up in heaven
    Her class lies late and snores,
While poor black cherubs rise at seven
    To do celestial chores.

1. What is Cullen's message?
2. How would you characterize the tone of this poem? Wrathful? Amused?

In some poems the poet's attitude may be plain enough; while in other poems attitudes may be so mingled that it is hard to describe them tersely without doing injustice to the poem. Does Andrew Marvell in "To His Coy Mistress" (page 780) take a serious or playful attitude toward the fact that he and his lady are destined to be food for worms? No one-word answer will suffice. And what of T. S. Eliot's "Love Song of J. Alfred Prufrock" (page 746)? In his attitude toward his redemption-seeking hero who wades with trousers rolled, Eliot is seriously funny. Such a mingled tone may be seen in the following poem by the wife of a governor of the Massachusetts Bay Colony and the earliest American poet of note. Anne Bradstreet's first book, *The Tenth Muse Lately Sprung Up in America* (1650), had been published in England without her consent. She wrote these lines to preface a second edition:

Anne Bradstreet (1612?–1672)
THE AUTHOR TO HER BOOK   1678

Thou ill-formed offspring of my feeble brain,
Who after birth did'st by my side remain,
Till snatched from thence by friends, less wise than true,
Who thee abroad exposed to public view;
Made thee in rags, halting, to the press to trudge,   5
Where errors were not lessened, all may judge.
At thy return my blushing was not small,
My rambling brat (in print) should mother call;
I cast thee by as one unfit for light,
Thy visage was so irksome in my sight;   10
Yet being mine own, at length affection would
Thy blemishes amend, if so I could:
I washed thy face, but more defects I saw,
And rubbing off a spot, still made a flaw.
I stretched thy joints to make thee even feet,   15
Yet still thou run'st more hobbling than is meet;
In better dress to trim thee was my mind,
But nought save homespun cloth in the house I find.
In this array, 'mongst vulgars may'st thou roam;
In critics' hands beware thou dost not come;   20
And take thy way where yet thou are not known.
If for thy Father asked, say thou had'st none;
And for thy Mother, she alas is poor,
Which caused her thus to send thee out of door.

In the author's comparison of her book to an illegitimate ragamuffin, we may be struck by the details of scrubbing and dressing a child: details that might well occur to a mother who had scrubbed and dressed many. As she might feel toward such a child, so she feels toward her book. She starts by deploring it but, as the poem goes on, cannot deny it her affection. Humor enters (as in the pun in line 15). She must dress the creature in *homespun cloth*, something both crude and serviceable. By the end of her poem, Mrs. Bradstreet seems to regard her book-child with tenderness, amusement, and a certain indulgent awareness of its faults. To read this poem is to sense its mingling of several attitudes. Simultaneously, a poet can be merry and in earnest.

Walt Whitman (1819–1892)

To a Locomotive in Winter   1881

Thee for my recitative,
Thee in the driving storm even as now, the snow, the winter-day
    declining,
Thee in thy panoply°, thy measur'd dual throbbing and thy   *suit of*
    beat convulsive,   *armor*
Thy black cylindric body, golden brass and silvery steel,
Thy ponderous side-bars, parallel and connecting rods, gyrating,
    shuttling at thy sides,   5
Thy metrical, now swelling pant and roar, now tapering in the distance,
Thy great protruding head-light fix'd in front,
Thy long, pale, floating vapor-pennants, tinged with delicate purple,
The dense and murky clouds out-belching from thy smoke-stack,
Thy knitted frame, thy springs and valves, the tremulous twinkle of
    thy wheels,   10
Thy train of cars behind, obedient, merrily following,
Through gale or calm, now swift, now slack, yet steadily careering;
Type of the modern—emblem of motion and power—pulse of the continent,
For once come serve the Muse and merge in verse, even as here I
    see thee,
With storm and buffeting gusts of wind and falling snow,   15
By day thy warning ringing bell to sound its notes,
By night thy silent signal lamps to swing.

Fierce-throated beauty!
Roll through my chant with all thy lawless music, thy swinging lamps
    at night,
Thy madly-whistled laughter, echoing, rumbling like an earthquake,
    rousing all,   20
Law of thyself complete, thine own track firmly holding,
(No sweetness debonair of tearful harp or glib piano thine,)
Thy trills of shrieks by rocks and hills return'd,
Launch'd o'er the prairies wide, across the lakes,
To the free skies unpent and glad and strong.   25

Emily Dickinson (1830–1886)

I like to see it lap the Miles

(about 1862)

I like to see it lap the Miles–
And lick the Valleys up–
And stop to feed itself at Tanks–
And then–prodigious step

Around a Pile of Mountains–   5
And supercilious peer
In Shanties–by the sides of Roads–
And then a Quarry pare

To fit its Ribs
And crawl between   10
Complaining all the while
In horrid–hooting stanza–
Then chase itself down Hill–

And neigh like Boanerges–
Then–punctual as a Star   15
Stop–docile and omnipotent
At its own stable door–

Questions

1. What differences in tone do you find between Whitman's and Emily Dickinson's poems? Point out in each poem whatever contributes to these differences.
2. *Boanerges* in Emily Dickinson's last stanza means "sons of thunder," a name given by Christ to the disciples John and James (see Mark 3:17). How far should the reader work out the particulars of this comparison? Does it make the tone of the poem serious?
3. In Whitman's opening line, what is a *recitative*? What other specialized terms from the vocabulary of music and poetry does each poem contain? How do they help underscore Whitman's theme?
4. Poets and song-writers probably have regarded the locomotive with more affection than they have shown most other machines. Why do you suppose this to be? Can you think of any other poems or songs for example?
5. What do these two poems tell you about locomotives that you would not be likely to find in a technical book on railroading?
6. Are the subjects of the two poems identical? Discuss.

THE PERSON IN THE POEM

The tone of a poem, we said, is like tone of voice in that both communicate feelings. Still, this comparison raises a question: when we read a poem, whose "voice" speaks to us?

"The poet's" is one possible answer; and in the case of many a poem, that answer may be right. Reading Anne Bradstreet's "The Author to Her Book," we can be reasonably sure that the poet speaks of her very own book, and of her own experiences. In order to read a poem, we seldom need to read a poet's biography; but in truth there are certain poems whose full effect depends upon our knowing at least a fact or two of the poet's life. In this poem, surely the poet refers to himself:

Trumbull Stickney (1874–1904)

SIR, SAY NO MORE   1905

Sir, say no more,
Within me 'tis as if
The green and climbing eyesight of a cat
Crawled near my mind's poor birds.

The subject of Stickney's poem is not some nightmare or hallucination. The poem may mean more to you if you know that Stickney, who wrote it shortly before his death, had been afflicted by cancer of the brain. But the poem is not a prosaic entry in the diary of a dying man, nor is it a good poem because a dying man wrote it. Not only does it tell truth from experience, it speaks in memorable words.

Most of us can tell the difference between a person we meet in life and a person we meet in a work of art—unlike the moviegoer in the Philippines who, watching a villain in an exciting film, pulled out a revolver and peppered the screen. And yet, in reading poems, we are liable to temptation. When the poet says "I," we may want to assume that he, like Trumbull Stickney, is making a personal statement. But reflect: do all poems have to be personal? Here is a brief poem inscribed on the tombstone of an infant in Burial Hill cemetery, Plymouth, Massachusetts:

Since I have been so quickly done for,
I wonder what I was begun for.

We do not know who wrote those lines, but it is clear that the poet was not a short-lived infant writing from personal experience. In other poems, the speaker is obviously a fictitious character. As a grown man William Blake, a skilled professional engraver, wrote a poem in the voice of a boy, an illiterate chimney sweeper. (The poem appears on page 438.) No law decrees that the speaker in a poem even has to be human: good poems have been uttered by clouds, pebbles, and cats. A **dramatic monologue** is a poem written as a speech made at some decisive or revealing moment. It is usually addressed by the speaker to some other character (who remains silent). Robert Browning, who developed the form, liked to put words into the mouths of characters stupider, weaker, or nastier than he: for instance see "My Last Duchess" (page 726), in which the speaker is an arrogant Renaissance duke. Browning himself, from all reports, was neither domineering nor merciless.

Let's consider a poem spoken by a fictitious character—in this case, a child. To understand the poem, you need to pay attention not only to what the child says, but also to how the poet seems to feel about it.

Randall Jarrell (1914–1965)
A SICK CHILD

[handwritten margin note: speaker is the child / postman - imagination]

1951

The postman comes when I am still in bed.
"Postman, what do you have for me today?"
I say to him. (But really I'm in bed.)
Then he says—what shall I have him say?

"This letter says that you are president   5
Of—this word here; it's a republic."
Tell them I can't answer right away.
"It's your duty." No, I'd rather just be sick.

[handwritten margin note: the child is bored!]

Then he tells me there are letters saying everything
That I can think of that I want for them to say.   10
I say, "Well, thank you very much. Good-bye."
He is ashamed, and turns and walks away.

If I can think of it, it isn't what I want.
I want . . . I want a ship from some near star
To land in the yard, and beings to come out   15
And think to me: "So this is where you are!

[handwritten margin note: postman is disappointed because can't satisfy boy.]

Come." Except that they won't do,
I thought of them. . . . And yet somewhere there must be
Something that's different from everything.
All that I've never thought of—think of me!

QUESTIONS

1. Would you call the speaker unfeeling or sensitive? Unimaginative or imaginative? How do you know?
2. Why is the postman *ashamed*?
3. Besides sickness, what is bothering the child? What does the child long for?
4. Do you think Jarrell sympathizes with the child's wishes and longings? By what means does he indicate his own attitude?

We tend to think of a poem as simply an expression of the feelings a poet had while writing it. And yet, as the following comic poem indicates, sometimes a poet in the process of writing a poem has feelings that the poem doesn't mention.

Alden Nowlan (b. 1933)

The Loneliness of the Long Distance Runner
1967

My wife bursts into the room
where I'm writing well
of my love for her

and because now
the poem is lost

I silently curse her.

Humorously, Nowlan suggests that loving his wife isn't the same as writing a poem about loving her. A good poem (if the poet can finish it) is a fixed and changeless thing; but evidently a living, changing poet with various emotions had to take a certain length of time in writing it.

In a famous definition, William Wordsworth calls poetry "the spontaneous overflow of powerful feelings . . . recollected in tranquillity." But in the case of the following poem, Wordsworth's feelings weren't all his; they didn't just overflow spontaneously; and the process of tranquil recollection had to go on for years.

William Wordsworth (1770–1850)

I Wandered Lonely as a Cloud

I wandered lonely as a cloud
  That floats on high o'er vales and hills,
When all at once I saw a crowd,
  A host, of golden daffodils,
Beside the lake, beneath the trees,
Fluttering and dancing in the breeze.
                5

Continuous as the stars that shine
  And twinkle on the milky way,
They stretched in never-ending line
  Along the margin of a bay:
Ten thousand saw I at a glance,
Tossing their heads in sprightly dance.
                10

The waves beside them danced; but they
  Out-did the sparkling waves in glee;
A poet could not but be gay,
  In such a jocund company;
I gazed—and gazed—but little thought
What wealth the show to me had brought:
                15

For oft, when on my couch I lie
  In vacant or in pensive mood,
They flash upon that inward eye   20
  Which is the bliss of solitude;
And then my heart with pleasure fills,
And dances with the daffodils.

Between the first printing of the poem in 1807 and the version of 1815 given here, Wordsworth made several deliberate improvements. He changed *dancing* to *golden* in line 4, *Along* to *Beside* in line 5, *Ten thousand* to *Fluttering and* in line 6, *laughing* to *jocund* in line 16, and he added a whole stanza (the second). In fact, the writing of the poem was unspontaneous enough for Wordsworth, at a loss for lines 21–22, to take them from his wife Mary. It is likely that the experience of daffodil-watching was not entirely his to begin with but was derived in part from the recollections his sister Dorothy Wordsworth had set down in her journal of April 15, 1802, two years before he first drafted his poem:

> When we were in the woods beyond Gowbarrow Park we saw a few daffodils close to the water-side. We fancied that the lake had floated the seeds ashore, and that the little colony had so sprung up. But as we went along there were more and yet more; and at last, under the boughs of the trees, we saw that there was a long belt of them along the shore, about the breadth of a country turnpike road. I never saw daffodils so beautiful. They grew among the mossy stones about and about them; some rested their heads upon these stones as on a pillow for weariness; and the rest tossed and reeled and danced, and seemed as if they verily laughed with the wind, that flew upon them over the Lake; they looked so gay, ever glancing, ever changing. This wind blew directly over the Lake to them. There was here and there a little knot, and a few stragglers a few yards higher up; but they were so few as not to disturb the simplicity, unity, and life of that one busy highway.

Notice that Wordsworth's poem echoes a few of his sister's observations. Weaving poetry out of their mutual memories, Wordsworth has offered the experience as if altogether his own, made himself lonely, and left Dorothy out. The point is not that Wordsworth is a liar or a plagiarist but that, like any other good poet, he has transformed ordinary life into art. A process of interpreting, shaping, and ordering had to intervene between the experience of looking at daffodils and the finished poem.

    We need not deny that a poet's experience can contribute to a poem nor that the emotion in the poem can indeed be the poet's. Still, to write a good poem one has to do more than live and feel. It seems a pity that, as Randall Jarrell has said, a cardinal may write verses worse than his youngest choirboy's. But writing poetry takes skill and imagination — qualities that extensive travel and wide experience do not necessarily give. For much of her life, Emily Dickinson seldom strayed from her family's house and grounds in Amherst, Massachusetts; yet her rimed lifestudies of a snake, a bee, and a hummingbird contain more poetry than we find in any firsthand description (so far) of the surface of the moon.

EXPERIMENT: *Reading with and without Biography*

Read the following poem and state what you understand from it. Then consider the circumstances in which it probably came to be written. (Some information is offered in a note at the end of this chapter.) Does the meaning of the poem change? To what extent does an appreciation of the poem need the support of biography?

William Carlos Williams (1883–1963)

THE RED WHEELBARROW   1923

so much depends
upon

a red wheel
barrow

glazed with rain
water

beside the white
chickens.

IRONY

To see a distinction between the poet and the words of a fictitious character — between Randall Jarrell and "A Sick Child" — is to be aware of **irony:** a manner of speaking that implies a discrepancy. If the mask says one thing and we sense that the writer is in fact saying something else, the writer has adopted an **ironic point of view.** No finer illustration exists in English than Jonathan Swift's "A Modest Proposal," an essay in which Swift speaks as an earnest, humorless citizen who sets forth his reasonable plan to aid the Irish poor. The plan is so monstrous no sane reader can assent to it: the poor are to sell their children as meat for the tables of their landlords. From behind his falseface, Swift is actually recommending not cannibalism but love and Christian charity.

A poem is often made complicated and more interesting by another kind of irony. **Verbal irony** occurs whenever words say one thing but mean something else, usually the opposite. The word *love* means *hate* here: "I just *love* to stay home and do my hair on a Saturday night!" If the verbal irony is conspicuously bitter, heavy-handed, and mocking, it is **sarcasm:** "Oh, he's the biggest spender in the world, all right!" (The sarcasm, if that statement were spoken, would be underscored by the speaker's tone of voice.) A famous instance of sarcasm is Mark Antony's line in his oration over the body of slain Julius Caesar: "Brutus is an honorable man." Antony repeats this line until the enraged populace begins shouting exactly what he means to call Brutus and the other conspirators: traitors, villains, murderers. We had best be alert for irony on the printed page, for if we miss it, our interpretations of a poem may go wild.

Robert Creeley (b. 1926)

Oh No   1959

If you wander far enough
you will come to it
and when you get there
they will give you a place to sit

for yourself only, in a nice chair,
and all your friends will be there
with smiles on their faces
and they will likewise all have places.

This poem is rich in verbal irony. The title helps point out that between the speaker's words and attitude lie deep differences. In line 2, what is *it*? Old age? The wandering suggests a conventional metaphor: the journey of life. Is *it* literally a rest home for "senior citizens," or perhaps some naïve popular concept of heaven (such as we meet in comic strips: harps, angels with hoops for halos) in which the saved all sit around in a ring, smugly congratulating one another? We can't be sure, but the speaker's attitude toward this final sitting-place is definite. It is a place for the selfish, as we infer from the phrase *for yourself only*. And *smiles on their faces* may hint that the smiles are unchanging and forced. There is a difference between saying "They had smiles on their faces" and "They smiled": the latter suggests that the smiles came from within. The word *nice* is to be regarded with distrust. If we see through this speaker, as Creeley implies we can do, we realize that, while pretending to be sweet-talking us into a seat, actually he is revealing the horror of a little hell. And the title is the poet's reaction to it (or the speaker's unironic, straightforward one): "Oh no! Not *that!*"

Dramatic irony, like verbal irony, contains an element of contrast, but it usually refers to a situation in a play wherein a character, whose knowledge is limited, says, does, or encounters something of greater significance than he or she knows. We, the spectators, realize the meaning of this speech or action, for the playwright has afforded us superior knowledge. In Sophocles' *King Oedipus*, when Oedipus vows to punish whoever has brought down a plague upon the city of Thebes, we know — as he does not — that the man he would punish is himself. (Referring to such a situation that precedes the downfall of a hero in a tragedy, some critics speak of **tragic irony** instead of dramatic irony.) Superior knowledge can be enjoyed not only by spectators in a theater but by readers of poetry as well. In *Paradise Lost*, we know in advance that Adam will fall into temptation, and we recognize his overconfidence when he neglects a warning. The situation of Oedipus contains also **cosmic irony,** or **irony of fate:** some Fate with a grim sense of humor seems cruelly to trick a human being. Cosmic irony clearly exists in poems in which fate or the Fates are personified and seen as hostile, as in Thomas Hardy's "The Convergence of the Twain" (p. 757); and it may be said to occur too in a poem such as Robinson's "Richard Cory" (p. 514) and in MacLeish's "The End of the World" (p. 779). Evidently it is a twist of fate for the most envied man in town to kill himself and another twist of fate for spectators at a circus to find themselves suddenly beholding a greater and more horrific show than they had paid for: the end of the world.

To sum up: the effect of irony depends upon the reader's noticing some incongruity or discrepancy between two things. In *verbal irony*, there is a contrast between the speaker's words and meaning; in an *ironic point of view*, between the writer's attitude and what is spoken by a fictitious character; in *dramatic irony*, between the limited knowledge of a character and the fuller knowledge of the reader or spectator; in *cosmic irony*, between a character's aspiration and the treatment he or she receives at the hands of Fate. Although in the work of an inept poet irony can be crude and obvious sarcasm, it is invaluable to a poet of more complicated mind, who imagines more than one perspective.

W. H. Auden (1907–1973)

The Unknown Citizen   1940

(To JS/07/M/378
This Marble Monument
Is Erected by the State)

— someone who knows the citizen

He was found by the Bureau of Statistics to be
One against whom there was no official complaint,
And all the reports on his conduct agree
That, in the modern sense of an old-fashioned word, he was a saint,
For in everything he did he served the Greater Community.   5
Except for the War till the day he retired
He worked in a factory and never got fired,
But satisfied his employers, Fudge Motors Inc.

Yet he wasn't a scab or odd in his views,
For his Union reports that he paid his dues,
(Our report on his Union shows it was sound)
And our Social Psychology workers found
That he was popular with his mates and liked a drink.
The Press are convinced that he bought a paper every day
And that his reactions to advertisements were normal in every way.
Policies taken out in his name prove that he was fully insured,
And his Health-card shows he was once in hospital but left it cured.
Both Producers Research and High-Grade Living declare
He was fully sensible to the advantages of the Installment Plan
And had everything necessary to the Modern Man,
A phonograph, a radio, a car and a frigidaire.
Our researchers into Public Opinion are content
That he held the proper opinions for the time of year;
When there was peace, he was for peace; when there was war, he went.
He was married and added five children to the population,   25
Which our Eugenist says was the right number for a parent of his
    generation,
And our teachers report that he never interfered with their education.
Was he free? Was he happy? The question is absurd:
Had anything been wrong, we should certainly have heard.

[handwritten margin notes: "Scott Hartlage called me yesterday - (Jim Cash's old roommate) he is going to night school no - Lisa is in Villa West + working at st. mary's"; line numbers 10, 15, 20]

Questions

1. Read the three-line epitaph at the beginning of the poem as carefully as you read what follows. How does the epitaph help establish the voice by which the rest of the poem is spoken?
2. Who is speaking?
3. What ironic discrepancies do you find between the speaker's attitude toward the subject and that of the poet himself? By what is the poet's attitude made clear?
4. In the phrase "The Unknown Soldier" (of which "The Unknown Citizen" reminds us), what does the word *unknown* mean? What does it mean in the title of Auden's poem?
5. What tendencies in our civilization does Auden satirize?
6. How would you expect the speaker to define a Modern Man, if a phonograph, a radio, a car, and a refrigerator are "everything" a Modern Man needs?

John Betjeman (b. 1906)

In Westminster Abbey   1940

Let me take this other glove off
    As the *vox humana* swells,
And the beauteous fields of Eden
    Bask beneath the Abbey bells.
Here, where England's statesmen lie,   5
Listen to a lady's cry.

[handwritten notes: "painting in ceiling", "woman is praying", "God will favor her + protect her preserve her position"]

Gracious Lord, oh bomb the Germans.
  Spare their women for Thy Sake,
And if that is not too easy
  We will pardon Thy Mistake.
But, gracious Lord, whate'er shall be,   10
Don't let anyone bomb me.

Keep our Empire undismembered,
  Guide our Forces by Thy Hand,
Gallant blacks from far Jamaica,   15
  Honduras and Togoland;
Protect them Lord in all their fights,
And, even more, protect the whites.

Think of what our Nation stands for:
  Books from Boots' and country lanes,   20
Free speech, free passes, class distinction,
  Democracy and proper drains.
Lord, put beneath Thy special care
One-eighty-nine Cadogan Square.

Although dear Lord I am a sinner,   25
  I have done no major crime;
Now I'll come to Evening Service
  Whensoever I have the time.
So, Lord, reserve for me a crown,
And do not let my shares° go down.   *stocks* 30

I will labor for Thy Kingdom,
  Help our lads to win the war,
Send white feathers to the cowards,
  Join the Women's Army Corps,
Then wash the Steps around Thy Throne   35
In the Eternal Safety Zone.

Now I feel a little better,
  What a treat to hear Thy Word,
Where the bones of leading statesmen
  Have so often been interred.   40
And now, dear Lord, I cannot wait
Because I have a luncheon date.

IN WESTMINSTER ABBEY. First printed during World War II. 2. *vox humana:* an organ stop that makes tones similar to those of the human voice. 20. *Boots':* a cut-rate pharmacy.

QUESTIONS

1. Who is the speaker? What do we know about her life style? About her prejudices?
2. Point out some of the places in which she contradicts herself.

3. How would you describe the speaker's attitude toward religion?
4. Through the medium of irony, what positive points do you believe Betjeman makes?

Sarah N. Cleghorn (1876–1959)

THE GOLF LINKS   1917

The golf links lie so near the mill
   That almost every day
The laboring children can look out
   And see the men at play.

QUESTIONS

1. Is this brief poem satiric? Does it contain any verbal irony? Is the poet making a matter-of-fact statement in words that mean just what they say?
2. What other kind of irony is present in the poem?
3. Sarah N. Cleghorn's poem dates from before the enactment of legislation against child labor. Is it still a good poem, or is it hopelessly outdated?
4. How would you state its theme?

EXERCISE: *Detecting Irony*

Point out the kinds of irony that occur in the following poem.

Thomas Hardy (1840–1928)

THE WORKBOX   1914

"See, here's the workbox, little wife,
   That I made of polished oak."
He was a joiner°, of village life;   *carpenter*
   She came of borough folk.

He holds the present up to her   5
   As with a smile she nears
And answers to the profferer,
   " 'Twill last all my sewing years!"

"I warrant it will. And longer too.
   'Tis a scantling that I got   10
Off poor John Wayward's coffin, who
   Died of they knew not what.

"The shingled pattern that seems to cease
   Against your box's rim
Continues right on in the piece   15
   That's underground with him.

"And while I worked it made me think
  Of timber's varied doom:
One inch where people eat and drink,
  The next inch in a tomb.   20

"But why do you look so white, my dear,
  And turn aside your face?
You knew not that good lad, I fear,
  Though he came from your native place?"

"How could I know that good young man,   25
  Though he came from my native town,
When he must have left far earlier than
  I was a woman grown?"

"Ah, no. I should have understood!
  It shocked you that I gave   30
To you one end of a piece of wood
  Whose other is in a grave?"

"Don't, dear, despise my intellect,
  Mere accidental things
Of that sort never have effect   35
  On my imaginings."

Yet still her lips were limp and wan,
  Her face still held aside,
As if she had known not only John,
  But known of what he died.   40

FOR REVIEW AND FURTHER STUDY

Ted Hughes (b. 1930)

SECRETARY   1957

If I should touch her she would shriek and weeping
Crawl off to nurse the terrible wound: all
Day like a starling under the bellies of bulls
She hurries among men, ducking, peeping,

Off in a whirl at the first move of a horn.   5
At dusk she scuttles down the gauntlet of lust
Like a clockwork mouse. Safe home at last
She mends her socks with holes, shirts that are torn

For father and brother, and a delicate supper cooks:
Goes to bed early, shuts out with the light   10
Her thirty years, and lies with buttocks tight,
Hiding her lovely eyes until day break.

1. Comment on the phrase in line 2, *the terrible wound.* Would the speaker himself regard the offense as "terrible"?
2. What traits has the secretary in common with *a starling* (line 3) and *a clockwork mouse* (line 7)?
3. Does the poet express one attitude toward his subject or is the tone of his poem a mingling of more than one ? Explain, referring to particulars in the poem.

John Berryman (1914–1972)

LIFE, FRIENDS, IS BORING. WE MUST NOT SAY SO   1964

Life, friends, is boring. We must not say so.
After all, the sky flashes, the great sea yearns,
we ourselves flash and yearn,
and moreover my mother told me as a boy
(repeatedly) "Ever to confess you're bored   5
means you have no

Inner Resources." I conclude now I have no
inner resources, because I am heavy bored.
Peoples bore me,
literature bores me, especially great literature,   10
Henry bores me, with his plights & gripes
as bad as achilles,

who loves people and valiant art, which bores me.
And the tranquil hills, & gin, look like a drag
and somehow a dog   15
has taken itself & its tail considerably away
into mountains or sea or sky, leaving
behind: me, wag.

QUESTIONS

1. Henry (line 11) is the central figure of Berryman's *77 Dream Songs.* Achilles (line 12), Greek hero of the Trojan war, was portrayed by Shakespeare as a sulking malcontent. Is a comparison of Henry, a rather ordinary American citizen, to Achilles likely to result in a heightening of Henry's importance or in a sense of ironic discrepancy? Discuss.
2. What is confused or self-contradictory in the precept "Ever to confess you're bored means you have no Inner Resources"?
3. What could the poet be trying to indicate by capitalizing *Inner Resources* in line 7 but not in line 8? By writing *achilles* with a small letter?
4. In line 14, what discrepancy do you find between the phrases *the tranquil hills* and *a drag*?
5. In the last line, what double meaning is there in the word *wag*?
6. True or false? "In comparing 'ourselves' to the sky and to the 'great sea,' the

speaker takes the attitude that he and his readers have dignity and grandeur, their emotions being as powerful as lightningbolts and tides." Do you find this paraphrase consistent or inconsistent with the tone of the poem? Why?

EXERCISE: *Telling Tone*

Here are two radically different poems on a similar subject. Try stating the theme of each poem in your own words. How is tone (the speaker's attitude) different in the two poems?

Richard Lovelace (1618–1658)

TO LUCASTA   1649

On Going to the Wars

Tell me not, Sweet, I am unkind
   That from the nunnery
Of thy chaste breast and quiet mind,
   To war and arms I fly.

True, a new mistress now I chase,   5
   The first foe in the field;
And with a stronger faith embrace
   A sword, a horse, a shield.

Yet this inconstancy is such
   As you too shall adore;   10
I could not love thee, Dear, so much,
   Loved I not Honor more.

Wilfred Owen (1893–1918)

DULCE ET DECORUM EST   1920

Bent double, like old beggars under sacks,
Knock-kneed, coughing like hags, we cursed through sludge,
Till on the haunting flares we turned our backs
And towards our distant rest began to trudge.
Men marched asleep. Many had lost their boots   5
But limped on, blood-shod. All went lame; all blind;
Drunk with fatigue; deaf even to the hoots
Of tired, outstripped Five-Nines° that dropped behind.   *gas-shells*

Gas! Gas! Quick, boys!—An ecstasy of fumbling,
Fitting the clumsy helmets just in time;   10
But someone still was yelling out and stumbling
And flound'ring like a man in fire or lime . . .

Dim, through the misty panes and thick green light,
As under a green sea, I saw him drowning.
In all my dreams, before my helpless sight,   15
He plunges at me, guttering, choking, drowning.

If in some smothering dreams you too could pace
Behind the wagon that we flung him in,
And watch the white eyes writhing in his face,
His hanging face, like a devil's sick of sin;   20
If you could hear, at every jolt, the blood
Come gargling from the froth-corrupted lungs,
Obscene as cancer, bitter as the cud
Of vile, incurable sores on innocent tongues, —
My friend, you would not tell with such high zest   25
To children ardent for some desperate glory,
The old Lie: Dulce et decorum est
Pro patria mori.

Dulce et Decorum Est. A British infantry officer in World War I, Owen was killed in action. 17. *you too:* Some manuscript versions of this poem carry the dedication "To Jessie Pope" (a writer of patriotic verse) or "To a certain Poetess." 27–28. *Dulce et . . . mori:* a quotation from the Latin poet Horace, "It is sweet and fitting to die for one's country."

James Stephens (1882–1950)

A Glass of Beer   1918

The lanky hank of a she in the inn over there
Nearly killed me for asking the loan of a glass of beer;
May the devil grip the whey-faced slut by the hair,
And beat bad manners out of her skin for a year.

That parboiled ape, with the toughest jaw you will see   5
On virtue's path, and a voice that would rasp the dead,
Came roaring and raging the minute she looked at me,
And threw me out of the house on the back of my head!

If I asked her master he'd give me a cask a day;
But she, with the beer at hand, not a gill° would arrange!   *quarter-pint* 10
May she marry a ghost and bear him a kitten, and may
The High King of Glory permit her to get the mange.

Questions

1. Who do you take to be the speaker? Is it the poet? The speaker may be angry, but what is the tone of this poem?
2. Would you agree with a commentator who said, "To berate anyone in truly memorable language is practically a lost art in America"? How well does the speaker (an Irishman) succeed? Which of his epithets and curses strike you as particularly imaginative?

Jonathan Swift (1667–1745)

ON STELLA'S BIRTHDAY

(1718–1719)

Stella this day is thirty-four
(We shan't dispute a year or more)—
However, Stella, be not troubled,
Although thy size and years are doubled,
Since first I saw thee at sixteen,   5
The brightest virgin on the green,
So little is thy form declined,
Made up so largely in thy mind.
Oh, would it please the gods, to split
Thy beauty, size, and years, and wit,   10
No age could furnish out a pair
Of nymphs so graceful, wise, and fair,
With half the luster of your eyes,
With half your wit, your years, and size.
And then, before it grew too late,   15
How should I beg of gentle Fate
(That either nymph might have her swain)
To split my worship too in twain.

ON STELLA'S BIRTHDAY. For many years Swift made an annual birthday gift of a poem to his close friend Mrs. Esther Johnson, the degree of whose nearness to the proud and lonely Swift remains an enigma to biographers. 18. *my worship:* as Dean of St. Patrick's in Dublin, Swift was addressed as "Your Worship."

QUESTIONS

1. If you were Stella, would you be amused or insulted by the poet's references to your *size?*
2. According to Swift in lines 7–8, what has compensated Stella for what the years have taken away?
3. Comment on the last four lines. Does Swift exempt himself from growing old?
4. How would you describe the tone of this poem? Offensive (like the speaker's complaints in "A Glass of Beer")? Playfully tender? Sad over Stella's growing fat and old?

William Blake (1757–1827)

THE CHIMNEY SWEEPER

1789

When my mother died I was very young,
And my father sold me while yet my tongue
Could scarcely cry " 'weep! 'weep! 'weep! 'weep!"
So your chimneys I sweep, and in soot I sleep.

There's little Tom Dacre, who cried when his head,   5
That curled like a lamb's back, was shaved: so I said
"Hush, Tom! never mind it, for when your head's bare
You know that the soot cannot spoil your white hair."

And so he was quiet, and that very night,
As Tom was a-sleeping, he had such a sight!   10
That thousands of sweepers, Dick, Joe, Ned, and Jack,
Were all of them locked up in coffins of black.

And by came an Angel who had a bright key,
And he opened the coffins and set them all free;
Then down a green plain leaping, laughing, they run,   15
And wash in a river, and shine in the sun.

Then naked and white, all their bags left behind,
They rise upon clouds and sport in the wind;
And the Angel told Tom, if he'd be a good boy,
He'd have God for his father, and never want joy.   20

And so Tom awoke; and we rose in the dark,
And got with our bags and our brushes to work.
Though the morning was cold, Tom was happy and warm;
So if all do their duty they need not fear harm.

QUESTIONS

1. What does Blake's poem reveal about conditions of life in the London of his day?
2. What does this poem have in common with "The Golf Links" (page 433)?
3. How does "The Chimney Sweeper" resemble "A Sick Child" (page 425)? In what ways does Blake's poem seem much different?
4. Sum up your impressions of the speaker's character. What does he say and do that displays it to us?
5. What pun do you find in line 3? Is its effect comic or serious?
6. In Tom Dacre's dream (lines 11–20), what wishes come true? Do you understand them to be the wishes of the chimney sweepers, of the poet, or of both?
7. In the last line, what is ironic in the speaker's assurance that the dutiful *need not fear harm*? What irony is there in his urging all to *do their duty*? (Who have failed in their duty to *him*?)
8. What is the tone of Blake's poem? Angry? Hopeful? Sorrowful? Compassionate? (Don't feel obliged to sum it up in a single word.)

INFORMATION FOR EXPERIMENT: *Reading with and without Biography*

THE RED WHEELBARROW (p. 428). Dr. Williams's poem reportedly contains a personal experience: he was gazing from the window of the house where one of his patients, a small girl, lay suspended between life and death. (This account, from the director of the public library in Williams's native Rutherford, N.J., is given by Geri M. Rhodes in "The Paterson Metaphor in William Carlos Williams' *Paterson*," master's essay, Tufts University, June 1965.)

14 Words

LITERAL MEANING: WHAT A POEM SAYS FIRST

Although successful as a painter, Edgar Degas struggled to produce sonnets, and found poetry discouragingly hard to write. To his friend, the poet Stéphane Mallarmé, he complained, "What a business! My whole day gone on a blasted sonnet, without getting an inch further . . . and it isn't ideas I'm short of . . . I'm full of them, I've got too many . . ."

"But Degas," said Mallarmé, "you can't make a poem with ideas — you make it with *words!*"[1]

Like the celebrated painter, some people assume that all it takes to make a poem is a bright idea. Poems state ideas, to be sure, and sometimes the ideas are invaluable; and yet the most impressive idea in the world will not make a poem unless its words are selected and arranged with loving art. Some poets take great pains to find the right word. Unable to fill a two-syllable gap in an unfinished line that went, "The seal's wide — — gaze toward Paradise," Hart Crane paged through an unabridged dictionary. When he reached *S,* he found the object of his quest in *spindrift:* "spray skimmed from the sea by a strong wind." The word is exact and memorable. Any word can be the right word, however, if artfully chosen and placed. It may be a word ordinary as *from.* Consider the difference between "The sedge is withered *on* the lake" (a misquotation of a line by Keats) and "The sedge is withered *from* the lake" (what Keats in fact wrote). Keats's original line suggests, as the altered line doesn't, that because the sedge (a growth of grasslike plants) has withered *from* the lake, it has withdrawn mysteriously.

In reading a poem, some people assume that its words can be skipped over rapidly, and they try to leap at once to the poem's general theme. It is as if they fear being thought clods unless they can find huge ideas in the poem (whether or not there are any). Such readers often ig-

---

[1] Paul Valéry, *Degas . . . Manet . . . Morisot,* translated by David Paul (New York: Pantheon, 1960), page 62.

nore the literal meanings of words: the ordinary, matter-of-fact sense to be found in a dictionary. (As you will see in Chapter Sixteen, "Saying and Suggesting," words possess not only dictionary meanings — **denotations** — but also many associations and suggestions — **connotations**.) Consider the following poem and see what you make of it.

William Carlos Williams (1883–1963)

THIS IS JUST TO SAY   1934

I have eaten
the plums
that were in
the icebox
and which   5
you were probably
saving
for breakfast

Forgive me
they were delicious   10
so sweet
and so cold

Some readers distrust a poem so simple and candid. They think, "What's wrong with me? There has to be more to it than this!" But poems seldom are puzzles in need of solutions. We can begin by accepting the poet's statements, without suspecting him of trying to hoodwink us. On later reflection, of course, we might possibly decide that the poet is playfully teasing or being ironic; but Williams gives us no reason to think that. There seems no need to look beyond the literal sense of his words, no profit in speculating that the plums symbolize worldly joys and that the icebox stands for the universe. Clearly, a reader who held such a grand theory would have overlooked (in eagerness to find a significant idea) the plain truth that the poet makes clear to us: that ice-cold plums are a joy to taste, especially if one knows they'll be missed the next morning.

To be sure, Williams's small poem is simpler than most poems are; and yet in reading any poem, no matter how complicated, you will do well to reach slowly and reluctantly for generalizations. An adept reader of poetry reads with open mind — with (in Richard L. McGuire's phrase) "as much innocence as he can muster." For in order to experience a poem, you first have to pay attention to its words; and only if you see what the words are saying are you likely to come to the poem's true theme. Recall Housman's "Loveliest of trees" (page 413): a poem that contains a message (how rapidly life passes, how vital it is to make the most of every spring). Yet before you can realize that theme, you have to notice the color, the quantity, and the weight (*hung with bloom*) of Housman's imagined cherry blossoms.

Poets often strive for words that point to physical details and solid objects. They may do so even when speaking of an abstract idea:

> Beauty is but a flower
> Which wrinkles will devour;
> Brightness falls from the air,
> Queens have died young and fair,
> Dust hath closed Helen's eye.
> I am sick, I must die:
>   Lord, have mercy on us!

In these lines by Thomas Nashe, the abstraction *beauty* has grown petals that shrivel. Brightness may be a general name for light, but Nashe succeeds in giving it the weight of a falling body.

If a poem reads *daffodils* instead of *vegetation, diaper years* instead of *infancy,* and *eighty-four* instead of *numerous,* we call its **diction** — its choice of words — particular and concrete, rather than general and abstract. In an apt criticism, William Butler Yeats once took to task the poems of W. E. Henley for being "abstract, as even an actor's movement can be when the thought of doing is plainer to his mind than the doing itself: the straight line from cup to lip, let us say, more plain than the hand's own sensation weighed down by that heavy spillable cup."[2] To convey the sense of that heavy spillable cup was to Yeats a goal, one that surely he attained in "Among School Children" by describing a woman's stark face: "Hollow of cheek as though it drank the wind / And took a mess of shadows for its meat." A more abstract-minded poet might have written "Her hollow cheek and wasted, hungry look." Ezra Pound gave a famous piece of advice to his fellow poets: "Go in fear of abstractions." This is not to say that a poet cannot employ abstract words, nor that all poems have to be about physical things. Much of T. S. Eliot's *Four Quartets* is concerned with time, eternity, history, language, reality, and other things that cannot be handled. But Eliot, however high he may soar for a general view, keeps returning to earth. He makes us aware of *things,* as Thomas Carlyle said a good writer has to do: "Wonderful it is with what cutting words, now and then, he severs asunder the confusion; shears it down, were it furlongs deep, into the true center of the matter; and there not only hits the nail on the head, but with crushing force smites it home, and buries it." Like other good

---

[2] *The Trembling of the Veil* (1922), reprinted in *The Autobiography of William Butler Yeats* (New York: Macmillan, 1953), p. 177.

writers, good poets remind us of that smitten nail and that spillable cup. "Perhaps indeed," wrote Walt Whitman in *Specimen Days*, "the efforts of the true poets, founders, religions, literatures, all ages, have been, and ever will be, our time and times to come, essentially the same — to bring people back from their persistent strayings and sickly abstractions, to the costless, average, divine, original concrete."

Knute Skinner (b. 1929)
THE COLD IRISH EARTH   1968

I shudder thinking
of the cold Irish earth.
The firelighter flares
in the kitchen range,
but a cold rain falls   5
all around Liscannor.
It scours the Hag's face
on the Cliffs of Moher.
It runs through the bog
and seeps up into mounds   10
of abandoned turf.
My neighbor's fields are chopped
by the feet of cattle
sinking down to the roots
of winter grass.   15
That coat hangs drying now
by the kitchen range,
but down at Healy's cross
the Killaspuglonane graveyard
is wet to the bone.   20

QUESTIONS
1. To what familiar phrase does Skinner's poem lend fresh meaning? What is its usual meaning?
2. What details in the poem show us that, in using the old phrase, Skinner literally means what he says?

Henry Taylor (b. 1942)
RIDING A ONE-EYED HORSE   1975

One side of his world is always missing.
You may give it a casual wave of the hand
or rub it with your shoulder as you pass,
but nothing on his blind side ever happens.

Hundreds of trees slip past him into darkness,   5
drifting into a hollow hemisphere
whose sounds you will have to try to explain.
Your legs will tell him not to be afraid

if you learn never to lie. Do not forget
to turn his head and let what comes come seen: 10
he will jump the fences he has to if you swing
toward them from the side that he can see

and hold his good eye straight. The heavy dark
will stay beside you always; let him learn
to lean against it. It will steady him   15
and see you safely through diminished fields.

QUESTION

Do you read this poem as a fable in which the horse stands for something, or as
a set of instructions for riding a one-eyed horse?

Robert Graves (b. 1895)
DOWN, WANTON, DOWN!   1933

Down, wanton, down! Have you no shame
That at the whisper of Love's name,
Or Beauty's, presto! up you raise
Your angry head and stand at gaze?

Poor bombard-captain, sworn to reach   5
The ravelin and effect a breach —
Indifferent what you storm or why,
So be that in the breach you die!

Love may be blind, but Love at least
Knows what is man and what mere beast;   10
Or Beauty wayward, but requires
More delicacy from her squires.

Tell me, my witless, whose one boast
Could be your staunchness at the post,
When were you made a man of parts   15
To think fine and profess the arts?

Will many-gifted Beauty come
Bowing to your bald rule of thumb,
Or Love swear loyalty to your crown?
Be gone, have done! Down, wanton, down!   20

DOWN, WANTON, DOWN! 5. *bombard-captain:* officer in charge of a bombard, an early type of
cannon that hurled stones. 6. *ravelin:* fortification with two faces that meet in a protruding
angle. *effect a breach:* break an opening through (a fortification). 15. *man of parts:* man of
talent or ability.

1. How do you define a wanton?
2. What wanton does the poet address?
3. Explain the comparison drawn in the second stanza.
4. In line 14, how many meanings do you find in *staunchness at the post*?
5. Explain any other puns you find in lines 15–19.
6. Do you take this to be a cynical poem making fun of Love and Beauty, or is Graves making fun of stupid, animal lust?

Peter Davison (b. 1928)

THE LAST WORD   1970

When I saw your head bow, I knew I had beaten you.
You shed no tears — not near me — but held your neck
Bare for the blow I had been too frightened
Ever to deliver, even in words. And now,
In spite of me, plummeting it came.   5
Frozen we both waited for its fall.

Most of what you gave me I have forgotten
With my mind but taken into my body,
But this I remember well: the bones of your neck
And the strain in my shoulders as I heaved up that huge   10
Double blade and snapped my wrists to swing
The handle down and hear the axe's edge
Nick through your flesh and creak into the block.

QUESTIONS

1. "The Last Word" stands fourth in a series titled "Four Love Poems." Sum up what happens in this poem. Do you take this to be *merely* a literal account of an execution? Explain the comparison.
2. Which words embody concrete things and show us physical actions? Which words have sounds that especially contribute to the poem's effectiveness?

David B. Axelrod (b. 1943)

ONCE IN A WHILE A PROTEST POEM   1976

Over and over again the papers print
the dried-out tit of an African woman
holding her starving child. Over
and over, cropping it each time to one
prominent, withered tit, the feeble   5
infant face. Over and over to toughen
us, teach us to ignore the foam turned
dusty powder on the infant's lips,
the mother's sunken face (is cropped)
and filthy dress. The tit remains;   10

the tit held out for everyone to see,
reminding us only that we are not so hungry
ogling the tit, admiring it and in our
living rooms, making it a symbol of starving
millions; our sympathy as real as silicone.   15

QUESTIONS

1. Why is the last word in this poem especially meaningful?
2. What does the poet protest?

Miller Williams (b. 1930)

ON THE SYMBOLIC CONSIDERATION OF HANDS
AND THE SIGNIFICANCE OF DEATH   1973

Watch people stop by bodies in funeral homes.
You know their eyes will fix on the hands and they do.
Because a hand that has no desire to make
a fist again or cut bread or lay stones
is among those things most difficult to believe.
It is believed for a fact by a very few
old nuns in France who carve beads out of knuckle bones.

QUESTIONS

1. Why, according to the poet, is it hard for us to believe in the literal fact of
   death? Why isn't such belief a problem for the nuns?
2. From just the title of the poem, would you expect the poem to be written in
   plain, simple language, or in very abstract, general language? In what kind of
   language *is* it written?
3. What possible reason could the poet have for choosing such a title? (Besides
   being a poet, Miller Williams is a critic and teacher of poetry. He probably
   knows many readers and students of poetry who expect poems *necessarily* to
   deal in symbolic considerations and large significances.)

John Donne (1572–1631)

BATTER MY HEART, THREE-PERSONED GOD, FOR YOU   1633

Batter my heart, three-personed God, for You
As yet but knock, breathe, shine, and seek to mend.
That I may rise and stand, o'erthrow me, and bend
Your force to break, blow, burn, and make me new.
I, like an usurped town to another due,   5
Labor to admit You, but Oh! to no end.
Reason, Your viceroy in me, me should defend,
But is captived, and proves weak or untrue.

446   Words

Yet dearly I love You, and would be lovèd fain,
But am betrothed unto Your enemy;
Divorce me, untie or break that knot again;
Take me to You, imprison me, for I,
Except You enthrall me, never shall be free,   10
Nor ever chaste, except You ravish me.

QUESTIONS

1. In the last line of this sonnet, to what does Donne compare the onslaught of
   God's love? Do you think the poem weakened by the poet's comparing a
   spiritual experience to something so grossly carnal? Discuss.
2. Explain the seeming contradiction in the last line: in what sense can a
   ravished person be *chaste*? Explain the seeming contradictions in lines 3–4
   and 12–13: how can a person thrown down and destroyed be enabled to *rise
   and stand*; an imprisoned person be *free*?
3. In lines 5–6 the speaker compares himself to a *usurped town* trying to throw
   off its conqueror by admitting an army of liberation. Who is the "usurper" in
   this comparison?
4. Explain the comparison of *Reason* to a *viceroy* (lines 7–8).
5. Sum up in your own words the message of Donne's poem. In stating its
   theme, did you have to read the poem for literal meanings, figurative comparisons, or both?

THE VALUE OF A DICTIONARY

If a poet troubles to seek out the best words available, the least we can
do is to find out what the words mean. The dictionary is a firm ally in
reading poems; if the poems are more than a century old, it is indispensable. Meanings change. When the Elizabethan poet George Gas-
coigne wrote, "O Abraham's brats, O brood of blessed seed," the word
brats implied neither irritation nor contempt. When in the seventeenth
century Andrew Marvell imagined two lovers' "vegetable love," he
referred to a vegetative or growing love, not one resembling a lettuce.
And when King George III called a building an "awful artificial spectacle," he was not condemning it but praising it as an awe-inspiring
work of art.

   In reading poetry, there is nothing to be done about this inevitable
tendency of language except to watch out for it. If you suspect that a
word has shifted in meaning over the years, most standard desk dictionaries will be helpful, an unabridged dictionary more helpful yet,
and most helpful of all the *Oxford English Dictionary (OED)*, which gives,
for each definition, successive examples of the word's written use down
through the past thousand years. You need not feel a grim obligation to
keep interrupting a poem in order to rummage the dictionary; but if the
poem is worth reading very closely, you may wish any aid you can find.

One of the valuable services of poetry is to recall for us the concrete, physical sense that certain words once had, but since have lost. As the English critic H. Coombes has remarked in *Literature and Criticism*,

> We use a word like *powerful* without feeling that it is really "power-full." We do not seem today to taste the full flavor of words as we feel that Falstaff (and Shakespeare, and probably his audience) tasted them when he was applauding the virtues of "good sherris-sack," which makes the brain "apprehensive, quick, forgetive, full of nimble, fiery, and delectable shapes." And being less aware of the life and substantiality of words, we are probably less aware of the things . . . that these words stand for.

"Every word which is used to express a moral or intellectual fact," said Emerson in *The Conduct of Life*, "if traced to its root, is found to be borrowed from some material appearance. *Right* means straight; *wrong* means twisted. *Spirit* primarily means wind; *transgression*, the crossing of a line; *supercilious*, the raising of an eyebrow." Browse in a dictionary and you will discover such original concretenesses. These are revealed in your dictionary's etymologies, or brief notes on the derivation of words, given in most dictionaries near the beginning of an entry on a word; in some dictionaries, at the end of the entry. Look up *squirrel*, for instance, and you will find it comes from two Greek words meaning "shadow-tail." For another example of a common word that originally contained a poetic metaphor, look up the origin of the word *daisy*.

EXPERIMENT: *Seeing Words' Origins*

Much of the effect of the following poem depends upon our awareness of the precision with which the poet has selected his words. We can better see this by knowing their derivations. For instance, *potpourri* comes from French: *pot* plus *pourri*. What do these words mean? (If you do not know French, look up the etymology of the word in a dictionary.) Look up the definitions and etymologies of *revenance, circumstance, inspiration, conceptual, commotion, cordial,* and *azure*; and try to state the meanings these words have in Wilbur's poem.

Richard Wilbur (b. 1921)
IN THE ELEGY SEASON   1950

Haze, char, and the weather of All Souls':
A giant absence mopes upon the trees:
Leaves cast in casual potpourris
Whisper their scents from pits and cellar-holes.

Or brewed in gulleys, steeped in wells, they spend   5
In chilly steam their last aromas, yield

From shallow hells a revenance of field
And orchard air. And now the envious mind

Which could not hold the summer in my head
While bounded by that blazing circumstance   10
Parades these barrens in a golden trance,
Remembering the wealthy season dead,

And by an autumn inspiration makes
A summer all its own. Green boughs arise
Through all the boundless backward of the eyes,   15
And the soul bathes in warm conceptual lakes.

Less proud than this, my body leans an ear
Past cold and colder weather after wings'
Soft commotion, the sudden race of springs,
The goddess' tread heard on the dayward stair,   20

Longs for the brush of the freighted air, for smells
Of grass and cordial lilac, for the sight
Of green leaves building into the light
And azure water hoisting out of wells.

An **allusion** is an indirect reference to any person, place, or thing
—fictitious, historical, or actual. Sometimes, to understand an allusion
in a poem, we have to find out something we didn't know before. But
usually the poet asks of us only common knowledge. When Edgar Allan
Poe refers to "the glory that was Greece / And the grandeur that was
Rome," he assumes that we have heard of those places, and that we will
understand his allusion to the cultural achievement of those nations
(implicit in *glory* and *grandeur*).

Allusions not only enrich the meaning of a poem, they also save
space. In "The Love Song of J. Alfred Prufrock" (page 746), T. S. Eliot, by
giving a brief introductory quotation from the speech of a damned soul
in Dante's *Inferno*, is able to suggest that his poem will be the confession of a soul in torment, who sees no chance of escape.

Often in reading a poem you will meet a name you don't recognize, on which the meaning of a line (or perhaps a whole poem) seems
to depend. In this book, most such unfamiliar references and allusions
are glossed or footnoted, but when you venture out on your own in
reading poems, you may find yourself needlessly perplexed unless you
look up such names, the way you look up any other words. Unless the
name is one that the poet made up, you will probably find it in one of
the larger desk dictionaries, such as *Webster's New Collegiate Dictionary*,
The American Heritage Dictionary, or *The American College Dictionary*. If
you don't solve your problem there, try an encyclopedia, a world atlas,
or *The New Century Cyclopedia of Names*.

Some allusions are quotations from other poems. In L. E. Sissman's "In and Out: A Home Away from Home," the narrator, a male college student, describes his sleeping love,

> This Sally now does like a garment wear
> The beauty of the evening; silent, bare,
> Hips, shoulders, arms, tresses, and temples lie.

(For the source of these lines, see Wordsworth's "Composed upon Westminster Bridge," page 824.)

EXERCISE: *Catching Allusions*

From your knowledge, supplemented by a dictionary or other reference work if need be, explain the allusions in the following poems.

Cid Corman (b. 1924)

THE TORTOISE   1964

Always to want to
go back, to correct
an error, ease a

guilt, see how a friend
is doing. And yet   5
one doesnt, except

in memory, in
dreams. The land remains
desolate. Always

the feeling is of   10
terrible slowness
overtaking haste.

J. V. Cunningham (b. 1911)

FRIEND, ON THIS SCAFFOLD THOMAS MORE LIES DEAD   1960

Friend, on this scaffold Thomas More lies dead
Who would not cut the Body from the Head.

Herman Melville (1819–1891)

THE PORTENT   (1859)

Hanging from the beam,
  Slowly swaying (such the law),
Gaunt the shadow on your green,
  Shenandoah!

The cut is on the crown
    (Lo, John Brown),
And the stabs shall heal no more.

Hidden in the cap
    Is the anguish none can draw;
So your future veils its face,   10
    Shenandoah!

But the streaming beard is shown
    (Weird John Brown),
The meteor of the war.

John Clare (1793–1864)

MOUSE'S NEST   (about 1835)

I found a ball of grass among the hay
And progged it as I passed and went away;
And when I looked I fancied something stirred,
And turned again and hoped to catch the bird—
When out an old mouse bolted in the wheats   5
With all her young ones hanging at her teats;
She looked so odd and so grotesque to me,
I ran and wondered what the thing could be,
And pushed the knapweed bunches where I stood;
Then the mouse hurried from the craking° brood.   *crying*   10
The young ones squeaked, and as I went away
She found her nest again among the hay.
The water o'er the pebbles scarce could run
And broad old cesspools glittered in the sun.

QUESTIONS

1. "To prog" (line 2) means "to poke about for food, to forage." In what ways
   does this word fit more exactly here than *prodded, touched,* or *searched*?
2. Is *craking* (line 10) better than *crying*? Which word better fits the poem? Why?
3. What connections do you find between the last two lines and the rest of the
   poem? To what are water that *scarce could run* and *broad old cesspools* (lines 13
   and 14) likened?

Lewis Carroll
[Charles Lutwidge Dodgson] (1832–1898)

JABBERWOCKY   1871

'Twas brillig, and the slithy toves
    Did gyre and gimble in the wabe:
All mimsy were the borogoves,
    And the mome raths outgrabe.

"Beware the Jabberwock, my son!
    The jaws that bite, the claws that catch!
Beware the Jubjub bird, and shun
    The frumious Bandersnatch!"

He took his vorpal sword in hand;
    Long time the manxome foe he sought—
So rested he by the Tumtum tree
    And stood awhile in thought.

And, as in uffish thought he stood,
    The Jabberwock, with eyes of flame,
Came whiffling through the tulgey wood,
    And burbled as it came!

One, two! One, two! And through and through
    The vorpal blade went snicker-snack!
He left it dead, and with its head
    He went galumphing back.

"And hast thou slain the Jabberwock?
    Come to my arms, my beamish boy!
O frabjous day! Callooh, Callay!"
    He chortled in his joy.

'Twas brillig, and the slithy toves
    Did gyre and gimble in the wabe:
All mimsy were the borogoves,
    And the mome raths outgrabe.

QUESTIONS

1. Look up *chortled* (line 24) in your dictionary and find out its definition and origin.
2. In *Through the Looking-Glass,* Alice seeks the aid of Humpty Dumpty to decipher the meaning of this nonsense poem. "*Brillig,*" he explains, "means four o'clock in the afternoon—the time when you begin *broiling* things for dinner." Does *brillig* sound like any other familiar word?
3. "*Slithy,*" the explanation goes on, "means 'lithe and slimy.' 'Lithe' is the same as 'active.' You see it's like a portmanteau—there are two meanings packed up into one word." *Mimsy* is supposed to pack together both "flimsy" and "miserable." In the rest of the poem, what other portmanteau— or packed suitcase—words can you find?

Wallace Stevens (1879–1955)

METAMORPHOSIS   1942

Yillow, yillow, yillow,
Old worm, my pretty quirk,
How the wind spells out
Sep - tem - ber. . . .

Summer is in bones.
Cock-robin's at Caracas.
Make o, make o, make o,
Oto - otu - bre.

And the rude leaves fall.
The rain falls. The sky
Falls and lies with the worms.
The street lamps

Are those that have been hanged.
Dangling in an illogical
To and to and fro   15
Fro Niz - nil - imbo.

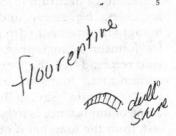

QUESTIONS

1. Explain the title. Of the several meanings of *metamorphosis* given in a dictionary, which best applies to the process that Stevens sees in the natural
   world?
2. What metamorphosis is also taking place in the *language* of the poem? How
   does it continue from line 4 to line 8 to line 16?
3. In the last line, which may recall the thickening drone of a speaker lapsing
   into sleep, *Niz - nil - imbo* seems not only a pun on the name of a
   month, but also a portmanteau word into which at least two familiar words
   are packed. Say it aloud. What are they?
4. What dictionary definitions of the word *quirk* seem relevant to line 2? How
   can a worm be a quirk? What else in this poem seems quirky?

J. V. Cunningham (b. 1911)

MOTTO FOR A SUN DIAL   1947

I who by day am function of the light
Am constant and invariant by night.

QUESTION

In mathematics, what do the words *function* and *constant* mean?

WORD CHOICE AND WORD ORDER

Even if Samuel Johnson's famous *Dictionary* of 1755 had been as thick as
Webster's unabridged, an eighteenth-century poet searching through it
for words to use would have had a narrower choice. For in English literature of the **neoclassical period** or **Augustan age**—that period from
about 1660 into the late eighteenth century—many poets subscribed to
a belief in **poetic diction:** "A system of words," said Dr. Johnson,
"refined from the grossness of domestic use." The system admitted into
a serious poem only certain words and subjects, excluding others as

violations of **decorum** (propriety). Accordingly such common words as *rat, cheese, big, sneeze,* and *elbow,* although admissible to satire, were thought inconsistent with the loftiness of tragedy, epic, ode, and elegy. Dr. Johnson's biographer, James Boswell, tells how a poet writing an epic reconsidered the word "rats" and instead wrote "the whiskered vermin race." Johnson himself objected to Lady Macbeth's allusion to her "keen knife," saying that "we do not immediately conceive that any crime of importance is to be committed with a knife; or who does not, at last, from the long habit of connecting a knife with sordid offices, feel aversion rather than terror?" Probably Johnson was here the victim of his age, and Shakespeare was right, but Johnson in one of his assumptions was right too: there are inappropriate words as well as appropriate ones.

Neoclassical poets chose their classical models more often from Roman writers than from Greek, as their diction suggests by the frequency of Latin derivatives. For example, a *net,* according to Dr. Johnson's dictionary, is "any thing reticulated or decussated, at equal distances, with interstices between the intersections." In company with Latinate words often appeared fixed combinations of adjective and noun ("finny prey" for "fish"), poetic names (a song to a lady named Molly might rechristen her Parthenia), and allusions to classical mythology. Neoclassical poetic diction was evidently being abused when, instead of saying "uncork the bottle," a poet could write,

> Apply thine engine to the spongy door,
> Set *Bacchus* from his glassy prison free,

in some bad lines ridiculed by Alexander Pope in *Peri Bathous, or, Of the Art of Sinking in Poetry.*

Not all poetic diction is excess baggage. To a reader who knew at first hand both living sheep and the pastoral poems of Virgil—as most readers nowadays do not—such a fixed phrase as "the fleecy care," which seems stilted to us, conveyed pleasurable associations. But "fleecy care" was more than a highfalutin way of saying "sheep"; as one scholar has pointed out, "when they wished, our poets could say 'sheep' as clearly and as often as anybody else. In the first place, 'fleecy' drew attention to wool, and demanded the appropriate visual image of sheep; for aural imagery the poets would refer to 'the bleating kind'; it all depended upon what was happening in the poem."[3]

Other poets have found some special kind of poetic language valuable: Anglo-Saxon poets, with their standard figures of speech, or **kennings** ("whale-road" for the sea, "ring-giver" for a ruler); makers of folk ballads who, no less than neoclassicists, love fixed epithet-noun combi-

[3] Bonamy Dobrée, *English Literature in the Early Eighteenth Century, 1700–1740* (New York: Oxford University Press, 1959), p. 161.

nations ("milk-white steed," "blood-red wine," "steel-driving man"); and Edmund Spenser, whose example made popular the adjective ending in -y (*fleecy, grassy, milky*).

When Wordsworth, in his Preface to *Lyrical Ballads*, asserted that "the language really spoken by men," especially by humble rustics, is plainer, more emphatic, and conveys "elementary feelings . . . in a state of greater simplicity," he was, in effect, advocating a new poetic diction. Wordsworth's ideas invited freshness into English poetry and, by admitting words that neoclassical poets would have called "low" ("His poor old *ankles* swell"), helped rid poets of the fear of being thought foolish for mentioning a commonplace.

This theory of the superiority of rural diction was, as Coleridge pointed out, hard to adhere to, and, in practice, Wordsworth was occasionally to write a language as Latinate and citified as these lines on yew trees:

> Huge trunks!—and each particular trunk a growth
> Of intertwisted fibers serpentine
> Up-coiling, and inveterately convolved . . .

Language so Latinate sounds pedantic to us, especially the phrase *inveterately convolved*. In fact, some poets, notably Gerard Manley Hopkins, have subscribed to the view that English words derived from Anglo-Saxon (Old English) have more force and flavor than their Latin equivalents. *Kingly*, one may feel, has more power than *regal*. One argument for this view is that so many words of Old English origin—*man, wife, child, house, eat, drink, sleep*—are basic to our living speech. It may be true that a language closer to Old English is particularly fit for rendering abstract notions concretely—as does the memorable title of a medieval work of piety, the *Ayenbite of Inwit* ("again-bite of inner wit" or "remorse of conscience"). And yet this view, if accepted at all, must be accepted with reservations. Some words of Latin origin carry meanings both precise and physical. In the King James Bible is the admonition, "See then that ye walk circumspectly, not as fools, but as wise" (Ephesians 5:15). To be *circumspect* (a word from two Latin roots meaning "to look" and "around") is to be watchful on all sides—a meaning altogether lost in a modernized wording of the passage once printed on a subway poster for a Bible society: "Be careful how you live, not thoughtlessly but thoughtfully."

When E. E. Cummings begins a poem, "mr youse needn't be so spry / concernin questions arty," we recognized another kind of diction available to poetry: **vulgate** (speech not much affected by schooling). Handbooks of grammar sometimes distinguish various **levels of usage.** A sort of ladder is imagined, on whose rungs words, phrases, and sentences may be ranked in an ascending order of formality, from the curses of an illiterate thug to the commencement-day address of a doctor of divinity. These levels range from vulgate through **colloquial** (the casual conversation or informal writing of literate people) and **general English** (most literate speech and writing, more studied than colloquial but not pretentious), up to **formal English** (the impersonal language of educated persons, usually only written, possibly spoken on dignified occasions). Recently, however, lexicographers have been shunning such labels. The designation *colloquial* has been expelled (*bounced* would be colloquial; *trun out*, vulgate) from *Webster's Third New International Dictionary* on the grounds that "it is impossible to know whether a word out of context is colloquial or not" and that the diction of Americans nowadays is more fluid than the labels suggest. Aware that we are being unscientific, we may find the labels useful. They may help roughly to describe what happens when, as in the following poem, a poet shifts from one level of usage to another. This poem employs, incidentally, a colloquial device throughout: omitting the subjects of sentences. In keeping the characters straight, it may be helpful to fill in the speaker for each *said* and for the verbs *saw* and *ducked* (lines 9 and 10).

Josephine Miles (b. 1911)

REASON

1955

Said, Pull her up a bit will you, Mac, I want to unload there.
Said, Pull her up my rear end, first come first serve.
Said, Give her the gun, Bud, he needs a taste of his own bumper.

Then the usher came out and got into the act:
Said, Pull her up, pull her up a bit, we need this space, sir.   5
Said, For God's sake, is this still a free country or what?
You go back and take care of Gary Cooper's horse
And leave me handle my own car.

Saw them unloading the lame old lady,
Ducked out under the wheel and gave her an elbow,   10
Said, All you needed to do was just explain;
Reason, Reason is my middle name.

Language on more than one level enlivens this miniature comedy; the vulgate of the resentful driver ("Pull her up my rear end," "leave me handle my own car") and the colloquial of the bystander ("Give her the gun"). There is also a contrast in formality between the old lady's driver, who says "Mac," and the usher, who says "sir." These varied levels of language distinguish the speakers in the poem from one another.

The diction of "Reason" is that of speech; that of Coleridge's "Kubla Khan" (p. 730) is more bookish. Coleridge is not at fault, however: the language of Josephine Miles's reasonable driver might not have contained Kubla Khan's stately pleasure dome. At present, most poetry in English appears to be shunning expressions such as "fleecy care" in favor of general English and the colloquial. In Scotland, there has been an interesting development: the formation of an active group of poets who write in Scots, a **dialect** (variety of language spoken by a social group or spoken in a certain locality). Perhaps, whether poets write in language close to speech or in language of greater formality, their poems will ring true if they choose appropriate words.

EXPERIMENT: *Wheeshts into Hushes*

Reword the following poem from Scots dialect into general English, using the closest possible equivalents. Then try to assess what the poem has gained or lost. (In line 4, a "ploy," as defined by *Webster's Third New International Dictionary*, is a pursuit or activity, "especially one that requires eagerness or finesse.")

Hugh MacDiarmid
[Christopher Murray Grieve] (1892–1978)

WHEESHT, WHEESHT   1926

Wheest°, wheesht, my foolish hert,   *hush*
For weel ye ken°   *know*
I widna ha'e ye stert
Auld ploys again.

It's guid to see her lie
Sae snod° an' cool,   *smooth*
A' lust o' lovin' by —
Wheesht, wheesht, ye fule!

Not only the poet's choice of words makes a poem seem more formal, or less, but also the way the words are arranged into sentences. Compare these lines,

> Jack and Jill went up the hill
> To fetch a pail of water.
> Jack fell down and broke his crown
> And Jill came tumbling after.

with Milton's account of a more significant downfall:

> Earth trembled from her entrails, as again
> In pangs, and Nature gave a second groan;
> Sky loured, and, muttering thunder, some sad drops
> Wept at completing of the mortal sin
> Original; while Adam took no thought

Eating his fill, nor Eve to iterate
Her former trespass feared, the more to soothe
Him with her loved society, that now
As with new wine intoxicated both
They swim in mirth, and fancy that they feel
Divinity within them breeding wings
Wherewith to scorn the Earth.

Not all the words in Milton's lines are bookish: indeed, many of them can be found in nursery rimes. What helps, besides diction, to distinguish this account of the Biblical fall from "Jack and Jill" is that Milton's nonstop sentence seems farther removed from usual speech in its length (83 words), in its complexity (subordinate clauses), and in its word order ("with new wine intoxicated both" rather than "both intoxicated with new wine"). Should we think less (or more highly) of Milton for choosing a style so elaborate and formal? No judgment need be passed: both Mother Goose and the author of *Paradise Lost* use language appropriate to their purposes.

Among the languages of humankind, English is by no means the most flexible. English words must be used in fairly definite and inviolable patterns, and whoever departs too far from them will not be understood. In the sentence "Cain slew Abel," if you change the word order, you change the meaning: "Abel slew Cain." Such inflexibility was not true of Latin, in which a poet could lay down words in almost any sequence and, because their endings (inflections) showed what parts of speech they were, could trust that no reader would mistake a subject for an object or a noun for an adjective. (E. E. Cummings has striven, in certain of his poems, for the freedom of Latin. One such poem, "anyone lived in a pretty how town," appears on page 459.)

The rigidity of English word order invites the poet to defy it and to achieve unusual effects by inverting it. It is customary in English to place adjective in front of noun (*a blue mantle, new pastures*). But an unusual emphasis is achieved when Milton ends "Lycidas" by reversing the pattern:

At last he rose, and twitched his mantle blue:
Tomorrow to fresh woods, and pastures new.

Perhaps the inversion in *mantle blue* gives more prominence to the color associated with heaven (and in "Lycidas," heaven is of prime importance). Perhaps the inversion in *pastures new*, stressing the *new*, heightens the sense of a rebirth.

Coleridge offered two "homely definitions of prose and poetry; that is, *prose:* words in their best order; *poetry:* the best words in the best order." If all goes well, a poet may fasten the right word into the right place, and the result may be—as T. S. Eliot said in "Little Gidding"—a "complete consort dancing together."

Reed Whittemore (b. 1919)

THE FALL OF THE HOUSE OF USHER

1970

It was a big boxy wreck of a house
Owned by a classmate of mine named Rod Usher,
Who lived in the thing with his twin sister.
He was a louse and she was a souse.

While I was visiting them one wet summer, she died.   5
We buried her,
Or rather we stuck her in a back room for a bit, meaning to bury her
When the graveyard dried.

But the weather got wetter.
One night we were both waked by a twister,   10
Plus a screeching and howling outside that turned out to be sister
Up and dying again, making it hard for Rod to forget her.

He didn't. He and she died in a heap, and I left quick,
Which was lucky since the house fell in right after,
                            Like a ton of brick.   15

QUESTIONS

1. Identify the story to which this poem makes allusion.
2. How is the tone of the original version of the Usher tragedy (if you know the story) different from that of Whittemore's retelling of it?
3. To say that something falls "like a ton of brick" is ordinarily to use a cliché. Does Whittemore's last line seem a cliché? What is novel about it?
4. How formal is the language of Whittemore's speaker? Why is the diction of this poem essential to its effectiveness?

E. E. Cummings (1894–1962)

ANYONE LIVED IN A PRETTY HOW TOWN

1940

anyone lived in a pretty how town
(with up so floating many bells down)
spring summer autumn winter
he sang his didn't he danced his did.

Women and men(both little and small)   5
cared for anyone not at all
they sowed their isn't they reaped their same
sun moon stars rain

children guessed(but only a few
and down they forgot as up they grew   10
autumn winter spring summer)
that noone loved him more by more

when by now and tree by leaf
she laughed his joy she cried his grief
bird by snow and stir by still   15
anyone's any was all to her

someones married their everyones
laughed their cryings and did their dance
(sleep wake hope and then)they
said their nevers they slept their dream   20

stars rain sun moon
(and only the snow can begin to explain
how children are apt to forget to remember
with up so floating many bells down)

one day anyone died i guess   25
(and noone stooped to kiss his face)
busy folk buried them side by side
little by little and was by was

all by all and deep by deep
and more by more they dream their sleep   30
noone and anyone earth by april
wish by spirit and if by yes.

Women and men(both dong and ding)
summer autumn winter spring
reaped their sowing and went their came   35
sun moon stars rain

QUESTIONS

1. Summarize the story told in this poem. Who are the main characters?
2. Rearrange the words in the two opening lines into the order you would expect them usually to follow. What effect does Cummings obtain by his unconventional word order?
3. Another of Cummings's strategies is to use one part of speech as if it were another; for instance, in line 4, *didn't* and *did* ordinarily are verbs, but here they are used as nouns. What other words in the poem perform functions other than their expected ones?

Richard Eberhart (b. 1904)
THE FURY OF AERIAL BOMBARDMENT   1947

You would think the fury of aerial bombardment
Would rouse God to relent; the infinite spaces
Are still silent. He looks on shock-pried faces.
History, even, does not know what is meant.

You would feel that after so many centuries   5
God would give man to repent; yet he can kill

Cannot blame God for war

As Cain could, but with multitudinous will,
No farther advanced than in his ancient furies.

Was man made stupid to see his own stupidity?
Is God by definition indifferent, beyond us all?   10
Is the eternal truth man's fighting soul
Wherein the Beast ravens in its own avidity?

Of Van Wettering I speak, and Averill,
Names on a list, whose faces I do not recall
But they are gone to early death, who late in school   15
Distinguished the belt feed lever from the belt holding pawl.

QUESTIONS

1. As a naval officer during World War II, Richard Eberhart was assigned for a time as an instructor in a gunnery school. How has this experience apparently contributed to the diction of his poem?
2. In his *Life of John Dryden*, complaining about a description of a sea fight Dryden had filled with nautical language, Samuel Johnson argued that technical terms should be excluded from poetry. Is this criticism applicable to Eberhart's last line? Can a word succeed for us in a poem, even though we may not be able to define it? (For more evidence, see also the technical terms in Henry Reed's "Naming of Parts," p. 794.)
3. Some readers have found a contrast in tone between the first three stanzas of this poem and the last stanza. How would you describe this contrast? What does diction contribute to it?

EXERCISE: *Different Kinds of English*

Read the following poems and see what kinds of diction and word order you find in them. Which poems are least formal in their language and which most formal? Is there any use of vulgate English? Any dialect? What does each poem achieve that its own kind of English makes possible?

Anonymous (American)

AS I WAS LAYING ON THE GREEN   (late nineteenth century)

As I was laying on the green,
A small English book I seen.
Carlyle's *Essay on Burns* was the edition,
So I left it laying in the same position.

A. R. Ammons (b. 1926)

SPRING COMING   1970

The caryophyllaceae
like a scroungy
frost are
rising through the lawn:

many-fingered as leggy
   copepods:
a suggestive delicacy,
lacework, like
the scent of wild plum
   thickets:
also the grackles
with their incredible
vertical, horizontal,
reversible
tails have arrived:
such nice machines.

William Wordsworth (1770–1850)

MY HEART LEAPS UP WHEN I BEHOLD 1807

My heart leaps up when I behold
  A rainbow in the sky:
So was it when my life began;
So is it now I am a man;
So be it when I shall grow old,
  Or let me die!
The Child is father of the Man;
And I could wish my days to be
Bound each to each by natural piety.

William Wordsworth (1770–1850)

MUTABILITY 1822

From low to high doth dissolution climb,
And sink from high to low, along a scale
Of awful notes, whose concord shall not fail;
A musical but melancholy chime,
Which they can hear who meddle not with crime,   5
Nor avarice, nor over-anxious care.
Truth fails not; but her outward forms that bear
The longest date do melt like frosty rime°,   *frozen dew*
That in the morning whitened hill and plain
And is no more; drop like the tower sublime   10
Of yesterday, which royally did wear
His crown of weeds, but could not even sustain
Some casual shout that broke the silent air,
Or the unimaginable touch of Time.

Anonymous

SCOTTSBORO

1936

Paper come out—done strewed de news
Seven po' chillun moan deat' house blues,
Seven po' chillun moanin' deat' house blues.
Seven nappy° heads wit' big shiny eye   *kinky*
All boun' in jail and framed to die,   5
All boun' in jail and framed to die.

Messin' white woman—snake lyin' tale
Hang and burn and jail wit' no bail.
Dat hang and burn and jail wit' no bail.
Worse ol' crime in white folks' lan'   10
Black skin coverin' po' workin' man,
Black skin coverin' po' workin' man.

Judge and jury—all in de stan'
Lawd, biggety name for same lynchin' ban',
Lawd, biggety name for same lynchin' ban'.   15
White folks and nigger in great co't house
Like cat down cellar wit' nohole mouse.
Like cat down cellar wit' nohole mouse.

SCOTTSBORO. This folk blues, collected by Lawrence Gellert in *Negro Songs of Protest* (New York: Carl Fischer, Inc., 1936), is a comment on the Scottsboro case. In 1931 nine black youths of Scottsboro, Alabama, were arrested and charged with the rape of two white women. Though eventually, after several trials, they were found not guilty, some of them at the time this song was composed had been convicted and sentenced to death.

15 Imagery

Ezra Pound (1885–1972)
IN A STATION OF THE METRO   1916

The apparition of these faces in the crowd;
Petals on a wet, black bough.

Pound said he wrote this poem to convey an experience: emerging one day from a train in the Paris subway (*Métro*), he beheld "suddenly a beautiful face, and then another and another." Originally he had described his impression in a poem thirty lines long. In this final version, each line contains an **image,** which, like a picture, may take the place of a thousand words.

Though the term *image* suggests a thing seen, when speaking of images in poetry we generally mean *a word or sequence of words that refers to any sensory experience.* Often this experience is a sight (**visual imagery,** as in Pound's poem), but it may be a sound (**auditory imagery**) or a touch (**tactile imagery,** as a perception of roughness or smoothness). It may be an odor or a taste or perhaps a bodily sensation such as pain, the prickling of gooseflesh, the quenching of thirst, or—as in the following brief poem—the perception of something cold.

Taniguchi Buson (1715–1783)
THE PIERCING CHILL I FEEL   (about 1760)

The piercing chill I feel:
  my dead wife's comb, in our bedroom,
    under my heel . . .

— Translated by Harold G. Henderson

As in this **haiku** (in Japanese, a poem of seventeen syllables) an image can convey — in a flash — understanding. Had he wished, the poet might have spoken of the dead woman, of the contrast between her death and his memory of her, of his feelings toward death in general. But such a discussion would be quite different from the poem he actually wrote. Striking his bare foot against the comb, now cold and motionless but associated with the living wife (perhaps worn in her hair), the widower feels a shock as if he had touched the woman's corpse. A literal, physical sense of death is conveyed; the abstraction "death" is understood through the senses. To render the abstract in concrete terms is what poets often try to do; in this attempt, an image can be valuable.

An image may occur in a single word, a phrase, a sentence, or, as in this case, an entire short poem. To speak of the **imagery** of a poem — all its images taken together — is often more useful than to speak of separate images. To divide Buson's haiku into five images — *chill, wife, comb, bedroom, heel* — is possible, for any noun that refers to a visible object or a sensation is an image, but this is to draw distinctions that in themselves mean little and to disassemble a single experience.

Does an image cause a reader to experience a sense impression? Not quite. Reading the word *petals*, no one literally sees petals; but the occasion is given for imagining them. The image asks to be seen with the mind's eye. And although "In a Station of the Metro" records what Ezra Pound saw, it is of course not necessary for a poet actually to have lived through a sensory experience in order to write it. Keats may never have seen a newly discovered planet through a telescope, despite the image in his sonnet on Chapman's Homer (p. 771).

It is tempting to think of imagery as mere decoration, particularly when we read Keats, who fills his poems with an abundance of sights, sounds, odors, and tastes. But a successful image is not just a dab of paint or a flashy bauble. When Keats opens "The Eve of St. Agnes" with what have been called the coldest lines in literature, he evokes by a series of images a setting and a mood:

> St. Agnes' eve — Ah, bitter chill it was!
> The owl, for all his feathers, was a-cold;
> The hare limped trembling through the frozen grass,
> And silent was the flock in woolly fold:
> Numb were the Beadsman's fingers, while he told
> His rosary, and while his frosted breath,
> Like pious incense from a censer old,
> Seemed taking flight for heaven, without a death, . . .

Indeed, some literary critics look for much of the meaning of a poem in its imagery, wherein they expect to see the mind of the poet more truly revealed than in whatever the poet explicitly claims to believe. In his investigation of Wordsworth's "Ode: Intimations of Immortality," the critic Cleanth Brooks devotes his attention to the imagery of light and darkness, which he finds carries on and develops Wordsworth's thought.[1]

Though Shakespeare's Theseus (in *A Midsummer Night's Dream*) accuses poets of being concerned with "airy nothings," poets are usually very much concerned with what is in front of them. This concern is of use to us. Perhaps, as Alan Watts has remarked, Americans are not the materialists they are sometimes accused of being. How could anyone taking a look at an American city think that its inhabitants deeply cherish material things? Involved in our personal hopes and apprehensions, anticipating the future so hard that much of the time we see the present through a film of thought across our eyes, perhaps we need a poet occasionally to remind us that even the coffee we absentmindedly sip comes in (as Yeats put it) a "heavy spillable cup."

"The greatest poverty," wrote Wallace Stevens, "is not to live / In a physical world." In his own poems, Stevens makes us aware of our world's richness. He can take even a common object sold by the pound in supermarkets and, with precise imagery, recall to us what we had forgotten we ever knew about it.

Wallace Stevens (1879–1955)

STUDY OF TWO PEARS   1942

I

Opusculum paedagogum°.   *a little work that teaches*
The pears are not viols,
Nudes or bottles.
They resemble nothing else.

II

They are yellow forms   5
Composed of curves
Bulging toward the base.
They are touched red.

III

They are not flat surfaces
Having curved outlines.   10
They are round
Tapering toward the top.

IV

In the way they are modeled
There are bits of blue.

[1] "Wordsworth and the Paradox of the Imagination," in *The Well Wrought Urn* (New York: Harcourt Brace Jovanovich, 1956).

A hard dry leaf hangs   15
From the stem.

V

The yellow glistens.
It glistens with various yellows,
Citrons, oranges and greens
Flowering over the skin.   20

VI

The shadows of the pears
Are blobs on the green cloth.
The pears are not seen
As the observer wills.

QUESTIONS

1. What is Stevens's point in paying so much attention to what pears *don't* look
   like? Comment in particular on his poem's last two lines.
2. How hard is it to visualize the two pears? How clear are the poet's descriptions?

EXPERIMENT: *Illustrating a Poem*

Let an artist in the class sketch Steven's two pears in color, following the poem
as faithfully as possible, trying to add little that the poem doesn't call for. Then
let the class compare poem and picture. A question for the artist: in rendering
which details was it necessary to use your own imagination?

Theodore Roethke (1908–1963)

ROOT CELLAR   1948

Nothing would sleep in that cellar, dank as a ditch,
Bulbs broke out of boxes hunting for chinks in the dark,
Shoots dangled and drooped,
Lolling obscenely from mildewed crates,
Hung down long yellow evil necks, like tropical snakes.   5
And what a congress of stinks!—
Roots ripe as old bait,
Pulpy stems, rank, silo-rich,
Leaf-mold, manure, lime, piled against slippery planks.
Nothing would give up life: 10
Even the dirt kept breathing a small breath.

QUESTIONS

1. As a boy growing up in Saginaw, Michigan, Theodore Roethke spent much
   of his time in a large commercial greenhouse run by his family. What details
   in his poem show more than a passing acquaintance with growing things?
2. What varieties of image does "Root Cellar" contain? Point out examples.

3. Which lines contain personifications, metaphors, or similes? How large a part of this poem is composed of these figures of speech?
4. What do you understand to be Roethke's attitude toward the root cellar? Does he view it as a disgusting chamber of horrors? Pay special attention to the last two lines.

Elizabeth Bishop (b. 1911)

THE FISH   1946

I caught a tremendous fish
and held him beside the boat
half out of water, with my hook
fast in a corner of his mouth.
He didn't fight.   5
He hadn't fought at all.
He hung a grunting weight,
battered and venerable
and homely. Here and there
his brown skin hung in strips   10
like ancient wall-paper,
and its pattern of darker brown
was like wall-paper:
shapes like full-blown roses
stained and lost through age.   15
He was speckled with barnacles,
fine rosettes of lime,
and infested
with tiny white sea-lice,
and underneath two or three   20
rags of green weed hung down.
While his gills were breathing in
the terrible oxygen
—the frightening gills,
fresh and crisp with blood,   25
that can cut so badly—
I thought of the coarse white flesh
packed in like feathers,
the big bones and the little bones,
the dramatic reds and blacks   30
of his shiny entrails,
and the pink swim-bladder
like a big peony.
I looked into his eyes
which were far larger than mine   35
but shallower, and yellowed,
the irises backed and packed
with tarnished tinfoil
seen through the lenses

of old scratched isinglass. 40
They shifted a little, but not
to return my stare.
—It was more like the tipping
of an object toward the light.
I admired his sullen face, 45
the mechanism of his jaw,
and then I saw
that from his lower lip
—if you could call it a lip—
grim, wet, and weapon-like, 50
hung five old pieces of fish-line,
or four and a wire leader
with the swivel still attached,
with all their five big hooks
grown firmly in his mouth. 55
A green line, frayed at the end
where he broke it, two heavier lines,
and a fine black thread
still crimped from the strain and snap
when it broke and he got away. 60
Like medals with their ribbons
frayed and wavering,
a five-haired beard of wisdom
trailing from his aching jaw.
I stared and stared 65
and victory filled up
the little rented boat,
from the pool of bilge
where oil had spread a rainbow
around the rusted engine 70
to the bailer rusted orange,
the sun-cracked thwarts,
the oarlocks on their strings,
the gunnels—until everything
was rainbow, rainbow, rainbow! 75
And I let the fish go.

QUESTIONS

1. How many abstract words does this poem contain? What proportion of the poem is imagery?
2. What is the speaker's attitude toward the fish? Comment in particular on lines 61–64.
3. What attitude do the images of the rainbow of oil (line 69), the orange bailer (bailing bucket, line 71), the *sun-cracked thwarts* (line 72) convey? Does the poet expect us to feel mournful because the boat is in such sorry condition?
4. What is meant by *rainbow, rainbow, rainbow*?
5. How do these images prepare us for the conclusion? Why does the speaker let the fish go?

MORE ABOUT HAIKU

> On the one-ton temple bell
> a moonmoth, folded into sleep,
> sits still.
>
> —Taniguchi Buson

Few words, many suggestions. By its nature, a haiku starts us thinking and feeling. Its name means "beginning-verse," perhaps because the haiku form may have originated in a game: players, given a haiku, were supposed to extend its three lines into a longer poem. Haiku tend to consist mainly of imagery, but as we saw in Buson's lines on the cold comb, their imagery is not always pictorial.

> Heat-lightning streak—
> through darkness pierces
> the heron's shriek.
>
> —Matsuo Basho

In the poet's account of his experience, are sight and sound neatly distinguished from each other?

Note that a haiku has little room for abstract thoughts or general observations. The following attempt, though in seventeen syllables, is far from haiku in spirit:

> Now that our love is gone
> I feel within my soul
> a nagging distress.

Unlike the author of those lines, haiku poets look out upon a literal world, seldom looking inward to *discuss* their feelings. Japanese haiku tend to be seasonal in subject, but because they are so highly compressed, they usually just *imply* a season: a blossom indicates spring; a crow on a branch, autumn; snow, winter. Not just pretty little sketches of nature (as some Westerners think), haiku assume a view of the universe in which observer and nature are not separated.

A haiku in Japanese is rimeless, its seventeen syllables arranged in a five-seven-five pattern. Haiku written in English frequently ignore any strict syllable-count; they may be rimed or unrimed as the poet likes.

If you care to try your hand at haiku-writing, here are a few suggestions. Make every word matter. Include few adjectives; shun needless conjunctions. Set your haiku in the present moment. Confine your poem to what can be seen, heard, smelled, tasted, or touched. Mere sensory reports, however, will be meaningless unless they make the reader feel something—as a contemporary American writer points out in this spoof.

Richard Brautigan (b. 1935)

HAIKU AMBULANCE   1968

A piece of green pepper
    fell
off the wooden salad bowl:
    so what?

     Here, freely translated, are two more Japanese haiku to inspire
you. Both are by Basho (1644–1694), the greatest master of the form.
Classic haiku sometimes gain from our knowing when and where they
were written: the first was composed on Basho's finding the site of a
famous castle, which the hero Yoshitsune and his warriors had died trying to storm, reduced to wilderness.

    Green weeds of summer
    grow where swordsmen's dreams
    once used to shimmer.

    In the old stone pool
    a frogjump:
    splishhhhh.

     Finally, here are four more untitled haiku written in English, of
recent origin.

Sprayed with strong poison   Clap!
my roses are crisp this year   the coffin lid
  in the crystal vase   shelters the fly
       —Paul Goodman   —Raymond Roseliep

A great freight truck   After weeks of watching the roof leak
     lit like a town   I fixed it tonight
through the dark stony desert   by moving a single board
     —Gary Snyder   —Gary Snyder

FOR REVIEW AND FURTHER STUDY

Jean Toomer (1894–1967)

REAPERS   1923

Black reapers with the sound of steel on stones
Are sharpening scythes. I see them place the hones
In their hip-pockets as a thing that's done,
And start their silent swinging, one by one.

Black horses drive a mower through the weeds,
And there, a field rat, startled, squealing bleeds,
His belly close to ground. I see the blade,
Blood-stained, continue cutting weeds and shade.

QUESTIONS

1. Imagine the scene Jean Toomer describes. Which particulars most vividly strike the mind's eye?
2. What kind of image is *silent swinging*?
3. Read the poem aloud. Notice especially the effect of the words *sound of steel on stones* and *field rat, startled, squealing bleeds*. What interesting sounds are present in the very words that contain these images?
4. What feelings do you get from this poem as a whole? Would you agree with someone who said, "This poem gives us a sense of happy, carefree life down on the farm, close to nature"? Exactly what in "Reapers" makes you feel the way you do? Besides appealing to our auditory and visual imagination, what do the images contribute?

Gerard Manley Hopkins (1844–1889)

PIED BEAUTY   (1877)

Glory be to God for dappled things—
   For skies of couple-color as a brinded° cow;   *streaked*
     For rose-moles all in stipple upon trout that swim;
Fresh-firecoal chestnut-falls; finches' wings;
   Landscape plotted and pieced—fold, fallow, and plow;   5
     And áll trádes, their gear and tackle and trim°.   *equipment*

All things counter, original, spare, strange;
   Whatever is fickle, freckled (who knows how?)
     With swift, slow; sweet, sour; adazzle, dim;
He fathers-forth whose beauty is past change: 10
         Praise him.

QUESTIONS

1. What does the word *pied* mean? (Hint: what does a Pied Piper look like?)
2. According to Hopkins, what do *skies, cow, trout, ripe chestnuts, finches' wings,* and *landscapes* all have in common? What landscapes can the poet have in mind? (Have you ever seen any *dappled* landscape while looking down from an airplane, or from a mountain or high hill?)
3. What do you make of line 6: what can carpenters' saws and ditch-diggers' spades possibly have in common with the dappled things in lines 2–4?
4. Does Hopkins refer only to contrasts that meet the eye? What other kinds of variation interest him?
5. Try to state in your own words the theme of this poem. How essential to our understanding of this theme are Hopkins's images?

John Keats (1795–1821)

Bright star! would I were steadfast as thou art (1819)

Bright star! would I were steadfast as thou art—
  Not in lone splendor hung aloft the night,
And watching, with eternal lids apart,
  Like nature's patient, sleepless Eremite°   *hermit*
The moving waters at their priest-like task   5
  Of pure ablution round earth's human shores,
Or gazing on the new soft-fallen mask
  Of snow upon the mountains and the moors—
No—yet still steadfast, still unchangeable,
  Pillowed upon my fair love's ripening breast,   10
To feel for ever its soft fall and swell,
  Awake for ever in a sweet unrest,
Still, still to hear her tender-taken breath,
And so live ever—or else swoon to death.

QUESTIONS

1. Stars are conventional symbols for love and a loved one. (Love, Shakespeare tells us in a sonnet, "is the star to every wandering bark.") In this sonnet, why is it not possible for the star to have this meaning? How does Keats use it?
2. What seems concrete and particular in the speaker's observations?
3. Suppose Keats had said *slow and easy* instead of *tender-taken* in line 13? What would have been lost?

Carl Sandburg (1878–1967)

Fog 1916

The fog comes
on little cat feet.
It sits looking
over harbor and city
on silent haunches
and then moves on.

QUESTION

In lines 15–22 of "The Love Song of J. Alfred Prufrock" (p. 746), T. S. Eliot also likens fog to a cat. Compare Sandburg's lines and Eliot's. Which passage tells us more about fogs and cats?

EXPERIMENT: *Writing with Images*

Taking the following poems as examples from which to start rather than as models to be slavishly copied, try to compose a brief poem that consists largely of imagery.

Walt Whitman (1819–1892)

THE RUNNER 1867

On a flat road runs the well-train'd runner;
He is lean and sinewy, with muscular legs;
He is thinly clothed—he leans forward as he runs,
With lightly closed fists, and arms partially rais'd.

T. E. Hulme (1883–1917)

IMAGE (about 1910)

Old houses were scaffolding once
                    and workmen whistling.

William Carlos Williams (1883–1963)

THE GREAT FIGURE 1921

Among the rain
and lights
I saw the figure 5
in gold
on a red   5
firetruck
moving
tense
unheeded
to gong clangs   10
siren howls
and wheels rumbling
through the dark city.

Robert Bly (b. 1926)

DRIVING TO TOWN LATE TO MAIL A LETTER 1962

It is a cold and snowy night. The main street is deserted.
The only things moving are swirls of snow.
As I lift the mailbox door, I feel its cold iron.
There is a privacy I love in this snowy night.
Driving around, I will waste more time.

H. D. [Hilda Doolittle] (1886–1961)

HEAT

1916

O wind, rend open the heat,
cut apart the heat,
rend it to tatters.

Fruit cannot drop
through this thick air— 5
fruit cannot fall into heat
that presses up and blunts
the points of pears
and rounds the grapes.

Cut the heat— 10
plough through it,
turning it on either side
of your path.

16 Saying and Suggesting

To write so clearly that they might bring "all things as near the mathematical plainness" as possible—that was the goal of scientists according to Bishop Thomas Sprat, who lived in the seventeenth century. Such an effort would seem bound to fail, because words, unlike numbers, are ambiguous indicators. Although it may have troubled Bishop Sprat, the tendency of a word to have multiplicity of meaning rather than mathematical plainness opens broad avenues to poetry.

Every word has at least one **denotation:** a meaning as defined in a dictionary. But the English language has many a common word with so many denotations that a reader may need to think twice to see what it means in a specific context. The noun *field*, for instance, can denote a piece of ground, a sports arena, the scene of a battle, part of a flag, a profession, and a number system in mathematics. Further, the word can be used as a verb ("he fielded a grounder") or an adjective ("field trip," "field glasses").

A word also has **connotations:** overtones or suggestions of additional meaning that it gains from all the contexts in which we have met it in the past. The word *skeleton*, according to a dictionary, denotes "the bony framework of a human being or other vertebrate animal, which supports the flesh and protects the organs." But by its associations, the word can rouse thoughts of war, of disease and death, or (possibly) of one's plans to go to medical school. Think, too, of the difference between "Old Doc Jones" and "Abner P. Jones, M.D." In the mind's eye, the former appears in his shirtsleeves; the latter has a gold nameplate on his door. That some words denote the same thing but have sharply different connotations is pointed out in this anonymous Victorian jingle:

> Here's a little ditty that you really ought to know:
> Horses "sweat" and men "perspire," but ladies only "glow."

The terms *druggist, pharmacist,* and *apothecary* all denote the same occupation, but apothecaries lay claim to special distinction.

Poets aren't the only people who care about the connotations of language. Advertisers know that connotations make money. Recently a Boston automobile dealer advertised his secondhand cars not as "used" but as "pre-owned," as if fearing that "used car" would connote an old heap with soiled upholstery and mysterious engine troubles that somebody couldn't put up with. "Pre-owned," however, suggests that the previous owner has taken the trouble of breaking in the car for you. Not long ago prune-packers, alarmed by a slump in sales, sponsored a survey to determine the connotations of prunes in the public consciousness. Asked, "What do you think of when you hear the word *prunes*?" most people replied, "dried up," "wrinkled," or "constipated." Dismayed, the packers hired an advertising agency to create a new image for prunes, in hopes of inducing new connotations. Soon, advertisements began to show prunes in brightly colored settings, in the company of bikinied bathing beauties.[1]

In imaginative writing, connotations are as crucial as they are in advertising. Consider this sentence: "A new brand of journalism is being born, or spawned" (Dwight Macdonald writing in *The New York Review of Books*). The last word, by its associations with fish and crustaceans, suggests that this new journalism is scarcely the product of human beings. And what do we make of Romeo's assertion that Juliet "is the sun"? Surely even a lovesick boy cannot mean that his sweetheart is "the incandescent body of gases about which the earth and other planets revolve" (a dictionary definition). He means, of course, that he thrives in her sight, that he feels warm in her presence or even at the thought of her, that she illumines his world and is the center of his universe. Because in the mind of the hearer these and other suggestions are brought into play, Romeo's statement, literally absurd, makes excellent sense.

Here is a famous poem that groups together things with similar connotations: certain ships and their cargoes. (A quinquireme, by the way, was an ancient Assyrian vessel propelled by sails and oars.)

John Masefield (1878–1967)

CARGOES   1902

Quinquireme of Nineveh from distant Ophir,
Rowing home to haven in sunny Palestine,
With a cargo of ivory,
And apes and peacocks,
Sandalwood, cedarwood, and sweet white wine.   5

---

[1] For this and other instances of connotation-engineering, see Vance Packard's *The Hidden Persuaders* (New York: McKay, 1958), chap. 13.

Stately Spanish galleon coming from the Isthmus,
Dipping through the Tropics by the palm-green shores,
With a cargo of diamonds,
Emeralds, amethysts,
Topazes, and cinnamon, and gold moidores°.   *Portuguese coins* 10

Dirty British coaster with a salt-caked smoke stack,
Butting through the Channel in the mad March days,
With a cargo of Tyne coal,
Road-rails, pig-lead,
Firewood, iron-ware, and cheap tin trays.   15

To us, as well as to the poet's original readers, the place-names in the
first two stanzas suggest the exotic and faraway. Ophir, a vanished
place, may have been in Arabia; according to the Bible, King Solomon
sent there for its celebrated pure gold, also for ivory, apes, peacocks,
and other luxury items. (See I Kings 9–10.) In his final stanza, Masefield
groups commonplace things (mostly heavy and metallic), whose
suggestions of crudeness, cheapness, and ugliness he deliberately contrasts with those of the precious stuffs he has listed earlier. For British
readers, the Tyne is a stodgy and familiar river; the English Channel in
March, choppy and likely to upset a stomach. The quinquireme is *rowing*, the galleon is *dipping*, but the dirty British freighter is *butting*,
aggressively pushing. Conceivably, the poet could have described
firewood and even coal as beautiful, but evidently he wants them to
convey sharply different suggestions here, to go along with the rest of
the coaster's cargo. In drawing such a sharp contrast between past and
present, Masefield does more than merely draw up bills-of-lading.
Perhaps he even implies a wry and unfavorable comment upon life in
the present day. His meaning lies not so much in the dictionary definitions of his words ("*moidores:* Portuguese gold coins formerly worth approximately five pounds sterling") as in their rich and vivid connotations.

William Blake (1757–1827)
LONDON   1794

I wander through each chartered street,
Near where the chartered Thames does flow,
And mark in every face I meet
Marks of weakness, marks of woe.

In every cry of every man,   5
In every infant's cry of fear,
In every voice, in every ban,
The mind-forged manacles I hear.

How the chimney-sweeper's cry
Every black'ning church appalls;   10
And the hapless soldier's sigh
Runs in blood down palace walls.

But most through midnight streets I hear
How the youthful harlot's curse
Blasts the new born infant's tear,   15
And blights with plagues the marriage hearse.

Here are only a few of the possible meanings of four of Blake's
words:

chartered (lines 1, 2)
> Denotations: Established by a charter (a written grant or a certifi-
> cate of incorporation); leased or hired.
>
> Connotations: Defined, limited, restricted, channeled, mapped,
> bound by law; bought and sold (like a slave or an inanimate ob-
> ject); Magna Charta; charters given crown colonies by the King.
>
> Other Words in the Poem with Similar Connotations: *Ban; man-
> acles; chimney-sweeper, soldier, harlot* (all hirelings).
>
> Interpretation of the Lines: The street has had mapped out for it
> the direction in which it must go; the Thames has had laid down
> to it the course it must follow. Street and river are channeled,
> imprisoned, enslaved (like every inhabitant of London).

black'ning (line 10)
> Denotation: Becoming black.
>
> Connotations: The darkening of something once light, the defile-
> ment of something once clean, the deepening of guilt, the gath-
> ering of darkness at the approach of night.
>
> Other Words in the Poem with Similar Connotations: Objects
> becoming marked or smudged (*marks of weakness, marks of woe*
> in the faces of passers-by; bloodied walls of a palace; marriage
> blighted with plagues); the word *appalls* (suggesting not only
> "to overcome with horror" but "to cast a pall or shroud over
> something"); *midnight streets.*
>
> Interpretation of the Line: Literally, every London church grows
> black from soot and hires a chimney-sweeper (a small boy) to
> help clean it. But Blake suggests too that by profiting from the
> suffering of the child laborer, the church is soiling its original
> purity.

Blasts, blights (lines 15–16)
> Denotations: Both *blast* and *blight* mean "to cause to wither" or "to
> ruin and destroy." Both are terms from horticulture. Frost *blasts*
> a bud and kills it; disease *blights* a growing plant.

Connotations: Sickness and death; gardens shriveled and dying; gusts of wind and the ravages of insects; things blown to pieces or rotted and warped.

Other Words in the Poem with Similar Connotations: Faces marked with weakness and woe; the child become a chimney-sweep; the soldier killed by war; blackening church and blood-ied palace; young girl turned harlot; wedding carriage transformed into a hearse.

Interpretation of the Lines: Literally, the harlot spreads the plague of syphilis, which, carried into marriage, can cause a baby to be born blind. In a larger and more meaningful sense, Blake sees the prostitution of even one young girl corrupting the entire institution of matrimony and endangering every child.

Some of these connotations are more to the point than others; the reader of a poem nearly always has the problem of distinguishing relevant associations from irrelevant ones. We need to read a poem in its entirety and, when a word leaves us in doubt, look for other things in the poem to corroborate or refute what we think it means. Relatively simple and direct in its statement, Blake's account of his stroll through the city at night becomes an indictment of a whole social and religious order. The indictment could hardly be this effective if it were "mathematically plain," its every word restricted to one denotation clearly spelled out.

Wallace Stevens (1879–1955)
DISILLUSIONMENT OF TEN O'CLOCK   1923

The houses are haunted
By white night-gowns.
None are green,
Or purple with green rings,
Or green with yellow rings,   5
Or yellow with blue rings.
None of them are strange,
With socks of lace
And beaded ceintures.
People are not going   10
To dream of baboons and periwinkles.
Only, here and there, an old sailor,
Drunk and asleep in his boots,
Catches tigers
In red weather.   15

QUESTIONS

1. What are *beaded ceintures*? What does the phrase suggest?

2. What meanings do you find in the colors mentioned in this poem?
3. What contrast does Stevens draw between the people who live in these houses and the old sailor? What do the connotations of *white night-gowns* and *sailor* add to this contrast?
4. What is lacking in these people who wear white night-gowns? Why should the poet's view of them be a "disillusionment"?

Guy Owen (b. 1925)

THE WHITE STALLION   1969

The Runaway

A white horse came to our farm once
Leaping like dawn the backyard fence.
In dreams I heard his shadow fall
Across my bed. A miracle,
I woke beneath his mane's surprise;   5
I saw my face within his eyes,
The dew ran down his nose and fell
Upon the bleeding window quince. . . .

But long before I broke the spell
My father's curses sped him on,   10
Four flashing hooves that bruised the lawn.
And as I stumbled into dawn
I saw him scorn a final hedge,
I heard his pride upon the bridge,
Then through the wakened yard I went   15
To read the rage the stallion spent.

QUESTIONS

1. What do these words denote in Owen's poem: *scorn, pride, wakened, rage*? (What does the stallion do when he *scorns* the hedge? How can *pride* be heard? What has *wakened* in the yard? From what evidence can the stallion's *rage* be read?)
2. What words in the poem seem especially rich in connotations?
3. Here is one paraphrase of the poem: "A runaway horse wakes a boy up and does some damage." Make a better paraphrase, one that more accurately reflects the feelings you are left with after reading the poem.

Samuel Johnson (1709–1784)

A SHORT SONG OF CONGRATULATION   (1780)

Long-expected one and twenty
  Ling'ring year at last is flown,
Pomp and pleasure, pride and plenty,
  Great Sir John, are all your own.

Loosened from the minor's tether;
   Free to mortgage or to sell,
Wild as wind, and light as feather
   Bid the slaves of thrift farewell.   5

Call the Bettys, Kates, and Jennys
   Every name that laughs at care,
Lavish of your grandsire's guineas,   10
   Show the spirit of an heir.

All that prey on vice and folly
   Joy to see their quarry fly:
Here the gamester light and jolly,   15
   There the lender grave and sly.

Wealth, Sir John, was made to wander,
   Let it wander as it will;
See the jockey, see the pander,
   Bid them come, and take their fill.   20

When the bonny blade carouses,
   Pockets full, and spirits high,
What are acres? What are houses?
   Only dirt, or° wet or dry.   *either*

If the guardian or the mother
   Tell the woes of willful waste,   25
Scorn their counsel and their pother,
   You can hang or drown at last.

Questions

1. In line 5, what does *tether* denote? What does the word suggest?
2. Why are *Bettys, Kates,* and *Jennys* more meaningful names as Johnson uses them than Elizabeths, Katherines, and Genevieves would be?
3. Johnson states in line 24 the connotations that *acres* and *houses* have for the young heir. What connotations might these terms have for Johnson himself?

Denise Levertov (b. 1923)

Sunday Afternoon   1958

After the First Communion
and the banquet of mangoes and
bridal cake, the young daughters
of the coffee merchant lay down
for a long siesta, and their white dresses   5
lay beside them in quietness
and the white veils floated
in their dreams as the flies buzzed.
But as the afternoon
burned to a close they rose   10

and ran about the neighborhood
among the halfbuilt villas
alive, alive, kicking a basketball, wearing
other new dresses, of bloodred velvet.

QUESTIONS

1. What contrasts do you find between the scene in lines 1–8 and that in the rest of this poem?
2. What suggestions do you derive from *white dresses* and *white veils*? From *other new dresses, of bloodred velvet*?
3. In line 10, what is interesting in the word *burned*? Why is it a more meaningful word than *drew*, or *came to a close*, or *closed*?

James Camp (b. 1923)

AT THE FIRST AVENUE REDEMPTION CENTER   1975

I enter the Plaidland Redemption Center
And, whistling a descant on a Handel theme,
Look for a sign.

The sign says:
"There is only one line.
Wait here."

AT THE FIRST AVENUE REDEMPTION CENTER. 1. *Plaidland:* a brand of trading stamps. 2. *descant:* in music, a melody or counterpoint played at the same time as a theme. *Handel:* George Frederick Handel (1685–1759), German-born composer of oratorios, musical dramas based on Bible stories. *Messiah* is Handel's best-known oratorio, in which solo voices and choruses sing of the annunciation, birth, life, death, and resurrection of Christ. 3. *Look for a sign:* In both Old and New Testaments, many persons look for some visible message from God: Noah, whose dove brings back an olive branch (Genesis 8); the doubting Pharisees who ask Christ to perform a miracle: "Master, we would see a sign from thee" (Matthew 12:38).

QUESTIONS

1. What suggestions do you find in the phrase *Redemption Center*?
2. What do the allusions to Handel and to the Bible lend to the poem? How do they help the message on the sign to appear more meaningful?

Richard Snyder (b. 1925)

A MONGOLOID CHILD HANDLING SHELLS ON THE BEACH   1971

She turns them over in her slow hands,
as did the sea sending them to her;
broken bits from the mazarine maze,
they are the calmest things on this sand.

The unbroken children splash and shout,
rough as surf, gay as their nesting towels.
But she plays soberly with the sea's
small change and hums back to it its slow vowels.

QUESTIONS

1. In what ways is the phrase *the mazarine maze* more valuable to this poem than if the poet had said "the deep blue sea"?
2. What is suggested by calling the other children *unbroken*? By saying that their towels are *nesting*?
3. How is the mongoloid child like the sea? How are the other children like the surf? What do the differences between sea and surf contribute to Richard Snyder's poem?
4. What is the poet's attitude toward the mongoloid child? How can you tell?

Elizabeth Bishop (b. 1911)

LATE AIR   1946

From a magician's midnight sleeve
  the radio-singers
distribute all their love-songs
over the dew-wet lawns.
  And like a fortune-teller's   5
their marrow-piercing guesses are whatever you believe.

But on the Navy-Yard aerial I find
  better witnesses
for love on summer nights.
Five remote red lights   10
  keep their nests there; Phoenixes
burning quietly, where the dew cannot climb.

QUESTIONS

1. To what kind of air, besides the kind we breathe, does the title refer?
2. What do you recall about phoenixes and their habits that lends meaning to this poem?
3. In the first stanza, what suggestions do you find in the *magician* and the *fortune-teller*? What do the two have in common? Are they likened to—or contrasted with—the *phoenixes* in stanza two?
4. Does line 4 contain a literal fact, a meaningful suggestion, or both? Comment also on the poet's reference to *dew* in the last line.
5. What can lights on an aerial in a shipyard possibly have to do with love?
6. Comment on this comment: "In 'Late Air' Elizabeth Bishop doesn't like vague, soggy language that can mean just any old thing the hearer wants it to—the language of pop songs and penny-in-the-slot fortune tickets. She likes language to be precise and mechanical, like an aerial. She doesn't want language to be rich in suggestions."

W. S. Merwin (b. 1927)

DEAD HAND

1963

Temptations still nest in it like basilisks.
Hang it up till the rings fall.

DEAD HAND. The basilisk, a fabled lizard of the Sahara, could crack rock with its look and (according to the Roman poet Lucan) could poison the hand of an attacker and cause death unless the hand was quickly severed from the body. (For more details see Jorge Luis Borges, *The Book of Imaginary Beings*. New York: E. P. Dutton, 1969.)

QUESTIONS

1. What are we told about the owner of the hand?
2. What is suggested?

Geoffrey Hill (b. 1932)

MERLIN

1959

I will consider the outnumbering dead:
For they are the husks of what was rich seed.
Now, should they come together to be fed,
They would outstrip the locusts' covering tide.

Arthur, Elaine, Mordred; they are all gone
Among the raftered galleries of bone.
By the long barrows of Logres they are made one,
And over their city stands the pinnacled corn.

MERLIN. In medieval legend, Merlin was a powerful magician and a seer, an aide of King Arthur. 5. *Elaine:* in Arthurian romance, the beloved of Sir Launcelot. *Mordred:* Arthur's treacherous nephew by whose hand the king died. 7. *barrows:* earthworks for burial of the dead. *Logres:* name of an ancient British kingdom, according to the twelfth-century historian Geoffrey of Monmouth, who gathered legends of King Arthur.

QUESTIONS

1. What does the title "Merlin" contribute to this poem? Do you prefer to read the poem as though it is Merlin who speaks to us — or the poet?
2. Line 4 alludes to the plague of locusts that God sent upon Egypt (Exodus 10): "For they covered the face of the whole earth, so that the land was darkened . . ." With this allusion in mind, explain the comparison of the dead to locusts.
3. Why are the suggestions inherent in the names of *Arthur, Elaine,* and *Mordred* more valuable to this poem than those we might find in the names of other dead persons called, say, Gus, Tessie, and Butch?
4. Explain the phrase in line 6: *the raftered galleries of bone.*
5. In the last line, what *city* does the poet refer to? Does he mean some particular city, or is he making a comparison?
6. What is interesting in the adjective *pinnacled*? How can it be applied to corn?

Wallace Stevens (1879–1955)

THE EMPEROR OF ICE-CREAM

1923

Call the roller of big cigars,
The muscular one, and bid him whip
In kitchen cups concupiscent curds.
Let the wenches dawdle in such dress
As they are used to wear, and let the boys 5
Bring flowers in last month's newspapers.
Let be be finale of seem.
The only emperor is the emperor of ice-cream.

Take from the dresser of deal,
Lacking the three glass knobs, that sheet 10
On which she embroidered fantails once
And spread it so as to cover her face.
If her horny feet protrude, they come
To show how cold she is, and dumb.
Let the lamp affix its beam. 15
The only emperor is the emperor of ice-cream.

THE EMPEROR OF ICE-CREAM. 9. *deal:* fir or pine wood used to make cheap furniture.

QUESTIONS

1. What scene is taking place in the first stanza? Describe it in your own words. What are your feelings about it?
2. Who do you suppose to be the dead person in the second stanza? What can you infer about her? What do you know about her for sure?
3. Make a guess about this mysterious emperor. Who do you take him to be?
4. What does ice cream mean to you? In this poem, what do you think it means to Stevens?

Robert Frost (1874–1963)

FIRE AND ICE

1923

Some say the world will end in fire,
Some say in ice.
From what I've tasted of desire
I hold with those who favor fire.
But if it had to perish twice,
I think I know enough of hate
To say that for destruction ice
Is also great
And would suffice.

QUESTIONS

1. To whom does Frost refer in line 1? In line 2?
2. What connotations of *fire* and *ice* contribute to the richness of Frost's comparison?

17 Figures of Speech

WHY SPEAK FIGURATIVELY?

"I will speak daggers to her, but use none," says Hamlet, preparing to confront his mother. His statement makes sense only because we realize that *daggers* is to be taken two ways: literally (denoting sharp, pointed weapons) and nonliterally (referring to something that can be used *like* weapons—namely, words). Reading poetry, we often meet comparisons between two things whose similarity we have never noticed before. When Marianne Moore observes that a fir tree has "an emerald turkey-foot at the top," the result is a pleasure that poetry richly affords: the sudden recognition of likenesses.

A treetop like a turkey-foot, words like daggers—such comparisons are called **figures of speech.** In its broadest definition, a figure of speech may be said to occur whenever a speaker or writer, for the sake of freshness or emphasis, departs from the usual denotations of words. Certainly, when Hamlet says he will speak daggers, no one expects him to release pointed weapons from his lips, for *daggers* is not to be read solely for its denotation. Its connotations—sharp, stabbing, piercing, wounding—also come to mind, and we see ways in which words and daggers work alike. (Words too can hurt: by striking through pretenses, possibly, or by wounding their hearer's self-esteem.) In the statement "A razor is sharper than an ax," there is no departure from the usual denotations of *razor* and *ax,* and no figure of speech results. Both objects are of the same class; the comparison is not offensive to logic. But in "How sharper than a serpent's tooth it is to have a thankless child," the objects—snake's tooth (fang) and ungrateful offspring—are so unlike that no reasonable comparison may be made between them. To find similarity, we attend to the connotations of *serpent's tooth*—biting, piercing, pain—rather than to its denotations. If we are aware of the connotations of *red rose* (beauty, softness, freshness, and so forth), then the line "My love is like a red, red rose" need not call to mind a woman with a scarlet face and a thorny neck.

Figures of speech are not devices to state what is demonstrably untrue. Indeed they often state truths that more literal language cannot communicate; they call attention to such truths; they lend them emphasis.

Alfred, Lord Tennyson (1809–1892)

THE EAGLE 1851

He clasps the crag with crooked hands;
Close to the sun in lonely lands,
Ringed with the azure world, he stands.

The wrinkled sea beneath him crawls;
He watches from his mountain walls,
And like a thunderbolt he falls.

This brief poem is rich in figurative language. In the first line, the phrase *crooked hands* may surprise us. An eagle does not have hands, we might protest; but the objection would be a quibble, for evidently Tennyson is indicating exactly how an eagle clasps a crag, in the way that human fingers clasp a thing. By implication, too, the eagle is a person. *Close to the sun,* if taken literally, is an absurd exaggeration, the sun being a mean distance of 93,000,000 miles from the earth. For the eagle to be closer to it by the altitude of a mountain is an approach so small as to be insignificant. But figuratively, Tennyson conveys that the eagle stands above the clouds, perhaps silhouetted against the sun, and for the moment belongs to the heavens rather than to the land and sea. The word *ringed* makes a circle of the whole world's horizons and suggests that we see the world from the eagle's height; the sea becomes an aged, sluggish animal; *mountain walls,* possibly literal, also suggests a fort or castle; and finally the eagle itself is likened to a thunderbolt in speed and in power, perhaps also in that its beak is — like our abstract conception of a lightning bolt — pointed. How much of the poem can be taken literally? Only *he clasps the crag, he stands, he watches, he falls.* (And even *he* is scarcely literal, for the poet cannot know the sex of the eagle; *it* would be the more likely word in an ornithologist's description of the bird.) The rest is made of figures of speech. The result is that, reading Tennyson's poem, we gain a bird's-eye view of sun, sea, and land — and even of bird. Like imagery, figurative language refers us to the physical world.

William Shakespeare (1564–1616)

SHALL I COMPARE THEE TO A SUMMER'S DAY? 1609

Shall I compare thee to a summer's day?
Thou art more lovely and more temperate.

Rough winds do shake the darling buds of May,
And <u>summer's</u> lease hath all too short a date.   5
Sometime too hot the eye of heaven shines,
And often is his gold complexion dimmed;
And every fair from fair sometimes declines,
By chance, or nature's changing course, untrimmed.
But thy eternal summer shall not fade,_   *end, change over*
Nor lose possession of that fair thou ow'st°;   *ownest, have*   10
Nor shall <u>death brag</u> thou wand'rest in his shade,_ } *eternal summer — perfection*
When in eternal lines to time thou grow'st.   *will not die*
   So long as men can breathe or eyes can see, }
   So long lives this, and this gives life to thee. } *reinforce*

Howard Moss (b. 1922)

SHALL I COMPARE THEE TO A SUMMER'S DAY?   1976

Who says you're like one of the dog days?
You're nicer. And better.
Even in May, the weather can be gray,
And a summer sub-let doesn't last forever.
Sometimes the sun's too hot;   5
Sometimes it is not.
Who can stay young forever?
People break their necks or just drop dead!
But you? Never!
If there's just one condensed reader left   10
Who can figure out the abridged alphabet,
   After you're dead and gone,
   In this poem you'll live on!

QUESTIONS

1. In Howard Moss's streamlined version of Shakespeare, from a series called "Modified Sonnets (Dedicated to adapters, abridgers, digesters, and condensers everywhere)," to what extent does he use figurative language? In Shakespeare's original sonnet, how high a proportion of Shakespeare's language is figurative?

2. Compare some of Moss's lines to the corresponding lines in Shakespeare's sonnet. Why is *Even in May, the weather can be gray* less interesting than the original? In the lines on the sun (5–6 in both versions), what has Moss's modification deliberately left out? Why is Shakespeare's seeing death as a braggart memorable? Why aren't you greatly impressed by Moss's last two lines?

3. Can you explain Shakespeare's play on the word *untrimmed* (line 8)? Evidently the word can mean "divested of trimmings," but what other suggestions do you find in it?

4. How would you answer someone who argued, "Maybe Moss's language isn't as good as Shakespeare's, but the meaning is still there. What's wrong with putting Shakespeare into up-to-date words that can be understood by everybody?"

METAPHOR AND SIMILE

> Life, like a dome of many-colored glass,
> Stains the white radiance of Eternity.

The first of these lines (from Shelley's "Adonais") is a **simile:** a comparison of two things, indicated by some connective, usually *like, as, than,* or a verb such as *resembles.* The things compared have to be dissimilar in kind for a simile to exist: it is no simile to say "Your fingers are like mine"; it is a literal observation. But to say "Your fingers are like sausages" is to use a simile. Omit the connective—say "Your fingers are sausages"—and the result is a **metaphor,** a statement that one thing *is* something else, which, in a literal sense, it is not. In the second of Shelley's lines, it is *assumed* that Eternity is light or radiance, and we have an **implied metaphor,** one that uses neither a connective nor the verb *to be.* Here are examples:

Oh, my love is like a red, red rose.	*Simile*
Oh, my love resembles a red, red rose.	*Simile*
Oh, my love is redder than a rose.	*Simile*
Oh, my love is a red, red rose.	*Metaphor*
Oh, my love has red petals and sharp thorns.	*Implied metaphor*
Oh, I placed my love into a long-stem vase	
And I bandaged my bleeding thumb.	*Implied metaphor*

Often you can tell a metaphor from a simile by much more than just the presence or absence of a connective. In general, a simile refers to only one characteristic that two things have in common, while a metaphor is not plainly limited in the number of resemblances it may indicate. To use the simile "He eats like a pig" is to compare man and animal in one respect: eating habits. But to say "He's a pig" is to use a metaphor that might involve comparisons of appearance and morality as well.

In everyday speech, simile and metaphor occur frequently. We use metaphors ("She's a doll"), and similes ("The tickets are selling like hotcakes") without being fully conscious of them. If, however, we are aware that words possess literal meanings as well as figurative ones, we do not write *died in the wool* for *dyed in the wool* or *tow the line* for *toe the line,* nor do we use **mixed metaphors** as did the writer who advised, "Water the spark of knowledge and it will bear fruit," or the speaker who urged, "To get ahead, keep your nose to the grindstone, your shoulder to the wheel, your ear to the ground, and your eye on the ball." Perhaps the unintended humor of these statements comes from our seeing that the writer, busy stringing together stale metaphors, was not aware that they had any physical reference.

Unlike a writer who thoughtlessly mixes metaphors, a good poet can join together incongruous things and still keep the reader's respect.

In his ballad "Thirty Bob a Week," John Davidson has a British working-man tell how it feels to try to support a large family on small wages:

> It's a naked child against a hungry wolf;
>   It's playing bowls upon a splitting wreck;
> It's walking on a string across a gulf
>   With millstones fore-and-aft about your neck;
> But the thing is daily done by many and many a one;
>   And we fall, face forward, fighting, on the deck.

Like the man with his nose to the grindstone, Davidson's wage-earner is in an absurd fix; but his balancing act seems far from merely nonsensical. For every one of the poet's comparisons—of workingman to child, to bowler, to tight-rope walker, and to seaman—offer suggestions of a similar kind. All help us see (and imagine) the workingman's hard life: a brave and unyielding struggle against impossible odds.

A poem may make a series of comparisons, like Davidson's, or the whole poem may be one extended comparison:

Richard Wilbur (b. 1917)
A SIMILE FOR HER SMILE   1950

Your smiling, or the hope, the thought of it,
Makes in my mind such pause and abrupt ease
As when the highway bridgegates fall,
Balking the hasty traffic, which must sit
On each side massed and staring, while   5
Deliberately the drawbridge starts to rise:

Then horns are hushed, the oilsmoke rarifies,
Above the idling motors one can tell
The packet's smooth approach, the slip,
Slip of the silken river past the sides,   10
The ringing of clear bells, the dip
And slow cascading of the paddle wheel.

    How much life metaphors bring to poetry may be seen by comparing two poems by Tennyson and Blake.

Alfred, Lord Tennyson (1809–1892)
FLOWER IN THE CRANNIED WALL   1869

Flower in the crannied wall,
I pluck you out of the crannies,
I hold you here, root and all, in my hand,
Little flower—but if I could understand
What you are, root and all, and all in all,
I should know what God and man is.

How many metaphors does this poem contain? None. Compare it with a briefer poem on a similar theme: the quatrain that begins Blake's "Auguries of Innocence." (We follow here the opinion of W. B. Yeats who, in editing Blake's poems, thought the lines ought to be printed separately.)

William Blake (1757–1827)

To see a world in a grain of sand   (about 1803)

To see a world in a grain of sand
And a heaven in a wild flower,
Hold infinity in the palm of your hand
And eternity in an hour.

Set beside Blake's poem, Tennyson's — short though it is — seems lengthy. What contributes to the richness of "To see a world in a grain of sand" is Blake's use of a metaphor in every line. And every metaphor is loaded with suggestion. Our world does indeed resemble a grain of sand: in being round, in being stony, in being one of a myriad (the suggestions go on and on). Like Blake's grain of sand, a metaphor holds much, within a small circumference.

Sylvia Plath (1932–1963)

Metaphors   1960

I'm a riddle in nine syllables,
An elephant, a ponderous house,
A melon strolling on two tendrils.
O red fruit, ivory, fine timbers!
This loaf's big with its yeasty rising.
Money's new-minted in this fat purse.
I'm a means, a stage, a cow in calf.
I've eaten a bag of green apples,
Boarded the train there's no getting off.

Questions

1. To what central fact do all the metaphors in this poem refer?
2. In the first line, what has the speaker in common with a riddle? Why does she say she has *nine* syllables?
3. How would you describe the tone of this poem? (Perhaps the poet expresses more than one attitude.) What attitude is conveyed in the metaphors of an elephant, "a ponderous house," "a melon strolling on two tendrils"? By the metaphors of red fruit, ivory, fine timbers, new-minted money? By the metaphor in the last line?

Emily Dickinson (1830–1886)

IT DROPPED SO LOW—IN MY REGARD (about 1863)

It dropped so low—in my Regard—
I heard it hit the Ground—
And go to pieces on the Stones
At bottom of my Mind—

Yet blamed the Fate that flung it—*less*
Than I denounced Myself,
For entertaining Plated Wares
Upon My Silver Shelf—

QUESTIONS

1. What is *it*? What two things are compared?
2. How much of the poem develops and amplifies this comparison?

Anonymous (English)

THERE WAS A MAN OF DOUBLE DEED 1783

There was a man of double deed
Who sowed his garden full of seed.
When the seed began to grow
'Twas like a garden full of snow,
When the snow began to melt   5
'Twas like a ship without a belt,
When the ship began to sail
'Twas like a bird without a tail,
When the bird began to fly
'Twas like an eagle in the sky,   10
When the sky began to roar
'Twas like a lion at the door,
When the door began to crack
'Twas like a stick across my back,
When my back began to smart   15
'Twas like a penknife in my heart,
And when my heart began to bleed
'Twas death and death and death indeed.

THERE WAS A MAN OF DOUBLE DEED. This traditional nursery rime may have originated as a chant to the rhythm of a bouncing ball. Its opening lines echo an old proverb: "A man of words and not of deeds is like a garden full of weeds." 6. *belt:* a series of armored plates at a ship's water line.

QUESTION

Does this seem no more than rigmarole or do you find it making any sense? Consider possible meanings of the phrase *double deed* and ways in which the objects joined in similes might be truly similar.

Ruth Whitman (b. 1922)

CASTOFF SKIN

1973

She lay in her girlish sleep at ninety-six,
small as a twig.
Pretty good figure

for an old lady, she said to me once.
Then she crawled away, leaving
a tiny stretched transparence

behind her. When I kissed her paper cheek
I thought of the snake,
of his quick motion.

QUESTIONS

1. Explain the central metaphor in "Castoff Skin."
2. What other figures of speech does the poem contain?

Denise Levertov (b. 1923)

LEAVING FOREVER

1964

He says the waves in the ship's wake
are like stones rolling away.
I don't see it that way.
But I see the mountain turning,
turning away its face as the ship
takes us away.

QUESTIONS

1. What do you understand to be the man's feelings about leaving forever? How does the speaker feel? With what two figures of speech does the poet express these conflicting views?
2. Suppose that this poem had ended in another simile (instead of its three last lines):

   I see the mountain as a suitcase
   left behind on the shore
   as the ship takes us away.

   How is Denise Levertov's choice of a figure of speech a much stronger one?

EXERCISE: *What Is Similar?*

Each of these quotations contains a simile or a metaphor. In each of these figures of speech, what two things is the poet comparing? Try to state exactly what you understand the two things to have in common: the most striking similarity or similarities that the poet sees.

1. Think of the storm roaming the sky uneasily
   like a dog looking for a place to sleep in,
   listen to it growling.
   > —Elizabeth Bishop, "Little Exercise"

2. When the hounds of spring are on winter's traces . . .
   > —Algernon Charles Swinburne, "Atalanta in Calydon"

3. The scarlet of the maples can shake me like a cry
   Of bugles going by.
   > —Bliss Carman, "A Vagabond Song"

4. "Hope" is the thing with feathers–
   That perches in the soul–
   And sings the tune without the words–
   And never stops–at all–
   > —Emily Dickinson, an untitled poem

5. Work without Hope draws nectar in a sieve . . .
   > —Samuel Taylor Coleridge, "Work Without Hope"

6. The finish of his hands
   shows oil, grain, knots
   where his growth scarred him.
   > —Carolyn Forché, "Dulcimer Maker"

OTHER FIGURES

When Shakespeare asks, in a sonnet,

> O! how shall summer's honey breath hold out
> Against the wrackful siege of batt'ring days,

it might seem at first that he mixes metaphors. How can a *breath* confront the battering ram of an invading army? But it is summer's breath and, by giving it to summer, Shakespeare makes the season a man or woman. It is as if the fragrance of summer were the breath within a person's body, and winter were the onslaught of old age.

Such is one instance of **personification**: a figure of speech in which a thing, an animal, or an abstract term (*truth, nature*) is made human. A personification extends throughout this whole short poem:

James Stephens (1882–1950)

THE WIND   1915

The wind stood up and gave a shout.
He whistled on his fingers and

Kicked the withered leaves about
And thumped the branches with his hand

And said he'd kill and kill and kill,
And so he will and so he will.

The wind is a wild man, and evidently it is not just any autumn breeze but a hurricane or at least a stiff gale. In poems that do not work as well as this one, personification may be employed mechanically. Hollow-eyed personifications walk the works of lesser English poets of the eighteenth century: Coleridge has quoted the beginning of one such neoclassical ode, "Inoculation! heavenly Maid, descend!" It is hard for the contemporary reader to be excited by William Collins's "The Passions, An Ode for Music" (1747), which personifies, stanza by stanza, Fear, Anger, Despair, Hope, Revenge, Pity, Jealousy, Love, Hate, Melancholy, and Cheerfulness, and has them listen to Music, until even "Brown Exercise rejoiced to hear, / And Sport leapt up, and seized his beechen spear." Still, the portraits of the Seven Deadly Sins in the four-teenth-century *Vision of Piers Plowman* remain memorable: "Thanne come Slothe al bislabered, with two slimy eiyen. . . ." In "Two Sonnets on Fame" John Keats makes an abstraction come alive in seeing Fame as "a wayward girl."

Hand in hand with personification often goes **apostrophe:** a way of addressing someone or something invisible or not ordinarily spoken to. In an apostrophe, a poet (in these examples Wordsworth) may address an inanimate object ("Spade! with which Wilkinson hath tilled his lands"), some dead or absent person ("Milton! thou shouldst be living at this hour"), an abstract thing ("Return, Delights!"), or a spirit ("Thou Soul that art the eternity of thought"). More often than not, the poet uses apostrophe to anounce a lofty and serious tone. An "O" may even be put in front of it ("O moon!") since, according to W. D. Snodgrass, every poet has a right to do so at least once in a lifetime. But apostrophe doesn't have to be highfalutin. It is a means of giving life to the inanimate. It is a way of giving body to the intangible, a way of speaking to it person to person, as in the words of a moving American spiritual: "Death, ain't you got no shame?"

Most of us, from time to time, emphasize a point with a statement containing exaggeration: "Faster than greased lightning," "I've told him a thousand times." We speak, then, not literal truth but use a figure of speech called **overstatement** (or **hyperbole**). Poets too, being fond of emphasis, often exaggerate for effect. Instances are Marvell's profession of a love that should grow "Vaster than empires, and more slow" and Burgon's description of Petra: "A rose-red city, half as old as Time." Overstatement can be used also for humorous purposes, as in a fat woman's boast (from a blues song): "Every time I shake, some skinny gal loses her home."[1] The opposite is **understatement,** implying more than is said. Mark Twain in *Life on the Mississippi* recalls how, as an ap-

---

[1] Quoted by LeRoi Jones in *Blues People* (New York: Wm. Morrow, 1963).

prentice steamboat-pilot asleep when supposed to be on watch, he was roused by the pilot and sent clambering to the pilot house: "Mr. Bixby was close behind, commenting." Another example is Robert Frost's line "One could do worse than be a swinger of birches" — the conclusion of a poem that has suggested that to swing on a birch tree is one of the most deeply satisfying activities in the world.

In **metonymy,** the name of a thing is substituted for that of another closely associated with it. For instance, we say "The White House decided," and mean the president did. When John Dyer writes in "Grongar Hill,"

> A little rule, a little sway,
> A sun beam on a winter's day,
> Is all the proud and might have
> Between the cradle and the grave,

we recognize that *cradle* and *grave* signify birth and death. A kind of metonymy, **synecdoche** is the use of a part of a thing to stand for the whole of it or vice versa. We say "She lent a hand," and mean that she lent her entire presence. Similarly, Milton in "Lycidas" refers to greedy clergymen as "blind mouths." Another kind of metonymy is the **transferred epithet:** a device of emphasis in which the poet attributes some characteristic of a thing to another thing closely associated with it. When Thomas Gray observes that, in the evening pastures, "drowsy tinklings lull the distant folds," he well knows that sheep's bells do not drowse, but sheep do. When Hart Crane, describing the earth as seen from an airplane, speaks of "nimble blue plateaus," he attributes the airplane's motion to the earth.

Paradox occurs in a statement that at first strikes us as self-contradictory but that on reflection makes some sense. "The peasant," said G. K. Chesterton, "lives in a larger world than the globe-trotter." Here, two different meanings of *larger* are contrasted: "greater in spiritual values" versus "greater in miles." Some paradoxical statements, however, are much more than plays on words. In a moving sonnet, the blind John Milton tells how one night he dreamed he could see his dead wife. The poem ends in a paradox:

> But oh, as to embrace me she inclined,
> I waked, she fled, and day brought back my night.

EXERCISE: *Paradox*

What paradoxes do you find in the following poem? For each, explain the sense that underlies the statement.

Chidiock Tichborne (1558?–1586)

ELEGY, WRITTEN WITH HIS OWN HAND
IN THE TOWER BEFORE HIS EXECUTION

1586

My prime of youth is but a frost of cares,
  My feast of joy is but a dish of pain,
My crop of corn is but a field of tares°,   *weeds*
  And all my good is but vain hope of gain:
The day is past, and yet I saw no sun,   5
And now I live, and now my life is done.

My tale was heard, and yet it was not told,
  My fruit is fall'n, and yet my leaves are green,
My youth is spent, and yet I am not old,
  I saw the world, and yet I was not seen: 10
My thread is cut, and yet it is not spun,
And now I live, and now my life is done.

I sought my death, and found it in my womb,
  I looked for life, and saw it was a shade,
I trod the earth, and knew it was my tomb,
  And now I die, and now I was but made: 15
My glass is full, and now my glass is run,
And now I live, and now my life is done.

Asked to define the difference between men and women, Samuel Johnson replied, "I can't conceive, madam, can you?" The great dictionary-maker was using a figure of speech known to classical rhetoricians as *paranomasia*, better known to us as a **pun** or play on words. How does a pun operate? It reminds us of another word (or other words) of similar or identical sound but of very different denotation. Although puns at their worst can be mere piddling quibbles, at best they can sharply point to surprising but genuine resemblances. The name of a dentist's country estate, Tooth Acres, is accurate: aching teeth paid for the land. In poetry, a pun may be facetious, as in Thomas Hood's ballad of "Faithless Nelly Gray":

Ben Battle was a soldier bold,
  And used to war's alarms;
But a cannon-ball took off his legs,
  So he laid down his arms!

Or it may be serious, as in these lines on war by E. E. Cummings:

the bigness of cannon
is skilful,

(*is skilful* becoming *is kill-ful* when read aloud), or perhaps, as in

Shakespeare's song in *Cymbeline*, "Fear no more the heat o' th' sun," both facetious and serious at once:

> Golden lads and girls all must,
> As chimney-sweepers, come to dust.

George Herbert (1593–1633)

THE PULLEY   1633

When God at first made man,
Having a glass of blessings standing by—
Let us (said he) pour on him all we can;
Let the world's riches, which dispersèd lie,
    Contract into a span.   5

So strength first made a way,
Then beauty flowed, then wisdom, honor, pleasure:
When almost all was out, God made a stay,
Perceiving that, alone of all His treasure,
    Rest in the bottom lay.   10

For if I should (said he)
Bestow this jewel also on My creature,
He would adore My gifts instead of Me,
And rest in Nature, not the God of Nature:
    So both should losers be.   15

Yet let him keep the rest,
But keep them with repining restlessness;
Let him be rich and weary, that at least,
If goodness lead him not, yet weariness
    May toss him to My breast.   20

QUESTIONS

1. What different senses of the word *rest* does Herbert bring into this poem?
2. How do God's words in line 16, *Yet let him keep the rest,* seem paradoxical?
3. What do you feel to be the tone of Herbert's poem? Does the punning make the poem seem comic?
4. Why is the poem called "The Pulley"? What is its implied metaphor?

To sum up: even though figures of speech are not to be taken *only* literally, they refer us to a tangible world. By *personifying* an eagle, Tennyson reminds us that the bird and humankind have certain characteristics in common. Through *metonymy*, a poet can focus our attention on a particular detail in a larger object; through *hyperbole* and *understatement*, make us see the physical actuality in back of words. *Pun* and *paradox* cause us to realize this actuality, too, and probably surprise us enjoyably at the same time. Through *apostrophe*, the poet animates the inanimate and asks it to listen — speaks directly to an immediate god or to the revivified dead. Put to such uses, figures of speech have power. They are more than just ways of playing with words.

Edmund Waller (1606–1687)

On a Girdle   1645

That which her slender waist confined,
Shall now my joyful temples bind;
No monarch but would give his crown,
His arms might do what this has done.

It was my heaven's extremest sphere,   5
The pale° which held that lovely deer;   *enclosure*
My joy, my grief, my hope, my love,
Did all within this circle move!

A narrow compass! and yet there
Dwelt all that's good, and all that's fair!   10
Give me but what this riband bound,
Take all the rest the sun goes round!

On a Girdle. Lines 1–2. *That which . . . temples bind*: A courtly lover might bind his brow with a lady's ribbon, to signify he was hers. 5. *extremest sphere*: In Ptolemaic astronomy, the outermost of the concentric spheres that surround the earth. In its wall the farthest stars are set.

Questions

1. To what things is the girdle compared?
2. Explain the pun in line 4. What effect does it have upon the tone of the poem?
3. Why is the effect of this pun different from that of Thomas Hood's play on the same word in "Faithless Nelly Gray" (quoted on p. 498)?
4. What does *compass* denote in line 9?
5. What paradox occurs in lines 9–10?
6. How many of the poem's statements are hyperbolic? Is the compliment the speaker pays his lady too grandiose to be believed? Explain.

John Donne (1572–1631)

A Hymn to God the Father   (1623)

Wilt Thou forgive that sin where I begun,
  Which is my sin, though it were done before?
Wilt Thou forgive those sins through which I run,
  And do them still, though still I do deplore?
    When Thou hast done, Thou hast not done,   5
      For I have more.

[handwritten annotations:] categorizing of sins 1. original he has lead otherpeople to sin by 2. sins that he has given up for a year or so 3. sins 4. sin of fear

Wilt Thou forgive that sin by which I have won
  Others to sin? and made my sin their door?
Wilt Thou forgive that sin which I did shun
  A year or two, but wallowed in a score?
    When Thou hast done, Thou hast not done,   *pun on word done*   10
        For I have more.

I have a sin of fear, that when I have spun
  My last thread, I shall perish on the shore;
Swear by Thyself that at my death Thy Sun - *Son*   15
  Shall shine as it shines now, and heretofore;
    And, having done that, Thou hast done,
        I have no more.

A HYMN TO GOD THE FATHER. According to his biographer Izaak Walton, Donne wrote this poem during an illness which brought him close to death.

QUESTIONS

1. Donne's wife, who had died in 1617, was named Anne More. Do you think he is punning on her name? Would that interpretation make sense?
2. For what different meanings can we read lines 5–6, 11–12, 17–18?
3. Discuss how fairly it can be charged that, because of its puns, Donne's poem is not serious.

Theodore Roethke (1908–1963)

I KNEW A WOMAN   1958

I knew a woman, lovely in her bones,
When small birds sighed, she would sigh back at them;
Ah, when she moved, she moved more ways than one:
The shapes a bright container can contain!
Of her choice virtues only gods should speak,   5
Or English poets who grew up on Greek
(I'd have them sing in chorus, cheek to cheek).

How well her wishes went! She stroked my chin,
She taught me Turn, and Counter-turn, and Stand;
She taught me Touch, that undulant white skin;   10
I nibbled meekly from her proffered hand;
She was the sickle; I, poor I, the rake,
Coming behind her for her pretty sake
(But what prodigious mowing we did make).

Love likes a gander, and adores a goose: 15
Her full lips pursed, the errant note to seize;
She played it quick, she played it light and loose;
My eyes, they dazzled at her flowing knees;
Her several parts could keep a pure repose,
Or one hip quiver with a mobile nose   20
(She moved in circles, and those circles moved).

Let seed be grass, and grass turn into hay:
I'm martyr to a motion not my own;
What's freedom for? To know eternity.
I swear she cast a shadow white as stone.   25
But who would count eternity in days?
These old bones live to learn her wanton ways:
(I measure time by how a body sways).

QUESTIONS

1. What outrageous puns do you find in Roethke's poem? Describe the effect of them.
2. What kind of figure of speech occurs in all three lines: *Of her choice virtues only gods should speak; My eyes, they dazzled at her flowing knees;* and *I swear she cast a shadow white as stone?*
3. What sort of figure is the poet's reference to himself as *old bones?*
4. Do you take *Let seed be grass, and grass turn into hay* as figurative language, or literal statement?
5. If you agree that the tone of this poem is witty and playful, do you think the poet is making fun of the woman? What is his attitude toward her? What part do figures of speech play in communicating it?

FOR REVIEW AND FURTHER STUDY

Robert Frost (1874–1963)
TREE AT MY WINDOW   1928

Tree at my window, window tree,
My sash is lowered when night comes on;
But let there never be curtain drawn
Between you and me.

Vague dream-head lifted out of the ground,   5
And thing next most diffuse to cloud,
Not all your light tongues talking aloud
Could be profound.

But, tree, I have seen you taken and tossed,
And if you have seen me when I slept,   10
You have seen me when I was taken and swept
And all but lost.

That day she put our heads together,
Fate had her imagination about her,
Your head so much concerned with outer,   15
Mine with inner, weather.

QUESTIONS

1. What is the central metaphor of this poem? Is it explicit or implied?

2. What is meant by *light tongues* (line 7)? What resemblances does this comparison point out?
3. What do you understand from the *inner weather* (line 16) by which the speaker was *taken and swept*?
4. What use does Frost make of personification? What does it contribute to the poem?

James C. Kilgore (b. 1928)

THE WHITE MAN PRESSED THE LOCKS   1970

Driving down the concrete vein,
Away from the smoky heart,
Through the darkening, blighted body,
Pausing at clotted arteries,
The white man pressed the locks
  on all the sedan's doors,
Sped toward the white corpuscles
  in the white arms
    hugging the black city.

QUESTIONS

1. Explain the two implied metaphors in this poem: what are the two bodies?
2. How do you take the word *hugging*? Is this a loving embrace or a stranglehold?
3. What, in your own words, is the poet's theme?

Elizabeth Jennings (b. 1926)

DELAY   1953

The radiance of that star that leans on me
Was shining years ago. The light that now
Glitters up there my eye may never see
And so the time lag teases me with how

Love that loves now may not reach me until
Its first desire is spent. The star's impulse
Must wait for eyes to claim it beautiful
And love arrived may find us somewhere else.

QUESTIONS

1. What is the poet comparing in this metaphor?
2. Why would the metaphor not have been available to a poet in Shakespeare's time?
3. What is the tone of the poem? How does the speaker feel about the *radiance of that star* — simply joyous and glad, as we might expect?

4. What connotations has the word *impulse* (line 6)? What is the implied metaphor here?

EXERCISE: *Figure Spotting*

In each of these poems, what figures of speech do you notice? For each metaphor or simile, try to state what is compared. In any use of metonymy, what is represented?

Richard Wilbur (b. 1921)
SLEEPLESS AT CROWN POINT   1976

All night, this headland
Lunges into the rumpling
Capework of the wind.

Anonymous (English)
THE FORTUNES OF WAR, I TELL YOU PLAIN   (1854–1856)

The fortunes of war, I tell you plain,
Are a wooden leg—or a golden chain.

A. E. Housman (1859–1936)
FROM THE WASH THE LAUNDRESS SENDS   1922

From the wash the laundress sends
My collars home with raveled ends:
I must fit, now these are frayed,
My neck with new ones London-made.

Homespun collars, homespun hearts,
Wear to rags in foreign parts.
Mine at least's as good as done,
And I must get a London one.

Robert Frost (1874–1963)
THE SECRET SITS   1936

We dance round in a ring and suppose,
But the Secret sits in the middle and knows.

Charles Simic (b. 1938)

FORK

1971

This strange thing must have crept
Right out of hell.
It resembles a bird's foot
Worn around the cannibal's neck.

As you hold it in your hand,
As you stab with it into a piece of meat,
It is possible to imagine the rest of the bird:
Its head which like your fist
Is large, bald, beakless and blind.

Ishmael Reed (b. 1938)

.05

1973

If i had a nickel
For all the women who've
Rejected me in my life
I would be the head of the
World Bank with a flunkie 5
To hold my derby as i
Prepared to fly chartered
Jet to sign a check
Giving India a new lease
On life 10

If i had a nickel for
All the women who've loved
Me in my life i would be
The World Bank's assistant
Janitor and wouldn't need 15
To wear a derby
All i'd think about would
Be going home

A. R. Ammons (b. 1926)

AUTO MOBILE

1971

For the bumps bangs & scratches of
collisive encounters
madam
I through time's ruts and weeds
sought you, metallic, your 5

stainless steel flivver:
I have banged you, bumped
and scratched, side-swiped,
momocked & begommed you &
your little flivver still
works so well.

10

W. S. Merwin (b. 1927)
Song of Man Chipping an Arrowhead

1973

Little children you will all go
but the one you are hiding
will fly

Robert Burns (1759–1796)
Oh, my love is like a red, red rose

(about 1788)

Oh, my love is like a red, red rose
   That's newly sprung in June;
My love is like the melody
   That's sweetly played in tune.

So fair art thou, my bonny lass,
   So deep in love am I;
And I will love thee still, my dear,
   Till a' the seas gang° dry.

5

go

Till a' the seas gang dry, my dear,
   And the rocks melt wi' the sun;
And I will love thee still, my dear,
   While the sands o' life shall run.

10

And fare thee weel, my only love!
   And fare thee weel awhile!
And I will come again, my love
   Though it were ten thousand mile.

15

Ogden Nash (1902–1971)
Very Like a Whale

1934

One thing that literature would be greatly the better for
Would be a more restricted employment by authors of simile and meta-
    phor.
Authors of all races, be they Greeks, Romans, Teutons or Celts,
Can't seem just to say that anything is the thing it is but have to go out of
    their way to say that it is like something else.

What does it mean when we are told   5
That the Assyrian came down like a wolf on the fold?
In the first place, George Gordon Byron had had enough experience
To know that it probably wasn't just one Assyrian, it was a lot of As-
    syrians.
However, as too many arguments are apt to induce apoplexy and thus
    hinder longevity,
We'll let it pass as one Assyrian for the sake of brevity.   10
Now then, this particular Assyrian, the one whose cohorts were gleaming
    in purple and gold,
Just what does the poet mean when he says he came down like a wolf on
    the fold?
In heaven and earth more than is dreamed of in our philosophy there are a
    great many things,
But I don't imagine that among them there is a wolf with purple and gold
    cohorts or purple and gold anythings.
No, no, Lord Byron, before I'll believe that this Assyrian was actually like
    a wolf I must have some kind of proof;   15
Did he run on all fours and did he have a hairy tail and a big red mouth
    and big white teeth and did he say Woof woof woof?
Frankly I think it very unlikely, and all you were entitled to say, at the
    very most,
Was that the Assyrian cohorts came down like a lot of Assyrian cohorts
    about to destroy the Hebrew host.
But that wasn't fancy enough for Lord Byron, oh dear me no, he had to in-
    vent a lot of figures of speech and then interpolate them,
With the result that whenever you mention Old Testament soldiers to
    people they say Oh yes, they're the ones that a lot of wolves dressed
    up in gold and purple ate them.   20
That's the kind of thing that's being done all the time by poets, from
    Homer to Tennyson;
They're always comparing ladies to lilies and veal to venison.
How about the man who wrote,
Her little feet stole in and out like mice beneath her petticoat?
Wouldn't anybody but a poet think twice   25
Before stating that his girl's feet were mice?
Then they always say things like that after a winter storm
The snow is a white blanket. Oh it is, is it, all right then, you sleep under a
    six-inch blanket of snow and I'll sleep under a half-inch blanket of
    unpoetical blanket material and we'll see which one keeps warm,
And after that maybe you'll begin to comprehend dimly
What I mean by too much metaphor and simile.   30

VERY LIKE A WHALE. The title is from *Hamlet* (Act III, scene 2): Feigning madness, Hamlet
likens the shape of a cloud to a whale. "Very like a whale," says Polonius, who, to humor
his prince, will agree to the accuracy of any figure at all. Nash's art has been described by
Max Eastman in *Enjoyment of Laughter* (New York: Simon and Schuster, 1936):

> If you have ever tried to write rimed verse, you will recognize in Nash's writing
> every naïve crime you were ever tempted to commit—artificial inversions, pre-
> tended rimes, sentences wrenched and mutilated to bring the rime-word to the end

of the line, words assaulted and battered into riming whether they wanted to or not, ideas and whole dissertations dragged in for the sake of a rime, the metrical beat delayed in order to get all the necessary words in, the metrical beat speeded up unconscionably because there were not enough words to put in.

Questions

1. Nash alludes to the opening lines of Byron's poem "The Destruction of Sennacherib" (see page 562):

The Assyrian came down like the wolf on the fold,
And his cohorts were gleaming in purple and gold;

and to Sir John Suckling's portrait of a bride in "A Ballad Upon a Wedding":

Her feet beneath her petticoat,
Like little mice stole in and out,
As if they feared the light: . . . .

How can these metaphors be defended against Nash's quibbles?
2. What valuable functions of simile and metaphor in poetry is Nash pretending to ignore?

18 Song

SINGING AND SAYING

Most poems are more memorable than most ordinary speech, and when music is combined with poetry the result can be more memorable still. The differences between speech, poetry, and song may appear if we consider, first of all, this fragment of an imaginary conversation between two lovers:

> Let's not drink; let's just sit here and look at each other. Or put a kiss inside my goblet and I won't want anything to drink.

Forgettable language, we might think; but let's try to make it a little more interesting:

> Drink to me only with your eyes, and I'll pledge my love to you with my
> eyes;
> Or leave a kiss within the goblet, that's all I'll want to drink.

The passage is closer to poetry, but still has a distance to go. At least we now have a figure of speech—the metaphor that love is wine, implied in the statement that one lover may salute another by lifting an eye as well as by lifting a goblet. But the sound of the words is not yet especially interesting. Here is another try, by Ben Jonson:

> Drink to me only with thine eyes,
>   And I will pledge with mine;
> Or leave a kiss but in the cup,
>   And I'll not ask for wine.

In these opening lines from Jonson's poem "To Celia," the improvement is noticeable. These lines are poetry; their language has become special. For one thing, the lines rime (with an additional rime sound on *thine*). There is interest, too, in the proximity of the words *kiss* and *cup*: the repetition (or alliteration) of the *k* sound. The rhythm of the lines has become regular; generally every other word (or syllable) is stressed:

> DRINK to me ON-ly WITH thine EYES,
>   And I will PLEDGE with MINE;
> OR LEAVE a KISS but IN the CUP,
>   And I'LL not ASK for WINE.

All these devices of sound and rhythm, together with metaphor, produce a pleasing effect — more pleasing than the effect of "Let's not drink; let's look at each other." But the words became more pleasing still when later set to music:

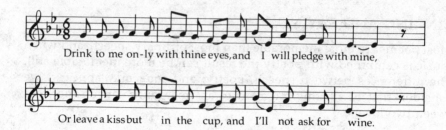

Drink to me on-ly with thine eyes, and I will pledge with mine,

Or leave a kiss but in the cup, and I'll not ask for wine.

In this memorable form, the poem is still alive today.

Ben Jonson (1573?–1637)

To Celia   1616

Drink to me only with thine eyes,
    And I will pledge with mine;
Or leave a kiss but in the cup,
    And I'll not ask for wine.
The thirst that from the soul doth rise   5
    Doth ask a drink divine;
But might I of Jove's nectar sup,
    I would not change for thine.

I sent thee late a rosy wreath,
    Not so much honoring thee   10
As giving it a hope that there
    It could not withered be.
But thou thereon didst only breathe,
    And sent'st it back to me;
Since when it grows, and smells, I swear,   15
    Not of itself but thee.

A compliment to a lady has rarely been put in language more graceful, more wealthy with interesting sounds. Other figures of speech besides metaphor make them unforgettable: for example, the hyperbolic tributes to the power of the lady's sweet breath, which can start picked roses growing again, and her kisses, which even surpass the nectar of the gods.

This song falls into stanzas—as many poems that resemble songs also do. A **stanza** (Italian for "station," "stopping-place," or "room") is a group of lines whose pattern is repeated throughout the poem. Most songs have more than one stanza. When printed, the stanzas of songs and poems usually are set off from one another by space. When sung, stanzas of songs are indicated by a pause or by the introduction of a refrain, or chorus (a line or lines repeated). The word **verse,** which strictly refers to one line of a poem, is sometimes loosely used to mean a whole stanza: "All join in and sing the second verse!" In speaking of a stanza, whether sung or read, it is customary to indicate by a convenient algebra its **rime scheme,** the order in which rimed words recur. For instance, the rime scheme of this stanza by Herrick is *a b a b;* the first and third lines rime and so do the second and fourth:

> Round, round, the roof doth run;
>   And being ravished thus,
> Come, I will drink a tun
>   To my Propertius.

Refrains are words, phrases, or lines repeated at intervals in a song or songlike poem. A refrain usually follows immediately after a stanza, and when it does, it is called **terminal refrain.** A refrain whose words change slightly with each recurrence is called an **incremental refrain,** as in "Frankie and Johnny" (p. 522). Sometimes we also hear an **internal refrain:** one that appears within a stanza, generally in a position that stays fixed throughout a poem. Both internal refrains and terminal refrains are used to great effect in the traditional song "The Cruel Mother":

Anonymous (traditional Scottish ballad)

THE CRUEL MOTHER

> She sat down below a thorn,
>   *Fine flowers in the valley,*
> And there she has her sweet babe born
>   *And the green leaves they grow rarely.*
>
> "Smile na sae° sweet, my bonny babe,"   *so* 5
>   *Fine flowers in the valley,*
> "And° ye smile sae sweet, ye'll smile me dead."   *if*
>   *And the green leaves they grow rarely.*

She's taen out her little pen-knife,
   Fine flowers in the valley,
And twinned° the sweet babe o' its life,   10   severed
   And the green leaves they grow rarely.

She's howket° a grave by the light o' the moon,   dug
   Fine flowers in the valley,
And there she's buried her sweet babe in   15
   And the green leaves they grow rarely.

As she was going to the church,
   Fine flowers in the valley,
She saw a sweet babe in the porch
   And the green leaves they grow rarely.   20

"O sweet babe, and thou were mine,"
   Fine flowers in the valley,
"I wad cleed° thee in the silk so fine."   dress
   And the green leaves they grow rarely.

"O mother dear, when I was thine,"   25
   Fine flowers in the valley,
"You did na prove to me sae kind."
   And the green leaves they grow rarely.

Taken by themselves, the refrain lines might seem mere pretty nonsense. But interwoven with the story of the murdered child, they form a
terrible counterpoint. What do they come to mean? Possibly that Nature
keeps going about her chores, unmindful of sin and suffering. The effect is an ironic contrast. It is the repetitiveness of a refrain, besides,
that helps to give it power.

Songs tend to be written in language simple enough to be understood on first hearing. Recently, however, song-writers have been able
to assume that their audiences would pay close attention to their words.
Bob Dylan, Leonard Cohen, Don McLean, and others have employed
words more complicated and difficult than have most previous writers
of popular songs, requiring listeners sometimes to play their recordings
many times over, with trebles turned up all the way.

Many poems began life as songs but today, their tunes forgotten,
survive in poetry anthologies. Shakespeare studded his plays with
songs, and many of his contemporaries wrote verse to fit existing tunes.
Some poets, themselves musicians (like Thomas Campion), composed
both words and music. In Shakespeare's day, **madrigals,** short secular
songs for three or more voice-parts arranged in counterpoint, enjoyed
great favor. A madrigal by Chidiock Tichborne is given on page 498;
and another, an anonymous English madrigal, "The Silver Swan," on
page 525.

Some poets who were not composers printed their work in madrigal books for others to set to music. In the seventeenth century, however, poetry and song seem to have fallen away from each other. By the end of the century, much new poetry, other than songs for plays, was written to be printed and to be silently read. Poets who wrote popular songs—like Thomas D'Urfey, compiler of the collection *Pills to Purge Melancholy*—were considered somewhat disreputable. With the notable exceptions of John Gay, who took existing popular tunes for *The Beggar's Opera*, and Robert Burns, who rewrote folk songs or made completely new words for them, few important English poets since Campion have been first-rate song-writers.

Occasionally, a poet has learned a thing or two from music. "But for the opera I could never have written *Leaves of Grass*," said Walt Whitman, who loved the Italian art form for its expansiveness. Coleridge, Hardy, Auden, and many others have learned from folk ballads, and T. S. Eliot patterned his thematically repetitive *Four Quartets* after the structure of a quartet in classical music. "Poetry," said Ezra Pound, "begins to atrophy when it gets too far from music." Still, even in the twentieth century, the poet has been more often a corrector of printer's proofs than a tunesmith or performer.

Some people think that to make a poem and to travel about singing it, as many rock singer-composers now do, is a return to the venerable tradition of the **troubadours**, minstrels of the late Middle Ages. But there are differences. No doubt the troubadours had to please their patrons, but for better or worse their songs were not affected by a stopwatch in a producer's hand or by the technical resources of a sound studio. Bob Dylan has denied that he is a poet, and Paul Simon once told an interviewer, "If you want poetry read Wallace Stevens." Nevertheless, much has been made lately of current song lyrics as poetry.[1] Are rock songs poems? Clearly some, but not all, are. That the lyrics of a song cannot stand the scrutiny of a reader does not necessarily invalidate them, though; song-writers do not usually write in order to be read. Pete Seeger has quoted a saying of his father: "A printed folk song is like a photograph of a bird in flight." Still there is no reason not to photograph birds, or to read song lyrics. If the words seem rich and interesting, we may possibly increase our enjoyment of them and perhaps be able to sing them more accurately. Like most poems and songs of the past, most current songs may end in the trash can of time. And yet, certain memorable rimed and rhythmic lines may live on, especially if music has served them for a base and if singers have given them wide exposure.

[1] See the paperback anthologies *The Poetry of Rock*, Richard Goldstein, ed. (New York: Bantam, 1969), and *Rock Is Beautiful*, Stephanie Spinner, ed. (New York: Dell, 1970).

Compare the following poem by Edwin Arlington Robinson and a popular song lyric based on it. Notice what Paul Simon had to do to Robinson's original in order to make it into a song, and how Simon altered Robinson's conception.

Edwin Arlington Robinson (1869–1935)

RICHARD CORY   1897

Whenever Richard Cory went down town,
We people on the pavement looked at him:
He was a gentleman from sole to crown,
Clean favored, and imperially slim.

And he was always quietly arrayed,   5
And he was always human when he talked;
But still he fluttered pulses when he said,
"Good-morning," and he glittered when he walked.

And he was rich — yes, richer than a king —
And admirably schooled in every grace: 10
In fine°, we thought that he was everything   *in short*
To make us wish that we were in his place.

So on we worked, and waited for the light,
And went without the meat, and cursed the bread;
And Richard Cory, one calm summer night,   15
Went home and put a bullet through his head.

Paul Simon (b. 1942)

RICHARD CORY   1966

With Apologies to E. A. Robinson

They say that Richard Cory owns
One half of this old town,
With elliptical connections
To spread his wealth around.
Born into Society,   5
A banker's only child,
He had everything a man could want:
Power, grace and style.

Refrain:

But I, I work in his factory
And I curse the life I'm livin'   10

RICHARD CORY, by Paul Simon. If possible, listen to the ballad sung by Simon and Garfunkel on *Sounds of Silence* (Columbia recording CL 2469, stereo CS 9269).
    © 1966 by Paul Simon. Used by permission.

And I curse my poverty
And I wish that I could be
Oh I wish that I could be
Oh I wish that I could be
Richard Cory.   15

The papers print his picture
Almost everywhere he goes:
Richard Cory at the opera,
Richard Cory at a show
And the rumor of his party   20
And the orgies on his yacht—
Oh he surely must be happy
With everything he's got.   *(Refrain.)*

He really gave to charity,
He had the common touch,   25
And they were grateful for his patronage
And they thanked him very much,
So my mind was filled with wonder
When the evening headlines read:
  "Richard Cory went home last night   30
  And put a bullet through his head."   *(Refrain.)*

BALLADS

Any narrative song, like Paul Simon's "Richard Cory," may be called a **ballad.** In English, some of the most famous ballads are **folk ballads,** loosely defined as anonymous story-songs transmitted orally before they were ever written down. Sir Walter Scott, a pioneer collector of Scottish folk ballads, drew the ire of an old woman whose songs he had transcribed: "They were made for singing and no' for reading, but ye ha'e broken the charm now and they'll never be sung mair." The old singer had a point. Print freezes songs and tends to hold them fast to a single version. However, if Scott and others had not written them down, many would have been lost.

In his monumental work *The English and Scottish Popular Ballads* (1882–1898), the American scholar Francis J. Child winnowed out 305 folk ballads he considered authentic—that is, creations of illiterate or semiliterate people who had preserved them orally. Child, who worked by insight as well as by learning, did such a good job of telling the difference between folk ballads and other kinds that later scholars have added only about a dozen ballads to his count. Often called **Child ballads,** his texts include "The Three Ravens," "Sir Patrick Spence," "The Twa Corbies," "Edward," "The Cruel Mother," and many others still on the lips of singers. Here is one of the best-known Child ballads.

Anonymous (traditional Scottish ballad)

Bonny Barbara Allan

It was in and about the Martinmas time,
   When the green leaves were afalling,
That Sir John Graeme, in the West Country,
   Fell in love with Barbara Allan.

He sent his men down through the town,   5
   To the place where she was dwelling:
"O haste and come to my master dear,
   Gin° ye be Barbara Allan."   *if*

O hooly°, hooly rose she up,   *slowly*
   To the place where he was lying,   10
And when she drew the curtain by:
   "Young man, I think you're dying."

"O it's I'm sick, and very, very sick,
   And 'tis a' for Barbara Allan." —
"O the better for me ye's never be,   15
   Tho your heart's blood were aspilling.

"O dinna ye mind°, young man," said she,   *don't you remember*
   "When ye was in the tavern adrinking,
That ye made the health° gae round and round,   *toasts*
   And slighted Barbara Allan?"   20

He turned his face unto the wall,
   And death was with him dealing:
"Adieu, adieu, my dear friends all,
   And be kind to Barbara Allan."

And slowly, slowly raise she up,   25
   And slowly, slowly left him,
And sighing said she could not stay,
   Since death of life had reft him.

She had not gane a mile but twa,
   When she heard the dead-bell ringing,   30
And every jow° that the dead-bell geid,   *stroke*
   It cried, "Woe to Barbara Allan!"

"O mother, mother, make my bed!
   O make it saft and narrow!
Since my love died for me today,   35
   I'll die for him tomorrow."

Bonny Barbara Allan. 1. *Martinmas:* Saint Martin's day, November 11.

Questions

1. In any line does the Scottish dialect cause difficulty? If so, try reading the line
aloud.

2. Without ever coming out and explicitly calling Barbara hard-hearted, this ballad reveals that she is. In which stanza and by what means is her cruelty demonstrated?
3. At what point does Barbara evidently have a change of heart? Again, how does the poem dramatize this change without explicitly talking about it?
4. In many American versions of this ballad, noble knight John Graeme becomes an ordinary citizen. The gist of the story is the same, but at the end are these further stanzas, incorporated from a different ballad:

They buried Willie in the old churchyard
    And Barbara in the choir;
And out of his grave grew a red, red rose,
    And out of hers a briar.

They grew and grew to the steeple top
    Till they could grow no higher;
And there they locked in a true love's knot,
    The red rose round the briar.

Do you think this appendage heightens or weakens the final impact of the story? Can the American ending be defended as an integral part of a new song? Explain.
5. Paraphrase lines 9, 15–16, 22, 25–28. By putting these lines into prose, what has been lost?

As you can see from "Bonny Barbara Allan," in a traditional English or Scottish folk ballad the storyteller speaks of the lives and feelings of others. Even if the pronoun "I" occurs, it rarely has much personality. Characters often exchange dialogue, but no one character speaks all the way through. Events move rapidly, perhaps because some of the dull transitional stanzas have been forgotten. The events themselves, as ballad scholar Albert B. Friedman has said, are frequently "the stuff of tabloid journalism—sensational tales of lust, revenge and domestic crime. Unwed mothers slay their newborn babes; lovers unwilling to marry their pregnant mistresses brutally murder the poor women, for which, without fail, they are justly punished."[2] There are also many ballads about people who converse with the dead ("The Unquiet Grave") or with supernatural beings ("Thomas the Rimer") and about gallant knights ("Sir Patrick Spence"), and there are a few humorous ballads, usually about unhappy marriages.

The ballad-spinner has at hand a fund of ready-made epithets: steeds are usually "milk-white" or "berry-brown," lips "rosy" or "ruby-red," corpses and graves "clay-cold," beds (like Barbara Allan's) "soft and narrow." At the least, these conventional phrases are terse and understandable. Sometimes they add meaning: the king who sends Sir Patrick Spence to his doom drinks "blood-red wine." The clothing,

[2] Introduction to *The Viking Book of Folk Ballads of the English-Speaking World*, edited by Albert B. Friedman (New York: Viking Press, 1956).

steeds, and palaces of ladies and lords are always luxurious: a queen may wear "grass-green silk" or "Spanish leather" and ride a horse with "fifty silver bells and nine." Such descriptions are naive, for as Friedman points out, ballad-singers were probably peasants imagining what they had seen only from afar: the life of the nobility. This may be why the skin of ladies in folk ballads is ordinarily "milk-white," "lily-white," or "snow-white." In an agrarian society, where most people worked in the fields, not to be suntanned was a sign of gentility.

A favorite pattern of ballad-makers is the so-called **ballad stanza,** four lines rimed *a b c b,* tending to fall into 8, 6, 8, and 6 syllables:

> Clerk Saunders and Maid Margaret
>   Walked owre yon garden green,
> And deep and heavy was the love
>   That fell thir twa between°.   *between those two*

Though not the only possible stanza for a ballad, this easily singable quatrain has continued to attract poets since the Middle Ages. Close kin to the ballad stanza is **common meter,** a stanza found in hymns, such as "Amazing Grace," by the eighteenth-century English hymnist John Newton:

> Amazing grace! how sweet the sound
>   That saved a wretch like me!
> I once was lost, but now am found,
>   Was blind, but now I see.

Notice that its pattern is that of the ballad stanza except for its *two* pairs of rimes. That all its lines rime is probably a sign of more literate artistry than we usually hear in folk ballads. Another sign of schoolteachers' influence is that Newton's rimes are exact. (Rimes in folk ballads are often rough-and-ready, as if made by ear, rather than polished and exact, as if the riming words had been matched for their similar spellings. In "Barbara Allan," for instance, the hard-hearted lover's name rimes with *afalling, dwelling, aspilling, dealing,* and even with *ringing* and *adrinking.*) That so many hymns were written in common meter may have been due to convenience. If a congregation didn't know the tune to a hymn in common meter, they readily could sing its words to the tune of another such hymn they knew. Besides hymnists, many poets have favored common meter, among them A. E. Housman and Emily Dickinson.

Obviously, whatever stanza a folk ballad may have is determined not by any printed shape its poet wishes for it but by the demands of music. Here, for instance, is a folk ballad (one of the few Child overlooked) with a stanza much more complicated than the ballad stanza.[3]

---

[3] Collected by Cecil Sharp in *Folksongs from Somerset* (London: Novello & Co., Ltd., 1904–09).

Anonymous (traditional English ballad)

Still Growing

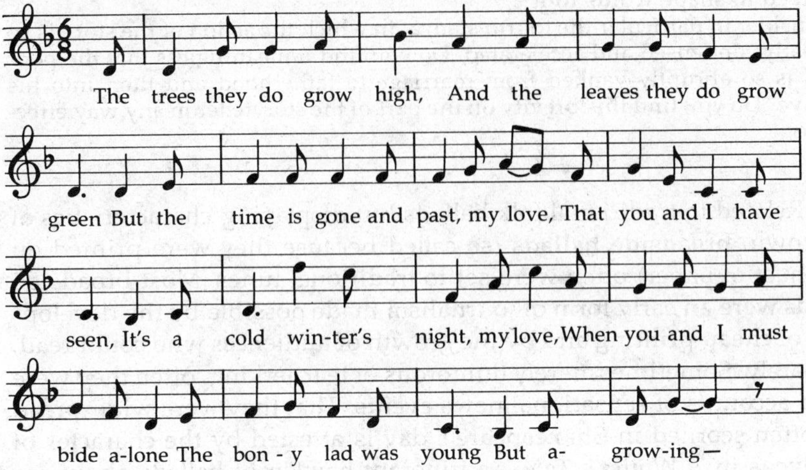

The trees they do grow high, and the leaves they do grow green;
  But the time is gone and past, my love, that you and I have seen:
It's a cold winter's night, my love, when you and I must bide alone.
  The bonny lad was young,
    But a-growing.

"O father, dear father, I'm feared you've done me harm
  You've married me a boy and I fear he is too young."
"O daughter, dear daughter, and if you stay at home and wait along o' me
  A lady you shall be,
    While he's a-growing.

"We'll send him to the college for one year or two
  And then perhaps in time, my love, a man he will grow.
I will buy you a bunch of white ribbons to tie about his bonny, bonny
    waist
  To let the ladies know
    That he's married."

At the age of sixteen, he was a married man,
  At the age of seventeen, she brought him a son;
At the age of eighteen, my love, O his grave was growing green,
  And so she put an end
    To his growing.

"I made my love a shroud of the holland so fine,"
  And every stitch she put in it the tears came trickling down;
"O once I had a sweetheart, but now I have got never a one
  So fare you well my own true love
    For ever."

1. What are the features of this stanza pattern?
2. If you know music, sing or hum the melody. How has this tune apparently helped to shape words to it?
3. Consider in particular the fourth stanza, in which the action of the story is so greatly condensed and accelerated. Do you find it meaningless that the poor lad is so abruptly yanked from marriage to fatherhood and then into his grave? Do you find this brevity on the part of the storyteller in any way effective?

Related to traditional folk ballads but displaying characteristics of their own, **broadside ballads** (so called because they were printed on one sheet of paper) often were set to traditional tunes. Most broadside ballads were an early form of journalism made possible by the development of cheap printing and by the growth of audiences who could read, just barely. Sometimes merely humorous or tear-jerking, often they were rimed accounts of sensational news events. That they were widespread and often scorned in Shakespeare's day is attested by the character of Autolycus in *A Winter's Tale,* an itinerant hawker of ballads about sea monsters and strange pregnancies ("a usurer's wife was brought to bed of twenty money-bags"). Although many broadsides tend to be **doggerel** (verse full of irregularities due not to skill but to incompetence), many excellent poets had their work taken up and peddled in the streets — among them Marvell, Swift, and Byron.[4]

Because they stick in the mind and because they were inexpensive to publish and to purchase, broadsides in the nineteenth century often were used to convey social or political messages. Some of the best are **protest songs,** like "Song of the Lower Classes" (about 1848) by Ernest Jones. A stanza follows:

> We're low — we're low — we're very very low,
>   Yet from our fingers glide
> The silken flow — and the robes that glow
>   Round the limbs of the sons of pride.
> And what we get — and what we give —
>   We know, and we know our share;
> We're not too low the cloth to weave,
>   But too low the Cloth to wear!

Compare those lines with this modern protest ballad:

[4] A generous collection of broadsides has been assembled by Vivian de Sola Pinto and A. E. Rodway in *The Common Muse: An Anthology of Popular British Ballad Poetry, XVth-XXth Century* (St. Clair Shores, Mich.: Scholarly Press, 1957). See also *Irish Street Ballads,* edited by Colm O. Lochlainn (New York: Corinth Books, 1960), and Olive Woolley Burt, *American Murder Ballads and Their Stories* (New York: Oxford University Press, 1958).

Woody Guthrie (1912–1967)

PLANE WRECK AT LOS GATOS (DEPORTEE)   1961

The crops are all in and the peaches are rotting,
The oranges are piled in their creosote dumps;
You're flying them back to the Mexican border
To pay all their money to wade back again.

Refrain:

Goodbye to my Juan, Goodbye Rosarita;   5
Adiós mes amigos, Jesús and Marie,
You won't have a name when you ride the big airplane:
All they will call you will be deportee.

My father's own father he waded that river;
They took all the money he made in his life;   10
My brothers and sisters come working the fruit trees
And they rode the truck till they took down and died.

Some of us are illegal and some are not wanted,
Our work contract's out and we have to move on;
Six hundred miles to that Mexico border,   15
They chase us like outlaws, like rustlers, like thieves.

We died in your hills, we died in your deserts,
We died in your valleys and died on your plains;
We died neath your trees and we died in your bushes,
Both sides of this river we died just the same.   20

The sky plane caught fire over Los Gatos Canyon,
A fireball of lightning and shook all our hills.
Who are all these friends all scattered like dry leaves?
The radio says they are just deportees.

Is this the best way we can grow our big orchards?   25
Is this the best way we can grow our good fruit?
To fall like dry leaves to rot on my top soil
And be called by no name except deportees?

In making a song out of a news event, "Plane Wreck at Los Gatos"
resembles a broadside ballad; but it is more like a folk ballad in that the
singer, instead of sticking around to comment on the action, disappears

and lets the characters speak for themselves. That is the way of most Child ballads: people in them may wail and mourn, but not the singer, who usually remains impersonal.

Literary ballads, not meant for singing, are written by sophisticated poets for book-educated readers who enjoy being reminded of folk ballads. Literary ballads imitate certain features of folk ballads: they may tell of tragic love affairs or of mortals who confront the supernatural; they may use conventional figures of speech, old-fangled diction, or ballad stanzas. Well-known poems of this kind include Keats's "La Belle Dame sans Merci" (page 632) and Coleridge's "Rime of the Ancient Mariner."

Anonymous (American ballad)

Frankie and Johnny

Frankie she was a good woman, Johnny he was her man,
And every silver dollar Frankie made went straight to her Johnny's hand.
He was her man, but he done her wrong.

Frankie and Johnny went walking, Johnny in a brand new suit.
"Cost me a hundred," says Frankie, "but don't my Johnny look cute?"   5
He was her man, but he done her wrong.

Frankie went down to the corner, she called for a thimble of gin,
She says to the fat bartender, "Has my lovin' Johnny been in?
I can't believe he's been doing me wrong."

"Ain't going to tell you no story, ain't going to tell you no lie,   10
Mister Johnny was in her 'bout an hour ago with a floozy named Ella Fly.
He is your man, but I believe he's doing you wrong."

Frankie ran down to the pawn shop, she didn't go there for fun.
She turned in her doorknob diamonds, she took out a forty-four gun.
He was her man, but he done her wrong.   15

Frankie ran down to the parlor-house, she leaned on the parlor-house bell.
"Stand out of my way, you floozies, or I'll splash you all over Hell!
I want my man, he's been doing me wrong."

Frankie looked over the transom, the tears ran out of her eyes.
There was her lovin' Johnny a-lovin' up Ella Fly.   20
He was her man, but he was doing her wrong.

She threw back her red silk kimono, she whipped out that old forty-four.
Rooty-toot-toot, three times she did shoot, right through that hardwood door.
He was her man, but he done her wrong.

Johnny grabbed off his Stetson, "O Lord no, Frankie, don't shoot!"   25
But Frankie squeezed the trigger three times more and he fell down like a
    stick of wood.
He was her man, but he done her wrong.

The first shot, Johnny staggered; the second shot, he fell;
The third shot took him through the heart and his face started coming out
    in Hell.
He was her man, but he done her wrong.   30

"O roll me over easy, roll me over slow,
Roll me over on my right side, honey, so my heart don't overflow.
I was your man, but I done you wrong."

Bring on your rubber-tired hearses, bring on your rubber-tired hacks.
There's eight men going to the burying yard and only seven of 'em com-
    ing back.   35
He was her man, but he done her wrong.

The judge look hard at the jury, says, "It's plain as plain can be.
This woman put some daylight through her man, it's murder in the sec-
    ond degree.
He was her man, and she done him wrong."

Now it wasn't murder in the second degree, it wasn't murder in the third,   40
All Frankie did was drop her man like a hunter drops a bird.
He was her man, but he done her wrong.

The jury went out on Frankie, sat under an electric fan,
Came back and said, "You're a free woman, go kill yourself another man
If he does you wrong, if he does you wrong."   45

"O put me away in a dungeon, put me in a cold, cold cell,
Put me where the north wind blows from the southeast corner of Hell.
I shot my man, 'cause he done me wrong."

Frankie she heard a rumbling, away down under the ground.
Maybe it was little Johnny where she had shot him down.   50
He was her man, but he done her wrong.

Frankie went out to the burying yard, just to look her Johnny in the face.
"Ain't it hard to see you, Johnny, in this lonesome place?"
He was her man, but he done her wrong.

Well, I looked down the lonesome street, Lord, as far off as I could see,   55
All I could hear was a two-string fiddle playing "Nearer, My God, to
    Thee."
He was her man, but he done her wrong.

FRANKIE AND JOHNNY. Hundreds of versions of this ballad exist; this one is a composite of
many. In the 1890s a murder that took place either in St. Louis or in Kansas City, Missouri,
became famous in folk song as the story of Frankie and Albert. About 1911, vaudeville
singers changed Albert's name to Johnny and introduced other elements. 16. *parlor-house*:
a brothel fancy enough to have a waiting room.

1. How would you describe the tone of this ballad?
2. Compare its account of Frankie's trial with these stanzas from an earlier "Frankie and Albert" version:

They took little Frankie to the courthouse,
They sat her in a big arm chair.
She was waiting for the judge to say,
"We will give her ninety-nine year,
Because she killed her man in the first degree."

But the judge he said to the jury,
"It's plain as plain can be
Why she shot the man she loved.
I think she ought to go free
Because a gambling man won't treat you right."

Frankie walked out on the scaffold
As brave as she could be:
"When I shot the man I loved
I murdered in the first degree.
He was my man and I loved him so."

How is this earlier version different in tone?
3. How can it be claimed that "Frankie and Johnny" is composed in the ballad stanza (illustrated on page 518)? It is hardly likely that whoever wrote it knew Child ballads. Why do you suppose this stanza has been so popular for five hundreds years or more?

EXPERIMENT: *Seeing the Traits of Ballads*

In the anthology at the back of this book, read the Child ballads "Edward," "Sir Patrick Spence," "The Three Ravens," and "The Twa Corbies" (pages 713–716). With these ballads in mind, consider one or more of these modern poems:

W. H. Auden, "As I Walked Out One Evening" (page 720)
E. E. Cummings, "All in green went my love riding" (page 733)
Walter de la Mare, "The Listeners" (page 734)
Bob Dylan, "Subterranean Homesick Blues" (page 743)
Dudley Randall, "Ballad of Birmingham" (page 792)
William Jay Smith, "American Primitive" (page 808)
William Butler Yeats, "Crazy Jane Talks with the Bishop" (page 828).

What characteristics of folk ballads do you find in them? In what ways do these modern poets depart from the traditions of folk ballads of the Middle Ages?

FOR REVIEW AND FURTHER STUDY

EXERCISE: *Songs or Poems or Both?*

Consider each of the following song lyrics. Which do you think can stand not only to be sung but to be read as poetry? Which probably should not be seen but only heard?

Anonymous (English madrigal)

FA, MI, FA, RE, LA, MI
1609

Fa, mi, fa, re, la, mi,
Begin, my son, and follow me;
Sing flat, fa mi,
So shall we well agree.
Hey tro loly lo.
Hold fast, good son,
With hey tro lily lo.
O sing this once again, lustily.

Anonymous (English madrigal)

THE SILVER SWAN, WHO LIVING HAD NO NOTE
1612

The silver swan, who living had no note,
When death approached unlocked her silent throat;
Leaning her breast against the reedy shore,
Thus sung her first and last, and sung no more.
Farewell, all joys; O death, come close mine eyes;
More geese than swans now live, more fools than wise.

Ern Alpaugh (b. 1914)
Dewey G. Pell (b. 1917)

SWINGING CHICK
1968

Swinging chick
You know she does the trick
Sho ba ba dee ba
She's so swinging
Always singing   5
She's my swinging chick

Swinging chick
Boy are we ever nice and thick
When she starts to doin' that swing and sway
The man in the moon's gotta get out of her way   10

Oh, swinging chick
Sho ba ba dee ba
She's my swing it
Pick it up and fling it
Swinging hum-a-dinging chick   15

John Lennon (b. 1940)
Paul McCartney (b. 1942)

ELEANOR RIGBY   1966

Ah, look at all the lonely people!
Ah, look at all the lonely people!

Eleanor Rigby
Picks up the rice in the church where a wedding has been,
Lives in a dream,
Waits at the window   5
Wearing the face that she keeps in a jar by the door.
Who is it for?

All the lonely people,
Where do they all come from?
All the lonely people,   10
Where do they all belong?

Father McKenzie,
Writing the words of a sermon that no one will hear,
No one comes near   15
Look at him working,
Darning his socks in the night when there's nobody there.
What does he care?

All the lonely people
Where do they all come from?
All the lonely people   20
Where do they all belong?

Eleanor Rigby
Died in the church and was buried along with her name.
Nobody came.   25
Father McKenzie,
Wiping the dirt from his hands as he walks from the grave,
No one was saved.

All the lonely people,
Where do they all come from?
All the lonely people,   30
Where do they all belong?

Ah, look at all the lonely people!
Ah, look at all the lonely people!

Joni Mitchell (b. 1943)

Black Crow

There's a crow flying
Dark and ragged
Tree to tree
He's black as the highway that's leading me
Now he's diving down   5
To pick up on something shiny
I feel like that black crow
Flying
In a blue sky.

I took a ferry to the highway   10
Then I drove to a pontoon plane
I took a plane to a taxi
And a taxi to a train
I've been travelling so long
How'm I ever going to know my home   15
When I see it again
I'm like a black crow flying
In a blue, blue sky.

In search of love and music
My whole life has been   20
Illumination
Corruption
And diving, diving, diving, diving,
Diving down to pick up on every shiny thing
Just like that black crow flying   25
In a blue sky.

I looked at the morning
After being up all night
I looked at my haggard face in the bathroom light
I looked out the window   30
And I saw that ragged soul take flight
I saw a black crow flying
In a blue sky
Oh I'm like a black crow flying
In a blue sky.   35

Anonymous (American song)

Good Mornin', Blues

1959

I woke up this mornin' with the blues all round my bed,
Yes, I woke up this morning with the blues all round my bed,
Went to eat my breakfast, had the blues all in my bread.

"Good mornin', blues, blues, how do you do?" (2)
"I'm feelin' pretty well, but, pardner, how are you?" 5

Yes, I woke up this morning, 'bout an hour 'fore day, (2)
Reached and grabbed the pillow where my baby used to lay.

If you ever been down, you know just how I feel, (2)
Feel like an engine, ain't got no drivin' wheel.

If I feel tomorrow, like I feel today, (2) 10
I'll stand right here, look a thousand miles away.

If the blues was whisky, I'd stay drunk all the time, (2)
Stay drunk, baby, just to wear you off my mind.

I got the blues so bad, it hurts my feet to walk, (2)
I got the blues so bad, it hurts my tongue to talk. 15

The blues jumped a rabbit, run him a solid mile, (2)
When the blues overtaken him, he hollered like a newborn child.

Good Mornin', Blues. This folk song has been adapted by Alan Lomax from a version by
singer Huddie Ledbetter (Leadbelly). The number (2) indicates a line to be sung twice.

19 Sound

SOUND AS MEANING

Isak Dinesen, in a memoir of her life on a plantation in East Africa, tells how some Kikuyu tribesmen reacted to their first hearing of rimed verse:

> The Natives, who have a strong sense of rhythm, know nothing of verse, or at least did not know anything before the times of the schools, where they were taught hymns. One evening out in the maize-field, where we had been harvesting maize, breaking off the cobs and throwing them on to the ox-carts, to amuse myself, I spoke to the field laborers, who were mostly quite young, in Swahili verse. There was no sense in the verses, they were made for the sake of rime — "Ngumbe na-penda chumbe, Malaya mbaya. Wakamba na-kula mamba." The oxen like salt — whores are bad — The Wakamba eat snakes. It caught the interest of the boys, they formed a ring round me. They were quick to understand that meaning in poetry is of no consequence, and they did not question the thesis of the verse, but waited eagerly for the rime, and laughed at it when it came. I tried to make them themselves find the rime and finish the poem when I had begun it, but they could not, or would not, do that, and turned away their heads. As they had become used to the idea of poetry, they begged: "Speak again. Speak like rain." Why they should feel verse to be like rain I do not know. It must have been, however, an expression of applause, since in Africa rain is always longed for and welcomed.[1]

What the tribesmen had discovered is that poetry, like music, appeals to the ear. However limited it may be in comparison with the sound of an orchestra — or a tribal drummer — the sound of words in itself gives pleasure. However, we might doubt Isak Dinesen's assumption that "meaning in poetry is of no consequence." "Hey nonny-nonny" and such nonsense has a place in song lyrics and other poems, and we might take pleasure in hearing rimes in Swahili; but most good poetry has meaningful sound as well as musical sound. Certainly the words of a song have an effect different from that of wordless music: they go along

[1] Isak Dinesen, *Out of Africa* (New York: Random House, 1972).

with their music and, by making statements, add more meaning. The French poet Isodore Isou, founder of a literary movement called *lettrisme*, maintained that poems can be written not only in words but in letters (sample lines: *xyl, xyl, / prprali dryl / znglo trpylo pwi*). But the sound of letters alone, without denotation and connotation, has not been enough to make Letterist poems memorable. In the response of the Kikuyu tribesmen, there may have been not only the pleasure of hearing sounds but also the agreeable surprise of finding that things not usually associated had been brought together.

More powerful when in the company of meaning, not apart from it, the sounds of consonants and vowels can contribute greatly to a poem's effect. The sound of *s*, which can suggest the swishing of water, has rarely been used more accurately than in Surrey's line "Calm is the sea, the waves work less and less." When, in a poem, the sound of words working together with meaning pleases mind and ear, the effect is **euphony,** as in the following lines from Tennyson's "Come down, O maid":

> Myriads of rivulets hurrying through the lawn,
> The moan of doves in immemorial elms,
> And murmuring of innumerable bees.

Its opposite is **cacophony:** a harsh, discordant effect. It too is chosen for the sake of meaning. We hear it in Milton's scornful reference in "Lycidas" to corrupt clergymen whose songs "Grate on their scrannel pipes of wretched straw." (Read that line and one of Tennyson's aloud and see which requires lips, teeth, and tongue to do more work.) But note that although Milton's line is harsh in sound, the line (when we meet it in his poem) is pleasing because it is artful. Pope has illustrated both euphony and cacophony in his *Essay on Criticism*, insisting that sound must echo sense:

> Soft is the strain when Zephyr gently blows,
> And the smooth stream in smoother numbers° flows;   *metrical rhythm*
> But when loud surges lash the sounding shore,
> The harsh, rough verse should like the torrent roar . . .

Not merely sound but also rhythm contributes to the effect of this passage.

Is sound in those examples identical with meaning? Not quite. In Tennyson's lines, for instance, the cooing of doves is not *exactly* a moan. As John Crowe Ransom has pointed out, the sound would be almost the same but the meaning entirely different in "The murdering of innumerable beeves." While it is true that the consonant sound *sl-* will often begin a word that conveys ideas of wetness and smoothness — *slick, slimy, slippery, slush* — we are so used to hearing it in words that convey nothing of the kind — *slave, sledgehammer, sleeve, slow* — that it is doubtful that the sound all by itself communicates anything very definite. Asked to nominate the most beautiful word in the English language, a wit once suggested not *sunrise* or *silvery* but *syphilis*.

Relating sound more closely to meaning, the device called **onomatopoeia** is an attempt to represent a thing or action by a word that imitates the sound associated with it: *zoom, whiz, crash, bang, ding-dong, pitter-patter, yakety-yak*. Onomatopoeia is often effective in poetry, as in Emily Dickinson's line about the fly with its "uncertain stumbling Buzz," in which the nasal sounds *n, m, ng* and the sibilants *c, s,* help make a droning buzz, and in Robert Lowell's transciption of a birdcall, "yuck-a, yuck-a, yuck-a" (in "Falling Asleep over the Aeneid").

Like the Kikuyu tribesmen, others who care for poetry have discovered in the sound of words something of the refreshment of cool rain. Dylan Thomas, telling how he began to write poetry, said that from early childhood words were to him "as the notes of bells, the sounds of musical instruments, the noises of wind, sea, and rain, the rattle of milkcarts, the clopping of hooves on cobbles, the fingering of branches on the window pane, might be to someone, deaf from birth, who has miraculously found his hearing."[2] For readers, too, the sound of words can have a magical spell, most powerful when it points to meaning. James Weldon Johnson in *God's Trombones* has told of an old-time preacher who began his sermon, "Brothers and sisters, this morning I intend to explain the unexplainable — find out the indefinable — ponder over the imponderable — and unscrew the inscrutable!" The repetition of sound in *unscrew* and inscrutable has appeal, but the magic of the words is all the greater if they lead us to imagine the mystery of all Creation as an enormous screw that the preacher's mind, like a screw-driver, will loosen. Though the sound of a word or the meaning of a word may have value all by itself, both become more memorable when taken together.

William Butler Yeats (1865–1939)

WHO GOES WITH FERGUS?   1892

Who will go drive with Fergus now,
And pierce the deep wood's woven shade,
And dance upon the level shore?
Young man, lift up your russet brow,

---

[2] "Notes on the Art of Poetry," *The Texas Quarterly,* 1961; reprinted in *Modern Poetics,* James Scully, ed. (New York: McGraw-Hill, 1965).

And lift your tender eyelids, maid,   5
And brood on hopes and fear no more.

And no more turn aside and brood
Upon love's bitter mystery;
For Fergus rules the brazen cars,
And rules the shadows of the wood,   10
And the white breast of the dim sea
And all dishevelled wandering stars.

WHO GOES WITH FERGUS? *Fergus:* Irish king who gave up his throne to be a wandering
poet.

QUESTIONS

1. In what lines do you find euphony?
2. In what line do you find cacophony?
3. How do the sounds of these lines stress what is said in them?

EXERCISE: *Listening to Meaning*

Read aloud the following brief poems. In the sounds of which particular words
are meanings well captured? In which of the poems below do you find onomatopoeia?

John Updike (b. 1932)

WINTER OCEAN   1960

Many-maned scud-thumper, tub
of male whales, maker of worn wood, shrub-
ruster, sky-mocker, rave!
portly pusher of waves, wind-slave.

Frances Cornford (1886–1960)

THE WATCH   1923

I wakened on my hot, hard bed,
Upon the pillow lay my head;
Beneath the pillow I could hear
My little watch was ticking clear.
I thought the throbbing of it went   5
Like my continual discontent.
I thought it said in every tick:
I am so sick, so sick, so sick.
O death, come quick, come quick, come quick,
Come quick, come quick, come quick, come quick!   10

William Wordsworth (1770–1850)

A Slumber Did My Spirit Seal   1800

A slumber did my spirit seal;
  I had no human fears—
She seemed a thing that could not feel
  The touch of earthly years.

No motion has she now, no force;
  She neither hears nor sees;
Rolled round in earth's diurnal course,
  With rocks, and stones, and trees.

Emanuel diPasquale (b. 1943)

Rain   1971

Like a drummer's brush,
the rain hushes the surface of tin porches.

ALLITERATION AND ASSONANCE

Listening to a symphony in which themes are repeated throughout each movement, we enjoy both their recurrence and their variation. We take similar pleasure in the repetition of a phrase or a single chord. Something like this pleasure is afforded us frequently in poetry.

Analogies between poetry and wordless music, it is true, tend to break down when carried far, since poetry—to mention a single difference—has denotation. But like musical compositions, poems have patterns of sounds. Among such patterns long popular in English poetry is **alliteration,** which has been defined as a succession of similar sounds. Alliteration occurs in the repetition of the same consonant sound at the beginning of successive words—"round and round the rugged rocks the ragged rascal ran"—or inside the words, as in Milton's description of the gates of Hell:

> On a sudden open fly
> With impetuous recoil and jarring sound
> The infernal doors, and on their hinges grate
> Harsh thunder, that the lowest bottom shook
> Of Erebus.

The former kind is called **initial alliteration,** the latter **internal alliteration** or **hidden alliteration.** We recognize alliteration by sound, not by spelling: *know* and *nail* alliterate, *know* and *key* do not. In a line by E. E. Cummings, "colossal hoax of clocks and calendars," the sound of *x* within *hoax* alliterates with the *cks* in clocks. Incidentally, the letter *r* does not *always* lend itself to cacophony: elsewhere in *Paradise Lost* Milton said that

> Heaven opened wide
> Her ever-during gates, harmonious sound
> On golden hinges moving . . .

By itself, a letter-sound has no particular meaning. This is a truth forgotten by people who would attribute the effectiveness of Milton's lines on the Heavenly Gates to, say, "the mellow *o*'s and liquid *l* of *harmonious* and *golden*." Mellow *o*'s and liquid *l*'s occur also in the phrase *moldy cold oatmeal*, which may have a quite different effect. Meaning depends on larger units of language than letters of the alphabet.

Today good prose writers usually avoid alliteration; in the past, some cultivated it. "There is nothing more swifter than time, nothing more sweeter," wrote John Lyly in *Euphues* (1579), and he went on— playing especially with the sounds of *v, n, t, s, l,* and *b*—"we have not, as Seneca saith, little time to live, but we lose much; neither have we a short life by nature, but we make it shorter by naughtiness." Poetry, too, formerly contained more alliteration than it usually contains today. In Old English verse, each line was held together by alliteration, a basic pattern still evident in the fourteenth century, as in the following description of the world as a "fair field" in *Piers Plowman:*

> A feir feld ful of folk fond I ther bi-twene,
> Of alle maner of men, the mene and the riche . . .

(For modern imitations of Old English verse, see Ezra Pound's "The Seafarer," page 790, and Richard Wilbur's "Junk," page 820.) Most poets nowadays save alliteration for special occasions. They may use it to give emphasis, as Edward Lear does: "Far and *few, far* and *few,* / Are the *lands* where the Jumblies *live.*" With its aid they can point out the relationship between two things placed side by side, as in Pope's line on things of little worth: "The courtier's *promises,* and sick man's *prayers.*" Alliteration, too, can be a powerful aid to memory. It is hard to forget such tongue twisters as "Peter Piper picked a peck of pickled peppers," or common expressions like "green as grass," "tried and true," and "from stem to stern." In fact, because alliteration directs our attention to something, it had best be used neither thoughtlessly nor merely for decoration, lest it call attention to emptiness. A case in point may be a line by Philip James Bailey, a reaction to a lady's weeping: "I saw, but *spared* to *speak.*" If the poet chose the word *spared* for any meaningful reason other than that it alliterates with *speak,* the reason is not clear.

As we have seen, to repeat the sound of a consonant is to produce alliteration, but to repeat the sound of a *vowel* is to produce **assonance.** Like alliteration, assonance may occur either initially—"*all* the *awful* auguries"[3] — or internally — Spenser's "Her goodly *eyes* like sapphires shining bright, / Her forehead *ivory* white . . ." and it can help make common phrases unforgettable: "eager beaver," "holy smoke." Like alliteration, it slows the reader down and focuses attention.

A. E. Housman (1859–1936)
Eight O'Clock

1922

He stood, and heard the steeple
  Sprinkle the quarters on the morning town.
One, two, three, four, to market-place and people
  It tossed them down.

Strapped, noosed, nighing his hour,
  He stood and counted them and cursed his luck;
And then the clock collected in the tower
  Its strength, and struck.

Questions

1. Why does the protagonist in this brief drama curse his luck? What is his situation?
2. For so short a poem, "Eight O'Clock" carries a great weight of alliteration. What patterns of initial alliteration do you find? What patterns of internal alliteration? What effect is created by all this heavy emphasis?

Alexander Pope (1688–1744)
Epitaph, Intended for Sir Isaac Newton in Westminster Abbey

1730

Nature and Nature's laws lay hid in night.
God said, *Let Newton be!* and all was light.

Questions

1. What patterns of alliteration and assonance does Pope employ?
2. How are they useful to his poem?

J. C. Squire (1884–1958)
It did not last

1933

It did not last: the Devil, howling *Ho!*
Let Einstein be! restored the status quo.

[3] Some prefer to call the repetition of an initial vowel-sound by the name of alliteration: "apt alliteration's artful aid."

Which of these translations of the same passage from Petrarch do you think is better poetry? Why? What do assonance and alliteration have to do with your preference?

1. Love that liveth and reigneth in my thought,
   That built his seat within my captive breast,
   Clad in the arms wherein with me he fought,
   Oft in my face he doth his banner rest.
                    —Henry Howard, Earl of Surrey (1517?–1547)

2. The long love that in my thought doth harbor,
   And in mine heart doth keep his residence,
   Into my face presseth with bold pretense
   And therein campeth, spreading his banner.
                    —Sir Thomas Wyatt (1503?–1542)

EXPERIMENT: *Reading for Assonance*

Try reading aloud as rapidly as possible the following poem by Tennyson. From the difficulties you encounter, you may be able to sense the slowing effect of assonance. Then read the poem aloud a second time, with consideration.

Alfred, Lord Tennyson (1809–1892)

THE SPLENDOR FALLS ON CASTLE WALLS   1850

The splendor falls on castle walls
    And snowy summits old in story;
The long light shakes across the lakes,
    And the wild cataract leaps in glory.
Blow, bugle, blow, set the wild echoes flying,   5
Blow, bugle; answer, echoes, dying, dying, dying.

O hark, O hear! how thin and clear,
    And thinner, clearer, farther going!
O sweet and far from cliff and scar
    The horns of Elfland faintly blowing!   10
Blow, let us hear the purple glens replying:
Blow, bugle; answer, echoes, dying, dying, dying.

O love, they die in yon rich sky,
    They faint on hill or field or river;
Our echoes roll from soul to soul,   15
    And grow for ever and for ever.
Blow, bugle, blow, set the wild echoes flying,
And answer, echoes, answer, dying, dying, dying.

RIME

Isak Dinesen's tribesmen, to whom rime was a new phenomenon, recognized at once that rimed language is special language. So do we, for, although much English poetry is unrimed, rime is one means to set poetry apart from ordinary conversation and bring it closer to music. A **rime** (or rhyme), defined most narrowly, occurs when two or more words or phrases contain an identical or similar vowel-sound, usually accented, and the consonant-sounds (if any) that follow the vowel-sound are identical: *hay* and *sleigh, prairie schooner* and *piano tuner.*[4] From these examples it will be seen that rime depends not on spelling but on sound.

Excellent rimes surprise. It is all very well that a reader may anticipate which vowel-sound is coming next, for patterns of rime give pleasure by satisfying expectations; but riming becomes dull clunking if, at the end of each line, the reader can predict the word that will end the next. Hearing many a jukebox song for the first time, a listener can do so: *charms* lead to *arms, skies above* to *love.* As Alexander Pope observes of the habits of dull rimesters,

> Where'er you find "the cooling western breeze,"
> In the next line it "whispers through the trees";
> If crystal streams "with pleasing murmurs creep,"
> The reader's threatened (not in vain) with "sleep" . . .

But who — given the opening line of this children's jingle — could predict the lines that follow?

Anonymous (English)

JULIUS CAESAR   (about 1940?)

Julius Caesar,
The Roman geezer,
Squashed his wife with a lemon-squeezer.

Here rimes combine things unexpectedly. Robert Herrick, too, made good use of rime to indicate a startling contrast:

> Then while time serves, and we are but decaying,
> Come, my Corinna, come, let's go a-Maying.

Though good rimes seem fresh, not all will startle, and probably few will call to mind things so unlike as *May* and *decay, Caesar* and *lemon-squeezer.* Some masters of rime often link words that, taken out of context, might seem common and unevocative. Here, for instance, is Alexander Pope's comment on a trifling and effeminate courtier:

> Yet let me flap this bug with gilded wings,
> This painted child of dirt, that stinks and stings;

---

[4] Some definitions of *rime* would apply the term to the repetition of any identical or similar sound, not only a vowel-sound. In this sense, assonance is a kind of rime; so is alliteration (called **initial rime**).

Whose buzz the witty and the fair annoys,
Yet wit ne'er tastes, and beauty ne'er enjoys:
So well-bred spaniels civilly delight
In mumbling of the game they dare not bite.
Eternal smiles his emptiness betray,
As shallow streams run dimpling all the way.

Pope's rime-words are not especially memorable — and yet these lines are, because (among other reasons) they rime. Wit may be driven home without rime, but it is rime that rings the doorbell. Admittedly, some rimes wear thin from too much use. More difficult to use freshly than before the establishment of Tin Pan Alley, rimes such as *moon, June, croon* seem leaden and to ring true would need an extremely powerful context. *Death* and *breath* are a rime that poets have used with wearisome frequency; another is *birth, earth, mirth.* And yet we cannot exclude these from the diction of poetry, for they might be the very words a poet would need in order to say something new and original. Both the following brief poems seem fresher than their rimes (if taken out of context) would lead us to expect.

William Blake (1757–1827)

THE ANGEL THAT PRESIDED O'ER MY BIRTH (1808–1811)

The Angel that presided o'er my birth
Said, "Little creature, formed of Joy and Mirth,
Go love without the help of any thing on earth."

John Frederick Nims (b. 1914)

PERFECT RHYME 1967

Life, that struck up his cocky tune with *breath,*
Finds, to conclude in music, only *death.*

What matters to rime is freshness — not of a word but of the poet's way of seeing.

Good poets, said John Dryden, learn to make their rime "so properly a part of the verse, that it should never mislead the sense, but itself be led and governed by it." The comment may remind us that skillful rime — unlike poor rime — is never a distracting ornament. "Rime the rudder is of verses, / With which, like ships, they steer their courses," wrote the seventeenth-century poet Samuel Butler. Like other patterns of sound, rime can help a poet to group ideas, emphasize particular words, and weave a poem together. It can start reverberations between words and can point to connections of meaning.

To have an **exact rime,** sounds following the vowel sound have to be the same: *red* and *bread, wealthily* and *stealthily, walk to her* and *talk to her.* If final consonant sounds are the same but the vowel sounds are different, the result is **slant rime,** also called **near rime, off rime,** or **partial rime:** *stone* riming with *sun, moon, rain, green, gone, thin.* By not satisfying the reader's expectation of an exact chime, but instead giving a clunk, a slant rime can help a poet say some things in a particular way. It works especially well for disappointed let-downs, negations, and denials, as in Blake's couplet:

> He who the ox to wrath has moved
> Shall never be by woman loved.

Consonance, a kind of slant rime, occurs when the rimed words or phrases have the same consonant sounds but a different vowel, as in *chitter* and *chatter.* It is used in a traditional nonsense poem, "The Cutty Wren": " 'O where are you going?' says *Milder* to *Malder.*" (W. H. Auden wrote a variation on it that begins, " 'O where are you going?' said *reader* to *rider,*" thus keeping the consonance.)

End rime, as its name indicates, comes at the ends of lines, **internal rime** within them. Most rime tends to be end rime. Few recent poets have used internal rime so heavily as Wallace Stevens in the beginning of "Bantams in Pine-Woods": "Chieftain Iffucan of Azcan in caftan / Of tan with henna hackles, halt!" (lines also heavy on alliteration). A poet may employ both end rime and internal rime in the same poem, as in Robert Burn's satiric ballad "The Kirk's Alarm":

> Orthodox, Orthodox, wha believe in John Knox,
>   Let me sound an alarm to your conscience:
> There's a heretic blast has been blawn i' the wast°,   *west*
> "That what is not sense must be nonsense."

Masculine rime is a rime of one-syllable words (*jail, bail*) or (in words of more than one syllable) stressed final syllables: *di-VORCE, re-MORSE,* or *horse, re-MORSE.* **Feminine rime** is a rime of two or more syllables, with stress on a syllable other than the last: *TUR-tle, FER-tile,* or (to take an example from Byron) *in-tel-LECT-u-al, hen-PECKED you all.* Often it lends itself to comic verse, but can occasionally be valuable to serious poems, as in Wordsworth's "Resolution and Independence":

> We poets in our youth begin in gladness,
> But thereof come in the end despondency and madness.

or as in Anne Sexton's "Eighteen Days Without You":

> and of course we're not married, we are a pair of scissors
> who come together to cut, without towels saying His. Hers.

Serious poems containing feminine rimes of three syllables have been attempted, notably by Thomas Hood in "The Bridge of Sighs":

Take her up tenderly,
Lift her with care;
Fashioned so slenderly,
Young, and so fair!

But the pattern is hard to sustain without lapsing into unintended comedy, as in the same poem:

Still, for all slips of hers,
One of Eve's family—
Wipe those poor lips of hers,
Oozing so clammily.

It works better when comedy is wanted:

Hilaire Belloc (1870–1953)

THE HIPPOPOTAMUS   1896

I shoot the Hippopotamus
    with bullets made of platinum,
Because if I use leaden ones
    his hide is sure to flatten 'em.

In **eye rime,** spellings look alike but pronunciations differ—*rough* and *dough, idea* and *flea*. Strictly speaking, eye rime is not rime at all.

In recent years American poetry has seen a great erosion of faith in rime, with Louis Simpson, James Wright, Robert Lowell, W. S. Merwin, and others quitting it for open forms. Indeed, it has been suggested that rime in the English language is exhausted. Such a view may be a reaction against the wearing-thin of rimes by overuse or the mechanical and meaningless application of a rime scheme. Yet anyone who listens to children skipping rope in the street, making up rimes to delight themselves as they go along, may doubt that the pleasures of rime are ended; and certainly the practice of Yeats and Emily Dickinson, to name only two, suggests that the possibilities of slant rime may be nearly infinite. If successfully employed, as it has been at times by a majority of English-speaking poets whose work we care to save, rime runs through its poem like a spine: the creature moves by means of it.

William Butler Yeats (1865–1939)

LEDA AND THE SWAN   1924

A sudden blow: the great wings beating still
Above the staggering girl, her thighs caressed
By the dark webs, her nape caught in his bill,
He holds her helpless breast upon his breast.

How can those terrified vague fingers push
The feathered glory from her loosening thighs?
And how can body, laid in that white rush,
But feel the strange heart beating where it lies?

A shudder in the loins engenders there
The broken wall, the burning roof and tower
And Agamemnon dead.
                                    Being so caught up,
So mastered by the brute blood of the air,
Did she put on his knowledge with his power
Before the indifferent beak could let her drop?

QUESTIONS

1. According to Greek mythology, the god Zeus in the form of a swan descended upon Leda, a Spartan queen. Among the offspring of this union were
   Clytemnestra, Agamemnon's unfaithful wife who conspired in his murder,
   and Helen, on whose account the Trojan war was fought. What does a knowledge of these allusions contribute to our understanding of the poem's last
   two lines?
2. The slant rime *up* / *drop* (lines 11, 14) may seem accidental or inept. Is it?
   Would this poem have ended nearly so well if Yeats had made an exact rime
   like *up* / *cup* or like *stop* / *drop*?

Allen Ginsberg (b. 1926)

POSTCARD TO D----   1975

Chuggling along in an old open bus
              past the green sugarfields
                    down a dusty dirt road
                          overlooking the ocean in Fiji,
thinking of your big Macdougal street house
              & the old orange peels
                    in your mail-garbage load,
                          smoggy windows you clean with a squeejee——

                                                              March 3, 1972

QUESTIONS

1. Which lines end in slant rimes and which end in exact rimes?
2. What is the effect of riming *Fiji* and *squeejee*? Comic or serious?
3. Who do you suppose D---- is?

Gerard Manley Hopkins (1844–1889)

GOD'S GRANDEUR   (1877)

The world is charged with the grandeur of God.
    It will flame out, like shining from shook foil;

It gathers to a greatness, like the ooze of oil
Crushed. Why do men then now not reck his rod?
Generations have trod, have trod, have trod;   5
   And all is seared with trade; bleared, smeared with toil;
   And wears man's smudge and shares man's smell: the soil
Is bare now, nor can foot feel, being shod.

And for all this, nature is never spent;
   There lives the dearest freshness deep down things;   10
And though the last lights off the black West went
   Oh, morning, at the brown brink eastward, springs—
Because the Holy Ghost over the bent
   World broods with warm breast and with ah! bright wings.

QUESTIONS

1. In a letter Hopkins explained *shook foil* (line 2): "I mean foil in its sense of leaf or tinsel . . . . Shaken goldfoil gives off broad glares like sheet lightning and also, and this is true of nothing else, owing to its zigzag dints and creasings and network of small many cornered facets, a sort of fork lightning too." What do you think he meant by *ooze of oil* (line 3)? Is this phrase an example of alliteration?
2. What instances of internal rime does the poem contain? How would you describe their effects?
3. Point out some of the poet's uses of alliteration and assonance. Does Hopkins go too far in his heavy use of devices of sound, or would you defend his practice?
4. Why do you suppose Hopkins, in the last two lines, says *over the bent / World* instead of (as we might expect) *bent over the world*? How can the world be bent? Can you make any sense out of this wording, or is Hopkins just trying to get his rime scheme to work out?

READING AND HEARING POEMS ALOUD

Thomas Moore's "The light that lies in women's eyes"—a line rich in internal rime, alliteration, and assonance—is harder to forget than "The light burning in the gaze of a woman." Because of sound, it is possible to remember the obscure line Christopher Smart wrote while in an insane asylum: "Let Ross, house of Ross rejoice with the Great Flabber Dabber Flat Clapping Fish with hands." Such lines, striking as they are even when read silently, become still more effective when said out loud. Reading poems aloud is a way to understand them. For this reason, practice the art of lending poetry your voice.

Before trying to read a poem aloud to other people, understand its meaning as thoroughly as possible. If you know what the poet is saying and the poet's attitude toward it, you will be able to find an appropriate tone of voice and to give each part of the poem a proper emphasis.

Except in the most informal situations and in some class exercises, read a poem to yourself before trying it on an audience. No actor goes before the footlights without first having studied the script, and the language of poems usually demands even more consideration than the language of most contemporary plays. Prepare your reading in advance. Check pronunciations you are not sure of. Underline things to be emphasized.

Read deliberately, more slowly than you would read aloud from a newspaper. Keep in mind that you are saying something to somebody. Don't race through the poem as if you are eager to get it over with.

Don't lapse into singsong. A poem may have a definite swing, but swing should never be exaggerated at the cost of sense. If you understand what the poem is saying and utter the poem as if you do, the temptation to fall into such a mechanical intonation should not occur. Observe the punctuation, making slight pauses for commas, longer pauses for full stops (periods, question marks, exclamation points).

If the poem is rimed, don't raise your voice and make the rimes stand out unnaturally. They should receive no more volume than other words in the poem, though a faint pause at the end of each line will call the listener's attention to them. This advice is contrary to a school that holds that, if a line does not end in any punctuation, one should not pause but run it together with the line following. The trouble is that, from such a reading, a listener may not be able to identify the rimes; besides, the line, that valuable unit of rhythm, is destroyed.

In some older poems rimes that look like slant rimes may have been exact rimes in their day:

Still so perverse and opposite,
As if they worshiped God for spite.
— Samuel Butler, *Hudibras* (1663)

Soft yielding minds to water glide away,
And sip, with nymphs, their elemental tea.
— Alexander Pope, "The Rape of the Lock" (1714)

You may wish to establish a consistent policy toward such shifting usage: is it worthwhile to distort current pronunciation for the sake of the rime?

Listening to a poem, especially if it is unfamiliar, calls for concentration. Merciful people seldom read poetry uninterruptedly to anyone for more than a few minutes at a time. Robert Frost, always kind to his audiences, used to intersperse poems with many silences and seemingly casual remarks — shrewdly giving his hearers a chance to rest from their labors and giving his poems a chance to settle in.

If, in first listening to a poem, you don't take in all its meaning, don't be discouraged. With more practice in listening, your attention span and your ability to understand poems read aloud will increase. Incidentally, following the text of poems in a book while hearing them read aloud may increase your comprehension, but it may not necessarily help you to *listen*. At least some of the time, close your book and let your ears make the poems welcome. That way, their sounds may better work for you.

Hearing recordings of poets reading their work can help both your ability to read aloud and your ability to listen. Not all poets read their poems well, but there is much to be relished in both the highly dramatic reading style of a Dylan Thomas and the quiet underplay of a Robert Frost. You need feel no obligation, of course, to imitate the poet's reading of a poem. You have to feel about the poem in your own way, in order to read it with conviction and naturalness.

Even if you don't have an audience, the act of speaking poetry can have its own rewards. Perhaps that is what James Wright is driving at in the following brief prose poem.

James Wright (b. 1927)
SAYING DANTE ALOUD   1976

You can feel the muscles and veins rippling in widening and rising circles, like a bird in flight under your tongue.

EXERCISE: *Reading for Sound and Meaning*
Read these two brief poems aloud. What devices of sound do you find in each of them? Try to explain what sound contributes to the total effect of the poem and how it reinforces what the poet is saying.

A. E. Housman (1859–1936)
WITH RUE MY HEART IS LADEN   1896

With rue my heart is laden
  For golden friends I had,
For many a rose-lipt maiden
  And many a lightfoot lad.

By brooks too broad for leaping
  The lightfoot boys are laid;
The rose-lipt girls are sleeping
  In fields where roses fade.

T. S. Eliot (1888–1965)
VIRGINIA   1934

Red river, red river,
Slow flow heat is silence

No will is still as a river
Still. Will heat move
Only through the mocking-bird
Heard once? Still hills
Wait. Gates wait. Purple trees,
White trees, wait, wait,
Delay, decay. Living, living,
Never moving. Ever moving
Iron thoughts came with me
And go with me:
Red river, river, river.

VIRGINIA. This poem is one of a series entitled "Landscapes."

20 Rhythm

STRESSES AND PAUSES

Rhythms affect us powerfully. We are lulled by a hammock's sway, awakened by an alarm clock's repeated yammer. Long after we come home from a beach, the rising and falling of waves and tides continue in memory. How powerfully the rhythms of poetry also move us may be felt in folk songs of railroad workers and chain gangs whose words were chanted in time to the lifting and dropping of a sledgehammer, and in verse that marching soldiers shout, putting a stress on every word that coincides with a footfall:

> Your LEFT! TWO! THREE! FOUR!
> Your LEFT! TWO! THREE! FOUR!
> You LEFT your WIFE and TWEN-ty-one KIDS
> And you LEFT! TWO! THREE! FOUR!
> You'll NEV-er get HOME to-NIGHT!

A rhythm is produced by a series of recurrences: the returns and departures of the seasons, the repetitions of an engine's stroke, the beats of the heart. A rhythm may be produced by the recurrence of a sound (the throb of a drum, a telephone's busy-signal), but rhythm and sound are not identical. A totally deaf man at a parade can sense rhythm from the motions of the marchers' arms and feet, from the shaking of the pavement as they tramp. Rhythms inhere in the motions of the moon and stars, even though they move without a sound.

In poetry, several kinds of recurrent *sound* are possible, including (as we saw in the last chapter) rime, alliteration, and assonance. But most often when we speak of the **rhythm** of a poem we mean the recurrence of stresses and pauses in it. When we hear a poem read aloud, stresses and pauses are, of course, part of its sound. It is possible to be aware of rhythms in poems read silently, too.

A **stress** (or **accent**) is a greater amount of force given to one syllable in speaking than is given to another. We favor a stressed syllable with a little more breath and emphasis, with the result that it comes out slightly louder, higher in pitch, or longer in duration than other syllables. In this manner we place a stress on the first syllable of words such as *eagle, impact, open,* and *statue,* and on the second syllable in *cigar, mystique, precise,* and *until.* Each word in English carries at least one stress, except (usually) for the articles *a, an,* and *the,* and one-syllable prepositions: *at, by, for, from, of, to, with.* Even these, however, take a stress once in a while: "Get WITH it!" "You're not THE Farrah Fawcett-Majors?" One word by itself is seldom long enough for us to notice a rhythm in it. Usually a sequence of at least a few words is needed for stresses to establish their pattern: a line, a passage, a whole poem. Strong rhythms may be seen in most Mother Goose rimes, to which children have been responding for hundreds of years. This rime is for an adult to chant while jogging a child up and down on a knee:

> Here goes my lord
> A trot, a trot, a trot, a trot!
> Here goes my lady
> A canter, a canter, a canter, a canter!
> Here goes my young master
> Jockey-hitch, jockey-hitch, jockey-hitch, jockey-hitch!
> Here goes my young miss
> An amble, an amble, an amble, an amble!
> The footman lags behind to tipple ale and wine
> And goes gallop, a gallop, a gallop, to make up his time.

More than one rhythm occurs in these lines, as the make-believe horse changes pace. How do these rhythms differ? From one line to the next, the interval between stresses lengthens or grows shorter. In "a TROT a TROT a TROT a TROT," the stress falls on every other syllable. But in the middle of the line "A CAN-ter a CAN-ter a CAN-ter a CAN-ter," the stress falls on every third syllable. When stresses recur at fixed intervals as in these lines, the resulting pattern is called a **meter.** The line "A trot a trot a trot a trot" is in **iambic** meter, a pattern of alternate unstressed and stressed syllables.[1] Of all patterns of rhythm in the English language, this one is most familiar; most of our traditional poetry is written in it and ordinary speech tends to resemble it. Most poems, less obvious in rhythm than nursery rimes are, rarely stick to their meters with such jog-trot regularity. The following lines also contain a horse-back-riding rhythm. (The poet, Gerard Manley Hopkins, is comparing the pell-mell plunging of a burn—Scottish word for a brook—to the motion of a wild horse.)

> This darksome burn, horseback brown,
> His rollrock highroad roaring down,

---

[1] Another kind of meter is possible, in which the intervals between stresses vary. This is **accentual** meter, not often found in contemporary poetry. It is discussed in the second section of this chapter.

In coop and in comb the fleece of his foam
Flutes and low to the lake falls home.

In the third line, when the brook courses through coop and comb ("hollow" and "ravine"), the passage breaks into a gallop; then, with the two-beat *falls home*, almost seems reined to a sudden halt.

Stresses embody meanings. Whenever two or more fall side by side, words gain in emphasis. Consider these hard-hitting lines from John Donne, in which accent marks have been placed, dictionary-fashion, to indicate the stressed syllables:

Bat'ter my heart', three'-per'soned God', for You'
As yet' but knock', breathe', shine', and seek' to mend';
That I may rise' and stand', o'er'throw' me, and bend'
Your force' to break', blow', burn', and make' me new'.

Unstressed (or **slack**) syllables also can direct our attention to what the poet means. In a line containing few stresses and a great many un-stressed syllables, there can be an effect not of power and force but of hesitation and uncertainty. Yeats asks in "Among School Children" what young mother, if she could see her baby grown to be an old man, would think him

A com'pen·sa'tion for the pang' of his birth'
Or the un·cer'tain·ty of his set'ting forth'?

When unstressed syllables recur in pairs, the result is a rhythm that trips and bounces, as in Robert Service's rollicking line:

A bunch' of the boys' were whoop'ing it up' in the Mal'a·mute sa·loon'. . .

or in Poe's lines—also light but probably supposed to be serious:

For the moon' nev'er beams' with·out' bring'ing me dreams'
Of the beau'ti·ful An'na·bel Lee'.

Apart from the words that convey it, the rhythm of a poem has no meaning. There are no essentially sad rhythms, nor any essentially happy ones. But some rhythms enforce certain meanings better than others do. The bouncing rhythm of Service's line seems fitting for an ac-count of a merry night in a Klondike saloon; but it may be distracting when encountered in Poe's wistful elegy.

EXERCISE: *Appropriate and Inappropriate Rhythms*

In each of the following passages, decide whether rhythm enforces meaning and tone or works against these elements and consequently against the poem's effectiveness.

1. Alfred, Lord Tennyson, "Break, break, break":

Break, break, break,
On thy cold gray stones, O Sea!

2. Edgar Allan Poe, "Ulalume":

> Then my heart it grew ashen and sober
> As the leaves that were crispèd and sere —
> As the leaves that were withering and sere,
> And I cried: "It was surely October
> On *this* very night of last year
> That I journey — I journeyed down here —
> That I brought a dread burden down here —
> On this night of all nights in the year,
> Ah, what demon has tempted me here?"

3. A. A. Milne, "Disobedience":

> James James
> Morrison Morrison
> Weatherby George Dupree
> Took great
> Care of his Mother,
> Though he was only three.
> James James
> Said to his Mother,
> "Mother," he said, said he;
> "You must never go down to the end of the town, if you don't go
> down with me."

4. Eliza Cook, "Song of the Sea-Weed":

> Many a lip is gaping for drink,
> And madly calling for rain;
> And some hot brains are beginning to think
> Of a messmate's opened vein.

5. William Shakespeare, song from *The Tempest*:

> The master, the swabber, the boatswain, and I,
> The gunner and his mate
> Loved Moll, Meg, and Marian, and Margery,
> But none of us cared for Kate;
> For she had a tongue with a tang
> Would cry to a sailor "Go hang!" —
> She loved not the savor of tar nor of pitch
> Yet a tailor might scratch her where'er she did itch;
> Then to sea, boys, and let her go hang!

Rhythms in poetry are due not only to stresses but also to pauses. "Every nice ear," observed Alexander Pope (*nice* meaning "finely tuned"), "must, I believe, have observed that in any smooth English verse of ten syllables, there is naturally a pause either at the fourth, fifth, or sixth syllable." Such a light but definite pause within a line is called a **cesura** (or caesura), "a cutting." More liberally than Pope, we apply the name to any pause in a line of any length, after any word in the line. In studying a poem, we often indicate a cesura by double lines (‖). Usually, a cesura will occur at a mark of punctuation, but there can be a cesura even if no punctuation is present. Sometimes you will find it at the end of a phrase or clause or, as in these lines by William Blake, after an internal rime:

> And priests in black gowns‖were walking their rounds
> And binding with briars‖my joys and desires.

Lines of ten or twelve syllables (as Pope knew) tend to have just one cesura, though sometimes there are more:

> Cover her face:‖mine eyes dazzle:‖she died young.

Pauses also tend to recur at more prominent places—namely, after each line. At the end of a verse (from *versus*, "a turning"), the reader's eye, before turning to go on to the next line, makes a pause, however brief. If a line ends in a full pause—usually indicated by some mark of punctuation—we call it **end-stopped**. All the lines in this stanza by Theodore Roethke are end-stopped:

> Let seed be grass and grass turn into hay:
> I'm martyr to a motion not my own;
> What's freedom for? To know eternity.
> I swear she cast a shadow white as stone.
> But who would count eternity in days?
> These old bones live to learn her wanton ways:
> (I measure time by how a body sways).[2]

A line that does not end in punctuation and that therefore is read with only a slight pause after it is called **run-on;** the running-on of its thought into the next line is **enjambment**. A run-on line gives us only part of a phrase, clause, or sentence. All these lines from Robert Browning are run-on lines, despite the fact that the lines are pairs of rimes:

> . . . Sir, 'twas not
> Her husband's presence only, called that spot
> Of joy into the Duchess' cheek: perhaps
> Frà Pandolf chanced to say "Her mantle laps
> Over my lady's wrist too much," or "Paint
> Must never hope to reproduce the faint
> Half-flush that dies along her throat." Such stuff
> Was courtesy, she thought . . .[3]

A passage in run-on lines has a rhythm different from that of a passage like Roethke's in end-stopped lines. When emphatic pauses occur in the quotation from Browning, they fall within a line rather than at the end of one. The passage by Roethke and that by Browning are in lines of the same meter (iambic) and the same length (ten syllables). What makes the big difference in their rhythms is enjambment, or lack of it.

[2] The complete poem, "I Knew a Woman," appears on page 501.
[3] The complete poem, "My Last Duchess," appears on page 726.

To sum up: rhythm is recurrence. In poems, it is made of stresses and pauses. The poet can produce it by doing any of several things: making the intervals between stresses fixed or varied, long or short; indicating pauses (cesuras) within lines; end-stopping lines or running them over; writing in short or long lines. Rhythm in itself cannot convey meaning. And yet if a poet's words have meaning, their rhythm must be one with it.

Gwendolyn Brooks (b. 1917)

We Real Cool   1960

The Pool Players.
Seven at the Golden Shovel.

We real cool. We
Left school. We

Lurk late. We
Strike straight. We

Sing sin. We
Thin gin. We

Jazz June. We
Die soon.

QUESTION

Describe the rhythms of this poem. By what techniques are they produced?

Robert Frost (1874–1963)

Never Again Would Birds' Song Be the Same   1942

He would declare and could himself believe
That the birds there in all the garden round
From having heard the daylong voice of Eve
Had added to their own an oversound,
Her tone of meaning but without the words.   5
Admittedly an eloquence so soft
Could only have had an influence on birds
When call or laughter carried it aloft.
Be that as may be, she was in their song.
Moreover her voice upon their voices crossed   10
Had now persisted in the woods so long
That probably it never would be lost.
Never again would birds' song be the same.
And to do that to birds was why she came.

1. Who is *he*?
2. In reading aloud line 9, do you stress *may*? (Do you say "as MAY be" or "as may BE"?) What guide do we have to the poet's wishes here?
3. Which lines does Frost cast mostly or entirely into monosyllables? How would you describe the impact of these lines?
4. In his *Essay on Criticism*, Alexander Pope made fun of poets who wrote mechanically, without wit: "And ten low words oft creep in one dull line." Do you think this criticism applicable to Frost's lines of monosyllables? Explain.

Ben Jonson (1573?–1637)

Slow, slow, fresh fount, keep time with my salt tears

1600

Slow, slow, fresh fount, keep time with my salt tears;
   Yet slower yet, oh faintly, gentle springs;
List to the heavy part the music bears,
    Woe weeps out her division° when she sings.   *a part in a song*
      Droop herbs and flowers,   5
      Fall grief in showers;
      Our beauties are not ours;
        Oh, I could still,
Like melting snow upon some craggy hill,
   Drop, drop, drop, drop,   10
Since nature's pride is now a withered daffodil.

SLOW, SLOW, FRESH FOUNT. The nymph Echo sings this lament over the youth Narcissus in Jonson's play *Cynthia's Revels*. In mythology, Nemesis, goddess of vengeance, to punish Narcissus for loving his own beauty, caused him to pine away and then transformed him into a narcissus (another name for a *daffodil*, line 11).

QUESTIONS

1. Read the first line aloud rapidly. Why is it difficult to do so?
2. Which lines rely most heavily on stressed syllables?
3. In general, how would you describe the rhythm of this poem? How is it appropriate to what is said?

Robert Lowell (1917–1977)

At the Altar

1946

I sit at a gold table with my girl
Whose eyelids burn with brandy. What a whirl
Of Easter eggs is colored by the lights,
As the Norwegian dancer's crystalled tights
Flash with her naked leg's high-booted skate,   5
Like Northern Lights upon my watching plate.

The twinkling steel above me is a star;
I am a fallen Christmas tree. Our car
Races through seven red-lights — then the road
Is unpatrolled and empty, and a load   10
Of ply-wood with a tail-light makes us slow.
I turn and whisper in her ear. You know
I want to leave my mother and my wife,
You wouldn't have me tied to them for life . . .
Time runs, the windshield runs with stars. The past   15
Is cities from a train, until at last
Its escalating and black-windowed blocks
Recoil against a Gothic church. The clocks
Are tolling. I am dying. The shocked stones
Are falling like a ton of bricks and bones   20
That snap and splinter and descend in glass
Before a priest who mumbles through his Mass
And sprinkles holy water; and the Day
Breaks with its lightning on the man of clay,
Dies amara valde. Here the Lord   25
Is Lucifer in harness: hand on sword,
He watches me for Mother, and will turn
The bier and baby-carriage where I burn.

AT THE ALTAR. In a public reading of this poem, Robert Lowell made some remarks cited
by George P. Elliott in *Fifteen Modern American Poets* (New York: Holt, Rinehart & Winston, 1956). Lit up like a Christmas tree, the speaker finds himself in a Boston nightclub,
watching a skating floorshow. Then he and his girl drive (or does he only dream they
drive?) to a church where a priest saying a funeral Mass sprinkles a corpse with holy
water. 23. *the Day:* the Day of Judgment. 25. *Dies amara valde:* "day bitter above all
others," a phrase from a funeral hymn, the *Dies Irae,* in which sinners are warned to fear
God's wrath. 28. *baby-carriage:* the undertaker's silver dolly, supporting a coffin.

QUESTIONS

1. Which lines in this poem are end-stopped?
2. What effects does Lowell obtain by so much enjambment?
3. What besides enjambment contributes to the rhythm of the poem?
4. How is this rhythm appropriate to what the poet is saying? Explain.

Alexander Pope (1688–1744)

ATTICUS   1735

How did they fume, and stamp, and roar, and chafe!
And swear, not Addison himself was safe.
  Peace to all such! but were there one whose fires
True genius kindles, and fair fame inspires;
Blest with each talent, and each art to please,   5
And born to write, converse, and live with ease,
Should such a man, too fond to rule alone,

Bear, like the Turk, no brother near the throne,
View him with scornful, yet with jealous eyes,
And hate for arts that caused himself to rise;   10
Damn with faint praise, assent with civil leer,
And, without sneering, teach the rest to sneer;
Willing to wound, and yet afraid to strike,
Just hint a fault, and hesitate dislike;
Alike reserved to blame, or to commend,   15
A timorous foe, and a suspicious friend;
Dreading e'en fools, by flatterers besieged,
And so obliging, that he ne'er obliged;
Like Cato, give his little Senate laws,
And sit attentive to his own applause: 20
While wits and Templars every sentence raise,
And wonder with a foolish face of praise —
Who but must laugh, if such a man there be?
Who would not weep, if Atticus were he?

ATTICUS. In this selection from "An Epistle to Dr. Arbuthnot," Pope has been referring to
dull versifiers and their angry reception of his satiric thrusts at them. With *Peace to all
such!* (line 3) he turns to his celebrated portrait of a rival man of letters, Joseph Addison.
19. *Cato:* Roman senator about whom Addison had written a tragedy. 21. *Templars:* London lawyers who dabbled in literature.

QUESTIONS

1. In these lines — one of the most famous damnations in English poetry — what
   positive virtues, in Pope's view, does Addison lack?
2. Read aloud from Robert Lowell's "At the Altar," then read aloud a few lines
   from Pope. Although both poets write in rimed couplets, in lines ten syllables long, how do the rhythms of the two poems compare? To what do you
   attribute the differences?

EXERCISE: *Two Kinds of Rhythm*

The following compositions in verse have lines of similar length, yet they differ
greatly in rhythm. Explain how they differ and why.

Sir Thomas Wyatt (1503?–1542)

WITH SERVING STILL   (1528–1536)

With serving still°   *continually*
   This have I won,
For my goodwill
   To be undone;

And for redress   5
   Of all my pain,

Disdainfulness
  I have again;

And for reward
  Of all my smart 10
Lo, thus unheard,
  I must depart!

Wherefore all ye
  That after shall
By fortune be, 15
  As I am, thrall,

Example take
  What I have won,
Thus for her sake
  To be undone! 20

Dorothy Parker (1893–1967)
RÉSUMÉ 1926

Razors pain you;
Rivers are damp;
Acids stain you;
And drugs cause cramp.
Guns aren't lawful;
Nooses give;
Gas smells awful;
You might as well live.

METER

To enjoy the rhythms of a poem, no special knowledge of meter is necessary. All you need do is pay attention to stresses and where they fall;
and you will perceive the basic pattern, if there is any. However, there
is nothing occult about the study of meter. Most people find they can
master its essentials in no more time than it takes to learn a complicated
game such as chess. If you take the time, you will then have the pleasure
of knowing what is happening in the rhythms of many a fine poem, and
pleasurable knowledge may even deepen your insight into poetry.

Far from being artificial constructions found only in the minds of
poets, meters occur in everyday speech and prose. As the following example will show, they may need only a poet to recognize them. The
English satirist Max Beerbohm, after contemplating the title page of his
first book, took his pen and added two more lines.

Max Beerbohm (1872–1956)

ON THE IMPRINT OF THE FIRST ENGLISH EDITION OF "THE WORKS OF MAX BEERBOHM"

(1896)

"London: JOHN LANE, *The Bodley Head*
  New York: CHARLES SCRIBNER'S SONS."
This plain announcement, nicely read,
  Iambically runs.

In everyday life, nobody speaks or writes in perfect iambic rhythm, except in occasional brief remarks: "a HAM on RYE." (As we have seen, iambic rhythm consists of a series of syllables alternately unstressed and stressed.) Poets rarely speak in it for very long either, and seldom with exactitude. If you read aloud Max Beerbohm's lines, you will hear an iambic rhythm but not an absolutely invariable one. And yet all of us speak with a rising and falling of stress somewhat like iambic meter. Perhaps, as the poet and scholar John Thompson has maintained, "The iambic metrical pattern has dominated English verse because it provides the best symbolic model of our language."[4]

A meter supplies a pattern for a poet's speech to depart from or to follow. To make ourselves aware of this pattern, we can **scan** a line or a poem by indicating the stresses in it. **Scansion,** the art of so doing, is not just a matter of pointing to syllables; it is also a matter of listening to a poem and making sense of it. To scan a poem is one way to indicate how to read it aloud; in order to see where stresses fall, you have to see the places where the poet wishes to put emphasis. That is why, when scanning a poem, you may find yourself suddenly understanding it.

An objection might be raised against scanning: isn't it too simple to pretend that all language (and poetry) can be divided neatly into stressed syllables and unstressed syllables? Indeed it is. As the linguist Otto Jespersen has said, "In reality there are infinite gradations of stress, from the most penetrating scream to the faintest whisper."[5] However, the idea in scanning a poem is not to reproduce the sound of a human voice. For that we would do better to buy a tape recorder. To scan a poem, rather, is to make a diagram of the stresses (and absences of stress) we find in it. Various marks are used in scansion; in this book we use ' for a stressed syllable and ‿ for an unstressed syllable. Some scanners, wishing a little more precision, also use the **half-stress** ('); this device can be helpful in many instances when a syllable usually not

---

[4] *The Founding of English Metre* (New York: Columbia University Press, 1966), p. 12.
[5] "Notes on Metre," (1933), reprinted in *The Structure of Verse: Modern Essays on Prosody,* edited by Harvey Gross (Greenwich, Conn.: Fawcett, 1966).

stressed comes at a place where it takes some emphasis, as in the last syllable in a line:

Bound each to each with nat·u·ral pi·e·ty.

Here, with examples, are some of the principal meters we find in English poetry. For each is given its basic **foot,** or molecule (usually one stressed and one or two unstressed syllables);

1. **Iambic** (foot: the **iamb,** ⌣ ′):

   The fall·ing out of faith·ful friends, re·new·ing is of love

2. **Anapestic** (foot: the **anapest,** ⌣ ⌣ ′):

   I am mon·arch of all I sur·vey

3. **Trochaic** (foot: the **trochee,** ′ ⌣):

   Dou·ble, dou·ble, toil and trou·ble

4. **Dactylic** (foot: the **dactyl,** ′ ⌣ ⌣):

   Take her up ten·der·ly

Iambic and anapestic meters are called **rising** meters because their movement rises from unstressed syllable (or syllables) to stress; trochaic and dactylic meters are called **falling.** In the twentieth century, the bouncing meters—anapestic and dactylic—have been used more often for comic verse than for serious poetry. Called feet, though they contain no unaccented syllables, are the **monosyllabic foot** (′) and the **spondee** (″). Meters are not ordinarily made up of them; if one were, it would be like the steady impact of nails being hammered into a board—no pleasure to hear or to dance to. But inserted now and then, they can lend emphasis and variety to a meter, as Yeats well knew when he broke up the predominantly iambic rhythm of "Who Goes with Fergus?" (p. 531) with the line,

And the white breast of the dim sea,

in which occur two spondees.

Metrical patterns are classified also by line lengths: **trochaic monometer,** for instance, is a line one trochee long, as in this anonymous brief comment on microbes:

Adam
Had 'em.

A frequently heard metrical description is **iambic pentameter:** a line of five iambs, a pattern especially familiar because it occurs in all blank verse (such as Shakespeare's plays and Milton's *Paradise Lost*), heroic couplets, and sonnets. The commonly used names for line lengths follow:

monometer	one foot	**pentameter**	five feet
dimeter	two feet	**hexameter**	six feet
trimeter	three feet	**heptameter**	seven feet
tetrameter	four feet	**octameter**	eight feet

Lines of more than eight feet are possible but are rare. They tend to break up into shorter lengths in the listening ear.

When Yeats chose the spondees *white breast* and *dim sea*, he was doing what poets who write in meter do frequently for variety — using a foot other than the expected one. Often such a substitution will be made at the very beginning of a line, as in the third line of this passage from Christopher Marlowe's *Tragical History of Doctor Faustus*:

Was this the face that launched a thou·sand ships
And burnt the top·less tow'rs of Il·i·um?
Sweet Hel·en, make me im·mor·tal with a kiss.

How, we might wonder, can that last line be called iambic at all? But it is, just as a waltz that includes an extra step or two, or leaves a few steps out, remains a waltz. In the preceding lines the basic iambic pentameter is established, and though in the third line the pattern is varied from, it does not altogether disappear. It continues for a while to run on in the reader's mind, where (if the poet does not stay away from it for too long) the meter will be there when the poem comes back to it.

Like a basic dance step, a metrical pattern is not to be slavishly adhered to. The fun in reading a metrical poem often comes from watching the poet continually departing from a pattern, giving a few heel-kicks to display a bit of joy or ingenuity, then easing back into the basic step again. Because meter is orderly and the rhythms of living speech are unruly, poets can play one against the other, in a sort of counterpoint. Robert Frost, a master at pitting a line of iambs against a very natural-sounding and irregular sentence, declared, "I am never more pleased than when I can get these into strained relation. I like to drag and break the intonation across the meter as waves first comb and then break stumbling on a shingle."[6]

Evidently Frost's skilled effects would be lost to a reader who, scanning a Frost poem or reading it aloud, distorted its rhythms to fit the words exactly to the meter. With rare exceptions, a good poem can

[6] Letter to John Cournos in 1914, in *Selected Letters of Robert Frost*, edited by Lawrance Thompson (New York: Holt, Rinehart & Winston, 1964), p. 128.

be read and scanned the way we would speak its sentences if they were ours. This, for example, is an unreal scansion:

˘ ´ ˘ ´ ˘ ´ ˘ ´ ˘ ´
That's my last Duch·ess paint·ed on the wall.

—because no speaker of English would say that sentence in that way. We are likely to stress *That's* and *last*.

Departure from metrical pattern is not merely desirable in poetry, it is a necessity: woe be to the poet who fails to depart from pattern often enough. Allowing the beat of words to slip into mechanical regularity, the poet sets a poem marching robot-like right over a precipice. Luckily, few poets, except writers of greeting cards, favor rhythms that go "a TROT a TROT a TROT a TROT" for very long. Robert Frost told an audience one time that if when writing a poem he found its rhythm becoming monotonous, he knew that the poem was going wrong and that he himself didn't believe what it was saying.

Although in good poetry we seldom meet a very long passage of absolute metrical regularity, we sometimes find (in a line or so) a monotonous rhythm that is effective. Words fall meaningfully in Macbeth's famous statement of world-weariness: "Tomorrow and tomorrow and tomorrow . . ." and in the opening lines of Thomas Gray's "Elegy":

˘ ´ ˘ ´ ˘ ´ ˘ ´ ˘ ´
The cur·few tolls the knell of part·ing day,
˘ ´ ˘ ´ ´ ´ ˘ ´ ˘ ´
The low·ing herd wind slow·ly o'er the lea,
˘ ´ ˘ ´ ˘ ´ ˘ ´ ˘ ´
The plow·man home·ward plods his wear·y way,
˘ ´ ˘ ´ ˘ ´ ˘ ´ ˘ ´
And leaves the world to dark·ness and to me.[7]

Here the almost unvarying iambic rhythm seems appropriate to convey the tolling of a bell and the weary setting down of one foot after the other.

Besides the two rising meters (iambic, anapestic) and the two falling meters (trochaic, dactylic), English poets have another valuable meter. It is **accentual meter,** in which the poet does not write in feet (as in the other meters) but instead counts accents (stresses). The idea is to have the same number of stresses in every line. The poet may place them anywhere in the line and may include practically any number of unstressed syllables, which do not count. In "Christabel," for instance, Coleridge keeps four stresses to a line, though the first line has only eight syllables and the last line has eleven:

´ ´ ´ ´
There is not wind e·nough to twirl
´ ´ ´ ´
The one red leaf, the last of its clan,

[7] The complete poem, "Elegy Written in a Country Churchyard," appears on page 668.

That dán·ces as óf·ten as dánce it cán,

Háng·ing so líght, and háng·ing so hígh,

On the tóp-most twíg that looks úp at the ský.

The history of accentual meter is long and honorable. Old English poetry was written in a kind of accentual meter, but its line was more rule-bound than Coleridge's: four stresses arranged two on either side of a cesura, plus alliteration of three of the stressed syllables. In "Junk" (p. 820), Richard Wilbur revives the pattern:

An áxe án·gles ‖ from my néigh·bor's ásh·can . . .

Many poets, from the authors of Mother Goose rimes to Gerard Manley Hopkins, have sometimes found accentual meters congenial.

It has been charged that the importation of Greek names for meters and of the classical notion of feet was an unsuccessful attempt to make a Parthenon out of English wattles. The charge is open to debate, but at least it is certain that Greek names for feet cannot mean to us what they meant to Aristotle. Greek and Latin poetry is measured not by stressed and unstressed syllables but by long and short vowel sounds. An iamb in classical verse is one short vowel followed by a long vowel. Such a meter constructed on the principle of vowel length is called a **quantitative** meter. Campion's "Rose-cheeked Laura" was an attempt to demonstrate it in English, but probably we enjoy the rhythm of the poem's well-placed stresses whether or not we notice its pattern of vowel sounds.

Thomas Campion (1567–1620)

ROSE-CHEEKED LAURA, COME   1602

Rose-cheeked Laura, come,
Sing thou smoothly with thy beauty's
Silent music, either other
    Sweetly gracing.

Lovely forms do flow   5
From concent° divinely framèd;   *harmony*
Heav'n is music, and thy beauty's
    Birth is heavenly.

These dull notes we sing
Discords need for helps to grace them;   10
Only beauty purely loving
    Knows no discord,

But still moves delight,
Like clear springs renewed by flowing,
Ever perfect, ever in them-   15
    Selves eternal.

Less popular among poets today than formerly, the use of meter endures. Major poets from Shakespeare through Yeats have fashioned their poems by it, and if we are to read their work with full enjoyment, we need to be aware of it. Another argument in favor of meter is expressed in an old jazz song: "It don't mean a thing if you ain't got that swing." Or, as critic Paul Fussell, Jr., has put it: "No element of a poem is more basic—and I mean physical—in its effect upon the reader than the metrical element, and perhaps no technical triumphs reveal more readily than the metrical the poet's sympathy with that universal human nature . . . which exists outside his own."[8]

Walter Savage Landor (1775–1864)

ON SEEING A HAIR OF LUCRETIA BORGIA   (1825)

Borgia, thou once wert almost too august
And high for adoration; now thou'rt dust.
All that remains of thee these plaits unfold,
Calm hair, meandering in pellucid gold.

QUESTIONS

1. Who was Lucretia Borgia and when did she live? What connotations that add meaning to Landor's poem has her name?
2. What does *meander* mean? How can a hair meander?
3. Scan the poem, indicating stressed syllables. What is the basic meter of most of the poem? What happens to this meter in the last line? Note especially *meandering in pel-*. How many light, unstressed syllables are there in a row? Does rhythm in any way reinforce what Landor is saying?

EXERCISE: *Meaningful Variation*

At what place or places in each of these passages does the poet depart from basic iambic meter? How does each departure help underscore the meaning?

1. John Dryden, "Mac Flecknoe" (speech of Flecknoe, prince of Nonsense, referring to Thomas Shadwell, poet and playwright):

    Shadwell alone of all my sons is he
    Who stands confirmed in full stupidity.
    The rest to some faint meaning make pretense,
    But Shadwell never deviates into sense.

[8] Paul Fussell, Jr., *Poetic Meter and Poetic Form* (New York: Random House, 1965), p. 110.

2. Alexander Pope, *An Essay on Criticism:*

> A needless Alexandrine ends the song
> That, like a wounded snake, drags its slow length along.

3. Henry King, "The Exequy" (an apostrophe to his wife):

> 'Tis true, with shame and grief I yield,
> Thou like the van° first tookst the field,   *vanguard*
> And gotten hath the victory
> In thus adventuring to die
> Before me, whose more years might crave
> A just precedence in the grave.
> But hark! my pulse like a soft drum
> Beats my approach, tells thee I come;
> And slow howe'er my marches be,
> I shall at last sit down by thee.

4. Henry Wadsworth Longfellow, "Mezzo Cammin":

>   Half-way up the hill, I see the Past
> Lying beneath me with its sounds and sights,—
>   A city in the twilight dim and vast,
> With smoking roofs, soft bells, and gleaming lights,—
>   And hear above me on the autumnal blast
> The cataract of Death far thundering from the heights.

5. Wallace Stevens, "Sunday Morning":

> Deer walk upon our mountains, and the quail
> Whistle about us their spontaneous cries;
> Sweet berries ripen in the wilderness;
> And, in the isolation of the sky,
> At evening, casual flocks of pigeons make
> Ambiguous undulations as they sink,
> Downward to darkness, on extended wings.

EXERCISE: *Recognizing Rhythms*

Which of the following poems contain predominant meters? Which poems are not wholly metrical, but are metrical in certain lines? Point out any such lines. What reasons do you see, in such places, for the poet's seeking a metrical effect?

George Gordon, Lord Byron (1788–1824)

THE DESTRUCTION OF SENNACHERIB   1815

The Assyrian came down like the wolf on the fold,
And his cohorts were gleaming in purple and gold;
And the sheen of their spears was like stars on the sea,
When the blue wave rolls nightly on deep Galilee.

Like the leaves of the forest when summer is green,   5
That host with their banners at sunset were seen:
Like the leaves of the forest when autumn hath blown,
That host on the morrow lay withered and strown.

For the Angel of Death spread his wings on the blast,
And breathed in the face of the foe as he passed;   10
And the eyes of the sleepers waxed deadly and chill,
And their hearts but once heaved—and for ever grew still!

And there lay the steed with his nostril all wide,
But through it there rolled not the breath of his pride;
And the foam of his gasping lay white on the turf,   15
And cold as the spray of the rock-beating surf.

And there lay the rider distorted and pale,
With the dew on his brow, and the rust on his mail;
And the tents were all silent, the banners alone,
The lances unlifted, the trumpet unblown.   20

And the widows of Ashur are loud in their wail,
And the idols are broke in the temple of Baal;
And the might of the Gentile, unsmote by the sword,
Hath melted like snow in the glance of the Lord!

THE DESTRUCTION OF SENNACHERIB. Byron retells the Bible story of King Sennacherib of Assyria who, while leading an invasion of Jerusalem, suddenly lost his army: "And it came to pass that night, that the angel of the Lord went out, and smote in the camp of the Assyrians a hundred fourscore and five thousand: and when they arose early in the morning, behold, they were all dead corpses" (II Kings 19:35). 21–22: *Ashur . . . Baal:* Assyria and the Assyrian deity. 23. *Gentile:* Sennacherib (a non-Hebrew).

Edna St. Vincent Millay (1892–1950)

COUNTING-OUT RHYME   1928

Silver bark of beech, and sallow
Bark of yellow birch and yellow
   Twig of willow.

Stripe of green in moosewood maple,
Colour seen in leaf of apple,   5
   Bark of popple.

Wood of popple pale as moonbeam,
Wood of oak for yoke and barn-beam,
   Wood of hornbeam.

Silver bark of beech, and hollow   10
Stem of elder, tall and yellow
   Twig of willow.

A. E. Housman (1859–1936)

WHEN I WAS ONE-AND-TWENTY   1896

When I was one-and-twenty
   I heard a wise man say,

"Give crowns and pounds and guineas
  But not your heart away;
Give pearls away and rubies
  But keep your fancy free."
But I was one-and-twenty,
  No use to talk to me.

When I was one-and-twenty
  I heard him say again,
"The heart out of the bosom
  Was never given in vain;
'Tis paid with sighs a plenty
  And sold for endless rue."
And I am two-and-twenty,
  And oh, 'tis true, 'tis true.

William Carlos Williams (1883–1963)

THE DESCENT OF WINTER (SECTION 10/30)   1934

To freight cars in the air

all the slow
    clank, clank
    clank, clank
moving about the treetops

the
    wha, wha
of the hoarse whistle

    pah, pah, pah
    pah, pah, pah, pah, pah
    piece and piece
    piece and piece
moving still trippingly
through the morningmist

long after the engine
has fought by
            and disappeared
in silence
            to the left

Walt Whitman (1819–1892)

BEAT! BEAT! DRUMS!   (1861)

Beat! beat! drums!—blow! bugles! blow!
Through the windows—through doors—burst like a ruthless force,
Into the solemn church, and scatter the congregation,
Into the school where the scholar is studying;

Leave not the bridegroom quiet—no happiness must he have now with
    his bride,   5
Nor the peaceful farmer any peace, ploughing his field or gathering his
    grain,
So fierce you whirr and pound you drums—so shrill you bugles blow.

Beat! beat! drums!—blow! bugles! blow!
Over the traffic of cities—over the rumble of wheels in the streets;
Are beds prepared for sleepers at night in the houses? no sleepers must
    sleep in those beds,   10
No bargainer's bargains by day—no brokers or speculators—would they
    continue?
Would the talkers be talking? would the singer attempt to sing?
Would the lawyer rise in the court to state his case before the judge?
Then rattle quicker, heavier drums—you bugles wilder blow.

Beat! beat! drums!—blow! bugles! blow!   15
Make no parley—stop for no expostulation,
Mind not the timid—mind not the weeper or prayer,
Mind not the old man beseeching the young man,
Let not the child's voice be heard, nor the mother's entreaties,
Make even the trestles to shake the dead where they lie awaiting the
    hearses.   20
So strong you thump O terrible drums—so loud you bugles blow.

21 Closed Form, Open Form

Form, as a general idea, is the design of a thing as a whole, the configuration of all its parts. No poem can escape having some kind of form, whether its lines are as various in length as broomstraws, or all in hexameter. To put this point another way: if you were to listen to a poem read aloud in a language unknown to you, or if you saw the poem printed in that foreign language, whatever in the poem you could see or hear would be the form of it.[1]

Of late, poets and critics debating the relative merits of "closed" and "open" form have worn out many miles of typewriter ribbon. Writing in **closed form,** a poet follows (or finds) some sort of pattern, such as that of a sonnet with its rime scheme and its fourteen lines of iambic pentameter. On a page, poems in closed form tend to look regular and symmetrical. Along with William Butler Yeats, who held that a successful poem will "come shut with a click, like a closing box," the poet who writes in closed form apparently strives for a kind of perfection—seeking, perhaps, to lodge words so securely in place that no word can be budged without a worsening.

The poet who writes in **open form** usually seeks no final click. Often, such a poet views the writing of a poem as a process, rather than a quest for an absolute. Free to use white space for emphasis, able to shorten or lengthen lines as the sense seems to require, the poet lets the poem discover its shape as it goes along, moving as water flows downhill, adjusting to its terrain, engulfing obstacles.

Right now, most American poets prefer open form to closed. But although less fashionable than they were, rime and meter are still in evidence. Most poetry of the past is in closed form. The reader who seeks a wide understanding of poetry will want to know both closed and open varieties.

---

[1] For a good summary of the uses of the term **form** in criticism of poetry, see the article "Form" by G. N. G. Orsini in *Princeton Encyclopedia of Poetry and Poetics*, 2nd ed., eds. Preminger, Warnke, and Hardison (Princeton: Princeton University Press, 1975).

CLOSED FORM:
BLANK VERSE, STANZA, SONNET

Closed form gives some poems a valuable advantage: it makes them more easily memorable. The **epic** poems of nations—long narratives tracing the adventures of popular heroes: the Greek *Iliad* and *Odyssey*, the French *Song of Roland*, the Spanish *Cid*—tend to occur in patterns of fairly consistent line length or number of stresses because these works were sometimes transmitted orally. Sung to the music of a lyre or chanted to a drumbeat, they may have been easier to memorize because of their patterns. If a singer forgot something, the song would have a noticeable hole in it, so rime or fixed meter probably helped prevent an epic from deteriorating when passed along from one singer to another. It is no coincidence that so many English playwrights of Shakespeare's day favored iambic pentameter. Companies of actors, often called upon to perform a different play daily, could count on a fixed line length to aid their burdened memories.

Some poets complain that closed form is a straitjacket, a limit to free expression. Other poets, however, feel that, like fires held fast in a narrow space, thoughts stated in a tightly binding form may take on a heightened intensity. "Limitation makes for power," according to one contemporary practitioner of closed form, Richard Wilbur; "the strength of the genie comes of his being confined in a bottle." Compelled by some strict pattern to arrange and rearrange words, delete, and exchange them, poets must focus on them the keenest attention. Often they stand a chance of discovering words more meaningful than the ones they started out with. And at times, in obedience to a rime scheme, the poet may be surprised by saying something quite unexpected. Composing a poem is like walking blindfolded down a dark road, with one's hand in the hand of an inexorable guide. With the conscious portion of the mind, the poet may wish to express what seems to be a good idea. But a line ending in *year* must be followed by another ending in *atmosphere, beer, bier, bombardier, cashier, deer, friction-gear, frontier*, or some other rime word that otherwise might not have entered the poem. That is why rime schemes and stanza patterns can be mighty allies and valuable disturbers of the unconscious. As Rolfe Humphries has said about a strict form: "It makes you think of better things than you would all by yourself."

The best-known one-line pattern for a poem in English is **blank verse**: unrimed iambic pentameter. (This pattern is not a stanza: stanzas have more than one line.) Most portions of Shakespeare's plays are in blank verse, and so are Milton's *Paradise Lost*, Tennyson's "Ulysses," certain dramatic monologues of Browning and Frost, and thousands of other poems. Here is a poem in blank verse that startles us by dropping out of its pattern in the final line. Keats appears to have written it late in his life to his fiancée Fanny Brawne.

John Keats (1795–1821)
THIS LIVING HAND, NOW WARM AND CAPABLE (1819?)

This living hand, now warm and capable
Of earnest grasping, would, if it were cold
And in the icy silence of the tomb,
So haunt thy days and chill thy dreaming nights
That thou wouldst wish thine own heart dry of blood
So in my veins red life might stream again,
And thou be conscience-calmed — see here it is —
I hold it towards you.

The **couplet** is a two-line stanza, usually rimed. Its lines often tend to be equal in length, whether short or long. Here are two examples:

Blow,
Snow!

As I in hoary winter's night stood shivering in the snow,
Surprised I was with sudden heat which made my heart to glow.

(Actually, any pair of rimed lines that contains a complete thought is called a couplet, even if it is not a stanza, such as the couplet that ends a sonnet by Shakespeare.) Unlike other stanzas, couplets are often printed solid, not separated one couplet from the next by white space. This practice is usual in printing the **heroic couplet** — or **closed couplet** — two rimed lines of iambic pentameter, the first ending in a light pause, the second more heavily end-stopped. George Crabbe, in *The Parish Register*, described a shotgun wedding:

Next at our altar stood a luckless pair,
Brought by strong passions and a warrant there:
By long rent cloak, hung loosely, strove the bride,
From every eye, what all perceived, to hide;
While the boy bridegroom, shuffling in his place,
Now hid awhile and then exposed his face.
As shame alternately with anger strove
The brain confused with muddy ale to move,
In haste and stammering he performed his part,
And looked the rage that rankled in his heart.

Though employed by Chaucer, the heroic couplet was named from its later use by Dryden and others in poems, translations of classical epics, and verse plays of epic heroes. It continued in favor through most of the eighteenth century. Much of our pleasure in reading good heroic couplets comes from the seemingly easy precision with which a skilled poet unites statements and strict pattern. In doing so, the poet may place a pair of words, phrases, clauses, or sentences side by side in agreement or similarity, forming a **parallel,** or in contrast and opposition, forming an **antithesis.** The effect is neat. For such skill in manipulating parallels and antitheses, John Denham's lines on the river Thames were much admired:

> O could I flow like thee, and make thy stream
> My great example, as it is my theme!
> Though deep, yet clear; though gentle, yet not dull;
> Strong without rage, without o'erflowing full.

These lines were echoed by Pope, ridiculing a poetaster, in two heroic couplets in *The Dunciad:*

> Flow, Welsted, flow! like thine inspirer, Beer:
> Though stale, not ripe; though thin, yet never clear;
> So sweetly mawkish, and so smoothly dull;
> Heady, not strong; o'erflowing, though not full.

Reading long poems in so exact a form, one may feel like a spectator at a ping-pong match unless the poet skillfully keeps varying rhythms. (Among much else, this skill distinguishes the work of Dryden and Pope from that of a lockstep horde of coupleteers who followed them.) One way of escaping such metronome-like monotony is to keep the cesura (see p. 549) shifting about from place to place—now happening early in a line, now happening late—and at times unexpectedly to hurl in a second or third cesura. Try working through George Crabbe's lines (on p. 568) and observe where the cesuras fall.

The **tercet** is a three-line stanza that, if rimed, usually keeps to one rime sound. **Terza rima,** the form Dante employs for *The Divine Comedy,* is made of tercets linked together by the rime scheme *a b a, b c b, c d c, d e d, e f e,* and so on. Harder to do in English than in Italian—with its greater resources of riming words—the form nevertheless has been managed by Shelley in "Ode to the West Wind" (with the aid of some slant rimes):

> Make me thy lyre, even as the forest is:
> What if my leaves are falling like its own!
> The tumult of thy mighty harmonies
>
> Will take from both a deep, autumnal tone,
> Sweet though in sadness. Be thou, spirit fierce,
> My spirit! Be thou me, impetuous one![2]

The workhorse of English stanzas is the **quatrain,** used for more

---

[2] The complete poem appears on pages 804–806.

rimed poems than any other form. It comes in many line lengths, and sometimes contains lines of varying length, as in the ballad stanza (see Chapter Eighteen).

Longer and more complicated stanzas are, of course, possible, but couplet, tercet, and quatrain have been called the building blocks of our poetry because most longer stanzas are made up of them. What short stanzas does John Donne mortar together to make the longer stanza of his "Song"?

John Donne (1572–1631)

Song

1633

Go and catch a falling star
  Get with child a mandrake root,
Tell me where all past years are,
  Or who cleft the Devil's foot,
Teach me to hear mermaids singing,   5
  Or to keep off envy's stinging,
    And find
    What wind
Serves to advance an honest mind.

If thou be'st borne to strange sights,   10
  Things invisible to see,
Ride ten thousand days and nights,
  Till age snow white hairs on thee,
Thou, when thou return'st, wilt tell me
  All strange wonders that befell thee,   15
    And swear
    Nowhere
Lives a woman true, and fair.

If thou findst one, let me know,
  Such a pilgrimage were sweet—   20
Yet do not, I would not go,
  Though at next door we might meet;
Though she were true, when you met her,
  And last, till you write your letter,
    Yet she   25
    Will be
False, ere I come, to two, or three.

Recently in vogue is a form known as **syllabic verse** in which the poet establishes a pattern of a certain number of syllables to a line. Either rimed or rimeless but usually stanzaic, syllabic verse has been hailed as a way for poets to escape "the tyranny of the iamb" and discover less conventional rhythms, since, if they take as their line length an *odd* number of syllables, then iambs, being feet of *two* syllables, cannot fit perfectly into it. Offbeat victories have been scored in syllabics by such poets as W. H. Auden, W. D. Snodgrass, Donald Hall, Thom Gunn, and Marianne Moore. A well-known syllabic poem is Dylan Thomas's "Fern Hill" (page 817). Notice its shape on the page, count the syllables in its lines, and you'll perceive its perfect symmetry. Although like playing a game, the writing of such a poem is apparently more than finger exercise: the discipline can help a poet to sing well, though (with Thomas) singing "in . . . chains like the sea."

Poets who write in demanding forms seem to enjoy taking on an arbitrary task for the fun of it, as ballet dancers do, or weightlifters. Much of our pleasure in reading such poems comes from watching words fall into a shape. It is the pleasure of seeing any hard thing done skillfully—a leap executed in a dance, a basketball swished through a basket. Still, to be excellent, a poem needs more than skill; and to enjoy a poem it isn't always necessary for the reader to be aware of the skill that went into it. Unknowingly, the editors of *The New Yorker* once printed an **acrostic**—a poem in which the initial letter of each line, read downwards, spells out a word or words—that named (and insulted) a well-known anthologist. Evidently, besides being ingenious, the acrostic was a printable poem. In the Old Testament book of Lamentations, profoundly moving songs tell of the sufferings of the Jews after the destruction of Jerusalem. Four of the songs are written as an alphabetical acrostic, every stanza beginning with a letter of the Hebrew alphabet. However ingenious, such sublime poetry cannot be dismissed as merely witty; nor can it be charged that a poet who writes in such a form does not express deep feeling.

Patterns of sound and rhythm can, however, be striven after in a dull mechanical way, for which reason many poets today think them dangerous. Swinburne, who loved alliterations and tripping meters, had enough detachment to poke fun at his own excessive patterning:

> From the depth of the dreamy decline of the dawn through a notable
>   nimbus of nebulous noonshine,
> Pallid and pink as the palm of the flag-flower that flickers with fear of
>   the flies as they float,
> Are the looks of our lovers that lustrously lean from a marvel of mystic mi-
>   raculous moonshine,
> These that we feel in the blood of our blushes that thicken and threaten
>   with throbs through the throat?

This is bad, but bad deliberately. If any good at all, a poem in a fixed pattern, such as a sonnet, is created not only by the craftsman's chipping away at it but by the explosion of a sonnet-shaped *idea*. Viewed mechanically, as so many empty boxes somehow to be filled up, stanzas can impose the most hollow sort of discipline, and a poem written in these stanzas becomes no more than finger-exercise. This comment (although on fiction) may be appropriate:

Roy Campbell (1901–1957)
ON SOME SOUTH AFRICAN NOVELISTS

1930

You praise the firm restraint with which they write—
  I'm with you there, of course.
They use the snaffle and the curb all right;
  But where's the bloody horse?

Not only firm restraint marks the rimed poems of Shakespeare, Emily Dickinson, and William Butler Yeats, but also strong emotion. Such poets ride with certain hand upon a sturdy horse.

Ronald Gross (b. 1935)
YIELD

1967

Yield.
No Parking.
Unlawful to Pass.
Wait for Green Light.
Yield.   5

Stop.
Narrow Bridge.
Merging Traffic Ahead
Yield.

Yield.   10

QUESTIONS

1. This poem by Ronald Gross is a "found poem." After reading it, how would you define **found poetry**?
2. Does "Yield" have a theme? If so, how would you state it?
3. What makes "Yield" mean more than traffic signs ordinarily mean to us?

EXPERIMENT: *Finding a Poem*

In a newspaper, magazine, catalogue, textbook, or advertising throwaway, find a sentence or passage that (with a little artistic manipulation on your part) shows promise of becoming a poem. Copy it into lines like poetry, being careful to place what seem to be the most interesting words at the ends of lines to give them greatest emphasis. According to the rules of found poetry, you may excerpt, delete, repeat, and rearrange elements but not add anything. What does this experiment tell you about poetric form? About ordinary prose?

Ronald Gross, who produces his "found poetry" by arranging prose from such unlikely places as traffic signs and news stories into poem-like lines, has told of making a discovery:

> As I worked with labels, tax forms, commercials, contracts, pin-up captions, obituaries, and the like, I soon found myself rediscovering all the traditional verse forms in found materials: ode, sonnet, epigram, haiku, free verse. Such finds made me realize that these forms are not mere artifices, but shapes that language naturally takes when carrying powerful thoughts or feelings.[3]

Though Gross is a playful experimenter, his remark is true of serious poetry. Traditional verse forms like sonnets and haiku aren't a lot of hollow pillowcases for a poet to stuff with verbiage. At best, in the hands of a skilled poet, they can be shapes into which living language seems to fall naturally.

It is fun to see words tumble gracefully into such a shape. Consider, for instance, one famous "found poem," a sentence discovered in a physics textbook: "And so no force, however great, can stretch a cord, however fine, into a horizontal line which shall be absolutely straight."[4] What a good clear sentence containing effective parallels ("however great . . . however fine"), you might say, taking pleasure in it. Yet this plain statement gives extra pleasure if arranged like this:

> And so no force, however great,
> Can stretch a cord, however fine,
> Into a horizontal line
> Which shall be absolutely straight.

So spaced, in lines that reveal its built-in rimes and rhythms, the sentence would seem one of those "shapes that language naturally takes" that Ronald Gross finds everywhere. (It is possible, of course, that the textbook writer was gleefully planting a quatrain for someone to find; but perhaps it is more likely that he knew much rimed, metrical poetry by heart and couldn't help writing it unconsciously.)

When we speak, with Ronald Gross, of "traditional verse forms," we usually mean **fixed forms.** If written in a fixed form, a poem inherits from other poems certain familiar elements of structure: an unvarying number of lines, say, or a stanza pattern. In addition, it may display certain **conventions:** expected features such as themes, subjects, attitudes, or figures of speech. In medieval folk ballads a "milk-white steed" is a

---

[3] "Speaking of Books: Found Poetry," *The New York Times Book Review*, June 11, 1967. Inspired by pop artists who reveal fresh vistas in Brillo boxes and comic strips, found poetry has had a recent vogue. Earlier practitioners include William Carlos Williams, whose long poem *Paterson* (New York: New Directions, 1963) quotes historical documents and statistics. Prose, said Williams in a letter, can be a "laboratory" for poetry: "It throws up jewels which may be cleaned and grouped."

[4] William Whewell, *Elementary Treatise on Mechanics* (Cambridge, England, 1819).

conventional figure of speech; and if its rider be a cruel and beautiful witch who kidnaps mortals, she is a conventional character. (*Conventional* doesn't necessarily mean uninteresting.)

In the poetry of western Europe and America, the **sonnet** is the fixed form that has attracted for the longest time the largest number of noteworthy practitioners. Originally an Italian form (*sonnetto:* "little song"), the sonnet owes much of its prestige to Petrarch (1304–1374), who wrote in it of his love for the unattainable Laura. So great was the vogue for sonnets in England at the end of the sixteenth century that a gentleman might have been thought a boor if he couldn't turn out a decent one. Not content to adopt merely the sonnet's fourteen-line pattern, English poets also tried on its conventional mask of the tormented lover. They borrowed some of Petrarch's similes (a lover's heart, for instance, is like a storm-tossed boat) and invented others. (If you would like more illustrations of Petrarchan conventions, see pages 664–666.)

Soon after English poets imported the sonnet in the middle of the sixteenth century, they worked out their own rime scheme—one easier for them to follow than Petrarch's, which calls for a greater number of riming words than English can readily provide. (In Italian, according to an exaggerated report, practically everything rimes.) In the following **English sonnet,** sometimes called a **Shakespearean sonnet,** the rimes cohere in four clusters: *a b a b, c d c d, e f e f, g g.* Because a rime scheme tends to shape the poet's statements to it, the English sonnet has three places where the procession of thought is likely to turn in another direction. Within its form, a poet may pursue one idea throughout the three quatrains and then in the couplet end with a surprise.

Michael Drayton (1563–1631)

Since there's no help, come let us kiss and part

1619

Since there's no help, come let us kiss and part;
Nay, I have done, you get no more of me,
And I am glad, yea, glad with all my heart
That thus so cleanly I myself can free;
Shake hands for ever, cancel all our vows,   5
And when we meet at any time again,
Be it not seen in either of our brows
That we one jot of former love retain.
Now at the last gasp of Love's latest breath,
When, his pulse failing, Passion speechless lies,   10
When Faith is kneeling by his bed of death,
And Innocence is closing up his eyes,
    Now if thou wouldst, when all have given him over,
    From death to life thou mightst him yet recover.

Less frequently met in English poetry, the **Italian sonnet,** or **Petrarchan sonnet,** follows the rime scheme *a b b a, a b b a* in its first eight lines, the **octave,** and then adds new rime sounds in the last six lines, the **sestet.** The sestet may rime *c d c d c d, c d e c d e, c d c c d c,* or in almost any other variation that doesn't end in a couplet. This organization into two parts sometimes helps arrange the poet's thoughts. In the octave, the poet may state a problem, and then, in the sestet, may offer a resolution. A lover, for example, may lament all octave long that a loved one is neglectful, then in line 9 begin to foresee some outcome: the speaker will die, or accept unhappiness, or trust that the beloved will have a change of heart.

Elizabeth Barrett Browning (1806–1861)

GRIEF   1844

I tell you, hopeless grief is passionless;
   That only men incredulous of despair,
   Half-taught in anguish, through the midnight air
Beat upward to God's throne in loud access
Of shrieking and reproach. Full desertness   5
   In souls, as countries, lieth silent-bare
   Under the blanching, vertical eye-glare
Of the absolute Heavens. Deep-hearted man, express
Grief for the Dead in silence like to death:
   Most like a monumental statue set   10
In everlasting watch and moveless woe
Till itself crumble to the dust beneath.
   Touch it: the marble eyelids are not wet—
If it could weep, it could arise and go.

In this Italian sonnet, the division in thought comes a bit early—in the middle of line 8. Few English-speaking poets who have used the form seem to feel strictly bound by it.

    "The sonnet," in the view of Robert Bly, a modern critic, "is where old professors go to die." And yet the use of the form by such twentieth-century poets as Yeats, Frost, Auden, Thomas, Pound, Cummings, Berryman, and Lowell suggests that it may be far from exhausted. Like the hero of the popular ballad "Finnegan's Wake," literary forms (though not professors) declared dead have a habit of springing up again.

EXERCISE: *Knowing Two Kinds of Sonnet*
Find other sonnets in this book. Which are English in form? Which are Italian?

Which are variations on either form or combinations of the two? You may wish to try your hand at writing both kinds of sonnet and experience the difference for yourself.

Oscar Wilde said that a cynic is "a man who knows the price of everything and the value of nothing." Such a terse, pointed statement is called an epigram. In poetry, however, an **epigram** is a form: "A short poem ending in a witty or ingenious turn of thought, to which the rest of the composition is intended to lead up" (according to the *Oxford English Dictionary*). Often it is a malicious gibe with an unexpected stinger in the final line—perhaps in the very last word:

Alexander Pope (1688–1744)

Epigram Engraved on the Collar of a Dog Which I Gave to His Royal Highness   1738

I am his Highness' dog at Kew;
Pray tell me, sir, whose dog are you?

Cultivated by the Roman poet Martial—for whom the epigram was a short poem, sometimes satiric but not always—this form has been especially favored by English poets who love Latin. Few characteristics of the English epigram seem fixed. Its pattern tends to be brief and rimed, its tone playfully merciless.

Martial (A.D. 40?–102?)

You serve the best wines always, my dear sir   A.D. 90

You serve the best wines always, my dear sir,
And yet they say your wines are not so good.
They say you are four times a widower.
They say . . . A drink? I don't believe I would.

—Translated by J. V. Cunningham

Sir John Harrington (1561?–1612)

Of Treason   1618

Treason doth never prosper; what's the reason?
For if it prosper, none dare call it treason.

William Blake (1757–1827)
HER WHOLE LIFE IS AN EPIGRAM

(1793)

Her whole life is an epigram: smack smooth°, and   *perfectly smooth*
    neatly penned,
Platted° quite neat to catch applause, with a sliding   *plaited, woven*
    noose at the end.

E. E. Cummings (1894–1962)
A POLITICIAN

1944

a politician is an arse upon
which everyone has sat except a man

J. V. Cunningham (b. 1911)
THIS HUMANIST WHOM NO BELIEFS CONSTRAINED

1947

This *Humanist* whom no beliefs constrained
Grew so broad-minded he was scatter-brained.

Keith Waldrop (b. 1932)
ON MEASURE

1968

The delicate foot of
Phoebe Isolde Farmer
taps meters acceptable to, among others, the
* * * Poetry Journal and the
University of * * * * * * Review and to   5
her brother, a minister, who is paying
for the printing of a small
volume—while he should be
praying, "Lord, grant her
wings."   10

EXPERIMENT: *Expanding an Epigram*

Rewrite any of the preceding epigrams, taking them out of rime (if they are in rime) and adding a few more words to them. See if your revisions have nearly the same effect as the originals.

EXERCISE: *Reading for Couplets*

Read all the sonnets by Shakespeare in this book. How do the final couplets of some of them resemble epigrams? Does this similarity diminish their effect of "seriousness"?

In English the only other fixed form to rival the sonnet and the epigram in favor is the **limerick:** five anapestic lines usually riming *a a b b a.*

> There was an old man of Pantoum
> Who kept a live sheep in his room.
> "It reminds me," he said,
> "Of a loved one long dead,
> But I never can quite recall whom."

The limerick was made popular by Edward Lear (1812–1888), English humorist and painter, whose own practice was to make the last line hark back to the first: "That oppressive old man of Pantoum."

EXPERIMENT: *Contriving a Clerihew*

The **clerihew,** a fixed form named for its inventor, Edmund Clerihew Bentley (1875–1956), has straggled behind the limerick in popularity. Here are four examples: how would you define the form and what are its rules? Who or what is its conventional subject matter? Try writing your own example.

James Watt
Was the hard-boiled kind of Scot:
He thought any dream
Sheer waste of steam.

— W. H. Auden

Sir Christopher Wren
Said, "I am going to dine with some men.
If anybody calls
Say I am designing St. Paul's."

— Edmund Clerihew Bentley

Etienne de Silhouette
(It's a good bet)
Has the shadiest claim
To fame.

— Cornelius J. Ter Maat

Dylan Thomas
Showed early promise.
His name's no dimmer, man,
On old Bob Zimmerman.

— T. O. Maglow

Dylan Thomas (1914–1953)

DO NOT GO GENTLE INTO THAT GOOD NIGHT

1952

Do not go gentle into that good night,
Old age should burn and rave at close of day;
Rage, rage against the dying of the light.

Though wise men at their end know dark is right,
Because their words had forked no lightning they   5
Do not go gentle into that good night.

Good men, the last wave by, crying how bright
Their frail deeds might have danced in a green bay,
Rage, rage against the dying of the light.

Wild men who caught and sang the sun in flight,   10
And learn, too late, they grieved it on its way,
Do not go gentle into that good night.

Grave men, near death, who see with blinding sight
Blind eyes could blaze like meteors and be gay,
Rage, rage against the dying of the light.   15

And you, my father, there on the sad height,
Curse, bless, me now with your fierce tears, I pray,
Do not go gentle into that good night.
Rage, rage against the dying of the light.

QUESTIONS

1. "Do not go gentle into that good night" is a **villanelle:** a fixed form originated by French courtly poets of the Middle Ages. (For another villanelle, see Theodore Roethke's "The Waking," page 799.) What are its rules?
2. Is Thomas's poem, like many another villanelle, just an elaborate and trivial exercise? Whom does the poet address? What is he saying?

OPEN FORM

Writing in **open form,** a poet seeks to discover a fresh and individual arrangement for words in every poem. Such a poem, generally speaking, has neither a rime scheme nor a basic meter informing the whole of it. Doing without those powerful (some would say hypnotic) elements, the poet who writes in open form relies on other means to engage and to sustain the reader's attention. Novice poets often think that open form looks easy, not nearly so hard as riming everything; but in truth, formally open poems are easy to write only if written carelessly. To compose lines with keen awareness of open form's demands, and of its infinite possibilities, calls for skill: at least as much as that needed to write in meter and rime, if not more. Should the poet succeed, then the discovered arrangement will seem exactly right for what the poem is saying. Words will seem at home in their positions, as naturally as the words of a decent sonnet.

Denise Levertov (b. 1923)
SIX VARIATIONS (PART III)   1961

Shlup, shlup, the dog
as it laps up
water
makes intelligent
music, resting
now and then to take breath in irregular
measure.

Open form, in this brief poem, affords Denise Levertov certain advantages. Able to break off a line at whatever point she likes (a privilege not available to the poet writing, say, a conventional sonnet, who has to break off each line after its tenth syllable), she selects her pauses artfully. Line-breaks lend emphasis: a word or phrase at the end of a line takes a little more stress (and receives a little more attention), because the ending of the line compels the reader to make a slight pause, if only for the brief moment it takes to sling back one's eyes (like a typewriter carriage) and fix them on the line following. Slight pauses, then, follow the words and phrases *the dog / laps up / water / intelligent / resting / irregular / measure*—all of these being elements that apparently the poet wishes to call our attention to. (The pause after a line-break also casts a little more weight upon the *first* word or phrase of each succeeding line.) Levertov makes the most of white space—another means of calling attention to things, as any good picture-framer knows. By setting a word all alone on a line (*water / measure*), she makes it stand out more than it would do in a line of pentameter. She feels free to include a bit of rime (*Shlup, shlup / up*). She creates rhythms: if you will read aloud the phrases *intelligent / music* and *irregular / measure*, you will sense that in each phrase the arrangement of pauses and stresses is identical. Like the dog's halts to take breath, the lengths of the lines seem naturally irregular. The result is a fusion of meaning and form: indeed, an "intelligent music."

Poetry in open form used to be called **free verse** (from the French *vers libre*), suggesting a kind of verse liberated from the shackles of rime and meter. "Writing free verse," said Robert Frost, who wasn't interested in it, "is like playing tennis with the net down." And yet, as Denise Levertov and many other poets demonstrate, high scores can be made in such an unconventional game, provided it doesn't straggle all over the court. For a successful poem in open form, the term *free verse* seems inaccurate. "Being an art form," said William Carlos Williams, "verse cannot be 'free' in the sense of having *no* limitations or guiding principles."[5] Various substitute names have been suggested: organic poetry, composition by field, raw (as against cooked) poetry, open form poetry. "But what does it matter what you call it?" remark the editors of an anthology called *Naked Poetry*. The best poems of the last twenty years "don't rhyme (usually) and don't move on feet of more or less equal duration (usually). That nondescription moves toward the only technical principle they all have in common."[6]

And yet many poems in open form have much more in common than absences and lacks. One positive principle has been Ezra Pound's famous suggestion that poets "compose in the sequence of the musical phrase, not in the sequence of the metronome" — good advice, perhaps, even for poets who write inside fixed forms. In Charles Olson's influential theory of **projective verse,** poets compose by listening to their own breathing. On paper, they indicate the rhythms of a poem by using a little white space or a lot, a slight indentation or a deep one, depending on whether a short pause or a long one is intended. Words can be grouped in clusters on the page (usually no more words than a lungful of air can accommodate). Heavy cesuras are sometimes shown by breaking a line in two and lowering the second part of it.[7] (An Olson poem appears on page 596.)

To the poet working in open form, no less than to the poet writing a sonnet, line length can be valuable. Walt Whitman, who loved to expand vast sentences for line after line, knew well that an impressive rhythm can accumulate if the poet will keep long lines approximately the same length, causing a pause to recur at about the same interval after every line. Sometimes, too, Whitman repeats the same words at each line's opening. An instance is the masterful sixth section of "When Lilacs Last in the Dooryard Bloom'd," an elegy for Abraham Lincoln:

> Coffin that passes through lanes and streets,
> Through day and night with the great cloud darkening the land,
> With the pomp of the inloop'd flags with the cities draped in black,
> With the show of the States themselves as of crape-veil'd women standing,
> With processions long and winding and the flambeaus of the night,
> With the countless torches lit, with the silent sea of faces and the unbared heads,

[5] "Free Verse," article in *Princeton Encyclopedia of Poetry and Poetics*.
[6] Stephen Berg and Robert Mezey, eds., foreword to *Naked Poetry: Recent American Poetry in Open Forms* (Indianapolis: Bobbs-Merrill, 1969).
[7] See Olson's essays "Projective Verse" and "Letter to Elaine Feinstein" in *Selected Writings*, edited by Robert Creeley (New York: New Directions, 1966). Olson's letters to Cid Corman are fascinating: *Letters for Origin, 1950–1955*, edited by Albert Glover (New York: Grossman, 1970).

With the waiting depot, the arriving coffin, and the somber faces,
With dirges through the night, with the thousand voices rising strong and
  solemn,
With all the mournful voices of the dirges pour'd around the coffin,
The dim-lit churches and the shuddering organs—where amid these you
  journey,
With the tolling tolling bells' perpetual clang,
Here, coffin that slowly passes,
I give you my sprig of lilac.

There is music in such solemn, operatic arias. Whitman's lines echo another model: the Hebrew **psalms,** or sacred songs, as translated in the
King James Version of the Bible. In Psalm 150, repetition also occurs inside of lines:

> Praise ye the Lord. Praise God in his sanctuary: praise him in the
> firmament of his power.
> Praise him for his mighty acts: praise him according to his excellent
> greatness.
> Praise him with the sound of the trumpet: praise him with the psaltery
> and harp.
> Praise him with the timbrel and dance: praise him with stringed in-
> struments and organs.
> Praise him upon the loud cymbals: praise him upon the high sounding
> cymbals.
> Let every thing that hath breath praise the Lord. Praise ye the Lord.

In Biblical Psalms, we are in the presence of (as Robert Lowell has said)
"supreme poems, written when their translators merely intended prose
and were forced by the structure of their originals to write poetry."[8]

Whitman was a more deliberate craftsman than he let his readers
think, and to anyone interested in writing in open form, his work will
repay close study. He knew that repetitions of any kind often make
memorable rhythms, as in this passage from "Song of Myself," with
every line ending on an -*ing* word (a stressed syllable followed by an
unstressed syllable):

> Here and there with dimes on the eyes walking,
> To feed the greed of the belly the brains liberally spooning,
> Tickets buying, taking, selling, but in to the feast never once going,
> Many sweating, ploughing, thrashing, and then the chaff for payment
>   receiving,
> A few idly owning, and they the wheat continually claiming.

Much more than simply repetition, of course, went into the music of
those lines—the internal rime *feed, greed,* the use of assonance, the

---

[8] "On Freedom in Poetry," in Berg and Mezey, *Naked Poetry*.

trochees that begin the third and fourth lines, whether or not they were calculated.

In such classics of open form poetry, sound and rhythm are positive forces. When speaking a poem in open form, you often may find that it makes a difference for the better if you pause at the end of each line. Try pausing there, however briefly; but don't allow your voice to drop. Read just as you would normally read a sentence in prose (except for the pauses, of course). Why do the pauses matter? Open form poetry usually has no meter to lend it rhythm. *Some* lines in an open form poem, as we have seen in Whitman's "dimes on the eyes" passage, do fall into metrical feet; sometimes the whole poem does. Usually lacking meter's aid, however, open form, in order to have more and more noticeable rhythms, has need of all the recurring pauses it can get. When reading their own work aloud, open form poets like Robert Creeley and Allen Ginsberg often pause very definitely at each line break. Such a habit makes sense only in reading artful poems.

No law requires a poet to split thoughts into irregular lines at all. Charles Baudelaire, Rainer Maria Rilke, Jorge Luis Borges, Alexander Solzhenitsyn, T. S. Eliot, and many others have written **prose poems,** in which, without caring that eye appeal and some of the rhythm of a line structure may be lost, the poet prints words in a block like a prose paragraph. For an example see Karl Shapiro's "The Dirty Word" (page 804).[9]

The great majority of poems appearing at present in American literary magazines are in open form. "Farewell, pale skunky pentameters (the only honest English meter, gloop! gloop!)," Kenneth Koch has gleefully exclaimed. Many poets have sought reasons for turning away from patterns and fixed forms. Some hold that it is wrong to fit words into any pattern that already exists and instead believe in letting a poem seek its own shape as it goes along. (Traditionalists might say that that is what all good poems do anyway: sonnets rarely know they are going to be sonnets until the third line has been written. However, there is no doubt that the sonnet form already exists, at least in the back of the head of any poet who has ever read sonnets.) Some open form poets offer a historical motive: they want to reflect the nervous, staccato, disconnected pace of our bumper-to-bumper society. Others see open form as an attempt to suit thoughts and words to a more spontaneous order than the traditional verse forms allow. "Better," says Gary Snyder, quoting from Zen, "the perfect, easy discipline of the swallow's dip and swoop, 'without east or west.' "[10]

[9] For more examples see *The Prose Poem, An International Anthology,* edited by Michael Benedikt (New York: Dell, 1976).
[10] "Some Yips & Barks in the Dark," in Berg and Mezey, *Naked Poetry.*

E. E. Cummings (1894–1962)

BUFFALO BILL'S

1923

```
Buffalo Bill's
defunct
          who used to
          ride a watersmooth-silver
                              stallion
and break onetwothreefourfive pigeonsjustlikethat
                                        Jesus

he was a handsome man
                    and what i want to know is
how do you like your blueeyed boy
Mister Death
```

5

10

QUESTION

Cummings's poem would look like this if given conventional punctuation and set in a solid block like prose:

Buffalo Bill's defunct, who used to ride a water-smooth silver stallion and break one, two, three, four, five pigeons just like that. Jesus, he was a handsome man. And what I want to know is: "How do you like your blue-eyed boy, Mister Death?"

If this were done, by what characteristics would it still be recognizable as poetry? But what would be lost?

Emily Dickinson (1830–1886)

VICTORY COMES LATE

(1861)

```
Victory comes late–
And is held low to freezing lips–
Too rapt with frost
To take it–
How sweet it would have tasted–
Just a Drop–
Was God so economical?
His Table's spread too high for Us–
Unless We dine on tiptoe–
Crumbs–fit such little mouths–
Cherries–suit Robins–
The Eagle's Golden Breakfast strangles–Them–
God keep His Oath to Sparrows–
Who of little Love–know how to starve–
```

5

10

QUESTIONS

1. In this specimen of poetry in open form, can you see any other places at which the poet might have broken off any of her lines? To place a word last in

a line gives it a greater emphasis; she might, for instance, have ended line 12 with *Breakfast* and begun a new line with the word *strangles*. Do you think she knows what she is doing here or does the pattern of this poem seem decided by whim? Discuss.

2. Read the poem aloud. Try pausing for a fraction of a second at every dash. Is there any justification for the poet's unorthodox punctuation?

William Carlos Williams (1883–1963)

The Dance   1944

In Breughel's great picture, The Kermess,
the dancers go round, they go round and
around, the squeal and the blare and the
tweedle of bagpipes, a bugle and fiddles
tipping their bellies (round as the thick-   5
sided glasses whose wash they impound)
their hips and their bellies off balance
to turn them. Kicking and rolling about
the Fair Grounds, swinging their butts, those
shanks must be sound to bear up under such   10
rollicking measures, prance as they dance
in Breughel's great picture, The Kermess.

The Dance. Pieter Breughel (1520?–1569), a Flemish painter known for his scenes of peasant activities, represented in "The Kermess" a celebration on the feast day of a local patron saint.

1. Scan this poem and try to describe the effect of its rhythms.
2. Williams, widely admired for his free verse, insisted for many years that what he sought was a form not in the least bit free. What effect does he achieve by ending lines on such weak words as the articles *and* and *the*? By splitting *thick-* / *sided*? By splitting a prepositional phrase with the break at the end of line 8? By using line breaks to split *those* and *such* from what they modify? What do you think he is trying to convey?
3. Is there any point in his making line 12 a repetition of the opening line?
4. Look at the reproduction of Breughel's painting "The Kermess" (also called "Peasants Dancing"). Aware that the rhythms of dancers, the rhythms of a painting, and the rhythms of a poem are not all the same, can you put in your own words what Breughel's dancing figures have in common with Williams's descriptions of them?

Robert Herrick (1591–1674)

UPON A CHILD THAT DIED

1648

Here she lies, a pretty bud,
Lately made of flesh and blood.
Who as soon fell fast asleep
As her little eyes did peep.
Give her strewings, but not stir
The earth that lightly covers her.

Saint Geraud [Bill Knott] (b. 1940)

POEM

1968

The only response
to a child's grave is
to lie down before it and play dead

QUESTION

What differences do you find between the effect of Herrick's poem and that of Saint Geraud's? Try to explain how the pattern (or lack of pattern) in each poem contributes to these differences.

Stephen Crane (1871–1900)

THE HEART

1895

In the desert
I saw a creature, naked, bestial,
Who, squatting upon the ground,
Held his heart in his hands,
And ate of it.   5

I said, "Is it good, friend?"
"It is bitter—bitter," he answered;
"But I like it
Because it is bitter,
And because it is my heart."   10

Walt Whitman (1819–1892)

CAVALRY CROSSING A FORD   (1865)

A line in long array where they wind betwixt green islands,
They take a serpentine course, their arms flash in the sun—hark to the
    musical clank,
Behold the silvery river, in it the splashing horses loitering stop to drink,
Behold the brown-faced men, each group, each person a picture, the
    negligent rest on the saddles,
Some emerge on the opposite bank, others are just entering the ford—
    while,
Scarlet and blue and snowy white,
The guidon flags flutter gayly in the wind.

QUESTIONS

The following nit-picking questions are intended to help you see exactly what
makes these two open form poems by Crane and Whitman so different in their
music.

1. What devices of sound occur in Whitman's phrase *silvery river* (line 3)?
   Where else in his poem do you find these devices?
2. Does Crane use any such devices? Try picking out, for instance, all syllables
   that end with the sound of the letter *t*.(There are a surprising number for a
   poem so short.)
3. In number of syllables, Whitman's poem is almost twice as long as Crane's.
   Which poem has more pauses in it? (Count pauses at the ends of lines, at
   marks of punctuation.)
4. Read the two poems aloud. In general, how would you describe the effect of
   their sounds and rhythms? Is Crane's poem necessarily an inferior poem for
   having less music?

Gary Gildner (b. 1938)

FIRST PRACTICE   1969

After the doctor checked to see
we weren't ruptured,
the man with the short cigar took us
under the grade school,
where we went in case of attack   5
or storm, and said

he was Clifford Hill, he was
a man who believed dogs
ate dogs, he had once killed
for his country, and if
there were any girls present
for them to leave now.
                            No one
left. OK, he said, he said I take
that to mean you are hungry
men who hate to lose as much
as I do. OK. Then
he made two lines of us
facing each other,
and across the way, he said,
is the man you hate most
in the world,
and if we are to win
that title I want to see how.
But I don't want to see
any marks when you're dressed,
he said. He said, *Now.*

10

15

20

25

Questions

1. What do you make of Hill and his world-view?
2. How does the speaker reveal his own view? Why, instead of quoting Hill directly ("This is a dog-eat-dog world"), does he call him *a man who believed dogs ate dogs* (lines 8–9)?
3. What effect is made by breaking off and lowering *No one* at the end of line 12?
4. What is gained by having a rime on the poem's last word?
5. For the sake of understanding how right the form of Gildner's poem is for it, imagine the poem in meter and a rime scheme, and condensed into two stanzas:

   Then he made two facing lines of us
   And he said, Across the way,
   Of all the men there are in the world
   Is the man you most want to slay,

   And if we are to win that title, he said,
   I want you to show me how.
   But I don't want to see any marks when you're dressed,
   He said. Go get him. *Now.*

   Why would that rewrite be so unfaithful to what Gildner is saying?
6. How would you answer someone who argued, "This can't be a poem—its subject is ugly and its language isn't beautiful"?

FOR REVIEW AND FURTHER STUDY

Leigh Hunt (1784–1859)

RONDEAU 1838

Jenny kissed me when we met,
   Jumping from the chair she sat in;
Time, you thief, who love to get
   Sweets into your list, put that in:
Say I'm weary, say I'm sad,
   Say that health and wealth have missed me,
Say I'm growing old, but add,
   Jenny kissed me.

QUESTION

Here is a fresh contemporary version of Hunt's "Rondeau" that yanks open the
form of the rimed original:

Jenny kissed me when we met,
jumping from her chair;
Time, you thief, who love to add
sweets into your list, put that in:
say I'm weary, say I'm sad,
say I'm poor and in ill health,
say I'm growing old—but note, too,
Jenny kissed me.

That revised version says approximately the same thing as Hunt's original,
doesn't it? Why is it less effective?

Frank Sidgwick (1879–1939)

THE AERONAUT TO HIS LADY 1921

I
   Through
   Blue
Sky
Fly   5
   To
   You.
Why?

Sweet
   Love,   10
Feet
   Move
      So
      Slow!

1. Describe the form in which this poem is written.
2. Would you guess that anybody could dash off a poem in this form with ease, or that Sidgwick is a skilled poet who had to overcome difficulty? (To find out, try writing a poem in this form and see what difficulties you meet.)
3. An opinion in a recent little magazine: "The form of a poem is the poet's business, not the reader's. Reading a poem, all you have to do is get the message." How well does this opinion apply to "The Aeronaut to his Lady"? Would you take as much pleasure from this poem if you weren't aware of its form? How important is its message?
4. How highly would you rate this poem in comparison to other poems you know? Do you think it a bit of trash? A clever doodad? A deathless masterpiece?
5. Here is a larger question to mull, if you didn't think Sidgwick's poem a masterpiece. What, *in addition to* mastery of form (whether open or closed), do you expect of the finest poetry?

Stevie Smith (1902–1971)

I REMEMBER

1957

It was my bridal night I remember,
An old man of seventy-three
I lay with my young bride in my arms,
A girl with t.b.
It was wartime, and overhead   5
The Germans were making a particularly heavy raid on Hampstead.
What rendered the confusion worse, perversely
Our bombers had chosen that moment to set out for Germany.
Harry, do they ever collide?
I do not think it has ever happened,   10
Oh my bride, my bride.

QUESTIONS

1. From the opening three lines, you might expect a rollicking, roughly metrical ballad or song. But as this poem goes on, how does its form surprise you?
2. What besides form, by the way, is odd or surprising here? Why can't this be called a conventional love lyric?
3. Lewis Turco has proposed the name *Nashers* for a certain kind of line (or couplet) found in the verse of Ogden Nash (whose "Very Like a Whale" appears on page 506). Nashers, according to Turco, are "usually long, of flat free verse or prose with humorous, often multisyllabic endings utilizing wrenched rhymes" (Lewis Turco, *The Book of Forms*, New York: E. P. Dutton, 1968). What Nashers can you find in "I Remember"?
4. What does the poet achieve by ending her poem in an exact rime (*collide/bride*)? Suppose she had ended it with another long, sprawling, unrimed line; for example, "As far as I know from reading the newspapers, O my poor coughing dear." What would be lost?
5. What do you understand to be the *tone* of this poem (the poet's implied attitude toward her material)? Would you call it tender and compassionate? Sorrowful? Grim? Playful and humorous? Earnest?

6. How does noticing the form of this poem help you to understand the tone of it?

Thomas Hardy (1840–1928)

AT A HASTY WEDDING   1901

If hours be years the twain are blest,
For now they solace swift desire
By bonds of every bond the best,
If hours be years. The twain are blest
Do eastern stars slope never west,
Nor pallid ashes follow fire:
If hours be years the twain are blest,
For now they solace swift desire.

QUESTIONS

1. A challenge that a poet faces in writing a **triolet** (another French courtly form) is that, obliged to devote five out of eight lines to repetitions, the poet has little room to say anything. In this triolet, what has Hardy succeeded in saying? Sum up his theme.
2. Why is the image of fire that dies to "pallid ashes" especially appropriate? (Compare the effect of this image to that of other images of pale things in Hardy's "Neutral Tones," page 612, a poem about the aftermath of a love affair.)

Geoffrey Chaucer (1340?–1400)

YOUR YEN TWO WOL SLEE ME SODENLY   (late fourteenth century)

Your yen° two wol slee° me sodenly;   *eyes, slay*
I may the beautee of hem° not sustene°,   *them, resist*
So woundeth hit thourghout my herte kene.

And but° your word wol helen° hastily   *unless, heal*
My hertes wounde, while that hit is grene°,   *new*   5
    Your yen two wol slee me sodenly;
    I may the beautee of hem not sustene.

Upon my trouthe° I sey you feithfully   *word*
That ye ben of my lyf and deeth the quene;
For with my deeth the trouthe° shal be sene.   *truth*   10
    Your yen two wol slee me sodenly;
    I may the beautee of hem not sustene,
    So woundeth it thourghout my herte kene.

YOUR YEN TWO WOL SLEE ME SODENLY. This poem is one of a group of three in the same fixed form, entitled "Merciles Beaute." 3. *so woundeth . . . kene:* "So deeply does it wound me through the heart."

1. This is a **roundel** (or **rondel**), an English form. What are its rules? How does it remind you of French courtly forms such as the villanelle and the triolet?
2. Try writing a roundel of your own in modern English. Although tricky, the form isn't extremely difficult: write only three lines and your poem is already eight-thirteenths finished. Here are some possible opening lines:

Baby, your eyes will slay me. Shut them tight.
Against their glow, I can't hold out for long. . . .

Your eyes present a pin to my balloon:
One pointed look and I start growing small. . . .

Since I escaped from love, I've grown so fat,
I barely can remember being thin. . . .

Wallace Stevens (1879–1955)

THIRTEEN WAYS OF LOOKING AT A BLACKBIRD   1923

I

Among twenty snowy mountains,
The only moving thing
Was the eye of the blackbird.

II

I was of three minds,
Like a tree   5
In which there are three blackbirds.

III

The blackbird whirled in the autumn winds.
It was a small part of the pantomime.

IV

A man and a woman
Are one.   10
A man and a woman and a blackbird
Are one.

V

I do not know which to prefer,
The beauty of inflections
Or the beauty of innuendoes,   15
The blackbird whistling
Or just after.

VI

Icicles filled the long window
With barbaric glass.
The shadow of the blackbird   20

Crossed it, to and fro.
The mood
Traced in the shadow
An indecipherable cause.

VII

O thin men of Haddam,   25
Why do you imagine golden birds?
Do you not see how the blackbird
Walks around the feet
Of the women about you?

VIII

I know noble accents   30
And lucid, inescapable rhythms;
But I know, too,
That the blackbird is involved
In what I know.

IX

When the blackbird flew out of sight,   35
It marked the edge
Of one of many circles.

X

At the sight of blackbirds
Flying in a green light,
Even the bawds of euphony   40
Would cry out sharply.

XI

He rode over Connecticut
In a glass coach.
Once, a fear pierced him,
In that he mistook   45
The shadow of his equipage
For blackbirds.

XII

The river is moving.
The blackbird must be flying.

XIII

It was evening all afternoon.   50
It was snowing
And it was going to snow.
The blackbird sat
In the cedar-limbs.

THIRTEEN WAYS OF LOOKING AT A BLACKBIRD. 25. *Haddam:* This Biblical-sounding name is
that of a town in Connecticut.

1. What is the speaker's attitude toward the men of Haddam? What attitude toward this world does he suggest they lack? What is implied by calling them *thin* (line 25)?
2. What do the landscapes of winter contribute to the poem's effectiveness? If Stevens had chosen images of summer lawns, what would have been lost?
3. In which sections of the poem does Stevens suggest that a unity exists between human being and blackbird, between blackbird and the entire natural world? Can we say that Stevens "philosophizes"? What role does imagery play in Steven's statement of his ideas?
4. What sense can you make of Part X? Make an enlightened guess.
5. Consider any one of the thirteen parts. What patterns of sound and rhythm do you find in it? What kind of structure does it have?
6. If the thirteen parts were arranged in some different order, would the poem be just as good? Or can we find a justification for its beginning with Part I and ending with Part XIII?
7. Does the poem seem an arbitrary combination of thirteen separate poems? Or is there any reason to call it a whole?

EXERCISE: *Seeing the Logic of Open Form Verse*

Read the following poems in open form silently to yourself, noticing what each poet does with white space, repetitions, line breaks, and indentations. Then read the poems aloud, trying to indicate by slight pauses where lines end and also pausing slightly at any space inside a line. Can you see any reasons for the poet's placing his words in this arrangement rather than in a prose paragraph? Do any of these poets seem to care also about visual effect? (As is the case with other kinds of poetry, there may not be any obvious logical reason for everything that happens in these poems.)

E. E. Cummings (1894–1962)

IN JUST-   1923

in Just-
spring   when the world is mud-
luscious the little
lame balloonman

whistles   far   and wee   5

and eddieandbill come
running from marbles and
piracies and it's
spring

when the world is puddle-wonderful   10

the queer
old balloonman whistles
far   and   wee
and bettyandisbel come dancing

from hop-scotch and jump-rope and   15

                    it's
                    spring
                    and
                        the

                            goat-footed   20

balloonMan   whistles
far
and
wee

Myra Cohn Livingston (b. 1926)

DRIVING   1972

Smooth it feels
        wheels
        in the groove of the gray
                roadway
                speedway   5
                freeway

long along the in and out
of gray car
    red car
    blue car   10

catching up and overtaking into
                one lane
                two lane
                three lane

                    it feels   15

over and over and ever and along

Donald Finkel (b. 1929)

GESTURE   1970

My arm sweeps down
    a pliant arc
        whatever I am
            streams through my
                negligent wrist: 5

the poem
        uncoils
                like a
                    whip, and
snaps   10
softly   an inch from your enchanted face.

Charles Olson (1910–1970)

LA CHUTE

my drum, hollowed out thru the thin slit,
carved from the cedar wood, the base I took
when the tree was felled

o my lute, wrought from the tree's crown

my drum, whose lustiness   5
was not to be resisted
                              my lute,
from whose pulsations
not one could turn away

                                        They   10
are where the dead are, my drum fell
where the dead are, who
will bring it up, my lute
who will bring it up where it fell in the face of them
where they are, where my lute and drum have fallen?   15

LA CHUTE. The French title means "The Fall."

22 Poems for the Eye

Let's look at a famous poem with a distinctive visible shape. In the seventeenth century, ingenious poets trimmed their lines into the silhouettes of altars and crosses, pillars and pyramids. Here is one. Is it anything more than a demonstration of ingenuity?

George Herbert (1593–1633)

EASTER WINGS

Lord, who createdst man in wealth and store,
Though foolishly he lost the same,
Decaying more and more
Till he became
Most poor;
With thee
Oh, let me rise
As larks, harmoniously,
And sing this day thy victories;
Then shall the fall further the flight in me.

My tender age in sorrow did begin;
And still with sicknesses and shame
Thou didst so punish sin,
That I became
Most thin.
With thee
Let me combine,
And feel this day thy victory;
For if I imp my wing on thine,
Affliction shall advance the flight in me.

In the next-to-last line, *imp* is a term from falconry meaning to repair the wing of an injured bird by grafting feathers into it.

If we see it merely as a picture, we will have to admit that Herbert's word design does not go far. It renders with difficulty shapes that a sketcher's pencil could set down in a flash. The pencil sketch might have more detail, might be more accurate. Was Herbert's effort wasted? It might have been, were there not more to his poem than meets the eye. The mind, too, is engaged by the visual pattern, by the realization that the words *most thin* are given emphasis by their narrow form. Here, visual pattern points out meaning. Heard aloud, too, "Easter Wings" takes on additional depths. Its rimes, its pattern of rhythm are perceptible. It gives pleasure as any poem in a symmetrical stanza may do: by establishing a pattern that leads the reader to anticipate when another rime or a pause will arrive and then fulfilling that expectation.

Ever since the invention of the alphabet, poems have existed not only as rhythmic sounds upon the air but also as visual patterns made of words. At least some of our pleasure in silently reading a poem derives from the way it looks upon its page. A poem in an open form can engage the eye with snowfields of white space and thickets of close-set words. A poem in stanzas can please us by its visual symmetry. And, far from being merely decorative, the visual devices of a poem can be meaningful, too. White space — as poets demonstrate who work in open forms — can indicate pauses. If white space entirely surrounds a word or phrase or line, then that portion of the poem obviously takes special emphasis. Typographical devices such as capital letters and italics also can lay stress upon words. In most traditional poems, a capital letter at the beginning of each new line helps indicate the importance the poet places upon line-divisions, whose regular intervals make a rhythm out of pauses. And the poet may be trying to show us that certain lines rime by indenting them.

Ever since George Herbert's day, writers have continued to experiment with the appearances of printed poetry. Notable efforts to entertain the eye are Lewis Carroll's rimed mouse's tail in *Alice in Wonderland*; and the *Calligrammes* of Guillaume Apollinaire, who arranged words in the shapes of a necktie, of the Eiffel Tower, and of spears of falling rain. Here is a shaped poem of more recent inspiration:

John Hollander (b. 1929)

SKELETON KEY

1969

Opening and starting key for a
1954 Dodge junked last year.

```
        O with what key
      shall I unlock this
     heart Tight in a coffer
  of chest something awaits a
jab a click a sharp turn yes an
opening Out with it then Let it
pour into forms it molds itself
Much like an escape of dreaming
prisoners taking shape out in a
relenting air in bright volumes
unimaginable even amid anterior
blacknesses let mine run out in
   the sunny roads Let them be
     released by modulations
       of point by bend of
        line too tiny for
        planning out back
         in hopeful dark
         times or places
         How to hold on
         to a part flat
         or wide enough
          to grasp was
          not too hard
          formerly and
           patterned
           edges cut
           themselves
         What midget
         forms shall
           fall in
           line or
          row beyond
          this wall
          of self A
          key can
        open a car
        Why not me
         O let me
           get in
```

Poems for the Eye   599

Evidently the shape of Hollander's car key agrees with what is said in it. A whole poem, of course, does not need to be such a verbal silhouette to have a meaningful appearance. In part of a longer poem, William Carlos Williams has conveyed the way a bellhop runs downstairs:

```
ta tuck a
        ta tuck a
                ta tuck a
                        ta tuck a
                                ta tuck a
```

This is not only good onomatopoeia and an accurate description of a rhythm; the steplike appearance of the lines goes together with their meaning.

Sometimes an unconventional-looking poem represents no familiar object but is an attempt to make the eye follow an unaccustomed path, as in this experiment by E. E. Cummings.

E. E. Cummings (1894–1962)

R-P-O-P-H-E-S-S-A-G-R   1935

```
                        r-p-o-p-h-e-s-s-a-g-r
                who
a)s w(e loo)k
upnowgath
                PPEGORHRASS
                                        eringint(o-
aThe):l
            eA
                !p:
S                                                       a
                        (r
    rIvInG               .gRrEaPsPhOs)
                                        to
rea(be)rran(com)gi(e)ngly
,grasshopper;
```

However startling it may be to eyes accustomed to poems in conventional line arrangements, this experiment is not a shaped poem. What matters is the grasshopperish leaps and backtracks that our eyes must make in unscrambling letters and words, rearranging them into a more usual order.

Though too much importance can be given to the visual element of poetry and though many poets seem hardly to care about it, it can be

another dimension that sets apart poetry from prose. It is at least argua-
ble that some of Walt Whitman's long-line, page-filling descriptions of
the wide ocean, open landscapes, and broad streets of his America,
which meet the eye as wide expanses of words, would lose something —
besides rhythm — if couched in lines only three or four syllables long.
Another poet who deeply cared about visual appearance was William
Blake, graphic artist and engraver as well as a master artist in words. By
publishing his *Songs of Innocence* and *Songs of Experience* (among other
works) with illustrations and accompanying hand-lettered poems, often
interwoven with the lines of the poems, Blake apparently strove to
make poem and appearance of poem a unity, striking mind and eye at
the same time.

The way a poem looks, while significant, is hardly enough in itself to make a poem succeed. To pour just any old words into a silhouette of the Taj Mahal would be as likely to result in a dismal poem as to
arrange them into the pattern of a sonnet. Like other good poems, good
shaped poems appeal not only to sight but to our other faculties, and
they depend upon sound, rhythm, imagery, denotation, and connotation. May Swenson, a poet who has written poems of both kinds, has
insisted that for her the visual arrangement of a poem can be discovered
only after the poem's "whole language structure and behavior" have
been completed: "What the poems say or show, their way of doing it
with *language*, is the main thing."[1] Clearly, if a poem has other virtues,
its visual pattern can be one more means for the poet to speak to us.

May Swenson (b. 1919)
STONE GULLETS   1970

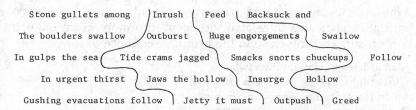

QUESTIONS

1. What do the three curving lines drawn into this poem suggest?
2. Besides depicting something, do they have any other uses to the poem?
3. Read "Stone Gullets" aloud. By what other devices (besides visual ones) does
   the poet communicate meanings?

[1] From an explanatory note at the end of her book of poems, *Iconographs* (New York: Scrib-
ners, 1970).

Some poets who write in English have envied poets who write in Chinese, a language in which certain words look like the things they represent. Consider this Chinese poem:

Wang Wei (701–761)
BIRD-SINGING STREAM
(about 750)

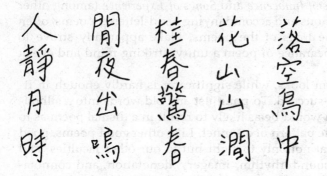

Substituting English words for ideograms, the poem becomes:

man	leisure	cassia	flower	fall
quiet	night	spring	mountain	empty
moon	rise	startle	mountain	bird
at times	sing	spring	stream	middle

Even without the aid of English crib-notes, all of us can read some Chinese if we can recognize a picture of a man. What resemblances can you see between any of the other ideograms and the things they stand for?[2]

Wai-lim Yip, the poet and critic who provided the Chinese text and translation, has also translated the poem into more usual English word order, still keeping close to the original sequence of ideas:

Man at leisure. Cassia flowers fall.
Quiet night. Spring mountain is empty.
Moon rises. Startles—a mountain bird.
It sings at times in the spring stream.

One envious Western poet was Ezra Pound, who included a few Chinese ideograms in his *Cantos* as illustrations. From the scholar Ernest Fenollosa, Pound said he had come to understand why a language written in ideograms "simply *had to stay poetic;* simply couldn't help being and staying poetic in a way that a column of English type might

[2] To help you compare English and Chinese, the Chinese original has been arranged in Western word-order. (Ordinarily, in Chinese, the word for "man" would appear at the upper right.)

very well not stay poetic."[3] Having an imperfect command of Chinese, Pound greatly overestimated the tendency of the language to depict things. (Only a small number of characters in modern Chinese are pictures; Chinese characters, like Western alphabets, also indicate the sounds of words.) Still, Pound's misunderstanding was fruitful. Thanks to his influence, many other recent poets were encouraged to consider the appearance of words.[4] E. E. Cummings, in a poem that begins "mOOn Over tOwns mOOn," has reveled in the fact that O's are moon-shaped. Aram Saroyan, in a poem entitled "crickets," makes capital of the fact that the word *cricket* somewhat resembles the snub-nosed insect of approximately the same length. The poem begins,

    crickets
    crickets
    crickets
    crickets

and goes on down its page like that, for thirty-seven lines. (Read aloud, by the way, the poem sounds somewhat like crickets chirping!) In recent years, a movement called **concrete poetry** has traveled far and wide. Though practitioners of the art disagree over its definition, what most concretists seem to do is make designs out of letters and words.

Reinhard Döhl (b. 1934)

1965

```
        ,pfelApfelApfelApfein
      ,felApfelApfelApfelApfelA,
     ,felApfelApfelApfelApfelApfe
    ApfelApfelApfelApfelApfelApf
    pfelApfelApfelApfelApfelApfel
    lApfelApfelApfelApfelApfelApfe
    pfelApfelApfelApfelApfelApfelA
    ApfelApfelApfelApfelApfelApfe
    felApfelApfelApfelApfelApfel
    \pfelApfelApfelApfelApfelApf
     elApfelApfelApfelWurmAp
     felApfelApfelApfelApfel
      ofelApfelApfelApfel
       felApfelApfelA
        felApfel
```

[3] *The ABC of Reading* (Norfolk, Conn., 1960), p. 22.
[4] For a good brief discussion of Pound's misunderstanding and its influence, see Milton Klonsky's introduction to his anthology *Speaking Pictures: A Gallery of Pictorial Poetry from the Sixteenth Century to the Present* (New York: Harmony, 1975).

1. Translate this concrete poem.
2. Do you think we should call it a poem? Why? Or why not?

Other concrete poets wield typography like a brush dipped in paint, using such techniques as blow-up, montage, and superimposed elements (the same words printed many times on top of the same impression, so that the result is blurriness). They may even keep words in a usual order, perhaps employing white space as freely as any writer of open form verse. According to Mary Ellen Solt, an American concretist, we can tell a concrete poem by its "concentration upon the physical material from which the poem or text is made."[5] Still another practitioner, Richard Kostelanetz, has suggested that a more accurate name for concrete poetry might be "word-imagery." He sees it occupying an area somewhere between conventional poetry and visual art.[6]

What makes concretism look foolish or impossible to understand (to those who approach it as if it ought to be traditional poetry) may be that concretists often use words without placing them in context with any other words. Aram Saroyan has a concrete poem consisting of a page blank except for one word: *oxygen*.

Much concrete poetry is clearly "something to look at rather than to read," Louis Untermeyer has said unsympathetically. And yet certain concrete poems can please as good poems always do: by their connotations, figures of speech, sounds, and metaphors—not to mention their rewards to the eye.

Ian Hamilton Finlay (b. 1925)

THE HORIZON OF HOLLAND   1963

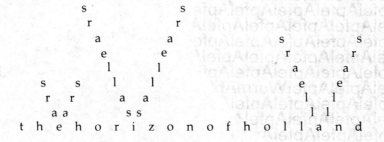

[5] Introduction to her anthology *Concrete Poetry: A World View* (Bloomington, Ind.: Indiana University Press, 1969).
[6] Introduction to his anthology *Imaged Words and Worded Images* (New York: Outerbridge and Dienstfrey, 1970).

Like E. E. Cummings's grasshoppers (p. 600), Finlay's verbal windmills make us search out a familiar word order. But in Finlay's poem our pleasure lies not only in puzzling out a sentence ("The horizon of Holland is all ears"), but also in beholding a shape that strikes the eye and in making a connection between it and an image that the title brings to mind. This is something other than what happens in a shaped poem such as "Skeleton Key" (p. 599) and "Easter Wings" (p. 597), where individual letters of the alphabet are not in themselves especially important.

Admittedly, some concrete poems mean less than meets the eye. In this fact, they seem more rigidly confined to the printed page than shaped poems such as "Easter Wings." A good shaped poem, though it would lose much if heard and not seen, still might be a satisfying poem. That many pretentious doodlers have taken up concretism may have caused a *Time* writer to sneer: did Joyce Kilmer miss all that much by never having seen a poem lovely as a

```
        t
       ttt
      rrrrr
     rrrrrrr
    eeeeeeeee
      ???
```

However, like other structures of language, concrete poems evidently can have the effect of poetry, if written by poets. Whether or not it ought to be dubbed "poetry," this art can do what poems traditionally have done: use language in delightful ways that reveal meanings to us.

Edwin Morgan (b. 1920)
Siesta of a Hungarian Snake   1968

s sz sz SZ sz SZ sz ZS zs ZS zs zs z

Questions

1. What do you suppose Morgan is trying to indicate by reversing the order of the two letters in mid line?
2. What, if anything, about this snake seems Hungarian?
3. Does the sound of its consonants matter?

Dorthi Charles (b. 1960)

CONCRETE CAT   1971

QUESTIONS

1. What does this writer indicate by capitalizing the *a* in *ear*? The *y* in *eye*? The *u* in mouth? By using spaces between the letters in the word *tail*?
2. Why is the word *mouse* upside down?
3. What possible pun might be seen in the cat's middle stripe?
4. What is the tone of "Concrete Cat"? How is it made evident?
5. Do these words seem chosen for their connotations or only for their denotations? Would you call this work of art a poem?

EXPERIMENT: *Do It Yourself*

Make a concrete poem of your own. If you need inspiration, pick some familiar object or animal and try to find words that look like it. For more ideas, study the typography of a magazine or newspaper; cut out interesting letters and numerals and try pasting them into arrangements. What (if anything) do your experiments tell you about familiar letters and words? You might also find it helpful to read a book of concrete poetry. Some are mentioned in this chapter. Another useful anthology is that of Emmett Williams, *Anthology of Concrete Poetry* (New York: Something Else Press, 1967).

23 Symbol

The national flag is supposed to bestir our patriotic feelings. When a black cat crosses his path, a superstitious man shivers, foreseeing bad luck. To each of these, by custom, our society expects a standard response. A flag, a black cat's crossing one's path — each is a **symbol:** a visible object or action that suggests some further meaning in addition to itself. In literature, a symbol might be the word *flag* or the words *a black cat crossed his path* or every description of flag or cat in an entire novel, story, play, or poem.

A flag and the crossing of a black cat may be called **conventional symbols,** since they can have a conventional or customary effect on us. Conventional symbols are also part of the language of poetry, as we know when we meet the red rose, emblem of love, in a lyric, or the Christian cross in the devotional poems of George Herbert. More often, however, symbols in literature have no conventional, long-established meaning, but particular meanings of their own. In Melville's novel *Moby Dick,* to take a rich example, whatever we associate with the great white whale is *not* attached unmistakably to white whales by custom. Though Melville tells us that men have long regarded whales with awe and relates Moby Dick to the celebrated fish that swallowed Jonah, the reader's response is to one particular whale, the creature of Herman Melville. Only the experience of reading the novel in its entirety can give Moby Dick his particular meaning.

We should say *meanings,* for as Eudora Welty has observed, it is a good thing Melville made Moby Dick a whale, a creature large enough to contain all that critics have found in him. A symbol in literature, if not conventional, has more than just one meaning. In "The Raven," by Edgar Allan Poe, the appearance of a strange black bird in the narrator's study is sinister; and indeed, if we take the poem seriously, we may even respond with a sympathetic shiver of dread. Does the bird mean death, fate, melancholy, the loss of a loved one, knowledge in the service of evil? All these, perhaps. Like any well-chosen symbol, Poe's raven sets going within the reader an unending train of feelings and associations.

We miss the value of a symbol, however, if we think it can mean absolutely anything we wish. If a poet has any control over our reactions, the poem will guide our responses in a certain direction.

T. S. Eliot (1888–1965)

THE BOSTON EVENING TRANSCRIPT   1917

The readers of the *Boston Evening Transcript*
Sway in the wind like a field of ripe corn.

When evening quickens faintly in the street,
Wakening the appetites of life in some
And to others bringing the *Boston Evening Transcript*,
I mount the steps and ring the bell, turning
Wearily, as one would turn to nod good-bye to La Rochefoucauld,
If the street were time and he at the end of the street,
And I say, "Cousin Harriet, here is the *Boston Evening Transcript*."

The newspaper, whose name Eliot purposely repeats so monotonously, indicates what this poem is about. Now defunct, the *Transcript* covered in detail the slightest activity of Boston's leading families and was noted for the great length of its obituaries. Eliot, then, uses the newspaper as a symbol for an existence of boredom, fatigue (*Wearily*), petty and unvarying routine (since an evening newspaper, like night, arrives on schedule). The *Transcript* evokes a way of life without zest or passion, for, opposed to people who read it, Eliot sets people who do not: those whose desires revive, not expire, when the working day is through. Suggestions abound in the ironic comparison of the *Transcript*'s readers to a cornfield late in summer. To mention only a few: the readers sway because they are sleepy; they vegetate; they are drying up; each makes a rattling sound when turning a page. It is not necessary that we know the remote and similarly disillusioned friend to whom the speaker might nod: La Rochefoucauld, whose cynical *Maxims* entertained Parisian society under Louis XIV (sample: "All of us have enough strength to endure the misfortunes of others"). We understand that the nod is symbolic of an immense weariness of spirit. We know nothing about Cousin Harriet, whom the speaker addresses, but imagine from the greeting she inspires that she is probably a bore.

If Eliot wishes to say that certain Bostonians lead lives of sterile boredom, why does he couch his meaning in symbols? Why doesn't he tell us directly what he means? These questions imply two assumptions not necessarily true: first, that Eliot has a message to impart; second, that he is concealing it. We have reason to think that Eliot did not usually have a message in mind when beginning a poem, for as he once told a critic: "The conscious problems with which one is concerned in the actual writing are more those of a quasi musical nature . . . than of a conscious exposition of ideas." Poets sometimes discover what they have to say while in the act of saying it. And it may be that in his *Transcript* poem, Eliot is saying exactly what he means. By communicating his meaning through symbols instead of statements, he may be choosing the only kind of language appropriate to an idea of great subtlety and complexity. (The paraphrase "Certain Bostonians are bored" hardly begins to describe the poem in all its possible meaning.) And by his use of symbolism, Eliot affords us the pleasure of finding our own entrances to his poem. Another great strength of a symbol is that, like some figures of speech, it renders the abstract in concrete terms, and, like any other image, refers to what we can perceive — an object like a newspaper, a gesture like a nod. Eliot might, like Robert Frost, have called himself a "synecdochist." Frost explained: "Always a larger significance. A little thing touches a larger thing."

This power of suggestion that a symbol contains is, perhaps, its greatest advantage. Sometimes, as in the following poem by Emily Dickinson, a symbol will lead us from a visible object to something too vast to be perceived.

Emily Dickinson (1830–1886)

THE LIGHTNING IS A YELLOW FORK (about 1870)

The Lightning is a yellow Fork
From Tables in the sky
By inadvertent fingers dropt
The awful Cutlery

Of mansions never quite disclosed
And never quite concealed
The Apparatus of the Dark
To ignorance revealed.

If the lightning is a fork, then whose are the fingers that drop it, the table from which it slips, the household to which it belongs? The poem implies this question without giving an answer. An obvious answer is "God," but can we be sure? We wonder, too, about these partially lighted mansions: if our vision were clearer, what would we behold?[1]

---

[1] In its suggestion of an infinite realm that mortal eyes cannot quite see, but whose nature can be perceived fleetingly through things visible, Emily Dickinson's poem, by coincidence, resembles the work of late-nineteenth-century French poets called **symbolists.** To a symbolist the shirt-tail of Truth is continually seen disappearing around a corner. With their Neoplatonic view of ideal realities existing in a great beyond, whose corresponding symbols are the perceptible cats that bite us and tangible stones we stumble over, French poets such as Charles Baudelaire, Jules Laforgue, and Stéphane Mallarmé were profoundly to affect poets writing in English, notably Yeats (who said a poem "entangles . . . a part of the Divine essence") and Eliot. But we consider in this chapter symbolism as an element in certain poems, not Symbolism, the literary movement.

"But how am I supposed to know a symbol when I see one?" The best approach is to read poems closely, taking comfort in the likelihood that it is better not to notice symbols at all than to find significance in every literal stone and huge meanings in every thing. In looking for the symbols in a poem, pick out all the references to concrete objects — newspapers, black cats, twisted pins. Consider these with special care. Note any that the poet emphasizes by detailed description, by repetition, or by placing at the very beginning or end of the poem. Ask: What is the poem about, what does it add up to? If, when the poem is paraphrased, the paraphrase depends primarily upon the meaning of certain concrete objects, these richly suggestive objects may be the symbols.

There are some things a literary symbol usually is *not*. A symbol is not an abstraction. Such terms as *truth, death, love,* and *justice* cannot work as symbols (unless personified, as in the traditional figure of Justice holding a scale). Most often, a symbol is something we can see in the mind's eye: a newspaper, a lightning bolt, a gesture of nodding good-bye.

In narratives, a well-developed character who speaks much dialogue and is not the least bit mysterious is usually not a symbol. But watch out for an executioner in a black hood; a character, named for a Biblical prophet, who does little but utter a prophecy; a trio of old women who resemble the Three Fates. (It has been argued, with good reason, that Milton's fully rounded character of Satan in *Paradise Lost* is a symbol embodying evil and human pride, but a narrower definition of symbol is more frequently useful.) A symbol *may* be a part of a person's body (the baleful eye of the murder victim in Poe's story "The Tell-Tale Heart") or a look, a voice, a mannerism.

A symbol usually is not the second term of a metaphor. In the line "The lightning is a yellow fork," the symbol is the lightning, not the fork.

Sometimes a symbol addresses a sense other than sight: the sound of a mysterious harp at the end of Chekhov's play *The Cherry Orchard;* or, in William Faulkner's tale "A Rose for Emily," the odor of decay that surrounds the house of the last survivor of a town's leading family — suggesting not only physical dissolution but also the decay of a social order. A symbol is a special kind of image, for it exceeds the usual image in the richness of its connotations. The dead wife's cold comb in the haiku of Buson (discussed on p. 464) works symbolically, suggesting among other things the chill of the grave, the contrast between the living and the dead.

Holding a narrower definition than that used in this book, some readers of poetry prefer to say that a symbol is always a concrete object, never an act. They would deny the label "symbol" to Ahab's breaking his tobacco pipe before setting out to pursue Moby Dick (suggesting, perhaps, his determination to allow no pleasure to distract him from the chase) or to any large motion (as Ahab's whole quest). This distinction, while confining, does have the merit of sparing one from seeing all motion to be possibly symbolic. Some would call Ahab's gesture not a symbol but a **symbolic act.**

To sum up: a symbol radiates hints or casts long shadows (to use Henry James's metaphor). We are unable to say it "stands for" or "represents" a meaning. It evokes, it suggests, it manifests. It demands no single necessary interpretation, such as the interpretation a driver gives to a red traffic light. Rather, like Emily Dickinson's lightning bolt, it points toward an indefinite meaning, which may lie in part beyond the reach of words. In a symbol, as Thomas Carlyle said in *Sartor Resartus*, "the Infinite is made to blend with the Finite, to stand visible, and as it were, attainable there."

Emily Dickinson (1830–1886)

I HEARD A FLY BUZZ — WHEN I DIED   (about 1862)

I heard a Fly buzz–when I died–
The Stillness in the Room
Was like the Stillness in the Air–
Between the Heaves of Storm–

The Eyes around–had wrung them dry–
And Breaths were gathering firm
For that last Onset–when the King
Be witnessed–in the Room–

I willed my Keepsakes–Signed away
What portion of me be   10
Assignable–and then it was
There interposed a Fly–

With Blue–uncertain stumbling Buzz–
Between the light–and me–
And when the Windows failed–and then   15
I could not see to see–

QUESTIONS

1. Why is the poem written in the past tense? Where is the speaker at present?
2. What do you understand from the repetition of the word *see* in the last line?
3. What does the poet mean by *Eyes around* (line 5), *that last Onset* (line 7), *the King* (line 7), and *What portion of me be / Assignable* (lines 10–11)?
4. In line 13, how can a sound be called *Blue* and *stumbling*?
5. What further meaning might *the Windows* (line 15) suggest, in addition to denoting the windows of the room?
6. What connotations of the word *fly* seem relevant to an account of a death?
7. Summarize your interpretation of the poem. What does the fly mean?

Thomas Hardy (1840–1928)

NEUTRAL TONES

1898

We stood by a pond that winter day,
And the sun was white, as though chidden of God,
And a few leaves lay on the starving sod;
  — They had fallen from an ash, and were gray.

Your eyes on me were as eyes that rove   5
Over tedious riddles of years ago;
And some words played between us to and fro
  On which lost the more by our love.

The smile on your mouth was the deadest thing
Alive enough to have strength to die;   10
And a grin of bitterness swept thereby
  Like an ominous bird a-wing. . . .

Since then, keen lessons that love deceives,
And wrings with wrong, have shaped to me
Your face, and the God-curst sun, and a tree,   15
  And a pond edged with grayish leaves.

QUESTIONS

1. Sum up the story told in this poem. In lines 1–12, what is the dramatic situation? What has happened in the interval between the experience related in these lines and the reflection in the last stanza?
2. What meanings do you find in the title?
3. Explain in your own words the metaphor in line 2.
4. What connotations appropriate to this poem does the *ash* (line 4) have, that *oak* or *maple* would lack?
5. What visible objects in the poem function symbolically? What actions or gestures?

If we read of a ship, its captain, its sailors, and the rough seas, and we realize we are reading about a commonwealth and how its rulers and workers keep it going even in difficult times, then we are reading an **allegory**. Closely akin to symbolism, allegory is a description — usually narrative — in which persons, places, and things are employed in a continuous system of equivalents.

Although more strictly limited in its suggestions than symbolism, allegory need not be thought inferior. Few poems continue to interest readers more than Dante's allegorical *Divine Comedy*. Sublime evidence of the appeal of allegory may be found in Christ's use of the **parable:** a brief narrative — usually allegorical but sometimes not — that teaches a moral.

Matthew 13:24–30 (Authorized or King James Version, 1611)

THE PARABLE OF THE GOOD SEED

The kingdom of heaven is likened unto a man which sowed good seed in his field:

But while men slept, his enemy came and sowed tares among the wheat, and went his way.

But when the blade was sprung up, and brought forth fruit, then appeared the tares also.

So the servants of the householder came and said unto him, Sir, didst not thou sow good seed in thy field? From whence then hath it tares?

He said unto them, An enemy hath done this. The servants said unto him, Wilt thou then that we go and gather them up?

But he said, Nay; lest while ye gather up the tares, ye root up also the wheat with them.

Let both grow together until the harvest: and in the time of harvest I will say to the reapers, Gather ye together first the tares, and bind them in bundles to burn them: but gather the wheat into my barn.

The sower is the Son of man, the field is the world, the good seed are the children of the Kingdom, the tares are the children of the wicked one, the enemy is the devil, the harvest is the end of the world, the reapers are angels. "As therefore the tares are gathered and burned in the fire; so shall it be in the end of this world" (Matthew 13:36–42).

Usually, as in this parable, the meanings of an allegory are plainly labeled or thinly disguised. In John Bunyan's allegorical narrative *The Pilgrim's Progress*, it is clear that the hero Christian, on his journey through places with such pointed names as Vanity Fair, the Valley of the Shadow of Death, and Doubting Castle, is the soul, traveling the road of life on the way toward Heaven. An allegory, when carefully built, is systematic. It makes one principal comparison, the working out of whose details may lead to further comparisons, then still further comparisons: Christian, thrown by Giant Despair into the dungeon of Doubting Castle, escapes by means of a key called Promise. Such a complicated design may take great length to unfold, as in Spenser's *Faerie Queene*; but, the method may be seen in a short poem:

George Herbert (1593–1633)

REDEMPTION

1633

Having been tenant long to a rich Lord,
  Not thriving, I resolvèd to be bold,
And make a suit unto him to afford
  A new small-rented lease and cancel th' old.

In Heaven at his manor I him sought.   5
    They told me there that he was lately gone
About some land which he had dearly bought
    Long since on earth, to take possession.
I straight returned, and knowing his great birth,
    Sought him accordingly in great resorts,   10
    In cities, theaters, gardens, parks, and courts.
At length I heard a ragged noise and mirth
    Of thieves and murderers; there I him espied,
    Who straight "Your suit is granted," said, and died.

QUESTIONS

1. In this allegory, what equivalents does Herbert give each of these terms:
   *tenant, Lord, not thriving, suit, new lease, old lease, manor, land, dearly bought,
   take possession, his great birth?*
2. What scene is depicted in the last three lines?

     An object in allegory is like a bird whose cage is clearly lettered
with its identity—"RAVEN, *Corvus corax*; habitat of specimen, Maine."
A symbol, by contrast, is a bird with piercing eyes that mysteriously appears one evening in your library. It is there; you can touch it. But what
does it mean? You look at it. It continues to look at you.

     Whether an object in literature is a symbol, part of an allegory, or
no such thing at all, it has at least one sure meaning. Moby Dick is first a
whale, the *Boston Evening Transcript* a newspaper. Besides deriving a
multitude of intangible suggestions from the title symbol in Eliot's long
poem *The Waste Land*, its readers cannot fail to carry away a sense of the
land's physical appearance: a river choked with sandwich papers and
cigarette ends, London Bridge "under the brown fog of a winter dawn."
A virtue of *The Pilgrim's Progress* is that its walking abstractions are no
mere abstractions but are also human: Giant Despair is a henpecked
husband. The most vital element of a literary work may pass us by,
unless before seeking further depths in a thing, we look to the thing itself.

Sir Philip Sidney (1554–1586)

YOU THAT WITH ALLEGORY'S CURIOUS FRAME   1591

You that with allegory's curious frame
    Of others' children changelings use to make,
    With me those pains, for God's sake, do not take;
    I list not° dig so deep for brazen fame.   *I do not choose to*
When I say Stella, I do mean the same   5
    Princess of beauty for whose only sake
    The reins of love I love, though never slake,
    And joy therein, though nations count it shame.

I beg no subject to use eloquence,
  Nor in hid ways do guide philosophy;   10
  Look at my hands for no such quintessence,
But know that I in pure simplicity
  Breathe out the flames which burn within my heart,
  Love only reading unto me this art.

Mina Loy (1881–1966)
OMEN OF VICTORY   1958

Women in uniform

relaxed for tea

under a shady garden tree

discover

a dove's feather

fallen in the sugar.

QUESTIONS
1. What does the conventional symbol of a dove usually indicate?
2. What do you understand from the symbol of the dove's feather in the sugar bowl? Do you take it to be an omen of something desirable, an evil omen of something the women in uniform don't wish, or aren't you sure?

Hart Crane (1899–1932)
BLACK TAMBOURINE   1926

The interests of a black man in a cellar
Mark tardy judgment on the world's closed door.
Gnats toss in the shadow of a bottle,
And a roach spans a crevice in the floor.

Aesop, driven to pondering, found
Heaven with the tortoise and the hare;
Fox brush and sow ear top his grave
And mingling incantations on the air.

The black man, forlorn in the cellar,
Wanders in some mid-kingdom, dark, that lies,   10
Between his tambourine, stuck on the wall,
And, in Africa, a carcass quick with flies.

QUESTIONS
1. According to tradition, Aesop, the Greek author of fables, was a slave. Do you think Crane means that Aesop's condition and the black man's are iden-

tical? What suggestions arise from the animals that Aesop "found Heaven with"? From the creatures that keep the black man company (lines 3–4)?

2. What do you make of the symbol of the tambourine? Of the symbol in the last line: the slain animal?

3. What *mid-kingdom* do you think the poet means? What do you understand by *the world's closed door*? If the black man is being kept in the cellar, what is this house?

EXERCISE: *Symbol Hunting*

After you have read each of these poems, decide which description best suits it:
1. The poem has a central symbol.
2. The poem contains no symbolism, but is to be taken literally.

William Carlos Williams (1883–1963)

POEM
1934

As the cat
climbed over
the top of

the jamcloset
first the right
forefoot
5

carefully
then the hind
stepped down

into the pit of
the empty
flowerpot
10

Theodore Roethke (1908–1963)

NIGHT CROW
1948

When I saw that clumsy crow
Flap from a wasted tree,
A shape in the mind rose up:
Over the gulfs of dream
Flew a tremendous bird
Further and further away
Into a moonless black,
Deep in the brain, far back.

John Donne (1572–1631)

A BURNT SHIP

1633

Out of a fired ship which by no way
But drowning could be rescued from the flame
Some men leaped forth, and ever as they came
Near the foe's ships, did by their shot decay;
So all were lost, which in the ship were found,
    They in the sea being burnt, they in the burnt ship drowned.

Wallace Stevens (1879–1955)

ANECDOTE OF THE JAR

1923

I placed a jar in Tennessee,
And round it was, upon a hill.
It made the slovenly wilderness
Surround that hill.

The wilderness rose up to it,   5
And sprawled around, no longer wild.
The jar was round upon the ground
And tall and of a port in air.

It took dominion everywhere.
The jar was gray and bare.   10
It did not give of bird or bush,
Like nothing else in Tennessee.

T. S. Eliot (1888–1965)

RHAPSODY ON A WINDY NIGHT

1917

Twelve o'clock.
Along the reaches of the street
Held in a lunar synthesis,
Whispering lunar incantations
Dissolve the floors of memory   5
And all its clear relations
Its divisions and precisions,
Every street-lamp that I pass
Beats like a fatalistic drum,
And through the spaces of the dark   10
Midnight shakes the memory
As a madman shakes a dead geranium.

Half-past one,
The street-lamp sputtered,
The street-lamp muttered,
The street-lamp said, "Regard that woman   15
Who hesitates toward you in the light of the door
Which opens on her like a grin.
You see the border of her dress
Is torn and stained with sand,   20
And you see the corner of her eye
Twists like a crooked pin."

The memory throws up high and dry
A crowd of twisted things;
A twisted branch upon the beach   25
Eaten smooth, and polished
As if the world gave up
The secret of its skeleton,
Stiff and white.
A broken spring in a factory yard,   30
Rust that clings to the form that the strength has left
Hard and curled and ready to snap.

Half-past two,
The street-lamp said,
"Remark the cat which flattens itself in the gutter,   35
Slips out its tongue
And devours a morsel of rancid butter."
So the hand of the child, automatic,
Slipped out and pocketed a toy that was running along the quay.
I could see nothing behind that child's eye.   40
I have seen eyes in the street
Trying to peer through lighted shutters,
And a crab one afternoon in a pool,
An old crab with barnacles on his back,
Gripped the end of a stick which I held him.   45

Half-past three,
The lamp sputtered,
The lamp muttered in the dark.
The lamp hummed:
"Regard the moon,   50
La lune ne garde aucune rancune,
She winks a feeble eye,
She smiles into corners.
She smooths the hair of the grass.
The moon has lost her memory.   55

A washed-out smallpox cracks her face,
Her hand twists a paper rose,
That smells of dust and eau de Cologne,

She is alone
With all the old nocturnal smells   60
That cross and cross across her brain."
The reminiscence comes
Of sunless dry geraniums
And dust in crevices,
Smells of chestnuts in the streets,   65
And female smells in shuttered rooms,
And cigarettes in corridors
And cocktail smells in bars.

The lamp said,
"Four o'clock,   70
Here is the number on the door.
Memory!
You have the key,
The little lamp spreads a ring on the stair.
Mount.   75
The bed is open; the tooth-brush hangs on the wall,
Put your shoes at the door, sleep, prepare for life."

The last twist of the knife.

Questions

1. Comment on the title. What sort of utterance is a rhapsody? What does the term mean in musical composition? Is it any more appropriate that the speaker's experience occurs on a windy night instead of on, say, a clear day at noon?
2. What happens to *memory* in the first twelve lines? What uses of memory are made throughout the remainder of the poem?
3. Into what sections or episodes can the poem clearly be divided? What marks the beginning of each episode?
4. In each episode, what happens? What parallel organization do the second and succeeding episodes have?
5. In general, how would you describe the process by which, in the second and each succeeding episode, one image leads to others?
6. In lines 33–45, what do cat, child, peering eyes, and crab have in common?
7. The description of a street lamp in lines 8–9 is not a hallucination. Gas-burning street lamps *did* pulsate and make a drumming sound. What other symbols in the poem also seem products of exact observation?
8. How do you visualize the comparison in lines 21–22?
9. Line 51 is a quotation from the French symbolist poet Laforgue: "The moon holds no grudge." What does the moon, as personified in this episode, have in common with the woman in the doorway (lines 16–22)? What does it have in common with the street lamp?
10. What patterns of sound and rhythm help bind the poem together?
11. What do you make of the tooth-brush on the wall (line 76)? What does it have to do with the *last twist of the knife* (line 78)?
12. Compare this poem with "The *Boston Evening Transcript*" (p. 608) and with "The Love Song of J. Alfred Prufrock" (p. 746). Do the symbols in these poems point to any mutual themes?

24 Myth

Poets have long been fond of retelling **myths,** narrowly defined as traditional stories of immortal beings. Such stories taken collectively may also be called **myth** or **mythology.** In one of the most celebrated collections of myth ever assembled, the *Metamorphoses*, the poet Ovid has told — to take one example from many — how Phaeton, child of the sun god, rashly tried to drive his father's fiery chariot on its daily round, lost control of the horses, and caused disaster both to himself and to the world. Our use of the term *myth* in discussing poetry, then, differs from its use in expressions such as "the myth of communism" and "the myth of democracy." In these examples, myth, in its broadest sense, is any idea people believe in, whether true or false. Nor do we mean — to take another familiar use of the word — a cock-and-bull story: "Judge Rapp doesn't roast speeders alive; that's just a *myth.*" In the following discussion, *myth* will mean — as critic Northrop Frye has put it — "the imitation of actions near or at the conceivable limits of desire." Myths tell us of the exploits of the gods — their battles, the ways in which they live, love, and perhaps suffer — all on a scale of magnificence larger than our life. We envy their freedom and power; they enact our wishes and dreams. Whether we believe in them or not, their adventures are myths: Ovid, it seems, placed no credence in the stories he related, for he declared, "I prate of ancient poets' monstrous lies."

And yet it is characteristic of a myth that it *can* be believed. Throughout history, myths have accompanied religious doctrines and rituals. They have helped sanction or recall the reasons for religious observances. A sublime instance is the New Testament account of the Last Supper. Because of it and its record of the words of Jesus, "This do in remembrance of Me," Christians have continued to re-enact the offering and partaking of the body and blood of their Lord, under the appearances of bread and wine. It is essential to recall that, just because a myth narrates the acts of a god, we do not necessarily mean by the term a false or fictitious narrative. When we speak of the "myth of Islam" or "the Christian myth," we do so without implying either belief or disbelief. Myths can also help sanction customs and institutions other than religious ones. At the same time the baking of bread was introduced to ancient Greece—one theory goes—there was introduced the myth of Demeter, goddess of grain, who had kindly sent her emissary Triptolemus to teach humankind this valuable art—thus helping to persuade the distrustful that bread was a good thing. Some myths seem made to divert and regale, not to sanction anything. Such may be the story of the sculptor Pygmalion, who fell in love with his statue of a woman; so exquisite was his work, so deep was his feeling, that Aphrodite brought the statue to life. And yet perhaps the story goes deeper than mere diversion: perhaps it is a way of saying that works of art achieve a reality of their own, that love can transform or animate its object.

How does a myth begin? Several theories have been proposed, none universally accepted. One is that a myth is a way to explain some natural phenomenon. Winter comes and the vegetation perishes because Persephone, child of Demeter, must return to the underworld for four months every year. This theory, as classical scholar Edith Hamilton has pointed out, may lead us to think incorrectly that Greek mythology was the creation of a primitive people. Tales of the gods of Mount Olympus may reflect an earlier inheritance, but Greek myths known to us were transcribed in an era of high civilization. Anthropologists have questioned whether primitive people generally find beauty in the mysteries of nature. "From my own study of living myths among savages," wrote Bronislaw Malinowski, "I should say that primitive man has to a very limited extent the purely artistic or scientific interest in nature; there is but little room for symbolism in his ideas and tales; and myth, in fact, is not an idle rhapsody . . . but a hard-working, extremely important cultural force."[1] Such a practical function was seen by Sir James Frazer in *The Golden Bough:* myths were originally expressions of human hope that nature would be fertile. Still another theory is that, once upon a time, heroes of myth were human prototypes. The Greek philosopher Euhemerus declared myths to be tales of real persons, which poets had exaggerated. Most present-day historians of myth would seek no general explanation but would say that different myths probably have different origins.

Poets have many coherent mythologies on which to draw; perhaps those most frequently consulted by British and American poets are the classical, the Christian, the Norse, and folk myth of the American frontier (embodying the deeds of superhuman characters such as Paul Bunyan). Some poets have taken inspiration from other myths as well: T. S. Eliot's *The Waste Land,* for example, is enriched by allusions to Buddhism and to pagan vegetation-cults.

As a tour through any good art museum will demonstrate, myth

---

[1] Bronislaw Malinowski, *Myth in Primitive Psychology* (1926); reprinted in *Magic, Science and Religion* (New York: Doubleday, 1954), p. 97.

pervades much of the graphic art of Western civilization. In literature, one evidence of its continuing value to recent poets and storytellers is the frequency with which myths — both primitive and civilized — are retold. William Faulkner's story "The Bear" recalls tales of Indian totem animals; John Updike's novel *The Centaur* presents the horse-man Chiron as a modern high school teacher; Hart Crane's poem "For the Marriage of Faustus and Helen" unites two figures of different myths, who dance to jazz; T. S. Eliot's plays bring into the drawing-room the myths of Alcestis (*The Cocktail Party*) and the Eumenides (*The Family Reunion*); Jean Cocteau's film *Orphée* shows us Eurydice riding to the underworld with an escort of motorcycles. Popular interest in such works may testify to the profound appeal myths continue to hold for us. Like any other large body of knowledge that can be alluded to, myth offers the poet an instant means of communication — if the reader also knows the particular myth cited. Writing "Lycidas," John Milton could depend upon his readers — mostly persons of similar classical learning — to understand him without footnotes. Today, a poet referring to a traditional myth must be sure to choose a reasonably well known one, or else write as well as T. S. Eliot, whose work has compelled his readers to single out his allusions and look them up. Like other varieties of poetry, myth is a kind of knowledge, not at odds with scientific knowledge but existing in addition to it.

D. H. Lawrence (1885–1930)

Bavarian Gentians

1932

Not every man has gentians in his house
In soft September, at slow, sad Michaelmas.

Bavarian gentians, big and dark, only dark
darkening the daytime, torch-like with the smoking blueness of Pluto's
    gloom,
ribbed and torch-like, with their blaze of darkness spread blue   5
down flattening into points, flattened under the sweep of white day
torch-flower of the blue-smoking darkness, Pluto's dark-blue daze,
black lamps from the halls of Dis, burning dark blue,
giving off darkness, blue darkness, as Demeter's pale lamps give off light,
lead me then, lead the way.   10

Reach me a gentian, give me a torch!
let me guide myself with the blue, forked torch of this flower
down the darker and darker stairs, where blue is darkened on blueness
even where Persephone goes, just now, from the frosted September
to the sightless realm where darkness is awake upon the dark   15

and Persephone herself is but a voice
or a darkness invisible enfolded in the deeper dark
of the arms Plutonic, and pierced with the passion of dense gloom,
among the splendor of torches of darkness, shedding darkness on the lost
      bride and her groom.

BAVARIAN GENTIANS. 4. *Pluto:* Roman name for Hades, in Greek mythology the ruler of the underworld, who abducted Persephone to be his bride. Each spring Persephone returns to earth and is welcomed by her mother Demeter, goddess of fruitfulness; each winter she departs again, to dwell with her husband below. 8. *Dis:* Pluto's realm.

QUESTIONS

1. Read this poem aloud. What devices of sound do you hear in it?
2. What characteristics of gentians appear to remind Lawrence of the story of Persephone? What significance do you attach to the poem's being set in September? How does the fact of autumn matter to the gentians and to Persephone?

Thomas Hardy (1840–1928)

THE OXEN   1915

Christmas Eve, and twelve of the clock.
   "Now they are all on their knees,"
An elder said as we sat in a flock
   By the embers in hearthside ease.

We pictured the meek mild creatures where
   They dwelt in their strawy pen,   5
Nor did it occur to one of us there
   To doubt they were kneeling then.

So fair a fancy few would weave
   In these years! Yet, I feel,   10
If someone said on Christmas Eve,
   "Come; see the oxen kneel

"In the lonely barton° by yonder coomb°   *farmyard; a hollow*
   Our childhood used to know,"
I should go with him in the gloom,   15
   Hoping it might be so.

THE OXEN. This ancient belief has had wide currency among peasants and farmers of western Europe. Some also say that on Christmas eve the beasts can speak.

QUESTIONS

1. What body of myth is Hardy's subject and what are his speaker's attitudes toward it? Perhaps, in Hardy's view, the pious report about oxen is only part of it.

2. Read this poem aloud and notice its sound and imagery. What contrast do you find between the sounds of the first stanza and the sounds of the last stanza? Which words make the difference? What images enforce a contrast in tone between the beginning of the poem and its ending?
3. G. K. Chesterton, writing as a defender of Christian faith, called Hardy's writings "the mutterings of the village atheist." See other poems by Hardy (particularly "Channel Firing," p. 755). What do you think Chesterton might have meant? Can "The Oxen" be called a hostile mutter?

William Wordsworth (1770–1850)

THE WORLD IS TOO MUCH WITH US   1807

The world is too much with us; late and soon,
Getting and spending, we lay waste our powers;
Little we see in Nature that is ours;
We have given our hearts away, a sordid boon!
This Sea that bares her bosom to the moon;   5
The winds that will be howling at all hours,
And are up-gathered now like sleeping flowers;
For this, for everything, we are out of tune;
It moves us not. Great God! I'd rather be
A Pagan suckled in a creed outworn;   10
So might I, standing on this pleasant lea,
Have glimpses that would make me less forlorn;
Have sight of Proteus rising from the sea;
Or hear old Triton blow his wreathèd horn.

QUESTIONS

1. In this sonnet by Wordsworth what condition does the poet complain about? To what does he attribute this condition?
2. How does it affect him as an individual?

When Plato in *The Republic* relates the Myth of Er, he introduces supernatural characters he himself originated. Poets, too, have been inspired to make up myths of their own, for their own purposes. "I must create a system or be enslaved by another man's," said William Blake, who in his "prophetic books" peopled the cosmos with supernatural beings having names like Los, Urizen, and Vala (side by side with recognizable figures from the Old Testament and New Testament). This kind of system-making probably has advantages and drawbacks. T. S. Eliot, in his essay on Blake, wishes that the author of *The Four Zoas* had accepted traditional myths, and he compares Blake's thinking to a piece of home-made furniture whose construction diverted valuable energy from the writing of poems. Others have found Blake's untraditional cosmos an achievement — notably William Butler Yeats, himself the author of an elaborate personal mythology. Although we need not know all of Yeats's mythology to enjoy his poems, to know of its existence can make a few great poems deeper for us and less difficult.

William Butler Yeats (1865–1939)

THE SECOND COMING   1921

Turning and turning in the widening gyre°   *spiral*
The falcon cannot hear the falconer;
Things fall apart; the center cannot hold;
Mere anarchy is loosed upon the world,
The blood-dimmed tide is loosed, and everywhere   5
The ceremony of innocence is drowned;
The best lack all conviction, while the worst
Are full of passionate intensity.

Surely some revelation is at hand;
Surely the Second Coming is at hand;   10
The Second Coming! Hardly are those words out
When a vast image out of *Spiritus Mundi*
Troubles my sight: somewhere in sands of the desert
A shape with lion body and the head of a man,
A gaze blank and pitiless as the sun,   15
Is moving its slow thighs, while all about it
Reel shadows of the indignant desert birds.
The darkness drops again; but now I know
That twenty centuries of stony sleep
Were vexed to nightmare by a rocking cradle,   20
And what rough beast, its hour come round at last,
Slouches towards Bethlehem to be born?

What kind of Second Coming does Yeats expect? Evidently it is not to be a Christian one. Yeats saw human history as governed by the turning of a Great Wheel, whose phases influence events and determine human personalities — rather like the signs of the Zodiac in astrology. Every two thousand years comes a horrendous moment: the Wheel completes a turn; one civilization ends and another begins. Strangely, a new age is always announced by birds and by acts of violence. Thus the Greek-Roman world arrives with the descent of Zeus in swan's form and the burning of Troy, the Christian era with the descent of the Holy Spirit — traditionally depicted as a dove — and the Crucifixion. In 1919 when Yeats wrote "The Second Coming," his Ireland was in the midst of turmoil and bloodshed; the Western Hemisphere had been severely shaken by World War I. A new millennium seemed imminent. What sphinxlike, savage deity would next appear, with birds proclaiming it angrily? Yeats thinks he imagines it emerging from *Spiritus Mundi*, Soul of the World, a collective unconscious from which a human being (since the individual soul touches it) receives dreams, nightmares, and racial memories.[2]

It is hard to say whether a poet who discovers a personal myth does so to have something to live by or to have something to write about. Robert Graves, who professes his belief in a White Goddess ("Mother of All Living, the ancient power of love and terror"), has said that he has written poetry in a trance, inspired by his Goddess-Muse.[3] Luckily, we do not have to know a poet's religious affiliation before we can read the poems. Perhaps most personal myths that enter poems are not acts of faith but works of art: stories that resemble traditional mythology.

John Heath-Stubbs (b. 1918)

A CHARM AGAINST THE TOOTHACHE   1954

Venerable Mother Toothache
Climb down from the white battlements,
Stop twisting in your yellow fingers
The fourfold rope of nerves;
And tomorrow I will give you a tot of whiskey   5
To hold in your cupped hands,
A garland of anise-flowers,
And three cloves like nails.
And tell the attendant gnomes
It is time to knock off now,   10
To shoulder their little pick-axes,
Their cold-chisels and drills.
And you may mount by a silver ladder
Into the sky, to grind
In the cracked polished mortar   15
Of the hollow moon.

By the lapse of warm waters,
And the poppies nodding like red coals,
The paths on the granite mountains,
And the plantation of my dreams.   20

QUESTIONS

1. This poem shows us a poet inventing a mythology. What powers and characteristics does he attribute to Mother Toothache? What facts of common experience does she help account for?

[2] Yeats fully explains his system in *A Vision* (1938; reprinted New York: Macmillan, 1956).
[3] See Graves's *The White Goddess*, rev. ed. (New York: Farrar, Straus & Giroux, 1966), or for a terser statement of his position, see his lecture "The Personal Muse" in *On Poetry: Collected Talks and Essays* (New York: Doubleday, 1969).

2. What is the tone of the poem?
3. In what ways does the poem recall any existing myths and rituals?

Earlier, looking at symbols, we saw that certain concrete objects in poetry can convey suggestions to which we respond without quite being able to tell why. Such, perhaps, are Emily Dickinson's forked lightning bolt dropped from celestial tables and her buzzing fly that arrives with death. Indefinite power may be present also in an **archetype** (Greek: "first-molded"), which can mean "an original model or pattern from which later things are made." The word acquired a special denotation through the work of the Swiss psychologist Carl Gustav Jung (1875–1961). Recently, it has occurred so frequently in literary criticism that students of poetry may wish to be aware of it.

An archetype, in Jung's view, is generally a story, character, symbol, or situation that recurs again and again in worldwide myth, literature, and dream. Some of these — as defined by Jung and others — might be figures such as the cruel mother (Cinderella's stepmother), the creature half human and half animal (centaurs, satyrs, mermaids), the beautiful garden (Eden, Arcadia, the myth of the Golden Age), the story of the hero who by slaying a monster delivers a country from its curse (the romance of Parsifal, the Old English heroic narrative *Beowulf*, the myth of Perseus, the legend of Saint George and the dragon), the story of the beast who yearns for the love of a woman (the fairy tale of "Beauty and the Beast," the movie *King Kong*), the story of the fall from innocence and initiation into life (the account in Genesis of the departure from Eden, J. D. Salinger's novel *The Catcher in the Rye*).

Like Sigmund Freud, Jung saw myth as an aid to the psychiatrist seeking to understand patients' dreams. But Jung went further and postulated the existence of a "collective unconscious" or racial memory in which archetypes lie. "These fantasy-images," said Jung, referring to dreams not traceable to anything a patient has ever experienced, "correspond to certain *collective* (not personal) structural elements in the human psyche in general, and, like the morphological elements of the human body, are *inherited*. . . . The archetype — let us never forget this — is a psychic organ present in all of us."[4]

What this means to the study of poetry is that, if we accept Jung's view, poems containing recognizable archetypes are likely to stir us more profoundly than those that do not. Archetypes being our inheritance from what Shakespeare called "the dark backward and abysm of time," most people can perceive them and respond to them. Some critics have found Jung's theory helpful in fathoming poems. In *Archetypal Patterns in Poetry* (1934), Maud Bodkin found similar archetypes in such dissimilar poems as "Kubla Khan" and *Paradise Lost*.

[4] Carl Jung, "The Psychology of the Child Archetype," in *Psyche and Symbol*, edited by Violet S. de Laszlo (New York: Doubleday, 1958), pp. 117, 123.

Recall Yeats's poem "The Second Coming," only one manifestation of the monstrous Sphinx in literature. There are clear resemblances between the *Spiritus Mundi* in Yeats's poem and Jung's idea of the collective unconscious. As early as 1900, Yeats felt sure of the existence of symbols much like archetypes:

> Any one who has any experience of any mystical state of the soul knows how there float up in the mind profound symbols, whose meaning, if indeed they do not delude one into the dream that they are meaningless, one does not perhaps understand for years. Nor I think has anyone, who has known that experience with any constancy, failed to find some day, in some old book or on some old monument, a strange or intricate image that had floated up before him, and to grow perhaps dizzy with the sudden conviction that our little memories are but part of some great Memory that renews the world and men's thoughts age after age, and that our thoughts are not, as we suppose, the deep, but a little foam upon the deep.[5]

Not all psychologists and students of literature agree with Jung. Some maintain that archetypes, because they tend to disappear with the disintegration of a culture in which they had prospered, are transmitted by word of mouth, not by racial memory.[6] Not all poets are as fond of the notion of great Memory as Yeats was. Recently the English poet Philip Larkin has observed:

> As a guiding principle I believe that every poem must be its own sole freshly created universe, and therefore have no belief in "tradition" or a common myth-kitty. . . . To me the whole of the ancient world, the whole of classical and biblical mythology means very little, and I think that using them today not only fills poems full of dead spots but dodges the writer's duty to be original.[7]

Larkin is probably reacting against bookishness. However, even readers who took no stock in Jung's theories may find *archetype* a useful name for something that, since antiquity, has exerted appeal to makers of myth—including some poets and storytellers.

David Wagoner (b. 1926)

MUSE   1974

Cackling, smelling of camphor, crumbs of pink icing
Clinging to her lips, her lipstick smeared
Halfway around her neck, her cracked teeth bristling

[5] William B. Yeats, "The Philosophy of Shelley's Poetry," *Essays and Introductions* (New York: Macmillan, 1968), pp. 78–79.
[6] See J. S. Lincoln, *The Dream in Primitive Cultures* (1935, p. 24; reprinted New York: Johnson Reprints, 1970).
[7] Statements made on two different occasions, quoted by John Press, *A Map of Modern English Verse* (New York: Oxford University Press, 1969), pp. 258–59.

With bloody splinters, she leans over my shoulder.
Oh my only hope, my lost dumfounding baggage,
My gristle-breasted, slack-jawed zealot, kiss me again.

QUESTIONS

1. To what ancient belief about the source of a poet's inspiration does Wagoner
   refer?
2. In what respects does his version of this myth seem untraditional?

Edward Allen (b. 1948)

THE BEST LINE YET   1972

In Stamford, at the edge of town, a giant statue stands:
An iron eagle sternly clasps the crag with crooked hands.
His pedestal is twenty feet, full thirty feet is he.
His head alone weighs many times as much as you or me.
All day, all night he keeps his watch and never stirs a feather.   5
His frowning brow glares straight ahead into the foulest weather.
They say this noble bird will spread his iron wings and fly
The day a virgin graduates from Stamford Senior High.
O, evil day when he shall rise above the peaceful town,
Endanger airplanes, frighten children, drop foul tonnage down!   10
So let not this accipiter° desert his silent vigil,   *bird of prey*
But yield to me my darling, Stamford's finest, Susan Kitchell.

QUESTIONS

1. How would you describe the tone of this myth-making poem (written when
   the author was a high school student)? Is it humorous, half-serious, or
   serious? How is the tone indicated?
2. What does it have in common with John Heath-Stubbs's "A Charm Against
   the Toothache" (page 626)?

Anonymous (traditional Scottish ballad)

THOMAS THE RIMER

True Thomas lay on Huntlie bank,
  A ferlie° he spied wi' his ee,   *wondrous thing*
And there he saw a lady bright,
  Come riding down by the Eildon Tree.

Her shirt was o' the grass-green silk,   5
  Her mantle o' the velvet fine,
At ilka tett° of her horse's mane   *every lock*
  Hang fifty siller bells and nine.

True Thomas, he pulled aff his cap,
    And louted° low down to his knee: *bowed* 10
"All hail, thou mighty Queen of Heaven!
    For thy peer on earth I never did see."

"O no, O no, Thomas," she said,
    "That name does not belang to me;
I am but the queen of fair Elfland,   15
    That am hither come to visit thee.

"Harp and carp°, Thomas," she said,   *sing ballads*
    "Harp and carp along wi' me,
And if ye dare to kiss my lips,
    Sure of your body I will be."   20

"Betide me weal, betide me woe,
    That weird° shall never daunton me";   *fate*
Syne° he has kissed her rosy lips,   *then*
    All underneath the Eildon Tree.

"Now, ye maun° go wi' me," she said,   *must* 25
    "True Thomas, ye maun go wi' me,
And ye maun serve me seven years,
    Thro weal or woe, as may chance to be."

She mounted on her milk-white steed,
    She's taen True Thomas up behind,   30
And aye° whene'er her bridle rung,   *always*
    The steed flew swifter than the wind.

O they rade on, and farther on—
    The steed gaed swifter than the wind—
Until they reached a desart wide,   35
    And living land was left behind.

"Light down, light down, now, True Thomas,
    And lean your head upon my knee;
Abide and rest a little space,
    And I will shew you ferlies three.
                                       40

"O see ye not yon narrow road,
    So thick beset with thorns and briars?
That is the path of righteousness,
    Though after it but few enquires.

"And see not ye that braid° braid road,   *broad* 45
    That lies across that lily leven°?   *lovely lawn*
That is the path of wickedness,
    Though some call it the road to heaven.

"And see not ye that bonny road,
    That winds about the ferny brae°?   *hillside* 50

That is the road to fair Elfland,
    Where thou and I this night maun gae.

"But, Thomas, ye maun hold your tongue,
    Whatever ye may hear or see,
For, if you speak word in Elfyn land,   55
    Ye'll ne'er get back to your ain countrie."

O they rade on, and farther on,
    And they waded thro rivers aboon the knee,
And they saw neither sun nor moon,
    But they heard the roaring of the sea.   60

It was mirk° mirk night, and there was nae stern° light,   *murky; star*
    And they waded thro red blude to the knee;
For a' the blude that's shed on earth
    Rins thro the springs o' that countrie.

Syne they came on to a garden green,   65
    And she pu'd an apple frae a tree:
"Take this for thy wages, True Thomas,
    It will give the tongue that can never lie."

"My tongue is mine ain," True Thomas said;
    "A gudely gift ye wad gie to me!   70
I neither dought° to buy or sell,   *would be able*
    At fair or tryst° where I may be.   *market*

"I dought neither speak to prince or peer,
    Nor ask of grace from fair ladye":
"Now hold thy peace," the lady said,   75
    "For as I say, so must it be."

He has gotten a coat of the even cloth,
    And a pair of shoes of velvet green,
And till seven years were gane and past
    True Thomas on earth was never seen.   80

THOMAS THE RIMER. Thomas of Erceldoune, popularly called True Thomas or Thomas the
Rimer, was an actual Scottish minstrel of the thirteenth century. He was said to have received the power of prophecy as a gift from the queen of the elves.

QUESTIONS

1. From what kinds of traditional myth does the poem derive? Point out Christian and pagan elements.
2. What impression do we receive of the queen? Is she benevolent or sinister?
   What popular attitudes toward the supernatural might this characterization
   reveal?
3. What do you make of the magic apple in lines 66--68? What other celebrated
   apples does it recall?
4. What statements seem ironies?

John Keats (1795–1821)

LA BELLE DAME SANS MERCI

O what can ail thee, knight-at-arms,
  Alone and palely loitering?
The sedge has withered from the lake,
  And no birds sing.

O what can ail thee, knight-at-arms,   5
  So haggard and so woe-begone?
The squirrel's granary is full,
  And the harvest's done.

I see a lily on thy brow
  With anguish moist and fever dew,   10
And on thy cheek a fading rose
  Fast withereth too.

"I met a lady in the meads,
  Full beautiful — a faery's child;
Her hair was long, her foot was light,   15
  And her eyes were wild.

"I made a garland for her head,
  And bracelets too, and fragrant zone°;   *belt, sash*
She looked at me as she did love,
  And made sweet moan.   20

"I set her on my pacing steed,
  And nothing else saw all day long,
For sidelong would she bend, and sing
  A faery's song.

"She found me roots of relish sweet,   25
  And honey wild, and manna dew,
And sure in language strange she said —
  'I love thee true!'

"She took me to her elfin grot,
  And there she wept and sighed full sore,   30
And there I shut her wild wild eyes
  With kisses four.

"And there she lullèd me asleep,
  And there I dreamed — ah! woe betide!
The latest dream I ever dreamed   35
  On the cold hill's side.

"I saw pale kings and princes too,
  Pale warriors, death-pale were they all;
They cried — 'La Belle Dame sans Merci
  Hath thee in thrall!'   40

"I saw their starved lips in the gloam,
　With horrid warning gaped wide,
And I awoke and found me here,
　On the cold hill's side.

"And this is why I sojourn here,   45
　Alone and palely loitering,
Though the sedge is withered from the lake
　And no birds sing."

LA BELLE DAME SANS MERCI. Keats borrowed this title, "The Lovely Merciless Beauty,"
from a medieval French poem. The text given above is his earliest version.

QUESTIONS

1. What happens in this ballad? What is indicated by the contrast between the
   imagery from nature in lines 17, 18, 25, and 26 and that in lines 3–4, 7–8, 44,
   and 47–48? How do you interpret the knight's *latest dream* (line 35)?
2. What do we know about this beautiful lady without pity? What supernatural
   powers does she possess?
3. In what respects does she resemble the Queen of Elfland in the ballad of
   "Thomas the Rimer"? In what respects does she differ?
4. What other *dames sans merci* do you find in other poems in this book? In what
   respects are they similar? In what respects, if any, is Keats's lady an individual?
5. What other relentless beauties with supernatural powers do you know from
   myth, folklore, literature, movies, or television? In what respects, if any, do
   they resemble the *Belle Dame* or Thomas the Rimer's queen?

John Milton (1608–1674)

LYCIDAS   1637

*In this monody the author bewails a learned friend, unfortunately drowned in his passage
from Chester on the Irish Seas, 1637. And by occasion foretells the ruin of our corrupted
clergy then in their height.*

Yet once more, O ye laurels, and once more,
Ye myrtles brown°, with ivy never sere,   *dark*
I come to pluck your berries harsh and crude°,   *immature*
And with forced fingers rude
Shatter your leaves before the mellowing year.   5
Bitter constraint and sad occasion dear
Compels me to disturb your season due;

LYCIDAS. Milton's "learned friend" was Edward King, scholar and poet, a fellow student
at Cambridge, who had planned to enter the ministry. In calling him Lycidas, Milton
employs a conventional name for a young shepherd in **pastoral poetry** (which either portrays the world of shepherds with some realism, as in Virgil's *Eclogues*, or makes it a pret-
tified Eden, as in Marlowe's "The Passionate Shepherd to His Love"). A *monody*, in the
epigraph, is a song for a single voice. 1–2. *laurels, myrtles:* Evergreens in the crowns traditionally bestowed upon poets.

For Lycidas is dead, dead ere his prime,
Young Lycidas, and hath not left his peer.
Who would not sing for Lycidas? he knew   10
Himself to sing, and build the lofty rhyme.
He must not float upon his wat'ry bier
Unwept, and welter° to the parching wind,   *toss about*
Without the meed° of some melodious tear.   *tribute*
    Begin, then, Sisters of the Sacred Well   15
That from beneath the seat of Jove doth spring,
Begin, and somewhat loudly sweep the string.
Hence with denial vain and coy excuse:
So may some gentle Muse°   *poet*
With lucky words favor my destined urn,   20
And, as he passes, turn,
And bid fair peace be to my sable shroud!
For we were nursed upon the self-same hill,
Fed the same flocks, by fountain, shade, and rill;
    Together both, ere the high lawns appeared   25
Under the opening eyelids of the Morn,
We drove a-field, and both together heard
What time the gray-fly winds° her sultry horn,   *sounds*
Batt'ning° our flocks with the fresh dews of night,   *feeding*
Oft till the star that rose at evening bright   30
Toward Heav'n's descent had sloped his westering wheel.
Meanwhile the rural ditties were not mute,
Tempered to the oaten° flute,   *made of an oat stalk*
Rough satyrs danced, and fauns with cloven heel
From the glad sound would not be absent long;   35
And old Damoetas loved to hear our song.
    But, O the heavy change, now thou art gone,
Now thou art gone, and never must return!
Thee, Shepherd, thee the woods and desert caves,
With wild thyme and the gadding° vine o'ergrown,   *wandering* 40
And all their echoes mourn.
The willows, and the hazel copses green,
Shall now no more be seen
Fanning their joyous leaves to thy soft lays.
As killing as the canker to the rose,   45
Or taint-worm to the weanling herds that graze,
Or frost to flowers, that their gay wardrobe wear
When first the white thorn blows°;   *blossoms*
Such, Lycidas, thy loss to shepherd's ear.
    Where were ye, Nymphs, when the remorseless deep 50
Closed o'er the head of your loved Lycidas?
For neither were ye playing on the steep
Where your old bards, the famous Druids, lie,

36. *Damoetas:* Perhaps some Cambridge tutor.
53. *Druids:* priests and poets of the Celts in pre-Christian Britain.

Nor on the shaggy top of Mona high,
Nor yet where Deva spreads her wizard stream.   55
Ay me! I fondly° dream!   *foolishly*
"Had ye been there"—for what could that have done?
What could the Muse herself that Orpheus bore,
The Muse herself, for her enchanting son,
Whom universal Nature did lament,   60
When, by the rout° that made the hideous roar,   *mob*
His gory visage down the stream was sent,
Down the swift Hebrus to the Lesbian shore?

    Alas! What boots it° with uncessant care   *what good does it do*
To tend the homely, slighted shepherd's trade,   65
And strictly meditate the thankless Muse?
Were it not better done, as others use°,   *do*
To sport with Amaryllis in the shade,
Or with the tangles of Neaera's hair?
Fame is the spur that the clear spirit doth raise   70
(That last infirmity of noble mind)
To scorn delights and live laborious days;
But the fair guerdon when we hope to find,
And think to burst out into sudden blaze,
Comes the blind Fury with th' abhorrèd shears,   75
And slits the thin-spun life. "But not the praise,"
Phoebus replied, and touched my trembling ears:
"Fame is no plant that grows on mortal soil,
Nor in the glistering° foil,   *glittering*
Set off to the world, nor in broad rumor° lies,   *reputation*   80
But lives and spreads aloft by those pure eyes
And perfect witness of all-judging Jove;
As he pronounces lastly on each deed,
Of so much fame in Heav'n expect thy meed."

    O fountain Arethuse, and thou honored flood,   85
Smooth-sliding Mincius, crowned with vocal reeds,
That strain I heard was of a higher mood:
But now my oat proceeds,
And listens to the Herald of the Sea,
That came in Neptune's plea.   90
He asked the waves, and asked the felon winds,
What hard mishap hath doomed this gentle swain?
And questioned every gust of rugged wings
That blows from off each beakèd promontory:

54. *Mona*: Roman name for the Isle of Man, near which King was drowned. 55. *Deva*: the River Dee, flowing between England and Wales. Its shifts in course were said to augur good luck for one country or the other. 68–69. *Amaryllis, Neaera*: conventional names for shepherdesses. 70. *the clear spirit doth raise*: doth raise the clear spirit. 77. *touched . . . ears*: gesture signifying "Remember!" 79. *foil*: a setting of gold or silver leaf, used to make a gem appear more brilliant. 85–86. *Arethuse, Minicius*: a fountain and river near the birthplaces of Theocritus and Virgil, respectively, hence recalling the most celebrated writer of pastorals in Greek and the most celebrated in Latin. 90. *in Neptune's plea*: bringing the sea-god's plea, "not guilty."

They knew not of his story;   95
And sage Hippotades their answer brings,
That not a blast was from his dungeon strayed:
The air was calm, and on the level brine
Sleek Panope with all her sisters played.
It was that fatal and perfidious bark,   100
Built in th' eclipse, and rigged with curses dark,
That sunk so low that sacred head of thine.
   Next, Camus, reverend sire, went footing slow,
His mantle hairy, and his bonnet sedge,
Inwrought with figures dim, and on the edge   105
Like to that sanguine flower inscribed with woe.
"Ah! who hath reft," quoth he, "my dearest pledge?"
Last came, and last did go,
The pilot of the Galilean lake;
Two massy keys he bore of metals twain   110
(The golden opes, the iron shuts amain°).   *with force*
He shook his mitered locks, and stern bespake:—
"How well could I have spared for thee, young swain,
Enow° of such as for their bellies' sake,   *enough*
Creep, and intrude, and climb into the fold!   115
Of other care they little reck'ning make
Than how to scramble at the shearers' feast,
And shove away the worthy bidden guest.
Blind mouths! that scarce themselves know how to hold
A sheep-hook, or have learned aught else the least   120
That to the faithful herdsman's art belongs!
What recks it them? What need they? they are sped°;   *prosperous*
And, when they list°, their lean and flashy songs   *so incline*
Grate on their scrannel° pipes of wretched straw;   *feeble, harsh*
The hungry sheep look up, and are not fed,   125
But, swoll'n with wind and the rank mist they draw,
Rot inwardly, and foul contagion spread;
Besides what the grim wolf with privy° paw   *stealthy*
Daily devours apace, and nothing said;
But that two-handed engine at the door   130
Stands ready to smite once, and smite no more."

99. *Panope:* a sea nymph. Her name means "one who sees all." 101. *eclipse:* thought to be
an omen of evil fortune. 103. *Camus:* spirit of the river Cam and personification of
Cambridge University. 109–112. *pilot:* Saint Peter, once a fisherman in Galilee, to whom
Christ gave the *keys* of Heaven (Matthew 16:19). As first Bishop of Rome, he wears the
miter, a bishop's emblematic head-covering. 115. *fold:* the Church of England. 120.
sheep-hook: a bishop's staff or crozier, which resembles a shepherd's crook. 128. *wolf:* probably the Church of Rome. Jesuits in England at the time were winning converts. 130. *two-
handed engine:* This disputed phrase may refer (among other possibilities) to the punishing sword of The Word of God (Revelation 19:13–15 and Hebrews 4:12). Perhaps Milton
sees it as a lightning bolt, as does Spenser, to whom Jove's wrath is a "three-forked
engine" (*Faerie Queene*, VIII, 9). 131. *smite once . . . no more:* Because, in the proverb, lightning never strikes twice in the same place?

Return, Alpheus; the dread voice is past
That shrunk thy streams; return, Sicilian Muse,
And call the vales, and bid them hither cast
Their bells and flow'rets of a thousand hues.   135
Ye valleys low, where the mild whispers use°   *resort*
Of shades, and wanton winds, and gushing brooks,
On whose fresh lap the swart star sparely looks,
Throw hither all your quaint enameled eyes,
That on the green turf suck the honied showers,   140
And purple all the ground with vernal flowers.
Bring the rathe° primrose that forsaken dies,   *early*
The tufted crow-toe, and pale jessamine,
The white pink, and the pansy freaked° with jet,   *streaked*
The glowing violet,   145
The musk-rose, and the well-attired woodbine,
With cowslips wan that hang the pensive head,
And every flower that sad embroidery wears;
Bid amaranthus all his beauty shed,
And daffadillies fill their cups with tears,   150
To strew the laureate hearse where Lycid lies.
For so, to interpose a little ease,
Let our frail thoughts dally with false surmise,
Ay me! whilst thee the shores and sounding seas
Wash far away, where'er thy bones are hurled;   155
Whether beyond the stormy Hebrides,
Where thou, perhaps, under the whelming tide
Visit'st the bottom of the monstrous° world;   *full of sea monsters*
Or whether thou, to our moist vows° denied,   *prayers*
Sleep'st by the fable of Bellerus old,   160
Where the great Vision of the guarded mount
Looks toward Namancos and Bayona's hold°:   *stronghold*
Look homeward, angel, now, and melt with ruth°;   *pity*
And, O ye dolphins, waft the hapless youth.
      Weep no more, woeful shepherds, weep no more,   165
For Lycidas, your sorrow, is not dead,
Sunk though he be beneath the wat'ry floor:
So sinks the day-star in the ocean bed
And yet anon repairs his drooping head,
And tricks° his beams, and with new-spangled ore°   *arrays; gold* 170
Flames in the forehead of the morning sky:
So Lycidas sunk low, but mounted high,
Through the dear might of Him that walked the waves,

133. *Sicilian Muse:* who inspired Theocritus, a native of Sicily. 138. *swart star:* Sirius, at its
zenith in summer, was thought to turn vegetation black. 153. *false surmise:* futile hope that
the body of Lycidas could be recovered. 160. *Bellerus:* legendary giant of Land's End, the
far tip of Cornwall. 161. *guarded mount:* Saint Michael's Mount, off Land's End, said to be
under the protection of the archangel. 162. *Namancos, Bayona:* on the coast of Spain. 164.
dolphins: In Greek legend, these kindly fish carried the spirits of the dead to the Blessed
Isles.

Where, other groves and other streams along,
With nectar pure his oozy locks he laves,   175
And hears the unexpressive nuptial song,
In the blest kingdoms meek of Joy and Love.
There entertain him all the Saints above,
In solemn troops, and sweet societies,
That sing, and singing in their glory move,   180
And wipe the tears forever from his eyes.
Now, Lycidas, the shepherds weep no more;
Henceforth thou art the Genius° of the shore,   *guardian spirit*
In thy large recompense, and shalt be good
To all that wander in that perilous flood.   185

  Thus sang the uncouth° swain to th' oaks and rills,   *rustic (or little-known)*
While the still Morn went out with sandals gray;
He touched the tender stops of various quills°,   *reeds of a shepherd's pipe*
With eager thought warbling his Doric lay:
And now the sun had stretched out all the hills,   190
And now was dropped into the western bay.
At last he rose, and twitched° his mantle blue: *donned*
Tomorrow to fresh woods and pastures new.

176. *unexpressive nuptial song:* inexpressibly beautiful song for the marriage feast of the
Lamb (Revelation 19:9). 189. *Doric lay:* pastoral poem. Doric is the dialect of Greek
employed by Theocritus.

QUESTIONS AND EXERCISES
1. With the aid of an encyclopedia or a handbook of classical mythology (such
   as Bulfinch's *Mythology,* Edith Hamilton's *Mythology,* or H. J. Rose's *Handbook of Greek Mythology*) learn more about the following myths or mythical figures and places to which Milton alludes:

   Line 15 Sisters of the Sacred Well (Muses)
        16 seat of Jove (Mount Olympus)
        58 the Muse . . . that Orpheus bore (Calliope)
     61–63 (the death of Orpheus)
        75 Fury with the . . . shears (Atropos, one of the three Fates)
        77 Phoebus
        89 Herald of the Sea (Triton)
        90 Neptune
        96 Hippotades
       106 (Hyacinthus)
       132 Alpheus

   Then reread Milton's poem. As a result of your familiarity with these myths,
   what details become clear?
2. Read the parable of the Good Shepherd (John 10:1–18). What relationships
   does Milton draw between the Christian idea of the shepherd and pastoral
   poetry?

3. "With these trifling fictions [allusions to classical mythology]," wrote Samuel Johnson about "Lycidas," "are mingled the most awful and sacred truths, such as ought never to be polluted with such irreverend combinations." Does this mingling of paganism and Christianity detract from Milton's poem? Discuss.
4. In "Lycidas" does Milton devise any new myth or myths?

25 Evaluating Poetry

"The bulk of English poetry is bad," a critic has said,[1] referring to all verse printed over the past six hundred years, not only that which survives in anthologies. As his comment reminds us, excellent poetry is at least as scarce as gold. Though readers who seek it for themselves can expect to pan through much shale, such labor need not discourage them from prospecting. Only the naïve reader assumes, "This poem must be good, or else why would it appear in a leading magazine?" Only the reader whose mind is coasting in neutral says, "Who knows if this poem is good? Who cares? It all depends upon your point of view." Open-minded, skeptical, and alert, the critical reader will make independent evaluations.

Why do we call some poems "bad"? We are not talking about their moral implications. Rather, we mean that, for one or more of many possible reasons, the poem has failed to move us or to engage our sympathies. Instead, it has made us doubt that the poet is in control of language and vision; perhaps it has aroused our antipathies or unwittingly appealed to our sense of the comic, though the poet is serious. Some poems can be said to succeed despite burdensome faults. But in general such faults are symptoms of deeper malady: some weakness in a poem's basic conception or in the poet's competence.

Nearly always, a bad poem reveals only a dim and distorted awareness of its probable effect on an alert reader. Perhaps the sound of words may clash with what a poem is saying, as in the jarring last word of this opening line of a tender lyric (author unknown, quoted by Richard Wilbur): "Come into the tent, my love, and close the flap." Perhaps a metaphor may fail by calling to mind more differences than similarities, as in Emily Dickinson's lines "Our lives are Swiss-- / So still--so cool." A bad poem usually overshoots or falls short of its mark by the poet's thinking too little or too much. Thinking much, a poet contrives such an excess of ingenuity as that quoted by Alexander Pope in

[1] Christopher Adams in the preface to his anthology, *The Worst English Poets* (London: Allan Wingate, 1958).

Peri Bathous, or *Of the Art of Sinking in Poetry:* a hounded stag who "Hears his own feet, and thinks they sound like more; / And fears the hind feet will o'ertake the fore." Thinking little, a poet writes redundantly, as Wordsworth in "The Thorn": "And they had fixed the wedding-day, / The morning that must wed them both."

In a poem that has a rime scheme or a set line length, when all is well, pattern and structure move inseparably with the rest of their poem, the way a tiger's skin and bones move with their tiger. But sometimes, in a poem that fails, the poet evidently has had difficulty in persuading statements to fit a formal pattern. English poets have long felt free to invert word order for a special effect, but the poet having trouble keeping to a rime scheme may invert words for no apparent reason but convenience. Needing a rime for *barge* may lead to ending a line with a *policedog large* instead of *a large policedog.* Another sign of trouble is a profusion of adjectives. If a line of iambic pentameter reads, "Her lovely skin, like dear sweet white old silk," we suspect the poet of stuffing the line to make it long enough. Whenever two or more adjectives stand together (in poetry or in good prose), they need to be charged with meaning. No one suspects Matthew Arnold of padding the last line of "To Marguerite": "The unplumbed, salt, estranging sea."

Because, over his dead body, even a poet's slightest and feeblest efforts may be collected, some lines in the canon of celebrated bards make us wonder, "How could he have written this?" Wordsworth, Shelley, Whitman, and Browning are among the great whose failures can be painful, and lapses of awareness may occur even in poems that, taken entire, are excellent. To be unwilling to read them, though, would be as ill advised as to refuse to see Venice just because the Grand Canal is said to contain impurities. The seasoned reader of poetry thinks no less of Tennyson for having written, "Form, Form, Riflemen Form! . . . Look to your butts, and take good aims!" The collected works of a duller poet may contain no such lines of unconscious double meaning, but neither do they contain, perhaps, any poem as good as "Ulysses." If the duller poet never had a spectacular failure, it may be because of failure to take risks.

We flatter ourselves if we think all imprecise poetry the work of times gone by. Poetry editors of current magazines find that about nine hundred out of a thousand unsolicited poems are, at a glance, unworthy of a second reading. Although editors may have nightmares in which they ignorantly reject the poems of some new Gerard Manley Hopkins or Emily Dickinson, they nonetheless send them back with a printed "thank you" slip, then turn to the hundred that look interesting. How are the poems winnowed so quickly? Often, inept poems fall into familiar categories. At one extreme is the poem written entirely in conventional diction, dimly echoing Shakespeare, Wordsworth, and the Bible, but garbling them. Couched in a rhythm that ticks along like a metronome, this kind of poem shows no sign that its author has ever taken a hard look at anything that can be tasted, handled, and felt. It employs loosely and thoughtlessly the most abstract of words: *love, beauty, life, death, time, eternity*. Littered with old-fashioned contractions (*'tis, o'er, where'er*), it may end in a simple platitude or preachment, as if the poet' expected us to profit from his or her wisdom and moral superiority. George Orwell's complaint against much contemporary writing (not only poetry) is applicable: "As soon as certain topics are raised"—and one thinks of such standard topics for poetry as spring, a first kiss, and stars—"the concrete melts into the abstract and no one seems able to think of turns of speech that are not hackneyed." Writers, Orwell charged, too often make their sentences out of tacked-together phrases "like the sections of a prefabricated hen-house."[2] Versifiers often do likewise.

At the opposite extreme is the poem that displays no acquaintance with poetry of the past but manages, instead, to fabricate its own clichés. Slightly paraphrased, a manuscript once submitted to *The Paris Review* began:

> Vile
> > rottenflush
> > > o   —*screaming*—
> > > f CORPSEBLOOD!!   ooze
> > STRANGLE my
> > > *eyes* . . .   HELL's
> > > O, ghastly   stench**!!!

At most, such a work has only a private value. The writer has vented personal frustrations upon words, instead of kicking stray dogs. In its way, "Vile Rottenflush" is as self-indulgent as the oldfangled "first kiss in spring" kind of poem. Both offend, both inspire distrust. "I dislike," said John Livingston Lowes, "poems that black your eyes, or put up their mouths to be kissed."

As jewelers tell which of two diamonds is fine by seeing which scratches the other, two poems may be tested by comparing them. This method works only on poems similar in length and kind: an epigram cannot rival an epic. Most poems we meet are neither sheer trash nor obvious masterpieces. Since, however, good diamonds to be proven need softer ones to scratch, in this chapter you will find a few clear-cut gems and a few clinkers. "In poetry," said Ronsard, "mediocrity is the greatest vice."

[2] George Orwell, "Politics and the English Language," from *Shooting an Elephant and Other Essays* (New York: Harcourt Brace Jovanovich, 1945).

Anonymous (English)

O Moon, when I gaze on thy beautiful face (about 1900)

O Moon, when I gaze on thy beautiful face,
Careering along through the boundaries of space,
The thought has often come into my mind
If I ever shall see thy glorious behind.

O Moon. Sir Edmund Gosse, the English critic (1849–1928), offered this quatrain as the
work of his maidservant, but there is reason to suspect him of having written it.

Questions

1. To what fact of astronomy does the last line refer?
2. Which words seem chosen with too little awareness of their denotations and
   connotations?
3. Even if you did not know that these lines probably were deliberately bad,
   how would you argue with someone who maintained that the opening *O* in
   the poem was admirable as a bit of concrete poetry? (See the quotation from
   E. E. Cummings on page 603.)

Grace Treasone

Life (about 1963)

Life is like a jagged tooth
that cuts into your heart;
fix the tooth and save the root,
and laughs, not tears, will start.

William Ernest Henley (1849–1903)

Madam Life's a piece in bloom 1908

Madam Life's a piece in bloom
  Death goes dogging everywhere:
She's the tenant of the room,
  He's the ruffian on the stair.

You shall see her as a friend,
  You shall bilk him once or twice;   5
But he'll trap you in the end,
  And he'll stick you for her price.

With his kneebones at your chest,
  And his knuckles in your throat,
You would reason – plead – protest!   10
  Clutching at her petticoat;

But she's heard it all before,
   Well she knows you've had your fun,
Gingerly she gains the door,   15
   And your little job is done.

QUESTIONS

1. Try to paraphrase the two preceding poems. What is the theme of each?
2. Which statement of theme do you find more convincing? Why?
3. Which poem is the more consistent in working out its metaphor?

Stephen Tropp (b. 1930)
MY WIFE IS MY SHIRT   1960

My wife is my shirt
I put my hands through her armpits
slide my head through her mouth
& finally button her blood around my hands

QUESTIONS

1. How consistently is the metaphor elaborated?
2. Why can this metaphor be said to work in exactly the opposite way from a
   personification?
3. A paraphrase might discover this simile: "My wife is as intimate, familiar,
   and close to me as the shirt on my back." If this is the idea and the poem is
   supposed to be a love poem, how precisely is its attitude expressed?

M. Krishnamurti (b. 1912)
THE SPIRIT'S ODYSSEY   1951

I saw her first in gleams,
As one might see in dreams
   A moonmaiden undrape
   Her opalescent shape
Midst moveless lunar streams!   5

Now fierce and sudden-truth'd,
She smites me, sabre-tooth'd:
   As sunlight, snarling, crawls
   Into the bower and mauls
The waker, slumber-sooth'd!   10

QUESTIONS

1. Can you explain the moonmaiden's abrupt transformation from a beautiful
   stripteaser to a ferocious beast? Does the title of the poem help?

2. Read this poem aloud and comment on the effectiveness of its sounds—particularly the rimes in the second stanza.

EXERCISE: *Seeing What Went Wrong*

Here is a small anthology of bad moments in poetry. For what reasons does each selection fail? In which passages do you attribute the failure to inappropriate sound or diction? To awkward word order? To inaccurate metaphor? To excessive overstatement? To forced rime? To monotonous rhythm? To redundancy? To simple-mindedness or excessive ingenuity?

1. From Sir Richard Blackmore's *Paraphrase of the Book of Job:*

   I cannot stifle this gigantic woe,
   Nor on my raging grief a muzzle throw.

2. "I'm Glad," in its entirety, author unknown:

   I'm glad the sky is painted blue,
   And the earth is painted green,
   With such a lot of nice fresh air
   All sandwiched in between.

3. A lover's lament from Harry Edward Mills's *Select Sunflowers:*

   I see her in my fondest moods,
       She haunts the parlor hallway;
   And yet her form my clasp eludes,
       Her lips my kisses alway.

4. A suffering swain makes a vow, from "the poem of a young tradesman" quoted by Coleridge in *Biographia Literaria:*

   No more will I endure love's pleasing pain,
   Or round my heart's leg tie his galling chain.

5. From an elegy for Queen Victoria by one of her subjects:

   Dust to dust, and ashes to ashes,
   Into the tomb the Great Queen dashes.

6. The opening lines of Alice Meynell's "The Shepherdess":

   She walks—the lady of my delight—
   A shepherdess of sheep.

7. From a juvenile poem of John Dryden, "Upon the Death of the Lord Hastings" (a victim of smallpox):

   Blisters with pride swelled; which through's flesh did sprout
   Like rose-buds, stuck i' th'lily-skin about.
   Each little pimple had a tear in it,
   To wail the fault its rising did commit . . .

8. A poet discusses the pity he feels for the newborn, from J. W. Scholl's *The Light-Bearer of Liberty:*

   Gooing babies, helpless pygmies,
   Who shall solve your Fate's enigmas?
   Who shall save you from Earth's stigmas?

9. A metaphor from Edgar A. Guest's "The Crucible of Life":

Sacred and sweet is the joy that must come
From the furnace of life when you've poured off the scum.

10. A stanza composed by Samuel Johnson as a deliberately bad example:

I put my hat upon my head
And walked into the Strand;
And there I met another man
Whose hat was in his hand.

11. A lover describes his lady, from Thomas Holley Chivers's "Rosalie Lee":

Many mellow Cydonian suckets,
   Sweet apples, anthosmial, divine,
From the ruby-rimmed beryline buckets,
   Star-gemmed, lily-shaped, hyaline:
Like the sweet golden goblet found growing
   On the wild emerald cucumber-tree,
Rich, brilliant, like chrysoprase glowing,
   Was my beautiful Rosalie Lee.

12. Lines on a sick gypsy, author unknown, quoted in *The Stuffed Owl, an Anthology of Bad Verse*, edited by D. B. Wyndham Lewis and Charles Lee:

There we leave her,
There we leave her,
Far from where her swarthy kindred roam,
In the Scarlet Fever,
Scarlet Fever,
Scarlet Fever Convalescent Home.

Sentimentality is the failure of writers who imply that they feel great emotion but who fail to give us sufficient grounds for sharing it. The emotion may be an anger greater than its object seems to call for, as in these lines to a girl who caused scandal (the exact nature of her act never being specified): "The gossip in each hall / Will curse your name . . . / Go! better cast yourself right down the falls!"[3] Or it may be an enthusiasm quite unwarranted by its subject: in *The Fleece* John Dyer temptingly describes the pleasures of life in a workhouse for the poor. The sentimental poet is especially prone to tenderness. Great tears fill this poet's eyes at a glimpse of an aged grandmother sitting by a hearth. For all the poet knows, she may be the well-to-do manager of a casino in Las Vegas, who would be startled to find herself an object of pity, but the sentimentalist seems not to care to know much about the woman herself. She is employed as a general excuse for feeling maudlin. Any other conventional object will serve as well: a faded valentine, the strains of an old song, a baby's cast-off pacifier. A celebrated instance of such

[3] Ali. S. Hilmi, "The Preacher's Sermon," in *Verse at Random* (Larnaca, Cyprus: Ohanian Press, 1953).

emotional self-indulgence is "The Old Oaken Bucket," by Samuel Woodworth, a stanza of which goes:

> How sweet from the green, mossy brim to receive it,
>   As, poised on the curb, it inclined to my lips!
> Not a full-flushing goblet could tempt me to leave it,
>   Tho' filled with the nectar that Jupiter sips.
> And now, far removed from the loved habitation,
>   The tear of regret will intrusively swell,
> As fancy reverts to my father's plantation,
>   And sighs for the bucket that hung in the well.

As a symbol, the bucket might conceivably be made to hold the significance of the past and the speaker's regret at being caught in the destroying grip of time. But the staleness of the phrasing and imagery (Jove's nectar, *tear of regret*) suggests that the speaker is not even seeing the actual physical bucket, and the tripping meter of the lines is inappropriate to an expression of tearful regret. Perhaps the poet's nostalgia is genuine. We need not doubt it; indeed, as Keith Waldrop has put it, "a bad poem is always sincere." However sincere in their feelings, sentimental poets are insincere in their art — otherwise, wouldn't they trouble to write better poems, or at least not print the ones they write? Woodworth, by the vagueness of his language and the monotony of his rhythms, fails to persuade us that we ought to care. Wet-eyed and sighing for a bucket, he achieves not pathos but **bathos:** a description that can move us to laughter instead of tears.[4]

Tears, of course, can be shed for good reason. A piece of sentimentality is not be confused with a well-wrought poem whose tone is tenderness. At first glance, the following poem by Burns might strike you as sentimental. If so, your suspicions are understandable, for it is a rare poet who can speak honestly or effectively on the theme that love grows deeper as lovers grow old. Many a popular song-writer has seen the process of aging as valuable: "Darling, I am growing old, / Silver threads among the gold." According to such songs, to grow decrepit is a privilege. What is fresh in Burns's poem, however, is that no attempt is made to gloss over the ravages of age and the inevitability of death. The speaker expresses no self-pity, no comment *about* her feelings, only a simple account of what has befallen her and her John and what is still to follow.

---

[4] *Bathos* in poetry can also mean an abrupt fall from the sublime to the trivial or incongruous. A sample, from Nicholas Rowe's play *The Fair Penitent:* "Is it the voice of thunder, or my father?" Another, from John Close, a minor Victorian: "Around their heads a dazzling halo shone, / No need of mortal robes, or any hat." When, however, such a letdown is used for a *desirable* effect of humor or contrast, it is usually called an **anticlimax:** as in Alexander Pope's lines on the queen's palace, "Here thou, great Anna! whom three realms obey, / Dost sometimes counsel take — and sometimes tea."

Robert Burns (1759–1796)

JOHN ANDERSON MY JO, JOHN

1790

John Anderson my jo°, John,   *dear*
  When we were first acquent°,   *acquainted*
Your locks were like the raven,
  Your bonny brow was brent°;   *unwrinkled*
But now your brow is beld°, John,   *bald* 5
  Your locks are like the snaw;
But blessings on your frosty pow°,   *head*
  John Anderson my jo.

John Anderson my jo, John,
  We clamb the hill thegither;   10
And mony a canty° day, John,   *happy*
  We've had wi' ane anither:
Now we maun° totter down, John,   *must*
  And hand in hand we'll go,
And sleep together at the foot,   15
  John Anderson my jo.

EXERCISE: *Fine or Shoddy Tenderness*

Which of the following two poems do you find sentimental? Which one would you defend? Why? At least one kind of evidence to look for is minute, detailed observation of physical objects. In a successful poem, the poet is likely at least occasionally to notice the world beyond his or her own skin; in a sentimental poem, this world is likely to be ignored while the poet looks inward. So that the poet's reputation (or lack of reputation) will not distract you, the poems are printed without by-lines.

THE OLD ARM-CHAIR

1838

I love it, I love it! and who shall dare
To chide me for loving that old arm-chair?
I've treasured it long as a sainted prize,
I've bedewed it with tears, I've embalmed it with sighs,
'Tis bound by a thousand bands to my heart;   5
Not a tie will break, not a link will start.
Would you know the spell?—a mother sat there!
And a sacred thing is that old arm-chair.

In childhood's hour I lingered near
The hallowed seat with listening ear;   10
And gentle words that mother would give
To fit me to die and teach me to live.

She told me that shame would never betide
With truth for my creed, and God for my guide;
She taught me to lisp my earliest prayer,   15
As I knelt beside that old arm-chair.

I sat and watched her many a day,
When her eyes grew dim, and her locks were gray;
And I almost worshipped her when she smiled,
And turned from her Bible to bless her child.   20
Years rolled on, but the last one sped, —
My idol was shattered, my earth-star fled!
I learned how much the heart can bear,
When I saw her die in her old arm-chair.

'Tis past, 'tis past! but I gaze on it now,   25
With quivering breath and throbbing brow;
'Twas there she nursed me, 'twas there she died,
And memory flows with a lava tide.
Say it is folly, and deem me weak,
Whilst scalding drops start down my cheek;   30
But I love it, I love it! and cannot tear
My soul from a mother's old arm-chair.

PIANO   1918

Softly, in the dusk, a woman is singing to me;
Taking me back down the vista of years, till I see
A child sitting under the piano, in the boom of the tingling strings
And pressing the small, poised feet of a mother who smiles as she sings.

In spite of myself, the insidious mastery of song   5
Betrays me back, till the heart of me weeps to belong
To the old Sunday evenings at home, with winter outside
And hymns in the cozy parlor, the tinkling piano our guide.

So now it is vain for the singer to burst into clamor
With the great black piano appassionato. The glamor   10
Of childish days is upon me, my manhood is cast
Down in the flood of remembrance, I weep like a child for the past.

Rod McKuen (b. 1933)
THOUGHTS ON CAPITAL PUNISHMENT   1954

There ought to be capital punishment for cars
that run over rabbits and drive into dogs
and commit the unspeakable, unpardonable crime
of killing a kitty cat still in his prime.

Purgatory, at the very least
        should await the driver
    driving over a beast.

Those hurrying headlights coming out of the dark
that scatter the scampering squirrels in the park
should await the best jury that one might compose
of fatherless chipmunks and husbandless does.

And then found guilty, after too fair a trial
should be caged in a cage with a hyena's smile
or maybe an elephant with an elephant gun
should shoot out his eyes when the verdict is done.

There ought to be something, something that's fair
to avenge Mrs. Badger as she waits in her lair
for her husband who lies with his guts spilling out
cause he didn't know what automobiles are about.

Hell on the highway, at the very least
        should await the driver
    driving over a beast.

Who kills a man kills a bit of himself
But a cat too is an extension of God.

William Stafford (b. 1914)

TRAVELING THROUGH THE DARK

1962

Traveling through the dark I found a deer
dead on the edge of the Wilson River road.
It is usually best to roll them into the canyon:
that road is narrow; to swerve might make more dead.

By glow of the tail-light I stumbled back of the car
and stood by the heap, a doe, a recent killing;
she had stiffened already, almost cold.
I dragged her off; she was large in the belly.

My fingers touching her side brought me the reason —
her side was warm; her fawn lay there waiting,
alive, still, never to be born.
Beside that mountain road I hesitated.

The car aimed ahead its lowered parking lights;
under the hood purred the steady engine.
I stood in the glare of the warm exhaust turning red;
around our group I could hear the wilderness listen.

I thought hard for us all — my only swerving —
then pushed her over the edge into the river.

1. Compare these poems by Rod McKuen and William Stafford. How are they similar in subject?
2. Explain Stafford's title. Who are all those traveling through the dark?
3. Comment on McKuen's use of language: how consistent is it? Consider especially: *unspeakable, unpardonable crime* (line 3), *kitty cat* (4), *scatter the scampering squirrels* (9), and *cause he didn't know* (19).
4. Compare the meaning of Stafford's last two lines and McKuen's last two. Does either poem have a moral? Can either poem be said to moralize?
5. How just is McKuen's justice? How well does the punishment fit the crime?
6. Which poem might be open to the charge of sentimentality? Why?

Ralph Waldo Emerson (1803–1882)

DAYS   1867

Daughters of Time, the hypocritic Days,
Muffled and dumb like barefoot dervishes,
And marching single in an endless file,
Bring diadems and fagots in their hands.
To each they offer gifts after his will,   5
Bread, kingdom, stars, and sky that holds them all.

I, in my pleachèd garden, watched the pomp°,   *solemn procession*
Forgot my morning wishes, hastily
Took a few herbs and apples, and the Day
Turned and departed silent. I, too late,   10
Under her solemn fillet° saw the scorn.   *headband*

DAYS. 1. *hypocritic:* Our word *hypocrite* comes from Greek: "one who plays a part" (as in a play or a procession). 2. *dervishes:* members of a Moslem religious order, whose vows of poverty obliged them to give away their possessions. 7. *pleachèd:* To pleach is to bend and interweave—a stylized, artificial method of prettifying natural branches.

Philip Larkin (b. 1922)

DAYS   1964

What are days for?
Days are where we live.
They come, they wake us
Time and time over.
They are to be happy in: 5
Where can we live but days?

Ah, solving that question
Brings the priest and the doctor
In their long coats
Running over the fields.   10

O. Emil Rauter (b. 1950)

OUR MINTED DAYS

1978

Each day is a shiny penny
Which Jove drops in our piggy bank's slot.
Spend them wisely, O you humans,
Or they will be gone but not forgot—
    gone but not forgot—
        And then you'll REALLY be sorry!!!

QUESTIONS

1. What has each poet to say on the subject of days? Sum up the theme of each poem.
2. To which of these three poems does each of the following student-written critical descriptions seem to refer? With which points of the description do you agree, or disagree?
   a. The entire poem sustains one metaphor. The poem goes into vivid detail and has memorable images.
   b. This poem makes one ootsy-cutesy comparison, expressed in stale clichés, unnecessary words, and excess punctuation.
   c. The poem is written in beautifully speakable language and has a beautiful simplicity. It gently kids those who believe in ignoring the simple pleasures that days bring.
   d. This poem is poverty-stricken. Its first six lines have no figures of speech and no imagery. Its language is as dull as dishwater. The poet sort of thumbs his nose at religion and science as if he is better than they are, and thinks them slightly ridiculous.
   e. Starting with a truly beautiful comparison involving the bright copper of the morning sun, this poem ends up speaking in the real everyday language of modern America.

In the collected writings of Abraham Lincoln, the earliest lines are these, which Lincoln as a boy set down in his arithmetic copybook:

> Abraham Lincoln
> his hand and pen
> he will be good but
> god knows When

That the lines are original with Lincoln is uncertain, but we do know that, even as a young man embarked on a busy political career, Lincoln now and again entertained a desire to write poetry. Referring to a poem he admired, Lincoln told a friend, "I would give all I am worth, and go in debt, to be able to write so fine a piece as I think that is." (The poem that so impressed him was by one William Knox, whom the world has little noted, nor long remembered.) In 1846 Lincoln sent three versions or partial versions of the following poem to the same friend, who had it printed in Quincy (Illinois) *Whig*, a local newspaper. Lincoln explained how he had come to write it:

In the fall of 1844, thinking I might aid some to carry the State of Indiana for Mr. Clay, I went into the neighborhood in that State in which I was raised, where my mother and only sister were buried, and from which I had been absent about fifteen years. That part of the country is, within itself, as unpoetical as any spot of the earth; but still, seeing it and its objects and inhabitants aroused feelings in me which were certainly poetry; though whether my expression of those feelings is poetry is quite another question.[5]

Abraham Lincoln (1809–1865)

MY CHILDHOOD-HOME I SEE AGAIN   (1844–1846)

My childhood-home I see again,
  And gladden with the view;
And still as mem'ries crowd my brain,
  There's sadness in it too.

O memory! thou mid-way world   5
  'Twixt Earth and Paradise,
Where things decayed, and loved ones lost
  In dreamy shadows rise.

And freed from all that's gross or vile,
  Seem hallowed, pure, and bright,   10
Like scenes in some enchanted isle,
  All bathed in liquid light.

As distant mountains please the eye,
  When twilight chases day—
As bugle-tones, that, passing by,   15
  In distance die away—

As leaving some grand water-fall
  We ling'ring, list its roar,
So memory will hallow all
  We've known, but know no more.   20

Now twenty years have passed away,
  Since here I bid farewell
To woods, and fields, and scenes of play
  And school-mates loved so well.

Where many were, how few remain   25
  Of old familiar things!
But seeing these to mind again
  The lost and absent brings.

[5] Letter of April 18, 1846, to Andrew Johnston, *The Collected Works of Abraham Lincoln*, ed. Roy P. Basler (New Brunswick, N.J.: Rutgers University Press, 1953), 1:378.

The friends I left that parting day—
　　How changed, as time has sped!
Young childhood grown, strong manhood grey,
　　And half of all are dead.

I hear the lone survivors tell
　　How nought from death could save,
Till every sound appears a knell,
　　And every spot a grave.

I range the fields with pensive tread,
　　And pace the hollow rooms;
And feel (companions of the dead)
　　I'm living in the tombs.

And here's an object more of dread,
　　Than aught the grave contains—
A human-form, with reason fled,
　　While wretched life remains.

Poor Matthew! Once of genius bright,—
　　A fortune-favored child
Now locked for aye, in mental night,
　　A haggard mad-man wild.

Poor Matthew! I have ne'er forgot
　　When first with maddened will,
Yourself you maimed, your father fought,
　　And mother strove to kill;

And terror spread, and neighbors ran,
　　Your dang'rous strength to bind;
And soon a howling crazy man,
　　Your limbs were fast confined.

How then you writhed and shrieked aloud,
　　Your bones and sinews bared;
And fiendish on the gaping crowd,
　　With burning eyeballs glared.

And begged, and swore, and wept, and prayed,
　　With maniac laughter joined—
How fearful are the signs displayed,
　　By pangs that kill the mind!

And when at length, tho' drear and long,
　　Time soothed your fiercer woes—
How plaintively your mournful song
　　Upon the still night rose.

I've heard it oft, as if I dreamed,
　　Far-distant, sweet, and lone;
The funeral dirge it ever seemed
　　Of reason dead and gone.

To drink its strains, I've stole away,
    All silently and still,
Ere yet the rising god of day   75
    Had streaked the Eastern hill.

Air held his breath; the trees all still
    Seemed sorr'wing angels round.
Their swelling tears in dew-drops fell
    Upon the list'ning ground.   80

But this is past, and naught remains
    That raised you o'er the brute.
Your mad'ning shrieks and soothing strains
    Are like forever mute.

Now fare thee well: more thou the cause   85
    Than subject now of woe.
All mental pangs, but time's kind laws,
    Hast lost the power to know.

And now away to seek some scene
    Less painful than the last —   90
With less of horror mingled in
    The present and the past.

The very spot where grew the bread
    That formed my bones, I see.
How strange, old field, on thee to tread,   95
    And feel I'm part of thee!

My Childhood-Home I See Again. The "mad-man" portrayed in lines 41–88 is Matthew Gentry; as boys, he and Lincoln had gone to school together. "He was rather a bright lad," Lincoln explained to Johnston, "and the son of *the* rich man in our very poor neighborhood. At the age of nineteen he unaccountably became furiously mad, from which condition he gradually settled down into harmless insanity. When, as I told you . . . I visited my old home in the fall of 1844, I found him still lingering in this wretched condition" (letter of Sept. 6, 1846).

Questions

1. At one point during the composition of this poem, Lincoln apparently saw the first 40 lines as one distinct section and the Matthew portrait (lines 41–88) as another. "When I got to writing," he told Johnston, "the change of subjects divided the thing into four little divisions or cantos." But either Lincoln did not write the other two cantos or they have not survived. Does the poem seem to you complete and self-contained as it stands? How does the Matthew portrait follow from the beginning? Do the two parts of the poem go together?
2. After you have formed your own opinion of Lincoln's poem, see which of the following statements comes nearest to it:

   This is an amateurish poem of some merit, but it is spoiled by too many inept and sentimental things in it.

   This is a flawed poem, but it contains memorable lines, and as a whole it succeeds for me.

This is an excellent poem that places Lincoln among the world's
noteworthy poets.

This is a bad poem that deserves no charity just because Lincoln wrote it.
Support your judgment of the poem by pointing to particulars.

Fred Emerson Brooks (1850–1923)

PAT'S OPINION OF FLAGS   1894

Every man in the world thinks his banner the best,
    And his national song
    Is often too long,
Yet in praising his flag he makes sport of the rest,
Though there's many a truth that is spoken in jest,   5
    Save wid malice prepense
    There should be no offense.

There's the Hawaiian kingdom stuck out in the ocean;
    'Twas made as a site
    For the seabirds to light;   10
There they worship their colors wid colored devotion,
And they never have war, but internal commotion,
    For those islands contain, O,
    Queen Lilli's volcano.

      . . .

There's the flag of the Chinese, as everywan knows,   15
    Cut three-cornered wid care,
    Like they'd no cloth to spare;
Yet they seem to have plenty when makin' their clothes;
Havin' no fashion plate, they've cut big, I suppose;
    Hangin' loose roundabout   20
    So the fleas will drop out.

You can judge of those men by the wardrobe they wear:
    They don't look to get fits
    For a "dollar six bits."
Their flag was made yellow, as people declare,   25
Because they've the smallpox so much over there;
    Be warned, if ye're wise,
    By the dragon it flies.

But one of the prettiest flags that I know
    Is the great oroflam   30
    Of our old Uncle Sam;
Wid the red and white bars all laid out in a row,
And a nice pasture blue for the bright stars to grow;
    Wid the eagle above
    And around it the dove.   35

Of the Star-spangled Banner alone, it is said
        She has earned this renown—
        She was niver pulled down.
With the green on my grave and that flag overhead
I think I'll rest aisy! But wait till I'm dead!   40
        Wid that flag in the sky
        I'm in no haste to die.

Anthony Hecht (b. 1923)

JAPAN   1954

It was a miniature country once
To my imagination; Home of the Short,
And also the academy of stunts
        Where acrobats are taught
        The famous secrets of the trade: 5
        To cycle in the big parade
While spinning plates upon their parasols,
Or somersaults that do not touch the ground,
        Or tossing seven balls
In Most Celestial Order round and round.   10

A child's quick sense of the ingenious stamped
All their invention: toys I used to get
At Christmastime, or the peculiar, cramped
        Look of their alphabet.
        Fragile and easily destroyed,   15
        Those little boats of celluloid
Driven by camphor round the bathroom sink,
And delicate the folded paper prize
        Which, dropped into a drink
Of water, grew up right before your eyes.   20

Now when we reached them it was with a sense
Sharpened for treachery compounding in their brains
Like mating weasels; our Intelligence
        Said: The Black Dragon reigns
        Secretly under yellow skin,   25
        Deeper than dyes of atabrine
And deadlier. The War Department said:
Remember you are Americans; forsake
        The wounded and the dead
At your own cost; remember Pearl and Wake.   30

And yet they bowed us in with ceremony,
Told us what brands of Sake were the best,
Explained their agriculture in a phony
        Dialect of the West,

Meant vaguely to be understood   35
As a shy sign of brotherhood
In the old human bondage to the facts
Of day-to-day existence. And like ants,
    Signaling tiny pacts
With their antennae, they would wave their hands.   40

At last we came to see them not as glib
Walkers of tightropes, worshipers of carp,
Nor yet a species out of Adam's rib
    Meant to preserve its warp
In Cain's own image. They had learned   45
That their tough eye-born goddess burned
Adoring fingers. They were very poor.
The holy mountain was not moved to speak.
    Wind at the paper door
Offered them snow out of its hollow peak.   50

Human endeavor clumsily betrays
Humanity. Their excrement served in this;
For, planting rice in water, they would raise
    Schistosomiasis
Japonica, that enters through   55
    The pores into the avenue
And orbit of the blood, where it may foil
The heart and kill, or settle in the brain.
    This fruit of their nightsoil
Thrives in the skull, where it is called insane.   60

Now the quaint early image of Japan
That was so charming to me as a child
Seems like a bright design upon a fan,
    Of water rushing wild
On rocks that can be folded up,   65
    A river which the wrist can stop
With a neat flip, revealing merely sticks
And silk of what had been a fan before,
    And like such winning tricks,
It shall be buried in excelsior.   70

JAPAN. 24. *The Black Dragon:* militarist organization that had urged the expansion of the
Japanese empire. 26. *atabrine:* a drug used against malaria. A side effect of it is that it gives
a yellow tinge to the user's skin. 30. *Pearl and Wake:* Pearl Harbor and Wake Island, attacked by the Japanese on December 7, 1941. Wake fell after a prolonged defense by a
small garrison of Marines. 54–55. *Schistosomiasis Japonica:* a disease caused by parasitic
worms in the bloodstream.

QUESTIONS

1. The preceding two poems by Brooks and Hecht have something in common:
   an American speaker's view of foreigners. Who is the speaker in each poem?

2. Pat opens with an apology for what he is about to say. Do you find this apology satisfactory? Why or why not?
3. Consider Pat's attitude toward flags in Brooks's lines 1–7 and his attitude toward Old Glory in the last two stanzas. What contradiction do you notice between these two attitudes?
4. A word worth knowing is *jingoism*, from a patriotic ditty sung in English music halls in 1878, when a British fleet was sent into Turkish waters to resist Russian advances: "We don't want to fight, but by jingo, if we do / We've got the ships, we've got the men, and got the money, too!" For what reasons might Brooks's poem be called jingoistic?
5. In Hecht's poem, what is the speaker's attitude toward the Japanese at the beginning of the poem? At the end? What changes it?
6. What is the effect of Hecht's references to medicine and disease? How does the speaker feel toward victims of Schistosomiasis Japonica? Compare this with Pat's reference to smallpox (line 33).
7. What is the theme of each poem? To what extent does each poet make us see his theme in concrete terms, using imagery and detailed observation?
8. These two poems point toward a larger topic for discussion. What does the quality of a poem have to do with the poet's ability to understand people and to sympathize with them?

26 Knowing Excellence

How can we tell an excellent poem from any other? To give reasons for excellence in poetry is harder than to give reasons for failure in poetry (so often due to familiar, old-hat sorts of imprecision and sentimentality). A bad poem tends to be stereotyped, an excellent poem unique. In judging either, we can have no absolute preexisting specifications. A poem is not a simple mechanism like an electric toaster that an inspector in a factory can test by a check-off list. It has to be judged on the basis of what it evidently is trying to be and how well it succeeds in its effort. Nor is excellence simply due to regularity and symmetry. For the sake of meaning, a competent poet often will depart from a pattern. There is satisfaction, said Robert Frost, in things not mechanically straight: "We enjoy the straight crookedness of a good walking stick."

To judge a poem, we first have to understand it. At least, we need to understand it *almost* all the way; there is, to be sure, a poem such as Hopkins's "The Windhover" (p. 762), which most readers probably would call excellent even though its meaning is still being debated. While it is a good idea to give a poem at least a couple of considerate readings before judging it, sometimes our first encounter with a poem starts turning into an act of evaluation. Moving along into the poem, becoming more deeply involved in it, we may begin forming an opinion. In general, the more a poem contains for us to understand, the more rewarding we are likely to find it. This does not mean that an obscure and highly demanding poem is always to be preferred to a relatively simple one. Difficult poems can be pretentious and incoherent, but there is something to be said for the poem complicated enough to leave us something to discover on our fifteenth reading (unlike most limericks, which yield their all at a single look). Here is such a poem, one not readily fathomed and exhausted.

William Butler Yeats (1865–1939)

SAILING TO BYZANTIUM   1927

That is no country for old men. The young
In one another's arms, birds in the trees

—Those dying generations—at their song,
The salmon-falls, the mackerel-crowded seas,
Fish, flesh, or fowl, commend all summer long   5
Whatever is begotten, born, and dies.
Caught in that sensual music all neglect
Monuments of unaging intellect.

An aged man is but a paltry thing,
A tattered coat upon a stick, unless   10
Soul clap its hands and sing, and louder sing
For every tatter in its mortal dress,
Nor is there singing school but studying
Monuments of its own magnificence;
And therefore I have sailed the seas and come   15
To the holy city of Byzantium.

O sages standing in God's holy fire
As in the gold mosaic of a wall,
Come from the holy fire, perne in a gyre°,   *spin down a spiral*
And be the singing-masters of my soul.   20
Consume my heart away; sick with desire
And fastened to a dying animal
It knows not what it is; and gather me
Into the artifice of eternity.

Once out of nature I shall never take   25
My bodily form from any natural thing,
But such a form as Grecian goldsmiths make
Of hammered gold and gold enameling
To keep a drowsy Emperor awake;
Or set upon a golden bough to sing   30
To lords and ladies of Byzantium
Of what is past, or passing, or to come.

SAILING TO BYZANTIUM. Byzantium was the capital of the Byzantine Empire, the city now called Istanbul. Yeats means, though, not merely the physical city. Byzantium is also a name for his conception of paradise.

Though *salmon-falls* (line 4) suggests Yeats's native Ireland, the poem, as we find out in line 25, is about escaping from the entire natural world. If the poet desires this escape, then probably the *country* mentioned in the opening line is no political nation but the cycle of birth and death in which human beings are trapped; and, indeed, the poet says his heart is "fastened to a dying animal." Imaginary landscapes, it would seem, are merging with the historical Byzantium. Lines 17-18 refer to mosaic images, adornments of the Byzantine cathedral of St. Sophia, in which the figures of saints are inlaid against backgrounds of gold. The clockwork bird of the last stanza is also a reference to something actual. Yeats noted: "I have read somewhere that in the Emperor's palace at Byzantium was a tree made of gold and silver, and artificial birds that sang." This description of the role the poet would seek—that of a changeless, immortal singer—directs us back to the earlier references to music and singing. Taken all together, they point toward the central metaphor of the poem: the craft of poetry can be a kind of singing. One kind of everlasting monument is a great poem. To study masterpieces of poetry is the only "singing school"—the only way to learn to write a poem.

We have no more than skimmed through a few of this poem's suggestions, enough to show that, out of allusion and imagery, Yeats has woven at least one elaborate metaphor. Surely one thing the poem achieves is that, far from merely puzzling us, it makes us aware of relationships between what a person can imagine and the physical world. There is the statement that a human heart is bound to the body that perishes, and yet it is possible to see consciousness for a moment independent of flesh, to sing with joy at the very fact that the body is crumbling away. Expressing a similar view of mortality, the Japanese artist Hokusai has shown a withered tree letting go of its few remaining leaves, while under it two graybeards shake with laughter. Like Hokusai's view, that of Yeats is by no means simple. Much of the power of Yeats's poem comes from the physical terms with which he states the ancient quarrel between body and spirit, body being a "tattered coat upon a stick." There is all the difference in the world between the work of the poet like Yeats whose eye is on the living thing and whose mind is awake and passionate, and that of the slovenly poet whose dull eye and sleepy mind focus on nothing more than some book read hastily long ago. The former writes a poem out of compelling need, the latter as if it seems a nice idea to write something.

Yeats's poem has the three qualities essential to beauty, according to the definition of Thomas Aquinas: wholeness, harmony, and radiance. The poem is all one; its parts move in peace with one another; it shines with emotional intensity. There is an orderly progression going on in it: from the speaker's statement of his discontent with the world of "sensual music," to his statement that he is quitting this world, to his prayer that the sages will take him in, and his vision of future immortality. And the images of the poem relate to one another—*dying generations* (line 3), *dying animal* (line 22), and the undying golden bird (lines 27-32) —to mention just one series of related things. "Sailing to Byzantium" is not the kind of poem that has, in Pope's words, "One simile, that solitary shines / In the dry desert of a thousand lines." Rich in figurative language, Yeats's whole poem develops a metaphor, with further metaphors as its tributaries.

"Sailing to Byzantium" has a theme that matters to us. What human being does not long, at times, to shed timid, imperfect flesh, to live in a state of absolute joy, unperishing? Being human, perhaps we too are stirred by Yeats's prayer: "Consume my heart away, sick with desire / And fastened to a dying animal. . . ." If it is true that in poetry (as Ezra Pound declared) "only emotion endures," then Yeats's poem ought to endure. (No reasons to be moved by a poem, however, can be of much use. If you happen not to feel moved by this particular poem, try another—but come back to "Sailing to Byzantium" after a while.)

Most excellent poems, it might be argued, contain significant themes, as does "Sailing to Byzantium." But the presence of such a theme is not enough to render a poem excellent. That classic tear-jerker "The Old Arm-Chair" (p. 648) expresses in its way, too, faith in a kind of immortality. Not theme alone makes an excellent poem, but how well a theme is stated.

Yeats's poem, some would say, is the match of any lyric in our language. Some might call it inferior to an epic (to Milton's *Paradise Lost*, say, or to the *Iliad*), but this is to lead us into a different argument: whether certain genres are innately better than others. Such an argument usually leads to a dead end. Evidently, *Paradise Lost* has greater range, variety, matter, length, and ambitiousness. But any poem—whether an epic or an epigram—may be judged by how well it fulfills the design it undertakes. God, who created both fleas and whales, pronounced all good. Fleas, like epigrams, have no reason to feel inferior.

EXERCISE: *Two Poems to Compare*

Here are two poems with a similar theme. Which contains more qualities of excellent poetry? Decide whether the other is bad or whether it may be praised for achieving something different.

Arthur Guiterman (1871–1943)
ON THE VANITY OF EARTHLY GREATNESS   1936

The tusks that clashed in mighty brawls
Of mastodons, are billiard balls.

The sword of Charlemagne the Just
Is ferric oxide, known as rust.

The grizzly bear whose potent hug
Was feared by all, is now a rug.

Great Caeser's bust is on the shelf,
And I don't feel so well myself.

Percy Bysshe Shelley (1792–1822)
OZYMANDIAS   1818

I met a traveler from an antique land
Who said: Two vast and trunkless legs of stone
Stand in the desert. Near them, on the sand,
Half sunk, a shattered visage lies, whose frown,

And wrinkled lip, and sneer of cold command, 5
Tell that its sculptor well those passions read
Which yet survive, stamped on these lifeless things,
The hand that mocked° them and the heart that fed; *imitated*
And on the pedestal these words appear:
"My name is Ozymandias, king of kings: 10
Look on my works, ye Mighty, and despair!"
Nothing beside remains. Round the decay
Of that colossal wreck, boundless and bare
The lone and level sands stretch far away.

Some excellent poems of the past will remain sealed to us unless
we are willing to sympathize with their conventions. Pastoral poetry,
for instance—Marlowe's "Passionate Shepherd" and Milton's "Lycidas"—asks us to accept certain conventions and situations that may
seem old-fashioned: idle swains, oaten flutes. We are under no grim
duty, of course, to admire poems whose conventions do not appeal to
us. But there is no point in blaming a poet for playing a particular game
or for observing its rules.

There are, however, inferior poems that appear to be pieced together from conventions: patchwork quilts of old unwanted words.

John Lyly (1554–1606?)

DAPHNE 1590

My Daphne's hair is twisted gold,
Bright stars apiece her eyes do hold;
My Daphne's brow enthrones the graces,
My Daphne's beauty stains all faces;
On Daphne's cheek grow rose and cherry, 5
On Daphne's lip a sweeter berry;
Daphne's snowy hand but touched does melt,
And then no heavenlier warmth is felt;
My Daphne's voice tunes all the spheres,
My Daphne's music charms all ears. 10
Fond° am I thus to sing her praise; *foolish*
These glories now are turned to bays.

DAPHNE. 12. *bays:* evergreen leaves in crowns traditionally awarded to poets; hence, poetic
fame.

Lyly's poem isn't worthless: a woman whose beauty *stains* all other
women's faces by comparison may be hard to forget. Still, "Daphne" is
a mediocre specimen of a kind of poetry that swept England in the sixteenth century, when the influence of Italian sonnets reached its height.

(See the discussion of the sonnet on page 574.) The result was a surplus of Petrarchan **conceits,** or elaborate comparisons (from the Italian *concetto:* concept, bright idea). Shakespeare, who at times helped himself generously from the Petrarchan stockpile, in the following famous sonnet pokes fun at poets who use such handed-down figures of speech thoughtlessly. Which traits of Lyly's Daphne do you find him kidding here?

William Shakespeare (1564–1616)

MY MISTRESS' EYES ARE NOTHING LIKE THE SUN   1609

My mistress' eyes are nothing like the sun;
Coral is far more red than her lips' red;
If snow be white, why then her breasts are dun;
If hairs be wires, black wires grow on her head.
I have seen roses damasked red and white,   5
But no such roses see I in her cheeks;
And in some perfumes is there more delight
Than in the breath that from my mistress reeks.
I love to hear her speak, yet well I know
That music hath a far more pleasing sound;   10
I grant I never saw a goddess go:
My mistress, when she walks, treads on the ground.
   And yet, by heaven, I think my love as rare
   As any she°, belied with false compare.   *woman*

Contrary to what you might expect, for years after Shakespeare's time, poets continued to write fine poems with the aid of such conventions.

Thomas Campion (1567–1620)

THERE IS A GARDEN IN HER FACE   1617

There is a garden in her face
Where roses and white lilies grow;
   A heav'nly paradise is that place
Wherein all pleasant fruits do flow.
   There cherries grow which none may buy   5
   Till "Cherry-ripe" themselves do cry.

Those cherries fairly do enclose
Of orient pearl a double row,
   Which when her lovely laughter shows,
They look like rose-buds filled with snow;   10
   Yet them nor° peer nor prince can buy,   *neither*
   Till "Cherry-ripe" themselves do cry.

Her eyes like angels watch them still;
Her brows like bended bows do stand,
   Threat'ning with piercing frowns to kill   15
All that attempt, with eye or hand
    Those sacred cherries to come nigh
    Till "Cherry-ripe" themselves do cry.

THERE IS A GARDEN IN HER FACE. 6. *"Cherry-ripe"*: cry of fruit-peddlers in London streets.

QUESTIONS

1. What does Campion's song owe to Petrarchan tradition?
2. What in it strikes you as fresh observation of actual life?
3. Comment in particular on the last stanza. Does the comparison of eyebrows to threatening bowmen seem too silly or far-fetched? What sense do you find in it?
4. Try to describe the tone of this poem. What do you understand, from this portrait of a young girl, to be the poet's feelings?

Excellent poetry might be easier to recognize if each poet had a fixed position on the slopes of Mount Parnassus, but from one century to the next, the reputations of some poets have taken humiliating slides, or made impressive clambers. We decide for ourselves which poems to call excellent, but readers of the future may reverse our opinions. Most of us no longer would share this popular view of Walt Whitman by one of his contemporaries:

> Walt Whitman (1819-1892), by some regarded as a great poet; by others, as no poet at all. Most of his so-called poems are mere catalogues of things, without meter or rime, but in a few more regular poems and in lines here and there he is grandly poetical, as in "O Captain! My Captain!"[1].

Walt Whitman (1819–1892)
O CAPTAIN! MY CAPTAIN!   1865

O Captain! my Captain! our fearful trip is done,
The ship has weather'd every rack, the prize we sought is won,
The port is near, the bells I hear, the people all exulting,
While follow eyes the steady keel, the vessel grim and daring;
    But O heart! heart! heart!   5
      O the bleeding drops of red,
        Where on the deck my Captain lies,
        Fallen cold and dead.

O Captain! my Captain! rise up and hear the bells;
Rise up — for you the flag is flung — for you the bugle trills,   10

[1] J. Willis Westlake, A.M., in *Common-school Literature, English and American, with Several Hundred Extracts to be Memorized* (Philadelphia, 1898).

For you bouquets and ribbon'd wreaths — for you the shores a-crowding,
For you they call, the swaying mass, their eager faces turning;
    Here Captain! dear father!
      This arm beneath your head!
        It is some dream that on the deck,   15
          You've fallen cold and dead.

My Captain does not answer, his lips are pale and still,
My father does not feel my arm, he has no pulse nor will,
The ship is anchor'd safe and sound, its voyage closed and done,
From fearful trip the victor ship comes in with object won;   20
    Exult O shores, and ring O bells!
      But I with mournful tread,
        Walk the deck my Captain lies,
          Fallen cold and dead.

O Captain! My Captain! Written soon after the death of Abraham Lincoln, this was, in
Whitman's lifetime, by far the most popular of his poems.

Questions

1. Compare this with other Whitman poems. (See another elegy for Lincoln,
   "When Lilacs Last in the Dooryard Bloom'd," quoted in part on page 581.) In
   what ways is "O Captain! My Captain!" uncharacteristic of his works? Do
   you agree with J. Willis Westlake that this is one of the few occasions on
   which Whitman is "grandly poetical"?
2. Comment on the appropriateness to its subject of the poem's rhythms.
3. Do you find any evidence in this poem than an excellent poet wrote it?

There is nothing to do but commit ourselves and praise or blame
and, if need be, let time erase our error. In a sense, all readers of poetry
are constantly reexamining the judgments of the past by choosing those
poems they care to go on reading. In the end, we have to admit that the
critical principles set forth in this chapter are all very well for admiring
excellent poetry we already know, but they cannot be carried like a
yardstick in the hand, to go out looking for it. As Ezra Pound said in his
ABC of Reading, "A classic is classic not because it conforms to certain
structural rules, or fits certain definitions (of which its author had quite
probably never heard). It is classic because of a certain eternal and irre-
pressible freshness."

The best poems, like "Sailing to Byzantium," may offer a kind of
religious experience. In the eighth decade of the twentieth century,
some of us rarely set foot outside an artificial environment. Whizzing
down four-lane superhighways, we observe lakes and trees in the distance. In a way our cities are to us as anthills are to ants, as Frost
reminds us in "Departmental." No less than anthills, they are "natural"
structures. But the "unnatural" world of school or business is, as Wordsworth says, too much with us. Locked in the shells of our ambitions,
our self-esteem, we forget our kinship to earth and sea. We fabricate

self-justifications. But a great poem shocks us into another order of perception. It points beyond language to something still more essential. It ushers us into an experience so moving and true that we feel (to quote King Lear) "cut to the brain." In bad or indifferent poetry, words are all there is.

Matthew Arnold (1822–1888)
BELOW THE SURFACE-STREAM, SHALLOW AND LIGHT   1869

Below the surface-stream, shallow and light,
Of what we *say* we feel—below the stream,
As light, of what we *think* we feel—there flows
With noiseless current strong, obscure and deep,
The central stream of what we feel indeed.

QUESTIONS

1. Speaking of himself and his fellow poets, W. D. Snodgrass has expressed the opinion that:

   our only hope as artists is to continually ask ourselves, "Am I writing what I *really* think? Not what is acceptable; not what my favorite intellectual would think in this situation; not what I wish I felt. Only what I cannot help thinking." ("Finding a Poem," *In Radical Pursuit*, New York, Harper & Row, 1974.)

   Compare Snodgrass's statement and the statement that Arnold makes in his brief poem.
2. Of what value is Arnold's observation to readers of poetry?

Thomas Gray (1716–1771)
ELEGY WRITTEN IN A COUNTRY CHURCHYARD   1753

The curfew tolls the knell of parting day,
  The lowing herd wind slowly o'er the lea,
The plowman homeward plods his weary way,
  And leaves the world to darkness and to me.

Now fades the glimmering landscape on the sight,   5
  And all the air a solemn stillness holds,
Save where the beetle wheels his droning flight,
  And drowsy tinklings lull the distant folds;

Save that from yonder ivy-mantled tow'r
  The moping owl does to the moon complain   10
Of such, as wand'ring near her secret bow'r,
  Molest her ancient solitary reign.

Beneath those rugged elms, that yew tree's shade,
　　Where heaves the turf in many a mold'ring heap,
Each in his narrow cell forever laid,　　　　　　　　　　　　　　15
　　The rude forefathers of the hamlet sleep.

The breezy call of incense-breathing morn,
　　The swallow twitt'ring from the straw-built shed,
The cock's shrill clarion, or the echoing horn°,　　　　*fox-hunters' horn*
　　No more shall rouse them from their lowly bed.　　　　　20

For them no more the blazing hearth shall burn,
　　Or busy housewife ply her evening care;
No children run to lisp their sire's return,
　　Or climb his knees the envied kiss to share.

Oft did the harvest to their sickle yield,　　　　　　　　　　　25
　　Their furrow oft the stubborn glebe° has broke;　　　　　　　*turf*
How jocund did they drive their team afield!
　　How bowed the woods beneath their sturdy stroke!

Let not Ambition mock their useful toil,
　　Their homely joys, and destiny obscure;　　　　　　　　　　30
Nor Grandeur hear with a disdainful smile
　　The short and simple annals of the poor.

The boast of heraldry, the pomp of pow'r,
　　And all that beauty, all that wealth e'er gave,
Awaits alike th' inevitable hour.　　　　　　　　　　　　　　35
　　The paths of glory lead but to the grave.

Nor you, ye proud, impute to these the fault,
　　If Mem'ry o'er their tomb no trophies raise,
Where through the long-drawn aisle and fretted° vault　　*decorated*
　　The pealing anthem swells the note of praise.　　　　　　40

Can storied° urn or animated bust　　　　　　　　　　　*inscribed*
　　Back to its mansion call the fleeting breath?
Can Honor's voice provoke the silent dust,
　　Or Flatt'ry soothe the dull cold ear of Death?

Perhaps in this neglected spot is laid　　　　　　　　　　　45
　　Some heart once pregnant with celestial fire;
Hands that the rod of empire might have swayed,
　　Or waked to ecstasy the living lyre.

But knowledge to their eyes her ample page
　　Rich with the spoils of time did ne'er unroll;　　　　　　50
Chill Penury repressed their noble rage,
　　And froze the genial current of the soul.

Full many a gem of purest ray serene,
　　The dark unfathomed caves of ocean bear:
Full many a flower is born to blush unseen,　　　　　　　55
　　And waste its sweetness on the desert air.

Some village Hampden, that with dauntless breast
    The little tyrant of his field withstood;
Some mute inglorious Milton here may rest,
    Some Cromwell guiltless of his country's blood.   60

Th' applause of list'ning senates to command,
    The threats of pain and ruin to despise,
To scatter plenty o'er a smiling land,
    And read their hist'ry in a nation's eyes,

Their lot forbade: nor circumscribed alone   65
    Their growing virtues, but their crimes confined;
Forbade to wade through slaughter to a throne,
    And shut the gates of mercy on mankind,

The struggling pangs of conscious truth to hide,
    To quench the blushes of ingenuous shame,   70
Or heap the shrine of Luxury and Pride
    With incense kindled at the Muse's flame.

Far from the madding° crowd's ignoble strife,   *frenzied*
    Their sober wishes never learned to stray;
Along the cool sequestered vale of life   75
    They kept the noiseless tenor of their way.

Yet ev'n these bones from insult to protect
    Some frail memorial still erected nigh,
With uncouth rhymes and shapeless sculpture decked,
    Implores the passing tribute of a sigh.   80

Their name, their years, spelt by th' unlettered Muse,
    The place of fame and elegy supply:
And many a holy text around she strews,
    That teach the rustic moralist to die.

For who to dumb Forgetfulness a prey,   85
    This pleasing anxious being e'er resigned,
Left the warm precincts of the cheerful day,
    Nor cast one longing ling'ring look behind?

On some fond breast the parting soul relies,
    Some pious drops the closing eye requires;   90
Ev'n from the tomb the voice of Nature cries,
    Ev'n in our ashes live their wonted° fires.   *customary*

For thee, who mindful of th' unhonored dead
    Dost in these lines their artless tale relate;
If chance, by lonely contemplation led,   95
    Some kindred spirit shall inquire thy fate,

Haply some hoary-headed swain° may say,   *shepherd*
    "Oft have we seen him at the peep of dawn
Brushing with hasty steps the dews away
    To meet the sun upon the upland lawn.   100

"There at the foot of yonder nodding beech
    That wreathes its old fantastic roots so high,
His listless length at noontide would he stretch,
    And pore upon the brook that babbles by.

"Hard by yon wood, now smiling as in scorn,   105
    Mutt'ring his wayward fancies he would rove,
Now drooping, woeful wan, like one forlorn,
    Or crazed with care, or crossed in hopeless love.

"One morn I missed him, on the customed hill,
    Along the heath and near his fav'rite tree;   110
Another came; not yet beside the rill,
    Nor up the lawn, nor at the wood was he;

"The next with dirges due in sad array
    Slow though the churchway path we saw him borne.
Approach and read (for thou canst read) the lay,   115
    Graved on the stone beneath yon aged thorn."

The Epitaph

Here rests his head upon the lap of Earth
    A youth to Fortune and to Fame unknown.
Fair Science° frowned not on his humble birth,   *Knowledge*
    And Melancholy marked him for her own.   120

Large was his bounty, and his soul sincere,
    Heav'n did a recompense as largely send:
He gave to Mis'ry all he had, a tear,
    He gained from Heav'n ('twas all he wished) a friend.

No farther seek his merits to disclose,   125
    Or draw his frailties from their dread abode,
(There they alike in trembling hope repose),
    The bosom of His Father and his God.

ELEGY WRITTEN IN A COUNTRY CHURCHYARD. 57. *Hampden:* John Hampden, who had
resisted illegal taxes imposed by Charles I.

QUESTIONS

1. In contrasting the unknown poor buried in this village churchyard and
   famous men buried in cathedrals (in *fretted vault,* line 39), what is Gray's
   theme? What do you understand from the line, *The paths of glory lead but to
   the grave?*
2. Carl J. Weber thinks that Gray's compassion for the village poor anticipates
   the democratic sympathies of the American Revolution: "Thomas Gray is
   the pioneer literary spokesman for the Ordinary Man." But another critic,
   Lyle Glazier, argues that the "Elegy" isn't political at all: that we misread if
   we think the poet meant "to persuade the poor and obscure that their barren lives are meaningful"; and also misread if we think he meant to assure
   the privileged classes "in whose ranks Gray was proud to consider himself"

that they need not worry about the poor, "who have already all essential riches." How much truth do you find in either of these views?

3. Cite lines and phrases that show Gray's concern for the musical qualities of words.

4. Who is the *youth* of the closing Epitaph? By *thee* (line 93) does Gray mean himself? Does he mean some fictitious poet supposedly writing the "Elegy" —the first-person speaker (line 4)? Does he mean some village stonecutter, a crude poet whose illiterate Muse (line 81) inspired him to compose tombstone epitaphs? Or could the Epitaph possibly refer to Gray's close friend of school and undergraduate days, the promising poet Richard West, who had died in 1742? Which interpretation seems to you the most reasonable? (Does our lack of absolute certainty negate the value of the poem?)

5. Walter Savage Landor called the Epitaph a tin kettle tied to the tail of a noble dog. Do you agree that the Epitaph is inferior to what has gone before it? What is its function in Gray's poem?

6. Many sources for Gray's phrases and motifs have been found in earlier poets: Virgil, Horace, Dante, Milton, and many more. Even if it could be demonstrated that Gray's poem has not one original line in it, would it be possible to dismiss the "Elegy" as a mere rag-bag of borrowings, like John Lyly's "Daphne"?

7. Gray's poem, a pastoral elegy, is in the same genre as another famous English poem: John Milton's "Lycidas." What conventions are common to both?

8. In the earliest surviving manuscript of Gray's poem, lines 73–76 read:

> No more with Reason and thyself at strife;
> Give anxious cares and endless wishes room
> But through the cool sequester'd vale of Life
> Pursue the silent tenor of thy doom.

In what ways does the final version of those lines seem superior?

9. Perhaps the best-known poem in English, Gray's "Elegy" has inspired hundreds of imitations, countless parodies, and translations into eighteen or more languages. (Some of these languages contain dozens of attempts to translate it.) To what do you attribute the poem's fame? What do you suppose has proved so universally appealing in it?

10. Compare Gray's "Elegy" with Shelley's "Ozymandias" and Arthur Guiterman's "On the Vanity of Earthly Greatness." What do the three poems have in common? How would you rank them in order of excellence?

27 Alternatives

THE POET'S REVISIONS

"He / Who casts to write a living line must sweat, / . . . and strike the second heat / Upon the Muse's anvil," wrote Ben Jonson. Indeed, few if any immortal poems can have been perfected with the first blow. The labor of revising seems the usual practice of most bards (other than the Bard of Avon, if we believe the famous rumor that in "whatsoever he penned, he never blotted out line"). As a result, a poet may leave us two or more versions of a poem — perhaps (as Robert Graves has said of his work drafts) "hatched and cross-hatched by puzzling layers of ink."

We need not, of course, rummage the poet's wastebasket in order to assess a poem. If we wish, we can follow a suggestion of the critic Austin Warren: take any fine poem and make changes in it. Then compare the changes with the original. We may then realize why the poem is as it is instead of something else. However, there is a certain undeniable pleasure in watching a poem go through its growth stages. Some readers have claimed that the study of successive versions gives them insight into the process by which poems come to be. More important to a reader whose concern is to read poems with appreciation, we stand to learn something about the rightness of a finished poem from seeing what alternatives occurred to the poet. To a critic who protested two lines in Wordsworth's "The Thorn," a painfully flat description of an infant's grave,

> I've measured it from side to side;
> 'Tis three feet long and two feet wide,

Wordsworth retorted, "They ought to be liked." However, he thought better of them and later made this change:

> Though but of compass small, and bare
> To thirsty suns and parching air.

A novice poet who regards a first draft as inviolable sometimes loses interest in the poem if anyone suggests that more work be done on it. Others have found high excitement in the task. "Months of re-writing! What happiness!" exclaimed William Butler Yeats in a letter to a friend. In fact, Yeats so much enjoyed revision that late in life he kept trying to improve the poems of his youth. The end results seem more youthful and spontaneous than the originals. A merciless self-critic, Yeats discarded lines that a lesser poet would have been grateful for. In some cases his final version was practically a new poem:

William Butler Yeats (1865–1939)

THE OLD PENSIONER   1890

I had a chair at every hearth,
When no one turned to see
With "Look at that old fellow there;
And who may he be?"
And therefore do I wander on,   5
And the fret is on me.

The road-side trees keep murmuring —
Ah, wherefore murmur ye
As in the old days long gone by,
Green oak and poplar tree!   10
The well-known faces are all gone,
And the fret is on me.

THE LAMENTATION OF THE OLD PENSIONER   1939

Although I shelter from the rain
Under a broken tree
My chair was nearest to the fire
In every company
That talked of love or politics,   5
Ere Time transfigured me.

Though lads are making pikes again
For some conspiracy,
And crazy rascals rage their fill
At human tyranny,   10
My contemplations are of Time
That has transfigured me.

There's not a woman turns her face
Upon a broken tree,
And yet the beauties that I loved   15
Are in my memory;
I spit into the face of Time
That has transfigured me.

QUESTIONS

1. "The Old Pensioner" is this poem's first printed version; "Lamentation," its last. From the original, what elements has Yeats in the end retained?

2. What does the final version add to our knowledge of the old man (his character, attitudes, circumstances)?
3. Compare in sound and rhythm the refrain in the "Lamentation" with the original refrain.
4. Why do the statements in the final version seem to follow one another more naturally, and the poem as a whole seem more tightly woven together?

Yeats's practice seems to document the assertion of critic A. F. Scott that "the work of correction is often quite as inspired as the first onrush of words and ideas." Yeats made a revealing comment on his methods of revision:

> In dream poetry, in "Kubla Khan," . . . every line, every word can carry its unanalyzable, rich associations; but if we dramatize some possible singer or speaker we remember that he is moved by one thing at a time, certain words must be dull and numb. Here and there in correcting my early poems I have introduced such numbness and dullness, turned, for instance, the "curd-pale moon" into the "brilliant moon," that all might seem, as it were, remembered with indifference, except some one vivid image. When I began to rehearse a play I had the defects of my early poetry; I insisted upon obvious all-pervading rhythm. Later on I found myself saying that only in those lines or words where the beauty of the passage came to its climax, must rhythm be obvious.[1]

In changing words for "dull and numb" ones, in breaking up and varying rhythms, Yeats evidently is trying for improvement not necessarily in a particular line, but in an entire poem.

Not all revisions are successful. An instance might be the alterations Keats made in "La Belle Dame sans Merci," in which the stanza with the "wild wild eyes" and the exactly counted kisses,

> She took me to her elfin grot,
>   And there she wept and sighed full sore,
> And there I shut her wild wild eyes
>   With kisses four.

was scrapped in favor of:

> She took me to her elfin grot,
>   And there she gazed and sighèd deep,
> And there I shut her wild sad eyes —
>   So kissed to sleep.

When Mark Antony begins his funeral oration, "Friends, Romans, countrymen: lend me your ears," Shakespeare makes him ask something quite different from the modernized version in one high school English textbook: "Friends, Romans, countrymen: listen to me." Strictly speaking, any revised version of a poem is a different poem, even if its only change is a single word.

---

[1] "Dramatis Personae, 1896–1902," in *The Autobiography of William Butler Yeats* (New York: Macmillan, 1953).

In each of the following pairs, which details of the revised version show an improvement of the earlier one? Exactly what makes the poet's second thoughts seem better (if you agree that they are)? Italics indicate words of one text not found in the other. Notice that in some cases, the poet has also changed word order.

1. Samuel Taylor Coleridge, "The Rime of the Ancient Mariner," from Part III:

   a. One after one, by the hornèd Moon
       (Listen, O Stranger! to me)
       Each turn'd his face with a ghastly pang
       And curs'd me with his *ee.*   *(1799 version)*

   b. One after one, by the *star-dogged* Moon,
       Too quick for groan or sigh,
       Each turned his face with a ghastly pang
       And cursed me with his *eye.*   *(1817 version)*

2. William Blake, last stanza of "London" (complete poem given on page 68):

   a. But most the midnight harlot's curse
       From every *dismal* street I hear,
       Weaves around the marriage hearse
       And blasts the new born infant's tear. *(first draft, 1793)*

   b. But most *through* midnight streets I hear
       How the *youthful* harlot's curse
       Blasts the new born infant's tear
       And *blights with plagues* the marriage hearse. *(1794 version)*

3. Edward FitzGerald, *The Rubáiyát of Omar Khayyám*, a quatrain:

   a. *For in and out, above, about, below,*
       'Tis nothing but a Magic Shadow-show,
           Play'd in a Box whose Candle is the Sun,
       Round *which* we *Phantom Figures* come and go.

                                      (first version, 1859 edition)

   b. We *are no other than a moving row*
       Of Magic Shadow-*shapes that* come and go
           Round *with* the Sun-*illumined Lantern held*
       In Midnight by the Master of the Show; . . .

                                      (fifth version, 1889 edition)

Walt Whitman (1819–1892)

A NOISELESS PATIENT SPIDER

A noiseless patient spider,
I mark'd where on a little promontory it stood isolated,
Mark'd how to explore the vacant vast surrounding,
It launch'd forth filament, filament, filament, out of itself,
Ever unreeling them, ever tirelessly speeding them.   5

And you O my soul where you stand,
Surrounded, detached, in measureless oceans of space,
Ceaselessly musing, venturing, throwing, seeking the spheres to connect
     them,
Till the bridge you will need be form'd, till the ductile anchor hold,
Till the gossamer thread you fling catch somewhere, O my soul.   10

THE SOUL, REACHING, THROWING OUT FOR LOVE

The Soul, reaching, throwing out for love,
As the spider, from some little promontory, throwing out filament after
     filament, tirelessly out of itself, that one at least may catch and form
     a link, a bridge, a connection
O I saw one passing along, saying hardly a word—yet full of love I de-
     tected him, by certain signs
O eyes wishfully turning! O silent eyes!
For then I thought of you o'er the world,
O latent oceans, fathomless oceans of love!
O waiting oceans of love! yearning and fervid! and of you sweet souls
     perhaps in the future, delicious and long:
But Death, unknown on the earth—ungiven, dark here, unspoken, never
     born:
You fathomless latent souls of love—you pent and unknown oceans of
     love!

QUESTIONS

1. One of these two versions of a poem by Whitman is an early draft from the
 poet's notebook. The other is the final version completed in 1871, about ten
 years later. Which is the final version?
2. In the final version, what has Whitman done to render his central metaphor
 (the comparison of soul and spider) more vivid and exact? What proportion
 of the final version is devoted to this metaphor?
3. In the early draft, what lines seem distracting or nonessential?

Donald Hall (b. 1928)

MY SON, MY EXECUTIONER   1955

My son, my executioner,
   I take you in my arms,
Quiet and small and just astir,
   And whom my body warms.

Sweet death, small son, our instrument   5
   Of immortality,
Your cries and hungers document
   Our bodily decay.

We twenty-five and twenty-two,
    Who seemed to live forever,   10
Observe enduring life in you
    And start to die together.

QUESTIONS

1. The first line introduces a paradoxical truth, the basic theme of the poem.
   How would you sum up this truth in your own words?
2. Exactly what do these words denote: *instrument* (line 5), *document* (line 7)?
3. When first published, this poem had a fourth stanza:

    I take into my arms the death
        Maturity exacts,
    And name with my imperfect breath
        The mortal paradox.

Do you think the poet right or wrong to omit this stanza? Explain.

TRANSLATIONS

Poetry, said Robert Frost, is what gets lost in translation. If absolutely
true, the comment is bad news for most of us, who have to depend on
translations for our only knowledge of great poems in some other languages. However, some translators seem able to save a part of their
originals and bring it across the language gap. At times they may even
add more poetry of their own, as if to try to compensate for what is lost.

Unlike the writer of an original poem, the translator begins with a
meaning that already exists. To convey it, the translator may decide to
stick closely to the denotations of the original words or else to depart
from them, more or less freely, after something he or she values more.
The latter aim is evident in the *Imitations* of Robert Lowell, who said he
had been "reckless with literal meaning" and instead had "labored
hard to get the tone." Particularly defiant of translation are poems in
dialect, uneducated speech, and slang: what can be used for English
equivalents? Ezra Pound, in a bold move, translates the song of a
Chinese peasant in *The Classic Anthology Defined by Confucius:*

    Yaller bird, let my corn alone,
    Yaller bird, let my crawps alone,
    These folks here won't let me eat,
    I wanna go back whaar I can meet
    the folks I used to know at home,
                I got a home an' I wanna' git goin'.

Here, it is our purpose to judge a translation not by its fidelity to
its original, but by the same standards we apply to any other poem
written in English. To do so may be another way to see the difference
between appropriate and inappropriate words.

EXERCISE: *Comparing Two Translations*

Here are two versions of a famous poem by Callimachus from the Greek (or Palatine) Anthology, a collection of lyrics and epigrams written between 700 B.C. and A.D. 1000. Cory's translation reflects the era of Tennyson; that by Fitts is clearly from the era of Eliot and Pound. What are their differences? Which of these two modes in translation do you prefer? Why? One mode is not intrinsically superior to the other.

William Cory (1832–1892)

HERACLITUS   1858

They told me, Heraclitus, they told me you were dead,
They brought me bitter news to hear and bitter tears to shed.
I wept as I remembered how often you and I
Had tired the sun with talking and sent him down the sky.

And now that thou art lying, my dear Old Carian guest,
A handful of grey ashes, long, long ago at rest,
Still are thy pleasant voices, thy nightingales, awake;
For Death, he taketh all away, but them he cannot take.

Dudley Fitts (1903–1968)

ELEGY ON HERAKLEITOS   1938

One brought me the news of your death, O Herakleitos my friend,
And I wept for you, remembering
How often we had watched the sun set as we talked.

And you are ashes now, old friend from Halikarnassos,
Ashes now:
                    but your nightingale songs live on,
And Death, the destroyer of every lovely thing,
Shall not touch them with his blind all-canceling fingers.

Federico García Lorca (1899–1936)

LA GUITARRA   (1921)   GUITAR   1967

Empieza el llanto	Begins the crying
de la guitarra.	of the guitar.
Se rompen las copas	From earliest dawn
de la madrugada.	the strokes are breaking.
Empieza el llanto	Begins the crying
de la guitarra.	of the guitar.
Es inútil	It is futile
callarla.	to stop its sound.
Es imposible	It is impossible
callarla.	to stop its sound.

Llora monótona	It is crying a monotone
como llora el agua,	like the crying of water,
como llora el viento	like the crying of wind
sobre la nevada.	over fallen snow.
Es imposible	It is impossible 15
callarla.	to stop its sound.
Llora por cosas	It is crying over things
lejanas.	far off.
Arena del Sur caliente	Burning sand of the South
que pide camelias blancas.	which covets white camelias. 20
Llora flecha sin blanco,	It is crying the arrow without aim,
la tarde sin mañana,	the evening without tomorrow,
y el primer pájaro muerto	and the first dead bird on the branch.
sobre la rama.	O guitar!
¡Oh, guitarra!	Heart heavily wounded 25
Corazón malherido	by five sharp swords.
por cinco espadas.	

— Translated by Keith Waldrop

Questions

1. Someone who knows Spanish should read aloud the original and the translation. Although it is impossible for any translation fully to capture the resonance of García Lorca's poem, in what places is the English version most nearly able to approximate it?
2. Another translation renders line 21: "It mourns for the targetless arrow." What is the difference between mourning for something and being the cry of it?
3. Throughout his translation, Waldrop closely follows the line divisions of the original, but in line 23 he combines García Lorca's lines 23 and 24. Can you see any point in his doing so? Would "on the branch" by itself be a strong line of English poetry?

Exercise: *Comparing Translations*

Which English translation of each of the following poems is the best poetry? The originals may be of interest to some. For those who do not know the foreign language, the editor's line-by-line prose paraphrases may help indicate what the translator had to work with and how much of the translation is the translator's own idea. In which do you find the diction most felicitous? In which do pattern and structure best move as one? What differences in tone are apparent? It is doubtful that any one translation will surpass the others in every detail.

Horace (65–8 B.C.)

Odes I (38)   (about 20 B.C.)

Persicos odi, puer, apparatus,
Displicent nexae philyra coronae;
Mitte sectari, rosa quo locorum
      Sera moretur.

Simplici myrto nihil allabores
Sedulus curo: neque te ministrum
Dedecet myrtus neque me sub arta
    Vite bibentem.

ODES I (38). Prose translation: (1) Persian pomp, boy, I detest, (2) garlands woven of lin-den bark displease me; (3–4) give up searching for the place where the late-blooming rose is. (5–6) Put no laborious trimmings on simple myrtle: (6–7) for myrtle is unbecoming nei-ther to you, a servant, nor to me, under the shade of this (8) vine, drinking.

1. SIMPLICITY   (about 1782)

    Boy, I hate their empty shows,
        Persian garlands I detest,
    Bring me not the late-blown rose
        Lingering after all the rest:
    Plainer myrtle pleases me
        Thus outstretched beneath my vine,
    Myrtle more becoming thee,
        Waiting with thy master's wine.

                                        —William Cowper

2. FIE ON EASTERN LUXURY!   (about 1830)

    Nay, nay, my boy—'tis not for me,
        This studious pomp of Eastern luxury;
    Give me no various garlands—fine
        With linden twine,
    Nor seek, where latest lingering blows,
        The solitary rose.

    Earnest I beg—add not with toilsome pain,
    One far-sought blossom to the myrtle plain,
    For sure, the fragrant myrtle bough
        Looks seemliest on thy brow;
    Nor me mis-seems, while, underneath the vine,
    Close interweaved, I quaff the rosy wine.

                                        —Hartley Coleridge

3. THE PREFERENCE DECLARED   1892

    Boy, I detest the Persian pomp;
        I hate those linden-bark devices;
    And as for roses, holy Moses!
        They can't be got at living prices!
    Myrtle is good enough for us,—
        For *you*, as bearer of my flagon;
    For *me*, supine beneath this vine,
        Doing my best to get a jag on!

                                        —Eugene Field

Charles Baudelaire (1821–1867)

RECUEILLEMENT   1866

Sois sage, ô ma Douleur, et tiens-toi plus tranquille.
Tu réclamais le Soir; il descend; le voici:
Une atmosphère obscure enveloppe la ville,
Aux uns portant la paix, aux autres le souci.

Pendant que des mortels la multitude vile,   5
Sous le fouet du Plaisir, ce bourreau sans merci,
Va cueillir des remords dans la fête servile,
Ma Douleur, donne-moi la main; viens par ici,

Loin d'eux. Vois se pencher les défuntes Années,
Sur les balcons du ciel, en robes surannées;   10
Surgir du fond des eaux le Regret souriant;

Le Soleil moribond s'endormir sous une arche,
Et, comme un long linceul trainant à l'Orient,
Entends, ma chère, entends la douce Nuit qui marche.

"MEDITATION." Prose translation: (1) Behave yourself [as a mother would say to her
child], O my Sorrow, and keep calmer. (2) You called for Evening; it descends; here it is:
(3) a dim atmosphere envelops the city, (4) Bringing peace to some; to others anxiety. (5)
While the vile multitude of mortals (6) under the whip of Pleasure, that merciless executioner, (7) go to gather remorse in the servile festival, (8) my Sorrow, give me your hand;
come this way, (9) far from them. See the dead years lean (10) on the balconies of the sky,
in old-fashioned dresses; (11) [see] Regret, smiling, emerge from the depths of the waters;
(12) [see] the dying Sun go to sleep under an arch; (13) and like a long shroud trailing in
the East, (14) hear, my darling, hear the soft Night who is walking.

1. PEACE, BE AT PEACE, O THOU MY HEAVINESS   1919

Peace, be at peace, O thou my heaviness,
Thou callèdst for the evening, lo! 'tis here,
The City wears a somber atmosphere
That brings repose to some, to some distress.
Now while the heedless throng make haste to press   5
Where pleasure drives them, ruthless charioteer,
To pluck the fruits of sick remorse and fear,
Come thou with me, and leave their fretfulness.
See how they hang from heaven's high balconies,
The old lost years in faded garments dressed,
And see Regret with faintly smiling mouth;
And while the dying sun sinks in the west,
Hear how, far off, Night walks with velvet tread,
And her long robe trails all about the south.

                                                             —Lord Alfred Douglas

2. INWARD CONVERSATION   1961

Be reasonable, my pain, and think with more detachment.
You asked to see the dusk; it descends; it is here:
A sheath of dark light robes the city,
To some bringing peace, to some the end of peace.

Now while the rotten herds of mankind,   5
Flogged by pleasure, that lyncher without touch,
Go picking remorse in their filthy holidays,
Let us join hands, my pain; come this way,

Far from them. Look at the dead years that lean on
The balconies of the sky, in their clothes long out of date;   10
The sense of loss that climbs from the deep waters with a smile;

The sun, nearly dead, that drops asleep beneath an arch;
And listen to the night, like a long shroud being dragged
Toward the east, my love, listen, the soft night is moving.

                                                             —Robert Bly

Calm down, my Sorrow, we must move with care.
You called for evening; it descends; it's here.
The town is coffined in its atmosphere,
bringing relief to some, to others care.

Now while the common multitude strips bare,   5
feels pleasure's cat o' nine tails on its back,
and fights off anguish at the great bazaar,
give me your hand, my Sorrow. Let's stand back;

back from these people! Look, the dead years dressed
in old clothes crowd the balconies of the sky.   10
Regret emerges smiling from the sea,

the sick sun slumbers underneath an arch,
and like a shroud strung out from east to west,
listen, my Dearest, hear the sweet night march!

—Robert Lowell

PARODY

In a **parody,** one writer imitates — and pokes fun at — another. Skillfully wrought, a parody can be a devastating form of literary criticism. Usually the parodist imitates the characteristic tone, form, language, and other elements of the original model, but sometimes applies them to a ludicrously uncharacteristic subject — as in E. B. White's parody of Walt Whitman, "A Classic Waits for Me" (page 686).

Rather than merely flinging abuse at another poet, the wise parodist imitates with understanding — perhaps with sympathy. The many crude parodies of T. S. Eliot's difficult poem *The Waste Land* show parodists mocking what they cannot fathom, with the result that, instead of illuminating the original, they belittle it (and themselves). Parody can be aimed at poems good or bad; yet there are poems of such splendor and dignity that no parodist seems able to touch them without looking like a small dog defiling a cathedral, and others so illiterate that parody would be squandered on them. In the following original by T. E. Brown, what failings does the parodist, J. A. Lindon, jump upon? (*God wot,* by the way, is an archaism for "God knows.")

T. E. Brown (1830–1897)	**J. A. Lindon** (b. 1914)
MY GARDEN 1887	MY GARDEN 1959

A garden is a lovesome thing,   A garden is a *lovesome* thing?
  God wot!   What rot!
Rose plot,   Weed plot,
Fringed pool,   Scum pool,
Ferned grot —   Old pot,   5
The veriest school   Snail-shiny stool

Of peace; and yet the fool
Contends that God is not—
Not God! in gardens! when the eve
   is cool?
Nay, but I have a sign;
'Tis very sure God walks in mine.

In pieces; yet the fool
Contends that snails are not—
Not snails! in gardens! when the
   eve is cool?
Nay, but I see their trails!   10
'Tis very sure *my* garden's full of
   snails!

Hugh Kingsmill
[Hugh Kingsmill Lunn] (1889–1949)
WHAT, STILL ALIVE AT TWENTY-TWO   (about 1920)

What, still alive at twenty-two,
A clean, upstanding chap like you?
Sure, if your throat 'tis hard to slit,
Slit your girl's, and swing for it.

Like enough, you won't be glad   5
When they come to hang you, lad:
But bacon's not the only thing
That's cured by hanging from a string.

So, when the spilt ink of the night
Spreads o'er the blotting-pad of light,   10
Lads whose job is still to do
Shall whet their knives, and think of you.

QUESTIONS

1. A. E. Housman considered this the best of many parodies of his poetry. Read
his poems in this book, particularly "Terence, this,is stupid stuff" and "To an
Athlete Dying Young" (pp. 763–765). What characteristics of theme, form,
and language does Hugh Kingsmill's parody convey?
2. What does Kingsmill exaggerate?

Kenneth Koch (b. 1925)
MENDING SUMP   1960

"Hiram, I think the sump is backing up.
The bathroom floor boards for above two weeks
Have seemed soaked through. A little bird, I think,
Has wandered in the pipes, and all's gone wrong."
"Something there is that doesn't hump a sump,"   5
He said; and through his head she saw a cloud
That seemed to twinkle. "Hiram, well," she said,

"Smith is come home! I saw his face just now
While looking through your head. He's come to die
Or else to laugh, for hay is dried-up grass   10
When you're alone." He rose, and sniffed the air.
"We'd better leave him in the sump," he said.

Questions

1. What poet is the object of this parody? Which of his poems are echoed in it?
2. Koch gains humor by making outrageous statements in the tone and language of his original. Looking at other poems in this book by the poet being parodied, how would you describe their tone? Their language?
3. Suppose, instead of casting his parody into blank verse, Koch had written:

   "Hiram, the sump is backing up.
   The bathroom floor boards
   For above two weeks
   Have been soaking through. A little bird,
   I think, has wandered in
   The pipes, and all's gone wrong."

   Why would the biting edge of his parody have been blunted?
4. What, by the way, is a *sump*?

John Frederick Nims (b. 1914)
Old Bethinkings of a Day of "Showers Likely" at Beansey Ridge   1971

Half twice some ninety-odd and more spans back
   Love oncewhile came.
Sweet Pheena Mente, now seventy years en-graved, 's
   Lesswise the same.

How blithe we picknicked us 'mid showers, throughdrenched   5
   In ditch and field.
Howe'ersowise the sane folk, pointing, snicked
   Our "wig-pates reeled."

How blithe on Beansey Ridge, foam-yodelling scarp,
   We jumped at rope.   10
Old Romans near-entombed-us outgrowled, "They
   Should plotz, we hope."

Alas, 'tis Sooth a drear Hap smote us thwart;
   Gap-grinned to see:
I, old Plutt Hodd, being (year wise-way-like) five;   15
   She, eighty-three.

Questions

1. Of what poet's work is this a parody? (Beansey Ridge, by the way, is a place-name the poet actually employed.)

2. What features of the poet's style is Nims poking fun at? Compare the parody with poems by the poet in this book. Notice especially the poet's choice of words and arrangement of them. (Suggestion: You might find it helpful to translate some of Nims's lines into ordinary conversational English.)
3. What theme or subject matter usual to the poet's work does this parody echo?

E. B. White (b. 1899)
A CLASSIC WAITS FOR ME   1944

(With apologies to Walt Whitman, plus a trial membership in the Classics Club)

A classic waits for me, it contains all, nothing is lacking,
Yet all were lacking if taste were lacking, or if the endorsement of the right
    man were lacking.
O clublife, and the pleasures of membership,
O volumes for sheer fascination unrivalled.
Into an armchair endlessly rocking,   5
Walter J. Black my president,
I, freely invited, cordially welcomed to membership,
My arm around John Kieran, Pearl S. Buck,
My taste in books guarded by the spirits of William Lyon Phelps, Hendrik
    Willem van Loon,
(From your memories, sad brothers, from the fitful risings and callings I
    heard),   10
I to the classics devoted, brother of rough mechanics, beauty-parlor tech-
    nicians, spot welders, radio-program directors
(It is not necessary to have a higher education to appreciate these books),
I, connoisseur of good reading, friend of connoisseurs of good reading ev-
    erywhere,
I, not obliged to take any specific number of books, free to reject any vol-
    ume, perfectly free to reject Montaigne, Erasmus, Milton,
I, in perfect health except for a slight cold, pressed for time, having only a
    few more years to live,   15
Now celebrate this opportunity.
Come, I will make the club indissoluble,
I will read the most splendid books the sun ever shone upon,
I will start divine magnetic groups,
    With the love of comrades,   20
    With the life-long love of distinguished
      committees.

I strike up for an Old Book.
Long the best-read figure in America, my dues paid, sitter in armchairs
    everywhere, wanderer in populous cities, weeping with Hecuba
    and with the late William Lyon Phelps,
Free to cancel my membership whenever I wish,
Turbulent, fleshy, sensible,   25

Never tiring of clublife,
Always ready to read another masterpiece provided it has the approval of
    my president, Walter J. Black,
Me imperturbe, standing at ease among writers,
Rais'd by a perfect mother and now belonging to a perfect book club,
Bearded, sunburnt, gray-neck'd, astigmatic,   30
Loving the masters and the masters only
(I am mad for them to be in contact with me),
My arm around Pearl S. Buck, only American woman to receive the Nobel
    Prize for Literature,
I celebrate this opportunity.
And I will not read a book nor the least part of a book but has the approval
    of the Committee,   35
For all is useless without that which you may guess at many times and not
    hit, that which they hinted at,
All is useless without readability.
By God! I will accept nothing which all cannot have their counterpart of
    on the same terms (89¢ for the Regular Edition or $1.39 for the De
    Luxe Edition, plus a few cents postage).
I will make inseparable readers with their arms around each other's necks,
    By the love of classics,   40
    By the manly love of classics.

A CLASSIC WAITS FOR ME. Advertisements for the Classics Club used to proclaim that its books were selected by a committee of the popular writers and interpreters of culture named in lines 8–9. 10. *your memories, sad brothers:* Phelps and van Loon had died shortly before White's satire was first printed in 1944. 23. *Hecuba:* in Homer's *Iliad,* the wife of Priam, defeated king of Troy, and mother of Hector, Trojan hero slain by Achilles. 28. *Me imperturbe:* Whitman's poem by this title begins, "Me imperturbe, standing at ease in Nature . . ." (The Latinate phrase could be roughly translated, "I, the unflappable.")

QUESTIONS

1. What is E. B. White making fun of, besides Walt Whitman's poetry? How timely does White's satire remain? (Have you noticed any recent book club ads?)
2. Compare White's opening lines with those of Whitman's "A Woman Waits for Me," a celebration of the joys of reproduction:

    A woman waits for me, she contains all, nothing is lacking,
    Yet all were lacking if sex were lacking, or if the
        moisture of the right man were lacking.

    In White's lines, how does the phrase *nothing is lacking* change in meaning? The phrase *the right man?*
3. What traits of Whitman's style does White imitate? (See other poems by Whitman in this book.)
4. The more you read of Whitman, the more you will appreciate White's parody. Look up "A Woman Waits for Me" in Whitman's *Leaves of Grass.* See also "Out of the Cradle Endlessly Rocking" and "Song of Myself." What further echoes of Whitman do you find in White's take-off? How closely does White remind you of Whitman's attitudes toward himself and toward the world?

EXPERIMENT: *Writing an Imitation or a Parody*

Write a poem in the manner of Emily Dickinson, William Carlos Williams, E. E. Cummings, or any other modern poet whose work interests you and which you feel able to imitate. Decide, before you start, whether to write a serious imitation (that could be slipped into the poet's *Collected Poems* without anyone being the wiser), or a humorous parody. Read all the poet's poems included in this book; perhaps you will find it helpful also to consult a larger selection or collection of the poet's work. It might be simplest to choose a particular poem as your model; but, if you like, you may echo any number of poems. Choose a model within the range of your own skill: to imitate a sonnet, for instance, you need to be able to rime and to write in meter. Probably, if your imitation is serious, and not a parody like E. B. White's parody of Whitman, it is a good idea to pick a subject or theme characteristic of the poet. This is a difficult project, but if you can do it even fairly well, you will know a great deal more about poetry and your poet.

28 Writing about Poetry

Assignment: a paper about a poem. You can approach it as a grim duty, of course: any activity can so be regarded. For Don Juan, in Spanish legend, even the act of love became a chore. But the act of writing, like the act of love, is much easier if your feelings take part in it. Write about anything you dislike and don't understand, and you not only set yourself the labors of Hercules, but you guarantee your reader discouragingly hard labor, too.

To write about a poem informatively, you need first of all to experience it. It helps to live with the poem for as long as possible: there is little point in trying to encompass the poem in a ten-minute tour of inspection on the night before the paper falls due. However challenging, writing about poetry has immediate rewards, and to mention just one, the poem you spend time with and write about is going to mean much more to you than poems skimmed quickly ever do.

Most of the problems you will meet in writing about a poem will be the same ones you meet in writing about a play or a story: finding a topic, organizing your thoughts, writing, revising. For general advice on writing papers about any kind of literature, see the Appendix at the back of this book. There are, however, a few ways in which a poem requires a different approach. This chapter will deal briefly with some of them, and it will offer a few illustrations of papers that students have written. These papers may not be works of inimitable genius, but they are pretty good papers, the likes of which most students can write with a modest investment of time and care.

Briefer than most stories and most plays, lyric poems *look* easier to write about. They call, however, for your keenest attention. You may find that, before you can discuss a short poem, you will have to read it slowly and painstakingly, with your mind (like your pencil) sharp and ready. Unlike a play or a short story, a lyric poem tends to have very little plot, and perhaps you will find little to say about what happens in it. In order to understand a poem, you'll need to notice elements other than narrative: the connotations or suggestions of its words, surely, and the rhythm of phrases and lines. The subtleties of language, almost apart from story, are so essential to a poem (and so elusive) that Robert

Frost was moved to say, "Poetry is what gets lost in translation." Once in a while, of course, you'll read a story whose prose abounds in sounds, rhythms, figures of speech, imagery, and other elements you expect of poetry. Certain novels of Herman Melville and William Faulkner contain paragraphs that, if extracted, seem in themselves prose-poems—so lively are they in their word-play, so rich in metaphor. But such writing is exceptional, and the main business of most fiction is to get a story told. To take an extreme case of a fiction writer who didn't want his prose to sound poetic, Georges Simenon, best known for his mystery novels, said that whenever he noticed in his manuscript any word or phrase that called attention to itself, he struck it out. That method of writing would never do for a poet, who revels in words and phrases that fix themselves in memory. It is safe to say that, in order to write well about a poem, you have to read it carefully enough to remember at least part of it word for word.

Let's consider three commonly useful approaches to writing about poetry.

EXPLICATION

In an **explication** (literally, "an unfolding") of a poem, a writer explains the entire poem in detail, unraveling any particular complexities to be found in it. This method is a valuable one in approaching a lyric poem, especially if the poem is rich in complexities (or in suggestions worth rendering explicit). Most poems that you'll ever be asked to explicate are short enough to discuss thoroughly within a limited time; fully to explicate a long and involved work, such as John Milton's epic *Paradise Lost,* might require a lifetime. (To explicate a short passage of Milton's long poem would be a more usual course assignment.)

All the details or suggestions in a poem that a sensitive and intelligent reader might consider, the writer of an explication considers and tries to unfold. These might include allusions, the denotations or connotations of words, the possible meanings of symbols, the effects of certain sounds and rhythms and formal elements (rime schemes, for instance), the sense of any statements that contain irony, and other particulars. Not intent on ripping a poem to pieces, the author of a useful explication instead tries to show how each part contributes to the whole.

An explication is easy to organize. You can start with the first line of the poem and keep working straight on through. An explication should not be confused with a paraphrase. A paraphrase simply puts the words of the poem into other words; it is a sort of translation, useful in getting at the plain prose sense and therefore especially helpful in clarifying a poem's main theme. Perhaps in writing an explication you will wish to do some paraphrasing; but an explication (unlike a paraphrase) does not simply restate: it explains a poem, in great detail.

Here, for example, is a famous poem by Robert Frost, followed by a student's concise explication. (The assignment was to explain whatever in "Design" seemed most essential, in not more than 750 words.)

Robert Frost (1874–1963)

DESIGN   1936

I found a dimpled spider, fat and white,
On a white heal-all, holding up a moth
Like a white piece of rigid satin cloth—
Assorted characters of death and blight
Mixed ready to begin the morning right,   5
Like the ingredients of a witches' broth—
A snow-drop spider, a flower like a froth,
And dead wings carried like a paper kite.

What had that flower to do with being white,
The wayside blue and innocent heal-all?   10
What brought the kindred spider to that height,
Then steered the white moth thither in the night?
What but design of darkness to appall?—
If design govern in a thing so small.

An Unfolding of Robert Frost's "Design"

Starting with the title, "Design," any reader of this poem will find it full of meaning. As Webster's New World Dictionary defines design, the word can denote among other things a plan, or "purpose; intention; aim." Some arguments for the existence of God (I remember from Sunday School) are based on the "argument from design": that because the world shows a systematic order, there must be a Designer who made it. But the word design can also mean "a secret or sinister scheme" -- such as we attribute to a "designing person." As we shall see, Frost's poem incorporates all of these meanings. His poem raises the question of whether there is a Designer, or an evil Designer, or no Designer at all.

Like many other sonnets, the poem is divided into two parts. The first eight lines draw a picture centering on the spider, who at first seems almost jolly. It is _dimpled_ and _fat_ like a baby, or Santa Claus. It stands on a wild flower whose name, _heal-all_, seems an irony: a heal-all is supposed to cure any disease, but it certainly has no power to restore life to the dead moth. (Later, in line ten, we learn that the heal-all used to be blue. Presumably it has died and become bleached-looking.) In this second line we discover, too, that the spider has hold of another creature. Right away we might feel sorry for the moth, were it not for the simile applied to it in line three: "Like a white piece of rigid satin cloth." Suddenly the moth becomes not a creature but a piece of fabric -- lifeless and dead -- and yet _satin_ has connotations also beautiful. For me satin, used in rich ceremonial costumes such as coronation gowns and brides' dresses, has a formality and luxury about it. Besides, there is great accuracy in the word: the smooth and slightly plush surface of satin is like the powder-smooth surface of moths' wings. But this "cloth," rigid and white, could be the lining to Dracula's coffin. Like the spider, with its snow-drop-shaped body, the moth reminds us both of beauty and of grim death. Spider, flower, and moth are indeed "assorted characters."

In the fifth line an invisible hand enters. The characters are "mixed" like ingredients in an evil potion. Some force doing the mixing is behind the scene. The characters in themselves are innocent enough, but when brought together and concocted, their whiteness and look of _rigor mortis_ are overwhelming. There is something diabolical in the spider's feast. The "morning right" echoes the word _rite_, a ritual -- in this case apparently a Black Mass or a Witches' Sabbath. The simile in line seven ("a flower like a froth") is more ambiguous and harder to describe. A froth is white, foamy, and delicate -- something found on a brook in the woods or on a beach after a wave recedes. However, in the natural world, froth also can be ugly: the foam on a dead dog's mouth. The dualism in nature -- its beauty and its horror -- is there in that one simile.

So far, the poem has portrayed a small, frozen scene, with the dimpled killer holding its victim as innocently as a boy holds a kite. Already, Frost has hinted that Nature may be, as Radcliffe Squires suggests, "nothing but an ash-white plain without love or faith or hope, where ignorant appetites cross by chance."[1] Now, in the last six lines of the sonnet, Frost comes out and directly states his theme. What else could bring these deathly pale, stiff things together "but design of darkness to appall?" The question is clearly rhetorical, meant to be answered, "Why, nothing but that, of course!" I take the next-to-last line to mean, "What except a design so dark and sinister that we're appalled by it." "Appall," by the way, is the second pun in the poem: it sounds like a pall or shroud. Steered carries the suggestion of a steering-wheel or rudder that some pilot had to control. Like the word brought, it implies that some Captain charted the paths of spider, heal-all, and moth, so that they arrived together.

Having suggested that the universe is in the hands of that sinister Captain (Fate? the Devil?), Frost adds a final note of doubt. The Bible tells us that "His eye is on the sparrow," but at the moment the poet doesn't seem sure. Maybe, he hints, when things in the universe drop below a certain size, they pass completely out of the Designer's notice. When creatures are that little, maybe He doesn't bother to govern them, but just lets them run wild. And possibly the same mindless chance is all that governs human lives. Maybe we're not even "sinners in the hands of an angry God,"[2] but are nothing but little dice being slung. And that -- because it is even more senseless -- is the worst suspicion of all.

1 The Major Themes of Robert Frost (Ann Arbor, Mich.: University of Michigan Press, 1963), p. 87.

2 Title of an early American sermon by Jonathan Edwards.

This excellent paper, while finding something worth unfolding in every line in Frost's poem, does so without seeming mechanical. Notice that, although the student proceeds through the poem from the title to the last line, she takes up points when necessary, in any sequence. In paragraph one, the writer looks ahead to the end of the poem and briefly states its main theme. (She does so in order to relate this theme to the poem's title.) In the second paragraph, she deals with the poem's *later* image of the heal-all, relating it to the first image. Along the way, she comments on the form of the poem ("Like many other sonnets"), on its similes and puns, its denotations and connotations.

Incidentally, this paper demonstrates good use of manuscript form. Each word in a quotation is reproduced faithfully. The student is within her rights to give Frost's *steered* a capital letter when beginning her own sentence with it. The critic she quotes (Radcliffe Squires) is identified in the essay and his book is given a footnote. Another footnote proves useful to give Jonathan Edwards credit for a memorable phrase. This paper demonstrates, too, how to make final corrections without retyping. In the last paragraph, notice how the student legibly added a word and neatly changed another word by crossing it out and writing a substitute above it. In her next-to-last sentence, the writer clearly transposes two letters with a handy mark (∿), deletes a word, and strikes out a superfluous letter.

It might seem that to work through a poem line by line is a lock-step task; and yet there can be high excitement in it. Randall Jarrell once wrote an explication of "Design" in which he managed to convey such excitement. In the following passage taken from it, see if you can sense the writer's joy in his work. (Don't, incidentally, feel obliged to compare the quality of your own insights with Jarrell's, nor the quality of your own prose. Be fair to yourself: unlike most students, Jarrell had the advantage of being an excellent poet and a gifted critic; besides, he had read and pondered Frost for years before he wrote his essay, and as a teacher he probably had taught "Design" many times.)

> Frost's details are so diabolically good that it seems criminal to leave some unremarked; but notice how *dimpled, fat,* and *white* (all but one; all but one) come from our regular description of any baby; notice how the *heal-all,* because of its name, is the one flower in all the world picked to be the altar for this Devil's Mass; notice how *holding up* the moth brings something ritual and hieratic, a ghostly, ghastly formality, to this priest and its sacrificial victim; notice how terrible to the fingers, how full of the stilling rigor of death, that *white piece of rigid satin cloth* is. And *assorted characters of death and blight* is, like so many things in this poem, sharply ambiguous: *a mixed bunch of actors* or *diverse representative signs.* The tone of the phrase *assorted characters of death and blight* is beautifully developed in the ironic Breakfast-Club-calisthenics, Radio-Kitchen heartiness of *mixed ready to begin the morning right* (which assures us, so unreassuringly, that this isn't any sort of Strindberg *Spook Sonata,* but hard fact), and con-

cludes in the *ingredients* of the witches' broth, giving the soup a sort of cuddly shimmer that the cauldron in *Macbeth* never had; the *broth*, even, is brought to life—we realize that witches' broth *is* broth, to be supped with a long spoon.[1]

Evidently, Jarrell's cultural interests are broad: ranging from August Strindberg's ground-breaking modern classic down to the Breakfast Club (a once-popular radio program that cheerfully exhorted its listeners to march around their tables). And yet breadth of knowledge, however much it deepens and enriches Jarrell's writing, isn't all that he brings to the reading of poetry. For him, an explication isn't a dull plod, but a voyage of discovery. His prose—full of figures of speech (*diabolically good, cuddly shimmer*)—conveys the apparent delight he takes in showing off his findings. Such a joy, of course, can't be acquired deliberately. But it can grow, the more you read and study poetry.

ANALYSIS

An **analysis** of a poem, like a news commentator's analysis of a crisis in the Middle East or a chemist's analysis of an unknown fluid, separates its subject into elements, as a means to understand that subject—to see what composes it. Usually, the writer of such an essay singles out one of those elements for attention: "Imagery of Light and Darkness in Frost's 'Design' "; "The Character of Satan in *Paradise Lost*."

Like explication, analysis can be particularly useful in dealing with a short poem. Unlike explication (which inches through a poem line by line), analysis often suits a long poem too, because it allows the writer to discuss just one manageable element in the poem. A good analysis casts intense light upon a poem from one direction. If you care enough about a poem, and about some perspective on it—its theme, say, or its symbolism, or its singability—writing an analysis can enlighten and give pleasure.

In this book you probably have met a few brief analyses: the discussion of connotations in John Masefield's "Cargoes" (page 477), for instance, or the examination of symbols in T. S. Eliot's "The *Boston Evening Transcript*" (page 608). In fact, most of the discussions in this book are analytic. Temporarily, we have separated the whole art of poetry into elements such as tone, irony, literal meaning, suggestions, imagery, figures of speech, sound, rhythm, and so on. No element of a poem, of course, exists apart from all the other elements. Still, by taking a closer look at particular elements, one at a time, we see them more clearly and more easily study them.

---

[1] From *Poetry and the Age* (New York: Alfred A. Knopf, 1953).

Long analyses of metrical feet, rime schemes, and indentations tend to make ponderous reading: such formal and technical elements are perhaps the hardest to discuss engagingly. And yet formal analysis (at least a little of it) can be interesting and illuminating: it can measure the very pulsebeat of lines. If you do care about the technical side of poetry, then write about it, by all means. You will probably find it helpful to learn the terms for the various meters, stanzas, fixed forms, and other devices, so that you can summon them to your aid with confidence. Here is a short formal analysis of "Design" by a student who evidently cares for technicalities yet who manages not to be a bore in talking about them. Concentrating on the sonnet form of Frost's poem, the student actually casts light upon the poem in its entirety.

The Design of "Design"

For "Design," the sonnet form has at least two advantages. First, as in most strict Italian sonnets, the argument of the poem falls into two parts. In the octave Frost draws his pale still-life of spider, flower, and moth; then in the sestet he contemplates the meaning of it. The sestet deals with a more general idea: the possible existence of a vindictive deity who causes the spider to catch the moth, and no doubt also causes other suffering. Frost weaves his own little web. The unwary reader is led into the poem by its opening story, and pretty soon is struggling with more than he expected. Even the rime scheme, by the way, has something to do with the poem's meaning. The word white ends the first line of the sestet. The same sound is echoed in the rimes that follow. All in all, half the lines in the poem end in an "ite." It seems as if Frost places great weight on the whiteness of his little scene, for the riming words both introduce the term white and keep reminding us of it.

A sonnet has a familiar design, and that is its second big advantage to this particular poem. In a way, writing "Design" as a sonnet almost seems a foxy joke. (I can just imagine Frost chuckling to himself, wondering if anyone will get it.) A sonnet, being a classical form, is an orderly world with certain laws in it. There is ready-made irony in its containing a meditation on whether there is any order in the universe at large. Obviously there's design in back of the poem, but is there any design to insect life, or human life? Whether or not the poet can answer this question (and it seems he can't), at least he discovers an order *while* writing the poem. Actually, that is just what Frost said a poet achieves: "a momentary stay against confusion."[1]

Although design clearly governs in this poem -- in "this thing so small" -- the design isn't entirely predictable. The poem starts out as an Italian sonnet, with just two riming sounds; then (unlike an Italian sonnet) it keeps the "ite" rimes going. It ends in a couplet, like a Shakespearean sonnet. From these unexpected departures from the pattern of the Italian sonnet announced in the opening lines, I get the impression that Frost's poem is somewhat like the larger universe. It looks perfectly orderly, until you notice the small details in it.

[1]"The Figure a Poem Makes," preface to Complete Poems of Robert Frost (New York: Holt, Rinehart and Winston, 1949), p. vi.

COMPARISON AND CONTRAST

To write a **comparison** of two poems, you place them side by side and point out their likenesses; to write a **contrast,** you point out their differences. If you wish, you can combine the two methods in the same paper. For example, even though you may emphasize similarities you may also call attention to differences, or vice versa.

Such a paper makes most sense if you pair two poems that have much in common. It would be possible to compare Ern Alpaugh and Dewey G. Pell's trivial pop song lyric "Swinging Chick" with Milton's profound "Lycidas," but comparison would be difficult, perhaps futile. Though both poems are in English, the two seem hopelessly remote from each other in diction, in tone, in complexity, and in worth.

Having found, however, a couple of poems that throw light on each other, you then go on in your paper to show further, unsuspected resemblances — not just the ones that are obvious (" 'Design' and 'Wing-Spread' are both about bugs"). The interesting resemblances are ones that take thinking to discover. Similarly, you may want to show noteworthy differences — besides those your reader will see without any help.

In comparing two poems, you may be tempted to discuss one of them and be done with it, then spend the latter half of your paper discussing the other. This simple way of organizing an essay can be dangerous if it leads you to keep the two poems in total isolation from each other. The whole idea of such an assignment, of course, is to get you to do some comparing. There is nothing wrong in discussing all of poem A first, then discussing poem B — if in discussing B you keep looking back at A. Another procedure is to keep comparing the two poems all the way through your paper — dealing first, let's say, with their themes; then with their metaphors; and finally, with their respective merits.

More often than not, a comparison is an analysis: a study of a theme common to two poems, for instance; or of two poets' similar fondness for the myth of Eden. But you also can evaluate poems by comparing and contrasting them: placing them side by side in order to decide which poet deserves the brighter laurels. Here, for example, is a paper that considers "Design" and "Wing-Spread," a poem of Abbie Huston Evans (first printed in 1938, two years later than Frost's poem). By comparing and contrasting the two poems for (1) their language and (2) their themes, this student shows us reasons for his evaluation.

"Wing-Spread" Does a Dip

The midge spins out to safety

Through the spider's rope;

But the moth, less lucky,

Has to grope.

Mired in glue-like cable   5

See him foundered swing

By the gap he opened

With his wing,

Dusty web enlacing

All that blue and beryl.   10

In a netted universe

Wing-spread is peril.

-- Abbie Huston Evans

"Wing-Spread," quoted above, is a good poem, but it is not in the
same class with "Design." Both poets show us a murderous spider and an
unlucky moth, but there are two reasons for Robert Frost's superiority.
One is his more suggestive use of language, the other is his more
memorable theme.

Let's start with language. "Design" is full of words and phrases
rich in suggestions. "Wing-Spread," by comparison, contains few. To
take just one example, Frost's "dimpled spider, fat and white" is
certainly a more suggestive description. Actually, Evans doesn't
describe her spider; she just says, "the spider's rope." (I have to
hand Evans the palm for showing us the spider and moth in action. In
Frost's view, they are dead and petrified -- but I guess that is the
impression he is after.) In "Design," the spider's dimples show that it
is like a chubby little kid, who further turns out to be a kite-flier.
This seems an odd, almost freaky way to look at a spider. I find it
more refreshing than Evans's view (although I like her word cable,
suggesting that the spider's web is a kind of suspension bridge). Frost's
word-choice -- his harping on white -- paints a more striking scene than
Evans's slightly vague "All that blue and beryl." Except for her
personification of the moth in her second stanza, Evans doesn't go in
for any figures of speech, and even that one isn't a clear personification -- she simply gives the moth a sex by referring to it as "him."
Frost's striking metaphors, similes, and even puns (right, appall) show him,

as usual, to be a master of figures of speech. He calls the moth's wings "satin cloth" and "a paper kite"; Evans just refers in line 8 to a moth's wing. As far as the language of the two poems goes, you might as well compare a vase ~~full of~~ brimming with flowers and a single flower stuck in a vase. (That is a poor metaphor, since Frost's poem contains only one flower, but I hope you will know what I mean.)

In fairness to Evans, I would say that she picks a pretty good solitary flower. And her poem has powerful sounds: short lines with the riming words coming at us again and again very frequently. In theme, however, "Wing-Spread" seems much more narrow than "Design." The first time I read Evans's poem all I felt was: Ho hum, the moth too was wide and got stuck. The second time I read it, I figured that she is saying something with a universal application. This message comes out in line 11, in "a netted universe." That is the most interesting phrase in her poem, one that you can think about. Netted makes me imagine the universe as being full of nets rigged by someone who is fishing for us. Maybe, like Frost, Evans sees an evil plan operating. She does not, though, investigate it. She says that the midge escapes because it is tiny. On the other hand, things with wide wing-spreads get stuck. Her theme as I read it is, "Be small and inconspicuous if you want to survive," or maybe, "Isn't it too bad that in this world the big beautiful types crack up and die, while the miserable little puny punks keep sailing?" Now, that is a valuable idea. I have often thought that very same thing myself. But Frost's closing note ("If design govern in a thing so small") is really devastating, because it raises a huge uncertainty. "Wing-Spread" leaves us with not much besides a moth stuck in a web, and a moral. In both language and theme, "Design" climbs to a higher altitude.

HOW TO QUOTE A POEM

Preparing to discuss a short poem, it is a good idea to emulate the student who wrote on "Wing-Spread" and to quote the whole text of the poem at the beginning of your paper, with its lines numbered. Then you can refer to it with ease, and your instructor, without having to juggle a book, can follow you.

Quoted to illustrate some point, memorable lines can add interest to your paper, and good commentators on poetry tend to be apt quoters, helping their readers to experience a word, a phrase, a line, or a passage that otherwise might be neglected. However, to quote from poetry is slightly more awkward than to quote from prose. There are lines to think about—important and meaningful units whose shape you will need to preserve. If you are quoting more than a couple of lines, it is good policy to arrange your quotation just as its lines occur in the poem, white space and all:

```
At the outset, the poet tells us of his discovery of

              a dimpled spider, fat and white,
        On a white heal-all, holding up a moth
        Like a white piece of rigid satin cloth --

and implies that the small killer is both childlike and sinister.
```

But if you are quoting less than two lines of verse, it would seem wasteful of paper to write:

```
The color white preoccupies Frost.  The spider is

                        fat and white,
        On a white heal-all

and even the victim moth is pale, too.
```

In such a case, it saves space to transform Frost's line arrangement into prose:

```
The color white preoccupies Frost.  The spider is "fat and white, /

On a white heal-all" -- and even the victim moth is pale, too.
```

Here, a diagonal (/) indicates the writer's respect for where the poet's lines begin and end. Some writers prefer to note line-breaks without diagonals, just by keeping the initial capital letter of a line (if there is any): "fat and white, On a white heal-all. . . ." Incidentally, the ellipsis (. . .) in that last remark indicates that words are omitted from the end of Frost's sentence; the fourth dot is a period. Some writers—meticulous souls—also stick in an ellipsis at the *beginning* of a quotation, if they're leaving out words from the beginning of a sentence in the original:

The color white preoccupies Frost in his description of the spider

" . . .fat and white, / On a white heal-all. . . ."

Surely there's no need for an initial ellipsis, though, if you begin quoting at the beginning of a sentence. No need for a final ellipsis, either, if your quotation goes right to the end of a sentence in the original. If it is obvious that only a phrase is being quoted, no need for an ellipsis in any case:

The speaker says he "found a dimpled spider" and he goes on to

portray it as a kite-flying boy.

If you leave out whole lines, indicate the omission by an ellipsis all by itself on a line:

The midge spins out to safety
Through the spider's rope;
. . .
In a netted universe
Wing-spread is peril.

BEFORE YOU BEGIN

Ready at last to write, you will have spent considerable time in reading, thinking, and feeling. After having chosen your topic, you probably will have taken a further look at the poem or poems you have picked, letting further thoughts and feelings come to you. The quality of your paper will depend, above all, upon the quality of your readiness to write.

Exploring a poem, a sensitive writer handles it with care and affection as though it were a living animal, and, done with it, leaves it still alive. The unfeeling writer, on the other hand, disassembles the poem in a dull, mechanical way, like someone with a blunt ax filling an order for one horse-skeleton. Again, to write well is a matter of engaging your feelings. Writing to a deadline, on an assigned topic, you easily can sink into a drab, workaday style, especially if you regard the poet as some uninspired builder of chicken-coops who hammers themes and images into place, and then slaps the whole thing with a coat of words. Certain expressions, if you lean on them habitually, may tempt you to think of the poet in that way. Here, for instance, is a discussion — by a plodding writer — of Robert Frost's poem.

The symbols Frost _uses_ in "Design" are very successful. Frost

makes the spider _stand for_ Nature. He _wants_ us to see Nature as

```
blind and cruel.  He also employs good sounds.  He uses a lot of

i's because he is trying to make you think of falling rain.
```

(Underscored words are worth questioning.) What's wrong with that comment? While understandable, the words *uses* and *employs* seem to lead the writer to see Frost only as a conscious tool-manipulator. To be sure, Frost in a sense "uses" symbols, but did he grab hold of them and lay them into his poem? For all we know, perhaps the symbols arrived quite unbidden, and used the poet. To write a good poem, Frost maintained, a poet himself has to be surprised. (How, by the way, can we hope to know what a poet *wants* to do? And there isn't much point in saying that the poet is *trying to* do something. He has already done it, if he has written a good poem.) At least, it is likely that Frost didn't plan to fulfill a certain quota of *i*-sounds. Writing his poem, not by following a blueprint but probably by bringing it slowly to the surface of his mind (like Elizabeth Bishop's hooked fish), Frost no doubt had enough to do without trying to engineer the reactions of his possible audience. Like all true symbols, Frost's spider doesn't *stand for* anything. The writer would be closer to the truth to say that the spider *suggests* or *reminds us* of Nature, or of certain forces in the natural world. (Symbols just hint, they don't indicate.)

After the student discussed the paper in a conference, he rewrote the first two sentences like this:

```
The symbols in Frost's "Design" are highly effective.  The

spider, for instance, suggests the blindness and cruelty of Nature.

Frost's word-sounds, too, are part of the meaning of his poem, for

the i's remind the reader of falling rain.
```

Not every reader of "Design" will hear rain falling, but the student's revision probably comes closer to describing the experience of the poem most of us know.

In writing about poetry, an occasional note of self-doubt can be useful: now and then a *perhaps* or a *possibly*, an *it seems* or a modest *I suppose*. Such expressions may seem timid shilly-shallying, but at least they keep the writer from thinking, "I know all there is to know about this poem."

Facing the showdown with your empty sheaf of paper, however, you can't worry forever about your critical vocabulary. To do so is to risk the fate of the centipede in a bit of comic verse, who was running along efficiently until someone asked, "Pray, which leg comes after which?," whereupon "He lay distracted in a ditch / Considering how to run." It is a safe bet that your instructor is human. Your main task as a writer is to communicate to another human being your sensitive reading of a poem.

TOPICS FOR WRITING

TOPICS FOR BRIEF PAPERS (250–500 WORDS)

1. Write a concise *explication* of a short poem of your choice, or one suggested by your instructor. In a paper this brief, probably you won't have room to explain everything in the poem; explain what you think most needs explaining. (An illustration of one such explication appears on page 691.)

2. Write an *analysis* of a short poem, first deciding which one of its elements to deal with. (An illustration of such an analysis appears on page 696.) For examples, here are a few specific topics:

   "Language of the Street: What It Contributes to Dylan's 'Subterranean Homesick Blues' "

   "Kinds of Irony in Hardy's 'The Workbox' "

   "The Attitude of the Speaker in Marvell's 'To His Coy Mistress' "

   "Folk Ballad Traits in Randall's 'Ballad of Birmingham' "

   "An Extended Metaphor in Levertov's 'Ways of Conquest' " (Explain the one main comparison that the poem makes and show how the whole poem makes it. Other likely possibilities for a paper on extended metaphor: Rich's "Diving into the Wreck," Dickinson's "Because I could not stop for Death.")

   "What the Skunks Mean in Lowell's 'Skunk Hour' "

   "The Rhythms of Plath's 'Daddy' "

   (To locate any of these poems, see the Index of Authors, Titles, and Quotations at the back of this book.)

3. Select a poem in which the main speaker is a character who for any reason interests you. You might consider, for instance, Betjeman's "In Westminster Abbey," Browning's "My Last Duchess" or "Soliloquy of the Spanish Cloister," Eliot's "Love Song of J. Alfred Prufrock," Frost's "Witch of Coös," or Jarrell's "Woman at the Washington Zoo." Then write a brief profile of this character, drawing only on what the poem tells you (or reveals). What is the character's approximate age? Situation in life? Attitude toward self? Attitude toward others? General personality? Do you find this character admirable?

4. Although each of these poems tells a story, what happens in the poem isn't necessarily obvious: Cummings's "anyone lived in a pretty how town," Eliot's "Love Song of J. Alfred Prufrock," Lawrence's "A Youth Mowing," Stafford's "At the Klamath Berry Festival," Winter's "At the San Francisco Airport," James Wright's "A Blessing." Choose one of these poems and in a paragraph sum up what you think happens in it. Then in a second paragraph ask yourself: what, *besides* the element of story, did you consider in order to understand the poem?

5. Think of someone you know (or someone you can imagine) whose attitude toward poetry in general is dislike. Suggest a particular poem for that person to read—a poem that you personally like—and, addressing your skeptical reader, point out whatever you find to enjoy in it, that you think the skeptic just might enjoy too.

TOPICS FOR MORE EXTENSIVE PAPERS (600–1,000 WORDS)

1. Write an explication of a poem short enough for you to work through line by line — for instance, Judith Wright's "Woman to Man" or "Woman to Child," or Williams's "Spring and All," or a sonnet. As though offering the benefit of your reading experience to a friend who hadn't read the poem before, try to point out all the leading difficulties you encountered in your own reading, and set forth in detail your understanding of any lines that contain such difficulties.

2. Write an explication of a longer poem — for instance, Eliot's "Rhapsody on a Windy Night," Frost's "Witch of Coös," Hardy's "Convergence of the Twain," or Rich's "Diving into the Wreck." Although you will not be able to go through every line of the poem, explain what you think most needs explaining.

3. In this book, you will find six to ten poems by each of these poets: Blake, Cummings, Dickinson, Donne, Frost, Hardy, Housman, Keats, Roethke, Shakespeare, Stevens, Whitman, William Carlos Williams, Wordsworth, and Yeats; and multiple selections for many more. (See Index of Authors, Titles, and Quotations.) After you have read a few specimens of the work of a poet who interests you, write an analysis of *more than one* of the poet's poems. To do this, you will need to select just one characteristic theme (or other element) to deal with — something typical of the poet's work, not found only in a single poem. Here are a few specific topics for such an analysis:

   "What Angers William Blake? A Look at Three Poems of Protest"

   "Elements of Song in Lyrics of Emily Dickinson"

   "The Humor of Robert Frost"

   "John Keats's Sensuous Imagery"

   "The Vocabulary of Music in Poems of Wallace Stevens"

   "Non-free Verse: Patterns of Sound in Three Poems of William Carlos Williams"

   "The Moment of Illumination in Elizabeth Bishop's 'Fish,' 'Filling Station,' and 'Five Flights Up' "

   "Yeats as a Poet of Love"

4. Compare and contrast two poems in order to evaluate them: which is more satisfying and effective poetry? To make a meaningful comparison, be sure to choose two poems that genuinely have much in common: perhaps a similar theme or subject. (For an illustration of such a paper, see the one given in this chapter. For suggestions of poems to compare, see Poems for Further Study.)

5. Evaluate by the method of comparison two different versions of a poem: early and late drafts, perhaps, or two translations from another language. For parallel versions to work on, see Chapter Twenty-seven, "Alternatives."

6. If the previous topic appeals to you, consider this. In 1912, twenty-four years before he printed "Design," Robert Frost sent a correspondent this early version:

   IN WHITE

   A dented spider like a snow drop white
   On a white Heal-all, holding up a moth
   Like a white piece of lifeless satin cloth —
   Saw ever curious eye so strange a sight? —

Portent in little, assorted death and blight   5
Like ingredients of a witches' broth?—
The beady spider, the flower like a froth,
And the moth carried like a paper kite.

What had that flower to do with being white,
The blue prunella every child's delight.   10
What brought the kindred spider to that height?
(Make we no thesis of the miller's plight.)
What but design of darkness and of night?
Design, design! Do I use the word aright?

Compare "In White" with "Design." In what respects is the finished poem
superior?

Topics for Long Papers (1,500 words or More)

1. Write a line-by-line explication of a poem rich in matters to explain, or a
   longer poem that offers ample difficulty. While relatively short, Donne's
   "Valediction: Forbidding Mourning" or Hopkins's "The Windhover" are
   poems that will take a good bit of time to explicate; but even a short, apparently simple poem such as Frost's "Stopping by Woods on a Snowy Evening" can provide more than enough to explicate thoughtfully in a longer
   paper.
2. Write an analysis of the work of one poet (as suggested above, in the third
   topic for more extensive papers) in which you go beyond this book to read an
   entire collection of that poet's work.
3. Write an analysis of a certain theme (or other element) that you find in the
   work of two or more poets. It is probable that in your conclusion you will
   want to set the poets' work side by side, comparing or contrasting it, and
   perhaps making some evaluation. Sample topics:

   "The Myth of Eden as Interpreted by James Dickey, Theodore Roethke, and
   Gary Snyder"

   "What It Is to Be a Woman: The Special Knowledge of Sylvia Plath and
   Judith Wright"

   "Language of Science in Some Poems of Eberhart, Merrill, and Ammons"

29 What Is Poetry?

Archibald MacLeish (b. 1892)

Ars Poetica
1926

A poem should be palpable and mute
As a globed fruit,

Dumb
As old medallions to the thumb,

Silent as the sleeve-worn stone
5
Of casement ledges where the moss has grown—

A poem should be wordless
As the flight of birds.

A poem should be motionless in time
As the moon climbs,
10

Leaving, as the moon releases
Twig by twig the night-entangled trees,

Leaving, as the moon behind the winter leaves,
Memory by memory the mind—

A poem should be motionless in time
15
As the moon climbs.

A poem should be equal to:
Not true.

For all the history of grief
An empty doorway and a maple leaf.
20

For love
The leaning grasses and two lights above the sea—

A poem should not mean
But be.

What is poetry? By now, perhaps, you have formed your own idea, whether or not you feel able to define it. Just in case further efforts at definition can be useful, here are a few memorable ones (including, for a second look, some given earlier):

> the art of uniting pleasure with truth by calling imagination to the help of reason.
>
> —Samuel Johnson

> the imaginative expression of strong feeling, usually rhythmical . . . the spontaneous overflow of powerful feelings recollected in tranquility.
>
> —William Wordsworth

> the best words in the best order.
>
> —Samuel Taylor Coleridge

> musical Thought.
>
> —Thomas Carlyle

> If I read a book and it makes my whole body so cold no fire can ever warm me, I know that it is poetry. If I feel physically as if the top of my head were taken off, I know that it is poetry. Is there any other way?
>
> —Emily Dickinson

> speech framed . . . to be heard for its own sake and interest even over and above its interest of meaning.
>
> —Gerard Manley Hopkins

> a revelation in words by means of the words.
>
> —Wallace Stevens

> not the assertion that something is true, but the making of that truth more fully real to us.
>
> —T. S. Eliot

> the clear expression of mixed feelings.
>
> —W. H. Auden

A poem differs from most prose in several ways. For one, both writer and reader tend to regard it differently. The poet's attitude is something like this: I offer this piece of writing to be read not as prose but as a poem—that is, more perceptively, thoughtfully, and considerately, with more attention to sounds and connotations. This is a great deal to expect, but in return, the reader, too, has a right to certain expectations. Approaching the poem in the anticipation of out-of-the-ordinary knowledge and pleasure, the reader assumes that the poet may use certain enjoyable devices not available to prose: rime, alliteration, meter, and rhythms—definite, various, or emphatic. (The poet may not *always* choose to employ these things.) The reader expects the poet to make greater use, perhaps, of resources of meaning such as figurative language, allusion, symbol, and imagery. As readers of prose we might seek no more than meaning: no more than what could be paraphrased without serious loss. Meeting any figurative language or graceful turns of word order, we think them pleasant extras. But in poetry all these "extras" matter as much as the paraphraseable content, if not more. For, when we finish reading a good poem, we cannot explain precisely to ourselves of what we have experienced — without repeating, word for word, the language of the poem itself.

It is doubtful that anyone can draw an immovable boundary between poetry and prose, nor does such an attempt seem necessary. Certain prose needs only to be arranged in lines to be seen as poetry — especially prose that conveys strong emotion in vivid, physical imagery and in terse, figurative, rhythmical language. Even in translation the words of Chief Joseph of the Nez Percé tribe, at the moment of his surrender to the U.S. Army in 1877, still move us and are memorable:

> Hear me, my warriors, my heart is sick and sad:
> Our chiefs are killed,
> The old men all are dead,
> It is cold and we have no blankets.
>
> The little children freeze to death.
>
> Hear me, my warriors, my heart is sick and sad:
> From where the sun now stands I will fight no more forever.

It may be that a poem can point beyond words to something still more essential. Language has its limits, and probably Edgar Allan Poe was the only poet ever to claim he could always find words for whatever he wished to express. For, of all a human being can experience and imagine, words say only part. "Human speech," said Flaubert, who strove after the best of it, "is like a cracked kettle on which we hammer out tunes to make bears dance, when what we long for is the compassion of the stars."

Like Yeats's chestnut-tree in "Among School Children" (which when asked whether it is leaf, blossom, or bole, has no answer), a poem is to be seen not as a confederation of form, rime, image, metaphor, tone, and theme, but as a whole. We study a poem one element at a time because the intellect best comprehends what it can separate. But only our total attention, involving the participation of our blood and marrow, can see all elements in a poem fused, all dancing together. Yeats knew how to make poems and how to read them:

> God guard me from those thoughts men think
> In the mind alone;
> He that sings a lasting song
> Thinks in a marrow-bone.

Throughout this book, we have been working on the assumption that the patient and conscious explication of poems will sharpen unconscious perceptions. We can only hope that it will; the final test lies in whether you care to go on by yourself, reading other poems, finding in them pleasure and enlightenment. Pedagogy must have a stop; so must the viewing of poems as if their elements fell into chapters. For the total experience of reading a poem surpasses the mind's categories. The wind in the grass, says a proverb, cannot be taken into the house.

30 Poems for Further Study

Sit a while dear son,
Here are biscuits to eat and here is milk to drink,
But as soon as you sleep and renew yourself in sweet clothes,
I kiss you with a good-by kiss and open the gates for your egress hence.

Long enough have you dream'd contemptible dreams,
Now I wash the gum from your eyes,
You must habit yourself to the dazzle of the light and of every moment of
    your life.

Long have you timidly waded holding a plank by the shore,
Now I will you to be a bold swimmer,
To jump off in the midst of the sea, rise again, nod to me, shout, and
    laughingly dash with your hair.

                   —Walt Whitman, "Song of Myself"

Anonymous (traditional Scottish ballad)

EDWARD

"Why dois your brand° sae° drap wi' bluid,   *sword; so*
     Edward, Edward?
Why dois your brand sae drap wi' bluid?
  And why sae sad gang° yee, O?"   *go*
"O, I hae killed my hauke sae guid,   5
     Mither, mither,
O, I hae killed my hauke sae guid,
  And I had nae mair bot° hee, O."   *but*

"Your haukis bluid was nevir sae reid,
     Edward, Edward,   10
Your haukis bluid was nevir sae reid,
  My deir son I tell thee, O."
"O, I hae killed my reid-roan steid,
     Mither, mither,
O, I hae killed my reid-roan steid,   15
  That erst° was sa fair and frie°, O."   *once; free*

"Your steid was auld, and ye hae gat mair,
     Edward, Edward,
Your steid was auld, and ye hae gat mair,
  Sum other dule° ye drie°, O."   *sorrow; suffer* 20
"O, I hae killed my fadir deir,
     Mither, mither,
O, I hae killed my fadir deir,
  Alas, and wae° is mee, O!"   *woe*

"And whatten penance wul ye drie for that,   25
     Edward, Edward?
And whatten penance will ye drie for that?
  My deir son, now tell me, O."
"Ile set my feit in yonder boat,
     Mither, mither,   30
Ile set my feit in yonder boat,
  And Ile fare ovir the sea, O."

"And what wul ye doe wi' your towirs and your ha'°,   *hall*
     Edward, Edward,
And what wul ye doe wi' your towirs and your ha',   35
  That were sae fair to see, O?"
"Ile let thame stand tul they doun fa',
     Mither, mither,
Ile let thame stand tul they doun fa',
  For here nevir mair maun° I bee, O."   *must* 40

"And what wul ye leive to your bairns° and your wife,   *children*
     Edward, Edward?

And what wul ye leive to your bairns and your wife,
    When ye gang ovir the sea, O?"
"The warldis° room, late° them beg thrae° life,   *world's; let; through* 45
      Mither, mither
The warldis room, late them beg thrae life,
    For thame nevir mair wul I see, O."

"And what wul ye leive to your ain° mither deir,   *own*
      Edward, Edward?
                                                50
And what wul ye leive to your ain mither deir?
    My deir son, now tell me, O."
"The curse of hell frae me sall ye beir,
      Mither, mither,
The curse of hell frae me sall ye beir,   55
    Sic° counseils° ye gave to me, O."   *such; counsel*

Anonymous (traditional Scottish ballad)

Sir Patrick Spence

The king sits in Dumferling toune,
    Drinking the blude-reid wine:
"O whar will I get guid sailor
    To sail this schip of mine?"

Up and spak an eldern knicht,   5
    Sat at the kings richt kne:
"Sir Patrick Spence is the best sailor
    That sails upon the se."

The king has written a braid letter,
    And signed it wi' his hand,
                                      10
And sent it to Sir Patrick Spence,
    Was walking on the sand.

The first line that Sir Patrick red,
    A loud lauch lauchèd he;
The next line that Sir Patrick red,
                                      15
    The teir blinded his ee.

"O wha° is this has don this deid,   *who*
    This ill deid don to me,
To send me out this time o' the yeir,
    To sail upon the se!
                                      20

"Mak haste, mak haste, my mirry men all,
    Our guid schip sails the morne."
"O say na sae°, my master deir,   *so*
    For I feir a deadlie storme.

"Late late yestreen I saw the new moone,   25
   Wi' the auld moone in hir arme,
And I feir, I feir, my deir master,
   That we will cum to harme."

O our Scots nobles wer richt laith°   *loath*
   To weet° their cork-heild schoone°;   *wet; shoes*   30
Bot lang owre° a' the play wer playd,   *before*
   Their hats they swam aboone°.   *above (their heads)*

O lang, lang may their ladies sit,
   Wi' their fans into their hand,
Or ere° they se Sir Patrick Spence   *long before*   35
   Cum sailing to the land.

O lang, lang may the ladies stand,
   Wi' their gold kems° in their hair,   *combs*
Waiting for their ain° deir lords,   *own*
   For they'll se thame na mair.   40

Haf owre°, haf owre to Aberdour,   *halfway over*
   It's fiftie fadom deip,
And thair lies guid Sir Patrick Spence,
   Wi' the Scots lords at his feit.

SIR PATRICK SPENCE. 9. *braid:* Broad, but broad in what sense? Among guesses are *plain-spoken, official,* and *on wide paper.*

Anonymous (traditional English ballad)

THE THREE RAVENS

There were three ravens sat on a tree,
   Down a down, hay down, hay down,
There were three ravens sat on a tree,
   With a down,
There were three ravens sat on a tree,   5
They were as black as they might be.
   With a down derry, derry, derry, down, down.

The one of them said to his mate,
"Where shall we our breakfast take?"

"Down in yonder greene field,   10
There lies a knight slain under his shield.

"His hounds they lie down at his feet,
So well they can their master keep.

"His hawks they fly so eagerly,
There's no fowl dare him come nigh."   15

Down there comes a fallow doe,
As great with young as she might go.

She lift up his bloody head,
And kist his wounds that were so red.

She got him up upon her back,   20
And carried him to earthen lake°.   *the grave*

She buried him before the prime,
She was dead herself ere evensong time.

God send every gentleman
Such hawks, such hounds, and such a leman°.   *lover*   25

THE THREE RAVENS. The lines of refrain are repeated in each stanza. "Perhaps in the folk
mind the doe is the form the soul of a human mistress, now dead, has taken," Albert B.
Friedman has suggested (in *The Viking Book of Folk Ballads*). "Most probably the knight's
beloved was understood to be an enchanted woman who was metamorphosed at certain
times into an animal." 22–23. *prime, evensong:* two of the canonical hours set aside for
prayer and worship. Prime is at dawn, evensong at dusk.

Anonymous (traditional Scottish ballad)

THE TWA CORBIES

As I was walking all alane,
I heard twa corbies° making a mane°;   *ravens; moan*
The tane° unto the t'other say,   *one*
"Where sall we gang° and dine today?"   *go*

"In behint yon auld fail dyke°,   *turf wall*   5
I wot° there lies a new slain knight;   *know*
And naebody kens° that he lies there,   *knows*
But his hawk, his hound, and lady fair.

"His hound is to the hunting gane,
His hawk to fetch the wild-fowl hame,   10
His lady's ta'en another mate,
So we may mak our dinner sweet.

"Ye'll sit on his white hause-bane°,   *neck bone*
And I'll pike out his bonny blue een;
Wi' ae° lock o' his gowden hair   *one*   15
We'll theek° our nest when it grows bare.   *thatch*

"Mony a one for him makes mane,
But nane sall ken where he is gane;
O'er his white banes, when they are bare,
The wind sall blaw for evermair."   20

THE TWA CORBIES. Sir Walter Scott, the first to print this ballad in his *Minstrelsy of the
Scottish Border* (1802–1803), calls it "rather a counterpart than a copy" of "The Three
Ravens." M. J. C. Hodgart and other scholars think he may have written most of it himself.

COMPARE:

"The Three Ravens" and "The Twa Corbies" with "All in green went my love riding" by E. E. Cummings (page 733).

Anonymous (English song)

WESTERN WIND   (about 1500)

Western wind, when wilt thou blow,
The° small rain down can rain?   (so that) the
Christ, if my love were in my arms,
And I in my bed again!

James Agee (1909–1955)

SUNDAY: OUTSKIRTS OF KNOXVILLE, TENNESSEE   1937

There, in the earliest and chary spring, the dogwood flowers.

Unharnessed in the friendly sunday air
By the red brambles, on the river bluffs,
Clerks and their choices pair.

Thrive by, not near, masked all away by shrub and juniper,   5
The ford v eight, racing the chevrolet.

They can not trouble her:

Her breasts, helped open from the afforded lace,
Lie like a peaceful lake;
And on his mouth she breaks her gentleness: 10

Oh, wave them awake!

They are not of the birds. Such innocence
Brings us whole to break us only.
Theirs are not happy words.

We that are human cannot hope.   15
Our tenderest joys oblige us most.
No chain so cuts the bone; and sweetest silk most shrewdly strangles.

How this must end, that now please love were ended,
In kitchens, bedfights, silences, women's-pages,
Sickness of heart before goldlettered doors,   20
Stale flesh, hard collars, agony in antiseptic corridors,
Spankings, remonstrances, fishing trips, orange juice,
Policies, incapacities, a chevrolet,

Scorn of their children, kind contempt exchanged,
Recalls, tears, second honeymoons, pity,   25
Shouted corrections of missed syllables,
Hot water bags, gallstones, falls down stairs,
Stammerings, soft foods, confusion of personalities,
Oldfashioned christmases, suspicions of theft,
Arrangements with morticians taken care of by sons in law,   30
Small rooms beneath the gables of brick bungalows,
The tumbler smashed, the glance between daughter and husband,
The empty body in the lonely bed
And, in the empty concrete porch, blown ash
Grandchildren wandering the betraying sun   35

Now, on the winsome crumbling shelves of the horror
God show, God blind these children!

Maya Angelou (b. 1928)
HARLEM HOPSCOTCH   1971

One foot down, then hop! It's hot.
    Good things for the ones that's got.
Another jump, now to the left.
    Everybody for hisself.

In the air, now both feet down.   5
    Since you black, don't stick around.
Food is gone, the rent is due,
    Curse and cry and then jump two.

All the people out of work,
    Hold for three, then twist and jerk.   10
Cross the line, they count you out.
    That's what hopping's all about.

Both feet flat, the game is done.
They think I lost. I think I won.

COMPARE:

"Harlem Hopscotch" with "We Real Cool" by Gwendolyn Brooks (page 551).

Matthew Arnold (1822–1888)
DOVER BEACH   1867

The sea is calm tonight.
The tide is full, the moon lies fair
Upon the straits;—on the French coast the light
Gleams and is gone; the cliffs of England stand,

Glimmering and vast, out in the tranquil bay.   5
Come to the window, sweet is the night-air!
Only, from the long line of spray
Where the sea meets the moon-blanched land,
Listen! you hear the grating roar
Of pebbles which the waves draw back, and fling,   10
At their return, up the high strand,
Begin, and cease, and then again begin,
With tremulous cadence slow, and bring
The eternal note of sadness in.

Sophocles long ago   15
Heard it on the Aegean, and it brought
Into his mind the turbid ebb and flow
Of human misery; we
Find also in the sound a thought,
Hearing it by this distant northern sea.   20

The Sea of Faith
Was once, too, at the full, and round earth's shore
Lay like the folds of a bright girdle furled.
But now I only hear
Its melancholy, long, withdrawing roar,   25
Retreating, to the breath
Of the night-wind, down the vast edges drear
And naked shingles° of the world.   *gravel beaches*

Ah, love, let us be true
To one another! for the world, which seems   30
To lie before us like a land of dreams,
So various, so beautiful, so new,
Hath really neither joy, nor love, nor light,
Nor certitude, nor peace, nor help for pain;
And we are here as on a darkling° plain   *darkened or darkening*   35
Swept with confused alarms of struggle and flight,
Where ignorant armies clash by night.

John Ashbery (b. 1927)

CITY AFTERNOON   1975

A veil of haze protects this
Long-ago afternoon forgotten by everybody
In this photograph, most of them now
Sucked screaming through old age and death.

If one could seize America   5
Or at least a fine forgetfulness
That seeps into our outline
Defining our volumes with a stain
That is fleeting too

But commemorates   10
Because it does define, after all:
Gray garlands, that threesome
Waiting for the light to change,
Air lifting the hair of one
Upside down in the reflecting pool.   15

W. H. Auden (1907–1973)
As I Walked Out One Evening   1940

As I walked out one evening,
  Walking down Bristol Street,
The crowds upon the pavement
  Were fields of harvest wheat.

And down by the brimming river   5
  I heard a lover sing
Under an arch of the railway:
  "Love has no ending.

"I'll love you, dear, I'll love you
  Till China and Africa meet,   10
And the river jumps over the mountain
  And the salmon sing in the street,

"I'll love you till the ocean
  Is folded and hung up to dry
And the seven stars go squawking   15
  Like geese about the sky.

"The years shall run like rabbits,
  For in my arms I hold
The Flower of the Ages,
  And the first love of the world."   20

But all the clocks in the city
  Began to whirr and chime:
"O let not Time deceive you,
  You cannot conquer Time.

"In the burrows of the Nightmare   25
  Where Justice naked is,
Time watches from the shadow
  And coughs when you would kiss.

"In headaches and in worry
  Vaguely life leaks away,   30
And Time will have his fancy
  Tomorrow or today.

"Into many a green valley
  Drifts the appalling snow;

Time breaks the threaded dances
    And the diver's brilliant bow.   35

"O plunge your hands in water,
    Plunge them in up to the wrist;
Stare, stare in the basin
    And wonder what you've missed.   40

"The glacier knocks in the cupboard,
    The desert sighs in the bed,
And the crack in the teacup opens
    A lane to the land of the dead.

"Where the beggars raffle the banknotes   45
    And the Giant is enchanting to Jack,
And the Lily-white Boy is a Roarer,
    And Jill goes down on her back.

"O look, look in the mirror,
    O look in your distress;   50
Life remains a blessing
    Although you cannot bless.

"O stand, stand at the window
    As the tears scald and start;
You shall love your crooked neighbor   55
    With your crooked heart."

It was late, late in the evening,
    The lovers they were gone;
The clocks had ceased their chiming,
    And the deep river ran on.   60

W. H. Auden (1907–1973)
Musée des Beaux Arts   1940

About suffering they were never wrong,
The Old Masters: how well they understood
Its human position; how it takes place
While someone else is eating or opening a window or just walking dully
        along;
How, when the aged are reverently, passionately waiting   5
For the miraculous birth, there always must be
Children who did not specially want it to happen, skating
On a pond at the edge of the wood:
They never forgot
That even the dreadful martyrdom must run its course   10
Anyhow in a corner, some untidy spot
Where the dogs go on with their doggy life and the torturer's horse
Scratches its innocent behind on a tree.

In Brueghel's *Icarus,* for instance: how everything turns away
Quite leisurely from the disaster; the ploughman may 15
Have heard the splash, the forsaken cry,
But for him it was not an important failure; the sun shone
As it had to on the white legs disappearing into the green
Water; and the expensive delicate ship that must have seen
Something amazing, a boy falling out of the sky, 20
Had somewhere to get to and sailed calmly on.

Elizabeth Bishop (b. 1911)

Filling Station 1965

Oh, but it is dirty!
—this little filling station,
oil-soaked, oil-permeated
to a disturbing, over-all
black translucency. 5
Be careful with that match!

Father wears a dirty,
oil-soaked monkey suit
that cuts him under the arms,
and several quick and saucy 10
and greasy sons assist him
(it's a family filling station),
all quite thoroughly dirty.

Do they live in the station?
It has a cement porch
behind the pumps, and on it
a set of crushed and grease-
impregnated wickerwork;
on the wicker sofa
a dirty dog, quite comfy.

Some comic books provide
the only note of color—
of certain color. They lie
upon a big dim doily
draping a taboret
(part of the set), beside
a big hirsute begonia.

Why the extraneous plant?
Why the taboret?
Why, oh why, the doily?
(Embroidered in daisy stitch
with marguerites, I think,
and heavy with gray crochet.)

Somebody embroidered the doily.
Somebody waters the plant,
or oils it, maybe. Somebody
arranges the rows of cans
so that they softly say:
ESSO—SO—SO—SO
to high-strung automobiles.
Somebody loves us all.

15

20

25

30

35

40

Elizabeth Bishop (b. 1911)
FIVE FLIGHTS UP   1976

Still dark.
The unknown bird sits on his usual branch.
The little dog next door barks in his sleep
inquiringly, just once.
Perhaps in his sleep, too, the bird inquires
once or twice, quavering.
Questions—if that is what they are—
answered directly, simply,
by day itself.

Enormous morning, ponderous, meticulous;
gray light streaking each bare branch,

5

10

each single twig, along one side,
making another tree, of glassy veins . . .
The bird still sits there. Now he seems to yawn.

The little black dog runs in his yard.   15
His owner's voice arises, stern,
"You ought to be ashamed!"
What has he done?
He bounces cheerfully up and down;
he rushes in circles in the fallen leaves.   20

Obviously, he has no sense of shame.
He and the bird know everything is answered,
all taken care of,
no need to ask again.
—Yesterday brought to today so lightly!   25
(A yesterday I find almost impossible to lift.)

William Blake (1757–1827)

Long John Brown and Little Mary Bell   (about 1803)

Little Mary Bell had a fairy in a nut,
Long John Brown had the Devil in his gut;
Long John Brown loved Little Mary Bell,
And the fairy drew the Devil into the nut-shell.

Her fairy skipped out and her fairy skipped in;   5
He laughed at the Devil saying "Love is a sin."
The Devil he raged and Devil he was wroth,
And the Devil entered into the young man's broth.

He was soon in the gut of the loving young swain,
For John eat and drank to drive away love's pain;   10
But all he could do he grew thinner and thinner,
Though he eat and drank as much as ten men for his dinner.

Some said he had a wolf in his stomach day and night,
Some said he had the Devil and they guessed right;
The fairy skipped about in his glory, joy and pride,   15
And he laughed at the Devil till poor John Brown died.

Then the fairy skipped out of the old nut-shell,
And woe and alack for pretty Mary Bell!
For the Devil crept in when the fairy skipped out,
And there goes Miss Bell with her fusty old nut.   20

William Blake (1757–1827)
THE SICK ROSE

1794

O Rose, thou art sick!
The invisible worm
That flies in the night,
In the howling storm,

Has found out thy bed
Of crimson joy,
And his dark secret love
Does thy life destroy.

William Blake (1757–1827)
THE TYGER

1794

Tyger! Tyger! burning bright
In the forests of the night,
What immortal hand or eye
Could frame thy fearful symmetry?

In what distant deeps or skies   5
Burnt the fire of thine eyes?
On what wings dare he aspire?
What the hand dare seize the fire?

And what shoulder, and what art,
Could twist the sinews of thy heart?   10
And when thy heart began to beat,
What dread hand? and what dread feet?

What the hammer? what the chain?
In what furnace was thy brain?
What the anvil? what dread grasp   15
Dare its deadly terrors clasp?

When the stars threw down their spears,
And watered heaven with their tears,
Did he smile his work to see?
Did he who made the Lamb make thee?   20

Tyger! Tyger! burning bright
In the forests of the night,
What immortal hand or eye
Dare frame thy fearful symmetry?

Gwendolyn Brooks (b. 1917)

THE BEAN EATERS

1960

They eat beans mostly, this old yellow pair.
Dinner is a casual affair.
Plain chipware on a plain and creaking wood,
Tin flatware.

Two who are Mostly Good.   5
Two who have lived their day,
But keep on putting on their clothes
And putting things away.

And remembering . . .
Remembering, with tinklings and twinges,   10
As they lean over the beans in their rented back room that is full of beads
        and receipts and dolls and cloths, tobacco crumbs, vases and
        fringes.

Robert Browning (1812–1889)

MY LAST DUCHESS

1842

Ferrara

That's my last Duchess painted on the wall,   *He put her to death upstairs*
Looking as if she were alive. I call
That piece a wonder, now; Frà Pandolf's hands
Worked busily a day, and there she stands.
Will 't please you sit and look at her? I said   5
"Frà Pandolf" by design, for never read
Strangers like you that pictured countenance,   *nobody can see duchess only a picture*
The depth and passion of its earnest glance,
But to myself they turned (since none puts by
The curtain I have drawn for you, but I)   10
And seemed as they would ask me, if they durst,
How such a glance came there; so, not the first
Are you to turn and ask thus. Sir, 'twas not
Her husband's presence only, called that spot   *Duke was in love w/ Duchess but only wanted her for himself - not to even smile at anyone*
Of joy into the Duchess' cheek; perhaps   15
Frà Pandolf chanced to say, "Her mantle laps
Over my lady's wrist too much," or "Paint
Must never hope to reproduce the faint
Half-flush that dies along her throat." Such stuff
Was courtesy, she thought, and cause enough
For calling up that spot of joy. She had   20
A heart—how shall I say?—too soon made glad,   *His ego is hurt that she liked other simple things as much as she like his gifts*
Too easily impressed; she liked whate'er
She looked on, and her looks went everywhere.

Sir, 'twas all one! My favor at her breast, 25
The dropping of the daylight in the West,
The bough of cherries some officious fool
Broke in the orchard for her, the white mule
She rode with round the terrace—all and each
Would draw from her alike the approving speech,
Or blush, at least. She thanked men,—good! but thanked 30
Somehow—I know not how—as if she ranked
My gift of a nine-hundred-years' old name
With anybody's gift. Who'd stoop to blame
This sort of trifling? Even had you skill
In speech—which I have not—to make your will 35
Quite clear to such an one, and say "Just this
Or that in you disgusts me; here you miss,
Or there exceed the mark"—and if she let
Herself be lessoned so, nor plainly set
Her wits to yours, forsooth, and made excuse— 40
E'en then would be some stooping; and I choose
Never to stoop. Oh, sir, she smiled, no doubt,
Whene'er I passed her; but who passed without
Much the same smile? This grew; I gave commands; 45
Then all smiles stopped together. There she stands
As if alive. Will 't please you rise? We'll meet
The company below, then. I repeat,
The Count your master's known munificence
Is ample warrant that no just pretense 50
Of mine for dowry will be disallowed;
Though his fair daughter's self, as I avowed
At starting, is my object. Nay, we'll go
Together down, sir. Notice Neptune, though,
Taming a sea-horse, thought a rarity, 55
Which Claus of Innsbruck cast in bronze for me!

Duke was overbearing

He wants her to be more appreciative of him but won't stoop low enough to tell her.

innocent

Her actions are trifling her.

He kills her?

smile at everyone

generosity guarantee

not of same position - servant

Duke wants to marry the daughter of the Count get dowry

MY LAST DUCHESS. Ferrara, a city in northern Italy, is the scene. Browning may have modeled his speaker after Alonzo, Duke of Ferrara (1533-1598). 3. *Frà Pandolf* and 56. *Claus of Innsbruck*: fictitious names of artists.

Robert Browning (1812–1889)
SOLILOQUY OF THE SPANISH CLOISTER 1842

Brother Lawrence is good man
Bad brother speaks

Gr-r-r—there go, my heart's abhorrence!
　Water your damned flower-pots, do!
If hate killed men, Brother Lawrence,
He hates Law.
　God's blood, would not mine kill you!
What? your myrtle-bush wants trimming? 5
　Oh, that rose has prior claims—
Needs its leaden vase filled brimming?
　Hell dry you up with its flames!

At the meal we sit together;
    Salve tibi!° I must hear   *Hail to thee!*   10
Wise talk of the kind of weather,
    Sort of season, time of year:
Not a plenteous cork-crop: scarcely
    Dare we hope oak-galls, I doubt;
What's the Latin name for "parsley"?   15
    What's the Greek name for "swine's snout"?

Whew! We'll have our platter burnished,
    Laid with care on our own shelf!
With a fire-new spoon we're furnished,
    And a goblet for ourself,   20
Rinsed like something sacrificial
    Ere 'tis fit to touch our chaps —
Marked with <u>L. for our initial</u>!
    (He-he! There his lily snaps!)

Saint, forsooth! While Brown Dolores   25
    Squats outside the Convent bank
With Sanchicha, telling stories,
    Steeping tresses in the tank,
Blue-black, lustrous, thick like horsehairs,
    — Can't I see his dead eye glow,   30
Bright as 'twere a Barbary corsair's?
    (That is, if he'd let it show!)

When he finishes refection,
    Knife and fork he never lays
Cross-wise, to my recollection,   35
    As I do, in Jesu's praise.
I the Trinity illustrate,
    Drinking watered orange-pulp —
In three sips the Arian frustrate;
    While he drains his at one gulp!   40

Oh, those melons! if he's able
    We're to have a feast; so nice!
One goes to the Abbot's table,
    All of us get each a slice.
How go on your flowers? None double?   45
    Not one fruit-sort can you spy?
Strange! — And I, too, at such trouble,
    Keep them close-nipped on the sly!

There's a great text in Galatians,
    Once you trip on it, entails   50
Twenty-nine distinct damnations,
    One sure, if another fails;
If I trip him just a-dying,
    Sure of heaven as sure can be,
Spin him round and send him flying   55
    Off to hell, a Manichee?

Or, my scrofulous French novel
  On grey paper with blunt type!
Simply glance at it, you grovel
  Hand and foot in Belial's gripe;   *Lustful*   60
If I double down its pages
  At the woeful sixteenth print,
When he gathers his greengages,
  Ope a sieve and slip it in't?

Or, there's Satan! — one might venture   65
  Pledge one's soul to him, yet leave
Such a flaw in the indenture   *Hates him + wants to*
  As he'd miss till, past retrieve,   *make contract with*
Blasted lay that rose-acacia   *devil.*
  We're so proud of! *Hy, Zy, Hine.* . . .   70
'St, there's Vespers! *Plena gratia*
Ave, Virgo!° Gr-r-r — you swine!   *Hail, Virgin, full of grace!*

SOLILOQUY OF THE SPANISH CLOISTER. 3. *Brother Lawrence:* one of the speaker's fellow monks. 31. *Barbary corsair:* a pirate operating off the Barbary coast of Africa. 39. *Arian:* a follower of Arius, heretic who denied the doctrine of the Trinity. 49. *a great text in Galatians:* a difficult verse in this book of the Bible. Brother Lawrence will be damned as a heretic if he wrongly interprets it. 56. *Manichee:* another kind of heretic, one who (after the Persian philosopher Mani) sees in the world a constant struggle between good and evil, neither able to win. 60. *Belial:* Here, not specifically Satan but (as used in the Old Testament) a name for wickedness. 70. *Hy, Zy, Hine:* Possibly the sound of a bell to announce evening devotions, possibly the beginning of a formula to summon the Devil.

Fred Chappell (b. 1936)

SKIN FLICK   1971

The selfsame surface that billowed once with
The shapes of Trigger and Gene. New faces now
Are in the saddle. Tits and buttocks
Slide rattling down the beam as down
A coal chute; in the splotched light   5
The burning bush strikes dumb.
Different sort of cattle drive:
No water for miles and miles.

In the aisles, new bugs and rats
Though it's the same Old Paint.   10
Audience of lepers, hopeless and homeless,
Or like the buffalo, at home
In the wind only. No
Mushy love stuff for them.

They eye the violent innocence they always knew.   15
Is that the rancher's palomino daughter?
Is this her eastern finishing school?

Same old predicament:
No water for miles and miles,
The horizon breeds no cavalry.   20

Men, draw your wagons in a circle. Be ready.

G. K. Chesterton (1874–1936)
THE DONKEY   1900

When fishes flew and forests walked
   And figs grew upon thorn,
Some moment when the moon was blood
   Then surely I was born;

With monstrous head and sickening cry   5
   And ears like errant wings,
The devil's walking parody
   On all four-footed things.

The tattered outlaw of the earth,
   Of ancient crooked will;   10
Starve, scourge, deride me: I am dumb,
   I keep my secret still.

Fools! For I also had my hour;
   One far fierce hour and sweet:
There was a shout about my ears,   15
   And palms before my feet.

THE DONKEY. For more details of the donkey's hour of triumph see Matthew 21:1–8.

Samuel Taylor Coleridge (1772–1834)
KUBLA KHAN   (1797-1798)

Or, a Vision in a Dream. A Fragment.

In Xanadu did Kubla Khan
A stately pleasure-dome decree:
Where Alph, the sacred river, ran
Through caverns measureless to man
   Down to a sunless sea.   5
So twice five miles of fertile ground
With walls and towers were girdled round;
And there were gardens bright with sinuous rills,
Where blossomed many an incense-bearing tree;
And here were forests ancient as the hills,
Enfolding sunny spots of greenery.   10

But oh! that deep romantic chasm which slanted
Down the green hill athwart a cedarn cover!
A savage place! as holy and enchanted
As e'er beneath a waning moon was haunted
By woman wailing for her demon-lover!
And from this chasm, with ceaseless turmoil seething,
As if this earth in fast thick pants were breathing,
A mighty fountain momently was forced:
Amid whose swift half-intermitted burst
Huge fragments vaulted like rebounding hail,
Or chaffy grain beneath the thresher's flail:
And 'mid these dancing rocks at once and ever
It flung up momently the sacred river.
Five miles meandering with a mazy motion
Through wood and dale the sacred river ran,
Then reached the caverns measureless to man,
And sank in tumult to a lifeless ocean:
And 'mid this tumult Kubla heard from far
Ancestral voices prophesying war!

   The shadow of the dome of pleasure
   Floated midway on the waves;
   Where was heard the mingled measure
   From the fountain and the caves.
It was a miracle of rare device,
A sunny pleasure-dome with caves of ice!

   A damsel with a dulcimer
   In a vision once I saw:
   It was an Abyssinian maid,
   And on her dulcimer she played,
   Singing of Mount Abora.
   Could I revive within me
   Her symphony and song,
   To such a deep delight 'twould win me,
That with music loud and long,
I would build that dome in air,
That sunny dome! those caves of ice!
And all who heard should see them there,
And all should cry, Beware! Beware!
His flashing eyes, his floating hair!
Weave a circle round him thrice,
And close your eyes with holy dread,
For he on honey-dew hath fed,
And drunk the milk of Paradise.

KUBLA KHAN. There was an actual Kublai Khan, a thirteenth-century Mongol emperor, and a Chinese city of Xamdu; but Coleridge's dream vision also borrows from travelers' descriptions of such other exotic places as Abyssinia and America. 51. *circle:* a magic circle drawn to keep away evil spirits.

Robert Creeley (b. 1926)

NAUGHTY BOY

1959

When he brings home a whale,
she laughs and says, that's not for real.

And if he won the Irish sweepstakes,
she would say, where were you last night?

Where are you now, for that matter? Am   5
I always (she says) to be looking

at you? She says,
if I thought it would get any better I

would shoot you, you
nut, you. Then pats her hair   10

into place, and waits
for Uncle Jim's deep-fired, all-fat, real gone

whale steaks.

Countee Cullen (1903–1946)

SATURDAY'S CHILD

1925

Some are teethed on a silver spoon,
With the stars strung for a rattle;
I cut my teeth as the black racoon —
for implements of battle.

Some are swaddled in silk and down,   5
And heralded by a star;
They swathed my limbs in a sackcloth gown
On a night that was black as tar.

For some, godfather and goddame
The opulent fairies be;   10
Dame Poverty gave me my name,
And Pain godfathered me.

For I was born on Saturday —
"Bad time for planting a seed,"
Was all my father had to say,   15
And, "One mouth more to feed."

Death cut the strings that gave me life,
And handed me to Sorrow,

The only kind of middle wife
My folks could beg or borrow.   20

COMPARE:

"Saturday's Child" with "Dream Deferred" by Langston Hughes (page 765) and
"Ballad of Birmingham" by Dudley Randall (page 792).

E. E. Cummings (1894–1962)
ALL IN GREEN WENT MY LOVE RIDING   1923

All in green went my love riding
on a great horse of gold
into the silver dawn.

four lean hounds crouched low and smiling
the merry deer ran before.   5

Fleeter be they than dappled dreams
the swift sweet deer
the red rare deer.

Four red roebuck at a white water
the cruel bugle sang before.   10

Horn at hip went my love riding
riding the echo down
into the silver dawn.

four lean hounds crouched low and smiling
the level meadows ran before.   15

Softer be they than slippered sleep
the lean lithe deer
the fleet flown deer.

Four fleet does at a gold valley
the famished arrow sang before.   20

Bow at belt went my love riding
riding the mountain down
into the silver dawn.

four lean hounds crouched low and smiling
the sheer peaks ran before.   25

Paler be they than daunting death
the sleek slim deer
the tall tense deer.

Four tall stags at a green mountain
the lucky hunter sang before.   30

All in green went my love riding
on a great horse of gold
into the silver dawn.

four lean hounds crouched low and smiling
my heart fell dead before.

35

COMPARE:

"All in green went my love riding" with the ballads "The Three Ravens" and
"The Twa Corbies" (pages 715–716).

Walter de la Mare (1873–1956)

THE LISTENERS
1912

"Is there anybody there?" said the Traveler,
   Knocking on the moonlit door;
And his horse in the silence champed the grasses
   Of the forest's ferny floor:
And a bird flew up out of the turret,   5
   Above the Traveler's head:
And he smote upon the door again a second time;
   "Is there anybody there?" he said.
But no one descended to the Traveler;
   No head from the leaf-fringed sill   10
Leaned over and looked into his grey eyes,
   Where he stood perplexed and still.
But only a host of phantom listeners
   That dwelt in the lone house then
Stood listening in the quiet of the moonlight   15
   To that voice from the world of men:
Stood thronging the faint moonbeams on the dark stair,
   That goes down to the empty hall,
Hearkening in an air stirred and shaken
   By the lonely Traveler's call.   20
And he felt in his heart their strangeness,
   Their stillness answering his cry,
While his horse moved, cropping the dark turf,
   'Neath the starred and leafy sky;
For he suddenly smote on the door, even   25
   Louder, and lifted his head:—
"Tell them I came, and no one answered,
   That I kept my word," he said.
Never the least stir made the listeners,
   Though every word he spake   30
Fell echoing through the shadowiness of the still house
   From the one man left awake:

Ay, they heard his foot upon the stirrup,
  And the sound of iron on stone,
And how the silence surged softly backward,   35
  When the plunging hoofs were gone.

James Dickey (b. 1923)
CHERRYLOG ROAD   1963

Off Highway 106
At Cherrylog Road I entered
The '34 Ford without wheels,
Smothered in kudzu,
With a seat pulled out to run   5
Corn whiskey down from the hills,

And then from the other side
Crept into an Essex
With a rumble seat of red leather
And then out again, aboard   10
A blue Chevrolet, releasing
The rust from its other color,

Reared up on three building blocks.
None had the same body heat;
I changed with them inward, toward   15
The weedy heart of the junkyard,
For I knew that Doris Holbrook
Would escape from her father at noon

And would come from the farm
To seek parts owned by the sun   20
Among the abandoned chassis,
Sitting in each in turn
As I did, leaning forward
As in a wild stock-car race

In the parking lot of the dead.   25
Time after time, I climbed in
And out the other side, like
An envoy or movie star
Met at the station by crickets.
A radiator cap raised its head,   30

Become a real toad or a kingsnake
As I neared the hub of the yard,
Passing through many states,
Many lives, to reach
Some grandmother's long Pierce-Arrow   35
Sending platters of blindness forth

From its nickel hubcaps
And spilling its tender upholstery
On sleepy roaches,
The glass panel in between
Lady and colored driver
Not all the way broken out,

The back-seat phone
Still on its hook.
I got in as though to exclaim,
"Let us go to the orphan asylum,
John; I have some old toys
For children who say their prayers."

I popped with sweat as I thought
I heard Doris Holbrook scrape
Like a mouse in the southern-state sun
That was eating the paint in blisters
From a hundred car tops and hoods.
She was tapping like code,

Loosening the screws,
Carrying off headlights,
Sparkplugs, bumpers,
Cracked mirrors and gear-knobs,
Getting ready, already,
To go back with something to show

Other than her lips' new trembling
I would hold to me soon, soon,
Where I sat in the ripped back seat
Talking over the interphone,
Praying for Doris Holbrook
To come from her father's farm

And to get back there
With no trace of me on her face
To be seen by her red-haired father
Who would change, in the squalling barn,
Her back's pale skin with a strop,
Then lay for me

In a bootlegger's roasting car
With a string-triggered 12-gauge shotgun
To blast the breath from the air.
Not cut by the jagged windshields,
Through the acres of wrecks she came
With a wrench in her hand,

Through dust where the blacksnake dies
Of boredom, and the beetle knows
The compost has no more life.

Someone outside would have seen
The oldest car's door inexplicably
Close from within:

I held her and held her and held her,   85
Convoyed at terrific speed
By the stalled, dreaming traffic around us,
So the blacksnake, stiff
With inaction, curved back
Into life, and hunted the mouse   90

With deadly overexcitement,
The beetles reclaimed their field
As we clung, glued together,
With the hooks of the seat springs
Working through to catch us red-handed   95
Amidst the gray breathless batting

That burst from the seat at our backs.
We left by separate doors
Into the changed, other bodies
Of cars, she down Cherrylog Road   100
And I to my motorcycle
Parked like the soul of the junkyard

Restored, a bicycle fleshed
With power, and tore off
Up Highway 106, continually   105
Drunk on the wind in my mouth,
Wringing the handlebar for speed,
Wild to be wreckage forever.

Emily Dickinson (1830–1886)
Because I could not stop for Death   (1863)

Because I could not stop for Death–
He kindly stopped for me–
The Carriage held but just Ourselves–
And Immortality.

We slowly drove–He knew no haste   5
And I had put away
My labor and my leisure too,
For His Civility–

We passed the School, where Children strove
At Recess–in the Ring–   10
We passed the Fields of Gazing Grain–
We passed the Setting Sun–

Or rather–He passed Us–
The Dews drew quivering and chill–
For only Gossamer, my Gown–   15
My Tippet°–only Tulle–   *cape*

We paused before a House that seemed
A Swelling of the Ground–
The Roof was scarcely visible–
The Cornice — in the Ground–   20

Since then–'tis Centuries–and yet
Feels shorter than the Day
I first surmised the Horses' Heads
Were toward Eternity–

BECAUSE I COULD NOT STOP FOR DEATH. In the version of this poem printed by Emily
Dickinson's first editors in 1890, stanza four was left out. In line 9 *strove* was replaced by
played; line 10 was made to read "Their lessons scarcely done"; line 20, "The cornice but a
mound"; line 21, "Since then 'tis centuries, but each"; and capitalization and punctuation
were made conventional.

Emily Dickinson (1830–1886)

I STARTED EARLY — TOOK MY DOG   (1862)

I started Early–Took my Dog–
And visited the Sea–
The Mermaids in the Basement
Came out to look at me–

And Frigates–in the Upper Floor   5
Extended Hempen Hands–
Presuming Me to be a Mouse–
Aground–upon the Sands–

But no Man moved Me–till the Tide
Went past my simple Shoe–   10
And past my Apron–and my Belt
And past my Bodice–too–

And made as He would eat me up–
As wholly as a Dew
Upon a Dandelion's Sleeve–   15
And then–I started–too–

And He–He followed–close behind–
I felt His Silver Heel
Upon my Ankle–Then my Shoes
Would overflow with Pearl–   20

Until We met the Solid Town–
No One He seemed to know–
And bowing–with a Mighty look–
At me–The Sea withdrew–

Emily Dickinson (1830–1886)

THE SOUL SELECTS HER OWN SOCIETY

(1862)

The Soul selects her own Society–
Then–shuts the Door–
To her divine Majority–
Present no more–

Unmoved–she notes the Chariots–pausing–   5
At her low Gate–
Unmoved–an Emperor be kneeling
Upon her Mat–

I've known her–from an ample nation–
Choose One–   10
Then–close the Valves of her attention–
Like Stone–

John Donne (1572–1631)

THE BAIT

1633

Come live with me and be my love,
And we will some new pleasures prove,
Of golden sands and crystal brooks,
With silken lines and silver hooks.

There will the river whispering run,   5
Warmed by thy eyes more than the sun;
And there the enamored fish will stay,
Begging themselves they may betray.

When thou wilt swim in that live bath,
Each fish, which every channel hath,   10
Will amorously to thee swim,
Gladder to catch thee, than thou him.

If thou to be so seen be'st loath,
By sun or moon, thou dark'nest both;
And if myself have leave to see,   15
I need not their light, having thee.

Let others freeze with angling reeds°,   rods
And cut their legs with shells and weeds,
Or treacherously poor fish beset
With strangling snare or windowy net.   20

Let coarse bold hands from slimy nest
The bedded fish in banks out-wrest,
Or curious traitors, sleave-silk flies,
Bewitch poor fishes' wand'ring eyes.

For thee, thou need'st no such deceit,   25
For thou thyself art thine own bait;
That fish that is not catched thereby,
Alas, is wiser far than I.

COMPARE:

"The Bait" with "The Passionate Shepherd to His Love" by Christopher
Marlowe (page 780).

John Donne (1572–1631)
THE FLEA   1633

Mark but this flea, and mark in this
How little that which thou deny'st me is;
It sucked me first, and now sucks thee,
And in this flea our two bloods mingled be;
Thou know'st that this cannot be said   5
A sin, nor shame, nor loss of maidenhead,
   Yet this enjoys before it woo,
     And pampered swells with one blood made of two,
     And this, alas, is more than we would do.

Oh stay, three lives in one flea spare,   10
Where we almost, yea more than married are.
This flea is you and I, and this
Our marriage bed, and marriage temple is;
Though parents grudge, and you, we're met
And cloistered in these living walls of jet.   15
   Though use° make you apt to kill me,   *custom*
     Let not to that, self-murder added be,
     And sacrilege, three sins in killing three.

Cruel and sudden, hast thou since
Purpled thy nail in blood of innocence?   20
Wherein could this flea guilty be,
Except in that drop it sucked from thee?
Yet thou triumph'st, and say'st that thou
Find'st not thyself, nor me, the weaker now;
   'Tis true; then learn how false, fears be;   25
     Just so much honor, when thou yield'st to me,
     Will waste, as this flea's death took life from thee.

COMPARE:

"The Flea" with "The Best Line Yet" by Edward Allen (page 629).

John Donne (1572–1631)

A Valediction: Forbidding Mourning   — don't cry   1633

[handwritten: farewell speech]

As virtuous men pass mildly away,
  And whisper to their souls to go,
Whilst some of their sad friends do say
  The breath goes now, and some say no:

So let us melt, and make no noise,   5
  No tear-floods, nor sigh-tempests move;
'Twere profanation of our joys
  To tell the laity our love.

Moving of th' earth° brings harms and fears;
  Men reckon what it did and meant;   10
But trepidation of the spheres,
  Though greater far, is innocent°.   *earthquake*   *harmless*

Dull sublunary lovers' love
  (Whose soul is sense) cannot admit
Absence, because it doth remove
  Those things which elemented° it.   15   *constituted*

But we, by a love so much refined
  That ourselves know not what it is,
Inter-assurèd of the mind,
  Care less, eyes, lips, and hands to miss.   20

Our two souls, therefore, which are one,
  Though I must go, endure not yet
A breach, but an expansiòn,
  Like gold to airy thinness beat.

If they be two, they are two so   25
  As stiff twin compasses are two:
Thy soul, the fixed foot, makes no show
  To move, but doth, if th' other do.

And though it in the center sit,
  Yet when the other far doth roam,   30
It leans and harkens after it,
  And grows erect as that comes home.

Such wilt thou be to me, who must,
  Like th' other foot, obliquely run;
Thy firmness makes my circle just°,   *perfect*   35
  And makes me end where I begun.

[Handwritten annotations in margins: similie; virtuous men pass quietly; Dies so peacefully you can't tell the actual moment; peaceful death compared to parting; parting of the lovers; parting; parting; parting sob.; constituted; main sob.; parting lovers; desire to make parting peaceful; used to draw circles; don't cry; together]

A Valediction: Forbidding Mourning. 11. *spheres:* In Ptolemaic astronomy, the concentric spheres surrounding the earth. The trepidation or motion of the ninth sphere was thought to change the date of the equinox.

John Dryden (1631–1700)
TO THE MEMORY OF MR. OLDHAM 1684

Farewell, too little and too lately known,
Whom I began to think and call my own;
For sure our souls were near allied, and thine
Cast in the same poetic mold with mine.
One common note on either lyre did strike, 5
And knaves and fools we both abhorred alike.
To the same goal did both our studies drive:
The last set out the soonest did arrive.
Thus Nissus fell upon the slippery place,
While his young friend performed and won the race. 10
O early ripe! to thy abundant store
What could advancing age have added more?
It might (what Nature never gives the young)
Have taught the numbers° of thy native tongue. *meters*
But satire needs not those, and wit will shine 15
Through the harsh cadence of a rugged line.
A noble error, and but seldom made,
When poets are by too much force betrayed.
Thy gen'rous fruits, though gathered ere their prime,
Still showed a quickness; and maturing time 20
But mellows what we write to the dull sweets of rhyme.
Once more, hail, and farewell! farewell, thou young
But ah! too short, Marcellus of our tongue!
Thy brows with ivy and with laurels bound;
But fate and gloomy night encompass thee around. 25

TO THE MEMORY OF MR. OLDHAM. John Oldham, poet best remembered for his *Satires upon the Jesuits*, had died at thirty. *9–10. Nissus; his young friend:* These two close friends, as Virgil tells us in the *Aeneid*, ran a race for the prize of an olive crown. *23. Marcellus:* Had he not died in his twentieth year, he would have succeeded the Roman emperor Augustus. *25.* This line echoes the *Aeneid* (VI, 886), in which Marcellus is seen walking under the black cloud of his impending doom.

COMPARE:

"To the Memory of Mr. Oldham" with "To an Athlete Dying Young" by A. E. Housman (page 764).

Alan Dugan (b. 1923)
LOVE SONG: I AND THOU 1961

Nothing is plumb, level or square:
    the studs are bowed, the joists
are shaky by nature, no piece fits
    any other piece without a gap

or pinch, and bent nails
    dance all over the surfacing
like maggots. By Christ
    I am no carpenter, I built
the roof for myself, the walls
    for myself, the floors
for myself, and got
    hung up in it myself. I
danced with a purple thumb
    at this house-warming, drunk
with my prime whiskey: rage.
    Oh I spat rage's nails
into the frame-up of my work:
    it held. It settled plumb,
level, solid, square and true
    for that great moment. Then
it screamed and went on through,
    skewing as wrong the other way.
God damned it. This is hell,
    but I planned it, I sawed it,
I nailed it, and I
    will live in it until it kills me.
I can nail my left palm
    to the left-hand cross-piece but
I can't do everything myself.
    I need a hand to nail the right,
a help, a love, a you, a wife.

COMPARE:

"Love Song: I and Thou" with "The Kiss" by Anne Sexton (page 801).

Bob Dylan (b. 1941)

SUBTERRANEAN HOMESICK BLUES 1965

Johnny's in the basement
Mixing up the medicine
I'm on the pavement
Thinking about the government
The man in the trenchcoat
Badge out, laid off
Says he's got a bad cough
Wants to get paid off
Look out kid

It's something you did
God knows when
But you're doin' it again
You better duck down the alley way
Lookin' for a new friend
The man in the coonskin cap   15
By the pig pen
Wants eleven dollar bills
You only got ten.

Maggie comes fleet foot
Face full of black soot   20
Talkin' that the heat put
Plants in the bed but
The phone's tapped anyway
Maggie says that many say
They must bust in early May   25
Orders from the D.A.
Look out kid
Don't matter what you did
Walk on your tip toes
Don't try No-Doz   30
Better stay away from those
That carry around a fire hose
Keep a clean nose
Watch the plain clothes
You don't need a weather man   35
To tell which way the wind blows.

Get sick get well
Hang around an ink well
Ring bell, hard to tell
If anything is goin' to sell   40
Try hard, get barred
Get back, write braille
Get jailed, jump bail
Join the army, if you fail
Look out kid, you're gonna get hit   45
But users, cheaters
Six time losers
Hang around the theatres
Girl by the whirl pool's
Lookin' for a new fool   50
Don't follow leaders
Watch the parkin' meters.

Ah, get born, keep warm
Short pants, romance, learn to dance
Get dressed, get blessed   55
Try to be a success

Please her, please him, buy gifts
Don't steal, don't lift
Twenty years of schoolin'
And they put you on the day shift   60
Look out kid, they keep it all hid
Better jump down a manhole
Light yourself a candle, don't wear sandals
Try to avoid the scandals
Don't wanna be a bum   65
You better chew gum
The pump don't work
'Cause the vandals took the handles.

T. S. Eliot (1888–1965)

JOURNEY OF THE MAGI   1927

"A cold coming we had of it,
Just the worst time of the year
For a journey, and such a long journey:
The ways deep and the weather sharp,
The very dead of winter."   5
And the camels galled, sore-footed, refractory,
Lying down in the melting snow.
There were times we regretted
The summer palaces on slopes, the terraces,
And the silken girls bringing sherbet.   10
Then the camel men cursing and grumbling
And running away, and wanting their liquor and women,
And the night-fires going out, and the lack of shelters,
And the cities hostile and the towns unfriendly
And the villages dirty and charging high prices: 15
A hard time we had of it.
At the end we preferred to travel all night,
Sleeping in snatches,
With the voices singing in our ears, saying
That this was all folly.   20

Then at dawn we came down to a temperate valley,
Wet, below the snow line, smelling of vegetation;
With a running stream and a water-mill beating the darkness,
And three trees on the low sky,
And an old white horse galloped away in the meadow.   25
Then we came to a tavern with vine-leaves over the lintel,
Six hands at an open door dicing for pieces of silver,
And feet kicking the empty wine-skins.
But there was no information, and so we continued
And arrived at evening, not a moment too soon   30
Finding the place; it was (you may say) satisfactory.

All this was a long time ago, I remember,
And I would do it again, but set down
This set down
This: were we led all that way for   35
Birth or Death? There was a Birth, certainly,
We had evidence and no doubt. I had seen birth and death,
But had thought they were different; this Birth was
Hard and bitter agony for us, like Death, our death.
We returned to our places, these Kingdoms,   40
But no longer at ease here, in the old dispensation,
With an alien people clutching their gods.
I should be glad of another death.

JOURNEY OF THE MAGI. The story of the Magi, the three wise men who traveled to
Bethlehem to behold the Christ child, is told in Matthew 2:1–12. That the three were kings
is a later tradition. 1–5. *A cold coming . . . winter:* Eliot quotes with slight changes from a
sermon preached on Christmas day, 1622, by Bishop Lancelot Andrewes. 24. *three times:*
foreshadowing the three crosses on Calvary (see Luke 23:32–33). 25. *white horse:* perhaps
the steed that carried the conquering Christ in the vision of St. John the Divine (Revelation 19:11–16). 41. *old dispensation:* older, pagan religion about to be displaced by Christianity.

COMPARE:

"Journey of the Magi" with "The Magi" by William Butler Yeats (page 830)

T. S. Eliot (1888–1965)
THE LOVE SONG OF J. ALFRED PRUFROCK   1917

S'io credessi che mia risposta fosse
A persona che mai tornasse al mondo,
Questa fiamma staria senza piu scosse.
Ma perciocche giammai di questo fondo
Non torno vivo alcun, s'i'odo il vero,
Senza tema d'infamia ti rispondo.

Let us go then, you and I,
When the evening is spread out against the sky
Like a patient etherized upon a table;
Let us go, through certain half-deserted streets,
The muttering retreats   5
Of restless nights in one-night cheap hotels
And sawdust restaurants with oyster-shells:
Streets that follow like a tedious argument
Of insidious intent
To lead you to an overwhelming question . . .   10
Oh, do not ask, "What is it?"
Let us go and make our visit.

In the room the women come and go
Talking of Michelangelo.

The yellow fog that rubs its back upon the window-panes, 15
The yellow smoke that rubs its muzzle on the window-panes
Licked its tongue into the corners of the evening,
Lingered upon the pools that stand in drains,
Let fall upon its back the soot that falls from chimneys,
Slipped by the terrace, made a sudden leap, 20
And seeing that it was a soft October night,
Curled once about the house, and fell asleep.

And indeed there will be time
For the yellow smoke that slides along the street,
Rubbing its back upon the window-panes; 25
There will be time, there will be time
To prepare a face to meet the faces that you meet;
There will be time to murder and create,
And time for all the works and days of hands
That lift and drop a question on your plate; 30
Time for you and time for me,
And time yet for a hundred indecisions,
And for a hundred visions and revisions,
Before the taking of a toast and tea.

In the room the women come and go 35
Talking of Michelangelo.

And indeed there will be time
To wonder, "Do I dare?" and, "Do I dare?"
Time to turn back and descend the stair,
With a bald spot in the middle of my hair— 40
[They will say: "How his hair is growing thin!"]
My morning coat, my collar mounting firmly to the chin,
My necktie rich and modest, but asserted by a simple pin—
[They will say: "But how his arms and legs are thin!"]
Do I dare 45
Disturb the universe?
In a minute there is time
For decisions and revisions which a minute will reverse.

For I have known them all already, known them all:—
Have known the evenings, mornings, afternoons, 50
I have measured out my life with coffee spoons;
I know the voices dying with a dying fall
Beneath the music from a farther room.
   So how should I presume?

And I have known the eyes already, known them all— 55
The eyes that fix you in a formulated phrase,
And when I am formulated, sprawling on a pin,
When I am pinned and wriggling on the wall,
Then how should I begin
To spit out all the butt-ends of my days and ways? 60
   And how should I presume?

And I have known the arms already, known them all —
Arms that are braceleted and white and bare
[But in the lamplight, downed with light brown hair!]
Is it perfume from a dress   65
That makes me so digress?
Arms that lie along a table, or wrap about a shawl.
   And should I then presume?
   And how should I begin?

     . . . . .

Shall I say, I have gone at dusk through narrow streets   70
And watched the smoke that rises from the pipes
Of lonely men in shirt-sleeves, leaning out of windows? . . .

I should have been a pair of ragged claws
Scuttling across the floors of silent seas.

     . . . . .

And the afternoon, the evening, sleeps so peacefully!   75
Smoothed by long fingers,
Asleep . . . tired . . . or it malingers,
Stretched on the floor, here beside you and me.
Should I, after tea and cakes and ices,
Have the strength to force the moment to its crisis?   80
But though I have wept and fasted, wept and prayed,
Though I have seen my head [grown slightly bald] brought in upon a plat-
    ter,
I am no prophet — and here's no great matter;
I have seen the moment of my greatness flicker,
And I have seen the eternal Footman hold my coat, and snicker,   85
And in short, I was afraid.

And would it have been worth it, after all,
After the cups, the marmalade, the tea,
Among the porcelain, among some talk of you and me,
Would it have been worth while,   90
To have bitten off the matter with a smile,
To have squeezed the universe into a ball
To roll it toward some overwhelming question,
To say: "I am Lazarus, come from the dead,
Come back to tell you all, I shall tell you all" —   95
If one, settling a pillow by her head,
   Should say: "That is not what I meant at all.
   That is not it, at all."

And would it have been worth it, after all,
Would it have been worth while,   100
After the sunsets and the dooryards and the sprinkled streets,
After the novels, after the teacups, after the skirts that trail along the
    floor —
And this, and so much more? —
It is impossible to say just what I mean!

But as if a magic lantern threw the nerves in patterns on a screen: 105
Would it have been worth while
If one, settling a pillow or throwing off a shawl,
And turning toward the window, should say:
  "That is not it at all,
  That is not what I meant, at all."   110

      . . . . .

No! I am not Prince Hamlet, nor was meant to be;
Am an attendant lord, one that will do
To swell a progress, start a scene or two,
Advise the prince; no doubt, an easy tool,
Deferential, glad to be of use,   115
Politic, cautious, and meticulous;
Full of high sentence, but a bit obtuse;
At times, indeed, almost ridiculous—
Almost, at times, the Fool.

I grow old . . . I grow old . . .   120
I shall wear the bottoms of my trousers rolled.

Shall I part my hair behind? Do I dare to eat a peach?
I shall wear white flannel trousers, and walk upon the beach.
I have heard the mermaids singing, each to each.

I do not think that they will sing to me.   125

I have seen them riding seaward on the waves
Combing the white hair of the waves blown back
When the wind blows the water white and black.

We have lingered in the chambers of the sea
By sea-girls wreathed with seaweed red and brown   130
Till human voices wake us, and we drown.

THE LOVE SONG OF J. ALFRED PRUFROCK. The epigraph, from Dante's *Inferno*, is the speech
of one dead and damned, who thinks that his hearer also is going to remain in Hell. Count
Guido da Montefeltro, whose sin has been to give false counsel after a corrupt prelate had
offered him prior absolution and whose punishment is to be wrapped in a constantly
burning flame, offers to tell Dante his story: "If I thought my reply were to someone who
could ever return to the world, this flame would waver no more. But since, I'm told, nobody ever escapes from this pit, I'll tell you without fear of ill fame." 29. *works and days:*
title of a poem by Hesiod (eighth century B.C.), depicting his life as a hard-working Greek
farmer and exhorting his brother to be like him. 82. *head . . . platter:* like that of John the
Baptist, prophet and praiser of chastity, whom King Herod beheaded at the demand of
Herodias, his unlawfully wedded wife (see Mark 6:17–28). 92–93. *squeezed . . . To roll it:* an
echo from Marvell's "To His Coy Mistress," lines 41–42 (see p. 371). 94. *Lazarus:* Probably
the Lazarus whom Christ called forth from the tomb (John 11:1–44), but possibly the
beggar seen in Heaven by the rich man in Hell (Luke 16:19–25).

Robert Frost (1874–1963)

MENDING WALL

1914

Something there is that doesn't love a wall,
That sends the frozen-ground-swell under it,
And spills the upper boulders in the sun;
And makes gaps even two can pass abreast.
The work of hunters is another thing: 5
I have come after them and made repair
Where they have left not one stone on a stone,
But they would have the rabbit out of hiding,
To please the yelping dogs. The gaps I mean,
No one has seen them made or heard them made,   10
But at spring-mending time we find them there.
I let my neighbor know beyond the hill;
And on a day we meet to walk the line
And set the wall between us once again.
We keep the wall between us as we go.   15
To each the boulders that have fallen to each.
And some are loaves and some so nearly balls
We have to use a spell to make them balance:
'Stay where you are until our backs are turned!'
We wear our fingers rough with handling them.   20
Oh, just another kind of outdoor game,
One on a side. It comes to little more:
There where it is we do not need the wall:
He is all pine and I am apple orchard.
My apple trees will never get across   25
And eat the cones under his pines, I tell him.
He only says, 'Good fences make good neighbors.'
Spring is the mischief in me, and I wonder
If I could put a notion in his head:
'Why do they make good neighbors? Isn't it   30
Where there are cows? But here there are no cows.
Before I built a wall I'd ask to know
What I was walling in or walling out,
And to whom I was like to give offense.
Something there is that doesn't love a wall,   35
That wants it down.' I could say 'Elves' to him,
But it's not elves exactly, and I'd rather
He said it for himself. I see him there
Bringing a stone grasped firmly by the top
In each hand, like an old-stone savage armed.   40
He moves in darkness as it seems to me,
Not of woods only and the shade of trees.
He will not go behind his father's saying,
And he likes having thought of it so well
He says again, 'Good fences make good neighbors.'   45

Compare:

"Mending Wall" with "Mending Sump" by Kenneth Koch (page 684).

Robert Frost (1874–1963)
Stopping by Woods on a Snowy Evening   1923

Whose woods these are I think I know.
His house is in the village though;
He will not see me stopping here
To watch his woods fill up with snow.

My little horse must think it queer   5
To stop without a farmhouse near
Between the woods and frozen lake
The darkest evening of the year.

He gives his harness bells a shake
To ask if there is some mistake.   10
The only other sound's the sweep
Of easy wind and downy flake.

The woods are lovely, dark and deep,
But I have promises to keep,
And miles to go before I sleep,   15
And miles to go before I sleep.

Robert Frost (1874–1963)
The Witch of Coös   1923

I stayed the night for shelter at a farm
Behind the mountain, with a mother and son,
Two old-believers. They did all the talking.

MOTHER. Folks think a witch who has familiar spirits
She could call up to pass a winter evening,   5
But won't, should be burned at the stake or something.
Summoning spirits isn't 'Button, button,
Who's got the button,' I would have them know.

SON. Mother can make a common table rear
And kick with two legs like an army mule.   10

MOTHER. And when I've done it, what good have I done?
Rather than tip a table for you, let me
Tell you what Ralle the Sioux Control once told me.
He said the dead had souls, but when I asked him
How could that be—I thought the dead were souls,   15
He broke my trance. Don't that make you suspicious
That there's something the dead are keeping back?
Yes, there's something the dead are keeping back.

SON. You wouldn't want to tell him what we have
Up attic, mother?   20

MOTHER. Bones — a skeleton.

SON. But the headboard of mother's bed is pushed
Against the attic door: the door is nailed.
It's harmless. Mother hears it in the night
Halting perplexed behind the barrier   25
Of door and headboard. Where it wants to get
Is back into the cellar where it came from.

MOTHER. We'll never let them, will we, son! We'll never!

SON. It left the cellar forty years ago
And carried itself like a pile of dishes   30
Up one flight from the cellar to the kitchen,
Another from the kitchen to the bedroom,
Another from the bedroom to the attic,
Right past both father and mother, and neither stopped it.
Father had gone upstairs; mother was downstairs.   35
I was a baby: I don't know where I was.

MOTHER. The only fault my husband found with me —
I went to sleep before I went to bed,
Especially in winter when the bed
Might just as well be ice and the clothes snow.   40
The night the bones came up the cellar-stairs
Toffile had gone to bed alone and left me,
But left an open door to cool the room off
So as to sort of turn me out of it.
I was just coming to myself enough   45
To wonder where the cold was coming from,
When I heard Toffile upstairs in the bedroom
And thought I heard him downstairs in the cellar.
The board we had laid down to walk dry-shod on
When there was water in the cellar in spring   50
Struck the hard cellar bottom. And then someone
Began the stairs, two footsteps for each step,
The way a man with one leg and a crutch,
Or a little child, comes up. It wasn't Toffile:
It wasn't anyone who could be there.   55
The bulkhead double-doors were double-locked
And swollen tight and buried under snow.
The cellar windows were banked up with sawdust
And swollen tight and buried under snow.
It was the bones. I knew them — and good reason.   60
My first impulse was to get to the knob
And hold the door. But the bones didn't try
The door; they halted helpless on the landing,
Waiting for things to happen in their favor.
The faintest restless rustling ran all through them.   65

I never could have done the thing I did
If the wish hadn't been too strong in me
To see how they were mounted for this walk.
I had a vision of them put together
Not like a man, but like a chandelier.   70
So suddenly I flung the door wide on him.
A moment he stood balancing with emotion,
And all but lost himself. (A tongue of fire
Flashed out and licked along his upper teeth.
Smoke rolled inside the sockets of his eyes.)   75
Then he came at me with one hand outstretched,
The way he did in life once; but this time
I struck the hand off brittle on the floor,
And fell back from him on the floor myself.
The finger-pieces slid in all directions.   80
(Where did I see one of those pieces lately?
Hand me my button-box — it must be there.)
I sat up on the floor and shouted. "Toffile,
It's coming up to you.' It had its choice
Of the door to the cellar or the hall.   85
It took the hall door for the novelty,
And set off briskly for so slow a thing,
Still going every which way in the joints, though,
So that it looked like lightning or a scribble,
From the slap I had just now given its hand.   90
I listened till it almost climbed the stairs
From the hall to the only finished bedroom,
Before I got up to do anything;
Then ran and shouted, "Shut the bedroom door,
Toffile, for my sake!' 'Company?' he said,   95
'Don't make me get up; I'm too warm in bed.'
So lying forward weakly on the handrail
I pushed myself upstairs, and in the light
(The kitchen had been dark) I had to own
I could see nothing. 'Toffile, I don't see it.   100
It's with us in the room though. It's the bones.'
'What bones?' 'The cellar bones — out of the grave.'
That made him throw his bare legs out of bed
And sit up by me and take hold of me.
I wanted to put out the light and see   105
If I could see it, or else mow the room,
With our arms at the level of our knees,
And bring the chalk-pile down. 'I'll tell you what —
It's looking for another door to try.
The uncommonly deep snow has made him think   110
Of his old song, *The Wild Colonial Boy*,
He always used to sing along the tote road.
He's after an open door to get outdoors.
Let's trap him with an open door up attic.'
Toffile agreed to that, and sure enough,   115

Almost the moment he was given an opening,
The steps began to climb the attic stairs.
I heard them. Toffile didn't seem to hear them.
'Quick!' I slammed to the door and held the knob.
'Toffile, get nails.' I made him nail the door shut   120
And push the headboard of the bed against it.
Then we asked was there anything
Up attic that we'd ever want again.
The attic was less to us than the cellar.
If the bones liked the attic, let them have it.   125
Let them stay in the attic. When they sometimes
Come down the stairs at night and stand perplexed
Behind the door and headboard of the bed,
Brushing their chalky skull with chalky fingers,
With sounds like the dry rattling of a shutter,   130
That's what I sit up in the dark to say—
To no one any more since Toffile died.
Let them stay in the attic since they went there.
I promised Toffile to be cruel to them
For helping them to be cruel once to him.   135

SON. We think they had a grave down in the cellar.

MOTHER. We know they had a grave down in the cellar.

SON. We never could find out whose bones they were.

MOTHER. Yes, we could too, son. Tell the truth for once.
They were a man's his father killed for me.   140
I mean a man he killed instead of me.
The least I could do was to help dig their grave.
We were about it one night in the cellar.
Son knows the story: but 'twas not for him
To tell the truth, suppose the time had come.   145
Son looks surprised to see me end a lie
We'd kept all these years between ourselves
So as to have it ready for outsiders.
But tonight I don't care enough to lie—
I don't remember why I ever cared.   150
Toffile, if he were here, I don't believe
Could tell you why he ever cared himself. . . .

She hadn't found the finger-bone she wanted
Among the buttons poured out in her lap.
I verified the name next morning: Toffile.   155
The rural letter box said Toffile Lajway.

THE WITCH OF COÖS. Coös is the northernmost county in New Hampshire. 13. *Ralle the Sioux Control:* the spirit of a dead Indian. In spiritualism, a control is a spirit who serves as a contact between a medium and other spirits of the departed.

Donald Hall (b. 1928)

THE TOWN OF HILL

1975

Back of the dam, under
a flat pad

of water, church
bells ring

in the ears of lilies,   5
a child's swing

curls in the current
of a yard, horned

pout sleep
in a green   10

mailbox, and
a boy walks

from a screened
porch beneath

the man-shaped   15
leaves of an oak

down the street looking
at the town

of Hill that water
covered forty   20

years ago,
and the screen

door shuts
under dream water.

Thomas Hardy (1840–1928)

CHANNEL FIRING

1914

That night your great guns, unawares,
Shook all our coffins as we lay,
And broke the chancel window-squares,
We thought it was the Judgment-day

And sat upright. While drearisome
Arose the howl of wakened hounds:
The mouse let fall the altar-crumb,
The worms drew back into the mounds,

The glebe cow drooled. Till God called, "No;
It's gunnery practice out at sea
Just as before you went below;
The world is as it used to be:

"All nations striving strong to make
Red war yet redder. Mad as hatters
They do no more for Christés sake
Than you who are helpless in such matters.

"That this is not the judgment-hour
For some of them's a blessed thing,
For if it were they'd have to scour
Hell's floor for so much threatening . . .

"Ha, ha. It will be warmer when
I blow the trumpet (if indeed
I ever do; for you are men,
And rest eternal sorely need)."

So down we lay again. "I wonder,
Will the world ever saner be,"
Said one, "than when He sent us under
In our indifferent century!"

And many a skeleton shook his head.
"Instead of preaching forty year,"
My neighbor Parson Thirdly said,
"I wish I had stuck to pipes and beer."

Again the guns disturbed the hour,
Roaring their readiness to avenge,
As far inland as Stourton Tower,
And Camelot, and starlit Stonehenge.

CHANNEL FIRING. 9. *glebe:* land belonging to the church, used for grazing. 35. *Stourton Tower:* a monument to the defeat of the Danes by Alfred the Great in 879 A.D. 36. *Camelot:* where King Arthur held court; *Stonehenge:* circle of huge stones thought to be the ruins of a prehistoric place of worship.

COMPARE:

"Channel Firing" with "The Fury of Aerial Bombardment" by Richard Eberhart (page 460).

Thomas Hardy (1840–1928)

THE CONVERGENCE OF THE TWAIN

1912

Lines on the Loss of the "Titanic"

I

    In a solitude of the sea
    Deep from human vanity,
And the Pride of Life that planned her, stilly couches she.

II

    Steel chambers, late the pyres
    Of her salamandrine fires,
Cold currents thrid°, and turn to rhythmic tidal lyres.   5   *thread*

III

    Over the mirrors meant
    To glass the opulent
The sea-worm crawls—grotesque, slimed, dumb, indifferent.

IV

    Jewels in joy designed   10
    To ravish the sensuous mind
Lie lightless, all their sparkles bleared and black and blind.

V

    Dim moon-eyed fishes near
    Gaze at the gilded gear
And query: "What does this vaingloriousness down here?"   15

VI

    Well: while was fashioning
    This creature of cleaving wing,
The Immanent Will that stirs and urges everything

VII

    Prepared a sinister mate
    For her—so gaily great—
A Shape of Ice, for the time far and dissociate.   20

VIII

    And as the smart ship grew
    In stature, grace, and hue,
In shadowy silent distance grew the Iceberg too.

IX

    Alien they seemed to be: 25
    No mortal eye could see
The intimate welding of their later history,

X

      Or sign that they were bent
      By paths coincident
On being anon twin halves of one august event.   30

XI

      Till the Spinner of the Years
      Said "Now!" And each one hears,
And consummation comes, and jars two hemispheres.

THE CONVERGENCE OF THE TWAIN. The luxury liner *Titanic*, supposedly unsinkable, went down in 1912 after striking an iceberg, on its first Atlantic voyage. 5. *salamandrine:* like the salamander, a lizard that supposedly thrives in fires, or like a spirit of the same name that inhabits fire (according to alchemists).

Robert Hayden (b. 1913)

A ROAD IN KENTUCKY   1966

And when that ballad lady went
   to ease the lover whose life she broke,
oh surely this is the real road she took,
   road all hackled through barberry fire,
through cedar and alder and sumac and thorn.   5

Red clay stained her flounces
   and stones cut her shoes
and the road twisted on to his loveless house
   and his cornfield dying
in the scarecrow's arms.   10

And when she had left her lover lying
   so stark and so stark, with the Star-of-Hope
drawn over his eyes, oh this is the road
   that lady walked in the cawing light,
so dark and so dark in the briary light.   15

COMPARE:

"A Road in Kentucky" with the anonymous ballad "Bonny Barbara Allan" (page 516).

Seamus Heaney (b. 1939)

DIGGING   1966

Between my finger and my thumb
The squat pen rests; snug as a gun.

Under my window, a clean rasping sound
When the spade sinks into gravelly ground:
My father, digging. I look down   5

Till his straining rump among the flowerbeds
Bends low, comes up twenty years away
Stooping in rhythm through potato drills
Where he was digging.

The coarse boot nestled on the lug, the shaft   10
Against the inside knee was levered firmly.
He rooted out tall tops, buried the bright edge deep
To scatter new potatoes that we picked
Loving their cool hardness in our hands.

By God, the old man could handle a spade.   15
Just like his old man.

My grandfather cut more turf in a day
Than any other man on Toner's bog.
Once I carried him milk in a bottle
Corked sloppily with paper. He straightened up   20
To drink it, then fell to right away

Nicking and slicing neatly, heaving sods
Over his shoulder, going down and down
For the good turf. Digging.

The cold smell of potato mould, the squelch and slap   25
Of soggy peat, the curt cuts of an edge
Through living roots awaken in my head.
But I've no spade to follow men like them.

Between my finger and my thumb
The squat pen rests.   30
I'll dig with it.

Anthony Hecht (b. 1923)

THE VOW   1967

In the third month, a sudden flow of blood.
The mirth of tabrets ceaseth, and the joy
Also of the harp. The frail image of God
Lay spilled and formless. Neither girl nor boy,
But yet blood of my blood, nearly my child.   5
       All that long day
Her pale face turned to the window's mild
       Featureless grey.

And for some nights she whimpered as she dreamed
The dead thing spoke, saying: "Do not recall   10
Pleasure at my conception. I am redeemed
From pain and sorrow. Mourn rather for all
Who breathlessly issue from the bone gates,
      The gates of horn,
For truly it is best of all the fates   15
      Not to be born.

"Mother, a child lay gasping for bare breath
On Christmas Eve when Santa Claus had set
Death in the stocking, and the lights of death
Flamed in the tree. O, if you can, forget   20
You were the child, turn to my father's lips
      Against the time
When his cold hand puts forth its fingertips
      Of jointed lime."

Doctors of Science, what is man that he   25
Should hope to come to a good end? *The best
Is not to have been born.* And could it be
That Jewish diligence and Irish jest
The consent of flesh and a midwinter storm
      Had reconciled,   30
Was yet too bold a mixture to inform
      A simple child?

Even as gold is tried, Gentile and Jew.
If that ghost was a girl's, I swear to it:
Your mother shall be far more blessed than you.   35
And if a boy's, I swear: The flames are lit
That shall refine us; they shall not destroy
      A living hair.
Your younger brothers shall confirm in joy
      This that I swear.   40

THE VOW. 2. *tabrets:* small drums used to accompany traditional Jewish dances. 14. *gates of horn:* According to Homer and Virgil pleasant, lying dreams emerge from the underworld through gates of ivory; ominous, truth-telling dreams, through gates of horn.

George Herbert (1593–1633)

LOVE   1633

Love bade me welcome; yet my soul drew back,
      Guilty of dust and sin.
But quick-eyed Love, observing me grow slack
      From my first entrance in,
Drew nearer to me, sweetly questioning   5
      If I lacked anything.

"A guest," I answered, "worthy to be here";
    Love said, "You shall be he."
"I, the unkind, ungrateful? Ah, my dear,
    I cannot look on Thee."   10
Love took my hand, and smiling did reply,
    "Who made the eyes but I?"

"Truth, Lord, but I have marred them; let my shame
    Go where it doth deserve."
"And know you not," says Love, "who bore the blame?"   15
    "My dear, then I will serve."
"You must sit down," says Love, "and taste My meat."
    So I did sit and eat.

COMPARE

"Love" with "Batter my heart, three-personed God, for You" by John Donne
(page 446).

Robert Herrick (1591–1674)
DELIGHT IN DISORDER   1633

A sweet disorder in the dress
Kindles in clothes a wantonness.
A lawn° about the shoulders thrown   *linen*
Into a fine distractión;
An erring lace, which here and there   5
Enthralls the crimson stomacher;
A cuff neglectful, and thereby
Ribbons to flow confusedly;
A winning wave, deserving note,
In the tempestuous petticoat;   10
A careless shoestring, in whose tie
I see a wild civility;
Do more bewitch me than when art
Is too precise in every part.

Robert Herrick (1591–1674)
TO THE VIRGINS, TO MAKE MUCH OF TIME   1648

Gather ye rose-buds while ye may,
    Old Time is still a-flying;
And this same flower that smiles today,
    Tomorrow will be dying.

The glorious lamp of heaven, the sun,   5
    The higher he's a-getting,
The sooner will his race be run,
    And nearer he's to setting.

That age is best which is the first,
    When youth and blood are warmer;   10
But being spent, the worse, and worst
    Times still succeed the former.

Then be not coy, but use your time,
  . And while ye may, go marry;   15
For having lost but once your prime,
    You may for ever tarry.

COMPARE:

"To the Virgins, to Make Much of Time" with "To His Coy Mistress" by
Andrew Marvell (page 780).

Gerard Manley Hopkins (1844–1889)

THE WINDHOVER   (1877)

To Christ Our Lord

I caught this morning morning's minion, king-
    dom of daylight's dauphin, dapple-dawn-drawn Falcon, in his riding
Of the rolling level underneath him steady air, and striding
High there, how he rung upon the rein of a wimpling wing
In his ecstasy! then off, off forth on swing,
    As a skate's heel sweeps smooth on a bow-bend: the hurl and gliding
    Rebuffed the big wind. My heart in hiding
Stirred for a bird,—the achieve of, the mastery of the thing!

Brute beauty and valor and act, oh, air, pride, plume, here
    Buckle! and the fire that breaks from thee then, a billion   10
Times told lovelier, more dangerous, O my chevalier!

    No wonder of it: shéer plód makes plow down sillion°   *furrow*
Shine, and blue-bleak embers, ah my dear,
    Fall, gall themselves, and gash gold-vermilion.

THE WINDHOVER. A windhover is a kestrel, or small falcon, so called because it can hover
upon the wind. 4. *rung ... wing:* A horse is "rung upon the rein" when its trainer holds
the end of a long rein and has the horse circle him. The possible meanings of *wimpling*
include (1) curving; (2) pleated, arranged in many little folds one on top of another; (3)
rippling or undulating like the surface of a flowing stream.

A. E. Housman (1859–1936)

TERENCE, THIS IS STUPID STUFF

1896

"Terence, this is stupid stuff:
You eat your victuals fast enough;
There can't be much amiss, 'tis clear,
To see the rate you drink your beer.
But oh, good Lord, the verse you make,   5
It gives a chap the belly-ache.
The cow, the old cow, she is dead;
It sleeps well, the horned head:
We poor lads, 'tis our turn now
To hear such tunes as killed the cow.   10
Pretty friendship 'tis to rhyme
Your friends to death before their time
Moping melancholy mad:
Come, pipe a tune to dance to, lad."

Why, if 'tis dancing you would be,   15
There's brisker pipes than poetry.
Say, for what were hop-yards meant,
Or why was Burton built on Trent?
Oh many a peer of England brews
Livelier liquor than the Muse,   20
And malt does more than Milton can
To justify God's ways to man.
Ale, man, ale's the stuff to drink
For fellows whom it hurts to think:
Look into the pewter pot   25
To see the world as the world's not.
And faith, 'tis pleasant till 'tis past:
The mischief is that 'twill not last.
Oh I have been to Ludlow fair
And left my necktie God knows where,   30
And carried half-way home, or near,
Pints and quarts of Ludlow beer:
Then the world seemed none so bad,
And I myself a sterling lad;
And down in lovely muck I've lain,   35
Happy till I woke again.
Then I saw the morning sky:
Heigho, the tale was all a lie;
The world, it was the old world yet,
I was I, my things were wet,   40
And nothing now remained to do
But begin the game anew.

Therefore, since the world has still
Much good, but much less good than ill,

Poems for Further Study   763

And while the sun and moon endure   45
Luck's a chance, but trouble's sure,
I'd face it as a wise man would,
And train for ill and not for good.
'Tis true, the stuff I bring for sale
Is not so brisk a brew as ale: 50
Out of a stem that scored the hand
I wrung it in a weary land.
But take it: if the smack is sour,
The better for the embittered hour;
It should do good to heart and head   55
When your soul is in my soul's stead;
And I will friend you, if I may,
In the dark and cloudy day.

     There was a king reigned in the East:
There, when kings will sit to feast,   60
They get their fill before they think
With poisoned meat and poisoned drink.
He gathered all that springs to birth
From the many-venomed earth;
First a little, thence to more,   65
He sampled all her killing store;
And easy, smiling, seasoned sound,
Sate the king when healths went round.
They put arsenic in his meat
And stared aghast to watch him eat;   70
They poured strychnine in his cup
And shook to see him drink it up:
They shook, they stared as white's their shirt:
Them it was their poison hurt.
—I tell the tale that I heard told.   75
Mithridates, he died old.

TERENCE, THIS IS STUPID STUFF. 1. *Terence:* As a name for himself, Housman takes that of a
Roman poet, author of satiric comedies. 18. *why was Burton built on Trent?* The answer is:
to use the river's water in the town's brewing industry.

A. E. Housman (1859–1936)

To an Athlete Dying Young   1896

The time you won your town the race
We chaired you through the market-place;
Man and boy stood cheering by,
And home we brought you shoulder-high.

Today, the road all runners come,   5
Shoulder-high we bring you home,
And set you at your threshold down,
Townsman of a stiller town.

Smart lad, to slip betimes away
From fields where glory does not stay,   10
And early though the laurel grows
It withers quicker than the rose.

Eyes the shady night has shut
Cannot see the record cut,
And silence sounds no worse than cheers   15
After earth has stopped the ears.

Now you will not swell the rout
Of lads that wore their honors out,
Runners whom renown outran
And the name died before the man.   20

So set, before its echoes fade,
The fleet foot on the sill of shade,
And hold to the low lintel up
The still-defended challenge-cup.

And round that early-laureled head   25
Will flock to gaze the strengthless dead,
And find unwithered on its curls
The garland briefer than a girl's.

COMPARE:

"To an Athlete Dying Young" with "To the Memory of Mr. Oldham" by John
Dryden (page 742).

Langston Hughes (1902–1967)

DREAM DEFERRED   1951

What happens to a dream deferred?

  Does it dry up
  like a raisin in the sun?
  Or fester like a sore—
  And then run?   5
  Does it stink like rotten meat?
  Or crust and sugar over—
  like a syrupy sweet?

  Maybe it just sags
  like a heavy load.   10

  Or does it explode?

COMPARE:

"Dream Deferred" with "Black Tambourine" by Hart Crane (page 615), "Saturday's Child" by Countee Cullen (page 732), and "Ballad of Birmingham" by
Dudley Randall (page 792).

Ted Hughes (b. 1930)
EXAMINATION AT THE WOMB-DOOR

1972

Who owns these scrawny little feet? *Death.*
Who owns this bristly scorched-looking face? *Death.*
Who owns these still-working lungs? *Death.*
Who owns this utility coat of muscles? *Death.*
Who owns these unspeakable guts? *Death.*   5
Who owns these questionable brains? *Death.*
All this messy blood? *Death.*
These minimum-efficiency eyes? *Death.*
This wicked little tongue? *Death.*
This occasional wakefulness? *Death.*   10

Given, stolen, or held pending trial?
Held.

Who owns the whole rainy, stony earth? *Death.*
Who owns all of space? *Death.*

Who is stronger than hope? *Death.*
Who is stronger than the will? *Death.*   15
Stronger than love? *Death.*
Stronger than life? *Death.*

But who is stronger than death?
                              Me, evidently.

Pass, Crow.
                                                                20

EXAMINATION AT THE WOMB-DOOR. This poem and the following two are from *Crow*, a book-length series of songs and fables whose central character, like some figures in African and American Indian legend, seems part bird, part human being, and part supernatural hero.

CROW'S FIRST LESSON

1972

God tried to teach Crow how to talk.
'Love,' said God. 'Say, Love.'
Crow gaped, and the white shark crashed into the sea
And went rolling downwards, discovering its own depth.

'No, no,' said God, 'Say Love. Now try it. LOVE.'   5
Crow gaped, and a bluefly, a tsetse, a mosquito
Zoomed out and down
To their sundry flesh-pots.

'A final try,' said God. 'Now, LOVE.'
Crow convulsed, gaped, retched and   10

Man's bodiless prodigious head
Bulbed out onto the earth, with swivelling eyes,
Jabbering protest—

And Crow retched again, before God could stop him.
And woman's vulva dropped over man's neck and tightened.   15
The two struggled together on the grass.
God struggled to part them, cursed, wept—

Crow flew guiltily off.

CROW AND STONE   1972

Crow was nimble but had to be careful
Of his eyes, the two dewdrops.
Stone, champion of the globe, lumbered towards him.

No point in detailing a battle
Where stone battered itself featureless   5
While Crow grew perforce nimbler.

The subnormal arena of space, agog,
Cheered these gladiators many aeons.
Still their struggle resounds.

But by now the stone is a dust—flying in vain,   10
And Crow has become a monster—his mere eyeblink
Holding the very globe in terror.

And still he who never has been killed
Croaks helplessly
And is only just born.   15

David Ignatow (b. 1914)
GET THE GASWORKS   1948

Get the gasworks into a poem,
and you've got the smoke and smokestacks,
the mottled red and yellow tenements,
and grimy kids who curse with the pungency
of the odor of gas. You've got America, boy.   5

Sketch in the river and barges,
all dirty and slimy.
How do the seagulls stay so white?
And always cawing like little mad geniuses?
You've got the kind of living   10
that makes the kind of thinking we do:

gaswork smokestack whistle tooting wisecracks.
They don't come because we like it that way,
but because we find it outside our window each morning,
in soot on the furniture,
and trucks carrying coal for gas, 15
the kid hot after the ball under the wheel.
He gets it over the belly, all right.
He dies there.

So the kids keep tossing the ball around
after the funeral. 20
So the cops keep chasing them,
so the mamas keep hollering,
and papa flings his newspaper outward,
in disgust with discipline. 25

Randall Jarrell (1914–1965)

THE DEATH OF THE BALL TURRET GUNNER 1945

From my mother's sleep I fell into the State
And I hunched in its belly till my wet fur froze.
Six miles from earth, loosed from its dream of life,
I woke to black flak and the nightmare fighters.
When I died they washed me out of the turret with a hose.

THE DEATH OF THE BALL TURRET GUNNER. Mr. Jarrell has written: "A ball turret was a plexiglass sphere set into the belly of a B-17 or B-24, and inhabited by two .50 caliber machineguns and one man, a short small man. When this gunner tracked with his machine-guns a fighter attacking his bomber from below, he revolved with the turret; hunched upside-down in his little sphere, he looked like the fetus in the womb. The fighters which attacked him were armed with cannon firing explosive shells. The hose was a steam hose."

COMPARE:

"The Death of the Ball Turret Gunner" with "Dulce et Decorum Est" by Wilfred Owen (page 436).

Randall Jarrell (1914–1965)

THE WOMAN AT THE WASHINGTON ZOO 1960

The saris go by me from the embassies.

Cloth from the moon. Cloth from another planet.
They look back at the leopard like the leopard.

And I. . . .
            this print of mine, that has kept its color
Alive through so many cleanings; this dull null 5

Navy I wear to work, and wear from work, and so
To my bed, so to my grave, with no
Complaints, no comment: neither from my chief,
The Deputy Chief Assistant, nor his chief—
Only I complain. . . . this serviceable   10
Body that no sunlight dyes, no hand suffuses
But, dome-shadowed, withering among columns,
Wavy beneath fountains—small, far-off, shining
In the eyes of animals, these beings trapped
As I am trapped but not, themselves, the trap,   15
Aging, but without knowledge of their age,
Kept safe here, knowing not of death, for death—
Oh, bars of my own body, open, open!

The world goes by my cage and never sees me.
And there come not to me, as come to these,   20
The wild beasts, sparrows pecking the llamas' grain,
Pigeons settling on the bears' bread, buzzards
Tearing the meat the flies have clouded. . . .
                              Vulture,
When you come for the white rat that the foxes left,
Take off the red helmet of your head, the black   25
Wings that have shadowed me, and step to me as man:
The wild brother at whose feet the white wolves fawn,
To whose hand of power the great lioness
Stalks, purring. . . .
                    You know what I was,
You see what I am: change me, change me!   30

John Keats (1795–1821)

ODE ON A GRECIAN URN   1820

Thou still unravished bride of quietness,
    Thou foster-child of silence and slow time,
Sylvan historian, who canst thus express
    A flowery tale more sweetly than our rhyme:
What leaf-fringed legend haunts about thy shape   5
    Of deities or mortals, or of both,
        In Tempe or the dales of Arcady?
    What men or gods are these? What maidens loth?
What mad pursuit? What struggle to escape?
        What pipes and timbrels? What wild ecstasy?   10

Heard melodies are sweet, but those unheard
    Are sweeter; therefore, ye soft pipes, play on;
Not to the sensual° ear, but, more endeared,   *physical*
    Pipe to the spirit ditties of no tone:

[handwritten annotations: "looking at characters on Grecian Urn" / "uses questions to describe" / "unwilling maidens"]

Fair youth, beneath the trees, thou canst not leave   15
    Thy song, nor ever can those trees be bare;
        Bold Lover, never, never canst thou kiss,
Though winning near the goal—yet, do not grieve;
        She cannot fade, though thou hast not thy bliss,
    For ever wilt thou love, and she be fair!   20

Ah, happy, happy boughs! that cannot shed
    Your leaves, nor ever bid the Spring adieu;
And, happy melodist, unwearièd,
    For ever piping songs for ever new;
More happy love! more happy, happy love!   25
    For ever warm and still to be enjoyed,
        For ever panting, and for ever young;
All breathing human passion far above,
    That leaves a heart high-sorrowful and cloyed,
        A burning forehead, and a parching tongue.   30

Who are these coming to the sacrifice?
    To what green altar, O mysterious priest,
Lead'st thou that heifer lowing at the skies,
    And all her silken flanks with garlands drest?
What little town by river or sea shore,   35
    Or mountain-built with peaceful citadel,
        Is emptied of this folk, this pious morn?
And, little town, thy streets for evermore
    Will silent be; and not a soul to tell
        Why thou art desolate, can e'er return.   40

O Attic shape! Fair attitude! with brede°   design
    Of marble men and maidens overwrought,
With forest branches and the trodden weed;
    Thou, silent form, dost tease us out of thought
As doth Eternity: Cold Pastoral!   45
    When old age shall this generation waste,
        Thou shalt remain, in midst of other woe
    Than ours, a friend to man, to whom thou say'st,
Beauty is truth, truth beauty,—that is all
        Ye know on earth, and all ye need to know.   50

ODE ON A GRECIAN URN. 7. *Tempe, dales of Arcady:* valleys in Greece. 41. *Attic:* Athenian, possessing a classical simplicity and grace. 49–50: If Keats had put the urn's words in quotation marks, critics might have been spared much ink. Does the urn say just "beauty is truth, truth beauty," or does its statement take in the whole of the last two lines?

COMPARE:

"Ode on a Grecian Urn" with "Lapis Lazuli" by William Butler Yeats (page 829) and "Anecdote of the Jar" by Wallace Stevens (page 617).

John Keats (1795–1821)

ON FIRST LOOKING INTO CHAPMAN'S HOMER 1816

Much have I traveled in the realms of gold,
  And many goodly states and kingdoms seen;
  Round many western islands have I been
Which <u>bards</u> in fealty to Apollo hold.   *poets*
Oft of one wide expanse had I been told   5
  That deep-browed Homer ruled as his demesne°,   *domain*
  Yet did I never breathe its pure serene
Till I heard Chapman speak out loud and bold.
Then felt I like some watcher of the skies
  When a new planet swims into his ken;   10
Or like stout Cortez when with eagle eyes
  He stared at the Pacific—and all his men
Looked at each other with a wild surmise—
  Silent, upon a peak in Darien.

[Handwritten annotations: "I have read many works of literature" near line 1; "Italian sonnet"; "metaphor (illiad & odessey)"; "of the works of Homer"; "never read until translation (illiad & odyssey)"]

ON FIRST LOOKING INTO CHAPMAN'S HOMER. When one evening in October 1816 Keats's friend and former teacher Cowden Clarke introduced the young poet to George Chapman's vigorous Elizabethan translations of the *Iliad* and the *Odyssey*, Keats stayed up all night reading and discussing them in high excitement; then went home at dawn to compose this sonnet, which Clarke received at his breakfast table. 4. *fealty:* in feudalism, the loyalty of a vassal to his lord; *Apollo:* classical god of poetic inspiration. 11. *stout Cortez:* the best-known boner in English poetry. (What Spanish explorer *was* the first European to view the Pacific?) 14. *Darien:* old name for the Isthmus of Panama.

John Keats (1795–1821)

TO AUTUMN 1820

I

Season of mists and mellow fruitfulness,
  Close bosom-friend of the maturing sun;
Conspiring with him how to load and bless
  With fruit the vines that round the thatch-eves run;
To bend with apples the mossed cottage-trees,   5
  And fill all fruit with ripeness to the core;
    To swell the gourd, and plump the hazel shells
With a sweet kernel; to set budding more,
  And still more, later flowers for the bees,
  Until they think warm days will never cease,   10
    For Summer has o'er-brimmed their clammy cells.

II

Who hath not seen thee oft amid thy store?
  Sometimes whoever seeks abroad may find
Thee sitting careless on a granary floor,
  Thy hair soft-lifted by the winnowing wind;   15

Or on a half-reaped furrow sound asleep,
    Drowsed with the fume of poppies, while thy hook
        Spares the next swath and all its twinèd flowers:
And sometimes like a gleaner thou dost keep
    Steady thy laden head across a brook;
    Or by a cider-press, with patient look,   20
        Thou watchest the last oozings hours by hours.

III

Where are the songs of Spring? Ay, where are they?
    Think not of them, thou hast thy music too,—
While barrèd clouds bloom the soft-dying day,   25
    And touch the stubble-plains with rosy hue;
Then in a wailful choir the small gnats mourn
    Among the river sallows°, borne aloft   *willows*
        Or sinking as the light wind lives or dies;
And full-grown lambs loud bleat from hilly bourn;   30
    Hedge-crickets sing; and now with treble soft
    The red-breast whistles from a garden-croft°;   *garden plot*
        And gathering swallows twitter in the skies.

COMPARE:

"To Autumn" with "In the Elegy Season" by Richard Wilbur (page 448).

Maxine Kumin (b. 1925)

WOODCHUCKS   1972

Gassing the woodchucks didn't turn out right.
The knockout bomb from the Feed and Grain Exchange
was featured as merciful, quick at the bone
and the case we had against them was airtight,
both exits shoehorned shut with puddingstone,   5
but they had a sub-sub-basement out of range.

Next morning they turned up again, no worse
for the cyanide than we for our cigarettes
and state-store Scotch, all of us up to scratch.
They brought down the marigolds as a matter of course   10
and then took over the vegetable patch
nipping the broccoli shoots, beheading the carrots.

The food from our mouths, I said, righteously thrilling
to the feel of the .22, the bullets' neat noses.
I, a lapsed pacifist fallen from grace   15
puffed with Darwinian pieties for killing,
now drew a bead on the littlest woodchuck's face.
He died down in the everbearing roses.

Ten minutes later I dropped the mother. She
flipflopped in the air and fell, her needle teeth   20
still hooked in a leaf of early Swiss chard.
Another baby next. O one-two-three
the murderer inside me rose up hard,
the hawkeye killer came on stage forthwith.

There's one chuck left. Old wily fellow, he keeps   25
me cocked and ready day after day after day.
All night I hunt his humped-up form. I dream
I sight along the barrel in my sleep.
If only they'd all consented to die unseen
gassed underground the quiet Nazi way.   30

COMPARE:

"Woodchucks" with "The Bull Calf" by Irving Layton (page 775) and "Janet
Waking" by John Crowe Ransom (page 793).

Philip Larkin (b. 1922)
VERS DE SOCIÉTÉ   1974

My wife and I have asked a crowd of craps
To come and waste their time and ours: perhaps
You'd care to join us? In a pig's arse, friend.
Day comes to an end.
The gas fire breathes, the trees are darkly swayed.   5
And so *Dear Warlock-Williams: I'm afraid—*

Funny how hard it is to be alone.
I could spend half my evenings, if I wanted,
Holding a glass of washing sherry, canted
Over to catch the drivel of some bitch   10
Who's read nothing but *Which;*
Just think of all the spare time that has flown

Straight into nothingness by being filled
With forks and faces, rather than repaid
Under a lamp, hearing the noise of wind,   15
And looking out to see the moon thinned
To an air-sharpened blade.
A life, and yet how sternly it's instilled

All solitude is selfish. No one now
Believes the hermit with his gown and dish   20
Talking to God (who's gone too); the big wish
Is to have people nice to you, which means
Doing it back somehow.
Virtue is social. Are, then, these routines

Playing at goodness, like going to church?   25
Something that bores us, something we don't do well
(Asking that ass about his fool research)
But try to feel, because, however crudely,
It shows us what should be?
Too subtle, that. Too decent, too. Oh hell,   30

Only the young can be alone freely.
The time is shorter now for company,
And sitting by a lamp more often brings
Not peace, but other things.
Beyond the light stand failure and remorse   35
Whispering *Dear Warlock-Williams: Why, of course* —

Vers de Société. The title is a French term for light verse, especially that written for social occasions. 9. *washing sherry:* sherry the quality of washing liquid, or dish detergent. 11. *Which:* British equivalent of *Consumer Reports.*

Philip Larkin (b. 1922)
Wedding-Wind
                                                                              1955

The wind blew all my wedding-day,
And my wedding-night was the night of the high wind;
And a stable door was banging, again and again,
That he must go and shut it, leaving me
Stupid in candlelight, hearing rain,   5
Seeing my face in the twisted candlestick,
Yet seeing nothing. When he came back
He said the horses were restless, and I was sad
That any man or beast that night should lack
The happiness I had.   10

                    Now in the day
All's raveled under the sun by the wind's blowing.
He has gone to look at the floods, and I
Carry a chipped pail to the chicken-run,
Set it down, and stare. All is the wind
Hunting through clouds and forests, thrashing   15
My apron and the hanging cloths on the line.
Can it be borne, this bodying-forth by wind
Of joy my actions turn on, like a thread
Carrying beads? Shall I be let to sleep
Now this perpetual morning shares my bed?   20
Can even death dry up .
These new delighted lakes, conclude
Our kneeling as cattle by all-generous waters?

Compare:

"Wedding-Wind" with "The River Merchant's Wife: a Letter" by Ezra Pound (page 789).

D. H. Lawrence (1885–1930)
A Youth Mowing   1917

There are four men mowing down by the Isar;
I can hear the swish of the scythe-strokes, four
Sharp breaths taken: yea, and I
Am sorry for what's in store.

The first man out of the four that's mowing   5
Is mine, I claim him once and for all;
Though it's sorry I am, on his young feet, knowing
None of the trouble he's led to stall.

As he sees me bringing the dinner, he lifts
His head as proud as a deer that looks   10
Shoulder-deep out of the corn; and wipes
His scythe-blade bright, unhooks

The scythe-stone and over the stubble to me.
Lad, thou hast gotten a child in me,
Laddie, a man thou'lt ha'e to be,   15
Yea, though I'm sorry for thee.

A YOUTH MOWING. 1. *Isar:* river in Austria and Germany that flows into the Danube.

Irving Layton (b. 1912)
The Bull Calf   1959

The thing could barely stand. Yet taken
from his mother and the barn smells
he still impressed with his pride,
with the promise of sovereignty in the way
his head moved to take us in.   5
The fierce sunlight tugging the maize from the ground
licked at his shapely flanks.
He was too young for all that pride.
I thought of the deposed Richard II.

"No money in bull calves," Freeman had said.   10
The visiting clergyman rubbed the nostrils
now snuffing pathetically at the windless day.
"A pity," he sighed.
My gaze slipped off his hat toward the empty sky
that circled over the black knot of men,   15
over us and the calf waiting for the first blow.

Struck,
the bull calf drew in his thin forelegs
as if gathering strength for a mad rush . . .
tottered . . . raised his darkening eyes to us,   20
and I saw we were at the far end

of his frightened look, growing smaller and smaller
till we were only the ponderous mallet
that flicked his bleeding ear
and pushed him over on his side, stiffly,   25
like a block of wood.

Below the hill's crest
the river snuffled on the improvised beach.
We dug a deep pit and threw the dead calf into it.
It made a wet sound, a sepulchral gurgle,   30
as the warm sides bulged and flattened.
Settled, the bull calf lay as if asleep,
one foreleg over the other,
bereft of pride and so beautiful now,
without movement, perfectly still in the cool pit,   35
I turned away and wept.

Compare:

"The Bull Calf" with "Woodchucks" by Maxine Kumin (page 772) and "Janet
Waking" by John Crowe Ransom (page 793)

Denise Levertov (b. 1923)
Ways of Conquest   1975

You invaded my country by accident,
not knowing you had crossed the border.
Vines that grew there touched you.
                              You ran past them,
shaking raindrops off the leaves — you or the wind.   5
It was toward the hills you ran,
inland —

I invaded your country with all my
'passionate intensity,'
pontoons and parachutes of my blindness.   10
But living now in the suburbs of the capital
incognito,
              my will to take the heart of the city
              has dwindled. I love
its unsuspecting life,   15
its adolescents who come to tell me their dreams in the dusty park
among the rocks and benches,
I the stranger who will listen.
I love
the wild herons who return each year to the marshy outskirts.   20
What I invaded has
invaded me.

Ways of Conquest. 9. *'passionate intensity'*: For the source of this phrase, see William
Butler Yeats's "The Second Coming," page 625.

Philip Levine (b. 1928)

To a Child Trapped in a Barber Shop 1966

You've gotten in through the transom
    and you can't get out
till Monday morning or, worse,
    till the cops come.

That six-year-old red face   5
    calling for mama
is yours; it won't help you
    because your case

is closed forever, hopeless.
    So don't drink   10
the Lucky Tiger, don't
    fill up on grease

because that makes it a lot worse,
    that makes it a crime
against property and the state   15
    and that costs time.

We've all been here before,
    we took our turn
under the electric storm
    of the vibrator   20

and stiffened our wills to meet
    the close clippers
and heard the true blade mowing
    back and forth

on a strip of dead skin,   25
    and we stopped crying.
You think your life is over?
    It's just begun.

Vachel Lindsay (1879–1931)

Factory Windows Are Always Broken 1914

Factory windows are always broken.
Somebody's always throwing bricks,
Somebody's always heaving cinders,
Playing ugly Yahoo tricks.

Factory windows are always broken.   5
Other windows are let alone.
No one throws through the chapel-window
The bitter, snarling, derisive stone.

Factory windows are always broken.
Something or other is going wrong.
Something is rotten—I think, in Denmark.
End of the factory-window song.

10

FACTORY WINDOWS ARE ALWAYS BROKEN. 4. *Yahoo:* In *Gulliver's Travels* by Jonathan Swift, yahoos are apelike creatures, vicious and destructive—Swift's caricatures of humankind. 11. *Something . . . Denmark:* "Something is rotten in the state of Denmark."—Marcellus in *Hamlet* I, iv, 90.

Robert Lowell (1917–1977)

SKUNK HOUR

1959

For Elizabeth Bishop

Nautilus Island's hermit
heiress still lives through winters in her Spartan cottage;
her sheep still graze above the sea.
Her son's a bishop. Her farmer
is first selectman in our village;
she's in her dotage.

5

Thirsting for
the hierarchic privacy
of Queen Victoria's century,
she buys up all
the eyesores facing her shore,
and lets them fall.

10

The season's ill—
we've lost our summer millionaire,
who seemed to leap from an L. L. Bean
catalogue. His nine-knot yawl
was auctioned off to lobstermen.
A red fox stain covers Blue Hill.

15

And now our fairy
decorator brightens his stop for fall;
his fishnet's filled with orange cork,
orange, his cobbler's bench and awl;
there is no money in his work,
he'd rather marry.

20

One dark night,
my Tudor Ford climbed the hill's skull;
I watched for love-cars. Lights turned down,
they lay together, hull to hull,
where the graveyard shelves on the town. . . .
My mind's not right.

25

30

A car radio bleats,
"Love, O careless Love. . . ." I hear
my ill-spirit sob in each blood cell,
as if my hand were at its throat. . . .
I myself am hell;   35
nobody's here—

only skunks, that search
in the moonlight for a bite to eat.
They march on their soles up Main Street:
white stripes, moonstruck eyes' red fire   40
under the chalk-dry and spar spire
of the Trinitarian Church.

I stand on top
of our back steps and breathe the rich air—
a mother skunk with her column of kittens swills the garbage pail.   45
She jabs her wedge-head in a cup
of sour cream, drops her ostrich tail,
and will not scare.

Archibald MacLeish (b. 1892)

THE END OF THE WORLD   1926

Quite unexpectedly as Vasserot
The armless ambidextrian was lighting
A match between his great and second toe,
And Ralph the lion was engaged in biting
The neck of Madame Sossman while the drum   5
Pointed, and Teeny was about to cough
In waltz-time swinging Jocko by the thumb—
Quite unexpectedly the top blew off:

And there, there overhead, there, there hung over
Those thousands of white faces, those dazed eyes,   10
There in the starless dark the poise, the hover,
There with vast wings across the canceled skies,
There in the sudden blackness the black pall
Of nothing, nothing, nothing—nothing at all.

COMPARE:
"The End of the World" with "Fire and Ice" by Robert Frost (page 486).

Christopher Marlowe (1564–1593)

THE PASSIONATE SHEPHERD TO HIS LOVE

Come live with me and be my love,
And we will all the pleasures prove
That valleys, groves, hills, and fields,
Woods, or steepy mountain yields.

And we will sit upon the rocks,   5
Seeing the shepherds feed their flocks
By shallow rivers, to whose falls
Melodious birds sing madrigals.

And I will make thee beds of roses
And a thousand fragrant posies,   10
A cap of flowers and a kirtle°   *skirt*
Embroidered all with leaves of myrtle;

A gown made of the finest wool
Which from our pretty lambs we pull;
Fair-linèd slippers for the cold,   15
With buckles of the purest gold;

A belt of straw and ivy buds,
With coral clasps and amber studs.
And if these pleasures may thee move,
Come live with me and be my love.   20

The shepherds' swains shall dance and sing
For thy delight each May morning.
If these delights thy mind may move,
Then live with me and be my love.

COMPARE:

"The Passionate Shepherd to His Love" with "The Bait" by John Donne (page 739).

Andrew Marvell (1621–1678)

TO HIS COY MISTRESS

1681

Had we but world enough, and time,
This coyness°, lady, were no crime.   *modesty, reluctance*
We would sit down and think which way
To walk, and pass our long love's day.
Thou by the Indian Ganges' side   5
Should'st rubies find; I by the tide
Of Humber would complain°. I would   *sing sad songs*
Love you ten years before the Flood,

And you should, if you please, refuse
Till the conversion of the Jews.   10
My vegetable° love should grow   *vegetative, flourishing*
Vaster than empires, and more slow.
An hundred years should go to praise
Thine eyes, and on thy forehead gaze,
Two hundred to adore each breast,   15
But thirty thousand to the rest.
An age at least to every part,
And the last age should show your heart.
For, lady, you deserve this state,
Nor would I love at lower rate.   20
    But at my back I always hear
Time's wingèd chariot hurrying near;
And yonder all before us lie
Deserts of vast eternity.
Thy beauty shall no more be found,   25
Nor in thy marble vault shall sound
My echoing song; then worms shall try
That long preserved virginity,
And your quaint honor turn to dust,
And into ashes all my lust.   30
The grave's a fine and private place,
But none, I think, do there embrace.
    Now therefore, while the youthful hue
Sits on thy skin like morning glew°   *glow*
And while thy willing soul transpires   35
At every pore with instant° fires,   *eager*
Now let us sport us while we may;
And now, like am'rous birds of prey,
Rather at once our time devour,
Than languish in his slow-chapped power,   40
Let us roll all our strength, and all
Our sweetness, up into one ball;
And tear our pleasures with rough strife
Thorough° the iron gates of life.   *through*
Thus, though we cannot make our sun   45
Stand still, yet we will make him run.

To His Coy Mistress. 7. *Humber:* a river that flows by Marvell's town of Hull (on the side
of the world opposite from the Ganges). 10. *conversion of the Jews:* an event that, according to St. John the Divine, is to take place just before the end of the world.

Compare:

"To His Coy Mistress" with "To the Virgins, to Make Much of Time" by Robert
Herrick (page 761).

James Merrill (b. 1926)

LABORATORY POEM

1958

Charles used to watch Naomi, taking heart
And a steel saw, open up turtles, live.
While she swore they felt nothing, he would gag
At blood, at the blind twitching, even after
The murky dawn of entrails cleared, revealing   5
Contours he knew, egg-yellows like lamps paling.

Well then. She carried off the beating heart
To the kymograph and rigged it there, a rag
In fitful wind, now made to strain, now stopped
By her solutions tonic or malign   10
Alternately in which it would be steeped.
What the heart bore, she noted on a chart,

For work did not stop only with the heart.
He thought of certain human hearts, their climb
Through violence into exquisite disciplines   15
Of which, as it now appeared, they all expired.
Soon she would fetch another and start over,
Easy in the presence of her lover.

LABORATORY POEM. 8. *kymograph:* device to record wavelike motions or pulsations on a piece of paper fastened to a revolving drum.

W. S. Merwin (b. 1927)

FOR THE ANNIVERSARY OF MY DEATH

1967

Every year without knowing it I have passed the day
When the last fires will wave to me
And the silence will set out
Tireless traveller
Like the beam of a lightless star   5

Then I will no longer
Find myself in life as in a strange garment
Surprised at the earth
And the love of one woman
And the shamelessness of men   10
As today writing after three days of rain
Hearing the wren sing and the falling cease
And bowing not knowing to what

John Milton (1608–1674)

WHEN I CONSIDER HOW MY LIGHT IS SPENT (1652?)

When I consider how my light is spent,
  Ere half my days in this dark world and wide,
  And that one talent which is death to hide
  Lodged with me useless, though my soul more bent
To serve therewith my Maker, and present   5
  My true account, lest He returning chide;
  "Doth God exact day-labor, light denied?"
  I fondly° ask. But Patience, to prevent   *foolishly*
That murmur, soon replies, "God doth not need
  Either man's work or His own gifts. Who best   10
  Bear His mild yoke, they serve Him best. His state
Is kingly: thousands at His bidding speed,
  And post o'er land and ocean without rest;
  They also serve who only stand and wait."

WHEN I CONSIDER HOW MY LIGHT IS SPENT. 1–2. *my light is spent / Ere half my days:* Milton had become blind before he was fifty (when half his life was spent out of a possible hundred years). 3. *that one talent:* For Christ's parable of the talents (measures of money), see Matthew 25:14–30.

Marianne Moore (1887–1972)

THE MIND IS AN ENCHANTING THING 1944

is an enchanted thing
  like the glaze on a
katydid-wing
    subdivided by sun
    till the nettings are legion.   5
Like Gieseking playing Scarlatti;

like the apteryx-awl
  as a beak, or the
kiwi's rain-shawl
    of haired feathers, the mind   10
    feeling its way as though blind,
walks along with its eyes on the ground.

It has memory's ear
  that can hear without
having to hear.   15
    Like the gyroscope's fall,
    truly unequivocal
because trued by regnant certainty,

it is a power of
    strong enchantment. It
is like the dove-
      neck animated by
      sun; it is memory's eye;
it's conscientious inconsistency.   20

It tears off the veil; tears   25
    the temptation, the
mist the heart wears,
      from its eyes,—if the heart
      has a face; it takes apart
dejection. It's fire in the dove-neck's   30

iridescence; in the
    inconsistencies
of Scarlatti.
      Unconfusion submits
its confusion to proof; it's   35
not a Herod's oath that cannot change.

THE MIND IS AN ENCHANTING THING. 6. *Gieseking . . . Scarlatti:* Walter Gieseking (1895–1956), German pianist, was a celebrated performer of the difficult sonatas of Italian composer Domenico Scarlatti (1685–1757). 7. *apteryx-awl:* awl-shaped beak of the apteryx, one of the kiwi family. (An awl is a pointed tool for piercing wood or leather.) 36. *Herod's oath:* King Herod's order condemning to death all infants in Bethlehem (Matthew 2:1–16). In one medieval English version of the Herod story, a pageant play, the king causes the death of his own child by refusing to withdraw his command.

Sylvia Plath (1932–1963)

DADDY   1965

You do not do, you do not do
Any more, black shoe
In which I have lived like a foot
For thirty years, poor and white,
Barely daring to breathe or Achoo.   5

Daddy, I have had to kill you.
You died before I had time—
Marble-heavy, a bag full of God,
Ghastly statue with one grey toe
Big as a Frisco seal   10

And a head in the freakish Atlantic
Where it pours bean green over blue
In the waters off beautiful Nauset.
I used to pray to recover you.
Ach, du.   15

In the German tongue, in the Polish town
Scraped flat by the roller

Of wars, wars, wars.
But the name of the town is common.
My Polack friend   20

Says there are a dozen or two.
So I never could tell where you
Put your foot, your root,
I never could talk to you.
The tongue stuck in my jaw.   25

It stuck in a barb wire snare.
Ich, ich, ich, ich,
I could hardly speak.
I thought every German was you.
And the language obscene   30

An engine, an engine
Chuffing me off like a Jew.
A Jew to Dachau, Auschwitz, Belsen.
I began to talk like a Jew.
I think I may well be a Jew.   35

The snows of the Tyrol, the clear beer of Vienna
Are not very pure or true.
With my gypsy ancestress and my weird luck
And my Taroc pack and my Taroc pack
I may be a bit of a Jew.   40

I have always been scared of *you*,
With your Luftwaffe, your gobbledygoo.
And your neat moustache
And your Aryan eye, bright blue.
Panzer-man, panzer-man, O You—   45

Not God but a swastika
So black no sky could squeak through.
Every woman adores a Fascist,
The boot in the face, the brute
Brute heart of a brute like you.   50

You stand at the blackboard, daddy,
In the picture I have of you,
A cleft in your chin instead of your foot
But no less a devil for that, no not
Any less the black man who   55

Bit my pretty red heart in two.
I was ten when they buried you.
At twenty I tried to die
And get back, back, back at you.
I thought even the bones will do.   60

But they pulled me out of the sack,
And they stuck me together with glue.

And then I knew what to do.
I made a model of you,
A man in black with a Meinkampf look

65

And a love of the rack and the screw.
And I said I do, I do.
So daddy, I'm finally through.
The black telephone's off at the root,
The voices just can't worm through.

70

If I've killed one man, I've killed two—
The vampire who said he was you
And drank my blood for a year,
Seven years, if you want to know.
Daddy, you can lie back now.

75

There's a stake in your fat black heart
And the villagers never liked you.
They are dancing and stamping on you.
They always *knew* it was you.
Daddy, daddy, you bastard, I'm through.

80

DADDY. Introducing this poem in a reading, Sylvia Plath remarked:

The poem is spoken by a girl with an Electra complex. Her father died while she thought
he was God. Her case is complicated by the fact that her father was also a Nazi and her
mother very possibly part Jewish. In the daughter the two strains marry and paralyze
each other—she has to act out the awful little allegory before she is free of it.

(Quoted by A. Alvarez, *Beyond All This Fiddle*, New York, 1971.) In some details "Daddy"
is autobiography: the poet's father, Otto Plath, a German, had come to the United States
from Grabow, Poland. He had died following amputation of a gangrened foot and leg,
when Sylvia was eight years old. Politically, Otto Plath was a Republican, not a Nazi; but
was apparently a somewhat domineering head of the household. (See the recollections of
the poet's mother, Aurelia Schober Plath, in her edition of *Letters Home* by Sylvia Plath,
New York, 1975.) 15. *Ach, du:* Oh, you. 27. *Ich, ich, ich, ich:* I, I, I, I. 51. *blackboard:* Otto
Plath had been a professor of biology at Boston University. 65. *Meinkampf:* Adolf Hitler
entitled his autobiography *Mein Kampf* ("My Life").

COMPARE:

"Daddy" with "American Primitive" by William Jay Smith (page 808) and
"Confession to Settle a Curse" by Rosmarie Waldrop (page 819).

Sylvia Plath (1932–1963)
MORNING SONG   1965

Love set you going like a fat gold watch.
The midwife slapped your footsoles, and your bald cry
Took its place among the elements.

Our voices echo, magnifying your arrival. New statue.
In a drafty museum, your nakedness
Shadows our safety. We stand round blankly as walls.

5

I'm no more your mother
Than the cloud that distils a mirror to reflect its own slow
Effacement at the wind's hand.

All night your moth-breath   10
Flickers among the flat pink roses. I wake to listen:
A far sea moves in my ear.

One cry, and I stumble from bed, cow-heavy and floral
In my Victorian nightgown.
Your mouth opens clean as a cat's. The window square   15

Whitens and swallows its dull stars. And now you try
Your handful of notes;
The clear vowels rise like balloons.

COMPARE:

"Morning Song" with "My Son, My Executioner" by Donald Hall (page 677)
and "Woman to Child" by Judith Wright (page 827).

Sylvia Plath (1932–1963)
POPPIES IN OCTOBER   1965

Even the sun-clouds this morning cannot manage such skirts.
Nor the woman in the ambulance
Whose red heart blooms through her coat so astoundingly—

A gift, a love gift
Utterly unasked for   5
By a sky

Palely and flamily
Igniting its carbon monoxides, by eyes
Dulled to a halt under bowlers.

O my god, what am I   10
That these late mouths should cry open
In a forest of frost, in a dawn of cornflowers.

COMPARE:

"Poppies in October" with "Bavarian Gentians" by D. H. Lawrence (page 622).

Alexander Pope (1688–1744)

AN ESSAY ON MAN (EPISTLE II, PART 1)   1733

Know then thyself, presume not God to scan°;   *scrutinize*
The proper study of Mankind is Man.
Placed on this isthmus of a middle state,
A being darkly wise, and rudely great:
With too much knowledge for the Sceptic side,   5
With too much weakness for the Stoic's pride,
He hangs between; in doubt to act, or rest;
In doubt to deem himself a god, or beast;
In doubt his mind or body to prefer;
Born but to die, and reasoning but to err;   10
Alike in ignorance, his reason such,
Whether he thinks too little, or too much:
Chaos of thought and passion, all confused;
Still by himself abused, or disabused;
Created half to rise, and half to fall;   15
Great lord of all things, yet a prey to all;
Sole judge of truth, in endless error hurled:
The glory, jest, and riddle of the world!
Go, wondrous creature! mount where Science guides,
Go, measure earth, weigh air, and state the tides;   20
Instruct the planets in what orbs° to run,   *orbits*
Correct old Time, and regulate the sun;
Go, soar with Plato to th' empyreal sphere,
To the first good, first perfect, and first fair;
Or tread the mazy round his followers trod,   25
And quitting sense call imitating God;
As Eastern priests in giddy circles run,
And turn their heads to imitate the sun.
Go, teach Eternal Wisdom how to rule—
Then drop into thyself, and be a fool!   30
Superior beings, when of late they saw
A mortal man unfold all Nature's law,
Admired such wisdom in an earthly shape,
And showed a Newton as we show an ape.
Could he, whose rules the rapid Comet bind,   35
Describe or fix one movement of his mind?
Who saw its fires here rise, and there descend,
Explain his own beginning, or his end?
Alas what wonder! Man's superior part
Unchecked may rise, and climb from art to art;   40
But when his own great work is but begun,
What Reason weaves, by Passion is undone.
Trace Science then, with Modesty thy guide;
First strip off all her equipage of pride;
Deduct what is but vanity, or dress,   45
Or learning's luxury, or idleness;

Or tricks to show the stretch of human brain,
Mere curious pleasure, or ingenious pain;
Expunge the whole, or lop th' excrescent° parts   *superfluous*
Of all, our vices have created arts;   50
Then see how little the remaining sum,
Which served the past, and must the times to come!

AN ESSAY ON MAN (EPISTLE II, PART 1). Pope entitles his second epistle "Of the Nature and State of Man as an Individual." His summary of the argument of this part: "The business of Man not to pry into God, but to study himself. His middle nature, his powers, frailties, and the limits of his capacity." 5–6: *Sceptic . . . Stoic's pride:* In Pope's view, both these ancient Greek philosophical schools were in error: the Sceptics in denying that man can attain any knowledge of reality; the Stoics in affirming that man, by ridding himself of his passions, can achieve Godlike calm. 23. *empyreal sphere:* the farthest sphere of the universe, the highest Heaven. 25. *his followers:* Plotinus and other followers of Plato were said to have conversed with the divine while in a state of trance. 34. *as we show an ape:* In eighteenth century London, apes were sometimes displayed as curiosities, made to perform in human clothes. The point is that Newton is to the gods as an ape is to human beings: inferior, but a remarkable imitation. (For another tribute to Newton, see Pope's epigram on page 535.)

Ezra Pound (1885–1972)

THE RIVER-MERCHANT'S WIFE: A LETTER   1915

While my hair was still cut straight across my forehead
I played about the front gate, pulling flowers.
You came by on bamboo stilts, playing horse,
You walked about my seat, playing with blue plums.
And we went on living in the village of Chokan: 5
Two small people, without dislike or suspicion.
At fourteen I married My Lord you.
I never laughed, being bashful.
Lowering my head, I looked at the wall.
Called to, a thousand times, I never looked back.   10

At fifteen I stopped scowling,
I desired my dust to be mingled with yours
Forever and forever and forever.
Why should I climb the lookout?

At sixteen you departed,   15
You went into far Ku-to-yen, by the river of swirling eddies,
And you have been gone five months.
The monkeys make sorrowful noise overhead.

You dragged your feet when you went out.
By the gate now, the moss is grown, the different mosses,   20
Too deep to clear them away!
The leaves fall early this autumn, in wind.
The paired butterflies are already yellow with August
Over the grass in the West garden;

They hurt me. I grow older.   25
If you are coming down through the narrows of the river Kiang,
Please let me know beforehand,
And I will come out to meet you
        As far as Cho-fu-sa.

THE RIVER-MERCHANT'S WIFE: A LETTER. A free translation from the Chinese poet Li Po
(eighth century).

COMPARE:

"The River Merchant's Wife: a Letter" with "Wedding-Wind" by Philip Larkin
(page 774).

Ezra Pound (1885–1972)

THE SEAFARER   1912

From the Anglo-Saxon

May I for my own self song's truth reckon,
Journey's jargon, how I in harsh days
Hardship endured oft.
Bitter breast-cares have I abided,
Known on my keel many a care's hold,   5
And dire sea-surge, and there I oft spent
Narrow nightwatch nigh the ship's head
While she tossed close to cliffs. Coldly afflicted,
My feet were by frost benumbed.
Chill its chains are; chafing sighs   10
Hew my heart round and hunger begot
Mere-weary mood. Lest man know not
That he on dry land loveliest liveth,
List how I, care-wretched, on ice-cold sea,
Weathered the winter, wretched outcast   15
Deprived of my kinsmen;
Hung with hard ice-flakes, where hail-scur flew,
There I heard naught save the harsh sea
And ice-cold wave, at whiles the swan cries,
Did for my games the gannet's clamour,   20
Sea-fowls' loudness was for me laughter,
The mews' singing all my mead-drink.
Storms, on the stone-cliffs beaten, fell on the stern
In icy feathers; full oft the eagle screamed
With spray on his pinion.
                        Not any protector   25
May make merry man faring needy.
This he little believes, who aye in winsome life
Abides 'mid burghers some heavy business,

Wealthy and wine-flushed, how I weary oft
Must bide above brine.   30
Neareth nightshade, snoweth from north,
Frost froze the land, hail fell on earth then,
Corn of the coldest. Nathless° there knocketh now   *nevertheless*
The heart's thought that I on high streams
The salt-wavy tumult traverse alone.   35
Moaneth alway my mind's lust
That I fare forth, that I afar hence
Seek out a foreign fastness.
For this there's no mood-lofty man over earth's midst,
Not though he be given his good, but will have in his youth greed;   40
Nor his deed to the daring, nor his king to the faithful
But shall have his sorrow for sea-fare
Whatever his lord will.
He hath not heart for harping, nor in ring-having
Nor winsomeness to wife, nor world's delight   45
Nor any whit else save the wave's slash,
Yet longing comes upon him to fare forth on the water.
Bosque° taketh blossom, cometh beauty of berries,   *bush*
Fields to fairness, land fares brisker,
All this admonisheth man eager of mood,   50
The heart turns to travel so that he then thinks
On flood-ways to be far departing.
Cuckoo calleth with gloomy crying,
He singeth summerward, bodeth sorrow,
The bitter heart's blood. Burgher knows not—   55
He the prosperous man—what some perform
Where wandering them widest draweth.
So that but now my heart burst from my breastlock,
My mood 'mid the mere-flood,
Over the whale's acre, would wander wide.   60
On earth's shelter cometh oft to me,
Eager and ready, the crying lone-flyer,
Whets for the whale-path the heart irresistibly,
O'er tracks of ocean; seeing that anyhow
My lord deems to me this dead life   65
On loan and on land, I believe not
That any earth-weal eternal standeth
Save there be somewhat calamitous
That, ere a man's tide go, turn it to twain.
Disease or oldness or sword-hate   70
Beats out the breath from doom-gripped body.
And for this, every earl whatever, for those speaking after—
Laud of the living, boasteth some last word,
That he will work ere he pass onward,
Frame on the fair earth 'gainst foes his malice,   75
Daring ado, . . .
So that all men shall honour him after
And his laud beyond them remain 'mid the English,

Aye, for ever, a lasting life's-blast,
Delight 'mid the doughty.

                          Days little durable, 80
And all arrogance of earthen riches,
There come now no kings nor Cæsars
Nor gold-giving lords like those gone.
Howe'er in mirth most magnified,
Whoe'er lived in life most lordliest, 85
Drear all this excellence, delights undurable!
Waneth the watch, but the world holdeth.
Tomb hideth trouble. The blade is layed low.
Earthly glory ageth and seareth.
No man at all going the earth's gait, 90
But age fares against him, his face paleth,
Grey-haired he groaneth, knows gone companions,
Lordly men, are to earth o'ergiven,
Nor may he then the flesh-cover, whose life ceaseth,
Nor eat the sweet nor feel the sorry, 95
Nor stir hand nor think in mid heart,
And though he strew the grave with gold,
His born brothers, their buried bodies
Be an unlikely treasure hoard.

COMPARE:

"The Seafarer" with "Junk" by Richard Wilbur (page 820).

Dudley Randall (b. 1914)

BALLAD OF BIRMINGHAM   1966

*(On the Bombing of a Church in
Birmingham, Alabama, 1963)*

"Mother dear, may I go downtown
Instead of out to play,
And march the streets of Birmingham
In a Freedom March today?"

"No, baby, no, you may not go, 5
For the dogs are fierce and wild,
And clubs and hoses, guns and jail
Aren't good for a little child."

"But, mother, I won't be alone.
Other children will go with me, 10
And march the streets of Birmingham
To make our country free."

"No, baby, no, you may not go,
For I fear those guns will fire.

But you may go to church instead
And sing in the children's choir."

She has combed and brushed her night-dark hair,
And bathed rose petal sweet,
And drawn white gloves on her small brown hands,
And white shoes on her feet.   20

The mother smiled to know her child
Was in the sacred place,
But that smile was the last smile
To come upon her face.

For when she heard the explosion,   25
Her eyes grew wet and wild.
She raced through the streets of Birmingham
Calling for her child.

She clawed through bits of glass and brick,
Then lifted out a shoe.   30
"O here's the shoe my baby wore,
But, baby, where are you?"

COMPARE:

"Ballad of Birmingham" with the anonymous ballads "Edward" (page 713) and
"The Cruel Mother" (page 511). Compare its theme with the themes of "Satur-
day's Child" by Countee Cullen (page 732) and "Dream Deferred" by Langston
Hughes (page 765).

John Crowe Ransom (1888–1974)
JANET WAKING   1927

Beautifully Janet slept
Till it was deeply morning. She woke then
And thought about her dainty-feathered hen,
To see how it had kept.

One kiss she gave her mother,   5
Only a small one gave she to her daddy
Who would have kissed each curl of his shining baby;
No kiss at all for her brother.

"Old Chucky, Old Chucky!" she cried,
Running on little pink feet upon the grass   10
To Chucky's house, and listening. But alas,
Her Chucky had died.

It was a transmogrifying° bee   *change-working*
Came droning down on Chucky's old bald head
And sat and put the poison. It scarcely bled,   15
But how exceedingly

And purply did the knot
Swell with the venom and communicate
Its rigor! Now the poor comb stood up straight
But Chucky did not.   20

So there was Janet
Kneeling on the wet grass, crying her brown hen
(Translated far beyond the daughters of men)
To rise and walk upon it.

And weeping fast as she had breath   25
Janet implored us, "Wake her from her sleep!"
And would not be instructed in how deep
Was the forgetful kingdom of death.

COMPARE:

"Janet Waking" with "Woodchucks" by Maxine Kumin (page 772) and "The
Bull Calf" by Irving Layton (page 775).

Henry Reed (b. 1914)
NAMING OF PARTS   1946

Today we have naming of parts. Yesterday,
We had daily cleaning. And tomorrow morning,
We shall have what to do after firing. But today,
Today we have naming of parts. Japonica
Glistens like coral in all of the neighboring gardens,   5
        And today we have naming of parts.

This is the lower sling swivel. And this
Is the upper sling swivel, whose use you will see,
When you are given your slings. And this is the piling swivel,
Which in your case you have not got. The branches   10
Hold in the gardens their silent, eloquent gestures,
        Which in our case we have not got.

This is the safety-catch, which is always released
With an easy flick of the thumb. And please do not let me
See anyone using his finger. You can do it quite easy   15
If you have any strength in your thumb. The blossoms
Are fragile and motionless, never letting anyone see
        Any of them using their finger.

And this you can see is the bolt. The purpose of this
Is to open the breech, as you see. We can slide it   20
Rapidly backwards and forwards: we call this
Easing the spring. And rapidly backwards and forwards
The early bees are assaulting and fumbling the flowers:
        They call it easing the Spring.

They call it easing the Spring: it is perfectly easy 25
If you have any strength in your thumb: like the bolt,
And the breech, and the cocking-piece, and the point of balance,
Which in our case we have not got; and the almond-blossom
Silent in all of the gardens and the bees going backwards and forwards,
      For today we have naming of parts. 30

COMPARE:

"Naming of Parts" with "The Fury of Aerial Bombardment" by Richard
Eberhart (page 460).

Adrienne Rich (b. 1929)

DIVING INTO THE WRECK 1973

First having read the book of myths,
and loaded the camera,
and checked the edge of the knife-blade,
I put on
the body-armor of black rubber 5
the absurd flippers
the grave and awkward mask.
I am having to do this
not like Cousteau with his
assiduous team 10
aboard the sun-flooded schooner
but here alone.

There is a ladder.
The ladder is always there
hanging innocently 15
close to the side of the schooner.
We know what it is for,
we who have used it.
Otherwise
it's a piece of maritime floss 20
some sundry equipment.

I go down.
Rung after rung and still
the oxygen immerses me
the blue light 25
the clear atoms
of our human air.
I go down.
My flippers cripple me,
I crawl like an insect down the ladder 30
and there is no one
to tell me when the ocean
will begin.

First the air is blue and then
it is bluer and then green and then   35
black I am blacking out and yet
my mask is powerful
it pumps my blood with power
the sea is another story
the sea is not a question of power   40
I have to learn alone
to turn my body without force
in the deep element.

And now: it is easy to forget
what I came for   45
among so many who have always
lived here
swaying their crenellated fans
between the reefs
and besides   50
you breathe differently down here.

I came to explore the wreck.
The words are purposes.
The words are maps.
I came to see the damage that was done   55
and the treasures that prevail.
I stroke the beam of my lamp
slowly along the flank
of something more permanent
than fish or weed   60

the thing I came for:
the wreck and not the story of the wreck
the thing itself and not the myth
the drowned face always staring
toward the sun   65
the evidence of damage
worn by salt and sway into this threadbare beauty
the ribs of the disaster
curving their assertion
among the tentative haunters.   70

This is the place.
And I am here, the mermaid whose dark hair
streams black, the merman in his armored body
We circle silently
about the wreck   75
we dive into the hold.
I am she: I am he

whose drowned face sleeps with open eyes
whose breasts still bear the stress
whose silver, copper, vermeil cargo lies   80

obscurely inside barrels
half-wedged and left to rot
we are the half-destroyed instruments
that once held to a course
the water-eaten log   85
the fouled compass

We are, I am, you are
by cowardice or courage
the one who find our way
back to this scene   90
carrying a knife, a camera
a book of myths
in which
our names do not appear.

Edwin Arlington Robinson (1869–1935)

MR. FLOOD'S PARTY   1921

Old Eben Flood, climbing alone one night
Over the hill between the town below
And the forsaken upland hermitage
That held as much as he should ever know
On earth again of home, paused warily.   5
The road was his with not a native near;
And Eben, having leisure, said aloud,
For no man else in Tilbury Town to hear:

"Well, Mr. Flood, we have the harvest moon
Again, and we may not have many more;   10
The bird is on the wing, the poet says,
And you and I have said it here before.
Drink to the bird." He raised up to the light
The jug that he had gone so far to fill,
And answered huskily: "Well, Mr. Flood,   15
Since you propose it, I believe I will."

Alone, as if enduring to the end
A valiant armor of scarred hopes outworn,
He stood there in the middle of the road
Like Roland's ghost winding° a silent horn.   *blowing*   20
Below him, in the town among the trees,
Where friends of other days had honored him,
A phantom salutation of the dead
Rang thinly till old Eben's eyes were dim.

Then, as a mother lays her sleeping child   25
Down tenderly, fearing it may awake,
He set the jug down slowly at his feet
With trembling care, knowing that most things break;

And only when assured that on firm earth
It stood, as the uncertain lives of men
Assuredly did not, he paced away,
And with his hand extended paused again:

"Well, Mr. Flood, we have not met like this
In a long time; and many a change has come
To both of us, I fear, since last it was
We had a drop together. Welcome home!"
Convivially returning with himself,
Again he raised the jug up to the light;
And with an acquiescent quaver said:
"Well, Mr. Flood, if you insist, I might.

"Only a very little, Mr. Flood—
For auld lang syne. No more, sir; that will do."
So, for the time, apparently it did,
And Eben evidently thought so too;
For soon amid the silver loneliness
Of night he lifted up his voice and sang,
Secure, with only two moons listening,
Until the whole harmonious landscape rang—

"For auld lang syne." The weary throat gave out,
The last word wavered; and the song being done,
He raised again the jug regretfully
And shook his head, and was again alone.
There was not much that was ahead of him,
And there was nothing in the town below—
Where strangers would have shut the many doors
That many friends had opened long ago.

MR. FLOOD'S PARTY. 11. *the poet:* Omar Khayyám, Persian poet, a praiser of wine, whose *Rubáiyát,* translated by Edward FitzGerald, included the lines:

> Come, fill the Cup, and in the fire of Spring
> Your Winter-garment of Repentance fling:
>   The Bird of Time has but a little way
>   To flutter and the Bird is on the Wing.

20. *Roland's ghost . . . horn:* In the battle of Roncesvalles (eighth century), Roland fought to his death, refusing to sound his horn for help until all hope was gone.

Theodore Roethke (1908–1963)
FRAU BAUMAN, FRAU SCHMIDT, AND FRAU SCHWARTZE   1953

Gone the three ancient ladies
Who creaked on the greenhouse ladders,
Reaching up white strings
To wind, to wind

The sweet-pea tendrils, the smilax,
Nasturtiums, the climbing
Roses, to straighten
Carnations, red
Chrysanthemums; the stiff
Stems, jointed like corn,
They tied and tucked, —
These nurses of nobody else.
Quicker than birds, they dipped
Up and sifted the dirt;
They sprinkled and shook;
They stood astride pipes,
Their skirts billowing out wide into tents,
Their hands twinkling with wet;
Like witches they flew along rows
Keeping creation at ease;
With a tendril for needle
They sewed up the air with a stem;
They teased out the seed that the cold kept asleep, —
All the coils, loops, and whorls.
They trellised the sun; they plotted for more than themselves.

I remember how they picked me up, a spindly kid,
Pinching and poking my thin ribs
Till I lay in their laps, laughing,
Weak as a whiffet,
Now, when I'm alone and cold in my bed,
They still hover over me,
These ancient leathery crones,
With their bandannas stiffened with sweat,
And their thorn-bitten wrists,
And their snuff-laden breath blowing lightly over me in my first sleep.

FRAU BAUMAN, FRAU SCHMIDT, AND FRAU SCHWARTZE. Roethke's father ran a commercial greenhouse in Saginaw, Michigan. 29. *whiffet:* a little puff of air; also, a small dog.

Theodore Roethke (1908–1963)

THE WAKING   1953

I wake to sleep, and take my waking slow.
I feel my fate in what I cannot fear.
I learn by going where I have to go.

We think by feeling. What is there to know?
I hear my being dance from ear to ear.
I wake to sleep, and take my waking slow.

Of those so close beside me, which are you?
God bless the Ground! I shall walk softly there,
And learn by going where I have to go.

Light takes the Tree; but who can tell us how?   10
The lowly worm climbs up a winding stair;
I wake to sleep, and take my waking slow.

Great Nature has another thing to do
To you and me; so take the lively air,
And, lovely, learn by going where to go.   15

This shaking keeps me steady. I should know.
What falls away is always. And is near.
I wake to sleep, and take my waking slow.
I learn by going where I have to go.

COMPARE:

"The Waking" with "Do not go gentle into that good night" by Dylan Thomas
(page 579).

Anne Sexton (1928–1975)
THE FURY OF OVERSHOES   1974

They sit in a row
outside the kindergarten,
black, red, brown, all
with those brass buckles.
Remember when you couldn't   5
buckle your own
overshoe
or tie your own
shoe
or cut your own meat   10
and the tears
running down like mud
because you fell off your
tricycle?
Remember, big fish,   15
when you couldn't swim
and simply slipped under
like a stone frog?
The world wasn't
yours.   20
It belonged to
the big people.
Under your bed
sat the wolf
and he made a shadow   25
when cars passed by
at night.

They made you give up
your nightlight
and your teddy   30
and your thumb.
Oh overshoes,
don't you
remember me,
pushing you up and down   35
in the winter snow?
Oh thumb,
I want a drink,
it is dark,
where are the big people,   40
when will I get there,
taking giant steps
all day,
each day
and thinking   45
nothing of it?

Anne Sexton (1928–1975)
The Kiss   1969

My mouth blooms like a cut.
I've been wronged all year, tedious
nights, nothing but rough elbows in them
and delicate boxes of Kleenex calling *crybaby*
crybaby, you fool!   5

Before today my body was useless.
Now it's tearing at its square corners.
It's tearing old Mary's garments off, knot by knot
and see—Now it's shot full of these electric bolts.
Zing! A resurrection!   10

Once it was a boat, quite wooden
and with no business, no salt water under it
and in need of some paint. It was no more
than a group of boards. But you hoisted her, rigged her.
She's been elected.   15

My nerves are turned on. I hear them like
musical instruments. Where there was silence
the drums, the strings are incurably playing. You did this.
Pure genuis at work. Darling, the composer has stepped
into fire.   20

Compare:

"The Kiss" with "Love Song: I and Thou" by Alan Dugan (page 742).

William Shakespeare (1564–1616)

THAT TIME OF YEAR THOU MAYST IN ME BEHOLD

1609

That time of year thou mayst in me behold
When yellow leaves, or none, or few, do hang
Upon those boughs which shake against the cold,
Bare ruined choirs where late the sweet birds sang.
In me thou see'st the twilight of such day   5
As after sunset fadeth in the west,
Which by-and-by black night doth take away,
Death's second self that seals up all in rest.
In me thou see'st the glowing of such fire
That on the ashes of his youth doth lie,   10
As the deathbed whereon it must expire,
Consumed with that which it was nourished by.
    This thou perceiv'st, which makes thy love more strong,
    To love that well which thou must leave ere long.

[handwritten annotations: use 3 comparisons to make point; sunset tree – fall; end of day; fire goes out; the speaker is in later part of life; simile; can't live without destroying what makes it live]

William Shakespeare (1564–1616)

WHEN, IN DISGRACE WITH FORTUNE AND MEN'S EYES

1609

When, in disgrace with Fortune and men's eyes,
I all alone beweep my outcast state,
And trouble deaf heaven with my bootless° cries,   *futile*
And look upon myself and curse my fate,
Wishing me like to one more rich in hope,   5
Featured like him, like him with friends possessed,
Desiring this man's art, and that man's scope,
With what I most enjoy contented least,
Yet in these thoughts myself almost despising,
Haply° I think on thee, and then my state,   *luckily*   10
Like to the lark at break of day arising
From sullen earth, sings hymns at heaven's gate;
    For thy sweet love rememb'red such wealth brings
    That then I scorn to change my state with kings.

William Shakespeare (1564–1616)

WHEN DAISIES PIED AND VIOLETS BLUE

1598

When daisies pied and violets blue
    And lady-smocks all silver-white
And cuckoo-buds° of yellow hue   *buttercups*
    Do paint the meadows with delight,

The cuckoo then, on every tree,   5
Mocks married men; for thus sings he,
              "Cuckoo,
Cuckoo, cuckoo!" — O word of fear,
Unpleasing to a married ear!

When shepherds pipe on oaten straws,   10
    And merry larks are ploughmen's clocks,
When turtles tread°, and rooks, and daws,   *turtledoves mate*
    And maidens bleach their summer smocks,
The cuckoo then, on every tree,
Mocks married men; for thus sings he,   15
              "Cuckoo,
Cuckoo, cuckoo!" — O word of fear,
Unpleasing to a married ear!

WHEN DAISIES PIED. This song and "When icicles hang by the wall" conclude the play
Love's Labor's Lost. 2. *lady-smocks*: also named cuckoo-flowers. 8. *O word of fear*: because it
sounds like the sound *cuckold*.

William Shakespeare (1564–1616)

WHEN ICICLES HANG BY THE WALL   1598

When icicles hang by the wall,
    And Dick the shepherd blows his nail,
And Tom bears logs into the hall,
    And milk comes frozen home in pail,
When blood is nipped and ways° be foul,   *roads*   5
    Then nightly sings the staring owl:
        "Tu-whit, to-who!"
            A merry note,
While greasy Joan doth keel° the pot.   *cool (as by skimming*
                                                                                       or stirring)

When all aloud the wind doth blow,   10
    And coughing drowns the parson's saw°,   *old saw, platitude*
And birds sit brooding in the snow,
    And Marian's nose looks red and raw,
When roasted crabs° hiss in the bowl,   *crab apples*
    Then nightly sings the staring owl: 15
        "Tu-whit, to-who!"
            A merry note,
While greasy Joan doth keel the pot.

Karl Shapiro (b. 1913)

THE DIRTY WORD   1947

The dirty word hops in the cage of the mind like the Pondicherry
vulture, stomping with its heavy left claw on the sweet meat of the brain
and tearing it with its vicious beak, ripping and chopping the flesh.
Terrified, the small boy bears the big bird of the dirty word into the
house, and grunting, puffing, carries it up the stairs to his own room in   5
the skull. Bits of black feather cling to his clothes and his hair as he locks
the staring creature in the dark closet.

All day the small boy returns to the closet to examine and feed the
bird, to caress and kick the bird, that now snaps and flaps its wings
savagely whenever the door is opened. How the boy trembles and delights   10
at the sight of the white excrement of the bird! How the bird leaps and
rushes against the walls of the skull, trying to escape from the zoo of the
vocabulary! How wildly snaps the sweet meat of the brain in its rage.

And the bird outlives the man, being freed at the man's death-
funeral by a word from the rabbi.   15

(But I one morning went upstairs and opened the door and entered
the closet and found in the cage of my mind the great bird dead. Softly
I wept it and softly removed it and softly buried the body of the bird in
the hollyhock garden of the house I lived in twenty years before. And out
of the worn black feathers of the wing have I made these pens to write   20
these elegies, for I have outlived the bird, and I have murdered it in my
early manhood.)

Percy Bysshe Shelley (1792–1822)

ODE TO THE WEST WIND   1820

It is a prayer

I

O wild West Wind, thou breath of Autumn's being,
Thou, from whose unseen presence the leaves dead
Are driven, like ghosts from an enchanter fleeing,

Yellow, and black, and pale, and hectic red,
Pestilence-stricken multitudes: O thou,   5
Who chariotest to their dark wintry bed

The wingèd seeds, where they lie cold and low,
Each like a corpse within its grave, until
Thine azure sister of the spring shall blow

giving time of dieing

Her clarion o'er the dreaming earth, and fill   10
(Driving sweet buds like flocks to feed in air)
With living hues and odors plain and hill:

Wild Spirit, which art moving everywhere;
Destroyer and preserver; hear, O, hear!

II

Thou on whose stream, 'mid the steep sky's commotion,   15
Loose clouds like earth's decaying leaves are shed,
Shook from the tangled boughs of Heaven and Ocean,

Angels of rain and lightning: there are spread
On the blue surface of thine airy surge,
Like the bright hair uplifted from the head   20

Of some fierce Maenad, even from the dim verge
Of the horizon to the zenith's height,
The locks of the approaching storm. Thou dirge

Of the dying year, to which this closing night
Will be the dome of a vast sepulcher,   25
Vaulted with all thy congregated might

Of vapors, from whose solid atmosphere
Black rain, and fire, and hail will burst: O, hear!

III

Thou who didst waken from his summer dreams
The blue Mediterranean, where he lay,   30
Lulled by the coil of his crystalline streams,

Beside a pumice isle in Baiae's bay,
And saw in sleep old palaces and towers
Quivering within the wave's intenser day,

All overgrown with azure moss, and flowers   35
So sweet, the sense faints picturing them! Thou
For whose path the Atlantic's level powers

Cleave themselves into chasms, while far below
The sea-blooms and the oozy woods which wear
The sapless foliage of the ocean, know   40

Thy voice, and suddenly grow gray with fear,
And tremble and despoil themselves: O, hear!

IV

If I were a dead leaf thou mightest bear;
If I were a swift cloud to fly with thee;
A wave to pant beneath thy power, and share   45

The impulse of thy strength, only less free
Than thou, O uncontrolable! If even
I were as in my boyhood, and could be

The comrade of thy wanderings over heaven;
As then, when to outstrip thy skiey speed
Scarce seemed a vision; I would ne'er have striven   50

As thus with thee in prayer in my sore need.
Oh! lift me as a wave, a leaf, a cloud!
I fall upon the thorns of life! I bleed!

A heavy weight of hours has chained and bowed   55
One too like thee: tameless, and swift, and proud.

V

Make me thy lyre, even as the forest is:
What if my leaves are falling like its own!
The tumult of thy mighty harmonies

Will take from both a deep, autumnal tone,   60
Sweet though in sadness. Be thou, spirit fierce,
My spirit! Be thou me, impetuous one!

Drive my dead thoughts over the universe
Like withered leaves, to quicken a new birth!
And, by the incantation of this verse,   65

Scatter, as from an unextinguished hearth
Ashes and sparks, my words among mankind!
Be through my lips to unawakened earth

The trumpet of a prophecy! O wind,
If Winter comes, can Spring be far behind?   70

ODE TO THE WEST WIND. 10. *clarion:* narrow-tubed trumpet once used on the battlefield because its shrill, clear call could be heard afar. 21. *Maenad:* in ancient Greece, a woman of the cult of the god Dionysus who would show her devotion by dancing herself into a frenzy. 32. *pumice isle in Baiae's bay:* an island of solidified lava in the bay of Naples, Italy. At Baiae are the ruins of villas of the Roman emperors. 57. *lyre:* Shelley is probably thinking of an Aeolian harp, which placed in a window produces deep strumming sounds when the wind blows over it.

Christopher Smart (1722–1771)

FOR I WILL CONSIDER MY CAT JEOFFRY   (1759–1763)

For I will consider my Cat Jeoffry.
For he is the servant of the Living God, duly and daily serving him.
For at the first glance of the glory of God in the East he worships in his
    way.
For is this done by wreathing his body seven times round with elegant
    quickness.
For then he leaps up to catch the musk°, which is the   *catnip*
    blessing of God upon his prayer.   5

For he rolls upon prank to work it in.

For having done duty and received blessing he begins to consider himself.

For this he performs in ten degrees.

For first he looks upon his fore-paws to see if they are clean.

For secondly he kicks up behind to clear away there.   10

For thirdly he works it upon stretch° with the fore-paws   *he works his*
extended.   *muscles, stretching*

For fourthly he sharpens his paws by wood.

For fifthly he washes himself.

For sixthly he rolls upon wash.

For seventhly he fleas himself, that he may not be interrupted upon the
beat°.   *his patrol*   15

For eighthly he rubs himself against a post.

For ninthly he looks up for his instructions.

For tenthly he goes in quest of food.

For having considered God and himself he will consider his neighbor.

For if he meets another cat he will kiss her in kindness.   20

For when he takes his prey he plays with it to give it a chance.

For one mouse in seven escapes by his dallying.

For when his day's work is done his business more properly begins.

For he keeps the Lord's watch in the night against the Adversary.

For he counteracts the powers of darkness by his electrical skin and glaring eyes.   25

For he counteracts the Devil, who is death, by brisking about the life.

For in his morning orisons he loves the sun and the sun loves him.

For he is of the tribe of Tiger.

For the Cherub Cat is a term of the Angel Tiger.

For he has the subtlety and hissing of a serpent, which in goodness he
suppresses.   30

For he will not do destruction if he is well-fed, neither will he spit without
provocation.

For he purrs in thankfulness when God tells him he's a good Cat.

For he is an instrument for the children to learn benevolence upon.

For every house is incomplete without him, and a blessing is lacking in
the spirit.

For the Lord commanded Moses concerning the cats at the departure of
the Children of Israel from Egypt.   35

For every family had one cat at least in the bag.

For the English cats are the best in Europe.

For he is the cleanest in the use of his fore-paws of any quadruped.

For the dexterity of his defense is an instance of the love of God to him exceedingly.

For he is the quickest to his mark of any creature.   40

For he is tenacious of his point.

For he is a mixture of gravity and waggery.

For he knows that God is his Savior.

For there is nothing sweeter than his peace when at rest.

For there is nothing brisker than his life when in motion.   45
For he is of the Lord's poor, and so indeed is he called by benevolence
     perpetually—Poor Jeoffry! poor Jeoffry! the rat has bit thy throat.
For I bless the name of the Lord Jesus that Jeoffry is better.
For the divine spirit comes about his body to sustain it in complete cat.
For his tongue is exceeding pure so that it has in purity what it wants in
     music.
For he is docile and can learn certain things.   50
For he can sit up with gravity which is patience upon approbation.
For he can fetch and carry, which is patience in employment.
For he can jump over a stick which is patience upon proof positive.
For he can spraggle upon waggle at the word of command.
For he can jump from an eminence into his master's bosom.   55
For he can catch the cork and toss it again.
For he is hated by the hypocrite and miser.
For the former is afraid of detection.
For the latter refuses the charge.
For he camels his back to bear the first notion of business.   60
For he is good to think on, if a man would express himself neatly.
For he made a great figure in Egypt for his signal services.
For he killed the Icneumon-rat, very pernicious by land.
For his ears are so acute that they sting again.
For from this proceeds the passing quickness of his attention.   65
For by stroking of him I have found out electricity.
For I perceived God's light about him both wax and fire.
For the electrical fire is the spiritual substance which God sends from
     heaven to sustain the bodies both of man and beast.
For God has blessed him in the variety of his movements.
For, though he cannot fly, he is an excellent clamberer.   70
For his motions upon the face of the earth are more than any other quad-
     ruped.
For he can tread to all the measures upon the music.
For he can swim for life.
For he can creep.

FOR I WILL CONSIDER MY CAT JEOFFRY. This is a self-contained extract from Smart's long poem *Jubilate Agno* ("Rejoice in the Lamb"), written during his confinement for insanity. 35. *For the Lord commanded Moses concerning the cats:* No such command is mentioned in Scripture. 54. *spraggle upon waggle:* W. F. Stead, in his edition of Smart's poem, suggests that this means Jeoffry will sprawl when his master waggles a finger or a stick. 59. *the charge:* perhaps the cost of feeding a cat.

William Jay Smith (b. 1918)

AMERICAN PRIMITIVE   1953

Look at him there in his stovepipe hat,
His high-top shoes, and his handsome collar;
Only my Daddy could look like that,
And I love my Daddy like he loves his Dollar.

The screen door bangs, and it sounds so funny —   5
There he is in a shower of gold;
His pockets are stuffed with folding money,
His lips are blue, and his hands feel cold.

He hangs in the hall by his black cravat,
The ladies faint, and the children holler: 10
Only my Daddy could look like that,
And I love my Daddy like he loves his Dollar.

COMPARE:

"American Primitive" with "Daddy" by Sylvia Plath (page 784).

W. D. Snodgrass (b. 1926)
THE OPERATION   1959

From stainless steel basins of water
They brought warm cloths and they washed me,
From spun aluminum bowls, cold Zephiran sponges, fuming;
Gripped in the dead yellow glove, a bright straight razor
Inched on my stomach, down my groin,   5
Paring the brown hair off. They left me
White as a child, not frightened. I was not
Ashamed. They clothed me, then,
In the thin, loose, light, white garments,
The delicate sandals of poor Pierrot,   10
A schoolgirl first offering her sacrament.

I was drifting, inexorably, on toward sleep.
In skullcaps, masked, in blue-green gowns, attendants
Towed my cart, afloat in its white cloths,
The body with its tributary poisons borne   15
Down corridors of the diseased, thronging:
The scrofulous faces, contagious grim boys,
The huddled families, weeping, a staring woman
Arched to her gnarled stick, — a child was somewhere
Screaming, screaming — then, blind silence, the elevator rising 20
To the arena, humming, vast with lights; blank hero,
Shackled and spellbound, to enact my deed.

Into flowers, into women, I have awakened.
Too weak to think of strength, I have thought all day,
Or dozed among standing friends. I lie in night, now,   25
A small mound under linen like the drifted snow.
Only by nurses visited, in radiance, saying, Rest.
Opposite, ranked office windows glare; headlamps, below,
Trace out our highways; their cargoes under dark tarpaulins,

Trucks climb, thundering, and sirens may   30
Wail for the fugitive. It is very still. In my brandy bowl
Of sweet peas at the window, the crystal world
Is inverted, slow and gay.

THE OPERATION. 3. *Zephiran:* like Zephirus, Greek personification of the west wind:
gentle, cool and soothing. Also the name of an antiseptic used in hospitals. 10. *Pierrot:*
traditional clown in French pantomime, white-faced, wearing loose pantaloons.

Gary Snyder (b. 1930)

MILTON BY FIRELIGHT   1959

Piute Creek, August 1955

"O hell, what do mine eyes
   with grief behold?"
Working with an old
Singlejack miner, who can sense
The vein and cleavage   5
In the very guts of rock, can
Blast granite, build
Switchbacks that last for years
Under the beat of snow, thaw, mule-hooves.
What use, Milton, a silly story   10
Of our lost general parents,
    eaters of fruit?

The Indian, the chainsaw boy,
And a string of six mules
Came riding down to camp   15
Hungry for tomatoes and green apples.
Sleeping in saddle-blankets
Under a bright night-sky
Han River slantwise by morning.
Jays squall   20
Coffee boils

In ten thousand years the Sierras
Will be dry and dead, home of the scorpion.
Ice-scratched slabs and bent trees.
No paradise, no fall,   25
Only the weathering land
The wheeling sky,
Man, with his Satan
Scouring the chaos of the mind.
Oh Hell!   30

Fire down
Too dark to read, miles from a road
The bell-mare clangs in the meadow

That packed dirt for a fill-in
Scrambling through loose rocks
On an old trail
All of a summer's day.

MILTON BY FIRELIGHT. 1–2. *"O hell, what do mine eyes with grief behold?"* Satan's envious words as he looks upon Adam and Eve in the Garden of Eden (Book IV, line 358 in Milton's *Paradise Lost*).

William Stafford (b. 1914)
AT THE KLAMATH BERRY FESTIVAL
1966

The war chief danced the old way —
the eagle wing he held before his mouth —
and when he turned the boom-boom
stopped. He took two steps. A sociologist
was there; the Scout troop danced.
I envied him the places where he had not been.

The boom began again. Outside he heard
the stick game, and the Blackfoot gamblers
arguing at poker under lanterns.
Still-moccasined and bashful, holding
the eagle wing before his mouth,
listening and listening, he danced after others stopped.

He took two steps, the boom caught up,
the mountains rose, the still deep river
slid but never broke its quiet.
I looked back when I left:
he took two steps, he took two steps,
past the sociologist.

AT THE KLAMATH BERRY FESTIVAL. The Klamath Indians have a reservation at the base of the Cascade Range in southern Oregon.

William Stafford (b. 1914)
WRITTEN ON THE STUB OF THE FIRST PAYCHECK
1966

Gasoline makes game scarce.
In Elko, Nevada, I remember a stuffed wildcat
someone had shot on Bing Crosby's ranch.
I stood in the filling station
breathing fumes and reading the snarl of a map.

There were peaks to the left so high
they almost got away in the heat;

Reno and Las Vegas were ahead.
I had promise of the California job,
and three kids with me.   10

It takes a lot of miles to equal one wildcat
today. We moved into a housing tract.
Every dodging animal carries my hope in Nevada.
It has been a long day, Bing.
Wherever I go is your ranch.   15

Wallace Stevens (1879–1955)

PETER QUINCE AT THE CLAVIER   1923

I

Just as my fingers on these keys
Make music, so the selfsame sounds
On my spirit make a music, too.

Music is feeling, then, not sound;
And thus it is that what I feel,   5
Here in this room, desiring you,

Thinking of your blue-shadowed silk,
Is music. It is like the strain
Waked in the elders by Susanna.

Of a green evening, clear and warm,   10
She bathed in her still garden, while
The red-eyed elders watching, felt

The basses of their beings throb
In witching chords, and their thin blood
Pulse pizzicati of Hosanna.   15

II

In the green water, clear and warm,
Susanna lay.
She searched
The touch of springs,
And found   20
Concealed imaginings.
She sighed,
For so much melody.

Upon the bank, she stood
In the cool   25
Of spent emotions.
She felt, among the leaves,
The dew
Of old devotions.

She walked upon the grass,
Still quavering.
The winds were like her maids,
On timid feet,
Fetching her woven scarves,
Yet wavering.

30

35

A breath upon her hand
Muted the night.
She turned—
A cymbal crashed,
And roaring horns.

40

III

Soon, with a noise like tambourines,
Came her attendant Byzantines.

They wondered why Susanna cried
Against the elders by her side;

And as they whispered, the refrain
Was like a willow swept by rain.

45

Anon, their lamps' uplifted flame
Revealed Susanna and her shame.

And then, the simpering Byzantines
Fled, with a noise like tambourines.

50

IV

Beauty is momentary in the mind—
The fitful tracing of a portal;
But in the flesh it is immortal.

The body dies; the body's beauty lives.
So evenings die, in their green going,
A wave, interminably flowing.
So gardens die, their meek breath scenting
The cowl of winter, done repenting.
So maidens die, to the auroral
Celebration of a maiden's choral.

55

60

Susanna's music touched the bawdy strings
Of those white elders; but, escaping,
Left only Death's ironic scraping.
Now, in its immortality, it plays
On the clear viol of her memory,
And makes a constant sacrament of praise.

65

PETER QUINCE AT THE CLAVIER. In Shakespeare's *Midsummer Night's Dream*, Peter Quince is a clownish carpenter who stages a mock-tragic play. In The Book of Susanna in the Apocrypha, two lustful elders who covet Susanna, a virtuous married woman, hide in her garden, spy on her as she bathes, then threaten to make false accusations against her unless she submits to them. When she refuses, they cry out, and her servants come running. All ends well when the prophet Daniel cross-examines the elders and proves them liars. 15. *pizzicati:* thin notes made by plucking a stringed instrument. 42. *Byzantines:* Susanna's maidservants.

Mark Strand (b. 1934)

EATING POETRY 1968

Ink runs from the corners of my mouth.
There is no happiness like mine.
I have been eating poetry.

The librarian does not believe what she sees.
Her eyes are sad 5
and she walks with her hands in her dress.

The poems are gone.
The light is dim.
The dogs are on the basement steps and coming up.

Their eyeballs roll, 10
their blond legs burn like brush.
The poor librarian begins to stamp her feet and weep.

She does not understand.
When I get on my knees and lick her hand,
she screams. 15

I am a new man.
I snarl at her and bark.
I romp with joy in the bookish dark.

James Tate (b. 1943)

FLIGHT 1967

For K.

Like a glum cricket
the refrigerator is singing
and just as I am convinced

that it is the only noise
in the building, a pot falls 5
in 2 B. The neighbors on

both sides of me suddenly
realize that they have not
made love to their wives

since 1947. The racket 10
multiplies. The man downhall
is teaching his dog to fly.

The fish are disgusted
and beat their heads blue
against a cold aquarium. I too   15

lose control and consider
the dust huddled in the corner
a threat to my endurance.

Were you here, we would not
tolerate mongrels in the air,   20
nor the conspiracies of dust.

We would drive all night,
your head tilted on my shoulder.
At dawn, I would nudge you

with my anxious fingers and say,   25
Already we are in Idaho.

Alfred, Lord Tennyson (1809–1892)
DARK HOUSE, BY WHICH ONCE MORE I STAND   1850

Dark house, by which once more I stand
  Here in the long unlovely street,
  Doors, where my heart was used to beat
So quickly, waiting for a hand,

A hand that can be clasped no more —   5
  Behold me, for I cannot sleep,
  And like a guilty thing I creep
At earliest morning to the door.

He is not here; but far away
  The noise of life begins again,   10
  And ghastly through the drizzling rain
On the bald street breaks the blank day.

DARK HOUSE. This poem is one part of the series *In Memoriam*, an elegy for Tennyson's
friend Arthur Henry Hallam.

Alfred, Lord Tennyson (1809–1892)
ULYSSES   (1833)

It little profits that an idle king,
By this still hearth, among these barren crags,
Matched with an agèd wife, I mete and dole
Unequal laws unto a savage race
That hoard, and sleep, and feed, and know not me.   5
I cannot rest from travel; I will drink
Life to the lees. All times I have enjoyed

Greatly, have suffered greatly, both with those
That loved me, and alone; on shore, and when
Through scudding drifts the rainy Hyades
Vexed the dim sea. I am become a name;
For always roaming with a hungry heart
Much have I seen and known—cities of men
And manners, climates, councils, governments,
Myself not least, but honored of them all—
And drunk delight of battle with my peers,
Far on the ringing plains of windy Troy.
I am a part of all that I have met;
Yet all experience is an arch wherethrough
Gleams that untraveled world whose margin fades
Forever and forever when I move.
How dull it is to pause, to make an end,
To rust unburnished, not to shine in use!
As though to breathe were life! Life piled on life
Were all too little, and of one to me
Little remains; but every hour is saved
From that eternal silence, something more,
A bringer of new things; and vile it were
For some three suns to store and hoard myself,
And this grey spirit yearning in desire
To follow knowledge like a sinking star,
Beyond the utmost bound of human thought.
    This is my son, mine own Telemachus,
To whom I leave the scepter and the isle—
Well-loved of me, discerning to fulfill
This labor, by slow prudence to make mild
A rugged people, and through soft degrees
Subdue them to the useful and the good.
Most blameless is he, centered in the sphere
Of common duties, decent not to fail
In offices of tenderness, and pay
Meet adoration to my household gods,
When I am gone. He works his work, I mine.
    There lies the port; the vessel puffs her sail;
There gloom the dark, broad seas. My mariners,
Souls that have toiled, and wrought, and thought with me—
That ever with a frolic welcome took
The thunder and the sunshine, and opposed
Free hearts, free foreheads—you and I are old;
Old age hath yet his honor and his toil.
Death closes all; but something ere the end,
Some work of noble note, may yet be done,
Not unbecoming men that strove with Gods.
The lights begin to twinkle from the rocks;
The long day wanes; the low moon climbs; the deep
Moans round with many voices. Come, my friends,
'Tis not too late to seek a newer world.

Push off, and sitting well in order smite
The sounding furrows; for my purpose holds
To sail beyond the sunset, and the baths   60
Of all the western stars, until I die.
It may be that the gulfs will wash us down;
It may be we shall touch the Happy Isles,
And see the great Achilles, whom we knew.
Though much is taken, much abides; and though   65
We are not now that strength which in old days
Moved earth and heaven, that which we are, we are—
One equal temper of heroic hearts,
Made weak by time and fate, but strong in will
To strive, to seek, to find, and not to yield.   70

ULYSSES. 10. *Hyades:* daughters of Atlas, who were transformed into a group of stars. Their
rising with the sun was thought to be a sign of rain. 63. *Happy Isles:* Elysium, a paradise
believed to be attainable by sailing west.

Dylan Thomas (1914–1953)

FERN HILL   1946

Now as I was young and easy under the apple boughs
About the lilting house and happy as the grass was green,
        The night above the dingle° starry,   *wooded valley*
            Time let me hail and climb
        Golden in the heydays of his eyes,   5
And honored among wagons I was prince of the apple towns
And once below a time I lordly had the trees and leaves
            Trail with daisies and barley
        Down the rivers of the windfall light.

And as I was green and carefree, famous among the barns   10
About the happy yard and singing as the farm was home,
        In the sun that is young once only,
            Time let me play and be
        Golden in the mercy of his means,
And green and golden I was huntsman and herdsman, the calves   15
Sang to my horn, the foxes on the hills barked clear and cold,
            And the sabbath rang slowly
        In the pebbles of the holy streams.

All the sun long it was running, it was lovely, the hay
Fields high as the house, the tunes from the chimneys, it was air   20
        And playing, lovely and watery
            And fire green as grass.
        And nightly under the simple stars
As I rode to sleep the owls were bearing the farm away,
All the moon long I heard, blessed among stables, the nightjars   25
        Flying with the ricks, and the horses
            Flashing into the dark.

And then to awake, and the farm, like a wanderer white
With the dew, come back, the cock on his shoulder: it was all
       Shining, it was Adam and maiden, 30
          The sky gathered again
       And the sun grew round that very day.
So it must have been after the birth of the simple light
In the first, spinning place, the spellbound horses walking warm
       Out of the whinnying green stable 35
          On to the fields of praise.

And honored among foxes and pheasants by the gay house
Under the new made clouds and happy as the heart was long,
       In the sun born over and over,
          I ran my heedless ways, 40
       My wishes raced through the house high hay
And nothing I cared, at my sky blue trades, that time allows
In all his tuneful turning so few and such morning songs
       Before the children green and golden
          Follow him out of grace, 45

Nothing I cared, in the lamb white days, that time would take me
Up to the swallow thronged loft by the shadow of my hand,
       In the moon that is always rising,
          Nor that riding to sleep
       I should hear him fly with the high fields 50
And wake to the farm forever fled from the childless land.
Oh as I was young and easy in the mercy of his means,
       Time held me green and dying
       Though I sang in my chains like the sea.

Dylan Thomas (1914–1953)

TWENTY-FOUR YEARS 1939

Twenty-four years remind the tears of my eyes.
(Bury the dead for fear that they walk to the grave in labor.)
In the groin of the natural doorway I crouched like a tailor
Sewing a shroud for a journey
By the light of the meat-eating sun.
Dressed to die, the sensual strut begun,
With my red veins full of money,
In the final direction of the elementary town
I advance for as long as forever is.

Rosmarie Waldrop (b. 1935)

CONFESSION TO SETTLE A CURSE 1972

You don't
know
who I am
because
you don't know   5
my mother
she's always been an exemplary mother
told me so herself
there were reasons she
had to lock   10
everything that could be locked
there's much can be
locked
in a good German household crowded
with wardrobes dressers sideboards   15
bookcases cupboards chests bureaus
desks trunks caskets coffers all with lock
and key
and locked
it was lots of trouble   20
for her
just carry that enormous key ring
be bothered all the time
I wanted scissors stationery
my winter coat and she had to unlock   25
the drawer get it out and lock
all up again
me she reproached for lacking
confidence not being open
I have a mother I can tell everything   30
she told me so
I've
been bound
made fast
locked   35
by the key witch
but a small
winner
I'm not
in turn locking   40
a child
in my arms.

COMPARE:

"Confession to Settle a Curse" with "Daddy" by Sylvia Plath (page 784).

Walt Whitman (1819–1892)
I Saw in Louisiana a Live-Oak Growing   1867

I saw in Louisiana a live-oak growing,
All alone stood it and the moss hung down from the branches,
Without any companion it grew there uttering joyous leaves of dark
   green,
And its look, rude, unbending, lusty, made me think of myself,
But I wonder'd how it could utter joyous leaves standing alone there
   without its friend near, for I knew I could not,   5
And I broke off a twig with a certain number of leaves upon it, and twined
   around it a little moss,
And brought it away, and I have placed it in sight in my room,
It is not needed to remind me as of my own dear friends,
(For I believe lately I think of little else than of them,)
Yet it remains to me a curious token, it makes me think of manly love;   10
For all that, and though the live-oak glistens there in Louisiana solitary in
   a wide flat space,
Uttering joyous leaves all its life without a friend a lover near,
I know very well I could not.

Walt Whitman (1819–1892)
When I Heard the Learn'd Astronomer   1865

When I heard the learn'd astronomer,
When the proofs, the figures, were ranged in columns before me,
When I was shown the charts and diagrams, to add, divide, and measure
   them
When I sitting heard the astronomer where he lectured with much
   applause in the lecture-room,
How soon unaccountable I became tired and sick,
Till rising and gliding out I wander'd off by myself,
In the mystical moist night-air, and from time to time,
Look'd up in perfect silence at the stars.

Richard Wilbur (b. 1921)
Junk   1961

Huru Welandes
                    worc ne geswiceð
monna ænigum
                    ðara ðe Mimming can
heardne gehealdan.
                    Waldere

An axe angles
                    from my neighbor's ashcan;
It is hell's handiwork,
                    the wood not hickory,
The flow of the grain
                    not faithfully followed.
The shivered shaft
                    rises from a shellheap
Of plastic playthings,
                    paper plates,   5
And the sheer shards
                    of shattered tumblers
That were not annealed
                    for the time needful.
At the same curbside,
                    a cast-off cabinet
Of wavily-warped
                    unseasoned wood
Waits to be trundled
                    in the trash-man's truck.   10
Haul them off! Hide them!
                         The heart winces
For junk and gimcrack,
                    for jerrybuilt things
And the men who make them
                         for a little money,
Bartering pride
               like the bought boxer
Who pulls his punches,
                    or the paid-off jockey   15
Who in the home stretch
                    holds in his horse.
Yet the things themselves
                    in thoughtless honor
Have kept composure,
                    like captives who would not
Talk under torture.
                    Tossed from a tailgate
Where the dump displays
                    its random dolmens°,   *prehistoric* 20
Its black barrows   *gravestones*
                    and blazing valleys,
They shall waste in the weather
                    toward what they were.
The sun shall glory
                    in the glitter of glass-chips,
Foreseeing the salvage
                    of the prisoned sand,
And the blistering paint
                    peel off in patches,   25

That the good grain
                    be discovered again.
Then burnt, bulldozed,
                    they shall all be buried
To the depths of diamonds,
                    in the making dark
Where halt Hephaestus
                    keeps his hammer
And Wayland's work
                    is worn away.   30

JUNK. Richard Wilbur notes: "The epigraph, taken from a fragmentary Anglo-Saxon poem, concerns the legendary smith Wayland, and may roughly be translated: 'Truly, Wayland's handiwork—the sword Mimming which he made—will never fail any man who knows how to use it bravely.'" 29. *Hephaestus:* another smith and artisan, the Greek god of fire, said to have forged armor for Achilles.

COMPARE:

"Junk" with "The Seafarer" by Ezra Pound (page 790).

William Carlos Williams (1883–1963)
SPRING AND ALL   1923

By the road to the contagious hospital
under the surge of the blue
mottled clouds driven from the
northeast—a cold wind. Beyond, the
waste of broad, muddy fields   5
brown with dried weeds, standing and fallen

patches of standing water
the scattering of tall trees

All along the road the reddish
purplish, forked, upstanding, twiggy   10
stuff of bushes and small trees
with dead, brown leaves under them
leafless vines—

Lifeless in appearance, sluggish
dazed spring approaches—   15

They enter the new world naked,
cold, uncertain of all
save that they enter. All about them
the cold, familiar wind—

Now the grass, tomorrow   20
the stiff curl of wildcarrot leaf

One by one objects are defined —
It quickens: clarity, outline of leaf

But now the stark dignity of
entrance — Still, the profound change   25
has come upon them: rooted, they
grip down and begin to awaken

COMPARE:

"Spring and All" with "in Just-" by E. E. Cummings (page 594) and "Root
Cellar" by Theodore Roethke (page 467).

William Carlos Williams (1883–1963)
TO WAKEN AN OLD LADY   1921

Old age is
a flight of small
cheeping birds
skimming
bare trees   5
above a snow glaze.
Gaining and failing
they are buffeted
by a dark wind —
But what?   10
On harsh weedstalks
the flock has rested,
the snow
is covered with broken
seedhusks   15
and the wind tempered
by a shrill
piping of plenty.

COMPARE:

"To Waken an Old Lady" with "Castoff Skin" by Ruth Whitman (page 494).

Yvor Winters (1900–1968)
AT THE SAN FRANCISCO AIRPORT   1952

To My Daughter, 1954

This is the terminal: the light
Gives perfect vision, false and hard;
The metal glitters, deep and bright.

Great planes are waiting in the yard—
They are already in the night.   5

And you are here beside me, small,
Contained and fragile, and intent
On things that I but half recall—
Yet going whither you are bent.
I am the past, and that is all.   10

But you and I in part are one:
The frightened brain, the nervous will,
The knowledge of what must be done,
The passion to acquire the skill
To face that which you dare not shun.   15

The rain of matter upon sense
Destroys me momently. The score:
There comes what will come. The expense
Is what one thought, and something more—
One's being and intelligence.   20

This is the terminal, the break.
Beyond this point, on lines of air,
You take the way that you must take;
And I remain in light and stare—
In light, and nothing else, awake.   25

William Wordsworth (1770–1850)

COMPOSED UPON WESTMINSTER BRIDGE   1807

Earth has not anything to show more fair:
Dull would he be of soul who could pass by
A sight so touching in its majesty:
This City now doth, like a garment, wear
The beauty of the morning; silent, bare,   5
Ships, towers, domes, theatres, and temples lie
Open unto the fields, and to the sky;
All bright and glittering in the smokeless air.
Never did sun more beautifully steep
In his first splendor, valley, rock, or hill;   10
Ne'er saw I, never felt, a calm so deep!
The river glideth at his own sweet will:
Dear God! the very houses seem asleep;
And all that mighty heart is lying still!

William Wordsworth (1770–1850)

Stepping Westward

1807

While my Fellow-traveler and I were walking by the side of Lock° Ket- *Lake*
terine, one fine evening after sunset, in our road to a hut where, in the
course of our tour, we had been hospitably entertained some weeks before,
we met, in one of the loneliest parts of that solitary region, two well-
dressed women, one of whom said to us, by way of greeting, "What, are
you stepping westward?"

"What, are you stepping westward?" — "Yea."
—'Twould be a *wildish* destiny,
If we, who thus together roam
In a strange land, and far from home,
Were in this place the guests of Chance;   5
Yet who would stop, or fear to advance,
Though home or shelter he had none,
With such a sky to lead him on?

The dewy ground was dark and cold;
Behind, all gloomy to behold;   10
And stepping westward seemed to be
A kind of *heavenly* destiny:
I liked the greeting; 'twas a sound
Of something without place or bound
And seemed to give me spiritual right   15
To travel through that region bright.

The voice was soft, and she who spake
Was walking by her native lake;
The salutation had to me
The very sound of courtesy: 20
Its power was felt; and while my eye
Was fixed upon the glowing sky,
The echo of the voice enwrought
A human sweetness with the thought
Of traveling through the world that lay   25
Before me in my endless way.

Stepping Westward. Wordsworth's "Fellow-traveler" was his sister Dorothy, with
whom in 1803 he made a tour of the Highlands of Scotland.

James Wright (b. 1927)

A Blessing

1961

Just off the highway to Rochester, Minnesota,
Twilight bounds softly forth on the grass.
And the eyes of those two Indian ponies
Darken with kindness.

They have come gladly out of the willows 5
To welcome my friend and me.
We step over the barbed wire into the pasture
Where they have been grazing all day, alone.
They ripple tensely, they can hardly contain their happiness
That we have come. 10
They bow shyly as wet swans. They love each other.
There is no loneliness like theirs.
At home once more,
They begin munching the young tufts of spring in the darkness.
I would like to hold the slenderer one in my arms, 15
For she has walked over to me
And nuzzled my left hand.
She is black and white,
Her mane falls wild on her forehead,
And the light breeze moves me to caress her long ear 20
That is delicate as the skin over a girl's wrist.
Suddenly I realize
That if I stepped out of my body I would break
Into blossom.

James Wright (b. 1927)
AUTUMN BEGINS IN MARTINS FERRY, OHIO 1963

In the Shreve High football stadium,
I think of Polacks nursing long beers in Tiltonsville,
And gray faces of Negroes in the blast furnace at Benwood,
And the ruptured night watchman of Wheeling Steel,
Dreaming of heroes. 5

All the proud fathers are ashamed to go home.
Their women cluck like starved pullets,
Dying for love.

Therefore,
Their sons grow suicidally beautiful 10
At the beginning of October,
And gallop terribly against each other's bodies.

Judith Wright (b. 1915)
WOMAN TO MAN 1971

The eyeless laborer in the night,
the selfless, shapeless seed I hold,
builds for its resurrection day —
silent and swift and deep from sight
foresees the unimagined light. 5

This is no child with a child's face;
this has no name to name it by;
yet you and I have known it well.
This is our hunter and our chase,
the third who lay in our embrace.   10

This is the strength that your arm knows,
the arc of flesh that is my breast,
the precise crystals of our eyes.
This is the blood's wild tree that grows
the intricate and folded rose.   15

This is the maker and the made;
this is the question and reply;
the blind head butting at the dark,
the blaze of light along the blade.
Oh hold me, for I am afraid.   20

Judith Wright (b. 1915)

WOMAN TO CHILD   1971

You who were darkness warmed my flesh
where out of darkness rose the seed.
Then all a world I made in me:
all the world you hear and see
hung upon my dreaming blood.   5

There moved the multitudinous stars,
and colored birds and fishes moved.
There swam the sliding continents.
All time lay rolled in me, and sense,
and love that knew not its beloved.   10

O node and focus of the world—
I hold you deep within that well
you shall escape and not escape—
that mirrors still your sleeping shape,
that nurtures still your crescent cell.   15

I wither and you break from me;
yet though you dance in living light,
I am the earth, I am the root,
I am the stem that fed the fruit,
the link that joins you to the night.   20

COMPARE:

"Woman to Child" with "Metaphors" (page 492) and "Morning Song" (page 786) by Sylvia Plath.

William Butler Yeats (1865–1939)

CRAZY JANE TALKS WITH THE BISHOP

1933

I met the Bishop on the road
And much said he and I.
"Those breasts are flat and fallen now,
Those veins must soon be dry;
Live in a heavenly mansion,   5
Not in some foul sty.

"Fair and foul are near of kin,
And fair needs foul," I cried.
"My friends are gone, but that's a truth
Nor° grave nor bed denied,   neither   10
Learned in bodily lowliness
And in the heart's pride.

"A woman can be proud and stiff
When on love intent;
But Love has pitched his mansion in   15
The place of excrement;
For nothing can be sole or whole
That has not been rent."

William Butler Yeats (1865–1939)

THE LAKE ISLE OF INNISFREE

1892

I will arise and go now, and go to Innisfree,
And a small cabin build there, of clay and wattles made:
Nine bean-rows will I have there, a hive for the honey-bee,
And live alone in the bee-loud glade.

And I shall have some peace there, for peace comes dropping slow,   5
Dropping from the veils of the morning to where the cricket sings;
There midnight's all a glimmer, and noon a purple glow,
And evening full of the linnet's wings.

I will arise and go now, for always night and day
I hear lake water lapping with low sounds by the shore;   10
While I stand on the roadway, or on the pavements grey,
I hear it in the deep heart's core.

THE LAKE ISLE OF INNISFREE. Yeats refers to an island in Lough (Lake) Gill, in County Sligo
in the west of Ireland. 2. *wattles:* frameworks of interwoven sticks or branches, used to
make walls and roofs.

COMPARE:

"The Lake Isle of Innisfree" with Yeats's "Sailing to Byzantium" (page 660).

William Butler Yeats (1865–1939)

LAPIS LAZULI

1938

For Harry Clifton

I have heard that hysterical women say
They are sick of the palette and fiddle-bow,
Of poets that are always gay,
For everybody knows or else should know
That if nothing drastic is done   5
Aeroplane and Zeppelin will come out,
Pitch like King Billy bomb-balls in
Until the town lie beaten flat.

All perform their tragic play,
There struts Hamlet, there is Lear,   10
That's Ophelia, that Cordelia;
Yet they, should the last scene be there,
The great stage curtain about to drop,
If worthy their prominent part in the play,
Do not break up their lines to weep.   15
They know that Hamlet and Lear are gay;
Gaiety transfiguring all that dread.
All men have aimed at, found and lost;
Black out; Heaven blazing into the head:
Tragedy wrought to its uttermost.   20
Though Hamlet rambles and Lear rages,
And all the drop-scenes drop at once
Upon a hundred thousand stages,
It cannot grow by an inch or an ounce.

On their own feet they came, or on shipboard,   25
Camel-back, horse-back, ass-back, mule-back,
Old civilizations put to the sword.
Then they and their wisdom went to rack:
No handiwork of Callimachus,
Who handled marble as if it were bronze,   30
Made draperies that seemed to rise
When sea-wind swept the corner, stands;
His long lamp-chimney shaped like the stem
Of a slender palm, stood but a day;
All things fall and are built again,   35
And those that build them again are gay.

Two Chinamen, behind them a third,
Are carved in lapis lazuli,
Over them flies a long-legged bird,
A symbol of longevity;   40
The third, doubtless a serving-man,
Carries a musical instrument.

Every discoloration of the stone,
Every accidental crack or dent,
Seems a water-course or an avalanche,   45
Or lofty slope where it still snows
Though doubtless plum or cherry-branch
Sweetens the little half-way house
Those Chinamen climb towards, and I
Delight to imagine them seated there;   50
There, on the mountain and the sky,
On all the tragic scene they stare.
One asks for mournful melodies;
Accomplished fingers begin to play.
Their eyes mid many wrinkles, their eyes,   55
Their ancient, glittering eyes, are gay.

LAPIS LAZULI. Lapis lazuli is a deep blue semiprecious stone. A friend had given Yeats the carving made from it, which he describes in lines 37-56. 7. *King Billy:* William of Orange, king of England who used cannon against the Irish in the Battle of the Boyne, 1690. Yeats also may have in mind Kaiser Wilhelm II of Germany, who sent zeppelins to bomb London in World War I. 29. *Callimachus:* Athenian sculptor, fifth century B.C.

COMPARE:

"Lapis Lazuli" with "Ode on a Grecian Urn" by John Keats (page 769) and "Anecdote of the Jar" by Wallace Stevens (page 617).

William Butler Yeats (1865–1939)
THE MAGI   1914

Now as at all times I can see in the mind's eye,
In their stiff, painted clothes, the pale unsatisfied ones
Appear and disappear in the blue depth of the sky
With all their ancient faces like rain-beaten stones,
And all their helms of silver hovering side by side,
And all their eyes still fixed, hoping to find once more,
Being by Calvary's turbulence unsatisfied,
The uncontrollable mystery on the bestial floor.

COMPARE:

"The Magi" with "Journey of the Magi" by T. S. Eliot (page 745).

DRAMA

Most plays, those literary works to which we give the collective name **drama,** are written not to be read in schoolbooks but to be performed. Finding plays in a literature anthology, the student may well ask, isn't there something wrong with the idea of reading plays on the printed page? To do so — to treat them as literature — isn't that a perversion of their nature?

True, plays are meant to be seen on stage, but equally true, reading a play may afford certain advantages. One advantage is that it is better to know some masterpieces by reading them than never to know them at all. Even if you live in a large city with many theaters, even if you attend a college where there are many theatrical productions, to succeed in your lifetime in witnessing, say, all the plays of Shakespeare might well be impossible. In print, they are as near-to-hand as a book on a shelf, ready to be enacted (if you like) on the stage of the mind.

After all, a play is literature before it exists in a theater; and it might be argued that when we read an unfamiliar play, we meet it in the same basic form in which it first appears to its actors and its director. If a play is rich and complex, or if it dates from the remote past and contains difficulties of language and allusion, to read it on the page enables us to study it at our leisure, to return to those parts that demand greater scrutiny. Some playwrights pay special heed to the silent reader. George Bernard Shaw and Edward Albee are among the modern playwrights who have sometimes prefaced their plays with remarks aimed only at the reading public, while Shaw occasionally rounded out his remarks with an epilogue besides. Shaw was fond of nuances lost upon the mere spectator. In *Pygmalion,* for instance, occurs this stage direction: *"He goes to the central window, through which, with his back to the company, he contemplates the river and the flowers in Battersea Park on the opposite bank as if they were a frozen desert."* The "frozen desert," of course, cannot appear on stage, while to display the flowers of Battersea Park would surpass a set designer's ingenuity.

Sometimes, reading a play in print is our only means of knowing it in its entirety. Producers, far from regarding Shakespeare's words as holy writ, sometimes omit speeches or shorten them. Every actor who undertakes the role of Iago in *Othello* finds it necessary to make his own interpretation of the character. Some regard Iago as a figure of pure evil; others, as a madman; still others, as a human being consumed by hatred, jealousy, and pride. And the director of a production of *Othello* has to make certain decisions — shall Othello dress as a Moor, or as a jet-set contemporary? Every stage version of the play is an interpretation; and so, after all, is each reader's silent reading of it. Read a play alertly and appreciatively, pausing sometimes to reflect — and to imagine. Then, perhaps, the play will come alive — and so will your interpretation.

31 What Is Drama?

THE PLAY AS PERFORMANCE

Unlike a short story or a novel, a **play** is a work of storytelling in which the characters are represented by actors. A play differs from a work of fiction in another essential: a play is addressed not to a solitary reader (nor to many solitary readers) but to a group of people seated together in a theater. To belong to such an audience is an experience far different from the experience of reading a story in solitude. Seated in a theater, the stage lights on and the house lights dimmed, we become members of a community whose responses affect our own responses. We, too, contribute to the community's response whenever we catch our breaths in excitement, murmur in surprise, laugh, sigh, or applaud. In contrast, when we watch, by ourselves, a movie shown on television — for instance, a slapstick comedy — we probably are moved to laughter less often than we would be if we watched the same film in a movie theater, surrounded by an appreciative, roaring crowd. In a theater of live actors, still another rapport exists: a sensitive give-and-take between actors and audience. While a professional actor may aim for a top performance on all occasions, it is, nonetheless, natural for an actor to feel inspired in proportion to the responsiveness (perhaps also in proportion to the size) of the audience.

The performance of a play, however, is much more than an occasion for the exchange of emotions between performers and audience. A play is a work of art composed of words (like fiction and poetry), and the words, of course, remain essential. Someone (presumably the playwright) devoted thought to the selection and the arrangement of those words. Watching a play, of course, we do not notice a playwright standing between us and the characters.[1] If the play is excellent, it flows along before our eyes; we are not aware that it is the product of conscious art (how ever it may be). In a silent reading, the usual play

---

[1] The word *playwright*, by the way, invites misspelling: note that it is not *playwrite*. From the Old English, the suffix *-wright* means "one who makes" (as a *boatwright*), a worker in a particular trade.

consists mainly of **dialogue,** exchanges of speech, punctuated by stage directions.[2] In performance, however, stage directions disappear. And although the thoughtful efforts of perhaps a hundred people — actors, director, producer, stage designer, costumer, make-up artist, technicians — may have gone into a production, a successful play is likely to make us forget its artifice. Perhaps we may even forget that the play exists as literature: gestures, facial expressions, bodily stance, lighting, and special effects may seem as essential as the playwright's words. Even though the words are not all there is to the living play, they are the organized bones of it. And the whole play, the finished production, is the total of whatever transpires upon the stage.

The sense of immediacy we derive from drama is suggested by the root meaning of the word. *Drama* means "action" or "deed" (from the Greek *dran,* "to do"). We use *drama* as a synonym for *plays,* but the word has several meanings. Sometimes it refers to a single play ("a stirring drama"); or to the work of a playwright, or **dramatist** ("Ibsen's drama"); or perhaps to a body of plays written in a particular time or place ("Elizabethan drama," "French drama of the seventeenth century"). In yet another familiar sense, *drama* often means a series of events that elicit high excitement: "A real-life drama," a news story might begin, "was enacted today before lunchtime crowds in downtown Manhattan as firemen battled to free two children trapped on the sixteenth floor of a burning building." In this sense, whatever is "dramatic" implies suspense, tension, or conflict. Plays, as we shall see, frequently contain such "dramatic" chains of events; and yet, if we expect all plays to be crackling with suspense or conflict, we may be disappointed. Some plays, such as Harold Pinter's strange comedy *The Dumb Waiter,* create little suspense and involve little conflict. However, they may compel our attention: perhaps we watch them for no reason other than to satisfy our curiosity. "Good drama," said critic George Jean Nathan, "is anything that interests an intelligently emotional group of persons assembled together in an illuminated hall."

THE PLAY AS LITERATURE

It might be added that drama, in that it exists in written form and may be read, has an additional dimension: it is also literature. Like a novel or a short story, a play usually has a theme and usually introduces us to characters whose futures we care about. Like many a lyric poem, a

[2] Not all plays employ dialogue. Generally, **pantomime** refers to any play without words (sometimes also called a **dumb show),** but originally, in ancient Rome, a pantomime meant an actor who single-handedly played all the parts in a play. Such a modern master of pantomime is the French stage and screen actor Marcel Marceau. In England, pantomime is something else again: a musical comedy for children performed at Christmas time, based on a fairy tale, and usually featuring elaborate costumes and female impersonation.

play often will embody suggestive objects and landscapes that provoke emotional responses. Boundaries between drama and other literary forms cannot be drawn absolutely: a play may contain passages of poetry. Plays may be written, wholly or partly, in some poetic measure such as *blank verse*,[3] favored by Shakespeare for many of the speeches of his principal characters. Many poems employ devices we might expect to find in a play: in a *dramatic monologue* (Robert Browning's "My Last Duchess," Tennyson's "Ulysses") the whole poem is presented as if spoken by one character addressing another. Some dramatic poems resemble a stage **soliloquy,** a speech in which a solitary character voices his thoughts: for instance, Robert Browning's "Soliloquy of the Spanish Cloister" (page 727). A long poem called a **poetic drama** resembles a printed play: speeches are assigned to named characters and parts of the poem are sometimes divided into acts and scenes. John Milton's magnificent *Samson Agonistes* (published in 1671), one such poetic drama, was declaredly never intended for the stage.

A play destined to be read but not acted (whatever the intentions of its author) is sometimes called a **closet drama** — "closet" meaning a small, private room. The works of Keats, Wordsworth, Byron, Coleridge, Tennyson, and other nineteenth-century English Romantic poets abound in examples. Percy Bysshe Shelley's neo-Shakespearean tragedy *The Cenci* (1819) has seldom escaped from its closet, though Shelley himself tried without luck to have it performed at Covent Garden. Perhaps too rich in lengthy oratory to suit the stage, and too sparse in opportunities for actors to use their hands and feet, such works nevertheless may lead long, respectable lives of their own, solely as literature.

HOW TO READ A PLAY

Some readers, when silently reading a play to themselves, try to visualize a stage, imagining the characters in costume and under lights. If such a reader is an actor or a director and is reading the play with an eye to staging it, then that reader may try to imagine every detail of a possible production, even shades of makeup and loudness of sound effects. But the nonprofessional reader, who regards the play as literature, need not attempt such exhaustive imagining. While some readers find it enjoyable to imagine the play taking place upon a stage, others prefer to imagine the people and events that the play brings vividly to mind. Sympathetically following the tangled life of Nora in *A Doll House* by Henrik Ibsen, we forget that we are reading printed stage directions and instead find ourselves in the presence of human conflict. Regarded in this light, a play becomes a form of storytelling, and the playwright's instructions to the actors and the director become a con-

---

[3] See the discussion of *blank verse* on page 567.

ventional mode of narrative that we accept in much the way that we accept the methods of a novel or short story. In reading *A Doll House* with more concern for Nora's fate than for the imagined appearance of an actress portraying her, we speed through an ordinary passage such as this (from a scene when Nora's husband hears the approach of an unwanted caller, Dr. Rank):

> Helmer *(with quiet irritation):* Oh, what does he want now? *(Aloud.)* Hold on. *(Goes and opens the door.)* Oh, how nice that you didn't just pass us by!

We read the passage, if the story absorbs us, as though we were reading a novel whose author, employing the conventional devices for recording speech in fiction, might have written:

> "Oh, what does he want now?" said Helmer under his breath, in annoyance. Aloud, he called, "Hold on," then walked to the door and opened it and greeted Rank with all the cheer he could muster — "Oh, how nice that you didn't just pass us by!"

Such is the power of an excellent play to make us ignore the playwright's artistry that it becomes a window through which the reader's gaze, given focus, encompasses more than language and typography, and beholds a scene of imagined life.

Most plays, whether seen in a theater or in print, employ *some* **conventions:** customary methods of presenting an action, usual and recognizable devices that an audience is willing to accept. In reading a great play from the past, such as *Oedipus Rex* or *Hamlet,* it will help us to know some of the conventions of the classical Greek theater or the Elizabethan theater. When in *Oedipus Rex,* for instance, we encounter a character called the Choragos, it may be useful to be aware that he is not exactly a participant in the action, but a leader of the chorus who stands to one side of the action, conversing with the principal character and offering comment. Nor can we expect the theater of the ancient Greeks to confine itself to the literal representation of the routine lives of ordinary people in everyday situations. Classical Greek tragedy, according to Aristotle, its leading theorist, represents an "action of supreme importance," an extraordinary moment in the life of a king or queen or other person of high estate. So accustomed are we to realism (which may include the faithful reproduction of every teaspoon on a table), and to realistic methods of play production (familiar to us from the typical television situation comedy that takes place in an upper-middle-class livingroom, with one wall removed), that a nonrealistic playwright such as Sophocles or Tom Stoppard may place unexpected demands upon us. Still, to meet such demands may give deep pleasure.

Whether we read a play or see it in a theater, playwrights ask us to participate. One reason for the long survival of the plays of Sophocles and Shakespeare may be that generations of playgoers have enjoyed actively exerting their imaginations. Certain plays expect a great deal from the audience, who are not allowed merely to sit passively. In the classic Nō theater of Japan, spectators have to recognize certain familiar agreed-on properties and to fill in details: a simple framework stands for a boat; four posts and a roof indicate any building from a palace to a peasant's hut; an actor's fan serves as a paintbrush, or a knife. In such a nonrealistic theater, the playwright, unhampered by stage sets, can change his scene or his century as rapidly as the spectators can imagine.

In our century, new media such as television and the film have brought profound changes to dramatic production. Lately, too, there have been stirrings of changes in attitudes toward the nature of drama itself. A traditional definition of *drama* has been "an illusion of life"; recently, however, some experimental acting companies have tried bringing into their productions moments of life itself. In the guerilla street theaters, lately prominent in cities of the east and west coasts, actors have taken the theater outdoors and have performed in streets, in front of factories, and in shopping centers. Included in many of their plays have been accidental or impromptu actions; some plays have been entirely improvised, not foreordained by a written script.

Such efforts, usually designed to convey a political message, go back to ancient modes. To seek to confirm the beliefs of a people has been one of drama's oldest functions. In partaking of the nature of ritual — something to be repeated in front of an audience on a special occasion — drama is akin to a festival (whether a religious festival or a rock festival) or a church service. Twice in the history of Europe drama has sprung forth as a part of worship: when in ancient Greece, plays were performed on feast days; and when in the Christian church of the Middle Ages, a play was introduced as an adjunct to the Easter mass with the enactment of the meeting between the three Marys and the angel at Christ's empty tomb. Evidently something in the nature of drama remains constant over the years — something as old, perhaps, as the deepest desires and highest aspirations of mankind.

32 Elements of a Play

Watching a play in a theater, held captive as its plot unfolds, we do not ordinarily see it as a contrivance. We could notice (if we wanted to) that it is the aggregate of script, acting, direction, lighting, sets, costumes, makeup, properties, sound effects, and much more. But probably, if the play is a good one, we do not stop to analyze it but take it in as one simultaneous experience.

Similarly, when we read a play on the printed page and find ourselves swept forward with the motion of its story, we need not wonder how — and out of what ingredients — the playwright put it together. Still, to analyze the structure of a play is one way to understand and appreciate a playwright's art. Analysis is complicated, however, by the fact that in an excellent play, the elements (including plot, theme, and characters) do not exist in isolation. Often, deeds clearly follow from the kinds of people the characters are, and from those deeds it is left to the reader to infer the **theme** of the play — whatever general point or truth about human beings may be drawn from it. Perhaps the most meaningful way to study the elements of a play (and certainly the most enjoyable) is to consider a play in its entirety.

Here is a short play worth reading for the boldness of its elements — and for its own sake. Its author, Isabella Augusta Persse Gregory, was born of an English family in rural County Galway, Ireland. At the turn of the century, with the poet William Butler Yeats, she worked to establish an Irish national theater, with the aim of offering new plays on Irish themes. She helped to manage (and finance) this theater company, best known after its move to the Abbey Theatre in Dublin, for some twenty-five years. Lady Gregory's devotion to the cause of Irish drama led her to try her own hand at writing plays. She achieved a fine short tragedy, *The Gaol Gate;* a serious comedy, *The Rising of the Moon;* and some hilarious farces: *Hyacinth Halvey* and *Spreading the News.* But her comic masterpiece is undoubtedly *The Workhouse Ward.* In it, her keen ear for Irish country speech enabled her to draw to perfection a trio of memorable characters. As you will discover, the principals are talkative. Their colorful, image-laden blarney, part of the fun, tells us many things about them. *The Workhouse Ward* makes profound comedy out of some highly unlikely material. As the curtain rises, two old men, decrepit and bedridden, are lying in the hospital ward of a public workhouse. Now what could be less promising of any joy, or wisdom, or surprise?

Lady Gregory (1859–1932)

THE WORKHOUSE WARD

1908

Persons

Mike McInerney
Michael Miskell } paupers
Mrs. Donohoe, a countrywoman

Scene. *A ward in Cloon Workhouse. The two old men in their beds.*

Michael Miskell: Isn't it a hard case, Mike McInerney, myself and yourself to be left here in the bed, and it the feast day of Saint Colman, and the rest of the ward attending on the Mass.

Mike McInerney: Is it sitting up by the hearth you are wishful to be, Michael Miskell, with cold in the shoulders and with speckled shins? Let you rise up so, and you well able to do it, not like myself that has pains the same as tin-tacks within in my inside.

Michael Miskell: If you have pains within in your inside there is no one can see it or know of it the way they can see my own knees that are swelled up with the rheumatism, and my hands that are twisted in ridges the same as an old cabbage stalk. It is easy to be talking about soreness and about pains, and they maybe not to be in it at all.

Mike McInerney: To open me and to analyze me you would know what sort of a pain and a soreness I have in my heart and in my chest. But I'm not one like yourself to be cursing and praying and tormenting the time the nuns are at hand, thinking to get a bigger share than myself of the nourishment and of the milk.

Michael Miskell: That's the way you do be picking at me and faulting me. I had a share and a good share in my early time, and it's well you know that, and the both of us reared in Skehanagh.

Mike McInerney: You may say that, indeed, we are both of us reared in Skehanagh. Little wonder you to have good nourishment the time we were both rising, and you bringing away my rabbits out of the snare.

Michael Miskell: And you didn't bring away my own eels, I suppose, I was after spearing in the Turlough? Selling them to the nuns in the convent you did, and letting on they to be your own. For you were always a cheater and a schemer, grabbing every earthly thing for your own profit.

Mike McInerney: And you were no grabber yourself, I suppose, till your land and all you had grabbed wore away from you!

Michael Miskell: If I lost it itself, it was through the crosses I met with and I going through the world. I never was a rambler and a card-player like yourself, Mike McInerney, that ran through all and lavished it unknown to your mother!

Mike McInerney: Lavished it, is it? And if I did was it you yourself led me to lavish it or some other one? It is on my own floor I would be today and in the face of my family, but for the misfortune I had to be put with a bad next door neighbor that was yourself. What way did my means go from me is it? Spending on fencing, spending on walls, making up gates, putting up doors, that would keep your hens and your ducks from coming in through starvation on my floor, and every four-footed beast you had from preying and trespassing on my oats and my mangolds° and my little lock of hay!

Michael Miskell: O to listen to you! And I striving to please you and to be kind to you and to close my ears to the abuse you would be calling and letting out of your mouth. To trespass on your crops is it? It's little temptation there was for my poor beasts to ask to cross the mering°. My God Almighty! What had you but a little corner of a field!

Mike McInerney: And what do you say to my garden that your two pigs had destroyed on me the year of the big tree being knocked, and they making gaps in the wall.

Michael Miskell: Ah, there does be a great deal of gaps knocked in a twelve-month. Why wouldn't they be knocked by thunder, the same as the tree, or some storm that came up from the west?

Mike McInerney: It was the west wind, I suppose, that devoured my green cabbage? And that rooted up my Champion potatoes? And that ate the gooseberries themselves from off the bush?

Michael Miskell: What are you saying? The two quietest pigs ever I had, no way wicked and well ringed. They were not ten minutes in it. It would be hard for them eat strawberries in that time, let alone gooseberries that's full of thorns.

Mike McInerney: They were not quiet, but very ravenous pigs you had that time, as active as a fox they were, killing my young ducks. Once they had blood tasted you couldn't stop them.

Michael Miskell: And what happened myself the fair day of Esserkelly, the time I was passing your door? Two brazened dogs that rushed out and took a piece of me. I never was the better of it or of the start I got, but wasting from then till now!

Mike McInerney: Thinking you were a wild beast they did, that had made his escape out of the travelling show, with the red eyes of you and the ugly face of you, and the two crooked legs of you that wouldn't hardly stop a pig in a gap. Sure any dog that had any life in it at all would be roused and stirred seeing the like of you going the road!

Michael Miskell: I did well taking out a summons against you that time. It is a great wonder you not to have been bound over° through your lifetime, but the laws of England is queer.

mangolds: beets.
mering: property line.
bound over: required by law to pay an indemnity.

Mike McInerney: What ailed me that I did not summons yourself after you stealing away the clutch of eggs I had in the barrel, and I away in Ardrahan searching out a clocking° hen.

Michael Miskell: To steal your eggs is it? Is that what you are saying now? *(Holds up his hands.)* The Lord is in heaven, and Peter and the saints, and yourself that was in Ardrahan that day put a hand on them as soon as myself! Isn't it a bad story for me to wearing out my days beside you the same as a spancelled° goat. Chained I am and tethered I am to a man that is ramsacking his mind for lies!

Mike McInerney: If it is a bad story for you, Michael Miskell, it is a worse story again for myself. A Miskell to be next and near me through the whole of the four quarters of the year. I never heard there to be any great name on the Miskells as there was on my own race and name.

Michael Miskell: You didn't, is it? Well, you could hear it if you had but ears to hear it. Go across to Lisheen Crannagh and down to the sea and to Newtown Lynch and the mills of Duras and you'll find a Miskell, and as far as Dublin!

Mike McInerney: What signifies Crannagh and the mills of Duras? Look at all my own generations that are buried at the Seven Churches. And how many generations of the Miskells are buried in it? Answer me that!

Michael Miskell: I tell you but for the wheat that was to be sowed there would be more side cars and more common cars° at my father's funeral (God rest his soul!) than at any funeral ever left your own door. And as to my mother, she was a Cuffe from Claregalway, and it's she had the purer blood!

Mike McInerney: And what do you say to the banshee°? Isn't she apt to have knowledge of the ancient race? Was ever she heard to screech or to cry for the Miskells? Or the Cuffes from Claregalway? She was not, but for the six families, the Hyneses, the Foxes, the Faheys, the Dooleys, the McInerneys. It is of the nature of the McInerneys she is I am thinking, crying them the same as a king's children.

Michael Miskell: It is a pity the banshee not to be crying for yourself at this minute, and giving you a warning to quit your lies and your chat and your arguing and your contrary ways; for there is no one under the rising sun could stand you. I tell you you are not behaving as in the presence of the Lord!

Mike McInerney: Is it wishful for my death you are? Let it come and meet me now and welcome so long as it will part me from yourself! And I say, and I would kiss the book on it, I to have one request only to be granted, and I leaving it in my will, it is what I would request, nine furrows of the field, nine ridges of the hills, nine waves of the ocean to be put between your grave and my own grave the time we will be laid in the ground!

Michael Miskell: Amen to that! Nine ridges, is it? No, but let the whole ridge

---

clocking: setting.

spancelled: tied fast by a span of rope or chain.

side cars . . . common cars: horse-drawn carts. The fancier side cars (also called *jaunting cars*) seat the passengers facing either side of the road. Miskell means that important persons would have come to the funeral.

banshee: spirit whose strange wail foretells death.

of the world separate us till the Day of Judgment! I would not be laid anear you at the Seven Churches, I to get Ireland without a divide!

Mike McInerney: And after that again! I'd sooner than ten pound in my hand, I to know that my shadow and my ghost will not be knocking about with your shadow and your ghost, and the both of us waiting our time. I'd sooner be delayed in Purgatory! Now, have you anything to say?

Michael Miskell: I have everything to say, if I had but the time to say it!

Mike McInerney (sitting up): Let me up out of this till I'll choke you!

Michael Miskell: You scolding pauper you!

Mike McInerney (shaking his fist at him): Wait a while!

Michael Miskell (shaking his fist): Wait a while yourself!

Mrs. Donohoe comes in with a parcel. She is a countrywoman with a frilled cap and a shawl. She stands still a minute. The two old men lie down and compose themselves.

Mrs. Donohoe: They bade me come up here by the stair. I never was in this place at all. I don't know am I right. Which now of the two of ye is Mike McInerney?

Mike McInerney: Who is it is calling me by my name?

Mrs. Donohoe: Sure amn't I your sister, Honor McInerney that was, that is now Honor Donohoe.

Mike McInerney: So you are, I believe. I didn't know you till you pushed anear me. It is time indeed for you to come see me, and I in this place five year or more. Thinking me to be no credit to you, I suppose, among that tribe of the Donohoes. I wonder they to give you leave to come ask am I living yet or dead?

Mrs. Donohoe: Ah, sure, I buried the whole string of them. Himself was the last to go. (Wipes her eyes.) The Lord be praised he got a fine natural death. Sure we must go through our crosses. And he got a lovely funeral; it would delight you to hear the priest reading the Mass. My poor John Donohoe! A nice clean man, you couldn't but be fond of him. Very severe on the tobacco he was, but he wouldn't touch the drink.

Mike McInerney: And is it in Curranroe you are living yet?

Mrs. Donohoe: It is so. He left all to myself. But it is a lonesome thing the head of a house to have died!

Mike McInerney: I hope that he has left you a nice way of living?

Mrs. Donohoe: Fair enough, fair enough. A wide lovely house I have; a few acres of grass land . . . the grass does be very sweet that grows among the stones. And as to the sea, there is something from it every day of the year, a handful of periwinkles to make kitchen, or cockles maybe. There is many a thing in the sea is not decent, but cockles is fit to put before the Lord!

Mike McInerney: You have all that! And you without ere a man in the house?

Mrs. Donohoe: It is what I am thinking, yourself might come and keep me company. It is no credit to me a brother of my own to be in this place at all.

Mike McInerney: I'll go with you! Let me out of this! It is the name of the McInerneys will be rising on every side!

Mrs. Donohoe: I don't know. I was ignorant of you being kept to the bed.

Mike McInerney: I am not kept to it, but maybe an odd time when there is a colic rises up within me. My stomach always gets better the time there is a change in the moon. I'd like well to draw anear you. My heavy blessing on you, Honor Donohoe, for the hand you have held out to me this day.

Mrs. Donohoe: Sure you could be keeping the fire in, and stirring the pot with the bit of Indian meal for the hens, and milking the goat and taking the tacklings off the donkey at the door; and maybe putting out the cabbage plants in their time. For when the old man died the garden died.

Mike McInerney: I could to be sure, and be cutting the potatoes for seed. What luck could there be in a place and a man not to be in it? Is that now a suit of clothes you have brought with you?

Mrs. Donohoe: It is so, the way you will be tasty coming in among the neighbors at Curranroe.

Mike McInerney: My joy you are! It is well you earned me! Let me up out of this! (*He sits up and spreads out the clothes and tries on the coat.*) That now is a good frieze coat° . . . and a hat in the fashion. . . . (*He puts on hat.*)

Michael Miskell (alarmed): And is it going out of this you are, Mike McInerney?

Mike McInerney: Don't you hear I am going? To Curranroe I am going. Going I am to a place where I will get every good thing!

Michael Miskell: And is it to leave me here after you, you will?

Mike McInerney (in a rising chant): Every good thing! The goat and the kid are there, the sheep and the lamb are there, the cow does be running and she coming to be milked! Ploughing and seed sowing, blossom at Christmas time, the cuckoo speaking through the dark days of the year! Ah, what are you talking about? Wheat high in the hedges, no talk about the rent! Salmon in the rivers as plenty as turf! Spending and getting and nothing scarce! Sport and pleasure, and music on the strings! Age will go from me and I will be young again. Geese and turkeys for the hundreds and drinks for the whole world!

Michael Miskell: Ah, Mike, is it truth you are saying, you to go from me and to leave me with rude people and with townspeople, and with people of every parish in the union, and they having no respect for me or no wish for me at all!

Mike McInerney: Whist now and I'll leave you . . . my pipe (*hands it over*); and I'll engage it is Honor Donohoe won't refuse to be sending you a few ounces of tobacco an odd time, and neighbors coming to the fair in November or in the month of May.

Michael Miskell: Ah, what signifies tobacco? All that I am craving is the talk. There to be no one at all to say out to whatever thought might be rising in my innate mind! To be lying here and no conversible person in it would be the abomination of misery!

Mike McInerney: Look now, Honor. . . . It is what I often heard said, two to be better than one. . . . Sure if you had an old trouser was full of holes . . . or a skirt . . . wouldn't you put another in under it that might be as tattered as itself, and the two of them together would make some sort of a decent show?

frieze coat: coat made of Frisian cloth, a coarse woolen material.

Mrs. Donohoe: Ah, what are you saying? There is no holes in that suit I brought you now, but as sound it is as the day I spun it for himself.

Mike McInerney: It is what I am thinking, Honor . . . I do be weak an odd time . . . any load I would carry, it preys upon my side . . . and this man does be weak an odd time with the swelling in his knees . . . but the two of us together it's not likely it is at the one time we would fail. Bring the both of us with you, Honor, and the height of the castle of luck on you, and the both of us together will make one good hardy man!

Mrs. Donohoe: I'd like my job! Is it queer in the head you are grown asking me to bring in a stranger off the road?

Michael Miskell: I am not, ma'am, but an old neighbor I am. If I had forecasted this asking I would have asked it myself. Michael Miskell I am, that was in the next house to you in Skehanagh!

Mrs. Donohoe: For pity's sake! Michael Miskell is it? That's worse again. Yourself and Mike that never left fighting and scolding and attacking one another like two young pups you were, and threatening one another after like two grown dogs!

Mike McInerney: All the quarrelling was ever in the place it was myself did it. Sure his anger rises fast and goes away like the wind. Bring him out with myself now, Honor Donohoe, and God bless you.

Mrs. Donohoe: Well, then, I will not bring him out, and I will not bring yourself out, and you not to learn better sense. Are you making yourself ready to come?

Mike McInerney: I am thinking, maybe . . . it is a mean thing for a man that is shivering into seventy years to go changing from place to place.

Mrs. Donohoe: Well, take your luck or leave it. All I asked was to save you from the hurt and the harm of the year.

Mike McInerney: Bring the both of us with you or I will not stir out of this.

Mrs. Donohoe: Give me back my fine suit so (*begins gathering up the clothes*), till I'll go look for a man of my own!

Mike McInerney: Let you go so, as you are so unnatural and so disobliging, and look for some man of your own, God help him! For I will not go with you at all!

Mrs. Donohoe: It is too much time I lost with you, and dark night waiting to overtake me on the road. Let the two of you stop together, and the back of my hand to you. It is I will leave you there the same as God left the Jews!

She goes out. The old men lie down and are silent for a moment.

Michael Miskell: Maybe the house is not so wide as what she says.

Mike McInerney: Why wouldn't it be wide?

Michael Miskell: Ah, there does be a good deal of middling poor houses down by the sea.

Mike McInerney: What would you know about wide houses? Whatever sort of a house you had yourself it was too wide for the provision you had into it.

Michael Miskell: Whatever provision I had in my house it was wholesome provision and natural provision. Herself and her periwinkles! Periwinkles is a hungry sort of food.

Mike McInerney: Stop your impudence and your chat or it will be the worse for you. I'd bear with my own father and mother as long as any man would, but if they'd vex me I would give them the length of a rope as soon as another!

Michael Miskell: I would never ask at all to go eating periwinkles.

Mike McInerney (sitting up): Have you anyone to fight me?

Michael Miskell (whimpering): I have not, only the Lord!

Mike McInerney: Let you leave putting insults on me so, and death picking at you!

Michael Miskell: Sure I am saying nothing at all to displease you. It is why I wouldn't go eating periwinkles, I'm in dread I might swallow the pin.

Mike McInerney: Who in the world wide is asking you to eat them? You're as tricky as a fish in the full tide!

Michael Miskell: Tricky is it! Oh, my curse and the curse of the four and twenty men upon you!

Mike McInerney: That the worm may chew you from skin to marrow bone! *(Seizes his pillow.)*

Michael Miskell (seizing his own pillow): I'll leave my death on you, you scheming vagabone!

Mike McInerney: By cripes! I'll pull out your pin feathers! *(Throwing pillow.)*

Michael Miskell (throwing pillow): You tyrant! You big bully you!

Mike McInerney (throwing pillow and seizing mug): Take this so, you stobbing ruffian you!

They throw all within their reach at one another, mugs, prayer books, pipes, etc.

CURTAIN

Certain plays survive, perhaps because (among other reasons) actors take pleasure in performing them. *The Workhouse Ward* is this kind of play: a fine showcase for the skills of the two principal comedians. Fixed in the center of a practically naked stage, the two men declaim, shake their fists, do "slow burns" (simulate gradually rising anger), hold up their hands toward heaven. Throughout, they enjoy the undistracted attention of the audience, their dialogue interrupted only briefly by the visit of Honor Donohoe.

Some critics say that the essence of drama is conflict. Evidently, Lady Gregory's one-act play is richly laden with this essential. But as the playwright touchingly shows, there is more to drama than conflict alone. Although *The Workhouse Ward* is mainly the story of a lifelong battle between Michael and Mike, the fleeting appearance of Mrs. Donohoe serves to reveal something more: the depths of the two men's bondage to each other. What is the *theme* of the play? Surely it has to do with human love, men's need for one another, fear of loneliness, the difficulty of changing one's life in old age. As was true for fiction and poetry, we can express the theme of a play in general terms, in a sentence. We do not, of course, have to make any such statement to enjoy the play. But by stating a theme, we acknowledge that the play (like all excellent works of literature) not only passes the time agreeably but leaves us slightly more wise. For *The Workhouse Ward*, there are many possible ways of stating the point the play leaves us with. One might be, "However bitterly they may quarrel, men, if they need each other, can remain brothers." Another might be, "Men who think they hate each other deeply may be bound together by love." But, of course, the play touches on truth so deep and fundamental that our one-sentence statement of its theme is, like all such simplifications, only partially applicable. The reader may be left thinking about the nature of love and of hate, wondering whether the relationship between Miskell and McInerney can fairly be called hate indeed. Perhaps their perpetual quarrel is a game, one that gives their barren lives both purpose and rich enjoyment.

Triumphantly, Lady Gregory has portrayed two splendid characters. Michael and Mike are not merely specimens of local eccentrics but show traits common to mankind at large. Like most of us, Mike McInerney is prone to exaggerate his hopes ("Age will go from me and I will be young again"), and Michael Miskell, when he loses his chance to escape the workhouse, is given to speak of his loss as "sour grapes" ("Maybe the house is not so wide as what she says").

Like a carefully wrought short story, *The Workhouse Ward* has a **plot,** sometimes taken to mean whatever happens in a story, more exactly referring to the author's particular *arrangement* of events.[1] (Told in chronological order, the story of Oedipus [see Chapter Thirty-three] might begin with the infant Oedipus taken out into the wilderness to perish. But as Sophocles arranges the events in the legend to make a play of it, the plot begins with Oedipus grown to manhood and king of Thebes.) Plot in *The Workhouse Ward* seems one with character. What happens from opening to outcome seems to follow from the kind of person Mike McInerney is (and, to a lesser extent, from the kinds of persons Michael Miskell and Mrs. Donohoe are, too). If the play may be said to have a **protagonist** — a term usually reserved for the hero of a larger and more eventful play, such as a tragedy — then Mike is the one: the central character who, more than the others, has a responsibility to act, to choose, to decide. As the playwright takes pains to show, Mike is impulsive. He is easily kindled to wrath, but he is also deeply loyal, as we can tell from his hesitation when Michael Miskell pleads with him not to leave, and from his final choice.

An important element of most plays is an **exposition,** in which we first meet the characters and find out what has previously happened, or is now happening. For a one-act play, *The Workhouse Ward* devotes a large segment to its exposition: from its opening line until the entrance of Mrs. Donohoe. By comparison, Shakespeare's far longer and more complicated *Tragedy of Richard III* begins almost abruptly, with its protagonist, a duke who longs to be king, summing up recent history in the play's very first speech and revealing his own character ("And

[1] For further discussion of *plot,* see pages 8–10.

therefore, since I cannot prove a lover . . . I am determined to prove a villain"). But the playwright knows her craft. The effectiveness of Lady Gregory's play requires that we understand and sympathetically accept the two leading characters; and so the exposition takes its time, carefully and thoroughly acquainting us with them. It is essential that we know the feud between Mike and Michael to be no fleeting spat but a fight that has lasted for decades. And because we understand this, we will realize, later in the play when Mike begs his sister to make a home for Michael, that there is humorous contrast between Mike's verbal abuse of his crony and his deep attachment to him — that, contrary to his words, Mike enjoys this fight and doesn't want to be done with it.

With the unexpected arrival of Mrs. Donohoe, the exposition ends and developments move rapidly. Passing on from the verbal battles between the two paupers, the playwright introduces a subtler and more interesting conflict: the moral struggle inside Mike McInerney over the question, Will he go away and leave his lifelong enemy? This is the play's major **dramatic question**.[2] Whether or not we actually state such a question in our minds (and it is doubtful that we do), our interest is heightened when we sense that now there is an element of uncertainty. (Granted, for us to guess the answer to the question might not be difficult.) When Mike starts trying on his new clothes and imagining an idyllic life ("Sport and pleasure, and music on the strings!"), it would seem that his departure is imminent. But there are negative **foreshadowings,** hints of the outcome, in Honor Donohoe's doubts about taking her brother home with her, in her complaint that she had not known he was a bed patient. Grander events have greater fore-shadowings: in Shakespeare's *Julius Caesar,* for instance, Caesar's assassination is foreshadowed in the soothsayer's warning to beware the ides of March, in reports of strange phenomena ("ghosts did shriek and squeal about the streets"), and in Calpurnia's dream of blood that spouts from Caesar's statue.

When Mike's sister flatly refuses to take Michael Miskell home, the plot gains a **complication,** an obstacle in the path of the central character. The **climax,** the moment when tension is at its greatest height and when the major dramatic question is about to be answered,[3] occurs in Mike's final stand: "Bring the both of us with you or I will not stir

---

[2] Some plays have more than one dramatic question. This is especially true of plays that have a **double plot** (or **subplot**), a secondary arrangement of incidents. In Ibsen's *A Doll House,* for instance, the main plot concerns Nora and her husband. But there is a second couple, Mrs. Linde and Krogstad, whose fortunes we also follow with interest and whose futures pose a second dramatic question.

[3] *Climax* is sometimes used to indicate any **crisis,** a moment of tension when one or another outcome is possible. This definition is easy to remember if you think of *crisis* in its medical sense: the turning point in the course of a disease when it becomes clear that a patient will either die or recover. But in talking about plays, a distinction between *crisis* and *climax* may be useful. A play may be said to have more than one crisis, perhaps several, in which case the last and most decisive crisis is the climax.

out of this." The **resolution,** also called the **conclusion** or **denouement** (French: the "untying of a knot"), swiftly ensues as Honor departs, condemning Mike to end his days in the workhouse. This resolution is not the end of the plot, of course, for we still are to be treated to the closing battle — an inspired piece of **stage business** (a term for any small nonverbal action that an audience finds interesting).

Some critics maintain that the incidents in a plot can be arranged in the outline of a pyramid.[4] In this view, a play begins with a **rising action,** the part of the plot, including the exposition, in which the sequence of events starts moving. At the climax, the plot reaches its peak, then tapers to a close in a **falling action,** usually marked by a sharp drop in the protagonist's fortunes. Some plays have demonstrable pyramids. In *The Workhouse Ward,* although there is little physical action, we might claim that there is a rising action in the first half of the play, including Honor Donohoe's offer and her brother's initial warm response to it. There is a climax ("Bring the both of us with you, Honor") and a falling action (Honor's refusal, her angry departure, and the two men's return to their quarrel). However, to erect such a pyramid out of so concise a play seems grandiose. The pyramid metaphor seems to apply more meaningfully to certain longer plays, among them some classic tragedies. Try it on *Oedipus Rex* (Chapter Thirty-three) or for an even neater fit, on Shakespeare's *Julius Caesar,* an unusual play in that its climax, the assassination of Caesar, occurs precisely in the middle (act III, scene 1), right where a good pyramid's point ought to be. But in most other plays, especially in contemporary drama, usually no pyramids can be discerned, or only lopsided ones.

Brief as it is, *The Workhouse Ward* has the main elements found in more complex drama. There is even a **symbol,** a thing that suggests meanings larger than itself: Mike's pipe, which he offers to Michael, being the one valuable object he owns and the object most dear to him. Perhaps, too, the suit of new clothes conveys a few suggestions: trying on coat and hat, Mike decks himself out in dreams of a new life, but when there is no more hope for his dreams, Honor gathers up the clothes again. Symbols in drama may be as large and portentous as the figure of a soothsayer croaking, "Beware the ides of March"; or they may be small, as in *The Workhouse Ward.*[5]

With these elements of a play in mind, look for them in a longer and more thickly populated play, such as the one presented here — one of the celebrated works of the Norwegian dramatist Henrik Ibsen. Although Ibsen was capable of poetic symbolism in plays such as *Brand* and *Peer Gynt,* it was his realistic dramas of small-town life (also includ-

[4] The pyramid metaphor was invented by the German critic Gustav Freytag in his *Technique of the Drama* (1904 reprint ed. New York: Arno Press, 1968).
[5] There also can be symbolic settings or gestures. For more examples of symbolism, see the discussion on pages 113–115 and 607–611.

ing *Ghosts, Pillars of Society,* and *An Enemy of the People*) that made the greatest impression abroad and won him the name of the father of modern drama. (In the English-speaking world, his disciples included George Bernard Shaw, who championed him.) Full of suspense, carefully plotted with evident crisis, climax, and resolution, *A Doll House* shows that Ibsen had learned his art from the **well-made plays** of nineteenth-century French dramatists Eugène Scribe and Victorien Sardou, plays which emphasize neatly dovetailed plots and heightening tensions. But while most well-made plays have been forgotten ("clockwork mice," Shaw called Sardou's works), Ibsen's plays continue to be revived — a tribute, perhaps, to their intellectual energy and to the poetry in them.

Henrik Ibsen (1828–1906)

A Doll House

1879

Translated by Rolf Fjelde

Characters

Torvald Helmer, a lawyer
Nora, his wife
Dr. Rank
Mrs. Linde
Nils Krogstad, a bank clerk
The Helmers' three small children
Anne-Marie, their nurse
Helene, a maid
A Delivery Boy

The action takes place in Helmer's residence.

ACT I

A comfortable room, tastefully but not expensively furnished. A door to the right in the back wall leads to the entryway; another to the left leads to Helmer's study. Between these doors, a piano. Midway in the left-hand wall a door, and further back a window. Near the window a round table with an armchair and a small sofa. In the right-hand wall, toward the rear, a door, and nearer the foreground a procelain stove with two armchairs and a rocking chair beside it. Between the stove and the side door, a small table. Engravings on the walls. An etagère with china figures and other small art objects; a small bookcase with richly bound books; the floor carpeted; a fire burning in the stove. It is a winter day.

A bell rings in the entryway; shortly after we hear the door being unlocked. Nora comes into the room, humming happily to herself; she is wearing street clothes and carries an armload of packages, which she puts down on the table to the right. She has left the hall door open; and through it a Delivery Boy is seen, holding a Christmas tree and a basket, which he gives to the Maid who let them in.

Nora: Hide the tree well, Helene. The children mustn't get a glimpse of it till this evening, after it's trimmed. (*To the Delivery Boy, taking out her purse.*) How much?

Delivery Boy: Fifty, ma'am.

Nora: There's a crown. No, keep the change. (*The Boy thanks her and leaves. Nora shuts the door. She laughs softly to herself while taking off her street things. Drawing a bag of macaroons from her pocket, she eats a couple, then steals over and listens at her husband's study door.*) Yes, he's home. (*Hums again as she moves to the table right.*)

Helmer (from the study): Is that my little lark twittering out there?

Nora (busy opening some packages): Yes, it is.

Helmer: Is that my squirrel rummaging around?

Nora: Yes!

Helmer: When did my squirrel get in?

Nora: Just now. (*Putting the macaroon bag in her pocket and wiping her mouth.*) Do come in, Torvald, and see what I've bought.

Helmer: Can't be disturbed. (*After a moment he opens the door and peers in, pen in hand.*) Bought, you say? All that there? Has the little spendthrift been out throwing money around again?

Nora: Oh, but Torvald, this year we really should let ourselves go a bit. It's the first Christmas we haven't had to economize.

Helmer: But you know we can't go squandering.

Nora: Oh yes, Torvald, we can squander a little now. Can't we? Just a tiny, wee bit. Now that you've got a big salary and are going to make piles and piles of money.

Helmer: Yes — starting New Year's. But then it's a full three months till the raise comes through.

Nora: Pooh! We can borrow that long.

Helmer: Nora! (*Goes over and playfully takes her by the ear.*) Are your scatter-brains off again? What if today I borrowed a thousand crowns, and you squandered them over Christmas week, and then on New Year's Eve a roof tile fell on my head, and I lay there —

Nora (putting her hand on his mouth): Oh! Don't say such things!

Helmer: Yes, but what if it happened — then what?

Nora: If anything so awful happened, then it just wouldn't matter if I had debts or not.

Helmer: Well, but the people I'd borrowed from?

Nora: Them? Who cares about them! They're strangers.

Helmer: Nora, Nora, how like a woman! No, but seriously, Nora, you know what I think about that. No debts! Never borrow! Something of freedom's lost — and something of beauty, too — from a home that's founded on borrowing and debt. We've made a brave stand up to now, the two of us; and we'll go right on like that the little while we have to.

Nora (going toward the stove): Yes, whatever you say, Torvald.

Helmer (following her): Now, now, the little lark's wings mustn't droop. Come on, don't be a sulky squirrel. *(Taking out his wallet.)* Nora, guess what I have here.

Nora (turning quickly): Money!

Helmer: There, see. *(Hands her some notes.)* Good grief, I know how costs go up in a house at Christmastime.

Nora: Ten — twenty — thirty — forty. Oh, thank you, Torvald; I can manage no end on this.

Helmer: You really will have to.

Nora: Oh yes, I promise I will! But come here so I can show you everything I bought. And so cheap! Look, new clothes for Ivar here — and a sword. Here a horse and a trumpet for Bob. And a doll and a doll's bed here for Emmy; they're nothing much, but she'll tear them to bits in no time anyway. And here I have dress material and handkerchiefs for the maids. Old Anne-Marie really deserves something more.

Helmer: And what's in that package there?

Nora (with a cry): Torvald, no! You can't see that till tonight!

Helmer: I see. But tell me now, you little prodigal, what have you thought of for yourself?

Nora: For myself? Oh, I don't want anything at all.

Helmer: Of course you do. Tell me just what — within reason — you'd most like to have.

Nora: I honestly don't know. Oh, listen, Torvald —

Helmer: Well?

Nora (fumbling at his coat buttons, without looking at him): If you want to give me something, then maybe you could — you could —

Helmer: Come on, out with it.

Nora (hurriedly): You could give me money, Torvald. No more than you think you can spare; then one of these days I'll buy something with it.

Helmer: But Nora —

Nora: Oh, please, Torvald darling, do that! I beg you, please. Then I could hang the bills in pretty gilt paper on the Christmas tree. Wouldn't that be fun?

Helmer: What are those little birds called that always fly through their fortunes?

Nora: Oh yes, spendthrifts; I know all that. But let's do as I say, Torvald; then I'll have time to decide what I really need most. That's very sensible, isn't it?

Helmer (smiling): Yes, very — that is, if you actually hung onto the money I give you, and you actually used it to buy yourself something. But it goes for the house and for all sorts of foolish things, and then I only have to lay out some more.

Nora: Oh, but Torvald —

Helmer: Don't deny it, my dear little Nora. *(Putting his arm around her waist.)* Spendthrifts are sweet, but they use up a frightful amount of money. It's incredible what it costs a man to feed such birds.

Nora: Oh, how can you say that! Really, I save everything I can.

Helmer (laughing): Yes, that's the truth. Everything you can. But that's nothing at all.

Nora (humming, with a smile of quiet satisfaction): Hm, if you only knew what expenses we larks and squirrels have, Torvald.

Helmer: You're an odd little one. Exactly the way your father was. You're never at a loss for scaring up money; but the moment you have it, it runs right out through your fingers; you never know what you've done with it. Well, one takes you as you are. It's deep in your blood. Yes, these things are hereditary, Nora.

Nora: Ah, I could wish I'd inherited many of Papa's qualities.

Helmer: And I couldn't wish you anything but just what you are, my sweet little lark. But wait; it seems to me you have a very — what should I call it? — a very suspicious look today —

Nora: I do?

Helmer: You certainly do. Look me straight in the eye.

Nora (looking at him): Well?

Helmer (shaking an admonitory finger): Surely my sweet tooth hasn't been running riot in town today, has she?

Nora: No. Why do you imagine that?

Helmer: My sweet tooth really didn't make a little detour through the confectioner's?

Nora: No, I assure you, Torvald —

Helmer: Hasn't nibbled some pastry?

Nora: No, not at all.

Helmer: Nor even munched a macaroon or two?

Nora: No, Torvald, I assure you, really —

Helmer: There, there now. Of course I'm only joking.

Nora (going to the table, right): You know I could never think of going against you.

Helmer: No, I understand that; and you *have* given me your word. *(Going over to her.)* Well, you keep your little Christmas secrets to yourself, Nora darling. I expect they'll come to light this evening, when the tree is lit.

Nora: Did you remember to ask Dr. Rank?

Helmer: No. But there's no need for that; it's assumed he'll be dining with us. All the same, I'll ask him when he stops by here this morning. I've ordered some fine wine. Nora, you can't imagine how I'm looking forward to this evening.

Nora: So am I. And what fun for the children, Torvald!

Helmer: Ah, it's so gratifying to know that one's gotten a safe, secure job, and with a comfortable salary. It's a great satisfaction, isn't it?

Nora: Oh, it's wonderful!

Helmer: Remember last Christmas? Three whole weeks before, you shut yourself in every evening till long after midnight, making flowers for the Christmas tree, and all the other decorations to surprise us. Ugh, that was the dullest time I've ever lived through.

Nora: It wasn't at all dull for me.

Helmer (smiling): But the outcome *was* pretty sorry, Nora.

Nora: Oh, don't tease me with that again. How could I help it that the cat came in and tore everything to shreds.

Helmer: No, poor thing, you certainly couldn't. You wanted so much to please us all, and that's what counts. But it's just as well that the hard times are past.

Nora: Yes, it's really wonderful.

Helmer: Now I don't have to sit here alone, boring myself, and you don't have to tire your precious eyes and your fair little delicate hands —

Nora (clapping her hands): No, is it really true, Torvald, I don't have to? Oh, how wonderfully lovely to hear! (*Taking his arm.*) Now I'll tell you just how I've thought we should plan things. Right after Christmas — (*The doorbell rings.*) Oh, the bell. (*Straightening the room up a bit.*) Somebody would have to come. What a bore!

Helmer: I'm not at home to visitors, don't forget.

Maid (from the hall doorway): Ma'am, a lady to see you —

Nora: All right, let her come in.

Maid (to Helmer): And the doctor's just come too.

Helmer: Did he go right to my study?

Maid: Yes, he did.

Helmer *goes into his room. The* Maid *shows in* Mrs. Linde, *dressed in traveling clothes, and shuts the door after her.*

Mrs. Linde (in a dispirited and somewhat hesitant voice): Hello, Nora.

Nora (uncertain): Hello —

Mrs. Linde: You don't recognize me.

Nora: No, I don't know — but wait, I think — (*Exclaiming.*) What! Kristine! Is it really you?

Mrs. Linde: Yes, it's me.

Nora: Kristine! To think I didn't recognize you. But then, how could I? (*More quietly.*) How you've changed, Kristine!

Mrs. Linde: Yes, no doubt I have. In nine — ten long years.

Nora: Is it so long since we met! Yes, it's all of that. Oh, these last eight years have been a happy time, believe me. And so now you've come in to town, too. Made the long trip in the winter. That took courage.

Mrs. Linde: I just got here by ship this morning.

Nora: To enjoy yourself over Christmas, of course. Oh, how lovely! Yes, enjoy ourselves, we'll do that. But take your coat off. You're not still cold? (*Helping her.*) There now, let's get cozy here by the stove. No, the easy chair there! I'll take the rocker here. (*Seizing her hands.*) Yes, now you have your old look again; it was only in that first moment. You're a bit more pale, Kristine — and maybe a bit thinner.

Mrs. Linde: And much, much older, Nora.

Nora: Yes, perhaps a bit older; a tiny, tiny bit; not much at all. (*Stopping short; suddenly serious.*) Oh, but thoughtless me, to sit here, chattering away. Sweet, good Kristine, can you forgive me?

Mrs. Linde: What do you mean, Nora?

Nora (softly): Poor Kristine, you've become a widow.

Mrs. Linde: Yes, three years ago.

Nora: Oh, I knew it, of course: I read it in the papers. Oh, Kristine, you must believe me; I often thought of writing you then, but I kept postponing it, and something always interfered.

Mrs. Linde: Nora dear, I understand completely.

Nora: No, it was awful of me, Kristine, You poor thing, how much you must have gone through. And he left you nothing?

Mrs. Linde: No.

Nora: And no children?

Mrs. Linde: No.

Nora: Nothing at all, then?

Mrs. Linde: Not even a sense of loss to feed on.

Nora (looking incredulously at her): But Kristine, how could that be?

Mrs. Linde (smiling wearily and smoothing her hair): Oh, sometimes it happens, Nora.

Nora: So completely alone. How terribly hard that must be for you. I have three lovely children. You can't see them now; they're out with the maid. But now you must tell me everything —

Mrs. Linde: No, no, no, tell me about yourself.

Nora: No, you begin. Today I don't want to be selfish. I want to think only of you today. But there *is* something I must tell you. Did you hear of the wonderful luck we had recently?

Mrs. Linde: No, what's that?

Nora: My husband's been made manager in the bank, just think!

Mrs. Linde: Your husband? How marvelous!

Nora: Isn't it? Being a lawyer is such an uncertain living, you know, especially if one won't touch any cases that aren't clean and decent. And of course Torvald would never do that, and I'm with him completely there. Oh, we're simply delighted, believe me! He'll join the bank right after New Year's and start getting a huge salary and lots of commissions. From now on we can live quite differently — just as we want. Oh, Kristine, I feel so light and happy! Won't it be lovely to have stacks of money and not a care in the world?

Mrs. Linde: Well, anyway, it would be lovely to have enough for necessities.

Nora: No, not just for necessities, but stacks and stacks of money!

Mrs. Linde (smiling): Nora, Nora, aren't you sensible yet? Back in school you were such a free spender.

Nora (with a quiet laugh): Yes, that's what Torvald still says. *(Shaking her finger.)* But "Nora, Nora" isn't as silly as you all think. Really, we've been in no position for me to go squandering. We've had to work, both of us.

Mrs. Linde: You too?

Nora: Yes, at odd jobs — needlework, crocheting, embroidery, and such — *(casually)* and other things too. You remember that Torvald left the department when we were married? There was no chance of promotion in his office, and of course he needed to earn more money. But that first year he drove himself terribly. He took on all kinds of extra work that kept him going morning and night. It wore him down, and then he fell deathly ill. The doctors said it was essential for him to travel south.

Mrs. Linde: Yes, didn't you spend a whole year in Italy?

Nora: That's right. It wasn't easy to get away, you know. Ivar had just been born. But of course we had to go. Oh, that was a beautiful trip, and it saved Torvald's life. But it cost a frightful sum, Kristine.

Mrs. Linde: I can well imagine.

Nora: Four thousand, eight hundred crowns it cost. That's really a lot of money.

Mrs. Linde: But it's lucky you had it when you needed it.

Nora: Well, as it was, we got it from Papa.

Mrs. Linde: I see. It was just about the time your father died.

Nora: Yes, just about then. And, you know, I couldn't make that trip out to nurse him. I had to stay here, expecting Ivar any moment, and with my poor sick Torvald to care for. Dearest Papa, I never saw him again, Kristine. Oh, that was the worst time I've known in all my marriage.

Mrs. Linde: I know how you loved him. And then you went off to Italy?

Nora: Yes. We had the means now, and the doctors urged us. So we left a month after.

Mrs. Linde: And your husband came back completely cured?

Nora: Sound as a drum!

Mrs. Linde: But — the doctor?

Nora: Who?

Mrs. Linde: I thought the maid said he was a doctor, the man who came in with me.

Nora: Yes, that was Dr. Rank — but he's not making a sick call. He's our closest friend, and he stops by at least once a day. No, Torvald hasn't had a sick moment since, and the children are fit and strong, and I am, too. *(Jumping up and clapping her hands.)* Oh, dear God, Kristine, what a lovely thing to live and be happy! But how disgusting of me — I'm talking of nothing but my own affairs. *(Sits on a stool close by Kristine, arms resting across her knees.)* Oh, don't be angry with me! Tell me, is it really true that you weren't in love with your husband? Why did you marry him, then?

Mrs. Linde: My mother was still alive, but bedridden and helpless — and I had my two younger brothers to look after. In all conscience, I didn't think I could turn him down.

Nora: No, you were right there. But was he rich at the time?

Mrs. Linde: He was very well off, I'd say. But the business was shaky, Nora. When he died, it all fell apart, and nothing was left.

Nora: And then — ?

Mrs. Linde: Yes, so I had to scrape up a living with a little shop and a little teaching and whatever else I could find. The last three years have been like one endless workday without a rest for me. Now it's over, Nora. My poor mother doesn't need me, for she's passed on. Nor the boys, either; they're working now and can take care of themselves.

Nora: How free you must feel —

Mrs. Linde: No — only unspeakably empty. Nothing to live for now. *(Standing up anxiously.)* That's why I couldn't take it any longer out in that desolate hole. Maybe here it'll be easier to find something to do and keep my mind occupied. If I could only be lucky enough to get a steady job, some office work —

Nora: Oh, but Kristine, that's so dreadfully tiring, and you already look so tired. It would be much better for you if you could go off to a bathing resort.

Mrs. Linde (going toward the window): I have no father to give me travel money, Nora.

Nora (rising): Oh, don't be angry with me.

Mrs. Linde (going to her): Nora dear, don't you be angry with me. The worst of my kind of situation is all the bitterness that's stored away. No one to work for, and yet you're always having to snap up your opportunities. You have to live; and so you grow selfish. When you told me the happy change in your lot, do you know I was delighted less for your sakes than for mine?

Nora: How so? Oh, I see. You think maybe Torvald could do something for you.

Mrs. Linde: Yes, that's what I thought.

Nora: And he will, Kristine! Just leave it to me; I'll bring it up so delicately — find something attractive to humor him with. Oh, I'm so eager to help you.

Mrs. Linde: How very kind of you, Nora, to be so concerned over me — doubly kind, considering you really know so little of life's burdens yourself.

Nora: I — ? I know so little — ?

Mrs. Linde (smiling): Well, my heavens — a little needlework and such — Nora, you're just a child.

Nora (tossing her head and pacing the floor): You don't have to act so superior.

Mrs. Linde: Oh?

Nora: You're just like the others. You all think I'm incapable of anything serious —

Mrs. Linde: Come now —

Nora: That I've never had to face the raw world.

Mrs. Linde: Nora dear, you've just been telling me all your troubles.

Nora: Hm! Trivia! *(Quietly.)* I haven't told you the big thing.

Mrs. Linde: Big thing? What do you mean?

Nora: You look down on me so, Kristine, but you shouldn't. You're proud that you worked so long and hard for your mother.

Mrs. Linde: I don't look down on a soul. But it *is* true: I'm proud — and happy, too — to think it was given to me to make my mother's last days almost free of care.

Nora: And you're also proud thinking of what you've done for your brothers.

Mrs. Linde: I feel I've a right to be.

Nora: I agree. But listen to this, Kristine — I've also got something to be proud and happy for.

Mrs. Linde: I don't doubt it. But whatever do you mean?

Nora: Not so loud. What if Torvald heard! He mustn't, not for anything in the world. Nobody must know, Kristine. No one but you.

Mrs. Linde: But what is it, then?

Nora: Come here. *(Drawing her down beside her on the sofa.)* It's true — I've also got something to be proud and happy for. I'm the one who saved Torvald's life.

Mrs. Linde: Saved — ? Saved how?

Nora: I told you about the trip to Italy. Torvald never would have lived if he hadn't gone south —

Mrs. Linde: Of course; your father gave you the means —

Nora (smiling): That's what Torvald and all the rest think, but —

Mrs. Linde: But — ?

Nora: Papa didn't give us a pin. I was the one who raised the money.

Mrs. Linde: You? That whole amount?

Nora: Four thousand, eight hundred crowns. What do you say to that?

Mrs. Linde: But Nora, how was it possible? Did you win the lottery?

Nora (disdainfully): The lottery? Pooh! No art to that.

Mrs. Linde: But where did you get it from then?

Nora (humming, with a mysterious smile): Hmm, tra-la-la-la.

Mrs. Linde: Because you couldn't have borrowed it.

Nora: No? Why not?

Mrs. Linde: A wife can't borrow without her husband's consent.

Nora (tossing her head): Oh, but a wife with a little business sense, a wife who knows how to manage —

Mrs. Linde: Nora, I simply don't understand —

Nora: You don't have to. Whoever said I *borrowed* the money? I could have gotten it other ways. *(Throwing herself back on the sofa.)* I could have gotten it from some admirer or other. After all, a girl with my ravishing appeal —

Mrs. Linde: You lunatic.

Nora: I'll bet you're eaten up with curiosity, Kristine.

Mrs. Linde: Now listen here, Nora — you haven't done something indiscreet?

Nora (sitting up again): Is it indiscreet to save your husband's life?

Mrs. Linde: I think it's indiscreet that without his knowledge you —

Nora: But that's the point: he mustn't know! My Lord, can't you understand? He mustn't ever know the close call he had. It was to *me* the doctors came to say his life was in danger — that nothing could save him but a stay in the south. Didn't I try strategy then! I began talking about how lovely it would be for me to travel abroad like other young wives; I begged and I cried; I told him please to remember my condition, to be kind and indulge me; and then I dropped a hint that he could easily take out a loan. But at that, Kristine, he nearly exploded. He said I was frivolous, and it was his duty as man of the house not to indulge me in whims and fancies — as I think he called them. Aha, I thought, now you'll just have to be saved — and that's when I saw my chance.

Mrs. Linde: And your father never told Torvald the money wasn't from him?

Nora: No, never. Papa died right about then. I'd considered bringing him into my secret and begging him never to tell. But he was too sick at the time — and then, sadly, it didn't matter.

Mrs. Linde: And you've never confided in your husband since?

Nora: For heaven's sake, no! Are you serious? He's so strict on that subject. Besides — Torvald, with all his masculine pride — how painfully humiliating for him if he ever found out he was in debt to me. That would just ruin our relationship. Our beautiful, happy home would never be the same.

Mrs. Linde: Won't you ever tell him?

Nora (thoughtfully, half smiling): Yes — maybe sometime, years from now, when I'm no longer so attractive. Don't laugh! I only mean when Torvald loves me less than now, when he stops enjoying my dancing and dressing up and reciting for him. Then it might be wise to have something in reserve — *(Breaking off.)* How ridiculous! That'll never happen — Well, Kristine, what do you think of my big secret? I'm capable of something too, hm? You can imagine, of course, how this thing hangs over me. It really hasn't been easy meeting the payments on time. In the business world there's what they call quarterly interest and what they call amortization, and these are always so terribly hard to manage. I've had to skimp a little here and there, wherever I could, you know. I could hardly spare anything from my house allowance, because Torvald has to live well. I couldn't let the children go poorly dressed; whatever I got for them, I felt I had to use up completely — the darlings!

Mrs. Linde: Poor Nora, so it had to come out of your own budget, then?

Nora: Yes, of course. But I was the one most responsible, too. Every time Torvald gave me money for new clothes and such, I never used more than half; always bought the simplest, cheapest outfits. It was a godsend that everything looks so well on me that Torvald never noticed. But it did weigh me down at times, Kristine. It *is* such a joy to wear fine things. You understand.

Mrs. Linde: Oh, of course.

Nora: And then I found other ways of making money. Last winter I was lucky enough to get a lot of copying to do. I locked myself in and sat writing every evening till late in the night. Ah, I was tired so often, dead tired. But still it was wonderful fun, sitting and working like that, earning money. It was almost like being a man.

Mrs. Linde: But how much have you paid off this way so far?

Nora: That's hard to say, exactly. These accounts, you know, aren't easy to figure. I only know that I've paid out all I could scrape together. Time and again I haven't known where to turn. *(Smiling.)* Then I'd sit here dreaming of a rich old gentleman who had fallen in love with me —

Mrs. Linde: What! Who is he?

Nora: Oh, really! And that he'd died, and when his will was opened, there in big letters it said, "All my fortune shall be paid over in cash, immediately, to that enchanting Mrs. Nora Helmer."

Mrs. Linde: But Nora dear — who *was* this gentleman?

Nora: Good grief, can't you understand? The old man never existed; that was only something I'd dream up time and again whenever I was at my wits' end for money. But it makes no difference now; the old fossil can go where he pleases for all I care; I don't need him or his will — because now I'm free. *(Jumping up.)* Oh, how lovely to think of that, Kristine! Carefree! To know you're carefree, utterly carefree; to be able to romp and play with the children, and to keep up a beautiful, charming home — everything just the way Torvald likes it! And think, spring is coming, with big blue skies. Maybe we can travel a little then. Maybe I'll see the ocean again. Oh yes, it *is* so marvelous to live and be happy!

The front doorbell rings.

Mrs. Linde (rising): There's the bell. It's probably best that I go.

Nora: No, stay. No one's expected. It must be for Torvald.

Maid (from the hall doorway): Excuse me, ma'am — there's a gentleman here to see Mr. Helmer, but I didn't know — since the doctor's with him —

Nora: Who is the gentleman?

Krogstad (from the doorway): It's me, Mrs. Helmer.

Mrs. Linde starts and turns away toward the window.

Nora (stepping toward him, tense, her voice a whisper): You? What is it? Why do you want to speak to my husband?

Krogstad: Bank business — after a fashion. I have a small job in the investment bank, and I hear now your husband is going to be our chief —

Nora: In other words, it's —

Krogstad: Just dry business, Mrs. Helmer. Nothing but that.

Nora: Yes, then please be good enough to step into the study. *(She nods indifferently as she sees him out by the hall door, then returns and begins stirring up the stove.)*

Mrs. Linde: Nora — who was that man?

Nora: That was a Mr. Krogstad — a lawyer.

Mrs. Linde: Then it really was him.

Nora: Do you know that person?

Mrs. Linde: I did once — many years ago. For a time he was a law clerk in our town.

Nora: Yes, he's been that.

Mrs. Linde: How he's changed.

Nora: I understand he had a very unhappy marriage.

Mrs. Linde: He's a widower now.

Nora: With a number of children. There now, it's burning. *(She closes the stove door and moves the rocker a bit to one side.)*

Mrs. Linde: They say he has a hand in all kinds of business.

Nora: Oh? That may be true: I wouldn't know. But let's not think about business. It's so dull.

> *Dr. Rank enters from Helmer's study.*

Rank (still in the doorway): No, no, really — I don't want to intrude, I'd just as soon talk a little while with your wife. *(Shuts the door, then notices Mrs. Linde.)* Oh, beg pardon. I'm intruding here too.

Nora: No, not at all. *(Introducing him.)* Dr. Rank, Mrs. Linde.

Rank: Well now, that's a name much heard in this house. I believe I passed the lady on the stairs as I came.

Mrs. Linde: Yes, I take the stairs very slowly. They're rather hard on me.

Rank: Uh-hm, some touch of internal weakness?

Mrs. Linde: More overexertion, I'd say.

Rank: Nothing else? Then you're probably here in town to rest up in a round of parties?

Mrs. Linde: I'm here to look for work.

Rank: Is that the best cure for overexertion?

Mrs. Linde: One has to live, Doctor.

Rank: Yes, there's a common prejudice to that effect.

Nora: Oh, come on, Dr. Rank — you really do want to live yourself.

Rank: Yes, I really do. Wretched as I am, I'll gladly prolong my torment indefinitely. All my patients feel like that. And it's quite the same, too, with the morally sick. Right at this moment there's one of those moral invalids in there with Helmer —

Mrs. Linde (softly): Ah!

Nora: Who do you mean?

Rank: Oh, it's a lawyer, Krogstad, a type you wouldn't know. His character is rotten to the root — but even he began chattering all-importantly about how he had to *live.*

Nora: Oh? What did he want to talk to Torvald about?

Rank: I really don't know. I only heard something about the bank.

Nora: I didn't know that Krog — that this man Krogstad had anything to do with the bank.

Rank: Yes, he's gotten some kind of berth down there. *(To Mrs. Linde.)* I don't know if you also have, in your neck of the woods, a type of person who

Scene III all five characters gives christine the job

scuttles about breathlessly, sniffing out hints of moral corruption, and then maneuvers his victim into some sort of key position where he can keep an eye on him. It's the healthy these days that are out in the cold.

Mrs. Linde: All the same, it's the sick who most need to be taken in.

Rank (with a shrug): Yes, there we have it. That's the concept that's turning society into a sanatorium.

Nora, lost in her thoughts, breaks out into quiet laughter and claps her hands.

Rank: Why do you laugh at that? Do you have any real idea of what society is?

Nora: What do I care about dreary old society? I was laughing at something quite different — something terribly funny. Tell me, Doctor — is everyone who works in the bank dependent now on Torvald?

Rank: Is that what you find so terribly funny?

Nora (smiling and humming): Never mind, never mind! *(Pacing the floor.)* Yes, that's really immensely amusing: that we — that Torvald has so much power now over all those people. *(Taking the bag out of her pocket.)* Dr. Rank, a little macaroon on that?

Rank: See here, macaroons! I thought they were contraband here.

Nora: Yes, but these are some that Kristine gave me.

Mrs. Linde: What? I — ?

Nora: Now, now, don't be afraid. You couldn't possibly know that Torvald had forbidden them. You see, he's worried they'll ruin my teeth. But hmp! Just this once! Isn't that so, Dr. Rank? Help yourself! *(Puts a macaroon in his mouth.)* And you too, Kristine. And I'll also have one, only a little one — or two, at the most. *(Walking about again.)* Now I'm really tremendously happy. Now there's just one last thing in the world that I have an enormous desire to do.

Rank: Well! And what's that?

Nora: It's something I have such a consuming desire to say so Torvald could hear.

Rank: And why can't you say it?

Nora: I don't dare. It's quite shocking.

Mrs. Linde: Shocking?

Rank: Well, then it isn't advisable. But in front of us you certainly can. What do you have such a desire to say so Torvald could hear?

Nora: I have such a huge desire to say — to hell and be damned!

Rank: Are you crazy?

Mrs. Linde: My goodness, Nora!

Rank: Go on, say it. Here he is.

Nora (hiding the macaroon bag): Shh, shh, shh!

Helmer comes in from his study, hat in hand, overcoat over his arm.

Nora (going toward him): Well, Torvald dear, are you through with him?

Helmer: Yes, he just left.

Nora: Let me introduce you — this is Kristine, who's arrived here in town.

Helmer: Kristine — ? I'm sorry, but I don't know —

Nora: Mrs. Linde, Torvald dear. Mrs. Kristine Linde.

Helmer: Of course. A childhood friend of my wife's, no doubt?

Mrs. Linde: Yes, we knew each other in those days.

Nora: And just think, she made the long trip down here in order to talk with you.

Helmer: What's this?

Mrs. Linde: Well, not exactly —

Nora: You see, Kristine is remarkably clever in office work, and so she's terribly eager to come under a capable man's supervision and add more to what she already knows —

Helmer: Very wise, Mrs. Linde.

Nora: And then when she heard that you'd become a bank manager — the story was wired out to the papers — then she came in as fast as she could and — Really, Torvald, for my sake you can do a little something for Kristine, can't you?

Helmer: Yes, it's not at all impossible. Mrs. Linde, I suppose you're a widow?

Mrs. Linde: Yes.

Helmer: Any experience in office work?

Mrs. Linde: Yes, a good deal.

Helmer: Well, it's quite likely that I can make an opening for you —

Nora (clapping her hands): You see, you see!

Helmer: You've come at a lucky moment, Mrs. Linde.

Mrs. Linde: Oh, how can I thank you?

Helmer: Not necessary. *(Putting his overcoat on.)* But today you'll have to excuse me —

Rank: Wait, I'll go with you. *(He fetches his coat from the hall and warms it at the stove.)*

Nora: Don't stay out long, dear.

Helmer: An hour; no more.

Nora: Are you going too, Kristine?

Mrs. Linde (putting on her winter garments): Yes, I have to see about a room now.

Helmer: Then perhaps we can all walk together.

Nora (helping her): What a shame we're so cramped here, but it's quite impossible for us to —

Mrs. Linde: Oh, don't even think of it! Good-bye, Nora dear, and thanks for everything.

Nora: Good-bye for now. Of course you'll be back this evening. And you too, Dr. Rank. What? If you're well enough? Oh, you've got to be! Wrap up tight now.

In a ripple of small talk the company moves out into the hall; children's voices are heard outside on the steps.

Nora: There they are! There they are! *(She runs to open the door. The children come in with their nurse, Anne-Marie.)* Come in, come in! *(Bends down and kisses them.)* Oh, you darlings —! Look at them, Kristine. Aren't they lovely!

Rank: No loitering in the draft here.

Helmer: Come, Mrs. Linde — this place is unbearable now for anyone but mothers.

Dr. Rank, Helmer, and Mrs. Linde go down the stairs. Anne-Marie goes into the living room with the children. Nora follows, after closing the hall door.

Nora: How fresh and strong you look. Oh, such red cheeks you have! Like apples and roses. *(The children interrupt her throughout the following.)* And it was so much fun? That's wonderful. Really? You pulled both Emmy and Bob on the sled? Imagine, all together! Yes, you're a clever boy, Ivar. Oh, let me hold her a bit, Anne-Marie. My sweet little doll baby! *(Takes the smallest from the nurse and dances with her.)* Yes, yes, Mama will dance with Bob as well. What? Did you throw snowballs? Oh, if I'd only been there! No, don't bother, Anne-Marie — I'll undress them myself. Oh yes, let me. It's such fun. Go in and rest; you look half frozen. There's hot coffee waiting for you on the stove. *(The nurse goes into the room to the left. Nora takes the children's winter things off, throwing them about, while the children talk to her all at once.)* Is that so? A big dog chased you? But it didn't bite? No, dogs never bite little, lovely doll babies. Don't peek in the packages, Ivar! What is it? Yes, wouldn't you like to know. No, no, it's an ugly something. Well? Shall we play? What shall we play? Hide-and-seek? Yes, let's play hide-and-seek. Bob must hide first. I must? Yes, let me hide first. *(Laughing and shouting, she and the children play in and out of the living room and the adjoining room to the right. At last Nora hides under the table. The children come storming in, search, but cannot find her, then hear her muffled laughter, dash over to the table, lift the cloth up and find her. Wild shouting. She creeps forward as if to scare them. More shouts. Meanwhile, a knock at the hall door; no one has noticed it. Now the door half opens, and Krogstad appears. He waits a moment; the game goes on.)*

Krogstad: Beg pardon, Mrs. Helmer —

Nora (with a strangled cry, turning and scrambling to her knees): Oh! What do you want?

Krogstad: Excuse me. The outer door was ajar; it must be someone forgot to shut it —

Nora (rising): My husband isn't home, Mr. Krogstad.

Krogstad: I know that.

Nora: Yes — then what do you want here?

Krogstad: A word with you.

Nora: With — ? *(To the children, quietly.)* Go in to Anne-Marie. What? No, the strange man won't hurt Mama. When he's gone, we'll play some more. *(She leads the children into the room to the left and shuts the door after them. Then, tense and nervous):* You want to speak to me?

Krogstad: Yes, I want to.

Nora: Today? But it's not yet the first of the month —

Krogstad: No, it's Christmas Eve. It's going to be up to you how merry a Christmas you have.

Nora: What is it you want? Today I absolutely can't —

Krogstad: We won't talk about that till later. This is something else. You do have a moment to spare, I suppose?

Nora: Oh yes, of course — I do, except —

Krogstad: Good. I was sitting over at Olsen's Restaurant when I saw your husband go down the street —

Nora: Yes?

Krogstad: With a lady.

1st act

Scene 4 complication occurs

Nora: Yes. So?

Krogstad: If you'll pardon my asking: wasn't that lady a Mrs. Linde?

Nora: Yes.

Krogstad: Just now come into town?

Nora: Yes, today.

Krogstad: She's a good friend of yours?

Nora: Yes, she is. But I don't see —

Krogstad: I also knew her once.

Nora: I'm aware of that.

Krogstad: Oh? You know all about it. I thought so. Well, then let me ask you short and sweet: is Mrs. Linde getting a job in the bank?

Nora: What makes you think you can cross-examine me, Mr. Krogstad — you, one of my husband's employees? But since you ask, you might as well know — yes, Mrs. Linde's going to be taken on at the bank. And I'm the one who spoke for her, Mr. Krogstad. Now you know.

Krogstad: So I guessed right.

Nora (pacing up and down): Oh, one does have a tiny bit of influence, I should hope. Just because I am a woman, don't think it means that — When one has a subordinate position, Mr. Krogstad, one really ought to be careful about pushing somebody who — hm —

Krogstad: Who has influence?

Nora: That's right.

Krogstad (in a different tone): Mrs. Helmer, would you be good enough to use your influence on my behalf?

Nora: What? What do you mean?

Krogstad: Would you please make sure that I keep my subordinate position in the bank?

Nora: What does that mean? Who's thinking of taking away your position?

Krogstad: Oh, don't play the innocent with me. I'm quite aware that your friend would hardly relish the chance of running into me again; and I'm also aware now whom I can thank for being turned out.

Nora: But I promise you —

Krogstad: Yes, yes, yes, to the point: there's still time, and I'm advising you to use your influence to prevent it.

Nora: But Mr. Krogstad, I have absolutely no influence.

Krogstad: You haven't? I thought you were just saying —

Nora: You shouldn't take me so literally. I! How can you believe that I have any such influence over my husband?

Krogstad: Oh, I've known your husband from our student days. I don't think the great bank manager's more steadfast than any other married man.

Nora: You speak insolently about my husband, and I'll show you the door.

Krogstad: The lady has spirit.

Nora: I'm not afraid of you any longer. After New Year's, I'll soon be done with the whole business.

Krogstad (restraining himself): Now listen to me, Mrs. Helmer. If necessary, I'll fight for my little job in the bank as if it were life itself.

Nora: Yes, so it seems.

Krogstad: It's not just a matter of income; that's the least of it. It's something *else* — All right, out with it! Look, this is the thing. You know, just like all the others, of course, that once, a good many years ago, I did something rather rash.

Nora: I've heard rumors to that effect.

Krogstad: The case never got into court; but all the same, every door was closed in my face from then on. So I took up those various activities you know about. I had to grab hold somewhere; and I dare say I haven't been among the worst. But now I want to drop all that. My boys are growing up. For their sakes, I'll have to win back as much respect as possible here in town. That job in the bank was like the first rung in my ladder. And now your husband wants to kick me right back down in the mud again.

Nora: But for heaven's sake, Mr. Krogstad, it's simply not in my power to help you.

Krogstad: That's because you haven't the will to — but I have the means to make you.

Nora: You certainly won't tell my husband that I owe you money?

Krogstad: Hm — what if I told him that?

Nora: That would be shameful of you. *(Nearly in tears.)* This secret — my joy and my pride — that he should learn it in such a crude and disgusting way — learn it from you. You'd expose me to the most horrible unpleasantness —

Krogstad: Only unpleasantness?

Nora (vehemently): But go on and try. It'll turn out the worse for you, because then my husband will really see what a crook you are, and then you'll *never* be able to hold your job.

Krogstad: I asked if it was just domestic unpleasantness you were afraid of?

Nora: If my husband finds out, then of course he'll pay what I owe at once, and then we'd be through with you for good.

Krogstad (a step closer): Listen, Mrs. Helmer — you've either got a very bad memory, or else no head at all for business. I'd better put you a little more in touch with the facts.

Nora: What do you mean?

Krogstad: When your husband was sick, you came to me for a loan of four thousand, eight hundred crowns.

Nora: Where else could I go?

Krogstad: I promised to get you that sum —

Nora: And you got it.

Krogstad: I promised to get you that sum, on certain conditions. You were so involved in your husband's illness, and so eager to finance your trip, that I guess you didn't think out all the details. It might just be a good idea to remind you. I promised you the money on the strength of a note I drew up.

Nora: Yes, and that I signed.

Krogstad: Right. But at the bottom I added some lines for your father to guarantee the loan. He was supposed to sign down there.

Nora: Supposed to? He did sign.

Krogstad: I left the date blank. In other words, your father would have dated his signature himself. Do you remember that?

Nora: Yes, I think —

Krogstad: Then I gave you the note for you to mail to your father. Isn't that so?

Nora: Yes.

Krogstad: And naturally you sent it at once — because only some five, six days later you brought me the note, properly signed. And with that, the money was yours.

Nora: Well, then; I've made my payments regularly, haven't I?

Krogstad: More or less. But — getting back to the point — those were hard times for you then, Mrs. Helmer.

Nora: Yes, they were.

Krogstad: Your father was very ill, I believe.

Nora: He was near the end.

Krogstad: He died soon after?

Nora: Yes.

Krogstad: Tell me, Mrs. Helmer, do you happen to recall the date of your father's death? The day of the month, I mean.

Nora: Papa died the twenty-ninth of September.

Krogstad: That's quite correct; I've already looked into that. And now we come to a curious thing — *(taking out a paper)* which I simply cannot comprehend.

Nora: Curious thing? I don't know —

Krogstad: This is the curious thing: that your father co-signed the note for your loan three days after his death.

Nora: How — ? I don't understand.

Krogstad: Your father died the twenty-ninth of September. But look. Here your father dated his signature October second. Isn't that curious, Mrs. Helmer? *(Nora is silent.)* Can you explain it to me? *(Nora remains silent.)* It's also remarkable that the words "October second" and the year aren't written in your father's hand, but rather in one that I think I know. Well, it's easy to understand. Your father forgot perhaps to date his signature, and then someone or other added it, a bit sloppily, before anyone knew of his death. There's nothing wrong in that. It all comes down to the signature. And there's no question about *that*, Mrs. Helmer. It really *was* your father who signed his own name here, wasn't it?

Nora (after a short silence, throwing her head back and looking squarely at him): No, it wasn't. I signed Papa's name.

Krogstad: Wait, now — are you fully aware that this is a dangerous confession?

Nora: Why? You'll soon get your money.

Krogstad: Let me ask you a question — why didn't you send the paper to your father?

Nora: That was impossible. Papa was so sick. If I'd asked him for his signature, I also would have had to tell him what the money was for. But I couldn't tell him, sick as he was, that my husband's life was in danger. That was just impossible.

Krogstad: Then it would have been better if you'd given up the trip abroad.

Nora: I couldn't possibly. The trip was to save my husband's life. I couldn't give that up.

Krogstad: But didn't you ever consider that this was a fraud against me?

Nora: I couldn't let myself be bothered by that. You weren't any concern of mine. I couldn't stand you, with all those cold complications you made, even though you knew how badly off my husband was.

Krogstad: Mrs. Helmer, obviously you haven't the vaguest idea of what you've involved yourself in. But I can tell you this: it was nothing more and nothing worse than I once did — and it wrecked my whole reputation.

Nora: You? Do you expect me to believe that you ever acted bravely to save your wife's life?

Krogstad: Laws don't inquire into motives.

Nora: Then they must be very poor laws.

Krogstad: Poor or not — if I introduce this paper in court, you'll be judged according to law.

Nora: This I refuse to believe. A daughter hasn't a right to protect her dying father from anxiety and care? A wife hasn't a right to save her husband's life? I don't know much about laws, but I'm sure that somewhere in the books these things are allowed. And you don't know anything about it — you who practice the law? You must be an awful lawyer, Mr. Krogstad.

Krogstad: Could be. But business — the kind of business we two are mixed up in — don't you think I know about that? All right. Do what you want now. But I'm telling you *this:* if I get shoved down a second time, you're going to keep me company. (*He bows and goes out through the hall.*)

Nora (pensive for a moment, then tossing her head): Oh, really! Trying to frighten me! I'm not so silly as all that. (*Begins gathering up the children's clothes, but soon stops.*) But — ? No, but that's impossible! I did it out of love.

The Children (in the doorway, left): Mama, that strange man's gone out the door.

Nora: Yes, yes, I know it. But don't tell anyone about the strange man. Do you hear? Not even Papa!

The Children: No, Mama. But now will you play again?

Nora: No, not now.

The Children: Oh, but Mama, you promised.

Nora: Yes, but I can't now. Go inside; I have too much to do. Go in, go in, my sweet darlings. (*She herds them gently back in the room and shuts the door after them. Settling on the sofa, she takes up a piece of embroidery and makes some stitches, but soon stops abruptly.*) No! (*Throws the work aside, rises, goes to the hall door and calls out.*) Helene! Let me have the tree in here. (*Goes to the table, left, opens the table drawer, and stops again.*) No, but that's utterly impossible!

Maid (with the Christmas tree): Where should I put it, ma'am?

Nora: There. The middle of the floor.

Maid: Should I bring anything else?

Nora: No, thanks. I have what I need.

The Maid, who has set the tree down, goes out.

Nora (absorbed in trimming the tree): Candles here — and flowers here. That terrible creature! Talk, talk, talk! There's nothing to it at all. The tree's going to be lovely. I'll do anything to please you, Torvald. I'll sing for you, dance for you —

Helmer comes in from the hall, with a sheaf of papers under his arm.

Nora: Oh! You're back so soon?

Helmer: Yes. Has anyone been here?

scene 5
put off
problem

Nora: Here? No.

Helmer: That's odd. I saw Krogstad leaving the front door.

Nora: So? Oh yes, that's true. Krogstad was here a moment.

Helmer: Nora, I can see by your face that he's been here, begging you to put in a good word for him.

Nora: Yes.

Helmer: And it was supposed to seem like your own idea? You were to hide it from me that he'd been here. He asked you that, too, didn't he?

Nora: Yes, Torvald, but —

Helmer: Nora, Nora, and you could fall for that? Talk with that sort of person and promise him anything? And then in the bargain, tell me an untruth.

Nora: An untruth — ?

Helmer: Didn't you say that no one had been here? *(Wagging his finger.)* My little songbird must never do that again. A songbird needs a clean beak to warble with. No false notes. *(Putting his arm, about her waist.)* That's the way it should be, isn't it? Yes, I'm sure of it. *(Releasing her.)* And so, enough of that. *(Sitting by the stove.)* Ah, how snug and cozy it is here. *(Leafing among his papers.)*

Nora (busy with the tree, after a short pause): Torvald!

Helmer: Yes.

Nora: I'm so much looking forward to the Stenborgs' costume party, day after tomorrow.

Helmer: And I can't wait to see what you'll surprise me with.

Nora: Oh, that stupid business!

Helmer: What?

Nora: I can't find anything that's right. Everything seems so ridiculous, so inane.

Helmer: So my little Nora's come to *that* recognition?

Nora (going behind his chair, her arms resting on its back): Are you very busy, Torvald?

Helmer: Oh —

Nora: What papers are those?

Helmer: Bank matters.

Nora: Already?

Helmer: I've gotten full authority from the retiring management to make all necessary changes in personnel and procedure. I'll need Christmas week for that. I want to have everything in order by New Year's.

Nora: So that was the reason this poor Krogstad —

Helmer: Hm.

Nora (still leaning on the chair and slowly stroking the nape of his neck): If you weren't so very busy, I would have asked you an enormous favor, Torvald.

Helmer: Let's hear. What is it?

Nora: You know, there isn't anyone who has your good taste — and I want so much to look well at the costume party. Torvald, couldn't you take over and decide what I should be and plan my costume?

Helmer: Ah, is my stubborn little creature calling for a lifeguard?

Nora: Yes, Torvald, I can't get anywhere without your help.

Helmer: All right — I'll think it over. We'll hit on something.

Nora: Oh, how sweet of you. *(Goes to the tree again. Pause.)* Aren't the red flowers pretty — ? But tell me, was it really such a crime that this Krogstad committed?

Helmer: Forgery. Do you have any idea what that means?

Nora: Couldn't he have done it out of need?

Helmer: Yes, or thoughtlessness, like so many others. I'm not so heartless that I'd condemn a man categorically for just one mistake.

Nora: No, of course not, Torvald!

Helmer: Plenty of men have redeemed themselves by openly confessing their crimes and taking their punishment.

Nora: Punishment — ?

Helmer: But now Krogstad didn't go that way. He got himself out by sharp practices, and that's the real cause of his moral breakdown.

Nora: Do you really think that would — ?

Helmer: Just imagine how a man with that sort of guilt in him has to lie and cheat and deceive on all sides, has to wear a mask even with the nearest and dearest he has, even with his own wife and children. And with the children, Nora — that's where it's most horrible.

Nora: Why?

Helmer: Because that kind of atmosphere of lies infects the whole life of a home. Every breath the children take in is filled with the germs of something degenerate.

Nora (coming closer behind him): Are you sure of that?

Helmer: Oh, I've seen it often enough as a lawyer. Almost everyone who goes bad early in life has a mother who's a chronic liar.

Nora: Why just — the mother?

Helmer: It's usually the mother's influence that's dominant, but the father's works in the same way, of course. Every lawyer is quite familiar with it. And still this Krogstad's been going home year in, year out, poisoning his own children with lies and pretense; that's why I call him morally lost. *(Reaching his hands out toward her.)* So my sweet little Nora must promise me never to plead his cause. Your hand on it. Come, come, what's this? Give me your hand. There, now. All settled. I can tell you it'd be impossible for me to work alongside of him. I literally feel physically revolted when I'm anywhere near such a person.

Nora (withdraws her hand and goes to the other side of the Christmas tree): How hot it is here! And I've got so much to do.

Helmer (getting up and gathering his papers): Yes, and I have to think about getting some of these read through before dinner. I'll think about your costume, too. And something to hang on the tree in gilt paper, I may even see about that. *(Putting his hand on her head.)* Oh you, my darling little songbird. *(He goes into his study and closes the door after him.)*

Nora (softly, after a silence): Oh, really! It isn't so. It's impossible. It must be impossible.

Anne-Marie (in the doorway, left): The children are begging so hard to come in to Mama.

Nora: No, no, no, don't let them in to me! You stay with them, Anne-Marie.

Anne-Marie: Of course, ma'am. *(Closes the door.)*

Nora (pale with terror): Hurt my children — ! Poison my home? *(A moment's*

[handwritten in left margin, rotated: wants to run away]

pause; then she tosses her head.) That's not true. Never. Never in all the world.

ACT II *crisis*

Same room. Beside the piano the Christmas tree now stands stripped of orna-ment, burned-down candle stubs on its ragged branches. Nora's street clothes lie on the sofa. Nora, alone in the room, moves restlessly about; at last she stops at the sofa and picks up her coat.

Nora (dropping the coat again): Someone's coming! *(Goes toward the door, lis-tens.)* No — there's no one. Of course — nobody's coming today, Christ-mas Day — or tomorrow, either. But maybe — *(Opens the door and looks out.)* No, nothing in the mailbox. Quite empty. *(Coming forward.)* What nonsense! He won't do anything serious. Nothing terrible could happen. It's impossible. Why, I have three small children.

Anne-Marie, with a large carton, comes in from the room to the left.

Anne-Marie: Well, at last I found the box with the masquerade clothes.
Nora: Thanks. Put it on the table.
Anne-Marie (does so): But they're all pretty much of a mess.
Nora: Ahh! I'd love to rip them in a million pieces!
Anne-Marie: Oh, mercy, they can be fixed right up. Just a little patience.
Nora: Yes, I'll go get Mrs. Linde to help me.
Anne-Marie: Out again now? In this nasty weather? Miss Nora will catch cold — get sick.
Nora: Oh, worse things could happen — How are the children?
Anne-Marie: The poor mites are playing with their Christmas presents, but —
Nora: Do they ask for me much?
Anne-Marie: They're so used to having Mama around, you know.
Nora: Yes. But Anne-Marie, I *can't* be together with them as much as I was.
Anne-Marie: Well, small children get used to anything.
Nora: You think so? Do you think they'd forget their mother if she was gone for good?
Anne-Marie: Oh, mercy — gone for good!
Nora: Wait, tell me, Anne-Marie — I've wondered so often — how could you ever have the heart to give your child over to strangers?
Anne-Marie: But I had to, you know, to become little Nora's nurse.
Nora: Yes, but how could you *do* it?
Anne-Marie: When I could get such a good place? A girl who's poor and who's gotten in trouble is glad enough for that. Because that slippery fish, he didn't do a thing for me, you know.
Nora: But your daughter's surely forgotten you.
Anne-Marie: Oh, she certainly has not. She's written to me, both when she was confirmed and when she was married.
Nora (clasping her about the neck): You old Anne-Marie, you were a good mother for me when I was little.
Anne-Marie: Poor little Nora, with no other mother but me.

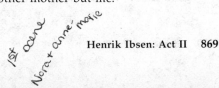
1st scene
Nora + anne-marie

Nora: And if the babies didn't have one, then I know that you'd — What silly talk! *(Opening the carton.)* Go in to them. Now I'll have to — Tomorrow you can see how lovely I'll look.

Anne-Marie: Oh, there won't be anyone at the party as lovely as Miss Nora. *(She goes off into the room, left.)*

Nora (begins unpacking the box, but soon throws it aside): Oh, if I dared to go out. If only nobody would come. If only nothing would happen here while I'm out. What craziness — nobody's coming. Just don't think. This muff — needs a brushing. Beautiful gloves, beautiful gloves. Let it go. Let it go! One, two, three, four, five, six — *(With a cry.)* Oh, there they are! *(Poises to move toward the door, but remains irresolutely standing. Mrs. Linde enters from the hall, where she has removed her street clothes.)*

Nora: Oh, it's you, Kristine. There's no one else out there? How good that you've come.

Mrs. Linde: I hear you were up asking for me.

Nora: Yes, I just stopped by. There's something you really can help me with. Let's get settled on the sofa. Look, there's going to be a costume party tomorrow evening at the Stenborgs' right above us, and now Torvald wants me to go as a Neapolitan peasant girl and dance the tarantella that I learned in Capri.

Mrs. Linde: Really, are you giving a whole performance?

Nora: Torvald says yes, I should. See, here's the dress. Torvald had it made for me down there; but now it's all so tattered that I just don't know —

Mrs. Linde: Oh, we'll fix that up in no time. It's nothing more than the trimmings — they're a bit loose here and there. Needle and thread? Good, now we have what we need.

Nora: Oh, how sweet of you!

Mrs. Linde (sewing): So you'll be in disguise tomorrow, Nora. You know what? I'll stop by then for a moment and have a look at you all dressed up. But listen, I've absolutely forgotten to thank you for that pleasant evening yesterday.

Nora (getting up and walking about): I don't think it was as pleasant as usual yesterday. You should have come to town a bit sooner, Kristine — Yes, Torvald really knows how to give a home elegance and charm.

Mrs. Linde: And you do, too, if you ask me. You're not your father's daughter for nothing. But tell me, is Dr. Rank always so down in the mouth as yesterday?

Nora: No, that was quite an exception. But he goes around critically ill all the time — tuberculosis of the spine, poor man. You know, his father was a disgusting thing who kept mistresses and so on — and that's why the son's been sickly from birth.

Mrs. Linde (lets her sewing fall to her lap): But my dearest Nora, how do you know about such things?

Nora (walking more jauntily): Hmp! When you've had three children, then you've had a few visits from — from women who know something of medicine, and they tell you this and that.

Mrs. Linde (resumes sewing; a short pause): Does Dr. Rank come here every day?

Nora: Every blessed day. He's Torvald's best friend from childhood, and *my* good friend, too. Dr. Rank almost belongs to this house.

Mrs. Linde: But tell me — is he quite sincere? I mean, doesn't he rather enjoy flattering people?

Nora: Just the opposite. Why do you think that?

Mrs. Linde: When you introduced us yesterday, he was proclaiming that he'd often heard my name in this house; but later I noticed that your husband hadn't the slightest idea who I really was. So how could Dr. Rank — ?

Nora: But it's all true, Kristine. You see, Torvald loves me beyond words, and, as he puts it, he'd like to keep me all to himself. For a long time he'd almost be jealous if I even mentioned any of my old friends back home. So of course I dropped that. But with Dr. Rank I talk a lot about such things, because he likes hearing about them.

Mrs. Linde: Now listen, Nora; in many ways you're still like a child. I'm a good deal older than you, with a little more experience. I'll tell you something: you ought to put an end to all this with Dr. Rank.

Nora: What should I put an end to?

Mrs. Linde: Both parts of it, I think. Yesterday you said something about a rich admirer who'd provide you with money —

Nora: Yes, one who doesn't exist — worse luck. So?

Mrs. Linde: Is Dr. Rank well off?

Nora: Yes, he is.

Mrs. Linde: With no dependents?

Nora: No, no one. But —

Mrs. Linde: And he's over here every day?

Nora: Yes, I told you that.

Mrs. Linde: How can a man of such refinement be so grasping?

Nora: I don't follow you at all.

Mrs. Linde: Now don't try to hide it, Nora. You think I can't guess who loaned you the forty-eight hundred crowns?

Nora: Are you out of your mind? How could you think such a thing! A friend of ours, who comes here every single day. What an intolerable situation that would have been!

Mrs. Linde: Then it really wasn't him.

Nora: No, absolutely not. It never even crossed my mind for a moment — And he had nothing to lend in those days; his inheritance came later.

Mrs. Linde: Well, I think that was a stroke of luck for you, Nora dear.

Nora: No, it never would have occurred to me to ask Dr. Rank — Still, I'm quite sure that if I had asked him —

Mrs. Linde: Which you won't, of course.

Nora: No, of course not. I can't see that I'd ever need to. But I'm quite positive that if I talked to Dr. Rank —

Mrs. Linde: Behind your husband's back?

Nora: I've got to clear up this other thing; *that's* also behind his back. I've *got* to clear it all up.

Mrs. Linde: Yes, I was saying that yesterday, but —

Nora (pacing up and down): A man handles these problems so much better than a woman —

Mrs. Linde: One's husband does, yes.

Nora: Nonsense. *(Stopping.)* When you pay everything you owe, then you get your note back, right?

Mrs. Linde: Yes, naturally.

Nora: And can rip it into a million pieces and burn it up — that filthy scrap of paper!

Mrs. Linde (looking hard at her, laying her sewing aside, and rising slowly): Nora, you're hiding something from me.

Nora: You can see it in my face?

Mrs. Linde: Something's happened to you since yesterday morning. Nora, what is it?

Nora (hurrying toward her): Kristine! *(Listening.)* Shh! Torvald's home. Look, go in with the children a while. Torvald can't bear all this snipping and stitching. Let Anne-Marie help you.

Mrs. Linde (gathering up some of the things): All right, but I'm not leaving here until we've talked this out. *(She disappears into the room, left, as Torvald enters from the hall.)*

Nora: Oh, how I've been waiting for you, Torvald dear.

Helmer: Was that the dressmaker?

Nora: No, that was Kristine. She's helping me fix up my costume. You know, it's going to be quite attractive.

Helmer: Yes, wasn't that a bright idea I had?

Nora: Brilliant! But then wasn't I good as well to give in to you?

Helmer: Good — because you give in to your husband's judgment? All right, you little goose, I know you didn't mean it like that. But I won't disturb you. You'll want to have a fitting, I suppose.

Nora: And you'll be working?

Helmer: Yes. *(Indicating a bundle of papers.)* See. I've been down to the bank. *(Starts toward his study.)*

Nora: Torvald.

Helmer (stops): Yes.

Nora: If your little squirrel begged you, with all her heart and soul, for something — ?

Helmer: What's that?

Nora: Then would you do it?

Helmer: First, naturally, I'd have to know what it was.

Nora: Your squirrel would scamper about and do tricks, if you'd only be sweet and give in.

Helmer: Out with it.

Nora: Your lark would be singing high and low in every room —

Helmer: Come on, she does that anyway.

Nora: I'd be a wood nymph and dance for you in the moonlight.

Helmer: Nora — don't tell me it's that same business from this morning?

Nora (coming closer): Yes, Torvald, I beg you, please!

Helmer: And you actually have the nerve to drag that up again?

Nora: Yes, yes, you've got to give in to me; you *have* to let Krogstad keep his job in the bank.

Helmer: My dear Nora, I've slated his job for Mrs. Linde.

Nora: That's awfully kind of you. But you could just fire another clerk instead of Krogstad.

Helmer: This is the most incredible stubbornness! Because you go and give an impulsive promise to speak up for him, I'm expected to —

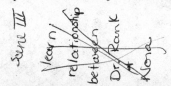

Nora: That's not the reason, Torvald. It's for your own sake. That man does writing for the worst papers; you said it yourself. He could do you any amount of harm. I'm scared to death of him —

Helmer: Ah, I understand. It's the old memories haunting you.

Nora: What do you mean by that?

Helmer: Of course, you're thinking about your father.

Nora: Yes, all right. Just remember how those nasty gossips wrote in the papers about Papa and slandered him so cruelly. I think they'd have had him dismissed if the department hadn't sent you up to investigate, and if you hadn't been so kind and open-minded toward him.

Helmer: My dear Nora, there's a notable difference between your father and me. Your father's official career was hardly above reproach. But mine is; and I hope it'll stay that way as long as I hold my position.

Nora: Oh, who can ever tell what vicious minds can invent? We could be so snug and happy now in our quiet, carefree home — you and I and the children, Torvald! That's why I'm pleading with you so —

Helmer: And just by pleading for him you make it impossible for me to keep him on. It's already known at the bank that I'm firing Krogstad. What if it's rumored around now that the new bank manager was vetoed by his wife —

Nora: Yes, what then — ?

Helmer: Oh yes — as long as our little bundle of stubbornness gets her way — ! I should go and make myself ridiculous in front of the whole office — give people the idea I can be swayed by all kinds of outside pressure. Oh, you can bet I'd feel the effects of that soon enough! Besides — there's something that rules Krogstad right out at the bank as long as I'm the manager.

Nora: What's that?

Helmer: His moral failings I could maybe overlook if I had to —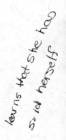

Nora: Yes, Torvald, why not?

Helmer: And I hear he's quite efficient on the job. But he was a crony of mine back in my teens — one of those rash friendships that crop up again and again to embarrass you later in life. Well, I might as well say it straight out: we're on a first-name basis. And that tactless fool makes no effort at all to hide it in front of others. Quite the contrary — he thinks that entitles him to take a familiar air around me, and so every other second he comes booming out with his "Yes, Torvald!" and "Sure thing, Torvald!" I tell you, it's been excruciating for me. He's out to make my place in the bank unbearable.

Nora: Torvald, you can't be serious about all this.

Helmer: Oh no? Why not?

Nora: Because these are such petty considerations.

Helmer: What are you saying? Petty? You think I'm petty!

Nora: No, just the opposite, Torvald dear. That's exactly why —

Helmer: Never mind. You call my motives petty; then I might as well be just that. Petty! All right! We'll put a stop to this for good. *(Goes to the hall door and calls.)* Helene!

Nora: What do you want?

Helmer (searching among his papers): A decision. *(The Maid comes in.)* Look here;

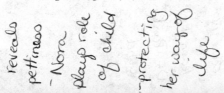

take this letter; go out with it at once. Get hold of a messenger and have him deliver it. Quick now. It's already addressed. Wait, here's some money.

Maid: Yes, sir. *(She leaves with the letter.)*

Helmer (straightening his papers): There, now, little Miss Willful.

Nora (breathlessly): Torvald, what was that letter?

Helmer: Krogstad's notice.

Nora: Call it back, Torvald! There's still time. Oh, Torvald, call it back! Do it for my sake — for your sake, for the children's sake! Do you hear, Torvald; do it! You don't know how this can harm us.

Helmer: Too late.

Nora: Yes, too late.

Helmer: Nora dear, I can forgive you this panic, even though basically you're insulting me. Yes, you are! Or isn't it an insult to think that *I* should be afraid of a courtroom hack's revenge? But I forgive you anyway, because this shows so beautifully how much you love me. *(Takes her in his arms.)* This is the way it should be, my darling Nora. Whatever comes, you'll see: when it really counts, I have strength and courage enough as a man to take on the whole weight myself.

Nora (terrified): What do you mean by that?

Helmer: The whole weight, I said.

Nora (resolutely): No, never in all the world.

Helmer: Good. So we'll share it, Nora, as man and wife. That's as it should be. *(Fondling her.)* Are you happy now? There, there, there — not these frightened dove's eyes. It's nothing at all but empty fantasies — Now you should run through your tarantella and practice your tambourine. I'll go to the inner office and shut both doors, so I won't hear a thing; you can make all the noise you like. *(Turning in the doorway.)* And when Rank comes, just tell him where he can find me. *(He nods to her and goes with his papers into the study, closing the door.)*

Nora (standing as though rooted, dazed with fright, in a whisper): He really could do it. He will do it. He'll do it in spite of everything. No, not that, never, never! Anything but that! Escape! A way out — *(The doorbell rings.)* Dr. Rank! Anything but that! *Anything,* whatever it is! *(Her hands pass over her face, smoothing it; she pulls herself together, goes over and opens the hall door. Dr. Rank stands outside, hanging his fur coat up. During the following scene, it begins getting dark.)*

Nora: Hello, Dr. Rank. I recognized your ring. But you mustn't go in to Torvald yet; I believe he's working.

Rank: And you?

Nora: For you, I always have an hour to spare — you know that. *(He has entered, and she shuts the door after him.)*

Rank: Many thanks. I'll make use of these hours while I can.

Nora: What do you mean by that? While you can?

Rank: Does that disturb you?

Nora: Well, it's such an odd phrase. Is anything going to happen?

Rank: What's going to happen is what I've been expecting so long — but I honestly didn't think it would come so soon.

Nora (gripping his arm): What is it you've found out? Dr. Rank, you have to tell me!

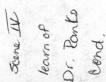

Rank (sitting by the stove): It's all over with me. There's nothing to be done about it.

Nora (breathing easier): Is it you — then — ?

Rank: Who else? There's no point in lying to one's self. I'm the most miserable of all my patients, Mrs. Helmer. These past few days I've been auditing my internal accounts. Bankrupt! Within a month I'll probably be laid out and rotting in the churchyard.

Nora: Oh, what a horrible thing to say.

Rank: The thing itself is horrible. But the worst of it is all the other horror before it's over. There's only one final examination left; when I'm finished with that, I'll know about when my disintegration will begin. There's something I want to say. Helmer with his sensitivity has such a sharp distaste for anything ugly. I don't want him near my sickroom.

Nora: Oh, but Dr. Rank —

Rank: I won't have him in there. Under no condition. I'll lock my door to him — As soon as I'm completely sure of the worst, I'll send you my calling card marked with a black cross, and you'll know then the wreck has started to come apart.

Nora: No, today you're completely unreasonable. And I wanted you so much to be in a really good humor.

Rank: With death up my sleeve? And then to suffer this way for somebody else's sins. Is there any justice in that? And in every single family, in some way or another, this inevitable retribution of nature goes on —

Nora (her hands pressed over her ears): Oh, stuff! Cheer up! Please — be gay!

Rank: Yes, I'd just as soon laugh at it all. My poor, innocent spine, serving time for my father's gay army days.

Nora (by the table, left): He was so infatuated with asparagus tips and *pâté de foie gras,* wasn't that it?

Rank: Yes — and with truffles.

Nora: Truffles, yes. And then with oysters, I suppose?

Rank: Yes, tons of oysters, naturally.

Nora: And then the port and champagne to go with it. It's so sad that all these delectable things have to strike at our bones.

Rank: Especially when they strike at the unhappy bones that never shared in the fun.

Nora: Ah, that's the saddest of all.

Rank (looks searchingly at her): Hm.

Nora (after a moment): Why did you smile?

Rank: No, it was you who laughed.

Nora: No, it was you who smiled, Dr. Rank!

Rank (getting up): You're even a bigger tease than I'd thought.

Nora: I'm full of wild ideas today.

Rank: That's obvious.

Nora (putting both hands on his shoulders): Dear, dear Dr. Rank, you'll never die for Torvald and me.

Rank: Oh, that loss you'll easily get over. Those who go away are soon forgotten.

Nora (looks fearfully at him): You believe that?

Rank: One makes new connections, and then —

Nora: Who makes new connections?

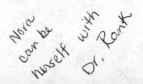
Nora can be herself with Dr. Rank

Rank: Both you and Torvald will when I'm gone. I'd say you're well under way already. What was that Mrs. Linde doing here last evening?

Nora: Oh, come — you can't be jealous of poor Kristine?

Rank: Oh yes, I am. She'll be my successor here in the house. When I'm down under, that woman will probably —

Nora: Shh! Not so loud. She's right in there.

Rank: Today as well. So you see.

Nora: Only to sew on my dress. Good gracious, how unreasonable you are. *(Sitting on the sofa.)* Be nice now, Dr. Rank. Tomorrow you'll see how beautifully I'll dance; and you can imagine then that I'm dancing only for you — yes, and of course for Torvald, too — that's understood. *(Takes various items out of the carton.)* Dr. Rank, sit over here and I'll show you something.

Rank (sitting): What's that?

Nora: Look here. Look.

Rank: Silk stockings.

Nora: Flesh-colored. Aren't they lovely? Now it's so dark here, but tomorrow — No, no, no, just look at the feet. Oh well, you might as well look at the rest.

Rank: Hm —

Nora: Why do you look so critical? Don't you believe they'll fit?

Rank: I've never had any chance to form an opinion on that.

Nora (glancing at him a moment): Shame on you. *(Hits him lightly on the ear with the stockings.)* That's for you. *(Puts them away again.)*

Rank: And what other splendors am I going to see now?

Nora: Not the least bit more, because you've been naughty. *(She hums a little and rummages among her things.)*

Rank (after a short silence): When I sit here together with you like this, completely easy and open, then I don't know — I simply can't imagine — whatever would have become of me if I'd never come into this house.

Nora (smiling): Yes, I really think you feel completely at ease with us.

Rank (more quietly, staring straight ahead): And then to have to go away from it all —

Nora: Nonsense, you're not going away.

Rank (his voice unchanged): — and not even be able to leave some poor show of gratitude behind, scarcely a fleeting regret — no more than a vacant place that anyone can fill.

Nora: And if I asked you now for — ? No —

Rank: For what?

Nora: For a great proof of your friendship —

Rank: Yes, yes?

Nora: No, I mean — for an exceptionally big favor —

Rank: Would you really, for once, make me so happy?

Nora: Oh, you haven't the vaguest idea what it is.

Rank: All right, then tell me.

Nora: No, but I can't, Dr. Rank — it's all out of reason. It's advice and help, too — and a favor —

Rank: So much the better. I can't fathom what you're hinting at. Just speak out. Don't you trust me?

Nora: Of course. More than anyone else. You're my best and truest friend, I'm sure. That's why I want to talk to you. All right, then, Dr. Rank: there's something you can help me prevent. You know how deeply, how inexpressibly dearly Torvald loves me; he'd never hesitate a second to give up his life for me.

Rank (leaning close to her): Nora — do you think he's the only one —

Nora (with a slight start): Who — ?

Rank: Who'd gladly give up his life for you.

Nora (heavily): I see.

Rank: I swore to myself you should know this before I'm gone. I'll never find a better chance. Yes, Nora, now you know. And also you know now that you can trust me beyond anyone else.

Nora (rising, natural and calm): Let me by.

Rank (making room for her, but still sitting): Nora —

Nora (in the hall doorway): Helene, bring the lamp in. *(Goes over to the stove.)* Ah, dear Dr. Rank, that was really mean of you.

Rank (getting up): That I've loved you just as deeply as somebody else? Was *that* mean?

Nora: No, but that you came out and told me. That was quite unnecessary —

Rank: What do you mean? Have you known — ?

The Maid comes in with the lamp, sets it on the table, and goes out again.

Rank: Nora — Mrs. Helmer — I'm asking you: have you known about it?

Nora: Oh, how can I tell what I know or don't know? Really, I don't know what to say — Why did you have to be so clumsy, Dr. Rank! Everything was so good.

Rank: Well, in any case, you now have the knowledge that my body and soul are at your command. So won't you speak out?

Nora (looking at him): After that?

Rank: Please, just let me know what it is.

Nora: You can't know anything now.

Rank: I have to. You mustn't punish me like this. Give me the chance to do whatever is humanly possible for you.

Nora: Now there's nothing you can do for me. Besides, actually, I don't need any help. You'll see — it's only my fantasies. That's what it is. Of course! *(Sits in the rocker, looks at him, and smiles.)* What a nice one you are, Dr. Rank. Aren't you a little bit ashamed, now that the lamp is here?

Rank: No, not exactly. But perhaps I'd better go — for good?

Nora: No, you certainly can't do that. You must come here just as you always have. You know Torvald can't do without you.

Rank: Yes, but *you?*

Nora: You know how much I enjoy it when you're here.

Rank: That's precisely what threw me off. You're a mystery to me. So many times I've felt you'd almost rather be with me than with Helmer.

Nora: Yes — you see, there are some people that one loves most and other people that one would almost prefer being with.

Rank: Yes, there's something to that.

Nora: When I was back home, of course I loved Papa most. But I always thought it was so much fun when I could sneak down to the maids' quarters, because they never tried to improve me, and it was always so amusing, the way they talked to each other.

Rank: Aha, so it's *their* place that I've filled.

Nora (jumping up and going to him): Oh, dear, sweet Dr. Rank, that's not what I mean at all. But you can understand that with Torvald it's just the same as with Papa —

The Maid enters from the hall.

Maid: Ma'am — please! *(She whispers to Nora and hands her a calling card.)*

Nora (glancing at the card): Ah! *(Slips it into her pocket.)*

Rank: Anything wrong?

Nora: No, no, not at all. It's only some — it's my new dress —

Rank: Really? But — there's your dress.

Nora: Oh, that. But this is another one — I ordered it — Torvald mustn't know —

Rank: Ah, now we have the big secret.

Nora: That's right. Just go in with him — he's back in the inner study. Keep him there as long as —

Rank: Don't worry. He won't get away. *(Goes into the study.)*

Nora (to the Maid): And he's standing waiting in the kitchen?

Maid: Yes, he came up by the back stairs.

Nora: But didn't you tell him somebody was here?

Maid: Yes, but that didn't do any good.

Nora: He won't leave?

Maid: No, he won't go till he's talked with you, ma'am.

Nora: Let him come in, then — but quietly. Helene, don't breathe a word about this. It's a surprise for my husband.

Maid: Yes, yes, I understand — *(Goes out.)*

Nora: This horror — it's going to happen. No, no, no, it can't happen, it mustn't. *(She goes and bolts Helmer's door. The Maid opens the hall door for Krogstad and shuts it behind him. He is dressed for travel in a fur coat, boots, and a fur cap.)*

Nora (going toward him): Talk softly. My husband's home.

Krogstad: Well, good for him.

Nora: What do you want?

Krogstad: Some information.

Nora: Hurry up, then. What is it?

Krogstad: You know, of course, that I got my notice.

Nora: I couldn't prevent it, Mr. Krogstad. I fought for you to the bitter end, but nothing worked.

Krogstad: Does your husband's love for you run so thin? He knows everything I can expose you to, and all the same he dares to —

Nora: How can you imagine he knows anything about this?

Krogstad: Ah, no — I can't imagine it either, now. It's not at all like my fine Torvald Helmer to have so much guts —

Nora: Mr. Krogstad, I demand respect for my husband!

Krogstad: Why, of course — all due respect. But since the lady's keeping it so

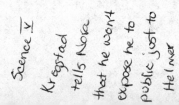

Scene V

Krogstad tells Nora that he won't expose he to public just to Helmer

carefully hidden, may I presume to ask if you're also a bit better informed than yesterday about what you've actually done?

Nora: More than you ever could teach me.

Krogstad: Yes, I *am* such an awful lawyer.

Nora: What is it you want from me?

Krogstad: Just a glimpse of how you are, Mrs. Helmer. I've been thinking about you all day long. A cashier, a night-court scribbler, a — well, a type like me also has a little of what they call a heart, you know.

Nora: Then show it. Think of my children.

Krogstad: Did you or your husband ever think of mine? But never mind. I simply wanted to tell you that you don't need to take this thing too seriously. For the present, I'm not proceeding with any action.

Nora: Oh no, really! Well — I knew that.

Krogstad: Everything can be settled in a friendly spirit. It doesn't have to get around town at all; it can stay just among us three.

Nora: My husband must never know anything of this.

Krogstad: How can you manage that? Perhaps you can pay me the balance?

Nora: No, not right now.

Krogstad: Or you know some way of raising the money in a day or two?

Nora: No way that I'm willing to use.

Krogstad: Well, it wouldn't have done you any good, anyway. If you stood in front of me with a fistful of bills, you still couldn't buy your signature back.

Nora: Then tell me what you're going to do with it.

Krogstad: I'll just hold onto it — keep it on file. There's no outsider who'll even get wind of it. So if you've been thinking of taking some desperate step —

Nora: I have.

Krogstad: Been thinking of running away from home —

Nora: I have!

Krogstad: Or even of something worse —

Nora: How could you guess that?

Krogstad: You can drop those thoughts.

Nora: How could you guess I was thinking of *that*?

Krogstad: Most of us think about *that* at first. I thought about it too, but I discovered I hadn't the courage —

Nora (lifelessly): I don't either.

Krogstad (relieved): That's true, you haven't the courage? You too?

Nora: I don't have it — I don't have it.

Krogstad: It would be terribly stupid, anyway. After that first storm at home blows out, why, then — I have here in my pocket a letter for your husband —

Nora: Telling everything?

Krogstad: As charitably as possible.

Nora (quickly): He mustn't ever get that letter. Tear it up. I'll find some way to get money.

Krogstad: Beg pardon, Mrs. Helmer, but I think I just told you —

Nora: Oh, I don't mean the money I owe you. Let me know how much you want from my husband, and I'll manage it.

Krogstad: I don't want any money from your husband.

Nora: What do you want, then?

Krogstad: I'll tell you what. I want to recoup, Mrs. Helmer; I want to get on in the world — and there's where your husband can help me. For a year and a half I've kept myself clean of anything disreputable — all that time struggling with the worst conditions; but I was satisfied, working my way up step by step. Now I've been written right off, and I'm just not in the mood to come crawling back. I tell you, I want to move on. I want to get back in the bank — in a better position. Your husband can set up a job for me —

Nora: He'll never do that!

Krogstad: He'll do it. I know him. He won't dare breathe a word of protest. And once I'm in there together with him, you just wait and see! Inside of a year, I'll be the manager's right-hand man. It'll be Nils Krogstad, not Torvald Helmer, who runs the bank.

Nora: You'll never see the day!

Krogstad: Maybe you think you can —

Nora: I have the courage now — for *that*.

Krogstad: Oh, you don't scare me. A smart, spoiled lady like you —

Nora: You'll see; you'll see!

Krogstad: Under the ice, maybe? Down in the freezing, coal-black water? There, till you float up in the spring, ugly, unrecognizable, with your hair falling out —

Nora: You don't frighten me.

Krogstad: Nor do you frighten me. One doesn't do these things, Mrs. Helmer. Besides, what good would it be? I'd still have him safe in my pocket.

Nora: Afterwards? When I'm no longer — ?

Krogstad: Are you forgetting that *I'll* be in control then over your final reputation? *(Nora stands speechless, staring at him.)* Good; now I've warned you. Don't do anything stupid. When Helmer's read my letter, I'll be waiting for his reply. And bear in mind that it's your husband himself who's forced me back to my old ways. I'll never forgive him for that. Good-bye, Mrs. Helmer. *(He goes out through the hall.)*

Nora (goes to the hall door, opens it a crack, and listens): He's gone. Didn't leave the letter. Oh no, no, that's impossible too! *(Opening the door more and more.)* What's that? He's standing outside — not going downstairs. He's thinking it over? Maybe he'll — ? *(A letter falls in the mailbox; then Krogstad's footsteps are heard, dying away down a flight of stairs. Nora gives a muffled cry and runs over toward the sofa table. A short pause.)* In the mailbox. *(Slips warily over to the hall door.)* It's lying there. Torvald, Torvald — now we're lost!

Mrs. Linde (entering with the costume from the room, left): There now, I can't see anything else to mend. Perhaps you'd like to try —

Nora (in a hoarse whisper): Kristine, come here.

Mrs. Linde (tossing the dress on the sofa): What's wrong? You look upset.

Nora: Come here. See that letter? *There!* Look — through the glass in the mailbox.

Mrs. Linde: Yes, yes, I see it.

Nora: That letter's from Krogstad —

Mrs. Linde: Nora — it's Krogstad who loaned you the money!

Nora: Yes, and now Torvald will find out everything.

Mrs. Linde: Believe me, Nora, it's best for both of you.

Nora: There's more you don't know. I forged a name.

Mrs. Linde: But for heaven's sake — ?

Nora: I only want to tell you that, Kristine, so that you can be my witness.

Mrs. Linde: Witness? Why should I — ?

Nora: If I should go out of my mind — it could easily happen —

Mrs. Linde: Nora!

Nora: Or anything else occurred — so I couldn't be present here —

Mrs. Linde: Nora, Nora, you aren't yourself at all!

Nora: And someone should try to take on the whole weight, all of the guilt, you follow me —

Mrs. Linde: Yes, of course, but why do you think — ?

Nora: Then you're the witness that it isn't true, Kristine. I'm very much myself; my mind right now is perfectly clear; and I'm telling you: nobody else has known about this; I alone did everything. Remember that.

Mrs. Linde: I will. But I don't understand all this.

Nora: Oh, how could you ever understand it? It's the miracle now that's going to take place.

Mrs. Linde: The miracle?

Nora: Yes, the miracle. But it's so awful, Kristine. It mustn't take place, not for anything in the world.

Mrs. Linde: I'm going right over and talk with Krogstad.

Nora: Don't go near him; he'll do you some terrible harm!

Mrs. Linde: There was a time once when he'd gladly have done anything for me.

Nora: He?

Mrs. Linde: Where does he live?

Nora: Oh, how do I know? Yes. (*Searches in her pocket.*) Here's his card. But the letter, the letter — !

Helmer (from the study, knocking on the door): Nora!

Nora (with a cry of fear): Oh! What is it? What do you want?

Helmer: Now, now, don't be so frightened. We're not coming in. You locked the door — are you trying on the dress?

Nora: Yes, I'm trying it. I'll look just beautiful, Torvald.

Mrs. Linde (who has read the card): He's living right around the corner.

Nora: Yes, but what's the use? We're lost. The letter's in the box.

Mrs. Linde: And your husband has the key?

Nora: Yes, always.

Mrs. Linde: Krogstad can ask for his letter back unread; he can find some excuse —

Nora: But it's just this time that Torvald usually —

Mrs. Linde: Stall him. Keep him in there. I'll be back as quick as I can. (*She hurries out through the hall entrance.*)

Nora (goes to Helmer's door, opens it, and peers in): Torvald!

Helmer (from the inner study): Well — does one dare set foot in one's own living room at last? Come on, Rank, now we'll get a look — (*In the doorway.*) But what's this?

Nora: What, Torvald dear?

Helmer: Rank had me expecting some grand masquerade.

Rank (in the doorway): That was my impression, but I must have been wrong.

Nora: No one can admire me in my splendor — not till tomorrow.

Helmer: But Nora dear, you look so exhausted. Have you practiced too hard?

Nora: No, I haven't practiced at all yet.

Helmer: You know, it's necessary —

Nora: Oh, it's absolutely necessary, Torvald. But I can't get anywhere without your help. I've forgotten the whole thing completely.

Helmer: Ah, we'll soon take care of that.

Nora: Yes, take care of me, Torvald, please! Promise me that? Oh, I'm so nervous. That big party — You must give up everything this evening for me. No business — don't even touch your pen. Yes? Dear Torvald, promise?

Helmer: It's a promise. Tonight I'm totally at your service — you little helpless thing. Hm — but first there's one thing I want to — *(Goes toward the hall door.)*

Nora: What are you looking for?

Helmer: Just to see if there's any mail.

Nora: No, no, don't do that, Torvald!

Helmer: Now what?

Nora: Torvald, please. There isn't any.

Helmer: Let me look, though. *(Starts out. Nora, at the piano, strikes the first notes of the tarantella. Helmer, at the door, stops.)* Aha!

Nora: I can't dance tomorrow if I don't practice with you.

Helmer (going over to her): Nora dear, are you really so frightened?

Nora: Yes, so terribly frightened. Let me practice right now; there's still time before dinner. Oh, sit down and play for me, Torvald. Direct me. Teach me, the way you always have.

Helmer: Gladly, if it's what you want. *(Sits at the piano.)*

Nora (snatches the tambourine up from the box, then a long, varicolored shawl, which she throws around herself, whereupon she springs forward and cries out): Play for me now! Now I'll dance!

Helmer plays and Nora dances. Rank stands behind Helmer at the piano and looks on.

Helmer (as he plays): Slower. Slow down.

Nora: Can't change it.

Helmer: Not so violent, Nora!

Nora: Has to be just like this.

Helmer (stopping): No, no, that won't do at all.

Nora (laughing and swinging her tambourine): Isn't that what I told you?

Rank: Let me play for her.

Helmer (getting up): Yes, go on. I can teach her more easily then.

Rank sits at the piano and plays; Nora dances more and more wildly. Helmer has stationed himself by the stove and repeatedly gives her directions; she seems not to hear them; her hair loosens and falls over her shoulders; she does not notice, but goes on dancing. Mrs. Linde enters.

Mrs. Linde (standing dumbfounded at the door): Ah — !

Nora (still dancing): See what fun, Kristine!

Helmer: But Nora darling, you dance as if your life were at stake.

Nora: And it is.

Helmer: Rank, stop! This is pure madness. Stop it, I say!

> *Rank breaks off playing, and Nora halts abruptly.*

Helmer (going over to her): I never would have believed it. You've forgotten everything I taught you.

Nora (throwing away the tambourine): You see for yourself.

Helmer: Well, there's certainly room for instruction here.

Nora: Yes, you see how important it is. You've got to teach me to the very last minute. Promise me that, Torvald?

Helmer: You can bet on it.

Nora: You mustn't, either today or tomorrow, think about anything else but me; you mustn't open any letters — or the mailbox —

Helmer: Ah, it's still the fear of that man —

Nora: Oh yes, yes, that too.

Helmer: Nora, it's written all over you — there's already a letter from him out there.

Nora: I don't know. I guess so. But you mustn't read such things now; there mustn't be anything ugly between us before it's all over.

Rank (quietly to Helmer): You shouldn't deny her.

Helmer (putting his arm around her): The child can have her way. But tomorrow night, after you've danced —

Nora: Then you'll be free.

Maid (in the doorway, right): Ma'am, dinner is served.

Nora: We'll be wanting champagne, Helene.

Maid: Very good, ma'am. *(Goes out.)*

Helmer: So — a regular banquet, hm?

Nora: Yes, a banquet — champagne till daybreak! *(Calling out.)* And some macaroons, Helene. Heaps of them — just this once.

Helmer (taking her hands): Now, now, now — no hysterics. Be my own little lark again.

Nora: Oh, I will soon enough. But go on in — and you, Dr. Rank. Kristine, help me put up my hair.

Rank (whispering, as they go): There's nothing wrong — really wrong, is there?

Helmer: Oh, of course not. It's nothing more than this childish anxiety I was telling you about. *(They go out, right.)*

Nora: Well?

Mrs. Linde: Left town.

Nora: I could see by your face.

Mrs. Linde: He'll be home tomorrow evening. I wrote him a note.

Nora: You shouldn't have. Don't try to stop anything now. After all, it's a wonderful joy, this waiting here for the miracle.

Mrs. Linde: What is it you're waiting for?

Nora: Oh, you can't understand that. Go in to them: I'll be along in a moment.

> *Mrs. Linde goes into the dining room. Nora stands a short while as if composing herself; then she looks at her watch.*

Nora: Five. Seven hours to midnight. Twenty-four hours to the midnight after, and then the tarantella's done. Seven and twenty-four? Thirty-one hours to live.

Helmer *(in the doorway, right):* What's become of the little lark?
Nora *(going toward him with open arms):* Here's your lark!

ACT III

Same scene. The table, with chairs around it, has been moved to the center of the room. A lamp on the table is lit. The hall door stands open. Dance music drifts down from the floor above. Mrs. Linde sits at the table, absently paging through a book, trying to read, but apparently unable to focus her thoughts. Once or twice she pauses, tensely listening for a sound at the outer entrance.

Mrs. Linde *(glancing at her watch):* Not yet — and there's hardly any time left. If only he's not — *(Listening again.)* Ah, there he is. *(She goes out in the hall and cautiously opens the outer door. Quiet footsteps are heard on the stairs. She whispers:)* Come in. Nobody's here.
Krogstad *(in the doorway):* I found a note from you at home. What's back of all this?
Mrs. Linde: I just *had* to talk to you.
Krogstad: Oh? And it just *had* to be here in this house?
Mrs. Linde: At my place it was impossible; my room hasn't a private entrance. Come in; we're all alone. The maid's asleep, and the Helmers are at the dance upstairs.
Krogstad *(entering the room):* Well, well, the Helmers are dancing tonight? Really?
Mrs. Linde: Yes, why not?
Krogstad: How true — why not?
Mrs. Linde: All right, Krogstad, let's talk.
Krogstad: Do we two have anything more to talk about?
Mrs. Linde: We have a great deal to talk about.
Krogstad: I wouldn't have thought so.
Mrs. Linde: No, because you've never understood me, really.
Krogstad: Was there anything more to understand — except what's all too common in life? A calculating woman throws over a man the moment a better catch comes by.
Mrs. Linde: You think I'm so thoroughly calculating? You think I broke it off lightly?
Krogstad: Didn't you?
Mrs. Linde: Nils — is that what you really thought?
Krogstad: If you cared, then why did you write me the way you did?
Mrs. Linde: What else could I do? If I had to break off with you, then it was my job as well to root out everything you felt for me.
Krogstad *(wringing his hands):* So that was it. And this — all this, simply for money!
Mrs. Linde: Don't forget I had a helpless mother and two small brothers. We couldn't wait for you, Nils; you had such a long road ahead of you then.
Krogstad: That may be; but you still hadn't the right to abandon me for somebody else's sake.

Mrs. Linde: Yes — I don't know. So many, many times I've asked myself if I did have that right.

Krogstad (more softly): When I lost you, it was as if all the solid ground dissolved from under my feet. Look at me; I'm a half-drowned man now, hanging onto a wreck.

Mrs. Linde: Help may be near.

Krogstad: It was near — but then you came and blocked it off.

Mrs. Linde: Without my knowing it, Nils. Today for the first time I learned that it's you I'm replacing at the bank.

Krogstad: All right — I believe you. But now that you know, will you step aside?

Mrs. Linde: No, because that wouldn't benefit you in the slightest.

Krogstad: Not "benefit" me, hm! I'd step aside anyway.

Mrs. Linde: I've learned to be realistic. Life and hard, bitter necessity have taught me that.

Krogstad: And life's taught me never to trust fine phrases.

Mrs. Linde: Then life's taught you a very sound thing. But you do have to trust in actions, don't you?

Krogstad: What does that mean?

Mrs. Linde: You said you were hanging on like a half-drowned man to a wreck.

Krogstad: I've good reason to say that.

Mrs. Linde: I'm also like a half-drowned woman on a wreck. No one to suffer with; no one to care for.

Krogstad: You made your choice.

Mrs. Linde: There wasn't any choice then.

Krogstad: So — what of it?

Mrs. Linde: Nils, if only we two shipwrecked people could reach across to each other.

Krogstad: What are you saying?

Mrs. Linde: Two on one wreck are at least better off than each on his own.

Krogstad: Kristine!

Mrs. Linde: Why do you think I came into town?

Krogstad: Did you really have some thought of me?

Mrs. Linde: I have to work to go on living. All my born days, as long as I can remember, I've worked, and it's been my best and my only joy. But now I'm completely alone in the world; it frightens me to be so empty and lost. To work for yourself — there's no joy in that. Nils, give me something — someone to work for.

Krogstad: I don't believe all this. It's just some hysterical feminine urge to go out and make a noble sacrifice.

Mrs. Linde: Have you ever found me to be hysterical? .

Krogstad: Can you honestly mean this? Tell me — do you know everything about my past?

Mrs. Linde: Yes.

Krogstad: And you know what they think I'm worth around here.

Mrs. Linde: From what you were saying before, it would seem that with me you could have been another person.

Krogstad: I'm positive of that.

Mrs. Linde: Couldn't it happen still?

Krogstad: Kristine — you're saying this in all seriousness? Yes, you are! I can see it in you. And do you really have the courage, then — ?

Mrs. Linde: I need to have someone to care for; and your children need a mother. We both need each other. Nils, I have faith that you're good at heart — I'll risk everything together with you.

Krogstad (gripping her hands): Kristine, thank you, thank you — Now I know I can win back a place in their eyes. Yes — but I forgot —

Mrs. Linde (listening): Shh! The tarantella. Go now! Go on!

Krogstad: Why? What is it?

Mrs. Linde: Hear the dance up there? When that's over, they'll be coming down.

Krogstad: Oh, then I'll go. But — it's all pointless. Of course, you don't know the move I made against the Helmers.

Mrs. Linde: Yes, Nils, I know.

Krogstad: And all the same, you have the courage to — ?

Mrs. Linde: I know how far despair can drive a man like you.

Krogstad: Oh, if I only could take it all back.

Mrs. Linde: You easily could — your letter's still lying in the mailbox.

Krogstad: Are you sure of that?

Mrs. Linde: Positive. But —

Krogstad (looks at her searchingly): Is that the meaning of it, then? You'll save your friend at any price. Tell me straight out. Is that it?

Mrs. Linde: Nils — anyone who's sold herself for somebody else once isn't going to do it again.

Krogstad: I'll demand my letter back.

Mrs. Linde: No, no.

Krogstad: Yes, of course. I'll stay here till Helmer comes down; I'll tell him to give me my letter again — that it only involves my dismissal — that he shouldn't read it —

Mrs. Linde: No, Nils, don't call the letter back.

Krogstad: But wasn't that exactly why you wrote me to come here?

Mrs. Linde: Yes, in that first panic. But it's been a whole day and night since then, and in that time I've seen such incredible things in this house. Helmer's got to learn everything; this dreadful secret has to be aired; those two have to come to a full understanding; all these lies and evasions can't go on.

Krogstad: Well, then, if you want to chance it. But at least there's one thing I can do, and do right away —

Mrs. Linde (listening): Go now, go, quick! The dance is over. We're not safe another second.

Krogstad: I'll wait for you downstairs.

Mrs. Linde: Yes, please do; take me home.

Krogstad: I can't believe it; I've never been so happy. *(He leaves by way of the outer door; the door between the room and the hall stays open.)*

Mrs. Linde (straightening up a bit and getting together her street clothes): How different now! How different! Someone to work for, to live for — a home to build. Well, it is worth the try! Oh, if they'd only come! *(Listening.)* Ah, there they are. Bundle up. *(She picks up her hat and coat. Nora's and Helmer's voices can be heard outside; a key turns in the lock, and Helmer brings Nora into*

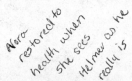

the hall almost by force. She is wearing the Italian costume with a large black shawl about her; he has on evening dress, with a black domino open over it.)

Nora (struggling in the doorway): No, no, no, not inside! I'm going up again. I don't want to leave so soon.

Helmer: But Nora dear —

Nora: Oh, I beg you, please, Torvald. From the bottom of my heart, *please* — only an hour more!

Helmer: Not a single minute, Nora darling. You know our agreement. Come on, in we go; you'll catch cold out here. *(In spite of her resistance, he gently draws her into the room.)*

Mrs. Linde: Good evening.

Nora: Kristine!

Helmer: Why, Mrs. Linde — are you here so late?

Mrs. Linde: Yes, I'm sorry, but I did want to see Nora in costume.

Nora: Have you been sitting here, waiting for me?

Mrs. Linde: Yes. I didn't come early enough; you were all upstairs; and then I thought I really couldn't leave without seeing you.

Helmer (removing Nora's shawl): Yes, take a good look. She's worth looking at, I can tell you that, Mrs. Linde. Isn't she lovely?

Mrs. Linde: Yes, I should say —

Helmer: A dream of loveliness, isn't she? That's what everyone thought at the party, too. But she's horribly stubborn — this sweet little thing. What's to be done with her? Can you imagine, I almost had to use force to pry her away.

Nora: Oh, Torvald, you're going to regret you didn't indulge me, even for just a half hour more.

Helmer: There, you see. She danced her tarantella and got a tumultuous hand — which was well earned, although the performance may have been a bit too naturalistic — I mean it rather overstepped the proprieties of art. But never mind — what's important is, she made a success, an overwhelming success. You think I could let her stay on after that and spoil the effect? Oh no; I took my lovely little Capri girl — my capricious little Capri girl, I should say — took her under my arm; one quick tour of the ballroom, a curtsy to every side, and then — as they say in novels — the beautiful vision disappeared. An exit should always be effective, Mrs. Linde, but that's what I can't get Nora to grasp. Phew, it's hot in here. *(Flings the domino on a chair and opens the door to his room.)* Why's it dark in here? Oh yes, of course. Excuse me. *(He goes in and lights a couple of candles.)*

Nora (in a sharp, breathless whisper): So?

Mrs. Linde (quietly): I talked with him.

Nora: And — ?

Mrs. Linde: Nora — you must tell your husband everything.

Nora (dully): I knew it.

Mrs. Linde: You've got nothing to fear from Krogstad, but you have to speak out.

Nora: I won't tell.

Mrs. Linde: Then the letter will.

Nora: Thanks, Kristine. I know now what's to be done. Shh!

Helmer (reentering): Well, then, Mrs. Linde — have you admired her?

Mrs. Linde: Yes, and now I'll say good night.

Helmer: Oh, come, so soon? Is this yours, this knitting?

Mrs. Linde: Yes, thanks. I nearly forgot it.

Helmer: Do you knit, then?

Mrs. Linde: Oh yes.

Helmer: You know what? You should embroider instead.

Mrs. Linde: Really? Why?

Helmer: Yes, because it's a lot prettier. See here, one holds the embroidery so, in the left hand, and then one guides the needle with the right — so — in an easy, sweeping curve — right?

Mrs. Linde: Yes, I guess that's —

Helmer: But, on the other hand, knitting — it can never be anything but ugly. Look, see here, the arms tucked in, the knitting needles going up and down — there's something Chinese about it. Ah, that was really a glorious champagne they served.

Mrs. Linde: Yes, good night, Nora, and don't be stubborn any more.

Helmer: Well put, Mrs. Linde!

Mrs. Linde: Good night, Mr. Helmer.

Helmer (accompanying her to the door): Good night, good night. I hope you get home all right. I'd be very happy to — but you don't have far to go. Good night, good night. (*She leaves. He shuts the door after her and returns.*) There, now, at last we got her out the door. She's a deadly bore, that creature.

Nora: Aren't you pretty tired, Torvald?

Helmer: No, not a bit.

Nora: You're not sleepy?

Helmer: Not at all. On the contrary, I'm feeling quite exhilarated. But you? Yes, you really look tired and sleepy.

Nora: Yes, I'm very tired. Soon now I'll sleep.

Helmer: See! You see! I was right all along that we shouldn't stay longer.

Nora: Whatever you do is always right.

Helmer (kissing her brow): Now my little lark talks sense. Say, did you notice what a time Rank was having tonight?

Nora: Oh, was he? I didn't get to speak with him.

Helmer: I scarcely did either, but it's a long time since I've seen him in such high spirits. (*Gazes at her a moment, then comes nearer her.*) Hm — it's marvelous, though, to be back home again — to be completely alone with you. Oh, you bewitchingly lovely young woman!

Nora: Torvald, don't look at me like that!

Helmer: Can't I look at my richest treasure? At all that beauty that's mine, mine alone — completely and utterly.

Nora (moving around to the other side of the table): You mustn't talk to me that way tonight.

Helmer (following her): The tarantella is still in your blood, I can see — and it makes you even more enticing. Listen. The guests are beginning to go. (*Dropping his voice.*) Nora — it'll soon be quiet through this whole house.

Nora: Yes, I hope so.

Helmer: You do, don't you, my love? Do you realize — when I'm out at a party like this with you — do you know why I talk to you so little, and keep such a distance away; just send you a stolen look now and then — you know why I do it? It's because I'm imagining then that you're my secret darling, my secret young bride-to-be, and that no one suspects there's anything between us.

Nora: Yes, yes; oh, yes, I know you're always thinking of me.

Helmer: And then when we leave and I place the shawl over those fine young rounded shoulders — over that wonderful curving neck — then I pretend that you're my young bride, that we're just coming from the wedding, that for the first time I'm bringing you into my house — that for the first time I'm alone with you — completely alone with you, your trembling young beauty! All this evening I've longed for nothing but you. When I saw you turn and sway in the tarantella — my blood was pounding till I couldn't stand it — that's why I brought you down here so early —

Nora: Go away, Torvald! Leave me alone. I don't want all this.

Helmer: What do you mean? Nora, you're teasing me. You will, won't you? Aren't I your husband — ?

A knock at the outside door.

Nora (startled): What's that?

Helmer (going toward the hall): Who is it?

Rank (outside): It's me. May I come in a moment?

Helmer (with quiet irritation): Oh, what does he want now? *(Aloud.)* Hold on. *(Goes and opens the door.)* Oh, how nice that you didn't just pass us by!

Rank: I thought I heard your voice, and then I wanted so badly to have a look in. *(Lightly glancing about.)* Ah, me, these old familiar haunts. You have it snug and cozy in here, you two.

Helmer: You seemed to be having it pretty cozy upstairs, too.

Rank: Absolutely. Why shouldn't I? Why not take in everything in life? As much as you can, anyway, and as long as you can. The wine was superb —

Helmer: The champagne especially.

Rank: You noticed that too? It's amazing how much I could guzzle down.

Nora: Torvald also drank a lot of champagne this evening.

Rank: Oh?

Nora: Yes, and that always makes him so entertaining.

Rank: Well, why shouldn't one have a pleasant evening after a well-spent day?

Helmer: Well spent? I'm afraid I can't claim that.

Rank (slapping him on the back): But I can, you see!

Nora: Dr. Rank, you must have done some scientific research today.

Rank: Quite so.

Helmer: Come now — little Nora talking about scientific research!

Nora: And can I congratulate you on the results?

Rank: Indeed you may.

Nora: Then they were good?

Rank: The best possible for both doctor and patient — certainty.

Nora (quickly and searchingly): Certainty?

Rank: Complete certainty. So don't I owe myself a gay evening afterwards?

Nora: Yes, you're right, Dr. Rank.

Helmer: I'm with you — just so long as you don't have to suffer for it in the morning.

Rank: Well, one never gets something for nothing in life.

Nora: Dr. Rank — are you very fond of masquerade parties?

Rank: Yes, if there's a good array of odd disguises —

Nora: Tell me, what should we two go as at the next masquerade?

Helmer: You little featherhead — already thinking of the next!

Rank: We two? I'll tell you what: you must go as Charmed Life —

Helmer: Yes, but find a costume for *that!*

Rank: Your wife can appear just as she looks every day.

Helmer: That was nicely put. But don't you know what you're going to be?

Rank: Yes, Helmer, I've made up my mind.

Helmer: Well?

Rank: At the next masquerade I'm going to be invisible.

Helmer: That's a funny idea.

Rank: They say there's a hat — black, huge — have you never heard of the hat that makes you invisible? You put it on, and then no one on earth can see you.

Helmer (suppressing a smile): Ah, of course.

Rank: But I'm quite forgetting what I came for. Helmer, give me a cigar, one of the dark Havanas.

Helmer: With the greatest pleasure. *(Holds out his case.)*

Rank: Thanks. *(Takes one and cuts off the tip.)*

Nora (striking a match): Let me give you a light.

Rank: Thank you. *(She holds the match for him; he lights the cigar.)* And now good-bye.

Helmer: Good-bye, good-bye, old friend.

Nora: Sleep well, Doctor.

Rank: Thanks for that wish.

Nora: Wish me the same.

Rank: You? All right, if you like — Sleep well. And thanks for the light. *(He nods to them both and leaves.)*

Helmer (his voice subdued): He's been drinking heavily.

Nora (absently): Could be. *(Helmer takes his keys from his pocket and goes out in the hall.)* Torvald — what are you after?

Helmer: Got to empty the mailbox; it's nearly full. There won't be room for the morning papers.

Nora: Are you working tonight?

Helmer: You know I'm not. Why — what's this? Someone's been at the lock.

Nora: At the lock — ?

Helmer: Yes, I'm positive. What do you suppose — ? I can't imagine one of the maids — ? Here's a broken hairpin. Nora, it's yours —

Nora (quickly): Then it must be the children —

Helmer: You'd better break them of that. Hm, hm — well, opened it after all. *(Takes the contents out and calls into the kitchen.)* Helene! Helene, would you put out the lamp in the hall. *(He returns to the room, shutting the hall door, then displays the handful of mail.)* Look how it's piled up. *(Sorting through them.)* Now what's this?

Nora (at the window): The letter! Oh, Torvald, no!

Helmer: Two calling cards — from Rank.

Nora: From Dr. Rank?

Helmer (examining them): "Dr. Rank, Consulting Physician." They were on top. He must have dropped them in as he left.

Nora: Is there anything on them?

Helmer: There's a black cross over the name. See? That's a gruesome notion. He could almost be announcing his own death.

Nora: That's just what he's doing.

Helmer: What! You've heard something? Something he's told you?

Nora: Yes. That when those cards came, he'd be taking his leave of us. He'll shut himself in now and die.

Helmer: Ah, my poor friend! Of course I knew he wouldn't be here much longer. But so soon — And then to hide himself away like a wounded animal.

Nora: If it has to happen, then it's best it happens in silence — don't you think so, Torvald?

Helmer (pacing up and down): He'd grown right into our lives. I simply can't imagine him gone. He with his suffering and loneliness — like a dark cloud setting off our sunlit happiness. Well, maybe it's best this way. For him, at least. *(Standing still.)* And maybe for us too, Nora. Now we're thrown back on each other, completely. *(Embracing her.)* Oh you, my darling wife, how can I hold you close enough? You know what, Nora — time and again I've wished you were in some terrible danger, just so I could stake my life and soul and everything, for your sake.

Nora (tearing herself away, her voice firm and decisive): Now you must read your mail, Torvald.

Helmer: No, no, not tonight. I want to stay with you, dearest.

Nora: With a dying friend on your mind?

Helmer: You're right. We've both had a shock. There's ugliness between us — these thoughts of death and corruption. We'll have to get free of them first. Until then — we'll stay apart.

Nora (clinging about his neck): Torvald — good night! Good night!

Helmer (kissing her on the cheek): Good night, little songbird. Sleep well, Nora. I'll be reading my mail now. *(He takes the letters into his room and shuts the door after him.)*

Nora (with bewildered glances, groping about, seizing Helmer's domino, throwing it around her, and speaking in short, hoarse, broken whispers): Never see him again. Never, never. *(Putting her shawl over her head.)* Never see the children either — them, too. Never, never. Oh, the freezing black water! The depths — down — Oh, I wish it were over — He has it now; he's reading it — now. Oh no, no, not yet. Torvald, good-bye, you and the children — *(She starts for the hall; as she does, Helmer throws open his door and stands with an open letter in his hand.)*

Helmer: Nora!

Nora (screams): Oh — !

Helmer: What is this? You know what's in this letter?

Nora: Yes, I know. Let me go! Let me out!

Helmer (holding her back): Where are you going?

Nora (struggling to break loose): You can't save me, Torvald!

Helmer (slumping back): True! Then it's true what he writes? How horrible! No, no, it's impossible — it can't be true.

Nora: It *is* true. I've loved you more than all this world.

Helmer: Ah, none of your slippery tricks.

Nora (taking one step toward him): Torvald — !

Helmer: What *is* this you've blundered into!

Nora: Just let me loose. You're not going to suffer for my sake. You're not going to take on my guilt.

Helmer: No more playacting. *(Locks the hall door.)* You stay right here and give me a reckoning. You understand what you've done? Answer! You understand?

Nora (looking squarely at him, her face hardening): Yes. I'm beginning to understand everything now.

Helmer (striding about): Oh, what an awful awakening! In all these eight years — she who was my pride and joy — a hypocrite, a liar — worse, worse — a criminal! How infinitely disgusting it all is! The shame! *(Nora says nothing and goes on looking straight at him. He stops in front of her.)* I should have suspected something of the kind. I should have known. All your father's flimsy values — Be still! All your father's flimsy values have come out in you. No religion, no morals, no sense of duty — Oh, how I'm punished for letting him off! I did it for your sake, and you repay me like this.

Nora: Yes, like this.

Helmer: Now you've wrecked all my happiness — ruined my whole future. Oh, it's awful to think of. I'm in a cheap little grafter's hands; he can do anything he wants with me, ask for anything, play with me like a puppet — and I can't breathe a word. I'll be swept down miserably into the depths on account of a featherbrained woman.

Nora: When I'm gone from this world, you'll be free.

Helmer: Oh, quit posing. Your father had a mess of those speeches too. What good would that ever do me if you were gone from this world, as you say? Not the slightest. He can still make the whole thing known; and if he does, I could be falsely suspected as your accomplice. They might even think that I was behind it — that I put you up to it. And all that I can thank you for — you that I've coddled the whole of our marriage. Can you see now what you've done to me?

Nora (icily calm): Yes.

Helmer: It's so incredible, I just can't grasp it. But we'll have to patch up whatever we can. Take off the shawl. I said, take it off! I've got to appease him somehow or other. The thing has to be hushed up at any cost. And as for you and me, it's got to seem like everything between us is just as it was — to the outside world, that is. You'll go right on living in this house, of course. But you can't be allowed to bring up the children; I don't dare trust you with them — Oh, to have to say this to someone I've loved so much! Well, that's done with. From now on happiness doesn't matter; all that matters is saving the bits and pieces, the appearance — *(The doorbell rings. Helmer starts.)* What's that? And so late. Maybe the worst — ? You think he'd — ? Hide, Nora! Say you're sick. *(Nora remains standing motionless. Helmer goes and opens the door.)*

Maid (half dressed, in the hall): A letter for Mrs. Helmer.

Helmer: I'll take it. *(Snatches the letter and shuts the door.)* Yes, it's from him. You don't get it; I'm reading it myself.

Nora: Then read it.

Helmer (by the lamp): I hardly dare. We may be ruined, you and I. But — I've got to know. *(Rips open the letter, skims through a few lines, glances at an enclosure, then cries out joyfully.)* Nora! *(Nora looks inquiringly at him.)* Nora! Wait — better check it again — Yes, yes, it's true. I'm saved. Nora, I'm saved!

Nora: And I?

Helmer: You too, of course. We're both saved, both of us. Look. He's sent back your note. He says he's sorry and ashamed — that a happy development in his life — oh, who cares what he says! Nora, we're saved! No one can hurt you. Oh, Nora, Nora — but first, this ugliness all has to go. Let me see — *(Takes a look at the note.)* No, I don't want to see it; I want the whole thing to fade like a dream. *(Tears the note and both letters to pieces, throws them into the stove and watches them burn.)* There — now there's nothing left — He wrote that since Christmas Eve you — Oh, they must have been three terrible days for you, Nora.

Nora: I fought a hard fight.

Helmer: And suffered pain and saw no escape but — No, we're not going to dwell on anything unpleasant. We'll just be grateful and keep on repeating: it's over now, it's over! You hear me, Nora? You don't seem to realize — it's over. What's it mean — that frozen look? Oh, poor little Nora, I understand. You can't believe I've forgiven you. But I have, Nora; I swear I have. I know that what you did, you did out of love for me.

Nora: That's true.

Helmer: You loved me the way a wife ought to love her husband. It's simply the means that you couldn't judge. But you think I love you any the less for not knowing how to handle your affairs? No, no — just lean on me; I'll guide you and teach you. I wouldn't be a man if this feminine helplessness didn't make you twice as attractive to me. You mustn't mind those sharp words I said — that was all in the first confusion of thinking my world had collapsed. I've forgiven you, Nora; I swear I've forgiven you.

Nora: My thanks for your forgiveness. *(She goes out through the door, right.)*

Helmer: No, wait — *(Peers in.)* What are you doing in there?

Nora (inside): Getting out of my costume.

Helmer (by the open door): Yes, do that. Try to calm yourself and collect your thoughts again, my frightened little songbird. You can rest easy now; I've got wide wings to shelter you with. *(Walking about close by the door.)* How snug and nice our home is, Nora. You're safe here; I'll keep you like a hunted dove I've rescued out of a hawk's claws. I'll bring peace to your poor, shuddering heart. Gradually it'll happen, Nora; you'll see. Tomorrow all this will look different to you; then everything will be as it was. I won't have to go on repeating I forgive you; you'll feel it for yourself. How can you imagine I'd ever conceivably want to disown you — or even blame you in any way? Ah, you don't know a man's heart, Nora. For a man there's something indescribably sweet and satisfying in knowing he's forgiven his wife — and forgiven her out of a full and open heart. It's as if she belongs to him in two ways now: in a sense he's given her fresh into the world again, and she's become his wife and his child as well. From now on that's what you'll be to me — you little, bewildered, helpless thing. Don't be afraid of anything, Nora; just open your heart to me, and I'll be conscience and will to you both — *(Nora enters in her regular clothes.)* What's this? Not in bed? You've changed your dress?

Nora: Yes, Torvald, I've changed my dress.

Helmer: But why now, so late?

Nora: Tonight I'm not sleeping.

Helmer: But Nora dear —

Nora (looking at her watch): It's still not so very late. Sit down, Torvald; we have a lot to talk over. *(She sits at one side of the table.)*

Helmer: Nora — what is this? That hard expression —

Nora: Sit down. This'll take some time. I have a lot to say.

Helmer (sitting at the table directly opposite her): You worry me, Nora. And I don't understand you.

Nora: No, that's exactly it. You don't understand me. And I've never understood you either — until tonight. No, don't interrupt. You can just listen to what I say. We're closing out accounts, Torvald.

Helmer: How do you mean that?

Nora (after a short pause): Doesn't anything strike you about our sitting here like this?

Helmer: What's that?

Nora: We've been married now eight years. Doesn't it occur to you that this is the first time we two, you and I, man and wife, have ever talked seriously together?

Helmer: What do you mean — seriously?

Nora: In eight whole years — longer even — right from our first acquaintance, we've never exchanged a serious word on any serious thing.

Helmer: You mean I should constantly go and involve you in problems you couldn't possibly help me with?

Nora: I'm not talking of problems. I'm saying that we've never sat down seriously together and tried to get to the bottom of anything.

Helmer: But dearest, what good would that ever do you?

Nora: That's the point right there: you've never understood me. I've been wronged greatly, Torvald — first by Papa, and then by you.

Helmer: What! By us — the two people who've loved you more than anyone else?

Nora (shaking her head): You never loved me. You've thought it fun to be in love with me, that's all.

Helmer: Nora, what a thing to say!

Nora: Yes, it's true now, Torvald. When I lived at home with Papa, he told me all his opinions, so I had the same ones too; or if they were different I hid them, since he wouldn't have cared for that. He used to call me his doll-child, and he played with me the way I played with my dolls. Then I came into your house —

Helmer: How can you speak of our marriage like that?

Nora (unperturbed): I mean, then I went from Papa's hands into yours. You arranged everything to your own taste, and so I got the same taste as you — or I pretended to; I can't remember. I guess a little of both, first one, then the other. Now when I look back, it seems as if I'd lived here like a beggar — just from hand to mouth. I've lived by doing tricks for you, Torvald. But that's the way you wanted it. It's a great sin what you and Papa did to me. You're to blame that nothing's become of me.

Helmer: Nora, how unfair and ungrateful you are! Haven't you been happy here?

Nora: No, never. I thought so — but I never have.

Helmer: Not — not happy!

Nora: No, only lighthearted. And you've always been so kind to me. But our home's been nothing but a playpen. I've been your doll-wife here, just as at home I was Papa's doll-child. And in turn the children have been my dolls. I thought it was fun when you played with me, just as they thought it fun when I played with them. That's been our marriage, Torvald.

Helmer: There's some truth in what you're saying — under all the raving exaggeration. But it'll all be different after this. Playtime's over; now for the schooling.

Nora: Whose schooling — mine or the children's?

Helmer: Both yours and the children's, dearest.

Nora: Oh, Torvald, you're not the man to teach me to be a good wife to you.

Helmer: And you can say that?

Nora: And I — how am I equipped to bring up children?

Helmer: Nora!

Nora: Didn't you say a moment ago that that was no job to trust me with?

Helmer: In a flare of temper! Why fasten on that?

Nora: Yes, but you were so very right. I'm not up to the job. There's another job I have to do first. I have to try to educate myself. You can't help me with that. I've got to do it alone. And that's why I'm leaving you now.

Helmer (jumping up): What's that?

Nora: I have to stand completely alone, if I'm ever going to discover myself and the world out there. So I can't go on living with you.

Helmer: Nora, Nora!

Nora: I want to leave right away. Kristine should put me up for the night —

Helmer: You're insane! You've no right! I forbid you!

Nora: From here on, there's no use forbidding me anything. I'll take with me whatever is mine. I don't want a thing from you, either now or later.

Helmer: What kind of madness is this!

Nora: Tomorrow I'm going home — I mean, home where I came from. It'll be easier up there to find something to do.

Helmer: Oh, you blind, incompetent child!

Nora: I must learn to be competent, Torvald.

Helmer: Abandon your home, your husband, your children! And you're not even thinking what people will say.

Nora: I can't be concerned about that. I only know how essential this is.

Helmer: Oh, it's outrageous. So you'll run out like this on your most scared vows.

Nora: What do you think are my most sacred vows?

Helmer: And I have to tell you that! Aren't they your duties to your husband and children?

Nora: I have other duties equally sacred.

Helmer: That isn't true. What duties are they?

Nora: Duties to myself.

Helmer: Before all else, you're a wife and a mother.

Nora: I don't believe in that any more. I believe that, before all else, I'm a human being, no less than you — or anyway, I ought to try to become one. I know the majority thinks you're right, Torvald, and plenty of books agree with you, too. But I can't go on believing what the majority says, or what's written in books. I have to think over these things myself and try to understand them.

Helmer: Why can't you understand your place in your own home? On a point like that, isn't there one everlasting guide you can turn to? Where's your religion?

Nora: Oh, Torvald, I'm really not sure what religion is.

Helmer: What — ?

Nora: I only know what the minister said when I was confirmed. He told me religion was this thing and that. When I get clear and away by myself, I'll go into that problem too. I'll see if what the minister said was right, or, in any case, if it's right for me.

Helmer: A young woman your age shouldn't talk like that. If religion can't move you, I can try to rouse your conscience. You do have some moral feeling? Or, tell me — has that gone too?

Nora: It's not easy to answer that, Torvald. I simply don't know. I'm all confused about these things. I just know I see them so differently from you. I find out, for one thing, that the law's not at all what I'd thought — but I can't get it through my head that the law is fair. A woman hasn't a right to protect her dying father or save her husband's life! I can't believe that.

Helmer: You talk like a child. You don't know anything of the world you live in.

Nora: No, I don't. But now I'll begin to learn for myself. I'll try to discover who's right, the world or I.

Helmer: Nora, you're sick; you've got a fever. I almost think you're out of your head.

Nora: I've never felt more clearheaded and sure in my life.

Helmer: And — clearheaded and sure — you're leaving your husband and children?

Nora: Yes.

Helmer: Then there's only one possible reason.

Nora: What?

Helmer: You no longer love me.

Nora: No. That's exactly it.

Helmer: Nora! You can't be serious!

Nora: Oh, this is so hard, Torvald — you've been so kind to me always. But I can't help it. I don't love you any more.

Helmer (struggling for composure): Are you also clearheaded and sure about that?

Nora: Yes, completely. That's why I can't go on staying here.

Helmer: Can you tell me what I did to lose your love?

Nora: Yes, I can tell you. It was this evening when the miraculous thing didn't come — then I knew you weren't the man I'd imagined.

Helmer: Be more explicit; I don't follow you.

Nora: I've waited now so patiently eight long years — for, my Lord, I know miracles don't come every day. Then this crisis broke over me, and such a certainty filled me: *now* the miraculous event would occur. While Krogstad's letter was lying out there, I never for an instant dreamed that you could give in to his terms. I was so utterly sure you'd say to him: go on, tell your tale to the whole wide world. And when he'd done that —

Helmer: Yes, what then? When I'd delivered my own wife into shame and disgrace — !

Nora: When he'd done that, I was so utterly sure that you'd step forward, take the blame on yourself and say: I am the guilty one.

Helmer: Nora — !

Nora: You're thinking I'd never accept such a sacrifice from you? No, of course not. But what good would my protests be against you? That was the miracle I was waiting for, in terror and hope. And to stave that off, I would have taken my life.

Helmer: I'd gladly work for you day and night, Nora — and take on pain and deprivation. But there's no one who gives up honor for love.

Nora: Millions of women have done just that.

Helmer: Oh, you think and talk like a silly child.

Nora: Perhaps. But you neither think nor talk like the man I could join myself to. When your big fright was over — and it wasn't from any threat against me, only for what might damage you — when all the danger was past, for you it was just as if nothing had happened. I was exactly the same, your little lark, your doll, that you'd have to handle with double care now that I'd turned out so brittle and frail. *(Gets up.)* Torvald — in that instant it dawned on me that for eight years I've been living here with a stranger, and that I'd even conceived three children — oh, I can't stand the thought of it! I could tear myself to bits.

Helmer (heavily): I see. There's a gulf that's opened between us — that's clear. Oh, but Nora, can't we bridge it somehow?

Nora: The way I am now, I'm no wife for you.

Helmer: I have the strength to make myself over.

Nora: Maybe — if your doll gets taken away.

Helmer: But to part! To part from you! No, Nora, no — I can't imagine it.

Nora (going out, right): All the more reason why it has to be. *(She reenters with her coat and a small overnight bag, which she puts on a chair by the table.)*

Helmer: Nora, Nora, not now! Wait till tomorrow.

Nora: I can't spend the night in a strange man's room.

Helmer: But couldn't we live here like brother and sister —

Nora: You know very well how long that would last. *(Throws her shawl about her.)* Good-bye, Torvald. I won't look in on the children. I know they're in better hands than mine. The way I am now, I'm no use to them.

Helmer: But someday, Nora — someday — ?

Nora: How can I tell? I haven't the least idea what'll become of me.

Helmer: But you're my wife, now and wherever you go.

Nora: Listen, Torvald — I've heard that when a wife deserts her husband's house just as I'm doing, then the law frees him from all responsibility. In any case, I'm freeing you from being responsible. Don't feel yourself bound, any more than I will. There has to be absolute freedom for us both. Here, take your ring back. Give me mine.

Helmer: That too?

Nora: That too.

Helmer: There it is.

Nora: Good. Well, now it's all over. I'm putting the keys here. The maids know all about keeping up the house — better than I do. Tomorrow, after I've left town, Kristine will stop by to pack up everything that's mine from home. I'd like those things shipped up to me.

Helmer: Over! All over! Nora, won't you ever think about me?

Nora: I'm sure I'll think of you often, and about the children and the house here.

Helmer: May I write you?

Nora: No — never. You're not to do that.

Helmer: Oh, but let me send you —

Nora: Nothing. Nothing.

Helmer: Or help you if you need it.

Nora: No. I accept nothing from strangers.

Helmer: Nora — can I never be more than a stranger to you?

Nora (picking up the overnight bag): Ah, Torvald — it would take the greatest miracle of all —

Helmer: Tell me the greatest miracle!

Nora: You and I both would have to transform ourselves to the point that — Oh, Torvald, I've stopped believing in miracles.

Helmer: But I'll believe. Tell me! Transform ourselves to the point that — ?

Nora: That our living together could be a true marriage. *(She goes out down the hall.)*

Helmer (sinks down on a chair by the door, face buried in his hands): Nora! Nora! *(Looking about and rising.)* Empty. She's gone. *(A sudden hope leaps in him.)* The greatest miracle — ?

From below, the sound of a door slamming shut.

Questions

1. How early in the play did you understand why Ibsen titled his work *A Doll House*? What speeches or actions gave you this understanding?
2. Sum up your impression of Nora's character. In what ways do you find her a victim, in what ways at fault?
3. Try to state the theme of the play. Does it involve women's rights? Self-fulfillment?
4. What central dramatic question does the play embody? At what point can this question be stated?
5. What is the crisis? In what way is this moment or event a "turning point"? (In what new direction does the action turn?)
6. What objects or actions in the play would you call symbolic? How effective are these symbols?
7. Eric Bentley, in an essay titled "Ibsen, Pro and Con" (*In Search of Theater*, New York: Knopf, 1953), criticizes the character of Krogstad, calling him "a mere pawn of the plot." "When convenient to Ibsen, he is a blackmailer. When inconvenient, he is converted." Do you agree or disagree?
8. Why is the play considered a work of realism? Is there anything in it that does not seem realistic?
9. In what respects does *A Doll House* seem to apply to life today? Is it in any way dated? Could there be a Nora in North America in the 1970s?

33 Tragedy

> A tragedy, then, is an imitation of an action that is serious, complete in itself, and of a certain magnitude; in a language embellished with each kind of artistry . . . cast in the form of drama, not narrative; accomplishing through incidents that arouse pity and fear the purgation of these emotions.
>
> —Aristotle, *Poetics*, Chapter VI

The form of drama we call **tragedy** was born in Greece in the fifth century B.C. Aristotle's famous definition, constructed in the fourth century B.C., has the authority of one who probably saw many classical tragedies performed. In making his observations, Aristotle does not seem to be laying down laws for what a tragedy ought to be. More likely, he is drawing — from tragedies he has seen or read — a general description of them.

Aristotle observes that the protagonist, the hero or chief character of a tragedy, is a person of "high estate," apparently a king or queen or other member of a royal family. In thus being as keenly interested as contemporary dramatists in the private lives of the powerful, Greek dramatists need not be accused of snobbery. It is the nature of tragedy that the protagonist must fall from power and from happiness; his high estate gives him a place of dignity to fall from and perhaps makes his fall seem all the more a calamity in that it involves an entire nation or people. Nor is the protagonist extraordinary merely in his position in society. Oedipus, in the play of Sophocles, is not only a king but a noble soul who suffers profoundly and who employs splendid speech to express his suffering.

But the tragic hero is not a superman; he is fallible. The hero's downfall is the result, to use Aristotle's term, of his *hamartia*: his error or transgression or (as some translators would have it) his flaw or weakness of character. The notion that a tragic hero has such a **tragic flaw** has often been attributed to Aristotle, but it is by no means clear that that is what Aristotle meant. According to this interpretation, every tragic hero has some fatal weakness, some moral Achilles' heel (pride, say, or lust for power) that brings him to a bad end. This interpretation does not fit every tragedy, nor does it unmistakably fit Aristotle's favorite example, *Oedipus Rex*, as we shall see.

Whatever Aristotle had in mind, however, many later critics find value in the idea of the tragic flaw. In this view, the downfall of a hero follows from his very nature. But whatever view we take — whether we find the hero's sufferings due to a flaw of character or to an error of judgment — we will probably find that his downfall results from acts for which he himself is responsible. In a Greek tragedy, the hero is a character amply capable of making choices — capable, too, of accepting the consequences.

It may be useful to take another look at Aristotle's definition of tragedy, with which we began. By **purgation** *(katharsis)*, did the ancient theorist mean that after witnessing a tragedy we feel relief, having released our pent-up emotions? Or did he mean that our feelings are purified, refined into something more ennobling? Scholars continue to argue. Whatever his exact meaning, clearly Aristotle implies that after witnessing a tragedy we feel better, not worse — not depressed, but somehow elated. We take a kind of pleasure in the spectacle of a noble man being abased, but surely this pleasure is a legitimate one. For tragedy, in the words of Edith Hamilton, affects us as "pain transmuted into exaltation by the alchemy of poetry."[1]

THE THEATER OF SOPHOCLES

For a citizen of Athens in the fifth century B.C., when the surviving classical Greek tragedies originated, a play was a religious occasion. Plays were given at the Lenaea, or feast of the winepress, in January; or during the Great Dionysia, or feast of Dionysus, god of wine and crops, in the spring. So well did the Athenians love contests that at the spring festival each playwright was to present — in competition — three tragedies on successive days, the last tragedy to be followed by a short comedy of a special sort. The comedy was a **satyr play,** a parody of a mythic story, containing a chorus of actors playing *satyrs,* creatures half goat or horse, half man. The costs of the plays (and presumably the prize money) were borne by a wealthy citizen chosen by the state.

Seated in the open air, in a hillside amphitheater, as many as fourteen thousand spectators could watch a performance that must have somewhat resembled an opera or a modern musical. The audience, arranged in rows, looked out across a rounded **orchestra** or dancing-place, where the chorus of fifteen (the number was fixed by Sophocles) sang passages of lyric poetry and executed dance movements. (It is also possible that actors and chorus sometimes shared the orchestra.) In

---

[1] "The Idea of Tragedy" in *The Greek Way to Western Civilization* (New York: Norton, 1942).

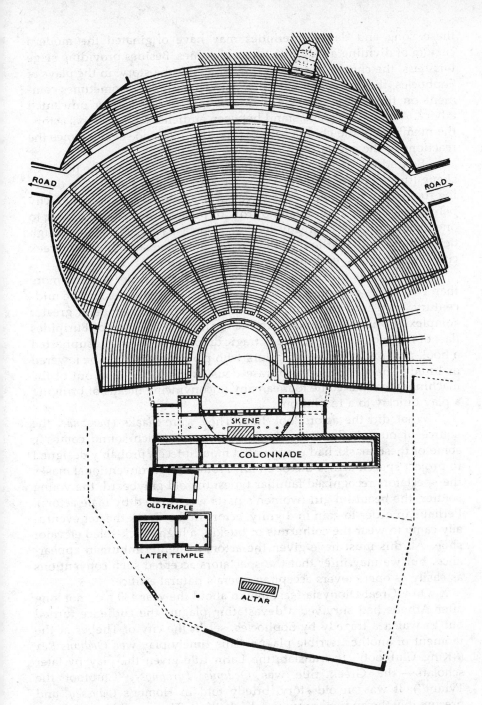

The theater of Dionysus at Athens in the time of Sophocles, a modern drawing based on scholarly guesswork. From R. C. Flickinger, *The Greek Theater and Its Drama* (1918).

these song and dance interludes may have originated the modern custom of dividing a play into acts and scenes. Besides providing stage business, the chorus had a function in telling the story: in the plays of Sophocles, they converse with the main character and sometimes comment on the action, offering words of warning and other unwanted advice. As they *physically* stand between audience and principal actors, the members of the chorus serve as middlemen who seem to voice the reactions of the spectators.

Behind the orchestra stood the actors, in front of a stage house or **skene** (the source of our word *scene*). Originally, the *skene* was a dressing room; later it is believed to have borne a painted backdrop. Directly behind the *skene,* a **colonnade** or row of pillars provided (according to one scholarly guess) a ready-made set for a palace. (This is a rough description of the Athenian theater of Dionysus; several other Greek cities had theaters, each unique in certain details.)

In the plays of Aeschylus in the early fifth century B.C., no more than two actors occupied the stage at any time. Sophocles, in the mid-century, increased the number to three, making situations of greater complexity possible. Still later in the century, in the time of Euripides (last of the trio of supreme Greek tragic dramatists), the *skene* supported a hook-and-pulley by which actors who played gods could be lowered or lifted — hence the Latin phrase **deus ex machina** ("god out of the machine") that has come to mean any unconvincing means of bringing a play quickly to a resolution.

What did the actors look like? They wore **masks** (*personae,* the source of our word *person:* "a thing through which sound comes"); some of these masks had exaggerated mouthpieces, probably designed to project speech across the open air. From certain conventional masks the spectators recognized familiar types: the old graybeard, the young soldier, the beautiful girl (women's parts were played by male actors). Perhaps in order to gain in dignity, actors in the Greek theater eventually came to wear the **cothurnus** or buskin, a high, thick-soled elevator shoe. All this must have given the actors a slightly inhuman appearance, but we may infer that the spectators accepted such conventions as easily as opera lovers accept an opera's natural artifice.

On a Great Dionysia feast day in about the year 430 B.C., not long after Athens had survived a devastating plague, the audience turned out to watch a tragedy by Sophocles, set in the city of Thebes at the moment of another terrible plague. This timely play was *Oedipus Rex* ("King Clubfoot," to translate the Latin title given the play by later scholars — the Greek title was *Oedipus Tyrannos,* "Clubfoot the Tyrant"). It was an old story, briefly told in Homer's *Odyssey,* and presumably the audience was familiar with it. They would have known the history of Oedipus who, because a prophecy had foretold that he would grow up to slay his father, had been taken out into the wilderness to perish. They would have known that before being left to die his feet had been pinned together, causing his clubfoot; and they would have known that later, adopted by King Polybos and grown to maturity, Oedipus won the throne of Thebes as a reward for ridding the city of the Sphinx, a winged, woman-headed lion. All comers to the Sphinx were asked a riddle, and failure to solve it meant death: "What goes on four legs in the morning, two at noon, and three at evening?" Oedipus correctly answered, "Man" (because as a baby he crawls on all fours, then as a man he walks erect, then as an old man he uses a cane). Chagrined, the Sphinx leaped from her rocky perch and dashed herself to death.

Sophocles (496?–406 B.C.)

OEDIPUS REX

An English Version by Dudley Fitts and Robert Fitzgerald

Characters°

Oedipus
A Priest
Creon
Teiresias
Iocastê
Messenger
Shepherd of Laïos
Second Messenger
Chorus of Theban Elders

The Scene: *Before the palace of Oedipus, King of Thebes. A central door and two lateral doors open onto a platform which runs the length of the façade. On the platform, right and left, are altars; and three steps lead down into the "orchestra," or chorus-ground. At the beginning of the action these steps are crowded by Suppliants° who have brought branches and chaplets of olive leaves and who lie in various attitudes of despair. Oedipus enters.*

PROLOGUE°

Oedipus: My children, generations of the living
    In the line of Kadmos°, nursed at his ancient hearth:

Characters: Some of these names are usually Anglicized: Jocasta, Laius. In this version, the translators prefer spelling names more nearly like the Greek.

Suppliants: persons come to ask some favor of the king.

Prologue: portion of the play containing the exposition.

² *line of Kadmos:* according to legend, the city of Thebes, where the play takes place, had been founded by the hero Cadmus.

Why have you strewn yourselves before these altars
In supplication, with your boughs and garlands?
The breath of incense rises from the city   5
With a sound of prayer and lamentation.

                              Children,
I would not have you speak through messengers,
And therefore I have come myself to hear you —
I, Oedipus, who bear the famous name.
    (To a Priest.) You, there, since you are eldest in the company,
Speak for them all, tell me what preys upon you,   10
Whether you come in dread, or crave some blessing:
Tell me, and never doubt that I will help you
In every way I can; I should be heartless
Were I not moved to find you suppliant here.

Priest: Great Oedipus, O powerful King of Thebes!   15
You see how all the ages of our people
Cling to your altar steps: here are boys
Who can barely stand alone, and here are priests
By weight of age, as I am a priest of God,
And young men chosen from those yet unmarried;   20
As for the others, all that multitude,
They wait with olive chaplets in the squares,
At the two shrines of Pallas°, and where Apollo°
Speaks in the glowing embers.

                          Your own eyes
Must tell you: Thebes is in her extremity   25
And can not lift her head from the surge of death.
A rust consumes the buds and fruits of the earth;
The herds are sick; children die unborn,
And labor is vain. The god of plague and pyre
Raids like detestable lightning through the city,   30
And all the house of Kadmos is laid waste,
All emptied, and all darkened: Death alone
Battens upon the misery of Thebes.

You are not one of the immortal gods, we know;
Yet we have come to you to make our prayer   35
As to the man of all men best in adversity
And wisest in the ways of God. You saved us
From the Sphinx, that flinty singer, and the tribute
We paid to her so long; yet you were never
Better informed than we, nor could we teach you: 40
It was some god breathed in you to set us free.

Therefore, O mighty King, we turn to you:
Find us our safety, find us a remedy,

---

²³ *Pallas:* title for Athena, goddess of wisdom.   ²³ *Apollo:* god of music, poetry, and
prophecy. At his shrine near Thebes, the ashes of fires were used to divine the future.

Whether by counsel of the gods or men.
A king of wisdom tested in the past   45
Can act in a time of troubles, and act well.
Noblest of men, restore
Life to your city! Think how all men call you
Liberator for your triumph long ago;
Ah, when your years of kingship are remembered,   50
Let them not say *We rose, but later fell —*
Keep the State from going down in the storm!
Once, years ago, with happy augury,
You brought us fortune; be the same again!
No man questions your power to rule the land: 55
But rule over men, not over a dead city!
Ships are only hulls, citadels are nothing,
When no life moves in the empty passageways.

Oedipus: Poor children! You may be sure I know
    All that you longed for in your coming here.   60
    I know that you are deathly sick; and yet,
    Sick as you are, not one is as sick as I.
    Each of you suffers in himself alone
    His anguish, not another's; but my spirit
    Groans for the city, for myself, for you.   65

    I was not sleeping, you are not waking me.
    No, I have been in tears for a long while
    And in my restless thought walked many ways.
    In all my search, I found one helpful course,
    And that I have taken: I have sent Creon,   70
    Son of Menoikeus, brother of the Queen,
    To Delphi, Apollo's place of revelation,
    To learn there, if he can,
    What act or pledge of mine may save the city.
    I have counted the days, and now, this very day,   75
    I am troubled, for he has overstayed his time.
    What is he doing? He has been gone too long.
    Yet whenever he comes back, I should do ill
    To scant whatever hint the god may give.

Priest: It is a timely promise. At this instant   80
    They tell me Creon is here.

Oedipus: O Lord Apollo!
    May his news be fair as his face is radiant!

Priest: It could not be otherwise: he is crowned with bay,
    The chaplet is thick with berries.

Oedipus: We shall soon know;
    He is near enough to hear us now.

    'Enter Creon.

                O Prince: 85

Brother: son of Menoikeus:
    What answer do you bring us from the god?
Creon: It is favorable. I can tell you, great afflictions
    Will turn out well, if they are taken well.
Oedipus: What was the oracle? These vague words   90
    Leave me still hanging between hope and fear.
Creon: Is it your pleasure to hear me with all these
    Gathered around us? I am prepared to speak,
    But should we not go in?
Oedipus: Let them all hear it.
    It is for them I suffer, more than for myself.   95
Creon: Then I will tell you what I heard at Delphi.

    In plain words
    The god commands us to expel from the land of Thebes
    An old defilement that it seems we shelter.
    It is a deathly thing, beyond expiation.   100
    We must not let it feed upon us longer.
Oedipus: What defilement? How shall we rid ourselves of it?
Creon: By exile or death, blood for blood. It was
    Murder that brought the plague-wind on the city.
Oedipus: Murder of whom? Surely the god has named him?   105
Creon: My lord: long ago Laïos was our king,
    Before you came to govern us.
Oedipus: I know;
    I learned of him from others; I never saw him.
Creon: He was murdered; and Apollo commands us now
    To take revenge upon whoever killed him.   110
Oedipus: Upon whom? Where are they? Where shall we find a clue
    To solve that crime, after so many years?
Creon: Here in this land, he said.
                            If we make enquiry,
    We may touch things that otherwise escape us.
Oedipus: Tell me: Was Laïos murdered in his house,   115
    Or in the fields, or in some foreign country?
Creon: He said he planned to make a pilgrimage.
    He did not come home again.
Oedipus: And was there no one,
    No witness, no companion, to tell what happened?
Creon: They were all killed but one, and he got away   120
    So frightened that he could remember one thing only.
Oedipus: What was that one thing? One may be the key
    To everything, if we resolve to use it.
Creon: He said that a band of highwaymen attacked them,
    Outnumbered them, and overwhelmed the King.   125
Oedipus: Strange, that a highwayman should be so daring —
    Unless some faction here bribed him to do it.
Creon: We thought of that. But after Laïos' death
    New troubles arose and we had no avenger.

Oedipus: What troubles could prevent your hunting down the killers?   130
Creon: The riddling Sphinx's song
    Made us deaf to all mysteries but her own.
Oedipus: Then once more I must bring what is dark to light.
    It is most fitting that Apollo shows,
    As you do, this compunction for the dead.   135
    You shall see how I stand by you, as I should,
    To avenge the city and the city's god,
    And not as though it were for some distant friend,
    But for my own sake, to be rid of evil.
    Whoever killed King Laïos might — who knows? —   140
    Decide at any moment to kill me as well.
    By avenging the murdered king I protect myself.
    Come, then, my children: leave the altar steps,
    Lift up your olive boughs!
                   One of you go
    And summon the people of Kadmos to gather here.   145
    I will do all that I can; you may tell them that.

    Exit a Page.

    So, with the help of God,
    We shall be saved — or else indeed we are lost.
Priest: Let us rise, children. It was for this we came,
    And now the King has promised it himself.   150
    Phoibos° has sent us an oracle; may he descend
    Himself to save us and drive out the plague.

    *Exeunt Oedipus and Creon into the palace by the central door. The Priest
    and the Suppliants disperse right and left. After a short pause the Chorus
    enters the orchestra.*

PARODOS°

                                            Strophe 1

Chorus: What is God singing in his profound
    Delphi of gold and shadow?
    What oracle for Thebes, the sunwhipped city?
    Fear unjoints me, the roots of my heart tremble.
    Now I remember, O Healer, your power, and wonder;   5
    Will you send doom like a sudden cloud, or weave it
    Like nightfall of the past?

---

¹⁵¹ *Phoibos:* the sun god Phoebus Apollo.
Parodos: part to be sung by the chorus on first entering. A *strophe* (according to theory)
was sung while the chorus danced from stage right to stage left; an *antistrophe*, while they
danced back again.

Speak, speak to us, issue of holy sound:
Dearest to our expectancy: be tender!

Let me pray to Athenê, the immortal daughter of Zeus,   10
And to Artemis her sister
Who keeps her famous throne in the market ring,
And to Apollo, bowman at the far butts of heaven —

O gods, descend! Like three streams leap against
The fires of our grief, the fires of darkness;   15
Be swift to bring us rest!

As in the old time from the brilliant house
Of air you stepped to save us, come again!

Now our afflictions have no end,
Now all our stricken host lies down   20
And no man fights off death with his mind;

The noble plowland bears no grain,
And groaning mothers can not bear —

See, how our lives like birds take wing,
Like sparks that fly when a fire soars,   25
To the shore of the god of evening.

The plague burns on, it is pitiless,
Though pallid children laden with death
Lie unwept in the stony ways,

And old gray women by every path   30
Flock to the strand about the altars

There to strike their breasts and cry
Worship of Phoibos in wailing prayers:
Be kind, God's golden child!

There are no swords in this attack by fire,   35
No shields, but we are ringed with cries.
Send the besieger plunging from our homes
Into the vast sea-room of the Atlantic
Or into the waves that foam eastward of Thrace —
For the day ravages what the night spares —   40

Destroy our enemy, lord of the thunder!
Let him be riven by lightning from heaven!

Phoibos Apollo, stretch the sun's bowstring,
That golden cord, until it sing for us,
Flashing arrows in heaven!
                              Artemis, Huntress,   45
Race with flaring lights upon our mountains!

O scarlet god, O golden-banded brow,
O Theban Bacchos in a storm of Maenads°,

Enter Oedipus, center.

Whirl upon Death, that all the Undying hate!
Come with blinding cressets, come in joy!   50

SCENE I

Oedipus: Is this your prayer? It may be answered. Come,
    Listen to me, act as the crisis demands,
    And you shall have relief from all these evils.

    Until now I was a stranger to this tale,
    As I had been a stranger to the crime.   5
    Could I track down the murderer without a clue?
    But now, friends,
    As one who became a citizen after the murder,
    I make this proclamation to all Thebans:
    If any man knows by whose hand Laïos, son of Labdakos,   10
    Met his death, I direct that man to tell me everything,
    No matter what he fears for having so long withheld it.
    Let it stand as promised that no further trouble
    Will come to him, but he may leave the land in safety.

    Moreover: If anyone knows the murderer to be foreign,   15
    Let him not keep silent: he shall have his reward from me.
    However, if he does conceal it; if any man
    Fearing for his friend or for himself disobeys this edict,
    Hear what I propose to do:

    I solemnly forbid the people of this country,   20
    Where power and throne are mine, ever to receive that man
    Or speak to him, no matter who he is, or let him
    Join in sacrifice, lustration, or in prayer.
    I decree that he be driven from every house,

---

⁴⁸ *Bacchos . . . Maenads:* god of wine with his attendant girl revelers.

Being, as he is, corruption itself to us: the Delphic 25
Voice of Zeus has pronounced this revelation.
Thus I associate myself with the oracle
And take the side of the murdered king.

As for the criminal, I pray to God —
Whether it be a lurking thief, or one of a number — 30
I pray that that man's life be consumed in evil and wretchedness.
And as for me, this curse applies no less
If it should turn out that the culprit is my guest here,
Sharing my hearth.
           You have heard the penalty.
I lay it on you now to attend to this 35
For my sake, for Apollo's, for the sick
Sterile city that heaven has abandoned.
Suppose the oracle had given you no command:
Should this defilement go uncleansed for ever?
You should have found the murderer: your king, 40
A noble king, had been destroyed!
               Now I,
Having the power that he held before me,
Having his bed, begetting children there
Upon his wife, as he would have, had he lived —
Their son would have been my children's brother, 45
If Laïos had had luck in fatherhood!
(But surely ill luck rushed upon his reign) —
I say I take the son's part, just as though
I were his son, to press the fight for him
And see it won! I'll find the hand that brought 50
Death to Labdakos' and Polydoros' child,
Heir of Kadmos' and Agenor's line.
And as for those who fail me,
May the gods deny them the fruit of the earth,
Fruit of the womb, and may they rot utterly! 55
Let them be wretched as we are wretched, and worse!

For you, for loyal Thebans, and for all
Who find my actions right, I pray the favor
Of justice, and of all the immortal gods.
Choragos°: Since I am under oath, my lord, I swear 60
    I did not do the murder, I can not name
    The murderer. Might not the oracle
    That has ordained the search tell where to find him?
Oedipus: An honest question. But no man in the world
    Can make the gods do more than the gods will. 65

<hr/>

60 *Choragos:* spokesman for the chorus.

Choragos: There is one last expedient —
Oedipus: Tell me what it is.
    Though it seem slight, you must not hold it back.
Choragos: A lord clairvoyant to the lord Apollo,
    As we all know, is the skilled Teiresias.
    One might learn much about this from him, Oedipus.   70
Oedipus: I am not wasting time:
    Creon spoke of this, and I have sent for him —
    Twice, in fact; it is strange that he is not here.
Choragos: The other matter — that old report — seems useless.
Oedipus: Tell me. I am interested in all reports.   75
Choragos: The King was said to have been killed by highwaymen.
Oedipus: I know. But we have no witnesses to that.
Choragos: If the killer can feel a particle of dread,
    Your curse will bring him out of hiding!
Oedipus: No.
    The man who dared that act will fear no curse.   80

Enter the blind seer Teiresias, led by a Page.

Choragos: But there is one man who may detect the criminal.
    This is Teiresias, this is the holy prophet
    In whom, alone of all men, truth was born.
Oedipus: Teiresias: seer: student of mysteries,
    Of all that's taught and all that no man tells,   85
    Secrets of Heaven and secrets of the earth:
    Blind though you are, you know the city lies
    Sick with plague; and from this plague, my lord,
    We find that you alone can guard or save us.

    Possibly you did not hear the messengers?   90
    Apollo, when we sent to him,
    Sent us back word that this great pestilence
    Would lift, but only if we established clearly
    The identity of those who murdered Laïos.
    They must be killed or exiled.
                                    Can you use   95
    Birdflight or any art of divination
    To purify yourself, and Thebes, and me
    From this contagion? We are in your hands.
    There is no fairer duty
    Than that of helping others in distress.   100
Teiresias: How dreadful knowledge of the truth can be
    When there's no help in truth! I knew this well,
    But did not act on it: else I should not have come.
Oedipus: What is troubling you? Why are your eyes so cold?
Teiresias: Let me go home. Bear your own fate, and I'll   105
    Bear mine. It is better so: trust what I say.

Oedipus: What you say is ungracious and unhelpful
    To your native country. Do not refuse to speak.
Teiresias: When it comes to speech, your own is neither temperate
    Nor opportune. I wish to be more prudent.   110
Oedipus: In God's name, we all beg you —
Teiresias: You are all ignorant.
    No; I will never tell you what I know.
    Now it is my misery; then, it would be yours.
Oedipus: What! You do know something, and will not tell us?
    You would betray us all and wreck the State?   115
Teiresias: I do not intend to torture myself, or you.
    Why persist in asking? You will not persuade me.
Oedipus: What a wicked old man you are! You'd try a stone's
    Patience! Out with it! Have you no feeling at all?
Teiresias: You call me unfeeling. If you could only see   120
    The nature of your own feelings . . .
Oedipus: Why,
    Who would not feel as I do? Who could endure
    Your arrogance toward the city?
Teiresias: What does it matter!
    Whether I speak or not, it is bound to come.
Oedipus: Then, if "it" is bound to come, you are bound to tell me.   125
Teiresias: No, I will not go on. Rage as you please.
Oedipus: Rage? Why not!
                  And I'll tell you what I think:
    You planned it, you had it done, you all but
    Killed him with your own hands: if you had eyes,
    I'd say the crime was yours, and yours alone.   130
Teiresias: So? I charge you, then,
    Abide by the proclamation you have made:
    From this day forth
    Never speak again to these men or to me;
    You yourself are the pollution of this country.   135
Oedipus: You dare say that! Can you possibly think you have
    Some way of going free, after such insolence?
Teiresias: I have gone free. It is the truth sustains me.
Oedipus: Who taught you shamelessness? It was not your craft.
Teiresias: You did. You made me speak. I did not want to.   140
Oedipus: Speak what? Let me hear it again more clearly.
Teiresias: Was it not clear before? Are you tempting me?
Oedipus: I did not understand it. Say it again.
Teiresias: I say that you are the murderer whom you seek.
Oedipus: Now twice you have spat out infamy. You'll pay for it!   145
Teiresias: Would you care for more? Do you wish to be really angry?
Oedipus: Say what you will. Whatever you say is worthless.
Teiresias: I say you live in hideous shame with those
    Most dear to you. You can not see the evil.
Oedipus: It seems you can go on mouthing like this for ever.   150
Teiresias: I can, if there is power in truth.

Oedipus: There is:
    But not for you, not for you,
    You sightless, witless, senseless, mad old man!
Teiresias: You are the madman. There is no one here
    Who will not curse you soon, as you curse me.   155
Oedipus: You child of endless night! You can not hurt me
    Or any other man who sees the sun.
Teiresias: True: it is not from me your fate will come.
    That lies within Apollo's competence,
    As it is his concern.
Oedipus: Tell me: 160
    Are you speaking for Creon, or for yourself?
Teiresias: Creon is no threat. You weave your own doom.
Oedipus: Wealth, power, craft of statesmanship!
    Kingly position, everywhere admired!
    What savage envy is stored up against these,   165
    If Creon, whom I trusted, Creon my friend,
    For this great office which the city once
    Put in my hands unsought — if for this power
    Creon desires in secret to destroy me!

    He has brought this decrepit fortune-teller, this   170
    Collector of dirty pennies, this prophet fraud —
    Why, he is no more clairvoyant than I am!
                              Tell us:
    Has your mystic mummery ever approached the truth?
    When that hellcat the Sphinx was performing here,
    What help were you to these people?   175
    Her magic was not for the first man who came along:
    It demanded a real exorcist. Your birds —
    What good were they? or the gods, for the matter of that?
    But I came by,
    Oedipus, the simple man, who knows nothing —   180
    I thought it out for myself, no birds helped me!
    And this is the man you think you can destroy,
    That you may be close to Creon when he's king!
    Well, you and your friend Creon, it seems to me,
    Will suffer most. If you were not an old man,   185
    You would have paid already for your plot.
Choragos: We can not see that his words or yours
    Have been spoken except in anger, Oedipus,
    And of anger we have no need. How can God's will
    Be accomplished best? That is what most concerns us.   190
Teiresias: You are a king. But where argument's concerned
    I am your man, as much a king as you.
    I am not your servant, but Apollo's.
    I have no need of Creon to speak for me.

    Listen to me. You mock my blindness, do you?   195

But I say that you, with both your eyes, are blind:
You can not see the wretchedness of your life,
Nor in whose house you live, no, nor with whom.
Who are your father and mother? Can you tell me?
You do not even know the blind wrongs   200
That you have done them, on earth and in the world below.
But the double lash of your parents' curse will whip you
Out of this land some day, with only night
Upon your precious eyes.
Your cries then — where will they not be heard?   205
What fastness of Kithairon will not echo them?
And that bridal-descant of yours — you'll know it then,
The song they sang when you came here to Thebes
And found your misguided berthing.
All this, and more, that you can not guess at now,   210
Will bring you to yourself among your children.

Be angry, then. Curse Creon. Curse my words.
I tell you, no man that walks upon the earth
Shall be rooted out more horribly than you.
Oedipus: Am I to bear this from him? — Damnation   215
    Take you! Out of this place! Out of my sight!
Teiresias: I would not have come at all if you had not asked me.
Oedipus: Could I have told that you'd talk nonsense, that
    You'd come here to make a fool of yourself, and of me?
Teiresias: A fool? Your parents thought me sane enough. 220
Oedipus: My parents again! — Wait: who were my parents?
Teiresias: This day will give you a father, and break your heart.
Oedipus: Your infantile riddles! Your damned abracadabra!
Teiresias: You were a great man once at solving riddles.
Oedipus: Mock me with that if you like; you will find it true. 225
Teiresias: It was true enough. It brought about your ruin.
Oedipus: But if it saved this town?
Teiresias (to the Page):   Boy, give me your hand.
Oedipus: Yes, boy; lead him away.
                — While you are here
    We can do nothing. Go; leave us in peace.
Teiresias: I will go when I have said what I have to say.   230
    How can you hurt me? And I tell you again:
    The man you have been looking for all this time,
    The damned man, the murderer of Laïos,
    That man is in Thebes. To your mind he is foreignborn,
    But it will soon be shown that he is a Theban,   235
    A revelation that will fail to please.
                    A blind man,
Who has his eyes now; a penniless man, who is rich now;
And he will go tapping the strange earth with his staff;
To the children with whom he lives now he will be
Brother and father — the very same; to her   240

Who bore him, son and husband — the very same
Who came to his father's bed, wet with his father's blood.

Enough. Go think that over.
If later you find error in what I have said,
You may say that I have no skill in prophecy.   245

Exit Teiresias, led by his Page. Oedipus goes into the palace.

ODE I°

Chorus: The Delphic stone of prophecies
    Remembers ancient regicide
    And a still bloody hand.
    That killer's hour of flight has come.
    He must be stronger than riderless   5
    Coursers of untiring wind,
    For the son of Zeus° armed with his father's thunder
    Leaps in lightning after him;
    And the Furies° follow him, the sad Furies.

    Holy Parnassos' peak of snow   10
    Flashes and blinds that secret man,
    That all shall hunt him down:
    Though he may roam the forest shade
    Like a bull gone wild from pasture
    To rage through glooms of stone.   15
    Doom comes down on him; flight will not avail him;
    For the world's heart calls him desolate,
    And the immortal Furies follow, for ever follow.

    But now a wilder thing is heard
    From the old man skilled at hearing Fate in the wingbeat of a bird.   20
    Bewildered as a blown bird, my soul hovers and can not find
    Foothold in this debate, or any reason or rest of mind.
    But no man ever brought — none can bring
    Proof of strife between Thebes' royal house,
    Labdakos' line,° and the son of Polybos°;   25

Ode: a choral song. Here again (as in the *parodos*) *strophe* and *antistrophe* probably indicate the movements of a dance.

⁷*son of Zeus:* Apollo.   ⁹*Furies:* three horrific female spirits whose task was to seek out and punish evil-doers.   ²⁵*Labdakos' line:* descendants of Laïos (true father of Oedipus, although the chorus does not know this).   ²⁵ *Polybos:* king who adopted the child Oedipus.

And never until now has any man brought word
Of Laïos' dark death staining Oedipus the King.

Divine Zeus and Apollo hold
Perfect intelligence alone of all tales ever told;
And well though this diviner works, he works in his own night;   30
No man can judge that rough unknown or trust in second sight,
For wisdom changes hands among the wise.
Shall I believe my great lord criminal
At a raging word that a blind old man let fall?
I saw him, when the carrion woman faced him of old,   35
Prove his heroic mind! These evil words are lies.

SCENE II

Creon: Men of Thebes:
    I am told that heavy accusations
    Have been brought against me by King Oedipus.

    I am not the kind of man to bear this tamely.

    If in these present difficulties   5
    He holds me accountable for any harm to him
    Through anything I have said or done — why, then,
    I do not value life in this dishonor.
    It is not as though this rumor touched upon
    Some private indiscretion. The matter is grave.   10
    The fact is that I am being called disloyal
    To the State, to my fellow citizens, to my friends.
Choragos: He may have spoken in anger, not from his mind.
Creon: But did you not hear him say I was the one
    Who seduced the old prophet into lying?   15
Choragos: The thing was said; I do not know how seriously.
Creon: But you were watching him! Were his eyes steady?
    Did he look like a man in his right mind?
Choragos: I do not know.
    I can not judge the behavior of great men.
    But here is the King himself.

    Enter Oedipus.

Oedipus: So you dared come back.   20
    Why? How brazen of you to come to my house,
    You murderer!
                    Do you think I do not know
    That you plotted to kill me, plotted to steal my throne?

Tell me, in God's name: am I coward, a fool,
That you should dream you could accomplish this?   25
A fool who could not see your slippery game?
A coward, not to fight back when I saw it?
You are the fool, Creon, are you not? hoping
Without support or friends to get a throne?
Thrones may be won or bought: you could do neither.   30
Creon: Now listen to me. You have talked; let me talk, too.
   You can not judge unless you know the facts.
Oedipus: You speak well: there is one fact; but I find it hard
   To learn from the deadliest enemy I have.
Creon: That above all I must dispute with you.   35
Oedipus: That above all I will not hear you deny.
Creon: If you think there is anything good in being stubborn
   Against all reason, then I say you are wrong.
Oedipus: If you think a man can sin against his own kind
   And not be punished for it, I say you are mad.   40
Creon: I agree. But tell me: what have I done to you?
Oedipus: You advised me to send for that wizard, did you not?
Creon: I did. I should do it again.
Oedipus: Very well. Now tell me:
   How long has it been since Laïos —
Creon: What of Laïos?
Oedipus: Since he vanished in that onset by the road?   45
Creon: It was long ago, a long time.
Oedipus: And this prophet,
   Was he practicing here then?
Creon: He was; and with honor, as now.
Oedipus: Did he speak of me at that time?
Creon: He never did;
   At least, not when I was present.
Oedipus: But . . . the enquiry?
   I suppose you held one?
Creon: We did, but we learned nothing. 50
Oedipus: Why did the prophet not speak against me then?
Creon: I do not know; and I am the kind of man
   Who holds his tongue when he has no facts to go on.
Oedipus: There's one fact that you know, and you could tell it.
Creon: What fact is that? If I know it, you shall have it. 55
Oedipus: If he were not involved with you, he could not say
   That it was I who murdered Laïos.
Creon: If he says that, you are the one that knows it! —
   But now it is my turn to question you.
Oedipus: Put your questions. I am no murderer.   60
Creon: First then: You married my sister?
Oedipus: I married your sister.
Creon: And you rule the kingdom equally with her?
Oedipus: Everything that she wants she has from me.
Creon: And I am the third, equal to both of you?

Oedipus: That is why I call you a bad friend.   65
Creon: No. Reason it out, as I have done.
    Think of this first. Would any sane man prefer
    Power, with all a king's anxieties,
    To that same power and the grace of sleep?
    Certainly not I.   70
    I have never longed for the king's power — only his rights.
    Would any wise man differ from me in this?
    As matters stand, I have my way in everything
    With your consent, and no responsibilities.
    If I were king, I should be a slave to policy.   75

    How could I desire a scepter more
    Than what is now mine — untroubled influence?
    No, I have not gone mad; I need no honors,
    Except those with the perquisites I have now.
    I am welcome everywhere; every man salutes me,   80
    And those who want your favor seek my ear,
    Since I know how to manage what they ask.
    Should I exchange this ease for that anxiety?
    Besides, no sober mind is treasonable.
    I hate anarchy   85
    And never would deal with any man who likes it.

    Test what I have said. Go to the priestess
    At Delphi, ask if I quoted her correctly.
    And as for this other thing: if I am found
    Guilty of treason with Teiresias,   90
    Then sentence me to death! You have my word
    It is a sentence I should cast my vote for —
    But not without evidence!
                        You do wrong
    When you take good men for bad, bad men for good.
    A true friend thrown aside — why, life itself   95
    Is not more precious!
                        In time you will know this well:
    For time, and time alone, will show the just man,
    Though scoundrels are discovered in a day.
Choragos: This is well said, and a prudent man would ponder it.
    Judgments too quickly formed are dangerous.   100
Oedipus: But is he not quick in his duplicity?
    And shall I not be quick to parry him?
    Would you have me stand still, hold my peace, and let
    This man win everything, through my inaction?
Creon: And you want — what is it, then? To banish me?   105
Oedipus: No, not exile. It is your death I want,
    So that all the world may see what treason means.

918   Tragedy

Creon: You will persist, then? You will not believe me?
Oedipus: How can I believe you?
Creon: Then you are a fool.
Oedipus: To save myself?
Creon: In justice, think of me.   110
Oedipus: You are evil incarnate.
Creon: But suppose that you are wrong?
Oedipus: Still I must rule.
Creon: But not if you rule badly.
Oedipus: O city, city!
Creon: It is my city, too!
Choragos: Now, my lords, be still. I see the Queen,
    Iocastê, coming from her palace chambers;   115
    And it is time she came, for the sake of you both.
    This dreadful quarrel can be resolved through her.

    Enter Iocastê.

Iocastê: Poor foolish men, what wicked din is this?
    With Thebes sick to death, is it not shameful
    That you should rake some private quarrel up?   120
    (To Oedipus.) Come into the house.
                                    — And you, Creon, go now:
    Let us have no more of this tumult over nothing.
Creon: Nothing? No, sister: what your husband plans for me
    Is one of two great evils: exile or death.
Oedipus: He is right.
                              Why, woman, I have caught him squarely   125
    Plotting against my life.
Creon: No! Let me die
    Accurst if ever I have wished you harm!
Iocastê: Ah, believe it, Oedipus!
    In the name of the gods, respect this oath of his
    For my sake, for the sake of these people here!   130

                                                    Strophe 1
Choragos: Open your mind to her, my lord. Be ruled by her, I beg
        you!
Oedipus: What would you have me do?
Choragos: Respect Creon's word. He has never spoken like a fool,
    And now he has sworn an oath.
Oedipus: You know what you ask?
Choragos: I do.
Oedipus: Speak on, then.
Choragos: A friend so sworn should not be baited so,   135
    In blind malice, and without final proof.
Oedipus: You are aware, I hope, that what you say
    Means death for me, or exile at the least.

Choragos: No, I swear by Helios, first in Heaven!
　　May I die friendless and accurst,
　The worst of deaths, if ever I meant that!
　　　It is the withering fields
　　　　That hurt my sick heart:
　　　　Must we bear all these ills,
　　　　　And now your bad blood as well?
Oedipus: Then let him go. And let me die, if I must,
　Or be driven by him in shame from the land of Thebes.
　It is your unhappiness, and not his talk,
　That touches me.
　　　　As for him —
　Wherever he is, I will hate him as long as I live.
Creon: Ugly in yielding, as you were ugly in rage!
　Natures like yours chiefly torment themselves.
Oedipus: Can you not go? Can you not leave me?
Creon:　　　　　　　　　　I can.
　You do not know me; but the city knows me,
　And in its eyes I am just, if not in yours.

Exit Creon.

Choragos: Lady Iocastê, did you not ask the King to go to his chambers?
Iocastê: First tell me what has happened.
Choragos: There was suspicion without evidence; yet it rankled
　As even false charges will.
Iocastê:　　　　　　On both sides?
Choragos:　　　　　　　　　On both.
Iocastê:　　　　　　　　　　But what was said?
Choragos: Oh let it rest, let it be done with!
　Have we not suffered enough?
Oedipus: You see to what your decency has brought you:
　You have made difficulties where my heart saw none.

Choragos: Oedipus, it is not once only I have told you —
　　You must know I should count myself unwise
　To the point of madness, should I now forsake you —
　　　You, under whose hand,
　　　　In the storm of another time,
　　　Our dear land sailed out free.
　　　　But now stand fast at the helm!
Iocastê: In God's name, Oedipus, inform your wife as well:
　Why are you so set in this hard anger?
Oedipus: I will tell you, for none of these men deserves

My confidence as you do. It is Creon's work,
His treachery, his plotting against me.

Iocastê: Go on, if you can make this clear to me.

Oedipus: He charges me with the murder of Laïos.

Iocastê: Has he some knowledge? Or does he speak from hearsay?

Oedipus: He would not commit himself to such a charge,
But he has brought in that damnable soothsayer
To tell his story.

Iocastê: Set your mind at rest.
If it is a question of soothsayers, I tell you
That you will find no man whose craft gives knowledge
Of the unknowable.

                     Here is my proof:

An oracle was reported to Laïos once
(I will not say from Phoibos himself, but from
His appointed ministers, at any rate)
That his doom would be death at the hands of his own son —
His son, born of his flesh and of mine!

Now, you remember the story: Laïos was killed
By marauding strangers where three highways meet;
But his child had not been three days in this world
Before the King had pierced the baby's ankles
And left him to die on a lonely mountainside.

Thus, Apollo never caused that child
To kill his father, and it was not Laïos' fate
To die at the hands of his son, as he had feared.
This is what prophets and prophecies are worth!
Have no dread of them.

                     It is God himself
Who can show us what he wills, in his own way.

Oedipus: How strange a shadowy memory crossed my mind,
Just now while you were speaking; it chilled my heart.

Iocastê: What do you mean? What memory do you speak of?

Oedipus: If I understand you, Laïos was killed
At a place where three roads meet.

Iocastê: So it was said;
We have no later story.

Oedipus: Where did it happen?

Iocastê: Phokis, it is called: at a place where the Theban Way
Divides into the roads toward Delphi and Daulia.

Oedipus: When?

Iocastê: We had the news not long before you came
And proved the right to your succession here.

Oedipus: Ah, what net has God been weaving for me?

Iocastê: Oedipus! Why does this trouble you?

Oedipus: Do not ask me yet.
First, tell me how Laïos looked, and tell me
How old he was.

Iocastê: He was tall, his hair just touched
With white; his form was not unlike your own.   215

Oedipus: I think that I myself may be accurst
By my own ignorant edict.

Iocastê: You speak strangely.
It makes me tremble to look at you, my King.

Oedipus: I am not sure that the blind man can not see.
But I should know better if you were to tell me —   220

Iocastê: Anything — though I dread to hear you ask it.

Oedipus: Was the King lightly escorted, or did he ride
With a large company, as a ruler should?

Iocastê: There were five men with him in all: one was a herald;
And a single chariot, which he was driving.   225

Oedipus: Alas, that makes it plain enough!

But who —
Who told you how it happened?

Iocastê: A household servant,
The only one to escape.

Oedipus: And is he still
A servant of ours?

Iocastê: No; for when he came back at last
And found you enthroned in the place of the dead king,   230
He came to me, touched my hand with his, and begged
That I would send him away to the frontier district
Where only the shepherds go —
As far away from the city as I could send him.
I granted his prayer; for although the man was a slave,   235
He had earned more than this favor at my hands.

Oedipus: Can he be called back quickly?

Iocastê: Easily.
But why?

Oedipus: I have taken too much upon myself
Without enquiry; therefore I wish to consult him.

Iocastê: Then he shall come.

But am I not one also   240
To whom you might confide these fears of yours?

Oedipus: That is your right; it will not be denied you,
Now least of all; for I have reached a pitch
Of wild foreboding. Is there anyone
To whom I should sooner speak?   245
Polybos of Corinth is my father.
My mother is a Dorian: Meropê.
I grew up chief among the men of Corinth
Until a strange thing happened —
Not worth my passion, it may be, but strange.   250

At a feast, a drunken man maundering in his cups
Cries out that I am not my father's son!

I contained myself that night, though I felt anger
And a sinking heart. The next day I visited
My father and mother, and questioned them. They stormed,   255
Calling it all the slanderous rant of a fool;
And this relieved me. Yet the suspicion
Remained always aching in my mind;
I knew there was talk; I could not rest;
And finally, saying nothing to my parents,   260
I went to the shrine at Delphi.
The god dismissed my question without reply;
He spoke of other things.
                          Some were clear,
Full of wretchedness, dreadful, unbearable:
As, that I should lie with my own mother, breed   265
Children from whom all men would turn their eyes;
And that I should be my father's murderer.

I heard all this, and fled. And from that day
Corinth to me was only in the stars
Descending in that quarter of the sky,   270
As I wandered farther and farther on my way
To a land where I should never see the evil
Sung by the oracle. And I came to this country
Where, so you say, King Laïos was killed.

I will tell you all that happened there, my lady.   275

There were three highways
Coming together at a place I passed;
And there a herald came towards me, and a chariot
Drawn by horses, with a man such as you describe
Seated in it. The groom leading the horses   280
Forced me off the road at his lord's command;
But as this charioteer lurched over towards me
I struck him in my rage. The old man saw me
And brought his double goad down upon my head
As I came abreast.
                   He was paid back, and more!   285
Swinging my club in this right hand I knocked him
Out of his car, and he rolled on the ground.
                                    I killed him.

I killed them all.
Now if that stranger and Laïos were — kin,
Where is a man more miserable than I?   290

More hated by the gods? Citizen and alien alike
Must never shelter me or speak to me —
I must be shunned by all.
                    And I myself
Pronounced this malediction upon myself!

Think of it: I have touched you with these hands,   295
These hands that killed your husband. What defilement!

Am I all evil, then? It must be so,
Since I must flee from Thebes, yet never again
See my own countrymen, my own country,
For fear of joining my mother in marriage   300
And killing Polybos, my father.
                              Ah,
If I was created so, born to this fate,
Who could deny the savagery of God?

O holy majesty of heavenly powers!
May I never see that day! Never!   305
Rather let me vanish from the race of men
Than know the abomination destined me!
Choragos: We too, my lord, have felt dismay at this.
    But there is hope: you have yet to hear the shepherd.
Oedipus: Indeed, I fear no other hope is left me.   310
Iocastê: What do you hope from him when he comes?
Oedipus: This much:
    If his account of the murder tallies with yours,
    Then I am cleared.
Iocastê: What was it that I said
    Of such importance?
Oedipus: Why, "marauders," you said,
    Killed the King, according to this man's story.   315
    If he maintains that still, if there were several,
    Clearly the guilt is not mine: I was alone.
    But if he says one man, singlehanded, did it,
    Then the evidence all points to me.
Iocastê: You may be sure that he said there were several;   320
    And can he call back that story now? He can not.
    The whole city heard it as plainly as I.
    But suppose he alters some detail of it:
    He can not ever show that Laïos' death
    Fulfilled the oracle: for Apollo said   325
    My child was doomed to kill him; and my child —
    Poor baby! — it was my child that died first.

No. From now on, where oracles are concerned,
I would not waste a second thought on any.

Oedipus: You may be right.
                                    But come: let someone go   330
    For the shepherd at once. This matter must be settled.
Iocastê: I will send for him.
    I would not wish to cross you in anything,
    And surely not in this. — Let us go in.

    Exeunt into the palace.

ODE II

Chorus: Let me be reverent in the ways of right,
        Lowly the paths I journey on;
        Let all my words and actions keep
        The laws of the pure universe
        From highest Heaven handed down.   5
        For Heaven is their bright nurse,
        Those generations of the realms of light;
        Ah, never of mortal kind were they begot,
        Nor are they slaves of memory, lost in sleep:
        Their Father is greater than Time, and ages not.   10

Antistrophe 1

        The tyrant is a child of Pride
        Who drinks from his great sickening cup
        Recklessness and vanity,
        Until from his high crest headlong
        He plummets to the dust of hope.   15
        That strong man is not strong.
        But let no fair ambition be denied;
        May God protect the wrestler for the State
        In government, in comely policy,
        Who will fear God, and on His ordinance wait.   20

Strophe 2

        Haughtiness and the high hand of disdain
        Tempt and outrage God's holy law;
        And any mortal who dares hold
        No immortal Power in awe
        Will be caught up in a net of pain: 25
        The price for which his levity is sold.
        Let each man take due earnings, then,
        And keep his hands from holy things,
        And from blasphemy stand apart —
        Else the crackling blast of heaven   30
        Blows on his head, and on his desperate heart;

Though fools will honor impious men,
In their cities no tragic poet sings.

Shall we lose faith in Delphi's obscurities,
We who have heard the world's core   35
Discredited, and the sacred wood
Of Zeus at Elis praised no more?
The deeds and the strange prophecies
Must make a pattern yet to be understood.
Zeus, if indeed you are lord of all,   40
Throned in light over night and day,
Mirror this in your endless mind:
Our masters call the oracle
Words on the wind, and the Delphic vision blind!
Their hearts no longer know Apollo,   45
And reverence for the gods has died away.

SCENE III

Enter Iocastê.

Iocastê: Princes of Thebes, it has occurred to me
To visit the altars of the gods, bearing
These branches as a suppliant, and this incense.
Our King is not himself: his noble soul
Is overwrought with fantasies of dread,   5
Else he would consider
The new prophecies in the light of the old.
He will listen to any voice that speaks disaster,
And my advice goes for nothing.

She approaches the altar, right.

                              To you, then, Apollo,
Lycean lord, since you are nearest, I turn in prayer.   10
Receive these offerings, and grant us deliverance
From defilement. Our hearts are heavy with fear
When we see our leader distracted, as helpless sailors
Are terrified by the confusion of their helmsman.

Enter Messenger.

Messenger: Friends, no doubt you can direct me: 15
Where shall I find the house of Oedipus,
Or, better still, where is the King himself?
Choragos: It is this very place, stranger; he is inside.
This is his wife and mother of his children.

Messenger: I wish her happiness in a happy house,   20
    Blest in all the fulfillment of her marriage.
Iocastê: I wish as much for you: your courtesy
    Deserves a like good fortune. But now, tell me:
    Why have you come? What have you to say to us?
Messenger: Good news, my lady, for your house and your husband.   25
Iocastê: What news? Who sent you here?
Messenger: I am from Corinth.
    The news I bring ought to mean joy for you,
    Though it may be you will find some grief in it.
Iocastê: What is it? How can it touch us in both ways?
Messenger: The people of Corinth, they say,   30
    Intend to call Oedipus to be their king.
Iocastê: But old Polybos — is he not reigning still?
Messenger: No. Death holds him in his sepulchre.
Iocastê: What are you saying? Polybos is dead?
Messenger: If I am not telling the truth, may I die myself.   35
Iocastê (to a Maidservant): Go in, go quickly; tell this to your master.

    O riddlers of God's will, where are you now!
    This was the man whom Oedipus, long ago,
    Feared so, fled so, in dread of destroying him —
    But it was another fate by which he died.   40

    Enter Oedipus, center.

Oedipus: Dearest Iocastê, why have you sent for me?
Iocastê: Listen to what this man says, and then tell me
    What has become of the solemn prophecies.
Oedipus: Who is this man? What is his news for me?
Iocastê: He has come from Corinth to announce your father's death!   45
Oedipus: Is it true, stranger? Tell me in your own words.
Messenger: I can not say it more clearly: the King is dead.
Oedipus: Was it by treason? Or by an attack of illness?
Messenger: A little thing brings old men to their rest.
Oedipus: It was sickness, then?
Messenger: Yes, and his many years.   50
Oedipus: Ah!
    Why should a man respect the Pythian hearth°, or
    Give heed to the birds that jangle above his head?
    They prophesied that I should kill Polybos,
    Kill my own father; but he is dead and buried,   55
    And I am here — I never touched him, never,
    Unless he died of grief for my departure,
    And thus, in a sense, through me. No. Polybos
    Has packed the oracles off with him underground.
    They are empty words.

---

⁵²*Pythian hearth:* the shrine at Delphi, whose priestess was famous for her prophecies.

Iocastê: Had I not told you so?   60
Oedipus: You had; it was my faint heart that betrayed me.
Iocastê: From now on never think of those things again.
Oedipus: And yet — must I not fear my mother's bed?
Iocastê: Why should anyone in this world be afraid,
    Since Fate rules us and nothing can be foreseen?   65
    A man should live only for the present day.

    Have no more fear of sleeping with your mother:
    How many men, in dreams, have lain with their mothers!
    No reasonable man is troubled by such things.
Oedipus: That is true; only —   70
    If only my mother were not still alive!
    But she is alive. I can not help my dread.
Iocastê: Yet this news of your father's death is wonderful.
Oedipus: Wonderful. But I fear the living woman.
Messenger: Tell me, who is this woman that you fear?   75
Oedipus: It is Meropê, man; the wife of King Polybos.
Messenger: Meropê? Why should you be afraid of her?
Oedipus: An oracle of the gods, a dreadful saying.
Messenger: Can you tell me about it or are you sworn to silence?
Oedipus: I can tell you, and I will.   80
    Apollo said through his prophet that I was the man
    Who should marry his own mother, shed his father's blood
    With his own hands. And so, for all these years
    I have kept clear of Corinth, and no harm has come —
    Though it would have been sweet to see my parents again.   85
Messenger: And is this the fear that drove you out of Corinth?
Oedipus: Would you have me kill my father?
Messenger: As for that
    You must be reassured by the news I gave you.
Oedipus: If you could reassure me, I would reward you.   90
Messenger: I had that in mind, I will confess: I thought
    I could count on you when you returned to Corinth.
Oedipus: No: I will never go near my parents again.
Messenger: Ah, son, you still do not know what you are doing —
Oedipus: What do you mean? In the name of God tell me!
Messenger: — If these are your reasons for not going home.   95
Oedipus: I tell you, I fear the oracle may come true.
Messenger: And guilt may come upon you through your parents?
Oedipus: That is the dread that is always in my heart.
Messenger: Can you not see that all your fears are groundless?
Oedipus: How can you say that? They are my parents, surely?   100
Messenger: Polybos was not your father.
Oedipus: Not my father?
Messenger: No more your father than the man speaking to you.
Oedipus: But you are nothing to me!
Messenger: Neither was he.
Oedipus: Then why did he call me son?

Messenger: I will tell you:
    Long ago he had you from my hands, as a gift.   105
Oedipus: Then how could he love me so, if I was not his?
Messenger: He had no children, and his heart turned to you.
Oedipus: What of you? Did you buy me? Did you find me by chance?
Messenger: I came upon you in the crooked pass of Kithairon.
Oedipus: And what were you doing there?
Messenger: Tending my flocks.   110
Oedipus: A wandering shepherd?
Messenger: But your savior, son, that day.
Oedipus: From what did you save me?
Messenger: Your ankles should tell you that.
Oedipus: Ah, stranger, why do you speak of that childhood pain?
Messenger: I cut the bonds that tied your ankles together.
Oedipus: I have had the mark as long as I can remember.   115
Messenger: That was why you were given the name you bear.
Oedipus: God! Was it my father or my mother who did it?
    Tell me!
Messenger: I do not know. The man who gave you to me
    Can tell you better than I.   120
Oedipus: It was not you that found me, but another?
Messenger: It was another shepherd gave you to me.
Oedipus: Who was he? Can you tell me who he was?
Messenger: I think he was said to be one of Laïos' people.
Oedipus: You mean the Laïos who was king here years ago?   125
Messenger: Yes; King Laïos; and the man was one of his herdsmen.
Oedipus: Is he still alive? Can I see him?
Messenger: These men here
    Know best about such things.
Oedipus: Does anyone here
    Know this shepherd that he is talking about?
    Have you seen him in the fields, or in the town?   130
    If you have, tell me. It is time things were made plain.
Choragos: I think the man he means is that same shepherd
    You have already asked to see. Iocastê perhaps
    Could tell you something.
Oedipus: Do you know anything
    About him, Lady? Is he the man we have summoned?   135
    Is that the man this shepherd means?
Iocastê: Why think of him?
    Forget this herdsman. Forget it all.
    This talk is a waste of time.
Oedipus: How can you say that,
    When the clues to my true birth are in my hands?
Iocastê: For God's love, let us have no more questioning!   140
    Is your life nothing to you?
    My own is pain enough for me to bear.
Oedipus: You need not worry. Suppose my mother a slave,
    And born of slaves: no baseness can touch you.

Iocastê: Listen to me, I beg you: do not do this thing!   145
Oedipus: I will not listen; the truth must be made known.
Iocastê: Everything that I say is for your own good!
Oedipus: My own good
    Snaps my patience, then; I want none of it.
Iocastê: You are fatally wrong! May you never learn who you are!
Oedipus: Go, one of you, and bring the shepherd here.   150
    Let us leave this woman to brag of her royal name.
Iocastê: Ah, miserable!
    That is the only word I have for you now.
    That is the only word I can ever have.

Exit into the palace.

Choragos: Why has she left us, Oedipus? Why has she gone   155
    In such a passion of sorrow? I fear this silence:
    Something dreadful may come of it.
Oedipus: Let it come!
    However base my birth, I must know about it.
    The Queen, like a woman, is perhaps ashamed
    To think of my low origin. But I   160
    Am a child of Luck; I can not be dishonored.
    Luck is my mother; the passing months, my brothers,
    Have seen me rich and poor.
                 If this is so,
    How could I wish that I were someone else?
    How could I not be glad to know my birth?   165

ODE III

                                          Strophe

Chorus: If ever the coming time were known
    To my heart's pondering,
    Kithairon, now by Heaven I see the torches
    At the festival of the next full moon,
    And see the dance, and hear the choir sing   5
    A grace to your gentle shade:
    Mountain where Oedipus was found,
    O mountain guard of a noble race!
    May the god who heals us lend his aid,
    And let that glory come to pass   10
    For our king's cradling-ground.

                                         Antistrophe

    Of the nymphs that flower beyond the years,
    Who bore you, royal child,
    To Pan of the hills or the timberline Apollo,
    Cold in delight where the upland clears,   15

Or Hermês for whom Kyllenê's° heights are piled?
Or flushed as evening cloud,
Great Dionysos, roamer of mountains,
He — was it he who found you there,
And caught you up in his own proud   20
Arms from the sweet god-ravisher
Who laughed by the Muses' fountains?

SCENE IV

Oedipus: Sirs: though I do not know the man,
    I think I see him coming, this shepherd we want:
    He is old, like our friend here, and the men
    Bringing him seem to be servants of my house.
    But you can tell, if you have ever seen him.   5

    Enter Shepherd escorted by servants.

Choragos: I know him, he was Laïos' man. You can trust him.
Oedipus: Tell me first, you from Corinth: is this the shepherd
    We were discussing?
Messenger: This is the very man.
Oedipus (to Shepherd): Come here. No, look at me. You must answer
    Everything I ask. — You belonged to Laïos?   10
Shepherd: Yes: born his slave, brought up in his house.
Oedipus: Tell me: what kind of work did you do for him?
Shepherd: I was a shepherd of his, most of my life.
Oedipus: Where mainly did you go for pasturage?
Shepherd: Sometimes Kithairon, sometimes the hills near-by.   15
Oedipus: Do you remember ever seeing this man out there?
Shepherd: What would he be doing there? This man?
Oedipus: This man standing here. Have you ever seen him before?
Shepherd: No. At least, not to my recollection.
Messenger: And that is not strange, my lord. But I'll refresh   20
    His memory: he must remember when we two
    Spent three whole seasons together, March to September,
    On Kithairon or thereabouts. He had two flocks;
    I had one. Each autumn I'd drive mine home
    And he would go back with his to Laïos' sheepfold. —   25
    Is this not true, just as I have described it?
Shepherd: True, yes; but it was all so long ago.
Messenger: Well, then: do you remember, back in those days
    That you gave me a baby boy to bring up as my own?
Shepherd: What if I did? What are you trying to say?   30
Messenger: King Oedipus was once that little child.

---

[16] *Kyllenê:* a sacred mountain, birthplace of Hermês, the deities' messenger. The chorus
assumes that the mountain was created in order to afford him birth.

Shepherd: Damn you, hold your tongue!

Oedipus: No more of that!

It is your tongue needs watching, not this man's.

Shepherd: My King, my Master, what is it I have done wrong?

Oedipus: You have not answered his question about the boy.   35

Shepherd: He does not know . . . He is only making trouble . . .

Oedipus: Come, speak plainly, or it will go hard with you.

Shepherd: In God's name, do not torture an old man!

Oedipus: Come here, one of you; bind his arms behind him.

Shepherd: Unhappy king! What more do you wish to learn?   40

Oedipus: Did you give this man the child he speaks of?

Shepherd: I did.

And I would to God I had died that very day.

Oedipus: You will die now unless you speak the truth.

Shepherd: Yet if I speak the truth, I am worse than dead.

Oedipus: Very well; since you insist upon delaying —   45

Shepherd: No! I have told you already that I gave him the boy.

Oedipus: Where did you get him? From your house? From somewhere
        else?

Shepherd: Not from mine, no. A man gave him to me.

Oedipus: Is that man here? Do you know whose slave he was?

Shepherd: For God's love, my King, do not ask me any more!   50

Oedipus: You are a dead man if I have to ask you again.

Shepherd: Then . . . Then the child was from the palace of Laïos.

Oedipus: A slave child? or a child of his own line?

Shepherd: Ah, I am on the brink of dreadful speech!

Oedipus: And I of dreadful hearing. Yet I must hear.   55

Shepherd: If you must be told, then . . .

                                        They said it was Laïos' child,

But it is your wife who can tell you about that.

Oedipus: My wife! — Did she give it to you?

Shepherd: My lord, she did.

Oedipus: Do you know why?

Shepherd: I was told to get rid of it.

Oedipus: An unspeakable mother!

Shepherd: There had been prophecies . . .   60

Oedipus: Tell me.

Shepherd: It was said that the boy would kill his own father.

Oedipus: Then why did you give him over to this old man?

Shepherd: I pitied the baby, my King,

And I thought that this man would take him far away

To his own country.

                        He saved him — but for what a fate!   65

For if you are what this man says you are,

No man living is more wretched than Oedipus.

Oedipus: Ah God!

It was true!

        All the prophecies!

                    — Now,

O Light, may I look on you for the last time!
I, Oedipus,
Oedipus, damned in his birth, in his marriage damned,
Damned in the blood he shed with his own hand!

He rushes into the palace.

70

ODE IV

Chorus: Alas for the seed of men.

What measure shall I give these generations
That breathe on the void and are void
And exist and do not exist?

Who bears more weight of joy
Than mass of sunlight shifting in images,
Or who shall make his thought stay on
That down time drifts away?

5

Your splendor is all fallen.

O naked brow of wrath and tears,
O change of Oedipus!
I who say your days call no man blest —
Your great days like ghósts góne.

10

Antistrophe 1

That mind was a strong bow.
Deep, how deep you drew it then, hard archer,
At a dim fearful range,
And brought dear glory down!

15

You overcame the stranger —
The virgin with her hooking lion claws —
And though death sang, stood like a tower
To make pale Thebes take heart.

20

Fortress against our sorrow!

Divine king, giver of laws,
Majestic Oedipus!
No prince in Thebes had ever such renown,
No prince won such grace of power.

25

Strophe 2

And now of all men ever known
Most pitiful is this man's story:

His fortunes are most changed, his state
Fallen to a low slave's   30
Ground under bitter fate.

O Oedipus, most royal one!
The great door that expelled you to the light
Gave at night — ah, gave night to your glory:
As to the father, to the fathering son.   35

All understood too late.

How could that queen whom Laïos won,
The garden that he harrowed at his height,
Be silent when that act was done?

Antistrophe 2

But all eyes fail before time's eye,   40
All actions come to justice there.
Though never willed, though far down the deep past,
Your bed, your dread sirings,
Are brought to book at last.
Child by Laïos doomed to die,   45
Then doomed to lose that fortunate little death,
Would God you never took breath in this air
That with my wailing lips I take to cry:

For I weep the world's outcast.

I was blind, and now I can tell why: 50
Asleep, for you had given ease of breath
To Thebes, while the false years went by.

EXODOS°

Enter, from the palace, Second Messenger.

Second Messenger: Elders of Thebes, most honored in this land,
What horrors are yours to see and hear, what weight
Of sorrow to be endured, if, true to your birth,
You venerate the line of Labdakos!
I think neither Istros nor Phasis, those great rivers,   5
Could purify this place of the corruption
It shelters now, or soon must bring to light —
Evil not done unconsciously, but willed.

The greatest griefs are those we cause ourselves.

Exodos: final scene, containing the resolution.

Choragos: Surely, friend, we have grief enough already;
      What new sorrow do you mean?
Second Messenger: The Queen is dead.
Choragos: Iocastê? Dead? But at whose hand?
Second Messenger: Her own.
      The full horror of what happened, you can not know,
      For you did not see it; but I, who did, will tell you
      As clearly as I can how she met her death.   15

      When she had left us,
      In passionate silence, passing through the court,
      She ran to her apartment in the house,
      Her hair clutched by the fingers of both hands.
      She closed the doors behind her; then, by that bed   20
      Where long ago the fatal son was conceived —
      That son who should bring about his father's death —
      We heard her call upon Laïos, dead so many years,
      And heard her wail for the double fruit of her marriage,
      A husband by her husband, children by her child.   25

      Exactly how she died I do not know:
      For Oedipus burst in moaning and would not let us
      Keep vigil to the end: it was by him
      As he stormed about the room that our eyes were caught.
      From one to another of us he went, begging a sword,   30
      Cursing the wife who was not his wife, the mother
      Whose womb had carried his own children and himself.
      I do not know: it was none of us aided him,
      But surely one of the gods was in control!
      For with a dreadful cry   35
      He hurled his weight, as though wrenched out of himself,
      At the twin doors: the bolts gave, and he rushed in.
      And there we saw her hanging, her body swaying
      From the cruel cord she had noosed about her neck.
      A great sob broke from him, heartbreaking to hear,   40
      As he loosed the rope and lowered her to the ground.

      I would blot out from my mind what happened next!
      For the King ripped from her gown the golden brooches
      That were her ornament, and raised them, and plunged them down
      Straight into his own eyeballs, crying, "No more,   45
      No more shall you look on the misery about me,
      The horrors of my own doing! Too long you have known
      The faces of those whom I should never have seen,
      Too long been blind to those for whom I was searching!
      From this hour, go in darkness!" And as he spoke,   50
      He struck at his eyes — not once, but many times;
      And the blood spattered his beard,
      Bursting from his ruined sockets like red hail.

So from the unhappiness of two this evil has sprung,
A curse on the man and woman alike. The old　　　　　　　　　55
Happiness of the house of Labdakos
Was happiness enough: where is it today?
It is all wailing and ruin, disgrace, death — all
The misery of mankind that has a name —
And it is wholly and for ever theirs.　　　　　　　　　　60

Choragos: Is he in agony still? Is there no rest for him?

Second Messenger: He is calling for someone to lead him to the gates
So that all the children of Kadmos may look upon
His father's murderer, his mother's — no,
I can not say it!

　　　　　　　　　　And then he will leave Thebes,　　　65
Self-exiled, in order that the curse
Which he himself pronounced may depart from the house.
He is weak, and there is none to lead him,
So terrible is his suffering.

　　　　　　　　　　But you will see:
Look, the doors are opening; in a moment　　　　　　　　70
You will see a thing that would crush a heart of stone.

The central door is opened; Oedipus, blinded, is led in.

Choragos: Dreadful indeed for men to see.
　　Never have my own eyes
　　Looked on a sight so full of fear.

　　Oedipus!　　　　　　　　　　　　　　　　　　　　75
　　What madness came upon you, what daemon
　　Leaped on your life with heavier
　　Punishment than a mortal man can bear?
　　No: I can not even
　　Look at you, poor ruined one.　　　　　　　　　　　80
　　And I would speak, question, ponder,
　　If I were able. No.
　　You make me shudder.

Oedipus: God. God.
　　Is there a sorrow greater?　　　　　　　　　　　　85
　　Where shall I find harbor in this world?
　　My voice is hurled far on a dark wind.
　　What has God done to me?

Choragos: Too terrible to think of, or to see.

　　　　　　　　　　　　　　　　　　　　　　Strophe 1

Oedipus: O cloud of night,　　　　　　　　　　　　　90
　　Never to be turned away: night coming on,
　　I can not tell how: night like a shroud!

　　My fair winds brought me here.
　　　　　　　　　　Oh God. Again

The pain of the spikes where I had sight,
The flooding pain   95
Of memory, never to be gouged out.
Choragos: This is not strange.
        You suffer it all twice over, remorse in pain,
        Pain in remorse.

Antistrophe 1

Oedipus: Ah dear friend   100
        Are you faithful even yet, you alone?
        Are you still standing near me, will you stay here,
        Patient, to care for the blind?
                                        The blind man!
        Yet even blind I know who it is attends me,
        By the voice's tone —   105
        Though my new darkness hide the comforter.
Choragos: Oh fearful act!
        What god was it drove you to rake black
        Night across your eyes?

Strophe 2

Oedipus: Apollo. Apollo. Dear   110
        Children, the god was Apollo.
        He brought my sick, sick fate upon me.
        But the blinding hand was my own!
        How could I bear to see
        When all my sight was horror everywhere?   115
Choragos: Everywhere; that is true.
Oedipus: And now what is left?
        Images? Love? A greeting even,
        Sweet to the senses? Is there anything?
        Ah, no, friends: lead me away.   120
        Lead me away from Thebes.
                                Lead the great wreck
        And hell of Oedipus, whom the gods hate.
Choragos: Your fate is clear, you are not blind to that.
        Would God you had never found it out!

Antistrophe 2

Oedipus: Death take the man who unbound   125
        My feet on that hillside
        And delivered me from death to life! What life?
        If only I had died,
        This weight of monstrous doom
        Could not have dragged me and my darlings down.   130
Choragos: I would have wished the same.
Oedipus: Oh never to have come here
        With my father's blood upon me! Never
        To have been the man they call his mother's husband!

Oh accurst! Oh child of evil,   135
To have entered that wretched bed —
                              the selfsame one!
More primal than sin itself, this fell to me.
Choragos: I do not know how I can answer you.
    You were better dead than alive and blind.
Oedipus: Do not counsel me any more. This punishment   140
    That I have laid upon myself is just.
    If I had eyes,
    I do not know how I could bear the sight
    Of my father, when I came to the house of Death,
    Or my mother: for I have sinned against them both   145
    So vilely that I could not make my peace
    By strangling my own life.
                        Or do you think my children,
    Born as they were born, would be sweet to my eyes?
    Ah never, never! Nor this town with its high walls,
    Nor the holy images of the gods.
                              For I,   150
    Thrice miserable! — Oedipus, noblest of all the line
    Of Kadmos, have condemned myself to enjoy
    These things no more, by my own malediction
    Expelling that man whom the gods declared
    To be a defilement in the house of Laïos.   155
    After exposing the rankness of my own guilt,
    How could I look men frankly in the eyes?
    No, I swear it,
    If I could have stifled my hearing at its source,
    I would have done it and made all this body   160
    A tight cell of misery, blank to light and sound:
    So I should have been safe in a dark agony
    Beyond all recollection.
                        Ah Kithairon!
    Why did you shelter me? When I was cast upon you,
    Why did I not die? Then I should never   165
    Have shown the world my execrable birth.

    Ah Polybos! Corinth, city that I believed
    The ancient seat of my ancestors: how fair
    I seemed, your child! And all the while this evil
    Was cancerous within me!
                        For I am sick   170
    In my daily life, sick in my origin.

    O three roads, dark ravine, woodland and way
    Where three roads met: you, drinking my father's blood,
    My own blood, spilled by my own hand: can you remember
    The unspeakable things I did there, and the things   175

I went on from there to do?

O marriage, marriage!
The act that engendered me, and again the act
Performed by the son in the same bed —

Ah, the net
Of incest, mingling fathers, brothers, sons,
With brides, wives, mothers: the last evil   180
That can be known by men: no tongue can say
How evil!

No. For the love of God, conceal me
Somewhere far from Thebes; or kill me; or hurl me
Into the sea, away from men's eyes for ever.

Come, lead me. You need not fear to touch me.   185
Of all men, I alone can bear this guilt.

Enter Creon.

Choragos: We are not the ones to decide; but Creon here
    May fitly judge of what you ask. He only
    Is left to protect the city in your place.
Oedipus: Alas, how can I speak to him? What right have I   190
    To beg his courtesy whom I have deeply wronged?
Creon: I have not come to mock you, Oedipus,
    Or to reproach you, either.
    (To Attendants.)   — You, standing there:
    If you have lost all respect for man's dignity,
    At least respect the flame of Lord Helios: 195
    Do not allow this pollution to show itself
    Openly here, an affront to the earth
    And Heaven's rain and the light of day. No, take him
    Into the house as quickly as you can.
    For it is proper   200
    That only the close kindred see his grief.
Oedipus: I pray you in God's name, since your courtesy
    Ignores my dark expectation, visiting
    With mercy this man of all men most execrable:
    Give me what I ask — for your good, not for mine.   205
Creon: And what is it that you would have me do?
Oedipus: Drive me out of this country as quickly as may be
    To a place where no human voice can ever greet me.
Creon: I should have done that before now — only,
    God's will had not been wholly revealed to me.   210
Oedipus: But his command is plain: the parricide
    Must be destroyed. I am that evil man.
Creon: That is the sense of it, yes; but as things are,
    We had best discover clearly what is to be done.
Oedipus: You would learn more about a man like me?   215
Creon: You are ready now to listen to the god.

Oedipus: I will listen. But it is to you
That I must turn for help. I beg you, hear me.

The woman in there —
Give her whatever funeral you think proper: 220
She is your sister.
             — But let me go, Creon!
Let me purge my father's Thebes of the pollution
Of my living here, and go out to the wild hills,
To Kithairon, that has won such fame with me,
The tomb my mother and father appointed for me,   225
And let me die there, as they willed I should.
And yet I know
Death will not ever come to me through sickness
Or in any natural way: I have been preserved
For some unthinkable fate. But let that be.   230
As for my sons, you need not care for them.
They are men, they will find some way to live.
But my poor daughters, who have shared my table,
Who never before have been parted from their father —
Take care of them, Creon; do this for me.   235
And will you let me touch them with my hands
A last time, and let us weep together?
Be kind, my lord,
Great prince, be kind!
             Could I but touch them,
They would be mine again, as when I had my eyes.   240

Enter Antigone and Ismene, attended.

Ah, God!
Is it my dearest children I hear weeping?
Has Creon pitied me and sent my daughters?
Creon: Yes, Oedipus: I knew that they were dear to you
In the old days, and know you must love them still.   245
Oedipus: May God bless you for this — and be a friendlier
Guardian to you than he has been to me!

Children, where are you?
Come quickly to my hands: they are your brother's —
Hands that have brought your father's once clear eyes   250
To this way of seeing —
             Ah dearest ones,
I had neither sight nor knowledge then, your father
By the woman who was the source of his own life!
And I weep for you — having no strength to see you —
I weep for you when I think of the bitterness   255
That men will visit upon you all your lives.

What homes, what festivals can you attend
Without being forced to depart again in tears?
And when you come to marriageable age,
Where is the man, my daughters, who would dare   260
Risk the bane that lies on all my children?
Is there any evil wanting? Your father killed
His father; sowed the womb of her who bore him;
Engendered you at the fount of his own existence!
That is what they will say of you.
                       Then, whom   265
Can you ever marry? There are no bridegrooms for you,
And your lives must wither away in sterile dreaming.
O Creon, son of Menoikeus!
You are the only father my daughters have,
Since we, their parents, are both of us gone for ever.   270
They are your own blood: you will not let them
Fall into beggary and loneliness;
You will keep them from the miseries that are mine!
Take pity on them; see, they are only children,
Friendless except for you. Promise me this,   275
Great Prince, and give me your hand in token of it.

Creon clasps his right hand.

Children:
I could say much, if you could understand me,
But as it is, I have only this prayer for you:
Live where you can, be as happy as you can —   280
Happier, please God, than God has made your father!
Creon: Enough. You have wept enough. Now go within.
Oedipus: I must; but it is hard.
Creon: Time eases all things.
Oedipus: But you must promise —
Creon: Say what you desire.
Oedipus: Send me from Thebes!
Creon: God grant that I may!   285
Oedipus: But since God hates me . . .
Creon: No, he will grant your wish.
Oedipus: You promise?
Creon: I can not speak beyond my knowledge.
Oedipus: Then lead me in.
Creon: Come now, and leave your children.
Oedipus: No! Do not take them from me!
Creon: Think no longer
That you are in command here, but rather think   290
How, when you were, you served your own destruction.

*Exeunt into the house all but the Chorus; the Choragos chants directly
to the audience.*

Choragos: Men of Thebes: look upon Oedipus.

> This is the king who solved the famous riddle
> And towered up, most powerful of men.
> No mortal eyes but looked on him with envy,   295
> Yet in the end ruin swept over him.
> Let every man in mankind's frailty
> Consider his last day; and let none
> Presume on his good fortune until he find
> Life, at his death, a memory without pain.   300

QUESTIONS

1. In scene I, how explicitly does the prophet Teiresias reveal the guilt of Oedipus? Does it seem to you stupidity on the part of Oedipus, or a defect in Sophocles' play, that the king takes so long to recognize his guilt and to admit to it?
2. How does Oedipus exhibit weakness of character? Point to scenes that reveal him as imperfectly noble in his words, deeds, or treatment of others.
3. "Oedipus is punished not for any fault in himself, but for his ignorance. Not knowing his family history, unable to recognize his parents on sight, he is blameless; and in slaying his father and marrying his mother, he behaves as any sensible person might behave in the same circumstances." Do you agree with this interpretation?
4. Besides the predictions of Teiresias, what other foreshadowings of the shepherd's revelation does the play contain?
5. Consider the character of Iocastê. Is she a "flat" character — a generalized queen figure — or an individual with distinctive traits of personality? Point to particular speeches or details in the play to back up your opinion.
6. Do the choral interludes merely interrupt the play with wordy poetry? Other than providing song, dance, and variety, do they have any value to the telling of the story?
7. What is dramatic irony? Besides the example given on page 1273, what other instances of dramatic irony do you find in *Oedipus Rex*? What do they contribute to the effectiveness of the play?
8. In the drama of Sophocles, violence and bloodshed take place offstage; thus, the suicide of Iocastê is only reported to us. Nor do we witness Oedipus' removal of his eyes; this horror is only given in the report by the second messenger. Of what advantage or disadvantage to the play is this limitation?
9. Does the play leave you with any definite attitude toward the gods? In inflicting a plague upon Thebes, in causing barrenness, in cursing a people as well as their king, do the gods seem to you cruel, unjust, or tyrannical? Is there any reverence displayed toward them?
10. Sigmund Freud, in *The Interpretation of Dreams*, made a famous and influential observation on the story of Oedipus: "His destiny moves us only because it might have been ours. . . . It is the fate of all of us to direct our first sexual impulses toward our mother and our first murderous hatred against our father." Is that why the play moves you?
11. How readily adaptable to the contemporary stage does *Oedipus Rex* appear? Suppose you were to stage a production of the play, with the aim of making it come alive for the present-day playgoer. What problems might you encounter? How would you deal with them?

In a great tragedy, we sense that some overpowering force is at work, closing in steadily upon the protagonist. Few spectators of *Oedipus Rex* wonder how the play will turn out, or ask themselves whether it will all end happily. As the French playwright Jean Anouilh has remarked,

> In a tragedy, nothing is in doubt and everyone's destiny is known. That makes for tranquility. There is a sort of fellow-feeling among characters in a tragedy: he who kills is as innocent as he who gets killed: it's all a matter of what part you are playing. Tragedy is restful; and the reason is that hope, that foul, deceitful thing, has no part in it. There isn't any hope. You're trapped. The whole sky has fallen on you, and all you can do about it is shout.[1]

Aristotle, in describing the workings of this inexorable force in *Oedipus Rex*, uses certain terms that later critics have found valuable. One is **recognition** or discovery (*anagnorisis*): the revelation of some fact not known before, or some person's true identity. Oedipus makes such a discovery: he recognizes that he himself was the child whom his mother had given over to be destroyed. Such a recognition also occurs in Shakespeare's *Macbeth* when Macduff reveals himself to have been "from his mother's womb / Untimely ripped," thus disclosing a double meaning in the witches' prophecy that Macbeth could be harmed by "none of woman born," and sweeping aside Macbeth's last shred of belief that he is infallible. Modern critics have taken the term to mean also the terrible enlightenment that accompanies such a recognition. "To see things plain — that is *anagnorisis*," Clifford Leech has observed, "and it is the ultimate experience we shall have if we have leisure at the point of death. . . . It is what tragedy ultimately is about: the realization of the unthinkable."[2]

Having made his discovery, Oedipus suffers a reversal in his fortunes: he goes off into exile, blinded and dethroned. Such a fall from happiness seems intrinsic to tragedy, but we should note that Aristotle has a more particular meaning for his term **reversal** (*peripeteia*, anglicized as **peripety**). He means an action that turns out to have the opposite effect from the effect its doer had intended. One of his illustrations of such an ironic reversal is from *Oedipus Rex*: the first messenger intends to cheer Oedipus with the partially good news that, contrary to the prophecy that Oedipus would kill his father, his father has died of old age. The reversal is in the fact that, when the messenger further reveals that old Polybos was Oedipus' father only by adoption, the king, instead of having his fears allayed, is stirred to new dread.

We are not altogether sorry, perhaps, to see an arrogant man such

---

[1] *Antigone*, translated by Lewis Galantière (New York: Random House, 1946).
[2] *Tragedy* (London: Methuen, 1969), p. 65.

as Oedipus humbled, and yet it is difficult not to feel that the punishment of Oedipus is greater than he deserves. Possibly this is what Aristotle meant in his observation that a tragedy arouses our pity and our fear: our compassion for Oedipus, and our terror as we sense the remorselessness of a universe in which a man is doomed.

Notice, however, that at the end of the play Oedipus does not curse God and die. Although such a complex play is open to many interpretations, it is probably safe to say that the play is not a bitter complaint against the universe. At last, Oedipus accepts the divine will, prays for blessings upon his children, and prepares to endure his exile — fallen from high estate, but uplifted in moral dignity.

Since the time of Sophocles, tragedy has been shaped by different theatrical conventions and by different philosophies. Still, some of the tragedies of Shakespeare resemble the tragedies of Sophocles in several ways. To mention one, Othello, like Oedipus, is a person of high estate: "a noble and valiant general." To mention another resemblance, *Othello*, like *Oedipus Rex*, conveys a sense that we are watching the inevitable.

THE THEATER OF SHAKESPEARE

Compared with the technical resources of a theater of today, those of a London public theater in the time of Queen Elizabeth I seem hopelessly limited. Plays had to be performed by daylight and scenery had to be kept simple: a table, a chair, a throne, perhaps an artificial tree or two to suggest a forest. But these limitations were in a sense advantages. What the theater of today can spell out for us realistically, with massive scenery and electric lighting, Elizabethan playgoers had to imagine and the playwright had to make vivid for them by means of language. Not having a lighting technician to work a panel, Shakespeare had to indicate the dawn by having Horatio, in *Hamlet,* say in a speech rich in metaphor and descriptive detail:

> But look, the morn in russet mantle clad
> Walks o'er the dew of yon high eastward hill.

And yet the theater of Shakespeare was not bare, for the playwright did have *some* valuable technical resources. Costumes could be elaborate, and apparently some costumes conveyed agreed-upon meanings: one theater manager's inventory included "a robe for to go invisible in." There could be musical accompaniment and sound effects such as gunpowder explosions and the beating of a pan to simulate thunder.

The stage itself was remarkably versatile. At its back were doors for exits and entrances and a curtained booth or alcove useful for hiding inside. Above the stage was a higher acting area — perhaps a porch or balcony — useful for a Juliet to stand upon and for a Romeo to raise his eyes to. And in the stage floor was a trapdoor leading to a "hell" or cellar, especially useful for ghosts or devils who had to emerge or disappear. The stage itself was a rectangular platform that projected into a yard enclosed by three-storied galleries.

Johannes de Witt, a Continental visitor to London, made a drawing of the Swan Theatre in about the year 1596. The original drawing is lost; this is Arend van Buchel's copy of it.

The building was round or octagonal: in *Henry V*, Shakespeare calls it a "wooden O." The audience sat in these galleries or else stood in the yard in front of the stage and at its sides. A roof or awning protected the stage and the high-priced gallery seats, but in case of sudden rain, the *groundlings*, who paid a penny to stand in the yard, must have been dampened.

Built by the theatrical company to which Shakespeare belonged, the Globe, the most celebrated of Elizabethan theaters, was actually situated not in the city of London itself but on the south bank of the Thames River. This location had been chosen because earlier, in 1574, public plays had been banished from the city by an ordinance that blamed them for "corruptions of youth and other enormities" (such as providing opportunities for prostitutes and purse-cutters).

A playwright had to please all members of the audience, not only the mannered and educated. This obligation may help to explain the wide range of matter and tone in an Elizabethan play: passages of subtle poetry, of deep philosophy, of coarse bawdry; scenes of sensational violence and of quiet psychological conflict (not that most members of the audience may not have enjoyed all of these elements). Because he was an actor as well as a playwright, Shakespeare well knew what his company could do, and what his audience wanted. In devising a play, he could write a part to take advantage of some actor's particular skills; or he could avoid straining the company's resources (certain of his plays have few female parts, perhaps because of a shortage of competent boy actors). The company might offer as many as thirty different plays in a season, customarily changing the program daily. This meant that the actors had to hold many parts in their heads, which may account for Elizabethan playwrights' fondness for blank verse. Lines of fixed length were easier for actors to commit to memory.

The Tragedy of Othello, here offered for study, may be (if you are fortunate) new to you. It is seldom taught in high school, since it is ablaze with passion and violence. But if you already know the play, we trust that you (like your instructor and your editor) still have much more to learn from it. Following his usual practice, Shakespeare based the play on a story he had appropriated — from a tale of "The Unfaithfulness of Husbands and Wives," by a sixteenth-century Italian writer, Giraldi Cinthio. And as he could not help but do, Shakespeare freely transformed his source material. In the original tale, the heroine Disdemona (whose name Shakespeare so hugely improved) is beaten to death with a stocking full of sand — a shoddier death than the Bard imagined for her.

Most critics agree that when he wrote *Othello*, in about 1604, Shakespeare was at the height of his imaginative powers. Surely no character in literature can touch us more than Desdemona, no character can shock and disgust us more than Iago. Between these two extremes stands Othello, a black man of courage and dignity — and yet human, capable of being fooled, a pushover for bad advice. Besides breathing life into these characters and a host of others, Shakespeare — as capable a writer as any the world has known — enables them to speak poetry. Sometimes, this poetry seems splendid and rich in imagery; at other times, quiet and understated. Always, it seems to grow naturally from the nature of Shakespeare's characters and from their situations. *The Tragedy of Othello* has never ceased to grip readers and beholders alike. It is a safe bet that it will triumphantly live as long as fathers dislike whomever their daughters marry, as long as husbands suspect their wives of cheating, as long as blacks remember slavery, and as long as the ambitious court favor and the jealous work deceit. The play may even make sense as long as public officials connive behind smiling faces (remember Watergate); and it may even endure as long as the world makes room for the kind, the true, the beautiful — the blessed pure in heart.

William Shakespeare (1564–1616)

THE TRAGEDY OF OTHELLO   1604?

The Moor of Venice

Edited by Alvin Kernan°

Characters

Othello, the Moor
Brabantio, father to Desdemona
Cassio, an honorable lieutenant
Iago, a villain
Roderigo, a gulled gentleman
Duke of Venice
Senators
Montano, Governor of Cyprus
Gentlemen of Cyprus
Lodovico and Gratiano, two noble Venetians
Sailors
Clown

Edited by Alvin Kernan: This text of *Othello* is based on that of the first Folio, or large collection, of Shakespeare's plays (1623). However, there are many differences between the Folio text and that of the play's first printing in the Quarto, or small volume, of 1621 (eighteen or nineteen years after the play's first performance). Some readings from the Quarto are included. For the reader's convenience, some material has been added by the editor (some indications of scene, some stage directions). Such additions are enclosed in brackets. Mr. Kernan's text and notes were prepared for the edition of *Othello* in the Signet Classic Shakespeare series (New York: New American Library, 1963), under the general editorship of Sylvan Barnet.

Desdemona, wife to Othello
Emilia, wife to Iago
Bianca, a courtesan
[*Messenger, Herald, Officers, Gentlemen, Musicians, Attendants*]

Scene. *Venice and Cyprus.*

ACT I

Scene I [*Venice. A street.*]

Roderigo: Tush! Never tell me? I take it much unkindly
    That thou, Iago, who hast had my purse
    As if the strings were thine, shouldst know of this.
Iago: 'Sblood°, but you'll not hear me! If ever I did dream
    Of such a matter, abhor me.
Roderigo: Thou told'st me   5
    Thou didst hold him in thy hate.
Iago: Despise me
    If I do not. Three great ones of the city,
    In personal suit to make me his lieutenant,
    Off-capped° to him; and, by the faith of man,
    I know my price; I am worth no worse a place.   10
    But he, as loving his own pride and purposes,
    Evades them with a bombast circumstance°,
    Horribly stuffed with epithets of war;
    Nonsuits° my mediators. For, "Certes," says he,
    "I have already chose my officer." And what was he?   15
    Forsooth, a great arithmetician°,
    One Michael Cassio, a Florentine,
    (A fellow almost damned in a fair wife)°
    That never set a squadron in the field,
    Nor the division of a battle knows   20
    More than a spinster; unless the bookish theoric,
    Wherein the tonguèd° consuls can propose
    As masterly as he. Mere prattle without practice
    Is all his soldiership. But he, sir, had th' election;
    And I, of whom his eyes had seen the proof   25
    At Rhodes, at Cyprus, and on other grounds
    Christian and heathen, must be belee'd and calmed
    By debitor and creditor. This counter-caster°,

I.i.   ⁴*'Sblood:* by God's blood.   ⁹*Off-capped:* doffed their caps — as a mark of respect.
¹²*bombast circumstance:* stuffed, roundabout speech.   ¹⁴*Nonsuits:* rejects.   ¹⁶*arithmetician:*
theorist (rather than practical).   ¹⁸*A . . . wife:* (a much-disputed passage, probably best
taken as a general sneer at Cassio as a dandy and a ladies' man. But in the story from
which Shakespeare took his plot the counterpart of Cassio is married, and it may be that
at the beginning of the play Shakespeare had decided to keep him married but later
changed his mind).   ²²*tonguèd:* eloquent.   ²⁸*counter-caster:* i.e., a bookkeeper who *casts*
(reckons up) figures on a *counter* (abacus).

He, in good time, must his lieutenant be,
And I — God bless the mark! — his Moorship's ancient°.   30
Roderigo: By heaven, I rather would have been his hangman.
Iago: Why, there's no remedy. 'Tis the curse of service:
Preferment goes by letter and affection°,
And not by old gradation°, where each second
Stood heir to th' first. Now, sir, be judge yourself,   35
Whether I in any just term am affined°
To love the Moor.
Roderigo: I would not follow him then.
Iago: O, sir, content you.
I follow him to serve my turn upon him.
We cannot all be masters, nor all masters   40
Cannot be truly followed. You shall mark
Many a duteous and knee-crooking° knave
That, doting on his own obsequious bondage,
Wears out his time, much like his master's ass,
For naught but provender; and when he's old, cashiered.   45
Whip me such honest knaves! Others there are
Who, trimmed in forms and visages of duty,
Keep yet their hearts attending on themselves,
And, throwing but shows of service on their lords,
Do well thrive by them, and when they have lined their coats,   50
Do themselves homage. These fellows have some soul;
And such a one do I profess myself. For, sir,
It is as sure as you are Roderigo,
Were I the Moor, I would not be Iago.
In following him, I follow but myself.   55
Heaven is my judge, not I for love and duty,
But seeming so, for my peculiar° end;
For when my outward action doth demonstrate
The native° act and figure of my heart
In complement extern°, 'tis not long after   60
But I will wear my heart upon my sleeve
For daws to peck at; I am not what I am.
Roderigo: What a full fortune does the thick-lips owe°
If he can carry't thus!
Iago: Call up her father,
Rouse him. Make after him, poison his delight,   65
Proclaim him in the streets, incense her kinsmen,
And though he in a fertile climate dwell,
Plague him with flies; though that his joy be joy,
Yet throw such chances of vexation on't
As it may lose some color.   70
Roderigo: Here is her father's house. I'll call aloud.

---

³⁰ *ancient:* standard-bearer; an under-officer.   ³³ *letter and affection:* recommendations
(from men of power) and personal preference.   ³⁴ *old gradation:* seniority.   ³⁶ *affined:*
bound.   ⁴² *knee-crooking:* bowing.   ⁵⁷ *peculiar:* personal.   ⁵⁹ *native:* natural, innate.
⁶⁰ *complement extern:* outward appearance.   ⁶³ *owe:* own.

Iago: Do, with like timorous° accent and dire yell
    As when, by night and negligence, the fire
    Is spied in populous cities.
Roderigo: What, ho, Brabantio! Signior Brabantio, ho!   75
Iago: Awake! What, ho, Brabantio! Thieves! Thieves!
    Look to your house, your daughter, and your bags!
    Thieves! Thieves!

    Brabantio above° [at a window].

Brabantio: What is the reason of this terrible summons?
    What is the matter there?   80
Roderigo: Signior, is all your family within?
Iago: Are your doors locked?
Brabantio: Why, wherefore ask you this?
Iago: Zounds, sir, y'are robbed! For shame. Put on your gown!
    Your heart is burst, you have lost half your soul.
    Even now, now, very now, an old black ram   85
    Is tupping your white ewe. Arise, arise!
    Awake the snorting citizens with the bell,
    Or else the devil will make a grandsire of you.
    Arise, I say!
Brabantio: What, have you lost your wits?
Roderigo: Most reverend signior, do you know my voice?   90
Brabantio: Not I. What are you?
Roderigo: My name is Roderigo.
Brabantio: The worser welcome!
    I have charged thee not to haunt about my doors.
    In honest plainness thou hast heard me say
    My daughter is not for thee; and now, in madness,   95
    Being full of supper and distemp'ring draughts°,
    Upon malicious knavery dost thou come
    To start° my quiet.
Roderigo: Sir, sir, sir —
Brabantio: But thou must needs be sure
    My spirits and my place° have in their power   100
    To make this bitter to thee.
Roderigo: Patience, good sir.
Brabantio: What tell'st thou me of robbing? This is Venice,
    My house is not a grange°.
Roderigo: Most grave Brabantio,
    In simple and pure soul I come to you.
Iago: Zounds, sir, you are one of those that will not serve God if the devil   105
    bid you. Because we come to do you service and you think we are
    ruffians, you'll have your daughter covered with a Barbary° horse,

---

⁷² *timorous:* frightening.   ⁷⁸ s.d. *above:* (i.e., on the small upper stage above and to the rear of the main platform stage, which resembled the projecting upper story of an Elizabethan house).   ⁹⁶ *distemp'ring draughts:* unsettling drinks.   ⁹⁸ *start:* disrupt.   ¹⁰⁰ *place:* rank, i.e., of senator.   ¹⁰³ *grange:* isolated house.   ¹⁰⁷ *Barbary:* Arabian, i.e., Moorish.

you'll have your nephews° neigh to you, you'll have coursers for
    cousins°, and gennets for germans°.
Brabantio: What profane wretch art thou?   110
Iago: I am one, sir, that comes to tell you your daughter and the Moor are
    making the beast with two backs.
Brabantio: Thou art a villain.
Iago: You are — a senator.
Brabantio: This thou shalt answer. I know thee, Roderigo.
Roderigo: Sir, I will answer anything. But I beseech you,   115
    If't be your pleasure and most wise consent,
    As partly I find it is, that your fair daughter,
    At this odd-even° and dull watch o' th' night,
    Transported, with no worse nor better guard
    But with a knave of common hire, a gondolier,   120
    To the gross clasps of a lascivious Moor —
    If this be known to you, and your allowance,
    We then have done you bold and saucy wrongs;
    But if you know not this, my manners tell me
    We have your wrong rebuke. Do not believe   125
    That from the sense of all civility°
    I thus would play and trifle with your reverence.
    Your daughter, if you have not given her leave,
    I say again, hath made a gross revolt,
    Tying her duty, beauty, wit, and fortunes   130
    In an extravagant° and wheeling stranger
    Of here and everywhere. Straight satisfy yourself.
    If she be in her chamber, or your house,
    Let loose on me the justice of the state
    For thus deluding you.
Brabantio: Strike on the tinder, ho!   135
    Give me a taper! Call up all my people!
    This accident° is not unlike my dream.
    Belief of it oppresses me already.
    Light, I say! Light!   *Exit [above].*
Iago: Farewell, for I must leave you.
    It seems not meet, nor wholesome to my place,   140
    To be produced — as, if I stay, I shall —
    Against the Moor. For I do know the State,
    However this may gall him with some check°,
    Cannot with safety cast° him; for he's embarked
    With such loud reason to the Cyprus wars,   145
    Which even now stands in act°, that for their souls
    Another of his fathom° they have none

---

[108] *nephews:* i.e., grandsons. [109] *cousins:* relations. [109] *gennets for germans:* Spanish
horses for blood relatives. [118] *odd-even:* between night and morning. [126] *sense of all
civility:* feeling of what is proper. [131] *extravagant:* vagrant, wandering (Othello is not
Venetian and thus may be considered a wandering soldier of fortune). [137] *accident:* happening. [143] *check:* restraint. [144] *cast:* dismiss. [146] *stands in act:* takes place. [147] *fathom:*
ability.

To lead their business; in which regard,
Though I do hate him as I do hell-pains,
Yet, for necessity of present life,   150
I must show out a flag and sign of love,
Which is indeed but sign. That you shall surely find him,
Lead to the Sagittary° that raisèd search:
And there will I be with him. So farewell.   [*Exit.*]

Enter Brabantio [in his nightgown], with Servants and torches.

Brabantio: It is too true an evil. Gone she is;   155
And what's to come of my despisèd time
Is naught but bitterness. Now, Roderigo,
Where didst thou see her? — O unhappy girl! —
With the Moor, say'st thou? — Who would be a father? —
How didst thou know 'twas she? — O, she deceives me   160
Past thought! — What said she to you? Get moe° tapers!
Raise all my kindred! — Are they married, think you?
Roderigo: Truly I think they are.
Brabantio: O heaven! How got she out? O treason of the blood!
Fathers, from hence trust not your daughters' minds   165
By what you see them act°. Is there not charms
By which the property° of youth and maidhood
May be abused? Have you not read, Roderigo,
Of some such thing?
Roderigo: Yes, sir, I have indeed.
Brabantio: Call up my brother. — O, would you had had her! —   170
Some one way, some another. — Do you know
Where we may apprehend her and the Moor?
Roderigo: I think I can discover him, if you please
To get good guard and go along with me.
Brabantio: Pray you lead on. At every house I'll call;   175
I may command at most. — Get weapons, ho!
And raise some special officers of night. —
On, good Roderigo; I will deserve your pains°.   [*Exeunt.*]

Scene II [*A street.*]

Enter Othello, Iago, Attendants with torches.

Iago: Though in the trade of war I have slain men,
Yet do I hold it very stuff° o' th' conscience
To do no contrived murder. I lack iniquity
Sometime to do me service. Nine or ten times
I had thought t' have yerked° him here, under the ribs.   5
Othello: 'Tis better as it is.
Iago: Nay, but he prated,

---

153 *Sagittary:* (probably the name of an inn).   161 *moe:* more.   166 *act:* do.   167 *property:*
true nature.   178 *deserve your pains:* be worthy of (and reward) your efforts.   I.ii.   2 *stuff:*
essence.   5 *yerked:* stabbed.

And spoke such scurvy and provoking terms
Against your honor, that with the little godliness I have
I did full hard forbear him. But I pray you, sir,
Are you fast married? Be assured of this,   10
That the magnifico° is much beloved,
And hath in his effect a voice potential
As double as the Duke's°. He will divorce you,
Or put upon you what restraint or grievance
The law, with all his might to enforce it on,   15
Will give him cable°.
Othello: Let him do his spite.
My services which I have done the Signiory°
Shall out-tongue his complaints. 'Tis yet to know° —
Which when I know that boasting is an honor
I shall promulgate — I fetch my life and being   20
From men of royal siege°, and my demerits°
May speak unbonneted to as proud a fortune
As this that I have reached°. For know, Iago,
But that I love the gentle Desdemona,
I would not my unhousèd° free condition   25
Put into circumscription and confine
For the seas' worth. But look, what lights come yond?

Enter Cassio, with [Officers and] torches.

Iago: Those are the raisèd father and his friends.
    You were best go in.
Othello: Not I. I must be found.
    My parts, my title, and my perfect soul°   30
    Shall manifest me rightly. Is it they?
Iago: By Janus, I think no.
Othello: The servants of the Duke? And my lieutenant?
    The goodness of the night upon you, friends.
    What is the news?
Cassio: The Duke does greet you, general;   35
    And he requires your haste-posthaste appearance
    Even on the instant.
Othello: What is the matter, think you?
Cassio: Something from Cyprus, as I may divine.
    It is a business of some heat. The galleys
    Have sent a dozen sequent° messengers   40
    This very night at one another's heels,
    And many of the consuls, raised and met,
    Are at the Duke's already. You have been hotly called for.

---

¹¹ *magnifico:* nobleman.   ¹²⁻¹³ *hath . . . Duke's:* i.e., can be as effective as the Duke.
¹⁶ *cable:* range, scope.   ¹⁷ *Signiory:* the rulers of Venice.   ¹⁸ *yet to know:* unknown as yet.
²¹ *siege:* rank.   ²¹ *demerits:* deserts.   ²²⁻²³ *May . . . reached:* i.e., are the equal of the family I
have married into.   ²⁵ *unhousèd:* unconfined.   ³⁰ *perfect soul:* clear, unflawed conscience.
⁴⁰ *sequent:* successive.

When, being not at your lodging to be found,
The Senate hath sent about three several° quests   45
To search you out.
Othello: 'Tis well I am found by you.
I will but spend a word here in the house,
And go with you.   [Exit.]
Cassio: Ancient, what makes he here?
Iago: Faith, he tonight hath boarded a land carack°.
If it prove lawful prize, he's made forever.   50
Cassio: I do not understand.
Iago: He's married.
Cassio: To who?

[Enter Othello.]

Iago: Marry°, to — Come captain, will you go?
Othello: Have with you.
Cassio: Here comes another troop to seek for you.

Enter Brabantio, Roderigo, with Officers and torches.

Iago: It is Brabantio. General, be advised.
He comes to bad intent.
Othello: Holla! Stand there!   55
Roderigo: Signior, it is the Moor.
Brabantio: Down with him, thief! [They draw swords.]
Iago: You, Roderigo? Come, sir, I am for you.
Othello: Keep up your bright swords, for the dew will rust them.
Good signior, you shall more command with years
Than with your weapons.   60
Brabantio: O thou foul thief, where hast thou stowed my daughter?
Damned as thou art, thou hast enchanted her!
For I'll refer me to all things of sense°,
If she in chains of magic were not bound,
Whether a maid so tender, fair, and happy,   65
So opposite to marriage that she shunned
The wealthy, curlèd darlings of our nation,
Would ever have, t'incur a general mock°,
Run from her guardage to the sooty bosom
Of such a thing as thou — to fear, not to delight.   70
Judge me the world if 'tis not gross in sense°
That thou hast practiced° on her with foul charms,
Abused her delicate youth with drugs or minerals
That weaken motion°. I'll have't disputed on;
'Tis probable, and palpable to thinking.   75

°45 several: separate. °49 carack: treasure ship. °52 Marry: By Mary (an interjection).
°63 refer . . . sense: i.e., base (my argument) on all ordinary understanding of nature.
°68 general mock: public shame. °71 gross in sense: obvious. °72 practiced: used tricks. °74 motion: thought, i.e., reason.

I therefore apprehend and do attach° thee
For an abuser of the world, a practicer
Of arts inhibited and out of warrant°.
Lay hold upon him. If he do resist,
Subdue him at his peril.

Othello: Hold your hands,   80
Both you of my inclining and the rest.
Were it my cue to fight, I should have known it
Without a prompter. Whither will you that I go
To answer this your charge?

Brabantio: To prison, till fit time
Of law and course of direct session   85
Call thee to answer.

Othello: What if I do obey?
How may the Duke be therewith satisfied,
Whose messengers are here about my side
Upon some present° business of the state
To bring me to him?

Officer: 'Tis true, most worthy signior.   90
The Duke's in council, and your noble self
I am sure is sent for.

Brabantio: How? The Duke in council?
In this time of the night? Bring him away.
Mine's not an idle cause. The Duke himself,
Or any of my brothers° of the state,   95
Cannot but feel this wrong as 'twere their own;
For if such actions may have passage free,
Bondslaves and pagans shall our statesmen be.   *Exeunt.*

Scene III   [*A council chamber.*]

Enter Duke, Senators, and Officers [set at a table, with lights and Attendants].

Duke: There's no composition° in this news
That gives them credit°.

First Senator: Indeed, they are disproportioned.
My letters say a hundred and seven galleys.

Duke: And mine a hundred forty.

Second Senator: And mine two hundred.
But though they jump° not on a just accompt° —   5
As in these cases where the aim° reports
'Tis oft with difference — yet do they all confirm
A Turkish fleet, and bearing up to Cyprus.

Duke: Nay, it is possible enough to judgment°.

---

⁷⁶ *attach:* arrest.   ⁷⁸ *inhibited . . . warrant:* prohibited and illegal (black magic).   ⁸⁹ *present:* immediate.   ⁹⁵ *brothers:* i.e., the other senators.   I.iii.   ¹ *composition:* agreement.   ² *gives them credit:* makes them believable.   ⁵ *jump:* agree.   ⁵ *just accompt:* exact counting. ⁶ *aim:* approximation.   ⁹ *to judgment:* when carefully considered.

I do not so secure me in the error,   10
But the main article I do approve
In fearful sense°.
Sailor (Within):   What, ho! What, ho! What, ho!

Enter Sailor.

Officer: A messenger from the galleys.
Duke: Now? What's the business?
Sailor: The Turkish preparation makes for Rhodes.
So was I bid report here to the State   15
By Signior Angelo.
Duke: How say you by this change?
First Senator: This cannot be
By no assay of reason. 'Tis a pageant°
To keep us in false gaze°. When we consider
Th' importancy of Cyprus to the Turk,   20
And let ourselves again but understand
That, as it more concerns the Turk than Rhodes,
So may he with more facile question° bear it,
For that it stands not in such warlike brace°,
But altogether lacks th' abilities   25
That Rhodes is dressed in. If we make thought of this,
We must not think the Turk is so unskillful
To leave that latest which concerns him first,
Neglecting an attempt of ease and gain
To wake and wage a danger profitless.   30
Duke: Nay, in all confidence he's not for Rhodes.
Officer: Here is more news.

Enter a Messenger.

Messenger: The Ottomites, reverend and gracious,
Steering with due course toward the isle of Rhodes,
Have there injointed them with an after° fleet.   35
First Senator: Ay, so I thought. How many, as you guess?
Messenger: Of thirty sail; and now they do restem
Their backward course, bearing with frank appearance
Their purposes toward Cyprus. Signior Montano,
Your trusty and most valiant servitor,   40
With his free duty° recommends° you thus,
And prays you to believe him.
Duke: 'Tis certain then for Cyprus.
Marcus Luccicos, is not he in town?
First Senator: He's now in Florence.   45
Duke: Write from us to him; post-posthaste dispatch.

10-12 *I do . . . sense:* i.e., just because the numbers disagree in the reports, I do not doubt
that the principal information (that the Turkish fleet is out) is fearfully true.   18 *pageant:*
show, pretense.   19 *in false gaze:* looking the wrong way.   23 *facile question:* easy struggle.
24 *warlike brace:* "military posture."   35 *after:* following.   41 *free duty:* unlimited respect.
41 *recommends:* informs.

First Senator: Here comes Brabantio and the valiant Moor.

Enter Brabantio, Othello, Cassio, Iago, Roderigo, and Officers.

Duke: Valiant Othello, we must straight° employ you
    Against the general° enemy Ottoman.
    [*To Brabantio*] I did not see you. Welcome, gentle signior.   50
    We lacked your counsel and your help tonight.
Brabantio: So did I yours. Good your grace, pardon me.
    Neither my place, nor aught I heard of business,
    Hath raised me from my bed; nor doth the general care
    Take hold on me; for my particular grief   55
    Is of so floodgate and o'erbearing nature
    That it engluts and swallows other sorrows,
    And it is still itself.
Duke: Why, what's the matter?
Brabantio: My daughter! O, my daughter!
Senators: Dead?
Brabantio: Ay, to me.
    She is abused, stol'n from me, and corrupted   60
    By spells and medicines bought of mountebanks;
    For nature so prepost'rously to err,
    Being not deficient, blind, or lame of sense,
    Sans° witchcraft could not.
Duke: Whoe'er he be that in this foul proceeding   65
    Hath thus beguiled your daughter of herself,
    And you of her, the bloody book of law
    You shall yourself read in the bitter letter
    After your own sense; yea, though our proper° son
    Stood in your action°.
Brabantio: Humbly I thank your Grace.   70
    Here is the man — this Moor, whom now, it seems,
    Your special mandate for the state affairs
    Hath hither brought.
All: We are very sorry for't.
Duke [*To Othello*]: What in your own part can you say to this?
Brabantio: Nothing, but this is so.   75
Othello: Most potent, grave, and reverend signiors,
    My very noble and approved° good masters,
    That I have ta'en away this old man's daughter,
    It is most true; true I have married her.
    The very head and front° of my offending   80
    Hath this extent, no more. Rude am I in my speech,
    And little blessed with the soft phrase of peace.
    For since these arms of mine had seven years' pith°
    Till now some nine moons wasted°, they have used

---

⁴⁸ *straight:* at once. ⁴⁹ *general:* universal. ⁶⁴ *Sans:* without. ⁶⁹ *proper:* own. ⁷⁰ *Stood in your action:* were the accused in your suit. ⁷⁷ *approved:* tested, proven by past performance. ⁸⁰ *head and front:* extreme form (*front* = forehead). ⁸³ *pith:* strength. ⁸⁴ *wasted:* past.

Their dearest° action in the tented field;   85
And little of this great world can I speak
More than pertains to feats of broils and battle;
And therefore little shall I grace my cause
In speaking for myself. Yet, by your gracious patience,
I will a round° unvarnished tale deliver   90
Of my whole course of love — what drugs, what charms,
What conjuration, and what mighty magic,
For such proceeding I am charged withal,
I won his daughter —
Brabantio: A maiden never bold,
Of spirit so still and quiet that her motion   95
Blushed at herself°, and she, in spite of nature,
Of years, of country, credit, everything,
To fall in love with what she feared to look on!
It is a judgment maimed and most imperfect
That will confess perfection so could err   100
Against all rules of nature, and must be driven
To find out practices of cunning hell
Why this should be. I therefore vouch again
That with some mixtures pow'rful o'er the blood,
Or with some dram, conjured to this effect,   105
He wrought upon her.
Duke: To vouch this is no proof,
Without more wider and more overt test
Than these thin habits° and poor likelihoods
Of modern° seeming do prefer against him.
First Senator: But, Othello, speak.   110
Did you by indirect and forcèd courses
Subdue and poison this young maid's affections?
Or came it by request, and such fair question°
As soul to soul affordeth?
Othello: I do beseech you,
Send for the lady to the Sagittary   115
And let her speak of me before her father.
If you do find me foul in her report,
The trust, the office, I do hold of you
Not only take away, but let your sentence
Even fall upon my life.
Duke: Fetch Desdemona hither.   120
Othello: Ancient, conduct them; you best know the place.

[*Exit Iago, with two or three Attendants.*]

And till she come, as truly as to heaven
I do confess the vices of my blood,

---

[85] *dearest:* most important.   [90] *round:* blunt.   [95-96] *her motion/Blushed at herself:* i.e., she was so modest that she blushed at every thought (and movement).   [108] *habits:* clothing.   [109] *modern:* trivial.   [113] *question:* discussion.

So justly to your grave ears I'll present
How I did thrive in this fair lady's love,   125
And she in mine.
Duke: Say it, Othello.
Othello: Her father loved me; oft invited me;
Still° questioned me the story of my life
From year to year, the battle, sieges, fortune
That I have passed.   130
I ran it through, even from my boyish days
To th' very moment that he bade me tell it.
Wherein I spoke of most disastrous chances,
Of moving accidents by flood and field,
Of hairbreadth scapes i' th' imminent° deadly breach,   135
Of being taken by the insolent foe
And sold to slavery, of my redemption thence
And portance° in my travel's history,
Wherein of anters° vast and deserts idle°,
Rough quarries, rocks, and hills whose heads touch heaven,   140
It was my hint to speak. Such was my process.
And of the Cannibals that each other eat,
The Anthropophagi°, and men whose heads
Grew beneath their shoulders. These things to hear
Would Desdemona seriously incline;   145
But still the house affairs would draw her thence;
Which ever as she could with haste dispatch,
She'd come again, and with a greedy ear
Devour up my discourse. Which I observing,
Took once a pliant hour, and found good means   150
To draw from her a prayer of earnest heart
That I would all my pilgrimage dilate°,
Whereof by parcels she had something heard,
But not intentively°. I did consent,
And often did beguile her of her tears   155
When I did speak of some distressful stroke
That my youth suffered. My story being done,
She gave me for my pains a world of kisses.
She swore in faith 'twas strange, 'twas passing° strange;
'Twas pitiful, 'twas wondrous pitiful.   160
She wished she had not heard it; yet she wished
That heaven had made her such a man. She thanked me,
And bade me, if I had a friend that loved her,
I should but teach him how to tell my story,
And that would woo her. Upon this hint I spake.   165
She loved me for the dangers I had passed,
And I loved her that she did pity them.
This only is the witchcraft I have used.

128 *Still:* regularly.   135 *imminent:* threatening.   138 *portance:* manner of acting.   139 *anters:*
caves.   139 *idle:* empty, sterile.   143 *Anthropophagi:* maneaters.   152 *dilate:* relate in full.
154 *intentively:* at length and in sequence.   159 *passing:* surpassing.

Here comes the lady. Let her witness it.

Enter Desdemona, Iago, Attendants.

Duke: I think this tale would win my daughter too.   170
    Good Brabantio, take up this mangled matter at the best°.
    Men do their broken weapons rather use
    Than their bare hands.
Brabantio: I pray you hear her speak.
    If she confess that she was half the wooer,
    Destruction on my head if my bad blame
    Light on the man. Come hither, gentle mistress.   175
    Do you perceive in all this noble company
    Where most you owe obedience?
Desdemona: My noble father,
    I do perceive here a divided duty.
    To you I am bound for life and education;   180
    My life and education both do learn me
    How to respect you. You are the lord of duty,
    I am hitherto your daughter. But here's my husband,
    And so much duty as my mother showed
    To you, preferring you before her father,   185
    So much I challenge° that I may profess
    Due to the Moor my lord.
Brabantio: God be with you. I have done.
    Please it your Grace, on to the state affairs.
    I had rather to adopt a child than get° it.
    Come hither, Moor.   190
    I here do give thee that with all my heart
    Which, but thou hast already, with all my heart
    I would keep from thee. For your sake°, jewel,
    I am glad at soul I have no other child,
    For thy escape would teach me tyranny,   195
    To hang clogs on them. I have done, my lord.
Duke: Let me speak like yourself and lay a sentence°
    Which, as a grise° or step, may help these lovers.
    When remedies are past, the griefs are ended
    By seeing the worst, which late on hopes depended°.   200
    To mourn a mischief that is past and gone
    Is the next° way to draw new mischief on.
    What cannot be preserved when fortune takes,
    Patience her injury a mock'ry makes.
    The robbed that smiles, steals something from the thief;   205
    He robs himself that spends a bootless° grief.
Brabantio: So let the Turk of Cyprus us beguile:
    We lose it not so long as we can smile.
    He bears the sentence well that nothing bears

---

171 *take . . . best:* i.e., make the best of this disaster.   186 *challenge:* claim as right.   189 *get:* beget.   193 *For your sake:* because of you.   197 *lay a sentence:* provide a maxim.   198 *grise:* step.   200 *late on hopes depended:* was supported by hope (of a better outcome) until lately.   202 *next:* closest, surest.   206 *bootless:* valueless.

But the free comfort which from thence he hears;
But he bears both the sentence and the sorrow
That to pay grief must of poor patience borrow.
These sentences, to sugar, or to gall,
Being strong on both sides, are equivocal.
But words are words. I never yet did hear
That the bruisèd heart was piercèd° through the ear
I humbly beseech you, proceed to th' affairs of state.

Duke: The Turk with a most mighty preparation makes for Cyprus.
Othello, the fortitude° of the place is best known to you; and though
we have there a substitute° of most allowed sufficiency°, yet opinion,
a more sovereign mistress of effects, throws a more safer voice on
you°. You must therefore be content to slubber° the gloss of your new
fortunes with this more stubborn and boisterous° expedition.

Othello: The tyrant Custom, most grave senators,
Hath made the flinty and steel couch of war
My thrice-driven° bed of down. I do agnize°
A natural and prompt alacrity
I find in hardness and do undertake
These present wars against the Ottomites.
Most humbly, therefore, bending to your state,
I crave fit disposition for my wife,
Due reference of place, and exhibition°,
With such accommodation and besort
As levels with° her breeding.

Duke: Why, at her father's.

Brabantio: I will not have it so.

Othello: Nor I.

Desdemona: Nor would I there reside,
To put my father in impatient thoughts
By being in his eye. Most gracious Duke,
To my unfolding° lend your prosperous° ear,
And let me find a charter° in your voice,
T' assist my simpleness.

Duke: What would you, Desdemona?

Desdemona: That I love the Moor to live with him,
My downright violence, and storm of fortunes,
May trumpet to the world. My heart's subdued
Even to the very quality of my lord.°

210

215

220

225

230

235

240

245

---

²¹⁶ *piercèd:* (some editors emend to *pieced,* i.e., "healed." But *piercèd* makes good sense: Brabantio is saying in effect that his heart cannot be further hurt [pierced] by the indignity of the useless, conventional advice the Duke offers him. *Pierced* can also mean, however, "lanced" in the medical sense, and would then mean "treated"). ²¹⁹ *fortitude:* fortification. ²²⁰ *substitute:* viceroy. ²²⁰ *most allowed sufficiency:* generally acknowledged capability. ²²⁰⁻²²² *opinion . . . you:* i.e., the general opinion, which finally controls affairs, is that you would be the best man in this situation. ²²² *slubber:* besmear. ²²³ *stubborn and boisterous:* rough and violent. ²²⁶ *thrice-driven:* i.e., softest. ²²⁶ *agnize:* know in myself. ²³² *exhibition:* grant of funds. ²³⁴ *levels with:* is suitable to. ²³⁹ *unfolding:* explanation. ²³⁹ *prosperous:* favoring. ²⁴⁰ *charter:* permission. ²⁴⁴⁻²⁴⁵ *My . . . lord:* i.e., I have become one in nature and being with the man I married (therefore, I too would go to the wars like a soldier).

I saw Othello's visage in his mind,
And to his honors and his valiant parts
Did I my soul and fortunes consecrate.
So that, dear lords, if I be left behind,
A moth of peace, and he go to the war,   250
The rites° for why I love him are bereft me,
And I a heavy interim shall support
By his dear absence. Let me go with him.
Othello: Let her have your voice°.
Vouch with me, heaven, I therefore beg it not   255
To please the palate of my appetite,
Nor to comply with heat° — the young affects°
In me defunct — and proper satisfaction°;
But to be free and bounteous to her mind;
And heaven defend° your good souls that you think   260
I will your serious and great business scant
When she is with me. No, when light-winged toys
Of feathered Cupid seel° with wanton° dullness
My speculative and officed instrument°,
That my disports corrupt and taint my business,   265
Let housewives make a skillet of my helm,
And all indign° and base adversities
Make head° against my estimation°! —
Duke: Be it as you shall privately determine,
Either for her stay or going. Th' affair cries haste,   270
And speed must answer it.
First Senator: You must away tonight.
Othello: With all my heart.
Duke: At nine i' th' morning here we'll meet again.
Othello, leave some officer behind,
And he shall our commission bring to you,   275
And such things else of quality and respect
As doth import you.
Othello: So please your grace, my ancient;
A man he is of honesty and trust.
To his conveyance I assign my wife,
With what else needful your good grace shall think   280
To be sent after me.
Duke: Let it be so.
Good night to every one. [*To Brabantio*] And, noble signior,
If virtue no delighted° beauty lack,
Your son-in-law is far more fair than black.
First Senator: Adieu, brave Moor. Use Desdemona well. 285
Brabantio: Look to her, Moor, if thou hast eyes to see:

251 *rites:* (may refer either to the marriage rites or to the rites, formalities, of war).   254 *voice:*
consent.   257 *heat:* lust.   257 *affects:* passions.   258 *proper satisfaction:* i.e., consummation
of the marriage.   260 *defend:* forbid.   263 *seel:* sew up.   263 *wanton:* lascivious.   264 *speculative . . . instrument:* i.e., sight (and, by extension, the mind).   267 *indign:* unworthy.
268 *Make head:* form an army, i.e., attack.   268 *estimation:* reputation.   283 *delighted:* delightful.

She has deceived her father, and may thee.

[Exeunt Duke, Senators, Officers, &c.]

Othello: My life upon her faith! Honest Iago,
My Desdemona must I leave to thee.
I prithee let thy wife attend on her, 290
And bring them after in the best advantage°.
Come, Desdemona. I have but an hour
Of love, of worldly matter, and direction
To spend with thee. We must obey the time.

Exit [Moor with Desdemona].

Roderigo: Iago? 295
Iago: What say'st thou, noble heart?
Roderigo: What will I do, think'st thou?
Iago: Why, go to bed and sleep.
Roderigo: I will incontinently° drown myself.
Iago: If thou dost, I shall never love thee after. Why, thou silly gentleman? 300
Roderigo: It is silliness to live when to live is torment; and then have we a
prescription to die when death is our physician.
Iago: O villainous! I have looked upon the world for four times seven
years, and since I could distinguish betwixt a benefit and an injury,
I never found man that knew how to love himself. Ere I would say I 305
would drown myself for the love of a guinea hen, I would change my
humanity with a baboon.
Roderigo: What should I do? I confess it is my shame to be so fond, but it
is not in my virtue° to amend it.
Iago: Virtue? A fig! 'Tis in ourselves that we are thus, or thus. Our bodies 310
are our gardens, to the which our wills are gardeners; so that if we
will plant nettles or sow lettuce, set hyssop and weed up thyme, supply it with one gender of herbs or distract° it with many — either to
have it sterile with idleness or manured with industry — why, the
power and corrigible° authority of this lies in our wills. If the bal- 315
ance of our lives had not one scale of reason to poise another of sensuality, the blood and baseness of our natures would conduct us to
most prepost'rous conclusions°. But we have reason to cool our
raging motions, our carnal sting or unbitted° lusts, whereof I take
this that you call love to be a sect or scion°. 320
Roderigo: It cannot be.
Iago: It is merely a lust of the blood and a permission of the will. Come,
be a man! Drown thyself? Drown cats and blind puppies! I have professed me thy friend, and I confess me knit to thy deserving with
cables of perdurable toughness. I could never better stead° thee than 325
now. Put money in thy purse. Follow thou the wars; defeat thy favor°
with an usurped° beard. I say, put money in thy purse. It cannot be

---

¹⁹¹ *advantage:* opportunity. ²⁹⁹ *incontinently:* at once. ³⁰⁹ *virtue:* strength (Roderigo is
saying that his nature controls him). ³¹³ *distract:* vary. ³¹⁵ *corrigible:* corrective. ³¹⁸ *conclusions:* ends. ³¹⁹ *unbitted:* i.e., uncontrolled. ³²⁰ *sect or scion:* off-shoot. ³²⁵ *stead:*
serve. ³²⁶ *defeat thy favor:* disguise your face. ³²⁷ *usurped:* assumed.

long that Desdemona should continue her love to the Moor. Put
money in thy purse. Nor he his to her. It was a violent commence-
ment in her and thou shalt see an answerable° sequestration — put   330
but money in thy purse. These Moors are changeable in their wills —
fill thy purse with money. The food that to him now is as luscious as
locusts° shall be to him shortly as bitter as coloquintida°. She must
change for youth; when she is sated with his body, she will find the
errors of her choice. Therefore, put money in thy purse. If thou wilt   335
needs damn thyself, do it a more delicate way than drowning. Make
all the money thou canst. If sanctimony° and a frail vow betwixt an
erring° barbarian and supersubtle Venetian be not too hard for my
wits, and all the tribe of hell, thou shalt enjoy her. Therefore, make
money. A pox of drowning thyself, it is clean out of the way. Seek   340
thou rather to be hanged in compassing° thy joy than to be drowned
and go without her.

Roderigo: Wilt thou be fast to my hopes, if I depend on the issue?

Iago: Thou art sure of me. Go, make money. I have told thee often, and I
retell thee again and again, I hate the Moor. My cause is hearted°;   345
thine hath no less reason. Let us be conjunctive° in our revenge
against him. If thou canst cuckold him, thou dost thyself a pleasure,
me a sport. There are many events in the womb of time, which will
be delivered. Traverse, go, provide thy money! We will have more of
this tomorrow. Adieu.   350

Roderigo: Where shall we meet i' th' morning?

Iago: At my lodging.

Roderigo: I'll be with thee betimes.

Iago: Go to, farewell. Do you hear, Roderigo?

Roderigo: I'll sell all my land.   *Exit.*   355

Iago: Thus do I ever make my fool my purse;
        For I mine own gained knowledge° should profane
        If I would time expend with such snipe
        But for my sport and profit. I hate the Moor,
        And it is thought abroad that 'twixt my sheets   360
        H'as done my office. I know not if't be true,
        But I, for mere suspicion in that kind,
        Will do, as if for surety°. He holds me well;
        The better shall my purpose work on him.
        Cassio's a proper° man. Let me see now: 365
        To get his place, and to plume up my will°
        In double knavery. How? How? Let's see.
        After some time, to abuse Othello's ears
        That he is too familiar with his wife.
        He hath a person and a smooth dispose°   370

---

³³⁰ *answerable:* similar. ³³³ *locusts:* (a sweet fruit). ³³³ *coloquintida:* a purgative derived
from a bitter apple. ³³⁷ *sanctimony:* sacred bond (of marriage). ³³⁸ *erring:* wandering.
³⁴¹ *compassing:* encompassing, achieving. ³⁴⁵ *hearted:* deepseated in the heart. ³⁴⁶ *con-
junctive:* joined. ³⁵⁷ *gained knowledge:* i.e., practical, worldly wisdom. ³⁶³ *surety:* certainty. ³⁶⁵ *proper:* handsome. ³⁶⁶ *plume up my will:* (many explanations have been
offered for this crucial line, which in Q₁ reads "make up my will." The general sense is
something like "to make more proud and gratify my ego"). ³⁷⁰ *dispose:* manner.

To be suspected — framed° to make women false.
The Moor is of a free and open nature
That thinks men honest that but seem to be so;
And will as tenderly be led by th' nose
As asses are.   375
I have't! It is engendered! Hell and night
Must bring this monstrous birth to the world's light.   [*Exit.*]

ACT II

Scene I   [*Cyprus.*]

    Enter Montano and two Gentlemen [one above]°.

Montano: What from the cape can you discern at sea?
First Gentleman: Nothing at all, it is a high-wrought flood.
    I cannot 'twixt the heaven and the main
    Descry a sail.
Montano: Methinks the wind hath spoke aloud at land;   5
    A fuller blast ne'er shook our battlements.
    If it hath ruffianed so upon the sea,
    What ribs of oak, when mountains melt on them,
    Can hold the mortise? What shall we hear of this?
Second Gentleman: A segregation° of the Turkish fleet.   10
    For do but stand upon the foaming shore,
    The chidden billow seems to pelt the clouds;
    The wind-shaked surge, with high and monstrous main°,
    Seems to cast water on the burning Bear
    And quench the guards of th' ever-fixèd pole.°   15
    I never did like molestation view
    On the enchafèd flood.
Montano: If that the Turkish fleet
    Be not ensheltered and embayed, they are drowned;
    It is impossible to bear it out.

    Enter a [third] Gentleman.

Third Gentleman: News, lads! Our wars are done.   20
    The desperate tempest hath so banged the Turks
    That their designment halts. A noble ship of Venice
    Hath seen a grievous wrack and sufferance°
    On most part of their fleet.
Montano: How? Is this true?

---

³⁷¹ *framed:* designed.   II.i. s.d. (the Folio arrangement of this scene requires that the First
Gentleman stand above — on the upper stage — and act as a lookout reporting sights
which cannot be seen by Montano standing below on the main stage).   ¹⁰ *segregation:*
separation.   ¹³ *main:* (both "ocean" and "strength").   ¹⁴⁻¹⁵ *Seems . . . pole:* (the constellation Ursa Minor contains two stars which are the *guards*, or companions, of the *pole*, or
North Star). ·   ²³ *sufferance:* damage.

Third Gentleman: The ship is here put in,   25
    A Veronesa; Michael Cassio,
    Lieutenant to the warlike Moor Othello,
    Is come on shore; the Moor himself at sea,
    And is in full commission here for Cyprus.
Montano: I am glad on't . 'Tis a worthy governor.   30
Third Gentleman: But this same Cassio, though he speak of comfort
    Touching the Turkish loss, yet he looks sadly
    And prays the Moor be safe, for they were parted
    With foul and violent tempest.
Montano: Pray heavens he be;
    For I have served him, and the man commands   35
    Like a full soldier. Let's to the seaside, ho!
    As well to see the vessel that's come in
    As to throw out our eyes for brave Othello,
    Even till we make the main and th' aerial blue
    An indistinct regard°.
Third Gentleman: Come, let's do so;   40
    For every minute is expectancy
    Of more arrivancie°.

    Enter Cassio.

Cassio: Thanks, you the valiant of the warlike isle,
    That so approve° the Moor. O, let the heavens
    Give him defense against the elements,
    For I have lost him on a dangerous sea.   45
Montano: Is he well shipped?
Cassio: His bark is stoutly timbered, and his pilot
    Of very expert and approved allowance°;
    Therefore my hopes, not surfeited to death°,   50
    Stand in bold cure°. (*Within:* A sail, a sail, a sail!)
Cassio: What noise?
First Gentleman: The town is empty; on the brow o' th' sea
    Stand ranks of people, and they cry, "A sail!"
Cassio: My hopes do shape him for the governor.   [*A shot.*]   55
Second Gentleman: They do discharge their shot of courtesy:
    Our friends at least.
Cassio: I pray you, sir, go forth
    And give us truth who 'tis that is arrived.
Second Gentleman: I shall.   [*Exit.*]   60
Montano: But, good lieutenant, is your general wived?
Cassio: Most fortunately. He hath achieved a maid

---

³⁹⁻⁴⁰ *the main . . . regard:* i.e., the sea and sky become indistinguishable.   ⁴² *arrivancie:*
arrivals.   ⁴⁴ *approve:* ("honor" or, perhaps, "are as warlike and valiant as your governor").
⁴⁹ *approved allowance:* known and tested.   ⁵⁰ *not surfeited to death:* i.e., not so great as to be
in danger.   ⁵¹ *Stand in bold cure:* i.e., are likely to be restored.

That paragons° description and wild fame°;
One that excels the quirks of blazoning pens°,
And in th' essential vesture of creation°
Does tire the ingener°.

Enter [Second] Gentleman.

How now? Who has put in?   65
Second Gentleman: 'Tis one Iago, ancient to the general.
Cassio: H'as had most favorable and happy speed:
Tempests themselves, high seas, and howling winds,
The guttered° rocks and congregated° sands,
Traitors ensteeped° to enclog the guiltless keel,   70
As having sense° of beauty, do omit
Their mortal° natures, letting go safely by
The divine Desdemona.
Montano: What is she?
Cassio: She that I spake of, our great captain's captain,
Left in the conduct of the bold Iago,   75
Whose footing° here anticipates our thoughts
A se'nnight's° speed. Great Jove, Othello guard,
And swell his sail with thine own pow'rful breath,
That he may bless this bay with his tall° ship,
Make love's quick pants in Desdemona's arms,   80
Give renewed fire to our extincted spirits.

Enter Desdemona, Iago, Roderigo, and Emilia.

O, behold! The riches of the ship is come on shore!
You men of Cyprus, let her have your knees.   [*Kneeling.*]
Hail to thee, lady! and the grace of heaven,
Before, behind thee, and on every hand,   85
Enwheel thee round.
Desdemona: I thank you, valiant Cassio.
What tidings can you tell of my lord?
Cassio: He is not yet arrived, nor know I aught
But that he's well and will be shortly here.
Desdemona: O but I fear. How lost you company?   90
Cassio: The great contention of sea and skies
Parted our fellowship. (*Within:* A sail, a sail!)   [*A shot.*]
But hark. A sail!
Second Gentleman: They give this greeting to the citadel;
This likewise is a friend.
Cassio: See for the news.   [*Exit Gentleman.*]   95

---

⁶²*paragons:* exceeds. ⁶² *wild fame:* extravagant report. ⁶³ *quirks of blazoning pens:* in-
genuities of praising pens. ⁶⁴ *essential vesture of creation:* essential human nature as
given by the Creator. ⁶⁵ *tire the ingener:* a difficult line that probably means something
like "outdo the human ability to imagine and picture." ⁶⁹ *guttered:* jagged. ⁶⁹ *congregated:* gathered. ⁷⁰ *ensteeped:* submerged. ⁷¹ *sense:* awareness. ⁷² *mortal:* deadly.
⁷⁶ *footing:* landing. ⁷⁷ *se'nnight's:* week's. ⁷⁹ *tall:* brave.

Good ancient, you are welcome. [*To Emilia*] Welcome, mistress.
Let it not gall your patience, good Iago,
That I extend° my manners. 'Tis my breeding°
That gives me this bold show of courtesy.   [*Kisses Emilia.*]

Iago: Sir, would she give you so much of her lips   100
As of her tongue she oft bestows on me,
You would have enough.

Desdemona: Alas, she has no speech.

Iago: In faith, too much.
I find it still when I have leave to sleep°.
Marry, before your ladyship°, I grant,   105
She puts her tongue a little in her heart
And chides with thinking.

Emilia: You have little cause to say so.

Iago: Come on, come on! You are pictures° out of door,
Bells in your parlors, wildcats in your kitchens,
Saints in your injuries°, devils being offended,   110
Players in your housewifery°, and housewives in your beds.

Desdemona: O, fie upon thee, slanderer!

Iago: Nay, it is true, or else I am a Turk:
You rise to play, and go to bed to work.

Emilia: You shall not write my praise.

Iago: No, let me not.   115

Desdemona: What wouldst write of me, if thou shouldst praise me?

Iago: O gentle lady, do not put me to't.
For I am nothing if not critical.

Desdemona: Come on, assay. There's one gone to the harbor?

Iago: Ay, madam.

Desdemona [*Aside*]: I am not merry; but I do beguile   120
The thing I am by seeming otherwise. —
Come, how wouldst thou praise me?

Iago: I am about it; but indeed my invention
Comes from my pate as birdlime° does from frieze° —
It plucks out brains and all. But my Muse labors,   125
And thus she is delivered:
If she be fair° and wise: fairness and wit,
The one's for use, the other useth it.

Desdemona: Well praised. How if she be black° and witty?

Iago: If she be black, and thereto have a wit,   130
She'll find a white that shall her blackness fit.

Desdemona: Worse and worse!

---

⁹⁸ *extend:* stretch. ⁹⁸ *breeding:* careful training in manners (Cassio is considerably more
than the polished gentleman than Iago, and aware of it). ¹⁰⁴ *still . . . sleep:* i.e., even when she
allows me to sleep she continues to scold. ¹⁰⁵ *before your ladyship:* in your presence.
¹⁰⁸ *pictures:* models (of virtue). ¹¹⁰ *in your injuries:* when you injure others. ¹¹¹ *house-
wifery:* this word can mean "careful, economical household management," and Iago
would then be accusing women of only pretending to be good housekeepers, while in
bed they are either [1] economical of their favors, or more likely [2] serious and dedicated
workers. ¹²⁴ *birdlime:* a sticky substance put on branches to catch birds. ¹²⁴ *frieze:*
rough cloth. ¹²⁷ *fair:* light-complexioned. ¹²⁹ *black:* brunette.

Emilia: How if fair and foolish?

Iago: She never yet was foolish that was fair,
For even her folly helped her to an heir. 135

Desdemona: Those are old fond° paradoxes to make fools laugh i' th'
alehouse. What miserable praise hast thou for her that's foul and
foolish?

Iago: There's none so foul, and foolish thereunto,
But does foul pranks which fair and wise ones do. 140

Desdemona: O heavy ignorance. Thou praisest the worst best. But what
praise couldst thou bestow on a deserving woman indeed — one
that in the authority of her merit did justly put on the vouch of very
malice itself°?

Iago: She that was ever fair, and never proud; 145
Had tongue at will, and yet was never loud;
Never lacked gold, and yet went never gay;
Fled from her wish, and yet said "Now I may";
She that being angered, her revenge being nigh,
Bade her wrong stay, and her displeasure fly; 150
She that in wisdom never was so frail
To change the cod's head for the salmon's tail°;
She that could think, and nev'r disclose her mind;
See suitors following, and not look behind:
She was a wight° (if ever such wights were) — 155

Desdemona: To do what?

Iago: To suckle fools and chronicle small beer°.

Desdemona: O most lame and impotent conclusion. Do not learn of him,
Emilia, though he be thy husband. How say you, Cassio? Is he not a
most profane and liberal° counselor? 160

Cassio: He speaks home°, madam. You may relish him more in° the soldier
than in the scholar. [*Takes Desdemona's hand.*]

Iago [*Aside*]: He takes her by the palm. Ay, well said, whisper! With as
little a web as this will I ensnare as great a fly as Cassio. Ay, smile
upon her, do! I will gyve° thee in thine own courtship. — You say 165
true; 'tis so, indeed! — If such tricks as these strip you out of your
lieutenantry, it had been better you had not kissed your three fingers
so oft — which now again you are most apt to play the sir° in. Very
good! Well kissed! An excellent curtsy°! 'Tis so, indeed. Yet again
your fingers to your lips? Would they were clyster pipes° for your 170
sake! [*Trumpets within.*] The Moor! I know his trumpet°.

Cassio: 'Tis truly so.

Desdemona: Let's meet him and receive him.

Cassio: Lo, where he comes.

---

¹³⁶ *fond:* foolish. ¹⁴²⁻⁴⁴ *one . . . itself:* i.e., a woman so honest and deserving that even
malice would be forced to approve of her. ¹⁵² *To . . . tail:* i.e., to exchange something
valuable for something useless. ¹⁵⁵ *wight:* person. ¹⁵⁷ *chronicle small beer:* i.e., keep
household accounts (the most trivial of occupations in Iago's opinion). ¹⁶⁰ *liberal:* licentious. ¹⁶¹ *speaks home:* thrusts deeply with his speech. ¹⁶¹ *relish him more in:* enjoy him
more as. ¹⁶⁵ *gyve:* bind. ¹⁶⁸ *the sir:* the fashionable gentleman. ¹⁶⁹ *curtsy:* courtesy, i.e.,
bow. ¹⁷⁰ *clyster pipes:* enema tubes. ¹⁷¹ *his trumpet:* (great men had their own distinctive
calls).

Enter Othello and Attendants.

Othello: O my fair warrior!
Desdemona: My dear Othello.   175
Othello: It gives me wonder great as my content
    To see you here before me. O my soul's joy!
    If after every tempest come such calms,
    May the winds blow till they have wakened death.
    And let the laboring bark climb hills of seas   180
    Olympus-high, and duck again as low
    As hell's from heaven. If it were now to die,
    'Twere now to be most happy; for I fear
    My soul hath her content so absolute
    That not another comfort like to this   185
    Succeeds in unknown fate.
Desdemona: The heavens forbid
    But that our loves and comforts should increase
    Even as our days do grow.
Othello: Amen to that, sweet powers!
    I cannot speak enough of this content:
    It stops me here [*touches his heart*]; it is too much of joy.   190
    And this, and this, the greatest discords be   [*They kiss.*]
    That e'er our hearts shall make!
Iago [*Aside*]:   O, you are well tuned now!
    But I'll set down the pegs° that make this music,
    As honest as I am.
Othello: Come, let us to the castle.
    News, friends! Our wars are done; the Turks are drowned.   195
    How does my old acquaintance of this isle?
    Honey, you shall be well desired in Cyprus;
    I have found great love amongst them. O my sweet,
    I prattle out of fashion, and I dote
    In mine own comforts. I prithee, good Iago,   200
    Go to the bay and disembark my coffers.
    Bring thou the master to the citadel;
    He is a good one and his worthiness
    Does challenge° much respect. Come, Desdemona,
    Once more well met at Cyprus.   205

Exit Othello and Desdemona [and all but Iago and Roderigo].

Iago [*To an Attendant*]: Do thou meet me presently at the harbor. [*To Roderigo*] Come hither. If thou be'st valiant (as they say base men being in love have then a nobility in their natures more than is native to them), list me. The lieutenant tonight watches on the court of guard°. First, I must tell thee this: Desdemona is directly in love with   210 him.

Roderigo: With him? Why, 'tis not possible.

---

¹⁹³ *set down the pegs:* loosen the strings (to produce discord).   ²⁰⁴ *challenge:* require, exact.
²¹⁰ *court of guard:* guardhouse.

Iago: Lay thy finger thus [*puts his finger to his lips*], and let thy soul be
instructed. Mark me with what violence she first loved the Moor but
for bragging and telling her fantastical lies. To love him still for prat- 215
ing? Let not thy discreet heart think it. Her eye must be fed. And
what delight shall she have to look on the devil? When the blood is
made dull with the act of sport, there should be a game° to inflame it
and to give satiety a fresh appetite, loveliness in favor°, sympathy
in years°, manners, and beauties; all which the Moor is defective in. 220
Now for want of these required conveniences°, her delicate tenderness will find itself abused, begin to heave the gorge°, disrelish and
abhor the Moor. Very nature will instruct her in it and compel her to
some second choice. Now sir, this granted — as it is a most pregnant°
and unforced position — who stands so eminent in the degree of this 225
fortune as Cassio does? A knave very voluble; no further conscion-
able° than in putting on the mere form of civil and humane° seeming
for the better compass of his salt° and most hidden loose° affection.
Why, none! Why, none! A slipper° and subtle knave, a finder of occasion, that has an eye can stamp and counterfeit advantages, though 230
true advantage never present itself. A devilish knave. Besides, the
knave is handsome, young, and hath all those requisites in him that
folly and green minds look after. A pestilent complete knave, and the
woman hath found him already.

Roderigo: I cannot believe that in her; she's full of most blessed condition. 235

Iago: Blessed fig's-end! The wine she drinks is made of grapes. If she had
been blessed, she would never have loved the Moor. Blessed pudding! Didst thou not see her paddle with the palm of his hand? Didst
not mark that?

Roderigo: Yes, that I did; but that was but courtesy. 240

Iago: Lechery, by this hand! [*Extends his index finger.*] An index° and obscure prologue to the history of lust and foul thoughts. They met so
near with their lips that their breaths embraced together. Villainous
thoughts, Roderigo. When these mutualities so marshal the way,
hard at hand comes the master and main exercise, th' incorporate° 245
conclusion: Pish! But, sir, be you ruled by me. I have brought you
from Venice. Watch you tonight; for the command, I'll lay't upon
you. Cassio knows you not. I'll not be far from you. Do you find some
occasion to anger Cassio, either by speaking too loud, or tainting°
his discipline, or from what other course you please which the time 250
shall more favorably minister.

Roderigo: Well.

Iago: Sir, he's rash and very sudden in choler°, and haply may strike at
you. Provoke him that he may; for even out of that will I cause these
of Cyprus to mutiny, whose qualification shall come into no true 255

---

²¹⁸ *game:* sport (with the added sense of "gamey," "rank"). ²¹⁹ *favor:* countenance, appearance. ²¹⁹⁻²⁰ *sympathy in years:* sameness of age. ²²¹ *conveniences:* advantages.
²²² *heave the gorge:* vomit. ²²⁴ *pregnant:* likely. ²²⁶⁻²⁷ *no further conscionable:* having no
more conscience. ²²⁷ *humane:* polite. ²²⁸ *salt:* lecherous. ²²⁸ *loose:* immoral. ²²⁹ *slipper:*
slippery. ²⁴¹ *index:* pointer. ²⁴⁵ *incorporate:* carnal. ²⁴⁹ *tainting:* discrediting. ²⁵³ *choler:*
anger.

taste° again but by the displanting of Cassio. So shall you have a
shorter journey to your desires by the means I shall then have to
prefer them; and the impediment most profitably removed without
the which there were no expectation of our prosperity.

Roderigo: I will do this if you can bring it to any opportunity.   260

Iago: I warrant thee. Meet me by and by at the citadel. I must fetch his
necessaries ashore. Farewell.

Roderigo: Adieu.   *Exit.*

Iago: That Cassio loves her, I do well believe't;
    That she loves him, 'tis apt and of great credit.   265
    The Moor, howbeit that I endure him not,
    Is of a constant, loving, noble nature,
    And I dare think he'll prove to Desdemona
    A most dear° husband. Now I do love her too;
    Not out of absolute° lust, though peradventure°   270
    I stand accountant for as great a sin,
    But partly led to diet° my revenge,
    For that I do suspect the lusty Moor
    Hath leaped into my seat; the thought whereof
    Doth, like a poisonous mineral, gnaw my inwards;   275
    And nothing can or shall content my soul
    Till I am evened with him, wife for wife.
    Or failing so, yet that I put the Moor
    At least into a jealousy so strong
    That judgment cannot cure. Which thing to do,   280
    If this poor trash of Venice, whom I trace°
    For his quick hunting, stand the putting on,
    I'll have our Michael Cassio on the hip,
    Abuse him to the Moor in the right garb°
    (For I fear Cassio with my nightcap too),   285
    Make the Moor thank me, love me, and reward me
    For making him egregiously an ass
    And practicing upon° his peace and quiet,
    Even to madness. 'Tis here, but yet confused:
    Knavery's plain face is never seen till used.   *Exit.*   290

Scene II   [*A street.*]

Enter Othello's Herald, with a proclamation.

Herald: It is Othello's pleasure, our noble and valiant general, that upon
certain tidings now arrived importing the mere perdition° of the
Turkish fleet, every man put himself into triumph. Some to dance, some
to make bonfires, each man to what sport and revels his addition°

---

²⁵⁵⁻⁵⁶ *qualification . . . taste:* i.e., appeasement will not be brought about (wine was "qualified" by adding water). ²⁶⁹ *dear:* expensive. ²⁷⁰ *out of absolute:* absolutely out of.
²⁷⁰ *peradventure:* perchance. ²⁷² *diet:* feed. ²⁸¹ *trace:* (most editors emend to "trash,"
meaning to hang weights on a dog to slow his hunting: but "trace" clearly means something like "put on the trace" or "set on the track"). ²⁸⁴ *right garb:* i.e., "proper fashion."
²⁸⁸ *practicing upon:* scheming to destroy. II.ii. ² *mere perdition:* absolute destruction.
⁴ *addition:* rank.

leads him. For, besides these beneficial news, it is the celebration of 5
his nuptial. So much was his pleasure should be proclaimed. All
offices° are open, and there is full liberty of feasting from this present
hour of five till the bell have told eleven. Bless the isle of Cyprus and
our noble general Othello!   *Exit.*

Scene III   [*The citadel of Cyprus.*]

    Enter Othello, Desdemona, Cassio, and Attendants.

Othello: Good Michael, look you to the guard tonight.
    Let's teach ourselves that honorable stop,
    Not to outsport direction.
Cassio: Iago hath discretion what to do;
    But notwithstanding, with my personal eye   5
    Will I look to't.
Othello: Iago is most honest.
    Michael, good night. Tomorrow with your earliest
    Let me have speech with you. [*To Desdemona*] Come, my dear love,
    The purchase made, the fruits are to ensue.
    That profit's yet to come 'tween me and you.   10
    Good night.   *Exit [Othello with Desdemona and Attendants].*

    Enter Iago.

Cassio: Welcome, Iago. We must to the watch.
Iago: Not this hour, lieutenant; 'tis not yet ten o' th' clock. Our general
    cast° us thus early for the love of his Desdemona; who let us not
    therefore blame. He hath not yet made wanton the night with her,   15
    and she is sport for Jove.
Cassio: She's a most exquisite lady.
Iago: And, I'll warrant her, full of game.
Cassio: Indeed, she's a most fresh and delicate creature.
Iago: What an eye she has! Methinks it sounds a parley to provocation.   20
Cassio: An inviting eye; and yet methinks right modest.
Iago: And when she speaks, is it not an alarum° to love?
Cassio: She is indeed perfection.
Iago: Well, happiness to their sheets! Come, lieutenant, I have a stoup°
    of wine, and here without are a brace of Cyprus gallants that would   25
    fain have a measure to the health of black Othello.
Cassio: Not tonight, good Iago. I have very poor and unhappy brains for
    drinking; I could well wish courtesy would invent some other cus-
    tom of entertainment.
Iago: O, they are our friends. But one cup! I'll drink for you.   30
Cassio: I have drunk but one tonight, and that was craftily qualified° too;
    and behold what innovation it makes here. I am unfortunate in the
    infirmity and dare not task my weakness with any more.
Iago: What, man! 'Tis a night of revels, the gallants desire it.

---

⁷ *offices:* kitchens and storerooms of food. II.iii.   ¹⁴ *cast:* dismissed.   ²² *alarum:* the call
to action, "general quarters."   ²⁴ *stoup:* two-quart tankard.   ³¹ *qualified:* diluted.

Cassio: Where are they?   35

Iago: Here, at the door. I pray you call them in.

Cassio: I'll do't, but it dislikes me.   *Exit.*

Iago: If I can fasten but one cup upon him
    With that which he hath drunk tonight already,
    He'll be as full of quarrel and offense   40
    As my young mistress' dog. Now, my sick fool Roderigo,
    Whom love hath turned almost the wrong side out,
    To Desdemona hath tonight caroused
    Potations pottle-deep°; and he's to watch.
    Three else° of Cyprus, noble swelling spirits,   45
    That hold their honors in a wary distance°,
    The very elements of this warlike isle,
    Have I tonight flustered with flowing cups,
    And they watch too. Now, 'mongst this flock of drunkards
    Am I to put our Cassio in some action   50
    That may offend the isle. But here they come.

Enter Cassio, Montano, and Gentlemen.

    If consequence do but approve my dream,
    My boat sails freely, both with wind and stream.

Cassio: 'Fore God, they have given me a rouse° already.

Montano: Good faith, a little one; not past a pint, as I am a soldier.   55

Iago: Some wine, ho!
    [*Sings*] And let me the canakin clink, clink;
        And let me the canakin clink.
          A soldier's a man;
          O man's life's but a span.
        Why then, let a soldier drink.   60
    Some wine, boys!

Cassio: 'Fore God, an excellent song!

Iago: I learned it in England, where indeed they are most potent in
    potting. Your Dane, your German, and your swag-bellied° Hollander   65
    — Drink, ho! — are nothing to your English.

Cassio: Is your Englishman so exquisite° in his drinking?

Iago: Why, he drinks you with facility your Dane dead drunk; he sweats
    not to overthrow your Almain; he gives your Hollander a vomit ere
    the next pottle can be filled.   70

Cassio: To the health of our general!

Montano: I am for it, lieutenant, and I'll do you justice.

Iago: O sweet England!
    [*Sings*] King Stephen was and a worthy peer;
        His breeches cost him but a crown;   75
        He held them sixpence all too dear,
        With that he called the tailor lown°.

---

⁴⁴ *pottle-deep:* to the bottom of the cup.   ⁴⁵ *else:* others.   ⁴⁶ *hold . . . distance:* are scrupulous
in maintaining their honor.   ⁵⁴ *rouse:* drink.   ⁶⁵ *swag-bellied:* pendulous-bellied.   ⁶⁷ *exquisite:* superb.   ⁷⁷ *lown:* lout.

He was a wight of high renown,
And thou art but of low degree:
'Tis pride that pulls the country down;   80
And take thine auld cloak about thee.

Some wine, ho!

Cassio: 'Fore God, this is a more exquisite song than the other.

Iago: Will you hear't again?

Cassio: No, for I hold him to be unworthy of his place that does those   85
    things. Well, God's above all; and there be souls must be saved, and
    there be souls must not be saved.

Iago: It's true, good lieutenant.

Cassio: For mine own part — no offense to the general, nor any man of
    quality — I hope to be saved.   90

Iago: And so do I too, lieutenant.

Cassio: Ay, but, by your leave, not before me. The lieutenant is to be saved
    before the ancient. Let's have no more of this; let's to our affairs. —
    God forgive us our sins! — Gentlemen, let's look to our business. Do
    not think, gentlemen, I am drunk. This is my ancient; this is my right   95
    hand, and this is my left. I am not drunk now. I can stand well
    enough, and I speak well enough.

Gentlemen: Excellent well!

Cassio: Why, very well then. You must not think then that I am drunk.
                                             Exit.

Montano: To th' platform, masters. Come, let's set the watch.   100

Iago: You see this fellow that is gone before.
He's a soldier fit to stand by Caesar
And give direction; and do but see his vice.
'Tis to his virtue a just equinox°,
The one as long as th' other. 'Tis pity of him.   105
I fear the trust Othello puts him in,
On some odd time of his infirmity,
Will shake this island.

Montano: But is he often thus?

Iago: 'Tis evermore his prologue to his sleep:
He'll watch the horologe a double set°   110
If drink rock not his cradle.

Montano: It were well
The general were put in mind of it.
Perhaps he sees it not, or his good nature
Prizes the virtue that appears in Cassio
And looks not on his evils. Is not this true?   115

    Enter Roderigo.

Iago [Aside]: How now, Roderigo?
I pray you after the lieutenant, go!   *[Exit Roderigo.]*

Montano: And 'tis great pity that the noble Moor
Should hazard such a place as his own second

---

104 *just equinox:* exact balance (of dark and light). 110 *watch . . . set:* stay awake twice
around the clock.

With one of an ingraft° infirmity.   120
It were an honest action to say so
To the Moor.

Iago: Not I, for this fair island!
I do love Cassio well and would do much
To cure him of this evil.   (Help! Help! *Within.*)
But hark! What noise?   125

Enter Cassio, pursuing Roderigo.

Cassio: Zounds, you rogue! You rascal!
Montano: What's the matter, lieutenant?
Cassio: A knave teach me my duty? I'll beat the knave into a twiggen°
   bottle.
Roderigo: Beat me?   130
Cassio: Dost thou prate, rogue?   [*Strikes him.*]
Montano: Nay, good lieutenant! I pray you, sir, hold your hand.

                                                        [*Stays him.*]

Cassio: Let me go, sir, or I'll knock you o'er the mazzard°.
Montano: Come, come, you're drunk!
Cassio: Drunk?   [*They fight.*] 135
Iago [*Aside to Roderigo*]: Away, I say! Go out and cry a mutiny!

                                                     [*Exit Roderigo.*]

Nay, good lieutenant. God's will, gentlemen!
Help, ho! Lieutenant. Sir. Montano.
Help, masters! Here's a goodly watch indeed!   [*A bell rung.*]
Who's that which rings the bell? Diablo, ho!   140
The town will rise. God's will, lieutenant,
You'll be ashamed forever.

Enter Othello and Attendants.

Othello: What is the matter here?
Montano: Zounds, I bleed still. I am hurt to the death.
   He dies.   [*He and Cassio fight again.*]
Othello: Hold for your lives!   145
Iago: Hold, ho! Lieutenant. Sir. Montano. Gentlemen!
   Have you forgot all place of sense and duty?
   Hold! The general speaks to you. Hold, for shame!
Othello: Why, how now, ho? From whence ariseth this?
   Are we turned Turks, and to ourselves do that   150
   Which heaven hath forbid the Ottomites°?
   For Christian shame put by this barbarous brawl!
   He that stirs next to carve for his own rage
   Holds his soul light°; he dies upon his motion.

---

¹²⁰ *ingraft:* ingrained.   ¹²⁸ *twiggen:* wicker-covered.   ¹³³ *mazzard:* head.   ¹⁵¹ *heaven . . .
Ottomites:* i.e., by sending the storm which dispersed the Turks.   ¹⁵⁴ *Holds his soul light:*
values his soul lightly.

Silence that dreadful bell! It frights the isle   155
From her propriety°. What is the matter, masters?
Honest Iago, that looks dead with grieving,
Speak. Who began this? On thy love, I charge thee.
Iago: I do not know. Friends all, but now, even now,
    In quarter° and in terms like bride and groom   160
    Devesting them for bed; and then, but now —
    As if some planet had unwitted men —
    Swords out, and tilting one at other's breasts
    In opposition bloody. I cannot speak
    Any beginning to this peevish odds°,   165
    And would in action glorious I had lost
    Those legs that brought me to a part of it!
Othello: How comes it, Michael, you are thus forgot?
Cassio: I pray you pardon me; I cannot speak.
Othello: Worthy Montano, you were wont to be civil;   170
    Thy gravity and stillness of your youth
    The world hath noted, and your name is great
    In mouths of wisest censure°. What's the matter
    That you unlace° your reputation thus
    And spend your rich opinion° for the name   175
    Of a night-brawler? Give me answer to it.
Montano: Worthy Othello, I am hurt to danger.
    Your officer, Iago, can inform you.
    While I spare speech, which something now offends° me,
    Of all that I do know; nor know I aught   180
    By me that's said or done amiss this night,
    Unless self-charity be sometimes a vice,
    And to defend ourselves it be a sin
    When violence assails us.
Othello: Now, by heaven,
    My blood begins my safer guides to rule,   185
    And passion, having my best judgment collied°,
    Assays to lead the way. If I once stir
    Or do but lift this arm, the best of you
    Shall sink in my rebuke. Give me to know
    How this foul rout began, who set it on;   190
    And he that is approved in this offense,
    Though he had twinned with me, both at a birth,
    Shall lose me. What? In a town of war
    Yet wild, the people's hearts brimful of fear,
    To manage° private and domestic quarrel?   195
    In night, and on the court and guard of safety?
    'Tis monstrous. Iago, who began't?
Montano: If partially affined, or leagued in office°,

---

¹⁵⁶ *propriety:* proper order. ¹⁶⁰ *In quarter:* on duty. ¹⁶⁵ *odds:* quarrel. ¹⁷³ *censure:* judgment. ¹⁷⁴ *unlace:* undo (the term refers specifically to the dressing of a wild boar killed in
the hunt). ¹⁷⁵ *opinion:* reputation. ¹⁷⁹ *offends:* harms, hurts. ¹⁸⁶ *collied:* darkened.
¹⁹⁵ *manage:* conduct. ¹⁹⁸ *If . . . office:* if you are partial because you are related ("affined")
or the brother officer (of Cassio).

Thou dost deliver more or less than truth,
Thou art no soldier.

Iago: Touch me not so near. 200
I had rather have this tongue cut from my mouth
Than it should do offense to Michael Cassio.
Yet I persuade myself to speak the truth
Shall nothing wrong him. This it is, general.
Montano and myself being in speech, 205
There comes a fellow crying out for help,
And Cassio following him with determined sword
To execute upon him. Sir, this gentleman
Steps in to Cassio and entreats his pause.
Myself the crying fellow did pursue, 210
Lest by his clamor — as it so fell out —
The town might fall in fright. He, swift of foot,
Outran my purpose; and I returned then rather
For that I heard the clink and fall of swords,
And Cassio high in oath; which till tonight 215
I ne'er might say before. When I came back —
For this was brief — I found them close together
At blow and thrust, even as again they were
When you yourself did part them.
More of this matter cannot I report; 220
But men are men; the best sometimes forget.
Though Cassio did some little wrong to him,
As men in rage strike those that wish them best,
Yet surely Cassio I believe received
From him that fled some strange indignity, 225
Which patience could not pass°.

Othello: I know, Iago,
Thy honesty and love doth mince° this matter,
Making it light to Cassio. Cassio, I love thee;
But never more be officer of mine.

Enter Desdemona, attended.

Look if my gentle love be not raised up. 230
I'll make thee an example.

Desdemona: What is the matter, dear?

Othello: All's well, sweeting; come away to bed.
[*To Montano*] Sir, for your hurts, myself will be your surgeon.
Lead him off.   [*Montano led off.*]
Iago, look with care about the town 235
And silence those whom this vile brawl distracted.
Come, Desdemona: 'tis the soldiers' life
To have their balmy slumbers waked with strife.

Exit [with all but Iago and Cassio].

---

226 *pass:* allow to pass.   227 *mince:* cut up (i.e., tell only part of).

Iago: What, are you hurt, lieutenant?

Cassio: Ay, past all surgery. 240

Iago: Marry, God forbid!

Cassio: Reputation, reputation, reputation! O, I have lost my reputation! I have lost the immortal part of myself, and what remains is bestial. My reputation, Iago, my reputation.

Iago: As I am an honest man, I had thought you had received some bodily 245 wound. There is more sense° in that than in reputation. Reputation is an idle and most false imposition°, oft got without merit and lost without deserving. You have lost no reputation at all unless you repute yourself such a loser. What, man, there are more ways to recover the general again. You are but now cast in his mood° — a punish- 250 ment more in policy° than in malice — even so as one would beat his offenseless dog to affright an imperious lion. Sue to him again, and he's yours.

Cassio: I will rather sue to be despised than to deceive so good a commander with so slight, so drunken, and so indiscreet an officer. 255 Drunk! And speak parrot°! And squabble! Swagger! Swear! and discourse fustian° with one's own shadow! O thou invisible spirit of wine, if thou hast no name to be known by, let us call thee devil!

Iago: What was he that you followed with your sword? What had he done to you? 260

Cassio: I know not.

Iago: Is't possible?

Cassio: I remember a mass of things, but nothing distinctly: a quarrel, but nothing wherefore. O God, that men should put an enemy in their mouths to steal away their brains! that we should with joy, pleasance, 265 revel, and applause transform ourselves into beasts!

Iago: Why, but you are now well enough. How came you thus recovered?

Cassio: It hath pleased the devil drunkenness to give place to the devil wrath. One unperfectness shows me another, to make me frankly despise myself. 270

Iago: Come, you are too severe a moraler. As the time, the place, and the condition of this country stands, I could heartily wish this had not befall'n; but since it is as it is, mend it for your own good.

Cassio: I will ask him for my place again: he shall tell me I am a drunkard. Had I as many mouths as Hydra, such an answer would stop them 275 all. To be now a sensible man, by and by a fool, and presently a beast! O strange! Every inordinate cup is unblest, and the ingredient is a devil.

Iago: Come, come, good wine is a good familiar creature if it be well used. Exclaim no more against it. And, good lieutenant, I think you think 280 I love you.

Cassio: I have well approved it, sir. I drunk?

---

²⁴⁶ *sense:* physical feeling. ²⁴⁷ *imposition:* external thing. ²⁵⁰ *cast in his mood:* dismissed because of his anger. ²⁵¹ *in policy:* politically necessary. ²⁵⁶ *speak parrot:* gabble without sense. ²⁵⁶⁻⁵⁷ *discourse fustian:* speak nonsense ("fustian" was a coarse cotton cloth used for stuffing).

Iago: You or any man living may be drunk at a time, man. I tell you what
you shall do. Our general's wife is now the general. I may say so in
this respect, for all he hath devoted and given up himself to the con- 285
templation, mark, and devotement of her parts° and graces. Confess
yourself freely to her; importune her help to put you in your place
again. She is of so free, so kind, so apt, so blessed a disposition she
holds it a vice in her goodness not to do more than she is requested.
This broken joint between you and her husband entreat her to splin- 290
ter°; and my fortunes against any lay° worth naming, this crack of
your love shall grow stronger than it was before.
Cassio: You advise me well.
Iago: I protest, in the sincerity of love and honest kindness.
Cassio: I think it freely; and betimes in the morning I will beseech the 295
virtuous Desdemona to undertake for me. I am desperate of my for-
tunes if they check° me.
Iago: You are in the right. Good night, lieutenant; I must to the watch.
Cassio: Good night, honest Iago.   *Exit Cassio.*
Iago: And what's he then that says I play the villain,   300
When this advice is free° I give, and honest,
Probal to° thinking, and indeed the course
To win the Moor again? For 'tis most easy
Th' inclining° Desdemona to subdue
In any honest suit; she's framed as fruitful°   305
As the free elements°. And then for her
To win the Moor — were't to renounce his baptism,
All seals and symbols of redeemèd sin —
His soul is so enfettered to her love
That she may make, unmake, do what she list,   310
Even as her appetite° shall play the god
With his weak function°. How am I then a villain
To counsel Cassio to this parallel course,
Directly to his good? Divinity of hell!
When devils will the blackest sins put on°,   315
They do suggest at first with heavenly shows°,
As I do now. For whiles this honest fool
Plies Desdemona to repair his fortune,
And she for him pleads strongly to the Moor,
I'll pour this pestilence into his ear: 320
That she repeals him° for her body's lust;
And by how much she strives to do him good,
She shall undo her credit with the Moor.
So will I turn her virtue into pitch,
And out of her own goodness make the net   325
That shall enmesh them all. How now, Roderigo?

---

²⁸⁶ *devotement of her parts:* devotion to her qualities. ²⁹⁰⁻⁹¹ *splinter:* splint. ²⁹¹ *lay:* wager.
²⁹⁷ *check:* repulse. ³⁰¹ *free:* generous and open. ³⁰² *Probal to:* provable by. ³⁰⁴ *inclining:*
inclined (to be helpful). ³⁰⁵ *framed as fruitful:* made as generous. ³⁰⁶ *elements:* i.e., basic
nature. ³¹¹ *appetite:* liking. ³¹² *function:* thought. ³¹⁵ *put on:* advance, further. ³¹⁶ *shows:*
appearances. ³²¹ *repeals him:* asks for (Cassio's reinstatement).

Enter Roderigo.

Roderigo: I do not follow here in the chase, not like a hound that hunts,
    but one that fills up the cry°. My money is almost spent; I have been
    tonight exceedingly well cudgeled; and I think the issue will be, I
    shall have so much experience for my pains; and so, with no money   330
    at all, and a little more wit, return again to Venice.

Iago: How poor are they that have not patience!
    What wound did ever heal but by degrees?
    Thou know'st we work by wit, and not by witchcraft;
    And wit depends on dilatory time.   335
    Does't not go well? Cassio hath beaten thee,
    And thou by that small hurt hath cashiered Cassio.
    Though other things grow fair against the sun,
    Yet fruits that blossom first will first be ripe.
    Content thyself awhile. By the mass, 'tis morning!   340
    Pleasure and action make the hours seem short.
    Retire thee, go where thou art billeted.
    Away, I say! Thou shalt know more hereafter.
    Nay, get thee gone!   *Exit Roderigo.*
                Two things are to be done: 345
    My wife must move° for Cassio to her mistress;
    I'll set her on;
    Myself awhile° to draw the Moor apart
    And bring him jump° when he may Cassio find
    Soliciting his wife. Ay, that's the way!   350
    Dull not device by coldness and delay.   *Exit.*

ACT III

Scene I   [*A street.*]

    Enter Cassio [and] Musicians.

Cassio: Masters, play here. I will content your pains°.
    Something that's brief; and bid "Good morrow, general." [*They play.*]

    [*Enter Clown°.*]

Clown: Why, masters, have your instruments been in Naples° that they
    speak i' th' nose thus?
Musician: How, sir, how?   5
Clown: Are these, I pray you, wind instruments?
Musician: Ay, marry, are they, sir.

---

³²⁸ *fills up the cry:* makes up one of the hunting pack, adding to the noise but not actually
tracking.   ³⁴⁶ *move:* petition.   ³⁴⁸ *awhile:* at the same time.   ³⁴⁹ *jump:* at the precise moment and place.   III.i.   ¹ *content your pains:* reward your efforts.   s.d. *Clown:* fool.   ³ *Naples:* this may refer either to the Neapolitan nasal tone, or to syphilis — rife in Naples —
which breaks down the nose.

Clown: O, thereby hangs a tale.

Musician: Whereby hangs a tale, sir?

Clown: Marry, sir, by many a wind instrument that I know. But, masters,   10
here's money for you; and the general so likes your music that he
desires you, for love's sake, to make no more noise with it.

Musician: Well, sir, we will not.

Clown: If you have any music that may not be heard, to't again. But, as
they say, to hear music the general does not greatly care.   15

Musician: We have none such, sir.

Clown: Then put up your pipes in your bag, for I'll away. Go, vanish into
air, away!   *Exit Musicians.*

Cassio: Dost thou hear me, mine honest friend?

Clown: No. I hear not your honest friend. I hear you.   20

Cassio: Prithee keep up thy quillets°. There's a poor piece of gold for
thee. If the gentlewoman that attends the general's wife be stirring,
tell her there's one Cassio entreats her a little favor of speech. Wilt
thou do this?

Clown: She is stirring, sir. If she will stir hither, I shall seem to notify unto   25
her°.   *Exit Clown.*

   Enter Iago.

Cassio: In happy time, Iago.

Iago: You have not been abed then?

Cassio: Why no, the day had broke before we parted.
I have made bold, Iago, to send in to your wife;
My suit to her is that she will to virtuous Desdemona   30
Procure me some access.

Iago: I'll send her to you presently,
And I'll devise a mean to draw the Moor
Out of the way, that your converse and business
May be more free.

Cassio: I humbly thank you for't.   *Exit [Iago].*   35
                          I never knew
A Florentine° more kind and honest.

   Enter Emilia.

Emilia: Good morrow, good lieutenant. I am sorry
For your displeasure°; but all will sure be well.
The general and his wife are talking of it,   40
And she speaks for you stoutly. The Moor replies
That he you hurt is of great fame in Cyprus
And great affinity°, and that in wholesome wisdom
He might not but refuse you. But he protests he loves you.
And needs no other suitor but his likings   45
To bring you in again.

---

²¹*quillets:* puns. ²⁵⁻²⁶*seem . . . her:* (the Clown is mocking Cassio's overly elegant manner
of speaking). ³⁷*Florentine:* i.e., Iago is as kind as if he were from Cassio's home town,
Florence. ³⁹*displeasure:* discomforting. ⁴³*affinity:* family.

Cassio: Yet I beseech you,
   If you think fit, or that it may be done,
   Give me advantage of some brief discourse
   With Desdemona alone.
Emilia: Pray you come in.
   I will bestow you where you shall have time   50
   To speak your bosom° freely.
Cassio: I am much bound to you.   *[Exeunt.]*

Scene II   *[The citadel.]*

   Enter Othello, Iago, and Gentlemen.

Othello: These letters give, Iago, to the pilot
   And by him do my duties to the Senate.
   That done, I will be walking on the works;
   Repair° there to me.
Iago: Well, my good lord, I'll do't.
Othello: This fortification, gentlemen, shall we see't?   5
Gentlemen: We'll wait upon your lordship.   *Exeunt.*

Scene III   *[The citadel.]*

   Enter Desdemona, Cassio, and Emilia.

Desdemona: Be thou assured, good Cassio, I will do
   All my abilities in thy behalf.
Emilia: Good madam, do. I warrant it grieves my husband
   As if the cause were his.
Desdemona: O, that's an honest fellow. Do not doubt, Cassio,   5
   But I will have my lord and you again
   As friendly as you were.
Cassio: Bounteous madam,
   Whatever shall become of Michael Cassio,
   He's never anything but your true servant.
Desdemona: I know't; I thank you. You do love my lord.   10
   You have known him long, and be you well assured
   He shall in strangeness stand no farther off
   Than in a politic distance.°
Cassio: Ay, but, lady,
   That policy may either last so long,
   Or feed upon such nice° and waterish diet,   15
   Or breed itself so out of circumstances°,
   That, I being absent, and my place supplied°,
   My general will forget my love and service.

---

[51] *bosom:* inmost thoughts.   III.ii.   [4] *Repair:* go.   III.iii.   [12-13] *He . . . distance:* i.e., he shall act no more distant to you than is necessary for political reasons.   [15] *nice:* trivial.   [16] *Or . . . circumstances:* i.e., or grow so on the basis of accidental happenings and political needs.   [17] *supplied:* filled.

Desdemona: Do not doubt° that; before Emilia here
      I give thee warrant of thy place. Assure thee,   20
      If I do vow a friendship, I'll perform it
      To the last article. My lord shall never rest;
      I'll watch him tame° and talk him out of patience;
      His bed shall seem a school, his board a shrift°;
      I'll intermingle everything he does   25
      With Cassio's suit. Therefore be merry, Cassio,
      For thy solicitor shall rather die
      Than give thy cause away.

      Enter Othello and Iago [at a distance].

Emilia: Madam, here comes my lord.
Cassio: Madam, I'll take my leave.   30
Desdemona: Why, stay, and hear me speak.
Cassio: Madam, not now. I am very ill at ease,
      Unfit for mine own purposes.
Desdemona: Well, do your discretion.   *Exit Cassio.*
Iago: Ha! I like not that.
Othello: What dost thou say?
Iago: Nothing, my lord; or if — I know not what.   35
Othello: Was not that Cassio parted from my wife?
Iago: Cassio, my lord? No, sure, I cannot think it
      That he would steal away so guilty-like,
      Seeing you coming.
Othello: I do believe 'twas he.   40
Desdemona [Coming to them]: How now, my lord?
      I have been talking with a suitor here,
      A man that languishes in your displeasure.
Othello: Who is't you mean?
Desdemona: Why, your lieutenant, Cassio. Good my lord,   45
      If I have any grace or power to move you,
      His present° reconciliation take.
      For if he be not one that truly loves you,
      That errs in ignorance, and not in cunning,
      I have no judgment in an honest face.   50
      I prithee call him back.
Othello: Went he hence now?
Desdemona: I' sooth so humbled
      That he hath left part of his grief with me
      To suffer with him. Good love, call him back.
Othello: Not now, sweet Desdemon; some other time.   55
Desdemona: But shall't be shortly?
Othello: The sooner, sweet, for you.
Desdemona: Shall't be tonight at supper?
Othello: No, not tonight.

---

19 *doubt:* imagine.   23 *watch him tame:* (animals were tamed by being kept awake).
24 *board a shrift:* table (seem) a confessional.   47 *present:* immediate.

Desdemona: Tomorrow dinner then?

Othello: I shall not dine at home;
    I meet the captains at the citadel.

Desdemona: Why then, tomorrow night, on Tuesday morn,   60
    On Tuesday noon, or night, on Wednesday morn.
    I prithee name the time, but let it not
    Exceed three days. In faith, he's penitent;
    And yet his trespass, in our common reason
    (Save that, they say, the wars must make example   65
    Out of her best), is not almost a fault
    T' incur a private check.° When shall he come?
    Tell me, Othello. I wonder in my soul
    What you would ask me that I should deny
    Or stand so mamm'ring° on. What? Michael Cassio,   70
    That came awooing with you, and so many a time,
    When I have spoke of you dispraisingly,
    Hath ta'en your part — to have so much to do
    To bring him in? By'r Lady, I could do much —

Othello: Prithee no more. Let him come when he will!   75
    I will deny thee nothing.

Desdemona: Why, this is not a boon;
    'Tis as I should entreat you wear your gloves,
    Or feed on nourishing dishes, or keep you warm,
    Or sue to you to do a peculiar profit°
    To your own person. Nay, when I have a suit   80
    Wherein I mean to touch your love indeed,
    It shall be full of poise° and difficult weight,
    And fearful to be granted.

Othello: I will deny thee nothing!
    Whereon I do beseech thee grant me this,
    To leave me but a little to myself.   85

Desdemona: Shall I deny you? No. Farewell, my lord.

Othello: Farewell, my Desdemona: I'll come to thee straight°.

Desdemona: Emilia, come. Be as your fancies teach you;
    Whate'er you be, I am obedient.   *Exit [with Emilia].*

Othello: Excellent wretch! Perdition catch my soul   90
    But I do love thee! And when I love thee not,
    Chaos is come again.

Iago: My noble lord —

Othello: What dost thou say, Iago?

Iago: Did Michael Cassio, when you wooed my lady,
    Know of your love?   95

Othello: He did, from first to last. Why dost thou ask?

Iago: But for a satisfaction of my thought,
    No further harm.

66-67 *is . . . check:* is almost not serious enough for a private rebuke (let alone a public disgrace). 70 *mamm'ring:* hesitating. 79 *peculiar profit:* particularly personal good. 82 *poise:* weight. 87 *straight:* at once.

Othello: Why of thy thought, Iago?

Iago: I did not think he had been acquainted with her.

Othello: O, yes, and went between us° very oft.   100

Iago: Indeed?

Othello: Indeed? Ay, indeed! Discern'st thou aught in that?
     Is he not honest?

Iago: Honest, my lord?

Othello: Honest? Ay, honest.

Iago: My lord, for aught I know.

Othello: What dost thou think?

Iago: Think, my lord?

Othello: Think, my lord?   105
     By heaven, thou echoest me,
     As if there were some monster in thy thought
     Too hideous to be shown. Thou dost mean something.
     I heard thee say even now, thou lik'st not that,
     When Cassio left my wife. What didst not like?   110
     And when I told thee he was of my counsel°
     Of my whole course of wooing, thou cried'st "Indeed?"
     And didst contract and purse thy brow together,
     As if thou then hadst shut up in thy brain
     Some horrible conceit°. If thou dost love me,   115
     Show me thy thought.

Iago: My lord, you know I love you.

Othello: I think thou dost;
     And, for I know thou'rt full of love and honesty
     And weigh'st thy words before thou giv'st them breath,
     Therefore these stops° of thine fright me the more;   120
     For such things in a false disloyal knave
     Are tricks of custom°; but in a man that's just
     They're close dilations°, working from the heart
     That passion cannot rule.

Iago: For Michael Cassio,
     I dare be sworn, I think that he is honest.   125

Othello: I think so too.

Iago: Men should be what they seem;
     Or those that be not, would they might seem none!

Othello: Certain, men should be what they seem.

Iago: Why then, I think Cassio's an honest man.

Othello: Nay, yet there's more in this?   130
     I prithee speak to me as to thy thinkings,
     As thou dost ruminate, and give thy worst of thoughts
     The worst of words.

Iago: Good my lord, pardon me:
     Though I am bound to every act of duty,

---

100 *between us:* i.e., as messenger.   111 *of my counsel:* in my confidence.   115 *conceit:* thought.   120 *stops:* interruptions.   122 *of custom:* customary.   123 *close dilations:* expressions of hidden thoughts.

I am not bound to that all slaves are free to.   135
Utter my thoughts? Why, say they are vile and false,
As where's that palace whereinto foul things
Sometimes intrude not? Who has that breast so pure
But some uncleanly apprehensions
Keep leets and law days°, and in sessions sit   140
With meditations lawful?
Othello: Thou dost conspire against thy friend, Iago,
If thou but think'st him wronged, and mak'st his ear
A stranger to thy thoughts.
Iago: I do beseech you —
Though I perchance am vicious in my guess   145
(As I confess it is my nature's plague
To spy into abuses, and of my jealousy
Shape faults that are not), that your wisdom
From one that so imperfectly conceits
Would take no notice, nor build yourself a trouble   150
Out of his scattering and unsure observance.
It were not for your quiet nor your good,
Nor for my manhood, honesty, and wisdom,
To let you know my thoughts.
Othello: What dost thou mean?
Iago: Good name in man and woman, dear my lord,   155
Is the immediate jewel of their souls.
Who steals my purse steals trash; 'tis something, nothing;
'Twas mine, 'tis his, and has been slave to thousands;
But he that filches from me my good name
Robs me of that which not enriches him   160
And makes me poor indeed.
Othello: By heaven, I'll know thy thoughts!
Iago: You cannot, if my heart were in your hand;
Nor shall not whilst 'tis in my custody.
Othello: Ha!
Iago: O, beware, my lord, of jealousy!   165
It is the green-eyed monster, which doth mock
The meat it feeds on. That cuckold lives in bliss
Who, certain of his fate, loves not his wronger;
But O, what damnèd minutes tells° he o'er
Who dotes, yet doubts — suspects, yet fondly° loves!   170
Othello: O misery.
Iago: Poor and content is rich, and rich enough;
But riches fineless° is as poor as winter
To him that ever fears he shall be poor.
Good God the souls of all my tribe defend   175
From jealousy!
Othello: Why? Why is this?

---

[140] *leets and law days:* meetings of local courts.   [169] *tells:* counts.   [170] *fondly:* foolishly.
[173] *fineless:* infinite.

Think'st thou I'd make a life of jealousy,
To follow still° the changes of the moon
With fresh suspicions? No! To be once in doubt
Is to be resolved. Exchange me for a goat   180
When I shall turn the business of my soul
To such exsufflicate and blown° surmises,
Matching thy inference. 'Tis not to make me jealous
To say my wife is fair, feeds well, loves company,
Is free of speech, sings, plays, and dances;   185
Where virtue is, these are more virtuous.
Nor from mine own weak merits will I draw
The smallest fear or doubt of her revolt,
For she had eyes, and chose me. No, Iago;
I'll see before I doubt; when I doubt, prove;   190
And on the proof there is no more but this:
Away at once with love or jealousy!
Iago: I am glad of this; for now I shall have reason
To show the love and duty that I bear you
With franker spirit. Therefore, as I am bound,   195
Receive it from me. I speak not yet of proof.
Look to your wife; observe her well with Cassio;
Wear your eyes thus: not jealous nor secure.
I would not have your free and noble nature
Out of self-bounty° be abused. Look to't.   200
I know our country disposition well:
In Venice they do let heaven see the pranks
They dare not show their husbands; their best conscience
Is not to leave't undone, but kept unknown.°
Othello: Dost thou say so?   205
Iago: She did deceive her father, marrying you;
And when she seemed to shake and fear your looks,
She loved them most.
Othello: And so she did.
Iago: Why, go to then!
She that so young could give out such a seeming
To seel° her father's eyes up close as oak° —   210
He thought 'twas witchcraft. But I am much to blame.
I humbly do beseech you of your pardon
For too much loving you.
Othello: I am bound to thee forever.
Iago: I see this hath a little dashed your spirits.
Othello: Not a jot, not a jot.
Iago: Trust me, I fear it has.   215
I hope you will consider what is spoke
Comes from my love. But I do see y' are moved.

---

[178] *To follow still:* to change always (as the phases of the moon). [182] *exsufflicate and blown:* inflated and flyblown. [200] *self-bounty:* innate kindness (which attributes his own motives to others). [203-4] *their . . . unknown:* i. e., their morality does not forbid adultery, but it does forbid being found out. [210] *seel:* hoodwink. [210] *oak:* (a close-grained wood).

I am to pray you not to strain° my speech
To grosser issues nor to larger reach°
Than to suspicion.   220
Othello: I will not.
Iago: Should you do so, my lord,
My speech should fall into such vile success
Which my thoughts aimed not. Cassio's my worthy friend —
My lord, I see y' are moved.
Othello: No, not much moved.
I do not think but Desdemona's honest.   225
Iago: Long live she so. And long live you to think so.
Othello: And yet, how nature erring from itself —
Iago: Ay, there's the point, as (to be bold with you)
Not to affect many proposèd matches
Of her own clime, complexion, and degree°,   230
Whereto we see in all things nature tends° —
Foh! one may smell in such a will most rank,
Foul disproportions, thoughts unnatural.
But, pardon me, I do not in position°
Distinctly° speak of her; though I may fear   235
Her will, recoiling to her better judgment,
May fall to match° you with her country forms°,
And happily° repent.
Othello: Farewell, farewell!
If more thou dost perceive, let me know more.
Set on thy wife to observe. Leave me, Iago.   240
Iago: My lord, I take my leave.   [*Going.*]
Othello: Why did I marry? This honest creature doubtless
Sees and knows more, much more, than he unfolds.
Iago [Returns]: My lord, I would I might entreat your honor
To scan this thing no farther. Leave it to time.   245
Although 'tis fit that Cassio have his place,
For sure he fills it up with great ability,
Yet, if you please to hold him off awhile,
You shall by that perceive him and his means.
Note if your lady strains his entertainment°   250
With any strong or vehement importunity;
Much will be seen in that. In the meantime
Let me be thought too busy in my fears
(As worthy cause I have to fear I am)
And hold her free, I do beseech your honor.   255
Othello: Fear not my government°.
Iago: I once more take my leave.   *Exit.*

---

²¹⁸ *strain:* enlarge the meaning.   ²¹⁹ *reach:* meaning.   ²³⁰ *degree:* social station.   ²³¹ *in . . .
tends:* i.e., all things in nature seek out their own kind.   ²³⁴ *position:* general argument.
²³⁵ *Distinctly:* specifically.   ²³⁷ *fall to match:* happen to compare.   ²³⁷ *country forms:* i.e., the
familiar appearance of her countrymen.   ²³⁸ *happily:* by chance.   ²⁵⁰ *strains his entertainment:* urge strongly that he be reinstated.   ²⁵⁶ *government:* self-control.

Othello: This fellow's of exceeding honesty,
And knows all qualities°, with a learnèd spirit
Of human dealings. If I do prove her haggard°,
Though that her jesses° were my dear heartstrings,   260
I'd whistle her off and let her down the wind°
To prey at fortune. Haply for° I am black
And have not those soft parts° of conversation
That chamberers° have, or for I am declined
Into the vale of years — yet that's not much —   265
She's gone. I am abused, and my relief
Must be to loathe her. O curse of marriage,
That we can call these delicate creatures ours,
And not their appetites! I had rather be a toad
And live upon the vapor of a dungeon   270
Than keep a corner in the thing I love
For others' uses. Yet 'tis the plague to great ones;
Prerogatived are they less than the base.
'Tis destiny unshunnable, like death.
Even then this forkèd° plague is fated to us   275
When we do quicken°. Look where she comes.

Enter Desdemona and Emilia.

If she be false, heaven mocked itself!
I'll not believe't.
Desdemona: How now, my dear Othello?
Your dinner, and the generous islanders
By you invited, do attend° your presence.   280
Othello: I am to blame.
Desdemona: Why do you speak so faintly?
Are you not well?
Othello: I have a pain upon my forehead, here°.
Desdemona: Why, that's with watching; 'twill away again,
Let me but bind it hard, within this hour   285
It will be well.
Othello: Your napkin° is too little;

[*He pushes the handkerchief away, and it falls.*]

Let it° alone. Come, I'll go in with you.
Desdemona: I am very sorry that you are not well.   *Exit* [*with Othello*].

---

²⁵⁸ *qualities:* natures, types of people. ²⁵⁹ *haggard:* a partly trained hawk which has gone wild again. ²⁶⁰ *jesses:* straps which held the hawk's legs to the trainer's wrist. ²⁶¹ *I'd . . . wind:* I would release her (like an untamable hawk) and let her fly free. ²⁶² *Haply for:* it may be because. ²⁶³ *soft parts:* gentle qualities and manners. ²⁶⁴ *chamberers:* courtiers — or, perhaps, accomplished seducers. ²⁷⁵ *forkèd:* horned (the sign of the cuckold was horns). ²⁷⁶ *do quicken:* are born. ²⁸⁰ *attend:* wait. ²⁸³ *here:* (he points to his imaginary horns). ²⁸⁶ *napkin:* elaborately worked handkerchief. ²⁸⁷ *it:* (it makes a considerable difference in the interpretation of later events whether this "it" refers to Othello's forehead or to the handkerchief; nothing in the text makes the reference clear).

Emilia: I am glad I have found this napkin;
　　This was her first remembrance from the Moor.　　　　　　　290
　　My wayward husband hath a hundred times
　　Wooed me to steal it; but she so loves the token
　　(For he conjured her she should ever keep it)
　　That she reserves it evermore about her
　　To kiss and talk to. I'll have the work ta'en out°　　　　　　295
　　And give't Iago. What he will do with it,
　　Heaven knows, not I; I nothing° but to please his fantasy°.

　　Enter Iago.

Iago: How now? What do you here alone?
Emilia: Do not you chide; I have a thing for you.
Iago: You have a thing for me? It is a common thing —　　　　300
Emilia: Ha?
Iago: To have a foolish wife.
Emilia: O, is that all? What will you give me now
　　For that same handkerchief?
Iago:　　　　　　　　　　What handkerchief?
Emilia: What handkerchief!　　　　　　　　　　　　　　　305
　　Why, that the Moor first gave to Desdemona,
　　That which so often you did bid me steal.
Iago: Hast stol'n it from her?
Emilia: No, but she let it drop by negligence,
　　And to th' advantage°, I, being here, took't up.　　　　　　310
　　Look, here 't is.
Iago:　　　　　　A good wench. Give it me.
Emilia: What will you do with't, that you have been so earnest
　　To have me filch it?
Iago:　　　　　　Why, what is that to you?　　　　*[Takes it.]*
Emilia: If it be not for some purpose of import°,
　　Give't me again. Poor lady, she'll run mad　　　　　　　315
　　When she shall lack° it.
Iago:　　　　　　　　Be not acknown on't°.
　　I have use for it. Go, leave me.　　　　　　*Exit Emilia.*
　　I will in Cassio's lodging lose this napkin
　　And let him find it. Trifles light as air
　　Are to the jealous confirmations strong　　　　　　　　320
　　As proofs of Holy Writ. This may do something.
　　The Moor already changes with my poison:
　　Dangerous conceits are in their natures poisons,
　　Which at the first are scarce found to distaste°,

---

²⁹⁵ *work ta'en out:* needlework copied.　²⁹⁷ *I nothing:* I wish nothing.　²⁹⁷ *fantasy:* fancy, whim.　³¹⁰ *to th' advantage:* being lucky.　³¹⁴ *import:* importance.　³¹⁶ *lack:* miss.　³¹⁶ *Be not acknown on't:* forget you ever saw it.　³²⁴ *are scarce found to distaste:* scarcely can be tasted.

But with a little°, act upon the blood,   325
Burn like the mines of sulfur. I did say so.

Enter Othello.

Look where he comes! Not poppy nor mandragora°,
Nor all the drowsy syrups of the world,
Shall ever medicine thee to that sweet sleep
Which thou owedst° yesterday.
Othello: Ha! ha! False to me?   330
Iago: Why, how now, general? No more of that.
Othello: Avaunt! be gone! Thou hast set me on the rack.
    I swear 'tis better to be much abused
    Than but to know't a little.
Iago: How now, my lord?
Othello: What sense had I of her stol'n hours of lust?   335
    I saw't not, thought it not, it harmed not me;
    I slept the next night well, fed well, was free and merry;
    I found not Cassio's kisses on her lips.
    He that is robbed, not wanting° what is stol'n,
    Let him not know't, and he's not robbed at all.   340
Iago: I am sorry to hear this.
Othello: I had been happy if the general camp,
    Pioners° and all, had tasted her sweet body,
    So I had nothing known. O now, forever
    Farewell the tranquil mind! Farewell content!   345
    Farewell the plumèd troops, and the big wars
    That make ambition virtue! O, farewell!
    Farewell the neighing steed and the shrill trump,
    The spirit-stirring drum, th' ear-piercing fife,
    The royal banner, and all quality,   350
    Pride, pomp, and circumstance° of glorious war!
    And O you mortal engines° whose rude throats
    Th' immortal Jove's dread clamors° counterfeit,
    Farewell! Othello's occupation's gone!
Iago: Is't possible, my lord?   355
Othello: Villain, be sure thou prove my love a whore!
    Be sure of it; give me the ocular proof;
    Or, by the worth of mine eternal soul,
    Thou hadst been better have been born a dog
    Than answer my waked wrath!
Iago: Is't come to this?   360
Othello: Make me to see't; or at the least so prove it
    That the probation° bear no hinge nor loop
    To hang a doubt on — or woe upon thy life!
Iago: My noble lord —

---

³²⁵ *with a little:* in a short time. ³²⁷ *poppy nor mandragora:* soporifics. ³³⁰ *owedst:* possessed. ³³⁹ *wanting:* missing. ³⁴³ *Pioners:* the basest manual laborers in the army, who dug trenches and mines. ³⁵¹ *circumstance:* pageantry. ³⁵² *mortal engines:* lethal weapons, i.e., cannon. ³⁵³ *clamors:* i.e., thunder. ³⁶² *probation:* proof.

Othello: If thou dost slander her and torture me,   365
    Never pray more; abandon all remorse;
    On horror's head horrors accumulate;
    Do deeds to make heaven weep, all earth amazed;
    For nothing canst thou to damnation add
    Greater than that.
Iago: O grace! O heaven forgive me!   370
    Are you a man? Have you a soul or sense?
    God b' wi' you! Take mine office. O wretched fool,
    That lov'st to make thine honesty a vice!
    O monstrous world! Take note, take note, O world,
    To be direct and honest is not safe.   375
    I thank you for this profit, and from hence
    I'll love no friend, sith° love breeds such offense.
Othello: Nay, stay. Thou shouldst be honest.
Iago: I should be wise; for honesty's a fool
    And loses that it works for.
Othello: By the world,   380
    I think my wife be honest, and think she is not;
    I think that thou art just, and think thou are not.
    I'll have some proof. My name, that was as fresh
    As Dian's° visage, is now begrimed and black
    As mine own face. If there be cords, or knives,   385
    Poison, or fire, or suffocating streams,
    I'll not endure it. Would I were satisfied!
Iago: I see you are eaten up with passion.
    I do repent me that I put it to you.
    You would be satisfied?
Othello: Would? Nay, and I will.   390
Iago: And may; but how? How satisfied, my lord?
    Would you, the supervisor°, grossly gape on?
    Behold her topped?
Othello: Death and damnation! O!
Iago: It were a tedious° difficulty, I think,
    To bring them to that prospect°. Damn them then,   395
    If ever mortal eyes do see them bolster°
    More than their own! What then? How then?
    What shall I say? Where's satisfaction?
    It is impossible you should see this,
    Were they as prime° as goats, as hot as monkeys,   400
    As salt° as wolves in pride°, and fools as gross
    As ignorance made drunk. But yet, I say,
    If imputation and strong circumstances
    Which lead directly to the door of truth
    Will give you satisfaction, you might hav't.   405

---

[377] *sith:* since.   [384] *Dian's:* Diana's (goddess of the moon and of chastity).   [392] *supervisor:* onlooker.   [394] *tedious:* hard to arrange.   [395] *prospect:* sight (where they can be seen). [396] *bolster:* go to bed with.   [400-01] *prime, salt:* lustful.   [401] *pride:* heat.

Othello: Give me a living reason she's disloyal.
Iago: I do not like the office°.
　　　But sith I am entered in this cause so far,
　　　Pricked° to't by foolish honesty and love,
　　　I will go on. I lay with Cassio lately, 　　　　　　　　　　410
　　　And being troubled with a raging tooth,
　　　I could not sleep.
　　　There are a kind of men so loose of soul
　　　That in their sleeps will mutter their affairs.
　　　One of this kind is Cassio. 　　　　　　　　　　　　　　415
　　　In sleep I heard him say, "Sweet Desdemona,
　　　Let us be wary, let us hide our loves!"
　　　And then, sir, would he gripe° and wring my hand,
　　　Cry "O sweet creature!" Then kiss me hard,
　　　As if he plucked up kisses by the roots 　　　　　　　　420
　　　That grew upon my lips; laid his leg o'er my thigh,
　　　And sigh, and kiss, and then cry, "Cursèd fate
　　　That gave thee to the Moor!"
Othello: O monstrous! monstrous!
Iago: 　　　　　　　　　　　　Nay, this was but his dream.
Othello: But this denoted a foregone conclusion°, 　　　　　425
　　　'Tis a shrewd doubt°, though it be but a dream.
Iago: And this may help to thicken other proofs
　　　That do demonstrate° thinly.
Othello: 　　　　　　　　　　I'll tear her all to pieces!
Iago: Nay, yet be wise. Yet we see nothing done;
　　　She may be honest yet. Tell me but this: 　　　　　　430
　　　Have you not sometimes seen a handkerchief
　　　Spotted with strawberries in your wife's hand?
Othello: I gave her such a one; 'twas my first gift.
Iago: I know not that; but such a handkerchief —
　　　I am sure it was your wife's — did I today 　　　　　435
　　　See Cassio wipe his beard with.
Othello: 　　　　　　　　　　If it be that ——
Iago: If it be that or any that was hers,
　　　It speaks against her with the other proofs.
Othello: O, that the slave had forty thousand lives!
　　　One is too poor, too weak for my revenge. 　　　　　440
　　　Now do I see 'tis true. Look here, Iago:
　　　All my fond love thus do I blow to heaven.
　　　'Tis gone.
　　　Arise, black vengeance, from the hollow hell!
　　　Yield up, O love, thy crown and hearted° throne 　　445
　　　To tyrannous hate! Swell, bosom, with thy fraught°,
　　　For 'tis of aspics'° tongues.
Iago: 　　　　　　　　　　Yet be content°.

---

⁴⁰⁷ *office:* duty. ⁴⁰⁹ *Pricked:* spurred. ⁴¹⁸ *gripe:* seize. ⁴²⁵ *foregone conclusion:* consummated fact. ⁴²⁶ *shrewd doubt:* penetrating guess. ⁴²⁸ *demonstrate:* show, appear. ⁴⁴⁵ *hearted:* seated in the heart. ⁴⁴⁶ *fraught:* burden. ⁴⁴⁷ *aspics':* asps'. ⁴⁴⁷ *content:* patient, quiet.

Othello: O, blood, blood, blood!

Iago: Patience, I say. Your mind may change.

Othello: Never, Iago. Like to the Pontic Sea°,   450
　　Whose icy current and compulsive course
　　Nev'r keeps retiring ebb, but keeps due on
　　To the Propontic and the Hellespont,
　　Even so my bloody thoughts, with violent pace,
　　Shall nev'r look back, nev'r ebb to humble love,   455
　　Till that a capable and wide° revenge
　　Swallow them up. [*He kneels.*] Now, by yond marble heaven,
　　In the due reverence of a sacred vow
　　I here engage my words.

Iago:　　　　　　　　　　Do not rise yet.   [*Iago kneels.*]
　　Witness, you ever-burning lights above,   460
　　You elements that clip° us round about,
　　Witness that here Iago doth give up
　　The execution° of his wit, hands, heart
　　To wronged Othello's service! Let him command,
　　And to obey shall be in me remorse°,   465
　　What bloody business ever°.   [*They rise.*]

Othello:　　　　　　　　　　I greet thy love,
　　Not with vain thanks but with acceptance bounteous°,
　　And will upon the instant put thee to 't°.
　　Within these three days let me hear thee say
　　That Cassio's not alive.   470

Iago: My friend is dead. 'Tis done at your request.
　　But let her live.

Othello:　　　　　　　　Damn her, lewd minx! O, damn her! Damn her!
　　Come, go with me apart. I will withdraw
　　To furnish me with some swift means of death
　　For the fair devil. Now art thou my lieutenant.   475

Iago: I am your own forever.   *Exeunt.*

Scene IV　[*A street.*]

　　Enter Desdemona, Emilia, and Clown.

Desdemona: Do you know, sirrah, where Lieutenant Cassio lies°?

Clown: I dare not say he lies anywhere.

Desdemona: Why, man?

Clown: He's a soldier, and for me to say a soldier lies, 'tis stabbing.

Desdemona: Go to. Where lodges he?   5

Clown: To tell you where he lodges is to tell you where I lie.

---

⁴⁵⁰ *Pontic Sea:* the Black Sea (famous for the strong and constant current with which it flows through the Bosporus into the Mediterranean, where the water level is lower). ⁴⁵⁶ *capable and wide:* sufficient and far-reaching. ⁴⁶¹ *clip:* enfold. ⁴⁶³ *execution:* workings, action. ⁴⁶⁵ *remorse:* pity. ⁴⁶⁶ *ever:* soever. ⁴⁶⁷ *bounteous:* absolute. ⁴⁶⁸ *to't:* i.e., to the work you have said you are prepared to do. III.iv. ¹ *lies:* lodges.

Desdemona: Can anything be made of this?

Clown: I know not where he lodges, and for me to devise a lodging, and say he lies here or he lies there, were to lie in mine own throat°.

Desdemona: Can you enquire him out, and be edified° by report?　　　10

Clown: I will catechize the world for him; that is, make questions, and by them answer.

Desdemona: Seek him, bid him come hither. Tell him I have moved° my lord on his behalf and hope all will be well.

Clown: To do this is within the compass° of man's wit, and therefore I　　15
will attempt the doing it.　　　　　　　　　　　　　　　*Exit Clown.*

Desdemona: Where should° I lose the handkerchief, Emilia?

Emilia: I know not, madam.

Desdemona: Believe me, I had rather have lost my purse
　　Full of crusadoes°. And but my noble Moor　　　　　20
　　Is true of mind, and made of no such baseness
　　As jealous creatures are, it were enough
　　To put him to ill thinking.

Emilia:　　　　　　　　　Is he not jealous?

Desdemona: Who? He? I think the sun where he was born
　Drew all such humors° from him.

Emilia:　　　　　　　　　Look where he comes.　　25

　　Enter Othello.

Desdemona: I will not leave him now till Cassio
　　Be called to him. How is't with you, my lord?

Othello: Well, my good lady. [*Aside*] O, hardness to
　　dissemble°! —
　　How do you, Desdemona?

Desdemona:　　　　　　　　Well, my good lord.

Othello: Give me your hand. This hand is moist°, my lady.　　30

Desdemona: It hath felt no age nor known no sorrow.

Othello: This argues° fruitfulness and liberal° heart.
　　Hot, hot, and moist. This hand of yours requires
　　A sequester° from liberty; fasting and prayer;
　　Much castigation; exercise devout;　　　　　35
　　For here's a young and sweating devil here
　　That commonly rebels. 'Tis a good hand,
　　A frank one.

Desdemona:　　　You may, indeed, say so;
　　For 'twas that hand that gave away my heart.

---

⁹ *lie in mine own throat:* (to lie in the throat is to lie absolutely and completely).　　¹⁰ *edified:* enlightened (Desdemona mocks the Clown's overly elaborate diction).　¹³ *moved:* pleaded with.　¹⁵ *compass:* reach.　¹⁷ *should:* might.　²⁰ *crusadoes:* Portuguese gold coins.　²⁵ *humors:* characteristics.　²⁸ *hardness to dissemble:* (Othello may refer here either to the difficulty he has in maintaining his appearance of composure, or to what he believes to be Desdemona's hardened hypocrisy).　³⁰ *moist:* (a moist, hot hand was taken as a sign of a lustful nature).　³² *argues:* suggests.　³² *liberal:* free, open (but also with a suggestion of "licentious"; from here on in this scene Othello's words bear a double meaning, seeming to be normal but accusing Desdemona of being unfaithful).　³⁴ *sequester:* separation.

Othello: A liberal hand! The hearts of old gave hands, 40
    But our new heraldry° is hands, not hearts.
Desdemona: I cannot speak of this. Come now, your promise!
Othello: What promise, chuck?
Desdemona: I have sent to bid Cassio come speak with you.
Othello: I have a salt and sorry rheum° offends me. 45
    Lend me thy handkerchief.
Desdemona: Here, my lord.
Othello: That which I gave you.
Desdemona: I have it not about me.
Othello: Not?
Desdemona: No, indeed, my lord.
Othello: That's a fault.
    That handkerchief 50
    Did an Egyptian to my mother give.
    She was a charmer°, and could almost read
    The thoughts of people. She told her, while she kept it
    'Twould make her amiable° and subdue my father
    Entirely to her love; but if she lost it 55
    Or made a gift of it, my father's eye
    Should hold her loathèd, and his spirits should hunt
    After new fancies. She, dying, gave it me,
    And bid me, when my fate would have me wived,
    To give it her. I did so; and take heed on't; 60
    Make it a darling like your precious eye.
    To lose't or give't away were such perdition
    As nothing else could match.
Desdemona: Is't possible?
Othello: 'Tis true. There's magic in the web° of it.
    A sibyl that had numbered in the world 65
    The sun to course two hundred compasses,
    In her prophetic fury° sewed the work;
    The worms were hallowed that did breed the silk,
    And it was dyed in mummy° which the skillful
    Conserved of maidens' hearts.
Desdemona: Indeed? Is't true? 70
Othello: Most veritable. Therefore look to't well.
Desdemona: Then would to God that I had never seen't!
Othello: Ha! Wherefore?
Desdemona: Why do you speak so startingly and rash?
Othello: Is't lost? Is't gone? Speak, is it out o' th' way? 75
Desdemona: Heaven bless us!
Othello: Say you?
Desdemona: It is not lost. But what an if it were?
Othello: How?
Desdemona: I say it is not lost. 80

---

⁴¹ *heraldry:* heraldic symbolism.   ⁴⁵ *a salt and sorry rheum:* a heavy, running head cold.
⁵² *charmer:* magician.   ⁵⁴ *amiable:* desirable.   ⁶⁴ *web:* weaving.   ⁶⁷ *prophetic fury:* seized
by the spirit and able to prophesy.   ⁶⁹ *mummy:* liquid drained from embalmed bodies.

Othello: Fetch't, let me see't!

Desdemona: Why, so I can; but I will not now.
　　This is a trick to put me from my suit:
　　Pray you let Cassio be received again.

Othello: Fetch me the handkerchief! My mind misgives.　　　　85

Desdemona: Come, come!
　　You'll never meet a more sufficient° man —

Othello: The handkerchief!

Desdemona: 　　　　　　　A man that all his time
　　Hath founded his good fortunes on your love,
　　Shared dangers with you —　　　　　　　　　　　　90

Othello: The handkerchief!

Desdemona: I'faith, you are to blame.

Othello: Away!　　　　　　　　　　　　　　*Exit Othello.*

Emilia: Is not this man jealous?

Desdemona: I nev'r saw this before.　　　　　　　　　　95
　　Sure there's some wonder in this handkerchief;
　　I am most unhappy in the loss of it.

Emilia: 'Tis not a year or two shows us a man.
　　They are all but stomachs, and we all but food;
　　They eat us hungerly, and when they are full,　　　　100
　　They belch us.

　　Enter Iago and Cassio.

　　　　　　　Look you, Cassio and my husband.

Iago: There is no other way; 'tis she must do't.
　　And lo the happiness! Go and importune her.

Desdemona: How now, good Cassio? What's the news with you?

Cassio: Madam, my former suit. I do beseech you　　　　105
　　That by your virtuous means I may again
　　Exist, and be a member of his love
　　Whom I with all the office° of my heart
　　Entirely honor. I would not be delayed.
　　If my offense be of such mortal kind　　　　　　110
　　That nor my service past, nor present sorrows,
　　Nor purposed merit in futurity,
　　Can ransom me into his love again,
　　But to know so must be my benefit°.
　　So shall I clothe me in a forced content,　　　　　115
　　And shut myself up in some other course
　　To fortune's alms.

Desdemona: 　　　　　　Alas, thrice-gentle Cassio,
　　My advocation° is not now in tune.
　　My lord is not my lord; nor should I know him
　　Were he in favor° as in humor altered.　　　　　120
　　So help me every spirit sanctified

---

⁸⁷ *sufficient:* complete, with all proper qualities.　　¹⁰⁸ *office:* duty.　　¹¹⁴ *benefit:* good.　　¹¹⁸ *advocation:* advocacy.　　¹²⁰ *favor:* countenance.

As I have spoken for you all my best
And stood within the blank° of his displeasure
For my free speech. You must awhile be patient.
What I can do I will; and more I will   125
Than for myself I dare. Let that suffice you.
Iago: Is my lord angry?
Emilia: He went hence but now,
And certainly in strange unquietness.
Iago: Can he be angry? I have seen the cannon
When it hath blown his ranks into the air   130
And, like the devil, from his very arm
Puffed his own brother. And is he angry?
Something of moment° then. I will go meet him.
There's matter in't indeed if he be angry.
Desdemona: I prithee do so.   *Exit [Iago.]*
                          Something sure of state°,   135
Either from Venice or some unhatched practice°
Made demonstrable here in Cyprus to him,
Hath puddled° his clear spirit; and in such cases
Men's natures wrangle with inferior things,
Though great ones are their object. 'Tis even so.   140
For let our finger ache, and it endues°
Our other, healthful members even to a sense
Of pain. Nay, we must think men are not gods,
Nor of them look for such observancy
As fits the bridal. Beshrew me much, Emilia,   145
I was, unhandsome warrior as I am,
Arraigning his unkindness with my soul;
But now I find I had suborned the witness,
And he's indicted falsely.
Emilia: Pray heaven it be
State matters, as you think, and no conception   150
Nor no jealous toy° concerning you.
Desdemona: Alas the day! I never gave him cause.
Emilia: But jealous souls will not be answered so;
They are not ever jealous for the cause,
But jealous for they're jealous. It is a monster   155
Begot upon itself, born on itself.
Desdemona: Heaven keep the monster from Othello's mind!
Emilia: Lady, amen.
Desdemona: I will go seek him. Cassio, walk here about.
If I do find him fit°, I'll move your suit   160
And seek to effect it to my uttermost.
Cassio: I humbly thank your ladyship.   *Exit [Desdemona with Emilia].*

   Enter Bianca.

---

123 *blank:* bull's-eye of a target.   133 *moment:* importance.   135 *of state:* state affairs.   136 *un-hatched practice:* undisclosed plot.   138 *puddled:* muddied.   141 *endues:* leads.   151 *toy:* trifle.
160 *fit:* receptive.

Bianca: Save you, friend Cassio!

Cassio: What make you from home?
How is't with you, my most fair Bianca?
I' faith, sweet love, I was coming to your house. 165

Bianca: And I was going to your lodging, Cassio.
What, keep a week away? Seven days and nights?
Eightscore eight hours? And lovers' absent hours
More tedious than the dial eightscore times?
O weary reck'ning°.

Cassio: Pardon me, Bianca. 170
I have this while with leaden thoughts been pressed,
But I shall in a more continuate° time
Strike off this score° of absence. Sweet Bianca,

[Gives her Desdemona's handkerchief.]

Take me this work out.

Bianca: O Cassio, whence came this?
This is some token from a newer friend. 175
To the felt absence now I feel a cause.
Is't come to this? Well, well.

Cassio: Go to, woman!
Throw your vile guesses in the devil's teeth,
From whence you have them. You are jealous now
That this is from some mistress, some remembrance. 180
No, by my faith, Bianca.

Bianca: Why, whose is it?

Cassio: I know not neither; I found it in my chamber.
I like the work well; ere it be demanded°,
As like enough it will, I would have it copied.
Take it and do't, and leave me for this time. 185

Bianca: Leave you? Wherefore?

Cassio: I do attend here on the general
And think it no addition, nor my wish,
To have him see me womaned.

Bianca: Why, I pray you?

Cassio: Not that I love you not.

Bianca: But that you do not love me! 190
I pray you bring° me on the way a little,
And say if I shall see you soon at night.

Cassio: 'Tis but a little way that I can bring you,
For I attend here; but I'll see you soon.

Bianca: 'Tis very good. I must be circumstanced°.   *Exeunt omnes.* 195

---

¹⁷⁰ *reck'ning:* addition.   ¹⁷² *continuate:* uninterrupted.   ¹⁷³ *Strike off this score:* i.e., pay this bill (the *score* being the account of drinks kept in a tavern).   ¹⁸³ *demanded:* asked for (by the person who lost it).   ¹⁹¹ *bring:* accompany.   ¹⁹⁵ *be circumstanced:* accept things as they are.

ACT IV

Scene I   [*A street.*]

    Enter Othello and Iago.

Iago: Will you think so?
Othello: Think so, Iago?
Iago: What,
    To kiss in private?
Othello: An unauthorized° kiss?
Iago: Or to be naked with her friend in bed
    An hour or more, not meaning any harm?
Othello: Naked in bed, Iago, and not mean harm?   5
    It is hypocrisy against the devil.
    They that mean virtuously, and yet do so,
    The devil their virtue tempts, and they tempt heaven.
Iago: If they do nothing, 'tis a venial slip.
    But if I give my wife a handkerchief —   10
Othello: What then?
Iago: Why, then 'tis hers, my lord; and being hers,
    She may, I think, bestow't on any man.
Othello: She is protectress of her honor too.
    May she give that?   15
Iago: Her honor is an essence that's not seen;
    They have it very oft that have it not.
    But for the handkerchief —
Othello: By heaven, I would most gladly have forgot it!
    Thou said'st — O, it comes o'er my memory   20
    As doth the raven° o'er the infected house,
    Boding to all — he had my handkerchief.
Iago: Ay, what of that?
Othello: That's not so good now.
Iago: What if I had said I had seen him do you wrong?
    Or heard him say — as knaves be such abroad°   25
    Who having, by their own importunate suit,
    Or voluntary dotage° of some mistress,
    Convincèd or supplied° them, cannot choose
    But they must blab —
Othello: Hath he said anything?
Iago: He hath, my lord; but be you well assured,   30
    No more than he'll unswear.
Othello: What hath he said?
Iago: Why, that he did — I know not what he did.
Othello: What? what?

IV.i.   ² *unauthorized:* illicit.   ²¹ *raven:* (a harbinger of death).   ²⁵ *abroad:* i.e., in the world.
²⁷ *voluntary dotage:* weakness of the will.   ²⁸ *Convincèd or supplied:* persuaded or gratified
(the mistress).

Iago: Lie —

Othello: With her?

Iago: With her, on her; what you will.   35

Othello: Lie with her? Lie on her? — We say lie on her when they belie
    her. — Lie with her! Zounds, that's fulsome°. — Handkerchief —
    confessions — handkerchief! — To confess, and be hanged for his
    labor — first to be hanged, and then to confess! I tremble at it. Na-
    ture would not invest herself in such shadowing passion without   40
    some instruction°. It is not words that shakes me thus. — Pish!
    Noses, ears, and lips? Is't possible? — Confess? — Handkerchief? —
    O devil!   *Falls in a trance.*

Iago: Work on.

    My med'cine works! Thus credulous fools are caught,   45
    And many worthy and chaste dames even thus,
    All guiltless, meet reproach°. What, ho! My lord!
    My lord, I say! Othello!

    Enter Cassio.

                    How now, Cassio?

Cassio: What's the matter?

Iago: My lord is fall'n into an epilepsy.   50
    This is his second fit; he had one yesterday.

Cassio: Rub him about the temples.

Iago: The lethargy° must have his quiet course.
    If not, he foams at mouth, and by and by
    Breaks out to savage madness. Look, he stirs.   55
    Do you withdraw yourself a little while.
    He will recover straight. When he is gone,
    I would on great occasion° speak with you.   *[Exit Cassio.]*
    How is it, general? Have you not hurt your head?

Othello: Dost thou mock° me?

Iago: I mock you not, by heaven.   60
    Would you would bear your fortune like a man.

Othello: A hornèd man's a monster and a beast.

Iago: There's many a beast then in a populous city,
    And many a civil° monster.

Othello: Did he confess it?

Iago: Good, sir, be a man.   65
    Think every bearded fellow that's but yoked
    May draw° with you. There's millions now alive
    That nightly lie in those unproper° beds

---

[37] *fulsome:* foul, repulsive.   [39-41] *Nature . . . instruction:* i.e., my mind would not become so
darkened (with anger) unless there were something in this (accusation); (it should be
remembered that Othello believes in the workings of magic and supernatural forces).
[47] *reproach:* shame.   [53] *lethargy:* coma.   [58] *great occasion:* very important matter.   [60] *mock:*
(Othello takes Iago's comment as a reference to his horns — which it is).   [64] *civil:* city-
dwelling.   [67] *draw:* i.e., like the horned ox.   [68] *unproper:* i.e., not exclusively the
husband's.

Which they dare swear peculiar.° Your case is better.
O, 'tis the spite of hell, the fiend's arch-mock,   70
To lip a wanton in a secure couch,
And to suppose her chaste. No, let me know;
And knowing what I am, I know what she shall be.
Othello: O, thou art wise! 'Tis certain.
Iago: Stand you awhile apart;
Confine yourself but in a patient list.°   75
Whilst you were here, o'erwhelmèd with your grief —
A passion most unsuiting such a man —
Cassio came hither. I shifted him away°
And laid good 'scuses upon your ecstasy°,
Bade him anon return, and here speak with me;   80
The which he promised. Do but encave° yourself
And mark the fleers°, the gibes, and notable° scorns
That dwell in every region of his face.
For I will make him tell the tale anew:
Where, how, how oft, how long ago, and when   85
He hath, and is again to cope your wife.
I say, but mark his gesture. Marry patience,
Or I shall say you're all in all in spleen°,
And nothing of a man.
Othello: Dost thou hear, Iago?
I will be found most cunning in my patience;   90
But — dost thou hear? — most bloody.
Iago: That's not amiss;
But yet keep time in all. Will you withdraw?

[*Othello moves to one side, where his remarks are not audible to Cassio and Iago.*]

Now will I question Cassio of Bianca,
A huswife° that by selling her desires
Buys herself bread and cloth. It is a creature   95
That dotes on Cassio, as 'tis the strumpet's plague
To beguile many and be beguiled by one.
He, when he hears of her, cannot restrain
From the excess of laughter. Here he comes.

Enter Cassio.

As he shall smile, Othello shall go mad:
And his unbookish° jealousy must conster°   100
Poor Cassio's smiles, gestures, and light behaviors

---

⁶⁹ *peculiar:* their own alone.   ⁷⁵ *a patient list:* the bounds of patience.   ⁷⁸ *shifted him away:* got rid of him by a stratagem.   ⁷⁹ *ecstasy:* trance (the literal meaning, "outside oneself," bears on the meaning of the change Othello is undergoing).   ⁸¹ *encave:* hide.   ⁸² *fleers:* mocking looks or speeches.   ⁸² *notable:* obvious.   ⁸⁸ *spleen:* passion, particularly anger.   ⁹⁴ *huswife:* housewife (but with the special meaning here of "prostitute").   ¹⁰¹ *unbookish:* ignorant.   ¹⁰¹ *conster:* construe.

Quite in the wrong. How do you, lieutenant?

Cassio: The worser that you give me the addition°
Whose want even kills me.

Iago: Ply Desdemona well, and you are sure on't.
Now, if this suit lay in Bianca's power,
How quickly should you speed!

Cassio: Alas, poor caitiff!°

Othello: Look how he laughs already!

Iago: I never knew woman love man so.

Cassio: Alas, poor rogue! I think, i' faith, she loves me.

Othello: Now he denies it faintly, and laughs it out.

Iago: Do you hear, Cassio?

Othello: Now he importunes him
To tell it o'er. Go to! Well said, well said!

Iago: She gives it out that you shall marry her.
Do you intend it?

Cassio: Ha, ha, ha!

Othello: Do ye triumph, Roman? Do you triumph?

Cassio: I marry? What, a customer°? Prithee bear some charity to my wit;
do not think it so unwholesome. Ha, ha, ha!

Othello: So, so, so, so. They laugh that win.

Iago: Why, the cry goes that you marry her.

Cassio: Prithee, say true.

Iago: I am a very villain else.

Othello: Have you scored° me? Well.

Cassio: This is the monkey's own giving out. She is persuaded I will
marry her out of her own love and flattery, not out of my promise.

Othello: Iago beckons me; now he begins the story.

[*Othello moves close enough to hear.*]

Cassio: She was here even now; she haunts me in every place. I was the
other day talking on the sea bank with certain Venetians, and thither
comes the bauble°, and falls me thus about my neck ——

Othello: Crying "O dear Cassio!" as it were. His gesture imports it.

Cassio: So hangs, and lolls, and weeps upon me; so shakes and pulls me!
Ha, ha, ha!

Othello: Now he tells how she plucked him to my chamber. O, I see that
nose of yours, but not that dog I shall throw it to.

Cassio: Well, I must leave her company.

Iago: Before me!° Look where she comes.

Enter Bianca.

Cassio: 'Tis such another fitchew!° Marry a perfumed one? What do you
mean by this haunting of me?

Bianca: Let the devil and his dam haunt you! What did you mean by that

---

¹⁰⁴ *addition:* title.   ¹⁰⁸ *caitiff:* wretch.   ¹¹⁹ *customer:* one who sells, a merchant (here, a prostitute).   ¹²⁵ *scored:* marked, defaced.   ¹³¹ *bauble:* plaything.   ¹³⁸ *Before me!:* (an exclamation
of surprise).   ¹³⁹ *fitchew:* polecat, i.e., strong-smelling creature.

same handkerchief you gave me even now? I was a fine fool to take it. I must take out the work? A likely piece of work that you should find it in your chamber and know not who left it there! This is some minx's token, and I must take out the work? There! [*She throws down the handkerchief.*] Give it your hobbyhorse°. Wheresoever you had it, I'll take out no work on't. 145

Cassio: How now, my sweet Bianca? How now? how now?

Othello: By heaven, that should be my handkerchief!

Bianca: If you'll come to supper tonight, you may; if you will not, come when you are next prepared for°. *Exit.* 150

Iago: After her, after her!

Cassio: Faith, I must; she'll rail in the streets else.

Iago: Will you sup there?

Cassio: Yes, I intend so. 155

Iago: Well, I may chance to see you, for I would very fain speak with you.

Cassio: Prithee come. Will you?

Iago: Go to, say no more. [*Exit Cassio.*]

Othello [Comes forward]: How shall I murder him, Iago?

Iago: Did you perceive how he laughed at his vice? 160

Othello: O Iago!

Iago: And did you see the handkerchief?

Othello: Was that mine?

Iago: Yours, by this hand! And to see how he prizes the foolish woman your wife! She gave it him, and he hath giv'n it his whore. 165

Othello: I would have him nine years a-killing! — A fine woman, a fair woman, a sweet woman?

Iago: Nay, you must forget that.

Othello: Ay, let her rot, and perish, and be damned tonight; for she shall not live. No, my heart is turned to stone; I strike it, and it hurts my 170 hand. O, the world hath not a sweeter creature! She might lie by an emperor's side and command him tasks.

Iago: Nay, that's not your way°.

Othello: Hang her! I do but say what she is. So delicate with her needle. An admirable musician. O, she will sing the savageness out of a 175 bear! Of so high and plenteous wit and invention° ——

Iago: She's the worse for all this.

Othello: O, a thousand, a thousand times. And then, of so gentle a condition°?

Iago: Ay, too gentle. 180

Othello: Nay, that's certain. But yet the pity of it, Iago. O Iago, the pity of it, Iago.

Iago: If you are so fond over her iniquity, give her patent to offend; for if it touch° not you, it comes near nobody.

Othello: I will chop her into messes°! Cuckold me! 185

Iago: O, 'tis foul in her.

---

¹⁴⁶ *hobbyhorse:* prostitute.   ¹⁵¹ *next prepared for:* next expected — i.e., never.   ¹⁷³ *way:* proper course.   ¹⁷⁶ *invention:* imagination.   ¹⁷⁸⁻⁷⁹ *gentle a condition:* (1) well born (2) of a gentle nature.   ¹⁸⁴ *touch:* affects.   ¹⁸⁵ *messes:* bits.

Othello: With mine officer!

Iago: That's fouler.

Othello: Get me some poison, Iago, this night. I'll not expostulate with her, lest her body and beauty unprovide my mind° again. This night, Iago!　　190

Iago: Do it not with poison. Strangle her in her bed, even the bed she hath contaminated.

Othello: Good, good! The justice of it pleases. Very good!

Iago: And for Cassio, let me be his undertaker°. You shall hear more by midnight.　　195

Othello: Excellent good!　　　　　　　　　　　　　　　*[A trumpet.]*

　　　　　　　　　　What trumpet is that same?

Iago: I warrant something from Venice.

　　　Enter Lodovico, Desdemona, and Attendants.

　　　　　　　　　　'Tis Lodovico.
This comes from the Duke. See, your wife's with him.

Lodovico: God save you, worthy general.

Othello:　　　　　　　　　　With° all my heart, sir.　　200

Lodovico: The Duke and the senators of Venice greet you.

　　　　　　　　　　　　　　[Gives him a letter.]

Othello: I kiss the instrument of their pleasures.

　　　　　　　　　　　　[Opens the letter and reads.]

Desdemona: And what's the news, good cousin Lodovico?

Iago: I am very glad to see you, signior.
　　　Welcome to Cyprus.　　　　　　　　　　　　　205

Lodovico: I thank you. How does Lieutenant Cassio?

Iago:　　　　　　　　　　　　　Lives, sir.

Desdemona: Cousin, there's fall'n between him and my lord
　　　An unkind° breach; but you shall make all well.

Othello: Are you sure of that?

Desdemona: My lord?　　　　　　　　　　　　　　　210

Othello [*Reads*]: "This fail you not to do, as you will — "

Lodovico: He did not call; he's busy in the paper.
　　　Is there division 'twixt my lord and Cassio?

Desdemona: A most unhappy one. I would do much
　　　T' atone° them, for the love I bear to Cassio.　　215

Othello: Fire and brimstone!

Desdemona:　　　　　　My lord?

Othello:　　　　　　　　　　Are you wise?

Desdemona: What, is he angry?

Lodovico:　　　　　　　May be th' letter moved him;
　　　For, as I think, they do command him home,
　　　Deputing Cassio in his government°.

---

¹⁹⁰ *unprovide my mind:* undo my resolution.　¹⁹⁵ *undertaker:* (not "burier" but "one who undertakes to do something").　²⁰⁰ *With:* i.e., I greet you with.　²⁰⁸ *unkind:* unnatural.　²¹⁵ *atone:* reconcile.　²¹⁹ *government:* office.

Desdemona: Trust me, I am glad on't.
Othello: Indeed?
Desdemona: My lord? 220
Othello: I am glad to see you mad.
Desdemona: Why, sweet Othello—
Othello: Devil! [*Strikes her.*]
Desdemona: I have not deserved this.
Lodovico: My lord, this would not be believed in Venice,
Though I should swear I saw't. 'Tis very much. 225
Make her amends; she weeps.
Othello: O devil, devil!
If that the earth could teem° with woman's tears,
Each drop she falls° would prove a crocodile°.
Out of my sight!
Desdemona: I will not stay to offend you. [*Going.*]
Lodovico: Truly, an obedient lady. 230
I do beseech your lordship call her back.
Othello: Mistress!
Desdemona: My lord?
Othello: What would you with her, sir?
Lodovico: Who? I, my lord?
Othello: Ay! You did wish that I would make her turn.
Sir, she can turn, and turn, and yet go on 235
And turn again; and she can weep, sir, weep;
And she's obedient; as you say, obedient.
Very obedient. Proceed you in your tears.
Concerning this, sir — O well-painted passion!
I am commanded home. — Get you away; 240
I'll send for you anon. — Sir, I obey the mandate
And will return to Venice. — Hence, avaunt! [*Exit Desdemona.*]
Cassio shall have my place. And, sir, tonight
I do entreat that we may sup together.
You are welcome, sir, to Cyprus. — Goats and monkeys! *Exit.* 245
Lodovico: Is this the noble Moor whom our full Senate
Call all in all sufficient? Is this the nature
Whom passion could not shake? whose solid virtue
The shot of accident nor dart of chance
Could neither graze nor pierce?
Iago: He is much changed. 250
Lodovico: Are his wits safe? Is he not light of brain?
Iago: He's that he is; I may not breathe my censure.
What he might be (if, what he might, he is not)
I would to heaven he were!
Lodovico: What, strike his wife?
Iago: Faith, that was not so well; yet would I knew 255
That stroke would prove the worst.

---

²²⁷ *teem:* conceive. ²²⁸ *falls:* drops. ²²⁸ *crocodile:* (the crocodile was supposed to shed false tears to lure its victims).

Lodovico: Is it his use?°
　　Or did the letters work upon his blood°
　　And new-create his fault?
Iago: Alas, alas!
　　It is not honesty in me to speak
　　What I have seen and known. You shall observe him,   260
　　And his own courses° will denote him so
　　That I may save my speech. Do but go after
　　And mark how he continues.
Lodovico: I am sorry that I am deceived in him.   *Exeunt.*

Scene II   [*The citadel.*]

　　Enter Othello and Emilia.

Othello: You have seen nothing then?
Emilia: Nor ever heard, nor ever did suspect.
Othello: Yes, you have seen Cassio and she together.
Emilia: But then I saw no harm, and then I heard
　　Each syllable that breath made up° between them.   5
Othello: What, did they never whisper?
Emilia: Never, my lord.
Othello: Nor send you out o' th' way?
Emilia: Never.
Othello: To fetch her fan, her gloves, her mask, nor nothing?
Emilia: Never, my lord.   10
Othello: That's strange.
Emilia: I durst, my lord, to wager she is honest,
　　Lay down my soul at stake°. If you think other,
　　Remove your thought. It doth abuse your bosom.
　　If any wretch have put this in your head,   15
　　Let heaven requite it with the serpent's curse°,
　　For if she be not honest°, chaste, and true,
　　There's no man happy. The purest of their wives
　　Is foul as slander.
Othello: Bid her come hither. Go.   *Exit Emilia.*
　　She says enough; yet she's a simple bawd°   20
　　That cannot say as much. This is a subtle whore,
　　A closet lock and key of villainous secrets,
　　And yet she'll kneel and pray; I have seen her do't.

　　Enter Desdemona and Emilia.

Desdemona: My lord, what is your will?
Othello: Pray you, chuck, come hither.
Desdemona: What is your pleasure?
Othello: Let me see your eyes.   25

---

²⁵⁶ *use:* habit.   ²⁵⁷ *blood:* passion.   ²⁶¹ *courses:* actions.   IV.ii.   ⁵ *that breath made up:*
spoken.   ¹³ *at stake:* as the wager.   ¹⁶ *serpent's curse:* (God's curse on the serpent after the
fall in Eden).   ¹⁷ *honest:* chaste.   ²⁰ *bawd:* procuress.

Look in my face.

Desdemona: What horrible fancy's this?

Othello [To Emilia]: Some of your function°, mistress:

    Leave procreants alone and shut the door;

    Cough or cry hem if anybody come.

    Your mystery°, your mystery! Nay, dispatch!   *Exit Emilia.*   30

Desdemona: Upon my knee, what doth your speech import?

    I understand a fury in your words°.

Othello: Why, what art thou?

Desdemona: Your wife, my lord; your true

    And loyal wife.

Othello: Come, swear it, damn thyself;

    Lest, being like one of heaven, the devils themselves   35

    Should fear to seize thee. Therefore be doubledamned:

    Swear thou art honest.

Desdemona: Heaven doth truly know it.

Othello: Heaven truly knows that thou art false as hell.

Desdemona: To whom, my lord? With whom? How am I false?

Othello: Ah, Desdemon! Away! Away! Away!   40

Desdemona: Alas the heavy day! Why do you weep?

    Am I the motive° of these tears, my lord?

    If haply° you my father do suspect

    An instrument of this your calling back,

    Lay not your blame on me. If you have lost him,   45

    I have lost him too.

Othello: Had it pleased heaven

    To try me with affliction, had they rained

    All kinds of sores and shames on my bare head,

    Steeped° me in poverty to the very lips,

    Given to captivity me and my utmost hopes,   50

    I should have found in some place of my soul

    A drop of patience. But alas, to make me

    The fixèd figure for the time of scorn°

    To point his slow and moving finger at.

    Yet could I bear that too, well, very well.   55

    But there where I have garnered up my heart,

    Where either I must live or bear no life,

    The fountain from the which my current runs

    Or else dries up — to be discarded thence,

    Or keep it as a cistern for foul toads   60

    To knot and gender° in — turn thy complexion there,

    Patience, thou young and rose-lipped cherubin!

    I here look grim as hell!°

---

[27] *Some of your function:* do your proper work (as the operator of a brothel).   [30] *mystery:* trade.   [32] *words:* (Q1 adds to this line, "But not the words").   [42] *motive:* cause.   [43] *haply:* by chance.   [49] *Steeped:* submerged.   [53] *The . . . scorn:* the very image of scorn in our time.   [61] *knot and gender:* twist in bunches and procreate.   [61-63] *turn . . . hell:* (the rough sense would seem to be "even Patience would grow pale, turn complexion, at Desdemona's perfidy, but that Othello looks grimly on").

Desdemona: I hope my noble lord esteems me honest.

Othello: O, ay, as summer flies are in the shambles°,   65
    That quicken even with blowing°. O thou weed,
    Who art so lovely fair, and smell'st so sweet,
    That the sense aches at thee, would thou hadst never been born!

Desdemona: Alas, what ignorant° sin have I committed?

Othello: Was this fair paper, this most goodly book,   70
    Made to write "whore" upon? What committed?
    Committed? O thou public commoner°,
    I should make very forges of my cheeks
    That would to cinders burn up modesty,
    Did I but speak thy deeds. What committed?   75
    Heaven stops the nose at it, and the moon winks°;
    The bawdy wind that kisses all it meets
    Is hushed within the hollow mine of earth
    And will not hear't. What committed?

Desdemona: By heaven, you do me wrong!   80

Othello: Are not you a strumpet?

Desdemona: No, as I am a Christian!
    If to preserve this vessel for my lord
    From any other foul unlawful touch
    Be not to be a strumpet, I am none.

Othello: What, not a whore?

Desdemona: No, as I shall be saved!   85

Othello: Is't possible?

Desdemona: O, heaven forgive us!

Othello: I cry you mercy° then.
    I took you for that cunning whore of Venice
    That married with Othello. [*Calling*] You, mistress,

Enter Emilia.

    That have the office opposite to Saint Peter   90
    And keep the gate of hell! You, you, ay, you!
    We have done our course; there's money for your pains.

                            [*Throws her some coins.*]

    I pray you turn the key and keep our counsel.   *Exit.*

Emilia: Alas, what does this gentleman conceive?
    How do you, madam? How do you, my good lady?   95

Desdemona: Faith, half asleep.

Emilia: Good madam, what's the matter with my lord?

Desdemona: With who?

Emilia: Why, with my lord, madam.

---

⁶⁵ *shambles:* abattoirs. ⁶⁶ *quicken even with blowing:* become impregnated as soon as they lay their eggs. ⁶⁹ *ignorant:* unknowing. ⁷² *commoner:* prostitute. ⁷⁶ *winks:* closes its eyes (the moon was the symbol of chastity). ⁸⁷ *cry you mercy:* ask your pardon.

Desdemona: Who is thy lord?

Emilia: He that is yours, sweet lady.   100

Desdemona: I have none. Do not talk to me, Emilia.
   I cannot weep, nor answers have I none
   But what should go by water°. Prithee tonight
   Lay on my bed my wedding sheets, remember;
   And call thy husband hither.

Emilia: Here's a change indeed!   *Exit.*   105

Desdemona: 'Tis meet I should be used so, very meet.
   How have I been behaved, that he might stick
   The small'st opinion on my least misuse°?

Enter Iago and Emilia.

Iago: What is your pleasure, madam? How is't with you?

Desdemona: I cannot tell. Those that do teach young babes   110
   Do it with gentle means and easy tasks.
   He might have chid me so; for, in good faith,
   I am a child to chiding.

Iago: What is the matter, lady?

Emilia: Alas, Iago, my lord hath so bewhored her,
   Thrown such despite° and heavy terms upon her   115
   That true hearts cannot bear it.

Desdemona: Am I that name, Iago?

Iago: What name, fair lady?

Desdemona: Such as she said my lord did say I was.

Emilia: He called her whore. A beggar in his drink
   Could not have laid such terms upon his callet°.   120

Iago: Why did he so?

Desdemona: I do not know; I am sure I am none such.

Iago: Do not weep, do not weep. Alas the day.

Emilia: Hath she forsook so many noble matches,
   Her father and her country, and her friends,   125
   To be called whore? Would it not make one weep?

Desdemona: It is my wretched fortune.

Iago: Beshrew° him for't!
   How comes this trick upon him?

Desdemona: Nay, heaven doth know.

Emilia: I will be hanged if some eternal villain,
   Some busy and insinuating rogue,   130
   Some cogging°, cozening slave, to get some office,
   Have not devised this slander. I will be hanged else.

Iago: Fie, there is no such man! It is impossible.

Desdemona: If any such there be, heaven pardon him.

Emilia A halter pardon him! And hell gnaw his bones!   135

---

¹⁰³ *water:* tears.   ¹⁰⁷⁻⁰⁸ *stick . . . misuse:* base any doubt on my smallest fault.   ¹¹⁵ *despite:* abuse.   ¹²⁰ *callet:* slut.   ¹²⁷ *Beshrew:* curse.   ¹³¹ *cogging:* cheating.

Why should he call her whore? Who keeps her company?
What place? What time? What form? What likelihood?
The Moor's abused by some most villainous knave,
Some base notorious knave, some scurvy fellow.
O heavens, that such companions° thou'dst unfold°,   140
And put in every honest hand a whip
To lash the rascals naked through the world
Even from the east to th' west!
Iago: Speak within door°.
Emilia: O, fie upon them! Some such squire° he was
That turned your wit the seamy side without   145
And made you to suspect me with the Moor.
Iago: You are a fool. Go to.
Desdemona   Alas, Iago,
What shall I do to win my lord again?
Good friend, go to him, for, by this light of heaven,
I know not how I lost him. Here I kneel: 150
If e'er my will did trespass 'gainst his love
Either in discourse of thought° or actual deed,
Or that mine eyes, mine ears, or any sense
Delighted them in any other form;
Or that I do not yet, and ever did,   155
And ever will (though he do shake me off
To beggarly divorcement) love him dearly,
Comfort forswear me. Unkindness may do much,
And his unkindness may defeat° my life,
But never taint my love. I cannot say "whore."   160
It does abhor me now I speak the word;
To do the act that might the addition earn
Not the world's mass of vanity could make me.
Iago: I pray you be content. 'Tis but his humor°.
The business of the state does him offense.   165
Desdemona: If 'twere no other.
Iago: It is but so, I warrant.   [*Trumpets within.*]
Hark how these instruments summon to supper.
The messengers of Venice stay the meat°.
Go in, and weep not. All things shall be well.

[*Exeunt Desdemona and Emilia.*]

Enter Roderigo.

How now, Roderigo?   170
Roderigo: I do not find that thou deal'st justly with me.
Iago: What in the contrary?

---

⁴⁰ *companions:* fellows, rogues. ¹⁴⁰ *unfold:* disclose. ¹⁴³ *within door:* more quietly and moderately. ¹⁴⁴ *squire:* (a term of contempt). ¹⁵² *discourse of thought:* thinking. ¹⁵⁹ *defeat:* destroy. ¹⁶⁴ *humor:* mood. ¹⁶⁸ *stay the meat:* await the meal.

Roderigo: Every day thou daff'st° me with some device°, Iago, and rather, as it seems to me now, keep'st from me all conveniency° than sup- 175 pliest me with the least advantage of hope. I will indeed no longer endure it; nor am I yet persuaded to put up° in peace what already I have foolishly suffered.

Iago: Will you hear me, Roderigo?

Roderigo: I have heard too much, and your words and performances are no kin together. 180

Iago: You charge me most unjustly.

Roderigo: With naught but truth. I have wasted myself out of my means. The jewels you have had from me to deliver Desdemona would half have corrupted a votarist°. You have told me she hath received them, and returned me expectations and comforts of sudden respect° and 185 acquaintance; but I find none.

Iago: Well, go to; very well.

Roderigo: Very well? Go to? I cannot go to, man; nor 'tis not very well. Nay, I think it is scurvy, and begin to find myself fopped° in it.

Iago: Very well. 190

Roderigo: I tell you 'tis not very well. I will make myself known to Desdemona. If she will return me my jewels, I will give over my suit and repent my unlawful solicitation. If not, assure yourself I will seek satisfaction of you.

Iago: You have said now? 195

Roderigo: Ay, and said nothing but what I protest° intendment of doing.

Iago: Why, now I see there's mettle° in thee, and even from this instant do build on thee a better opinion than ever before. Give me thy hand, Roderigo. Thou hast taken against me a most just exception°, but yet I protest I have dealt most directly° in thy affair. 200

Roderigo: It hath not appeared.

Iago: I grant indeed it hath not appeared, and your suspicion is not with- out wit and judgment. But, Roderigo, if thou hast that in thee indeed which I have greater reason to believe now than ever — I mean pur- pose, courage, and valor — this night show it. If thou the next night 205 following enjoy not Desdemona, take me from this world with treachery and devise engines for° my life.

Roderigo: Well, what is it? Is it within reason and compass°?

Iago: Sir, there is especial commission come from Venice to depute Cassio in Othello's place. 210

Roderigo Is that true? Why, then Othello and Desdemona return again to Venice.

Iago: O, no; he goes into Mauritania and taketh away with him the fair Desdemona, unless his abode be lingered here by some accident; wherein none can be so determinate° as the removing of Cassio. 215

Roderigo: How do you mean, removing him?

---

¹⁷³ *daff'st:* put off. ¹⁷³ *device:* scheme. ¹⁷⁴ *conveniency:* what is needful. ¹⁷⁶ *put up:* ac- cept. ¹⁸⁴ *votarist:* nun. ¹⁸⁵ *sudden respect:* immediate consideration. ¹⁸⁹ *fopped:* duped. ¹⁹⁶ *protest:* aver. ¹⁹⁷ *mettle:* spirit. ¹⁹⁹ *exception:* objection. ²⁰⁰ *directly:* straightforwardly. ²⁰⁷ *engines for:* schemes against. ²⁰⁸ *compass:* possibility. ²¹⁵ *determinate:* effective.

Iago: Why, by making him uncapable of Othello's place — knocking out his brains.

Roderigo: And that you would have me to do?

Iago: Ay, if you dare do yourself a profit and a right. He sups tonight with a harlotry°, and thither will I go to him. He knows not yet of his honorable fortune. If you will watch his going thence, which I will fashion to fall out° between twelve and one, you may take him at your pleasure. I will be near to second° your attempt, and he shall fall between us. Come, stand not amazed at it, but go along with me. I will show you such a necessity in his death that you shall think yourself bound to put it on him. It is now high supper time, and the night grows to waste. About it.

Roderigo: I will hear further reason for this.

Iago: And you shall be satisfied.   *Exeunt.*

Scene III   [*The citadel.*]

   Enter Othello, Lodovico, Desdemona, Emilia, and Attendants.

Lodovico: I do beseech you, sir, trouble yourself no further.

Othello: O, pardon me; 'twill do me good to walk.

Lodovico: Madam, good night. I humbly thank your ladyship.

Desdemona: Your honor is most welcome.

Othello: Will you walk, sir? O, Desdemona.

Desdemona: My lord?

Othello: Get you to bed on th' instant; I will be returned forthwith.
   Dismiss your attendant there. Look't be done.

Desdemona: I will, my lord.   *Exit [Othello, with Lodovico and Attendants].*

Emilia: How goes it now? He looks gentler than he did.

Desdemona: He says he will return incontinent°,
   And hath commanded me to go to bed.
   And bade me to dismiss you.

Emilia: Dismiss me?

Desdemona: It was his bidding; therefore, good Emilia,
   Give me my nightly wearing, and adieu.
   We must not now displease him.

Emilia: I would you had never seen him!

Desdemona: So would not I. My love doth so approve him
   That even his stubbornness, his checks°, his frowns —
   Prithee unpin me — have grace and favor.

Emilia: I have laid these sheets you bade me on the bed.

Desdemona: All's one°. Good Father, how foolish are our minds!
   If I do die before, prithee shroud me
   In one of these same sheets.

Emilia: Come, come! You talk.

Desdemona: My mother had a maid called Barbary.

---

²²¹ *harlotry:* female. ²²³ *fall out:* occur. ²²⁴ *second:* support. IV.iii. ¹¹ *incontinent:* at once. ¹⁹ *checks:* rebukes. ²² *All's one:* no matter.

She was in love; and he she loved proved mad
And did forsake her. She had a song of "Willow";
An old thing 'twas, but it expressed her fortune,
And she died singing it. That song tonight   30
Will not go from my mind; I have much to do
But to go hang my head all at one side
And sing it like poor Barbary. Prithee dispatch.
Emilia: Shall I go fetch your nightgown?
Desdemona: No, unpin me here.   35
This Lodovico is a proper man.
Emilia: A very handsome man.
Desdemona: He speaks well.
Emilia: I know a lady in Venice would have walked barefoot to Palestine
for a touch of his nether lip.   40
Desdemona [Sings]:
      "The poor soul sat singing by a sycamore tree,
            Sing all a green willow;
      Her hand on her bosom, her head on her knee,
            Sing willow, willow, willow.
      The fresh streams ran by her and murmured her moans;   45
            Sing willow, willow, willow;
      Her salt tears fell from her, and soft'ned the stones —
            Sing willow, willow, willow — "
      Lay by these.   [*Gives Emilia her clothes.*]
            "Willow, Willow" —   50
      Prithee hie° thee; he'll come anon°.
      "Sing all a green willow must be my garland
      Let nobody blame him; his scorn I approve" —
      Nay, that's not next. Hark! Who is't that knocks?
Emilia: It is the wind.   55
Desdemona [Sings]:
      "I called my love false love; but what said he then?
            Sing willow, willow, willow:
      If I court moe° women, you'll couch with moe men."
      So, get thee gone; good night. Mine eyes do itch.
      Doth that bode weeping?
Emilia: 'Tis neither here nor there. 60
Desdemona: I have heard it said so. O, these men, these men.
      Dost thou in conscience think, tell me, Emilia,
      That there be women do abuse their husbands
      In such gross kind?
Emilia: There be some such, no question.
Desdemona: Wouldst thou do such a deed for all the world?   65
Emilia: Why, would not you?
Desdemona: No, by this heavenly light!
Emilia: Nor I neither by this heavenly light.
      I might do't as well i' th' dark.

---

⁵¹ *hie:* hurry.   ⁵¹ *anon:* at once.   ⁵⁸ *moe:* more.

Desdemona: Wouldst thou do such a deed for all the world?

Emilia: The world's a huge thing; it is a great price for a small vice. 70

Desdemona: In troth, I think thou wouldst not.

Emilia: In troth, I think I should; and undo't when I had done. Marry, I would not do such a thing for a joint-ring°, nor for measures of lawn°, nor for gowns, petticoats, nor caps, nor any petty exhibition°, but for all the whole world? Why, who would not make her husband 75 a cuckold to make him a monarch? I should venture purgatory for't.

Desdemona: Beshrew me if I would do such a wrong for the whole world.

Emilia: Why, the wrong is but a wrong i' th' world; and having the world for your labor, 'tis a wrong in your own world, and you might quickly make it right. 80

Desdemona: I do not think there is any such woman.

Emilia: Yes, a dozen; and as many to th' vantage as would store° the world they played for.
But I do think it is their husbands' faults
If wives do fall. Say that they slack their duties 85
And pour our treasures into foreign° laps;
Or else break out in peevish jealousies,
Throwing restraint upon us; or say they strike us,
Or scant our former having in despite° —
Why, we have galls; and though we have some grace, 90
Yet have we some revenge. Let husbands know
Their wives have sense like them. They see, and smell,
And have their palates both for sweet and sour,
As husbands have. What is it that they do
When they change° us for others? Is it sport? 95
I think it is. And doth affection° breed it?
I think it doth. Is't frailty that thus errs?
It is so too. And have not we affections?
Desires for sport? and frailty? as men have?
Then let them use us well; else let them know, 100
The ills we do, their ills instruct us so°.

Desdemona: Good night, good night. Heaven me such uses° send,
Not to pick bad from bad, but by bad mend.   *Exeunt.*

ACT V

Scene I   [*A street.*]

Enter Iago and Roderigo.

Iago: Here, stand behind this bulk°; straight will he come.
Wear thy good rapier bare, and put it home.

---

73 *joint-ring:* (a ring with two interlocking halves).   74 *lawn:* fine linen.   74 *exhibition:* payment.   82 *to . . . store:* in addition as would fill.   86 *foreign:* alien, i.e., other than the wife.   89 *scant . . . despite:* reduce, in spite, our household allowance (?).   95 *change:* exchange.   96 *affection:* strong feeling, desire.   101 *instruct us so:* teach us to do likewise.   102 *uses:* practices.   V.i.   1 *bulk:* projecting stall of a shop.

Quick, quick! Fear nothing; I'll be at thy elbow.
It makes us, or it mars us, think on that,
And fix most firm thy resolution.   5
Roderigo: Be near at hand; I may miscarry in't.
Iago: Here, at thy hand. Be bold, and take thy stand.   [*Moves to one side.*]
Roderigo: I have no great devotion to the deed,
And yet he hath given me satisfying reasons.
'Tis but a man gone. Forth my sword! He dies!   10
Iago: I have rubbed this young quat° almost to the sense°,
And he grows angry. Now, whether he kill Cassio,
Or Cassio him, or each do kill the other,
Every way makes my gain. Live Roderigo,
He calls me to a restitution large   15
Of gold and jewels that I bobbed° from him
As gifts to Desdemona.
It must not be. If Cassio do remain,
He hath a daily beauty in his life
That makes me ugly; and besides, the Moor   20
May unfold me to him; there stand I in much peril.
No, he must die. But so, I hear him coming.

Enter Cassio.

Roderigo: I know his gait. 'Tis he. Villain, thou diest!   [*Thrusts at Cassio.*]
Cassio: That thrust had been mine enemy indeed
But that my coat° is better than thou know'st.   25
I will make proof of thine.   [*Fights with Roderigo.*]
Roderigo: O, I am slain!°
Cassio: I am maimed forever. Help, ho! Murder! Murder!

Enter Othello [to one side].

Othello: The voice of Cassio. Iago keeps his word.
Roderigo: O, villain that I am!
Othello: It is even so.
Cassio: O help, ho! Light! A surgeon!   30
Othello: 'Tis he. O brave Iago, honest and just,
That hast such noble sense of thy friend's wrong!
Thou teachest me. Minion°, your dear lies dead,
And your unblest° fate hies°. Strumpet, I come.
Forth of my heart those charms, thine eyes, are blotted.   35

---

¹¹ *quat:* pimple. ¹¹ *to the sense:* raw. ¹⁶ *bobbed:* swindled. ²⁵ *coat:* i.e., a mail shirt or
bulletproof vest. ²⁶ *slain:* most editors add here a stage direction that has Iago wounding
Cassio in the leg from behind, but remaining unseen. However, nothing in the text requires this, and Cassio's wound can be given him in the fight with Roderigo, for presumably when Cassio attacks Roderigo the latter would not simply accept the thrust but
would parry. Since Iago enters again at line 46, he must exit at some point after line
22. ³³ *Minion:* hussy, i.e., Desdemona. ³⁴ *unblest:* unsanctified. ³⁴ *hies:* approaches
swiftly.

Thy bed, lust-stained, shall with lust's blood be spotted.

Exit Othello.

Enter Lodovico and Gratiano.

Cassio: What, ho? No watch? No passage°? Murder! Murder!
Gratiano: 'Tis some mischance. The voice is very direful.
Cassio: O, help!
Lodovico: Hark! 40
Roderigo: O wretched villain!
Lodovico: Two or three groan. 'Tis heavy night.
    These may be counterfeits. Let's think't unsafe
    To come into the cry without more help.
Roderigo: Nobody come? Then shall I bleed to death. 45
Lodovico: Hark!

Enter Iago [with a light].

Gratiano: Here's one comes in his shirt, with light and weapons.
Iago: Who's there? Whose noise is this that cries on murder?
Lodovico: We do not know.
Iago: Do not you hear a cry?
Cassio: Here, here! For heaven's sake, help me!
Iago: What's the matter? 50
Gratiano: This is Othello's ancient, as I take it.
Lodovico: The same indeed, a very valiant fellow.
Iago: What are you here that cry so grievously?
Cassio: Iago? O, I am spoiled, undone by villains.
    Give me some help. 55
Iago: O me, lieutenant! What villains have done this?
Cassio: I think that one of them is hereabout
    And cannot make away.
Iago: O treacherous villains!
    [*To Lodovico and Gratiano*] What are you there?
    Come in, and give some help.
Roderigo: O, help me here! 60
Cassio: That's one of them.
Iago: O murd'rous slave! O villain!   [*Stabs Roderigo.*]
Roderigo: O damned Iago! O inhuman dog!
Iago: Kill men i' th' dark? — Where be these bloody thieves? —
    How silent is this town! — Ho! Murder! Murder! —
    What may you be? Are you of good or evil? 65
Lodovico: As you shall prove us, praise us.
Iago: Signior Lodovico?
Lodovico: He, sir.
Iago: I cry you mercy. Here's Cassio hurt by villains. 70
Gratiano: Cassio?
Iago: How is't, brother?

<hr>

[37] *passage:* passers-by.

Cassio: My leg is cut in two.

Iago: Marry, heaven forbid!
        Light, gentlemen. I'll bind it with my shirt.

        Enter Bianca.

Bianca: What is the matter, ho? Who is't that cried?   75
Iago: Who is't that cried?
Bianca: O my dear Cassio! My sweet Cassio!
        O Cassio, Cassio, Cassio!
Iago: O notable strumpet! — Cassio, may you suspect
        Who they should be that have thus mangled you?
Cassio: No.   80
Gratiano: I am sorry to find you thus. I have been to seek you.
Iago: Lend me a garter. So. O for a chair
        To bear him easily hence.
Bianca: Alas, he faints! O Cassio, Cassio, Cassio!
Iago: Gentlemen all, I do suspect this trash   85
        To be a party in this injury. —
        Patience awhile, good Cassio. — Come, come.
        Lend me a light. Know we this face or no?
        Alas, my friend and my dear countryman
        Roderigo? No. — Yes, sure. — Yes, 'tis Roderigo!   90
Gratiano: What, of Venice?
Iago: Even he, sir. Did you know him?
Gratiano: Know him? Ay.
Iago: Signior Gratiano? I cry your gentle pardon.
        These bloody accidents must excuse my manners
        That so neglected you.
Gratiano: I am glad to see you.   95
Iago: How do you, Cassio? — O, a chair, a chair!
Gratiano: Roderigo?
Iago: He, he, 'tis he! [*A chair brought in.*] O, that's well said°; the chair.
        Some good man bear him carefully from hence.
        I'll fetch the general's surgeon. [*To Bianca*] For you, mistress,   100
        Save you your labor. [*To Cassio*] He that lies slain here, Cassio,
        Was my dear friend. What malice was between you?
Cassio: None in the world; nor do I know the man.
Iago: What, look you pale? — O, bear him out o' th' air.

                                        [*Cassio is carried off.*]

        Stay you, good gentlemen. — Look you pale, mistress?   105
        Do you perceive the gastness° of her eye?
        Nay, if you stare, we shall hear more anon.
        Behold her well; I pray you look upon her.
        Do you see, gentlemen? Nay, guiltiness will speak,
        Though tongues were out of use°.   110

---

⁹⁸ *well said:* well done.   ¹⁰⁶ *gastness:* terror.   ¹¹⁰ *tongues were out of use:* men no longer
spoke.

[*Enter Emilia.*]

Emilia: Alas, what is the matter? What is the matter, husband?
Iago: Cassio hath here been set on in the dark
    By Roderigo and fellows that are scaped.
    He's almost slain, and Roderigo quite dead.
Emilia: Alas, good gentleman! Alas, good Cassio!   115
Iago: This is the fruits of whoring. Prithee, Emilia,
    Go know of Cassio where he supped tonight.
    [*To Bianca*] What, do you shake at that?
Bianca: He supped at my house; but I therefore shake not.
Iago: O, did he so? I charge° you go with me.   120
Emilia: Oh fie upon thee, strumpet!
Bianca: I am no strumpet, but of life as honest
    As you that thus abuse me.
Emilia: As I? Fie upon thee!
Iago: Kind gentlemen, let's go see poor Cassio dressed°.
    [*To Bianca*] Come, mistress, you must tell's another tale.   125
    Emilia, run you to the citadel
    And tell my lord and lady what hath happed   [*Exit Emilia.*]
    Will you go on afore?   *Exeunt* [*all but Iago*].
              This is the night
    That either makes me or fordoes me quite°.   [*Exit.*]

Scene II.   [*Desdemona's chamber.*]

   Enter Othello [*with a light*]; *and Desdemona in her bed.*

Othello: It is the cause, it is the cause, my soul.
    Let me not name it to you, you chaste stars.
    It is the cause. Yet I'll not shed her blood,
    Nor scar that whiter skin of hers than snow
    And smooth as monumental alabaster.   5
    Yet she must die, else she'll betray more men.
    Put out the light, and then put out the light.
    If I quench thee, thou flaming minister°,
    I can again thy former light restore,
    Should I repent me; but once put out thy light,   10
    Thou cunning'st° pattern of excelling nature,
    I know not where is that Promethean heat°
    That can thy light relume°. When I have plucked the rose,
    I cannot give it vital° growth again;
    It needs must wither. I'll smell thee on the tree.   [*He kisses her.*]   15
    O balmy breath, that dost almost persuade
    Justice to break her sword. One more, one more!

---

¹²⁰ *charge:* command.   ¹²⁴ *dressed:* bandaged.   ¹²⁹ *fordoes me quite:* completely ruins me.
V.ii.   ⁸ *minister:* worker, servant.   ¹¹ *cunning'st:* most intricate and skillfully wrought (by
nature excelling itself).   ¹² *Promethean heat:* divine fire (Prometheus is the Titan who
stole fire from heaven and gave it to man).   ¹³ *relume:* relight.   ¹⁴ *vital:* living.

Be thus when thou art dead, and I will kill thee,
And love thee after. One more, and that's the last!
So sweet was ne'er so fatal. I must weep,   20
But they are cruel tears. This sorrow's heavenly;
It strikes where it doth love. She wakes.

Desdemona: Who's there? Othello?

Othello: Ay, Desdemona.

Desdemona: Will you come to bed, my lord?

Othello: Have you prayed tonight, Desdemon?

Desdemona: Ay, my lord.   25

Othello: If you bethink yourself of any crime
Unreconciled as yet to heaven and grace,
Solicit for it straight.

Desdemona: Alack, my lord, what may you mean by that?

Othello: Well, do it, and be brief; I will walk by°.   30
I would not kill thy unpreparèd spirit.
No, heavens forfend! I would not kill thy soul.

Desdemona: Talk you of killing?

Othello: Ay, I do.

Desdemona: Then heaven
Have mercy on me!

Othello: Amen, with all my heart.

Desdemona: If you say so, I hope you will not kill me.   35

Othello: Humh.

Desdemona: And yet I fear you; for you're fatal then
When your eyes roll so. Why I should fear I know not,
Since guiltiness I know not; but yet I feel I fear.

Othello: Think on thy sins.

Desdemona: They are loves I bear to you.   40

Othello: Ay, and for that thou diest.

Desdemona: That death's unnatural that kills for loving.
Alas, why gnaw you so your nether lip?
Some bloody passion shakes your very frame.
These are portents; but yet I hope, I hope,   45
They do not point on me.

Othello: Peace and be still.

Desdemona: I will so. What's the matter?

Othello: That handkerchief which I so loved and gave thee,
Thou gav'st to Cassio.

Desdemona: No, by my life and soul!
Send for the man and ask him.

Othello: Sweet soul, take heed,   50
Take heed of perjury; thou art on thy deathbed.

Desdemona: Ay, but not yet to die.

Othello: Presently°.
Therefore confess thee freely of thy sin,

---

³⁰ *by:* nearby.   ⁵² *Presently:* immediately.

For to deny each article° with oath
Cannot remove nor choke the strong conception   55
That I do groan withal. Thou art to die.

Desdemona: Then Lord have mercy on me.

Othello: I say, amen.

Desdemona: And have you mercy too. I never did
Offend you in my life; never loved Cassio
But with such general warranty° of heaven   60
As I might love. I never gave him token.

Othello: By heaven, I saw my handkerchief in's hand!
O perjured woman! thou dost stone° my heart,
And mak'st me call what I intend to do
A murder, which I thought a sacrifice.   65
I saw the handkerchief.

Desdemona: He found it then.
I never gave it him. Send for him hither.
Let him confess a truth.

Othello: He hath confessed.

Desdemona: What, my lord?

Othello: That he hath used thee.

Desdemona: How? Unlawfully?

Othello: Ay.   70

Desdemona: He will not say so.

Othello: No, his mouth is stopped.
Honest Iago hath ta'en order for't°.

Desdemona: O, my fear interprets. What, is he dead?

Othello: Had all his hairs been lives, my great revenge
Had stomach° for them all.   75

Desdemona: Alas, he is betrayed, and I undone!

Othello: Out, strumpet! Weep'st thou for him to my face?

Desdemona: O, banish me, my lord, but kill me not!

Othello: Down, strumpet!

Desdemona: Kill me tomorrow; let me live tonight!   80

Othello: Nay, if you strive —

Desdemona: But half an hour!

Othello: Being done, there is no pause.

Desdemona: But while I say one prayer!

Othello: It is too late.   *Smothers her.*

   Emilia at the door.

Emilia [Calls within]: My lord, my lord! What, ho, my lord, my lord!

Othello: What noise is this? Not dead? Not yet quite dead?   85
I that am cruel am yet merciful;
I would not have thee linger in thy pain.

Emilia [Within]: What, ho! My lord, my lord!

---

⁵⁴ *article:* item (of the charge of adultery. Othello makes heavy use of legal terms in this scene). ⁶⁰ *warranty:* allowance. ⁶³ *stone:* turn to stone. ⁷² *ta'en order for't:* made sure of it. ⁷⁵ *stomach:* appetite.

Othello: So, so. Who's there?
Emilia [*Within*]: O, good my lord, I would speak a word with you.
Othello: Yes, 'tis Emilia. — By and by. — She's dead. —   90
    'Tis like she comes to speak of Cassio's death.
    The noise was high°. Ha! No more moving?
    Still as the grave. — Shall she come in? Were't good? —
    I think she stirs again. No. — What's best to do?
    If she come in, she'll sure speak to my wife.   95
    My wife! My wife! What wife? I have no wife.
    O, insupportable! O heavy hour!
    Methinks it should be now a huge eclipse
    Of sun and moon, and that th' affrighted globe
    Should yawn° at alteration.
Emilia [*Within*]:   I do beseech you   100
    That I may speak with you, O good my lord!
Othello: I had forgot thee. O, come in, Emilia.
    Soft, by and by. — Let me the curtains draw. —

        [*Draws the bed hangings and then opens the door.*]

    Where art thou?

    Enter Emilia.

        What's the matter with thee now?
Emilia: O my good lord, yonder's foul murders done!   105
Othello: What? Now?
Emilia: But now, my lord.
Othello: It is the very error° of the moon.
    She comes more nearer earth than she was wont
    And makes men mad.   110
Emilia: Cassio, my lord, hath killed a young Venetian
    Called Roderigo.
Othello: Roderigo killed?
    And Cassio killed?
Emilia: No, Cassio is not killed.
Othello: Not Cassio killed? Then murder's out of tune,   115
    And sweet revenge grows harsh.
Desdemona: O, falsely, falsely murdered!
Emilia: O Lord! What cry is that?
Othello: That? What?
Emilia: Out and alas! that was my lady's voice.
    Help! Help, ho! Help! O lady, speak again!
    Sweet Desdemona! O sweet mistress, speak!   120
Desdemona: A guiltless death I die.
Emilia: O, who hath done this deed?

---

⁹² *high*: loud (Q1 reads "here"). ⁹⁸⁻¹⁰⁰ *Methinks . . . alteration*: (the Elizabethans believed that great changes in human affairs were reflected by disorders in nature). ¹⁰⁰ *yawn*: gape open (as in an earthquake). ¹⁰⁸ *error*: wandering out of regular course (disorders in the heavens were believed by some to cause disorders on earth, as well as vice versa).

Desdemona: Nobody — I myself. Farewell.

    Commend me to my kind lord. O, farewell!   [*She dies.*]

Othello: Why, how should she be murd'red?

Emilia: Alas, who knows?   125

Othello: You heard her say herself, it was not I.

Emilia: She said so. I must needs report the truth.

Othello: She's like a liar gone to burning hell!

    'Twas I that killed her.

Emilia: O, the more angel she,

    And you the blacker devil!   130

Othello: She turned to folly, and she was a whore.

Emilia: Thou dost belie her, and thou art a devil.

Othello: She was false as water.

Emilia: Thou art rash as fire to say

    That she was false. O, she was heavenly true!

Othello: Cassio did top her. Ask thy husband else.   135

    O, I were damned beneath all depth in hell

    But that I did proceed upon just grounds

    To this extremity. Thy husband knew it all.

Emilia: My husband?

Othello: Thy husband.

Emilia: That she was false to wedlock?

Othello: Ay, with Cassio. Had she been true,   140

    If heaven would make me such another world

    Of one entire and perfect chrysolite°,

    I'd not have sold her for it.

Emilia: My husband?

Othello: Ay, 'twas he that told me on her first.

    An honest man he is, and hates the slime   145

    That sticks on filthy deeds.

Emilia: My husband?

Othello: What needs this iterance? Woman, I say thy husband.

Emilia: O mistress, villainy hath made mocks with love!

    My husband say she was false?

Othello: He, woman.

    I say, thy husband. Dost understand the word?   150

    My friend, thy husband; honest, honest Iago.

Emilia: If he say so, may his pernicious soul

    Rot half a grain a day! He lies to th' heart.

    She was too fond of her most filthy bargain.

Othello: Hah?   155

Emilia: Do thy worst.

    This deed of thine is no more worthy heaven

    Than thou wast worthy her.

Othello: Peace, you were best°.

Emilia: Thou hast not half that pow'r to do me harm

---

¹⁴² *chrysolite:* topaz.   ¹⁵⁸ *Peace, you were best:* i.e., you had better be silent.

As I have to be hurt. O gull! O dolt!   160
As ignorant as dirt! Thou hast done a deed —

[Othello moves to draw his sword.]

I care not for thy sword; I'll make thee known,
Though I lost twenty lives. Help! Help! Ho! Help!
The Moor hath killed my mistress! Murder! murder!

Enter Montano, Gratiano, and Iago [and Others].

Montano: What is the matter? How now, general?   165
Emilia: O, are you come, Iago? You have done well,
   That men must lay their murders on your neck.
Gratiano: What is the matter?
Emilia: Disprove this villain, if thou be'st a man.
   He says thou told'st him that his wife was false.   170
   I know thou didst not; thou'rt not such a villain.
   Speak, for my heart is full.
Iago: I told him what I thought, and told no more
   Than what he found himself was apt and true.
Emilia: But did you ever tell him she was false?   175
Iago: I did.
Emilia: You told a lie, an odious damnèd lie!
   Upon my soul, a lie! A wicked lie!
   She false with Cassio? Did you say with Cassio?
Iago: With Cassio, mistress. Go to, charm° your tongue.   180
Emilia: I will not charm my tongue; I am bound to speak:
   My mistress here lies murdered in her bed.
All: O heavens forfend!
Emilia: And your reports have set the murder on.
Othello: Nay, stare not, masters. It is true indeed.   185
Gratiano: 'Tis a strange truth.
Montano: O monstrous act!
Emilia: Villainy, villainy, villainy!
   I think upon't — I think I smell't! — O villainy!
   I thought so then. — I'll kill myself for grief. —
   O villainy, villainy!   190
Iago: What, are you mad? I charge you get you home.
Emilia: Good gentlemen, let me have leave to speak.
   'Tis proper I obey him, but not now.
   Perchance, Iago, I will ne'er go home.
Othello: O! O! O!   [Falls on the bed.]
Emilia: Nay, lay thee down and roar,   195
   For thou hast killed the sweetest innocent
   That e'er did lift up eye.
Othello: O, she was foul!   [Rises.]
   I scarce did know you, uncle. There lies your niece,

---

¹⁸⁰ charm: control.

Whose breath, indeed, these hands have newly stopped.
I know this act shows horrible and grim.   200
Gratiano: Poor Desdemon! I am glad thy father's dead.
Thy match was mortal to him, and pure grief
Shore his old thread in twain. Did he live now,
This sight would make him do a desperate turn;
Yea, curse his better angel from his side,   205
And fall to reprobation°.
Othello: 'Tis pitiful; but yet Iago knows
That she with Cassio hath the act of shame
A thousand times committed. Cassio confessed it;
And she did gratify his amorous works   210
With that recognizance and pledge of love,
Which I first gave her. I saw it in his hand.
It was a handkerchief, an antique token
My father gave my mother.
Emilia: O God! O heavenly God!   215
Iago: Zounds, hold your peace!
Emilia: 'Twill out, 'twill out! I peace?
No, I will speak as liberal as the north°.
Let heaven and men and devils, let them all,
All, all, cry shame against me, yet I'll speak.
Iago: Be wise, and get you home.
Emilia: I will not.   220

                    [*Iago draws and threatens Emilia.*]

Gratiano: Fie! Your sword upon a woman?
Emilia: O thou dull Moor, that handkerchief thou speak'st of
I found by fortune, and did give my husband;
For often with a solemn earnestness —
More than indeed belonged to such a trifle —   225
He begged of me to steal't.
Iago: Villainous whore!
Emilia: She give it Cassio? No, alas, I found it,
And I did give't my husband.
Iago: Filth, thou liest!
Emilia: By heaven, I do not, I do not, gentlemen.
O murd'rous coxcomb! What should such a fool   230
Do with so good a wife?
Othello: Are there no stones° in heaven
But what serves for the thunder? Precious villain!
[*The Moor runs at Iago, but is disarmed by Montano. Iago kills his wife.*]

Gratiano: The woman falls. Sure he hath killed his wife.
Emilia: Ay, ay. O, lay me by my mistress' side.   [*Exit Iago.*]

---

²⁰⁶ *reprobation:* damnation.   ²¹⁷ *liberal as the north:* freely (and bitingly) as the north wind blows.   ²³¹ *stones:* thunderbolts.

Gratiano: He's gone, but his wife's killed.

Montano: 'Tis a notorious° villain. Take you this weapon,

　　Which I have recovered from the Moor.

　　Come, guard the door without. Let him not pass,

　　But kill him rather. I'll after that same villain,

　　For 'tis a damnèd slave.　　　　*Exit [with all but Othello and Emilia].*

Othello:　　　　　　　I am not valiant neither;

　　But every puny whipster° gets my sword.

　　But why should honor outlive honesty?

　　Let it go all.

Emilia:　　　　What did thy song bode, lady?

　　Hark, canst thou hear me? I will play the swan,

　　And die in music. [*Sings*] "Willow, willow, willow."

　　Moor, she was chaste. She loved thee, cruel Moor,

　　So come my soul to bliss as I speak true.

　　So speaking as I think, alas, I die.　　　　　　[*She dies.*]

Othello: I have another weapon in this chamber;

　　It was a sword of Spain, the ice-brook's temper.

　　O, here it is. — Uncle, I must come forth.

Gratiano [Within]: If thou attempt it, it will cost thee dear.

　　Thou hast no weapon, and perforce must suffer.

Othello: Look in upon me then and speak with me,

　　Or, naked as I am, I will assault thee.

　　[*Enter Gratiano.*]

Gratiano: What is the matter?

Othello:　　　　　　　　　Behold, I have a weapon;

　　A better never did itself sustain

　　Upon a soldier's thigh. I have seen the day

　　That with this little arm and this good sword

　　I have made my way through more impediments

　　Than twenty times your stop. But O vain boast!

　　Who can control his fate? 'Tis not so now.

　　Be not afraid, though you do see me weaponed.

　　Here is my journey's end, here is my butt°,

　　And very seamark of my utmost sail°.

　　Do you go back dismayed? 'Tis a lost fear.

　　Man but a rush° against Othello's breast.

　　And he retires. Where should Othello go?

　　Now, how dost thou look now? O ill-starred wench!

　　Pale as thy smock! When we shall meet at compt°,

　　This look of thine will hurl my soul from heaven,

　　And fiends will snatch at it. Cold, cold, my girl?

235

240

245

250

255

260

265

270

---

236 *notorious:* out-and-out.　241 *puny whipster:* small top-whipping boy (?).　264 *butt:* target, stopping place.　265 *seamark of my utmost sail:* maker of my furthest journey. 267 *Man but a rush:* attack with only a reed.　270 *compt:* Judgment Day.

Even like thy chastity.
O cursèd, cursèd slave! Whip me, ye devils,
From the possession of° this heavenly sight!   275
Blow me about in winds! roast me in sulfur!
Wash me in steep-down gulfs of liquid fire!
O Desdemon! Dead Desdemon; dead. O! O!

Enter Lodovico, Cassio, Montano, and Iago [as prisoner,] with Officers.

Lodovico: Where is this rash and most unfortunate man?
Othello: That's he that was Othello? Here I am.   280
Lodovico: Where is that viper? Bring the villain forth.
Othello: I look down towards his feet° — but that's a fable.
   If that thou be'st a devil, I cannot kill thee.   [*Wounds Iago.*]
Lodovico: Wrench his sword from him.   [*Othello is disarmed.*]
Iago: I bleed, sir, but not killed.
Othello: I am not sorry neither. I'd have thee live;   285
   For in my sense, 'tis happiness to die.
Lodovico: O thou Othello that was once so good,
   Fall'n in the practice° of a cursèd slave,
   What shall be said to thee?
Othello: Why, anything:
   An honorable murderer, if you will;   290
   For naught I did in hate, but all in honor.
Lodovico: This wretch hath part confessed his villainy.
   Did you and he consent in Cassio's death?
Othello: Ay.
Cassio: Dear general, I never gave you cause.   295
Othello: I do believe it, and I ask your pardon.
   Will you, I pray, demand that demi-devil
   Why he hath thus ensnared my soul and body?
Iago: Demand me nothing. What you know, you know.
   From this time forth I never will speak word.   300
Lodovico: What, not to pray?
Gratiano: Torments will ope your lips.
Othello: Well, thou dost best.
Lodovico: Sir, you shall understand what hath befall'n,
   Which, as I think, you know not. Here is a letter
   Found in the pocket of the slain Roderigo;   305
   And here another. The one of them imports
   The death of Cassio to be undertook
   By Roderigo.
Othello: O villain!
Cassio: Most heathenish and most gross!
Lodovico: Now here's another discontented paper   310
   Found in his pocket too; and this, it seems,

---

²⁷⁵ *the possession of:* being possessed by.   ²⁸² *towards his feet:* i.e., for his cloven hoofs.
²⁸⁸ *practice:* plotting.

Roderigo meant t' have sent this damnèd villain;
But that, belike, Iago in the interim
Came in and satisfied him.
Othello: O thou pernicious caitiff!
How came you, Cassio, by that handkerchief   315
That was my wife's?
Cassio: I found it in my chamber;
And he himself confessed it but even now
That there he dropped it for a special purpose
Which wrought to his desire.
Othello: O fool! Fool! Fool!
Cassio: There is besides in Roderigo's letter,   320
How he upbraids Iago that he made him
Brave me upon the watch; whereon it came
That I was cast; and even but now he spake,
After long seeming dead — Iago hurt him,
Iago set him on.   325
Lodovico: You must forsake this room and go with us.
Your power and your command is taken off,
And Cassio rules in Cyprus. For this slave,
If there be any cunning cruelty
That can torment him much and hold him long,   330
It shall be his. You shall close prisoner rest
Till that the nature of your fault be known
To the Venetian state. Come, bring away.
Othello: Soft you, a word or two before you go.
I have done the state some service and they know't.   335
No more of that. I pray you, in your letters,
When you shall these unlucky deeds relate,
Speak of me as I am. Nothing extenuate,
Nor set down aught in malice. Then must you speak
Of one that loved not wisely, but too well;   340
Of one not easily jealous, but, being wrought,
Perplexed in the extreme; of one whose hand,
Like the base Judean°, threw a pearl away
Richer than all his tribe; of one whose subdued eyes,
Albeit unusèd to the melting mood,   345
Drops tears as fast as the Arabian trees
Their med'cinable gum. Set you down this.
And say besides that in Aleppo once,
Where a malignant and a turbaned Turk
Beat a Venetian and traduced the state,   350
I took by th' throat the circumcisèd dog
And smote him — thus.   [*He stabs himself.*]

---

[343] *Judean:* (most editors use the Q1 reading, "Indian," here, but F is clear: both readings point toward the infidel, the unbeliever.

Lodovico: O bloody period!°
Gratiano: All that is spoke is marred.
Othello: I kissed thee ere I killed thee. No way but this,
     Killing myself, to die upon a kiss.   [*He falls over Desdemona and dies.*]   355
Cassio: This did I fear, but thought he had no weapon;
     For he was great of heart.
Lodovico [*To Iago*]:   O Spartan dog,
     More fell° than anguish, hunger, or the sea!
     Look on the tragic loading of this bed.
     This is thy work. The object poisons sight;   360
     Let it be hid.   [*Bed curtains drawn.*]
                     Gratiano, keep° the house,
     And seize upon the fortunes of the Moor,
     For they succeed on you. To you, lord governor,
     Remains the censure of this hellish villain,
     The time, the place, the torture. O, enforce it!   365
     Myself will straight aboard, and to the state
     This heavy act with heavy heart relate.   *Exeunt.*

QUESTIONS

ACT I

1. What is Othello's position in society? How is he regarded by those who know him? By his own words, when we first meet him in Scene II, what traits of character does he manifest?
2. How do you account for Brabantio's dismay on learning of his daughter's marriage, despite the fact that Desdemona has married a man so generally honored and admired?
3. What is Iago's view of human nature? In his fondness for likening men to animals (as in I, i, 44–45, I, i, 85–86, and I, iii, 374–375), what does he tell us about himself?
4. What reasons does Iago give for his hatred of Othello?
5. In Othello's defense before the senators (Scene III), how does he explain Desdemona's gradual falling in love with him?
6. Is Brabantio's warning to Othello (I, iii, 286–287) an accurate or an inaccurate prophecy?
7. By what strategy does Iago enlist Roderigo in his plot against the Moor? In what lines do we learn Iago's true feelings toward Roderigo?

ACT II

1. What do the Cypriots think of Othello? Do their words (in Scene I) make him seem to us a lesser man, or a larger one?
2. What cruelty does Iago display toward Emilia? How well founded is his distrust of his wife's fidelity?
3. In II, iii, 227, Othello speaks of Iago's "honesty and love." How do you account for Othello's being so totally deceived?

³⁵³ *period:* end.   ³⁵⁸ *fell:* cruel.   ³⁶¹ *keep:* remain in.

4. For what major events does the merrymaking (proclaimed in Scene II) give opportunity?

ACT III

1. Trace the steps by which Iago rouses Othello to suspicion. Is there anything in Othello's character or circumstances that renders him particularly susceptible to Iago's wiles?
2. In III, iv, 96–97, Emilia knows of Desdemona's distress over the lost handkerchief. At this moment, how do you explain her failure to relieve Desdemona's mind? Is Emilia aware of her husband's villainy?

ACT IV

1. In this act, what circumstantial evidence is added to Othello's case against Desdemona?
2. How plausible do you find Bianca's flinging the handkerchief at Cassio just when Othello is looking on? How important is the handkerchief in this play? What does it represent? What suggestions or hints do you find in it?
3. What prevents Othello from being moved by Desdemona's appeal (IV, ii, 34–87)?
4. When Roderigo grows impatient with Iago (IV, ii, 171–196), how does Iago make use of his fellow plotter's discontent?
5. What does the conversation between Emilia and Desdemona (Scene III) tell us about the nature of each? Someone has called Emilia's concluding speech (84–101) a Renaissance plea for women's liberation. Do you agree? How timely is it?
6. In this act, what scenes (or speeches) have contained memorable dramatic irony?

ACT V

1. Summarize the events that lead to Iago's unmasking.
2. How does Othello's mistaken belief that Cassio is slain (V, i, 27–33) affect the outcome of the play?
3. What is Iago's motive in stabbing Roderigo?
4. In your interpretation of the play, exactly what impels Othello to kill Desdemona? Jealousy? Desire for revenge? Excess idealism? A wish to be a public avenger who punishes, "else she'll betray more men"?
5. What do you understand by Othello's calling himself "one that loved not wisely but too well" (V, ii, 340)?
6. In your view, does Othello's long speech in V, ii, 334–352 succeed in restoring his original dignity and nobility? Do you agree with Cassio (V, ii, 357) that Othello was "great of heart"?

GENERAL QUESTIONS

1. What motivates Iago to carry out his schemes? Do you find him a devil incarnate, a madman, or a rational human being?
2. Who besides Othello does Iago deceive? What is Desdemona's opinion of him? Emilia's? Cassio's (before Iago is found out)? To what do you attribute Iago's success as a deceiver?
3. How essential to the play is the fact that Othello is a black man, a Moor, and not a native of Venice?

4. In the introduction to his edition of the play in *The Complete Signet Classic Shakespeare* (New York: Harcourt Brace Jovanovich, 1972), Alvin Kernan has remarked:

Othello is probably the most neatly, the most formally constructed of Shakespeare's plays. Every character is, for example, balanced by another similar or contrasting character. Desdemona is balanced by her opposite, Iago; love and concern for others at one end of the scale, hatred and concern for self at the other.

Besides Desdemona and Iago, what other pairs of characters seem to strike balances?

5. "Never was any play fraught, like this of *Othello*, with improbabilities," wrote Thomas Rymer in a famous attack (*A Short View of Tragedy*, 1692). Although Othello is supposed to be a courageous general, he does nothing in the play that can be considered brave — "unless the killing himself, to avoid a death the Law was about to inflict upon him." When jealousy moves Othello to revenge himself on Cassio, he sends Iago to do his fighting for him, "and chooses himself to murder the silly woman his wife, that was like to make no resistance." Discuss.

6. Consider any passage of the play in which there is a shift from verse to prose, or from prose to verse. What is the effect of this shift?

7. Indicate a passage that you consider memorable for its poetry. Does the passage seem introduced for its own sake? Does it in any way advance the action of the play, express theme, or demonstrate character?

8. Does the play contain any *tragic recognition* — as discussed on page 943, a moment of terrible enlightenment, a "realization of the unthinkable"?

9. Does the downfall of Othello proceed from any flaw in his nature, or is his downfall entirely the work of Iago?

34 Comedy

Comedy, from the Greek *komos*, "a revel," is thought to have originated in festivities to celebrate spring: ritual performances in praise of Dionysus, god of fertility and wine. No one knows the origin of comedy for sure, but at least we do know that one ancient comic play, the *Cyclops* of Euripides, includes the jovial, drunken character of Silenus — the foster father of Dionysus — and a chorus garbed as goatlike satyrs, who tipple wine, sing, and dance. In drama, comedy may be broadly defined as whatever makes us laugh. A comedy may be a name for one entire play, or we may say that there is comedy in only part of a play — as in a comic character or a comic situation.

The best-known traditional emblem of drama — a pair of masks, one sorrowful (representing tragedy) and one smiling (representing comedy) — suggests that tragedy and comedy, although opposites, are close relatives. Often, comedy shows people getting into trouble through error or weakness; in this respect it is akin to tragedy. But an important difference between comedy and tragedy lies in the attitude toward human failing that is expected of us. When a main character in a comedy suffers from overweening pride, as does Oedipus, or if he fails to recognize that his bride-to-be is actually his mother, we laugh — something we would never do in watching a competent performance of *Oedipus Rex*. In a tragedy, some force — fate or the gods or the nature of things — relentlessly decrees suffering or death for the protagonist. In a comedy, the force impels the protagonist to realize, against all odds, eventual good fortune: success in love, sudden wealth, the humiliation of his enemies.

If Jean Anouilh is right in saying that one effect of a tragic situation is a certain serenity for the character or characters trapped in a hopeless bind,[1] then perhaps a comic situation generates serenity too — but certainly not for the characters embroiled in it. They may struggle as hard as Charles Chaplin trying to rescue a drunk from drowning, getting tangled in a rope, then slipping and falling into the water (to cite a classic film comedy, *City Lights*). In comedy, the char-

[1]See Anouilh's comment quoted in the discussion of tragedy, page 943.

acters usually achieve serenity only in the final moments, when at last the bullies are exposed, the money turns up, and the "nice guys" triumph. If we want to find serenity in comedy, we can probably find it in the audience, who know that somehow the character's struggles will turn out all right. Characters in silent movie comedies, for instance, lead a charmed existence. When the Keystone Kops whip their car across a railroad track a split second before a train roars by, the moviegoer does not worry about their safety. Even a horrible crash will not kill anyone, though it may turn tall men into midgets, or produce a few characters whose heads are interchanged.

"There are all kinds of humor," film comic Groucho Marx has declared. "Some is derisive, some sympathetic, and some merely whimsical. That is just what makes comedy so much harder to create than serious drama; people laugh in many different ways, and they cry only in one."[2] Whether or not it is correct to say that there is only one way of crying, the great film clown is right in saying that humor is various, and he accurately distinguishes one kind of comedy from another.

Derisive humor is basic to **satiric comedy**, in which human weakness or folly is ridiculed from a vantage point of supposedly enlightened superiority. Satiric comedy may be coolly malicious and gently biting, but it is always fundamentally hostile. An obvious illustration of hostility, from Ben Jonson's *Epicene; or, The Silent Woman* (1609), is this speech of the henpecked sea captain Otter, berating his wife:

> A most vile face! and yet she spends me forty pound a year in mercury and hogs' bones. All her teeth were made in the Blackfriars, both her eyebrows in the Strand, and her hair in Silver-street. Every part of the town owns a piece of her. . . . She takes herself asunder still when she goes to bed, into some twenty boxes; and about next day noon is put together again, like a great German clock: and so comes forth, and rings a tedious larum[3] to the whole house, and then is quiet again for an hour, but for her quarters.

The satirist is castigating not only some women's excessive reliance on makeup, but men's greed in marrying for money: Otter had previously revealed that he didn't love his wife; he loved her six thousand pounds in dowry.

Satiric comedy is at least as old as the classic plays of Aristophanes (about 448–380 B.C.), whose *Lysistrata* is another attack on human greed and on men who delude themselves that they wage war for unselfish reasons. Satiric playwrights, from Molière in seventeenth-century France to Bernard Shaw in twentieth-century Britain, have

---

[2] Statement contributed to Max Eastman, *The Enjoyment of Laughter* (New York: Simon and Schuster, 1936).
[3] alarm.

claimed that their satire has a corrective function: that by exposing vice or pretense they cause the spectators to avoid behavior of the sort pilloried on the stage. However, it is doubtful that very many playgoers have recognized their own follies in satiric plays and have then reformed.

Another traditional sort of comedy, **romantic comedy**, prefers sympathetic humor (to use another of Groucho Marx's categories). Its main characters are generally lovers, and its plot unfolds their successful attempt to be united. Unlike satiric comedy, romantic comedy portrays people with kindly indulgence, not withering contempt. It may take place in the everyday world or in some never-never land (such as the forest of Arden in Shakespeare's *As You Like It* or Prospero's island in *The Tempest*). Though a romantic comedy may depict folly and vice (especially in its villains and minor characters), entertainment, not moral correction, is usually its apparent concern. The writer of such a play seems to agree with George Meredith that "to love Comedy you must know the real world, and know men and women well enough not to expect too much of them, though you may still hope for good."[4]

COMEDY HIGH AND LOW

Comedy is sometimes divided into "high" and "low" categories. **High comedy** relies on wit and verbal humor rather than physical action. It appeals to a sophisticated audience fond of epigrams ("A fellow that lives in a windmill has not a more whimsical dwelling than the heart of a man that is lodged in a woman" — to quote an **epigram**, or short, sententious statement, from William Congreve's *The Way of the World*, 1700). A species of high comedy, the **comedy of manners,** or witty satire set in high society, was written by Congreve and other English playwrights of the **Restoration period** (the period following the year 1660, when Charles II, restored to the throne, reopened the London theaters, which had been closed by the Puritans). In more recent times, splendid comedies of manners have been written by Oscar Wilde — notably *The Importance of Being Earnest* (1895) — and by Bernard Shaw, whose play *Pygmalion* (1913), included in this chapter, contrasts life in the streets with life in aristocratic drawing-rooms and suggests that a flower-peddler differs from a duchess in little except manners and habits of speech.

Low comedy (to take the opposite extreme) places greater emphasis on physical action, and its verbal jokes do not require much

---

[4] "An Essay on Comedy" (1877), in *Comedy*, edited by Wylie Sypher (New York: Anchor Books, 1956).

intellect to appreciate. ("I've got a goat with no nose." — "No nose, eh? How does the poor thing smell?" — "Just terrible.") Low comedy includes several distinct types. One is the **burlesque,** a broadly humorous parody or travesty of another play or kind of play. (In America, *burlesque* is something else: a form of show business once popular featuring stripteases interspersed with bits of ribald low comedy.) Another valuable type of low comedy is the **farce,** generally a fast-moving play about extramarital relations. The master of farce was French playwright Georges Feydeau (1862–1921), whose plays are practically all plot, with only the flattest of characters: mindless ninnies who play frantic games of hide-and-seek in order not to be discovered by their spouses. **Slapstick comedy** (such as that of the Keystone Kops) is a kind of farce not necessarily involving adultery. Featuring practically all violent physical action, it takes its name from a device used by circus clowns: a bat with two boards that loudly clap together when one clown swats another. Although called "low," farce can have high-reaching implications. In a classic moment in a silent movie, *We Faw Down* (1928), when Laurel and Hardy's wives catch their husbands with two girl friends and chase the two clowns down a street lined with apartment houses, one wife fires a gun and the air is suddenly thick with dozens of pantsless men leaping out of every bedroom window. The joke reaches far (or as Henry James said of symbols, "casts long shadows"): it assumes a society in which infidelity is the norm, not the exception.

Many theories have been propounded to explain why we laugh; they tend to fall into certain familiar arguments. One school, maintained by French philosopher Henri Bergson, sees laughter as a form of ridicule, implying a feeling of disinterested superiority: all jokes are *on* somebody. In Bergson's view, laughter springs from situations in which we sense a conflict between some mechanical or rigid pattern of behavior and our sense of a more natural or "organic" kind of behavior that is possible.[5] An example might be the situation of silent film comic Buster Keaton in *The Admiral:* having launched a little boat that springs a leak, Keaton rigidly goes down with it, with frozen face. (The more natural and organic thing to do would be to swim for shore.) Other thinkers view laughter as our response to expectations fulfilled, or to expectations set up but then suddenly frustrated. Some hold it to be the expression of our delight in seeing our suppressed urges acted out (as when a comedian hurls an egg at a pompous stuffed shirt); some, to be our defensive reaction to a painful and disturbing truth. Perhaps Groucho Marx is right and we laugh for different reasons. At

[5] See Bergson's essay *Le Rire* (1900), translated as "Laughter" in Wylie Sypher's *Comedy* (previously cited).

least it seems certain that jokes, when theorists analyze them, cease to be funny — in fact, cease to exist.

Bernard Shaw (1856–1950)

PYGMALION   1913

PREFACE TO PYGMALION

A Professor of Phonetics°

As will be seen later on, Pygmalion needs, not a preface, but a sequel, which I have supplied in its due place.

The English have no respect for their language, and will not teach their children to speak it. They cannot spell it because they have nothing to spell it with but an old foreign alphabet of which only the consonants — and not all of them — have any agreed speech value. Consequently no man can teach himself what it should sound like from reading it; and it is impossible for an Englishman to open his mouth without making some other Englishman despise him. Most European languages are now accessible in black and white to foreigners: English and French are not thus accessible even to Englishmen and Frenchmen. The reformer we need most today is an energetic enthusiast: that is why I have made such a one the hero of a popular play.

There have been heroes of that kind crying in the wilderness for many years past. When I became interested in the subject towards the end of the eighteen-seventies, the illustrious Alexander Melville Bell, the inventor of Visible Speech, had emigrated to Canada, where his son invented the telephone; but Alexander J. Ellis was still a London Patriarch, with an impressive head always covered by a velvet skull cap, for which he would apologize to public meetings in a very courtly manner. He and Tito Pagliardini, another phonetic veteran, were men whom it was impossible to dislike. Henry Sweet, then a young man, lacked their sweetness of character: he was about as conciliatory to conventional mortals as Ibsen or Samuel Butler. His great ability as a phonetician (he was, I think, the best of them all at his job) would have entitled him to high official recognition, and perhaps enabled him to popularize his subject, but for his Satanic contempt for all academic dignitaries and persons in general who thought more of Greek than of phonetics. Once, in the days when the Imperial Institute rose in South Kensington, and Joseph Chamberlain was booming the Empire, I induced the editor of a leading monthly review to commission an article from Sweet on the imperial importance of his subject. When it arrived, it contained nothing but a savagely derisive attack on a professor of language and literature whose chair Sweet regarded as proper to a

A Professor of Phonetics: This professor is not a fictitious character. Shaw, who himself professed an interest in phonetic spelling and preached the need of reforming the English alphabet, is writing from his own experience.

phonetic expert only. The article, being libellous, had to be returned as impossible; and I had to renounce my dream of dragging its author into the limelight. When I met him afterwards, for the first time for many years, I found to my astonishment that he, who had been a quite tolerably presentable young man, had actually managed by sheer scorn to alter his personal appearance until he had become a sort of walking repudiation of Oxford and all its traditions. It must have been largely in his own despite that he was squeezed into something called a Readership of phonetics there. The future of phonetics rests probably with his pupils, who all swore by him; but nothing could bring the man himself into any sort of compliance with the university to which he nevertheless clung by divine right in an intensely Oxonian way. I daresay his papers, if he has left any, include some satires that may be published without too destructive results fifty years hence. He was, I believe, not in the least an ill-natured man: very much the opposite, I should say; but he would not suffer fools gladly; and to him all scholars who were not rabid phoneticians were fools.

Those who knew him will recognize in my third act the allusion to the Current Shorthand in which he used to write postcards. It may be acquired from a four and sixpenny manual published by the Clarendon Press. The postcards which Mrs. Higgins describes are such as I have received from Sweet. I would decipher a sound which a cockney would represent by *zerr*, and a Frenchman by *seu*, and then write demanding with some heat what on earth it meant. Sweet, with boundless contempt for my stupidity, would reply that it not only meant but obviously was the word Result, as no other word containing that sound, and capable of making sense with the context, existed in any language spoken on earth. That less expert mortals should require fuller indications was beyond Sweet's patience. Therefore, though the whole point of his Current Shorthand is that it can express every sound in the language perfectly, vowels as well as consonants, and that your hand has to make no stroke except the easy and current ones with which you write m, n, and u, l, p, and q, scribbling them at whatever angle comes easiest to you, his unfortunate determination to make this remarkable and quite legible script serve also as a shorthand reduced it in his own practice to the most inscrutable of cryptograms. His true objective was the provision of a full, accurate, legible script for our language; but he was led past that by his contempt for the popular Pitman system of shorthand, which he called the Pitfall system. The triumph of Pitman was a triumph of business organization: there was a weekly paper to persuade you to learn Pitman: there were cheap textbooks and exercise books and transcripts of speeches for you to copy, and schools where experienced teachers coached you up to the necessary proficiency. Sweet could not organize his market in that fashion. He might as well have been the Sybil who tore up the leaves of prophecy that nobody would attend to. The four and sixpenny manual, mostly in his lithographed handwriting, that was never vulgarly advertized, may perhaps some day be taken up by a syndicate and pushed upon the public as The Times pushed the Encyclopædia Britannica; but until then it will certainly not prevail against Pitman. I have bought three copies of it during my lifetime; and I am informed by the publishers that its cloistered existence is still a steady and healthy one. I actually learned the system two several times; and yet the shorthand in which I am writing these lines is Pitman's. And the reason is, that my secretary cannot transcribe Sweet, having been perforce taught in the schools of Pitman. In America I could use the commercially organized Gregg shorthand, which has taken a hint from Sweet by making its letters writable (current, Sweet would have called them) instead of having to be geometrically drawn like Pitman's; but all these systems, including Sweet's, are spoilt by making them available for verbatim reporting, in which complete and exact spelling and word division are impossible. A complete and exact phonetic script is neither practicable nor necessary for ordinary use; but if we enlarge our alphabet to the Russian size, and make our spelling as phonetic as Spanish, the advance will be prodigious.

Pygmalion Higgins is not a portrait of Sweet, to whom the adventure of Eliza Doolittle would have been impossible; still, as will be seen, there are touches of Sweet in the play. With Higgins's physique and temperament Sweet might have set the Thames on fire. As it was, he impressed himself professionally on Europe to an extent that made his comparative personal obscurity, and the failure of Oxford to do justice to his eminence, a puzzle to foreign specialists in his subject. I do not blame Oxford, because I think Oxford is quite right in demanding a certain social amenity from its nurslings (heaven knows it is not exorbitant in its requirement!); for although I well know how hard it is for a man of genius with a seriously underrated subject to maintain serene and kindly relations with the men who underrate it, and who keep all the best places for less important subjects which they profess without originality and sometimes without much capacity for them, still, if he overwhelms them with wrath and disdain, he cannot expect them to heap honors on him.

Of the later generations of phoneticians I know little. Among them towered Robert Bridges, to whom perhaps Higgins may owe his Miltonic sympathies, though here again I must disclaim all portraiture. But if the play makes the public aware that there are such people as phoneticians, and that they are among the most important people in England at present, it will serve its turn.

I wish to boast that Pygmalion has been an extremely successful play, both on stage and on screen, all over Europe and North America as well as at home. It is so intensely and deliberately didactic, and its subject is esteemed so dry, that I delight in throwing it at the heads of the wiseacres who repeat the parrot cry that art should never be didactic. It goes to prove my contention that great art can never be anything else.

Finally, and for the encouragement of people troubled with accents that cut them off from all high employment, I may add that the change wrought by Professor Higgins in the flower girl is neither impossible nor uncommon. The modern concierge's daughter who fulfills her ambition by playing the Queen of Spain in Ruy Blas at the Théâtre Français is only one of the many thousands of men and women who have sloughed off their native dialects and acquired a new tongue. Our West End shop assistants and domestic servants are bilingual. But the thing has to be done scientifically, or the last state of the aspirant may be worse than the first. An honest slum dialect is more tolerable than the attempts of phonetically untaught persons to imitate the plutocracy. Ambitious flower-girls who read this play must not imagine that they can pass themselves off as fine ladies by untutored imitation. They must learn their alphabet over again, and differently, from a phonetic expert. Imitation will only make them ridiculous.

> *Note for Technicians.* A complete representation of the play as printed in this edition is technically possible only on the cinema screen or on stages furnished with exceptionally elaborate machinery. For ordinary theatrical use the scenes separated by rows of asterisks are to be omitted.
>
> In the dialogue an e upside down indicates the indefinite vowel, sometimes called obscure or neutral, for which, though it is one of the commonest sounds in English speech, our wretched alphabet has no letter.

ACT I

> *London at 11.15 P.M. Torrents of heavy summer rain. Cab whistles blowing frantically in all directions. Pedestrians running for shelter into the portico of St. Paul's church (not Wren's cathedral but Inigo Jones's church in Covent Garden vegetable market), among them a lady and her daughter in evening dress. All are peering out gloomily at the rain, except one man with his back turned to the rest, wholly preoccupied with a notebook in which he is writing.*
> *The church clock strikes the first quarter.*

The Daughter (in the space between the central pillars, close to the one on her left): I'm getting chilled to the bone. What can Freddy be doing all this time? He's been gone twenty minutes.

The Mother (on her daughter's right): Not so long. But he ought to have got us a cab by this.

A Bystander (on the lady's right): He wont get no cab not until half-past eleven, missus, when they come back after dropping their theatre fares.

The Mother: But we must have a cab. We cant stand here until half-past eleven. It's too bad.

The Bystander: Well, it aint my fault, missus.

The Daughter: If Freddy had a bit of gumption, he would have got one at the theatre door.

The Mother: What could he have done, poor boy?

The Daughter: Other people got cabs. Why couldnt he?

> *Freddy rushes in out of the rain from the Southampton Street side, and comes between them closing a dripping umbrella. He is a young man of twenty, in evening dress, very wet round the ankles.*

The Daughter: Well, havnt you got a cab?

Freddy: Theres not one to be had for love or money.

The Mother: Oh, Freddy, there must be one. You cant have tried.

The Daughter: It's too tiresome. Do you expect us to go and get one ourselves?

Freddy: I tell you theyre all engaged. The rain was so sudden: nobody was prepared; and everybody had to take a cab. Ive been to Charing Cross one way and nearly to Ludgate Circus the other; and they were all engaged.

The Mother: Did you try Trafalgar Square?

Freddy: There wasn't one at Trafalgar Square.

The Daughter: Did you try?

Freddy: I tried as far as Charing Cross Station. Did you expect me to walk to Hammersmith?

The Daughter: You havnt tried at all.

The Mother: You really are very helpless, Freddy. Go again; and dont come back until you have found a cab.

Freddy: I shall simply get soaked for nothing.

The Daughter: And what about us? Are we to stay here all night in this draught, with next to nothing on? You selfish pig —

Freddy: Oh, very well: I'll go, I'll go. (*He opens his umbrella and dashes off Strandwards, but comes into collision with a flower girl who is hurrying in for shelter, knocking her basket out of her hands. A blinding flash of lightning, followed instantly by a rattling peal of thunder, orchestrates the incident.*)

The Flower Girl: Nah then, Freddy: look wh' y' gowin, deah.

Freddy: Sorry. (*He rushes off.*)

The Flower Girl (picking up her scattered flowers and replacing them in the basket): Theres menners f' yer! Tǝ-oo banches o voylets trod into the mad. (*She sits down on the plinth of the column, sorting her flowers, on the lady's right. She is not at all a romantic figure. She is perhaps eighteen, perhaps twenty, hardly older. She wears a little sailor hat of black straw that has long been exposed to the dust and soot of London and has seldom if ever been brushed. Her hair needs washing rather badly: its mousy color can hardly be natural. She wears a shoddy black coat that reaches nearly to her knees and is shaped to her waist. She has a brown skirt with a coarse apron. Her boots are much the worse for wear. She is no doubt as clean as she can afford to be; but compared to the ladies she is very dirty. Her features are no worse than theirs; but their condition leaves something to be desired; and she needs the services of a dentist.*)

The Mother: How do you know that my son's name is Freddy, pray?

The Flower Girl: Ow, eez yǝ-ooa san, is e? Wal, fewd dan y' dǝ-ooty bawmz a mather should, eed now bettern to spawl a pore gel's flahrzn than ran awy athaht pyin. Will ye-oo py me f'them? (*Here, with apologies, this desperate attempt to represent her dialect without a phonetic alphabet must be abandoned as unintelligible outside London.*)

The Daughter: Do nothing of the sort, mother. The idea!

The Mother: Please allow me, Clara. Have you any pennies?

The Daughter: No. Ive nothing smaller than sixpence.

The Flower Girl (hopefully): I can give you change for a tanner, kind lady.

The Mother (to Clara): Give it to me. (*Clara parts reluctantly.*) Now (*to the girl*). This is for your flowers.

The Flower Girl: Thank you kindly, lady.

The Daughter: Make her give you the change. These things are only a penny a bunch.

The Mother: Do hold your tongue, Clara. (*To the girl.*) You can keep the change.

The Flower Girl: Oh, thank you, lady.

The Mother: Now tell me how you know that young gentleman's name.

The Flower Girl: I didnt.

The Mother: I heard you call him by it. Dont try to deceive me.

The Flower Girl (protesting): Who's trying to deceive you? I called him Freddy or Charlie same as you might yourself if you was talking to a stranger and wished to be pleasant.

The Daughter: Sixpence thrown away! Really, mamma, you might have spared Freddy that. *(She retreats in disgust behind the pillar.)*

An elderly gentleman of the amiable military type rushes into the shelter, and closes a dripping umbrella. He is in the same plight as Freddy, very wet about the ankles. He is in evening dress, with a light overcoat. He takes the place left vacant by the daughter.

The Gentleman: Phew!

The Mother (to the gentleman): Oh, sir, is there any sign of its stopping?

The Gentleman: I'm afraid not. It started worse than ever about two minutes ago. *(He goes to the plinth beside the flower girl; puts up his foot on it; and stoops to turn down his trouser ends.)*

The Mother: Oh dear! *(She retires sadly and joins her daughter.)*

The Flower Girl (taking advantage of the military gentleman's proximity to establish friendly relations with him): If it's worse, it's a sign it's nearly over. So cheer up, Captain; and buy a flower off a poor girl.

The Gentleman: I'm sorry. I havnt any change.

The Flower Girl: I can give you change, Captain.

The Gentleman: For a sovereign? Ive nothing less.

The Flower Girl: Garn! Oh do buy a flower off me, Captain. I can change half-a-crown. Take this for tuppence.

The Gentleman: Now dont be troublesome: theres a good girl. *(Trying his pockets.)* I really havnt any change — Stop: heres three hapence, if thats any use to you. *(He retreats to the other pillar.)*

The Flower Girl (disappointed, but thinking three half-pence better than nothing): Thank you, sir.

The Bystander (to the girl): You be careful: give him a flower for it. Theres a bloke here behind taking down every blessed word youre saying. *(All turn to the man who is taking notes.)*

The Flower Girl (springing up terrified): I aint done nothing wrong by speaking to the gentleman. Ive a right to sell flowers if I keep off the kerb. *(Hysterically.)* I'm a respectable girl: so help me, I never spoke to him except to ask him to buy a flower off me.

General hubbub, mostly sympathetic to the flower girl, but deprecating her excessive sensibility. Cries of Dont start hollerin. Who's hurting you? Nobody's going to touch you. Whats the good of fussing? Steady on. Easy easy, etc., *come from the elderly staid spectators, who pat her comfortingly. Less patient ones bid her shut her head, or ask her roughly what is wrong with her. A remoter group, not knowing what the matter is, crowd in and increase the noise with question and answer:* Whats the row? What-she do? Where is he? A tec taking her down. What! him? Yes: him over there: Took money off the gentleman, *etc.*

The Flower Girl (breaking through them to the gentleman, crying wildly): Oh, sir, dont let him charge me. You dunno what it means to me. Theyll take away my character and drive me on the streets for speaking to gentlemen. They —

The Note Taker (coming forward on her right, the rest crowding after him): There! there! there! there! who's hurting you, you silly girl? What do you take me for?

The Bystander: It's aw rawt: e's a genleman: look at his bǝ-oots. *(Explaining to the note taker.)* She thought you was a copper's nark, sir.

The Note Taker (with quick interest): Whats a copper's nark?

The Bystander (inapt at definition): It's a — well, it's a copper's nark, as you might say. What else would you call it? A sort of informer.

The Flower Girl (still hysterical): I take my Bible oath I never said a word —

The Note Taker (overbearing but good-humored): Oh, shut up, shut up. Do I look like a policeman?

The Flower Girl (far from reassured): Then what did you take down my words for? How do I know whether you took me down right? You just shew me what youve wrote about me. *(The note taker opens his book and holds it steadily under her nose, though the pressure of the mob trying to read it over his shoulders would upset a weaker man.)* Whats that? That aint proper writing. I cant read that.

The Note Taker: I can. *(Reads, reproducing her pronunciation exactly.)* "Cheer ap, Keptin; n' baw ya flahr orf a pore gel."

The Flower Girl (much distressed): It's because I called him Captain. I meant no harm. *(To the gentleman.)* Oh, sir, dont let him lay a charge agen me for a word like that. You —

The Gentleman: Charge! I make no charge. *(To the note taker.)* Really, sir, if you are a detective, you need not begin protecting me against molestation by young women until I ask you. Anybody could see that the girl meant no harm.

The Bystanders Generally (demonstrating against police espionage): Course they could. What business is it of yours? You mind your own affairs. He wants promotion, he does. Taking down people's words! Girl never said a word to him. What harm if she did? Nice thing a girl cant shelter from the rain without being insulted, etc., etc., etc. *(She is conducted by the more sympathetic demonstrators back to her plinth, where she resumes her seat and struggles with her emotion.)*

The Bystander: He aint a tec. He's a blooming busybody: thats what he is. I tell you, look at his bǝ-oots.

The Note Taker (turning on him genially): And how are all your people down at Selsey?

The Bystander (suspiciously): Who told you my people come from Selsey?

The Note Taker: Never you mind. They did. *(To the girl.)* How do you come to be up so far east? You were born in Lisson Grove.

The Flower Girl (appalled): Oh, what harm is there in my leaving Lisson Grove? It wasnt fit for a pig to live in; and I had to pay four-and-six a week. *(In tears.)* Oh, boo — hoo — oo —

The Note Taker: Live where you like; but stop that noise.

The Gentleman (to the girl): Come, come! he cant touch you: you have a right to live where you please.

A Sarcastic Bystander (thrusting himself between the note taker and the gentleman): Park Lane, for instance. I'd like to go into the Housing Question with you, I would.

The Flower Girl (subsiding into a brooding melancholy over her basket, and talking very low-spiritedly to herself): I'm a good girl, I am.

The Sarcastic Bystander (not attending to her): Do you know where I come from?

The Note Taker (promptly): Hoxton.

Titterings. Popular interest in the note taker's performance increases.

The Sarcastic One (amazed): Well, who said I didnt? Bly me! you know everything, you do.

The Flower Girl (still nursing her sense of injury): Aint no call to meddle with me, he aint.

The Bystander (to her): Of course he aint. Dont you stand it from him. *(To the note taker.)* See here: what call have you to know about people what never offered to meddle with you?

The Flower Girl: Let him say what he likes. I dont want to have no truck with him.

The Bystander: You take us for dirt under your feet, dont you? Catch you taking liberties with a gentleman!

The Sarcastic Bystander: Yes: tell him where he come from if you want to go fortune-telling.

The Note Taker: Cheltenham, Harrow, Cambridge, and India.

The Gentleman: Quite right.

Great laughter. Reaction in the note taker's favor. Exclamations of He knows all about it. Told him proper. Hear him tell the toff where he come from? *etc.*

The Gentleman: May I ask, sir, do you do this for your living at a music hall?

The Note Taker: I've thought of that. Perhaps I shall some day.

The rain has stopped; and the persons on the outside of the crowd begin to drop off.

The Flower Girl (resenting the reaction): He's no gentleman, he aint, to interfere with a poor girl.

The Daughter (out of patience, pushing her way rudely to the front and displacing the gentleman, who politely retires to the other side of the pillar): What on earth is Freddy doing? I shall get pneumownia if I stay in this draught any longer.

The Note Taker (to himself, hastily making a note of her pronunciation of "monia"): Earlscourt.

The Daughter (violently): Will you please keep your impertinent remarks to yourself.

The Note Taker: Did I say that out loud? I didnt mean to. I beg your pardon. Your mother's Epsom, unmistakeably.

The Mother (advancing between the daughter and the note taker): How very curious! I was brought up in Largelady Park, near Epsom.

The Note Taker (uproariously amused): Ha! ha! What a devil of a name! Excuse me. *(To the daughter.)* You want a cab, do you?

The Daughter: Dont dare speak to me.

The Mother: Oh please, please, Clara. *(Her daughter repudiates her with an angry shrug and retires haughtily.)* We should be so grateful to you, sir, if you found us a cab. *(The note taker produces a whistle.)* Oh, thank you. *(She joins her daughter.)*

The note taker blows a piercing blast.

The Sarcastic Bystander: There! I knowed he was a plainclothes copper.

The Bystander: That aint a police whistle: thats a sporting whistle.

The Flower Girl *(still preoccupied with her wounded feelings):* He's no right to take away my character. My character is the same to me as any lady's.

The Note Taker: I dont know whether youve noticed it; but the rain stopped about two minutes ago.

The Bystander: So it has. Why didn't you say so before? and us losing our time listening to your silliness! *(He walks off towards the Strand.)*

The Sarcastic Bystander: I can tell where you come from. You come from Anwell. Go back there.

The Note Taker *(helpfully):* Hanwell.

The Sarcastic Bystander *(affecting great distinction of speech):* Thenk you, teacher. Haw haw! So long. *(He touches his hat with mock respect and strolls off.)*

The Flower Girl: Frightening people like that! How would he like it himself?

The Mother: It's quite fine now, Clara. We can walk to a motor bus. Come. *(She gathers her skirts above her ankles and hurries off towards the Strand.)*

The Daughter: But the cab — *(Her mother is out of hearing.)* Oh, how tiresome! *(She follows angrily.)*

All the rest have gone except the note taker, the gentleman, and the flower girl, who sits arranging her basket, and still pitying herself in murmurs.

The Flower Girl: Poor girl! Hard enough for her to live without being worried and chivied.

The Gentleman *(returning to his former place on the note taker's left):* How do you do it, if I may ask?

The Note Taker: Simply phonetics. The science of speech. Thats my profession: also my hobby. Happy is the man who can make a living by his hobby! You can spot an Irishman or a Yorkshireman by his brogue. *I* can place any man within six miles. I can place him within two miles in London. Sometimes within two streets.

The Flower Girl: Ought to be ashamed of himself, unmanly coward!

The Gentleman: But is there a living in that?

The Note Taker: Oh yes. Quite a fat one. This is an age of upstarts. Men begin in Kentish Town with £80 a year, and end in Park Lane with a hundred thousand. They want to drop Kentish Town; but they give themselves away every time they open their mouths. Now I can teach them —

The Flower Girl: Let him mind his own business and leave a poor girl —

The Note Taker *(explosively):* Woman: cease this detestable boohooing instantly; or else seek the shelter of some other place of worship.

The Flower Girl *(with feeble defiance):* Ive a right to be here if I like, same as you.

The Note Taker: A woman who utters such depressing and disgusting sounds has no right to be anywhere — no right to live. Remember that you are a human being with a soul and the divine gift of articulate speech: that your native language is the language of Shakespear and Milton and The Bible; and dont sit there crooning like a bilious pigeon.

The Flower Girl (quite overwhelmed, looking up at him in mingled wonder and deprecation without daring to raise her head): Ah-ah-ah-ow-ow-ow-oo!

The Note Taker (whipping out his book): Heavens! what a sound! *(He writes; then holds out the book and reads, reproducing her vowels exactly.)* Ah-ah-ah-ow-ow-ow-oo!

The Flower Girl (tickled by the performance, and laughing in spite of herself): Garn!

The Note Taker: You see this creature with her kerbstone English: the English that will keep her in the gutter to the end of her days. Well, sir, in three months I could pass that girl off as a duchess at an ambassador's garden party. I could even get her a place as lady's maid or shop assistant, which requires better English.

The Flower Girl: What's that you say?

The Note Taker: Yes, you squashed cabbage leaf, you disgrace to the noble architecture of these columns, you incarnate insult to the English language: I could pass you off as the Queen of Sheba. *(To the Gentleman.)* Can you believe that?

The Gentleman: Of course I can. I am myself a student of Indian dialects; and —

The Note Taker (eagerly): Are you? Do you know Colonel Pickering, the author of Spoken Sanscrit?

The Gentleman: I am Colonel Pickering. Who are you?

The Note Taker: Henry Higgins, author of Higgins's Universal Alphabet.

Pickering (with enthusiasm): I came from India to meet you.

Higgins: I was going to India to meet you.

Pickering: Where do you live?

Higgins: 27A Wimpole Street. Come and see me tomorrow.

Pickering: I'm at the Carlton. Come with me now and lets have a jaw over some supper.

Higgins: Right you are.

The Flower Girl (to Pickering, as he passes her): Buy a flower, kind gentleman. I'm short for my lodging.

Pickering: I really havnt any change. I'm sorry. *(He goes away.)*

Higgins (shocked at the girl's mendacity): Liar. You said you could change half-a-crown.

The Flower Girl (rising in desperation): You ought to be stuffed with nails, you ought. *(Flinging the basket at his feet.)* Take the whole blooming basket for sixpence.

The church clock strikes the second quarter.

Higgins (hearing in it the voice of God, rebuking him for his Pharisaic want of charity to the poor girl): A reminder. *(He raises his hat solemnly; then throws a handful of money into the basket and follows Pickering.)*

The Flower Girl (picking up a half-crown): Ah-ow-ooh! *(Picking up a couple of florins.)* Aaah-ow-ooh! *(Picking up several coins.)* Aaaaah-ow-ooh! *(Picking up a half-sovereign.)* Aaaaaaaaaaaah-ow-ooh!!!

Freddy (springing out of a taxicab): Got one at last. Hallo! *(To the girl.)* Where are the two ladies that were here?

The Flower Girl: They walked to the bus when the rain stopped.

Freddy: And left me with a cab on my hands! Damnation!

The Flower Girl (with grandeur): Never mind, young man. I'm going home in a taxi. *(She sails off to the cab. The driver puts his hand behind him and holds the door firmly shut against her. Quite understanding his mistrust, she shews him her handful of money.)* A taxi fare aint no object to me, Charlie. *(He grins and opens the door.)* Here. What about the basket?

The Taximan: Give it here. Tuppence extra.

Liza: No: I dont want nobody to see it. *(She crushes it into the cab and gets in, continuing the conversation through the window.)* Goodbye, Freddy.

Freddy (dazedly raising his hat): Goodbye.

Taximan: Where to?

Liza: Bucknam Pellis [Buckingham Palace].

Taximan: What d'ye mean — Bucknam Pellis?

Liza: Dont you know where it is? In the Green Park, where the King lives. Goodbye, Freddy. Dont let me keep you standing there. Goodbye.

Freddy: Goodbye. *(He goes.)*

Taximan: Here? Whats this about Bucknam Pellis? What business have you at Bucknam Pellis?

Liza: Of course I havnt none. But I wasn't going to let him know that. You drive me home.

Taximan: And wheres home?

Liza: Angel Court, Drury Lane, next Meiklejohn's oil shop.

Taximan: That sounds more like it, Judy. *(He drives off.)*

* * * * *

Let us follow the taxi to the entrance to Angel Court, a narrow little archway between two shops, one of them Meiklejohn's oil shop. When it stops there, Eliza gets out, dragging her basket with her.

Liza: How much?

Taximan (indicating the taximeter): Cant you read? A shilling.

Liza: A shilling for two minutes!!

Taximan: Two minutes or ten: it's all the same.

Liza: Well, I dont call it right.

Taximan: Ever been in a taxi before?

Liza (with dignity): Hundreds and thousands of times, young man.

Taximan (laughing at her): Good for you, Judy. Keep the shilling, darling, with best love from all at home. Good luck! *(He drives off.)*

Liza (humiliated): Impidence!

> She picks up the basket and trudges up the alley with it to her lodging: a small room with very old wall paper hanging loose in the damp places. A broken pane in the window is mended with paper. A portrait of a popular actor and a fashion plate of ladies' dresses, all wildly beyond poor Eliza's means, both torn from newspapers, are pinned up on the wall. A birdcage hangs in the window; but its tenant died long ago: it remains as a memorial only.
>
> These are the only visible luxuries: the rest is the irreducible minimum of poverty's needs: a wretched bed heaped with all sorts of coverings that have any

warmth in them, a draped packing case with a basin and jug on it and a little looking glass over it, a chair and table, the refuse of some suburban kitchen, and an American alarum clock on the shelf above the unused fireplace: the whole lighted with a gas lamp with a penny in the slot meter. Rent: four shillings a week.

Here Eliza, chronically weary, but too excited to go to bed, sits, counting her new riches and dreaming and planning what to do with them, until the gas goes out, when she enjoys for the first time the sensation of being able to put in another penny without grudging it. This prodigal mood does not extinguish her gnawing sense of the need for economy sufficiently to prevent her from calculating that she can dream and plan in bed more cheaply and warmly than sitting up without a fire. So she takes off her shawl and skirt and adds them to the miscellaneous bedclothes. Then she kicks off her shoes and gets into bed without any further change.

ACT II

Next day at 11 A.M. Higgins's laboratory in Wimpole Street. It is a room on the first floor, looking on the street, and was meant for the drawing room. The double doors are in the middle of the back wall; and persons entering find in the corner to their right two tall file cabinets at right angles to one another against the walls. In this corner stands a flat writing-table, on which are a phonograph, a laryngoscope, a row of tiny organ pipes with a bellows, a set of lamp chimneys for singing flames with burners attached to a gas plug in the wall by an indiarubber tube, several tuning-forks of different sizes, a life-size image of half a human head, shewing in section the vocal organs, and a box containing a supply of wax cylinders for the phonograph.

Further down the room, on the same side, is a fireplace, with a comfortable leather-covered easy-chair at the side of the hearth nearest the door, and a coal-scuttle. There is a clock on the mantelpiece. Between the fireplace and the phonograph table is a stand for newspapers.

On the other side of the central door, to the left of the visitor, is a cabinet of shallow drawers. On it is a telephone and the telephone directory. The corner beyond, and most of the side wall, is occupied by a grand piano, with the keyboard at the end furthest from the door, and a bench for the players extending the full length of the keyboard. On the piano is a dessert dish heaped with fruit and sweets, mostly chocolates.

The middle of the room is clear. Besides the easy-chair, the piano bench, and two chairs at the phonograph table, there is one stray chair. It stands near the fireplace. On the walls, engravings: mostly Piranesis and mezzotint portraits. No paintings.

Pickering is seated at the table, putting down some cards and a tuning-fork which he has been using. Higgins is standing up near him, closing two or three file drawers which are hanging out. He appears in the morning light as a robust, vital, appetizing sort of man of forty or thereabouts, dressed in a professional-looking black frock-coat with a white linen collar and black silk tie. He is of energetic, scientific type, heartily, even violently interested in everything that can be studied as a scientific subject, and careless about himself and other people, including their feelings. He is, in fact, but for his years and size, rather like a very impetuous baby "taking notice" eagerly and loudly, and requiring almost as much watching to keep him out of unintended mischief. His manner varies from genial bullying when he is in a good humor to stormy petulance when anything goes wrong; but he is so entirely frank and void of malice that he remains likeable even in his least reasonable moments.

Higgins (as he shuts the last drawer): Well, I think thats the whole show.

Pickering: It's really amazing. I havnt taken half of it in, you know.

Higgins: Would you like to go over any of it again?

Pickering (rising and coming to the fireplace, where he plants himself with his back to the fire): No, thank you: not now. I'm quite done up for this morning.

Higgins (following him, and standing beside him on his left): Tired of listening to sounds?

Pickering: Yes. It's a fearful strain. I rather fancied myself because I can pronounce twenty-four distinct vowel sounds; but your hundred and thirty beat me. I cant hear a bit of difference between most of them.

Higgins (chuckling, and going over to the piano to eat sweets): Oh, that comes with practice. You hear no difference at first; but you keep on listening, and presently you find theyre all as different as A from B. *(Mrs. Pearce looks in: she is Higgins's housekeeper.)* Whats the matter?

Mrs. Pearce (hesitating, evidently perplexed): A young woman asks to see you, sir.

Higgins: A young woman! What does she want?

Mrs. Pearce: Well, sir, she says youll be glad to see her when you know what she's come about. She's quite a common girl, sir. Very common indeed. I should have sent her away, only I thought perhaps you wanted her to talk into your machines. I hope Ive not done wrong; but really you see such queer people sometimes — youll excuse me, I'm sure, sir —

Higgins: Oh, thats all right, Mrs. Pearce. Has she an interesting accent?

Mrs. Pearce: Oh, something dreadful, sir, really. I dont know how you can take an interest in it.

Higgins (to Pickering): Lets have her up. Shew her up, Mrs. Pearce. *(He rushes across to his working table and picks out a cylinder to use on the phonograph.)*

Mrs. Pearce (only half resigned to it): Very well, sir. It's for you to say. *(She goes downstairs.)*

Higgins: This is rather a bit of luck. I'll shew you how I make records. We'll set her talking; and I'll take it down first in Bell's Visible Speech; then in broad Romic; and then we'll get her on the phonograph so that you can turn her on as often as you like with the written transcript before you.

Mrs. Pearce (returning): This is the young woman, sir.

The flower girl enters in state. She has a hat with three ostrich feathers, orange, sky-blue, and red. She has a nearly clean apron, and the shoddy coat has been tidied a little. The pathos of this deplorable figure, with its innocent vanity and consequential air, touches Pickering, who has already straightened himself in the presence of Mrs. Pearce. But as to Higgins, the only distinction he makes between men and women is that when he is neither bullying nor exclaiming to the heavens against some feather-weight cross, he coaxes women as a child coaxes its nurse when it wants to get anything out of her.

Higgins (*brusquely, recognizing her with unconcealed disappointment, and at once, babylike, making an intolerable grievance of it*): Why, this is the girl I jotted down last night. She's no use: I've got all the records I want of the Lisson Grove lingo; and I'm not going to waste another cylinder on it. (*To the girl.*) Be off with you: I dont want you.

The *Flower Girl*: Dont you be so saucy. You aint heard what I come for yet. (*To Mrs. Pearce, who is waiting at the door for further instructions.*) Did you tell him I come in a taxi?

Mrs. Pearce: Nonsense, girl! what do you think a gentleman like Mr. Higgins cares what you came in?

The *Flower Girl*: Oh, we are so proud! He aint above giving lessons, not him: I heard him say so. Well, I aint come here to ask for any compliment; and if my money's not good enough I can go elsewhere.

Higgins: Good enough for what?

The *Flower Girl*: Good enough for yə-oo. Now you know, dont you? I've come to have lessons, I am. And to pay for em tə-oo: make no mistake.

Higgins (*stupent*): Well!!! (*Recovering his breath with a gasp.*) What do you expect me to say to you?

The *Flower Girl*: Well, if you was a gentleman, you might ask me to sit down, I think. Dont I tell you I'm bringing you business?

Higgins: Pickering: shall we ask this baggage to sit down, or shall we throw her out of the window?

The *Flower Girl* (*running away in terror to the piano, where she turns at bay*): Ah-ah-oh-ow-ow-ow-oo! (*Wounded and whimpering.*) I wont be called a baggage when Ive offered to pay like any lady.

Motionless, the two men stare at her from the other side of the room, amazed.

Pickering (*gently*): But what is it you want?

The *Flower Girl*: I want to be a lady in a flower shop stead of sellin at the corner of Tottenham Court Road. But they wont take me unless I can talk more genteel. He said he could teach me. Well, here I am ready to pay him — not asking any favor — and he treats me zif I was dirt.

Mrs. Pearce: How can you be such a foolish ignorant girl as to think you could afford to pay Mr. Higgins?

The *Flower Girl*: Why shouldnt I? I know what lessons cost as well as you do; and I'm ready to pay.

Higgins: How much?

The *Flower Girl* (*coming back to him, triumphant*): Now youre talking! I thought youd come off it when you saw a chance of getting back a bit of what you chucked at me last night. (*Confidentially.*) Youd had a drop in, hadnt you?

Higgins (*peremptorily*): Sit down.

The *Flower Girl*: Oh, if youre going to make a compliment of it —

Higgins (*thundering at her*): Sit down.

Mrs. Pearce (*severely*): Sit down, girl. Do as youre told.

The *Flower Girl*: Ah-ah-ah-ow-ow-oo! (*She stands, half rebellious, half bewildered.*)

Pickering (very courteous): Wont you sit down? *(He places the stray chair near the hearthrug between himself and Higgins.)*

Liza (coyly): Dont mind if I do. *(She sits down. Pickering returns to the hearth-rug.)*

Higgins: Whats your name?

The Flower Girl: Liza Doolittle.

Higgins (declaiming gravely):

> Eliza, Elizabeth, Betsy and Bess,
> They went to the woods to get a bird's nes':

Pickering: They found a nest with four eggs in it:

Higgins: They took one apiece, and left three in it.

They laugh heartily at their own fun.

Liza: Oh, dont be silly.

Mrs. Pearce (placing herself behind Eliza's chair): You mustnt speak to the gentleman like that.

Liza: Well, why wont he speak sensible to me?

Higgins: Come back to business. How much do you propose to pay me for the lessons?

Liza: Oh, I know whats right. A lady friend of mine gets French lessons for eighteenpence an hour from a real French gentleman. Well, you wouldnt have the face to ask me the same for teaching me my own language as you would for French; so I wont give more than a shilling. Take it or leave it.

Higgins (walking up and down the room, rattling his keys and his cash in his pockets): You know, Pickering, if you consider a shilling, not as a simple shilling, but as a percentage of this girl's income, it works out as fully equivalent to sixty or seventy guineas from a millionaire.

Pickering: How so?

Higgins: Figure it out. A millionaire has about £150 a day. She earns about half-a-crown.

Liza (haughtily): Who told you I only —

Higgins (continuing): She offers me two-fifths of her day's income for a lesson. Two-fifths of a millionaire's income for a day would be somewhere about £60. It's handsome. By George, it's enormous! it's the biggest offer I ever had.

Liza (rising, terrified): Sixty pounds! What are you talking about? I never offered you sixty pounds. Where would I get —

Higgins: Hold your tongue.

Liza (weeping): But I aint got sixty pounds. Oh —

Mrs. Pearce: Dont cry, you silly girl. Sit down. Nobody is going to touch your money.

Higgins: Somebody is going to touch you, with a broomstick, if you dont stop snivelling. Sit down.

Liza (obeying slowly): Ah-ah-ah-ow-oo-o! One would think you was my father.

Higgins: If I decide to teach you, I'll be worse than two fathers to you. Here! *(He offers her his silk handkerchief.)*

Liza: Whats this for?

Higgins: To wipe your eyes. To wipe any part of your face that feels moist. Remember: thats your handkerchief; and thats your sleeve. Dont mistake the one for the other if you wish to become a lady in a shop.

> *Liza, utterly bewildered, stares helplessly at him.*

Mrs. Pearce: It's no use talking to her like that, Mr. Higgins: she doesnt understand you. Besides, youre quite wrong: she doesnt do it that way at all. *(She takes the handkerchief.)*

Liza (snatching it): Here! You give me that handkerchief. He gev it to me, not to you.

Pickering (laughing): He did. I think it must be regarded as her property, Mrs. Pearce.

Mrs. Pearce (resigning herself): Serve you right, Mr. Higgins.

Pickering: Higgins: I'm interested. What about the ambassador's garden party? I'll say youre the greatest teacher alive if you make that good. I'll bet you all the expenses of the experiment you cant do it. And I'll pay for the lessons.

Liza: Oh, you are real good. Thank you, Captain.

Higgins (tempted, looking at her): It's almost irresistible. She's so deliciously low — so horribly dirty —

Liza (protesting extremely): Ah-ah-ah-ah-ow-ow-oo-oo!!! I aint dirty: I washed my face and hands afore I come, I did.

Pickering: Youre certainly not going to turn her head with flattery, Higgins.

Mrs. Pearce (uneasy): Oh, dont say that, sir: theres more ways than one of turning a girl's head; and nobody can do it better than Mr. Higgins, though he may not always mean it. I do hope, sir, you wont encourage him to do anything foolish.

Higgins (becoming excited as the idea grows on him): What is life but a series of inspired follies? The difficulty is to find them to do. Never lose a chance: it doesnt come every day. I shall make a duchess of this draggletailed guttersnipe.

Liza (strongly deprecating this view of her): Ah-ah-ah-ow-ow-oo!

Higgins (carried away): Yes: in six months — in three if she has a good ear and a quick tongue — I'll take her anywhere and pass her off as anything. We'll start today: now! this moment! Take her away and clean her, Mrs. Pearce. Monkey Brand, if it wont come off any other way. Is there a good fire in the kitchen?

Mrs. Pearce (protesting): Yes; but —

Higgins (storming on): Take all her clothes off and burn them. Ring up Whitely or somebody for new ones. Wrap her up in brown paper til they come.

Liza: Youre no gentleman, youre not, to talk of such things. I'm a good girl, I am; and I know what the like of you are, I do.

Higgins: We want none of your Lisson Grove prudery here, young woman. Youve got to learn to behave like a duchess. Take her away, Mrs. Pearce. If she gives you any trouble, wallop her.

Liza (springing up and running between Pickering and Mrs. Pearce for protection): No! I'll call the police, I will.

Mrs. Pearce: But Ive no place to put her.

Higgins: Put her in the dustbin.

Liza: Ah-ah-ah-ow-ow-oo!

Pickering: Oh come, Higgins! be reasonable.

Mrs. Pearce (resolutely): You must be reasonable, Mr. Higgins: really you must. You cant walk over everybody like this.

Higgins, thus scolded, subsides. The hurricane is succeeded by a zephyr of amiable surprise.

Higgins (with professional exquisiteness of modulation): I walk over everybody! My dear Mrs. Pearce, my dear Pickering, I never had the slightest intention of walking over anyone. All I propose is that we should be kind to this poor girl. We must help her to prepare and fit herself for her new station in life. If I did not express myself clearly it was because I did not wish to hurt her delicacy, or yours.

Liza, reassured, steals back to her chair.

Mrs. Pearce (to Pickering): Well, did you ever hear anything like that, sir?

Pickering (laughing heartily): Never, Mrs. Pearce: never.

Higgins (patiently): Whats the matter?

Mrs. Pearce: Well, the matter is, sir, that you cant take a girl up like that as if you were picking up a pebble on the beach.

Higgins: Why not?

Mrs. Pearce: Why not! But you dont know anything about her. What about her parents? She may be married.

Liza: Garn!

Higgins: There! As the girl very properly says, Garn! Married indeed! Dont you know that a woman of that class looks a worn out drudge of fifty a year after she's married?

Liza: Whood marry me?

Higgins (suddenly resorting to the most thrillingly beautiful tones in his best elocutionary style): By George, Eliza, the streets will be strewn with the bodies of men shooting themselves for your sake before Ive done with you.

Mrs. Pearce: Nonsense, sir. You mustnt talk like that to her.

Liza (rising and squaring herself determinedly): I'm going away. He's off his chump, he is. I dont want no balmies teaching me.

Higgins (wounded in his tenderest point by her insensibility to his elocution): Oh, indeed! I'm mad, am I? Very well, Mrs. Pearce: you neednt order the new clothes for her. Throw her out.

Liza (whimpering): Nah-ow. You got no right to touch me.

Mrs. Pearce: You see now what comes of being saucy. *(Indicating the door.)* This way, please.

Liza (almost in tears): I didnt want no clothes. I wouldnt have taken them. *(She throws away the handkerchief.)* I can buy my own clothes.

Higgins (deftly retrieving the handkerchief and intercepting her on her reluctant way to the door): Youre an ungrateful wicked girl. This is my return for offering to take you out of the gutter and dress you beautifully and make a lady of you.

Mrs. Pearce: Stop, Mr. Higgins. I wont allow it. It's you that are wicked. Go home to your parents, girl; tell them to take better care of you.

Liza: I aint got no parents. They told me I was big enough to earn my own living and turned me out.

Mrs. Pearce: Wheres your mother?

Liza: I aint got no mother. Her that turned me out was my sixth stepmother. But I done without them. And I'm a good girl, I am.

Higgins: Very well, then, what on earth is all this fuss about? The girl doesnt belong to anybody — is no use to anybody but me. *(He goes to Mrs. Pearce and begins coaxing.)* You can adopt her, Mrs. Pearce: I'm sure a daughter would be a great amusement to you. Now dont make any more fuss. Take her downstairs; and —

Mrs. Pearce: But whats to become of her? Is she to be paid anything? Do be sensible, sir.

Higgins: Oh, pay her whatever is necessary: put it down in the housekeeping book. *(Impatiently.)* What on earth will she want with money? She'll have her food and clothes. She'll only drink if you give her money.

Liza (turning on him): Oh you are a brute. It's a lie: nobody ever saw the sign of liquor on me. *(To Pickering.)* Oh, sir: youre a gentleman: dont let him speak to me like that.

Pickering (in good-humored remonstrance): Does it occur to you, Higgins, that the girl has some feelings?

Higgins (looking critically at her): Oh no, I dont think so. Not any feelings that we need bother about. *(Cheerily.)* Have you, Eliza?

Liza: I got my feelings same as anyone else.

Higgins (to Pickering, reflectively): You see the difficulty?

Pickering: Eh? What difficulty?

Higgins: To get her to talk grammar. The mere pronunciation is easy enough.

Liza: I dont want to talk grammar. I want to talk like a lady in a flower-shop.

Mrs. Pearce: Will you please keep to the point, Mr. Higgins. I want to know on what terms the girl is to be here. Is she to have any wages? And what is to become of her when youve finished your teaching? You must look ahead a little.

Higgins (impatiently): Whats to become of her if I leave her in the gutter? Tell me that, Mrs. Pearce.

Mrs. Pearce: Thats her own business, not yours, Mr. Higgins.

Higgins: Well, when Ive done with her, we can throw her back into the gutter; and then it will be her own business again; so thats all right.

Liza: Oh, youve no feeling heart in you: you dont care for nothing but yourself. *(She rises and takes the floor resolutely.)* Here! Ive had enough of this. I'm going. *(Making for the door.)* You ought to be ashamed of yourself, you ought.

Higgins (snatching a chocolate cream from the piano, his eyes suddenly beginning to twinkle with mischief): Have some chocolates, Eliza.

Liza (halting, tempted): How do I know what might be in them? Ive heard of girls being drugged by the like of you.

Higgins whips out his penknife; cuts a chocolate in two; puts one half into his mouth and bolts it; and offers her the other half.

Higgins: Pledge of good faith, Eliza. I eat one half: you eat the other. *(Liza opens her mouth to retort: he pops the half chocolate into it.)* You shall have boxes of them, barrels of them, every day. You shall live on them. Eh?

Liza *(who has disposed of the chocolate after being nearly choked by it):* I wouldnt have ate it, only I'm too ladylike to take it out of my mouth.

Higgins: Listen, Eliza. I think you said you came in a taxi.

Liza: Well, what if I did? Ive as good a right to take a taxi as anyone else.

Higgins: You have, Eliza; and in future you shall have as many taxis as you want. You shall go up and down and round the town in a taxi every day. Think of that, Eliza.

Mrs. Pearce: Mr. Higgins: youre tempting the girl. It's not right. She should think of the future.

Higgins: At her age! Nonsense! Time enough to think of the future when you havnt any future to think of. No, Eliza: do as this lady does: think of other people's futures; but never think of your own. Think of chocolates, and taxis, and gold, and diamonds.

Liza: No: I dont want no gold and no diamonds. I'm a good girl, I am. *(She sits down again, with an attempt at dignity.)*

Higgins: You shall remain so, Eliza, under the care of Mrs. Pearce. And you shall marry an officer in the Guards, with a beautiful moustache: the son of a marquis, who will disinherit him for marrying you, but will relent when he sees your beauty and goodness —

Pickering: Excuse me, Higgins; but I really must interfere. Mrs. Pearce is quite right. If this girl is to put herself in your hands for six months for an experiment in teaching, she must understand thoroughly what she's doing.

Higgins: How can she? She's incapable of understanding anything. Besides, do any of us understand what we are doing? If we did, would we ever do it?

Pickering: Very clever, Higgins; but not to the present point. *(To Eliza.)* Miss Doolittle —

Liza *(overwhelmed):* Ah-ah-ow-oo!

Higgins: There! Thats all youll get out of Eliza. Ah-ah-ow-oo! No use explaining. As a military man you ought to know that. Give her her orders: thats enough for her. Eliza: you are to live here for the next six months, learning how to speak beautifully, like a lady in a florist's shop. If youre good and do whatever youre told, you shall sleep in a proper bedroom, and have lots to eat, and money to buy chocolates and take rides in taxis. If youre naughty and idle you will sleep in the back kitchen among the black beetles, and be walloped by Mrs. Pearce with a broomstick. At the end of six months you shall go to Buckingham Palace in a carriage, beautifully dressed. If the King finds out youre not a lady, you will be taken by the police to the Tower of London, where your head will be cut off as a warning to other presumptuous flower girls. If you are not found out, you shall have a present of seven-and-sixpence to start life with as a lady in a shop. If you refuse this offer you will be a most ungrateful wicked girl; and the angels will weep for you. *(To Pickering.)* Now are you satisfied, Pickering? *(To Mrs. Pearce.)* Can I put it more plainly and fairly, Mrs. Pearce?

Mrs. Pearce *(patiently):* I think youd better let me speak to the girl properly in private. I dont know that I can take charge of her or consent to the arrangement at all. Of course I know you dont mean her any harm; but when you get what you call interested in people's accents, you never think or care what may happen to them or you. Come with me, Eliza.

Higgins: Thats all right. Thank you, Mrs. Pearce. Bundle her off to the bathroom.

Liza (rising reluctantly and suspiciously): Youre a great bully, you are. I wont stay here if I dont like. I wont let nobody wallop me. I never asked to go to Bucknam Palace, I didnt. I was never in trouble with the police, not me. I'm a good girl —

Mrs. Pearce: Dont answer back, girl. You dont understand the gentleman. Come with me. *(She leads the way to the door, and holds it open for Eliza.)*

Liza (as she goes out): Well, what I say is right. I wont go near the King, not if I'm going to have my head cut off. If I'd known what I was letting myself in for, I wouldnt have come here. I always been a good girl; and I never offered to say a word to him; and I dont owe him nothing; and I dont care; and I wont be put upon; and I have my feelings the same as anyone else —

Mrs. Pearce shuts the door; and Eliza's plaints are no longer audible.

* * * * *

Eliza is taken upstairs to the third floor greatly to her surprise; for she expected to be taken down to the scullery. There Mrs. Pearce opens a door and takes her into a spare bedroom.

Mrs. Pearce: I will have to put you here. This will be your bedroom.

Liza: O-h, I couldnt sleep here, missus. It's too good for the likes of me. I should be afraid to touch anything. I aint a duchess yet, you know.

Mrs. Pearce: You have got to make yourself as clean as the room: then you wont be afraid of it. And you must call me Mrs. Pearce, not missus. *(She throws open the door of the dressingroom, now modernized as a bathroom.)*

Liza: Gawd! whats this? Is this where you wash clothes? Funny sort of copper I call it.

Mrs. Pearce: It is not a copper. This is where we wash ourselves, Eliza, and where I am going to wash you.

Liza: You expect me to get into that and wet myself all over! Not me. I should catch my death. I knew a woman did it every Saturday night; and she died of it.

Mrs. Pearce: Mr. Higgins has the gentlemen's bathroom downstairs; and he has a bath every morning, in cold water.

Liza: Ugh! He's made of iron, that man.

Mrs. Pearce: If you are to sit with him and the Colonel and be taught you will have to do the same. They wont like the smell of you if you dont. But you can have the water as hot as you like. There are two taps: hot and cold.

Liza (weeping): I couldnt. I dursnt. Its not natural: it would kill me. Ive never had a bath in my life: not what youd call a proper one.

Mrs. Pearce: Well, dont you want to be clean and sweet and decent, like a lady? You know you cant be a nice girl inside if youre a dirty slut outside.

Liza: Boohoo!!!!

Mrs. Pearce: Now stop crying and go back into your room and take off all your clothes. Then wrap yourself in this *(taking down a gown from its peg and handing it to her)* and come back to me. I will get the bath ready.

Liza (all tears): I cant. I wont. I'm not used to it. Ive never took off all my clothes before. It's not right: it's not decent.

Mrs. Pearce: Nonsense, child. Dont you take off all your clothes every night when you go to bed?

Liza (amazed): No. Why should I? I should catch my death. Of course I take off my skirt.

Mrs. Pearce: Do you mean that you sleep in the underclothes you wear in the daytime?

Liza: What else have I to sleep in?

Mrs. Pearce: You will never do that again as long as you live here. I will get you a proper nightdress.

Liza: Do you mean change into cold things and lie awake shivering half the night? You want to kill me, you do.

Mrs. Pearce: I want to change you from a frowzy slut to a clean respectable girl fit to sit with the gentlemen in the study. Are you going to trust me and do what I tell you or be thrown out and sent back to your flower basket?

Liza: But you dont know what the cold is to me. You dont know how I dread it.

Mrs. Pearce: Your bed won't be cold here: I will put a hot water bottle in it. *(Pushing her into the bedroom.)* Off with you and undress.

Liza: Oh, if only I'd known what a dreadful thing it is to be clean I'd never have come. I didnt know when I was well off. I —*(Mrs. Pearce pushes her through the door, but leaves it partly open lest her prisoner should take to flight.)*

Mrs. Pearce puts on a pair of white rubber sleeves, and fills the bath, mixing hot and cold, and testing the result with the bath thermometer. She perfumes it with a handful of bath salts and adds a palmful of mustard. She then takes a formidable looking long handled scrubbing brush and soaps it profusely with a ball of scented soap.

Eliza comes back with nothing on but the bath gown huddled tightly round her, a piteous spectacle of abject terror.

Mrs. Pearce: Now come along. Take that thing off.

Liza: Oh I couldnt, Mrs. Pearce: I reely couldnt. I never done such a thing.

Mrs. Pearce: Nonsense. Here: step in and tell me whether its hot enough for you.

Liza: Ah-oo! Ah-oo! It's too hot.

Mrs. Pearce (deftly snatching the gown away and throwing Eliza down on her back): It wont hurt you. *(She sets to work with the scrubbing brush.)*

Eliza's screams are heartrending.

*   *   *   *   *

Meanwhile the Colonel has been having it out with Higgins about Eliza. Pickering has come from the hearth to the chair and seated himself astride of it with his arms on the back to cross-examine him.

Pickering: Excuse the straight question, Higgins. Are you a man of good character where women are concerned?

Higgins (moodily): Have you ever met a man of good character where women are concerned?

Pickering: Yes: very frequently.

Higgins (dogmatically, lifting himself on his hands to the level of the piano, and sitting on it with a bounce): Well, I havnt. I find that the moment I let a woman make friends with me, she becomes jealous, exacting, suspicious, and a damned nuisance. I find that the moment I let myself make friends with a woman, I become selfish and tyrannical. Women upset everything. When you let them into your life, you find that the woman is driving at one thing and youre driving at another.

Pickering: At what, for example?

Higgins (coming off the piano restlessly): Oh, Lord knows! I suppose the woman wants to live her own life; and the man wants to live his; and each tries to drag the other on to the wrong track. One wants to go north and the other south; and the result is that both have to go east, though they both hate the east wind. *(He sits down on the bench at the keyboard.)* So here I am, a confirmed old bachelor, and likely to remain so.

Pickering (rising and standing over him gravely): Come, Higgins! You know what I mean. If I'm to be in this business I shall feel responsible for that girl. I hope it's understood that no advantage is to be taken of her position.

Higgins: What! That thing! Sacred, I assure you. *(Rising to explain.)* You see, she'll be a pupil; and teaching would be impossible unless pupils were sacred. Ive taught scores of American millionairesses how to speak English: the best looking women in the world. I'm seasoned. They might as well be a block of wood. It's —

Mrs. Pearce opens the door. She has Eliza's hat in her hand. Pickering retires to the easy-chair at the hearth and sits down.

Higgins (eagerly): Well, Mrs. Pearce: is it all right?

Mrs. Pearce (at the door): I just wish to trouble you with a word, if I may, Mr. Higgins.

Higgins: Yes, certainly. Come in. *(She comes forward.)* Dont burn that, Mrs. Pearce. I'll keep it as a curiosity. *(He takes the hat.)*

Mrs. Pearce: Handle it carefully, sir, please. I had to promise her not to burn it; but I had better put it in the oven for a while.

Higgins (putting it down hastily on the piano): Oh! thank you. Well, what have you to say to me?

Pickering: Am I in the way?

Mrs. Pearce: Not in the least, sir. Mr. Higgins: will you please be very particular what you say before the girl?

Higgins (sternly): Of course. I'm always particular about what I say. Why do you say this to me?

Mrs. Pearce (unmoved): No, sir: youre not at all particular when youve mislaid anything or when you get a little impatient. Now it doesnt matter before me: I'm used to it. But you really must not swear before the girl.

Higgins (indignantly): I swear! *(Most emphatically.)* I never swear. I detest the habit. What the devil do you mean?

Mrs. Pearce (stolidly): Thats what I mean, sir. You swear a great deal too much. I dont mind your damning and blasting, and what the devil and where the devil and who the devil —

Higgins: Mrs. Pearce: this language from your lips! Really!

Mrs. Pearce (not to be put off): — but there is a certain word° I must ask you not to use. The girl used it herself when she began to enjoy the bath. It begins with the same letter as bath. She knows no better: she learnt it at her mother's knee. But she must not hear it from your lips.

Higgins (loftily): I cannot charge myself with having ever uttered it, Mrs. Pearce. *(She looks at him steadfastly. He adds, hiding an uneasy conscience with a judicial air.)* Except perhaps in a moment of extreme and justifiable excitement.

Mrs. Pearce: Only this morning, sir, you applied it to your boots, to the butter, and to the brown bread.

Higgins: Oh, that! Mere alliteration, Mrs. Pearce, natural to a poet.

Mrs. Pearce: Well, sir, whatever you choose to call it, I beg you not to let the girl hear you repeat it.

Higgins: Oh, very well, very well. Is that all?

Mrs. Pearce: No, sir. We shall have to be very particular with this girl as to personal cleanliness.

Higgins: Certainly. Quite right. Most important.

Mrs. Pearce: I mean not to be slovenly about her dress or untidy in leaving things about.

Higgins (going to her solemnly): Just so. I intended to call your attention to that. *(He passes on to Pickering, who is enjoying the conversation immensely.)* It is these little things that matter, Pickering. Take care of the pence and the pounds will take care of themselves is as true of personal habits as of money. *(He comes to anchor on the hearthrug, with the air of a man in an unassailable position.)*

Mrs. Pearce: Yes, sir. Then might I ask you not to come down to breakfast in your dressing-gown, or at any rate not to use it as a napkin to the extent you do, sir. And if you would be so good as not to eat everything off the same plate, and to remember not to put the porridge saucepan out of your hand on the clean tablecloth, it would be a better example to the girl. You know you nearly choked yourself with a fishbone in a jam only last week.

Higgins (routed from the hearthrug and drifting back to the piano): I may do these things sometimes in absence of mind; but surely I dont do them habitually. *(Angrily.)* By the way: my dressing-gown smells most damnably of benzine.

Mrs. Pearce: No doubt it does, Mr. Higgins. But if you will wipe your fingers —

Higgins (yelling): Oh very well, very well: I'll wipe them in my hair in future.

Mrs. Pearce: I hope youre not offended, Mr. Higgins.

Higgins (shocked at finding himself thought capable of an unamiable sentiment): Not at all, not at all. Youre quite right, Mrs. Pearce: I shall be particularly careful before the girl. Is that all?

Mrs. Pearce: No, sir. Might she use some of those Japanese dresses you brought from abroad? I really cant put her back into her old things.

Higgins: Certainly. Anything you like. Is that all?

Mrs. Pearce: Thank you, sir. Thats all. *(She goes out.)*

Higgins: You know, Pickering, that woman has the most extraordinary ideas about me. Here I am, a shy, diffident sort of man. Ive never been able to

---

a certain word: bloody.

feel really grown-up and tremendous, like other chaps. And yet she's firmly persuaded that I'm an arbitrary overbearing bossing kind of person. I cant account for it.

Mrs. Pearce returns.

Mrs. Pearce: If you please, sir, the trouble's beginning already. Theres a dust-man downstairs, Alfred Doolittle, wants to see you. He says you have his daughter here.

Pickering (rising): Phew! I say!

Higgins (promptly): Send the blackguard up.

Mrs. Pearce: Oh, very well, sir. *(She goes out.)*

Pickering: He may not be a blackguard, Higgins.

Higgins: Nonsense. Of course he's a blackguard.

Pickering: Whether he is or not, I'm afraid we shall have some trouble with him.

Higgins (confidently): Oh, no: I think not. If theres any trouble he shall have it with me, not I with him. And we are sure to get something interesting out of him.

Pickering: About the girl?

Higgins: No. I mean his dialect.

Pickering: Oh!

Mrs. Pearce (at the door): Doolittle, sir. *(She admits Doolittle and retires).*

Alfred is an elderly but vigorous dustman°, clad in the costume of his profession, including a hat with a back brim covering his neck and shoulders. He has well marked and rather interesting features, and seems equally free from fear and conscience. He has a remarkably expressive voice, the result of a habit of giving vent to his feelings without reserve. His present pose is that of wounded honor and stern resolution.

Doolittle (at the door, uncertain which of the two gentlemen is his man): Professor Iggins?

Higgins: Here. Good morning. Sit down.

Doolittle: Morning, Governor. *(He sits down magisterially.)* I come about a very serious matter, Governor.

Higgins (to Pickering): Brought up in Hounslow. Mother Welsh, I should think. *(Doolittle opens his mouth, amazed. Higgins continues.)* What do you want, Doolittle?

Doolittle (menacingly): I want my daughter: thats what I want. See?

Higgins: Of course you do. Youre her father, arnt you? You dont suppose any-one else wants her, do you? I'm glad to see you have some spark of family feeling left. She's upstairs. Take her away at once.

Doolittle (rising, fearfully taken aback): What?

Higgins: Take her away. Do you suppose I'm going to keep your daughter for you?

Doolittle (remonstrating): Now, now, look here, Governor. Is this reasonable? Is it fairity to take advantage of a man like this? The girl belongs to me. You got her. Where do I come in? *(He sits down again.)*

dustman: a garbage collector.

Higgins: Your daughter had the audacity to come to my house and ask me to teach her to speak properly so that she could get a place in a flower-shop. This gentleman and my housekeeper have been here all the time. *(Bullying him.)* How dare you come here and attempt to blackmail me? You sent her here on purpose.

Doolittle (protesting): No, Governor.

Higgins: You must have. How else could you possibly know that she is here?

Doolittle: Don't take a man up like that, Governor.

Higgins: The police shall take you up. This is a plant — a plot to extort money by threats. I shall telephone for the police. *(He goes resolutely to the telephone and opens the directory.)*

Doolittle: Have I asked you for a brass farthing? I leave it to the gentleman here: have I said a word about money?

Higgins (throwing the book aside and marching down on Doolittle with a poser): What else did you come for?

Doolittle (sweetly): Well, what would a man come for? Be human, Governor.

Higgins (disarmed): Alfred: did you put her up to it?

Doolittle: So help me, Governor, I never did. I take my Bible oath I aint seen the girl these two months past.

Higgins: Then how did you know she was here?

Doolittle ("most musical, most melancholy"): I'll tell you, Governor, if youll only let me get a word in. I'm willing to tell you. I'm wanting to tell you. I'm waiting to tell you.

Higgins: Pickering: this chap has a certain natural gift of rhetoric. Observe the rhythm of his native woodnotes wild. "I'm willing to tell you: I'm wanting to tell you: I'm waiting to tell you." Sentimental rhetoric! thats the Welsh strain in him. It also accounts for his mendacity and dishonesty.

Pickering: Oh, please, Higgins: I'm west country myself. *(To Doolittle.)* How did you know the girl was here if you didnt send her?

Doolittle: It was like this, Governor. The girl took a boy in the taxi to give him a jaunt. Son of her landlady, he is. He hung about on the chance of her giving him another ride home. Well, she sent him back for her luggage when she heard you was willing for her to stop here. I met the boy at the corner of Long Acre and Endell Street.

Higgins: Public house. Yes?

Doolittle: The poor man's club, Governor: why shouldnt I?

Pickering: Do let him tell his story, Higgins.

Doolittle: He told me what was up. And I ask you, what was my feelings and my duty as a father? I says to the boy, "You bring me the luggage," I says—

Pickering: Why didnt you go for it yourself?

Doolittle: Landlady wouldnt have trusted me with it, Governor. She's that kind of woman: you know. I had to give the boy a penny afore he trusted me with it, the little swine. I brought it to her just to oblige you like, and make myself agreeable. Thats all.

Higgins: How much luggage?

Doolittle: Musical instrument, Governor. A few pictures, a trifle of jewelry, and a bird-cage. She said she didnt want no clothes. What was I to think from that, Governor? I ask you as a parent what was I to think?

Higgins: So you came to rescue her from worse than death, eh?

Doolittle (appreciatively: relieved at being so well understood): Just so, Governor. Thats right.

Pickering: But why did you bring her luggage if you intended to take her away?

Doolittle: Have I said a word about taking her away? Have I now?

Higgins (determinedly): Youre going to take her away, double quick. *(He crosses to the hearth and rings the bell.)*

Doolittle (rising): No, Governor. Dont say that. I'm not the man to stand in my girl's light. Heres a career opening for her, as you might say; and —

Mrs. Pearce opens the door and awaits orders.

Higgins: Mrs. Pearce: this is Eliza's father. He has come to take her away. Give her to him. *(He goes back to the piano, with an air of washing his hands of the whole affair.)*

Doolittle: No. This is a misunderstanding. Listen here —

Mrs. Pearce: He cant take her away, Mr. Higgins: how can he? You told me to burn her clothes.

Doolittle: Thats right. I cant carry the girl through the streets like a blooming monkey, can I? I put it to you.

Higgins: You have put it to me that you want your daughter. Take your daughter. If she has no clothes go out and buy her some.

Doolittle (desperate): Wheres the clothes she come in? Did I burn them or did your missus here?

Mrs. Pearce: I am the housekeeper, if you please. I have sent for some clothes for your girl. When they come you can take her away. You can wait in the kitchen. This way, please.

Doolittle, much troubled, accompanies her to the door; then hesitates; finally turns confidentially to Higgins.

Doolittle: Listen here, Governor. You and me is men of the world, aint we?

Higgins: Oh! Men of the world, are we? Youd better go, Mrs. Pearce.

Mrs. Pearce: I think so, indeed, sir. *(She goes, with dignity.)*

Pickering: The floor is yours, Mr. Doolittle.

Doolittle (to Pickering): I thank you, Governor. *(To Higgins, who takes refuge on the piano bench, a little overwhelmed by the proximity of his visitor; for Doolittle has a professional flavor of dust about him.)* Well, the truth is, I've taken a sort of fancy to you, Governor; and if you want the girl, I'm not so set on having her back home again but what I might be open to an arrangement. Regarded in the light of a young woman, she's a fine handsome girl. As a daughter she's not worth her keep; and so I tell you straight. All I ask is my rights as a father; and youre the last man alive to expect me to let her go for nothing; for I can see youre one of the straight sort, Governor. Well, whats a five-pound note to you? and whats Eliza to me? *(He returns to his chair and sits down judicially.)*

Pickering: I think you ought to know, Doolittle, that Mr. Higgins's intentions are entirely honorable.

Doolittle: Course they are, Governor. If I thought they wasn't, I'd ask fifty.

Higgins (revolted): Do you mean to say that you would sell your daughter for £50?

Doolittle: Not in a general way I would; but to oblige a gentleman like you I'd do a good deal, I do assure you.

Pickering: Have you no morals, man?

Doolittle (unabashed): Cant afford them, Governor. Neither could you if you was as poor as me. Not that I mean any harm, you know. But if Liza is going to have a bit out of this, why not me too?

Higgins (troubled): I dont know what to do, Pickering. There can be no question that as a matter of morals it's a positive crime to give this chap a farthing. And yet I feel a sort of rough justice in his claim.

Doolittle: Thats it, Governor. Thats all I say. A father's heart, as it were.

Pickering: Well, I know the feeling; but really it seems hardly right —

Doolittle: Dont say that, Governor. Dont look at it that way. What am I, Governors both? I ask you, what am I? I'm one of the undeserving poor: thats what I am. Think of what that means to a man. It means that he's up agen middle class morality all the time. If theres anything going, and I put in for a bit of it, it's always the same story: "Youre undeserving; so you cant have it." But my needs is as great as the most deserving widow's that ever got money out of six different charities in one week for the death of the same husband. I dont need less than a deserving man: I need more. I dont eat less hearty than him; and I drink a lot more. I want a bit of amusement, cause I'm a thinking man. I want cheerfulness and a song and a band when I feel low. Well, they charge me just the same for everything as they charge the deserving. What is middle class morality? Just an excuse for never giving me anything. Therefore, I ask you, as two gentlemen, not to play that game on me. I'm playing straight with you. I aint pretending to be deserving. I'm undeserving; and I mean to go on being undeserving. I like it; and thats the truth. Will you take advantage of a man's nature to do him out of the price of his own daughter what he's brought up and fed and clothed by the sweat of his brow until she's growed big enough to be interesting to you two gentlemen? Is five pounds unreasonable? I put it to you; and I leave it to you.

Higgins (rising, and going over to Pickering): Pickering: if we were to take this man in hand for three months, he could choose between a seat in the Cabinet and a popular pulpit in Wales.

Pickering: What do you say to that, Doolittle?

Doolittle: Not me, Governor, thank you kindly. Ive heard all the preachers and all the prime ministers — for I'm a thinking man and game for politics or religion or social reform same as all the other amusements — and I tell you it's a dog's life any way you look at it. Undeserving poverty is my line. Taking one station in society with another, it's — it's — well, it's the only one that has any ginger in it, to my taste.

Higgins: I suppose we must give him a fiver.

Pickering: He'll make a bad use of it, I'm afraid.

Doolittle: Not me, Governor, so help me I wont. Dont you be afraid that I'll save it and spare it and live idle on it. There wont be a penny of it left by Monday: I'll have to go to work same as if I'd never had it. It wont pauperize me, you bet. Just one good spree for myself and the missus, giving pleasure to ourselves and employment to others, and satisfaction to you to think it's not been throwed away. You couldnt spend it better.

Higgins (taking out his pocket book and coming between Doolittle and the piano):
This is irresistible. Lets give him ten. *(He offers two notes to the dustman.)*

Doolittle: No, Governor. She wouldnt have the heart to spend ten; and perhaps
I shouldnt neither. Ten pounds is a lot of money: it makes a man feel
prudent like; and then goodbye to happiness. You give me what I ask
you, Governor: not a penny more, and not a penny less.

Pickering: Why dont you marry that missus of yours? I rather draw the line
at encouraging that sort of immorality.

Doolittle: Tell her so, Governor: tell her so. I'm willing. It's me that suffers by
it. Ive no hold on her. I got to be agreeable to her. I got to give her presents.
I got to buy her clothes something sinful. I'm a slave to that woman,
Governor, just because I'm not her lawful husband. And she knows it too.
Catch her marrying me! Take my advice, Governor: marry Eliza while
she's young and dont know no better. If you dont you'll be sorry for it
after. If you do, she'll be sorry for it after; but better her than you, because
youre a man, and she's only a woman and dont know how to be happy
anyhow.

Higgins: Pickering: if we listen to this man another minute, we shall have no
convictions left. *(To Doolittle.)* Five pounds I think you said.

Doolittle: Thank you kindly, Governor.

Higgins: Youre sure you wont take ten?

Doolittle: Not now. Another time, Governor.

Higgins (handing him a five-pound note): Here you are.

Doolittle: Thank you, Governor. Good morning. *(He hurries to the door, anxious
to get away with his booty. When he opens it he is confronted with a dainty
and exquisitely clean young Japanese lady in a simple blue cotton kimono
printed cunningly with small white jasmine blossoms. Mrs. Pearce is with her.
He gets out of her way deferentially and apologizes.)* Beg pardon, miss.

The Japanese Lady: Garn! Dont you know your own daughter?

Doolittle: ⎰ *exclaiming* ⎱ Bly me! it's Eliza!
Higgins: ⎱ *simul-* ⎰ Whats that? This!
Pickering: ⎰ *taneously* ⎱ By Jove!

Liza: Dont I look silly?

Higgins: Silly?

Mrs. Pearce (at the door): Now, Mr. Higgins, please dont say anything to make
the girl conceited about herself.

Higgins (conscientiously): Oh! Quite right, Mrs. Pearce. *(To Eliza.)* Yes: damned
silly.

Mrs. Pearce: Please, sir.

Higgins (correcting himself): I mean extremely silly.

Liza: I should look all right with my hat on. *(She takes up her hat; puts it on; and
walks across the room to the fireplace with a fashionable air.)*

Higgins: A new fashion, by George! And it ought to look horrible!

Doolittle (with fatherly pride): Well, I never thought she'd clean up as good looking as that, Governor. She's a credit to me, aint she?

Liza: I tell you, it's easy to clean up here. Hot and cold water on tap, just as
much as you like, there is. Woolly towels, there is; and a towel horse so hot,
it burns your fingers. Soft brushes to scrub yourself, and a wooden bowl of

soap smelling like primroses. Now I know why ladies is so clean. Washing's a treat for them. Wish they could see what it is for the like of me!

Higgins: I'm glad the bathroom met with your approval.

Liza: It didnt: not all of it; and I dont care who hears me say it. Mrs. Pearce knows.

Higgins: What was wrong, Mrs. Pearce?

Mrs. Pearce (blandly): Oh, nothing, sir. It doesnt matter.

Liza: I had a good mind to break it. I didnt know which way to look. But I hung a towel over it, I did.

Higgins: Over what?

Mrs. Pearce: Over the looking-glass, sir.

Higgins: Doolittle: you have brought your daughter up too strictly.

Doolittle: Me! I never brought her up at all, except to give her a lick of a strap now and again. Dont put it on me, Governor. She aint accustomed to it, you see: thats all. But she'll soon pick up your free-and-easy ways.

Liza: I'm a good girl, I am; and I wont pick up no free-and-easy ways.

Higgins: Eliza: if you say again that youre a good girl, your father shall take you home.

Liza: Not him. You dont know my father. All he come here for was to touch you for some money to get drunk on.

Doolittle: Well, what else would I want money for? To put into the plate in church, I suppose. *(She puts out her tongue at him. He is so incensed by this that Pickering presently finds it necessary to step between them.)* Dont you give me none of your lip; and dont let me hear you giving this gentleman any of it neither, or youll hear from me about it. See?

Higgins: Have you any further advice to give her before you go, Doolittle? Your blessing, for instance.

Doolittle: No, Governor: I aint such a mug as to put up my children to all I know myself. Hard enough to hold them in without that. If you want Eliza's mind improved, Governor, you do it yourself with a strap. So long, gentlemen. *(He turns to go.)*

Higgins (impressively): Stop. Youll come regularly to see your daughter. It's your duty, you know. My brother is a clergyman; and he could help you in your talks with her.

Doolittle (evasively): Certainly, I'll come, Governor. Not just this week, because I have a job at a distance. But later on you may depend on me. Afternoon, gentlemen. Afternoon, maam. *(He touches his hat to Mrs. Pearce, who disdains the salutation and goes out. He winks at Higgins, thinking him probably a fellow-sufferer from Mrs. Pearce's difficult disposition, and follows her.)*

Liza: Dont you believe the old liar. He'd as soon you set a bulldog on him as a clergyman. You wont see him again in a hurry.

Higgins: I dont want to, Eliza. Do you?

Liza: Not me. I dont want never to see him again, I dont. He's a disgrace to me, he is, collecting dust, instead of working at his trade.

Pickering: What is his trade, Eliza?

Liza: Talking money out of other people's pockets into his own. His proper trade's a navvy; and he works at it sometimes too — for exercise — and earns good money at it. Aint you going to call me Miss Doolittle any more?

Pickering: I beg your pardon, Miss Doolittle. It was a slip of the tongue.

Liza: Oh, I dont mind; only it sounded so genteel. I should just like to take a taxi to the corner of Tottenham Court Road and get out there and tell it to wait for me, just to put the girls in their place a bit. I wouldnt speak to them, you know.

Pickering: Better wait til we get you something really fashionable.

Higgins: Besides, you shouldnt cut your old friends now that you have risen in the world. Thats what we call snobbery.

Liza: You dont call the like of them my friends now, I should hope. Theyve took it out of me often enough with their ridicule when they had the chance; and now I mean to get a bit of my own back. But if I'm to have fashionable clothes, I'll wait. I should like to have some. Mrs. Pearce says youre going to give me some to wear in bed at night different to what I wear in the daytime; but it do seem a waste of money when you could get something to shew. Besides, I never could fancy changing into cold things on a winter night.

Mrs. Pearce (coming back): Now, Eliza. The new things have come for you to try on.

Liza: Ah-ow-oo-ooh! *(She rushes out.)*

Mrs. Pearce (following her): Oh, dont rush about like that, girl. *(She shuts the door behind her.)*

Higgins: Pickering: we have taken on a stiff job.

Pickering (with conviction): Higgins: we have.

*   *   *   *   *

There seems to be some curiosity as to what Higgins's lessons to Eliza were like. Well, here is a sample: the first one.

Picture Eliza, in her new clothes, and feeling her inside put out of step by a lunch, dinner, and breakfast of a kind to which it is unaccustomed, seated with Higgins and the Colonel in the study, feeling like a hospital out-patient at a first encounter with the doctors.

Higgins, constitutionally unable to sit still, discomposes her still more by striding restlessly about. But for the reassuring presence and quietude of her friend the Colonel she would run for her life, even back to Drury Lane.

Higgins: Say your alphabet.

Liza: I know my alphabet. Do you think I know nothing? I dont need to be taught like a child.

Higgins (thundering): Say your alphabet.

Pickering: Say it, Miss Doolittle. You will understand presently. Do what he tells you; and let him teach you in his own way.

Liza: Oh well, if you put it like that — Ahyee, bəyee, cəyee, dəyee —

Higgins (with the roar of a wounded lion): Stop. Listen to this, Pickering. This is what we pay for as elementary education. This unfortunate animal has been locked up for nine years in school at our expense to teach her to speak and read the language of Shakespear and Milton. And the result is Ahyee, Bə-yee, Cə-yee, Dəyee. *(To Eliza.)* Say A, B, C, D.

Liza (almost in tears): But I'm sayin it. Ahyee, Bəyee, Cəyee —

Higgins: Stop. Say a cup of tea.

Liza: A cappətə-ee.

Higgins: Put your tongue forward until it squeezes against the top of your lower teeth. Now say cup.

Liza: C-c-c — I cant. C-Cup.

Pickering: Good. Splendid, Miss Doolittle.

Higgins: By Jupiter, she's done it the first shot. Pickering: we shall make a duchess of her. *(To Eliza.)* Now do you think you could possibly say tea? Not tə-yee, mind: if you ever say bə-yee cə-yee də-yee again you shall be dragged round the room three times by the hair of your head. *(Fortissimo.)* T, T, T, T.

Liza (weeping): I cant hear no difference cep that it sounds more genteel-like when you say it.

Higgins: Well, if you can hear that difference, what the devil are you crying for? Pickering: give her a chocolate.

Pickering: No, no. Never mind crying a little, Miss Doolittle: you are doing very well; and the lessons wont hurt. I promise you I wont let him drag you round the room by your hair.

Higgins: Be off with you to Mrs. Pearce and tell her about it. Think about it. Try to do it by yourself: and keep your tongue well forward in your mouth instead of trying to roll it up and swallow it. Another lesson at half-past four this afternoon. Away with you.

Eliza, still sobbing, rushes from the room.

And that is the sort of ordeal poor Eliza has to go through for months before we meet her again on her first appearance in London society of the professional class.

ACT III

It is Mrs. Higgins's at-home day. Nobody has yet arrived. Her drawing room, in a flat on Chelsea Embankment, has three windows looking on the river; and the ceiling is not so lofty as it would be in an older house of the same pretension. The windows are open, giving access to a balcony with flowers in pots. If you stand with your face to the windows, you have the fireplace on your left and the door in the righthand wall close to the corner nearest the windows.

Mrs. Higgins was brought up on Morris and Burne-Jones°; and her room, which is very unlike her son's room in Wimpole Street, is not crowded with furniture and little tables and nicknacks. In the middle of the room there is a big ottoman; and this, with the carpet, the Morris wall-papers, and the Morris chintz window curtains and brocade covers of the ottoman and its cushions, supply all the ornament, and are much too handsome to be hidden by odds and

---

Morris and Burne-Jones: Mrs. Higgins displays a somewhat old-fashioned taste in art and interior decoration. William Morris (1834–1896), poet and artist, in 1861 had founded a company using medieval craft techniques to turn out furniture (including the Morris chair), wallpaper, fabrics, and objects of art. Morris and Company produced stained glass designed by Sir Edward Burne-Jones (1833–1898), a painter and (like Morris) a critic of industrialism.

ends of useless things. A few good oil-paintings from the exhibitions in the Grosvenor Gallery thirty years ago (the Burne-Jones, not the Whistler side of them) are on the walls. The only landscape is a Cecil Lawson on the scale of a Rubens. There is a portrait of Mrs. Higgins as she was when she defied the fashion in her youth in one of the beautiful Rossettian costumes° which, when caricatured by people who did not understand, led to the absurdities of popular estheticism in the eighteen-seventies.

In the corner diagonally opposite the door Mrs. Higgins, now over sixty and long past taking the trouble to dress out of the fashion, sits writing at an elegantly simple writing-table with a bell button within reach of her hand. There is a Chippendale chair further back in the room between her and the window nearest her side. At the other side of the room, further forward, is an Elizabethan chair roughly carved in the taste of Inigo Jones. On the same side a piano in a decorated case. The corner between the fireplace and the window is occupied by a divan cushioned in Morris chintz.

It is between four and five in the afternoon.

The door is opened violently; and Higgins enters with his hat on.

Mrs. Higgins (dismayed): Henry! *(Scolding him.)* What are you doing here today? It is my at-home day: you promised not to come. *(As he bends to kiss her, she takes his hat off, and presents it to him.)*

Higgins: Oh bother! *(He throws the hat down on the table.)*

Mrs. Higgins: Go home at once.

Higgins (kissing her): I know, mother. I came on purpose.

Mrs. Higgins: But you mustnt. I'm serious, Henry. You offend all my friends: they stop coming whenever they meet you.

Higgins: Nonsense! I know I have no small talk; but people dont mind. *(He sits on the settee.)*

Mrs. Higgins: Oh! dont they? Small talk indeed! What about your large talk? Really, dear, you mustnt stay.

Higgins: I must. Ive a job for you. A phonetic job.

Mrs. Higgins: No use, dear. I'm sorry; but I cant get round your vowels; and though I like to get pretty postcards in your patent shorthand, I always have to read the copies in ordinary writing you so thoughtfully send me.

Higgins: Well, this isnt a phonetic job.

Mrs. Higgins: You said it was.

Higgins: Not your part of it. Ive picked up a girl.

Mrs. Higgins: Does that mean that some girl has picked you up?

Higgins: Not at all. I dont mean a love affair.

Mrs. Higgins: What a pity!

Higgins: Why?

Mrs. Higgins: Well, you never fall in love with anyone under forty-five. When will you discover that there are some rather nice-looking young women about?

Higgins: Oh, I cant be bothered with young women. My idea of a lovable woman

Rossettian costumes: long filmy dresses such as those worn by women in the paintings of Dante Gabriel Rossetti (1828–1882). Rossetti was a founder of the Pre-Raphaelite Brotherhood, a group of painters and poets who sought their inspiration in art of the Middle Ages.

is somebody as like you as possible. I shall never get into the way of seriously liking young women: some habits lie too deep to be changed. *(Rising abruptly and walking about, jingling his money and his keys in his trouser pockets.)* Besides, theyre all idiots.

Mrs. Higgins: Do you know what you would do if you really loved me, Henry?

Higgins: Oh bother! What? Marry, I suppose.

Mrs. Higgins: No. Stop fidgeting and take your hands out of your pockets. *(With a gesture of despair, he obeys and sits down again.)* Thats a good boy. Now tell me about the girl.

Higgins: She's coming to see you.

Mrs. Higgins: I dont remember asking her.

Higgins: You didnt. *I* asked her. If youd known her you wouldnt have asked her.

Mrs. Higgins: Indeed! Why?

Higgins: Well, it's like this. She's a common flower girl. I picked her off the kerbstone.

Mrs. Higgins: And invited her to my at-home!

Higgins (rising and coming to her to coax her): Oh, thatll be all right. Ive taught her to speak properly; and she has strict orders as to her behavior. She's to keep to two subjects: the weather and everybody's health — Fine day and How do you do, you know — and not to let herself go on things in general. That will be safe.

Mrs. Higgins: Safe! To talk about our health! about our insides! perhaps about our outsides! How could you be so silly, Henry?

Higgins (impatiently): Well, she must talk about something. *(He controls himself and sits down again.)* Oh, she'll be all right: dont you fuss. Pickering is in it with me. Ive a sort of bet on that I'll pass her off as a duchess in six months. I started on her some months ago; and she's getting on like a house on fire. I shall win my bet. She has a quick ear; and she's easier to teach than my middle-class pupils because she's had to learn a complete new language. She talks English almost as you talk French.

Mrs. Higgins: Thats satisfactory, at all events.

Higgins: Well, it is and it isnt.

Mrs. Higgins: What does that mean?

Higgins: You see, Ive got her pronunciation all right; but you have to consider not only how a girl pronounces, but what she pronounces; and that's where —

They are interrupted by the parlor-maid, announcing guests.

The Parlor-Maid: Mrs. and Miss Eynsford Hill. *(She withdraws.)*

Higgins: Oh Lord! *(He rises; snatches his hat from the table; and makes for the door; but before he reaches it his mother introduces him.)*

Mrs. and Miss Eynsford Hill are the mother and daughter who sheltered from the rain in Covent Garden. The mother is well bred, quiet, and has the habitual anxiety of straitened means. The daughter has acquired a gay air of being very much at home in society: the bravado of genteel poverty.

Mrs. Eynsford Hill (to Mrs. Higgins): How do you do? *(They shake hands.)*

Miss Eynsford Hill: How d'you do? *(She shakes.)*

Mrs. Higgins (introducing): My son Henry.

Mrs. Eynsford Hill: Your celebrated son! I have so longed to meet you, Professor Higgins.

Higgins (glumly, making no movement in her direction): Delighted. *(He backs against the piano and bows brusquely.)*

Miss Eynsford Hill (going to him with confident familiarity): How do you do?

Higgins (staring at her): Ive seen you before somewhere. I havnt the ghost of a notion where; but Ive heard your voice. *(Drearily.)* It doesnt matter. Youd better sit down.

Mrs. Higgins: I'm sorry to say that my celebrated son has no manners. You mustnt mind him.

Miss Eynsford Hill (gaily): I don't. *(She sits in the Elizabethan chair.)*

Mrs. Eynsford Hill (a little bewildered): Not at all. *(She sits on the ottoman between her daughter and Mrs. Higgins, who has turned her chair away from the writing-table.)*

Higgins: Oh, have I been rude? I didnt mean to be.

He goes to the central window, through which, with his back to the company, he contemplates the river and the flowers in Battersea Park on the opposite bank as if they were a frozen desert.

The parlor-maid returns, ushering in Pickering.

The Parlor-Maid: Colonel Pickering. *(She withdraws.)*

Pickering: How do you do, Mrs. Higgins?

Mrs. Higgins: So glad youve come. Do you know Mrs. Eynsford Hill — Miss Eynsford Hill? *(Exchange of bows. The Colonel brings the Chippendale chair a little forward between Mrs. Hill and Mrs. Higgins, and sits down.)*

Pickering: Has Henry told you what weve come for?

Higgins (over his shoulder): We were interrupted: damn it!

Mrs. Higgins: Oh Henry, Henry, really!

Mrs. Eynsford Hill (half rising): Are we in the way?

Mrs. Higgins (rising and making her sit down again): No, no. You couldnt have come more fortunately: we want you to meet a friend of ours.

Higgins (turning hopefully): Yes, by George! We want two or three people. You'll do as well as anybody else.

The parlor-maid returns, ushering Freddy.

The Parlor-Maid: Mr. Eynsford Hill.

Higgins (almost audibly, past endurance): God of Heaven! another of them.

Freddy (shaking hands with Mrs. Higgins): Ahdedo?

Mrs. Higgins: Very good of you to come. *(Introducing.)* Colonel Pickering.

Freddy (bowing): Ahdedo?

Mrs. Higgins: I dont think you know my son, Professor Higgins.

Freddy (going to Higgins): Ahdedo?

Higgins (looking at him much as if he were a pickpocket): I'll take my oath Ive met you before somewhere. Where was it?

Freddy: I dont think so.

Higgins (resignedly): It dont matter, anyhow. Sit down.

He shakes Freddy's hand, and almost slings him on to the ottoman with his face to the window; then comes round to the other side of it.

Higgins: Well, here we are, anyhow! *(He sits down on the ottoman next to Mrs. Eynsford Hill, on her left.)* And now, what the devil are we going to talk about until Eliza comes?

Mrs. Higgins: Henry: you are the life and soul of the Royal Society's soirées; but really youre rather trying on more commonplace occasions.

Higgins: Am I? Very sorry. *(Beaming suddenly.)* I suppose I am, you know. *(Uproariously.)* Ha, ha!

Miss Eynsford Hill (who considers Higgins quite eligible matrimonially): I sympathize. *I* havnt any small talk. If people would only be frank and say what they really think!

Higgins (relapsing into gloom): Lord forbid!

Mrs. Eynsford Hill (taking up her daughter's cue): But why?

Higgins: What they think they ought to think is bad enough, Lord knows; but what they really think would break up the whole show. Do you suppose it would be really agreeable if I were to come out now with what *I* really think?

Miss Eynsford Hill (gaily): Is it so very cynical?

Higgins: Cynical! Who the dickens said it was cynical? I mean it wouldnt be decent.

Mrs. Eynsford Hill (seriously): Oh! I'm sure you dont mean that, Mr. Higgins.

Higgins: You see, we're all savages, more or less. We're supposed to be civilized and cultured — to know all about poetry and philosophy and art and science, and so on; but how many of us know even the meanings of these names? *(To Miss Hill.)* What do you know of poetry? *(To Mrs. Hill.)* What do you know of science? *(Indicating Freddy.)* What does he know of art or science or anything else? What the devil do you imagine I know of philosophy?

Mrs. Higgins (warningly): Or of manners, Henry?

The Parlor-Maid (opening the door): Miss Doolittle. *(She withdraws.)*

Higgins (rising hastily and running to Mrs. Higgins): Here she is, mother. *(He stands on tiptoe and makes signs over his mother's head to Eliza to indicate to her which lady is her hostess.)*

Eliza, who is exquisitely dressed, produces an impression of such remarkable distinction and beauty as she enters that they all rise, quite fluttered. Guided by Higgins's signals, she comes to Mrs. Higgins with studied grace.

Liza (speaking with pedantic correctness of pronunciation and great beauty of tone): How do you do, Mrs. Higgins? *(She gasps slightly in making sure of the H in Higgins, but is quite successful.)* Mr. Higgins told me I might come.

Mrs. Higgins (cordially): Quite right: I'm very glad indeed to see you.

Pickering: How do you do, Miss Doolittle?

Liza (shaking hands with him): Colonel Pickering, is it not?

Mrs. Eynsford Hill: I feel sure we have met before, Miss Doolittle. I remember your eyes.

Liza: How do you do? *(She sits down on the ottoman gracefully in the place just left vacant by Higgins.)*

Mrs. Eynsford Hill (introducing): My daughter Clara.

Liza: How do you do?

Clara (impulsively): How do you do? *(She sits down on the ottoman beside Eliza, devouring her with her eyes.)*

Mrs. Eynsford Hill *(introducing):* My son Freddy.
Liza: How do you do?

>   *Freddy bows and sits down in the Elizabethan chair, infatuated.*

Higgins *(suddenly):* By George, yes: it all comes back to me! *(They stare at him.)* Covent Garden! *(Lamentably.)* What a damned thing!
Mrs. Higgins: Henry, please! *(He is about to sit on the edge of the table.)* Dont sit on my writing-table: youll break it.
Higgins *(sulkily):* Sorry.

>   *He goes to the divan, stumbling into the fender and over the fire-irons on his way; extricating himself with muttered imprecations; and finishing his disastrous journey by throwing himself so impatiently on the divan that he almost breaks it. Mrs. Higgins looks at him, but controls herself and says nothing.*
>   *A long and painful pause ensues.*

Mrs. Higgins *(at last, conversationally):* Will it rain, do you think?
Liza: The shallow depression in the west of these islands is likely to move slowly in an easterly direction. There are no indications of any great change in the barometrical situation.
Freddy: Ha! ha! how awfully funny!
Liza: What is wrong with that, young man? I bet I got it right.
Freddy: Killing!
Mrs. Eynsford Hill: I'm sure I hope it wont turn cold. Theres so much influenza about. It runs right through our whole family regularly every spring.
Liza *(darkly):* My aunt died of influenza: so they said.
Mrs. Eynsford Hill *(clicks her tongue sympathetically):* !!!
Liza *(in the same tragic tone):* But it's my belief they done the old woman in.
Mrs. Higgins *(puzzled):* Done her in?
Liza: Y-e-e-e-es, Lord love you! Why should she die of influenza? She come through diphtheria right enough the year before. I saw her with my own eyes. Fairly blue with it, she was. They all thought she was dead; but my father he kept ladling gin down her throat til she came to so sudden that she bit the bowl off the spoon.
Mrs. Eynsford Hill *(startled):* Dear me!
Liza *(piling up the indictment):* What call would a woman with that strength in her have to die of influenza? What become of her new straw hat that should have come to me? Somebody pinched it; and what I say is, them as pinched it done her in.
Mrs. Eynsford Hill: What does doing her in mean?
Higgins *(hastily):* Oh, thats the new small talk. To do a person in means to kill them.
Mrs. Eynsford Hill *(to Eliza, horrified):* You surely dont believe that your aunt was killed?
Liza: Do I not! Them she lived with would have killed her for a hat-pin, let alone a hat.
Mrs. Eynsford Hill: But it cant have been right for your father to pour spirits down her throat like that. It might have killed her.
Liza: Not her. Gin was mother's milk to her. Besides, he'd poured so much down his own throat that he knew the good of it.

Mrs. Eynsford Hill: Do you mean that he drank?

Liza: Drank! My word! Something chronic.

Mrs. Eynsford Hill: How dreadful for you!

Liza: Not a bit. It never did him no harm what I could see. But then he did not keep it up regular. *(Cheerfully.)* On the burst, as you might say, from time to time. And always more agreeable when he had a drop in. When he was out of work, my mother used to give him fourpence and tell him to go out and not come back until he'd drunk himself cheerful and loving-like. Theres lots of women has to make their husbands drunk to make them fit to live with. *(Now quite at her ease.)* You see, it's like this. If a man has a bit of conscience, it always takes him when he's sober; and then it makes him low-spirited. A drop of booze just takes that off and makes him happy. *(To Freddy, who is in convulsions of suppressed laughter.)* Here! what are you sniggering at?

Freddy: The new small talk. You do it so awfully well.

Liza: If I was doing it proper, what was you laughing at? *(To Higgins.)* Have I said anything I oughtnt?

Mrs. Higgins (interposing): Not at all, Miss Doolittle.

Liza: Well, thats a mercy, anyhow. *(Expansively.)* What I always say is —

Higgins (rising and looking at his watch): Ahem!

Liza (looking round at him; taking the hint; and rising): Well: I must go. *(They all rise. Freddy goes to the door.)* So pleased to have met you. Goodbye. *(She shakes hands with Mrs. Higgins.)*

Mrs. Higgins: Goodbye.

Liza: Goodbye, Colonel Pickering.

Pickering: Goodbye, Miss Doolittle. *(They shake hands.)*

Liza (nodding to the others): Goodbye, all.

Freddy (opening the door for her): Are you walking across the Park, Miss Doolittle? If so —

Liza (with perfectly elegant diction): Walk! Not bloody likely. *(Sensation.)* I am going in a taxi. *(She goes out.)*

Pickering gasps and sits down. Freddy goes out on the balcony to catch another glimpse of Eliza.

Mrs. Eynsford Hill (suffering from shock): Well, I really cant get used to the new ways.

Clara (throwing herself discontentedly into the Elizabethan chair): Oh, it's all right, mamma, quite right. People will think we never go anywhere or see anybody if you are so old-fashioned.

Mrs. Eynsford Hill: I daresay I am very old-fashioned; but I do hope you wont begin using that expression, Clara. I have got accustomed to hear you talking about men as rotters, and calling everything filthy and beastly; though I do think it horrible and unlady like. But this last is really too much. Dont you think so, Colonel Pickering?

Pickering: Dont ask me. Ive been away in India for several years; and manners have changed so much that I sometimes dont know whether I'm at a respectable dinnertable or in a ship's forecastle.

Clara: It's all a matter of habit. Theres no right or wrong in it. Nobody means anything by it. And it's so quaint, and gives such a smart emphasis to things that are not in themselves very witty. I find the new small talk delightful and quite innocent.

Mrs. Eynsford Hill (rising): Well, after that, I think it's time for us to go.

Pickering and Higgins rise.

Clara (rising): Oh yes: we have three at-homes to go to still. Goodbye, Mrs. Higgins. Goodbye, Colonel Pickering. Goodbye, Professor Higgins.

Higgins (coming grimly at her from the divan, and accompanying her to the door): Goodbye. Be sure you try on that small talk at the three at-homes. Dont be nervous about it. Pitch it in strong.

Clara (all smiles): I will. Goodbye. Such nonsense, all this early Victorian prudery!

Higgins (tempting her): Such damned nonsense!

Clara: Such bloody nonsense!

Mrs. Eynsford Hill (convulsively): Clara!

Clara: Ha! ha! *(She goes out radiant, conscious of being thoroughly up to date, and is heard descending the stairs in a stream of silvery laughter.)*

Freddy (to the heavens at large): Well, I ask you — *(He gives it up, and comes to Mrs. Higgins.)* Goodbye.

Mrs. Higgins (shaking hands): Goodbye. Would you like to meet Miss Doolittle again?

Freddy (eagerly): Yes, I should, most awfully.

Mrs. Higgins: Well, you know my days.

Freddy: Yes. Thanks awfully. Goodbye. *(He goes out.)*

Mrs. Eynsford Hill: Goodbye, Mr. Higgins.

Higgins: Goodbye. Goodbye.

Mrs. Eynsford Hill (to Pickering): It's no use. I shall never be able to bring myself to use that word.

Pickering: Dont. It's not compulsory, you know. Youll get on quite well without it.

Mrs. Eynsford Hill: Only, Clara is so down on me if I am not positively reeking with the latest slang. Goodbye.

Pickering: Goodbye. *(They shake hands.)*

Mrs. Eynsford Hill (to Mrs. Higgins): You mustnt mind Clara. *(Pickering, catching from her lowered tone that this is not meant for him to hear, discreetly joins Higgins at the window.)* We're so poor! and she gets so few parties, poor child! She doesnt quite know. *(Mrs. Higgins, seeing that her eyes are moist, takes her hand sympathetically and goes with her to the door.)* But the boy is nice. Dont you think so?

Mrs. Higgins: Oh, quite nice. I shall always be delighted to see him.

Mrs. Eynsford Hill: Thank you, dear. Goodbye. *(She goes out.)*

Higgins (eagerly): Well? Is Eliza presentable? *(He swoops on his mother and drags her to the ottoman, where she sits down in Eliza's place with her son on her left.)*

Pickering returns to his chair on her right.

Mrs. Higgins: You silly boy, of course she's not presentable. She's a triumph of your art and of her dressmaker's; but if you suppose for a moment that she doesn't give herself away in every sentence she utters, you must be perfectly cracked about her.

Pickering: But dont you think something might be done? I mean something to eliminate the sanguinary element from her conversation.

Mrs. Higgins: Not as long as she is in Henry's hands.

Higgins (aggrieved): Do you mean that my language is improper?

Mrs. Higgins: No, dearest: it would be quite proper — say on a canal barge; but it would not be proper for her at a garden party.

Higgins (deeply injured): Well I must say —

Pickering (interrupting him): Come, Higgins: you must learn to know yourself. I havent heard such language as yours since we used to review the volunteers in Hyde Park twenty years ago.

Higgins (sulkily): Oh, well, if you say so, I suppose I dont always talk like a bishop.

Mrs. Higgins (quieting Henry with a touch): Colonel Pickering: will you tell me what is the exact state of things in Wimpole Street?

Pickering (cheerfully: as if this completely changed the subject): Well, I have come to live there with Henry. We work together at my Indian Dialects; and we think it more convenient —

Mrs. Higgins: Quite so. I know all about that: it's an excellent arrangement. But where does this girl live?

Higgins: With us, of course. Where should she live?

Mrs. Higgins: But on what terms? Is she a servant? If not, what is she?

Pickering (slowly): I think I know what you mean, Mrs. Higgins.

Higgins: Well, dash me if *I* do! Ive had to work at the girl every day for months to get her to her present pitch. Besides, she's useful. She knows where my things are, and remembers my appointments and so forth.

Mrs. Higgins: How does your housekeeper get on with her?

Higgins: Mrs. Pearce? Oh, she's jolly glad to get so much taken off her hands; for before Eliza came, she used to have to find things and remind me of my appointments. But she's got some silly bee in her bonnet about Eliza. She keeps saying "You dont think, sir": doesnt she, Pick?

Pickering: Yes: thats the formula. "You dont think, sir." Thats the end of every conversation about Eliza.

Higgins: As if I ever stop thinking about the girl and her confounded vowels and consonants. I'm worn out, thinking about her, and watching her lips and her teeth and her tongue, not to mention her soul, which is the quaintest of the lot.

Mrs. Higgins: You certainly are a pretty pair of babies, playing with your live doll.

Higgins: Playing! The hardest job I ever tackled: make no mistake about that, mother. But you have no idea how frightfully interesting it is to take a human being and change her into a quite different human being by creating a new speech for her. It's filling up the deepest gulf that separates class from class and soul from soul.

Pickering (drawing his chair closer to Mrs. Higgins and bending over to her eagerly): Yes: it's enormously interesting. I assure you, Mrs. Higgins, we take Eliza very seriously. Every week — every day almost — there is some new change. *(Closer again.)* We keep records of every stage — dozens of gramophone disks and photographs —

Higgins (assailing her at the other ear): Yes, by George: it's the most absorbing
   experiment I ever tackled. She regularly fills our lives up: doesnt she, Pick?

Pickering: We're always talking Eliza.

Higgins: Teaching Eliza.

Pickering: Dressing Eliza.

Mrs. Higgins: What!

Higgins: Inventing new Elizas.

Higgins:	(speaking together)	You know, she has the most extraordinary quickness of ear:
Pickering:		I assure you, my dear Mrs. Higgins, that girl
Higgins:		just like a parrot. Ive tried her with every
Pickering:		is a genius. She can play the piano quite beautifully.
Higgins:		possible sort of sound that a human being can make —
Pickering:		We have taken her to classical concerts and to music
Higgins:		Continental dialects, African dialects, Hottentot
Pickering:		halls; and it's all the same to her: she plays everything
Higgins:		clicks, things it took me years to get hold of; and
Pickering:		she hears right off when she comes home, whether it's
Higgins:		she picks them up like a shot, right away, as if she had
Pickering:		Beethoven and Brahms or Lehar and Lionel Monckton;
Higgins:		been at it all her life.
Pickering:		though six months ago, she'd never as much as touched a piano —

Mrs. Higgins (putting her fingers in her ears, as they are by this time shouting one
   another down with an intolerable noise): Sh-sh-sh — sh! (They stop.)

Pickering: I beg your pardon. (He draws his chair back apologetically.)

Higgins: Sorry. When Pickering starts shouting nobody can get a word in edge-
   ways.

Mrs. Higgins: Be quiet, Henry. Colonel Pickering: dont you realize that when
   Eliza walked in Wimpole Street, something walked in with her?

Pickering: Her father did. But Henry soon got rid of him.

Mrs. Higgins: It would have been more to the point if her mother had. But as
   her mother didnt something else did.

Pickering: But what?

Mrs. Higgins (unconsciously dating herself by the word): A problem.

Pickering: Oh, I see. The problem of how to pass her off as a lady.

Higgins: I'll solve that problem. Ive half solved it already.

Mrs. Higgins: No, you two infinitely stupid male creatures: the problem of
   what is to be done with her afterwards.

Higgins: I dont see anything in that. She can go her own way, with all the advantages I have given her.

Mrs. Higgins: The advantages of that poor woman who was here just now!
   The manners and habits that disqualify a fine lady from earning her own
   living without giving her a fine lady's income! Is that what you mean?

Pickering (indulgently, being rather bored): Oh, that will be all right, Mrs. Higgins.
   (He rises to go.)

Higgins (rising also): We'll find her some light employment.

Pickering: She's happy enough. Dont you worry about her. Goodbye. (He
   shakes hands as if he were consoling a frightened child, and makes for the door.)

Higgins: Anyhow, theres no good bothering now. The thing's done. Goodbye, mother. (*He kisses her, and follows Pickering.*)

Pickering (turning for a final consolation): There are plenty of openings. We'll do whats right. Goodbye.

Higgins (to Pickering as they go out together): Lets take her to the Shakespear exhibition at Earls Court.

Pickering: Yes: lets. Her remarks will be delicious.

Higgins: She'll mimic all the people for us when we get home.

Pickering: Ripping. (*Both are heard laughing as they go downstairs.*)

Mrs. Higgins (rises with an impatient bounce, and returns to her work at the writing-table. She sweeps a litter of disarranged papers out of the way; snatches a sheet of paper from her stationery case; and tries resolutely to write. At the third time she gives it up; flings down her pen; grips the table angrily and exclaims): Oh, men! men!! men!!!

* * * * *

Clearly Eliza will not pass as a duchess yet; and Higgins's bet remains unwon. But the six months are not yet exhausted and just in time Eliza does actually pass as a princess. For a glimpse of how she did it imagine an Embassy in London one summer evening after dark. The hall door has an awning and a carpet across the sidewalk to the kerb, because a grand reception is in progress. A small crowd is lined up to see the guests arrive.

A Rolls-Royce car drives up. Pickering, in evening dress, with medals and orders, alights, and hands out Eliza, in opera cloak, evening dress, diamonds, fan, flowers and all accessories. Higgins follows. The car drives off; and the three go up the steps and into the house, the door opening for them as they approach.

Inside the house they find themselves in a spacious hall from which the grand staircase rises. On the left are the arrangements for the gentlemen's cloaks. The male guests are depositing their hats and wraps there.

On the right is a door leading to the ladies' cloakroom. Ladies are going in cloaked and coming out in splendor. Pickering whispers to Eliza and points out the ladies' room. She goes into it. Higgins and Pickering take off their overcoats and take tickets for them from the attendant.

One of the guests, occupied in the same way, has his back turned. Having taken his ticket, he turns round and reveals himself as an important looking young man with an astonishingly hairy face. He has an enormous moustache, flowing out into luxuriant whiskers. Waves of hair cluster on his brow. His hair is cropped closely at the back, and glows with oil. Otherwise he is very smart. He wears several worthless orders. He is evidently a foreigner, guessable as a whiskered Pandour from Hungary; but in spite of the ferocity of his moustache he is amiable and genially voluble.

Recognizing Higgins, he flings his arms wide apart and approaches him enthusiastically.

Whiskers: Maestro, maestro. (*He embraces Higgins and kisses him on both cheeks.*) You remember me?

Higgins: No I dont. Who the devil are you?

Whiskers: I am your pupil: your first pupil, your best and greatest pupil. I am little Nepommuck, the marvellous boy. I have made your name famous throughout Europe. You teach me phonetic. You cannot forget ME.

Higgins: Why dont you shave?

Nepommuck: I have not your imposing appearance, your chin, your brow. Nobody notice me when I shave. Now I am famous: they call me Hairy Faced Dick.

Higgins: And what are you doing here among all these swells?

Nepommuck: I am interpreter. I speak 32 languages. I am indispensable at these international parties. You are great cockney specialist: you place a man anywhere in London the moment he open his mouth. I place any man in Europe.

A footman hurries down the grand staircase and comes to Nepommuck.

Footman: You are wanted upstairs. Her excellency cannot understand the Greek gentleman.

Nepommuck: Thank you, yes, immediately.

The footman goes and is lost in the crowd.

Nepommuck (to Higgins): This Greek diplomatist pretends he cannot speak nor understand English. He cannot deceive me. He is the son of a Clerkenwell watchmaker. He speaks English so villainously that he dare not utter a word of it without betraying his origin. I help him to pretend; but I make him pay through the nose. I make them all pay. Ha ha! *(He hurries upstairs.)*

Pickering: Is this fellow really an expert? Can he find out Eliza and blackmail her?

Higgins: We shall see. If he finds her out I lose my bet.

Eliza comes from the cloakroom and joins them.

Pickering: Well, Eliza, now for it. Are you ready?

Liza: Are you nervous, Colonel?

Pickering: Frightfully. I feel exactly as I felt before my first battle. It's the first time that frightens.

Liza: It is not the first time for me, Colonel. I have done this fifty times — hundreds of times — in my little piggery in Angel Court in my daydreams. I am in a dream now. Promise me not to let Professor Higgins wake me; for if he does I shall forget everything and talk as I used to in Drury Lane.

Pickering: Not a word, Higgins. *(To Eliza.)* Now, ready?

Liza: Ready.

Pickering: Go.

They mount the stairs, Higgins last. Pickering whispers to the footman on the first landing.

First Landing Footman: Miss Doolittle, Colonel Pickering, Professor Higgins.

Second Landing Footman: Miss Doolittle, Colonel Pickering, Professor Higgins.

At the top of the staircase the Ambassador and his wife, with Nepommuck at her elbow, are receiving.

Hostess (taking Eliza's hand): How d'ye do?

Host (same play): How d'ye do? How d'ye do, Pickering?

Liza (with a beautiful gravity that awes her hostess): How do you do? *(She passes on to the drawingroom.)*

Hostess: Is that your adopted daughter, Colonel Pickering? She will make a sensation.

Pickering: Most kind of you to invite her for me. *(He passes on.)*

Hostess (to Nepommuck): Find out all about her.

Nepommuck (bowing): Excellency — *(He goes into the crowd.)*

Host: How d'ye do, Higgins? You have a rival here tonight. He introduced himself as your pupil. Is he any good?

Higgins: He can learn a language in a fortnight — knows dozens of them. A sure mark of a fool. As a phonetician, no good whatever.

Hostess: How d'ye do, Professor?

Higgins: How do you do? Fearful bore for you this sort of thing. Forgive my part in it. *(He passes on.)*

In the drawing room and its suite of salons the reception is in full swing. Eliza passes through. She is so intent on her ordeal that she walks like a somnambulist in a desert instead of a débutante in a fashionable crowd. They stop talking to look at her, admiring her dress, her jewels, and her strangely attractive self. Some of the younger ones at the back stand on their chairs to see.

The Host and Hostess come in from the staircase and mingle with their guests. Higgins, gloomy and contemptuous of the whole business, comes into the group where they are chatting.

Hostess: Ah, here is Professor Higgins: he will tell us. Tell us all about the wonderful young lady, Professor.

Higgins (almost morosely): What wonderful young lady?

Hostess: You know very well. They tell me there has been nothing like her in London since people stood on their chairs to look at Mrs. Langtry.

Nepommuck joins the group, full of news.

Hostess: Ah, here you are at last, Nepommuck. Have you found out all about the Doolittle lady?

Nepommuck: I have found out all about her. She is a fraud.

Hostess: A fraud! Oh no.

Nepommuck: YES, yes. She cannot deceive me. Her name cannot be Doolittle.

Higgins: Why?

Nepommuck: Because Doolittle is an English name. And she is not English.

Hostess: Oh, nonsense! She speaks English perfectly.

Nepommuck: Too perfectly. Can you shew me any English woman who speaks English as it should be spoken? Only foreigners who have been taught to speak it speak it well.

Hostess: Certainly she terrified me by the way she said How d'ye do. I had a schoolmistress who talked like that; and I was mortally afraid of her. But if she is not English what is she?

Nepommuck: Hungarian.

All the Rest: Hungarian!

Nepommuck: Hungarian. And of royal blood. I am Hungarian. My blood is royal.

Higgins: Did you speak to her in Hungarian?

Nepommuck: I did. She was very clever. She said "Please speak to me in English: I do not understand French." French! She pretend not to know the difference between Hungarian and French. Impossible: she knows both.

Higgins: And the blood royal? How did you find that out?

Nepommuck: Instinct, maestro, instinct. Only the Magyar races can produce that air of the divine right, those resolute eyes. She is a princess.

Host: What do you say, Professor?

Higgins: I say an ordinary London girl out of the gutter and taught to speak by an expert. I place her in Drury Lane.

Nepommuck: Ha ha ha! Oh, maestro, maestro, you are mad on the subject of cockney dialects. The London gutter is the whole world for you.

Higgins (to the Hostess): What does your Excellency say?

Hostess: Oh, of course I agree with Nepommuck. She must be a princess at least.

Host: Not necessarily legitimate, of course. Morganatic perhaps. But that is undoubtedly her class.

Higgins: I stick to my opinion.

Hostess: Oh, you are incorrigible.

The group breaks up, leaving Higgins isolated. Pickering joins him.

Pickering: Where is Eliza? We must keep an eye on her.

Eliza joins them.

Liza: I dont think I can bear much more. The people all stare so at me. An old lady has just told me that I speak exactly like Queen Victoria. I am sorry if I have lost your bet. I have done my best; but nothing can make me the same as these people.

Pickering: You have not lost it, my dear. You have won it ten times over.

Higgins: Let us get out of this. I have had enough of chattering to these fools.

Pickering: Eliza is tired; and I am hungry. Let us clear out and have supper somewhere.

ACT IV

The Wimpole Street laboratory. Midnight. Nobody in the room. The clock on the mantelpiece strikes twelve. The fire is not alight: it is a summer night. Presently Higgins and Pickering are heard on the stairs.

Higgins (calling down to Pickering): I say, Pick: lock up, will you? I shant be going out again.

Pickering: Right. Can Mrs. Pearce go to bed? We dont want anything more, do we?

Higgins: Lord, no!

Eliza opens the door and is seen on the lighted landing in all the finery in which she has just won Higgins's bet for him. She comes to the hearth, and switches on the electric lights there. She is tired: her pallor contrasts strongly with her dark eyes and hair; and her expression is almost tragic. She takes off her cloak; puts her fan and gloves on the piano; and sits down on the bench, brooding and silent. Higgins, in evening dress, with overcoat and hat, comes in, carrying a smoking jacket which he has picked up downstairs. He takes off the hat and overcoat; throws them carelessly on the newspaper stand; disposes of his coat in the same way; puts on the smoking jacket; and throws himself wearily into the easy-chair at the hearth. Pickering, similarly attired, comes in. He also takes off his hat and overcoat, and is about to throw them on Higgins's when he hesitates.

Pickering: I say: Mrs. Pearce will row if we leave these things lying about in the drawing room.

Higgins: Oh, chuck them over the bannisters into the hall. She'll find them there in the morning and put them away all right. She'll think we were drunk.

Pickering: We are, slightly. Are there any letters?

Higgins: I didnt look. (*Pickering takes the overcoats and hats and goes downstairs. Higgins begins half singing half yawning an air from La Fanciulla del Golden West. Suddenly he stops and exclaims:*) I wonder where the devil my slippers are!

Eliza looks at him darkly; then rises suddenly and leaves the room.
Higgins yawns again, and resumes his song.
Pickering returns, with the contents of the letter-box in his hand.

Pickering: Only circulars, and this coroneted billet-doux for you. (*He throws the circulars into the fender, and posts himself on the hearth-rug, with his back to the grate.*)

Higgins (glancing at the billet-doux): Money-lender. (*He throws the letter after the circulars.*)

Eliza returns with a pair of large down-at-heel slippers. She places them on the carpet before Higgins, and sits as before without a word.

Higgins (yawning again): Oh Lord! What an evening! What a crew! What a silly tomfoolery! (*He raises his shoe to unlace it, and catches sight of the slippers. He stops unlacing and looks at them as if they had appeared there of their own accord.*) Oh! theyre there, are they?

Pickering (stretching himself): Well, I feel a bit tired. It's been a long day. The garden party, a dinner party, and the reception! Rather too much of a good thing. But youve won your bet, Higgins. Eliza did the trick, and something to spare, eh?

Higgins (fervently): Thank God it's over!

Eliza flinches violently; but they take no notice of her; and she recovers herself and sits stonily as before.

Pickering: Were you nervous at the garden party? *I* was. Eliza didnt seem a bit nervous.

Higgins: Oh, she wasnt nervous. I knew she'd be all right. No: it's the strain of putting the job through all these months that has told on me. It was interesting enough at first, while we were at the phonetics; but after that I got deadly sick of it. If I hadnt backed myself to do it I should have chucked the whole thing up two months ago. It was a silly notion: the whole thing has been a bore.

Pickering: Oh come! the garden party was frightfully exciting. My heart began beating like anything.

Higgins: Yes, for the first three minutes. But when I saw we were going to win hands down, I felt like a bear in a cage, hanging about doing nothing. The dinner was worse: sitting gorging there for over an hour, with nobody but a damned fool of a fashionable woman to talk to! I tell you, Pickering, never again for me. No more artificial duchesses. The whole thing has been simple purgatory.

Pickering: Youve never been broken in properly to the social routine. *(Strolling over to the piano.)* I rather enjoy dipping into it occasionally myself: it makes me feel young again. Anyhow, it was a great success: an immense success. I was quite frightened once or twice because Eliza was doing it so well. You see, lots of the real people cant do it at all: theyre such fools that they think style comes by nature to people in their position; and so they never learn. Theres always something professional about doing a thing superlatively well.

Higgins: Yes: thats what drives me mad: the silly people dont know their own silly business. *(Rising.)* However, it's over and done with; and now I can go to bed at last without dreading tomorrow.

Eliza's beauty becomes murderous.

Pickering: I think I shall turn in too. Still, it's been a great occasion: a triumph for you. Goodnight. *(He goes.)*

Higgins (following him): Goodnight. *(Over his shoulder, at the door.)* Put out the lights, Eliza; and tell Mrs. Pearce not to make coffee for me in the morning: I'll take tea. *(He goes out.)*

Eliza tries to control herself and feel indifferent as she rises and walks across to the hearth to switch off the lights. By the time she gets there she is on the point of screaming. She sits down in Higgins's chair and holds on hard to the arms. Finally she gives way and flings herself furiously on the floor, raging.

Higgins (in despairing wrath outside): What the devil have I done with my slippers? *(He appears at the door.)*

Liza (snatching up the slippers, and hurling them at him one after the other with all her force): There are your slippers. And there. Take your slippers; and may you never have a day's luck with them!

Higgins (astounded): What on earth — ! *(He comes to her.)* Whats the matter? Get up. *(He pulls her up.)* Anything wrong?

Liza (breathless): Nothing wrong — with you. Ive won your bet for you, havnt I? Thats enough for you. *I* dont matter, I suppose.

Higgins: You won my bet! You! Presumptuous insect! *I* won it. What did you throw those slippers at me for?

Liza: Because I wanted to smash your face. I'd like to kill you, you selfish brute. Why didnt you leave me where you picked me out of — in the gutter? You thank God it's all over, and that now you can throw me back again there, do you? *(She crisps her fingers frantically.)*

Higgins (looking at her in cool wonder): The creature is nervous, after all.

Liza (gives a suffocated scream of fury, and instinctively darts her nails at his face): !!

Higgins (catching her wrists): Ah! would you? Claws in, you cat. How dare you shew your temper to me? Sit down and be quiet. *(He throws her roughly into the easy-chair.)*

Liza (crushed by superior strength and weight): Whats to become of me? Whats to become of me?

Higgins: How the devil do I know whats to become of you? What does it matter what becomes of you?

Liza: You dont care. I know you dont care. You wouldnt care if I was dead. I'm nothing to you — not so much as them slippers.

Higgins (thundering): Those slippers.

Liza (with bitter submission): Those slippers. I didnt think it made any difference now.

A pause. Eliza hopeless and crushed. Higgins a little uneasy.

Higgins (in his loftiest manner): Why have you begun going on like this? May I ask whether you complain of your treatment here?

Liza: No.

Higgins: Has anybody behaved badly to you? Colonel Pickering? Mrs. Pearce? Any of the servants?

Liza: No.

Higgins: I presume you dont pretend that *I* have treated you badly?

Liza: No.

Higgins: I am glad to hear it. *(He moderates his tone.)* Perhaps youre tired after the strain of the day. Will you have a glass of champagne? *(He moves towards the door.)*

Liza: No. *(Recollecting her manners.)* Thank you.

Higgins (good-humored again): This has been coming on you for some days. I suppose it was natural for you to be anxious about the garden party. But thats all over now. *(He pats her kindly on the shoulder. She writhes.)* Theres nothing more to worry about.

Liza: No. Nothing more for you to worry about. *(She suddenly rises and gets away from him by going to the piano bench, where she sits and hides her face.)* Oh God! I wish I was dead.

Higgins (staring after her in sincere surprise): Why? In heaven's name, why? *(Reasonably, going to her.)* Listen to me, Eliza. All this irritation is purely subjective.

Liza: I dont understand. I'm too ignorant.

Higgins: It's only imagination. Low spirits and nothing else. Nobody's hurting you. Nothing's wrong. You go to bed like a good girl and sleep it off. Have a little cry and say your prayers: that will make you comfortable.

Liza: I heard your prayers. "Thank God it's all over!"

Higgins (impatiently): Well, dont you thank God it's all over? Now you are free and can do what you like.

Liza (pulling herself together in desperation): What am I fit for? What have you left me fit for? Where am I to go? What am I to do? Whats to become of me?

Higgins (enlightened, but not at all impressed): Oh, thats whats worrying you, is it? *(He thrusts his hands into his pockets, and walks about in his usual manner, rattling the contents of his pockets, as if condescending to a trivial subject out of pure kindness.)* I shouldnt bother about it if I were you. I should imagine you wont have much difficulty in settling yourself somewhere or other, though I hadnt quite realized that you were going away. *(She looks quickly at him: he does not look at her, but examines the dessert stand on the piano and decides that he will eat an apple.)* You might marry, you know. *(He bites a large piece out of the apple and munches it noisily.)* You see, Eliza, all men are not confirmed old bachelors like me and the Colonel. Most men are the marrying sort (poor devils!); and youre not bad-looking: it's quite a pleasure to look at you sometimes — not now, of course, because youre crying and looking as ugly as the very devil; but when youre all right and quite yourself, youre what I should call attractive. That is, to the people in the marrying line, you understand. You go to bed and have a good nice rest; and then get up and look at yourself in the glass; and you wont feel so cheap.

Eliza again looks at him, speechless, and does not stir.
   The look is quite lost on him: he eats his apple with a dreamy expression of happiness, as it is quite a good one.

Higgins (a genial afterthought occurring to him): I daresay my mother could find some chap or other who would do very well.
Liza: We were above that at the corner of Tottenham Court Road.
Higgins (waking up): What do you mean?
Liza: I sold flowers. I didnt sell myself. Now youve made a lady of me I'm not fit to sell anything else. I wish youd left me where you found me.
Higgins (slinging the core of the apple decisively into the grate): Tosh, Eliza. Dont you insult human relations by dragging all this cant about buying and selling into it. You neednt marry the fellow if you dont like him.
Liza: What else am I to do?
Higgins: Oh, lots of things. What about your old idea of a florist's shop? Pickering could set you up in one: he has lots of money. *(Chuckling.)* He'll have to pay for all those togs you have been wearing today; and that, with the hire of the jewelry, will make a big hole in two hundred pounds. Why, six months ago you would have thought it the millennium to have a flower shop of your own. Come! youll be all right. I must clear off to bed: I'm devilish sleepy. By the way, I came down for something: I forget what it was.
Liza: Your slippers.
Higgins: Oh yes, of course. You shied them at me. *(He picks them up, and is going out when she rises and speaks to him.)*
Liza: Before you go, sir —
Higgins (dropping the slippers in his surprise at her calling him Sir): Eh?
Liza: Do my clothes belong to me or to Colonel Pickering?
Higgins (coming back into the room as if her question were the very climax of unreason): What the devil use would they be to Pickering?
Liza: He might want them for the next girl you pick up to experiment on.

Higgins (shocked and hurt): Is that the way you feel towards us?

Liza: I dont want to hear anything more about that. All I want to know is whether anything belongs to me. My own clothes were burnt.

Higgins: But what does it matter? Why need you start bothering about that in the middle of the night?

Liza: I want to know what I may take away with me. I dont want to be accused of stealing.

Higgins (now deeply wounded): Stealing! You shouldnt have said that, Eliza. That shews a want of feeling.

Liza: I'm sorry. I'm only a common ignorant girl; and in my station I have to be careful. There cant be any feelings between the like of you and the like of me. Please will you tell me what belongs to me and what doesnt?

Higgins (very sulky): You may take the whole damned houseful if you like. Except the jewels. Theyre hired. Will that satisfy you? *(He turns on his heel and is about to go in extreme dudgeon.)*

Liza (drinking in his emotion like nectar, and nagging him to provoke a further supply): Stop, please. *(She takes off her jewels.)* Will you take these to your room and keep them safe? I dont want to run the risk of their being missing.

Higgins (furious): Hand them over. *(She puts them into his hands.)* If these belonged to me instead of to the jeweller, I'd ram them down your ungrateful throat. *(He perfunctorily thrusts them into his pockets, unconsciously decorating himself with the protruding ends of the chains.)*

Liza (taking a ring off): This ring isnt the jeweller's: it's the one you bought me in Brighton. I dont want it now. *(Higgins dashes the ring violently into the fireplace, and turns on her so threateningly that she crouches over the piano with her hands over her face, and exclaims.)* Dont you hit me.

Higgins: Hit you! You infamous creature, how dare you accuse me of such a thing? It is you who have hit me. You have wounded me to the heart.

Liza (thrilling with hidden joy): I'm glad. Ive got a little of my own back, anyhow.

Higgins (with dignity, in his finest professional style): You have caused me to lose my temper: a thing that has hardly ever happened to me before. I prefer to say nothing more tonight. I am going to bed.

Liza (pertly): Youd better leave a note for Mrs. Pearce about the coffee; for she wont be told by me.

Higgins (formally): Damn Mrs. Pearce; and damn the coffee; and damn you; and *(wildly)* damn my own folly in having lavished my hard-earned knowledge and the treasure of my regard and intimacy on a heartless guttersnipe. *(He goes out with impressive decorum, and spoils it by slamming the door savagely.)*

Eliza goes down on her knees on the hearthrug to look for the ring. When she finds it she considers for a moment what to do with it. Finally she flings it down on the dessert stand and goes upstairs in a tearing rage.

*   *   *   *   *

The furniture of Eliza's room has been increased by a big wardrobe and a sumptuous dressing-table. She comes in and switches on the electric light. She goes to the wardrobe; opens it; and pulls out a walking dress, a hat, and a pair of shoes, which she throws on the bed. She takes off her evening dress and shoes;

then takes a padded hanger from the wardrobe; adjusts it carefully in the evening dress; and hangs it in the wardrobe, which she shuts with a slam. She puts on her walking shoes, her walking dress, and hat. She takes her wrist watch from the dressing table and fastens it on. She pulls on her gloves; takes her vanity bag; and looks into it to see that her purse is there before hanging it on her wrist. She makes for the door. Every movement expresses her furious resolution.

She takes a last look at herself in the glass.

She suddenly puts out her tongue at herself; then leaves the room, switching off the electric light at the door.

Meanwhile, in the street outside, Freddy Eynsford Hill, lovelorn, is gazing up at the second floor, in which one of the windows is still lighted.

The light goes out.

Freddy: Goodnight, darling, darling, darling.

Eliza comes out, giving the door a considerable bang behind her.

Liza: Whatever are you doing here?
Freddy: Nothing. I spend most of my nights here. It's the only place where I'm happy. Dont laugh at me, Miss Doolittle.
Liza: Dont you call me Miss Doolittle, do you hear? Liza's good enough for me. *(She breaks down and grabs him by the shoulders.)* Freddy: you dont think I'm a heartless guttersnipe, do you?
Freddy: Oh no, no, darling: how can you imagine such a thing? You are the loveliest, dearest —

He loses all self-control and smothers her with kisses. She, hungry for comfort, responds. They stand there in one another's arms.
An elderly police constable arrives.

Constable (scandalized): Now then! Now then!! Now then!!!

They release one another hastily.

Freddy: Sorry, constable. Weve only just become engaged.

They run away.

The constable shakes his head, reflecting on his own courtship and on the vanity of human hopes. He moves off in the opposite direction with slow professional steps.

The flight of the lovers takes them to Cavendish Square. There they halt to consider their next move.

Liza (out of breath): He didnt half give me a fright, that copper. But you answered him proper.
Freddy: I hope I havent taken you out of your way. Where were you going?
Liza: To the river.
Freddy: What for?
Liza: To make a hole in it.
Freddy (horrified): Eliza, darling. What do you mean? What's the matter?

Liza: Never mind. It doesnt matter now. There's nobody in the world now but you and me, is there?

Freddy: Not a soul.

They indulge in another embrace, and are again surprised by a much younger constable.

Second Constable: Now then, you two! What's this? Where do you think you are? Move along here, double quick.

Freddy: As you say, sir, double quick.

They run away again, and are in Hanover Square before they stop for another conference.

Freddy: I had no idea the police were so devilishly prudish.

Liza: It's their business to hunt girls off the streets.

Freddy: We must go somewhere. We cant wander about the streets all night.

Liza: Cant we? I think it'd be lovely to wander about for ever.

Freddy: Oh, darling.

They embrace again, oblivious of the arrival of a crawling taxi. It stops.

Taximan: Can I drive you and the lady anywhere, sir?

They start asunder.

Liza: Oh, Freddy, a taxi. The very thing.

Freddy: But, damn it, I've no money.

Liza: I have plenty. The Colonel thinks you should never go out without ten pounds in your pocket. Listen. We'll drive about all night; and in the morning I'll call on old Mrs. Higgins and ask her what I ought to do. I'll tell you all about it in the cab. And the police wont touch us there.

Freddy: Righto! Ripping. *(To the Taximan.)* Wimbledon Common. *(They drive off.)*

ACT V

Mrs. Higgins's drawing room. She is at her writing-table as before. The parlor-maid comes in.

The Parlor-Maid (at the door): Mr. Henry, maam, is downstairs with Colonel Pickering.

Mrs. Higgins: Well, shew them up.

The Parlor-Maid: Theyre using the telephone, maam. Telephoning to the police, I think.

Mrs. Higgins: What!

The Parlor-Maid (coming further in and lowering her voice): Mr. Henry is in a state, maam. I thought I'd better tell you.

Mrs. Higgins: If you had told me that Mr. Henry was not in a state it would have been more surprising. Tell them to come up when theyve finished with the police. I suppose he's lost something.

The Parlor-Maid: Yes, maam. *(Going.)*

Mrs. Higgins: Go upstairs and tell Miss Doolittle that Mr. Henry and the Colonel are here. Ask her not to come down til I send for her.

The Parlor-Maid: Yes, maam.

Higgins bursts in. He is, as the parlor-maid has said, in a state.

Higgins: Look here, mother: heres a confounded thing!

Mrs. Higgins: Yes, dear. Good morning. (*He checks his impatience and kisses her, whilst the parlor-maid goes out.*) What is it?

Higgins: Eliza's bolted.

Mrs. Higgins (calmly continuing her writing): You must have frightened her.

Higgins: Frightened her! nonsense! She was left last night, as usual, to turn out the lights and all that; and instead of going to bed she changed her clothes and went right off: her bed wasnt slept in. She came in a cab for her things before seven this morning; and that fool Mrs. Pearce let her have them without telling me a word about it. What am I to do?

Mrs. Higgins: Do without, I'm afraid, Henry. The girl has a perfect right to leave if she chooses.

Higgins (wandering distractedly across the room): But I cant find anything. I dont know what appointments Ive got. I'm — (*Pickering comes in. Mrs. Higgins puts down her pen and turns away from the writing-table.*)

Pickering (shaking hands): Good morning, Mrs. Higgins. Has Henry told you? (*He sits down on the ottoman.*)

Higgins: What does that ass of an inspector say? Have you offered a reward?

Mrs. Higgins (rising in indignant amazement): You dont mean to say you have set the police after Eliza.

Higgins: Of course. What are the police for? What else could we do? (*He sits in the Elizabethan chair.*)

Pickering: The inspector made a lot of difficulties. I really think he suspected us of some improper purpose.

Mrs. Higgins: Well, of course he did. What right have you to go to the police and give the girl's name as if she were a thief, or a lost umbrella, or something? Really! (*She sits down again, deeply vexed.*)

Higgins: But we want to find her.

Pickering: We cant let her go like this, you know, Mrs. Higgins. What were we to do?

Mrs. Higgins: You have no more sense, either of you, than two children. Why —

The parlor-maid comes in and breaks off the conversation.

The Parlor-Maid: Mr. Henry: a gentleman wants to see you very particular. He's been sent on from Wimpole Street.

Higgins: Oh, bother! I cant see anyone now. Who is it?

The Parlor-Maid: A Mr. Doolittle, sir.

Pickering: Doolittle! Do you mean the dustman?

The Parlor-Maid: Dustman! Oh no, sir: a gentleman.

Higgins (springing up excitedly): By George, Pick, it's some relative of hers that she's gone to. Somebody we know nothing about. (*To the parlor-maid.*) Send him up, quick.

The Parlor-Maid: Yes, sir. (*She goes.*)

Higgins (eagerly, going to his mother): Genteel relatives! now we shall hear something. *(He sits down in the Chippendale chair.)*
Mrs. Higgins: Do you know any of her people?
Pickering: Only her father: the fellow we told you about.
The Parlor-Maid (announcing): Mr. Doolittle. *(She withdraws.)*

Doolittle enters. He is resplendently dressed as for a fashionable wedding, and might, in fact, be the bridegroom. A flower in his buttonhole, a dazzling silk hat, and patent leather shoes complete the effect. He is too concerned with the business he has come on to notice Mrs. Higgins. He walks straight to Higgins, and accosts him with vehement reproach.

Doolittle (indicating his own person): See here! Do you see this? You done this.
Higgins: Done what, man?
Doolittle: This, I tell you. Look at it. Look at this hat. Look at this coat.
Pickering: Has Eliza been buying you clothes?
Doolittle: Eliza! not she. Why would she buy me clothes?
Mrs. Higgins: Good morning, Mr. Doolittle. Wont you sit down?
Doolittle (taken aback as he becomes conscious that he has forgotten his hostess): Asking your pardon, maam. *(He approaches her and shakes her proffered hand.)* Thank you. *(He sits down on the ottoman, on Pickering's right.)* I am that full of what has happened to me that I cant think of anything else.
Higgins: What the dickens has happened to you?
Doolittle: I shouldnt mind if it had only happened to me: anything might happen to anybody and nobody to blame but Providence, as you might say. But this is something that you done to me: yes, you, Enry Iggins.
Higgins: Have you found Eliza?
Doolittle: Have you lost her?
Higgins: Yes.
Doolittle: You have all the luck, you have. I aint found her; but she'll find me quick enough now after what you done to me.
Mrs. Higgins: But what has my son done to you, Mr. Doolittle?
Doolittle: Done to me! Ruined me. Destroyed my happiness. Tied me up and delivered me into the hands of middle class morality.
Higgins (rising intolerantly and standing over Doolittle): Youre raving. Youre drunk. Youre mad. I gave you five pounds. After that I had two conversations with you, at half-a-crown an hour. Ive never seen you since.
Doolittle: Oh! Drunk am I? Mad am I? Tell me this. Did you or did you not write a letter to an old blighter in America that was giving five millions to found Moral Reform Societies all over the world, and that wanted you to invent a universal language for him?
Higgins: What! Ezra D. Wannafeller! He's dead. *(He sits down again carelessly.)*
Doolittle: Yes: he's dead; and I'm done for. Now did you or did you not write a letter to him to say that the most original moralist at present in England, to the best of your knowledge, was Alfred Doolittle, a common dustman?
Higgins: Oh, after your first visit I remember making some silly joke of the kind.
Doolittle: Ah! you may well call it a silly joke. It put the lid on me right enough. Just give him the chance he wanted to shew that Americans is not like us:

that they reckonize and respect merit in every class of life, however humble. Them words is in his blooming will, in which, Henry Higgins, thanks to your silly joking, he leaves me a share in his Pre-digested Cheese Trust worth three thousand a year on condition that I lecture for his Wannafeller Moral Reform World League as often as they ask me up to six times a year.

Higgins: The devil he does! Whew! (*Brightening suddenly.*) What a lark!

Pickering: A safe thing for you, Doolittle. They wont ask you twice.

Doolittle: It aint the lecturing I mind. I'll lecture them blue in the face, I will, and not turn a hair. It's making a gentleman of me that I object to. Who asked him to make a gentleman of me? I was happy. I was free. I touched pretty nigh everybody for money when I wanted it, same as I touched you, Enry Iggins. Now I am worrited; tied neck and heels; and everybody touches me for money. It's a fine thing for you, says my solicitor. Is it? says I. You mean it's a good thing for you, I says. When I was a poor man and had a solicitor once when they found a pram in the dust cart, he got me off, and got shut of me and got me shut of him as quick as he could. Same with the doctors: used to shove me out of the hospital before I could hardly stand on my legs, and nothing to pay. Now they finds out that I'm not a healthy man and cant live unless they looks after me twice a day. In the house I'm not let do a hand's turn for myself: somebody else must do it and touch me for it. A year ago I hadnt a relative in the world except two or three that wouldnt speak to me. Now Ive fifty, and not a decent week's wages among the lot of them. I have to live for others and not for myself: thats middle class morality. You talk of losing Eliza. Dont you be anxious: I bet she's on my doorstep by this: she that could support herself easy by selling flowers if I wasnt respectable. And the next one to touch me will be you, Enry Iggins. I'll have to learn to speak middle class language from you, instead of speaking proper English. Thats where youll come in; and I daresay thats what you done it for.

Mrs. Higgins: But, my dear Mr. Doolittle, you need not suffer all this if you are really in earnest. Nobody can force you to accept this bequest. You can repudiate it. Isnt that so, Colonel Pickering?

Pickering: I believe so.

Doolittle (softening his manner in deference to her sex): Thats the tragedy of it, maam. It's easy to say chuck it; but I havnt the nerve. Which of us has? We're all intimidated. Intimidated, maam: thats what we are. What is there for me if I chuck it but the workhouse in my old age? I have to dye my hair already to keep my job as a dustman. If I was one of the deserving poor, and had put by a bit, I could chuck it; but then why should I, acause the deserving poor might as well be millionaires for all the happiness they ever has. They dont know what happiness is. But I, as one of the undeserving poor, have nothing between me and the pauper's uniform but this here blasted three thousand a year that shoves me into the middle class. (Excuse the expression, maam; youd use it yourself if you had my provocation.) Theyve got you every way you turn: it's a choice between the Skilly of the workhouse and the Char Bydis of the middle class; and I havnt the nerve for the workhouse. Intimidated: thats what I am.

Broke. Bought up. Happier men than me will call for my dust, and touch me for their tip; and I'll look on helpless, and envy them. And thats what your son brought me to. *(He is overcome by emotion.)*

Mrs. Higgins: Well, I'm very glad youre not going to do anything foolish, Mr. Doolittle. For this solves the problem of Eliza's future. You can provide for her now.

Doolittle (with melancholy resignation): Yes, maam: I'm expected to provide for everyone now, out of three thousand a year.

Higgins (jumping up): Nonsense! he cant provide for her. He shant provide for her. She doesnt belong to him. I paid him five pounds for her. Doolittle: either youre an honest man or a rogue.

Doolittle (tolerantly): A little of both, Henry, like the rest of us: a little of both.

Higgins: Well, you took money for the girl; and you have no right to take her as well.

Mrs. Higgins: Henry: dont be absurd. If you want to know where Eliza is, she is upstairs.

Higgins (amazed): Upstairs!!! Then I shall jolly soon fetch her downstairs. *(He makes resolutely for the door).*

Mrs. Higgins (rising and following him): Be quiet, Henry. Sit down.

Higgins: I —

Mrs. Higgins: Sit down, dear; and listen to me.

Higgins: Oh very well, very well, very well. *(He throws himself ungraciously on the ottoman, with his face towards the windows.)* But I think you might have told us this half an hour ago.

Mrs. Higgins: Eliza came to me this morning. She told me of the brutal way you two treated her.

Higgins (bounding up again): What!

Pickering (rising also): My dear Mrs. Higgins, she's been telling you stories. We didnt treat her brutally. We hardly said a word to her; and we parted on particularly good terms. *(Turning on Higgins.)* Higgins: did you bully her after I went to bed?

Higgins: Just the other way about. She threw my slippers in my face. She behaved in the most outrageous way. I never gave her the slightest provocation. The slippers came bang into my face the moment I entered the room — before I had uttered a word. And used perfectly awful language.

Pickering (astonished): But why? What did we do to her?

Mrs. Higgins: I think I know pretty well what you did. The girl is naturally rather affectionate, I think. Isnt she, Mr. Doolittle?

Doolittle: Very tender-hearted, maam. Takes after me.

Mrs. Higgins: Just so. She had become attached to you both. She worked very hard for you, Henry. I dont think you quite realize what anything in the nature of brain work means to a girl of her class. Well, it seems that when the great day of trial came, and she did this wonderful thing for you without making a single mistake, you two sat there and never said a word to her, but talked together of how glad you were that it was all over and how you had been bored with the whole thing. And then you were surprised because she threw your slippers at you! *I* should have thrown the fire-irons at you.

Higgins: We said nothing except that we were tired and wanted to go to bed. Did we, Pick?

Pickering (shrugging his shoulders): That was all.

Mrs. Higgins (ironically): Quite sure?

Pickering: Absolutely. Really, that was all.

Mrs. Higgins: You didnt thank her, or pet her, or admire her, or tell her how splendid she'd been.

Higgins (impatiently): But she knew all about that. We didnt make speeches to her, if thats what you mean.

Pickering (conscience stricken): Perhaps we were a little inconsiderate. Is she very angry?

Mrs. Higgins (returning to her place at the writing-table): Well, I'm afraid she wont go back to Wimpole Street, especially now that Mr. Doolittle is able to keep up the position you have thrust on her; but she says she is quite willing to meet you on friendly terms and let bygones be bygones.

Higgins (furious): Is she, by George? Ho!

Mrs. Higgins: If you promise to behave yourself, Henry, I'll ask her to come down. If not, go home; for you have taken up quite enough of my time.

Higgins: Oh, all right. Very well. Pick: you behave yourself. Let us put on our best Sunday manners for this creature that we picked out of the mud. *(He flings himself sulkily into the Elizabethan chair.)*

Doolittle (remonstrating): Now, now, Enry Iggins! Have some consideration for my feelings as a middle class man.

Mrs. Higgins: Remember your promise, Henry. *(She presses the bell-button on the writing-table.)* Mr. Doolittle: will you be so good as to step out on the balcony for a moment. I dont want Eliza to have the shock of your news until she has made it up with these two gentlemen. Would you mind?

Doolittle: As you wish, lady. Anything to help Henry to keep her off my hands. *(He disappears through the window.)*

The parlor-maid answers the bell. Pickering sits down in Doolittle's place.

Mrs. Higgins: Ask Miss Doolittle to come down, please.

The Parlor-Maid: Yes, maam. *(She goes out.)*

Mrs. Higgins: Now, Henry: be good.

Higgins: I am behaving myself perfectly.

Pickering: He is doing his best, Mrs. Higgins.

A pause. Higgins throws back his head; stretches out his legs; and begins to whistle.

Mrs. Higgins: Henry, dearest, you dont look at all nice in that attitude.

Higgins (pulling himself together): I was not trying to look nice, mother.

Mrs. Higgins: It doesnt matter, dear. I only wanted to make you speak.

Higgins: Why?

Mrs. Higgins: Because you cant speak and whistle at the same time.

Higgins groans. Another very trying pause.

Higgins (springing up, out of patience): Where the devil is that girl? Are we to wait here all day?

Eliza enters, sunny, self-possessed, and giving a staggeringly convincing exhibition of ease of manner. She carries a little workbasket, and is very much at home. Pickering is too much taken aback to rise.

Liza: How do you do, Professor Higgins? Are you quite well?

Higgins (choking): Am I — *(He can say no more.)*

Liza: But of course you are: you are never ill. So glad to see you again, Colonel Pickering. *(He rises hastily; and they shake hands.)* Quite chilly this morning, isnt it? *(She sits down on his left. He sits beside her.)*

Higgins: Dont you dare try this game on me. I taught it to you; and it doesnt take me in. Get up and come home; and dont be a fool.

Eliza takes a piece of needlework from her basket, and begins to stitch at it, without the least notice of this outburst.

Mrs. Higgins: Very nicely put, indeed, Henry. No woman could resist such an invitation.

Higgins: You let her alone, mother. Let her speak for herself. You will jolly soon see whether she has an idea that I havnt put into her head or a word that I havnt put into her mouth. I tell you I have created this thing out of the squashed cabbage leaves of Covent Garden; and now she pretends to play the fine lady with me.

Mrs. Higgins (placidly): Yes, dear; but youll sit down, wont you?

Higgins sits down again, savagely.

Liza (to Pickering, taking no apparent notice of Higgins, and working away deftly): Will you drop me altogether now that the experiment is over, Colonel Pickering?

Pickering: Oh dont. You mustnt think of it as an experiment. It shocks me, somehow.

Liza: Oh, I'm only a squashed cabbage leaf —

Pickering (impulsively): No.

Liza (continuing quietly): — but I owe so much to you that I should be very unhappy if you forgot me.

Pickering: It's very kind of you to say so, Miss Doolittle.

Liza: It's not because you paid for my dresses. I know you are generous to everybody with money. But it was from you that I learnt really nice manners; and that is what makes one a lady, isnt it? You see it was so very difficult for me with the example of Professor Higgins always before me. I was brought up to be just like him, unable to control myself, and using bad language on the slightest provocation. And I should never have known that ladies and gentlemen didnt behave like that if you hadnt been there.

Higgins: Well!!

Pickering: Oh, thats only his way, you know. He doesnt mean it.

Liza: Oh, *I* didnt mean it either, when I was a flower girl. It was only my way. But you see I did it; and thats what makes the difference after all.

Pickering: No doubt. Still, he taught you to speak, and I couldnt have done that, you know.

Liza (trivially): Of course: that is his profession.

Higgins: Damnation!

Liza (continuing): It was just like learning to dance in the fashionable way: there was nothing more than that in it. But do you know what began my real education?

Pickering: What?

Liza (stopping her work for a moment): Your calling me Miss Doolittle that day when I first came to Wimpole Street. That was the beginning of self-respect for me. *(She resumes her stitching.)* And there were a hundred little things you never noticed, because they came naturally to you. Things about standing up and taking off your hat and opening doors —

Pickering: Oh, that was nothing.

Liza: Yes: things that shewed you thought and felt about me as if I were something better than a scullery-maid; though of course I know you would have been just the same to a scullery-maid if she had been let into the drawing room. You never took off your boots in the dining room when I was there.

Pickering: You mustnt mind that. Higgins takes off his boots all over the place.

Liza: I know. I am not blaming him. It is his way, isnt it? But it made such a difference to me that you didnt do it. You see, really and truly, apart from the things anyone can pick up (the dressing and the proper way of speaking, and so on), the difference between a lady and a flower girl is not how she behaves, but how she's treated. I shall always be a flower girl to Professor Higgins, because he always treats me as a flower girl, and always will; but I know I can be a lady to you, because you always treat me as a lady, and always will.

Mrs. Higgins: Please dont grind your teeth, Henry.

Pickering: Well, this is really very nice of you, Miss Doolittle.

Liza: I should like you to call me Eliza, now, if you would.

Pickering: Thank you. Eliza, of course.

Liza: And I should like Professor Higgins to call me Miss Doolittle.

Higgins: I'll see you damned first.

Mrs. Higgins: Henry! Henry!

Pickering (laughing): Why dont you slang back at him? Dont stand it. It would do him a lot of good.

Liza: I cant. I could have done it once; but now I cant go back to it. You told me, you know, that when a child is brought to a foreign country, it picks up the language in a few weeks, and forgets its own. Well, I am a child in your country. I have forgotten my own language, and can speak nothing but yours. Thats the real break-off with the corner of Tottenham Court Road. Leaving Wimpole Street finishes it.

Pickering (much alarmed): Oh! but youre coming back to Wimpole Street, arnt you? Youll forgive Higgins?

Higgins (rising): Forgive! Will she, by George! Let her go. Let her find out how she can get on without us. She will relapse into the gutter in three weeks without me at her elbow.

Doolittle appears at the centre window. With a look of dignified reproach at Higgins, he comes slowly and silently to his daughter, who, with her back to the window, is unconscious of his approach.

Pickering: He's incorrigible, Eliza. You wont relapse, will you?

Liza: No: not now. Never again. I have learnt my lesson. I dont believe I could utter one of the old sounds if I tried. (*Doolittle touches her on the left shoulder. She drops her work, losing her self-possession utterly at the spectacle of her father's splendor.*) A-a-a-a-ah-ow-ooh!

Higgins (with a crow of triumph): Aha! Just so. A-a-a-a-ahowooh! A-a-a-a-ahowooh! A-a-a-a-ahowooh! Victory! Victory! (*He throws himself on the divan, folding his arms, and spraddling arrogantly.*)

Doolittle: Can you blame the girl? Dont look at me like that, Eliza. It aint my fault. Ive come into some money.

Liza: You must have touched a millionaire this time, dad.

Doolittle: I have. But I'm dressed something special today. I'm going to St. George's, Hanover Square. Your stepmother is going to marry me.

Liza (angrily): Youre going to let yourself down to marry that low common woman!

Pickering (quietly): He ought to, Eliza. (*To Doolittle.*) Why has she changed her mind?

Doolittle (sadly): Intimidated, Governor. Intimidated. Middle class morality claims its victim. Wont you put on your hat, Liza, and come and see me turned off?

Liza: If the Colonel says I must, I — I'll (*almost sobbing*) I'll demean myself. And get insulted for my pains, like enough.

Doolittle: Dont be afraid: she never comes to words with anyone now, poor woman! respectability has broke all the spirit out of her.

Pickering (squeezing Eliza's elbow gently): Be kind to them, Eliza. Make the best of it.

Liza (forcing a little smile for him through her vexation): Oh well, just to shew theres no ill feeling. I'll be back in a moment. (*She goes out.*)

Doolittle (sitting down beside Pickering): I feel uncommon nervous about the ceremony, Colonel. I wish youd come and see me through it.

Pickering: But youve been through it before, man. You were married to Eliza's mother.

Doolittle: Who told you that, Colonel?

Pickering: Well, nobody told me. But I concluded — naturally —

Doolittle: No: that aint the natural way, Colonel: it's only the middle class way. My way was always the undeserving way. But dont say nothing to Eliza. She dont know: I always had a delicacy about telling her.

Pickering: Quite right. We'll leave it so, if you dont mind.

Doolittle: And youll come to the church, Colonel, and put me through straight?

Pickering: With pleasure. As far as a bachelor can.

Mrs. Higgins: May I come, Mr. Doolittle? I should be very sorry to miss your wedding.

Doolittle: I should indeed be honored by your condescension, maam; and my poor old woman would take it as a tremenjous compliment. She's been very low, thinking of the happy days that are no more.

Mrs. Higgins (rising): I'll order the carriage and get ready. (*The men rise, except Higgins.*) I shant be more than fifteen minutes. (*As she goes to the door Eliza comes in, hatted and buttoning her gloves.*) I'm going to the church to see your father married, Eliza. You had better come in the brougham with me. Colonel Pickering can go on with the bridegroom.

Mrs. Higgins goes out. Eliza comes to the middle of the room between the centre window and the ottoman. Pickering joins her.

Doolittle: Bridegroom. What a word! It makes a man realize his position, somehow. *(He takes up his hat and goes towards the door.)*

Pickering: Before I go, Eliza, do forgive Higgins and come back to us.

Liza: I dont think dad would allow me. Would you, dad?

Doolittle (sad but magnanimous): They played you off very cunning, Eliza, them two sportsmen. If it had been only one of them, you could have nailed him. But you see, there was two; and one of them chaperoned the other, as you might say. *(To Pickering.)* It was artful of you, Colonel; but I bear no malice: I should have done the same myself. I been the victim of one woman after another all my life, and I dont grudge you two getting the better of Liza. I shant interfere. It's time for us to go, Colonel. So long, Henry. See you in St. George's, Eliza. *(He goes out.)*

Pickering (coaxing): Do stay with us, Eliza. *(He follows Doolittle.)*

Eliza goes out on the balcony to avoid being alone with Higgins. He rises and joins her there. She immediately comes back into the room and makes for the door; but he goes along the balcony and gets his back to the door before she reaches it.

Higgins: Well, Eliza, youve had a bit of your own back, as you call it. Have you had enough? and are you going to be reasonable? Or do you want any more?

Liza: You want me back only to pick up your slippers and put up with your tempers and fetch and carry for you.

Higgins: I havnt said I wanted you back at all.

Liza: Oh, indeed. Then what are we talking about?

Higgins: About you, not about me. If you come back I shall treat you just as I have always treated you. I cant change my nature; and I dont intend to change my manners. My manners are exactly the same as Colonel Pickering's.

Liza: Thats not true. He treats a flower girl as if she was a duchess.

Higgins: And I treat a duchess as if she was a flower girl.

Liza: I see. *(She turns away composedly, and sits on the ottoman, facing the window.)* The same to everybody.

Higgins: Just so.

Liza: Like father.

Higgins (grinning, a little taken down): Without accepting the comparison at all points, Eliza, it's quite true that your father is not a snob, and that he will be quite at home in any station of life to which his eccentric destiny may call him. *(Seriously.)* The great secret, Eliza, is not having bad manners or good manners or any other particular sort of manners, but having the same manner for all human souls: in short, behaving as if you were in Heaven, where there are no third-class carriages, and one soul is as good as another.

Liza: Amen. You are a born preacher.

Higgins (irritated): The question is not whether I treat you rudely, but whether you ever heard me treat anyone else better.

Liza (*with sudden sincerity*): I dont care how you treat me. I dont mind your swearing at me. I shouldnt mind a black eye: Ive had one before this. But (*standing up and facing him*) I wont be passed over.

Higgins: Then get out of my way; for I wont stop for you. You talk about me as if I were a motor bus.

Liza: So you are a motor bus: all bounce and go, and no consideration for anyone. But I can do without you: dont think I cant.

Higgins: I know you can. I told you you could.

Liza (*wounded, getting away from him to the other side of the ottoman with her face to the hearth*): I know you did, you brute. You wanted to get rid of me.

Higgins: Liar.

Liza: Thank you. (*She sits down with dignity.*)

Higgins: You never asked yourself, I suppose, whether *I* could do without you.

Liza (*earnestly*): Dont you try to get round me. Youll have to do without me.

Higgins (*arrogant*): I can do without anybody. I have my own soul: my own spark of divine fire. But (*with sudden humility*) I shall miss you, Eliza. (*He sits down near her on the ottoman.*) I have learnt something from your idiotic notions: I confess that humbly and gratefully. And I have grown accustomed to your voice and appearance. I like them, rather.

Liza: Well, you have both of them on your gramophone and in your book of photographs. When you feel lonely without me, you can turn the machine on. It's got no feelings to hurt.

Higgins: I cant turn your soul on. Leave me those feelings; and you can take away the voice and the face. They are not you.

Liza: Oh, you are a devil. You can twist the heart in a girl as easy as some could twist her arms to hurt her. Mrs. Pearce warned me. Time and again she has wanted to leave you; and you always got round her at the last minute. And you dont care a bit for her. And you dont care a bit for me.

Higgins: I care for life, for humanity; and you are a part of it that has come my way and been built into my house. What more can you or anyone ask?

Liza: I wont care for anybody that doesnt care for me.

Higgins: Commercial principles, Eliza. Like (*reproducing her Covent Garden pronunciation with professional exactness*) s'yollin voylets [selling violets], isnt it?

Liza: Dont sneer at me. It's mean to sneer at me.

Higgins: I have never sneered in my life. Sneering doesnt become either the human face or the human soul. I am expressing my righteous contempt for Commercialism. I dont and wont trade in affection. You call me a brute because you couldnt buy a claim on me by fetching my slippers and finding my spectacles. You were a fool: I think a woman fetching a man's slippers is a disgusting sight: did I ever fetch your slippers? I think a good deal more of you for throwing them in my face. No use slaving for me and then saying you want to be cared for: who cares for a slave? If you come back, come back for the sake of good fellowship; for youll get nothing else. Youve had a thousand times as much out of me as I have out of you; and if you dare to set up your little dog's tricks of fetching and carrying slippers against my creation of a Duchess Eliza, I'll slam the door in your silly face.

Liza: What did you do it for if you didnt care for me?

Higgins (heartily): Why, because it was my job.

Liza: You never thought of the trouble it would make for me.

Higgins: Would the world ever have been made if its maker had been afraid of making trouble? Making life means making trouble. Theres only one way of escaping trouble; and thats killing things. Cowards, you notice, are always shrieking to have troublesome people killed.

Liza: I'm no preacher: I dont notice things like that. I notice that you dont notice me.

Higgins (jumping up and walking about intolerantly): Eliza: youre an idiot. I waste the treasures of my Miltonic mind by spreading them before you. Once for all, understand that I go my way and do my work without caring twopence what happens to either of us. I am not intimidated, like your father and stepmother. So you can come back or go to the devil: which you please.

Liza: What am I to come back for?

Higgins (bouncing up on his knees on the ottoman and leaning over it to her): For the fun of it. Thats why I took you on.

Liza (with averted face): And you may throw me out tomorrow if I dont do everything you want me to?

Higgins: Yes; and you may walk out tomorrow if I dont do everything you want me to.

Liza: And live with my stepmother?

Higgins: Yes, or sell flowers.

Liza: Oh! if I only could go back to my flower basket! I should be independent of both you and father and all the world! Why did you take my independence from me? Why did I give it up? I'm a slave now, for all my fine clothes.

Higgins: Not a bit. I'll adopt you as my daughter and settle money on you if you like. Or would you rather marry Pickering?

Liza (looking fiercely round at him): I wouldnt marry you if you asked me; and youre nearer my age than what he is.

Higgins (gently): Than he is: not "than what he is."

Liza (losing her temper and rising): I'll talk as I like. Youre not my teacher now.

Higgins (reflectively): I dont suppose Pickering would, though. He's as confirmed an old bachelor as I am.

Liza: Thats not what I want; and dont you think it. I've always had chaps enough wanting me that way. Freddy Hill writes to me twice and three times a day, sheets and sheets.

Higgins (disagreeably surprised): Damn his impudence! *(He recoils and finds himself sitting on his heels.)*

Liza: He has a right to if he likes, poor lad. And he does love me.

Higgins (getting off the ottoman): You have no right to encourage him.

Liza: Every girl has a right to be loved.

Higgins: What! By fools like that?

Liza: Freddy's not a fool. And if he's weak and poor and wants me, may be he'd make me happier than my betters that bully me and dont want me.

Higgins: Can he make anything of you? That's the point.

Liza: Perhaps I could make something of him. But I never thought of us making anything of one another; and you never think of anything else. I only want to be natural.

Higgins: In short, you want me to be as infatuated about you as Freddy? Is that it?

Liza: No I dont. Thats not the sort of feeling I want from you. And dont you be too sure of yourself or of me. I could have been a bad girl if I'd liked. Ive seen more of some things than you, for all your learning. Girls like me can drag gentlemen down to make love to them easy enough. And they wish each other dead the next minute.

Higgins: Of course they do. Then what in thunder are we quarrelling about?

Liza (much troubled): I want a little kindness. I know I'm a common ignorant girl, and you a book-learned gentleman; but I'm not dirt under your feet. What I done *(correcting herself)* what I did was not for the dresses and the taxis: I did it because we were pleasant together and I come — came — to care for you; not to want you to make love to me, and not forgetting the difference between us, but more friendly like.

Higgins: Well, of course. Thats just how I feel. And how Pickering feels. Eliza: youre a fool.

Liza: Thats not a proper answer to give me. *(She sinks on the chair at the writing-table in tears.)*

Higgins: It's all youll get until you stop being a common idiot. If youre going to be a lady, youll have to give up feeling neglected if the men you know dont spend half their time snivelling over you and the other half giving you black eyes. If you cant stand the coldness of my sort of life, and the strain of it, go back to the gutter. Work til youre more a brute than a human being; and then cuddle and squabble and drink til you fall asleep. Oh, it's a fine life, the life of the gutter. It's real: it's warm: it's violent: you can feel it through the thickest skin: you can taste it and smell it without any training or any work. Not like Science and Literature and Classical Music and Philosophy and Art. You find me cold, unfeeling, selfish, dont you? Very well: be off with you to the sort of people you like. Marry some sentimental hog or other with lots of money, and a thick pair of lips to kiss you with and a thick pair of boots to kick you with. If you cant appreciate what youve got, youd better get what you can appreciate.

Liza (desperate): Oh, you are a cruel tyrant. I cant talk to you: you turn everything against me: I'm always in the wrong. But you know very well all the time that youre nothing but a bully. You know I cant go back to the gutter, as you call it, and that I have no real friends in the world but you and the Colonel. You know well I couldnt bear to live with a low common man after you two; and it's wicked and cruel of you to insult me by pretending I could. You think I must go back to Wimpole Street because I have nowhere else to go but father's. But dont you be too sure that you have me under your feet to be trampled on and talked down. I'll marry Freddy, I will, as soon as I'm able to support him.

Higgins (thunderstruck): Freddy!!! that young fool! That poor devil who couldnt get a job as an errand boy even if he had the guts to try for it! Woman: do you not understand that I have made you a consort for a king?

Liza: Freddy loves me: that makes him king enough for me. I dont want him to work: he wasnt brought up to it as I was. I'll go and be a teacher.

Higgins: Whatll you teach, in heaven's name?

Liza: What you taught me. I'll teach phonetics.

Higgins: Ha! ha! ha!

Liza: I'll offer myself as an assistant to that hairyfaced Hungarian.

Higgins (rising in a fury): What! That imposter! that humbug! that toadying ignoramus! Teach him my methods! my discoveries! You take one step in his direction and I'll wring your neck. *(He lays hands on her.)* Do you hear?

Liza (defiantly non-resistant): Wring away. What do I care? I knew youd strike me some day. *(He lets her go, stamping with rage at having forgotten himself, and recoils so hastily that he stumbles back into his seat on the ottoman.)* Aha! Now I know how to deal with you. What a fool I was not to think of it before! You cant take away the knowledge you gave me. You said I had a finer ear than you. And I can be civil and kind to people, which is more than you can. Aha! *(Purposely dropping her aitches to annoy him.)* Thats done you, Enry Iggins, it az. Now I dont care that *(snapping her fingers)* for your bullying and your big talk. I'll advertize it in the papers that your duchess is only a flower girl that you taught, and that she'll teach anybody to be a duchess just the same in six months for a thousand guineas. Oh, when I think of myself crawling under your feet and being trampled on and called names, when all the time I had only to lift up my finger to be as good as you, I could just kick myself.

Higgins (wondering at her): You damned impudent slut, you! But it's better than snivelling; better than fetching slippers and finding spectacles, isn't it? *(Rising.)* By George, Eliza, I said I'd make a woman of you; and I have. I like you like this.

Liza: Yes: you turn round and make up to me now that I'm not afraid of you, and can do without you.

Higgins: Of course I do, you little fool. Five minutes ago you were like a mill-stone round my neck. Now youre a tower of strength: a consort battleship. You and I and Pickering will be three old bachelors instead of only two men and a silly girl.

Mrs. Higgins returns, dressed for the wedding. Eliza instantly becomes cool and elegant.

Mrs. Higgins: The carriage is waiting, Eliza. Are you ready?

Liza: Quite. Is the Professor coming?

Mrs. Higgins: Certainly not. He cant behave himself in church. He makes remarks out loud all the time on the clergyman's pronunciation.

Liza. Then I shall not see you again, Professor. Goodbye. *(She goes to the door.)*

Mrs. Higgins (coming to Higgins): Goodbye, dear.

Higgins: Goodbye, mother. *(He is about to kiss her, when he recollects something.)* Oh, by the way, Eliza, order a ham and a Stilton cheese, will you? And buy me a pair of reindeer gloves, number eights, and a tie to match that new suit of mine. You can choose the color. *(His cheerful, careless, vigorous voice shews that he is incorrigible.)*

Liza (disdainfully): Number eights are too small for you if you want them lined with lamb's wool. You have three new ties that you have forgotten in the drawer of your washstand. Colonel Pickering prefers double Glouce-ster to Stilton; and you dont notice the difference. I telephoned Mrs.

Pearce this morning not to forget the ham. What you are to do without me I cannot imagine. *(She sweeps out.)*

Mrs. Higgins: I'm afraid youve spoilt that girl, Henry. I should be uneasy about you and her if she were less fond of Colonel Pickering.

Higgins: Pickering! Nonsense: she's going to marry Freddy. Ha ha! Freddy! Freddy!! Ha ha ha ha ha!!!!! *(He roars with laughter as the play ends.)*

The rest of the story need not be shown in action, and indeed, would hardly need telling if our imaginations were not so enfeebled by their lazy dependence on the ready-mades and reach-me-downs of the ragshop in which Romance keeps its stock of "happy endings" to misfit all stories. Now, the history of Eliza Doolittle, though called a romance because the transfiguration it records seems exceedingly improbable, is common enough. Such transfigurations have been achieved by hundreds of resolutely ambitious young women since Nell Gwynne set them the example by playing queens and fascinating kings in the theatre in which she began by selling oranges. Nevertheless, people in all directions have assumed, for no other reason than that she became the heroine of a romance, that she must have married the hero of it. This is unbearable, not only because her little drama, if acted on such a thoughtless assumption, must be spoiled, but because the true sequel is patent to anyone with a sense of human nature in general, and of feminine instinct in particular.

Eliza, in telling Higgins she would not marry him if he asked her, was not coquetting: she was announcing a well-considered decision. When a bachelor interests, and dominates, and teaches, and becomes important to a spinster, as Higgins with Eliza, she always, if she has character enough to be capable of it, considers very seriously indeed whether she will play for becoming that bachelor's wife, especially if he is so little interested in marriage that a determined and devoted woman might capture him if she set herself resolutely to do it. Her decision will depend a good deal on whether she is really free to choose; and that, again, will depend on her age and income. If she is at the end of her youth, and has no security for her livelihood, she will marry him because she must marry anybody who will provide for her. But at Eliza's age a good-looking girl does not feel that pressure: she feels free to pick and choose. She is therefore guided by her instinct in the matter. Eliza's instinct tells her not to marry Higgins. It does not tell her to give him up. It is not in the slightest doubt as to his remaining one of the strongest personal interests in her life. It would be very sorely strained if there was another woman likely to supplant her with him. But as she feels sure of him on that last point, she has no doubt at all as to her course, and would not have any, even if the difference of twenty years in age, which seems so great to youth, did not exist between them.

As our own instincts are not appealed to by her conclusion, let us see whether we cannot discover some reason in it. When Higgins excused his indifference to young women on the ground that they had an irresistible rival in his mother, he gave the clue to his inveterate old-bachelordom. The case is uncommon only to the extent that remarkable mothers are uncommon. If an imaginative boy has a sufficiently rich mother who has intelligence, personal grace, dignity of character without harshness, and a cultivated sense of the best art of her time to enable her to make her house beautiful, she sets a standard for him against which very few women can struggle, besides effecting for him a disengagement of his affections, his sense of beauty, and his idealism from his specifically sexual impulses. This makes him a standing puzzle to the huge number of uncultivated people who have been brought up in tasteless homes by commonplace or disagreeable parents, and to whom, consequently, literature, painting, sculpture, music, and affectionate personal relations come as modes of sex if they come at all. The word passion means nothing else to them; and that Higgins could have a passion for phonetics and idealize his mother instead of Eliza, would seem to them absurd and unnatural. Nevertheless, when we look round and see that hardly anyone is too ugly or disagreeable to find a wife or a husband if he or she wants one, whilst many old maids and bachelors are above the average in quality and culture, we cannot help suspecting that the disentanglement of sex from the associations with which it is so commonly confused, a disentanglement which persons of genius achieve by sheer intellectual analysis, is sometimes produced or aided by parental fascination.

Now, though Eliza was incapable of thus explaining to herself Higgins's formidable powers of resistance to the charm that prostrated Freddy at the first glance, she was instinctively aware that she could never obtain a complete grip of him, or come between him and his mother (the first necessity of the married woman). To put it shortly, she knew that for some mysterious reason he had not the makings of a married man in him, according to her conception of a husband as one to whom she would be his nearest and fondest and warmest interest. Even had there been no mother-rival, she would still have refused to accept an interest in herself that was secondary to philosophic interests. Had Mrs. Higgins died, there would still have been Milton and the Universal Alphabet. Landor's remark that to those who have the greatest power of loving, love is a secondary affair, would not have recommended Landor to Eliza. Put that along with her resentment of Higgins's domineering superiority, and her mistrust of his coaxing cleverness in getting round her and evading her wrath when he had gone too far with his impetuous bullying, and you will see that Eliza's instinct had good grounds for warning her not to marry her Pygmalion.

And now, whom did Eliza marry? For if Higgins was a predestinate old bachelor, she was most certainly not a predestinate old maid. Well, that can be told very shortly to those who have not guessed it from the indications she has herself given them.

Almost immediately after Eliza is stung into proclaiming her considered determination not to marry Higgins, she mentions the fact that young Mr. Frederick Eynsford Hill is pouring out his love for her daily through the post. Now Freddy is young, practically twenty years younger than Higgins: he is a gentleman (or, as Eliza would qualify him, a toff), and speaks like one. He is nicely dressed, is treated by the Colonel as an equal, loves her unaffectedly, and is not her master, nor ever likely to dominate her in spite of his advantage of social standing. Eliza has no use for the foolish romantic tradition that all women love to be mastered, if not actually bullied and beaten. "When you go to women," says Nietzsche, "take your whip with you." Sensible despots have never confined that precaution to women: they have taken their whips with them when they have dealt with men, and been slavishly idealized by the men over whom they have flourished the whip much more than by women. No doubt there are slavish women as well as slavish men; and women, like men, admire those that are stronger than themselves. But to admire a strong person and to live under that strong person's thumb are two different things. The weak may not be admired and hero-worshipped; but they are by no means disliked or shunned; and they never seem to have the least difficulty in marrying people who are too good for them. They may fail in emergencies; but life is not one long emergency: it is mostly a string of situations for which no exceptional strength is needed, and with which even rather weak people can cope if they have a stronger partner to help them out. Accordingly, it is a truth everywhere in evidence that strong people, masculine or feminine, not only do not marry stronger people, but do not show any preference for them in selecting their friends. When a lion meets another with a louder roar "the first lion thinks the last a bore." The man or woman who feels strong enough for two, seeks for every other quality in a partner than strength.

The converse is also true. Weak people want to marry strong people who do not frighten them too much; and this often leads them to make the mistake we describe metaphorically as "biting off more than they can chew." They want too much for too little; and when the bargain is unreasonable beyond all bearing, the union becomes impossible: it ends in the weaker party being either discarded or borne as a cross, which is worse. People who are not only weak, but silly or obtuse as well, are often in these difficulties.

This being the state of human affairs, what is Eliza fairly sure to do when she is placed between Freddy and Higgins? Will she look forward to a lifetime of fetching Higgins's slippers or to a lifetime of Freddy fetching hers? There can be no doubt about the answer. Unless Freddy is biologically repulsive to her, and Higgins biologically attractive to a degree that overwhelms all her other instincts, she will, if she marries either of them, marry Freddy.

And that is just what Eliza did.

Complications ensued; but they were economic, not romantic. Freddy had no money and no occupation. His mother's jointure, a last relic of the opulence of Largelady Park, had enabled her to struggle along in Earlscourt with an air of gentility, but not to procure any serious secondary education for her children, much less give the boy a profession. A clerkship at thirty shillings a week was beneath Freddy's dignity, and extremely distasteful to him besides. His prospects consisted of a hope that if he kept up appearances somebody would do something for him. The something appeared vaguely to his imagination as a private secretaryship or a sinecure of some sort. To his mother it perhaps appeared as a marriage to some lady of means who could not resist her boy's niceness. Fancy her feelings when he married a flower girl who had become disclassed under extraordinary circumstances which were now notorious!

It is true that Eliza's situation did not seem wholly ineligible. Her father, though formerly a dustman, and now fantastically disclassed, had become extremely popular in the smartest society by a social talent which triumphed over every prejudice and every disadvantage. Rejected by the middle class, which he loathed, he had shot up at once into the highest circles by his wit, his dustmanship (which he carried like a banner), and his Nietzschean transcendence of good and evil. At intimate ducal dinners he sat on the right hand of the Duchess; and in country houses he smoked in the pantry and was made much of by the butler when he was not feeding in the dining room and being consulted by cabinet ministers. But he found it almost as hard to do all this on four thousand a year as Mrs. Eynsford Hill to live in Earlscourt on an income so pitiably smaller that I have not the heart to disclose its exact figure. He absolutely refused to add the last straw to his burden by contributing to Eliza's support.

Thus Freddy and Eliza, now Mr. and Mrs. Eynsford Hill, would have spent a penniless honeymoon but for a wedding present of £500 from the Colonel to Eliza. It lasted a long time because Freddy did not know how to spend money, never having had any to spend, and Eliza, socially trained by a pair of old bachelors, wore her clothes as long as they held together and looked pretty, without the least regard to their being many months out of fashion. Still, £500 will not last two young people for ever; and they both knew, and Eliza felt as well, that they must shift for themselves in the end. She could quarter herself on Wimpole Street because it had come to be her home; but she was quite aware that she ought not to quarter Freddy there, and that it would not be good for his character if she did.

Not that the Wimpole Street bachelors objected. When she consulted them, Higgins declined to be bothered about her housing problem when that solution was so simple. Eliza's desire to have Freddy in the house with her seemed of no more importance than if she had wanted an extra piece of bedroom furniture. Pleas as to Freddy's character, and the moral obligation on him to earn his own living, were lost on Higgins. He denied that Freddy had any character, and declared that if he tried to do any useful work some competent person would have the trouble of undoing it: a procedure involving a net loss to the community, and great unhappiness to Freddy himself, who was obviously intended by Nature for such light work as amusing Eliza, which, Higgins declared, was a much more useful and honorable occupation than working in the city. When Eliza referred again to her project of teaching phonetics, Higgins abated not a jot of his violent opposition to it. He said she was not within ten years of being qualified to meddle with his pet subject; and as it was evident that the Colonel agreed with him, she felt she could not go against them in this grave matter, and that she had no right, without Higgins's consent, to exploit the knowledge he had given her; for his knowledge seemed to her as much his private property as his watch: Eliza was no communist. Besides, she was superstitiously devoted to them both, more entirely and frankly after her marriage than before it.

It was the Colonel who finally solved the problem, which had cost him much perplexed cogitation. He one day asked Eliza, rather shyly, whether she had quite given up her notion of keeping a flower shop. She replied that she had thought of it, but had put it out of her head, because the Colonel had said, that day at Mrs. Higgins's, that it would never do. The Colonel confessed that when he said that, he had not quite recovered from the dazzling impression of the day before. They broke the matter to Higgins that evening. The sole comment vouchsafed by him very nearly led to a serious quarrel with Eliza. It was to the effect that she would have in Freddy an ideal errand boy.

Freddy himself was next sounded on the subject. He said he had been thinking of a shop himself; though it had presented itself to his pennilessness as a small place in which Eliza should sell tobacco at one counter whilst he sold newspapers at the opposite one. But he agreed that it would be extraordinarily jolly to go early every morning with Eliza to Covent Garden and buy flowers on the scene of their first meeting: a sentiment which earned him many kisses from his wife. He added that he had always been afraid to propose anything of the sort, because Clara would make an awful row about a step that must damage her matrimonial chances, and his mother could not be expected to like it after clinging for so many years to that step of the social ladder on which retail trade is impossible.

This difficulty was removed by an event highly unexpected by Freddy's mother. Clara, in the course of her incursions into those artistic circles which were the highest within her reach, discovered that her conversational qualifications were expected to include a grounding in the novels of Mr. H. G. Wells. She borrowed them in various directions so energetically that she swallowed them all within two months. The result was a conversion of a kind quite common today. A modern Acts of the Apostles would fill fifty whole Bibles if anyone were capable of writing it.

Poor Clara, who appeared to Higgins and his mother as a disagreeable and ridiculous person, and to her own mother as in some inexplicable way a social failure, had never seen herself in either light; for, though to some extent ridiculed and mimicked in West Kensington like everybody else there, she was accepted as a rational and normal — or shall we say inevitable? — sort of human being. At worst they called her The Pusher; but to them no more than to herself had it ever occurred that she was pushing the air, and pushing it in a wrong direction. Still, she was not happy. She was growing desperate. Her one asset, the fact that her mother was what the Epsom greengrocer called a carriage lady, had no exchange value, apparently. It had prevented her from getting educated, because the only education she could have afforded was education with the Earlscourt greengrocer's daughter. It had led her to seek the society of her mother's class; and that class simply would not have her, because she was much poorer than the greengrocer, and, far from being able to afford a maid, could not afford even a housemaid, and had to scrape along at home with an illiberally treated general servant. Under such circumstances nothing could give her an air of being a genuine product of Largelady Park. And yet its tradition made her regard a marriage with anyone within her reach as an unbearable humiliation. Commercial people and professional people in a small way were odious to her. She ran after painters and novelists; but she did not charm them; and her bold attempts to pick up and practise artistic and literary talk irritated them. She was, in short, an utter failure, an ignorant, incompetent, pretentious, unwelcome, penniless, useless little snob; and though she did not admit these disqualifications (for nobody ever faces unpleasant truths of this kind until the possibility of a way out dawns on them) she felt their effects too keenly to be satisfied with her position.

Clara had a startling eyeopener when, on being suddenly wakened to enthusiasm by a girl of her own age who dazzled her and produced in her a gushing desire to take her for a model, and gain her friendship, she discovered that this exquisite apparition had graduated from the gutter in a few months time. It shook her so violently, that when Mr. H. G. Wells lifted her on the point of his puissant pen, and placed her at the angle of view from which the life she was leading and the society to which she clung appeared in its true relation to real human needs and worthy social structure, he effected a conversion and a conviction of sin comparable to the most sensational feats of General Booth or Gypsy Smith. Clara's snobbery went bang. Life suddenly began to move with her. Without knowing how or why, she began to make friends and enemies. Some of the acquaintances to whom she had been a tedious or indifferent or ridiculous affliction, dropped her: others became cordial. To her amazement she found that some "quite nice" people were saturated with Wells, and that this accessibility to ideas was the secret of their niceness. People she had thought deeply religious, and had tried to conciliate on that tack with disastrous results, suddenly took an interest in her, and revealed a hostility to conventional religion which she had never conceived possible except among the most desperate characters. They made her read Galsworthy; and Galsworthy exposed the vanity of Largelady Park and finished her. It exasperated her to think that the dungeon in which she had languished for so many unhappy years had been unlocked all the time, and that the impulses she had so carefully struggled with and stifled for the sake of keeping well with society, were precisely those by which alone she could have come into any sort of sincere human contact. In the radiance of these discoveries, and the tumult of their reaction, she made a fool of herself as freely and conspicuously as when she so rashly adopted Eliza's expletive in Mrs. Higgins's drawing room; for the new-born Wellsian had to find her bearings almost as ridiculously as a baby; but nobody hates a baby for its ineptitudes, or thinks the worse of it for trying to eat the matches; and Clara lost no friends by her follies. They laughed at her to her face this time; and she had to defend herself and fight it out as best she could.

When Freddy paid a visit to Earlscourt (which he never did when he could possibly help it) to make the desolating announcement that he and his Eliza were thinking of blackening the Largelady scutcheon by opening a shop, he found the little household already convulsed by a prior announcement from Clara that she also was going to work in an old furniture shop in Dover Street, which had been started by a fellow Wellsian. This appointment Clara owed, after all, to her old social accomplishment of Push. She had made up her mind that, cost what it might, she would see Mr. Wells in the flesh; and she had achieved her end at a garden party. She had better luck than so rash an enterprise deserved. Mr. Wells came up to her expectations. Age had not withered him, nor could custom stale his infinite variety in half an hour. His pleasant neatness and compactness, his small hands and feet, his teeming ready brain, his unaffected accessibility, and a certain fine apprehensiveness which stamped him as susceptible from his topmost hair to his tipmost toe, proved irresistible. Clara talked of nothing else for weeks and weeks afterwards. And as she happened to talk to the lady of the furniture shop, and that lady also desired above all things to know Mr. Wells and sell pretty things to him, she offered Clara a job on the chance of achieving that end through her.

And so it came about that Eliza's luck held, and the expected opposition to the flower shop melted away. The shop is in the arcade of a railway station not very far from the Victoria and Albert Museum; and if you live in that neighborhood you may go there any day and buy a buttonhole from Eliza.

Now here is a last opportunity for romance. Would you not like to be assured that the shop was an immense success, thanks to Eliza's charms and her early business experience in Covent Garden? Alas! the truth is the truth:

the shop did not pay for a long time, simply because Eliza and her Freddy did not know how to keep it. True, Eliza had not to begin at the very beginning: she knew the names and prices of the cheaper flowers; and her elation was unbounded when she found that Freddy, like all youths educated at cheap, pretentious, and thoroughly inefficient schools, knew a little Latin. It was very little, but enough to make him appear to her a Porson or Bentley, and to put him at his ease with botanical nomenclature. Unfortunately he knew nothing else; and Eliza, though she could count money up to eighteen shillings or so, and had acquired a certain familiarity with the language of Milton from her struggles to qualify herself for winning Higgins's bet, could not write out a bill without utterly disgracing the establishment. Freddy's power of stating in Latin that Balbus built a wall and that Gaul was divided into three parts did not carry with it the slightest knowledge of accounts or business: Colonel Pickering had to explain to him what a cheque book and a bank account meant. And the pair were by no means easily teachable. Freddy backed up Eliza in her obstinate refusal to believe that they could save money by engaging a bookkeeper with some knowledge of the business. How, they argued, could you possibly save money by going to extra expense when you already could not make both ends meet? But the Colonel, after making the ends meet over and over again, at last gently insisted; and Eliza, humbled to the dust by having to beg from him so often, and stung by the uproarious derision of Higgins, to whom the notion of Freddy succeeding at anything was a joke that never palled, grasped the fact that business, like phonetics, has to be learned.

On the piteous spectacle of the pair spending their evenings in shorthand schools and polytechnic classes, learning bookkeeping and typewriting with incipient junior clerks, male and female, from the elementary schools, let me not dwell. There were even classes at the London School of Economics, and a humble personal appeal to the director of that institution to recommend a course bearing on the flower business. He, being a humorist, explained to them the method of the celebrated Dickensian essay on Chinese Metaphysics by the gentleman who read an article on China and an article on Metaphysics and combined the information. He suggested that they should combine the London School with Kew Gardens. Eliza, to whom the procedure of the Dickensian gentleman seemed perfectly correct (as in fact it was) and not in the least funny (which was only her ignorance), took the advice with entire gravity. But the effort that cost her the deepest humiliation was a request to Higgins, whose pet artistic fancy, next to Milton's verse, was caligraphy, and who himself wrote a most beautiful Italian hand, that he would teach her to write. He declared that she was congenitally incapable of forming a single letter worthy of the least of Milton's words; but she persisted; and again he suddenly threw himself into the task of teaching her with a combination of stormy intensity, concentrated patience, and occasional bursts of interesting disquisition on the beauty and nobility, the august mission and destiny, of human handwriting. Eliza ended by acquiring an extremely uncommercial script which was a positive extension of her personal beauty, and spending three times as much on stationery as anyone else because certain qualities and shapes on paper became indispensable to her. She could not even address an envelope in the usual way because it made the margins all wrong.

Their commercial schooldays were a period of disgrace and despair for the young couple. They seemed to be learning nothing about flower shops. At last they gave it up as hopeless, and shook the dust of the shorthand schools, and the polytechnics, and the London School of Economics from their feet for ever. Besides, the business was in some mysterious way beginning to take care of itself. They had somehow forgotten their objections to employing other people. They came to the conclusion that their own way was the best, and that they had really a remarkable talent for business. The Colonel, who had been compelled for some years to keep a sufficient sum on current account at his bankers to make up their deficits, found that the provision was unnecessary: the young people were prospering. It is true that there was not quite fair play between them and their competitors in trade. Their weekends in the country cost them nothing, and saved them the price of their Sunday dinners; for the motor car was the Colonel's; and he and Higgins paid the hotel bills. Mr. F. Hill, florist and greengrocer (they soon discovered that there was money in asparagus; and asparagus led to other vegetables), had an air which stamped the business as classy; and in private life he was still Frederick Eynsford Hill, Esquire. Not that there was any swank about him: nobody but Eliza knew that he had been christened Frederick Challoner. Eliza herself swanked like anything.

That is all. That is how it has turned out. It is astonishing how much Eliza still manages to meddle in the housekeeping at Wimpole Street in spite of the shop and her own family. And it is notable that though she never nags her husband, and frankly loves the Colonel as if she were his favorite daughter, she has never got out of the habit of nagging Higgins that was established on the fatal night when she won his bet for him. She snaps his head off on the faintest provocation, or on none. He no longer dares to tease her by assuming an abysmal inferiority of Freddy's mind to his own. He storms and bullies and derides; but she stands up to him so ruthlessly that the Colonel has to ask her from time to time to be kinder to Higgins; and it is the only request of his that brings a mulish expression into her face. Nothing but some emergency or calamity great enough to break down all likes and dislikes, and throw them both back on their common humanity — and may they be spared any such trial! — will ever alter this. She knows that Higgins does not need her, just as her father did not need her. The very scrupulousness with which he told her that day that he had become used to having her there, and dependent on her for all sorts of little services, and that he should miss her if she went away (it would never have occurred to Freddy or the Colonel to say anything of the sort) deepens her inner certainty that she is "no more to him than them slippers"; yet she has a sense, too, that his indifference is deeper than the infatuation of commoner souls. She is immensely interested in him. She has even secret mischievous moments in which she wishes she could get him alone, on a desert island, away from all ties and with nobody else in the world to consider, and just drag him off his pedestal and see him making love like any common man. We all have private imaginations of that sort. But when it comes to business, to the life that she really leads as distinguished from the life of dreams and fancies, she likes Freddy and she likes the Colonel; and she does not like Higgins and Mr. Doolittle. Galatea never does quite like Pygmalion: his relation to her is too godlike to be altogether agreeable.

ACT I

1. How does the opening scene in the rainy street prepare us for what is to happen later? In the light of later developments, what is ironic in the first encounter between Freddy and the Flower Girl? How does this scene show us Liza's character: her pride in herself, her aspirations?
2. Translate the Flower Girl's first two speeches into standard English. (Try reading them aloud, if you have difficulty.)

ACT II

1. From Higgins's reasons for remaining "a confirmed old bachelor" (page 1058) and his exchanges with Liza, do you think him (as a student said) "a sexist pig in his attitude toward women in general and Liza in particular"?
2. Why is Alfred Doolittle so alarmed when Higgins offers to give over Liza to him? What seems to be the playwright's attitude toward Doolittle — is the man portrayed as a villain?
3. Comment on Higgins's methods as a teacher in the closing scene.

ACT III

1. Review the scene at the home of Mrs. Higgins, when Eliza makes her debut in society. For what reasons can the scene be called an illustration of comedy of manners at its best? To what differences between the customs and attitudes of one social class and those of another does Shaw point for comic effect?
2. In both the scene at his mother's home and the scene at the Embassy, how does Shaw define Henry Higgins's attitude toward the upper crust of society?
3. What kind of person is Nepommuck? How does his appearance at the reception pose a threat to Higgins's scheme? How does Nepommuck advance the action?
4. This act contains the central crisis of the play: the turning point from which events will proceed in a new direction. What is this moment of crisis?

ACT IV

1. Now that Higgins has won his bet, what is his attitude toward Liza? What is her reaction toward him? In this act, what fresh dramatic question (or questions) does Shaw introduce?
2. Do you find Higgins (as a critic has said) a cold-hearted idealist "to whom human material is raw material only"? In his argument with Liza, why is Higgins "shocked and hurt" and "deeply wounded"?
3. What meaning is attached to the ring that Higgins flings into the fireplace and that Liza reclaims?

ACT V

1. Why is sudden wealth so painful to Alfred Doolittle?
2. At the end, how does Liza emerge triumphant?

3. Shaw has been accused of dangling before us the prospect of marriage between Liza and Higgins, then at the end perversely withdrawing it. In your opinion, how effectively does Shaw (both in the final scene and in his afterword about "the rest of the story") justify his refusal to give the play a conventional romantic ending?

GENERAL QUESTIONS

1. After having her speech and manners corrected, does Liza Doolittle remain otherwise the same person, or does she undergo a change of character?
2. Briefly retell the classical story of Pygmalion and Galatea. (If it is unfamiliar, you can find it in an encyclopedia or in a handbook such as Thomas Bulfinch's *Mythology*.) How does Shaw's play embody the Greek myth? How does Shaw, in his version of the story, depart from it?
3. What parts of the play contain information addressed to the silent reader, not to the theater audience? How much does the audience have to miss? Can *Pygmalion* be called a "closet drama" — one to be read, not seen or heard?
4. Consider the scenes set off by rows of asterisks, supposed to be intended for a movie version or for a theater with elaborate machinery. If these scenes were left out of a stage production of the play, what if anything would be missed?
5. Shaw called this play "intensely and deliberately didactic." What lesson or lessons does it teach? What is Shaw saying about the English language? About the nature of society?
6. If you are familiar with the musical adaptation of the play — Alan Jay Lerner and Frederick Loewe's *My Fair Lady* — discuss some of the liberties taken with Shaw's original. In what respects is the musical a more (or less) conventional comedy than *Pygmalion*?
7. How much truth is there in the remark that Shaw's play is a modern version of the fairy tale of Cinderella?

Anton Chekhov (1860–1904)

THE MARRIAGE PROPOSAL   1889

Translated by Irina Prishvin and X. J. Kennedy

Characters

Stepan Stepanovich Chubukov, a rich landowner.
Ivan Vassilevich Lomov, a younger man, neighbor of Chubukov. Although he is in excellent health, he imagines himself to be ailing.
Natalia Stepanovna, Chubukov's unmarried daughter, twenty-five years old.

Scene. *The main room in Chubukov's mansion. Lomov enters in a tuxedo and white gloves.*

Chubukov (rising to greet him): Why, Lomov, you of all people! *(Pumps Lomov's hand.)* You're a sight for sore eyes, young fellow — how are you?

Lomov: Oh, no use complaining. And you?

Chubukov: We're still alive, my poor old daughter and me. Why haven't you been to see us? Pull up a chair. But what's this? What are you doing in that get-up? Look at you! Tuxedo, black tie, gloves, et cetera. What's happened? Are you going to be somebody's pall-bearer?

Lomov (sitting): No, no, nothing like that. I've dressed to come and see you.

Chubukov (incredulously): To see *me*? Then why the special get-up, old friend? You look like a caterer on New Year's Eve.

Lomov: You see, it's like this. *(He leans closer.)* I've come, Stepan Stepanovich, to ask a favor of you. Oh, I know you've helped me often in the past, but this is different. You see — oh, I'm so nervous I'm shaking. Excuse me, Stepan Stepanovich, I'll just drink a little water. *(Pours himself some water from a pitcher and gulps, gargling it.)*

Chubukov (to himself): Why, the sly dog, he's come to ask for a loan. Should I give it to him? Not a chance! *(Aloud.)* Well, what can I do for you, old friend?

Lomov: I'll tell you, old neighbor — forgive me, I don't mean you're *old*. I mean — oh, Lord, now I'm all mixed up. What I mean is, you're the only one that can help me. Oh, I know I'm a pitiful worm, I don't deserve it —

Chubukov: Don't deserve what? For God's sake, quit beating around the bush. Spit it out, man, spit it out!

Lomov: Very well. I'll spit it *right* out. I've come — I've come to ask you for Natalia's hand in marriage.

Chubukov: Ivan Vassilevich, are you serious? Say that again — I don't trust these old ears.

Lomov: I hereby request the hand . . . .

Chubukov (butting in): Son-in-law! Sweet boy! Et cetera! *(Jumping up and giving him a bear-hug.)* For years — years! — I've been waiting for this moment. I always said it would make sense for you and Natalia to tie the knot, seeing as our two properties abut. I'm so glad I could cry! *(Dabs a tear.)* God bless your marriage bed, have a whole army of children. Why am I standing here blithering? What news! You could knock me over with a feather. I've got to call Natalia.

Lomov: Oh dear. Tell me, Stepan Stepanovich, what do you think she'll say? Will she have me?

Chubukov: Have you? How could she possibly say no to a handsome, good-looking, et cetera? Why, she's crazy about you. Don't go away! I'll run and fetch her. *(He exits.)*

Lomov: Ugh, it's cold in here. I'm shaking like a leaf. I've got butterflies in my stomach as if I was going to take a final examination. Decisive, that's what I've got to be. Don't dare think. Think too long, keep waiting for the perfect woman, wait for true love to come along, and I'll never get married at all. Brrrr, it's like an ice-box. Natalia Stepanovna is a good housekeeper, she was always on the honor roll at school, and as for looks — well, I've seen worse. What more could anybody want? I'm so scared there's a buzzing in my ears. *(Gulps more water.)* Anyway, I absolutely have got to get married. Here I am, thirty-five — a dangerous age. If I don't get married now, I never will. Besides, I should settle down, quit running around, take better care of myself. This heart murmur of mine. The palpitations. I'm always getting excited and blowing up. One of these days I might keel right over. See, even now I can't hold my hand steady. And there's that twitch in my right eyebrow again. Trying to sleep at night, that's the worst. Every time I start to drop off — yow! pain shoots through my left side and wakes me up again. Ouch! It travels to my shoulder. It makes for my head. I have to jump out of bed like a crazy man and run around the room. I work the thing off and lie back down. I no sooner go back to sleep than — yow! there it goes again! Sometimes it hits me twenty times a night.

Natalia (entering): Oh. It's you. Papa told me there was a buyer here, come to pick up his goods. Hello, Ivan Vassilevich.

Lomov (rising): How — how are you, Natalia?

Natalia: Don't mind my apron. We've been shelling peas. Where have you been keeping yourself? Sit down. *(They sit.)* Will you have lunch?

Lomov: No thanks, I'm full.

Natalia: Smoke if you like. There are matches on the table. Nice weather we've been having. Better than yesterday, I mean — all that rain. Our men couldn't cut hay. How is it going at your place? How many stacks have you finished? The day before yesterday I got anxious to see it all done, so I had a whole field cut, and now I could just kick myself, because the hay got rained on and now it will probably rot. I should have let them wait. Say, why are you wearing that tuxedo? You look great in it. Come on, tell me, why are you all dressed up? Is there a party?

Lomov (agitatedly): Well you see it's this way, my dear Natalia Stepanovna. To make a long story short I've made up my mind to ask you to listen to me. Now perhaps this will come as a surprise to you, perhaps you won't like the idea at first, and you'll be angry. Anyway . . . . *(Aside.)* Damn! it's cold in here!

Natalia: What's the matter with you? *(Pause, while Lomov sits silently squirming.)* Will you please explain yourself?

Lomov: All right. I'll come to the point. You remember, Natalia Stepanovna, that ever since you and I were children, I've been proud to consider myself a friend of your family. My aunt that's now dead, and her husband — you know, the ones that left me their estate — always thought the world of your father and your mother when she was alive. In business, the Lomovs and the Chubukovs have always been thick as thieves, and I believe they think a lot of each other. And after all, my land borders yours. Why, my White Ox Meadows run right up to your birch woods, and . . . .

Natalia: Excuse me, did you say *your* White Ox Meadows?

Lomov: That's right. *My* meadows.

Natalia: What do you mean? The White Ox Meadows are ours, not yours.

Lomov: Now just hold on a minute, Natalia Stepanovna. You know they're mine, and they always will be.

Natalia: Well, that's news to me! What gives you the right to claim our meadows?

Lomov: What gives *me* . . .? See here now, it's the White Ox Meadows I'm talking about — the ones in between your birch woods and the swamp.

Natalia: That's what I thought you meant. They're ours.

Lomov: I'm sorry to have to put you straight, Natalia Stepanovna, but they're mine just as plain as the nose on your face.

Natalia: You're out of your mind. Since when have they been yours?

Lomov: Since when? Since as long as my family goes back. Since as long as I can remember.

Natalia: Stop talking nonsense, Ivan Vassilevich.

Lomov: You can look at the deed, my dear Natalia. It's true there was once an argument over those meadows, but now that's all past and the whole town knows they're mine. Why are you arguing? Listen, here's how it was — my aunt's grandmother let your great-grandfather's peasants graze their oxen on those meadows, rent free, for as long as they'd make bricks for her. Forty years went by, and your great-grandfather's peasants got so used to working those meadows, they forgot and thought they owned them, when the truth was . . . .

Natalia: No, no, that wasn't how it was at all. My grandfather and his father took a survey of that land, and they claimed it all the way to the swamp, which means the White Ox Meadows are ours. There's nothing to argue about. You're just being difficult.

Lomov: The deed, Natalia Stepanovna, I can show you the deed!

Natalia: You must be joking. For three hundred years that land has been in our family, and now you come along and say it isn't ours. What sort of fool do you take me for? It's not that those meadows are worth anything, really — maybe three, four hundred rubles — it's just that I can't stand cheating. I won't be cheated. I won't!

Lomov (losing his temper): Will you calm down and listen to me? Your great-grandfather's peasants baked my aunt's grandmother's bricks, and my aunt's grandmother, out of the goodness of her heart . . . .

Natalia: I don't care about your aunt's grandmother's bricks! The meadows belong to us and that's final!

Lomov: They're *my* meadows.

Natalia: They're ours! You can talk till you're blue in the face, you can go home and put on fifteen tuxedoes if you like, but you can't change a thing — those meadows are ours, ours, ours! I don't want anything of yours, and you're not going to get anything of mine!

Lomov: The meadows mean nothing to me, Natalia Stepanovna. I'm simply defending what belongs to me. You can take the meadows, if it'll make you happy — I'll make you a gift of them.

Natalia: You? Give them to *me?* I'm the one that ought to do the giving. I must say, Ivan Vassilevich, you're certainly acting strangely. Up till now I've always thought of you as a good neighbor, a true friend. Why, only last year didn't we lend you our only threshing machine even though it meant we couldn't thresh our own wheat till November? And now here you are treating us like a band of gypsies trying to rob you. Making me a present of my own family's land! What a neighbor you are! You've got a lot of nerve, if you ask me.

Lomov: What do you take me for, a swindler? I've never tried to take anybody else's land in my life, and I'm not going to stand for your accusations. (*Hurries to the pitcher, pours more water, and gulps.*) The White Ox Meadows are mine!

Natalia: That's a lie! They're ours!

Lomov: They're mine! Mine, mine, I say!

Natalia: Never! I'll show you — I'll send my men to mow those meadows before sundown!

Lomov: What's that you said?

Natalia: You'll see. My mowers will be out there in five minutes, swinging their scythes.

Lomov: I'll take a shotgun to them!

Natalia: Just you try it!

Lomov (clapping a hand to his heart): The White Ox Meadows are mine! Understand? Mine!

Natalia: Keep your voice down. When you're in your own house you can rant and rave and roar yourself hoarse, but when you're in my house you can talk like a human being.

Lomov: If it wasn't for these stabbing pains in my side and my splitting headache, I'd give you a roar that would blow your ears out. *(Shouts.)* The White Ox Meadows are mine!

Natalia: Ours!

Lomov: Mine!

Natalia: Ours!

Lomov: Mine! Mine!

Chubukov (entering): Here, here, what's all the shouting about?

Natalia: Papa, will you please explain to this gentleman who the White Ox Meadows belong to, us or him?

Chubukov (to Lomov): Why, they're ours, my friend, as you well know.

Lomov: Now see here, Stepan Stepanovich, will you listen to reason? My aunt's grandmother let your grandfather's peasants use those meadows for free, temporarily. The peasants used that land for forty years and started thinking it was their own. But after the Emancipation° . . . .

Chubukov: Oh come on now, old friend, aren't you forgetting something? The reason the peasants didn't pay rent to your aunt's grandmother was that nobody was sure the meadows belonged to her, and there was a big fuss, et cetera. But today, why even the pigs and goats know that that land is Chubukov's. I guess you haven't looked at the deed lately.

Lomov: I — I can prove to you those meadows are mine.

Chubukov: You'll have a hard time proving that.

Lomov: I can show it to you in black and white.

Chubukov: Well then what are you shouting for? Do you think you can have my meadows just by shouting for 'em? I'm not out to get anything of yours, and you're not going to get what's mine. If you're going to make a big fuss about those meadows, I'd sooner give 'em to the peasants than I'd give 'em to you. Got that straight, et cetera?

Lomov: Now wait a minute. Since when do you think you can steal somebody else's land and give it to your stinking peasants?

Chubukov: Leave that for me to decide. And you'd better get another thing clear, young fellow — I'm not used to anybody marching into my own house and

---

Emancipation: In 1861 the czar Alexander II had freed the serfs, who previously were bound to the land and considered property, and had given them land of their own.

bawling me out, et cetera. Not to mention the fact that I'm twice as old as you, and have a right to a little respect, et cetera. So you can just talk to me calmly, without flying off the handle.

Lomov: You think I'm still just a little boy you can twist around your finger. First you say my land is yours and then you expect me to lie back and be calm about it. Call yourself a neighbor? You're no neighbor, you're a land-shark.

Chubukov: How was that again?

Natalia: The mowers, Papa! Send the mowers out to cut the meadows, now!

Chubukov: Young man, would you mind repeating what you just called me?

Natalia: The White Ox Meadows are ours, and so they'll stay! He won't get 'em! Never, never!

Lomov: We'll see about that. I'm going to my lawyer. We'll let the judge decide.

Chubukov: Go ahead and see your lawyer, a lot I care. I know your kind — never happy unless you're suing somebody. You little weasel, your family always did have a weakness for lawyers, the whole damned crew of you.

Lomov: Keep your filthy mouth off of my family. The Lomovs have always been fine upstanding citizens. Not one of us ever got put in jail for embezzling, like your father.

Chubukov: Every last one of you Lomovs has been cuckoo in the head.

Natalia: That's right, every last one!

Chubukov: Why, your grandfather was a well-known lush, et cetera, and your youngest aunt ran away with an architect. Fact is fact.

Lomov: A hunchback, your mother was. *(Grabs his chest.)* O God, the pain is stabbing me! I'm seeing flashes! Help! Give me water!

Chubukov: And your old man was a vodka-soak that ate himself fat as a tick.

Natalia: And your aunt was the high priestess of dirty gossip!

Lomov: My left foot is paralyzed. And you're a schemer. Ah, ah, my heart! The whole town knows that on election day you were going around buying votes. I can see shooting-stars! My hat, where's my hat?

Natalia: It's a low trick you've tried to play on us, you crook.

Chubukov: Cheap double-crosser.

Lomov: Here's my hat. My heart . . . . Which way is the door? I think I'm dying. My foot's turned to stone. *(Staggers toward the door.)*

Chubukov (following him): Well, don't set your big stone foot in my house again!

Natalia: Go on, take us to court, see if we care!

Lomov goes out.

Chubukov: To hell with him! *(Paces up and down in agitation.)*

Natalia: That snake-in-the-grass. Oh, Papa, we can't even trust our neighbors any more.

Chubukov: That skunk. That overdressed scarecrow. Et cetera.

Natalia: That monster! Makes a pass at our land and then shoots off his mouth at us.

Chubukov: And on top of all that, that silly jackass had the nerve to make a proposal, et cetera. Can you imagine?

Natalia: A — proposal? What kind of proposal?

Chubukov: Why, he came over here to propose to you.

Natalia: To propose? To *me?* Why didn't you tell me that before?

Chubukov: Sure, why do you think he got all decked out in his monkey-suit? That underdone sausage, that — that ghost of a turnip!

Natalia: But — but — to *propose* to me! *(She gives a wail of anguish and plops herself into a chair.)* Bring him back, oh, Papa, bring him back! Bring him back — right now — here!

Chubukov: Bring back who?

Natalia: Hurry up, I'm telling you, will you hurry? I'm going to be sick! Don't let him get away! *(Whimpers and beats fists against her chair hysterically.)*

Chubukov: What's the matter with you? *(Claps a hand to his head.)* Now, if this isn't a fine kettle of fish! I could hang myself, I could put a bullet through my head. Her last chance, he was, and I went and ruined it.

Natalia: I'll die! Go, go, bring him back!

Chubukov: All right, all right, I'm going! Just don't howl like that! *(He dashes out.)*

Natalia (still moaning): What have they done to me? Bring him back! Bring him back!

A pause. Then Chubukov dashes in.

Chubukov: He's coming right away, damn him. You can talk to him yourself, I'm not going to.

Natalia (wails): Just bring him in!

Chubukov (shouting): Hold on, will you? I tell you he's coming. Lord, what agony it is to have a grown daughter! I could slash my throat. By heaven, I'm going to! To think of it! Here we insulted the man, called him names, threw him out, and it's all your fault.

Natalia: My fault? It was yours!

Chubukov: Your fault, you, you — *(Lomov appears at the door.)* All right, here he is, *you* talk to him.

Lomov enters as if exhausted.

Lomov: These awful palpitations in my chest . . . Oh, my leg has gone dead! There's this pain in my side . . .

Natalia: Now, Ivan Vassilevich, you'll just have to forgive us, we didn't know what we were saying. Why, now I remember perfectly — the White Ox Meadows are yours.

Lomov: My heart — it's jumping so! Of course they're my meadows. Oh dear, now *both* my brows are twitching!

Natalia: Just calm yourself. Come over here and sit down next to me. *(They sit, side by side.)* Oh, we were so wrong! We got carried away. The meadows are yours, really.

Lomov: I — I don't give a hoot about the land. It was the principle of the thing!

Natalia: I always knew you were a man of principle. Now do let's talk about something else.

Lomov: Anyhow, I can prove it. My aunt's grandmother let your grandfather's peasants use the land because they supplied her with bricks . . . .

Natalia: Oh, let's forget about all that! *(To herself.)* How am I going to get him off those meadows and on to the right track? *(Aloud.)* Are you going to go hunting this year?

Lomov: I guess I'll do a little grouse-shooting after the hay is in. And oh, Natalia

Stepanovna, did you hear about the bad luck I had? You know my dog Kuska? Well, he's gone lame.

Natalia: The poor old pooch, what happened to him?

Lomov: I don't know. Must have twisted a leg in a rabbit hole or maybe another dog took a bite of him. *(Sighs.)* My number one dog, he is. Not to mention what he cost me. Why, do you know, I gave Mironov a hundred and twenty-five rubles for him.

Natalia: You were robbed, Ivan Vassilevich.

Lomov: Do you think so? I call that a bargain. There's no dog like him.

Natalia: Well, Papa gave eighty-five rubles for our Puksa, and Puksa is a better dog than Kuska any day.

Lomov: Puksa? Better than Kuska? Are you crazy? *(Laughs.)* What a notion! Puksa better than Kuska!

Natalia: Why, of course he's better. Puksa isn't full-grown yet, it's true, but when it comes to brains and breeding, even Count Volchanyetsky hasn't got a better dog.

Lomov: Please excuse me, Natalia Stepanovna, but isn't there something you're leaving out? Puksa has an overshot jaw, and a dog with an overshot jaw can't ever amount to anything.

Natalia: Oh, sure, he has an overshot jaw, has he? That's news to me!

Lomov: Now, Natalia, I know all about these things, and I swear to you his lower jaw is a good inch shorter than his upper.

Natalia (sarcastically): And I suppose you got him down and measured him with a tape measure?

Lomov: That's just what I did. He can run, all right, but when it comes to hunting, he'll never get anywhere. He'll snap at a rabbit and it will just slip out.

Natalia: Now, look. In the first place, our Puksa is a thoroughbred, the son of Chisels and Harness. Your Kuska — what's he? Such a mixture there's no telling what he is. He's old and ugly as a worn-out nag.

Lomov: Are you out of your mind? He's mature, it's true, but I wouldn't take five of your Puksas for him. I wouldn't dream of it! Kuska is a real dog, but as for your Puksa — why, this whole discussion is just plain silly. Any dog's as good as Puksa. Twenty-five rubles for him would be highway robbery.

Natalia: Ivan Vassilevich, some perverse spirit has got into you. First you pretend you own the White Ox Meadows and now you claim Kuska is a better dog than Puksa. I just don't have any use for liars like you, because you know perfectly well that Puksa is a hundred times the dog your flearidden old Kuska is. Why are you arguing?

Lomov: You think I'm blind? You think I'm a fool? Won't you admit your Puksa has an overshot jaw?

Natalia: That's not true.

Lomov: It's true!

Natalia: It isn't!

Lomov: Lady, why are you shouting at me?

Natalia: And why are you talking a lot of rot? High time you put a bullet through your old Kuska and put him out of his misery. And you say he's better than Puksa!

Lomov: Please. I can't go on arguing. I'm having palpitations.

Natalia: Isn't that always the way! Hunters that talk the most are the ones that know the least!

Lomov: Lady, will you please be quiet? My heart is pounding. It's going to explode. *(Shouts.)* For God's sake, shut up!

Natalia: Not on your life. I'll keep right on talking until you admit that Puksa is a hundred times better than your Kuska.

Lomov: A hundred times worse! I wish he was dead, your Puksa. Oh, my head! My shoulder! My eyebrows!

Natalia: As for your mangy old Kuska, he's half dead already.

Lomov (practically in tears): Shut your mouth! My heart is blowing up!

Natalia: I will *not* shut up.

Chubukov (entering): What's the matter now?

Natalia: Papa, give us your word of honor, which is the better dog, his Kuska or our Puksa?

Lomov: Stepan Stepanovich, tell me the truth — does your Puksa have an overshot jaw or doesn't he? Yes or no?

Chubukov: So what if he does? Who cares? He's still the best dog in the district, et cetera.

Lomov: But isn't my Kuska better? Now, honestly, isn't he?

Chubukov: Don't get yourself in an uproar. All right, I'll admit your Kuska has his points. He's well bred, fast on his feet, has nice ribs, et cetera. But if the truth has to be told, that dog has two things wrong with him. He's old as the hills and his muzzle's too short.

Lomov: His muzzle's too short? Ah, ah, my heart! Will you look at the facts? Remember that hunt over at Marusinsky's? My Kuska ran neck-and-neck with the Count's best dog, while your Puksa was a whole mile in the rear!

Chubukov: That was only because the Count's huntsman hit him with a whip.

Lomov: Yes, and for good reason. All the other dogs took off after the fox, and your Puksa started chasing a sheep.

Chubukov: Listen, you, I'm going to lose my temper if you don't stop arguing. The huntsman gave Puksa a crack on the nose just because some people are always jealous of other people's dogs. That's how it is, that's how *you* are. You see some dog that's better than yours and right away you start finding things wrong with him — this, that, and the other thing, et cetera. Oh, don't tell *me* about that hunt. I remember how it went.

Lomov: Yes, and so do I.

Chubukov (mimicking him): "Yes, and so do I." What can *you* remember? You had such a jag on at the time.

Lomov: My — my heart! My foot's turning to stone again. I can't feel . . .

Natalia (mimicking him): "My heart, my foot!" Call yourself a hunter? You couldn't catch a cockroach on a kitchen sink, let alone a fox. "My heart! My foot!"

Chubukov: Some hunter you are! You ought to be home taking your blood pressure, not gallivanting around trying to catch dumb animals. The only reason you go hunting is to drink and give people a hard time about their dogs. Oh, let's get off this subject before I lose my temper and give you a poke, et cetera. I hate to tell you, boy, but as a hunter you aren't worth beans.

Lomov: And you? You think *you're* a hunter? The only reason you go hunting is to flatter the Count and pull shady deals and connive — oh, oh, my heart! You're a conniver, that's what you are!

Chubukov: Who, me, a conniver? *(Shouts.)* Shut up!

Lomov: Conniver!

Chubukov: Babyface! Sassy puppy!

Lomov: Old rat! Old slippery Jesuit!

Chubukov: Shut up before I fill you full of buckshot like a partridge!

Lomov: The whole town knows — oh, my heart! — how your dying wife used to beat you up. Oh, my foot! My eyebrows! Here come those shooting-stars again. I'm going to keel over. I'm falling . . . . *(He staggers about.)*

Chubukov: Yeah, the whole town knows how your housekeeper bosses you. How she won't let you out at night.

Lomov: Oh, oh, my heart's exploded! My shoulder — where's my shoulder? — can't find my shoulder. Shooting-stars! I'm passing out . . . . *(He sinks into a chair.)* A doctor, I've got to have a doctor. *(Swoons and goes limp.)*

Chubukov: You worm. You ninny. You make me sick to my stomach. *(Gulps water.)*

Natalia: Call yourself a hunter? You can't tell one end of a horse from the other. Papa — what's wrong with him? Look, look! *(Shrieks.)* He's dead!

Chubukov: I'm going to throw up. Give me room!

Natalia: He's gone! *(Tugs Lomov's sleeve.)* Ivan Vassilevich, Ivan Vassilevich, wake up! Don't run out on me! It's no use! He's dead! *(Drops into a chair.)* Doctor! Doctor!

Chubukov: Is something the matter?

Natalia (wailing): He's dead, dead, dead, that's all!

Chubukov: Who is? *(Stares at Lomov.)* Good Lord, I do believe he is. Good Lord. Should we call a doctor? House calls are twenty rubles. Let's try some water. *(Presses a glass of water to Lomov's lips.)* Drink up, old friend. He won't drink. Must be dead. Oh, if this isn't my rotten luck. Why don't I just blow my brains out, et cetera? I ought to have cut my throat ten years ago. What am I waiting for? Hand me a knife, give me a gun! *(Lomov stirs.)* Wait a minute. I think he's coming to. Here, drink this water. That's a good boy.

Lomov: Shooting-stars . . . everything's foggy . . . where am I?

Chubukov: Go on, get married, and then you can go to hell. She says yes! *(He places Lomov's hand in Natalia's.)* She says yes, she'll marry you, et cetera. I give you my blessing. Just get married and get out of my hair, the two of you!

Lomov: Huh? What? *(He stands up.)* Who says yes to me?

Chubukov: She does! Well, what are you waiting for? Pucker up and kiss her, damn it!

Natalia (wailing): He isn't dead! Yes, yes, I'm willing!

Chubukov: Quick, seal it with a kiss!

Lomov: What's that? Kiss who? *(They kiss.)* Oh, that feels rather good. Excuse me, what's all this about? Oh yes, now I remember. My heart . . . the shooting-stars . . . Natalia Stepanovna, I'm so happy. *(Kisses her hand.)* But my foot feels likes pins and needles.

Natalia: And I'm happy too.

Chubukov: Whew! what a weight off my back!

Natalia: Maybe now you'll admit that Kuska is worse than Puksa?

Lomov: Better!

Natalia: Worse!

Chubukov: This marriage is off to a great start. Let's have some champagne.

Lomov: He's better!

Natalia: Worse! Worse, worse, worse!

Chubukov (calling offstage to his servants): Champagne! Bring champagne! Champagne!

CURTAIN

Questions

1. Although as a rule we need not care what happens to the characters in a play after the final curtain, are you at all tempted to imagine Lomov and Natalia in their future life together? Do you agree that Chekhov invites us to make a guess about it? What is yours?
2. What major dramatic question is raised early in the play — the question to whose possible answer (whether yes or no) we look forward? At what moment does the question arise for you?
3. What is the crisis of the play? The climax? The resolution? Would you call *The Marriage Proposal* a "well-made play"? How carefully constructed is its action?
4. Does Chekhov imply any general observations on Russian society in the nineteenth century? What do you infer to be the usual position of an unmarried woman, the public attitude toward her?
5. Would you call the play a satiric comedy, a romantic comedy, or neither? What (as best you can tell) is the playwright's attitude toward his characters?
6. What moments in the play struck you as the most funny? Try to understand your own reactions. Exactly what appealed to your sense of comedy?

Neil Simon (b. 1927)

COME BLOW YOUR HORN   1961

Characters

Alan Baker
Peggy Evans
Buddy Baker, Alan's younger brother
Father
Connie
Mother
A Woman

Synopsis of Scenes:

Time: The present.
Place: Alan's apartment in the East Sixties, New York City.

Act I: Six o'clock in the evening, early fall.
Act II: Immediately after.
Act III: Late afternoon. Three weeks later.

ACT I

> *At rise: Alan Baker, in a short Italian suede ski jacket, is standing in the doorway being his charming, persuasive best in attempting to lure Peggy Evans into his bachelor apartment. Peggy is in a ski outfit that fits her so snugly it leaves little room for skiing. Alan puts down his valise, then slides Peggy's overnight bag out of her hand without her even noticing it and places it on the floor. Alan is very adept at this game. Being good-looking, bright, thirty-three and single against Peggy's twenty-two years of blissful ignorance and eagerness to please, it appears that Alan has all the marbles stacked on his side.*

Peggy: Alan, no!
Alan: Come on, honey.
Peggy: Alan, no.
Alan (Taking off her ski jacket): Just five more minutes. Come on.
Peggy: Alan, no. Please.

> *He pulls her into the living room.*

Alan: But you said you were cold.
Peggy: I am.
Alan (Embracing her): I'll start a fire. I'll have your blood going up and down in no time.
Peggy: Alan, I want to go upstairs and take a bath. I've got about an inch of the New York Thruway on me.
Alan: Honey, you can't go yet. We've got to have one last drink. To cap the perfect weekend.
Peggy: It was four days.
Alan: It's not polite to count . . . Don't you ever get tired of looking sensational?
Peggy: Do you think I do?
Alan: You saw what happened at the ski jump. They were looking at you and jumping into the parking lot . . . Come here.

> *He bites her on the neck.*

Peggy: Why do you always do that?
Alan: Do what?
Peggy: Bite me on the neck.
Alan: What's the matter? You don't think I'm a vampire, do you?
Peggy: Gee, I never thought of that.
Alan: If it'll make you feel safer, I'll chew on your ear lobe.

> *He does.*

Peggy (Giggles): Kiss me.
Alan: I'm not through with the hors d'oeuvres yet.

He kisses her.

Peggy (Sighs and sits on sofa): Now I feel warm again.
Alan: Good.
Peggy: Thank you for the weekend, Alan. I had a wonderful time.
Alan: Yeah, it was fun.

Crossing toward bar.

Peggy: Even though he didn't show up.
Alan (Stops and turns): Who?
Peggy: Your friend from M-G-M.
Alan (Continuing to bar. Quickly): Oh, Mr. Manheim. Yeah . . . Well, that's show
    biz.
Peggy: Did it say when he expects to be in New York again?
Alan: Did what?

Picks up carton containing scotch bottle.

Peggy: The telegram. From Hollywood.
Alan: Oh! Didn't I tell you? Next week. Early part.
Peggy: It's kind of funny now that you think of it, isn't it?
Alan: What is?
Peggy: Him wanting to meet me in a hotel.
Alan (Taking bottle out of carton): It was a ski lodge.
Peggy: Was it? Anyway, it was nice. I've never been to New Hampshire before.
Alan: It was Vermont.

Putting down carton.

Peggy: Oh, I'm terrible with names. I can't imagine why an important man like
    that wants to travel all the way up there just to meet me.
Alan (Puts bottle back on bar): I explained all that. Since this picture he's planning
    is all about a winter carnival, he figured the best place to meet you would
    be against the natural setting of the picture. To see how you photograph
    against the snow. That makes sense . . . *(Not too sure)* Doesn't it?

Crosses right.

Peggy: Oh, sure.
Alan: Sure.

Pulls Peggy up from couch and embraces her.

Peggy: We ought to go again sometime when it's not for business. Just for fun.
Alan: That should be a weekend.
Peggy: Maybe next time I could learn to ski.
Alan: I wouldn't be surprised.
Peggy: It's a shame we were cooped up in the room so long.
Alan: Yes. Well, I explained, we had that bad break in the weather.
Peggy: You mean all that snow.
Alan: Exactly . . . But you make the cutest little Saint Bernard . . .

He is just about to kiss her when the buzzer rings.

Peggy: That's the lobby.
Alan: I don't hear a thing.
Peggy: Maybe it's for me.
Alan: My buzzer? You live up in the penthouse.
Peggy: I know. But I'm always here.

He looks at her quizzically, then goes to wall phone and picks it up.

Alan (Into phone): Yes? . . . Who? . . . Buddy? . . . Hi, kid . . . Now? . . . Well, sure. Sure, if it's important. You know the apartment. *(He hangs up)* My kid brother.
Peggy: Oh. I'd better go.
Alan (Alan reaches for her again): This is the seventh floor. We still have over a minute.
Peggy (Eluding him): I want to go up and change anyway. *(She picks up her parka and goes to him, then says invitingly)* You think he'll be here long?
Alan: Not when you ask me like that.
Peggy: Why don't you come up in twenty minutes?
Alan: Why don't you come down in nineteen?
Peggy: All right. 'By, Alan.
Alan: 'By, Connie.
Peggy: Peggy!

She breaks from him.

Alan: What?
Peggy: Peggy! That's the third time this weekend you called me Connie.
Alan: I didn't say Connie. I said Honey!
Peggy: Oh!
Alan: Oh!
Peggy: Sorry.

Alan opens door. She smiles and exits. Alan breathes a sigh of relief. Picks up suitcase and goes into bedroom as the doorbell rings.

Alan (Offstage): Come on in, it's open.

Buddy Baker, his younger brother, enters with a valise in hand. Buddy is the complete opposite of Alan. Reserved, unsure, shy.

Buddy: Hello, Alan . . . Are you busy?

Enters apartment and looks around.

Alan (Offstage): No, no. Come on in, kid. *(Alan on)* What's up? *(Alan sees suitcase.)* What's in there?
Buddy: Pajamas, toothbrush, the works.
Alan: You're kidding.
Buddy: Nope.
Alan: You mean you left? *(Buddy nods.)* Permanently?
Buddy: I took eight pairs of socks. For me, that's permanently.

Alan: I don't believe it. You can't tell me you actually ran away from home.

Buddy: Well, I cheated a little. I took a taxi.

>*Takes off coat and places it on suitcase.*

Alan: You're serious. You mean my baby brother finally broke out of prison?

Buddy: We planned it long enough, didn't we?

Alan: Yes, but every time I brought it up you said you weren't ready. Why didn't you say something to me?

Buddy: When? You weren't at work since Thursday.

Alan: Hey, did Dad say anything? About my being gone?

Buddy: Not at the office. But at home he's been slamming doors. The chandelier in the foyer fell down. Where were you?

Alan: Vermont.

Buddy: Skiing?

Alan: Only during the day.

>*Sits on sofa and lights cigarette.*

Buddy: I don't know how you do it. If I'm at work one minute after nine, he docks my pay . . . and I get less to eat at home.

Alan: Because he expects it from you. From me he says he expects nothing, so that's what I give him.

Buddy: You're better off. At least you're not treated like a baby. You can talk with him.

Alan: We don't talk. We have heart to heart threatening . . .

Buddy: That's better than the subtle treatment I get. Last night I came home three o'clock in the morning. He didn't approve. What do you think he did? *(Alan shakes his head)* As I passed his bedroom door, he crowed like a rooster. Cock-a-doodle-doo.

Alan: You're kidding. What'd you say?

Buddy: Nothing. I wanted to cluck back like a chicken but I didn't have the nerve.

Alan: Oh, he's beautiful.

Buddy: And then yesterday was my birthday. *(Sits on sofa)* Twenty-one years old.

Alan: Oh, that's right. Gee, I'm sorry I wasn't there, Buddy. Happy birthday, kid.

>*He shakes Buddy's hand warmly.*

Buddy: Thanks.

Alan: I even forgot to get you a present.

Buddy: I got one. A beaut. From Mom and Dad.

Alan: What was it?

Buddy: A surprise party. Mom, Dad, and the Klingers.

Alan: Who are the Klingers?

Buddy: Oh, the Klingers are that lovely couple the folks met last summer at Lake Mahopac.

Alan: Why? They're not your friends.

Buddy: Think. Why would they have the Klingers to meet me?

Alan: They've got a daughter.

Buddy: Oh, have they got a daughter.

Alan: You mean they brought her with them?

Buddy: In a crate.

Alan: Let me guess. Naomi?

Buddy: Close. Renee.

Alan: Not much on looks but brilliant.

Buddy: A genius. An I.Q. of 170. Same as her weight.

Alan: And of course they had her dressed for the kill. They figured what she couldn't do, maybe Bergdorf could.

Buddy: Nothing could help. So I spent the night of my twenty-first birthday watching a girl devour an entire bowl of cashew nuts.

Alan: Oh, I'm sorry, kid.

Buddy (Rises, crosses right center): It's been getting worse and worse. He looks in my closets, my drawers. He listens to my phone calls. I don't know what it is I've done, Alan, but I swear he's going to turn me in.

Alan: Well, it's simple enough. He's afraid you're going to follow in my footsteps.

Buddy: I did. I thought it over all day and realized I had to leave . . . Well — here I am.

Alan: Oh, I'm so proud of you, Buddy. If you weren't twenty-one, I'd kiss you.

Buddy: You really think I did the right thing?

Alan: What did you do, rob a bank? You're only going to be living four subway stations away. You're still working for him, *aren't you?*

Buddy: Well, there's going to be trouble there too.

Alan: What do you mean?

Buddy: I know I'm going to be struck by lightning for saying this . . . but I'm thinking of leaving the business.

Alan: . . . On the level?

Buddy: I'm not happy there, Alan. I'm not like you. You're good in the business . . . I'm not.

Alan: It's just that you're inexperienced.

Buddy: It's not only that. It just doesn't interest me. Gee whiz, there's a million more important things going on in the world today. New countries are being born. They're getting ready to send men to the moon. I just can't get excited about making wax fruit.

Alan: Why not? It's a business like anything else.

Buddy: It's different for you, Alan. You're hardly ever there. *(He sits)* You're the salesman, you're outside all day. Meeting people. Human beings. But I'm inside looking at petrified apples and pears and plums. They never rot, they never turn brown, they never grow old . . . It's like the fruit version of *The Picture of Dorian Gray*°.

Alan (Follows): You know why you feel that way? Because you never get a chance to take the chains off. During the day it's all right. But at night you've got to bite into the *real* fruit of life, Buddy, not wax.

Buddy: Yeah, I guess so.

The Picture of Dorian Gray: In this novel of 1891 by Oscar Wilde, a young gentleman sinking deeper into depravity keeps a smooth, unblemished face, while his portrait grows steadily more rotten-looking.

Alan: But that's all behind you now, right?

Buddy (Crosses downstage left): Well . . . *(He looks at his watch.)* In a few minutes anyway.

Alan (Crosses downstage left): What do you mean?

Buddy: Dad should be coming home soon.

Alan: You mean you didn't tell him you were leaving?

Buddy: I couldn't, Alan.

Alan: Why not? Were you scared?

Buddy: You bet I was. With you out of work these last few days he hasn't been all smiles . . . And besides . . . I just didn't want to hurt him . . . Sure he's stubborn and old-fashioned . . . but he means well.

Alan: I know, kid. I understand.

Buddy: I left him at the plant and came home early tonight. Then I wrote him a long letter explaining how I felt and left it on his bed. And in the morning, I think I'll be able to reason with him. Don't you?

Crosses to Alan right.

Alan: Frankly no, but what's the difference? I'm proud of you. You walked out of Egypt, kid. How about a drink? To celebrate. Scotch or bourbon?

He crosses to bar.

Buddy (Sits on sofa): Sure . . .

Alan: Scotch, bourbon?

Buddy: Scotch.

Alan: Scotch it is.

Buddy: And ginger ale.

Alan (Stops): Scotch and ginger ale? . . . They must know you in every bar in town. *(He makes drinks)* Hey, how did Mom take all this?

Buddy (Crosses and sits on sofa): Oh, she's upset, of course. The most important thing to her is peace in the family.

Alan: And a clean apartment.

Buddy (Smiles): And a clean apartment.

Alan: By the way, how is the Museum of Expensive Furniture?

Buddy: Oh, the living room is still closed to the public!

Alan: Living room? I don't remember ever seeing a living room.

Buddy: Sure you did. The one that had the lamp shades wrapped in cellophane for the past twenty years.

Alan (Placing drinks on coffee table): Oh, yes. I was outlawed from that room years ago for putting a cigarette in an ash tray.

Buddy: . . . But you know why I really left home. I don't want to have milk and cake standing over the sink any more. I want to sit in a chair and eat like real people.

Alan: Whoa, boy. You've got to start easy otherwise you'll get the bends. Maybe tonight you can hang your coat on the doorknob. Then maybe in a few days you'll be ready for bigger things . . . like leaving your socks on the floor.

Buddy (Swings around right): Oh, it's going to be wonderful, just the two of us, Alan. *(He looks around)* Hey, I never realized it before, but this is a great apartment.

Alan: Yeah. It comes a little high, but you pay for the atmosphere.

Buddy: Oh, I almost forgot. How much is my rent?

Alan: What rent?

Buddy: For my share? I won't stay here unless I can pay my share.

Alan: All right, sport. Give me thirty dollars.

Buddy: Who are you kidding? This place is no sixty dollars a month.

Alan: Look, that's your rent. Thirty dollars. When the old man starts paying you more, you can pay *me* more.

Buddy: Well, just to start with. But we split everything else. The food and gas and electricity and everything. Agreed?

Alan (Crosses right to Buddy, bringing a drink): Agreed. *(Hands Buddy a drink)* Here. You owe me seventy-five cents. *(Raising his glass)* Well, here's to the Baker Brothers. The dream we've planned for years . . . You take all the girls on the West Side, I'll take the East Side . . . and I'll get in trouble afore ye. *(He winks affectionately at Buddy. Buddy drinks, Alan watches)* How is it?

Buddy (Not very happy): Different.

Alan: It should be. You just invented it. *(The phone rings)* Ten to one it's a gorgeous girl. *(Phone rings again. He picks up phone)* Hello? . . . Oh, Mom! . . . How are you, gorgeous? . . . We were just talking about you . . . Yes, about ten minutes ago . . . He's fine . . . Of course I'm going to take care of him . . . All right, sweetheart. *(He holds phone out to Buddy)* It's the Curator of the Museum.

Buddy (He takes the phone anxiously and sits on sofa. Alan goes to bar for refill): Hello, Mom? . . . How are you? . . . Fine . . . Fine . . . No, no. I'll have dinner soon . . . I don't know, some place in the neighborhood . . . Mom . . . Did Dad read the letter yet? . . . Oh, still at the plant. *(Alan crosses to Buddy. Buddy breathes a little easier)* What? . . . Mom, I don't want you to hide the letter . . . I *want* him to read it . . . He what? . . . Oh, boy!

Alan: What's wrong?

Buddy: Well, I know that just makes it worse, Mom, but I can't — Mom! . . . Mom! . . . Mom! . . .

Alan: She's crying?

Nods.

Buddy: She's crying.

Alan: Crying.

Buddy: (Back into phone): Mom, please calm down . . . No, Mom, that's not fair of you to ask me that.

Alan: What does she want you to do, come home?

Buddy (Jumping up): Mom, don't tear up the letter. I can't come home.

Alan (Crossing downstage left in front of table): Let me talk to her.

Buddy: But what about my life?

Alan: Let me talk to her.

Buddy: Mom, please-don't-tear-up-the-letter!

Alan (Reaching for phone): Give me the phone.

Buddy (Turns away): Alan, will you wait a minute. *(Back into phone)* All right, Mom. Let me think about it. I will. I'll call you back . . . Later . . . I promise . . . All right . . . Don't tear up the letter . . . Good-by.

He hangs up.

Alan: You'll think about what?

Buddy: Dad called Mom about ten minutes ago from the plant. Screaming. Some customer is angry at you! Because you didn't show up for a meeting today?

Alan: Oh, my gosh, Mr. Meltzer, I forgot.

Buddy: Anyway, Mom's afraid when he finds out that I left on top of this he'll go to pieces.

Alan: All right, all right. One thing has nothing to do with the other. I'll straighten him out.

Buddy: But he's going to let this all out on Mom. And you know when he starts to yell. You could get killed just from the fall-out.

Alan: Well, what do you want to do?

Buddy: I don't know. Maybe I should go home.

Picks up coat and suitcase.

Alan: Go home? Why?

Buddy: Why should Mother get the blame for something we've done?

Alan (Follows): Don't ask me. I don't crow like a rooster at three o'clock in the morning.

Buddy: What am I supposed to do?

Alan: Grow up. Be a man. You're twenty-one years old.

Takes his suitcase and coat and puts them down by sofa.

Buddy: You mean just forget about it?

Alan: Buddy, how long do you want to wait until you start enjoying life? When you're sixty-five you get social security, not girls.

Buddy: I don't know how we got all twisted around. I'm on your side. I want to leave. It's Dad who's against it.

Alan: Buddy, I know he means well. But he'll just never understand that things in life change. He's been in the wax-fruit business too long. *You've* changed.

Buddy: I know, but —

Alan: You're twenty-one years old now. You're ripe. Come on, kid. You've got one shoe off. Kick the other one off.

Buddy (Looks at Alan a moment, then shrugs): I — I guess you're right.

Alan: Then you'll stay?

Buddy (Nods): Yeah . . . Why not?

Alan (Puts arm around him): That's the kid brother I love and adore. Now go put your stuff in the bedroom.

Buddy: You sure I won't be in your way here or anything?

Picking up his coat and suitcase.

Alan: Of course not. We just may have to work out a traffic system. I've got a girl coming down in a few minutes.

Buddy: A girl? Why didn't you say so? Whenever you want to be alone, just say the word. I'll go out to a movie.

Alan: Don't worry. With my schedule, you won't miss a picture this year. *(The doorbell rings)* You hear that? She's here ten minutes ahead of time.

The doorbell rings again.

Buddy: I'd better put this in here and go.

Goes into bedroom.

Alan: No, no. I want you to see her first. *(He crosses to door)* Ready for the thrill of your life? *(He opens the door a crack as he says:)* . . . and my third wish, O Geni, is that when I open the door, the most beautiful girl in the world will be standing there. *(He motions Buddy to come out of bedroom. As he opens the door, there stands his Father, scowling disgustedly)* Dad!!

Buddy enters and immediately goes back into bedroom closing door quietly behind him.

Father (Steps in and looks at Alan and nods disgustedly. He walks into the room. Alan looks after him, dismayed, and seems puzzled when he doesn't see Buddy. The Father examines the room. It is obvious he approves of nothing in the apartment)

Alan (Meeting him downstage center): Gee, Dad . . . this is a . . . pleasant . . . surprise. *(The Father looks at him as if to say, "I'll bet")* How . . . how are you?

Father: How am I? . . . I'll tell you sometime . . . That's how I am.

He continues his inspection.

Alan: I've redecorated the place . . . How do you like it?

Father: Fancy . . . Very fancy . . . You must have some nice job.

Sniffs highball glass.

Alan: I just got in, Dad. I was about to call you.

Father: The phone company shouldn't have to depend on your business.

Alan: I wanted to explain what happened to me. Why I wasn't in the last two days.

Father: There's nothing to explain.

Alan: Yes, there is, Dad.

Father: Why? I understand. You work very hard two days a week and you need a five-day weekend. That's normal.

Alan: Dad, I'm not going to lie. I was up in Vermont skiing. I intended to be back Sunday night, but I twisted my bad ankle again. I couldn't drive. I thought it was broken.

Father: I'll send you a get-well card.

Alan: I'm sorry, Dad. I really am.

Father: You're sorry. I can't ask more than that.

Alan: I'll be in the office first thing in the morning.

Father: That's good news. You know the address, don't you?

Alan: Yes, Dad. I know the address.

Father: See. I always said you were smart. So I'll see you in the morning.

Alan: Right!

Alan starts upstage.

Father (Stops): Oh, by the way . . . How's the Meltzer account going?

Alan: The Meltzer account?

Alan comes back.

Father: From Atlantic City? The one you bragged about was all wrapped up?

Alan: Oh . . . er . . . fine.

Father: Fine? . . . I'm glad to hear that . . . Because he called today.

Alan (Surprised): Oh? . . . About an order?

Father: Yes. About an order.

Alan (A little skeptical): . . . Did . . . did we get one?

Father: Yes . . . We got one.

Alan: . . . How much?

Father: How much? — guess.

Alan: Well, Dad, I —

Father: Guess! Guess how much we got from Meltzer.

Alan: . . . Nothing?

Father: Bingo! Right on the button! . . . Bum!

Alan: Dad, wait a minute . . .

Father: Did you have a nice weekend, bum? Do you know what it costs to go skiing for four days? Three thousand dollars a day? Bum!

Alan: I tried to call him. I couldn't get a line through.

Father: On skis you tried to call him? You should be in the Olympics.

Alan (Crossing to phone): I'll call him right back. I'll explain everything.

Father: Where you gonna call him?

Alan: In Atlantic City.

Father: Who're you going to talk to? The Boardwalk? He's here!

Alan: In New York?

Father: In the Hotel Croyden. For two days he's sitting waiting while you're playing in the snow.

Alan: Dad, I promise you. I won't lose the account.

Father: Why? This would be the first one you ever lost? You want to see the list? You could ski *(gestures)* down your cancellations.

Alan: I couldn't get back in time, Dad. Skiing had nothing to do with it.

Father: I'm sorry. I forgot. I left out golf and sailing and sleeping and drinking and women. You're terrific. If I was in the bum business I would want ten like you.

Alan: That's not true. I put in plenty of time in the business.

Father: Two years. In six years you put in two years. I had my bookkeeper figure it out.

Alan: Thank you.

Father: My own son. I get more help from my competitors.

Starts to sit.

Alan: Well, why not? You treat me like one.

Father (Jumping up): I treat you? Do I wander in at eleven o'clock in the morning? Do I take three hours for lunch . . . in night clubs? . . . When are you there?

Alan: What do you mean, when?

Father: When? When? You take off legal holidays, Jewish holidays, Catholic holidays . . . Last year you took off Hallowe'en.

Alan: I was sick.

Father: When you came back to work you were sick. When you were sick you were dancing.

Alan: In the first place, it's not true. And in the second place, what good does it do coming in? You don't need me. You never ask my advice about the business, do you?

Father: What does a skier know about wax fruit?

Alan: You see? You see? You won't even listen.

Father (He sits): Come in early. I'll listen.

Alan: I did. For three years. Only then I was "too young" to have anything to say. And now that I've got my own apartment, I'm too much of a "bum" to have anything to say. Admit it, Dad. You don't give me the same respect you give the night watchman.

Father: At least I know where he is at night.

Alan: . . . You know where I am, too. Having fun. What's wrong with it? I think what I do at night should be my business.

Father: Not when it's nighttime four days in a row. Listen, what do I care? *(He rises and crosses right)* Do whatever you want. Go ahead and live like a bum.

Alan: Why am I a bum?

Father: Are you married?

Alan: No.

Father: Then you're a bum!

Alan: Give me a chance. I'll get married.

Father: I heard that for years. When you were twenty-six, twenty-seven, twenty-eight, even twenty-nine, you were a bachelor. But now you're over thirty and you're still not married, so you're a bum and that's all there is to it.

Turns away.

Alan: Who made thirty the closing date? All I want to do is have a little fun out of life like any other healthy, normal American boy.

Father: Healthy you are, American you are, normal you're not.

Alan: What do you mean?

Father: Look at your brother, that's what I mean. That's normal. He'll be something, that kid. He'll never be like you. Not in a million years.

Alan: Really? He might surprise you.

Father: That I'll bet my life on. He's in the plant the first thing in the morning, he puts in a whole day's work. No, that's one son I'll never have to worry about.

Alan: Have you read your mail lately?

Father: What?

Alan: Nothing.

Father: All right, I don't want to discuss anything more. I want to see you in the office tomorrow morning at eight o'clock.

Alan: Eight o'clock? There's no one there then.

Father: You'll be there. And you'll be there two nights a week and Saturdays, holidays, birthdays, and vacations. I'm sick and tired of being the father. From now on I'm the boss.

Alan: All right, Dad, but eight o'clock is silly. I have nothing to do until nine.

Father (Crossing up to foyer): You play solitaire all day anyway. You can get in three more games.

Alan: Okay. Okay, I'll be there.

Father: With the Meltzer account. If you haven't got it signed and in your pocket . . . you can ski *(gesturing)* right into the unemployment office.

Alan: I'll try, Dad. I'll really do my best.

Father: With your best, we're in trouble. From you I need a miracle. *(Alan sits downstage right center chair)* Eight o'clock with the Meltzer account . . .

Alan: Yes, Dad.

Father: The day your brother becomes like you, I throw myself in front of an airplane.

> *And with that he exits. As front door slams, Buddy comes rushing out of the bedroom door in a state of shock.*

Buddy: Did you hear that? I told you, Alan. I told you what he'd do.

Alan (Crosses to phone): What hotel did he say, the Croyden?

Buddy: Wait'll he reads that letter. He'll kill himself. He'll kill all of us. Like those stories in the *Daily News.* Alan, give me the phone.

> *Alan dials 411.*

Alan: Take it easy, will you. I've got to call Meltzer.

Buddy: Meltzer? We've got to get to Mom before he gets home. She's got to tear up that letter.

Alan: Will you relax. He's not going to kill anyone until he's had his supper . . . I'll straighten everything out.

Buddy: How?

Alan: All I've got to do is get Meltzer to sign. *(Into phone)* I'd like the number of the Hotel Croyden please.

Buddy: Suppose you don't?

Alan: There's no problem. He came to New York because I promised him a party . . . *(Into phone)* What was that? Thank you.

> *Dials number.*

Buddy: I sure picked a rotten time to leave. It's going to be murder up there. *(Starts to go)* I'm going home.

Alan: You walk out that door, I don't want you back.

Buddy (Coming back): Alan, why don't you help me?

Alan (Into phone): Mr. Martin Meltzer, please . . . Thank you. *(To Buddy)* I'm doing more than helping you. I'm saving you. It took you two years to get this far. Next time it'll take you five. *(Into phone and rises)* Hello? Mr. Meltzer? Hi? Alan Baker! . . . Where was I? . . . I'm too embarrassed to tell you . . . You ready? . . . Atlantic City . . . Yes. I thought you wanted me to come *there* . . . I just didn't think . . . Sure, I had the girls with me . . .

Buddy: You're a lunatic!

Alan (Covers phone quickly): Will you shut up? *(Back into phone)* What? . . . Well, can't you take the morning train back? . . . Can I still get in touch with the girls? . . . They're here with me right now.

Buddy: Where?

Alan (Covers phone again quickly): I'll shove you in the closet. *(Back into phone)* What was that? . . . Yes . . . That was one of the girls you heard . . . Pretty? *(He laughs. Turns head slightly from phone)* Honey, he wants to know if you're pretty . . . Mr. Meltzer, did you ever see an ugly girl in the Copacabana line? . . . No, they're off this week . . . Yes, they're dying to . . . Your hotel. Room 326 . . . Half hour? You have the drinks ready, I'll bring the drinkers. *(He laughs a phony laugh into the phone and hangs up)* I hate my-self.

He picks up book and thumbs through it quickly.

Buddy: I never saw anyone like you. Is it like this every night?

Alan: Well, it's always slow before Christmas. *(Reading from book)* "Married . . . Married . . . Europe . . . Pregnant . . ." *(Finds something in book)* Ahhh, here we are. Chickie Parker.

He dials.

Buddy: Chickie Parker?

Alan: And she looks just like she sounds. *(Into phone)* Hello? . . . Chickie? Don't you know you could be arrested for having such a sexy voice? . . . Alan . . . How could I? I just got in from Europe an hour ago . . . Switzerland . . . A specialist there told me if I don't see you within a half an hour, I'll die . . . Yes, tonight . . . A friend of mine is having a little party . . . Wonderful guy . . . Hundred laughs . . . Hey, Chickie, is your roommate free? The French girl? . . . Wonderful. Yes. Bring her . . . No, I can't. I've got to get the pretzels. Can you meet me there? The Hotel Croyden, Room 326, Marty Meltzer . . . A half hour . . . Marvelous. I just love you . . . What? . . . Yes, Alan *Baker.* *(He hangs up) Voilà!*

Buddy (He's flabbergasted): And it took me three months to get a date for my prom.

Alan: I'd better get going. *(He starts for bedroom when the buzzer rings. He stops)* Now what? *(He crosses quickly to intercom and speaks into it)* . . . Hello? . . . Who? *(Big surprise)* Connie!! . . . What are you doing here? . . . No, honey, no . . . Now? . . . Well, sure . . . sure, come on. *(He hangs up)* Of all the nights.

Buddy: Who's that?

Alan: A girl.

Buddy: Another one? Is she coming up?

Alan nods.

Alan (Half to himself): She wasn't due back in town till tomorrow. What a time to show up.

Buddy: Then why are you seeing her?

Alan: Oh, I can't give this girl the brush.

Buddy: I thought that part would be easy.

Alan: You don't understand. This girl is different. She's not like . . . well, she's different.

Buddy: You mean this one's for serious?

Alan: Who said serious? I just said different.

Buddy: Oh boy, would that solve everything at home if you got married. You know Mom's had an open line to the caterers for three years now.

Alan: Married? Me? With all this? Are you crazy?

Buddy: Well, I just thought — since she's a *nice* girl . . .

Alan: She's the *nicest* . . . but I'm working on it . . . Listen, you'd better blow. I want to see her alone.

Doorbell rings.

Buddy: Okay.

He starts for the door.

Alan: Oh! Hey, go out the service entrance in the kitchen . . . Come back in a few minutes.

Buddy *(He nods and goes to kitchen door):* Boy, no wonder you come in at eleven o'clock in the morning!

He exits. Alan crosses quickly to the door and opens it about an inch and says aloud:

Alan: And my third wish, O Geni, is that when I open my eyes, the most beautiful girl in the world will be standing there.

He opens door, turns and looks. Connie is standing there, holding an octagonal hat box. Alan crossing downstage right.

O Joy! My third wish has been granted. Enter, beautiful lady.

Connie enters.

Connie: Well, I guess it's safe as long as you've used up the other two wishes.

Alan: How are you, Connie?

Connie: Fine . . . now that I'm back.

Alan *(He embraces her):* Mmm. How does a girl get to smell like that?

Connie: She washes occasionally.

Holding package between them.

Alan: Come here. I've been thinking about this moment for two whole weeks. *(He tries to get closer)* Will you put down that package.

Connie *(She presents it to him):* After you open it.

Alan *(He takes it):* What is it?

Connie: A present.

Alan: For me? Why?

Connie *(She shrugs):* I like you! . . . And I missed you.

Alan: Well, I did too, but I didn't get you a present.

Connie: Well, don't get upset about it. I just like you six dollars and ninety-eight cents more than you like me . . . Open it.

Unbuttons jacket. He opens it.

Alan *(He looks in box. He is overwhelmed):* Connie! . . . My ski hat!

He takes it out of box.

Connie: It's like the one you lost, isn't it?

Alan *(He is really quite thrilled with it):* It's the same thing. *(He looks inside at the label)* It's the identical one I bought in Switzerland. I've looked all over New York for this. Where *(Puts box on fireplace chair)* did you ever get it?

Connie: In Montreal . . . It wasn't hard. Up there the newsstand dealers wear *(He puts hat on — She puts jacket on sofa)* them.

Alan: It even fits. How did you know my head size?

Connie: I've got an imprint on my neck.

Alan *(Throws hat on sofa):* Connie, you're wonderful. Only *you* would think of a thing like this.

Connie: Well, I *thought* of a watch, but I could afford this better.

Alan: Come here you.

> *He takes her in his arms.*

Connie (Coyly): Ah, the pay-off.
Alan: Thank you very much.

> *He kisses her.*

Connie: You're welcome — very much.

> *Alan moves to embrace her. She backs away.*

Connie: Alan relax.
Alan: I'm not through yet.

> *She crosses left.*

Connie: I've just come eight hundred miles in a prehistoric train and I'm tired, hungry, and too weak to be chased around the sofa.
Alan (Crosses to Connie): I'll carry you. We'll save lots of time and energy.

> *He moves after.*

Connie: Alan, please don't take advantage. I've got enough handicaps as it is.
Alan: Like what?
Connie (Wilting): Like being on your side. *(He grabs her and she swings around right of him)* It isn't fair. You and me against me is not fair. What is it you've got?
Alan: I don't know. Am I terribly good-looking?
Connie: Oh, God, no. You've got just enough things wrong with your face to make you very attractive . . . It's something else. Some strange power you have over me. But beware. The day I find out what it is, I'll have a gypsy destroy the spell with a dead chicken.
Alan: You little fool. Nothing can stop the Phantom Lover.

> *He starts after her.*

Connie: Alan, no!

> *Backs right.*

Alan (Stalking her): One kiss. If it leaves you cold, I'll stop. But if it gets you all crazy, we play house rules.
Connie (Moves so chair right is between them): Now, Alan, play fair.
Alan: I'll keep my hands behind my back. I'll spot you a five-point lead. I'll only be permitted to use my upper lip.

> *Steps up on chair.*

Connie: Alan, not now. Please. I haven't got the strength to put up an interesting fight. I just wanted to see you before I fell into bed for the next week and a half.
Alan: Okay. *(He pecks her)* A rough tour, heh?

> *Alan gets down off chair.*

Connie: This was the roughest.

Sits on right arm of chair.

Alan (He laughs): You poor kid. When does the show go out again?

Connie: They leave in two weeks.

Alan: They? . . . Not you?

Connie (Smiles): Not me.

Alan: Why not?

Connie: I just suddenly decided to quit.

Alan: Oh. Well, have you got another show lined up?

Connie: Well . . . it's not just the show I quit . . . It's show business.

Alan (He looks at her): . . . Are you serious?

Connie (She nods. She doesn't want to make a big thing of it now): I'll tell you all about it tomorrow. *(Starts left)* Will you call me, darling? . . . In the afternoon?

Alan: Wait a minute. I want to hear about this.

Connie: There's nothing to tell.

Alan: Nothing to tell? You're giving up your career and there's nothing to tell?

Connie (She laughs): Oh, Alan, darling . . . what career?

Alan: What do you mean, what career? You're a singer, aren't you?

Connie: Well, I wouldn't invest in it.

Alan: I don't get it. Things are going so well for you . . . All those musicals you do.

Connie (Sits on sofa): They're not musicals. They're industrial shows. Two-hour commercials completely uninterrupted by entertainment.

Alan (Sits on sofa and puts hat on table behind sofa): I'm serious.

Connie: I'm dead serious. This past month we did a show for the Consolidated Meat Packers. Have you any idea what it's like singing "Why not take all of me"° dressed as a sausage?

Alan (He smiles): It sounds funny.

Connie: Maybe to you. But I've seen butchers sit there and cry.

Alan: All right, so it's not *My Fair Lady.* You don't expect it to come easy, do you?

Connie: I don't expect it to come at all. Not now. Alan . . . *(Breaks left)* I'd work my throat to the bone if I thought I had a chance . . . or if I wanted it that much. But somehow lately I don't care any more . . . I guess it started when I met you.

Sits on left arm.

Alan: Honey, everyone gets discouraged. But you don't suddenly throw away a promising career.

Connie: Promising? Even you once said I was a lousy singer.

Alan: No, I didn't. I said you had a lousy voice. There's a big difference.

Connie: There is?

Alan: Of course. You've got looks, personality. That's all you need in the music business today. Hockey players are making albums.

Connie: It's *not* enough, Alan. You've got to have talent too.

Alan: Only if you want to be good. Not if you want to be a star.

Line from "All of Me" by Seymour Simons and Gerald Marks. © Copyright 1931 Bourne, Inc., New York, N.Y. Copyright renewed. Used by permission.

Connie: Well, it's pretty evident I'm not going to be either.

Alan: I just don't understand your attitude.

Connie: I don't understand *yours*. The world isn't losing one of its great artists.

Alan: What suddenly brought all this on?

Connie (Sits left of him): It's very simple. I just got tired of being away from you so long.

Alan (Withdrawing slightly): . . . Oh! . . . Well . . . if that's what you want.

Connie: That's it. No more traveling. No more buses and trains and long-distance phone calls. *(She moves closer)* I don't want to be more than a thirty-five cent taxi ride away from you.

Alan (Getting a little jittery): You . . . seem to have made up your mind.

Connie: Yes. And what a relief it is.

Alan: Well . . . What will you do now?

Connie: I'll manage. *(Alan rises — drifts right of center)* Girls are doing it every day. I'll maybe do a little modeling or become a secretary . . . or . . . a house-wife.

Alan (Turns to face her): What?

Connie: Housewife. You know . . . sleep-in maids.

Alan (Serious): What do you mean?

Connie: It was a joke . . . You didn't get it.

Alan (Deadpan): Yeah, I get it . . . It's funny. *(Looks at his watch)* Holy mackerel, look at the time. *(Starts upstage left)* Honey, I'm awfully sorry but I've got an important business appointment. Can I call you later?

Connie: No. I want to finish talking.

Alan: About what?

Connie: Housewives.

Alan: What about them?

Connie: You act as if you never heard of them.

Alan: Sure I did. My mother's a housewife. Connie, sweetheart . . . This is serious talk. Let's set aside a whole night for it. But right now I've really got to run.

Holds her jacket out for her.

Connie: How far?

Alan: What?

Connie: I must have touched a nerve or something.

Alan: That's not true. We've discussed marriage before, haven't we?

Connie: Yes. On this very couch. Or were they just campaign promises?

Alan: What difference did it make? I didn't win the election, did I?

Connie: The returns aren't all in yet.

Alan (He looks at his watch nervously): Connie, honey. *You're* tired and I've got a business appointment . . .

Holds jacket out again.

Connie: At seven o'clock?

Alan: It won't take long. I can be through by ten.

Connie: I'll bet you can.

Alan: What do you mean?

Connie: Oh, Alan, I'm a big girl. You've got a date.

Alan: It's a business appointment . . . And besides, I didn't expect you back until tomorrow.

Connie: You know, something just occurred to me. *(Rises.)* A few minutes ago I couldn't understand why you were fighting so hard to keep me in show business. It's suddenly very clear.

Alan: What is?

Connie: It's not *my* career you're worried about. It's *yours!*

Alan: My career??

Connie: As a lover. *(Grabs jacket and crosses right center)* That's why you want me to stay out on the road.

Alan: Why? I'm crazy about you.

Connie: Yes . . . when I'm here. The minute I leave . . . substitution. Oh, it's beautiful. A bachelor's dream. The two-platoon system.

> *Putting on jacket.*

Alan: What are you talking about?

Connie: You'll never grow stale, Alan. Or bored. Not as long as you keep rotating the crops every two weeks.

Alan: You're not being fair. *(Crossing downstage left)* I never said I didn't want to get married. But you come in here and make it sound like an emergency.

Connie: For some strange reason I thought you felt the same as I did. These past six months were . . .

Alan: They were wonderful. That's why I hate to see them end.

Connie: END! Getting married is the end?

Alan: I didn't mean it that way. Connie, you've got to understand, in a way a thirty-three-year-old guy is a lot younger than a twenty-four-year-old girl. That is, he may not be ready for marriage yet.

Connie: Let's leave the third person out of this. You mean you.

Alan: The point is, I didn't actually start my bachelor fling until late in life. And to tell the truth, I don't know if I'm flung out yet.

Connie: You would be if you were in love with me.

Alan: I am. Very much in love . . . only . . . I don't know. I'm like a kid with a few chocolates left in the box. I want to finish them first.

Connie: Will you stop twisting thoughts. Now you're making it sound as if I'm taking candy from a baby.

> *Crosses right and sits.*

Alan: No, I'm not. I'm leveling with you. Sure I see other girls. I'm only human but *(Crossing toward bar)* you must admit although these past six months were wonderful and exciting, I *have* made certain sacrifices that go against the very nature of man. *(Turns to her)* And you know from whence I speak.

Connie: The subject hasn't exactly been taboo.

Alan (Crosses left): True it was discussed. But it never got off the drawing board. If it were another girl, I'd be in Tahiti painting by now. But here I am. Still battling it out.

Connie: The war would be over if I knew just what it was we were fighting for.

Alan: I don't think I follow that.

Connie: All right, then, Alan, let's have the truth. Either you've said to yourself,

"I'm going to marry this girl," or, "I'm going to have an affair with her." All I ask is that you let me in on your decision. If marriage is out just say so. I won't run. I'll stay and fight for my honor the way a girl who's been properly brought up should. And I can truthfully tell you I'll lose the battle before long, because, damn it, I'm in love with you. But if you're really in love with me, you've got to tell me and be prepared to back it up with the rest of your life. (Rises) Well, which is it going to be, Alan? Do we march down the aisle or into the bedroom?

Alan (He stares at her unbelievingly a few seconds): That's the lousiest thing I ever heard . . . What am I supposed to say?

Starts right.

Connie: Say what you really feel.
Alan: You mean if I want to make love to you all I have to do is speak up?
Connie: Loud and clear.
Alan: You're a nut. (Breaks left) A sweet, beautiful nut!
Connie: I'm waiting, Alan.
Alan (Turning to her): For what? If I say I want you, you're mine. If I say I love you, I'm yours.
Connie: It's that simple.
Alan: Well, I'm not going to play. (Crosses left) It's more dangerous than Russian roulette.
Connie: It's just being honest with each other, Alan. That's what you're afraid of. You won't even be honest with yourself.
Alan: How can I be? I don't know what I want yet.
Connie: I didn't say you *had* to love me. I just want to know if you do.
Alan (Crossing right to center): If I want you I don't have to love you, but if I love you I shouldn't want you — I . . . I don't know. You've got to be an I.B.M. machine to figure out this affair.
Connie: I guess so. I forgot to make room for human failing.
Alan: Boy oh boy, for an innocent little girl you sure play rough.
Connie: I didn't choose the game, Alan.

She starts to go.

Alan: Where are you going?

He stops her.

Connie: I'd say you needed a chance to think.
Alan: No, I don't.
Connie: You mean you've made up your mind?
Alan: Yes . . . Yes, I've made up my mind.
Connie: . . . Well?
Alan: You mean, no matter what I say, you'll go along with it?
Connie: To the letter.
Alan: Okay . . . Okay, then . . . We march into the bedroom.
Connie (Stares at him): That's the lousiest thing I ever heard.
Alan: Uh huh. You see. You see. It's not so much fun when the *dentist* is sitting in the chair is it? You don't like it when I hold the drill.

Connie: I'm not complaining, Alan. I asked for it.

Alan: Oh, that you did. And I called your little bluff, didn't I?

Connie: You certainly did.

> *She goes up to door.*

Alan: Where are you going?

Connie: Back to my hotel.

Alan (Crossing up left of her): All right, wait a second, Connie. The joke is over. You're embarrassed because I made you lose face. I'm sorry. But when you pushed me into a corner like that I had no choice.

Connie: Oh, my face is still all there, Alan. I just figure if I'm going into business here I might as well get the rest of my merchandise.

> *She goes blowing him a kiss. Alan stares after her.*

Alan: . . . No . . . Never happen . . . Not her . . . *(The doorbell rings. Alan rushes to it. He opens it expectantly. It's Buddy)* Oh, it's you.

Buddy: Hey, was that her?

Alan: Where'd you go?

Buddy: Downstairs for a sandwich. Now that's what I call a pretty girl.

> *Alan gets coat from closet.*

Alan: You stay away from that kind. They're nothing but trouble.

Buddy: How did it go?

Alan: Oh, fine. Fine.

Buddy: I thought maybe the other girl walked in.

Alan: What other girl?

Buddy: The one you were expecting. From upstairs. Didn't you call her?

Alan: Peggy! O, my gosh, I forgot.

> *He crosses quickly to telephone. Throwing coat over sofa back.*

Buddy (Crosses downstage right center): You ought to get one of those maps with the stick pins so you know where they are all the time.

Alan (Dialing): I don't know what I'm doing tonight. What's that number again?

Buddy: Is she as pretty as the one that just left?

Alan: Peggy? Prettier. With none of the disadvantages.

Buddy: Boy, what a great place to live. And all for thirty bucks a month.

> *Sits right center chair.*

Alan (Hangs up): Hey, that's right. I forgot we're sharing everything. How would you like to meet her?

Buddy: Who?

Alan: Peggy. From upstairs.

Buddy (Jumps up): Me? Are you kidding?

Alan: Why? She's coming down anyway. No sense in sending her home empty-handed.

Buddy: But she's expecting you.

Alan: Turn the lights down low. She won't figure it out till she's going back up in the elevator.

Buddy: You're crazy.

Alan: No. That's how I met her. She rang the wrong bell one night. There's some poor guy in this building waiting for her since last July.

Buddy: You're not serious, Alan. She probably baby-sits for boys like me.

Alan: No. She's only twenty-two.

Buddy: I'm talking about experience, not age. I didn't realize it until I got here tonight, but I've been living in a convent all my life.

Alan: Buddy, trust me. She'll be crazy about you.

Buddy (Crossing away left): No, she won't. I don't want to meet her, Alan.

Alan (Crossing to him): I don't get you. Where's your spirit of adventure? You sound like an old man.

Buddy: An old man?

Alan: Sure, look at the way you dress. Why does a young boy like you wear a black suit?

Buddy: It's not black. It's charcoal gray.

Alan: Whatever it is, you look like Herbert Hoover.

Buddy: I'm sorry. I'll buy an all-white suit tomorrow.

Alan: Buddy, I don't do this for everyone. Just brothers I love.

Buddy: I'd like to, Alan, but gee, I had other plans.

Break away left.

Alan: What other plans?

Buddy: They've got that emergency UN meeting on television tonight, I'd really like to see it.

Alan (Crossing to him): The UN? Buddy, if I offered this to the Security Council, the meeting would be off tonight.

Buddy: Look, maybe you're not interested in what's going on in the world, but I am.

Alan: I'm interested in what's going on with you. What is it? Are you afraid?

Buddy: Yes — I mean, no.

Alan: You mean, yes.

Buddy: No, I don't.

Alan: You know, something just occurred to me. Is it possible that —

Buddy: You're going to be late, Alan.

Alan: I figured you were in the Army, overseas. Paris. I took it for granted —

Buddy (Crosses up left of sofa): I got around.

Alan: Where? In a sightseeing bus?

Buddy: What are you making such a fuss about? What's so damn important about it, anyway?

Alan (Crosses upstage right of sofa): It's plenty important.

Buddy (Evades him crossing downstage right): I'll get around to it soon enough.

Alan: Buddy, baby, why didn't you tell me? *(Crosses right to Buddy)* That's what big brothers are for. This is the answer to your problem.

Buddy: I haven't got a problem.

Alan: You haven't, huh?

Buddy: Look, there's a big difference between the way you and I operate. If I get a handshake from a girl I figure I had a good night.

Alan: With Peggy, all you have to do is say "Hello." From there on it's downhill.

Buddy: It can't be that easy. I know. I've tried.

Alan: Look kid, I wanted to get you a birthday present anyway. Now I found something you haven't got.

Buddy: I don't want it. I'm happy the way I am.

Alan: Buddy, please. If not for your sake, then for mine.

Buddy: For yours?

Alan: Ever since I moved out, I felt I haven't really been looking after you . . . the way a big brother should. I want to make it up to you, kid.

Buddy: I'm not complaining. You've been fine.

Alan: It would really give me pleasure, Buddy, to do this for you . . . It's something a father could never do.

Buddy: I'll say.

Alan: But brothers, well, it's different, Buddy . . . I feel that it's my duty and privilege to help you at this very important time of your life. What do you say, Buddy? . . . Please!

Buddy: Well . . . if it'll make you happy, all right.

Alan: Thanks, kid. *(Buddy shrugs. Alan crosses to phone and dials — Buddy crosses right)* You'll see. This'll be set up so perfectly, you won't even have to say a word to her . . .

Hums "In a Little Spanish Town." Into phone:

Hello? Peggy? . . . Yeah . . . No, no, wait a minute . . . *(He rises)* I have good and bad news . . . First the bad news. I've got to go out . . . No, most of the evening. Important business . . . You ready for the good news? . . . He's here . . . Manheim!

Buddy: Who?

Alan (Into phone): Oscar Manheim, the producer from M-G-M.

Buddy (Runs left of center): What?????

Alan: Just as you left . . . He's staying in my apartment tonight . . . He wants to meet you.

Buddy: I gotta get out of here.

He starts to go.

Alan (Into phone): Yes, now . . . I told him all about you.

Buddy: Please, Alan.

Alan (Into phone): Ten minutes? . . . Fine . . . Oh, don't dare thank me, honey. I'm really doing *him* the favor. *(He hangs up)* The ball's over the fence, kid. All you've got to do now is run the bases.

Buddy: Are you out of your mind? Me? A producer?

Alan: You want to be a director? I'll call her back.

Motions to phone.

Buddy: But why did you tell her that?

Alan: Just to make it easier for you.

Buddy: Easier?

Alan: Now the pressure's off you. It's all on her.

Buddy: What are you talking about?

Alan: She's got a bug about getting into pictures. Now's her chance to prove how really talented she is.

Buddy: How would I know?

Alan: Because you're a big producer from M-G-M, Oscar Manheim.

Buddy: Doesn't she know what he looks like?

Alan: No. I made him up. Sounds real, huh?

Buddy: Made it up? But she could call M-G-M and check.

Alan: She doesn't know how to dial. Look. She's been auditioning for years without making a picture. She's got more money than M-G-M. She's having too much fun being discovered.

Buddy: What am I supposed to do, make her a star?

Alan: No. Just give her a small part in the picture.

Buddy: What picture??

Alan: I Was a Teen-age Producer. I don't know. Can't you make up a picture?

Buddy (Breaking away right): No. Right now I can't even think of my own name.

Alan (Gets ready to leave): You're my brother. When the chips are down, you'll come through.

Buddy: A twenty-one-year-old movie producer. Holy cow!

Crosses left to sofa.

Alan: Well, I'd better get going.

Buddy: Wait a minute. When is she going to be here?

Alan: Ten minutes. She just lives upstairs.

Buddy: Ten minutes? I don't feel so good.

Alan: Look, if you're really too scared I'll call her back and cancel it.

Buddy: No. No, never mind.

Alan: You won't admit it, but you're glad I called. Is there anything you need?

Buddy: Yeah. A drink.

Alan: Here you are.

Hands drink to him. Then picks up trench coat.

Buddy: Well, here's to Oscar Wilhelm.

Alan: Manheim.

Buddy: Oh, jeez.

He drinks it all quickly.

Alan: Hey, take it easy with that stuff.

Crossing up to foyer; puts on trench coat.

Buddy: Can you imagine if I drop dead and she calls the police. They'll bury me in Hollywood.

Alan: It's going to be the greatest night of your life. You'll thank me for it some day.

He's at the door.

Buddy: Alan!

Alan: Yes?

Buddy: Will you call before you come home?

Alan: I'll call, I'll ring the doorbell and I'll cough loud as soon as I'm within two blocks of the house. *(He opens the door.)* So long, kid. And happy birthday! *(And he's gone.)*

Buddy stares after him a minute.

Buddy: Happy birthday! . . . Why¸couldn't he get me a tie like everyone else? . . .
How'd I get talked into this? *(He rubs his stomach as he apparently just got
a twinge of nervousness. He picks up both glasses and puts them on bar. Starts
right, gets a thought, looks at his own jacket. Runs up to hall closet, takes out
jacket, looks at it, puts it back. Then he takes out a bright blue smoking jacket,
runs down to sofa, takes off his jacket, throws it on sofa, throws hanger on sofa
table and puts on smoking jacket. Picks up cigarette holder from coffee table,
inserts cigarette and starts to light it. As he does so doorbell rings. He stands
paralyzed with fear. Screams)* Oh! . . . Just a sec . . . *(He looks around in a panic.
He starts upstage, sees his jacket on sofa and throws it under back of sofa. Then
he runs to the door and stops quickly to compose himself. He straightens himself up. Hell, he's going to go through with it. He opens the door. A small,
rather harassed woman in her late fifties stands there) (Yells)* Mom!

Woman *(Curtain falls as she speaks crossing downstage right)*: Oh, darling, I'm so
glad you're here.

Buddy *(Follows — in a state of shock)*: Mom! . . .

CURTAIN

ACT II

*The same. At rise: Buddy is frantically pacing back and forth. Buddy is about to
have his first experience and here sits his mother.*

    *Mrs. Baker is a woman who has managed to find a little misery in the best
of things. Sorrow and trouble are the only things that can make her happy. She
was born in this country, dresses in fine fashion and in general her speech and
appearance are definitely American. But she thinks Old World. Superstitions,
beliefs, customs still cling to her. Or rather she clings to them. Because of this,
we can't take her hysterics too seriously.*

Buddy: Mom, are you feeling all right?

Mother: Darling, can I have a cold glass of water? I almost fainted on the subway.

Buddy: Mom, what are you doing here?

Mother: I got such a dizzy spell. I never thought I'd get here.

Buddy: Mom . . . what did you want?

Mother: A glass of water, sweetheart.

Buddy: No, I meant —

*But maybe the water would be quicker. He rushes to the bar and pours a glass of
water.*

Mother: I've got no luck. I never had any and I never will.

Buddy *(Rushes back with glass)*: Here, Mom.

Mother *(Takes a sip)*: That just makes me nauseous. *(He takes glass and puts it on
    fireplace bench left)* Let me catch my breath.

Buddy: Maybe you need some fresh air, Mom. Outside?

Mother (Rises): Just let me sit a few minutes . . . Where's Alan?

Buddy: Out. On business. Do you feel any better?

Mother: When did I ever feel better?

Buddy: Mom, I hope you understand, but I've got this appointment tonight.

Mother: Did you have dinner yet?

Buddy: What? Dinner? Yes. Yes, I had a sandwich.

Mother: A sandwich? For supper? That's how you start the minute you're away?

Buddy: I'm not hungry, Mom. You see, I've got this appointment . . .

Mother: What'd you have, one of those greasy hamburgers?

Buddy: No. Roast beef. I had a big roast beef sandwich.

Mother: That's not enough for you. Let me make you some eggs.

Buddy: I don't want any eggs.

Mother: Look at this place. Look at the dirt.

Buddy: It's all right, Mom.

Mother: Sure. Boys. I'll bet no one's been in here to clean in a year.

Buddy (He might as well tell her): Mom, will you listen to me. I'm . . . I'm . . . I'm expecting a girl here in a few minutes.

Mother: To clean?

Buddy (Exasperated): No, not to clean . . . She's a friend of mine.

Mother: From our neighborhood?

Buddy: No, you don't know her. She's . . . er . . . a girl I knew in school. We're writing a story together.

Mother: Then let me make you some appetizers.

Buddy: We don't want any appetizers.

Mother: Buddy, I've got to talk to you about your father.

Buddy: Can't we do it tomorrow? She's going to be here any second.

Mother: What's the matter? She's more important than me?

Buddy: Mom, no one's more important than you.

Mother: How can you say that when you worry me like this? I know you. You won't eat unless the food's in front of you.

Buddy: No one eats unless the food's in front of them. Mom, I haven't got time . . .

Mother (Hurt): You want me to go, I'll go.

Buddy: Mom, please don't be hurt. I didn't want to have this meeting. It came up unexpectedly. But I have to go through with it.

Mother: Buddy, your father's going to be home in a few minutes. You should have heard him on the phone before about Alan. If the operator was listening, there'll be a man there in the morning to rip it off the wall.

Buddy: I can't discuss this with you now.

Mother: No, but for girls you've got time.

Sits right center chair.

Buddy: It's not a girl. It's . . . a . . . meeting. About a story we're writing. It may go on till two o'clock in the morning.

Mother: Without appetizers?

Buddy: We don't need appetizers!

Mother (Crosses to him): Wait'll he reads that letter. Wait'll he finds out you're gone. Remember what he did when Alan left?

Buddy: I know, Mom. He was very upset.

Mother: Upset? I'll never forget it. He came home from work at three o'clock, went into his room, put on his pajamas and got into bed to die . . . Four days he stayed in bed. He just laid there waiting to die.

Buddy: But he didn't die, Mom. He put on weight.

Mother: Don't think he wasn't disappointed . . . He was plenty hurt by Alan leaving, believe me. He thought by now Alan would be married, have a grandchild. Who knows if he'll ever get married. And now you.

Buddy: Mom, please —

Mother: I know what he's going to say tonight. He'll blame it all on me. He'll say I was too easy with the both of you. He'll say, "Because of you my sister Gussie has two grandchildren and all I've got is a bum and a letter" . . . I know him.

Buddy: Look, Mom. How about if I come home tomorrow night for dinner? And I'll have a long talk with Dad about everything. Okay?

Mother: Tomorrow? By tomorrow he'll be in bed again writing out his will. He'll be on the phone saying good-by to his family.

Buddy: He won't, Mom. He just gets very dramatic sometimes.

Mother: Maybe I am too easygoing. Maybe if I were like some mothers who forbid their children to do everything, I'd be better off today.

Buddy: No, Mom. You're the best mother I ever had . . . Do you feel any better?

Mother: How do I know? I feel too sick to tell.

Buddy: Really, a good night's sleep and you'll feel wonderful. Take something before you go to bed. Some warm milk.

Mother: Who buys milk now that you're not there.

Buddy: Then buy some.

Mother: Maybe I'll be better off if I take a hot bath.

Buddy: That's the girl.

Mother: I'll probably pass out right in the tub.

Buddy: No you won't. Why do you get so emotional all the time?

Mother: I don't look for it, believe me, darling.

Buddy: Mom, everything's going to be all right. *(He half lifts her to her feet)* Sleep tight.

> He kisses her forehead.

Mother: I feel better knowing at least you'll be there tomorrow.

Buddy: For dinner. I promise.

> He starts upstage.

Mother (She stops): . . . What'll I make?

Buddy (Coming down to her): What?

Mother: For dinner? What do you want to eat?

Buddy: Anything. I don't care. Good night, Mom.

Mother: I want to make something you like now that you're not home.

Buddy: I like everything. Roast beef, okay?

Mother: All right, good. *(He starts upstage. She starts, then stops)* You had roast beef tonight.

> He comes back.

Buddy (Beside himself with anxiety): I can eat it again.

Mother: I could get a turkey. A big turkey.

Buddy: Okay! Turkey! Wonderful!

Mother: It doesn't really pay for one night.

Buddy (He can't take it any more. He practically screams): Mom, for Pete's sakes, it doesn't matter.

Mother (Near tears): What are you yelling? I'm only trying to make you happy. Who do I cook for, myself? I haven't eaten anything besides coffee for ten years.

Buddy: I'm sorry, Mom.

Mother: Oh, I've got that stick in the heart again.

Sits right center chair.

Buddy: You're just upset.

Mother: No. I ate lamb chops tonight. They never agree with me.

Buddy: Oh, boy.

Mother: Darling, do you have an Alka-Seltzer?

Buddy: Alka-Seltzer? I don't know . . . Wait a minute. I'll look in the kitchen.

He rushes off madly to the kitchen right.

Mother (She rubs her stomach): She wished it on me. His sister Gussie wished it on me.

Buddy comes running back out.

Buddy: There isn't any here.

Mother: Sure. Boys. You wouldn't have water if you didn't have a faucet.

Buddy: Mom, make anything you want. Turkey. Roast beef. I'll be home tomorrow night. Now why don't you go home and relax. Take a cab.

Mother: It's starting to rain. Where am I going to get a cab?

Buddy: I'll get you one, okay?

Mother: All right. Let me sit a few minutes.

Buddy: A few minutes? *(He can't wait any longer)* Mom, I'll get the doorman to get you a cab. *(Runs up to door)* Do you want to wait in the lobby?

Mother: You don't have to run out.

Buddy: I'll be right back. In two minutes.

And he is gone in a flash.

Mother: Don't get overheated . . . Who am I talking to? *(She looks around the apartment and shakes her head disapprovingly. Puts bag on chair, unbuttons coat . . . She gets up, crosses to the coffee table, empties one ash tray into the other. Then starts to cross with the refuse into the kitchen when the phone rings. She turns and goes to the phone) (Into phone)* Hello? . . . Who? . . . No, he isn't. To whom am I speaking to, please? Meltzer? Martin Meltzer . . . No, this is Alan's mother . . . What? . . . Why should I kid about a thing like that? . . . No, I'm positive he's not here . . . A message? . . . Wait. I'll get a pencil. *(She looks for a pencil. There is none on the table, so she runs quickly to the left cabinet, then upstage cabinet, sofa, table and looks frantically for a pencil. There is none to be found. She runs back quickly to the phone)* Go on, I'll remember. Talk fast so I could write it down as soon as you're finished . . . "Extremely important. Your wife just came in unexpectedly from Atlantic

City and is on her way to the Hotel Croyden so Alan should be sure *not* to come with those certain parties." Yes, I have it . . . I do . . . I can't repeat it to you, I'm trying to remember it . . . Mr. Meltzer, Hotel Croyden . . . Yes . . . Don't talk any more, I'm going to write it down quick. Good-by. *(She hangs up)* Some message. That's a book, not a message. *(She starts to look for a pencil again)* Where's a pencil? They don't have Alka-Seltzer, they're gonna have a pencil? *(She crosses right toward counter) (The phone rings)* Suddenly I'm an answering service. *(She answers phone)* Hello? . . . No, he isn't . . . This is Alan's mother . . . Why should I kid about a thing like that? . . . To whom am I speaking to please? . . . Who? . . . Chickie? . . . That's a name? . . . Chickie Parker . . . You forgot whose hotel? . . . Mr. Meltzer's? Where do I know that name from? . . . Oh, for God sakes, he just called. With a message to Alan. Something about Atlantic City. I think he said Alan shouldn't go there . . . I don't know what it means either. I'm not a secretary. I'm a mother . . . without a pencil . . . The hotel? . . . Yes, he did mention it . . . I think it was the Parker . . . Oh, that's *your* name . . . Wait. Oh, yes. The Croyden . . . A message for Alan? I can only try, darling . . . "Chickie was detained but she's on her way to the Croyden now." Yes. You're welcome. Good-by. *(She hangs up. She crosses upstage to desk area, looking for a pencil)* There must be some carrying on here. Their father should only know . . . A businessman and a college boy and they don't have a pencil. *(She starts right and the phone rings again)* Oh, for God's sakes. *(The phone rings again)* All right, all right, what do you want from me? *(She rushes quickly to the phone and picks it up)* Yes? . . . Who? . . . Who did you want, please? . . . No, he's out. This is Alan's mother . . . Listen, don't start that with me . . . Who is this? . . . Connie what? . . . Again with a message . . . Miss, can't you write it down, I don't have a pencil . . . You what? . . . Yes . . . Yes . . . Yes . . . You're welcome . . . Good-by. *(She hangs up)* Good-by, go home, good luck, who knows what she said. *(Sits on sofa and cries)* Who tells him to have so many phone calls? . . . It's disgusting. *(The phone rings. She screams)* What do you want from my life? *(She just stares at the phone. It continues to ring)* I wouldn't pick it up now if it stood on its head. *(It continues to ring)* Oh, I'm so nauseous. *(She can't stand it any longer. She picks it up, but she yells at it angrily)* Hello? . . . What do you want? . . . Who is this? . . . Alan who? . . . Oh, Alan . . . *(She starts to cry)* It's Mother. *(She sits)* What am I doing here? . . . I'm answering your phone calls . . . He's outside getting me a subway . . . I mean a taxi . . . No, there's no one else here . . . Who called? . . . The whole world called . . . First a man called . . . Meltzer? . . . No, it didn't sound like that . . .

The door opens and Buddy rushes in.

Buddy: Okay, Mom.
Mother *(Into phone)*: Oh, I've got to go now. Buddy is here with the cab. Talk to Buddy.
Buddy: I've got the cab. It's waiting outside.
Mother: Here.

Hands him phone.

Buddy: Who is that?

Mother: Alan. *(She gets up and hands phone to Buddy and crosses right to get bag)* Here!

Buddy (Taking phone): Hello, Alan? . . . What's wrong? I don't know who called, I was outside. *(To Mother)* Mom, did someone call?

Mother: I gave all the messages to Alan. I don't want to keep the taxi waiting. Good-by, sweetheart.

She starts to door.

Buddy: Mom, who called? A girl?

Mother: Yes, darling. Good-by.

Buddy: What did she say?

Mother: I don't remember.

She opens door.

Buddy: Why didn't you write it down?

Mother: Don't *you* start with me . . . This must be costing a fortune. I only hope I don't pass out in the taxi!

She goes.

Buddy: Mom, wait . . . *(Into phone)* Hello, Alan . . . I don't know. I can't make head or tail out of her . . . Where are you? . . . No, she didn't get here yet . . . Lousy, that's how I feel . . . I already had a drink. It doesn't help . . . Hey, wait a minute. Who am I again? . . . Oscar *Wol*heim? . . . *Manheim!* Oscar Manheim . . . Oh, boy . . . Look, Alan. I changed my mind. I can't go through with it. I'm going out. Yes. Now. Well . . . I'll leave her a note from you . . . I'm sorry. Good-by. *(He hangs up)* That's it. I'll leave her a note. That's all. *(He quickly starts to search for a pencil and paper. He looks in the shelves under downstage left cabinet and takes out container with two dozen pencils)* Eight thousand pencils and no paper. *(He crosses to table behind sofa and finds piece of paper. He sits on sofa and starts to write and repeats aloud)* "Dear Peggy . . . More bad news . . . Paul . . . *(Momentarily forgets name)* Manheim . . . is . . . dead! . . . Love . . . Alan"

He puts down pencil, then crosses to door. Reads letter again as he bends down to leave it under door. The front bell rings. He gasps. The bell rings again. He throws up his hands in despair and then opens door. Peggy stands there ravishingly dressed. She looks utterly fantastic.

Peggy: Hi. I'm Peggy Evans. *(She walks in. He closes door)* I'm not disturbing you or anything, am I?

Buddy (He looks at her, overwhelmed by her pulchritude, follows her downstage): No . . . not at all.

He is in a state of semi-shock.

Peggy (Sitting on sofa): Alan said you wanted to meet me. I hope you forgive the way I look. I've been in a car all day . . . I must be a mess.

Buddy: No . . . You look . . . very neat.

He tears up the note and puts pieces in his pocket.

Peggy: Thanks . . . Coming from you, that's something. *(She crosses to him)* It's a shame you couldn't get up to the ski lodge.

Buddy: What ski lodge?

Peggy: In New Hampshire. Or Vermont. I'm not very good at names. In fact, I'm afraid I've forgotten yours.

Buddy: Oh . . . It's . . . *Manheim.*

Peggy: That's right. Mr. Manheim.

Buddy: Jack Man — heim . . . No, not Jack.

Peggy: That's right, Jack.

Buddy: Yes, Jack . . . won't you sit down?

Indicating right center chair.

Peggy: Thank you . . . *(She sits on sofa)* I understand you had some problem at the studio.

Buddy: Oh, yes . . . we did.

Peggy: What was it?

She takes a cigarette and lights it.

Buddy: It was . . . er . . . *(He sees flame)* Er . . . we had a . . . fire.

Peggy: Who?

Buddy: I beg your pardon?

Peggy: Who did you have to fire?

Buddy: No, no. *A* fire. Part of the studio burned down.

Peggy: Oh? Was anyone hurt?

Buddy: No . . . just a few extras . . . Say, would you like a drink?

Peggy: Oooh, like a transfusion. I don't mind admitting it, but I'm nervous.

Buddy: You're nervous? What would you like?

Peggy: What are you having?

Buddy (This one is easy. He tosses it off grandly): Oh . . . scotch and ginger ale.

Peggy: Oh, that's cute. I mean what are you *really* having?

Buddy (Embarrassed): I don't know. What are you having?

Peggy: Grand Marnier.

Buddy: Grandma who?

Peggy: Grand Marnier. It's French. You know, a liquoor.

Buddy: Oh . . . *(He crosses up to bar and looks for it. He picks up a scotch bottle)* No, I don't see any.

Peggy: Oh, scotch'll be fine. *(He pours drinks)* I suppose you've heard it before, but you look awfully young for a producer.

Buddy (Crossing left of her): Oh, do I?

Peggy: To look at you I'd say you were only about twenty-six, but I bet I'm way off.

Buddy: Oh, way off. *(Hands her drink and sits left of her)* Well, here we are.

Peggy: What should we drink to?

Buddy: Anything you like.

Peggy: Let's make a silent toast.

Buddy: Okay.

They both close their eyes, take a beat, she opens hers, nudges him, he opens his eyes, clink glasses and drink.

Peggy (Makes herself comfortable, puts down glass and snuffs out cigarette): Well, now . . . down to business.

Buddy: Huh?

Peggy: I suppose you want to know what I've done.

Buddy: Not necessarily.

Peggy: I'll be perfectly frank with you. I've never been in a picture before.

Buddy: Is that so?

Peggy: But I'm not totally inexperienced.

Buddy: So Alan told me.

Peggy: Last summer when I was on the Coast I did an "Untouchables."

Buddy: No kidding?

Peggy: I was a dead body. They fished me out of the river.

Buddy: I think I saw that.

Peggy: Lots of people did. I got loads of work from it. But it's not what I really want to do. That's why I'm taking acting class. With Felix Ungar. He lives in this building. Right under this apartment. In fact *that's* how I met Alan. *(She puts her hand on his right knee)* I rang the wrong bell one night.

Buddy looks down at his knee and laughs almost hysterically.

Buddy: How about that?

Peggy: And look how it turned out. Through a silly mistake, I'm being auditioned by one of the biggest producers *(taking hand off knee)* in the business. Life is funny, isn't it?

Buddy (Puts drink down and rises crossing right): Hysterical.

Peggy (Rises — crosses below coffee table): Well, is there anything you'd like me to do?

Buddy: What?

Peggy: Do. Read a scene? Or kind of take on a character like in class. Or is just talking like this enough?

Buddy: Oh, it's plenty. To tell the truth, I'm a little tired.

Sits right center chair.

Peggy: Oh, from the trip. Would you like me to massage your think muscle?

Buddy: Huh?

Peggy: Here! *(She indicates her temple. She goes to where he's sitting, and stands over him)* Just close your eyes and put your head back.

Buddy: I don't think . . .

Peggy: I'm very good at this. Now just relax . . . *(He does)* . . . and try and forget about the picture business. *(She massages)* No, I can feel it. You're still thinking about the studio.

Buddy: No, I'm not. I swear I'm not.

The phone rings. He jumps up.

Peggy: Are you expecting anyone?

Buddy: Me? No! No! *(It rings again, angrily)* No, I'll get it. I'll get it. *(He crosses to phone quickly and picks it up. Into phone)* Hello! . . . Dad!!! . . . I'm sorry. I didn't mean to yell . . . What? . . . now? . . . Look, Dad, I'll come downstairs, okay? . . . Dad? . . . Dad? . . . Oh, boy!

He hangs up.

Peggy: Is anything wrong?

Buddy: What? Oh, yeah . . . It's . . . it's someone I don't want to see . . . A writer . . .

Peggy: Dad? It sounded like it was your father.

Buddy: Oh! Oh, no. That's just a nickname. Dad. You know, like Ernest Hemingway is Poppa.

Peggy: Oh! Is Dad coming up?

Buddy: Yeah, Dad's coming up . . . Look would you do me a big, big favor? I've got to be alone with him for a few minutes . . . To talk about script changes.

Peggy: I understand. I could go up and get that bottle of Grand Marnier.

Buddy (That's inspirational): That's it. Would you do that?

Peggy: Of course.

> *She starts for the door.*

Buddy (He stops her): Not that way!

Peggy: What?

Buddy: I don't want him to know I'm auditioning someone else. He's already got someone in mind.

Peggy: Oh, I appreciate that. Thanks an awful lot, Mr. Manheim.

> *She kisses him and exits through the kitchen door. He starts right to make sure she has gone. He looks at his jacket, unbuttons it, takes it off, throws it into bedroom and closes door. He runs downstage, grabs the two glasses from coffee table and puts them on bar. He starts right, stops, looks at glasses. Picks one up and examines it for lipstick, takes out his handkerchief, wipes lipstick off, puts glass on bar. As he wipes his own mouth with handkerchief, doorbell rings. He frantically tries to jam handkerchief into pocket and can't. Doorbell rings again. Panicky, he throws handkerchief out window left. He grabs a large book from upstage bookshelf, opens it, goes to door, book in hand, composes himself as if he had been reading all evening and opens door. There stands his Father, with the letter in his hand.*

Buddy: Hello, Dad. *(The father walks in, holds up the letter to Buddy's face, to indicate he got it, then he walks into the apartment. Buddy follows left of him)* Are you all right, Dad? . . . Is anything wrong? *(The Father stares ahead speechless. He has taken letter out of envelope and now holds it in front of Buddy's face)* I — I didn't think you'd be coming down tonight . . . I was going to have a long talk with you in the morning . . . at the plant . . . and then I told Mother I'd be home for dinner tomorrow night . . . so you and I could sit down and talk some more . . . and I could explain how I . . . Dad, you're angry, aren't you? . . .

Father: Me? Angry. Why should I be angry?

Buddy: About the letter.

Father (Looks at him): What letter?

Buddy: This letter. The letter I wrote you.

Father: No, no. You didn't write this letter. Someone I don't know wrote this letter. Not you. You, I know. This person I never met.

Buddy: Dad, don't you think it would be better if we waited until tomorrow, when we're both — calmer? Dad, I meant to have a long talk with you about this.

Father: Talk? What's there to talk about? *(He still holds up letter)* It's signed, sealed and delivered. The Declaration of Independence . . . What's there to talk about?

Buddy: Dad, I think you're too upset now to discuss this logically.

Father: Oh, I expected it. *(Puts letter in envelope)* You hang around your brother long enough it was bound to happen. So what's the windup. My sister Gussie has two grandchildren and I have a bum and a letter.

Buddy: Dad, this didn't suddenly happen. I tried to explain how I felt the other night. But you wouldn't listen.

Father (He starts to sit and jumps up): Don't try and tell me I wouldn't listen. That's all I did was listen.

> *Crosses left.*

Buddy: But every time I would start to say something, you would walk out of the room.

Father: If you showed me a little respect, then maybe I would listen.

Buddy: Dad, you're not making any sense.

Father: *I'm* not making sense? Very nice. Very nice talk to a father.

Buddy: What do you want me to say?

Father: I want to hear from your own lips . . . nicely . . . why such a young boy can't live at home with his parents.

Buddy: Young boy?

Father (Holding up a warning finger): Nicely!

Buddy: Dad, I'm twenty-one.

Father (Noncommittal): You're twenty-one.

Buddy: You say it as if you don't believe me. I was twenty-one yesterday, wasn't I?

Father (Shrugs): Whatever you say.

Buddy: What do you mean whatever I say?

Father (Finger up again): Nicely!

Buddy: All right. I *say* I was twenty-one. That's old enough to make your own decision in life. When *you* were twenty-one, you were already married, weren't you?

Father: You were there?

Buddy: No, I wasn't there. You told me yourself.

Father: Those days were altogether different. *(Crosses away left)* I was working when I was eleven years old. *(Turns to him)* I didn't go to camp.

Buddy: What's camp got to do with all this???

Father (Threatening): I'll walk right out of here!

Buddy: Dad, all right. I don't mean to be disrespectful, but your answers never match my questions.

Father (Crossing above and right of Buddy): Oh, that too? I don't talk fancy enough for you like your brother and his show business friends.

Buddy: That's what I mean. Who said anything about show business?

Father: Well, that's where he is all day, isn't he? Backstage at some burlesque house.

Buddy: They haven't had burlesque in New York in twenty years.

Father: He hasn't put in a day's work in twenty years. And now I suppose I can expect that of you.

Buddy: No, Dad. I'll work there as long as you want me to . . . No matter how I feel about it.

Father: What do you mean, no matter how you feel?

Buddy: Well, Dad, I never had a chance to try anything else. I had two years of college, then the Army, and then right into the business. Maybe it's not the right field for me.

Father: Not the right field? *(He addresses an imaginary listener in right center chair)* I give the boy the biggest artificial fruit manufacturing house in the East, he tells me *not the right field.* Ha!

He sits right center chair.

Buddy: I don't know if I've got any talent . . . but . . . I've always toyed with the idea of becoming a writer.

Father: A writer? What kind of writer? Letters? *(He holds up letter)* Letters you write beautiful. I don't know who's going to buy them, but they're terrific.

Buddy: But supposing I'm good? I'm not even getting a chance to find out. Supposing I could write plays . . . for television or the theater?

Father: Plays can close. *(Crossing to him)* Television you turn off. Wax fruit lays in the bowl till you're a hundred.

Buddy: But business doesn't stimulate me, Dad. I don't have fun.

Father: You don't have fun? I'll put in music, you can dance while you work.

Buddy: Dad, forget about the business for now. I'll stay. All I want now is your permission for me to live here on my own.

Father (Puts letter in coat pocket): All right, let me ask you a question. If you were in my place, if you were my father, with conditions in the world as they are today, with juvenile delinquency, with the stories you read in the papers about the crazy parties that go on, the drinking and whatnot . . . would you let *your* son leave home?

Buddy: Yes!

Father: That's no answer!

Buddy: Dad, it just doesn't seem as if we're ever going to understand each other.

Father: How can we? You listen to your brother more than you listen to me.

Buddy: That's not true.

Father: Do you deny that he's the one who put this bug in your mouth about leaving home?

Buddy: In your ear, Dad.

Father: What?

Buddy: Bug in your ear.

Father: Excuse my ignorance, Mr. Writer.

Buddy: I wasn't making fun of you.

Father: Why not? Your brother does.

Buddy: No, he doesn't.

Father: He doesn't, heh? I can imagine the things he must tell you. You'll learn plenty from him, believe me, plenty. At least you I had hopes for. Alan I could never talk to. But you, you were always good. I could take you anywhere. I could take you visiting, you would sit on a chair for three hours, you wouldn't hear a peep out of you. I remember I used to say, give Aunt Gussie a kiss. You'd go right over and give Aunt Gussie a kiss. But the older one. I chased him all over Brooklyn one day because he wouldn't give Aunt Gussie a kiss . . . What was so terrible to give Aunt Gussie a kiss?

Buddy: I guess it was that hat she wore. You always had to kiss her through a veil.

Father: You see how you take his side.

Buddy: I wasn't taking his side.

Father: No, heh? What's the use talking to you. You'll do what he says in the end anyway. If you want to become a bum like him, that's your affair.

Buddy: Why is Alan a bum?

Father: Is he married?

Buddy: No.

Father: Then he's a bum!

Buddy: Dad, you really never had any problems with me before, have you? Won't you trust me now?

Father (He sighs): All right, you want trust. I'll give you trust.

Buddy: What do you mean?

Father: There's a disagreement here. A dispute. We'll arbitrate.

Buddy: That's all I've been asking of you.

Father: I've heard your side. You've heard my side. If you want, we'll give it a six-month trial period. Fairer than that, I can't be.

Buddy: I think that's very fair, Dad. Six months is fine.

Crossing left.

Father: Then it's settled. You'll come home and live for six months . . .

Buddy: Come home? *(Shouts, crossing to him)* You don't want to give me a trial. You don't want to be fair . . . You just — just —

Father (Rises and shakes upstage hand): Don't you raise your voice. You're not too big to get a good slap across the face.

Buddy: I'm sorry, Dad.

Father: I never thought I'd live to see this day. That a son would talk to his father like this. I've been some terrible father to you, haven't I?

Buddy: No, Dad. You've been a wonderful father. Just meet me halfway. Please . . . What do you say?

Father (Crosses left of him): I'll . . . I'll let you know.

Buddy: What do you mean, you'll let me know?

Father: I'm not rushing into any decision pell mell . . . I'll go home and think about it. If you want, you can stay here tonight, I won't argue. But tomorrow, you'll come home for dinner and we'll see what we'll see.

Buddy: All right, that'll be fine. Good night, Dad.

He starts upstage.

Father: You need any money?

Buddy: No, I've got plenty.

Comes back.

Father: Where are you going to sleep?

Buddy: On the sofa.

Father: That's some place to sleep.

Buddy: Dad, I'll be all right. I'll see you tomorrow. I promise.

Father: You don't have to promise. You say you'll be there, I trust you.

Buddy: Thanks, Dad. Good night.

  Starts up again.

Father (Just about to leave, when he stops and turns): Oh, wait a minute.
Buddy: What's the matter?
Father: I want to call your mother. Tell her everything's all right. I know she's worried.

  He crosses to phone.

Buddy (Crossing and sits down center chair): Oh, boy!

  The Father dials, sighing, in Buddy's direction.

Father (Into phone): Hello? . . . Jezebel? . . . Is Mrs. Baker home? . . . Oh! I wonder where she is? . . . Listen, Jezebel, before you go home, I want you to write down a message for her . . . All right, get a pencil . . .

  Suddenly Peggy comes out from the kitchen. She wears a topcoat. Buddy rises as she enters.

Peggy: Excuse me, but I'm all out of Grand Marnier too, I'll run down to the liquor store and get some. *(To Father)* Hello, Dad!

  She goes back out kitchen door. The Father stares after her dumfounded. Buddy is in a state of shock. The Father turns slowly back to the phone.

Father: Hello, Jezebel? . . . Tell Mrs. Baker I'm with the bum! . . . The twenty-one-year-old bum! *(He slams the phone down, turns and points an accusing finger at Buddy)* Bum!
Buddy: Dad . . .
Father: Bum!
Buddy: Let me explain . . .
Father: Bum!
Buddy: Please . . .
Father: Twenty-one years old! You're a bigger bum than your brother is right now and you've still got twelve years to go!
Buddy: Dad, please.

  The front door suddenly opens. Alan walks in and sees the Father.

Alan: Dad!!
Father: Ah, the other bum. Come on in. We're having a party.
Alan: What are you doing here?
Father: I was invited to dinner. That's some cook you have in there.
Alan: Where?
Buddy (Defeated): In the kitchen.
Alan: What? . . . *(To Buddy)* Well, didn't you explain? That she was waiting for me?
Father: I don't need you to make up stories. *(Crosses to Buddy)* I've got Tennessee Williams for that.

  The phone rings. Father starts out.

Alan: Dad, wait. I want to talk to you.

He crosses quickly to the phone.

Father: I've heard enough.

He starts to go.

Alan (Into phone): Hello? . . . Oh, Mr. Meltzer.

Father (Stops): Meltzer? What does he want?

Alan (Into phone): Now, please. Calm down. I tried to explain. There was a mixup somewhere.

Father: What's wrong?

Alan: Nothing, Dad. Nothing. *(Into phone)* What? . . . Well, how should I know your wife was coming in? . . . I didn't get any message from my mother.

Father (Crosses to him): What are you talking about?

Alan (Into phone): If I can just talk to your wife . . . Mr. Meltzer, there's no need for a lawsuit.

Father: Lawsuit? What lawsuit?

Alan: Dad, wait a minute . . . *(Into phone)* Mr. Meltzer . . .

Father: Give me that phone. *(Grabs phone and brightly says)* Hello? Meltzer? This is Mr. Baker, senior. What's the trouble?

Alan: He's hysterical, Dad. Don't listen to him.

Father: Your wife and *who* rang the doorbell together? What French girl? . . . But who arranged such a thing? . . . I see . . . *(Turns to Alan)* I see . . . Good-by.

He hands phone to Alan, who hangs up, and starts for door. Alan follows.

Alan: Dad, if you'd just listen for five minutes . . . Dad!!!!! Dad, Dad . . . please say something!

The Father crosses past them in silence. He turns on raised foyer and speaks calmly.

Father: May you and your brother live and be well. God bless you, all the luck in the world, you should know nothing but happiness. If I ever speak to either one of you again, my tongue should fall out!

He opens the door and goes. The two brothers stand there looking at each other helplessly.

Buddy (Crosses right to fireplace): I knew it. I knew this would happen.

Alan (Concerned): Do you think he means it?

Alan takes off coat and puts it on left handrail.

Buddy: Means it? In ten minutes he'll be home, giving the rest of my clothes to the janitor.

Alan (Crosses downstage right of sofa): I never saw him this mad. *(Crossing down)* Not since the day he chased me all over Brooklyn when I wouldn't give Aunt Gussie a kiss.

Buddy: Oh, he's mad all right. And he means it. *(Crosses left to him)* We're *fired.*

Alan (Musing): But how can he get along without us?

Buddy: And he was almost out the door. And then that fruitcake walks in and says, "Hello, Dad" . . . His mustache almost fell off.

Alan (Sits on sofa): I'm sorry, kid. I didn't mean to get you involved.

Buddy: It's not your fault.

Alan: I thought I was doing you a favor . . . Well, it's over with anyway.

Buddy: What's over? She's coming back with a French bottle to do silly little things.

Alan: She is?

Buddy: She gets me all crazy. Suppose I do something nutty, like signing her to a five-year contract? . . . *(Doorbell rings)* I can't face her again, Alan. Please.

Alan: All right, never mind. I'll take over. Go on out to a movie.

Buddy (Grabs his coat from under sofa): That's a great idea. Maybe one of my pictures is playing around.

Doorbell rings again. He exits through kitchen right. Alan opens door; Connie stands there with valise.

Alan: Connie!

Closes door. She puts down case and gives Alan long kiss interrupting his "Wha . . .," then when she releases him:

Connie: Me no Connie. Me Jane. You Tarzan. Jane come to swing with Tarzan in tree.

Alan: What's in that suitcase?

Connie: The rest of my merchandise.

She takes off her coat. Puts it on right handrail.

Alan: You're drunk.

Crossing away right.

Connie: On one martini?

Alan: You get loaded just ordering one.

Connie: Now, then, the bedroom. It's in that direction, isn't it?

She picks up suitcase and starts for bedroom.

Alan: You stay out of there. What's come over you?

Connie: Nothing, darling. I gave you a choice and you made it.

Alan: What?

Connie: Wonderful service, isn't it? You don't even have to pick it up. We deliver.

Alan: You're not drunk. You're crazy.

Connie (Puts down suitcase and crosses right stalking him as he backs away): Just think of it, darling? We're going to live together, love together. Fun, fun, fun. Sin, sin, sin.

Alan: Connie, you're scaring the hell out of me.

Connie: You don't even have to say you love me. And when you get bored, just kick me out and give me a letter of recommendation.

Alan: Will you cut it out? It's not funny any more.

Breaks away left.

Connie: I don't understand, Alan. Isn't this what you want? Isn't this what you asked for?

Alan: No.

Connie: No?

Alan: That's right, no. I said I could see nothing wrong for two young people who were very fond of each other to have a healthy, normal relationship. But I see no reason to turn this affair into a . . . foreign art movie.

Connie: Good heavens, sir. I must be in the wrong apartment.

Alan: Look, I told you before. I'm not denying anything. Six nights a week I'm Leonard Lover. But with you . . . well, you're different.

Connie: Careful, Alan. You're on the brink of committing yourself.

Alan: Who's keeping it a secret? I love you.

Connie: You weren't very sure.

Alan: I am now. If I can turn down an offer like this with a girl like you, I must be in love.

Connie: Well, then . . . where does that leave us?

Alan: . . . I don't know.

Connie (Sits right arm of right center chair): You don't know?

Alan (Crossing to her): Look honey, you've got to give me a chance to think. A lot of things have happened tonight. I just lost my job.

Connie: I thought you worked for your father.

Alan: We must be in a hell of a recession. He just let two sons go . . . Oh, Connie, don't you see . . .

Connie: No, I don't see. You love me but you won't marry me, and you love me too much to live with me.

Alan (Crosses around chair to right of it): I know. I can't figure it out either.

Connie (Angry): I see. Well, I'm sorry, Alan, but I can't spend the rest of my life waiting in the hallway.

She gets up and crosses to center.

Alan: Wait a minute.

Connie: For what? I either come in or go out. You want me or you don't. Yes or no.

Alan: Why can't things be like they were before?

Connie: It's too late. We've raised the stakes.

Alan: Who made you the dealer all of a sudden?

Connie: If the game is too big, Alan, get out.

Alan: I see. A brilliant maneuver, General. You've got me cornered. Very well, I surrender.

Connie: I don't take prisoners.

She goes to foyer.

Alan (Angry): I mean it. If that's what you want, I'll marry you.

Connie (Grabs coat. Puts over left arm): If that's the way you'll marry me, I don't want it.

Alan (Crossing to her): Connie, wait. Where are you going?

Connie (Putting on coat): Right now I want to be about a thirty-five-*dollar* taxi ride away from you.

Alan (Sincerely. Crossing to her): Connie, wait . . . I don't want you to leave.

Connie (She's made-up her mind): I'm sorry.

Alan: You mean I won't see you again?

Connie: I don't know. Maybe if you get lonely enough. *(The phone rings)* You probably won't have much chance tonight. Start in the morning.

Phone rings again. Picks up suitcase.

Alan: Connie, wait.

Connie: Answer your phone, Alan. It's the second platoon.

Phone rings again.

Alan (He picks up phone): Hello . . . Oh, Mom. *(To Connie)* Connie, it's my mother.

Connie: Your mother? Oh, come on, Alan.

She opens door.

Alan: Why should I kid about a thing like that?

Connie: Good-by.

And she's gone closing door behind her.

Alan: Connie . . . Connie, wait. *(Back into phone. He sits)* Hello, Mom? . . . What's wrong? Did Dad get home yet? . . . Aunt Gussie's? . . . Well, don't worry about it. He'll probably just sleep there tonight. He'll be home tomorrow when he calms down . . . Mom, please don't cry . . . All right, look, I'll come up and sleep there tonight . . . Yes, in my old room . . . I don't feel like being alone either . . . What? . . . No, not yet . . . Mom, please, I'm very upset . . . I've got a lot on my mind . . . I can't decide that now . . . Mom, I don't care — lamb chops, turkey, chicken salad, anything . . .

CURTAIN

ACT III

Three weeks later. At rise: Buddy has Alan's sports jacket in his arms, one sleeve draped over his shoulder. The jacket is putting in extra duty as Buddy's dancing partner.

This is a different Buddy from the one we've seen before. In a few weeks he seems to have blossomed. He now has the assurance and self-confidence that comes with independence. He has a bounce and vitality we haven't seen before.

He dances and chants his own rhythm.

Buddy: . . . One, two, cha-cha-cha . . . Very good, cha-cha-cha . . . And turn, cha-cha-cha . . . *(The telephone rings on "turn")* Answer phone, cha-cha-cha . . . Very good, cha-cha-cha . . . *(He places coat on sofa saying "Excuse me, my dear." He picks up phone)* Hello? . . . Snow? *(He sits on sofa)* . . . Don't you know you could get arrested for having such a sexy voice . . . No . . . I'm still trying to get tickets for the Ionesco play that's opening tonight . . . They're supposed to call me. Then I thought we might go up to the Palladium . . . for a little . . . cha-cha-cha. Oh, say . . . could you pick me up here? It would be easier. Wonderful . . . 42 East 63rd Street. About seven? . . . Make it five to. I'm only human. Good-by. *(He hangs up, slaps his hands, and gives a little giggle of joy. Then he resumes)* Do it right, cha-cha-cha . . . Tonight's the night, cha-cha-cha . . . (*The phone rings. He picks it up. Sits on upstage end of coffee table*) Hello?

At this moment, the door opens and Alan enters. Or better, he drags in. This is not the Alan of two weeks ago. He looks bedraggled. He seems to have lost a great deal of cockiness, his self-assurance. He hangs trench coat in closet and crosses downstage right to counter.

Buddy: Yes, it is . . . Yes? . . . Oh, wonderful . . . That's two tickets for tonight . . . Yes, I'll pick them up at the box office . . . In Alan Baker's name . . . Thank you very much. Good-by. (*He hangs up. He sees Alan*) Oh, hi, Aly. I didn't hear you come in. Gee, what a break. Your broker just got me two tickets for the Ionesco play tonight. I used your name. Is it all right?

Alan (*Staring ahead*): Why not? I'm not using it any more.

Buddy gets up, picks up his dancing partner, and resumes.

Buddy: And again, cha-cha-cha . . . To the right, cha-cha-cha . . . (*He keeps on dancing*) Where were you today?

Alan (*Staring ahead*): At the Polo Grounds waiting for the Giants to come back . . . Anyone call?

Buddy (*He's still dancing*): Yeah . . . a Mr. Copeland . . . and a Mr. Sampler . . . cha-cha-cha . . .

Alan (*Looks at him*): What'd they say?

Buddy: Nice and easy, cha-cha-cha . . .

Alan (*Angry*): Hey, Pupi, I'm talking to you.

Buddy (*He stops*): What's wrong?

Alan: I'd like to hear one sentence without the rhythm in it. What'd they say?

Buddy: Who?

Alan (*Crossing to him*): Copeland and Sampler, cha-cha-cha!

Buddy: Nothing. They'll call back later. What's eating you, Alan?

Pats Alan's shoulder and puts coat on sofa and sits.

Alan: It's just a little annoying to have to wait until the dance is over to get my messages.

He takes coat off sofa, brushes it and hangs it in closet upstage.

Buddy: Boy, you're jumpy lately. You've got a case of nerves, old boy.

Alan (*Crossing downstage to right center chair*): Thank you, doctor, is my hour up?

Buddy: What do you do all day, anyway? You're gone from ten to six. You come home bushed. You keep getting strange calls all day. What's all the mystery?

Alan: There's no mystery.

Buddy (*Accusingly*): Have you got a job?

Alan: No, I haven't got a job. Are you sure no one else called?

Buddy: You mean Connie?

Alan (*Expectantly*): Connie? Why? Did she . . . ?

Buddy: No, but you talk about her in your sleep.

Alan (*Sits right center chair*): Me? You're crazy.

Buddy: Last night you even walked in your sleep. You stretched out your arms and said, "Oh, Connie, darling" . . . I'm going to have to start locking my door.

Alan: Are you ribbing me?

Buddy: Why don't you call her, Alan?

Alan: What for? I'm not interested . . . Besides . . . she checked out of her hotel.

Buddy: Oh! Where'd she go?

Alan: How should I know. I didn't ask them.

Buddy: Maybe she left a forwarding address.

Alan: There's no forwarding address.

Buddy: How do you know?

Alan: I asked them . . . Look, will you forget about Connie.

Buddy: Subject closed. *(Alan rises and Buddy crosses to bar)* How about a drink?

Alan: I don't want a drink. *(Buddy pours one. Alan looks at him)* What are *you* drinking for?

Buddy: I like one at night now. Helps me unwind.

> *Crossing right of center. He drinks.*

Alan: What do *you* have to unwind from?

Buddy: Oh, the little everyday problems of life.

Alan (Rises and crosses to him): Problems? You never had it so good. You sleep till twelve o'clock. Lounge around until two. You go out every night. How do you fill up the rest of the day?

Buddy: Well, that's one of the little problems I have to unwind from. *(Alan turns away right disgustedly)* I'm just having a little fun. What's wrong, Alan?

Alan (Changing his attitude. Turns upstage): Nothing. Nothing, I'm sorry, kid. I don't know what's wrong with me lately. Listen, I don't feel like sitting in again tonight. You want to go to a movie? Just the two of us?

Buddy (Puts glass on sofa table): Oh, gee, I'd like to, Alan, but I've got a date.

Alan: Again? That's four times this week. Who's on tonight?

Buddy: This one's a dancer. Modern jazz. Her name is Snow.

Alan: Snow?

Buddy (Crosses to Alan): Snow Eskanazi!

Alan: Sounds like an Italian Eskimo.

Buddy: She's a real weirdo. Wears that white flour on her face like the Japanese Kabuki dancers. But I've got a hunch underneath she's very pretty.

Alan: Take her out in a strong wind, maybe you'll find out . . . Where do you collect these girls, anyway?

Buddy: I met Snow at that party I went to in the Village last Saturday.

Alan: The one you took the Greek interpreter to?

Buddy: Yeah. Snow was with an Indian exchange student. I was sitting on the floor next to her and she leans over and gives me her phone number. Just like that.

Alan: How did Sabu feel about all this?

Buddy: He loaned her the pencil. Besides, he made a date with the Greek interpreter.

Alan (Sits right center chair): No wonder they have emergency sessions at the UN.

Buddy: Like a jerk I went and left early. You know what I hear they played at three o'clock in the morning?

Alan: What?

Buddy: Strip Scrabble!

Alan: Strip Scrabble?? . . . I suddenly feel eight years old. Are you sure you're the same boy who was eating milk and cake over a sink three weeks ago?

Buddy: How about that, what's happened to me, Alan? You've given me a new lease on life. Three weeks here with no one telling me what to do and when to come home. Well, I'm a different person, aren't I?

Alan: Different? You're going to need identification before I let you in here again.

Buddy: That's why I hate to see you moping around like this. *(Crosses to him)* You're a different person too. It's not like you to let yourself go.

Pats his knee.

Alan (Indignant): What do you mean?

Buddy: Well, you've been sitting home every night, you haven't called a girl in three weeks, you're even getting to look seedy. Why don't you call Rocco tomorrow?

Crosses away left.

Alan: Rocco?

Buddy: My barber.

Alan (Rises and crosses to him): Your barber? What do you mean, *your* barber? *I* sent you there. He's *my* barber.

Buddy: I know. It was just a figure of speech. I didn't mean anything. You can have him back.

Fixes Alan's tie.

Alan: I don't want him back. I just want it clear that you only go there. But Rocco is *my* barber.

Turns away right, unfixes his tie.

Buddy: Sure, Alan, sure . . . Anyway, cheer up. *(He pats Alan's shoulder patronizingly)* Things'll get better. *(Alan sits right center chair. The doorbell rings)* That can't be Snow. It's too early. *(He hops over to door and opens it. It's Peggy in another crazy outfit)* Oh, hello.

Peggy: Hello, Mr. Manheim.

Buddy: Come on in. You know Alan Baker.

He no longer fears the masquerade.

Peggy: Oh, sure. Hi! *(Waves)* I heard you were back. Is everything all right in Hollywood?

Buddy: Oh, great. We're just about ready to roll on the picture.

Peggy: I never got a call. I guess you found someone else for my part.

Buddy: Not at all. We just have the male lead set. We're still looking for the girl.

Peggy: Oh? Who did you get?

Buddy: For what?

Peggy: The male lead.

Buddy: Oh. Someone new. An Italian actor.

Alan: Rocco La Barber.

Peggy: Oh, sure. I've heard of him.

Buddy: Well . . . if you'll excuse me, I've got to get dressed. I've got to look over some locations tonight.

Peggy: Of course.

Buddy: I'll call you. I'm still very interested. (*Looks at his watch and shoots his cuff*) Great Scot, it's nearly seven.

Smiles at Alan and prances into the bedroom.

Peggy: So young and so brilliant.

Alan: Eight colleges are after his brain.

Peggy: (*Crosses above Alan*): I can understand why *he* hasn't called. What's your excuse?

Alan (Rises and starts left): No excuse. I've just been busy.

Peggy (Stepping downstage): And I've been lonely, Alan . . . really lonely . . .

Alan: I haven't been doing much either.

Peggy (Crosses to him): You haven't called in nearly three weeks. You never answered my messages.

Alan: I'm sorry.

Peggy (Swings him around): Prove it. Let's go to Connecticut this weekend.

Alan: What's in Connecticut?

Peggy (Putting arm around him): The ski lodge.

Alan: It's Vermont.

Peggy: I don't care. As long as we're together. How about it?

Alan (Breaking left): Well, Peggy . . . I'm not working any more. I don't have much time for skiing.

Peggy (Angry. Crosses stage up right of him)

Alan (Stops her): Peggy, wait. It's nothing personal. I'm still crazy about you . . . All right, look. We'll go this weekend.

Peggy: That's more like my Alan. (*She puts his arm around her*) Bite me on the neck.

Alan: What?

Peggy: Bite me on the neck like you used to.

Alan: Well, Peggy, I don't really feel . . .

Peggy: Oh, come on.

Alan shrugs and bites her.

Peggy: Ow! You bit me. (*She breaks up to foyer, turns*) You really *must* be a vampire.

She opens door and exits. Alan crosses back down to sofa and sits. Buddy returns wearing a sports jacket. It's one of those multicolored jobs that they advertise every Sunday in the Times *but no one ever really buys.*

Buddy (He turns around, modeling it): Well? How do you like the sports jacket?

Alan: I like the lining. What's the jacket like?

Buddy: How do you think this will go at Sardi's?

Alan: What are you doing, going to Sardi's?

Buddy: I thought I'd make an impression on Snow. Hey, that reminds me. I'd better make a reservation.

Buddy picks up phone, and dials.

Alan (*Exaggeratively swings legs on sofa out of Buddy's way*): You certainly have blossomed into the Young Man about Town. The theater, the latest styles, Sardi's. I've created an Ivy League Frankenstein.

Buddy (*Into phone*): Hello? I'd like to reserve a table for two for tonight, please. Seven-thirty . . . Oh, you are? (*He covers phone with his hand*) He says they're all booked up. (*He snaps his fingers, back into phone*) Are you sure you don't have a reservation for me? Manheim? I'm with M-G-M.

Alan throws up his hands.

Buddy (*Into phone*): Yes, it was probably an oversight . . . Would you? I'd appreciate that . . . Thanks, so much. Good-by! (*He hangs up*) Voilà!

Alan (*Looks up to heaven*): What have I done?

Buddy (*Starts upstage and stops*): You think he believed me?

Alan: Why not? I did.

Buddy: I'd better get moving. (*Starts for foyer and stops and comes downstage right of Alan*) Oh, by the way, Alan. What are you doing about eleven-thirty tonight?

Alan: I'll be sitting in a shawl reading the Bible. Why?

Buddy: I hear there's a great picture at the Paris. Why don't you catch the last show. I think it lets out about one.

Alan: I don't want to be let out about one.

Buddy: Well, you see, I thought later on I might drop back here with Snow . . . for a nightcap.

Alan: You what?

Buddy: I hate to ask you, Alan, but this may be my night to conquer Mount Everest. You don't mind going to a movie, do you?

Alan (*Rises. Seething*): You're damned right I mind!

Buddy: What's wrong, Alan? That was our arrangement, wasn't it? If one fellow had a girl —

Alan: That was *my* arrangement. I did the arranging and *you* went to the movies. Where do you get this *our* stuff?

Buddy (*Quite innocently*): I thought we were splitting everything fifty-fifty?

Alan: We were, until you got all the fifties. (*Crosses right of him and turns*) Boy, what nerve. We're not splitting anything any more. Is that understood?

Buddy: Sure, Alan.

Alan: Except the rent. From now on your rent is a hundred forty-two dollars a month.

Buddy: Okay.

Alan (*Crosses right to counter*): I think I've been bighearted long enough.

Buddy: Alan, I never . . .

Alan: And buy your own food too. I'm sick and tired of bringing home cookies and watching you finish them reading *my* magazines and watching *my* television.

Buddy: You're kidding!

Alan (*Picks up box and shakes it at him*): The hell I am. Just keep away from my Fig Newtons!

Buddy (*Half chuckles at the ridiculousness of the situation*): I don't understand. I always give you some of my Yankee Doodles.

Alan (*But he's not kidding. Crossing to him*): And stop eating them all over the rug with your crumbs. I never saw anything like it. Clothes lying all over the place. It's disgusting.

Buddy: Alan, what's eating you? Is it because of this girl?

Alan (Crossing upstage left): Connie? She's got nothing to do with this.

Buddy (Sits on sofa): Well, something's bothering you. I'd like to know what.

Alan: Oh, you would, heh? Well, there's plenty bothering me. I happen to think you're pretty ungrateful.

Buddy: Ungrateful!

Alan (Crossing right of Buddy behind sofa): Yes, ungrateful. I took you in here, taught you how to dress and walk and talk. Now look at you. You're a big man.

Buddy: What's wrong, Alan? You said yourself I should grow up and become a man.

Alan: I said become a man. *(Points to himself)* Not this man. Don't take my place in life.

Buddy: How have I taken your place?

Alan: I run the water for a bath and five minutes later I hear you splashing in there. You're using my barber, my restaurants, my ticket broker, my apartment, and my socks. How's it going, kid, am I having fun?

Buddy: You're the one who suggested I do all these things. You said I should start having some fun.

Alan: I said fun. Have a good time. I didn't say anything about carrying on like this.

Crosses right of center.

Buddy: Like what?

Alan (Turns): Like a bum!

Buddy (Jumps up): A bum???

Alan: You heard me. What kind of crows are you running around with? *(Crosses to him)* Intellectual delinquents . . . Strip Scrabble! . . . You're lucky Interpol didn't rush in there and raid the joint.

Buddy: What kind of girls do you know? When did that kook upstairs get out of the Girl Scouts?

Alan: I'm talking to *you!* Where were you until four o'clock the other morning?

Buddy: What's the difference?

Alan (Crosses and sits right center chair): I want to know where you were until four o'clock in the morning?

Buddy: Cocka-doodle-doo! What's with you?

Alan (Jumps up): Don't cocka-doodle-doo me.

Buddy: When did you suddenly switch sides? *(Crosses to him)* When I moved in here you were carrying on like every night was New Year's Eve.

Alan: We're not talking about a thirty-three-year-old bum. We're talking about a twenty-one-year-old bum.

Buddy: Oh, you mean it's all right for you.

Alan: I mean, it's not all right for you. *(Crosses left to coffee table)* Three weeks ago you came in here heartsick over the fate of the world. When was the last time you picked up a newspaper or a book without a phone number in it? What happened to our young hope for a brave new world? We're losing half of South America and you're doing the cha-cha.

Buddy: What's dancing got to do with it?

Alan (Crosses to him): And what about looking for a job?

Buddy: I have been.

Alan: Since when is the employment office in an espresso joint in the Village? You're nothing but a clean-shaven beatnik.

Buddy: I haven't asked you for anything.

Alan: You'd have starved to death if Mom hadn't been smuggling pot-roast sandwiches through the enemy lines.

Buddy: I didn't notice you throwing yours in the garbage can.

Alan: At least I call her now and then. You're too busy to worry about her. And have you thought once of how Dad is getting along with the business without either of us there now?

Buddy: What brought all this on?

Alan: I'm seeing you for the first time.

Buddy: You mean you're seeing yourself for the first time. I'm just a carbon copy of you.

Alan: Well, whoever it is, I don't like it.

Buddy: Why do I get the blame? You go around committing murder and I get the chair.

Alan (He raises his arm threateningly): Don't get smart with me. You're not too big yet to get a good slap across the face.

Buddy: Holy mackerel, I got two fathers!

Alan: Cut that out. I'm nothing like him. Nothing at all.

Turns away left.

Buddy: Well, you certainly don't sound like yourself.

Alan (Turns to him): How can I? You're myself now.

Buddy: Well, maybe there's one too many of you around here.

Alan: Maybe there is. Which one of me is leaving?

Buddy: It's your apartment. In the meantime, I've got to shave. (Crosses to bedroom door and Alan crosses downstage center as Buddy goes up to door. Buddy stops and turns) By the way, which is my water, the hot or the cold?

He stalks out of the room.

Alan: How do you like the nerve of that kid? Well, we'll see how big an operator he is without me to supply him with everything. (Crosses left to bar and pours himself a drink. Tips glass to his mouth and realizes there's nothing in it. He picks up bottle and sees it's empty) A whole bottle of scotch! (He takes empty bottle, crosses angrily to bedroom door, waves empty bottle and shouts) Bum! (He starts to bar and the doorbell rings. Puts bottle on sofa table) Ah, that must be Nanook of the North! . . . This I've got to see. (He crosses to door and opens it. The Mother stands there with a heavy valise) Mom! Mom, what are you doing here?

Mother (She trudges into the room): I'm lucky I'm here at all. Six blocks I had to lug this from the subway. You'd think a stranger would help a woman.

She puts down valise and flops in a chair.

Alan (Follows left of her): Mom, what are you doing with a suitcase? Where are you going?

Mother: I'm not going any more. I'm here.

Alan: Here? Why?

Mother: For the same reason Buddy's here . . . I've run away from home.

Alan: Mom, you're not serious?

Mother: Don't think I'm not ashamed. A woman of my age running away from home. I was so humiliated. A woman from my building saw me in the subway with the suitcase. I had to lie to her. I said I was going to visit my brother in California. Then at 125th Street I had to change to a local to come here. She's not so dumb. For California you don't change at 125th Street. I should worry. My life is over anyway.

Alan: Why, Mom? What happened?

Mother: What happened? Ask America what happened? In Alaska they must have heard how that man has been carrying on with me. For three weeks now. Three weeks.

Alan: All right, Mom, he's very upset. But he'll get over it. He always does.

Mother: No, not this time. This time it's different. There's no making up now. I thought maybe there was a chance this morning. I was going to show him I could be bigger than he was. I wanted to show him *I* didn't forget.

Alan: Forget what?

Mother: Today. It's our thirty-seventh anniversary.

Alan (Kneels left of her): Oh, that's right. Happy anniversary, Mom.

He kisses her.

Mother: Thank you, darling. Anyway, I went over to him. I swear to you, I had a big smile on my face, like this: *(She gives a big smile. Then goes back to her sorrow)* And then as nice as I could possibly say it, I said, "Happy Anniversary, darling. I wish you all the happiness in the world." *(She sobs)* And what do you think he said to me?

Alan: What?

Mother: "Thank you . . . and I wish you what you wish me." *(She sobs)* For what? What did I do he should say such a thing?

Alan: But how do you know he meant anything wrong by that?

Mother: Because he knows what I was wishing him.

She cries.

Alan (Throws up his hands in futility. Crossing up right of her): Oh, boy!

Mother: All because of you two. He keeps blaming me. "Your bums. Your two bums!"

Buddy comes out of the bedroom.

Buddy (Crosses to left of Mother; leaves jacket on desk): Mom? What are you doing here?

Mother (Crosses right to Buddy. She starts right in on him): I'm lucky I'm here at all. Six blocks I had to lug this from the subway.

Buddy: Whose suitcase is that?

Alan: My new roommate's! . . . Mom, will you listen to me. You're just being emotional. You know you can't live here.

Buddy: Here?

Mother: Where else have I got to go? A hotel? Maybe I should move in with his sister Gussie? I'll join the Army first.

Alan: Mom, it's not that I don't want you. But you wouldn't be comfortable here. It's a small bachelor apartment.

Mother: So what am I now? I'm a bachelor too. *(She feels terribly sorry for herself)* A bachelor with two grown sons.

The doorbell rings.

Buddy (Runs up to door): Oh, that's probably Snow.

Mother: You're expecting company? *(She picks up suitcase and starts to bedroom)* I won't be in your way. I'll go in the bedroom with my sewing.

Alan: Mom, you don't have to do that.

Mother: You wouldn't hear me. I'll be like a dead person.

Alan: Mom, you don't need your suitcase.

Mother (Stopping at bedroom right door and turns): It's all right. I want to unpack my Alka-Seltzer. Oh, I'm so nauseous.

She holds her stomach and goes into the bedroom. The doorbell rings again twice.

Alan (Crossing to counter right. To Buddy): Well, answer it, lover.

Buddy crosses to door quickly and opens it. The Father stands there, steaming.

Buddy: Dad!

Father (He storms in on foyer. To Buddy): Where is she? I know she's here. *(To Alan)* Where's their mother?

Alan (Weakly): In the bedroom.

Father: Oh, they're hiding them in the bedroom now. What's the matter, the kitchen's being painted? *(He crosses to bedroom and opens door. He looks in)* Very nice. Very nice for a mother.

Buddy crosses downstage and sits on sofa.

Mother (From offstage): What do you want?

Father: What is she doing in there?

Mother (Offstage): She's drinking Alka-Seltzer.

Father (Crossing downstage below coffee table. Turns away): I thought I'd find her in here.

The Mother comes out with a glass in her hand. Crossing downstage center.

Mother: Where else should I be? They're still my children.

Father: She should be home. I'm still her husband.

Mother: Not when you treat your own children the way you do.

Father: This is something I will not discuss in front of strangers.

Mother: They're your sons.

Father (Crossing right center): They're *your* sons! They're my strangers! . . . Is she coming home?

Mother: She's home. This is where she lives now.

Father: This is where she lives? With bums?

Mother: That's right. So that makes me a bum too. All right? Now you're happy? Now you've got three bums.

Alan: Dad, can I say something?

Father: Who's he talking to? I'm not even here.

Buddy (Crossing downstage left of Father): Can I say something?

Father: Write it in a play. I'll be there opening night.

Alan: All right, Dad, please calm down. Will you talk to me for one minute?

Father (Crossing left below coffee table): Is she coming?

Alan: Dad, please. It's important.

Father: Did the woman hear what I said?

Alan: All right, don't answer me directly. If you understand, blink your eyes once for "yes" and twice for "no."

Father (To Mother): Did she listen to that? If I were here, I'd slap him in the mouth . . . Is she coming?

Buddy: Dad, we can't go on like this forever.

Father: Forever is over. They'll have no more parents to bother them. They should be very happy.

Alan (Crosses left): What do you mean, no more parents?

Father (To Mother): Tell him. Four months we'll be gone. I've got the tickets in my pocket.

Mother: You bought the tickets? I told you, I'm not going. Not until everything is all right with you and the boys.

Alan: Going where?

Father: Around the world. *(Crosses right center)* Tell him around the world we're going. Ask him if that's far enough?

Mother: I'm not going around any worlds.

Father: She's going. I've got the tickets in my pocket.

Alan: Do you mean it? Are you really going?

Father (Takes ticket out of pocket and holds it up): Here! In three weeks we'll be in China. They'll be here bumming around in peace, and we'll be in China . . . in the middle of a revolution. They'll worry a lot.

Alan (One step to Father): But how can you leave for four months? Who's going to take care of the business?

Father: What business? Tell him? Is she coming around the world . . . *(Crossing left below coffee table)* or do I take my sister Gussie?

Mother: I told you, I'm not going pleasure cruising with aggravation still on my heart.

Alan (Crosses left to center): Dad, what about the business???

Father: Is she coming?

Mother: Answer him!

Father: I answered him. Tomorrow there'll be no business. I'm selling the business. Is that an answer?

Alan: Selling the business?

Buddy: Are you serious?

Father: Look who's suddenly so shocked. The skier and the Pulitzer Prize winner.

Alan (Crossing left to him): Why are you selling it?

Father: Who should I save it for, his children?

Buddy: But who did you sell it to, Dad?

Father: Who? To Chiang Kai-shek. That's why I'm going to China.

Crosses right to counter.

Alan (Following): Why, Dad. Are you selling because of us?

Father: You? You think I need you two? I did bigger business in the three weeks you were gone than in the six years you were there.

The doorbell rings.

Buddy: Oh, boy!

Father (To Mother): I'm not waiting any more. If she wants, I'll meet her in Hong Kong.

Alan: Dad, wait. I've got to talk to you about this.

Doorbell rings.

Buddy (Looking upstage anxiously): Can't you talk later?

The doorbell rings again.

Mother: Buddy, the doorbell.

Buddy: Alan, what'll I do?

Alan: Will you take that girl and get out of here?

Buddy starts upstage.

Father (Crossing to Buddy): Girl? What girl??

Buddy: Just a girl, Dad. Do you think you could finish this conversation in the bedroom?

Father (He can't take any more): The bedroom? I'll break every bone in his body.

He raises his arm to hit Buddy.

Mother (Crossing downstage left): Harry!

Father (Follows imitating): Harry, Harry.

Buddy (Backing away): Dad, wait . . .

Suddenly the door opens and Connie enters.

Connie (On foyer): Oh, hello!

Alan (Crosses upstage to right of Connie. Stunned): Connie!

Mother: Harry, please, don't say anything.

Father: Don't *say* anything? No, I'll sit here and applaud.

Alan: Connie, where have you been?

Connie: Cincinnati.

Alan: Cincinnati?

Connie (Crossing downstage right to counter): With the Electrical Appliance Dealers of America.

Alan follows her.

Father: I don't have to listen to this kind of talk.

He starts for door left above sofa. Buddy stops him.

Buddy: Dad, wait a minute, please.

Alan: You mean you did another industrial show?

Connie: I was Miss Automatic Toaster. I popped up and sang . . . And after the show three salesmen tried to butter me.

Alan: But why did you take the job? You said you were quitting.

Connie: You changed my mind for me. Look, Alan, this doesn't seem to be the time to discuss this . . .

Alan: No, no. This is only my mother and father.

Father: Only??

Connie (Looks at her and says to Mother): Oh, hello.

Mother (Sweetly): How do you do?

Father (Crossing to left of her below sofa. To Mother): Are you crazy, "How do you do?"

Alan: What do you mean, I changed your mind?

Connie: You were right, Alan. I'm much too talented to quit. Besides, I'm beginning to enjoy my work.

Alan: What work?

Father: What do you think, what work? *(To Mother)* You're going to stay here while this is going on?

Buddy (Takes his arm): Dad, you don't know what you're saying.

Father (Lifts arm from shoulder exaggerating movement): Pushing? A father you're pushing?

Mother (Starts upstage behind sofa table): Harry, come in the bedroom.

Connie (Moves as if to go): Alan, call me later.

Alan (Stops her): No, tell me what you're talking about.

Connie: Well, I really came to say good-by.

Alan: Good-by?

Connie: The Electrical Dealers want me to go to Europe. With all expenses paid.

Father (Shrugs): She's not ashamed to say it.

Connie (Buddy and Father exchange places): It's a wonderful opportunity, Alan. And after all, it's about time I had a "fling."

Alan: A *fling??*

Connie: You know how it is with a twenty-four-year-old girl. She's really not ready to settle down yet.

Alan: Connie, listen to me.

The phone rings.

Father (Points to phone. Says to Mother): You hear? That's the cook. She'll be coming to work soon.

Phone rings.

Connie: I don't leave until Thursday. Call me, Alan.

Buddy (Grabs Father's arm): Dad, please come inside and talk to me.

Father: Again he's pushing.

The phone keeps ringing.

Alan: Connie, you can't go to Europe. I won't let you.

Phone rings.

Mother: Alan, your phone.

Connie: You won't *let* me?

Alan: Connie, I need you. *(Phone rings)* I didn't realize it until you were out of my life for three weeks. I couldn't stand it. I love *(phone rings)* you, sweetheart.

Mother (Crosses to right of center): Alan, your phone.

Connie: Alan, we've been through those words before.

Alan: I didn't really feel *(phone rings)* this way before. You've got to believe me. It's all over. I have flung!

Ring.

Mother (Crosses left to coffee table): Buddy, the phone.

Buddy: Dad . . .

Father (To Buddy): If he pushes me once more, he'll bleed from the nose.

Buddy: I wasn't pushing you.

The phone rings.

Mother: Maybe I'm crazy. No one hears a phone.

She picks it up.

Connie: Alan, are you sure?

Mother (Into phone): Hello?

Connie: Are you really sure?

Alan: I was never so sure of anything in my life.

Mother: Alan, it's for you.

Alan: I'm busy, Mom. Take a message.

Mother: Again with a message.

Buddy: Who is it, Mom?

Mother: Do I know? Do I have a pencil?

Buddy: All right, don't get excited.

Father: That's right. Yell at your mother. Push *her!*

Buddy (Crosses upstage above sofa table): I wasn't pushing!

Mother: Alan, it's a Mr. Kaplan or Koplon . . . Oh, I'm so nauseous.

Father: Copeland? From Begley's Department Store in Texas? . . . Give me that.

He grabs phone.

Alan (Crossing left): No, Dad —

Father (Into phone): Hello? . . . Mr. Copeland of Texas? . . . How do you do, sir . . . To what do I owe the honor of this phone call? . . . Order? What order? . . . Yes, of course it's Mr. Baker . . . No, his father . . . Oh . . . just a minute. *(He is bewildered. He looks front but hands him phone)* It's for him.

Alan (Into phone): Hello, Mr. Copeland . . . You what? . . . Oh, wonderful . . . The same order we talked about today? . . . Yes, I've got it. You'll have the shipment the first of the month . . . Not at all . . . Have a nice trip back . . . and thank you . . . Good-by.

He hangs up.

Father (Stares at him): How does he come to know Copeland of Texas?

Alan: I heard he was in town. I called him and took him out to lunch a few times . . . alone. *(He takes out paper from his pocket)* I guess *you'd* better take care of this order, Dad.

Father takes paper and looks at it in disbelief.

Father: Four years I'm after Copeland of Texas.

Buddy (Crosses downstage right of Alan): So that's what you've been doing every day. Working. And all those phone calls from Copeland and Sampler.

Father: Sampler too? . . . I just got a telegram for a big order tonight. For transparent grapes.

Alan: I thought I owed you that much, Dad.

Father (To Alan): Owed me? *(Then crosses left)* He owes me nothing. I don't need his orders.

Puts invoice in pocket.

Alan (Crosses left to him): Dad, please. Even if you don't want me to work for you, can't we at least be friends?

Father (Angry. Away from Alan): I don't need a bum for a friend.

Alan: Why am I a bum?

Father: Is he married?

Alan: Yes!

Father: Then he's a bu — *(He stops short and turns to Alan)* What????

Alan: That is . . . I will be if Connie says yes. *(He crosses right to Connie who steps to him)* Connie, I'll wake up a judge tonight. I'll get down on both knees. I'll do anything, but please . . . won't you marry me?

Connie: Oh, darling. *(They kiss)*

Connie nudges him.

Alan: Huh! *(Turns to others)* Mom, I guess you can call the caterers . . . This is Connie Dayton. The girl I'm going to marry.

Buddy: No kidding?

Connie crosses left to Mother. They meet right center.

Mother: Oh, darling.

She and Connie embrace.

Buddy (Crosses to Mother): Gee, congratulations.

They all look at Alan who then looks for approval from the Father. They all turn and look at Father.

Alan: Dad —

The Father turns away from them.

Mother: Harry, your son is going to get married.

Father: No one tells me nothing. All I get is pushed.

Alan (Crosses left to Father): Dad, I don't know how to say this to you . . . but . . . well, you were right about so many things. *(Father nods . . . huh . . . huh)* I was a bum. *(Father nods . . . huh . . . huh)* I guess every boy's got to be a bum even for a little while. I just ran into overtime. *(Father nods . . . huh . . . huh)* There's a lot more I want to say to you, Dad, but not now. Look, why don't we all go out to celebrate? To a night club.

Crosses right to Connie.

Father: He hasn't got a job, he's going to night clubs.

Mother: Harry, the children want to take us out.

Father: Let them save their money for furniture.

Alan (Afraid things are going to start all over again): Oh, Dad, can't you just once —

Connie: No, Alan, Alan. *(Leaping into the breach. Crosses left to Father)* Mr. Baker is right. It's impossible to talk in night clubs anyway. And tonight I'd like to talk. After all, I suddenly have a new family. *(To Mr. Baker, tenderly)* Please Mr. Baker . . . why don't we all have dinner together.

Father (He turns slowly to see who this girl is. She looks "nice." "Very nice." And suddenly he has no more sons. Now he's got a daughter. He smiles. Removes hat and places it over his heart and bows) Well . . . Maybe just for a cup of coffee.

Alan (Crosses left to Connie): Thanks, Dad.

Father (To Alan . . . warning): But we come home early. You've got to be at the plant eight o'clock in the morning and I don't want any excuses.

Alan: Do you mean that? Do you really want me back?

Father: No, I'm going to put the night watchman in charge while I'm in China.

Alan (Laughs — starts upstage taking Connie): Come on, everybody.

Connie (On way up stops at Buddy): Good night, Buddy.

> *She kisses him and continues to foyer.*

Buddy: Good night, Connie.

Mother (Crosses to Buddy): Buddy, darling, you do whatever you want, sweetheart. You're not a baby any more.

Buddy: Thanks, Mom.

> *He kisses her.*

Mother: But be up for dinner Friday night.

Buddy: I will.

Mother: And bring your laundry.

> *Crosses to bedroom to get valise and coat.*

Buddy (As Father starts toward door): Well, Dad, you still haven't said anything. Is it OK to leave home?

Father (Stops): No.

Buddy: Oh, Dad.

Father (Crosses to Buddy): So what are you asking me? *(Alan crosses left of Father behind sofa)* If I say "no" it's "yes" anyway. There was a time when my "no" was "no," but now you're twenty-one and "no" is "yes." So it's "yes" and forget the "no." *(Alan and Buddy exchange puzzled looks)*

> *He takes valise from Mother who has come out of bedroom and they all start out.*

Buddy (As Father goes off): Thanks, Dad.

Alan (Has put on coat): See you back here later? . . . About twelve?

Buddy: Make it one.

Alan (Smiles): Right, Mr. Manheim. *(He goes to door and turns)* So long . . . bum! *(He exits)*

> *Buddy looks after him, crosses to upstage left desk and gets jacket. Puts jacket on and looks around room. He crosses now to sofa and arranges pillows. Doorbell rings. Buddy crosses to downstage left lamp and turns it out.*

Buddy: Coming, my Snowflake! *(He goes to door, composes himself, then opens it. A Woman in her fifties stands there)* Aunt Gussie!

Curtain starts down.

Woman (She walks into room as curtain falls): I was in the neighborhood, so I thought I'd say hello.

CURTAIN

QUESTIONS

ACT I

1. For what reasons does Buddy Baker move in with his brother Alan? What are the brothers' feelings toward the home that both have fled? Do they bitterly resent their parents?
2. In what ways are Peggy Evans and Connie Dayton very different persons? Does either seem a **stock character** — a familiar stereotype that we recognize from certain outstanding traits?
3. Why does Alan stare in disbelief when Connie (on page 1139) offers him his choice? What is running through his mind?
4. In the confrontation between Alan and his father, how do the old man's expectations clash with Alan's plans for himself? What is ironic in the father's references to Buddy ("that's one son I'll never have to worry about")?
5. What dramatic questions does the playwright raise by the end of Act One? (Dramatic questions: problems or conflicts in whose outcome we become interested.) Which one of these questions seems to matter most?

ACT II

1. What is comic in the timing of Mrs. Baker's visit? What do we expect to happen as a result of her accepting the phone calls for Alan?
2. When Buddy confides his ambition to write for television or the theater, his father says, "Plays can close. Television you turn off. Wax fruit lays in the bowl till you're a hundred." Is the senior Baker supposed to be a Philistine? Do you feel that Neil Simon has any sympathy for him and his view?
3. Two *crises* occur in this act — moments of great tension, turning points from which the action may go off in one or another direction. What are these two crises? Whose future — Alan's or Buddy's — is more endangered by them?

ACT III

1. As this act begins, what changes have taken place in the lives and attitudes of the Baker brothers? Explain Alan's remark, "I've created an Ivy League Frankenstein." What does Alan's calling Buddy a bum reveal about Alan himself? (Where in this play have we heard this word before?)
2. When the father enters, why does he at first refer to his wife and sons only in the third person, struggling not to say *you?* (Suggested exercise: try to converse with someone in this non-you style. What are its difficulties?)
3. What is comic in the circumstances in the midst of which Alan asks Connie to marry him? (Compare this scene with Chekhov's *The Marriage Proposal* — are there any similarities?)

4. What concession to Buddy does the father make in the end? What brings about this sudden change of heart?
5. Why do you suppose the playwright instructs the curtain to start to fall before Aunt Gussie has even stepped into the room?

GENERAL QUESTIONS

1. How many times in this play does a Baker brother go to the door, expecting a beautiful woman, only to greet an unwelcome relative? Are these repetitions boring, or funny?
2. To what extent does our enjoyment of Neil Simon's play depend on our appreciation of verbal humor? Point out any lines that struck you as particularly comic. What do they tell us about the characters who utter them?
3. How can you tell from this play that for years Simon successfully wrote situation comedy for television? Does the play seem the worse for this experience?
4. Can we accurately call *Come Blow Your Horn* a *well-made play?* An example of a *farce?* A conventional *romantic comedy?*
5. In what ways does this play seem faithful to life? In what ways is it neater than life tends to be?

35 The Theater in the Twentieth Century

REALISM AND NONREALISM

As the twentieth century began, realism in the theaters of Western Europe, England, and America appeared to have won a resounding victory. (**Realism** in drama, like realism in fiction, may be broadly defined as an attempt to reproduce faithfully the surface appearance of life, especially that of ordinary people in everyday situations.) The theater had been slow to admit controversial or unpleasant themes, and slow to shed its trappings of Victorian romanticism. But now it was less often that actors declaimed their passions in oratorical style in front of backdrops painted with waterfalls and volcanoes, while stationed exactly at the center of the stage as if to sing "duets meant to bring forth applause" (as the Swedish playwright August Strindberg had complained). By 1891 even Victorian London had witnessed a production of a play that frankly portrayed a man dying from venereal disease — Henrik Ibsen's *Ghosts*.

In the theater of realism, a room was represented by a **box set** — three walls that joined in two corners and a ceiling that tilted as if seen in perspective — replacing drapery walls that had billowed and doors that had flapped, not slammed. Instead of posing at stage-center to deliver key speeches, actors were instructed to speak from wherever the dramatic situation placed them, and now and then turn their backs upon the audience. They were to behave as if they lived in a room with the fourth wall sliced away, unaware that they had any audience.

In such a realistic room, actors hardly could rant (or, in Hamlet's phrase, "tear a passion to tatters") without seeming foolish. Another effect of more lifelike direction was to discourage the use of such devices as the soliloquy and the **aside** (villain to audience: "Heh! heh! Now she's in me power!"). To encourage actors even further in imitating reality, the influential director Constantin Stanislavsky of the Moscow Art Theater developed his famous system to help actors feel at home inside a playwright's characters. One of Stanislavsky's exercises was to have the actors search their memories for personal experiences like those of the characters in the play; another was to have the actors act out things a character did *not* do in the play but might do in life. The system enabled Stanislavsky to bring a sense of authenticity to his productions of the plays of Chekhov and of Maxim Gorky's *The Lower Depths* (1902), a play that showed the tenants of a sordid lodging house drinking themselves to death (and hanging themselves) in surroundings of realistic squalor.

Gorky's play is a masterpiece of **naturalism,** a kind of realism in fiction and drama concerned with the more brutal or unpleasant aspects of reality. As codified by the French novelist and playwright Émile Zola, who influenced Ibsen, naturalism viewed a person as a creature whose acts are determined by heredity and environment; and Zola urged writers to study the behavior of their characters with the detachment of zoologists studying animals.

No sooner had realism and naturalism won the day than a reaction arose. One opposing force was the **Symbolist movement** in the French theater, most influentially expressed by the Belgian playwright Maurice Maeterlinck. Like the French Symbolist poets Charles Baudelaire and Stéphane Mallarmé, Maeterlinck assumes that the visible world reflects some spirit world we cannot directly perceive. Accordingly, his plays are filled with hints and portents: suggestive objects (jeweled rings, veils, distant candles), mysterious locales (crumbling castles, dim grottoes), vague sounds from afar, dialogue rich in silences and unfinished sentences. In *The Intruder,* (1890), a blind man sees the approach of Death. In *Pélléas and Mélisande* (1892) occurs a typical bit of Symbolist stage business: a small boy stands on his grandfather's shoulders to peer through a high window and speak of wonders invisible to the audience.[1]

Besides Maeterlinck's plays, and those of the Irish Symbolist poet William Butler Yeats, realism-defying plays emerged from unexpected quarters. Even the master of realism, Ibsen, whose plays had helped bring about a more lifelike theater, turned away from plots of middle-class people and small-town life. Some of Ibsen's earlier plays had been poetic fantasies *(Brand, Peer Gynt)*; and again, in his last plays, he returned to nonrealism with *John Gabriel Borkman* (1896) and *When We Dead Awaken* (1899). (Both plays contain symbolic mountains that heaven-assaulting protagonists try to climb.) In Russia, Anton Chekhov, whose plays appeared realistic on the surface, built drama around a central symbol *(The Seagull, The Cherry Orchard)*. In Sweden, August Strindberg, who earlier had won fame as a naturalist, reversed direction and, in *The Dream Play* (1902) and *The Ghost Sonata* (1907), introduced characters who change their identities and who move across dreamlike landscapes without regard for space or time. Strindberg anticipated the movement called **expressionism** in German theater after World War I.

[1] For more about symbolism and Symbolists, see the discussions in Chapters Six and Twenty-three.

Delighting in bizarre sets and exaggerated makeup and costuming, expressionist playwrights and producers sought to reflect intense states of emotion and, sometimes, to depict the world through lunatic eyes. A classic example (on film) is *The Cabinet of Dr. Caligari,* made in Berlin in 1919–1920, in which a hypnotist sends forth a subject to murder people. Garbed in jet black, the killer sleepwalks through a town of lop-sided houses, twisted streets, and railings that tilt at gravity-defying angles. In expressionist movies and plays, madness is objectified, and dreams become realities.

In 1893 Strindberg had complained of producers who represented a kitchen by a drapery painted with pictures of kettles; but by 1900, realistic play production had gone to opposite extremes. In the 1920s there was even a Broadway play whose curtain rose upon a detailed replica of Schrafft's restaurant, complete to the last fork and folded napkin. (Still, as the critic George Jean Nathan remarked, no matter how elaborate a stage dinner, the table never seemed to have any butter.) Theaters housed increasingly complicated machines, making it all the easier to present scenes full of realistic detail. Elevators lifted heavy sets swiftly and quietly into place; other sets, at the touch of a button, revolved on giant turntables. Theaters became warehouses for huge ready-made scenery.[2] By 1900, the **picture-frame stage** had come into general use: the type of stage on which the action is contained within the **proscenium,** or arch. By the turn of the century, too, the **apron,** or forestage projecting into the audience, had practically vanished; and the picture-frame stage with its box set had succeeded in more completely separating actors from audience. In effect, now the audience sat in one room, watching actors going through their motions in another.

Some playwrights fought the domination of the painstakingly realistic set. Bertolt Brecht in Germany and Luigi Pirandello in Italy conceived plays to be performed on bare stages — gas pipes and plaster in full view — as if to remind spectators that they beheld events in a theater, not events in the outside world. In reaction against the picture-frame stage, alternative theaters were designed, such as the **arena theater** or **theater in the round,** in which the audience is seated on all four sides of the performing area; and the **flexible theater,** in which the seats are movable. Such theaters usually are not commercial theaters (most of which maintain their traditional picture-frame stages, built decades ago). Rather, the alternative theaters are found in college and civic playhouses, in large cities, in storefronts, and in converted lofts. Proponents of arena staging claim that it brings actors and audience into a greater intimacy; opponents, that it keeps the actors artificially circulating like goldfish in a bowl. Perhaps it is safe to say only

[2] See Allardyce Nicoll, *The Development of the Theatre,* 3rd ed. (New York: Harcourt, Brace, 1946), pp. 218–220.

that some plays lend themselves to being seen head-on in a picture frame; others, to being surrounded.

In recent years, some theater companies in America have questioned not only the value of the picture-frame stage, but the value of any stage at all. Such experimental groups follow in the footsteps of Antonin Artaud, French poet and playwright, whose collected manifestos, *The Theater and Its Double* (1938), argue for a theater without a stage, in which the spectacle takes place all around (and in the midst of) the spectators.[3] In the 1960s, according to one historian of recent drama in America, "everything came into question: the place of the performer in the theater; the place of the audience; the function of the playwright and the usefulness of a written script; the structure of the playhouse, and later the need for any kind of playhouse; and finally, the continued existence of theater as a relevant force in a changing culture."[4]

Young actors and playwrights joined **ensembles** (companies of amateurs or semiprofessionals working together to create new plays, sometimes living together in a commune). Some ensembles offered plays anywhere they could: in streets, in parks, on rooftops, in parking lots, even in laundromats. In *The Laundromat Play* (1966), which enjoyed forty-three performances, two women argue over who owns some clothes; one throws bleach in the other's face, and the play ends with a chorus who emerge with signs, chanting that the war in Vietnam is similarly meaningless.[5] (The play was performed by the Pageant Players of New York, a **guerilla theater** ensemble, a group devoted to radical political propaganda, who specialized in setting up dramatic situations in public places without telling the spectators that the situation had been planned.) Unlike traditional plays, such works obviously seek to shatter the boundary between actors and audience, and to attain a degree of realism in which the play is hardly to be distinguished from the stream of passing life. At one performance of the Firehouse Theater, the audience was invited to take part:

> "Would you like to see Faust or be Faust?" Those who chose to "see" Faust kept their roles as spectators. Those who chose to "be" Faust were enclosed in a vast communal bedsheet, given a powdered soap with which to perform a ritual hand-washing of one another, and then brought into close physical contact for up to thirty minutes as they swayed back and forth to an om-like chant.[6]

[3] See especially "The Theater of Cruelty (First Manifesto)" in *The Theater and Its Double*, translated by Mary Caroline Richards (New York: Grove Press, 1958).

[4] Arthur Sainer, *The Radical Theatre Notebook* (New York: Avon Books, 1975), p. 15.

[5] The text of the play, with directions ("We make sure there is an empty machine") is given in *Guerilla Street Theater*, edited by Henry Lesnick (New York: Avon Books, 1973), pp. 160–162.

[6] Sainer, *The Radical Theatre Notebook*, p. 72.

Ensembles, though some have been pretentious, at least have recalled that drama can be a kind of ritual, with living participants. Yet such experiments raise vexing questions. Can a play break down the distinction between art and "real life" without losing whatever life that, in a conventional play, the playwright's art holds fast?

TRAGICOMEDY AND THE ABSURD

Fresh attitudes toward play production and theater design reflected fresh conceptions of drama. One of the more prominent developments in mid-twentieth-century drama has been the rise of **tragicomedy.** As the term implies, tragicomic plays are plays that not only stir us to pity and fear (to echo Aristotle's description of the effect of tragedy), but to laughter as well. Although tragicomedy is a kind of drama we think modern, it is by no means a new invention. The term was used (although jokingly) by the Roman writer of comedy Plautus in about 185 B.C., and later critics have applied it to certain plays of the classical Greek dramatist Euripides — notably, *Alcestis*, in which apparently tragic events jostle with snappy repartee and end happily.

Since classical times, many playwrights have mingled laughter and tears, in defiance of what was said to be Aristotle's doctrine of the **unities.** The unities were not actually Aristotle's idea, but a code of rules laid down by Italian critics who interpreted Aristotle in the seventeenth and eighteenth centuries. According to them, the action of a play (1) must not span more than twenty-four hours; (2) must take place in a single locale; and (3) must be wholly tragic or wholly comic, not a mixture. However, many great plays defy such rules: *Othello* defies all three. Shakespeare is particularly fond of the tragicomic mingling: in Hamlet's dialogue with a joking gravedigger, for instance, or in the suicide of the queen in *Antony and Cleopatra*, when asps are brought to her by a wisecracking clown. In the tragedies of Shakespeare and others, passages of clownish humor are sometimes called **comic relief,** meaning that the comedy introduces a sharp contrast. But such passages can do more than provide relief. In *Othello* (III, iv, 1–16), the clown's banter with Desdemona for a moment makes the surrounding tragedy seem, by comparison, more poignant and intense.

No one doubts that *Othello* is a tragedy, but some twentieth-century plays leave us bemused: should we laugh or cry? One of the most talked-about plays since World War II, Samuel Beckett's *Waiting for Godot*, portrays two clownish tramps who mark time in a wasteland, wistfully looking for a savior who never arrives. (Contemporary drama, by the way, has often featured such **antiheroes:** ordinary people, inglorious and inarticulate, who carry on not from bravery but from inertia.[7]) We cannot help laughing at the tramps' painful situation; or,

[7] The rise of the antihero in recent fiction is discussed briefly on page 45. These remarks apply to drama as well.

to put it the other way around, we feel deeply moved by their ridiculous plight. Surely, a modern tragicomedy like *Godot* does not show us great souls suffering greatly — as Edith Hamilton said we are shown in a classical tragedy.

But perhaps the effect of such a play takes time to sink in. As contemporary playwright Edward Albee has suggested, sometimes the spectator's sense of relief after experiencing pity and fear (what Aristotle calls *katharsis*) may be a delayed reaction: "I don't feel that catharsis in a play necessarily takes place during the course of a play. Often it should take place afterwards."[8] If Albee is right, then perhaps we may be amused while watching a tragicomedy, then go home and feel deeply stirred by it.

Straddling the fence between tragedy and comedy, Beckett portrays people whose suffering seems ridiculous. His play belongs to the **theater of the absurd:** a general name for a constellation of plays first staged in Paris in the 1950s. "For the modern critical spirit, nothing can be taken entirely seriously, nor entirely lightly," according to Eugène Ionesco, one of the movement's leading playwrights and chief voices. A human being, such playwrights assume, is a helpless waif alone in a universe that confronts him with ridiculous obstacles. In Ionesco's *Amédée* (1953), a couple share an apartment with a gigantic corpse that keeps swelling relentlessly; in his *Rhinoceros* (1958), the human race starts turning into rhinos, except for one man, who remains human and isolated. A favorite theme in the theater of the absurd is that communication between people is impossible. Language is therefore futile: Ionesco's *The Bald Soprano* (1948) accordingly pokes fun at polite social conversation in a scene whose dialogue consists entirely of illogical strings of catch-phrases. In *Endgame* (1957), Samuel Beckett also burlesques small talk, and dramatizes his sense of the present condition of mankind: the central character is blind and paralyzed and his legless parents live inside two garbage cans. Oddly, the effect of the play isn't total gloom: we leave the theater both amused and bemused by it.[9]

Fashions in drama change along with playwrights' convictions, and today the theater of the absurd seems no longer the dominant influence on new drama in America. Along with other protests of the 1960s, guerilla street theater seems to have spent its force. Of late, some loudly applauded new plays have been neither absurd nor revolutionary. David Mamet's *American Buffalo* (1975) realistically portrays three petty thieves in a junk shop as they plot to steal a coin collection. Albert Innaurato's *Gemini* (1977) takes a realistic (and comic) view of life in a Philadelphia neighborhood only a little less depressed than the rundown lodging house in Gorky's *The Lower Depths*. In both plays, the

---

[8] "The Art of the Theater," interview in *The Paris Review*, No. 39, Fall 1966.

[9] For an excellent study of the theater of the absurd, see Martin Esslin, *The Theatre of the Absurd*, revised edition (New York: Overlook Press, 1973).

dialogue shows high fidelity to ordinary speech (a lowbrow woman to her common-law spouse in *Gemini*: "I'll just pick out of your plate"). The American theater may have entered an era of "new naturalism," in the view of critic Richard Gilman.[10] At least it appears that, in many recent plays, fantasy and absurdity are out, straightforward realism is in, communication between human beings is still possible, and events on stage follow in logical (and chronological) order.

Bertolt Brecht (1898–1956)

MOTHER COURAGE AND HER CHILDREN 1941

A Chronicle of the Thirty Years' War°

English version by Eric Bentley

Characters

Mother Courage	*Old Colonel*
Kattrin, her dumb daughter	*Clerk*
Eilif, her elder son	*Young Soldier*
Swiss Cheese, her younger son	*Older Soldier*
Recruiting Officer	*Peasant*
Sergeant	*Peasant Woman*
Cook	*Young Man*
Swedish Commander	*Old Woman*
Chaplain	*Another Peasant*
Ordnance Officer	*Another Peasant Woman*
Yvette Pottier	*Young Peasant*
Man with the Bandage	*Lieutenant*
Another Sergeant	*Voice*

I

Spring, 1624, In Dalarna°, the Swedish Commander Oxenstierna is recruiting for the campaign in Poland. The canteen woman Anna Fierling, commonly known as Mother Courage, loses a son.

Highway outside a town. A Sergeant and a Recruiting Officer stand shivering.

---

[10] "Out Goes Absurdism — In Comes the New Naturalism," *The New York Times,* Sunday, March 19, 1978.

Thirty Years' War: This general European war was fought from 1618 to 1648, mainly in Germany. It was largely a struggle between certain Protestant German princes (supported by foreign powers, such as Denmark, Sweden, and France) and the Holy Roman Empire and the house of Hapsburg (which controlled Spain, Austria, Bohemia, Hungary, and most of Italy). When the war ended, the Empire was weakened and France emerged dominant in Europe. Germany was devastated, its populace thinned and reduced to starvation.

Dalarna: region and province in Central Sweden.

Recruiting Officer: How the hell can you line up a squadron in a place like this? You know what I keep thinking about, Sergeant? Suicide. I'm supposed to knock four platoons together by the twelfth — four platoons the Chief's asking for! And they're so friendly around here, I'm scared to go to sleep at night. Suppose I do get my hands on some character and squint at him so I don't notice he's pigeon-chested and has varicose veins. I get him drunk and relaxed, he signs on the dotted line. I pay for the drinks, he steps outside for a minute. I have a hunch I should follow him to the door, and am I right? Off he's shot like a louse from a scratch. You can't take a man's word any more, Sergeant. There's no loyalty left in the world, no trust, no faith, no sense of honor. I'm losing my confidence in mankind, Sergeant.

Sergeant: What they could use around here is a good war. What else can you expect with peace running wild all over the place? You know what the trouble with peace is? No organization. And when do you get organization? In a war. Peace is one big waste of equipment. Anything goes, no one gives a damn. See the way they eat? Cheese on pumpernickel, bacon on the cheese? Disgusting! How many horses have they got in this town? How many young men? Nobody knows! They haven't bothered to count 'em! That's peace for you! I've been in places where they haven't had a war for seventy years and you know what? The people haven't even been given names! They don't know who they are! It takes a war to fix that. In a war, everyone registers, everyone's name's on a list. Their shoes are stacked, their corn's in the bag, you count it all up — cattle, men, *et* cetera — and you take it away! That's the story: no organization, no war!

Recruiting Officer: It's the God's truth.

Sergeant: Of course, a war's like any good deal: hard to get going. But when it does get moving, it's a pisser, and they're all scared of peace, like a dice player who can't stop — 'cause when peace comes they have to pay up. Of course, *until* it gets going, they're just as scared of war, it's such a novelty!

Recruiting Officer: Hey, look, here's a canteen wagon. Two women and a couple of fellows. Stop the old lady, Sergeant. And if there's nothing doing this time, you won't catch me freezing my ass in the April wind any longer.

A harmonica is heard. A canteen wagon rolls on, drawn by two young fellows. Mother Courage is sitting on it with her dumb daughter, Kattrin.

Mother Courage: A good day to you, Sergeant!

Sergeant (barring the way): Good day to *you!* Who d'you think *you* are?

Mother Courage: Tradespeople.

She sings:

> Stop all the troops: here's Mother Courage!
> Hey, Captain, let them come and buy!
> For they can get from Mother Courage
> Boots they will march in till they die!
> Your marching men do not adore you
> (Packs on their backs, lice in their hair)
> But it's to death they're marching for you
> And so they need good boots to wear!
> Christians, awake! Winter is gone!

The snows depart! Dead men sleep on!
Let all of you who still survive
Get out of bed and look alive!

Your men will walk till they are dead, sir,
But cannot fight unless they eat.
The blood they spill for you is red, sir,
What fires that blood is my red meat.
Cannon is rough on empty bellies:
First with my meat they should be crammed.
Then let them go and find where hell is
And give my greetings to the damned!
Christians, awake! Winter is gone!
The snows depart! Dead men sleep on!
Let all of you who still survive
Get out of bed and look alive!

Sergeant: Halt! Where are you from, riffraff?

Eilif: Second Finnish Regiment!

Sergeant: Where are your papers?

Mother Courage: Papers?

Swiss Cheese: But this is Mother Courage!

Sergeant: Never heard of her. Where'd she get a name like that?

Mother Courage: They call me Mother Courage 'cause I was afraid I'd be ruined, so I drove through the bombardment of Riga like a madwoman, with fifty loaves of bread in my cart. They were going moldy, what else could I do?

Sergeant: No funny business! Where are your papers?

Mother Courage (rummaging among papers in a tin box and clambering down from her wagon): Here, Sergeant! Here's a missal — I got it in Altötting to wrap my cucumbers in. Here's a map of Moravia — God knows if I'll ever get there — the birds can have it if I don't. And here's a document saying my horse hasn't got hoof and mouth disease — pity he died on us, he cost fifteen guilders, thank God I didn't pay it. Is that enough paper?

Sergeant: Are you pulling my leg? Well, you've got another guess coming. You need a license and you know it.

Mother Courage: Show a little respect for a lady and don't go telling these grown children of mine I'm pulling anything of yours. What would I want with you? My license in the Second Protestant Regiment is an honest face. If *you* wouldn't know how to read it, that's not my fault, I want no rubber stamp on it anyhow.

Recruiting Officer: Sergeant, we have a case of insubordination on our hands. Do you know what we need in the army? Discipline!

Mother Courage: I was going to say sausages.

Sergeant: Name?

Mother Courage: Anna Fierling.

Sergeant: So you're all Fierlings.

Mother Courage: I was talking about me.

Sergeant: And I was talking about your children.

Mother Courage: Must they all have the same name? *(Pointing to the elder son:)* This fellow, for instance, I call him Eilif Noyocki. Why? He got the name from his father who told me he was called Koyocki. Or was it Moyocki?

Anyhow, the lad remembers him to this day. Only the man he remembers is someone else, a Frenchman with a pointed beard. But he certainly has his father's brains — that man could whip the breeches off a farmer's backside before he could turn around. So we all have our own names.

Sergeant: You're all called something different?

Mother Courage: Are you pretending you don't understand?

Sergeant (pointing at the younger son): He's Chinese, I suppose.

Mother Courage: Wrong again. Swiss.

Sergeant: After the Frenchman?

Mother Courage: Frenchman? What Frenchman? Don't confuse the issue, Sergeant, or we'll be here all day. He's Swiss, but he happens to be called Feyos, a name that has nothing to do with his father, who was called something else — a military engineer, if you please, and a drunkard.

Swiss Cheese nods, beaming; even Kattrin smiles.

Sergeant: Then how come his name's Feyos?

Mother Courage: Oh, Sergeant, you have no imagination. *Of course* he's called Feyos: when he came, I was with a Hungarian. He didn't mind. He had a floating kidney, though he never touched a drop. He was a very *honest* man. The boy takes after him.

Sergeant: But that wasn't his father!

Mother Courage: I said: he took after him. I call him Swiss Cheese. Why? Because he's good at pulling wagons. *(Pointing to her daughter:)* And that is Kattrin Haupt, she's half German.

Sergeant: A nice family, I must say!

Mother Courage: And we've seen the whole wide world together — this wagon-load and me.

Sergeant: We'll need all that in writing. *(He writes.)* You're from Bamberg in Bavaria. What are you doing *here?*

Mother Courage: I can't wait till the war is good enough to come to Bamberg.

Recruiting Officer: And you two oxen pull the cart. Jacob Ox and Esau Ox°! D'you ever get out of harness?

Eilif: Mother! May I smack him in the puss? I'd like to.

Mother Courage: I'd like *you* to stay where you are. And now, gentlemen, what about a brace of pistols? Or a belt? Sergeant? Yours is worn clean through.

Sergeant: It's something else *I'm* looking for. These lads of yours are straight as birch trees, strong limbs, massive chests. . . . What are such fine specimens doing out of the army?

Mother Courage (quickly): A soldier's life is not for sons of mine!

Recruiting Officer: Why not? It means money. It means fame. Peddling shoes is woman's work. *(To Eilif:)* Step this way and let's see if that's muscle or chicken fat.

Mother Courage: It's chicken fat. Give him a good hard look, and he'll fall right over.

Recruiting Officer: Yes, and kill a calf in the falling! *(He tries to hustle Eilif away.)*

Mother Courage: Let him alone! He's not for you!

Jacob Ox and Esau Ox: Jacob and Esau were twin brothers, the story of whose quarrel and reconciliation is told in Genesis.

Recruiting Officer: He called my face a puss. That is an insult. The two of us will now go and settle the affair on the field of honor.

Eilif: Don't worry, Mother, I can handle him.

Mother Courage: Stay here. You're never happy till you're in a fight. He has a knife in his boot and he knows how to use it.

Recruiting Officer: I'll draw it out of him like a milk tooth. Come on, young fellow!

Mother Courage: Officer, I'll report you to the Colonel, and he'll throw you in jail. His lieutenant is courting my daughter.

Sergeant: Go easy. *(To Mother Courage:)* What have you got against the service, wasn't his own father a soldier? Didn't you say he died a soldier's death?

Mother Courage: This one's just a baby. You'll lead him like a lamb to the slaughter. I know you, you'll get five guilders for him.

Recruiting Officer (to Eilif): First thing you know, you'll have a lovely cap and high boots, how about it?

Eilif: Not from you.

Mother Courage: "Let's you and me go fishing," said the angler to the worm. *(To Swiss Cheese:)* Run and tell everybody they're trying to steal your brother! *(She draws a knife.)* Yes, just you try, and I'll cut you down like dogs! We sell cloth, we sell ham, we are peaceful people!

Sergeant: You're peaceful all right: your knife proves that. Why, you should be ashamed of yourself. Give me that knife, you hag! You admit you live off the war, what else *could* you live off? Now tell me, how can we have a war without soldiers?

Mother Courage: Do they have to be mine?

Sergeant: So that's the trouble. The war should swallow the peach stone and spit out the peach, hm? Your brood should get fat off the war, but the poor war must ask nothing in return, it can look after itself, can it? Call yourself Mother Courage and then get scared of the war, your breadwinner? Your sons aren't scared, I know that much.

Eilif: Takes more than a war to scare me.

Sergeant: Correct! Take me. The soldier's life hasn't done *me* any harm, has it? I enlisted at seventeen.

Mother Courage: You haven't reached seventy.

Sergeant: I will, though.

Mother Courage: Above ground?

Sergeant: Are you trying to rile me, telling me I'll die?

Mother Courage: Suppose it's the truth? Suppose I see it's your fate? Suppose I *know* you're just a corpse on furlough?

Swiss Cheese: She can look into the future. Everyone says so.

Recruiting Officer: Then by all means look into the sergeant's future. It might amuse him.

Sergeant: I don't believe in that stuff.

Mother Courage: Helmet!

The Sergeant gives her his helmet.

Sergeant: It means less than a crap in the grass. Anything for a laugh.

Mother Courage (taking a sheet of parchment and tearing it in two): Eilif, Swiss Cheese, Kattrin! So shall we all be torn in two if we let ourselves get too deep into this war! (*To the Sergeant:*) I'll give you the bargain rate, and do it free. Watch! Death is black, so I draw a black cross.

Swiss Cheese: And the other she leaves blank, see?

Mother Courage: I fold them, put them in the helmet, and mix 'em up together, the way we're all mixed up together from our mother's womb on. Now draw!

The Sergeant hesitates.

Recruiting Officer (to Eilif): I don't take just anybody. I'm choosy. And you've got guts, I like that.

Sergeant (fishing around in the helmet): It's silly. Means as much as blowing your nose.

Swiss Cheese: The black cross! Oh, his number's up!

Recruiting Officer: Don't let them get under your skin. There aren't enough bullets to go around.

Sergeant (hoarsely): You cheated me!

Mother Courage: You cheated yourself the day you enlisted. And now we must drive on. There isn't a war every day in the week, we must get to work.

Sergeant: Hell, you're not getting away with this! We're taking that bastard of yours with *us!*

Eilif: I'd like that, Mother.

Mother Courage: Quiet — you Finnish devil, you!

Eilif: And Swiss Cheese wants to be a soldier, too.

Mother Courage: That's news to me. I see I'll have to draw lots for all three of you. (*She goes to the back to draw the crosses on bits of paper.*)

Recruiting Officer (to Eilif): People've been saying the Swedish soldier is religious. That kind of loose talk has hurt us a lot. One verse of a hymn every Sunday — and then only if you have a voice . . .

Mother Courage (returning with the slips and putting them in the Sergeant's helmet): So they'd desert their old mother, would they, the scoundrels? They take to war like a cat to cream. But I'll consult these slips, and they'll see the world's no promised land, with a "Join up, son, you're officer material!" Sergeant, I'm afraid for them, very afraid they won't get through this war. They have terrible qualities, all three. (*She holds the helmet out to Eilif.*) There. Draw your lot. (*Eilif fishes in the helmet, unfolds a slip. She snatches it from him.*) There you have it: a cross. Unhappy mother that I am, rich only in a mother's sorrows! He dies. In the springtime of his life, he must go. If he's a soldier, he must bite the dust, that's clear. He's too brave, like his father. And if he doesn't use his head, he'll go the way of all flesh, the slip proves it. (*Hectoring him:*) Will you use your head?

Eilif: Why not?

Mother Courage: It's using your head to stay with your mother. And when they make fun of you and call you a chicken, just laugh.

Recruiting Officer: If you're going to wet your pants, I'll try your brother.

Mother Courage: I told you to laugh. Laugh! Now it's your turn, Swiss Cheese. You should be a better bet, you're honest. (*He fishes in the helmet.*) Why are you giving that slip such a funny look? You've drawn a blank for sure. It can't be there's a cross on it. It can't be I'm going to lose *you.* (*She takes the slip.*) A cross? Him too! Could it be 'cause he's so simple? Oh, Swiss Cheese, you'll be a goner too, if you aren't honest, honest, honest the whole time, the way I always brought you up to be, the way you always bring me all the change when you buy me a loaf. It's the only way you can save yourself. Look, Sergeant, if it isn't a black cross!

Sergeant: It's a cross! I don't understand how *I* got one. I always stay well in the rear. *(To the Officer:)* But it can't be a trick: it gets *her* children too.

Swiss Cheese: It gets me too. But I don't accept it!

Mother Courage (to Kattrin): And now all I have left for certain is you, you're a cross in yourself, you have a good heart. *(She holds the helmet up high toward the wagon but takes the slip out herself.)* Oh, I could give up in despair! There must be some mistake, I didn't mix them right. Don't be too kind, Kattrin, just don't, there's a cross in your path too. Always be very quiet, it can't be hard, you can't speak. Well, so now you know, all of you: be careful, you'll need to be. Now let's climb on the wagon and move on. *(She returns the helmet to the Sergeant and climbs on the wagon.)*

Recruiting Officer (to the Sergeant): Do something!

Sergeant: I don't feel very well.

Recruiting Officer: Maybe you caught a chill when you handed over your helmet in this wind. Get her involved in a business transaction! *(Aloud.)* That belt, Sergeant, you could at least take a look at it. These good people live by trade, don't they? Hey, all of you, the sergeant wants to buy the belt!

Mother Courage: Half a guilder. A belt like that is worth two guilders. *(She clambers down again from the wagon.)*

Sergeant: It isn't new. But there's too much wind here. I'll go and look at it behind the wagon. *(He does so.)*

Mother Courage: I don't find it windy.

Sergeant: Maybe it's worth half a guilder at that. There's silver on it.

Mother Courage (following him behind the wagon): A solid six ounces worth!

Recruiting Officer (to Eilif): And we can have a drink, just us men. I'll advance you some money to cover it. Let's go.

Eilif stands undecided.

Mother Courage: Half a guilder, then.

Sergeant: I don't understand it. I always stay in the rear. There's no safer spot for a sergeant to be. You can send the others on ahead in quest of fame. My appetite is ruined. I can tell you right now: I won't be able to get anything down.

Mother Courage: You shouldn't take on so, just because you can't eat. Just stay in the rear. Here, take a slug of brandy, man. *(She gives him brandy.)*

Recruiting Officer (taking Eilif by the arm and making off toward the back): Ten guilders in advance and you're a soldier of the king and a stout fellow and the women will be mad about you. And you can give me a smack in the puss for insulting you.

Both leave. Dumb Kattrin jumps down from the wagon and lets out harsh cries.

Mother Courage: Coming, Kattrin, coming! The sergeant's just paying up. *(She bites the half guilder.)* I'm suspicious of all money, I've been badly burned, Sergeant. But this money's good. And now we'll be going. Where's Eilif?

Swiss Cheese: Gone with the recruiting officer.

Mother Courage (standing quite still, then): Oh, you simpleton! *(To Kattrin:)* You can't speak, I know. You are innocent.

Sergeant: That's life. Take a slug yourself, Mother. Being a soldier isn't the worst that could happen. You want to live off war and keep you and yours out of it, do you?

Mother Courage: You must help your brother now, Kattrin.

> *Brother and sister get into harness together and pull the wagon. Mother Courage walks at their side. The wagon gets under way.*

Sergeant (looking after them):
> When a war gives you all you earn
> One day it may claim something in return!

II

> *In the years 1625 and 1626 Mother Courage journeys through Poland in the baggage train of the Swedish army. She meets her son again before the fortified town of Wallhof. — Of the successful sale of a capon and great days for the brave son.*
>
> Tent of the Swedish Commander. Kitchen next to it. Thunder of cannon. The Cook is quarreling with Mother Courage, who is trying to sell him a capon.

Cook: Sixty hellers for that miserable bird?

Mother Courage: Miserable bird? This fat fowl? Your Commander is a glutton. Woe betide you if you've nothing for him to eat. This capon is worth sixty hellers to you.

Cook: They're ten hellers a dozen on every corner.

Mother Courage: A capon like this on every corner! With a siege going on and people all skin and bones? Maybe you can get a field rat! I said maybe. Because we're all out of *them* too. Don't you see the soldiers running five deep after one hungry little field rat? All right then, in a siege, my price for a giant capon is fifty hellers.

Cook: But we're not "in a siege," we're doing the besieging, it's the other side that's "in a siege," when will you get this into your head?

Mother Courage: A fat lot of difference that makes, *we* haven't got a thing to eat either. They took everything into the town with them before all this started, and now they've nothing to do but eat and drink, I hear. It's us I'm worried about. Look at the farmers around here, they haven't a thing.

Cook: Certainly they have. They hide it.

Mother Courage (triumphant): They have not! They're ruined, that's what. They're so hungry I've seen 'em digging up roots to eat. I could boil your leather belt and make their mouths water with it. That's how things are around here. And I'm expected to let a capon go for forty hellers!

Cook: Thirty. Not forty. I said thirty hellers.

Mother Courage: I say this is no ordinary capon. It was a talented animal, so I hear. It would only feed to music — one march in particular was its favorite. It was so intelligent it could count. Forty hellers is too much for all this? I know *your* problem: if you don't find something to eat and quick, the Chief will — cut — your — fat — head — off!

Cook: All right, just watch. (*He takes a piece of beef and lays his knife on it.*) Here's a piece of beef, I'm going to roast it. I give you one more chance.

Mother Courage: Roast it, go ahead, it's only one year old.

Cook: One *day* old! Yesterday it was a cow. I saw it running around.

Mother Courage: In that case it must have started stinking before it died.

Cook: I don't care if I have to cook it for five hours. We'll see if it's still hard after that. (*He cuts into it.*)

Mother Courage: Put plenty of pepper in, so the Commander won't smell the smell.

The Swedish Commander, a Chaplain, and Eilif enter the tent.

Commander (clapping Eilif on the shoulder): In the Commander's tent with you, my son! Sit at my right hand, you happy warrior! You've played a hero's part, you've served the Lord in his own Holy War, *that's* the thing! And you'll get a gold bracelet out of it when we take the town if *I* have any say in the matter! We come to save their souls and what do they do, the filthy, shameless peasant pigs? Drive their cattle away from *us*, while they stuff their priests with beef at both ends! But you showed 'em. So here's a can of red wine for you, we'll drink together! (*They do so.*) The chaplain gets the dregs, he's pious. Now what would you like for dinner, my hearty?

Eilif: How about a slice of meat?

Commander: Cook, meat!

Cook: Nothing to eat, so he brings company to eat it!

Mother Courage makes him stop talking; she wants to listen.

Eilif: Tires you out, skinning peasants. Gives you an appetite.

Mother Courage: Dear God, it's my Eilif!

Cook: Who?

Mother Courage: My eldest. It's two years since I saw him, he was stolen from me in the street. He must be in high favor if the Commander's invited him to dinner. And what do you have to eat? Nothing. You hear what the Commander's guest wants? Meat! Better take my advice, buy the capon. The price is one guilder.

The Commander has sat down with Eilif and the Chaplain.

Commander (roaring): Cook! Dinner, you pig, or I'll have your head!

Cook: This is blackmail. Give me the damn thing!

Mother Courage: A miserable bird like this?

Cook: You were right. Give it here. It's highway robbery, fifty hellers.

Mother Courage: I said one guilder. Nothing's too high for my eldest, the Commander's guest of honor.

Cook (giving her the money): Well, you might at least pluck it till I have a fire going.

Mother Courage (sitting down to pluck the capon): I can't wait to see his face when he sees me. This is my brave and clever son. I have a stupid one as well but he's honest. The daughter is nothing. At least, she doesn't talk: we must be thankful for small mercies.

Commander: Have another can, my son, it's my favorite Falernian. There's only one cask left — two at the most — but it's worth it to meet a soldier that still believes in God! The shepherd of our flock here just looks on, he only preaches, he hasn't a clue how anything gets done. So now, Eilif, my son, give us the details: tell us how you fixed the peasants and grabbed the twenty bullocks. And let's hope they'll soon be here.

Eilif: In one day's time. Two at the most.

Mother Courage: Now that's considerate of Eilif — to bring the oxen tomorrow — otherwise my capon wouldn't have been so welcome today.

Eilif: Well, it was like this. I found out that the peasants had hidden their oxen and — on the sly and chiefly at night — had driven them into a certain wood. The people from the town were to pick them up there. I let them get their oxen in peace — they ought to know better than me where they are, I said to myself. Meanwhile I made my men crazy for meat. Their rations were short and I made sure they got shorter. Their mouths'd water at the sound of any word beginning with MEA . . . , like measles.

Commander: Smart fella.

Eilif: Not bad. The rest was a snap. Only the peasants had clubs and outnumbered us three to one and made a murderous attack on us. Four of them drove me into a clump of trees, knocked my good sword from my hand, and yelled, "Surrender!" What now, I said to myself, they'll make mincemeat of me.

Commander: What did you do?

Eilif: I laughed.

Commander: You what?

Eilif: I laughed. And so we got to talking. I came right down to business and said: "Twenty guilders an ox is too much, I bid fifteen." Like I wanted to buy. That foxed 'em. So while they were scratching their heads, I reached for my good sword and cut 'em to pieces. Necessity knows no law, huh?

Commander: What do *you* say, shepherd of the flock?

Chaplain: Strictly speaking, that saying is not in the Bible. Our Lord made five hundred loaves out of five so that no such necessity would arise. When he told men to love their neighbors, their bellies were full. Things have changed since his day.

Commander (laughing): Things have changed! A swallow of wine for those wise words, you pharisee! *(To Eilif:)* You cut 'em to pieces in a good cause, our fellows were hungry and you gave 'em to eat. Doesn't it say in the Bible "Whatsoever thou doest for the least of these my children, thou doest for me?" And what *did* you do for 'em? You got 'em the best steak dinner they every tasted. Moldy bread is not what they're used to. They always ate white bread, and drank wine in their helmets, before going out to fight for God.

Eilif: I reached for my good sword and cut 'em to pieces.

Commander: You have the makings of a Julius Caesar, why, you should be presented to the King!

Eilif: I've seen him — from a distance of course. He seemed to shed a light all around. I must try to be like him!

Commander: I think you're succeeding, my boy! Oh, Eilif, you don't know how I value a brave soldier like you! I treat such a chap as my very own son. *(He takes him to the map.)* Take a look at our position, Eilif, it isn't all it might be, is it?

Mother Courage has been listening and is now plucking angrily at her capon.

Mother Courage: He must be a very bad Commander.

Cook: Just a gluttonous one. Why bad?

Mother Courage: Because he needs *brave* soldiers, that's why. If his plan of campaign was any good, why would he need *brave* soldiers, wouldn't plain, ordinary soldiers do? Whenever there are great virtues, it's a sure sign something's wrong.

Cook: You mean, it's a sure sign something's right.

Mother Courage: I mean what I say. Why? When a general or a king is stupid and leads his soldiers into a trap, they need this virtue of courage. When he's tightfisted and hasn't enough soldiers, the few he does have need the heroism of Hercules — another virtue. And if he's slovenly and doesn't give a damn about anything, they have to be as wise as serpents or they're finished. Loyalty's another virtue and you need plenty of it if the king's always asking too much of you. All virtues which a well-regulated country with a good king or a good general wouldn't need. In a good country virtues wouldn't be necessary. Everybody could be quite ordinary, middling, and, for all I care, cowards.

Commander: I bet your father was a soldier.

Eilif: I've heard he was a great soldier. My mother warned me. I know a song about that.

Commander: Sing it to us. *(Roaring:)* Bring that meat!

Eilif: It's called The Song of the Wise Woman and the Soldier.

He sings and at the same time does a war dance with his saber:

> A shotgun will shoot and a jackknife will knife,
> If you wade in the water, it will drown you,
> Keep away from the ice, if you want my advice,
> Said the wise woman to the soldier.
>
> But that young soldier, he loaded his gun,
> And he reached for his knife, and he started to run:
> For marching never could hurt him!
> From the north to the south he will march through the land
> With his knife at his side and his gun in his hand:
> That's what the soldiers told the wise woman.
>
> Woe to him who defies the advice of the wise!
> If you wade in the water, it will drown you!
> Don't ignore what I say or you'll rue it one day,
> Said the wise woman to the soldier.
>
> But that young soldier, his knife at his side
> And his gun in his hand, he steps into the tide:
> For water never could hurt him!
> When the new moon is shining on yonder church tower

We are all coming back: go and pray for that hour:
That's what the soldiers told the wise woman.

Mother Courage (continues the song from her kitchen, beating on a pan with a spoon):

Then the wise woman spoke: you will vanish like smoke
Leaving nothing but cold air behind you!
Just watch the smoke fly! Oh God, don't let him die!
Said the wise woman to the soldier.

Eilif: What's that?
Mother Courage (singing on):

And the lad who defied the wise woman's advice,
When the new moon shone, floated down with the ice:
He waded in the water and it drowned him.

The wise woman spoke, and they vanished like smoke,
And their glorious deeds did not warm us.
Your glorious deeds do not warm us!

Commander: What a kitchen I've got! There's no end to the liberties they take!

Eilif has entered the kitchen and embraced his mother.

Eilif: To see you again! Where are the others?
Mother Courage (in his arms): Happy as ducks in a pond. Swiss Cheese is paymaster with the Second Regiment, so at least he isn't in the fighting. I couldn't keep him out altogether.
Eilif: Are your feet holding up?
Mother Courage: I've a bit of trouble getting my shoes on in the morning.

The Commander has come over.

Commander: So you're his mother! I hope you have more sons for me like this fellow.
Eilif: If I'm not the lucky one: to be feasted by the Commander while you sit listening in the kitchen!
Mother Courage: Yes. I heard all right. *(She gives him a box on the ear.)*
Eilif (his hand on his cheek): Because I took the oxen?
Mother Courage: No. Because you didn't surrender when the four peasants let fly at you and tried to make mincemeat of you! Didn't I teach you to take care of yourself? You Finnish devil, you!

The Commander and the Chaplain stand laughing in the doorway.

III

Three years pass and Mother Courage, with parts of a Finnish regiment, is taken prisoner. Her daughter is saved, her wagon likewise, but her honest son dies.

A camp. The regimental flag is flying from a pole. Afternoon. All sorts of wares hanging on the wagon. Mother Courage's clothesline is tied to the wagon at one end, to a cannon at the other. She and Kattrin are folding the washing on the cannon. At the same time she is bargaining with an Ordnance Officer over a bag of bullets. Swiss Cheese, in paymaster's uniform now, looks on. Yvette Pottier, a very good-looking young person, is sewing at a colored hat, a glass of brandy before her. She is in stocking feet. Her red boots are near by.

Officer: I'm letting you have the bullets for two guilders. Dirt cheap. 'Cause I need the money. The Colonel's been drinking with the officers for three days and we're out of liquor.

Mother Courage: They're army property. If they find 'em on me, I'll be court-martialed. You sell your bullets, you bastards, and send your men out to fight with nothing to shoot with.

Officer: Oh, come on, you scratch my back, and I'll scratch yours.

Mother Courage: I won't take army stuff. Not at *that* price.

Officer: You can resell 'em for five guilders, maybe eight, to the Ordnance Officer of the Fourth Regiment. All you have to do is give him a receipt for twelve. He hasn't a bullet left.

Mother Courage: Why don't you do it yourself?

Officer: I don't trust him. We're friends.

Mother Courage (taking the bag): Give it here. *(To Kattrin:)* Take it around to the back and pay him a guilder and a half. *(As the Officer protests:)* I said a guilder and a half! *(Kattrin drags the bag away. The Officer follows. Mother Courage speaks to Swiss Cheese:)* Here's your underwear back, take care of it; it's October now, autumn may come at any time: I purposely don't say it must come, I've learned from experience there's nothing that must come, not even the seasons. But your books *must* balance now you're the regimental paymaster. *Do* they balance?

Swiss Cheese: Yes, Mother.

Mother Courage: Don't forget they made you paymaster because you're honest and so simple you'd never think of running off with the cash. Don't lose that underwear.

Swiss Cheese: No, mother. I'll put it under the mattress. *(He starts to go.)*

Officer: I'll go with you, paymaster.

Mother Courage: Don't teach him any monkey business.

Without a good-by the Officer leaves with Swiss Cheese.

Yvette (waving to him): You might at least say good-by!

Mother Courage (to Yvette): I don't like that. He's no sort of company for my Swiss Cheese. But the war's not making a bad start. Before all the different countries get into it, four or five years'll have gone by like nothing. If I look ahead and make no mistakes, business will be good. Don't you know you shouldn't drink in the morning with your illness?

Yvette: Who says I'm ill? That's libel!

Mother Courage: They all say so.

Yvette: They're all liars. I'm desperate, Mother Courage. They all avoid me like a stinking fish. Because of those lies. So what am I arranging my hat for? *(She throws it down.)* That's why I drink in the morning. I never used to, it gives you crow's feet. But what's the difference? Every man in the regiment knows me. I should have stayed at home when my first was unfaithful. But pride isn't for the likes of us, you eat dirt or down you go.

Mother Courage: Now don't you start again with your friend Peter and how it all happened — in front of my innocent daughter.

Yvette: She's the one that should hear it. So she'll get hardened against love.

Mother Courage: That's something no one ever gets hardened against.

Yvette: I'll tell you about it, and get it off my chest. I grew up in Flanders' fields, that's where it starts, or I'd never even have caught sight of him and I wouldn't be here in Poland today. He was an army cook, blond, a Dutchman, but thin. Kattrin, beware of thin men! I didn't. I didn't even know he'd had another girl before me and she called him Peter Piper because he never took his pipe out of his mouth the whole time, it meant so little to him.

She sings "The Fraternization Song":

> When I was almost seventeen
> The foe came to our land
> And laying aside his saber
> He took me gently by the hand.
>
>> First came the May Day Rite
>> Then came the May Day night.
>> The pipes played and the drums did beat.
>> The foe paraded down the street.
>> And then with us they took their ease
>> And fraternized behind the trees.
>
> Our foes they came in plenty.
> A cook was my own foe.
> I hated him by daylight
> But in the dark I loved him so.
>
>> First comes the May Day Rite
>> Then comes the May Day night.
>> The pipes play and the drums do beat.
>> The foe parades down every street.
>> And then with us they take their ease
>> And fraternize behind the trees.
>
> The heavens seemed to open
> Such passion did I feel.
> But my people never understood
> The love I felt was real.
>
>> One day the sun rose slow
>> On all my pain and woe.
>> My loved one, with the other men,
>> Presented arms and stood at ease
>> Then marched away past all those trees
>> And never did come back again.

I made the mistake of running after him, I never found him. It's five years ago now. *(With swaying gait she goes behind the wagon.)*

Mother Courage: You've left your hat.

Yvette: For the birds.

Mother Courage: Let this be a lesson to you, Kattrin, never start anything with a soldier. The heavens do seem to open, so watch out! Even with men who're not in the army life's no honeypot. He tells you he'd like to kiss the ground under your feet — did you wash 'em yesterday, while we're on the subject? — and then if you don't look out, your number's up, you're his slave for life. Be glad you're dumb, Kattrin: you'll never contradict yourself, you'll never want to bite your tongue off because you spoke out of turn. Dumbness is a gift from God. Here comes the Commander's cook, what's bothering *him?*

Enter the Cook and the Chaplain.

Chaplain: I bring a message from your son Eilif. The cook came with me. You've made, ahem, an impression on him.

Cook: I thought I'd get a little whiff of the balmy breeze.

Mother Courage: You're welcome to that if you behave yourself, and even if you don't I think I can handle you. But what does Eilif want? I don't have any money.

Chaplain: Actually, I have something to tell his brother, the paymaster.

Mother Courage: He isn't here. And he isn't anywhere else either. He's not his brother's paymaster, and I won't have him led into temptation. Let Eilif try it on with someone else! *(She takes money from the purse at her belt.)* Give him this. It's a sin. He's speculating in mother love, he ought to be ashamed of himself.

Cook: Not for long. He has to go with his regiment now — to his death maybe. Send some more money, or you'll be sorry. You women are hard — and sorry afterward. A glass of brandy wouldn't cost very much, but you refuse to provide it, and six feet under goes your man and you can't dig him up again.

Chaplain: All very touching, my dear cook, but to fall in this war is not a misfortune, it's a blessing. This is a war of religion. Not just any old war but a special one, a religious one, and therefore pleasing unto God.

Cook: Correct. In one sense it's a war because there's fleecing, bribing, plundering, not to mention a little raping, but it's different from all other wars because it's a war of religion. That's clear. All the same, it makes you thirsty.

Chaplain (to Mother Courage, pointing at the Cook): I tried to hold him off but he said you'd bewitched him. He dreams about you.

Cook (lighting a clay pipe): Brandy from the fair hand of a lady, that's for me. And don't embarrass me any more: the stories the chaplain was telling me on the way over still have me blushing.

Mother Courage: A man of his cloth! I must get you both something to drink or you'll be making improper advances out of sheer boredom.

Chaplain: That is indeed a temptation, said the court chaplain, and gave way to it. *(Turning toward Kattrin as he walks:)* And who is this captivating young person?

Mother Courage: She's not a captivating young person, she a respectable young person.

The Chaplain and the Cook go with Mother Courage behind the cart, and one hears them talk politics.

Mother Courage: The trouble here in Poland is that the Poles *would* keep meddling. It's true our King moved in on them with man, beast, and wagon, but instead of keeping the peace the Poles attacked the Swedish King when he was in the act of peacefully withdrawing. So they were guilty of a breach of the peace and their blood is on their own heads.

Chaplain: Anyway, our King was thinking of nothing but freedom. The Kaiser enslaved them all, Poles and Germans alike, so our King *had* to liberate them.

Cook: Just what *I* think. Your health! Your brandy is first-rate, I'm never mistaken in a face.

Kattrin looks after them, leaves the washing, goes to the hat, picks it up, sits down, and takes up the red boots.

And the war is a war of religion. *(Singing while Kattrin puts the boots on:)* "A mighty fortress is our God . . ." *(He sings a verse or so of Luther's hymn.)* And talking of King Gustavus, this freedom he tried to bring to Germany cost him a pretty penny. Back in Sweden he had to levy a salt tax, the poorer folks didn't like it a bit. Then, too, he had to lock up the Germans and even cut their heads off, they clung so to slavery and their Kaiser. Of course, if no one had *wanted* to be free, the King would have got quite mad. First it was just Poland he tried to protect from bad men, especially the Kaiser, then his appetite grew with eating, and he ended up protecting Germany too. Now Germany put up a pretty decent fight. So the good King had nothing but worries in return for his outlay and his goodness, and of course he had to get his money back with taxes, which made bad blood, but he didn't shrink even from that. For he had one thing in his favor anyway, God's Holy Word, which was all to the good, because otherwise they could have said he did it for profit. That's how he kept his conscience clear. He always put conscience first.

Mother Courage: It's plain you're no Swede, or you'd speak differently of the Hero King.

Chaplain: What's more, you eat his bread.

Cook: I don't eat his bread. I bake his bread.

Mother Courage: He's unbeatable. Why? His men believe in him. *(Earnestly:)* To hear the big fellows talk, they wage war from fear of God and for all things bright and beautiful, but just look into it, and you'll see they're not so silly: they want a good profit out of it, or else the little fellows like you and me wouldn't back 'em up.

Cook: That's right.

Chaplain: And as a Dutchman you'd do well to see which flag's flying here before you express an opinion!

Mother Courage: All good Protestants forever!

Cook: A health!

Kattrin has begun to strut about with Yvette's hat on, copying Yvette's sexy walk. Suddenly cannon and shots. Drums. Mother Courage, the Cook, and the

Chaplain rush around to the front of the cart, the last two with glasses in their hands. The Ordnance Officer and a Soldier come running to the cannon and try to push it along.

Mother Courage: What's the matter? Let me get my washing off that gun, you slobs! *(She tries to do so.)*

Officer: The Catholics! Surprise attack! We don't know if we can get away! *(To the Soldier:)* Get that gun! *(He runs off.)*

Cook: For heaven's sake! I must go to the Commander. Mother Courage, I'll be back in a day or two — for a short conversation. *(He rushes off.)*

Mother Courage: Hey, you've left your pipe!

Cook (off): Keep it for me, I'll need it!

Mother Courage: This *would* happen just when we were making money.

Chaplain: Well, I must be going too. Yes, if the enemy's so close, it can be dangerous. "Blessed are the peacemakers," a good slogan in war time! If only I had a cloak.

Mother Courage: I'm lending no cloaks. Not even to save a life, I'm not. I've had experience in that line.

Chaplain: But I'm in special danger. Because of my religion.

Mother Courage (bringing him a cloak): It's against my better judgment. Now run!

Chaplain: I thank you, you're very generous, but maybe I'd better stay and sit here. If I run, I might attract the enemy's attention, I might arouse suspicion.

Mother Courage (to the Soldier): Let it alone, you dolt, who's going to pay you for this? It'll cost you your life, let me hold it for you.

Soldier (running away): You're my witness: I tried!

Mother Courage: I'll swear to it! *(Seeing Kattrin with the hat:)* What on earth are you up to — with a whore's hat! Take it off this minute! Are you mad? With the enemy coming? *(She tears the hat off her head.)* Do you want them to find you and make a whore of you? And she has the boots on too, straight from Babylon. I'll soon fix that. *(She tries to get them off.)* Oh, God, Chaplain, help me with these boots, I'll be right back. *(She runs to the wagon.)*

Yvette (entering and powdering her face): What's that you say: the Catholics are coming? Where's my hat? Who's been trampling on it? I can't run around in that, what will they think of me? And I don't even have a mirror. *(To the Chaplain:)* How do I look — too much powder?

Chaplain: Just, er, right.

Yvette: And where are my red boots? *(She can't find them because Kattrin is hiding her feet under her skirt.)* I left them here! Now I've got to go barefoot to my tent, it's a scandal! *(Exit.)*

Swiss Cheese comes running in carrying a cash box. Mother Courage enters with her hands covered with ashes.

Mother Courage (to Kattrin): Ashes! *(To Swiss Cheese:)* What have you got there?

Swiss Cheese: The regimental cash box.

Mother Courage: Throw it away! Your paymastering days are over!

Swiss Cheese: It's a trust! *(He goes to the back.)*

Mother Courage (to the Chaplain): Off with your pastor's cloak, Chaplain, or they'll recognize you, cloak or no cloak. (*She is rubbing ashes into Kattrin's face.*) Keep still. A little dirt, and you're safe. A calamity! The sentries were drunk. Well, one must hide one's light under a bushel, as they say. When a soldier sees a clean face, there's one more whore in the world. Especially a Catholic soldier. For weeks on end, no grub. Then, when the plundering starts and they steal some, they jump on top of the womenfolk. That should do. Let me look at you. Not bad. Looks like you've been rolling in muck. Don't tremble. Nothing can happen to you now. (*To Swiss Cheese:*) Where've you left the cash box?

Swiss Cheese: I thought I'd just put it in the wagon.

Mother Courage (horrified): What! In my wagon? God punish you for a prize idiot! If I just look away for a moment! They'll hang all three of us!

Swiss Cheese: Then I'll put it somewhere else. Or escape with it.

Mother Courage: You'll stay where you are. It's too late.

Chaplain (still changing his clothes): For heaven's sake: the flag!

Mother Courage (taking down the flag): God in heaven! I don't notice it any more. I've had it twenty-five years.

The thunder of cannon grows.

Three days later. Morning. The cannon is gone. Mother Courage, Kattrin, the Chaplain, and Swiss Cheese sit anxiously eating.

Swiss Cheese: This is the third day I've been sitting here doing nothing, and the Sergeant, who's always been patient with me, may be slowly beginning to ask, "Where on earth is Swiss Cheese with that cash box?"

Mother Courage: Be glad they're not on the trail.

Chaplain: What about me? I can't hold a service here or I'll be in hot water. It is written, "Out of the abundance of the heart, the tongue speaketh." But woe is me if *my* tongue speaketh!

Mother Courage: That's how it is. Here you sit — one with his religion, the other with his cash box, I don't know which is more dangerous.

Chaplain: We're in God's hands now!

Mother Courage: I hope we're not *that* desperate, but it *is* hard to sleep nights. 'Course it'd be easier if *you* weren't here, Swiss Cheese, all the same I've not done badly. I told them I was against the Antichrist, who's a Swede with horns on his head. I told them I noticed his left horn's a bit threadbare. When they cross-examined me, I always asked where I could buy holy candles a bit cheaper. I know these things because Swiss Cheese's father was a Catholic and made jokes about it. They didn't quite believe me but they needed a canteen, so they turned a blind eye. Maybe it's all for the best. We're prisoners. But so are lice in fur.

Chaplain: The milk is good. As far as quantity goes, we may have to reduce our Swedish appetites somewhat. We are defeated.

Mother Courage: Who's defeated? The defeats and victories of the fellows at the top aren't always defeats and victories for the fellows at the bottom. Not at all. There've been cases where a defeat is a victory for the fellows at the bottom, it's only their honor that's lost, nothing serious. In Livonia once, our Chief took such a knock from the enemy, in the confusion I got a fine gray mare out of the baggage train, it pulled my wagon seven months —

till we won and there was an inventory. But in general both defeat and victory are a costly business for us that haven't got much. The best thing is for politics to get stuck in the mud. *(To Swiss Cheese:)* Eat!

Swiss Cheese: I don't like it. How will the Sergeant pay his men?

Mother Courage: Soldiers in flight don't get paid.

Swiss Cheese: Well, they could claim to be. No pay, no flight. They can refuse to budge.

Mother Courage: Swiss Cheese, your sense of duty worries me. I've brought you up to be honest because you're not very bright. But don't overdo it. And now I'm going with the chaplain to buy a Catholic flag and some meat. There's no one can hunt out meat like him, sure as a sleepwalker. He can tell a good piece of meat from the way his mouth waters. A good thing they let me stay in the business. In business you ask what price, not what religion. And Protestant trousers keep you just as warm.

Chaplain: As the mendicant monk said when there was talk of the Lutherans turning the whole world upside down: Beggars will *always* be needed. *(Mother Courage disappears into the wagon.)* She's worried about the cash box. Up to now they've ignored us — as if we were part of the wagon — but can it last?

Swiss Cheese: I can get rid of it.

Chaplain: That's almost *more* dangerous. Suppose you're seen. They have spies. Yesterday morning one jumped out of the very hole I was relieving myself in. I was so scared I almost broke out in prayer — *that* would have given me away all right! I believe their favorite way of finding a Protestant is smelling his excrement. The spy was a little brute with a bandage over one eye.

Mother Courage (clambering out of the wagon with a basket): I've found you out, you shameless hussy! *(She holds up Yvette's red boots in triumph.)* Yvette's red boots! She just swiped them — because you went and told her she was a captivating person. *(She lays them in the basket.)* Stealing Yvette's boots! But *she* disgraces herself for money, *you* do it for nothing — for pleasure! I told you, you must wait for the peace. No soldiers! Save your proud peacock ways for peacetime!

Chaplain: I don't find her proud.

Mother Courage: Prouder than she can afford to be. I like her when people say "I never noticed the poor thing." I like her when she's a stone in Dalarna, where there's nothing but stones. *(To Swiss Cheese:)* Leave the cash box where it is, do you hear? And pay attention to your sister, she needs it. Between the two of you, you'll be the death of me yet. I'd rather take care of a bag of fleas.

She leaves with the Chaplain. Kattrin clears the dishes away.

Swiss Cheese: Not many days more when you can sit in the sun in your shirtsleeves. *(Kattrin points to a tree.)* Yes, the leaves are yellow already. *(With gestures, Kattrin asks if he wants a drink.)* I'm not drinking, I'm thinking. *(Pause.)* She says she can't sleep. So I *should* take the cash box away. I've found a place for it. I'll keep it in the mole hole by the river till the time comes. I might get it tonight before sunrise and take it to the regiment. How far can they have fled in three days? The Sergeant's eyes'll pop out of his head. "I give you the cash box to take care of, and what do you do," he'll say, "but hand it right back to me: you've disappointed me most pleasantly, Swiss Cheese." Yes, Kattrin, I *will* have a glass now!

When Kattrin reappears behind the wagon two men confront her. One of them is a Sergeant. The other doffs his hat and flourishes it in a showy greeting. He has a bandage over one eye.

Man with the bandage: Good morning, young lady. Have you seen a man from the Second Protestant Regiment?

Terrified, Kattrin runs away, spilling her brandy. The two men look at each other and then withdraw after seeing Swiss Cheese.

Swiss Cheese (starting up from his reflection): You're spilling it! What's the matter with you, have you hurt your eye? I don't understand. Yes, and I must be going, too. I've decided it's the thing to do. (*He stands up. She does all she can to make him aware of the danger he is in. He only pushes her away.*) I'd like to know what you mean. I know you mean well, poor thing, you just can't get it out. And don't trouble yourself about the brandy, I'll live to drink so much of it, what's one glass? (*He takes the cash box out of the wagon and puts it under his coat.*) I'll be back right away. But don't hold me up or I'll have to scold you. Yes, I know you mean well. If you could only speak!

When she tries to hold him back he kisses her and pulls himself free. Exit. She is desperate and runs up and down, emitting little sounds. Mother Courage and the Chaplain return. Kattrin rushes at her mother.

Mother Courage: What *is* it, what *is* it, Kattrin? Control yourself! Has someone done something to you? Where is Swiss Cheese? (*To the Chaplain:*) Don't stand around, get that Catholic flag up! (*She takes a Catholic flag out of her basket and the Chaplain runs it up the pole.*)

Chaplain (bitterly): All good Catholics forever!

Mother Courage: Now, Kattrin, calm down and tell all about it, your mother understands you. What, that little bastard of mine's taken the cash box away? I'll box his ears for him, the rascal! Now take your time and don't try to talk, use your hands. I don't like it when you howl like a dog, what'll the chaplain think of you? You're giving him the creeps. A man with one eye was here?

Chaplain: That fellow with one eye is an informer! Have they caught Swiss Cheese? (*Kattrin shakes her head, shrugs her shoulders.*) This is the end.

Voices off. The two men bring in Swiss Cheese.

Swiss Cheese: Let me go. I've nothing on me. You're breaking my shoulder! I am innocent.

Sergeant: This is where he comes from. These are his friends.

Mother Courage: Us? Since when?

Swiss Cheese: I don't even know 'em. I was just getting my lunch here. Ten hellers it cost me. Maybe you saw me sitting on that bench. It was too salty.

Sergeant: Who *are* you people, anyway?

Mother Courage: Law-abiding citizens! It's true what he says. He bought his lunch here. And it was too salty.

Sergeant: Are you pretending you don't know him?

Mother Courage: I can't know all of them, can I? *I* don't ask, "What's your name and are you a heathen?" If they pay up, they're not heathens to me. Are you a heathen?

Swiss Cheese: Oh, no!

Chaplain: He sat there like a law-abiding fellow and never once opened his mouth. Except to eat. Which is necessary.

Sergeant: Who do you think *you* are?

Mother Courage: Oh, he's my barman. And you're thirsty, I'll bring you a glass of brandy. You must be footsore and weary!

Sergeant: No brandy on duty. *(To Swiss Cheese:)* You were carrying something. You must have hidden it by the river. We saw the bulge in your shirt.

Mother Courage: Sure it was him?

Swiss Cheese: I think you mean another fellow. There *was* a fellow with something under his shirt, I saw him. I'm the wrong man.

Mother Courage: I think so too. It's a misunderstanding. Could happen to anyone. Oh, I know what people are like, I'm Mother Courage, you've heard of me, everyone knows about me, and I can tell you this: he looks honest.

Sergeant: We're after the regimental cash box. And we know what the man looks like who's been keeping it. We've been looking for him two days. It's you.

Swiss Cheese: No, it's not!

Sergeant: And if you don't shell out, you're dead, see? Where is it?

Mother Courage (urgently): 'Course he'd give it to you to save his life. He'd up and say, *I've* got it, here it is, you're stronger than me. He's not *that* stupid. Speak, little stupid, the sergeant's giving you a chance!

Swiss Cheese: What if I haven't got it?

Sergeant: Come with us. We'll get it out of you. *(They take him off.)*

Mother Courage (shouting after them): He'd tell you! He's not *that* stupid! And don't you break his shoulder! *(She runs after them.)*

The same evening. The Chaplain and Kattrin are rinsing glasses and polishing knives.

Chaplain: Cases of people getting caught like this are by no means unknown in the history of religion. I am reminded of the Passion of Our Lord and Savior. There's an old song about it.

He sings "The Song of the Hours":

> In the first hour of the day
> Simple Jesus Christ was
> Presented as a murderer
> To the heathen Pilate.
>
> Pilate found no fault in him
> No cause to condemn him
> So he sent the Lord away.
> Let King Herod see him!

Hour the third: the Son of God
Was with scourges beaten
And they set a crown of thorns
On the head of Jesus.

And they dressed him as a king
Joked and jested at him
And the cross to die upon
He himself must carry.

Six: they stripped Lord Jesus bare.
To the cross they nailed him.
When the blood came gushing, he
Prayed and loud lamented.

Each upon his cross, two thieves
Mocked him like the others.
And the bright sun crept away
Not to see such doings.

Nine: Lord Jesus cried aloud
That he was forsaken!
In a sponge upon a pole
Vinegar was fed him.

Then the Lord gave up the ghost
And the earth did tremble.
Temple curtains split in twain.
Cliffs fell in the ocean.

Evening: they broke the bones
Of the malefactors.
Then they took a spear and pierced
The side of gentle Jesus.

And the blood and water ran
And they laughed at Jesus.
Of this simple son of man
Such and more they tell us.

Mother Courage (entering, excited): It's life and death. But the Sergeant will still listen to us. The only thing is, he mustn't know it's our Swiss Cheese, or they'll say we helped him. It's only a matter of money, but where can *we* get money? Isn't Yvette here yet? I talked to her on the way over. She's picked up a Colonel who may be willing to buy her a canteen business.

Chaplain: You'd sell the wagon, everything?

Mother Courage: Where else would I get the money for the Sergeant?

Chaplain: What are you to live off?

Mother Courage: That's just it.

Enter Yvette with a hoary old Colonel.

Yvette (embracing Mother Courage): Dear Mistress Courage, we meet again.

(Whispering:) He didn't say no. *(Aloud:)* This is my friend, my, um, business adviser. I happened to hear you might sell your wagon. Due to special circumstances, I'd like to think about it.

Mother Courage: I want to pawn it, not sell it. And nothing hasty. In war time you don't find another wagon like that so easy.

Yvette (disappointed): Only pawn it? I thought you wanted to sell. I don't know if I'm interested. *(To the Colonel:)* What do *you* think, my dear?

Colonel: I quite agree with you, bunny.

Mother Courage: It's only for pawn.

Yvette: I thought you *had* to have the money.

Mother Courage (firmly): I do have to have it. But I'd rather wear my feet off looking for an offer than just sell. Why? We live off the wagon. It's an opportunity for you, Yvette. Who knows when you'll have another such? Who knows when you'll find another business adviser?

Colonel: Take it, take it!

Yvette: My friend thinks I should go ahead, but I'm not sure, if it's only for pawn. You think we should buy it outright, don't you?

Colonel: I do, bunny, I do!

Mother Courage: Then you must go and find something that's for sale. Maybe you'll find it — if you have the time, and your friend goes with you, let's say in about a week, or two weeks, you may find the right thing.

Yvette: Yes, we can certainly look around for something. I love going around looking, I love going around with you, Poldy . . .

Colonel: Really? Do you?

Yvette: Oh, it's lovely! I could take two weeks of it!

Colonel: Really, could you?

Yvette: If you get the money, when are you thinking of paying it back?

Mother Courage: In two weeks. Maybe one.

Yvette: I can't make up my mind. Poldy, advise me, *chéri!* *(She takes the Colonel to one side.)* She'll *have* to sell, don't worry. That Lieutenant — the blond one, you know the one I mean — he'll lend me the money. He's *mad* about me, he says I remind him of someone. What do you advise?

Colonel: Oh, I have to warn you against *him.* He's no good. He'll exploit the situation. I told you, bunny, I told you I'd buy you something, didn't I tell you that?

Yvette: I simply can't let you!

Colonel: Oh, please, please!

Yvette: Well, if you think the Lieutenant might exploit the situation I *will* let you!

Colonel: I do think so.

Yvette: So you advise me to?

Colonel: I do, bunny, I do!

Yvette (returning to Mother Courage): My friend says all right. Write me out a receipt saying the wagon's mine when the two weeks are up — with everything in it. I'll just run through it all now, the two hundred guilders can wait. *(To the Colonel:)* You go ahead to the camp, I'll follow, I must go over all this so nothing'll be missing later from *my* wagon!

Colonel: Wait, I'll help you up! *(He does so.)* Come soon, honey bun! *(Exit.)*

Mother Courage: Yvette, Yvette!

Yvette: There aren't many boots left!

Mother Courage: Yvette, this is no time to go through the wagon, yours or not yours. You promised you'd talk to the Sergeant about Swiss Cheese. There isn't a minute to lose. He's up before the court-martial one hour from now.

Yvette: I just want to count these shirts again.

Mother Courage (dragging her down the steps by the skirt): You hyena, Swiss Cheese's life's at stake! And don't say who the money comes from. Pretend he's your sweetheart, for heaven's sake, or we'll all get it for helping him.

Yvette: I've arranged to meet One Eye in the bushes. He must be there by now.

Chaplain: And don't hand over all two hundred, a hundred and fifty's sure to be enough.

Mother Courage: Is it your money? I'll thank you to keep your nose out of this, I'm not doing you out of your porridge. Now run, and no haggling, remember his life's at stake. (She pushes Yvette off.)

Chaplain: I didn't want to talk you into anything, but what are we going to live on? You have an unemployable daughter around your neck.

Mother Courage: I'm counting on that cash box, smart aleck. They'll pay his expenses out of it.

Chaplain: You think she can work it?

Mother Courage: It's in her own interest: I pay the two hundred and she gets the wagon. She knows what she's doing, she won't have her Colonel on the string forever. Kattrin, go and clean the knives, use pumice stone. And don't you stand around like Jesus in Gethsemane. Get a move on, wash those glasses. There'll be over fifty cavalrymen here tonight, and you'll be saying you're not used to being on your feet. "Oh my poor feet, in church I never had to run around like this!" I think they'll let us have him. Thanks be to God they're corruptible. They're not wolves, they're human and after money. God is merciful, and men are bribable, that's how His will is done on earth as it is in Heaven. Corruption is our only hope. As long as there's corruption, there'll be merciful judges and even the innocent may get off.

Yvette comes in panting.

Yvette: They'll do it for two hundred if you make it snappy — these things change from one minute to the next. I'd better take One Eye to my Colonel at once. He confessed he had the cash box, they put the thumbscrews on him. But he threw it in the river when he noticed them coming up behind him. So it's gone. Shall I run and get the money from my Colonel?

Mother Courage: The cash box gone? How'll I ever get my two hundred back?

Yvette: So you thought you could get it from the cash box? I would have been sunk. Not a hope, Mother Courage. If you want your Swiss Cheese, you'll have to pay. Or should I let the whole thing drop, so you can keep your wagon?

Mother Courage: I wasn't figuring on this. But you needn't hound me, you'll get the wagon, it's yours already, and it's been mine seventeen years. I need a minute to think it over, it's all so sudden. What can I do? I can't pay two hundred. You should have haggled with them. I must hold on to something, or any passer-by can kick me in the ditch. Go and say I'll pay a hundred and twenty or the deal's off. Even then I lose the wagon.

Yvette: They won't do it. And anyway, One Eye's in a hurry. He keeps looking over his shoulder all the time, he's so worked up. Hadn't I better give them the whole two hundred?

Mother Courage (desperate): I can't pay it! I've been working thirty years. She's twenty-five and still no husband. I have her to think of. So leave me alone. I know what I'm doing. A hundred and twenty or no deal.

Yvette: You know best. *(She runs off.)*

Mother Courage turns away and slowly walks a few paces to the rear. Then she turns around, looks neither at the Chaplain nor her daughter, and sits down to help Kattrin polish the knives.

Mother Courage: Don't break the glasses, they're not ours. Watch what you're doing, you're cutting yourself. Swiss Cheese will be back, I'll give two hundred, if I have to. You'll get your brother back. With eighty guilders we could pack a hamper with goods and begin again. It wouldn't be the end of the world.

Chaplain: The Bible says: the Lord will provide.

Mother Courage: Rub them dry, I said.

They clean the knives in silence.

They say the war will stop soon. How would it? I ask. And no one can answer me. *(Slowly.)* The King and the Pope are mortal enemies, their Faith is different. They must go for each other till one of them drops dead, neither of them can relax till then. Even so they can't get on with it. Why not? The Emperor is in the way, and they both have something against him. They're not going to fight each other to the death with the Emperor lurking about till they're half dead so he can fall on both of 'em! No, they're banding together against the Emperor so he'll drop dead first and they can go for each other.

Suddenly Kattrin runs sobbing behind the wagon.

Someone once offered me five hundred guilders for the wagon. I didn't take it. My Eilif, wherever he may be, thought I'd taken it and cried all night.

Yvette comes running in.

Yvette: They won't do it. I warned you. One Eye was going to drop it then and there. There's no point, he said. He said the drums would roll any second now and that's the sign a verdict has been reached. I offered a hundred and fifty, he didn't even shrug. I could hardly get him to stay there while I came here.

Mother Courage: Tell him I'll pay two hundred. Run!

Yvette runs. Mother Courage sits, silent. The Chaplain has stopped doing the glasses.

I believe — I've haggled too long.

In the distance, a roll of drums. The Chaplain stands up and walks toward the rear. Mother Courage remains seated. It grows dark. It gets light again. Mother Courage has not moved. Yvette appears, pale.

Yvette: Now you've done it — with your haggling. You can keep the wagon now. He got eleven bullets in him. I don't know why I still bother about you, you don't deserve it, but I just happened to learn they don't think the cash box is really in the river. They suspect it's here, they think you're connected with him. I think they're going to bring him here to see if you'll give yourself away when you see him. You'd better not know him or we're in for it. And I'd better tell you straight, they're just behind me. Shall I keep Kattrin away? (*Mother Courage shakes her head.*) Does she know? Maybe she never heard the drums or didn't understand.

Mother Courage: She knows. Bring her.

Yvette brings Kattrin, who walks over to her mother and stands by her. Mother Courage takes her hand. Two men come on with a stretcher; there is a sheet on it and something underneath. Beside them, the Sergeant. They put the stretcher down.

Sergeant: Here's a man we can't identify. But he has to be registered to keep the records straight. He bought a meal from you. Look at him, see if you know him. (*He pulls back the sheet.*) Do you know him? (*Mother Courage shakes her head.*) What? You never saw him before he took that meal? (*Mother Courage shakes her head.*) Lift him up. Throw him in the carrion pit. He has no one that knows him.

They carry him off.

IV

Mother Courage sings "The Song of the Great Capitulation."
    Outside an officer's tent. Mother Courage waits. A Clerk looks out of the tent.

Clerk: I know you. You had a Protestant paymaster with you, he was hiding out with you. Better make no complaint.

Mother Courage: But I'm innocent and if I give up it'll look as if I had a bad conscience. They cut everything in my wagon to ribbons with their sabers and then claimed a fine of five thalers for nothing and less than nothing.

Clerk: For your own good, keep your trap shut. We haven't many canteens, so we let you stay in business, especially if you've a bad conscience and have to pay a fine now and then.

Mother Courage: I'm going to file a complaint.

Clerk: As you wish. Wait here till the Captain has time. (*He withdraws into the tent.*)

A Young Soldier comes storming in.

Young Soldier: Screw the Captain! Where *is* the son of a bitch? Swiping my reward, spending it on brandy for his whores, I'll rip his belly open!

An Older Soldier (*coming after him*): Shut your hole, you'll wind up in the stocks.

Young Soldier: Come out, you thief, I'll make lamb chops out of you! I was the only one in the squad who swam the river and *he* grabs my money, I can't even buy myself a beer. Come on out! And let me slice you up!

Older Soldier: Holy Christ, he'll destroy himself!

Young Soldier: Let me go or I'll run *you* down too. This has got to be settled!

Older Soldier: Saved the Colonel's horse and didn't get the reward. He's young, he hasn't been at it long.

Mother Courage: Let him go. He doesn't have to be chained, he's not a dog. Very reasonable to want a reward. Why else should he want to shine?

Young Soldier: He's in there pouring it down! You're all nice. I've done something special, I want the reward!

Mother Courage: Young man, don't scream at *me*, I have my own troubles. And go easy with your voice, you may need it when the Captain comes. The Captain'll come and you'll be hoarse and can't make a sound, so he'll have to deny himself the pleasure of sticking you in the stocks till you pass out. The screamers don't scream long, only half an hour, after which they have to be sung to sleep, they're all in.

Young Soldier: I'm not all in, and sleep's out of the question. I'm hungry. They're making their bread out of acorns and hempseed, and not even much of that. He's whoring on my money, and I'm hungry. I'll murder him!

Mother Courage: I understand: you're hungry. Last year your Commander ordered you people out of the streets and into the fields. So the crops got trampled down. I could have got ten guilders for boots, if anyone'd had ten guilders, and if I'd had any boots. He didn't expect to be around this year, but he is, and there's famine. I understand: you're angry.

Young Soldier: It's no use your talking. I won't stand for injustice!

Mother Courage: You're quite right. But how long? How long won't you stand for injustice? One hour? Or two? You haven't asked yourself that, have you? And yet it's the main thing. It's pure misery to sit in the stocks. Especially if you leave it till then to decide you do stand for injustice.

Young Soldier: I don't know why I listen to you. Screw that Captain! Where is he?

Mother Courage: You listen because you know I'm right. Your rage has calmed down already. It was a short one and you'd need a long one. But where would you find it?

Young Soldier: Are you trying to say it's not right to ask for the money?

Mother Courage: Just the opposite. I only say, your rage won't last. You'll get nowhere with it, it's a pity. If your rage was a long one, I'd urge you on. Slice him up, I'd advise you. But what's the use if you *don't* slice him up because you can feel your tail between your legs? You stand there and the Captain lets you have it.

Older Soldier: You're quite right, he's crazy.

Young Soldier: All right, we'll see whether I slice him up or not. *(He draws his sword.)* When he comes out, I slice him up!

Clerk (looking out): The Captain will be out in a minute. *(In the tone of military command:)* Be seated!

The Young Soldier sits.

Mother Courage: And he *is* seated. What did I tell you? You are seated. They know us through and through. They know how they must work it. Be seated! And we sit. And in sitting there's no revolt. Better not stand up again — not the way you did before — don't stand up again. And don't be embarrassed in front of me, I'm no better, not a scrap. They've drawn our teeth, haven't they? If we say boo, it's bad for business. Let me tell you about the great capitulation.

She sings "The Song of the Great Capitulation":

> Long ago when I was a green beginner
> I believed I was a special case.

(None of your ordinary run of the mill girls, with my looks and my talent, and my love of the higher things in life!)

> And if I picked a hair out of my dinner
> I would put the cook right in his place.

(All or nothing. Anyhow, never the second best. I am the master of my Fate. I'll take orders from no one.)

> Then a little bird whispered in my ear:
> "That's all very well, but wait a year
> And you will join the big brass band
> And with your trumpet in your hand
> You'll march in lockstep with the rest.
> Then one day, look! The battalions wheel!
> The whole thing swings from east to west!
> And falling on your knees, you'll squeal:
> The Lord God, He knows best!
> (But don't give *me* that!)"

> And a month or two before that year was over
> I had learned to drink their cup of tea.

(Two children round your neck, and the price of bread and what all!)

> And the day soon came when I was to discover
> They had me just where they wanted me.

(You must get in good with people. If you scratch my back, I'll scratch yours. Don't stick your neck out.)

> And that little bird whispered in my ear:
> "You didn't even take a year!
> And you have joined the big brass band
> And with your trumpet in your hand
> You marched in lockstep with the rest.
> But one day, look! The battalions wheeled!
> The whole thing swung from east to west!
> And falling on your knees, you squealed:
> The Lord God, He knows best!
> (But don't give *me* that!)"

> Yes, our hopes are high, our plans colossal!
> And we hitch our wagon to a star!

(Where there's a will there's a way. One can't hold a good man down.)

We can move mountains, says St. Paul the great Apostle
And yet: how heavy one cigar!

(We must cut our coat according to our cloth.)

For that little bird whispers in your ear:
"That's all very well but wait a year
And we will join the big brass band
And with our trumpet in our hand
We march in lockstep with the rest.
But one day, look! The battalions wheel!
The whole thing swings from east to west!
And falling on our knees, we squeal:
The Lord God, He knows best!
(But don't give *me* that!)"

And so I think you should stay here with your sword drawn if you're set on it and your anger is big enough. You have good cause, I admit. But if your anger is a short one, you'd better go.

Young Soldier: Kiss my ass. (*He stumbles off, the other Soldier following him.*)

Clerk (sticking his head out): The Captain is ready now. You can file your complaint.

Mother Courage: I've thought better of it. I'm not complaining. (*Exit.*)

The Clerk looks after her, shaking his head.

V

Two years have passed. The war covers wider and wider territory. Forever on the move, the little wagon crosses Poland, Moravia, Bavaria, Italy, and again Bavaria. 1631. Tilly's victory at Magdeburg costs Mother Courage four officers' shirts.

The wagon stands in a war-ravaged village. Faint military music from the distance. Two soldiers are being served at a counter by Kattrin and Mother Courage. One of them has a woman's fur coat about his shoulders.

Mother Courage: What, you can't pay? No money, no brandy! They can play victory marches, they should pay their men.

First Soldier: I want my brandy! I arrived too late for plunder. The Chief allowed one hour to plunder the town, it's a swindle. He's not inhuman, he says. So I suppose they bought him off.

Chaplain (staggering in): There are more in the farmhouse. A family of peasants. Help me someone. I need linen!

The second Soldier goes with him. Kattrin is getting very excited. She tries to get her mother to bring linen out.

Mother Courage: I have none. I sold all my bandages to the regiment. I'm not tearing up my officers' shirts for these people.

Chaplain (calling over his shoulder): I said I need linen!

Mother Courage (stopping Kattrin from entering the wagon): Not a thing! They can't pay, and why? They have nothing and they pay nothing!

Chaplain (to a woman he is carrying in): Why did you stay out there in the line of fire?

Woman: Our farm —

Mother Courage: Think they'd ever let go of *anything?* And now I'm supposed to pay. Well, I won't!

First Soldier: They're Protestants, why should they be Protestants?

Mother Courage: Protestant, Catholic, what do *they* care? Their farm's gone, that's what.

Second Soldier: They're not Protestants anyway, they're Catholics.

First Soldier: In a bombardment we can't pick and choose.

A Peasant (brought on by the Chaplain): My arm's gone.

Chaplain: Where's that linen?

All look at Mother Courage, who does not budge.

Mother Courage: I can't give you any. With all I have to pay out — taxes, duties, bribes. . . . (Kattrin takes up a board and threatens her mother with it, emitting gurgling sounds.) Are you out of your mind? Put that board down or I'll let you have one, you lunatic! I'm giving nothing, I don't dare, I have myself to think of. (The Chaplain lifts her bodily off the steps of the wagon and sets her down on the ground. He takes out shirts from the wagon and tears them in strips.) My shirts, my officers' shirts!

From the house comes the cry of a child in pain.

Peasant: The child's still in there.

Kattrin runs in.

Chaplain (to the Woman): Stay where you are. She's getting it for you.

Mother Courage: Hold her back, the roof may fall in!

Chaplain: I'm not going back in there!

Mother Courage (pulled in both directions): Go easy on my expensive linen.

The Second Soldier holds her back. Kattrin brings a baby out of the ruins.

Mother Courage: Another baby to drag around, you must be pleased with yourself. Give it to its mother this minute! Or do I have to fight you again for hours till I get it from you? Are you deaf? (To the Second Soldier:) Don't stand about gawking, go back there and tell 'em to stop that music, I can see their victory without it. I have nothing but losses from your victory!

Chaplain (bandaging): The blood's coming through.

Kattrin is rocking the child and half humming a lullaby.

Mother Courage: There she sits, happy as a lark in all this misery. Give the baby back, the mother is coming to! (She sees the First Soldier. He had been handling the drinks, and is now trying to make off with the bottle.) God's truth! You beast! You want another victory, do you? Then pay for it!

First Soldier: I have nothing.

Mother Courage (snatching the fur coat back): Then leave this coat, it's stolen goods anyhow.

Chaplain: There's still someone in there.

VI

*Before the city of Ingolstadt in Bavaria Mother Courage is present at the funeral
of the fallen commander, Tilly. Conversations take place about war heroes and
the duration of the war. The Chaplain complains that his talents are lying fallow
and Kattrin gets the red boots. The year is 1632.*

*The inside of a canteen tent. The inner side of a counter at the rear. Rain. In
the distance, drums and funeral music. The Chaplain and the regimental Clerk
are playing draughts. Mother Courage and her daughter are taking an inventory.*

Chaplain: The funeral procession is just starting out.

Mother Courage: Pity about the Chief — twenty-two pairs of socks — getting
killed that way. They say it was an accident. There was a fog over the fields
that morning, and the fog was to blame. The Chief called up another regiment, told 'em to fight to the death, rode back again, missed his way in the
fog, went forward instead of back, and ran smack into a bullet in the thick
of battle — only four lanterns left. (*A whistle from the rear. She goes to the
counter. To a Soldier:*) It's a disgrace the way you're all skipping your Commander's funeral! (*She pours a drink.*)

Clerk: They shouldn't have handed the money out before the funeral. Now the
men are all getting drunk instead of going to it.

Chaplain (to the Clerk): Don't you have to be there?

Clerk: I stayed away because of the rain.

Mother Courage: It's different for you, the rain might spoil your uniform. I hear
they wanted to ring the bells for his funeral, which is natural, but it came
out that the churches had been shot up by his orders, so the poor Commander won't be hearing any bells when they lower him in his grave. Instead, they'll fire off three shots so the occasion won't be *too* sober —
sixteen leather belts.

A Voice from the counter: Service! One brandy!

Mother Courage: Your money first. No, you *can't* come inside the tent, not with
those boots on. You can drink outside, rain or no rain. I only let officers in
here. (*To the Clerk:*) The Chief had his troubles lately, I hear. There was unrest in the Second Regiment because he didn't pay 'em. He said it was a
war of religion and they must fight it free of charge.

Funeral march. All look toward the rear.

Chaplain: Now they're filing past the body.

Mother Courage: I feel sorry for a Commander or an Emperor like that — when
he might have had something special in mind, something they'd talk about
in times to come, something they'd raise a statue to him for. The conquest
of the world now, *that's* a goal for a Commander, he wouldn't know any
better. . . . Lord, worms have got into the biscuits. . . . In short, he works
his hands to the bone and then it's all spoiled by the common riffraff that
only wants a jug of beer or a bit of company, not the higher things in life.
The finest plans have always been spoiled by the littleness of them that
should carry them out. Even Emperors can't do it all by themselves. They
count on support from their soldiers and the people round about. Am I
right?

Chaplain (laughing): You're right, Mother Courage, till you come to the soldiers. They do what they can. Those fellows outside, for example, drinking their brandy in the rain, I'd trust 'em to fight a hundred years, one war after another, two at a time if necessary. And I wasn't trained as a commander.

Mother Courage: . . . Seventeen leather belts. . . . Then you don't think the war might end?

Chaplain: Because a commander's dead? Don't be childish, they grow on trees. There are always heroes.

Mother Courage: Well, I wasn't asking for the sake of argument. I was wondering if I should buy up a lot of supplies. They happen to be cheap just now. But if the war ended, I might just as well throw them away.

Chaplain: I realize you are serious, Mother Courage. Well, there've always been people going around saying some day the war will end. I say, you can't be sure the war will *ever* end. Of course it may have to pause occasionally — for breath, as it were — it can even meet with an accident — nothing on this earth is perfect — a war of which we could say it left nothing to be desired will probably never exist. A war can come to a sudden halt — from unforeseen causes — you can't think of everything — a little oversight, and the war's in the hole, and someone's got to pull it out again! The someone is the Emperor or the King or the Pope. They're such friends in need, the war has really nothing to worry about, it can look forward to a prosperous future.

A Soldier (singing at the counter):

> One schnapps, mine host, make haste!
> We have no time to waste:
> We must be shooting, shooting, shooting
> Our Emperor's foes uprooting!

Make it a double. This is a holiday.

Mother Courage: If I was sure you're right . . .

Chaplain: Think it out for yourself: how *could* the war end?

Soldier (offstage):

> Two breasts, mine host, make haste!
> For we have no time to waste:
> We must be hating, hating, hating
> We cannot keep our Emperor waiting!

Clerk (suddenly): What about peace? Yes, peace. I'm from Bohemia. I'd like to get home once in a while.

Chaplain: Oh, you would, would you? Dear old peace! What happens to the hole when the cheese is gone?

Soldier (offstage):

> Your blessing, priest, make haste!
> For we have no time to waste:
> We must be dying, dying, dying
> Our Emperor's greatness glorifying!

Clerk: In the long run you can't live without peace!

Chaplain: Well, I'd say there's peace even in war, war has its islands of peace.

For war satisfies *all* needs, even those of peace, yes, they're provided for, or the war couldn't keep going. In war — as in the very thick of peace — you can take a crap, and between one battle and the next there's always a beer, and even on the march you can snatch a nap — on your elbow maybe, in a gutter — something can always be managed. Of course you can't play cards during an attack, but neither can you while ploughing the fields in peace time: it's when the victory's won that there are possibilities. You have your leg shot off, and at first you raise quite an outcry as if it *was* something, but soon you calm down or take a swig of brandy, and you end up hopping about, and the war is none the worse for your little misadventure. And can't you be fruitful and multiply in the thick of slaughter — behind a barn or somewhere? Nothing can keep you from it very long in any event. And so the war has your offspring and can carry on. War is like love, it always finds a way. Why *should* it end?

Kattrin has stopped working. She stares at the Chaplain.

Mother Courage: Then I *will* buy those supplies, I'll rely on you. (*Kattrin suddenly bangs a basket of glasses down on the ground and runs out. Mother Courage laughs.*) Kattrin! Lord, Kattrin's still going to wait for peace. I promised her she'll get a husband — when it's peace. (*She runs after her.*)
Clerk (standing up): I win. You were talking. You pay.
Mother Courage (returning with Kattrin): Be sensible, the war'll go on a bit longer, and we'll make a bit more money, then peace'll be all the nicer. Now you go into the town, it's not ten minutes' walk, and bring the things from the Golden Lion, just the more expensive ones, we can get the rest later in the wagon. It's all arranged, the clerk will go with you, most of the soldiers are at the Commander's funeral, nothing can happen to you. Do a good job, don't lose anything, Kattrin, think of your trousseau!

Kattrin ties a cloth around her head and leaves with the Clerk.

Chaplain: You don't mind her going with the clerk?
Mother Courage: She's not so pretty anyone would want to ruin her.
Chaplain: The way you run your business and always come through is highly commendable, Mother Courage — I see how you got your name.
Mother Courage: The poor need courage. Why? They're lost. That they even get up in the morning is something — in *their* plight. Or that they plough a field — in war time. Even their bringing children into the world shows they have courage, for they have no prospects. They have to hang each other one by one and slaughter each other in the lump, so if they want to look each other in the face once in a while, well, it takes courage. That they put up with an Emperor and a Pope, that takes an unnatural amount of courage, for *they* cost you your life. (*She sits, takes a small pipe from her pocket and smokes it.*) You might chop me a bit of firewood.
Chaplain (reluctantly taking his coat off and preparing to chop wood): Properly speaking, I'm a pastor of souls, not a woodcutter.
Mother Courage: But I don't have a soul. And I do need wood.
Chaplain: What's that little pipe you've got there?
Mother Courage: Just a pipe.

Chaplain: I think it's a very particular pipe.

Mother Courage: Oh?

Chaplain: The cook's pipe in fact. The cook from the Oxenstierna Regiment.

Mother Courage: If you know, why beat about the bush?

Chaplain: Because I don't know if you've been *aware* that's what you've been smoking. It was possible you just rummaged among your belongings and your fingers just lit on a pipe and you just took it. In pure absent-mindedness.

Mother Courage: How do you know that's not it?

Chaplain: It isn't. You *are* aware of it. (*He brings the ax down on the block with a crash.*)

Mother Courage: What if I was?

Chaplain: I must give you a warning, Mother Courage, it's my duty. You are unlikely to see the gentleman again but that's no pity, you're in luck. Mother Courage, he did not impress me as trustworthy. On the contrary.

Mother Courage: Really? He was such a nice man.

Chaplain: Well! So that's what you call a nice man. I do not. (*The ax falls again.*) Far be it from me to wish him ill, but I cannot — cannot — describe him as nice. No, no, he's a Don Juan, a cunning Don Juan. Just look at that pipe if you don't believe me. You must admit it tells all.

Mother Courage: I see nothing special in it. It's been used, of course.

Chaplain: It's bitten halfway through! He's a man of great violence! It is the pipe of a man of great violence, you can see *that* if you've any judgment left! (*He deals the block a tremendous blow.*)

Mother Courage: Don't bite my chopping block halfway through!

Chaplain: I told you I had no training as a woodcutter. The care of souls was my field. Around here my gifts and capabilities are grossly misused. In physical labor my God-given talents find no — um — adequate expression — which is a sin. You haven't heard me preach. Why, I can put such spirit into a regiment with a single sermon that the enemy's a mere flock of sheep to them and their own lives no more than smelly old shoes to be thrown away at the thought of final victory! God has given me the gift of tongues. I can preach you out of your senses!

Mother Courage: I need my senses. What would I do without them?

Chaplain: Mother Courage, I have often thought that — under a veil of plain speech — you conceal a heart. You are human, you need warmth.

Mother Courage: The best way of warming this tent is to chop plenty of firewood.

Chaplain: You're changing the subject. Seriously, my dear Courage, I sometimes ask myself how it would be if our relationship should be somewhat more firmly cemented. I mean, now the wild wind of war has whirled us so strangely together.

Mother Courage: The cement's pretty firm already. I cook your meals. And you lend a hand — at chopping firewood, for instance.

Chaplain (*going over to her, gesturing with the ax*): You know what I mean by a close relationship. It has nothing to do with eating and woodcutting and such base necessities. Let your heart speak!

Mother Courage: Don't come at me like that with your ax, that'd be *too* close a relationship!

Chaplain: This is no laughing matter, I am in earnest. I've thought it all over.

Mother Courage: Dear Chaplain, be a sensible fellow. I like you, and I don't want to heap coals of fire on your head. All I want is to bring me and my children through in that wagon. It isn't just mine, the wagon, and anyway I've no mind to start any adventures. At the moment I'm taking quite a risk buying these things when the Commander's fallen and there's all this talk of peace. Where would you go, if I was ruined? See? You don't even know. Now chop some firewood and it'll be warm of an evening, which is quite a lot in times like these. What was that? *(She stands up. Kattrin enters, breathless, with a wound across the eye and forehead. She is dragging all sorts of articles, parcels, leather goods, a drum, etc.)* What is it, were you attacked? On the way back? She was attacked on the way back! I'll bet it was that soldier who got drunk on my liquor. I should never have let you go. Dump all that stuff! It's not bad, the wound is only a flesh wound. I'll bandage it for you, it'll all be healed up in a week. They're worse than animals. *(She bandages the wound.)*

Chaplain: I reproach them with nothing. At home they never did these shameful things. The men who start the wars are responsible, they bring out the worst in people.

Mother Courage: Didn't the clerk walk you back home? That's because you're a respectable girl, he thought they'd leave you alone. The wound's not at all deep, it will never show. There: all bandaged up. Now, I've got something for you, rest easy. I've been keeping them secret. *(She digs Yvette's red boots out of a bag.)* Well, what do you see? You always wanted them. Now you have them. *(She helps her to put the boots on.)* Put them on quick, before I change my mind. It will never show, though it wouldn't bother *me* if it did. The ones they like fare worst. They drag them around till they're finished. Those they don't care for they leave alone. I've seen so many girls, pretty as they come in the beginning, then all of a sudden they're so ugly they'd scare a wolf. They can't even go behind a tree on the street without having something to fear from it. They lead a frightful life. Like with trees: the tall, straight ones are cut down for roof timber, and the crooked ones can enjoy life. So this wound here is really a piece of luck. The boots have kept well. I gave them a good cleaning before I put them away.

Kattrin leaves the boots and creeps into the wagon.

Chaplain (when she's gone): I hope she won't be disfigured?

Mother Courage: There'll be a scar. She needn't wait for peace now.

Chaplain: She didn't let them get any of the stuff.

Mother Courage: Maybe I shouldn't have made such a point of it. If only I ever knew what went on inside her head. Once she stayed out all night, once in all the years. Afterward she seemed much the same, except that she worked harder. I could never get out of her what happened. I worried about it for quite a while. *(She picks up the things Kattrin spilled and sorts them angrily.)* This is war. A nice source of income, I must say!

Cannon shots.

Chaplain: Now they're lowering the Commander into his grave! A historic moment.

Mother Courage: It's a historic moment to me when they hit my daughter over the eye. She's all but finished now, she'll never get a husband, and she's so mad about children! Even her dumbness comes from the war. A soldier stuck something in her mouth when she was little. I'll never see Swiss Cheese again, and where my Eilif is the Good Lord knows. Curse the war!

VII

Mother Courage at the height of her business career.

A highway. The Chaplain, Mother Courage, and her daughter Kattrin pull the wagon, and new wares are hanging from it. Mother Courage wears a necklace of silver coins.

Mother Courage: I won't let you spoil my war for me. Destroys the weak, does it? Well, what does peace do for 'em, huh? War feeds its people better.

She sings:

> If war don't suit your disposition
> When victory comes, you will be dead.
> War is a business proposition:
> But not with cheese, with steel instead!
> Christians, awake! Winter is gone!
> The snows depart! Dead men sleep on!
> Let all of you who still survive
> Get out of bed and look alive!

And staying in one place won't help either. Those who stay at home are the first to go.

She sings:

> Too many seek a bed to sleep in:
> Each ditch is taken, and each cave
> And he who digs a hole to creep in
> Finds he has dug an early grave.
> And many a man spends many a minute
> In hurrying toward some resting place.
> You wonder, when at last he's in it
> Just why the fellow forced the pace.

The wagon proceeds.

VIII

1632. In this same year Gustavus Adolphus fell in the battle of Lützen. The peace threatens Mother Courage with ruin. Her brave son performs one heroic deed too many and comes to a shameful end.

A camp. A summer morning. In front of the wagon, an Old Woman and her son. The son is dragging a large bag of bedding.

Mother Courage (from inside the wagon): Must you come at the crack of dawn?

Young Man: We've been walking all night, twenty miles it was, we have to be back today.

Mother Courage (still inside): What do I want with bed feathers? People don't even have houses.

Young Man: At least wait till you see 'em.

Old Woman: Nothing doing here either, let's go.

Young Man: And let 'em sign away the roof over our heads for taxes? Maybe she'll pay three guilders if you throw in that bracelet. *(Bells start ringing.)* You hear, mother?

Voices (from the rear): It's peace! The King of Sweden's been killed!

Mother Courage sticks her head out of the wagon. She hasn't done her hair yet.

Mother Courage: Bells! What are the bells for, middle of the week?

Chaplain (crawling out from under the wagon): What's that they're shouting?

Young Man: It's peace.

Chaplain: Peace!

Mother Courage: Don't tell me peace has broken out — when I've just gone and bought all these supplies!

Chaplain (calling, toward the rear): Is it peace?

Voice (from a distance): They say the war stopped three weeks ago. I've only just heard.

Chaplain (to Mother Courage): Or why would they ring the bells?

Voice: A great crowd of Lutherans have just arrived with wagons — they brought the news.

Young Man: It's peace, mother. *(The Old Woman collapses.)* What's the matter?

Mother Courage (back in the wagon): Kattrin, it's peace! Put on your black dress, we're going to church, we owe it to Swiss Cheese! Can it be true?

Young Man: The people here say so too, the war's over. Can you stand up? *(The Old Woman stands up, dazed.)* I'll get the harness shop going again now, I promise you. Everything'll be all right, father will get his bed back. . . . Can you walk? *(To the Chaplain:)* She felt ill, it was the news. She didn't believe there'd ever be peace again. Father always said there would. We're going home. *(They leave.)*

Mother Courage (off): Give her some brandy.

Chaplain: They've left already.

Mother Courage (still off): What's going on in the camp over there?

Chaplain: They're all getting together. I think I'll go over. Shall I put my pastor's coat on again?

Mother Courage: Better get the exact news first, and not risk being taken for the Antichrist. I'm glad about the peace even though I'm ruined. At least I've got two of my children through the war. Now I'll see my Eilif again.

Chaplain: And who may this be coming down from the camp? Well, if it isn't our Swedish Commander's cook!

Cook (somewhat bedraggled, carrying a bundle): Who's here? The chaplain!

Chaplain: Mother Courage, a visitor!

Mother Courage clambers out.

Cook: Well, I promised I'd come over for a brief conversation as soon as I had time. I didn't forget your brandy, Mrs. Fierling.

Mother Courage: Jesus, the Commander's cook! After all these years! Where is Eilif, my eldest?

Cook: Isn't he here yet? He went on ahead yesterday, he was on his way over.

Chaplain: I *will* put my pastor's coat on. I'll be back. *(He goes behind the wagon.)*

Mother Courage: He may be here any minute then. *(She calls toward the wagon:)* Kattrin, Eilif's coming! Bring a glass of brandy for the cook, Kattrin! *(Kattrin doesn't come.)* Just pull your hair over it. Mr. Lamb is no stranger. *(She gets the brandy herself.)* She won't come out. Peace is nothing to her, it was too long coming. They hit her right over the eye. You can hardly see it now. But she thinks people stare at her.

Cook: Ah yes, war! *(He and Mother Courage sit.)*

Mother Courage: Cook, you come at a bad time: I'm ruined.

Cook: What? That's terrible!

Mother Courage: The peace has broken my neck. On the chaplain's advice I've gone and bought a lot of supplies. Now everybody's leaving and I'm holding the baby.

Cook: How could you listen to the chaplain? If I'd had time — but the Catholics were too quick for me — I'd have warned you against him. He's a windbag. Well, so now he's the big man round here!

Mother Courage: He's been doing the dishes for me and helping with the wagon.

Cook: With the wagon — him! And I'll bet he's told you a few of his jokes. He has a most unhealthy attitude toward women. I tried to influence him but it was no good. He isn't sound.

Mother Courage: Are you sound?

Cook: If I'm nothing else, I'm sound. Your health!

Mother Courage: Sound! Only one person around here was ever sound, and I never had to slave as I did then. He sold the blankets off the children's beds in the spring, and he called my harmonica unchristian. You aren't recommending yourself if you *admit* you're sound.

Cook: You fight tooth and nail, don't you? I like that.

Mother Courage: Don't tell me you've been dreaming of my teeth and nails.

Cook: Well, here we sit, while the bells of peace do ring, and you pouring your famous brandy as only you know how!

Mother Courage: I don't think much of the bells of peace at the moment. I don't see how they can hand out all this pay that's in arrears. And then where shall I be with my famous brandy? Have you all been paid?

Cook (hesitating): Not exactly. That's why we disbanded. In the circumstances, I thought, why stay? For the time being, I'll look up a couple of friends. So here I sit — with you.

Mother Courage: In other words, you're broke.

Cook (annoyed by the bells): It's about time they stopped that racket! I'd like to set myself up in some business. I'm fed up with being their cook. I'm supposed to make do with tree roots and shoe leather, and then they throw my hot soup in my face! Being a cook nowadays is a dog's life. I'd sooner be a soldier, but of course, it's peace now. *(As the Chaplain turns up, wearing his old coat:)* We'll talk it over later.

Chaplain: The coat's pretty good. Just a few moth holes.

Cook: I don't know why you take the trouble. You won't find another pulpit.

Who could you incite now to earn an honest living or risk his life for a cause? Besides. I have a bone to pick with you.

Chaplain: Have you?

Cook: I have. You advised a lady to buy superfluous goods on the pretext that the war would never end.

Chaplain (hotly): I'd like to know what business it is of yours?

Cook: It's unprincipled behavior! How can you give unwanted advice? And interfere with the conduct of other people's business?

Chaplain: Who's interfering now, I'd like to know? *(To Mother Courage:)* I had no idea you were such a close friend of this gentleman and had to account to *him* for everything.

Mother Courage: Now don't get excited. The cook's giving his personal opinion. You can't deny your war was a flop.

Chaplain: You have no respect for peace, Courage. You're a hyena of the battle-field!

Mother Courage: A what?

Cook: Who insults my girl friend insults me!

Chaplain: I am *not* speaking to you, your intentions are only too transparent! *(To Mother Courage:)* But when I see *you* take peace between finger and thumb like a snotty old hanky, my humanity rebels! It shows that you want war, not peace, for what you get out of it. But don't forget the proverb: he who sups with the devil must use a long spoon!

Mother Courage: Remember what one fox said to another that was caught in a trap? "If you stay there, you're just asking for trouble!" There isn't much love lost between me and the war. And when it comes to calling me a hyena, you and I part company.

Chaplain: Then why all this grumbling about the peace just as everyone's heaving a sigh of relief? Is it for the junk in your wagon?

Mother Courage: My goods are not junk. I live off them. *You've* been living off them.

Chaplain: You live off war. Exactly.

Cook (to the Chaplain): As a grown man, you should know better than to go around advising people. *(To Mother Courage:)* Now, in your situation you'd be smart to get rid of certain goods at once — before the prices sink to nothing. Get ready and get going, there isn't a moment to lose!

Mother Courage: That's sensible advice, I think I'll take it.

Chaplain: Because the cook says so.

Mother Courage: Why didn't *you* say so? He's right, I must get to the market. *(She climbs into the wagon.)*

Cook: One up for me, Chaplain. You have no presence of mind. You should have said, "I gave you advice? Why, I was just talking politics!" And you shouldn't take me on as a rival. Cockfights are not becoming to your cloth.

Chaplain: If you don't shut your trap, I'll murder you, cloth or no cloth!

Cook (taking his boots off and unwinding the wrappings on his feet): If you hadn't degenerated into a godless tramp, you could easily get yourself a par-sonage, now it's peace. Cooks won't be needed, there's nothing to cook, but there's still plenty to believe, and people will go right on believing it.

Chaplain: Mr. Lamb, please don't drive me out! Since I became a tramp, I'm a somewhat better man. I couldn't preach to 'em any more.

Yvette Pottier enters, decked out in black, with a stick. She is much older, fatter, and heavily powdered. Behind her, a Servant.

Yvette: Hullo, everybody! Is this Mother Courage's establishment?

Chaplain: Quite right. And with whom have we the pleasure?

Yvette: I am Madame Colonel Starhemberg, good people. Where's Mother Courage?

Chaplain (calling to the wagon): Madame Colonel Starhemberg wants to speak to you!

Mother Courage (from inside): Coming!

Yvette (calling): It's Yvette!

Mother Courage (inside): Yvette!

Yvette: Just to see how you're getting on! *(As the Cook turns around in horror:)* Peter!

Cook: Yvette!

Yvette: Of all things! How did *you* get here?

Cook: On a cart.

Chaplain: Well! You know each other? Intimately?

Yvette: I'll say. *(Scrutinizing the Cook:)* You're fat.

Cook: For that matter, *you're* no beanpole.

Yvette: Anyway, it's lucky we've met, tramp. Now I can tell you what I think of you.

Chaplain: Do so, tell him all, but wait till Mother Courage comes out.

Cook: Now don't make a scene . . .

Mother Courage (coming out, laden with goods): Yvette! *(They embrace.)* But why are you in mourning?

Yvette: Doesn't it suit me? My husband, the colonel, died several years ago.

Mother Courage: The old fellow that nearly bought my wagon?

Yvette: His elder brother.

Mother Courage: So you're not doing badly. Good to see one person who got somewhere in the war.

Yvette: I've had my ups and downs.

Mother Courage: Don't let's speak ill of colonels. They make money like hay.

Chaplain (to the Cook): If I were you, I'd put my shoes on again. *(To Yvette:)* You promised to give us your opinion of this gentleman.

Cook: Now, Yvette, don't make a stink!

Mother Courage: He's a friend of mine, Yvette.

Yvette: He's — Peter Piper, that's who.

Mother Courage: What!

Cook: Cut the nicknames. My name's Lamb.

Mother Courage (laughing): Peter Piper? Who turned the women's heads? And I've been keeping your pipe for you.

Chaplain: And smoking it.

Yvette: Lucky I can warn you against him. He's a bad lot. You won't find worse on the whole coast of Flanders. He got more girls in trouble than . . .

Cook: That's a long time ago, it isn't true any more.

Yvette: Stand up when you talk to a lady! Oh, how I loved that man; and all the time he was having a little bowlegged brunette. He got *her* into trouble too, of course.

Cook: I seem to have brought *you* luck!

Yvette: Shut your trap, you hoary ruin! And you take care, Mother Courage, this type is still dangerous even in decay!

Mother Courage (to Yvette): Come with me, I must get rid of this stuff before the prices fall.

Yvette (concentrating on the Cook): Miserable cur!

Mother Courage: Maybe you can help me at army headquarters, you have contacts.

Yvette: Seducer!

Mother Courage (shouting into the wagon): Kattrin, church is all off, I'm going to market!

Yvette: Whore hunter!

Mother Courage (still to Kattrin): When Eilif comes, give him something to drink!

Yvette: That a man like him should have been able to turn me from the straight and narrow! I have my own star to thank that I rose none the less to the heights! But I've put an end to your tricks, Peter Piper, and one day — in a better life than this — the Lord God will reward me! Come, Mother Courage! *(She leaves with Mother Courage.)*

Chaplain: As our text this morning let us take the saying: the mills of God grind slowly. And you complain of my jokes!

Cook: I never have any luck. I'll be frank, I was hoping for a good hot dinner, I'm starving. And now they'll be talking about me, and she'll get a completely wrong picture. I think I should go before she comes back.

Chaplain: I think so too.

Cook: Chaplain, peace makes me sick. Mankind must perish by fire and sword, we're born and bred in sin! Oh, how I wish I was roasting a great fat capon for the Commander — God knows where *he's* got to — with mustard sauce and those little yellow carrots . . .

Chaplain: Red cabbage — with capon, red cabbage.

Cook: You're right. But he always wanted yellow carrots.

Chaplain: He never understood a thing.

Cook: You always put plenty away.

Chaplain: Under protest.

Cook: Anyway, you must admit, those were the days.

Chaplain: Yes, that I might admit.

Cook: Now you've called her a hyena, there's not much future for you here either. What are you staring at?

Chaplain: It's Eilif!

Followed by two soldiers with halberds, Eilif enters. His hands are fettered. He is white as chalk.

Chaplain: What's happened to you?

Eilif: Where's mother?

Chaplain: Gone to town.

Eilif: They said she was here. I was allowed a last visit.

Cook (to the Soldiers): Where are you taking him?

A Soldier: For a ride.

The other Soldier makes the gesture of throat cutting.

Chaplain: What has he done?

Soldier: He broke in on a peasant. The wife is dead.

Chaplain: Eilif, how could you?

Eilif: It's no different. It's what I did before.

Cook: That was in war time.

Eilif: Shut your hole. Can I sit down till she comes?

Soldier: No.

Chaplain: It's true. In war time they honored him for it. He sat at the Commander's right hand. It was bravery. Couldn't we speak with the military police?

Soldier: What's the use? Stealing cattle from a peasant, what's brave about that?

Cook: It was just stupid.

Eilif: If I'd been stupid, I'd have starved, smarty.

Cook: So you were bright and paid for it.

Chaplain: At least we must bring Kattrin out.

Eilif: Let her alone. Just give me some brandy.

Soldier: No.

Chaplain: What shall we tell your mother?

Eilif: Tell her it was no different. Tell her it was the same. Oh, tell her nothing.

The Soldiers take him away.

Chaplain: I'll come with you, I'll . . .

Eilif: I don't need a priest!

Chaplain: You don't know — yet. *(He follows him.)*

Cook (calling after him): I'll have to tell her, she'll want to see him!

Chaplain: Better tell her nothing. Or maybe just that he was here, and he'll return, maybe tomorrow. Meantime I'll be back and can break the news. *(He leaves quickly.)*

The Cook looks after him, shakes his head, then walks about uneasily. Finally, he approaches the wagon.

Cook: Hello! Won't you come out? You want to sneak away from the peace, don't you? Well, so do I! I'm the Swedish Commander's cook, remember me? I was wondering if you've got anything to eat in there — while we're waiting for your mother. I wouldn't mind a bit of bacon — or even bread — just to pass the time. *(He looks in.)* She's got a blanket over her head.

The thunder of cannon. Mother Courage runs in, out of breath, still carrying the goods.

Mother Courage: Cook, the peace is over, the war's on again, has been for three days! I didn't get rid of this stuff after all, thank God! There's a shooting match in the town already — with the Lutherans. We must get away with the wagon. Pack, Kattrin! What's on *your* mind? Something the matter?

Cook: Nothing.

Mother Courage: But there is. I see it in your face.

Cook: Because the war's on again, most likely. May it last till tomorrow evening, so I can get something in my belly!

Mother Courage: You're not telling me.

Cook: Eilif was here. Only he had to go away again.

Mother Courage: He was here? Then we'll see him on the march. I'll be with our side this time. How'd he look?

Cook: The same.

Mother Courage: He'll *never* change. And the war couldn't get *him*, he's bright. Help me with the packing. *(She starts it.)* Did he tell you anything? Is he well in with the Provost? Did he tell you about his heroic deeds?

Cook (darkly): He's done one of them again.

Mother Courage: Tell me about it later. *(Kattrin appears.)* Kattrin, the peace is over, we're on the move again. *(To the Cook:)* What *is* the matter with you?

Cook: I'll enlist.

Mother Courage: A good idea. Where's the Chaplain?

Cook: In the town. With Eilif.

Mother Courage: Stay with us a while, Lamb, I need a bit of help.

Cook: This matter of Yvette . . .

Mother Courage: Hasn't done you any harm at all in my eyes. Just the opposite. Where there's smoke, there's fire, they say. You'll come?

Cook: I may as well.

Mother Courage: The Twelfth Regiment's under way. Into harness with you! Maybe I'll see Eilif before the day is out, just think! That's what I like best. Well, it wasn't such a long peace, we can't grumble. Let's go!

The Cook and Kattrin are in harness.

Mother Courage sings:

> From Ulm to Metz, past dome and steeple
> My wagon always moves ahead.
> The war can care for all its people
> So long as there is steel and lead.
> Though steel and lead are stout supporters
> A war needs human beings too.
> Report today to your headquarters!
> If it's to last, this war needs you!

IX

The great war of religion has lasted sixteen years and Germany has lost half its inhabitants. Those who are spared in battle die by plague. Over once blooming countryside hunger rages. Towns are burned down. Wolves prowl the empty streets. In the autumn of 1634 we find Mother Courage in the Fichtelgebirge not far from the road the Swedish army is taking. Winter has come early and is hard. Business is bad. Only begging remains. The cook receives a letter from Utrecht and is sent packing.

In front of a half-ruined parsonage. Early winter. A gray morning. Gusts of wind. Mother Courage and the Cook at the wagon in shabby clothes.

Cook: There are no lights on. No one's up.

Mother Courage: But it's a parsonage. The parson'll have to leave his feather bed and ring the bells. Then he'll have some hot soup.

Cook: Where'll he get it from? The whole village is starving.

Mother Courage: The house is lived in. There was a dog barking.

Cook: If the parson has anything, he'll hang on to it.

Mother Courage: Maybe if we sang him something . . .

Cook: I've had enough. *(Suddenly:)* I didn't tell you, a letter came from Utrecht. My mother's died of cholera, the inn is mine. There's the letter, if you don't believe me. I'll show it to you, though my aunt's railing about me and my ups and downs is none of your business.

Mother Courage (reading): Lamb, I'm tired of wandering, too. I feel like a butcher's dog taking meat to my customers and getting none myself. I've nothing more to sell and people have nothing to pay with. In Saxony someone tried to force a chestful of books on me in return for two eggs. And in Württemberg they would have let me have their plough for a bag of salt. Nothing grows any more, only thorn bushes. In Pomerania I heard the villagers have been eating their younger children. Nuns have been caught committing robbery.

Cook: The world's dying out.

Mother Courage: Sometimes I see myself driving through hell with this wagon and selling brimstone. And sometimes I'm driving through heaven handing out provisions to wandering souls! If only we could find a place where there's no shooting, me and my children — what's left of 'em — we might rest a while.

Cook: We could open this inn together. Think about it, Courage. *My* mind's made up. With or without you, I'm leaving for Utrecht. And today too.

Mother Courage: I must talk to Kattrin, it's a bit sudden, and I don't like to make my decisions in the cold on an empty stomach. *(Kattrin emerges from the wagon.)* Kattrin, I've something to tell you. The cook and I want to go to Utrecht, he's been left an inn. You'd be able to stay put and get to know some people. Many a man'd be prepared to take on a girl with a position. Looks aren't everything. I like the idea. I get on well with the cook. I'll say this for him: he has a head for business. We'd be sure of our dinner, that would be all right, wouldn't it? You'd have your own bed, what do you think of *that?* In the long run, this is no life, on the road. You might be killed any time. You're eaten up with lice as it is. And we must decide now, because otherwise we go north with the Swedes. They must be over there somewhere. *(She points left.)* I think we'll decide to go, Kattrin.

Cook: Anna, I must have a word with you alone.

Mother Courage: Go back inside, Kattrin.

Kattrin does so.

Cook: I'm interrupting because there's a misunderstanding, Anna. I thought I wouldn't have to say it right out, but I see I must. If you're bringing *her,* it's all off. Do we understand each other?

Kattrin has her head out of the back of the wagon and is listening.

Mother Courage: You mean I leave Kattrin behind?

Cook: What do you think? There's no room in the inn, it isn't one of those places with three counters. If the two of us look lively we can earn a living, but three's too many. Let Kattrin keep your wagon.

Mother Courage: I was thinking we might find her a husband in Utrecht.

Cook: Don't make me laugh. With that scar? And old as she is? And dumb?

Mother Courage: Not so loud!

Cook: Loud or soft, what is, is. That's another reason I can't have her in the inn. Customers don't like having something like that always before their eyes. You can't blame them.

Mother Courage: Shut up. I told you not to talk so loud.

Cook: There's a light in the parsonage, we can sing now!

Mother Courage: Cook, how could she pull the wagon by herself? The war frightens her. She can't bear it. She has terrible dreams. I hear her groan at night, especially after battles. What she sees in her dreams I don't know. She suffers from sheer pity. The other day I found her with a hedgehog that we'd run over.

Cook: The inn's too small. *(Calling:)* Worthy Sir, menials, and all within! We now present the song of Solomon, Julius Caesar, and other great souls who came to no good, so you can see we're law-abiding folk too, and have a hard time getting by, especially in winter.

He sings "The Song of the Great Souls of this Earth":

> King Solomon was very wise,
> So what's his history?
> He came to view this life with scorn,
> Yes, he came to regret he ever had been born
> Declaring: all is vanity.
> King Solomon was very wise,
> But long before the day was out
> The consequence was clear, alas:
> His wisdom 'twas that brought him to this pass.
> A man is better off without.

For the virtues are dangerous in this world, as our fine song tells. You're better off without, you have a nice life, breakfast included — some good hot soup maybe . . . I'm an example of a man who's not had any, and I'd like some, I'm a soldier, but what good did my bravery do me in all those battles? None at all. I might just as well have wet my pants like a poltroon and stayed at home. For why?

> Old Julius Caesar, he was brave.
> His fame shall never cease.
> He sat like a god on an altar piece.
> Yet they tore brave old Julius limb from valiant limb
> And Brutus helped to slaughter him.
> Old Julius was very brave
> But long before the day was out
> The consequence was clear, alas:
> His bravery 'twas that brought him to this pass.
> A man is better off without.

(Under his breath:) They don't even look out. *(Aloud:)* Worthy Sir, menials, and all within! You could say, no, courage isn't the thing to fill a man's belly, try honesty, that should be worth a dinner, at any rate it must have *some* effect. Let's see.

You all know honest Socrates
Who always spoke the truth.
They owed him thanks for that, you'd think,
But what happened? Why, they put hemlock in his drink
And swore that he misled the youth.
How honest was this Socrates!
Yet long before the day was out
The consequence was clear, alas:
His honesty had brought him to this pass.
A man is better off without.

Yes, we're told to be unselfish and share what we have, but what if we have nothing? And those who do share it don't have an easy time either, for what's left when you're through sharing? Unselfishness is a very rare virtue — it doesn't pay.

Unselfish Martin could not bear
His fellow creatures' woes.
He met a poor man in the snows
And he gave this poor fellow half his cloak to wear:
So both of them fell down and froze.
His brothers' woes he could not bear,
So long before the day was out
The consequence was clear, alas:
Unselfishness had brought him to this pass.
A man is better off without.

That's how it is with us. We're law-abiding folk, we keep to ourselves, don't steal, don't kill, don't burn the place down. And in this way we sink lower and lower and the song proves true and there's no soup going. And if we were different, if we were thieves and killers, maybe we could eat our fill! For virtues bring no reward, only vices. Such is the world, need it be so?

God's ten commandments we have kept
And acted as we should.
It has not done us any good.
All you people who sit beside a roaring fire
O help us in our need so dire!
The ten commandments we have kept
And long before the day was out
The consequence was clear, alas:
Our godliness has brought us to this pass.
A man is better off without.

Voice (from above): You there! Come up! There's some soup here for you!

Mother Courage: Lamb, I couldn't swallow a thing. I don't say what you said is unreasonable, but was it your last word? We've always understood each other.

Cook: Yes, Anna. Think it over.

Mother Courage: There's nothing to think over. I'm not leaving her here.

Cook: You're going to be silly, but what can I do? I'm not inhuman, it's just that the inn's a small one. And now we must go up, or there'll be nothing doing here too, and we've been singing in the cold for nothing.

Mother Courage: I'll fetch Kattrin.

Cook: Better stick something in your pocket for her. If there are three of us, they'll get a shock.

Exeunt.

Kattrin clambers out of the wagon with a bundle. She makes sure they are both gone. Then, on a wagon wheel, she lays out a skirt of her mother's and a pair of the cook's trousers side by side and easy to see. She has just finished, and has picked up her bundle, when Mother Courage returns.

Mother Courage (with a plate of soup): Kattrin! Stay where you are, Kattrin! Where do you think you're going with that bundle? *(She examines the bundle.)* She's packed her things. Were you listening? I told him there was nothing doing, he can *have* Utrecht and his lousy inn, what would we want with a lousy inn? *(She sees the skirt and trousers.)* Oh, you're a stupid girl, Kattrin, what if I'd seen that and you gone? *(She takes hold of Kattrin who is trying to leave.)* And don't think I've sent him packing on your account. It was the wagon. You can't part us, I'm too used to it, it was the wagon. Now we're leaving and we'll put the cook's things here where he'll find 'em, the stupid man. *(She clambers up and throws a couple of things down to go with the trousers.)* There! He's fired. The last man I'll take into *this* business! Now let's be going, you and me. This winter'll pass, like all the others. Get into harness, it looks like snow.

They harness themselves to the wagon, turn it around, and start out. A gust of wind. Enter the Cook, still chewing. He sees his things.

X

During the whole of 1635 Mother Courage and Kattrin pull the wagon along the roads of central Germany in the wake of the ever more tattered armies.

On the highway. Mother Courage and Kattrin are pulling the wagon. They come to a prosperous farmhouse. Someone inside is singing.

Voice:

> In March a bush we planted
> To make the garden gay.
> In June we were enchanted:
> A lovely rose was blooming
> The balmy air perfuming!
> Blest are they
> Who have gardens gay!
> In June we were enchanted.
>
> When snow falls helter-skelter
> And loudly blows the storm

Our farmhouse gives us shelter.
The winter's in a hurry
But we've no cause to worry.
We are warm
In the midst of the storm!
Our farmhouse gives us shelter.

Mother Courage and Kattrin have stopped to listen. Then they start out again.

XI

January, 1636. Catholic troops threaten the Protestant town of Halle. The stone begins to speak. Mother Courage loses her daughter and journeys onward alone. The war is not yet near its end.

The wagon, very far gone now, stands near a farmhouse with a straw roof. It is night. Out of the woods come a Lieutenant and three Soldiers in full armor.

Lieutenant: And there mustn't be a sound. If anyone yells, cut him down.
First Soldier: But we'll have to knock — if we want a guide.
Lieutenant: Knocking's a natural noise, it's all right, could be a cow hitting the wall of the cowshed.

The Soldiers knock at the farmhouse door. An Old Peasant Woman opens. A hand is clapped over her mouth. Two Soldiers enter.

A Man's Voice: What is it?

The Soldiers bring out an Old Peasant and his son.

Lieutenant (pointing to the wagon on which Kattrin has appeared): There's one. *(A Soldier pulls her out.)* Is this everybody that lives here?
Peasants (alternating): That's our son. And that's a girl that can't talk. Her mother's in town buying up stocks because the shopkeepers are running away and selling cheap. They're canteen people.
Lieutenant: I'm warning you. Keep quiet. One sound and we'll crack you over the head with a pike. And I need someone to show us the path to the town. *(He points to the Young Peasant:)* You! Come here!
Young Peasant: I don't know any path!
Second Soldier (grinning): He don't know any path!
Young Peasant: I don't help Catholics.
Lieutenant (to the Second Soldier): Let him feel your pike in his side.
Young Peasant (forced to his knees, the pike at his throat): I'd rather die!
Second Soldier (again mimicking): He'd rather die!
First Soldier: I know how to change his mind. *(He walks over to the cowshed.)* Two cows and a bull. Listen, you. If you aren't going to be reasonable, I'll saber your cattle.
Young Peasant: Not the cattle!
Peasant Woman (weeping): Spare the cattle, Captain, or we'll starve!
Lieutenant: If he must be pigheaded!
First Soldier: I think I'll start with the bull.
Young Peasant (to the old one): Do I have to? *(The older one nods.)* I'll do it.

Peasant Woman: Thank you, thank you, Captain, for sparing us, for ever and ever, Amen.

The Old Man stops her going on thanking him.

First Soldier: I knew the bull came first all right!

Led by the Young Peasant, the Lieutenant and the Soldiers go on their way.

Old Peasant: I wish we knew what it was. Nothing good, I suppose.

Peasant Woman: Maybe they're just scouts. What are you doing?

Old Peasant (setting a ladder against the roof and climbing up): I'm seeing if they're alone. *(On the roof.)* Things are moving — all over. I can see armor. And cannon. There must be more than a regiment. God have mercy on the town and all within!

Peasant Woman: Are there lights in the town?

Old Peasant: No, they're all asleep. *(He climbs down.)* There'll be an attack, and they'll all be slaughtered in their beds.

Peasant Woman: The watchman'll give warning.

Old Peasant: They must have killed the watchman in the tower on the hill or he'd have sounded his horn before this.

Peasant Woman: If there were more of us . . .

Old Peasant: But being that we're alone with that cripple . . .

Peasant Woman: There's nothing we can do, is there?

Old Peasant: Nothing.

Peasant Woman: We can't get down there. In the dark.

Old Peasant: The whole hillside's swarming with 'em.

Peasant Woman: We could give a sign?

Old Peasant: And be cut down for it?

Peasant Woman: No, there's nothing we can do. *(To Kattrin:)* Pray, poor thing, pray! There's nothing we can do to stop this bloodshed, so even if you can't talk, at least pray! He hears, if no one else does. I'll help you. *(All kneel, Kattrin behind.)* Our Father, which art in Heaven, hear our prayer, let not the town perish with all that lie therein asleep and fearing nothing. Wake them, that they rise and go to the walls and see the foe that comes with fire and sword in the night down the hill and across the fields. *(Back to Kattrin:)* God protect our mother and make the watchman not sleep but wake ere it's too late. And save our son-in-law, too, O God, he's there with his four children, let them not perish, they're innocent, they know nothing — *(To Kattrin, who groans:)* — one of them's not two years old, the eldest is seven. *(Kattrin rises, troubled.)* Heavenly Father, hear us, only Thou canst help us or we die, for we are weak and have no sword nor nothing; we cannot trust our own strength but only Thine, O Lord; we are in Thy hands, our cattle, our farm, and the town too, we're all in Thy hands, and the foe is nigh unto the walls with all his power.

Kattrin, unperceived, has crept off to the wagon, has taken something out of it, put it under her apron, and has climbed up the ladder to the roof.

Be mindful of the children in danger, especially the little ones, be mindful of the old folk who cannot move, and of all Christian souls, O Lord.

Old Peasant: And forgive us our trespasses as we forgive them that trespass against us. Amen.

Sitting on the roof, Kattrin takes a drum from under her apron and starts to beat it.

Peasant Woman: Heavens, what's she doing?
Old Peasant: She's out of her mind!
Peasant Woman: Get her down, quick.

The Old Peasant runs to the ladder but Kattrin pulls it up on the roof.

She'll get us in trouble.
Old Peasant: Stop it this minute, you silly cripple!
Peasant Woman: The soldiers'll come!
Old Peasant (looking for stones): I'll stone you!
Peasant Woman: Have you no pity, have you no heart? We have relations there too, four grandchildren, but there's nothing we can do. If they find us now, it's the end, they'll stab us to death!

Kattrin is staring into the far distance, toward the town. She goes on drumming.

Peasant Woman (to the Peasant): I told you not to let that riffraff on your farm. What do *they* care if we lose our cattle?
Lieutenant (running back with Soldiers and the Young Peasant): I'll cut you all to bits!
Peasant Woman: We're innocent, sir, there's nothing we can do. She did it, a stranger!
Lieutenant: Where's the ladder?
Old Peasant: On the roof.
Lieutenant (calling): Throw down the drum. I order you! (*Kattrin goes on drumming.*) You're all in this, but you won't live to tell the tale.
Old Peasant: They've been cutting down fir trees around here. If we bring a tall enough trunk we can knock her off the roof . . .
First Soldier (to the Lieutenant): I beg leave to make a suggestion. (*He whispers something to the Lieutenant, who nods.*) Listen, you! We have an idea — for your own good. Come down and go with us to the town. Show us your mother and we'll spare her.

Kattrin goes on drumming.

Lieutenant (pushing him away): She doesn't trust you, no wonder with your face. (*He calls up to Kattrin:*) Hey, you! Suppose I give you my word? I'm an officer, my word's my bond!

Kattrin drums harder.

Nothing is sacred to her.
Young Peasant: Sir, it's not just because of her mother!
First Soldier: This can't go on, they'll hear it in the town as sure as hell.
Lieutenant: We must make another noise with something. Louder than that drum. What can we make a noise with?
First Soldier: But we mustn't make a noise!
Lieutenant: A harmless noise, fool, a peacetime noise!

Old Peasant: I could start chopping wood.

Lieutenant: That's it! *(The Peasant brings his ax and chops away.)* Chop! Chop harder! Chop for your life!

> *Kattrin has been listening, beating the drum less hard. Very upset, and peering around, she now goes on drumming.*

It's not enough. *(To the First Soldier:)* You chop too!

Old Peasant: I've only one ax. *(He stops chopping.)*

Lieutenant: We must set fire to the farm. Smoke her out.

Old Peasant: That's no good, Captain. When they see fire from the town, they'll know everything.

> *During the drumming Kattrin has been listening again. Now she laughs.*

Lieutenant: She's laughing at us, that's too much, I'll have her guts if it's the last thing I do. Bring a musket!

> *Two Soldiers off. Kattrin goes on drumming.*

Peasant Woman: I have it, Captain. That's their wagon over there, Captain. If we smash that, she'll stop. It's all they have, Captain.

Lieutenant (to the Young Peasant): Smash it! *(Calling:)* If you don't stop that noise, we'll smash your wagon!

> *The Young Peasant deals the wagon a couple of feeble blows with a board.*

Peasant Woman (to Kattrin): Stop, you little beast!

> *Kattrin stares at the wagon and pauses. Noises of distress come out of her. But she goes on drumming.*

Lieutenant: Where are those sons of bitches with that gun?

First Soldier: They can't have heard anything in the town or we'd hear their cannon.

Lieutenant (calling): They don't hear you. And now we're going to shoot you. I'll give you one more chance: throw down that drum!

Young Peasant (dropping the board, screaming to Kattrin): Don't stop now! Or they're all done for. Go on, go on, go on . . .

> *The Soldier knocks him down and beats him with his pike. Kattrin starts crying but goes on drumming.*

Peasant Woman: Not in the back, you're killing him!

> *The Soldiers arrive with the musket.*

Second Soldier: The Colonel's foaming at the mouth. We'll be court-martialed.

Lieutenant: Set it up! Set it up! *(Calling while the musket is set up on forks:)* Once and for all: stop that drumming!

> *Still crying, Kattrin is drumming as hard as she can.*

Fire!

> *The Soldiers fire. Kattrin is hit. She gives the drum another feeble beat or two, then slowly collapses.*

Lieutenant: That's an end to the noise.

> *But the last beats of the drum are lost in the din of cannon from the town. Mingled with the thunder of cannon, alarm bells are heard in the distance.*

First Soldier: She made it.

XII

> *Toward morning. The drums and pipes of troops on the march, receding. In front of the wagon Mother Courage sits by Kattrin's body. The Peasants of the last scene are standing near.*

Peasants: You must leave, woman. There's only one regiment to go. You can never get away by yourself.

Mother Courage: Maybe she's fallen asleep.

> *She sings:*

> Lullaby, baby, what's that in the hay?
> The neighbor's kids cry but mine are gay.
> The neighbor's kids are dressed in dirt:
> Your silks are cut from an angel's skirt.
> They are all starving: you have a pie.
> If it's too stale, you need only cry.
> Lullaby, baby, what's rustling there?
> One lad fell in Poland. The other is — where?

You shouldn't have told her about the children.

Peasants: If you hadn't gone off to the town to get your cut, maybe it wouldn't have happened.

Mother Courage: She's asleep now.

Peasants: She's not asleep, it's time you realized. She's gone. You must get away. There are wolves in these parts. And the bandits are worse.

Mother Courage: That's right. (*She goes and fetches a cloth from the wagon to cover up the body.*)

Peasant Woman: Have you no one now? Someone you can go to?

Mother Courage: There's one. My Eilif.

Peasant (while Mother Courage covers the body): Find him then. Leave *her* to us. We'll give her a proper burial. You needn't worry.

Mother Courage: Here's money for the expenses.

> *She pays the Peasant. The Peasant and his son shake her hand and carry Kattrin away.*

Peasant Woman (also taking her hand, and bowing, as she goes away): Hurry!

Mother Courage (harnessing herself to the wagon): I hope I can pull the wagon by myself. Yes, I'll manage, there's not much in it now. I must get back into business.

> *Another regiment passes at the rear with pipe and drum. Mother Courage starts pulling the wagon.*

Mother Courage: Hey! Take me with you!

Soldiers are heard singing:

> Dangers, surprises, devastations!
> The war moves on, but will not quit.
> And though it last three generations,
> We shall get nothing out of it.
> Starvation, filth, and cold enslave us.
> The army robs us of our pay.
> But God may yet come down and save us:
> His holy war won't end today.
>> Christians, awake! Winter is gone!
>> The snows depart! Dead men sleep on!
>> Let all of you who still survive
>> Get out of bed and look alive!

QUESTIONS

SCENE ONE

1. In the opening speech of the play, what is ironic in the recruiting officer's complaint that people have no trust in one another, no sense of honor any more?
2. What is your reaction to the story of how Mother Courage was given her name? Would you call her defying the bombardment an act of courage? What else about her character does the rest of this scene reveal?

SCENE TWO

1. By what deeds has Eilif risen in the favor of his commanding officer? How do the Commander and Mother Courage differ in their opinions of Eilif's "bravery"?
2. Mother Courage to the Cook: "In a good country virtues wouldn't be necessary." Why not? Explain what you understand her to mean by this statement.

SCENE THREE

1. Why does Kattrin covet Yvette's red boots?
2. What contrasting views of the war do the Cook and the Chaplain express? What view of the war do we receive from Mother Courage?
3. Why is Mother Courage so reluctant to part with her wagon?
4. Why does she not claim her son's body?

SCENE FOUR

1. When we first see Mother Courage waiting outside the Captain's tent, about what — besides the loss of her merchandise — do we expect her to plead?
2. What argument does she express in "The Song of the Great Capitulation"? How does this argument figure not only in this scene, but in the whole play?
3. Why does the young soldier depart in such bitterness, hurling an insult at Mother Courage?

4. For what reason does Mother Courage apparently decide not to file her complaint after all?

SCENE FIVE

1. What does this scene reveal about the characters of (a) Kattrin, (b) the Chaplain, and (c) Mother Courage?

SCENE SIX

1. Note the contrast between the burial of Tilly, the leader who has fallen in battle, and the wounding of Kattrin. What point do you think Brecht, by drawing this contrast, is trying to make?
2. After Kattrin has been attacked and wounded, why does Mother Courage make her a present of the red boots?

SCENE SEVEN

1. How does Mother Courage's praise for the war compare with her words at the end of Scene Six? Has she at all changed her thinking about the war since the play began?

SCENE EIGHT

1. Does Yvette's accusation against the Cook surprise you? In previous scenes, how has Brecht led up to it?
2. How does Mother Courage react to the news of peace?
3. What has the coming of peace to do with Eilif's death sentence? Compare the Soldier's comment in this scene ("Stealing cattle from a peasant, what's brave about that?") with the Commander's tributes to Eilif in Scene Two.
4. Why does the Chaplain go away with Eilif? (Despite his promise, the Chaplain will not return.)

SCENE NINE

1. What is the theme of the Cook's "Song of the Great Souls of the Earth"? Does it help explain his refusal to take along Kattrin to live at the inn?
2. Why does Kattrin want to run away? Why does Mother Courage choose to stay with her?

SCENE TEN

1. What can the prosperous farmhouse possibly mean to Mother Courage and Kattrin, as they briefly pause before it? What other suggestions do you get from the farmhouse, and from the song being sung within? What other character or characters in the play have expressed an attitude similar to the one expressed in the song?

SCENE ELEVEN

1. For what cause does Kattrin give her life? From what traits of character shown in earlier scenes does her sacrifice appear to follow naturally?
2. Comment on the theatrical effectiveness of Brecht's having a character who

cannot speak, and who has made almost no sounds until now, sound a loud warning on a drum?

3. Explain the First Soldier's remark in the last line: "She made it."

SCENE TWELVE

1. How is Mother Courage at least in part to blame for Kattrin's death?
2. What is ironic in Mother Courage's answer to the peasant that there is one person she can turn to?
3. With what impression of Mother Courage are you left as the play ends? Is she a fool? Is she magnificent?

GENERAL QUESTIONS

1. Did Brecht's summaries (preceding most of the scenes) spoil your reading of the play by giving away what would happen? What is their usefulness?
2. Brecht said that reviewers of the original production saw the play as demonstrating "the overwhelming vital strength of the mother animal." Accordingly, he made several changes in his script to render Mother Courage a less sympathetic character. Does he appear to have succeeded, or do you sympathize with her nevertheless?
3. Compare Mother Courage with Kattrin, especially in such qualities as courage and generosity.
4. What are a few opinions expressed by Mother Courage with which the playwright seems to agree?
5. Compare and contrast the characters of Eilif and Swiss Cheese.
6. What symbolism do you find in the play? Consider objects such as the Cook's pipe, Yvette's red boots, and the canteen wagon.
7. Which events or speeches seem foreshadowings?
8. What is the play's central theme? Is it simply, "War is Hell," or is the playwright making any more specific comment on war? In what scenes, speeches, and songs in this theme made clear? What does the play have to say about courage?
9. A student has observed, "Brecht's whole play is a bitter attack on people who passively accept evil and quietly live with it." Do you agree? Is Brecht in this play a cynic? An idealist?

Harold Pinter (b. 1930)

The Dumb Waiter

1959

Characters

Ben

Gus

Scene: *A basement room. Two beds, flat against the back wall. A serving hatch, closed, between the beds. A door to the kitchen and lavatory, left. A door to a passage, right.*

Ben is lying on a bed, left, reading a paper. Gus is sitting on a bed, right, tying his shoe-laces, with difficulty. Both are dressed in shirts, trousers and braces°.

braces: suspenders.

Silence.

Gus ties his laces, rises, yawns and begins to walk slowly to the door, left. He stops, looks down, and shakes his foot.

Ben lowers his paper and watches him. Gus kneels and unties his shoe-lace and slowly takes off the shoe. He looks inside it and brings out a flattened matchbox. He shakes it and examines it. Their eyes meet. Ben rattles his paper and reads. Gus puts the matchbox in his pocket and bends down to put on his shoe. He ties his lace, with difficulty. Ben lowers his paper and watches him. Gus walks to the door, left, stops, and shakes the other foot. He kneels, unties his shoe-lace, and slowly takes off the shoe. He looks inside it and brings out a flattened cigarette packet. He shakes it and examines it. Their eyes meet. Ben rattles his paper and reads. Gus puts the packet in his pocket, bends down, puts on his shoe and ties the lace.

He wanders off, left.

Ben slams the paper down on the bed and glares after him. He picks up the paper and lies on his back, reading.

Silence.

A lavatory chain is pulled twice off, left, but the lavatory does not flush.

Silence.

Gus re-enters, left, and halts at the door, scratching his head.

Ben slams down the paper.

Ben: Kaw!

He picks up the paper.

What about this? Listen to this!

He refers to the paper.

A man of eighty-seven wanted to cross the road. But there was a lot of traffic, see? He couldn't see how he was going to squeeze through. So he crawled under a lorry°.

Gus: He what?
Ben: He crawled under a lorry. A stationary lorry.
Gus: No?
Ben: The lorry started and ran over him.
Gus: Go on!
Ben: That's what it says here.
Gus: Get away.
Ben: It's enough to make you want to puke, isn't it?
Gus: Who advised him to do a thing like that?
Ben: A man of eighty-seven crawling under a lorry!
Gus: It's unbelievable.
Ben: It's down here in black and white.
Gus: Incredible.

Silence.

Gus shakes his head and exits. Ben lies back and reads. The lavatory chain is pulled once off left, but the lavatory does not flush. Ben whistles at an item in the paper. Gus re-enters.

I want to ask you something.

lorry: truck.

Ben: What are you doing out there?

Gus: Well, I was just —

Ben: What about the tea?

Gus: I'm just going to make it.

Ben: Well, go on, make it.

Gus: Yes, I will. (*He sits in a chair. Ruminatively.*) He's laid on some very nice crockery this time, I'll say that. It's sort of striped. There's a white stripe.

Ben reads.

It's very nice. I'll say that.

Ben turns the page.

You know, sort of round the cup. Round the rim. All the rest of it's black, you see. Then the saucer's black, except for right in the middle, where the cup goes, where it's white.

Ben reads.

Then the plates are the same, you see. Only they've got a black stripe — the plates — right across the middle. Yes, I'm quite taken with the crockery.

Ben (still reading): What do you want plates for? You're not going to eat.

Gus: I've brought a few biscuits.

Ben: Well, you'd better eat them quick.

Gus: I always bring a few biscuits. Or a pie. You know I can't drink tea without anything to eat.

Ben: Well, make the tea then, will you? Time's getting on.

Gus brings out the flattened cigarette packet and examines it.

Gus: You got any cigarettes? I think I've run out.

He throws the packet high up and leans forward to catch it.

I hope it won't be a long job, this one.

Aiming carefully, he flips the packet under his bed.

Oh, I wanted to ask you something.

Ben (slamming his paper down). Kaw!

Gus: What's that?

Ben: A child of eight killed a cat!

Gus: Get away.

Ben: It's a fact. What about that, eh? A child of eight killing a cat!

Gus: How did he do it?

Ben: It was a girl.

Gus: How did she do it?

Ben: She —

He picks up the paper and studies it.

It doesn't say.

Gus: Why not?

Ben: Wait a minute. It just says — Her brother, aged eleven, viewed the incident from the toolshed.

Gus: Go on!

Ben: That's bloody ridiculous.

Pause.

Gus: I bet he did it.
Ben: Who?
Gus: The brother.
Ben: I think you're right.

Pause.

(*Slamming down the paper.*) What about that, eh? A kid of eleven killing a cat and blaming it on his little sister of eight! It's enough to —

He breaks off in disgust and seizes the paper. Gus rises.

Gus: What time is he getting in touch?

Ben reads.

What time is he getting in touch?
Ben: What's the matter with you? It could be any time. Any time.
Gus (moves to the foot of Ben's bed): Well, I was going to ask you something.
Ben: What?
Gus: Have you noticed the time that tank takes to fill?
Ben: What tank?
Gus: In the lavatory.
Ben: No. Does it?
Gus: Terrible.
Ben: Well, what about it?
Gus: What do you think's the matter with it?
Ben: Nothing.
Gus: Nothing?
Ben: It's got a deficient ballcock, that's all.
Gus: A deficient what?
Ben: Ballcock.
Gus: No? Really?
Ben: That's what I should say.
Gus: Go on! That didn't occur to me.

Gus wanders to his bed and presses the mattress.

I didn't have a very restful sleep today, did you? It's not much of a bed. I could have done with another blanket too. (*He catches sight of a picture on the wall.*) Hello, what's this? (*Peering at it.*) 'The First Eleven.' Cricketers. You seen this, Ben?
Ben (reading): What?
Gus: The first eleven.
Ben: What?
Gus: There's a photo here of the first eleven.
Ben: What first eleven?
Gus (studying the photo): It doesn't say.
Ben: What about that tea?
Gus: They all look a bit old to me.

Gus wanders downstage, looks out front, then all about the room.

I wouldn't like to live in this dump. I wouldn't mind if you had a window, you could see what it looked like outside.

Ben: What do you want a window for?

Gus: Well, I like to have a bit of a view, Ben. It whiles away the time.

He walks about the room.

I mean, you come into a place when it's still dark, you come into a room you've never seen before, you sleep all day, you do your job, and then you go away in the night again.

Pause.

I like to get a look at the scenery. You never get the chance in this job.

Ben: You get your holidays, don't you?

Gus: Only a fortnight.

Ben (lowering the paper): You kill me. Anyone would think you're working every day. How often do we do a job? Once a week? What are you complaining about?

Gus: Yes, but we've got to be on tap though, haven't we? You can't move out of the house in case a call comes.

Ben: You know what your trouble is?

Gus: What?

Ben: You haven't got any interests.

Gus: I've got interests.

Ben: What? Tell me one of your interests.

Pause.

Gus: I've got interests.

Ben: Look at me. What have I got?

Gus: I don't know. What?

Ben: I've got my woodwork. I've got my model boats. Have you ever seen me idle? I'm never idle. I know how to occupy my time, to its best advantage. Then when a call comes, I'm ready.

Gus: Don't you ever get a bit fed up?

Ben: Fed up? What with?

Silence. Ben reads. Gus feels in the pocket of his jacket, which hangs on the bed.

Gus: You got any cigarettes? I've run out.

The lavatory flushes off left.

There she goes.

Gus sits on his bed.

No, I mean, I say the crockery's good. It is. It's very nice. But that's about all I can say for this place. It's worse than the last one. Remember that last place we were in? Last time, where was it? At least there was a wireless there. No, honest. He doesn't seem to bother much about our comfort these days.

Ben: When are you going to stop jabbering?

Gus: You'd get rheumatism in a place like this, if you stay long.

Ben: We're not staying long. Make the tea, will you? We'll be on the job in a minute.

Gus picks up a small bag by his bed and brings out a packet of tea. He examines it and looks up.

Gus: Eh, I've been meaning to ask you.

Ben: What the hell is it now?

Gus: Why did you stop the car this morning, in the middle of that road?

Ben *(lowering the paper):* I thought you were asleep.

Gus: I was, but I woke up when you stopped. You did stop, didn't you?

Pause.

In the middle of that road. It was still dark, don't you remember? I looked out. It was all misty. I thought perhaps you wanted to kip,° but you were sitting up dead straight, like you were waiting for something.

Ben: I wasn't waiting for anything.

Gus: I must have fallen asleep again. What was all that about then? Why did you stop?

Ben *(picking up the paper):* We were too early.

Gus: Early? *(He rises.)* What do you mean? We got the call, didn't we, saying we were to start right away. We did. We shoved out on the dot. So how could we be too early?

Ben *(quietly).* Who took the call, me or you?

Gus: You.

Ben: We were too early.

Gus: Too early for what?

Pause.

You mean someone had to get out before we got in?

He examines the bedclothes.

I thought these sheets didn't look too bright. I thought they ponged° a bit. I was too tired to notice when I got in this morning. Eh, that's taking a bit of a liberty, isn't it? I don't want to share my bed-sheets. I told you things were going down the drain. I mean, we've always had clean sheets laid on up till now. I've noticed it.

Ben: How do you know those sheets weren't clean?

Gus: What do you mean?

Ben: How do you know they weren't clean? You've spent the whole day in them, haven't you?

Gus: What, you mean it might be my pong? *(He sniffs sheets.)* Yes. *(He sits slowly on bed.)* It could be my pong, I suppose. It's difficult to tell. I don't really know what I pong like, that's the trouble.

Ben *(referring to the paper):* Kaw!

kip: nap.

ponged: smelled (of body odor).

Gus: Eh, Ben.

Ben: Kaw!

Gus: Ben.

Ben: What?

Gus: What town are we in? I've forgotten.

Ben: I've told you. Birmingham.

Gus: Go on!

> *He looks with interest about the room.*

That's in the Midlands. The second biggest city in Great Britain. I'd never have guessed.

> *He snaps his fingers.*

Eh, it's Friday today, isn't it? It'll be Saturday tomorrow.

Ben: What about it?

Gus (excited): We could go and watch the Villa.

Ben: They're playing away.

Gus: No, are they? Caarr! What a pity.

Ben: Anyway, there's no time. We've got to get straight back.

Gus: Well, we have done in the past, haven't we? Stayed over and watched a game, haven't we? For a bit of relaxation.

Ben: Things have tightened up, mate. They've tightened up.

> *Gus chuckles to himself.*

Gus: I saw the Villa get beat in a cup-tie once. Who was it against now? White shirts. It was one-all at half-time. I'll never forget it. Their opponents won by a penalty. Talk about drama. Yes, it was a disputed penalty. Disputed. They got beat two-one, anyway, because of it. You were there yourself.

Ben: Not me.

Gus: Yes, you were there. Don't you remember that disputed penalty?

Ben: No.

Gus: He went down just inside the area. Then they said he was just acting. I didn't think the other bloke touched him myself. But the referee had the ball on the spot.

Ben: Didn't touch him! What are you talking about? He laid him out flat!

Gus: Not the Villa. The Villa don't play that sort of game.

Ben: Get out of it.

> *Pause.*

Gus: Eh, that must have been here, in Birmingham.

Ben: What must?

Gus: The Villa. That must have been here.

Ben: They were playing away.

Gus: Because you know who the other team was? It was the Spurs. It was Tottenham Hotspur.

Ben: Well, what about it?

Gus: We've never done a job in Tottenham.

Ben: How do you know?

Gus: I'd remember Tottenham.

Ben turns on his bed to look at him.

Ben: Don't make me laugh, will you?

Ben turns back and reads. Gus yawns and speaks through his yawn.

Gus: When's he going to get in touch?

Pause.

Yes, I'd like to see another football match. I've always been an ardent football fan. Here, what about coming to see the Spurs tomorrow?

Ben *(tonelessly)*: They're playing away.

Gus: Who are?

Ben: The Spurs.

Gus: Then they might be playing here.

Ben: Don't be silly.

Gus: If they're playing away they might be playing here. They might be playing the Villa.

Ben *(tonelessly)*: But the Villa are playing away.

Pause. An envelope slides under the door, right. Gus sees it. He stands, looking at it.

Gus: Ben.

Ben: Away. They're all playing away.

Gus: Ben, look here.

Ben: What?

Gus: Look.

Ben turns his head and sees the envelope. He stands.

Ben: What's that?

Gus: I don't know.

Ben: Where did it come from?

Gus: Under the door.

Ben: Well, what is it?

Gus: I don't know.

They stare at it.

Ben: Pick it up.

Gus: What do you mean?

Ben: Pick it up!

Gus slowly moves towards it, bends and picks it up.

What is it?

Gus: An envelope.

Ben: Is there anything on it?

Gus: No.

Ben: Is it sealed?

Gus: Yes.

Ben: Open it.

Gus: What?

Ben: Open it!

Gus opens it and looks inside.

What's in it?

Gus empties twelve matches into his hand.

Gus: Matches.
Ben: Matches?
Gus: Yes.
Ben: Show it to me.

Gus passes the envelope. Ben examines it.

Nothing on it. Not a word.
Gus: That's funny, isn't it?
Ben: It came under the door?
Gus: Must have done.
Ben: Well, go on.
Gus: Go on where?
Ben: Open the door and see if you can catch anyone outside.
Gus: Who, me?
Ben: Go on!

Gus stares at him, puts the matches in his pocket, goes to his bed and brings a revolver from under the pillow. He goes to the door, opens it, looks out and shuts it.

Gus: No one.

He replaces the revolver.

Ben: What did you see?
Gus: Nothing.
Ben: They must have been pretty quick.

Gus takes the matches from his pocket and looks at them.

Gus: Well, they'll come in handy.
Ben: Yes.
Gus: Won't they?
Ben: Yes, you're always running out, aren't you?
Gus: All the time.
Ben: Well, they'll come in handy then.
Gus: Yes.
Ben: Won't they?
Gus: Yes, I could do with them. I could do with them too.
Ben: You could, eh?
Gus: Yes.
Ben: Why?
Gus: We haven't got any.
Ben: Well, you've got some now, haven't you?
Gus: I can light the kettle now.
Ben: Yes, you're always cadging matches. How many have you got there?

Gus: About a dozen.

Ben: Well, don't lose them. Red too. You don't even need a box.

Gus probes his ear with a match.

(Slapping his hand.) Don't waste them! Go on, go and light it.

Gus: Eh?

Ben: Go and light it.

Gus: Light what?

Ben: The kettle.

Gus: You mean the gas.

Ben: Who does?

Gus: You do.

Ben *(his eyes narrowing):* What do you mean, I mean the gas?

Gus: Well, that's what you mean, don't you? The gas.

Ben *(powerfully):* If I say go and light the kettle I mean go and light the kettle.

Gus: How can you light a kettle?

Ben: It's a figure of speech! Light the kettle. It's a figure of speech!

Gus: I've never heard it.

Ben: Light the kettle! It's common usage!

Gus: I think you've got it wrong.

Ben *(menacing):* What do you mean?

Gus: They say put on the kettle.

Ben *(taut):* Who says?

They stare at each other, breathing hard.

(Deliberately.) I have never in all my life heard anyone say put on the kettle.

Gus: I bet my mother used to say it.

Ben: Your mother? When did you last see your mother?

Gus: I don't know, about —

Ben: Well, what are you talking about your mother for?

They stare.

Gus, I'm not trying to be unreasonable. I'm just trying to point out something to you.

Gus: Yes, but —

Ben: Who's the senior partner here, me or you?

Gus: You.

Ben: I'm only looking after your interests, Gus. You've got to learn, mate.

Gus: Yes, but I've never heard —

Ben *(vehemently):* Nobody says light the gas! What does the gas light?

Gus: What does the gas — ?

Ben *(grabbing him with two hands by the throat, at arm's length):* THE KETTLE, YOU FOOL!

Gus takes the hands from his throat.

Gus: All right, all right.

Pause.

Ben: Well, what are you waiting for?

Gus: I want to see if they light.

Ben: What?

Gus: The matches.

He takes out the flattened box and tries to strike.

No.

He throws the box under the bed.
Ben stares at him.
Gus raises his foot.

Shall I try it on here?

Ben stares. Gus strikes a match on his shoe. It lights.

Here we are.

Ben (wearily): Put on the bloody kettle, for Christ's sake.

Ben goes to his bed, but, realizing what he has said, stops and half turns. They look at each other. Gus slowly exits, left. Ben slams his paper down on the bed and sits on it, head in hands.

Gus (entering): It's going.

Ben: What?

Gus: The stove.

Gus goes to his bed and sits.

I wonder who it'll be tonight.

Silence.

Eh, I've been wanting to ask you something.

Ben (putting his legs on the bed): Oh, for Christ's sake.

Gus: No. I was going to ask you something.

He rises and sits on Ben's bed.

Ben: What are you sitting on my bed for?

Gus sits.

What's the matter with you? You're always asking me questions. What's the matter with you?

Gus: Nothing.

Ben: You never used to ask me so many damn questions. What's come over you?

Gus: No, I was just wondering.

Ben: Stop wondering. You've got a job to do. Why don't you just do it and shut up?

Gus: That's what I was wondering about.

Ben: What?

Gus: The job.

Ben: What job?

Gus (tentatively): I thought perhaps you might know something.

Ben looks at him.

I thought perhaps you — I mean — have you got any idea — who it's going to be tonight?

Ben: Who what's going to be?

They look at each other.

Gus (at length): Who it's going to be.

Silence.

Ben: Are you feeling all right?
Gus: Sure.
Ben: Go and make the tea.
Gus: Yes, sure.

Gus exits, left, Ben looks after him. He then takes his revolver from under the pillow and checks it for ammunition. Gus re-enters.

The gas has gone out.
Ben: Well, what about it?
Gus: There's a meter.
Ben: I haven't got any money.
Gus: Nor have I.
Ben: You'll have to wait.
Gus: What for?
Ben: For Wilson.
Gus: He might not come. He might just send a message. He doesn't always come.
Ben: Well, you'll have to do without it, won't you?
Gus: Blimey.
Ben: You'll have a cup of tea afterwards. What's the matter with you?
Gus: I like to have one before.

Ben holds the revolver up to the light and polishes it.

Ben: You'd better get ready anyway.
Gus: Well, I don't know, that's a bit much, you know, for my money.

He picks up a packet of tea from the bed and throws it into the bag.

I hope he's got a shilling, anyway, if he comes. He's entitled to have. After all, it's his place, he could have seen there was enough gas for a cup of tea.
Ben: What do you mean, it's his place?
Gus: Well, isn't it?
Ben: He's probably only rented it. It doesn't have to be his place.
Gus: I know it's his place. I bet the whole house is. He's not even laying on any gas now either.

Gus sits on his bed.

It's his place all right. Look at all the other places. You go to this address, there's a key there, there's a teapot, there's never a soul in sight — (*He pauses.*) Eh, nobody ever hears a thing, have you ever thought of that? We never get any complaints, do we, too much noise or anything like that? You never see a soul, do you? — except the bloke who comes. You ever notice that? I wonder if the walls are sound-proof. *(He touches the wall above his bed.)* Can't tell. All you do is wait, eh? Half the time he doesn't even bother to put in an appearance, Wilson.

Ben: Why should he? He's a busy man.

Gus (thoughtfully): I find him hard to talk to, Wilson. Do you know that, Ben?

Ben: Scrub round it, will you?

Pause.

Gus: There are a number of things I want to ask him. But I can never get round to it, when I see him.

Pause.

I've been thinking about the last one.

Ben: What last one?

Gus: That girl.

Ben grabs the paper, which he reads.

(Rising, looking down at Ben.) How many times have you read that paper?

Ben slams the paper down and rises.

Ben (angrily): What do you mean?

Gus: I was just wondering how many times you'd —

Ben: What are you doing, criticizing me?

Gus: No, I was just —

Ben: You'll get a swipe round your earhole if you don't watch your step.

Gus: Now look here, Ben —

Ben: I'm not looking anywhere! *(He addresses the room.)* How many times have I — ! A bloody liberty!

Gus: I didn't mean that.

Ben: You just get on with it, mate. Get on with it, that's all.

Ben gets back on the bed.

Gus: I was just thinking about that girl, that's all.

Gus sits on his bed.

She wasn't much to look at, I know, but still. It was a mess though, wasn't it? What a mess. Honest, I can't remember a mess like that one. They don't seem to hold together like men, women. A looser texture, like. Didn't she spread, eh? She didn't half spread. Kaw! But I've been meaning to ask you.

Ben sits up and clenches his eyes.

Who clears up after we've gone? I'm curious about that. Who does the clearing up? Maybe they don't clear up. Maybe they just leave them there, eh? What do you think? How many jobs have we done? Blimey, I can't count them. What if they never clear anything up after we've gone.

Ben (pityingly): You mutt. Do you think we're the only branch of this organization? Have a bit of common. They got departments for everything.

Gus: What, cleaners and all?

Ben: You birk°!
Gus: No, it was that girl made me start to think —

> *There is a loud clatter and racket in the bulge of wall between the beds, of some-thing descending. They grab their revolvers, jump up and face the wall. The noise comes to a stop. Silence. They look at each other. Ben gestures sharply towards the wall. Gus approaches the wall slowly. He bangs it with his revolver. It is hollow. Ben moves to the head of his bed, his revolver cocked. Gus puts his revolver on his bed and pats along the bottom of the center panel. He finds a rim. He lifts the panel. Disclosed is a serving-hatch, a "dumb waiter." A wide box is held by pulleys. Gus peers into the box. He brings out a piece of paper.*

Ben: What is it?
Gus: You have a look at it.
Ben: Read it.
Gus (reading): Two braised steak and chips. Two sago puddings. Two teas with-out sugar.
Ben: Let me see that. *(He takes the paper.)*
Gus (to himself): Two teas without sugar.
Ben: Mmnn.
Gus: What do you think of that?
Ben: Well —

> *The box goes up. Ben levels his revolver.*

Gus: Give us a chance! They're in a hurry, aren't they?

> *Ben re-reads the note. Gus looks over his shoulder.*

That's a bit — that's a bit funny, isn't it?
Ben (quickly): No. It's not funny. It probably used to be a café here, that's all. Upstairs. These places change hands very quickly.
Gus: A café?
Ben: Yes.
Gus: What, you mean this was the kitchen, down here?
Ben: Yes, they change hands overnight, these places. Go into liquidation. The people who run it, you know, they don't find it a going concern, they move out.
Gus: You mean the people who ran this place didn't find it a going concern and moved out?
Ben: Sure.
Gus: WELL, WHO'S GOT IT NOW?

> *Silence.*

Ben: What do you mean, who's got it now?
Gus: Who's got it now? If they moved out, who moved in?
Ben: Well, that all depends —

> *The box descends with a clatter and bang. Ben levels his revolver. Gus goes to the box and brings out a piece of paper.*

birk: stupid idiot.

Gus (reading): Soup of the day. Liver and onions. Jam tart.

> *A pause. Gus looks at Ben. Ben takes the note and reads it. He walks slowly to the hatch. Gus follows. Ben looks into the hatch but not up it. Gus puts his hand on Ben's shoulder. Ben throws it off. Gus puts his finger to his mouth. He leans on the hatch and swiftly looks up it. Ben flings him away in alarm. Ben looks at the note. He throws his revolver on the bed and speaks with decision.*

Ben: We'd better send something up.
Gus: Eh?
Ben: We'd better send something up.
Gus: Oh! Yes. Yes. Maybe you're right.

> *They are both relieved at the decision.*

Ben (purposefully): Quick! What have you got in that bag?
Gus: Not much.

> *Gus goes to the hatch and shouts up it.*

Wait a minute!
Ben: Don't do that!

> *Gus examines the contents of the bag and brings them out, one by one.*

Gus: Biscuits. A bar of chocolate. Half a pint of milk.
Ben: That all?
Gus: Packet of tea.
Ben: Good.
Gus: We can't send the tea. That's all the tea we've got.
Ben: Well, there's no gas. You can't do anything with it, can you?
Gus: Maybe they can send us down a bob°.
Ben: What else is there?
Gus (reaching into bag): One Eccles cake.
Ben: One Eccles cake?
Gus: Yes.
Ben: You never told me you had an Eccles cake.
Gus: Didn't I?
Ben: Why only one? Didn't you bring one for me?
Gus: I didn't think you'd be keen.
Ben: Well, you can't send up one Eccles cake, anyway.
Gus: Why not?
Ben: Fetch one of those plates.
Gus: All right.

> *Gus goes towards the door, left, and stops.*

Do you mean I can keep the Eccles cake then?
Ben: Keep it?
Gus: Well, they don't know we've got it, do they?
Ben: That's not the point.
Gus: Can't I keep it?

bob: shilling.

Ben: No, you can't. Get the plate.

> *Gus exits, left. Ben looks in the bag. He brings out a packet of crisps°. Enter Gus with a plate.*

> (*Accusingly, holding up the crisps.*) Where did these come from?

Gus: What?

Ben: Where did these crisps come from?

Gus: Where did you find them?

Ben (hitting him on the shoulder): You're playing a dirty game, my lad!

Gus: I only eat those with beer!

Ben: Well, where were you going to get the beer?

Gus: I was saving them till I did.

Ben: I'll remember this. Put everything on the plate.

> *They pile everything on to the plate. The box goes up without the plate.*

> Wait a minute!

> *They stand.*

Gus: It's gone up.

Ben: It's all your stupid fault, playing about!

Gus: What do we do now?

Ben: We'll have to wait till it comes down.

> *Ben puts the plate on the bed, puts on his shoulder holster, and starts to put on his tie.*

> You'd better get ready.

> *Gus goes to his bed, puts on his tie, and starts to fix his holster.*

Gus: Hey, Ben.

Ben: What?

Gus: What's going on here?

> *Pause.*

Ben: What do you mean?

Gus: How can this be a café?

Ben: It used to be a café.

Gus: Have you seen the gas stove?

Ben: What about it?

Gus: It's only got three rings.

Ben: So what?

Gus: Well, you couldn't cook much on three rings, not for a busy place like this.

Ben (irritably): That's why the service is slow!

> *Ben puts on his waistcoat.*

Gus: Yes, but what happens when we're not here? What do they do then? All these menus coming down and nothing going up. It might have been going on like this for years.

crisps: potato chips.

Ben brushes his jacket.

What happens when we go?

Ben puts on his jacket.

They can't do much business.

The box descends. They turn about. Gus goes to the hatch and brings out a note.

Gus (*reading*): Macaroni Pastitsio. Ormitha Macarounada.
Ben: What was that?
Gus: Macaroni Pastitsio. Ormitha Macarounada.
Ben: Greek dishes.
Gus: No.
Ben: That's right.
Gus: That's pretty high class.
Ben: Quick before it goes up.

Gus puts the plate in the box.

Gus (*calling up the hatch*): Three McVitie and Price! One Lyons Red Label! One Smith's Crisps! One Eccles cake! One Fruit and Nut!
Ben: Cadbury's.
Gus (*up the hatch*): Cadbury's!
Ben (*handing the milk*): One bottle of milk.
Gus (*up the hatch*): One bottle of milk! Half a pint! (*He looks at the label.*) Express Dairy! (*He puts the bottle in the box.*)

The box goes up.

Just did it.
Ben: You shouldn't shout like that.
Gus: Why not?
Ben: It isn't done.

Ben goes to his bed.

Well, that should be all right, anyway, for the time being.
Gus: You think so, eh?
Ben: Get dressed, will you? It'll be any minute now.

Gus puts on his waistcoat. Ben lies down and looks up at the ceiling.

Gus: This is some place. No tea and no biscuits.
Ben: Eating makes you lazy, mate. You're getting lazy, you know that? You don't want to get slack on your job.
Gus: Who me?
Ben: Slack, mate, slack.
Gus: Who me? Slack?
Ben: Have you checked your gun? You haven't even checked your gun. It looks disgraceful, anyway. Why don't you ever polish it?

Gus rubs his revolver on the sheet. Ben takes out a pocket mirror and straightens his tie.

Gus: I wonder where the cook is. They must have had a few, to cope with that. Maybe they had a few more gas stoves. Eh! Maybe there's another kitchen along the passage.

Ben: Of course there is! Do you know what it takes to make an Ormitha Macarounada?

Gus: No, what?

Ben: An Ormitha — ! Buck your ideas up, will you?

Gus: Takes a few cooks, eh?

Gus puts his revolver in its holster.

The sooner we're out of this place the better.

He puts on his jacket.

Why doesn't he get in touch? I feel like I've been here years. *(He takes his revolver out of its holster to check the ammunition.)* We've never let him down though, have we? We've never let him down. I was thinking only the other day, Ben. We're reliable, aren't we?

He puts his revolver back in its holster.

Still, I'll be glad when it's over tonight.

He brushes his jacket.

I hope the bloke's not going to get excited tonight, or anything. I'm feeling a bit off. I've got a splitting headache.

Silence.
> *The box descends. Ben jumps up.*
> *Gus collects the note.*

(Reading.) One Bamboo Shoots, Water Chestnuts and Chicken. One Char Siu and Beansprouts.

Ben: Beansprouts?

Gus: Yes.

Ben: Blimey.

Gus: I wouldn't know where to begin.

He looks back at the box. The packet of tea is inside it. He picks it up.

They've sent back the tea.

Ben *(anxious):* What'd they do that for?

Gus: Maybe it isn't tea-time.

The box goes up. Silence.

Ben *(throwing the tea on the bed, and speaking urgently):* Look here. We'd better tell them.

Gus: Tell them what?

Ben: That we can't do it, we haven't got it.

Gus: All right then.

Ben: Lend us your pencil. We'll write a note.

Gus, turning for a pencil, suddenly discovers the speaking-tube, which hangs on the right wall of the hatch facing his bed.

Gus: What's this?
Ben: What?
Gus: This.
Ben (examining it): This? It's a speaking-tube.
Gus: How long has that been there?
Ben: Just the job. We should have used it before, instead of shouting up there.
Gus: Funny I never noticed it before.
Ben: Well, come on.
Gus: What do you do?
Ben: See that? That's a whistle.
Gus: What, this?
Ben: Yes, take it out. Pull it out.

Gus does so.

That's it.
Gus: What do we do now?
Ben: Blow into it.
Gus: Blow?
Ben: It whistles up there if you blow. Then they know you want to speak. Blow.

Gus blows. Silence.

Gus (tube at mouth): I can't hear a thing.
Ben: Now you speak! Speak into it!

Gus looks at Ben, then speaks into the tube.

Gus: The larder's bare!
Ben: Give me that!

He grabs the tube and puts it to his mouth.

(Speaking with great deference.) Good evening. I'm sorry to — bother you, but we just thought we'd better let you know that we haven't got anything left. We sent up all we had. There's no more food down here.

He brings the tube slowly to his ear.

What?

To mouth.

What?

To ear. He listens. To mouth.

No, all we had we sent up.

To ear. He listens. To mouth.

Oh, I'm very sorry to hear that.

To ear. He listens. To Gus.

The Eccles cake was stale.

He listens. To Gus.

The chocolate was melted.

He listens. To Gus.

The milk was sour.
Gus: What about the crisps?
Ben (listening): The biscuits were mouldy.

He glares at Gus. Tube to mouth.

Well, we're very sorry about that.

Tube to ear.

What?

To mouth.

What?

To ear.

Yes. Yes.

To mouth.

Yes certainly. Certainly. Right away.

To ear. The voice has ceased. He hangs up the tube.

(*Excitedly.*) Did you hear that?

Gus: What?
Ben: You know what he said? Light the kettle! Not put on the kettle! Not light the gas! But light the kettle!
Gus: How can we light the kettle?
Ben: What do you mean?
Gus: There's no gas.
Ben (clapping hand to head): Now what do we do?
Gus: What did he want us to light the kettle for?
Ben: For tea. He wanted a cup of tea.
Gus: *He* wanted a cup of tea! What about me? I've been wanting a cup of tea all night!
Ben (despairingly): What do we do now?
Gus: What are we supposed to drink?

Ben sits on his bed, staring.

What about us?

Ben sits.

I'm thirsty too. I'm starving. And he wants a cup of tea. That beats the band, that does.

Ben lets his head sink on to his chest.

I could do with a bit of sustenance myself. What about you? You look as if you could do with something too.

Gus sits on his bed.

We send him up all we've got and he's not satisfied. No, honest, it's enough to make the cat laugh. Why did you send him up all that stuff? *(Thoughtfully.)* Why did I send it up?

Pause.

Who knows what he's got upstairs? He's probably got a salad bowl. They must have something up there. They won't get much from down here. You notice they didn't ask for any salads? They've probably got a salad bowl up there. Cold meat, radishes, cucumbers. Watercress. Roll mops.

Pause.

Hardboiled eggs.

Pause.

The lot. They've probably got a crate of beer too. Probably eating my crisps with a pint of beer now. Didn't have anything to say about those crisps, did he? They do all right, don't worry about that. You don't think they're just going to sit there and wait for stuff to come up from down here, do you? That'll get them nowhere.

Pause.

They do all right.

Pause.

And he wants a cup of tea.

Pause.

That's past a joke, in my opinion.

He looks over at Ben, rises, and goes to him.

What's the matter with you? You don't look too bright. I feel like an Alka-Seltzer myself.

Ben sits up.

Ben *(in a low voice):* Time's getting on.
Gus: I know. I don't like doing a job on an empty stomach.
Ben *(wearily):* Be quiet a minute. Let me give you your instructions.
Gus: What for? We always do it the same way, don't we?
Ben: Let me give you your instructions.

Gus sighs and sits next to Ben on the bed. The instructions are stated and repeated automatically.

When we get the call, you go over and stand behind the door.
Gus: Stand behind the door.

Ben: If there's a knock on the door you don't answer it.
Gus: If there's a knock on the door I don't answer it.
Ben: But there won't be a knock on the door.
Gus: So I won't answer it.
Ben: When the bloke comes in —
Gus: When the bloke comes in —
Ben: Shut the door behind him.
Gus: Shut the door behind him.
Ben: Without divulging your presence.
Gus: Without divulging my presence.
Ben: He'll see me and come towards me.
Gus: He'll see you and come towards you.
Ben: He won't see you.
Gus (absently): Eh?
Ben: He won't see you.
Gus: He won't see me.
Ben: But he'll see me.
Gus: He'll see you.
Ben: He won't know you're there.
Gus: He won't know you're there.
Ben: He won't know *you're* there.
Gus: He won't know I'm there.
Ben: I take out my gun.
Gus: You take out your gun.
Ben: He stops in his tracks.
Gus: He stops in his tracks.
Ben: If he turns round —
Gus: If he turns round —
Ben: You're there.
Gus: I'm here.

   Ben frowns and presses his forehead.

   You've missed something out.
Ben: I know. What?
Gus: I haven't taken my gun out, according to you.
Ben: You take your gun out —
Gus: After I've closed the door.
Ben: After you've closed the door.
Gus: You've never missed that out before, you know that?
Ben: When he sees you behind him —
Gus: Me behind him —
Ben: And me in front of him —
Gus: And you in front of him —
Ben: He'll feel uncertain —
Gus: Uneasy.
Ben: He won't know what to do.
Gus: So what will he do?
Ben: He'll look at me and he'll look at you.
Gus: We won't say a word.

Ben: We'll look at him.
Gus: He won't say a word.
Ben: He'll look at us.
Gus: And we'll look at him.
Ben: Nobody says a word.

> *Pause.*

Gus: What do we do if it's a girl?
Ben: We do the same.
Gus: Exactly the same?
Ben: Exactly.

> *Pause.*

Gus: We don't do anything different?
Ben: We do exactly the same.
Gus: Oh.

> *Gus rises, and shivers.*

Excuse me.

> *He exits through the door on the left. Ben remains sitting on the bed, still. The lavatory chain is pulled once off left, but the lavatory does not flush.*
> *Silence. Gus re-enters and stops inside the door, deep in thought. He looks at Ben, then walks slowly across to his own bed. He is troubled. He stands, thinking. He turns and looks at Ben. He moves a few paces towards him.*

(Slowly in a low, tense voice.) Why did he send us matches if he knew there was no gas?

> *Silence. Ben stares in front of him. Gus crosses to the left side of Ben, to the foot of his bed, to get to his other ear.*

Why did he send us matches if he knew there was no gas?

> *Ben looks up.*

Why did he do that?
Ben: Who?
Gus: Who sent us those matches?
Ben: What are you talking about?

> *Gus stares down at him.*

Gus (thickly): Who is it upstairs?
Ben (nervously): What's one thing to do with another?
Gus: Who is it, though?
Ben: What's one thing to do with another?

> *Ben fumbles for his paper on the bed.*

Gus: I asked you a question.
Ben: Enough!

Gus (*with growing agitation*): I asked you before. Who moved in? I asked you. You said the people who had it before moved out. Well, who moved in?

Ben (*hunched*): Shut up.

Gus: I told you, didn't I?

Ben (*standing*): Shut up!

Gus (*feverishly*): I told you before who owned this place, didn't I? I told you.

Ben hits him viciously on the shoulder.

I told you who ran this place, didn't I?

Ben hits him viciously on the shoulder.

(*Violently.*) Well, what's he playing all these games for? That's what I want to know. What's he doing it for?

Ben: What games?

Gus (*passionately, advancing*): What's he doing it for? We've been through our tests, haven't we? We got right through our tests, years ago, didn't we? We took them together, don't you remember, didn't we? We've proved ourselves before now, haven't we? We've always done our job. What's he doing all this for? What's the idea? What's he playing these games for?

The box in the shaft comes down behind them. The noise is this time accompanied by a shrill whistle, as it falls. Gus rushes to the hatch and seizes the note.

(*Reading.*) Scampi!

He crumples the note, picks up the tube, takes out the whistle, blows and speaks.

WE'VE GOT NOTHING LEFT! NOTHING! DO YOU UNDERSTAND?

Ben seizes the tube and flings Gus away. He follows Gus and slaps him hard, back-handed, across the chest.

Ben: Stop it! You maniac!

Gus: But you heard!

Ben (*savagely*): That's enough! I'm warning you!

Silence.
    Ben hangs the tube. He goes to his bed and lies down. He picks up his paper and reads.
    Silence.
    The box goes up.
    They turn quickly, their eyes meet. Ben turns to his paper.
    Slowly Gus goes back to his bed, and sits.
    Silence.
    The hatch falls back into place.
    They turn quickly, their eyes meet. Ben turns back to his paper.
    Silence.
    Ben throws his paper down.

Ben: Kaw!

He picks up the paper and looks at it.

Listen to this!

Pause.

What about that, eh?

Pause.

Kaw!

Pause.

Have you ever heard such a thing?
Gus *(dully):* Go on!
Ben: It's true.
Gus: Get away.
Ben: It's down here in black and white.
Gus *(very low):* Is that a fact?
Ben: Can you imagine it.
Gus: It's unbelievable.
Ben: It's enough to make you want to puke, isn't it?
Gus *(almost inaudible):* Incredible.

Ben shakes his head. He puts the paper down and rises. He fixes the revolver in his holster.

  Gus stands up. He goes towards the door on the left.

Ben: Where are you going?
Gus: I'm going to have a glass of water.

He exits. Ben brushes dust off his clothes and shoes. The whistle in the speaking-tube blows. He goes to it, takes the whistle out and puts the tube to his ear. He listens. He puts it to his mouth.

Ben: Yes.

To ear. He listens. To mouth.

Straight away. Right.

To ear. He listens. To mouth.

Sure we're ready.

To ear. He listens. To mouth.

Understood. Repeat. He has arrived and will be coming in straight away. The normal method to be employed. Understood.

To ear. He listens. To mouth.

Sure we're ready.

To ear. He listens. To mouth.

Right.

He hangs the tube up.

Gus!

He takes out a comb and combs his hair, adjusts his jacket to diminish the bulge of the revolver. The lavatory flushes off left. Ben goes quickly to the door, left.

Gus!

The door right opens sharply. Ben turns, his revolver levelled at the door.
   Gus stumbles in.
   He is stripped of his jacket, waistcoat, tie, holster and revolver.
   He stops, body stooping, his arms at his sides.
   He raises his head and looks at Ben.
   A long silence.
   They stare at each other.

CURTAIN

QUESTIONS

1. Describe the job by which Ben and Gus earn their livings. What do you learn (or guess) about Wilson? About the "organization" the two men work for?
2. How would you describe each of the characters? Who is the "senior partner"? Who expresses more sympathy for their victims? What other traits or qualities do they reveal?
3. Indicate a few speeches in which Pinter appears to satirize (as critic Harold Clurman has put it) "the banality, repetitiousness, and emptiness of ordinary conversation."
4. What events in the play remain mysterious and unexplained?
5. What happens in the conclusion? How do you interpret it?
6. "This play is a bummer. Nothing much happens and we don't expect anything to happen, and so there is no interest or suspense." Do you agree? Or did you find yourself reading the play with any particular expectation? If so, what did you expect?
7. What additional meaning do you find in the title of the play (besides its denoting a small, hand-operated elevator)? Does *The Dumb Waiter* contain any other "dumb waiters"?
8. If you were to produce this play, would you stage it on a picture-frame stage, or in an arena theater? Why?
9. To what theatrical movement or movements discussed in this chapter does *The Dumb Waiter* seem akin? Would you call the play a work of realism? A tragicomedy?
10. The playwright has remarked:

We have heard many times that tired, grimy phrase, 'Failure of communication,' and this phrase has been fixed to my work quite consistently. I believe the contrary. I think that we communicate only too well, in our silence, in what is unsaid, and that what takes place is a continual evasion, desperate rear-guard attempts to keep ourselves to ourselves. Communication is too alarming. To enter into someone's life is too frightening. To disclose to others the poverty within us is too fearsome a possibility. ("Writing for the Theatre" [a talk given in 1962] in *Complete Works: One* [New York: Grove Press, 1976].)

How well does Pinter's remark apply to *The Dumb Waiter*? At what moments in the play do Gus and Ben exchange silent looks that perhaps reveal more than words?

36 Evaluating Drama

To **evaluate** a play is to decide whether the play is any good or not; and if it is good, how good it is in relation to other plays of its kind. In the theater, evaluation is usually thought to be the task of the play reviewer (or, to use a phrase with nobler connotations, "drama critic"), ordinarily a person who sees a new play on its first night and who then tells us, in print or over the air, what the play is about, how well it is done, and whether or not we ought to go to see it. Enthroned in an excellent free seat, the drama critic apparently plies a glamorous trade. What fun it must be to whittle a nasty epigram: to be able to observe, as did a critic of a faltering production of *Uncle Tom's Cabin*, that "The Siberian wolf hound was weakly supported."

However, unless you find a job on a large city newspaper or radio station, or write for a college paper, or broadcast on a campus FM station, the opportunities to be a drama critic today are probably few and strictly limited. Much more significant, for most of us, is the task of evaluation we undertake for our own satisfaction. We see a play, or a film or a drama on television, and then we make up our minds about it; and we often have to decide whether to recommend it to anyone else.

To evaluate new drama isn't easy. (And in this discussion, let us define *drama* broadly to include not only plays, but whatever actors perform in the movies or on television, since most of us see more movies and television programs than plays.) But at least a part of the process of evaluation has already been accomplished for us. To produce a new play, even in an amateur theater, or to produce a new drama for the movies or for television, is complicated and involves large sums of money and the efforts of many people. Sifted from a mountain of submitted playscripts, already subjected to long scrutiny and evaluation, a new play or film, whether or not it is of any deep interest, arrives with a certain built-in air of professional competence. It is probably seldom that a dull play written by the producer's relative or friend finds enough financial backers to reach the stage; only on the fictitious Broadway of Mel Brooks's movie *The Producers* could there be a musical comedy as awful as *Springtime for Hitler.* Nor do most college and civic theaters afford us much opportunity to see thoroughly inept plays; usually they give us new productions of *Oedipus Rex* or *Pygmalion;* or else (if they are less adventurous) new versions of whatever succeeded on Broadway in the recent past.

So new plays — the few that we do see — tend, like television drama, to be somebody's safe investment. More often than not, our powers of evaluation confront only slick, pleasant, and efficient mediocrity. We owe it to ourselves to discriminate; and here are a few suggestions designed to help you tell the difference between an ordinary, run-of-the-reel product, and a work of drama that may offer high reward.

1. Discard any inexorable rules you may have collected that affirm what a drama ought to be. (One such rule states that a tragedy is innately superior to a comedy, no matter how deep a truth a comedy may strike.) Never mind the misinterpreters of Aristotle who insist that a play must "observe the unities" — that is, must unfold its events in one day and in one place, and must keep tragedy and comedy strictly apart. (Shakespeare ignores such rules.) There is no sense in damning a play for lacking "realism" (what if it's an expressionist play, or a fantasy?), or in belaboring the failure of its plot to fit into a pyramid structure.

2. Instead, watch the play (or read it) alertly, with your mind and your senses open wide. Recall that certain theaters, such as the classic Greek theater of Sophocles, impose certain conventions. Do not condemn *Oedipus Rex* for the reason one spectator gave: "That damned chorus keeps sticking their noses in!" Do not complain that Hamlet utters soliloquies; nor that, in the same play, certain speeches (when the speakers exit) rime unnaturally.

3. Ask yourself if the characters are fully realized. Do their actions follow from the kinds of persons they are, or does the action seem to impose itself upon them, making the play seem falsely contrived? Does the resolution arrive (as in a satisfying play) because of the natures of the characters; or are the characters saved (or destroyed) merely by some *deus ex machina,* or nick-of-time arrival of the Marines?

4. Recognize drama that belongs to a certain family: a *farce,* say, or a *comedy of manners,* or a **melodrama** — a play in which suspense and physical action are the prime ingredients. Recognizing such a familiar type of drama may help make some things clear to you, and may save you from attacking a play for being what it is, in fact, supposed to be. After all, there can be satisfying melodramas, and excellent plays may

contain melodramatic elements. What is wrong with thrillers is not that they have suspense, but that suspense is all they have. Awhirl with furious action, they employ stick-figure characters.

5. If there are symbols, ask how well they belong to their surrounding worlds. Do they help to reveal meaning, or merely decorate? In Tennessee Williams's *The Glass Menagerie*, Laura's collection of figurines is much more than simply ornamental.

6. Test the play or film for **sentimentality,** the failure of a dramatist, actor, or director caused by expecting from us a greater emotional response than we are given reason to feel. (For further discussion of sentimentality, see Chapter Twenty-five.)

7. Decide what it is that you admire or dislike, and, in the case of a play, whether it is the play that you admire or dislike, or the production. (It is useful to draw this distinction if you are evaluating the play and not the production.)

8. Ask yourself what the theme is. What does the drama reveal? How far and how deeply does its statement go; how readily can we apply it beyond the play to the human world outside? Be slow, of course, to attribute to the playwright the opinions of the characters.

Do all this and you may find that evaluating plays, movies, and television plays is a richly meaningful activity. It may reveal wisdom and pleasure that had previously bypassed you. It may even help you decide what to watch in the future, how to choose those works of drama that help us to fulfill — not merely to spend — our waking lives.

37 Writing about Drama

METHODS

If you feel the need for any suggestions on how to select a topic, how to define it, take notes, organize your thoughts, write a rough draft, revise, and put your essay into finished form, please see the Appendix, "Writing about Literature" (page 1377). The scope of the following discussion is narrower.

How is writing about a play any different from writing about a short story or a poem? Differences will quickly emerge if you are writing about a play you have actually seen performed. Although, like a story or a poem, a play in print is usually the work of one person (and it is relatively fixed and changeless), a play on stage may be the joint effort of seventy or eighty people — actors, director, costumers, set designers, and technicians — and in its many details it may change from season to season, or even from night to night. Later on in this chapter, you will find some advice on reviewing a performance of a play, as you might do for a class assignment or for publication in, say, a campus newspaper. But in a literature course, for the most part, you will probably write about the plays you quietly read, and behold only in the theater of your mind. At least one advantage in writing about a printed play is that you can always go back and reread it, unlike the reviewer who, unless provided with a script, has nothing but memory to rely on.

Before you begin to write, it makes sense to read the *whole* play — not just the dialogue, but also everything in italics: descriptions of scenes, instructions to the actors, and other stage directions. This point may seem obvious, but the meaning of a scene, or even of an entire play, may depend on the tone of voice in which an actor is supposed to deliver a line. At the end of *A Doll House*, we need to pay attention to what Ibsen tells the actor playing Helmer — *"A sudden hope leaps in him"* — if we are to understand that, when Nora departs, she ignores Helmer's last desperate hope for a reconciliation, and she slams the door emphatically. And of course there is a resounding meaning in the final stage direction, in "the sound of a door slamming shut."

Taking notes on passages you will want to quote or refer to in your paper, you can use a concise method for keeping track of them. Jot down the numbers of act, scene, and line — for instance: I, ii, 42. Later, when you write, this handy shorthand will save space, and you can use it both in footnotes and in the body of your essay. Even if you do without footnotes, you can still indicate the exact lines you are quoting, or referring to:

Iago's hypocrisy, apparent in his famous defense of his good name (III, iii, 157-161), is aptly summed up by Roderigo, who accuses him: "Your words and performances are no kin together" (IV, ii, 180-181).

Any of the methods frequently applied in writing about fiction and poetry — explication, analysis, comparison and contrast — can serve in writing about a play. All three methods are discussed in Chapter Nine, "Writing about Fiction," and again in Chapter Twenty-eight, "Writing about Poetry." (For student papers that illustrate explication, see pages 216 and 691; analysis, pages 220 and 696; comparison and contrast, page 698.) For using these methods to write about plays in particular, here are a few suggestions.

A whole play is too much to cover in an ordinary **explication** — a detailed, line-by-line unfolding of meaning. An explication of *Othello* could take years; a more reasonable class assignment would be to explicate a single key speech or passage from a play: Iago's description of a "deserving woman" (*Othello*, II, i, 145–157); or the first song of the chorus in *Oedipus Rex*.

If you decide to write an essay by the method of **comparison** and **contrast** (two methods, actually, but they usually work together), you might set two plays side by side and point out their similarities and differences. Again, watch out: do not bite off more than you can chew. A profound topic — "The Self-deceptions of Othello and Oedipus" — might do for a three-hundred-page dissertation, but an essay of a mere thousand words could treat it only sketchily. Probably the dual methods of comparison and contrast are most useful for a long term paper on a large but finite topic: "Attitudes Toward Marriage in *A Doll House* and *Pygmalion*," "Sinister Humor in *The Real Inspector Hound* and *The Zoo Story*." In a shorter paper, you can readily compare and contrast two characters or situations within the same play: "The Two Quarrels in *The Marriage Proposal*," "The Different Sons of Mother Courage."

For writing about drama, **analysis** (a separation into elements) is an especially useful method. You can consider just one element in a play, and so your topic tends to be humanly manageable — "Animal Imagery in Some Speeches from *Othello*," or "The Theme of Fragility in *The Glass Menagerie*." Not all plays, however, contain every element you might find in fiction and poetry. Unlike a short story or a novel, a play does not ordinarily have a narrator. In most plays, the point of view is that of the audience, who see the events not through some narrator's eyes, but through their own.[1] And while it is usual for a short story to be written in an all-pervading style, some plays — *Pygmalion*, for instance — seem written in as many different styles as there are speaking characters. (But you might well argue that in the Fitts and Fitzgerald version of *Oedipus Rex*, a consistently elevated style informs all of the speeches, or that in Harold Pinter's *The Dumb Waiter* both characters speak the same language, however maundering and inarticulate.) Rime schemes and metrical patterns, elements familiar in traditional poetry, are seldom found in contemporary plays, which tend to sound like ordinary conversation. To be sure, some plays *are* written in poetic forms: the rimed couplets of the French plays of Molière (deftly captured in Richard Wilbur's English translations) and the blank verse of the greater portion of *Othello*. (If, by the way, you wish any advice to heed in quoting passages from *Othello*, or any other play in blank verse or in rime, see "How To Quote a Poem," on page 701.) Despite whatever some plays may lack, most plays contain more than enough elements for analysis, including characters, themes, tone, irony, imagery, figures of speech, symbols, myths, and conventions.

Ready to begin writing an analysis of a play, you might think at first that one element — the plot — ought to be particularly easy to detach from the rest, and write about. But beware. In a good play (as in a good novel or short story), plot and character and theme are likely to be one, not perfectly simple to tell apart. Besides, if in your essay you were to summarize the events in the play, and then stop, you wouldn't tell your readers much that they couldn't observe for themselves just by reading the play, or by seeing it. In a meaningful, informative analysis, the writer does not merely isolate an element, but also shows how it functions within its play and why it is necessary to the whole.

Say you intend to write an essay on the plot of Bertolt Brecht's *Mother Courage and Her Children* (Chapter Thirty-five). Dealing with a play so richly complex, you will probably find yourself with enough work to do if you take even one part of the plot, not necessarily the whole of it. You might consider, for instance, just the exposition — the

[1] Point of view in drama is a study in itself; this mere mention grossly simplifies the matter. Some playwrights attempt to govern what the spectator sees, trying to make the stage become the mind of a character. An obvious example is the classic German film *The Cabinet of Dr. Caligari*, in which the scenery is distorted as though perceived by a lunatic. Some plays contain characters who act as narrators, directly addressing the audience in much the way that first-person narrators in fiction often address the reader. In Tennessee Williams's *The Glass Menagerie*, Tom Wingfield behaves like such a narrator, introducing scenes, commenting on the action. So does the psychiatrist Martin Dysart in Peter Shaffer's *Equus* (1974). But such a character in a play does not alter our angle of vision, our physical point of view.

part that tells us whatever we need to know about events in the past and introduces the leading characters. (*Exposition* is discussed on page 846.) In most plays the exposition comes early, and in Brecht's play it occurs in Scene One, in the first appearance of Mother Courage and in her early conversation with the Sergeant and the Recruiting Officer — from the moment of her entrance until a new event takes place, when she tells the Sergeant's fortune. From this exposition we learn how she received her name, we meet her children, and hear of their three different fathers. An exposition can do even more than fill in facts. You could write an essay to show, for instance, that the exposition in Brecht's play also delineates Mother Courage, displays her driving ambition, portrays her family, indicates her contempt for local laws and national boundaries, and introduces at least one other important theme — that, for her, profit is to be held dearer than life itself. Like many other plays, Brecht's great work tells more than one story. Another valuable essay could demonstrate how a subplot, the story of Yvette Pottier and her rise in the world, closely relates to the main plot, the story of Mother Courage and her children, and indirectly comments on it.

Though you might wish to include some brief summarizing in your essay, you will probably find as you study the play thoughtfully that you are drawn from the question of "what happens" into the more absorbing question, "What do the events finally mean?" Here is Richard Gilman, a professional critic and teacher of drama, writing an analysis of *Mother Courage and Her Children* in which he will try to set forth the play's main theme. He begins with a short summary.

> To summarize the play's main line of action: Anna Fierling, called Mother Courage, . . . is a sutler who follows the shifting campaigns and battle lines of the Thirty Years' War, selling supplies to one or another of the armies. She is tough, salty, "indomitable," and her steadfast purpose is to preserve her life, for its own sake but that in turn for the sake of her three children, in the midst of unending devastation and death. One by one, however, the children die and the mother is left alone, hitched to her wagon, a survivor in only the narrowest bodily sense.
>
> From the very beginning the ironic perspective is present that will issue in this survival at the cost of everything that has seemed to matter. Mother Courage's own nickname has a grossly ironic origin; as she tells the story, she received it after driving madly through the bombardment of Riga "with fifty loaves of bread in my cart. They were going moldy . . . I was afraid I'd be ruined." Is her virtue therefore founded on a sham? The point Brecht is making is that it is founded on an overwhelming practicality, a business sense that dominates everything she does and that is seen throughout to be in mortal, insoluble conflict with all other "values," including, in the deepest irony of all, that of life itself.
>
> The deaths of her children all take place as more or less direct results of her making the living that is designed to sustain them. She loses one son to the blandishment of a recruiting officer when she lets him out of her sight in order to make a sale . . . and the other when she tries to

bargain over the ransom demanded of her after he has been captured by enemy soldiers. (Her only means of raising the money is to sell her wagon, which would mean that she could not provide for her other child.) And her mute, defenseless daughter is killed when she is off on business.[2]

In the first of these paragraphs, Gilman supplies a capsule summary of the whole play — at least, of what befalls the central characters. Notice, however, that he does not merely summarize. He gives us not only "the play's main line of action," but also a thumbnail description of the character of Anna Fierling, and he declares her "steadfast purpose." He says she is, at the end of the play, "a survivor in only the narrowest bodily sense." His second paragraph develops this telling remark, going on to state his understanding of Brecht's point, the play's essential theme. In making this statement, Gilman keeps the text of the play before him, and refers to the story of the bombardment of Riga. He quotes from a speech of Mother Courage, to show her belief that the loss of some bread would "ruin" her, not the loss of her life. Having set forth the theme — Brecht's comment on the terrible folly of living only by "business sense," by practicality — Gilman returns in his third paragraph to the method of summary. Again, he does much more than summarize: he tells why the deaths of the children occurred; and he demonstrates that, in these events, the play makes clear its theme.

Gilman's thematic analysis goes on, but this much of it may be enough to suggest its effectiveness. Someone has described a good writer (on any subject) as one who continually makes leaps from the specific to the general and back again — leaps as agile as those of a squirrel that lives in a tree, moving back and forth, up and down between lower and higher branches. An expert critic of drama, such as Gilman, proceeds with a similar ease and confidence. Your instructor will not expect you to write with so much knowledge and skill, but perhaps you can learn from Gilman's example. Gilman keeps pointing to details in the text of the play, going on to clarify (in more abstract terms) whatever he thinks they mean — now moving in for a closer look, now stepping back for a larger, more inclusive view. From the loftiest generalization — a statement of the play's main theme — he is perfectly capable of coming down again and again to specific events, to characters, to the playwright's very words.

THE CARD REPORT

Instead of an essay, some instructors like to assign a **card report**. If asked to write a card report on a play, you will find yourself writing a kind of analysis. To do so, you first single out certain elements of a play, then you list them on 5 x 8-inch index cards as concisely as possible.

[2] From "Brecht," a chapter in Gilman's *The Making of Modern Drama* (New York: Farrar, Straus and Giroux, 1974), pp. 224–225.

Such an exercise is often assigned in a class studying fiction; and one student's card report on the Edgar Allan Poe story, "The Tell-Tale Heart," appears on pages 225–226. In dealing with a play, however, you will need to include some elements different from those in a short story. And because a full-length play may take more room to summarize than a short story, your instructor may suggest that, if necessary, you take two cards (four sides) for your report. Still, in order to write a good card report, you have to be both brief and specific. Before you start, sort out your impressions of the play, and try to decide what characters, scenes, and lines of dialogue are the most important and memorable. Reducing your scattered impressions to essentials, you will have to reexamine what you have read; and when you get done, you will know the play much more thoroughly. It is not easy to write readable comments within so small a space; and you may find such a report taking as much thought and effort as any analysis you have ever written in essay form.

On the following three pages, you will find an example: a card report on Brecht's *Mother Courage and Her Children* — a complex, panoramic play spanning a period of thirteen years, and so, especially difficult to summarize. Nevertheless, the student, by including only those things that seemed crucial, managed to write a fair account of the play in only three card sides. He still managed to work in two or three pertinent quotations, and, at the end, to include some of his own sharp observations. An adequate report on *Mother Courage* hardly could be much briefer. If you were to report on a one-scene play with only two or three characters — Chekhov's *The Marriage Proposal*, say, or Pinter's *The Dumb Waiter* — you might find yourself able to confine your report to a single card. For the *Mother Courage* report, the student was asked to include:

1. The playwright's name, nationality, and dates.
2. The title of the play and the date of its first performance.
3. The central character, with a brief description that includes leading traits.
4. Other characters, also described.
5. The scene or scenes and, if the play does not take place in the present, the time of its action.
6. The major dramatic question. (This question is whatever the play leads us to ask ourselves: some conflict whose outcome we wonder about, some uncertainty. For instance, in Lady Gregory's *The Workhouse Ward*, the question is, "Will Mike McInerney part company with Michael Miskell?" A further discussion of dramatic questions appears in Chapter Thirty-two, "Elements of a Play.")
7. A brief summary of main events in the play, listed act by act (or scene by scene, in the case of *Mother Courage*).

Bertolt Brecht (German, 1898–1956)
Mother Courage and Her Children, 1941

Central character: Anna Fierling, ironically called Mother Courage,
petty war profiteer: a camp-following peddler. Shrewd and cunning, she
is in some ways perceptive (her seeing the "religious war" as actually
being fought for gain), in other ways obtuse (her belief that the war
can bring prosperity to her and her family). Though driven by greed,
she is somehow splendid in her determination to go on, no matter what.
Other characters: her daughter Kattrin, the play's true heroine: a mute,
generous and tender-hearted ("She suffers from sheer pity"). Mother
Courage's sons, each the other's opposite: Eilif, the elder, clever and
unscrupulous; Swiss Cheese, the younger, stupid and honest. Lamb, a
cook: in his youth a Don Juan, now just an ordinary sensual man -- frank
and down-to-earth, but selfish. Yvette Pottier: a prostitute, later an
officer's wife -- cynical and disappointed in love. The Chaplain: a
weak, fallible man of mere words (except for one moment when he seizes
Mother Courage's shirts to make bandages).
    Scene and time: Europe in 1624-1636, during the Thirty Years' War.
Scenes take place in Sweden, Poland, Germany -- wherever armies go:
towns and villages, encampments, highways.
    Major dramatic question: Will Mother Courage's prophecy (that her
children will die) be fulfilled?   Swedish
    Main events (numbers indicate scenes): (1) When/army recruiters try
to enlist Eilif, Mother Courage tells fortunes and predicts death for

(Front of first card)

8. As best one can describe it, the tone of the play: the playwright's apparent feelings toward the main character or the
   main events.
9. One or more situations of **dramatic irony,** if you find any such
   situations in the play. (Dramatic irony occurs when a character
   says, does, or meets something much more meaningful than
   he or she is aware. For instance, when Sophocles' hero
   Oedipus vows to punish the man responsible for bringing
   down a curse on Thebes, he does not know — as does the
   audience — that the man is himself. For a further discussion of
   this term see pages 429–430.)
10. The play's central theme. (If you find none, say so. On the
    other hand, plays often contain more than one theme — which
    of them seems most clearly borne out by the main events?)
11. Any symbols you feel to be centrally important. Try to state
    briefly what each suggests to you.
12. Either (a) a concise evaluation of the play; or (b) a recom-
    mendation for how to produce it. (If you choose to do the
    former, see Chapter Thirty-six, "Evaluating Drama," for spe-
    cific suggestions. If you choose the latter, first decide whether
    or not the play is a work of realism. Should sets, lighting, and

the recruiting sergeant and for her children. Eilif enlists. (2) Two
years later Mother Courage, while selling a capon to the Swedish commander's cook, finds Eilif risen in the army and, for having robbed
peasants, thought a "brave soldier." (3) Yvette relates her bad luck in
love; Kattrin envies her. Mother Courage, Kattrin, Swiss Cheese (now an
army paymaster), and the Chaplain are captured by the Catholics. Swiss
Cheese is executed when his mother haggles too long over his ransom.
She is afraid to claim his body. (4) Singing her "Song of the Great
Capitulation" to a disgruntled soldier, persuading him to accept things
as they are, she decides not to file a complaint against soldiers who
destroyed her goods. (5) After a battle she vainly tries to prevent the
Chaplain from using her shirts for bandages. Kattrin saves a baby's
life. (6) A head wound ruins Kattrin's chances for marriage. For a
moment Mother Courage curses the war, but (7) is soon plying her trade
again. (8) In a brief interlude of peace the Cook reappears; so does
Yvette, who identifies him as her seducer. Eilif, sentenced to die for
slaying a peasant, is granted a last visit to his mother, but finds her
gone to unload goods before prices fall. The Cook conceals the news of
Eilif's doom and replaces the Chaplain as a wagon-puller. (9) The Cook
inherits an inn, asks Mother Courage to join him in running it, but he
won't take Kattrin along. The girl overhears this proposal and tries
to run away, but her mother stops her and sends the Cook packing. (10)
Mother and daughter pull the wagon. (11) Hearing that children are
threatened by a surprise attack on a town, Kattrin mounts a rooftop and
beats a drum to give warning. She is shot to death. (12) Hauling her
wagon alone, Mother Courage goes on endlessly chasing the war.
    Dramatic irony: In (8) and (12), Mother Courage expects to see
Eilif, not knowing of his death. In (9), unknown to Mother Courage and
the Cook, Kattrin overhears their talk about her.

(Back of first card)

costumes be closely detailed and lifelike, or perhaps be extravagant or expressionistic? Would a picture-frame stage or
an arena best accommodate the play? What advice would you
offer the actors for interpreting their roles? What exactly
would you emphasize in the play if you were directing a production of it?)

THE PLAY REVIEW

Writing a **play review,** a brief critical account of an actual performance,
involves making an evaluation. To do so, you first have to decide what
to evaluate: the work of the playwright; the work of the actors, director,
and production staff; or the work of both. If the play is some classic of
Chekhov or Ibsen, then evidently the more urgent task for a reviewer
is not to evaluate the playwright's work, but to evaluate the success of
the actors, director, and production staff in interpreting it. To be sure, a
reviewer's personal feelings toward a play (even a towering classic) may
deserve mention. Writing of a certain Ibsen masterpiece, the critic
H. L. Mencken made a memorable comment when he remarked that,
next to being struck down by a taxicab and having his hat smashed, he
could think of no worse punishment than going to another production

Theme: "War is a business proposition," as Mother Courage declares in her song (7). The sergeant, at the close of (1), applies this theme to her and her family: "When a war gives you all you earn / One day it may claim something in return!"

Tone: indignation mingled with compassion (particularly for Kattrin) and bitter humor. Brecht seems to admire Mother Courage for her horse-sense and her ability to endure, yet he sharply condemns her naive trust in war and in the almighty guilder.

Symbols: the canteen wagon -- the heavy burden of war, the cross to which Mother Courage is finally harnessed without hope of salvation. The Cook's pipe, source of his nickname Peter Piper (another caster of spells?). It shows his nature as a lover: his violence and callousness. Yvette's red boots, which Kattrin covets: ability to attract men. To Mother Courage (6), they seem a way for Kattrin to dispose of her virtue. The wealthy farmhouse and the song within it (10): smug, selfish happiness that tries to ignore others' sufferings -- the attitude of Mother Courage herself.

Recommendation for a production: Exact realism isn't possible in staging a play that includes much of Europe and a period of thirteen years. Perhaps the wagon, the central symbol, should look as real as possible; but costumes can look timeless and abstract. Scenery should appear impermanent: shattered houses, pitched tents. Stage directions seem to call for a picture-frame stage to accommodate so many backgrounds ("In front of a half-ruined parsonage," "a prosperous farm house"), so many horizontal highways. The leading actress shouldn't sentimentalize Mother Courage as a brave, noble Mom, but instead should portray her as a fallible, stubborn human being. ###

(One side of second card)

of *Rosmersholm*. But a newer, less well-known play is probably more in need of an evaluation.

To judge a live performance is, in many ways, more of a challenge than to judge a play read in a book. Obviously there is much to consider besides the playwright's script: acting, direction, costumes, sets, lighting, perhaps music, anything else that contributes to one's total experience in the theater. Still, many students find that to write a play review is more stimulating — and even more fun — than most writing assignments. And although the student with experience in acting or in stagecraft may be a more knowing reviewer than the student without such experience, the latter may prove just as capable in responding to a play and in judging it fairly and perceptively.

In the previous chapter, "Evaluating Drama," we assumed that in order to judge a play one has to understand it, and be aware of its particular conventions. (For a list of things to consider in judging a play — whether staged or printed — see pages 1265–1266.) Some plays will evoke a stong positive or negative response in the reviewer, either at once or by the time the final curtain tumbles; others will need to be pondered. Incidentally, harsh evaluations sometimes tempt a reviewer to flashes of wit. One celebrated flash is Eugene Field's observation of an actor in a production of *Hamlet*, that "he played the king as though he were in constant fear that somebody else was going to play the ace." The comment isn't merely nasty; it implies that Field had closely watched the actor's performance and had discerned what was wrong with it. Readers, of course, have a right to expect that reviewers do not just sneer (or gush praise), but clearly set forth reasons for their feelings.

Reviewing plays seems an art with few fixed rules, but in general, an adequate play review usually gives us a small summary of the play — for the reader unacquainted with it — and perhaps also indicates what the play is about: its central theme. If the play is familiar and often performed, some comment on the director's whole approach to it may be useful. Is the production exactly what you'd expect, or are there any fresh and apparently original innovations? And if the production is fresh, does it achieve its freshness by violating the play? (The director of one college production of *Othello* — to mention an original, but not entirely successful, innovation — placed emphasis on the play's being partly set in Venice by staging it in the campus swimming pool, with the actors sometimes floating about on barges and on a homemade gondola.) In other respects, does the play seem firmly directed, so that the actors neither lag nor hurry, and so that they speak and gesture not in an awkward, stylized manner, but naturally? Are their roles well chosen for them? Usually, also, a reviewer pays particular attention to the performances of the leading actors, or principals; and to the costumes, sets, and lighting, if these are noteworthy. The theater itself may deserve mention. Is it distractingly uncomfortable? For a certain play, is it strikingly suitable or unsuitable? (*Othello* afloat might seem awkward and artificial. We may be so nervous about the gondola tipping over that we can't pay attention to the lines.) And if, all along, the reviewer has not been making clear an opinion of the play and its production, an opinion will probably emerge in the concluding paragraph.

For further pointers, read a few professional play reviews in magazines such as *The New Yorker, Time, Newsweek, Saturday Review, Hudson Review,* and others; or on the entertainment pages of a metropolitan newspaper. Here is a good concise review of an amateur production of *Mother Courage and Her Children,* written for a college newspaper, but similar to what your instructor might ask you to write for a course assignment.

Players As Peasants Are Moving
But Mother Shows Dearth of Earth

Bertolt Brecht's masterpiece <u>Mother Courage and Her Children</u>, the

final production in the Speech Department Players' spring series, began

a week's run in Soames Auditorium last night. The play takes in a lot

of time and world -- most of Central Europe over a long stretch of the

Thirty Years' War that wasted Germany. It would be a rough thing to stage realistically without a Hollywood budget, and the Players don't try. Still, they manage -- with the aid of Bea Lee and Mel Blaustein's stark, simple sets and Donna Marr's costumes (heavy on the burlap) -- to give you a sense of war-torn landscapes. It all looks like a seventeenth-century Waiting for Godot.

Nobody waits around long in this production, however. The play is full of action, and the Players are nothing if not energetic. I almost wished the peasants would drop their arms to their sides once in a while and stop bounding around like a bunch of jumping beans. The action mainly revolves around the character of Mother Courage, who follows the troops hawking food, brandy, and belts. She consumes lovers like peanuts and has a trio of children as assorted as the/General Assembly. She'll do any- thing to make her family secure in a world where security is scarce. But what she doesn't see is that the war is destroying her family, even though it is good for business, till in the end she is left to pull her wagon single-handedly.

As Mother, Mona Bermingham hits me as miscast, badly. I still remember her fine job as Nora in Ibsen's A Doll House last season. She shook with indignation and made a nineteenth-century Norwegian bluestocking look like a contemporary Libber. But Bermingham, though skilled, looks physically slight for the part of a big fat Bavarian earth mother. Though she shouts loud enough, she seems only shrill, and at the end when she goes off dragging her rolling store, it is a little like watching a dove trying to haul a cement-mixer. She has an annoying habit of turning her back on the audience every time she is supposed to be torn with emotion -- as when, after Swiss Cheese ends up full of holes, she doesn't dare claim his body. Maybe Professor Jan Merke, who directed, is trying to understate things, but I am left feeling that he didn't trust his leading actress to show any real passion. To her credit, Bermingham doesn't sentimentalize the part. She manages to put across a nasty, wheedling, money-grubbing quality that seems just right for a woman supposed to be a "hyena of the battlefield."

The support of the other Players helps what is left of Brecht's play to come on strong. As Swiss Cheese, Otto Uschold has a nice wide-eyed innocence. Annabel Stefanelli, as Kattrin, the daughter who dies a martyr makes a terrific mute, making every look and gesture get across as much as, or more than, words. I like Paul Fallowfield's Eilif (the swaggering other son). Bill-Joe Brenner plays the Chaplain as a stiff, poker-faced type, but according to Brecht, the Chaplain is more complicated, even sometimes likeable. All told, Mother Courage and Her Children is still a great, disturbing play. The Players' energetic production is worth going to.

TOPICS FOR WRITING

Finding a topic that you care to write about is, of course, the most important step in writing a meaningful paper. Specific advice on topic-finding is given on page 1379, in the Appendix: Writing about Literature. The following list of topics is not meant to replace your own ideas, but to get your ideas going, and to illustrate topics likely to result in valuable papers.

TOPICS FOR BRIEF PAPERS (250–500 WORDS)

1. When the curtain comes down on the conclusion of some plays, the audience is left to decide exactly what finally happened. In a short informal essay, state your interpretation of the conclusion of one of these plays: *A Doll House, The Dumb Waiter, The Glass Menagerie, The Real Inspector Hound.* Don't just give a plot summary; tell what you think the conclusion means.
2. Sum up the main suggestions you find in one of these meaningful objects (or actions): the handkerchief in *Othello;* the Christmas tree in *A Doll House* (or Nora's doing a wild tarantella); the dumb waiter in *The Dumb Waiter;* the park bench in *The Zoo Story;* Laura's collection of figurines in *The Glass Menagerie.*
3. Here is an exercise in being terse. Write a card report on a short, one-scene play such as *The Marriage Proposal* or *The Dumb Waiter*, and confine your remarks to both sides of one 5 x 8-inch card. (For further instructions see page 1271.)
4. Review a play you have seen within recent memory and have felt strongly about (or against). Give your opinion of *either* the performance or the playwright's piece of writing, with reasons for your evaluation.
5. Write an essay entitled, "Why I Prefer Plays to Films" (or vice versa). Cite some particular plays and films to support your argument. (If you have never seen any professional plays, pick some other topic.)

Topics for More Extended Papers (600–1,000 words)

1. From a play you have enjoyed, choose a passage that strikes you as difficult, worth reading closely. Try to pick a passage not longer than about 200 words, or twenty lines. Explicate it, working through it sentence by sentence or line by line. For instance, any of these passages might be considered memorable (and essential to their plays):

   Iago's soliloquy, "Thus do I ever make my fool my purse" (*Othello*, I, iii, 356–377).

   Oedipus to Teiresias, speech beginning, "Wealth, power, craft of statesmanship!" (*Oedipus Rex*, Scene I, 163–186).

   Tom Wingfield's opening speech, "Yes, I have tricks in my pocket," through "I think the rest of the play will explain itself . . . ." (*The Glass Menagerie*, Scene I).

   Jerry's passage beginning "It's just . . . it's just that . . . it's just that if you can't deal with people, you have to make a start somewhere. WITH ANIMALS!" (*The Zoo Story*, paragraph near the end of Jerry's dog story monologue).

2. Take just a single line or sentence from a play — one that stands out for some reason as centrally important. Perhaps it states a theme, reveals a character, or serves as a crisis (or turning point). Write an essay demonstrating its importance: how it functions, why it is necessary. Some possible lines:

   Iago to Roderigo: "I am not what I am" (*Othello*, I, i, 62).

   Liza to Pickering: "The difference between a lady and a flower girl is not how she behaves, but how she's treated" (*Pygmalion*, V).

   Amanda to Tom: "You live in a dream; you manufacture illusions!" (*The Glass Menagerie*, VII).

   Moon to Birdboot: "It will follow me to my grave and become my epitaph — Here lies Moon the second string" (*The Real Inspector Hound*, the opening conversation).

3. Write an essay in analysis, in which you single out one element of a play for examination — character, plot, setting, theme, dramatic irony, tone, language, symbolism, conventions, or any other element. Try to relate this element to the play as a whole. Sample topics: "Imagery of Poison in *A Doll House* (or in *Othello*)"; "The Character of Teiresias in *Oedipus Rex*"; "Varieties of Speech in *Pygmalion*"; "Dramatic Irony as Laugh-getter in *Come Blow Your Horn*"; "Tennessee Williams's Use of Magic-Lantern Slides in *The Glass Menagerie*"; "All the World's a Zoo: The Central Metaphor of a Play by Edward Albee."

4. Compare and contrast a character, theme, or situation in a play with a similar element in a work of fiction. For instance, taking *The Zoo Story* and Joseph Conrad's short novel in Chapter Ten, write an essay, "Jerry as Peter's Secret Sharer." Or find a similarity between Tom Stoppard's *The Real Inspector Hound* and A. Conan Doyle's story of Sherlock Holmes, "The Adventure of the Speckled Band."

Topics for Long Papers (1,500 words or more)

1. Choosing from among the Plays for Further Study, or taking some other modern or contemporary play your instructor suggests, report any diffi-

culties you encountered in reading and responding to it. Explicate any troublesome passages for the benefit of other readers.

2. After you have read the discussion of the theater of the absurd in Chapter Thirty-five, analyze for their element of absurdity *The Dumb Waiter, The Zoo Story,* and *The Real Inspector Hound.* What conventions of the theater of the absurd do the three plays contain?

3. Compare and contrast two plays — a play in this book and another play by the same author — with attention to one particular element. For instance: "The Theme of Woman's Independence in Ibsen's *A Doll House* and *Hedda Gabler*"; "Shaw's Criticism of Society in *Pygmalion* and *Major Barbara*"; "Antirealism in the Stagecraft of Tennessee Williams: *The Glass Menagerie* and *Camino Real.*"

4. Compare and contrast two plays by different authors — "*Come Blow Your Horn* and *The Zoo Story:* Two Concepts of 'Success' in Business and in Love."

5. Transform a short story that you admire into the script for a one-act play. Include a description of sets, lighting, and costumes; stage directions; and instructions for the actors wherever necessary. Some likely stories to work on: "A & P," "The Catbird Seat," "The Chaser," "The Minister's Black Veil," "A Dill Pickle," "The Tell-Tale Heart," "First Confession." After you have completed your play, write a brief account of the problems you encountered in trying to move the story to the stage, and what you did about them. (Or you might direct a classroom performance of your play, then discuss its problems with the class.)

6. If you have ever acted or taken part in staging plays, consult with your instructor and see whether you both find that your experience could enable you to write a substantial paper. With the aid of specific recollections, perhaps, you might sum up what you have learned about the nature of drama or about what makes an effective play.

38 Plays for Further Study

FROM A PROPOSED AGREEMENT BETWEEN THE PLAYWRIGHT AND THE SPECTATOR

It is also agreed that every man here exercise his own judgment and not censure by contagion, or upon trust, from another's voice or face that sits by him . . . that he be fixed and settled in his censure, that what he approves or not approves today he will do the same tomorrow; and, if tomorrow, the next day; and so the next week, if need be; and not be brought about by any that sits on the bench with him, though they indict and arraign plays daily.

— The Scrivener, in Ben Jonson's *Bartholomew Fair* (1614)

Tennessee Williams (b. 1914)

THE GLASS MENAGERIE

1945

Nobody, not even the rain, has such small hands.
                                    E. E. Cummings

Characters

Amanda Wingfield, the mother. A little woman of great but confused vitality clinging frantically to another time and place. Her characterization must be carefully created, not copied from type. She is not paranoiac, but her life is paranoia. There is much to admire in Amanda, and as much to love and pity as there is to laugh at. Certainly she has endurance and a kind of heroism, and though her foolishness makes her unwittingly cruel at times, there is tenderness in her slight person.

Laura Wingfield, her daughter. Amanda, having failed to establish contact with reality, continues to live vitally in her illusions, but Laura's situation is even graver. A childhood illness has left her crippled, one leg slightly shorter than the other, and held in a brace. This defect need not be more than suggested on the stage. Stemming from this, Laura's separation increases till she is like a piece of her own glass collection, too exquisitely fragile to move from the shelf.

Tom Wingfield, her son. And the narrator of the play. A poet with a job in a warehouse. His nature is not remorseless, but to escape from a trap he has to act without pity.

Jim O'Connor, the gentleman caller. A nice, ordinary, young man.

Scene. *An alley in St. Louis.*

Part I. *Preparation for a Gentleman Caller.*
Part II. *The Gentleman Calls.*

Time. *Now and the Past.*

SCENE I

The Wingfield apartment is in the rear of the building, one of those vast hive-like conglomerations of cellular living-units that flower as warty growths in overcrowded urban centers of lower middle-class population and are symptomatic of the impulse of this largest and fundamentally enslaved section of American society to avoid fluidity and differentiation and to exist and function as one interfused mass of automatism.

The apartment faces an alley and is entered by a fire-escape, a structure whose name is a touch of accidental poetic truth, for all of these huge buildings are always burning with the slow and implacable fires of human desperation. The fire-escape is included in the set — that is, the landing of it and steps descending from it.

The scene is memory and is therefore nonrealistic. Memory takes a lot of poetic license. It omits some details; others are exaggerated, according to the emotional value of the articles it touches, for memory is seated predominantly in the heart. The interior is therefore rather dim and poetic.

At the rise of the curtain, the audience is faced with the dark, grim rear wall of the Wingfield tenement. This building, which runs parallel to the footlights, is flanked on both sides by dark, narrow alleys which run into murky canyons of tangled clotheslines, garbage cans and the sinister latticework of neighboring fire-escapes. It is up and down these side alleys that exterior entrances and exits are made, during the play. At the end of Tom's opening commentary, the dark tenement wall slowly reveals (by means of a transparency) the interior of the ground floor Wingfield apartment.

Downstage is the living room, which also serves as a sleeping room for Laura, the sofa unfolding to make her bed. Upstage, center, and divided by a wide arch or second proscenium with transparent faded portieres (or second curtain), is the dining room. In an old-fashioned what-not in the living room are seen scores of transparent glass animals. A blown-up photograph of the father hangs on the wall of the living room, facing the audience, to the left of the archway. It is the face of a very handsome young man in a doughboy's First World War cap. He is gallantly smiling, ineluctably smiling, as if to say, "I will be smiling forever."

The audience hears and sees the opening scene in the dining room through both the transparent fourth wall of the building and the transparent gauze portieres of the dining-room arch. It is during this revealing scene that the fourth wall slowly ascends, out of sight. This transparent exterior wall is not brought down again until the very end of the play, during Tom's final speech.

The narrator is an undisguised convention of the play. He takes whatever license with dramatic convention as is convenient to his purposes.

Tom enters dressed as a merchant sailor from alley, stage left, and strolls across the front of the stage to the fire-escape. There he stops and lights a cigarette. He addresses the audience.

Tom: Yes, I have tricks in my pocket, I have things up my sleeve. But I am the opposite of a stage magician. He gives you illusion that has the appearance of truth. I give you truth in the pleasant disguise of illusion. To begin with, I turn back time. I reverse it to that quaint period, the thirties, when the huge middle class of America was matriculating in a school for the blind. Their eyes had failed them, or they had failed their eyes, and so they were having their fingers pressed forcibly down on the fiery Braille alphabet of a dissolving economy. In Spain there was revolution. Here there was only shouting and confusion. In Spain there was Guernica. Here there were disturbances of labor, sometimes pretty violent, in otherwise peaceful cities such as Chicago, Cleveland, Saint Louis. . . . This is the social background of the play.

(Music.)

The play is memory. Being a memory play, it is dimly lighted, it is sentimental, it is not realistic. In memory everything seems to happen to music. That explains the fiddle in the wings. I am the narrator of the play, and also a character in it. The other characters are my mother, Amanda, my sister, Laura, and a gentleman caller who appears in the final scenes. He is the most realistic character in the play, being an emissary from a world of reality that we were somehow set apart from. But since I have a poet's weakness for symbols, I am using this character also as a symbol; he is the long delayed but always expected something that we live for. There is a fifth character in the play who doesn't appear except in this larger-than-life photograph over the mantel. This is our father who left us a long time ago. He was a telephone man who fell in love with long distances; he gave up his job with the telephone company and skipped the light fantastic out of town . . . The last we heard of him was a picture post-card from Mazatlan, on the Pacific coast of Mexico, containing a message of two words — "Hello — Good-bye!" and an address. I think the rest of the play will explain itself. . . .

Amanda's voice becomes audible through the portieres.

(Legend on Screen: "Où Sont Les Neiges.")°

He divides the portieres and enters the upstage area.

    Amanda and Laura are seated at a drop-leaf table. Eating is indicated by gestures without food or utensils. Amanda faces the audience. Tom and Laura are seated in profile.

    The interior has lit up softly and through the scrim we see Amanda and Laura seated at the table in the upstage area.

Amanda (calling): Tom?
Tom: Yes, Mother.
Amanda: We can't say grace until you come to the table!
Tom: Coming, Mother. *(He bows slightly and withdraws, reappearing a few moments later in his place at the table.)*
Amanda (to her son): Honey, don't *push* with your *fingers.* If you have to push with something, the thing to push with is a crust of bread. And chew — chew! Animals have sections in their stomachs which enable them to digest food without mastication, but human beings are supposed to chew their food before they swallow it down. Eat food leisurely, son, and really enjoy it. A well-cooked meal has lots of delicate flavors that have to be held in the mouth for appreciation. So chew your food and give your salivary glands a chance to function!

Tom deliberately lays his imaginary fork down and pushes his chair back from the table.

Tom: I haven't enjoyed one bite of this dinner because of your constant directions on how to eat it. It's you that makes me rush through meals with your hawk-like attention to every bite I take. Sickening — spoils my appetite — all this discussion of animals' secretion — salivary glands — mastication!
Amanda (lightly): Temperament like a Metropolitan star! *(He rises and crosses downstage.)* You're not excused from the table.
Tom: I am getting a cigarette.
Amanda: You smoke too much.

(Legend . . . Neiges."): A slide bearing this line by the French poet François Villon, "Where are the snows (of yesteryear)?", is to be projected on a stage wall.

Laura rises.

Laura: I'll bring in the blanc mange.

He remains standing with his cigarette by the portieres during the following.

Amanda (rising): No, sister, no, sister — you be the lady this time and I'll be the darky.

Laura: I'm already up.

Amanda: Resume your seat, little sister — I want you to stay fresh and pretty — for gentlemen callers!

Laura: I'm not expecting any gentlemen callers.

Amanda (crossing out to kitchenette. Airily): Sometimes they come when they are least expected! Why, I remember one Sunday afternoon in Blue Mountain — *(Enters kitchenette.)*

Tom: I know what's coming!

Laura: Yes. But let her tell it.

Tom: Again?

Laura: She loves to tell it.

Amanda returns with bowl of dessert.

Amanda: One Sunday afternoon in Blue Mountain — your mother received — seventeen! — gentlemen callers! Why, sometimes there weren't chairs enough to accommodate them all. We had to send the nigger over to bring in folding chairs from the parish house.

Tom (remaining at portieres): How did you entertain those gentlemen callers?

Amanda: I understood the art of conversation!

Tom: I bet you could talk.

Amanda: Girls in those days *knew* how to talk, I can tell you.

Tom: Yes?

(Image: Amanda As A Girl On A Porch Greeting Callers.)

Amanda: They knew how to entertain their gentlemen callers. It wasn't enough for a girl to be possessed of a pretty face and a graceful figure — although I wasn't slighted in either respect. She also needed to have a nimble wit and a tongue to meet all occasions.

Tom: What did you talk about?

Amanda: Things of importance going on in the world! Never anything coarse or common or vulgar. *(She addresses Tom as though he were seated in the vacant chair at the table though he remains by portieres. He plays this scene as though he held the book.)* My callers were gentlemen — all! Among my callers were some of the most prominent young planters of the Mississippi Delta — planters and sons of planters!

Tom motions for music and a spot of light on Amanda. Her eyes lift, her face glows, her voice becomes rich and elegiac.

(Screen Legend: "Où Sont Les Neiges.")

There was young Champ Laughlin who later became vice-president of the Delta Planters Bank. Hadley Stevenson who was drowned in Moon Lake and left his widow one hundred and fifty thousand in Government bonds.

There were the Cutrere brothers, Wesley and Bates. Bates was one of my bright particular beaux! He got in a quarrel with that wild Wainright boy. They shot it out on the floor of Moon Lake Casino. Bates was shot through the stomach. Died in the ambulance on his way to Memphis. His widow was also well-provided for, came into eight or ten thousand acres, that's all. She married him on the rebound — never loved her — carried my picture on him the night he died! And there was that boy that every girl in the Delta had set her cap for! That beautiful, brilliant young Fitzhugh boy from Green County!

Tom: What did he leave his widow?

Amanda: He never married! Gracious, you talk as though all of my old admirers had turned up their toes to the daisies!

Tom: Isn't this the first you mentioned that still survives?

Amanda: That Fitzhugh boy went North and made a fortune — came to be known as the Wolf of Wall Street! He had the Midas touch, whatever he touched turned to gold! And I could have been Mrs. Duncan J. Fitzhugh, mind you! But — I picked your *father!*

Laura (rising): Mother, let me clear the table.

Amanda: No dear, you go in front and study your typewriter chart. Or practice your shorthand a little. Stay fresh and pretty! — It's almost time for our gentlemen callers to start arriving. (*She flounces girlishly toward the kitchenette.*) How many do you suppose we're going to entertain this afternoon?

Tom throws down the paper and jumps up with a groan.

Laura (alone in the dining room): I don't believe we're going to receive any, Mother.

Amanda (reappearing, airily): What? No one — not one? You must be joking! (*Laura nervously echoes her laugh. She slips in a fugitive manner through the half-open portieres and draws them gently behind her. A shaft of very clear light is thrown on her face against the faded tapestry of the curtains.*) **(Music: "The Glass Menagerie" Under Faintly.)** (*Lightly.*) Not one gentleman caller? It can't be true! There must be a flood, there must have been a tornado!

Laura: It isn't a flood, it's not a tornado, Mother. I'm just not popular like you were in Blue Mountain. . . . (*Tom utters another groan. Laura glances at him with a faint, apologetic smile. Her voice catching a little.*) Mother's afraid I'm going to be an old maid.

(The Scene Dims Out With "Glass Menagerie" Music.)

SCENE II

"Laura, Haven't You Ever Liked Some Boy?"

On the dark stage the screen is lighted with the image of blue roses.
    Gradually Laura's figure becomes apparent and the screen goes out.
    The music subsides.
    Laura is seated in the delicate ivory chair at the small clawfoot table.
    She wears a dress of soft violet material for a kimono — her hair tied back from her forehead with a ribbon.
    She is washing and polishing her collection of glass.

Amanda appears on the fire-escape steps. At the sound of her ascent, Laura catches her breath, thrusts the bowl of ornaments away and seats herself stiffly before the diagram of the typewriter keyboard as though it held her spellbound. Something has happened to Amanda. It is written in her face as she climbs to the landing: a look that is grim and hopeless and a little absurd.

She has on one of those cheap or imitation velvety-looking cloth coats with imitation fur collar. Her hat is five or six years old, one of those dreadful cloche hats that were worn in the late twenties, and she is clasping an enormous black patent-leather pocketbook with nickel clasp and initials. This is her fulldress outfit, the one she usually wears to the D.A.R.

Before entering she looks through the door.

She purses her lips, opens her eyes wide, rolls them upward and shakes her head.

Then she slowly lets herself in the door. Seeing her mother's expression Laura touches her lips with a nervous gesture.

Laura: Hello, Mother, I was — *(She makes a nervous gesture toward the chart on the wall. Amanda leans against the shut door and stares at Laura with a martyred look.)*

Amanda: Deception? Deception? *(She slowly removes her hat and gloves, continuing the swift suffering stare. She lets the hat and gloves fall on the floor — a bit of acting.)*

Laura (shakily): How was the D.A.R. meeting? *(Amanda slowly opens her purse and removes a dainty white handkerchief which she shakes out delicately and delicately touches to her lips and nostrils.)* Didn't you go the D.A.R. meeting, Mother?

Amanda (faintly, almost inaudibly): — No. — No. *(Then more forcibly.)* I did not have the strength — to go the D.A.R. In fact, I did not have the courage! I wanted to find a hole in the ground and hide myself in it forever! *(She crosses slowly to the wall and removes the diagram of the typewriter keyboard. She holds it in front of her for a second, staring at it sweetly and sorrowfully — then bites her lips and tears it in two pieces.)*

Laura (faintly): Why did you do that, Mother? *(Amanda repeats the same procedure with the chart of the Gregg Alphabet.)* Why are you —

Amanda: Why? Why? How old are you, Laura?

Laura: Mother, you know my age.

Amanda: I thought that you were an adult; it seems that I was mistaken. *(She crosses slowly to the sofa and sinks down and stares at Laura.)*

Laura: Please don't stare at me, Mother.

Amanda closes her eyes and lowers her head. Count ten.

Amanda: What are we going to do, what is going to become of us, what is the future?

Count ten.

Laura: Has something happened, Mother? *(Amanda draws a long breath and takes out the handkerchief again. Dabbing process.)* Mother, has — something happened?

Amanda: I'll be all right in a minute. I'm just bewildered — *(count five)* — by life. . . .

Laura: Mother, I wish that you would tell me what's happened.

Amanda: As you know, I was supposed to be inducted into my office at the D.A.R. this afternoon. **(Image: A Swarm of Typewriters.)** But I stopped off at Rubicam's Business College to speak to your teachers about your having a cold and ask them what progress they thought you were making down there.

Laura: Oh. . . .

Amanda: I went to the typing instructor and introduced myself as your mother. She didn't know who you were. Wingfield, she said. We don't have any such student enrolled at the school! I assured her she did, that you had been going to classes since early in January. "I wonder," she said, "if you could be talking about that terribly shy little girl who dropped out of school after only a few days' attendance?" "No," I said, "Laura, my daughter, has been going to school every day for the past six weeks!" "Excuse me," she said. She took the attendance book out and there was your name, unmistakably printed, and all the dates you were absent until they decided that you had dropped out of school. I still said, "No, there must have been some mistake! There must have been some mix-up in the records!" And she said, "No — I remember her perfectly now. Her hand shook so that she couldn't hit the right keys! The first time we gave a speed-test, she broke down completely — was sick at the stomach and almost had to be carried into the wash-room! After that morning she never showed up any more. We phoned the house but never got any answer" — while I was working at Famous and Barr, I suppose, demonstrating those — Oh! I felt so weak I could barely keep on my feet. I had to sit down while they got me a glass of water! Fifty dollars' tuition, all of our plans — my hopes and ambitions for you — just gone up the spout, just gone up the spout like that. *(Laura draws a long breath and gets awkwardly to her feet. She crosses to the victrola and winds it up.)* What are you doing?

Laura: Oh! *(She releases the handle and returns to her seat.)*

Amanda: Laura, where have you been going when you've gone out pretending that you were going to business college?

Laura: I've just been going out walking.

Amanda: That's not true.

Laura: It is. I just went walking.

Amanda: Walking? Walking? In winter? Deliberately courting pneumonia in that light coat? Where did you walk to, Laura?

Laura: It was the lesser of two evils, Mother. **(Image: Winter Scene In Park.)** I couldn't go back up. I — threw up — on the floor!

Amanda: From half past seven till after five every day you mean to tell me you walked around in the park, because you wanted to make me think that you were still going to Rubicam's Business College?

Laura: It wasn't as bad as it sounds. I went inside places to get warmed up.

Amanda: Inside where?

Laura: I went in the art museum and the bird-houses at the Zoo. I visited the penguins every day! Sometimes I did without lunch and went to the movies. Lately I've been spending most of my afternoons in the Jewel-box, that big glass house where they raise the tropical flowers.

Amanda: You did all this to deceive me, just for the deception? *(Laura looks down.)* Why?

Laura: Mother, when you're disappointed, you get that awful suffering look on your face, like the picture of Jesus' mother in the museum!

Amanda: Hush!

Laura: I couldn't face it.

Pause. A whisper of strings.

(Legend: "The Crust of Humility.")

Amanda (hopelessly fingering the huge pocketbook): So what are we going to do the rest of our lives? Stay home and watch the parades go by? Amuse ourselves with the glass menagerie, darling? Eternally play those worn-out phonograph records your father left as a painful reminder of him? We won't have a business career — we've given that up because it gave us nervous indigestion! *(Laughs wearily.)* What is there left but dependency all our lives? I know so well what becomes of unmarried women who aren't prepared to occupy a position. I've seen such pitiful cases in the South — barely tolerated spinsters living upon the grudging patronage of sister's husband or brother's wife! — stuck away in some little mouse-trap of a room — encouraged by one in-law to visit another — little birdlike women without any nest — eating the crust of humility all their life! Is that the future that we've mapped out for ourselves? I swear it's the only alternative I can think of! It isn't a very pleasant alternative, is it? Of course — some girls *do* marry. *(Laura twists her hands nervously.)* Haven't you ever liked some boy?

Laura: Yes I liked one once. *(Rises.)* I came across his picture a while ago.

Amanda (with some interest): He gave you his picture?

Laura: No, it's in the year-book.

Amanda (disappointed): Oh — a high-school boy.

(Screen Image: Jim As A High-School Hero Bearing A Silver Cup.)

Laura: Yes. His name was Jim. *(Laura lifts the heavy annual from the clawfoot table.)* Here he is in *The Pirates of Penzance.*

Amanda (absently): The what?

Laura: The operetta the senior class put on. He had a wonderful voice and we sat across the aisle from each other Mondays, Wednesdays and Fridays in the Aud. Here he is with the silver cup for debating! See his grin?

Amanda (absently): He must have had a jolly disposition.

Laura: He used to call me — Blue Roses.

(Image: Blue Roses.)

Amanda: Why did he call you such a name as that?

Laura: When I had that attack of pleurosis — he asked me what was the matter when I came back. I said pleurosis — he thought that I said Blue Roses! So that's what he always called me after that. Whenever he saw me, he'd holler, "Hello, Blue Roses!" I didn't care for the girl that he went out with. Emily Meisenbach. Emily was the best-dressed girl at Soldan. She never struck me, though, as being sincere . . . It says in the Personal Section — they're engaged. That's — six years ago! They must be married by now.

Amanda: Girls that aren't cut out for business careers usually wind up married to some nice man. *(Gets up with a spark of revival.)* Sister, that's what you'll do!.

Laura utters a startled, doubtful laugh. She reaches quickly for a piece of glass.

Laura: But, Mother —
Amanda: Yes? *(Crossing to photograph.)*
Laura (in a tone of frightened apology): I'm — crippled!

(Image: Screen.)

Amanda: Nonsense! Laura, I've told you never, never to use that word. Why, you're not crippled, you just have a little defect — hardly noticeable, even! When people have some slight disadvantage like that, they cultivate other things to make up for it — develop charm — and vivacity — and — *charm!* That's all you have to do! *(She turns again to the photograph.)* One thing your father had *plenty of* — was *charm!*

Tom motions to the fiddle in the wings.

(The Scene Fades Out With Music.)

SCENE III

(Legend On The Screen: "After The Fiasco — ")

Tom speaks from the fire-escape landing.

Tom: After the fiasco at Rubicam's Business College, the idea of getting a gentleman caller for Laura began to play a more important part in Mother's calculations. It became an obsession. Like some archetype of the universal unconscious, the image of the gentleman caller haunted our small apartment. . . . **(Image: Young Man At Door With Flowers.)** An evening at home rarely passed without some allusion to this image, this spectre, this hope. . . . Even when he wasn't mentioned, his presence hung in Mother's preoccupied look and in my sister's frightened, apologetic manner — hung like a sentence passed upon the Wingfields! Mother was a woman of action as well as words. She began to take logical steps in the planned direction. Late that winter and in the early spring — realizing that extra money would be needed to properly feather the nest and plume the bird — she conducted a vigorous campaign on the telephone, roping in subscribers to one of those magazines for matrons called *The Home-maker's Companion,* the type of journal that features the serialized sublimations of ladies of letters who think in terms of delicate cup-like breasts, slim, tapering waists, rich, creamy thighs, eyes like wood-smoke in autumn, fingers that soothe and caress like strains of music, bodies as powerful as Etruscan sculpture.

(Screen Image: Glamor Magazine Cover.)

Amanda enters with phone on long extension cord. She is spotted in the dim stage.

Amanda: Ida Scott? This is Amanda Wingfield! We *missed* you at the D.A.R. last Monday! I said to myself: She's probably suffering with that sinus condition! How is that sinus condition? Horrors! Heaven have mercy! — You're a Christian martyr, yes, that's what you are, a Christian martyr! Well, I just now happened to notice that your subscription to the *Companion's* about to expire! Yes, it expires with the next issue, honey! — just when that wonderful new serial by Bessie Mae Hopper is getting off to such an exciting start. Oh, honey, it's something that you can't miss! You remember how *Gone With the Wind* took everybody by storm? You simply couldn't go out if you hadn't read it. All everybody *talked* was Scarlett O'Hara. Well, this is a book that critics already compare to *Gone With the Wind.* It's the *Gone With the Wind* of the post-World War generation! — What? — Burning? — Oh, honey, don't let them burn, go take a look in the oven and I'll hold the wire! Heavens — I think she's hung up!

(Dim Out.)

(Legend On Screen: "You Think I'm In Love With Continental Shoemakers?")

Before the stage is lighted, the violent voices of Tom and Amanda are heard. They are quarreling behind the portieres. In front of them stands Laura with clenched hands and panicky expression.

A clear pool of light on her figure throughout this scene.

Tom: What in Christ's name am I —
Amanda (shrilly): Don't you use that —
Tom: Supposed to do!
Amanda: Expression! Not in my —
Tom: Ohhh!
Amanda: Presence! Have you gone out of your senses?
Tom: I have, that's true, *driven* out!
Amanda: What is the matter with you, you — big — big — IDIOT!
Tom: Look — I've got *no thing*, no single thing —
Amanda: Lower your voice!
Tom: In my life here that I can call my OWN! Everything is —
Amanda: Stop that shouting!
Tom: Yesterday you confiscated my books! You had the nerve to —
Amanda: I took that horrible novel back to the library — yes! That hideous book by that insane Mr. Lawrence. *(Tom laughs wildly.)* I cannot control the output of diseased minds or people who cater to them — *(Tom laughs still more wildly.)* BUT I WON'T ALLOW SUCH FILTH BROUGHT INTO MY HOUSE! No, no, no, no, no!
Tom: House, house! Who pays rent on it, who makes a slave of himself to —
Amanda (fairly screeching): Don't you DARE to —
Tom: No, no, I mustn't say things! *I've* got to just —

Amanda: Let me tell you —

Tom: I don't want to hear any more! (*He tears the portieres open. The upstage area is lit with a turgid smoky red glow.*)

Amanda's hair is in metal curlers and she wears a very old bathrobe, much too large for her slight figure, a relic of the faithless Mr. Wingfield.

An upright typewriter and a wild disarray of manuscripts are on the drop-leaf table. The quarrel was probably precipitated by Amanda's interruption of his creative labor. A chair lying overthrown on the floor.

Their gesticulating shadows are cast on the ceiling by the fiery glow.

Amanda: You *will* hear more, you —

Tom: No, I won't hear more, I'm going out!

Amanda: You come right back in —

Tom: Out, out out! Because I'm —

Amanda: Come back here, Tom Wingfield! I'm not through talking to you!

Tom: Oh, go —

Laura (desperately): Tom!

Amanda: You're going to listen, and no more insolence from you! I'm at the end of my patience! (*He comes back toward her.*)

Tom: What do you think I'm at? Aren't I supposed to have any patience to reach the end of, Mother? I know, I know. It seems unimportant to you, what I'm *doing* — what I *want* to do — having a little *difference* between them! You don't think that —

Amanda: I think you've been doing things that you're ashamed of. That's why you act like this. I don't believe that you go every night to the movies. Nobody goes to the movies night after night. Nobody in their right minds goes to the movies as often as you pretend to. People don't go to the movies at nearly midnight, and movies don't let out at two A.M. Come in stumbling. Muttering to yourself like a maniac! You get three hours' sleep and then go to work. Oh, I can picture the way you're doing down there. Moping, doping, because you're in no condition.

Tom (wildly): No, I'm in no condition!

Amanda: What right have you got to jeopardize your job? Jeopardize the security of us all? How do you think we'd manage if you were —

Tom: Listen! You think I'm crazy *about* the *warehouse*? (*He bends fiercely toward her slight figure.*) You think I'm in love with the Continental Shoemakers? You think I want to spend fifty-five *years* down there in that — *celotex interior!* with — *fluorescent* — *tubes!* Look! I'd rather somebody picked up a crowbar and battered out my brains — than go back mornings! I *go!* Every time you come in yelling that God damn *"Rise and Shine!" "Rise and Shine!"* I say to myself *"How lucky dead people are!"* But I get up. I *go!* For sixty-five dollars a month I give up all that I dream of doing and being *ever!* And you say self — *self's* all I ever think of. Why, listen, if self is what I thought of, Mother, I'd be where he is — GONE! (*Pointing to father's picture.*) As far as the system of transportation reaches! (*He starts past her. She grabs his arm.*) Don't grab at me, Mother!

Amanda: Where are you going?

Tom: I'm going to the *movies!*

Amanda: I don't believe that lie!

Tom (*crouching toward her, overtowering her tiny figure. She backs away, gasping*): I'm going to opium dens! Yes, opium dens, dens of vice and criminals' hang-outs, Mother. I've joined the Hogan gang, I'm a hired assassin, I carry a tommy-gun in a violin case! I run a string of cat-houses in the Valley! They call me Killer, Killer Wingfield, I'm leading a double-life, a simple, honest warehouse worker by day, by night a dynamic *czar* of the *underworld, Mother.* I go to gambling casinos, I spin away fortunes on the roulette table! I wear a patch over one eye and a false mustache, sometimes I put on green whiskers. On those occasions they call me — *El Diablo!* Oh, I could tell you things to make you sleepless! My enemies plan to dyna-mite this place. They're going to blow us all sky-high some night! I'll be glad, very happy, and so will you! You'll go up, up on a broomstick, over Blue Mountain with seventeen gentlemen callers! You ugly — babbling old — witch. . . . (*He goes through a series of violent, clumsy movements, seizing his overcoat, lunging to the door, pulling it fiercely open. The women watch him, aghast. His arm catches in the sleeve of the coat as he struggles to pull it on. For a moment he is pinioned by the bulky garment. With an out-raged groan he tears the coat off again, splitting the shoulders of it, and hurls it across the room. It strikes against the shelf of Laura's glass collection, there is a tinkle of shattering glass. Laura cries out as if wounded.*)

(Music Legend: "The Glass Menagerie.")

Laura (*shrilly*): My glass! — menagerie. . . . (*She covers her face and turns away.*)

But Amanda is still stunned and stupefied by the "ugly witch" so that she barely notices this occurrence. Now she recovers her speech.

Amanda (*in an awful voice*): I won't speak to you — until you apologize! (*She crosses through portieres and draws them together behind her. Tom is left with Laura. Laura clings weakly to the mantel with her face averted. Tom stares at her stupidly for a moment. Then he crosses to shelf. Drops awkwardly to his knees to collect the fallen glass, glancing at Laura as if he would speak but couldn't.*)

"The Glass Menagerie" steals in as

(The Scene Dims Out.)

SCENE IV

The interior is dark. Faint in the alley.

A deep-voiced bell in a church is tolling the hour of five as the scene com-mences.

Tom appears at the top of the alley. After each solemn boom of the bell in the tower, he shakes a little noise-maker or rattle as if to express the tiny spasm of man in contrast to the sustained power and dignity of the Almighty. This and the unsteadi-ness of his advance make it evident that he has been drinking.

As he climbs the few steps to the fire-escape landing light steals up inside. Laura appears in night-dress, observing Tom's empty bed in the front room.

Tom fishes in his pockets for the door-key, removing a motley assortment of articles in the search, including a perfect shower of movie-ticket stubs and an empty bottle. At last he finds the key, but just as he is about to insert it, it slips from his fingers. He strikes a match and crouches below the door.

Tom (bitterly): One crack — and it falls through!

Laura opens the door.

Laura: Tom! Tom, what are you doing?
Tom: Looking for a door-key.
Laura: Where have you been all this time?
Tom: I have been to the movies.
Laura: All this time at the movies?
Tom: There was a very long program. There was a Garbo picture and a Mickey Mouse and a travelogue and a newsreel and a preview of coming attractions. And there was an organ solo and a collection for the milk-fund — simultaneously — which ended up in a terrible fight between a fat lady and an usher!
Laura (innocently): Did you have to stay through everything?
Tom: Of course! And, oh, I forgot! There was a big stage show! The headliner on this stage show was Malvolio the Magician. He performed wonderful tricks, many of them, such as pouring water back and forth between pitchers. First it turned to wine and then it turned to beer and then it turned to whiskey. I know it was whiskey it finally turned into because he needed somebody to come up out of the audience to help him, and I came up — both shows! It was Kentucky Straight Bourbon. A very generous fellow, he gave souvenirs. *(He pulls from his back pocket a shimmering rainbow-colored scarf.)* He gave me this. This is his magic scarf. You can have it, Laura. You wave it over a canary cage and you get a bowl of gold-fish. You wave it over the gold-fish bowl and they fly away canaries. . . But the wonderfullest trick of all was the coffin trick. We nailed him into a coffin and he got out of the coffin without removing one nail. *(He has come inside.)* There is a trick that would come in handy for me — get me out of this 2 by 4 situation! *(Flops onto bed and starts removing shoes.)*
Laura: Tom — Shhh!
Tom: What you shushing me for?
Laura: You'll wake up Mother.
Tom: Goody, goody! Pay 'er back for all those "Rise an' Shines." *(Lies down, groaning.)* You know it don't take much intelligence to get yourself into a nailed-up coffin, Laura. But who in hell ever got himself out of one without removing one nail?

As if in answer, the father's grinning photograph lights up.

(Scene Dims Out.)

Immediately following: The church bell is heard striking six. At the sixth stroke the alarm clock goes off in Amanda's room, and after a few moments we hear her calling: "Rise and Shine! Rise and Shine! Laura, go tell your brother to rise and shine!"

Tom (*sitting up slowly*): I'll rise — but I won't shine.

The light increases.

Amanda: Laura, tell your brother his coffee is ready.

Laura slips into front room.

Laura: Tom! it's nearly seven. Don't make Mother nervous. (*He stares at her stupidly. Beseechingly.*) Tom, speak to Mother this morning. Make up with her, apologize, speak to her!

Tom: She won't to me. It's her that started not speaking.

Laura: If you just say you're sorry she'll start speaking.

Tom: Her not speaking — is that such a tragedy?

Laura: Please — please!

Amanda (*calling from kitchenette*): Laura, are you going to do what I asked you to do, or do I have to get dressed and go out myself?

Laura: Going, going — soon as I get on my coat! (*She pulls on a shapeless felt hat with nervous, jerky movement, pleadingly glancing at Tom. Rushes awkwardly for coat. The coat is one of Amanda's inaccurately made-over, the sleeves too short for Laura.*) Butter and what else?

Amanda (*entering upstage*): Just butter. Tell them to charge it.

Laura: Mother, they make such faces when I do that.

Amanda: Sticks and stones may break my bones, but the expression on Mr. Garfinkel's face won't harm us! Tell your brother his coffee is getting cold.

Laura (*at door*): Do what I asked you, will you, will you, Tom?

He looks sullenly away.

Amanda: Laura, go now or just don't go at all!

Laura (*rushing out*): Going — going! (*A second later she cries out. Tom springs up and crosses to the door. Amanda rushes anxiously in. Tom opens the door.*)

Tom: Laura?

Laura: I'm all right. I slipped, but I'm all right.

Amanda (*peering anxiously after her*): If anyone breaks a leg on those fire-escape steps, the landlord ought to be sued for every cent he possesses! (*She shuts door. Remembers she isn't speaking and returns to other room.*)

As Tom enters listlessly for his coffee, she turns her back to him and stands rigidly facing the window on the gloomy gray vault of the areaway. Its light on her face with its aged but childish features is cruelly sharp, satirical as a Daumier print.

(Music Under: "Ave Maria.")

Tom glances sheepishly but sullenly at her averted figure and slumps at the table. The coffee is scalding hot; he sips it and gasps and spits it back in the cup. At his gasp, Amanda catches her breath and half turns. Then catches herself and turns back to window.

Tom blows on his coffee, glancing sidewise at his mother. She clears her throat. Tom clears his. He starts to rise. Sinks back down again, scratches his head, clears his throat again. Amanda coughs. Tom raises his cup in both hands to blow on it, his eyes staring over the rim of it at his mother for several moments. Then he slowly sets the cup down and awkwardly and hesitantly rises from the chair.

Tom (hoarsely): Mother. I — I apologize. Mother. *(Amanda draws a quick, shuddering breath. Her face works grotesquely. She breaks into childlike tears.)* I'm sorry for what I said, for everything that I said, I didn't mean it.

Amanda (sobbingly): My devotion has made me a witch and so I make myself hateful to my children!

Tom: No, you *don't.*

Amanda: I worry so much, don't sleep, it makes me nervous!

Tom (gently): I understand that.

Amanda: I've had to put up a solitary battle all these years. But you're my right-hand bower! Don't fall down, don't fail!

Tom (gently): I try, Mother.

Amanda (with great enthusiasm): Try and you will SUCCEED! *(The notion makes her breathless.)* Why, you — you're just *full* of natural endowments! Both of my children — they're *unusual* children! Don't you think I know it? I'm so — *proud!* Happy and — feel I've — so much to be thankful for but — Promise me one thing, son!

Tom: What, Mother?

Amanda: Promise, son, you'll — never be a drunkard!

Tom (turns to her grinning): I will never be a drunkard, Mother.

Amanda: That's what frightened me so, that you'd be drinking! Eat a bowl of Purina!

Tom: Just coffee, Mother.

Amanda: Shredded wheat biscuit?

Tom: No. No, Mother, just coffee.

Amanda: You can't put in a day's work on an empty stomach. You've got ten minutes — don't gulp! Drinking too-hot liquids makes cancer of the stomach. . . . Put cream in.

Tom: No, thank you.

Amanda: To cool it.

Tom: No! No, thank you, I want it black.

Amanda: I know, but it's not good for you. We have to do all that we can to build ourselves up. In these trying times we live in, all that we have to cling to is — each other. . . . That's why it's so important to — Tom, I — I sent out your sister so I could discuss something with you. If you hadn't spoken I would have spoken to you. *(Sits down.)*

Tom (gently): What is it, Mother, that you want to discuss?

Amanda: Laura!

Tom puts his cup down slowly.

(Legend On Screen: "Laura.")

(Music: "The Glass Menagerie.")

Tom: — Oh. — Laura . . .

Amanda (touching his sleeve): You know how Laura is. So quiet but — still water runs deep! She notices things and I think she — broods about them. *(Tom looks up.)* A few days ago I came in and she was crying.

Tom: What about?

Amanda: You.

Tom: Me?

Amanda: She has an idea that you're not happy here.

Tom: What gave her that idea?

Amanda: What gives her any idea? However, you do act strangely. I — I'm not criticizing, understand *that!* I know your ambitions do not lie in the warehouse, that like everybody in the whole wide world — you've had to — make sacrifices, but — Tom — Tom — life's not easy, it calls for — Spartan endurance! There's so many things in my heart that I cannot describe to you! I've never told you but I — *loved* your father. . . .

Tom (gently): I know that, Mother.

Amanda: And you — when I see you taking after his ways! Staying out late — and — well, you *had* been drinking the night you were in that — terrifying condition! Laura says that you hate the apartment and that you go out nights to get away from it! Is that true, Tom?

Tom: No. You say there's so much in your heart that you can't describe to me. That's true of me, too. There's so much in my heart that I can't describe to *you!* So let's respect each other's —

Amanda: But, why — *why*, Tom — are you always so *restless?* Where do you go to, nights?

Tom: I — go to the movies.

Amanda: Why do you go to the movies so much, Tom?

Tom: I go to the movies because — I like adventure. Adventure is something I don't have much of at work, so I go to the movies.

Amanda: But, Tom, you go to the movies *entirely* too *much!*

Tom: I like a lot of adventure.

Amanda looks baffled, then hurt. As the familiar inquisition resumes he becomes hard and impatient again. Amanda slips back into her querulous attitude toward him.

(Image On Screen: Sailing Vessel With Jolly Roger.)

Amanda: Most young men find adventure in their careers.

Tom: Then most young men are not employed in a warehouse.

Amanda: The world is full of young men employed in warehouses and offices and factories.

Tom: Do all of them find adventure in their careers?

Amanda: They do or they do without it! Not everybody has a craze for adventure.

Tom: Man is by instinct a lover, a hunter, a fighter, and none of those instincts are given much play at the warehouse!

Amanda: Man is by instinct! Don't quote instinct to me! Instinct is something that people have got away from! It belongs to animals! Christian adults don't want it!

Tom: What do Christian adults want, then, Mother?

Amanda: Superior things! Things of the mind and the spirit! Only animals have to satisfy instincts! Surely your aims are somewhat higher than theirs! Than monkeys — pigs —

Tom: I reckon they're not.

Amanda: You're joking. However, that isn't what I wanted to discuss.

Tom (rising): I haven't much time.

Amanda (pushing his shoulders): Sit down.

Tom: You want me to punch in red at the warehouse, Mother?

Amanda: You have five minutes. I want to talk about Laura.

(Legend: "Plans And Provisions.")

Tom: All right! What about Laura?

Amanda: We have to be making plans and provisions for her. She's older than you, two years, and nothing has happened. She just drifts along doing nothing. It frightens me terribly how she just drifts along.

Tom: I guess she's the type that people call home girls.

Amanda: There's no such type, and if there is, it's a pity! That is unless the home is hers, with a husband!

Tom: What?

Amanda: Oh, I can see the handwriting on the wall as plain as I see the nose in front of my face! It's terrifying! More and more you remind me of your father! He was out all hours without explanation — Then *left! Goodbye!* And me with the bag to hold. I saw that letter you got from the Merchant Marine. I know what you're dreaming of. I'm not standing here blind-folded. Very well, then. Then *do* it! But not till there's somebody to take your place.

Tom: What do you mean?

Amanda: I mean that as soon as Laura has got somebody to take care of her, married, a home of her own, independent — why, then you'll be free to go wherever you please, on land, on sea, whichever way the wind blows! But until that time you've got to look out for your sister. I don't say me because I'm old and don't matter! I say for your sister because she's young and de-pendent. I put her in business college — a dismal failure! Frightened her so it made her sick to her stomach. I took her over to the Young People's League at the church. Another fiasco. She spoke to nobody, nobody spoke to her. Now all she does is fool with those pieces of glass and play those worn-out records. What kind of a life is that for a girl to lead!

Tom: What can I do about it?

Amanda: Overcome selfishness! Self, self, self is all that you ever think of! (*Tom springs up and crosses to get his coat. It is ugly and bulky. He pulls on a cap with earmuffs.*) Where is your muffler? Put your wool muffler on! (*He snatches it angrily from the closet and tosses it around his neck and pulls both ends tight.*) Tom! I haven't said what I had in mind to ask you.

Tom: I'm too late to —

Amanda (catching his arms — very importunately. Then shyly): Down at the ware-house, aren't there some — nice young men?

Tom: No!

Amanda: There *must* be — *some . . .*

Tom: Mother —

Gesture.

Amanda: Find out one that's clean-living — doesn't drink and — ask him out for sister!

Tom: What?

Amanda: For *sister!* To *meet!* Get *acquainted!*

Tom (stamping to door): Oh, my go-osh!

Amanda: Will you? *(He opens door. Imploringly.)* Will you? *(He starts down.)* Will you? *Will* you, dear?

Tom (calling back): YES!

Amanda closes the door hesitantly and with a troubled but faintly hopeful expression.

(Screen Image: Glamor Magazine Cover.)

Spot Amanda at phone.

Amanda: Ella Cartwright? This is Amanda Wingfield! How are you, honey? How is that kidney condition? *(Count five.)* Horrors! *(Count five.)* You're a Christian martyr, yes, honey, that's what you are, a Christian martyr! Well, I just happened to notice in my little red book that your subscription to the *Companion* has just run out! I knew that you wouldn't want to miss out on the wonderful serial starting in this new issue. It's by Bessie Mae Hopper, the first thing she's written since *Honeymoon for Three.* Wasn't that a strange and interesting story? Well, this one is even lovelier, I believe. It has a sophisticated society background. It's all about the horsey set on Long Island!

(Fade Out.)

SCENE V

(Legend On Screen: "Annunciation.") *Fade with music.*

It is early dusk of a spring evening. Supper has just been finished in the Wingfield apartment. Amanda and Laura in light colored dresses are removing dishes from the table, in the upstage area, which is shadowy, their movements formalized almost as a dance or ritual, their moving forms as pale and silent as moths.

Tom, in white shirt and trousers, rises from the table and crosses toward the fire-escape.

Amanda (as he passes her): Son, will you do me a favor?

Tom: What?

Amanda: Comb your hair! You look so pretty when your hair is combed! (*Tom slouches on sofa with evening paper. Enormous caption "Franco Triumphs."*) There is only one respect in which I would like you to emulate your father.

Tom: What respect is that?

Amanda: The care he always took of his appearance. He never allowed himself to look untidy. (*He throws down the paper and crosses to fire-escape.*) Where are you going?

Tom: I'm going out to smoke.

Amanda: You smoke too much. A pack a day at fifteen cents a pack. How much would that amount to in a month? Thirty times fifteen is how much, Tom? Figure it out and you will be astounded at what you could save. Enough to give you a night-school course in accounting at Washington U! Just think what a wonderful thing that would be for you, son!

Tom is unmoved by the thought.

Tom: I'd rather smoke. (*He steps out on landing, letting the screen door slam.*)

Amanda (sharply): I know! That's the tragedy of it. . . . (*Alone, she turns to look at her husband's picture.*)

(Dance Music: "All The World Is Waiting For the Sunrise!")

Tom (to the audience): Across the alley from us was the Paradise Dance Hall. On evenings in spring the windows and doors were open and the music came outdoors. Sometimes the lights were turned out except for a large glass sphere that hung from the ceiling. It would turn slowly about and filter the dusk with delicate rainbow colors. Then the orchestra played a waltz or a tango, something that had a slow and sensuous rhythm. Couples would come outside, to the relative privacy of the alley. You could see them kissing behind ash-pits and telephone poles. This was the compensation for lives that passed like mine, without any change or adventure. Adventure and change were imminent in this year. They were waiting around the corner for all these kids. Suspended in the mist over Berchtesgaden, caught in the folds of Chamberlain's umbrella — In Spain there was Guernica! But here there was only hot swing music and liquor, dance halls, bars, and movies, and sex that hung in the gloom like a chandelier and flooded the world with brief, deceptive rainbows. . . . All the world was waiting for bombardments!

Amanda turns from the picture and comes outside.

Amanda (sighing): A fire-escape landing's a poor excuse for a porch. (*She spreads a newspaper on a step and sits down, gracefully and demurely as if she were settling into a swing on a Mississippi veranda.*) What are you looking at?

Tom: The moon.

Amanda: Is there a moon this evening?

Tom: It's rising over Garfinkel's Delicatessen.

Amanda: So it is! A little silver slipper of a moon. Have you made a wish on it yet?

Tom: Um-hum.

Amanda: What did you wish for?

Tom: That's a secret.

Amanda: A secret, huh? Well, I won't tell mine either. I will be just as mysterious as you.

Tom: I bet I can guess what yours is.

Amanda: Is my head so transparent?

Tom: You're not a sphinx.

Amanda: No, I don't have secrets. I'll tell you what I wished for on the moon. Success and happiness for my precious children! I wish for that whenever there's a moon, and when there isn't a moon, I wish for it, too.

Tom: I thought perhaps you wished for a gentleman caller.

Amanda: Why do you say that?

Tom: Don't you remember asking me to fetch one?

Amanda: I remember suggesting that it would be nice for your sister if you brought home some nice young man from the warehouse. I think I've made that suggestion more than once.

Tom: Yes, you have made it repeatedly.

Amanda: Well?

Tom: We are going to have one.

Amanda: What?

Tom: A gentleman caller!

(The Annunciation Is Celebrated With Music.)

Amanda rises.

(Image on Screen: Caller With Bouquet.)

Amanda: You mean you have asked some nice young man to come over?

Tom: Yep. I've asked him to dinner.

Amanda: You really did?

Tom: I did!

Amanda: You did, and did he — *accept?*

Tom: He did!

Amanda: Well, well — well, well! That's — lovely!

Tom: I thought that you would be pleased.

Amanda: It's definite, then?

Tom: Very definite.

Amanda: Soon?

Tom: Very soon.

Amanda: For heaven's sake, stop putting on and tell me some things, will you?

Tom: What things do you want me to tell you?

Amanda: *Naturally* I would like to know when he's *coming!*

Tom: He's coming tomorrow.

Amanda: *Tomorrow?*

Tom: Yep. Tomorrow.

Amanda: But, Tom!

Tom: Yes, Mother?

Amanda: Tomorrow gives me no time!

Tom: Time for what?

Amanda: Preparations! Why didn't you phone me at once, as soon as you asked him, the minute that he accepted? Then, don't you see, I could have been getting ready!

Tom: You don't have to make any fuss.

Amanda: Oh, Tom, Tom, Tom, of course I have to make a fuss! I want things nice, not sloppy! Not thrown together. I'll certainly have to do some fast thinking, won't I?

Tom: I don't see why you have to think at all.

Amanda: You just don't know. We can't have a gentleman caller in a pig-sty! All my wedding silver has to be polished, the monogrammed table linen ought to be laundered! The windows have to be washed and fresh curtains put up. And how about clothes? We have to *wear* something, don't we?

Tom: Mother, this boy is no one to make a fuss over!

Amanda: Do you realize he's the first young man we've introduced to your sister? It's terrible, dreadful, disgraceful that poor little sister has never received a single gentleman caller! Tom, come inside! *(She opens the screen door.)*

Tom: What for?

Amanda: I want to ask you some things.

Tom: If you're going to make such a fuss, I'll call it off, I'll tell him not to come.

Amanda: You certainly won't do anything of the kind. Nothing offends people worse than broken engagements. It simply means I'll have to work like a Turk! We won't be brilliant, but we'll pass inspection. Come on inside. *(Tom follows, groaning.)* Sit down.

Tom: Any particular place you would like me to sit?

Amanda: Thank heavens I've got that new sofa! I'm also making payments on a floor lamp I'll have sent out! And put the chintz covers on, they'll brighten things up! Of course I'd hoped to have these walls re-papered. . . . What is the young man's name?

Tom: His name is O'Connor.

Amanda: That, of course, means fish — tomorrow is Friday! I'll have that salmon loaf — with Durkee's dressing! What does he do? He works at the warehouse?

Tom: Of course! How else would I —

Amanda: Tom, he — doesn't drink?

Tom: Why do you ask me that?

Amanda: Your father *did!*

Tom: Don't get started on that!

Amanda: He *does* drink, then?

Tom: Not that I know of!

Amanda: Make sure, be certain! The last thing I want for my daughter's a boy who drinks!

Tom: Aren't you being a little premature? Mr. O'Connor has not yet appeared on the scene!

Amanda: But will tomorrow. To meet your sister, and what do I know about his character? Nothing! Old maids are better off than wives of drunkards!

Tom: Oh, my God!

Amanda: Be still!

Tom (leaning forward to whisper): Lots of fellows meet girls whom they don't marry!

Amanda: Oh, talk sensibly, Tom — and don't be sarcastic! *(She has gotten a hairbrush.)*

Tom: What are you doing?

Amanda: I'm brushing that cow-lick down! What is this young man's position at the warehouse?

Tom (submitting grimly to the brush and the interrogation): This young man's position is that of a shipping clerk, Mother.

Amanda: Sounds to me like a fairly responsible job, the sort of a job *you* would be in if you just had more *get-up.* What is his salary? Have you got any idea?

Tom: I would judge it to be approximately eighty-five dollars a month.

Amanda: Well — not princely, but —

Tom: Twenty more than I make.

Amanda: Yes, how well I know! But for a family man, eighty-five dollars a month is not much more than you can just get by on. . . .

Tom: Yes, but Mr. O'Connor is not a family man.

Amanda: He might be, mightn't he? Some time in the future?

Tom: I see. Plans and provisions.

Amanda: You are the only young man that I know of who ignores the fact that the future becomes the present, the present the past, and the past turns into everlasting regret if you don't plan for it!

Tom: I will think that over and see what I can make of it.

Amanda: Don't be supercilious with your mother! Tell me some more about this — what do you call him?

Tom: James D. O'Connor. The D. is for Delaney.

Amanda: Irish on *both* sides! *Gracious!* And doesn't drink?

Tom: Shall I call him up and ask him right this minute?

Amanda: The only way to find out about those things is to make discreet inquiries at the proper moment. When I was a girl in Blue Mountain and it was suspected that a young man drank, the girl whose attentions he had been receiving, if any girl *was,* would sometimes speak to the minister of his church, or rather her father would if her father was living, and sort of feel him out on the young man's character. That is the way such things are discreetly handled to keep a young woman from making a tragic mistake!

Tom: Then how did you happen to make a tragic mistake?

Amanda: That innocent look of your father's had everyone fooled! He *smiled* — the world was *enchanted!* No girl can do worse than put herself at the mercy of a handsome appearance! I hope that Mr. O'Connor is not too good-looking.

Tom: No, he's not too good-looking. He's covered with freckles and hasn't too much of a nose.

Amanda: He's not right-down homely, though?

Tom: Not right-down homely. Just medium homely, I'd say.

Amanda: Character's what to look for in a man.

Tom: That's what I've always said, Mother.

Amanda: You've never said anything of the kind and I suspect you would never give it a thought.

Tom: Don't be suspicious of me.

Amanda: At least I hope he's the type that's up and coming.

Tom: I think he really goes in for self-improvement.

Amanda: What reason have you to think so?

Tom: He goes to night school.

Amanda (beaming): Splendid! What does he do, I mean study?

Tom: Radio engineering and public speaking!

Amanda: Then he has visions of being advanced in the world! Any young man who studies public speaking is aiming to have an executive job some day! And radio engineering? A thing for the future! Both of these facts are very illuminating. Those are the sort of things that a mother should know concerning any young man who comes to call on her daughter. Seriously or — not.

Tom: One little warning. He doesn't know about Laura. I didn't let on that we had dark ulterior motives. I just said, why don't you come have dinner with us? He said okay and that was the whole conversation.

Amanda: I bet it was! You're eloquent as an oyster. However, he'll know about Laura when he gets here. When he sees how lovely and sweet and pretty she is, he'll thank his lucky stars he was asked to dinner.

Tom: Mother, you mustn't expect too much of Laura.

Amanda: What do you mean?

Tom: Laura seems all those things to you and me because she's ours and we love her. We don't even notice she's crippled any more.

Amanda: Don't say crippled! You know that I never allow that word to be used!

Tom: But face facts, Mother. She is and — that's not all —

Amanda: What do you mean "not all"?

Tom: Laura is very different from other girls.

Amanda: I think the difference is all to her advantage.

Tom: Not quite all — in the eyes of others — strangers — she's terribly shy and lives in a world of her own and those things make her seem a little peculiar to people outside the house.

Amanda: Don't say peculiar.

Tom: Face the facts. She is.

(The Dance-hall Music Changes To A Tango That Has A Minor And Somewhat Ominous Tone.)

Amanda: In what way is she peculiar — may I ask?

Tom (gently): She lives in a world of her own — a world of — little glass ornaments, Mother. . . . *(Gets up. Amanda remains holding brush, looking at him, troubled.)* She plays old phonograph records and — that's about all — *(He glances at himself in the mirror and crosses to door.)*

Amanda (sharply): Where are you going?

Tom: I'm going to the movies. *(Out screen door.)*

Amanda: Not to the movies, every night to the movies! *(Follows quickly to screen door.)* I don't believe you always go to the movies! *(He is gone. Amanda looks worriedly after him for a moment. Then vitality and optimism return and she turns from the door. Crossing to portieres.)* Laura! Laura! *(Laura answers from kitchenette.)*

Laura: Yes, Mother.

Amanda: Let those dishes go and come in front! *(Laura appears with dish towel. Gaily.)* Laura, come here and make a wish on the moon!

Laura (entering): Moon — moon?

Amanda: A little silver slipper of a moon. Look over your left shoulder, Laura, and make a wish! *(Laura looks faintly puzzled as if called out of sleep. Amanda seizes her shoulders and turns her at an angle by the door.)* Now! Now, darling, wish!

Laura: What shall I wish for, Mother?

Amanda (her voice trembling and her eyes suddenly filling with tears): Happiness! Good Fortune!

The violin rises and the stage dims out.

SCENE VI

(Image: High School Hero.)

Tom: And so the following evening I brought Jim home to dinner. I had known Jim slightly in high school. In high school Jim was a hero. He had tremendous Irish good nature and vitality with the scrubbed and polished look of white chinaware. He seemed to move in a continual spotlight. He was a star in basketball, captain of the debating club, president of the senior class and the glee club and he sang the male lead in the annual light operas. He was always running or bounding, never just walking. He seemed always at the point of defeating the law of gravity. He was shooting with such velocity through his adolescence that you would logically expect him to arrive at nothing short of the White House by the time he was thirty. But Jim apparently ran into more interference after his graduation from Soldan. His speed had definitely slowed. Six years after he left high school he was holding a job that wasn't much better than mine.

(Image: Clerk.)

He was the only one at the warehouse with whom I was on friendly terms. I was valuable to him as someone who could remember his former glory, who had seen him win basketball games and the silver cup in debating. He knew of my secret practice of retiring to a cabinet of the washroom to work on poems when business was slack in the warehouse. He called me Shakespeare. And while the other boys in the warehouse regarded me with suspicious hostility, Jim took a humorous attitude toward me. Gradually his attitude affected the others, their hostility wore off and they also began to smile at me as people smile at an oddly fashioned dog who trots across their path at some distance.

I knew that Jim and Laura had known each other at Soldan, and I had heard Laura speak admiringly of his voice. I didn't know if Jim remembered her or not. In high school Laura had been as unobtrusive as Jim had been astonishing. If he did remember Laura, it was not as my sister, for when I asked him to dinner, he grinned and said, "You know, Shakespeare, I never thought of you as having folks!"

He was about to discover that I did. . . .

(Light Up Stage.)

(Legend On Screen: "The Accent Of A Coming Foot.")

Friday evening. It is about five o'clock of a late spring evening which comes "scattering poems in the sky."

A delicate lemony light is in the Wingfield apartment.

Amanda has worked like a Turk in preparation for the gentleman caller. The results are astonishing. The new floor lamp with its rose-silk shade is in place, a colored paper lantern conceals the broken light fixture in the ceiling, new billowing white curtains are at the windows, chintz covers are on chairs and sofa, a pair of new sofa pillows make their initial appearance.

Open boxes and tissue paper are scattered on the floor.

Laura stands in the middle with lifted arms while Amanda crouches before her, adjusting the hem of the new dress, devout and ritualistic. The dress is colored and designed by memory. The arrangement of Laura's hair is changed; it is softer and more becoming. A fragile, unearthly prettiness has come out in Laura: she is like a piece of translucent glass touched by light, given a momentary radiance, not actual, not lasting.

Amanda (impatiently): Why are you trembling?

Laura: Mother, you've made me so nervous!

Amanda: How have I made you nervous?

Laura: By all this fuss! You make it seem so important!

Amanda: I don't understand you, Laura. You couldn't be satisfied with just sitting home, and yet whenever I try to arrange something for you, you seem to resist it. *(She gets up.)* Now take a look at yourself. No, wait! Wait just a moment — I have an idea!

Laura: What is it now?

Amanda produces two powder puffs which she wraps in handkerchiefs and stuffs in Laura's bosom.

Laura: Mother, what are you doing?

Amanda: They call them "Gay Deceivers"!

Laura: I won't wear them!

Amanda: You will!

Laura: Why should I?

Amanda: Because, to be painfully honest, your chest is flat.

Laura: You make it seem like we were setting a trap.

Amanda: All pretty girls are a trap, a pretty trap, and men expect them to be. **(Legend: "A Pretty Trap.")** Now look at yourself, young lady. This is the prettiest you will ever be! I've got to fix myself now! You're going to be surprised by your mother's appearance! *(She crosses through portieres, humming gaily.)*

Laura moves slowly to the long mirror and stares solemnly at herself.

A wind blows the white curtains inward in a slow, graceful motion and with a faint, sorrowful sighing.

Amanda (offstage): It isn't dark enough yet. *(She turns slowly before the mirror with a troubled look.)*

(Legend On Screen: "This Is My Sister: Celebrate Her With Strings!" Music.)

Amanda (laughing, off): I'm going to show you something. I'm going to make a spectacular appearance!

Laura: What is it, Mother?

Amanda: Possess your soul in patience — you will see! Something I've resurrected from that old trunk! Styles haven't changed so terribly much after all. . . . *(She parts the portieres.)* Now just look at your mother! *(She wears a girlish frock of yellowed voile with a blue silk sash. She carries a bunch of jonquils — the legend of her youth is nearly revived. Feverishly.)* This is the dress in which I led the cotillion. Won the cakewalk twice at Sunset Hill, wore one spring to the Governor's ball in Jackson! See how I sashayed around the ballroom, Laura? *(She raises her skirt and does a mincing step around the room.)* I wore it on Sundays for my gentlemen callers! I had it on the day I met your father — I had malaria fever all that spring. The change of climate from East Tennessee to the Delta — weakened resistance — I had a little temperature all the time — not enough to be serious — just enough to make me restless and giddy! Invitations poured in — parties all over the Delta! — "Stay in bed," said Mother, "you have fever!" — but I just wouldn't. — I took quinine but kept on going, going! — Evenings, dances! — Afternoons, long, long rides! Picnics — lovely! — So lovely, that country in May. — All lacy with dogwood, literally flooded with jonquils! — That was the spring I had the craze for jonquils. Jonquils became an absolute obsession. Mother said, "Honey, there's no more room for jonquils." And still I kept bringing in more jonquils. Whenever, wherever I saw them, I'd say, "Stop! Stop! I see jonquils!" I made the young men help me gather the jonquils! It was a joke, Amanda and her jonquils! Finally there were no more vases to hold them, every available space was filled with jonquils. No vases to hold them? All right, I'll hold them myself! And then I — *(She stops in front of the picture.)* **(Music)** met your father! Malaria fever and jonquils and then — this — boy. . . . *(She switches on the rose-colored lamp.)* I hope they get here before it starts to rain. *(She crosses upstage and places the jonquils in bowl on table.)* I gave your brother a little extra change so he and Mr. O'Connor could take the service car home.

Laura (with altered look): What did you say his name was?

Amanda: O'Connor.

Laura: What is his first name?

Amanda: I don't remember. Oh, yes, I do. It was — Jim!

Laura sways slightly and catches hold of a chair.

(Legend On Screen: "Not Jim!")

Laura (faintly): Not — Jim!

Amanda: Yes, that was it, it was Jim! I've never known a Jim that wasn't nice!

(Music: Ominous.)

Laura: Are you sure his name is Jim O'Connor?

Amanda: Yes. Why?

Laura: Is he the one that Tom used to know in high school?

Amanda: He didn't say so. I think he just got to know him at the warehouse.

Laura: There was a Jim O'Connor we both knew in high school — *(Then, with effort.)* If that is the one that Tom is bringing to dinner — you'll have to excuse me, I won't come to the table.

Amanda: What sort of nonsense is this?

Laura: You asked me once if I'd ever liked a boy. Don't you remember I showed you this boy's picture?

Amanda: You mean the boy you showed me in the year book?

Laura: Yes, that boy.

Amanda: Laura, Laura, were you in love with that boy?

Laura: I don't know, Mother. All I know is I couldn't sit at the table if it was him!

Amanda: It won't be him! It isn't the least bit likely. But whether it is or not, you will come to the table. You will not be excused.

Laura: I'll have to be, Mother.

Amanda: I don't intend to humor your silliness, Laura. I've had too much from you and your brother, both! So just sit down and compose yourself till they come. Tom has forgotten his key so you'll have to let them in, when they arrive.

Laura (panicky): Oh, Mother — *you* answer the door!

Amanda (lightly): I'll be in the kitchen — busy!

Laura: Oh, Mother, please answer the door, don't make me do it!

Amanda (crossing into kitchenette): I've got to fix the dressing for the salmon. Fuss, fuss — silliness! — over a gentleman caller!

Door swings shut. Laura is left alone.

(Legend: "Terror!")

She utters a low moan and turns off the lamp — sits stiffly on the edge of the sofa, knotting her fingers together.

(Legend On Screen: "The Opening Of A Door!")

Tom and Jim appear on the fire-escape steps and climb to landing. Hearing their approach, Laura rises with a panicky gesture. She retreats to the portieres.
    The doorbell. Laura catches her breath and touches her throat. Low drums.

Amanda (calling): Laura, sweetheart! The door!

Laura stares at it without moving.

Jim: I think we just beat the rain.

Tom: Uh-huh. *(He rings again, nervously. Jim whistles and fishes for a cigarette.)*

Amanda (very, very gaily): Laura, that is your brother and Mr. O'Connor! Will you let them in, darling?

Laura crosses toward kitchenette door.

Laura (breathlessly): Mother — you go to the door!

Amanda steps out of kitchenette and stares furiously at Laura. She points imperiously at the door.

Laura: Please, please!

Amanda (in a fierce whisper): What is the matter with you, you silly thing?

Laura (desperately): Please, you answer it, *please!*

Amanda: I told you I wasn't going to humor you, Laura. Why have you chosen this moment to lose your mind?

Laura: Please, please, please, you go!

Amanda: You'll have to go to the door because I can't!

Laura (despairingly): I can't either!

Amanda: Why?

Laura: I'm *sick!*

Amanda: I'm sick, too — of your nonsense! Why can't you and your brother be normal people? Fantastic whims and behavior! *(Tom gives a long ring.)* Preposterous goings on! Can you give me one reason — *(Calls out lyrically.)* COMING! JUST ONE SECOND! — why should you be afraid to open a door? Now you answer it, Laura!

Laura: Oh, oh, oh . . . *(She returns through the portieres. Darts to the victrola and winds it frantically and turns it on.)*

Amanda: Laura Wingfield, you march right to that door!

Laura: Yes — yes, Mother!

A faraway, scratchy rendition of "Dardanella" softens the air and gives her strength to move through it. She slips to the door and draws it cautiously open. Tom enters with the caller, Jim O'Connor.

Tom: Laura, this is Jim. Jim, this is my sister, Laura.

Jim (stepping inside): I didn't know that Shakespeare had a sister!

Laura (retreating stiff and trembling from the door): How — how do you do?

Jim (heartily extending his hand): Okay!

Laura touches it hesitantly with hers.

Jim: Your hand's *cold,* Laura!

Laura: Yes, well — I've been playing the victrola. . . .

Jim: Must have been playing classical music on it! You ought to play a little hot swing music to warm you up!

Laura: Excuse me — I haven't finished playing the victrola. . . .

She turns awkwardly and hurries into the front room. She pauses a second by the victrola. Then catches her breath and darts through the portieres like a frightened deer.

Jim (grinning): What was the matter?

Tom: Oh — with Laura? Laura is — terribly shy.

Jim: Shy, huh? It's unusual to meet a shy girl nowadays. I don't believe you ever mentioned you had a sister.

Tom: Well, now you know. I have one. Here is the *Post Dispatch.* You want a piece of it?

Jim: Uh-huh.

Tom: What piece? The comics?

Jim: Sports! (*Glances at it.*) Ole Dizzy Dean is on his bad behavior.

Tom (disinterest): Yeah? (*Lights cigarette and crosses back to fire-escape door.*)

Jim: Where are *you* going?

Tom: I'm going out on the terrace.

Jim (goes after him): You know, Shakespeare — I'm going to sell you a bill of goods!

Tom: What goods?

Jim: A course I'm taking.

Tom: Huh?

Jim: In public speaking! You and me, we're not the warehouse type.

Tom: Thanks — that's good news. But what has public speaking got to do with it?

Jim: It fits you for — executive positions!

Tom: Awww.

Jim: I tell you it's done a helluva lot for me.

(Image: Executive At Desk.)

Tom: In what respect?

Jim: In every! Ask yourself what is the difference between you an' me and men in the office down front? Brains? — No! — Ability? — No! Then what? Just one little thing —

Tom: What is that one little thing?

Jim: Primarily it amounts to — social poise! Being able to square up to people and hold your own on any social level!

Amanda (offstage): Tom?

Tom: Yes, Mother?

Amanda: Is that you and Mr. O'Connor?

Tom: Yes, Mother.

Amanda: Well, you just make yourselves comfortable in there.

Tom: Yes, Mother.

Amanda: Ask Mr. O'Connor if he would like to wash his hands.

Jim: Aw — no — thank you — I took care of that at the warehouse. Tom —

Tom: Yes?

Jim: Mr. Mendoza was speaking to me about you.

Tom: Favorably?

Jim: What do you think?

Tom: Well —

Jim: You're going to be out of a job if you don't wake up.

Tom: I am waking up —

Jim: You show no signs.

Tom: The signs are interior.

(Image On Screen: The Sailing Vessel With Jolly Roger Again.)

Tom: I'm planning to change. (*He leans over the rail speaking with quiet exhilaration. The incandescent marquees and signs of the first-run movie houses light his face from across the alley. He looks like a voyager.*) I'm right at the point of committing myself to a future that doesn't include the warehouse and Mr. Mendoza or even a night-school course in public speaking.

Jim: What are you gassing about?

Tom: I'm tired of the movies.

Jim: Movies!

Tom: Yes, movies! Look at them — *(A wave toward the marvels of Grand Avenue.)* All of those glamorous people — having adventures — hogging it all, gobbling the whole thing up! You know what happens? People go to the *movies* instead of *moving!* Hollywood characters are supposed to have all the adventures for everybody in America, while everybody in America sits in a dark room and watches them have them! Yes, until there's a war. That's when adventure becomes available to the masses! *Everyone's* dish, not only Gable's! Then the people in the dark room come out of the dark room to have some adventures themselves — Goody, goody — It's our turn now, to go to the South Sea Island — to make a safari — to be exotic, far-off — But I'm not patient. I don't want to wait till then. I'm tired of the *movies* and I am *about* to move!

Jim (incredulously): Move?

Tom: Yes.

Jim: When?

Tom: Soon!

Jim: Where? Where?

Theme three music seems to answer the question, while Tom thinks it over. He searches among his pockets.

Tom: I'm starting to boil inside. I know I seem dreamy, but inside — well, I'm boiling! Whenever I pick up a shoe, I shudder a little thinking how short life is and what I am doing! — Whatever that means. I know it doesn't mean shoes — except as something to wear on a traveler's feet! *(Finds paper.)* Look —

Jim: What?

Tom: I'm a member.

Jim (reading): The Union of Merchant Seamen.

Tom: I paid my dues this month, instead of the light bill.

Jim: You will regret it when they turn the lights off.

Tom: I won't be here.

Jim: How about your mother?

Tom: I'm like my father. The bastard son of a bastard! See how he grins? And he's been absent going on sixteen years!

Jim: You're just talking, you drip. How does your mother feel about it?

Tom: Shhh — Here comes Mother! Mother is not acquainted with my plans!

Amanda (enters portieres): Where are you all?

Tom: On the terrace, Mother.

They start inside. She advances to them. Tom is distinctly shocked at her appearance. Even Jim blinks a little. He is making his first contact with girlish Southern vivacity and in spite of the night-school course in public speaking is somewhat thrown off the beam by the unexpected outlay of social charm.

Certain responses are attempted by Jim but are swept aside by Amanda's gay laughter and chatter. Tom is embarrassed but after the first shock Jim reacts very warmly. Grins and chuckles, is altogether won over.

(Image: Amanda As A Girl.)

Amanda (coyly smiling, shaking her girlish ringlets): Well, well, well, so this is Mr. O'Connor. Introductions entirely unnecessary. I've heard so much about you from my boy. I finally said to him, Tom — good gracious! — why don't you bring this paragon to supper? I'd like to meet this nice young man at the warehouse! — Instead of just hearing him sing your praises so much! I don't know why my son is so stand-offish — that's not Southern behavior! Let's sit down and — I think we could stand a little more air in here! Tom, leave the door open. I felt a nice fresh breeze a moment ago. Where has it gone? Mmm, so warm already! And not quite summer, even. We're going to burn up when summer really gets started. However, we're having — we're having a very light supper. I think light things are better fo' this time of year. The same as light clothes are. Light clothes an' light food are what warm weather calls fo'. You know our blood gets so thick during th' winter — it takes a while fo' us to *adjust* ou'selves! — when the season changes . . . It's come so quick this year. I wasn't prepared. All of a sudden — heavens! Already summer! — I ran to the trunk an' pulled out this light dress — Terribly old! Historical almost! But feels so good — so good an' co-ol, y'know. . . .

Tom: Mother —

Amanda: Yes, honey?

Tom: How about — supper?

Amanda: Honey, you go ask Sister if supper is ready! You know that Sister is in full charge of supper! Tell her you hungry boys are waiting for it. *(To Jim.)* Have you met Laura?

Jim: She —

Amanda: Let you in? Oh, good, you've met already! It's rare for a girl as sweet an' pretty as Laura to be domestic! But Laura is, thank heavens, not only pretty but also very domestic. I'm not at all. I never was a bit. I never could make a thing but angel-food cake. Well, in the South we had so many servants. Gone, gone, gone. All vestiges of gracious living! Gone completely! I wasn't prepared for what the future brought me. All of my gentlemen callers were sons of planters and so of course I assumed that I would be married to one and raise my family on a large piece of land with plenty of servants. But man proposes — and woman accepts the proposal! — To vary that old, old saying a little bit — I married no planter! I married a man who worked for the telephone company! — that gallantly smiling gentleman over there! *(Points to the picture.)* A telephone man who — fell in love with long-distance! — Now he travels and I don't even know where! — But what am I going on for about my — tribulations? Tell me yours — I hope you don't have any! Tom?

Tom (returning): Yes, Mother?

Amanda: Is supper nearly ready?

Tom: It looks to me like supper is on the table.

Amanda: Let me look — *(She rises prettily and looks through portieres.)* Oh, lovely — But where is Sister?

Tom: Laura is not feeling well and she says that she thinks she'd better not come to the table.

Amanda: What? — Nonsense! — Laura? Oh, Laura!
Laura (offstage, faintly): Yes, Mother.
Amanda: You really must come to the table. We won't be seated until you come to the table! Come in, Mr. O'Connor. You sit over there and I'll — Laura? Laura Wingfield! You're keeping us waiting, honey! We can't say grace until you come to the table!

The back door is pushed weakly open and Laura comes in. She is obviously quite faint, her lips trembling, her eyes wide and staring. She moves unsteadily toward the table.

(Legend: "Terror!")

Outside a summer storm is coming abruptly. The white curtains billow inward at the windows and there is a sorrowful murmur and deep blue dusk.
   Laura suddenly stumbles — She catches at a chair with a faint moan.

Tom: Laura!
Amanda: Laura! *(There is a clap of thunder.)* **(Legend: "Ah!")** *(Despairingly.)* Why, Laura, you *are* sick, darling! Tom, help your sister into the living room, dear! Sit in the living room, Laura — rest on the sofa. Well! *(To the gentleman caller.)* Standing over the hot stove made her ill! — I told her that it was just too warm this evening, but — *(Tom comes back in. Laura is on the sofa.)* Is Laura all right now?
Tom: Yes.
Amanda: What *is* that? Rain? A nice cool rain has come up! *(She gives the gentleman caller a frightened look.)* I think we may — have grace — now . . . *(Tom looks at her stupidly.)* Tom, honey — you say grace!
Tom: Oh . . . "For these and all thy mercies — " *(They bow their heads, Amanda stealing a nervous glance at Jim. In the living room Laura, stretched on the sofa, clenches her hand to her lips, to hold back a shuddering sob.)* God's Holy Name be praised —

(The Scene Dims Out.)

SCENE VII

(A Souvenir.)

Half an hour later. Dinner is just being finished in the upstage area which is concealed by the drawn portieres.
   As the curtain rises Laura is still huddled upon the sofa, her feet drawn under her, her head resting on a pale blue pillow, her eyes wide and mysteriously watchful. The new floor lamp with its shade of rose-colored silk gives a soft, becoming light to her face, bringing out the fragile, unearthly prettiness which usually escapes attention. There is a steady murmur of rain, but it is slackening and stops soon after the scene begins; the air outside becomes pale and luminous as the moon breaks out.
   A moment after the curtain rises, the lights in both rooms flicker and go out.

Jim: Hey, there, Mr. Light Bulb!

Amanda laughs nervously.

(Legend: "Suspension Of A Public Service.")

Amanda: Where was Moses when the lights went out? Ha-ha. Do you know the answer to that one, Mr. O'Connor?

Jim: No, Ma'am, what's the answer?

Amanda: In the dark! *(Jim laughs appreciatively.)* Everybody sit still. I'll light the candles. Isn't it lucky we have them on the table? Where's a match? Which of you gentlemen can provide a match?

Jim: Here.

Amanda: Thank you, sir.

Jim: Not at all, Ma'am!

Amanda: I guess the fuse has burnt out. Mr. O'Connor, can you tell a burnt-out fuse? I know I can't and Tom is a total loss when it comes to mechanics. **(Sound: Getting Up: Voices Recede A Little To Kitchenette.)** Oh, be careful you don't bump into something. We don't want our gentleman caller to break his neck. Now wouldn't that be a fine howdy-do?

Jim: Ha-ha! Where is the fuse-box?

Amanda: Right here next to the stove. Can you see anything?

Jim: Just a minute.

Amanda: Isn't electricity a mysterious thing? Wasn't it Benjamin Franklin who tied a key to a kite? We live in such a mysterious universe, don't we? Some people say that science clears up all the mysteries for us. In my opinion it only creates more! Have you found it yet?

Jim: No, Ma'am. All these fuses look okay to me.

Amanda: Tom!

Tom: Yes, Mother?

Amanda: That light bill I gave you several days ago. The one I told you we got the notices about?

Tom: Oh. — Yeah.

(Legend: "Ha!")

Amanda: You didn't neglect to pay it by any chance?

Tom: Why, I —

Amanda: Didn't! I might have known it!

Jim: Shakespeare probably wrote a poem on that light bill, Mrs. Wingfield.

Amanda: I might have known better than to trust him with it! There's such a high price for negligence in this world!

Jim: Maybe the poem will win a ten-dollar prize.

Amanda: We'll just have to spend the remainder of the evening in the nineteenth century, before Mr. Edison made the Mazda lamp!

Jim: Candlelight is my favorite kind of light.

Amanda: That shows you're romantic! But that's no excuse for Tom. Well, we got through dinner. Very considerate of them to let us get through dinner before they plunged us into everlasting darkness, wasn't it, Mr. O'Connor?

Jim: Ha-ha!

Amanda: Tom, as a penalty for your carelessness you can help me with the dishes.

Jim: Let me give you a hand.

Amanda: Indeed you will not!

Jim: I ought to be good for something.

Amanda: Good for something? *(Her tone is rhapsodic.)* You? Why, Mr. O'Connor, nobody, *nobody's* given me this much entertainment in years — as you have!

Jim: Aw, now, Mrs. Wingfield!

Amanda: I'm not exaggerating, not one bit! But Sister is all by her lonesome. You go keep her company in the parlor! I'll give you this lovely old candelabrum that used to be on the altar at the church of the Heavenly Rest. It was melted a little out of shape when the church burnt down. Lightning struck it one spring. Gypsy Jones was holding a revival at the time and he intimated that the church was destroyed because the Episcopalians gave card parties.

Jim: Ha-ha.

Amanda: And how about coaxing Sister to drink a little wine? I think it would be good for her! Can you carry both at once?

Jim: Sure. I'm Superman!

Amanda: Now, Thomas, get into this apron!

The door of kitchenette swings closed on Amanda's gay laughter; the flickering light approaches the portieres.

Laura sits up nervously as he enters. Her speech at first is low and breathless from the almost intolerable strain of being alone with a stranger.

(The Legend: "I Don't Suppose You Remember Me At All!")

In her first speeches in this scene, before Jim's warmth overcomes her paralyzing shyness, Laura's voice is thin and breathless as though she has run up a steep flight of stairs.

Jim's attitude is gently humorous. In playing this scene it should be stressed that while the incident is apparently unimportant, it is to Laura the climax of her secret life.

Jim: Hello, there, Laura.

Laura (faintly): Hello. *(She clears her throat.)*

Jim: How are you feeling now? Better?

Laura: Yes. Yes, thank you.

Jim: This is for you. A little dandelion wine. *(He extends it toward her with extravagant gallantry.)*

Laura: Thank you.

Jim: Drink it — but don't get drunk! *(He laughs heartily. Laura takes the glass uncertainly; laughs shyly.)* Where shall I set the candles?

Laura: Oh — oh, anywhere . . .

Jim: How about here on the floor? Any objections?

Laura: No.

Jim: I'll spread a newspaper under to catch the drippings. I like to sit on the floor. Mind if I do?

Laura: Oh, no.

Jim: Give me a pillow?

Laura: What?

Jim: A pillow!

Laura: Oh . . . *(Hands him one quickly.)*

Jim: How about you? Don't you like to sit on the floor?

Laura: Oh — yes.

Jim: Why don't you, then?

Laura: I — will.

Jim: Take a pillow! *(Laura does. Sits on the other side of the candelabrum. Jim crosses his legs and smiles engagingly at her.)* I can't hardly see you sitting way over there.

Laura: I can — see you.

Jim: I know, but that's not fair, I'm in the limelight. *(Laura moves her pillow closer.)* Good! Now I can see you! Comfortable?

Laura: Yes.

Jim: So am I. Comfortable as a cow. Will you have some gum?

Laura: No, thank you.

Jim: I think that I will indulge, with your permission. *(Musingly unwraps it and holds it up.)* Think of the fortune made by the guy that invented the first piece of chewing gum. Amazing, huh? The Wrigley Building is one of the sights of Chicago. — I saw it summer before last when I went up to the Century of Progress. Did you take in the Century of Progress?

Laura: No, I didn't.

Jim: Well, it was quite a wonderful exposition. What impressed me most was the Hall of Science. Gives you an idea of what the future will be in America, even more wonderful than the present time is! *(Pause. Smiling at her.)* Your brother tells me you're shy. Is that right, Laura?

Laura: I — don't know.

Jim: I judge you to be an old-fashioned type of girl. Well, I think that's a pretty good type to be. Hope you don't think I'm being too personal — do you?

Laura (hastily, out of embarrassment): I believe I *will* take a piece of gum, if you — don't mind. *(Clearing her throat.)* Mr. O'Connor, have you — kept up with your singing?

Jim: Singing? Me?

Laura: Yes. I remember what a beautiful voice you had.

Jim: When did you hear me sing?

(Voice Offstage In The Pause.)

Voice (offstage):
> O blow, ye winds, heigh-ho,
> A-roving I will go!
> I'm off to my love
> With a boxing glove —
> Ten thousand miles away!

Jim: You say you've heard me sing?

Laura: Oh, yes! Yes, very often . . . I — don't suppose you remember me — at all?

Jim (smiling doubtfully): You know I have an idea I've seen you before. I had that idea soon as you opened the door. It seemed almost like I was about to remember your name. But the name that I started to call you — wasn't a name! And so I stopped myself before I said it.

Laura: Wasn't it — Blue Roses?

Jim (springs up, grinning): Blue Roses! My gosh, yes — Blue Roses! That's what I had on my tongue when you opened the door! Isn't it funny what tricks your memory plays? I didn't connect you with the high school somehow or other. But that's where it was; it was high school. I didn't even know you were Shakespeare's sister! Gosh, I'm sorry.

Laura: I didn't expect you to. You — barely knew me!

Jim: But we did have a speaking acquaintance, huh?

Laura: Yes, we — spoke to each other.

Jim: When did you recognize me?

Laura: Oh, right away!

Jim: Soon as I came in the door?

Laura: When I heard your name I thought it was probably you. I knew that Tom used to know you a little in high school. So when you came in the door — Well, then I was — sure.

Jim: Why didn't you *say* something, then?

Laura (breathlessly): I didn't know what to say, I was — too surprised!

Jim: For goodness' sakes! You know, this sure is funny!

Laura: Yes! Yes, isn't it, though . . .

Jim: Didn't we have a class in something together?

Laura: Yes, we did.

Jim: What class was that?

Laura: It was — singing — Chorus!

Jim: Aw!

Laura: I sat across the aisle from you in the Aud.

Jim: Aw.

Laura: Mondays, Wednesdays and Fridays.

Jim: Now I remember — you always came in late.

Laura: Yes, it was so hard for me, getting upstairs. I had that brace on my leg — it clumped so loud!

Jim: I never heard any clumping.

Laura (wincing at the recollection): To me it sounded like — thunder!

Jim: Well, well, well. I never even noticed.

Laura: And everybody was seated before I came in. I had to walk in front of all those people. My seat was in the back row. I had to go clumping all the way up the aisle with everyone watching!

Jim: You shouldn't have been self-conscious.

Laura: I know, but I was. It was always such a relief when the singing started.

Jim: Aw, yes, I've placed you now! I used to call you Blue Roses. How was it that I got started calling you that?

Laura: I was out of school a little while with pleurosis. When I came back you asked me what was the matter. I said I had pleurosis — you thought I said Blue Roses. That's what you always called me after that!

Jim: I hope you didn't mind.

Laura: Oh, no — I liked it. You see, I wasn't acquainted with many — people. . . .

Jim: As I remember you sort of stuck by yourself.

Laura: I — I — never had much luck at — making friends.

Jim: I don't see why you wouldn't.

Laura: Well, I — started out badly.

Jim: You mean being —

Laura: Yes, it sort of — stood between me —

Jim: You shouldn't have let it!

Laura: I know, but it did, and —

Jim: You were shy with people!

Laura: I tried not to be but never could —

Jim: Overcome it?

Laura: No, I — I never could!

Jim: I guess being shy is something you have to work out of kind of gradually.

Laura (sorrowfully): Yes — I guess it —

Jim: Takes time!

Laura: Yes —

Jim: People are not so dreadful when you know them. That's what you have to remember! And everybody has problems, not just you, but practically everybody has got some problems. You think of yourself as having the only problems, as being the only one who is disappointed. But just look around you and you will see lots of people as disappointed as you are. For instance, I hoped when I was going to high school that I would be further along at this time, six years later, than I am now — You remember that wonderful write-up I had in *The Torch?*

Laura: Yes! *(She rises and crosses to table.)*

Jim: It said I was bound to succeed in anything I went into! *(Laura returns with the annual.)* Holy Jeez! *The Torch! (He accepts it reverently. They smile across it with mutual wonder. Laura crouches beside him and they begin to turn through it. Laura's shyness is dissolving in his warmth.)*

Laura: Here you are in *Pirates of Penzance!*

Jim (wistfully): I sang the baritone lead in that operetta.

Laura (rapidly): So — *beautifully!*

Jim (protesting): Aw —

Laura: Yes, yes — beautifully — beautifully!

Jim: You heard me?

Laura: All three times!

Jim: No!

Laura: Yes!

Jim: All three performances?

Laura (looking down): Yes.

Jim: Why?

Laura: I — wanted to ask you to — autograph my program.

Jim: Why didn't you ask me to?

Laura: You were always surrounded by your own friends so much that I never had a chance to.

Jim: You should have just —

Laura: Well, I — thought you might think I was —

Jim: Thought I might think you was — what?

Laura: Oh —

Jim (with reflective relish): I was beleaguered by females in those days.

Laura: You were terribly popular!

Jim: Yeah —

Laura: You had such a — friendly way —

Jim: I was spoiled in high school.

Laura: Everybody — liked you!

Jim: Including you?

Laura: I — yes, I — I did, too — *(She gently closes the book in her lap.)*

Jim: Well, well, well! — Give me that program, Laura. *(She hands it to him. He signs it with a flourish.)* There you are — better late than never!

Laura: Oh, I — what a — surprise!

Jim: My signature isn't worth very much right now. But some day — maybe — it will increase in value! Being disappointed is one thing and being discouraged is something else. I am disappointed but I'm not discouraged. I'm twenty-three years old. How old are you?

Laura: I'll be twenty-four in June.

Jim: That's not old age!

Laura: No, but —

Jim: You finished high school?

Laura (with difficulty): I didn't go back.

Jim: You mean you dropped out?

Laura: I made bad grades in my final examinations. *(She rises and replaces the book and the program. Her voice strained.)* How is — Emily Meisenbach getting along?

Jim: Oh, that kraut-head!

Laura: Why do you call her that?

Jim: That's what she was.

Laura: You're not still — going with her?

Jim: I never see her.

Laura: It said in the Personal Section that you were — engaged!

Jim: I know, but I wasn't impressed by that — propaganda!

Laura: It wasn't — the truth?

Jim: Only in Emily's optimistic opinion!

Laura: Oh —

(Legend: "What Have You Done Since High School?")

Jim lights a cigarette and leans indolently back on his elbows smiling at Laura with a warmth and charm which light her inwardly with altar candles. She remains by the table and turns in her hands a piece of glass to cover her tumult.

Jim (after several reflective puffs on a cigarette): What have you done since high school? *(She seems not to hear him.)* Huh? *(Laura looks up.)* I said what have you done since high school, Laura?

Laura: Nothing much.

Jim: You must have been doing something these six long years.

Laura: Yes.

Jim: Well, then, such as what?

Laura: I took a business course at business college —

Jim: How did that work out?

Laura: Well, not very — well — I had to drop out, it gave me — indigestion —

Jim laughs gently.

Jim: What are you doing now?

Laura: I don't do anything — much. Oh, please don't think I sit around doing nothing! My glass collection takes up a good deal of my time. Glass is something you have to take good care of.

Jim: What did you say — about glass?

Laura: Collection I said — I have one — *(She clears her throat and turns away again, acutely shy).*

Jim (abruptly): You know what I judge to be the trouble with you? Inferiority complex! Know what that is? That's what they call it when someone low-rates himself! I understand it because I had it, too. Although my case was not so aggravated as yours seems to be. I had it until I took up public speaking, developed my voice, and learned that I had an aptitude for science. Before that time I never thought of myself as being outstanding in any way whatsoever! Now I've never made a regular study of it, but I have a friend who says I can analyze people better than doctors that make a profession of it. I don't claim that to be necessarily true, but I can sure guess a person's psychology, Laura! *(Takes out his gum.)* Excuse me, Laura. I always take it out when the flavor is gone. I'll use this scrap of paper to wrap it in. I know how it is to get it stuck on a shoe. Yep — that's what I judge to be your principal trouble. A lack of confidence in yourself as a person. You don't have the proper amount of faith in yourself. I'm basing that fact on a number of your remarks and also on certain observations I've made. For instance that clumping you thought was so awful in high school. You say that you even dreaded to walk into class. You see what you did? You dropped out of school, you gave up an education because of a clump, which as far as I know was practically non-existent! A little physical defect is what you have. Hardly noticeable even! Magnified thousands of times by imagination! You know what my strong advice to you is? Think of yourself as *superior* in some way!

Laura: In what way would I think?

Jim: Why, man alive, Laura! Just look about you a little. What do you see? A world full of common people! All of 'em born and all of 'em going to die! Which of them has one-tenth of your good points! Or mine! Or anyone else's, as far as that goes — Gosh! Everybody excels in some one thing. Some in many! *(Unconsciously glances at himself in the mirror.)* All you've got to do is discover in *what!* Take me, for instance. *(He adjusts his tie at the mirror.)* My interest happens to lie in electro-dynamics. I'm taking a course in radio engineering at night school, Laura, on top of a fairly responsible job at the warehouse. I'm taking that course and studying public speaking.

Laura: Ohhhh.

Jim: Because I believe in the future of television! *(Turning back to her.)* I wish to be ready to go up right along with it. Therefore I'm planning to get in on the ground floor. In fact, I've already made the right connections and all that remains is for the industry itself to get under way! Full steam —

(His eyes are starry.) Knowledge — Zzzzzp! *Money* — Zzzzzzp! — *Power!* That's the cycle democracy is built on! *(His attitude is convincingly dynamic. Laura stares at him, even her shyness eclipsed in her absolute wonder. He suddenly grins.)* I guess you think I think a lot of myself!

Laura: No — o-o-o, I —

Jim: Now how about you? Isn't there something you take more interest in than anything else?

Laura: Well, I do — as I said — have my — glass collection —

A peal of girlish laughter from the kitchen.

Jim: I'm not right sure I know what you're talking about. What kind of glass is it?

Laura: Little articles of it, they're ornaments mostly! Most of them are little animals made out of glass, the tiniest little animals in the world. Mother calls them a glass menagerie! Here's an example of one, if you'd like to see it! This one is one of the oldest. It's nearly thirteen. *(He stretches out his hand.)* **(Music: "The Glass Menagerie.")** Oh, be careful — if you breathe, it breaks!

Jim: I'd better not take it. I'm pretty clumsy with things.

Laura: Go on, I trust you with him! *(Places it in his palm.)* There now — you're holding him gently! Hold him over the light, he loves the light! You see how the light shines through him?

Jim: It sure does shine!

Laura: I shouldn't be partial, but he is my favorite one.

Jim: What kind of a thing is this one supposed to be?

Laura: Haven't you noticed the single horn on his forehead?

Jim: A unicorn, huh?

Laura: Mmm-hmmm!

Jim: Unicorns, aren't they extinct in the modern world?

Laura: I know!

Jim: Poor little fellow, he must feel sort of lonesome.

Laura (smiling): Well, if he does he doesn't complain about it. He stays on a shelf with some horses that don't have horns and all of them seem to get along nicely together.

Jim: How do you know?

Laura (lightly): I haven't heard any arguments among them!

Jim (grinning): No arguments, huh? Well, that's a pretty good sign! Where shall I set him?

Laura: Put him on the table. They all like a change of scenery once in a while!

Jim (stretching): Well, well, well, well — Look how big my shadow is when I stretch!

Laura: Oh, oh, yes — it stretches across the ceiling!

Jim (crossing to door): I think it's stopped raining. *(Opens fire-escape door.)* Where does the music come from?

Laura: From the Paradise Dance Hall across the alley.

Jim: How about cutting the rug a little, Miss Wingfield?

Laura: Oh, I —

Jim: Or is your program filled up? Let me have a look at it. *(Grasps imaginary card.)* Why, every dance is taken! I'll just have to scratch some out. **(Waltz**

Music: "La Golondrina.") Ahhh, a waltz! (*He executes some sweeping turns by himself, then holds his arms toward Laura.*)

Laura (breathlessly): I — can't dance!

Jim: There you go, that inferiority stuff!

Laura: I've never danced in my life!

Jim: Come on, try!

Laura: Oh, but I'd step on you!

Jim: I'm not made out of glass.

Laura: How — how — how do we start?

Jim: Just leave it to me. You hold your arms out a little.

Laura: Like this?

Jim: A little bit higher. Right. Now don't tighten up, that's the main thing about it — relax.

Laura (laughing breathlessly): It's hard not to.

Jim: Okay.

Laura: I'm afraid you can't budge me.

Jim: What do you bet I can't? (*He swings her into motion.*)

Laura: Goodness, yes, you can!

Jim: Let yourself go, now, Laura, just let yourself go.

Laura: I'm —

Jim: Come on!

Laura: Trying!

Jim: Not so stiff — Easy does it!

Laura: I know but I'm —

Jim: Loosen th' backbone! There now, that's a lot better.

Laura: Am I?

Jim: Lots, lots better! (*He moves her about the room in a clumsy waltz.*)

Laura: Oh, my!

Jim: Ha-ha!

Laura: Goodness, yes you can!

Jim: Ha-ha-ha! (*They suddenly bump into the table. Jim stops.*) What did we hit on?

Laura: Table.

Jim: Did something fall off it? I think —

Laura: Yes.

Jim: I hope that it wasn't the little glass horse with the horn!

Laura: Yes.

Jim: Aw, aw, aw. Is it broken?

Laura: Now it is just like all the other horses.

Jim: It's lost its —

Laura: Horn! It doesn't matter. Maybe it's a blessing in disguise.

Jim: You'll never forgive me. I bet that that was your favorite piece of glass.

Laura: I don't have favorites much. It's no tragedy, Freckles. Glass breaks so easily. No matter how careful you are. The traffic jars the shelves and things fall off them.

Jim: Still I'm awfully sorry that I was the cause.

Laura (smiling): I'll just imagine he had an operation. The horn was removed to make him feel less — freakish! (*They both laugh.*) Now he will feel more at home with the other horses, the ones that don't have horns . . .

Jim: Ha-ha, that's very funny! (*Suddenly serious.*) I'm glad to see that you have a sense of humor. You know — you're — well — very different! Surprisingly different from anyone else I know! (*His voice becomes soft and hesitant with a genuine feeling.*) Do you mind me telling you that? (*Laura is abashed beyond speech.*) You make me feel sort of — I don't know how to put it! I'm usually pretty good at expressing things, but — This is something that I don't know how to say! (*Laura touches her throat and clears it — turns the broken unicorn in her hands.*) (*Even softer.*) Has anyone ever told you that you were pretty? (**Pause: Music.**) (*Laura looks up slowly, with wonder, and shakes her head.*) Well, you are! In a very different way from anyone else. And all the nicer because of the difference, too. (*His voice becomes low and husky. Laura turns away, nearly faint with the novelty of her emotions.*) I wish you were my sister. I'd teach you to have some confidence in yourself. The different people are not like other people, but being different is nothing to be ashamed of. Because other people are not such wonderful people. They're one hundred times one thousand. You're one times one! They walk all over the earth. You just stay here. They're common as — weeds, but —you — well, you're — *Blue Roses!*

(Image On Screen: Blue Roses.)

(Music Changes.)

Laura: But blue is wrong for — roses . . .
Jim: It's right for you — You're — pretty!
Laura: In what respect am I pretty?
Jim: In all respects — believe me! Your eyes — your hair — are pretty! Your hands are pretty! (*He catches hold of her hand.*) You think I'm making this up because I'm invited to dinner and have to be nice. Oh, I could do that! I could put on an act for you, Laura, and say lots of things without being very sincere. But this time I am. I'm talking to you sincerely. I happened to notice you had this inferiority complex that keeps you from feeling comfortable with people. Somebody needs to build your confidence up and make you proud instead of shy and turning away and — blushing — Somebody ought to — ought to — *kiss* you, Laura! (*His hand slips slowly up her arm to her shoulder.*) (**Music Swells Tumultuously.**) (*He suddenly turns her about and kisses her on the lips. When he releases her Laura sinks on the sofa with a bright, dazed look. Jim backs away and fishes in his pocket for a cigarette.*) (**Legend On Screen: "Souvenir."**) Stumble-john! (*He lights the cigarette, avoiding her look. There is a peal of girlish laughter from Amanda in the kitchen. Laura slowly raises and opens her hand. It still contains the little broken glass animal. She looks at it with a tender, bewildered expression.*) Stumble-john! I shouldn't have done that — That was way off the beam. You don't smoke, do you? (*She looks up, smiling, not hearing the question. He sits beside her a little gingerly. She looks at him speechlessly — waiting. He coughs decorously and moves a little farther aside as he considers the situation and senses her feelings, dimly, with perturbation. Gently.*) Would you — care for a — mint? (*She doesn't seem to hear him but her look grows brighter even.*) Peppermint — Life Saver? My pocket's a regular drug store — wherever I go . . . (*He pops a mint in his mouth. Then gulps and decides*

to make a clean breast of it. He speaks slowly and gingerly.) Laura, you know, if I had a sister like you, I'd do the same thing as Tom. I'd bring out fellows — introduce her to them. The right type of boys of a type to — appreciate her. Only — well — he made a mistake about me. Maybe I've got no call to be saying this. That may not have been the idea in having me over. But what if it was? There's nothing wrong about that. The only trouble is that in my case — I'm not in a situation to — do the right thing. I can't take down your number and say I'll phone. I can't call up next week and — ask for a date. I thought I had better explain the situation in case you misunderstood it and — hurt your feelings. . . . *(Pause. Slowly, very slowly, Laura's look changes, her eyes returning slowly from his to the ornament in her palm.)*

Amanda utters another gay laugh in the kitchen.

Laura *(faintly):* You — won't — call again?
Jim: No, Laura, I can't. *(He rises from the sofa.)* As I was just explaining, I've — got strings on me, Laura, I've — been going steady! I go out all the time with a girl named Betty. She's a home-girl like you, and Catholic, and Irish, and in a great many ways we — get along fine. I met her last summer on a moonlight boat trip up the river to Alton, on the *Majestic.* Well — right away from the start it was — love! **(Legend: Love!)** *(Laura sways slightly forward and grips the arm of the sofa. He fails to notice, now enrapt in his own comfortable being.)* Being in love has made a new man of me! *(Leaning stiffly forward, clutching the arm of the sofa, Laura struggles visibly with her storm. But Jim is oblivious, she is a long way off.)* The power of love is really pretty tremendous! Love is something that — changes the whole world, Laura! *(The storm abates a little and Laura leans back. He notices her again.)* It happened that Betty's aunt took sick, she got a wire and had to go to Centralia. So Tom — when he asked me to dinner — I naturally just accepted the invitation, not knowing that you — that he — that I — *(He stops awkwardly.)* Huh — I'm a stumble-john! *(He flops back on the sofa. The holy candles in the altar of Laura's face have been snuffed out! There is a look of almost infinite desolation. Jim glances at her uneasily.)* I wish that you would — say something. *(She bites her lip which was trembling and then bravely smiles. She opens her hand again on the broken glass ornament. Then she gently takes his hand and raises it level with her own. She carefully places the unicorn in the palm of his hand, then pushes his fingers closed upon it.)* What are you — doing that for? You want me to have him? — Laura? *(She nods.)* What for?
Laura: A — souvenir . . .

She rises unsteadily and crouches beside the victrola to wind it up.

(Legend On Screen: "Things Have A Way Of Turning Out So Badly.")

(Or Image: "Gentleman Caller Waving Good-bye! — Gaily.")

At this moment Amanda rushes brightly back in the front room. She bears a pitcher of fruit punch in an old-fashioned cut-glass pitcher and a plate of macaroons. The plate has a gold border and poppies painted on it.

Amanda: Well, well, well! Isn't the air delightful after the shower? I've made you children a little liquid refreshment. *(Turns gaily to the gentleman caller.)* Jim, do you know that song about lemonade?

> "Lemonade, lemonade
> Made in the shade and stirred with a spade —
> Good enough for any old maid!"

Jim (uneasily): Ha-ha! No — I never heard it.
Amanda: Why, Laura! You look so serious!
Jim: We were having a serious conversation.
Amanda: Good! Now you're better acquainted!
Jim (uncertainly): Ha-ha! Yes.
Amanda: You modern young people are much more serious-minded than my generation. I was so gay as a girl!
Jim: You haven't changed, Mrs. Wingfield.
Amanda: Tonight I'm rejuvenated! The gaiety of the occasion, Mr. O'Connor! *(She tosses her head with a peal of laughter. Spills lemonade.)* Oooo! I'm baptizing myself!
Jim: Here — let me —
Amanda (setting the pitcher down): There now. I discovered we had some maraschino cherries. I dumped them in, juice and all!
Jim: You shouldn't have gone to that trouble, Mrs. Wingfield.
Amanda: Trouble, trouble? Why it was loads of fun! Didn't you hear me cutting up in the kitchen? I bet your ears were burning! I told Tom how outdone with him I was for keeping you to himself so long a time! He should have brought you over much, much sooner! Well, now that you've found your way, I want you to be a very frequent caller! Not just occasional but all the time. Oh, we're going to have a lot of gay times together! I see them coming! Mmm, just breathe that air! So fresh, and the moon's so pretty! I'll skip back out — I know where my place is when young folks are having a — serious conversation!
Jim: Oh, don't go out, Mrs. Wingfield. The fact of the matter is I've got to be going.
Amanda: Going, now? You're joking! Why, it's only the shank of the evening, Mr. O'Connor!
Jim: Well, you know how it is.
Amanda: You mean you're a young workingman and have to keep workingmen's hours. We'll let you off early tonight. But only on the condition that next time you stay later. What's the best night for you? Isn't Saturday night the best night for you workingmen?
Jim: I have a couple of time-clocks to punch, Mrs. Wingfield. One at morning, another one at night!
Amanda: My, but you *are* ambitious! You work at night, too?
Jim: No, Ma'am, not work but — Betty! *(He crosses deliberately to pick up his hat. The band at the Paradise Dance Hall goes into a tender waltz.)*
Amanda: Betty? Betty? Who's — Betty! *(There is an ominous cracking sound in the sky.)*
Jim: Oh, just a girl. The girl I go steady with! *(He smiles charmingly. The sky falls.)*

(Legend: "The Sky Falls.")

Amanda (a long-drawn exhalation): Ohhhh . . . Is it a serious romance, Mr. O'Connor?

Jim: We're going to be married the second Sunday in June.

Amanda: Ohhhh — how nice! Tom didn't mention that you were engaged to be married.

Jim: The cat's not out of the bag at the warehouse yet. You know how they are. They call you Romeo and stuff like that. *(He stops at the oval mirror to put on his hat. He carefully shapes the brim and the crown to give a discreetly dashing effect.)* It's been a wonderful evening, Mrs. Wingfield. I guess this is what they mean by Southern hospitality.

Amanda: It really wasn't anything at all.

Jim: I hope it don't seem like I'm rushing off. But I promised Betty I'd pick her up at the Wabash depot, an' by the time I get my jalopy down there her train'll be in. Some women are pretty upset if you keep 'em waiting.

Amanda: Yes, I know — The tyranny of women! *(Extends her hand.)* Goodbye, Mr. O'Connor. I wish you luck — and happiness — and success! All three of them, and so does Laura! — Don't you, Laura?

Laura: Yes!

Jim (taking her hand): Goodbye, Laura. I'm certainly going to treasure that souvenir. And don't you forget the good advice I gave you. *(Raises his voice to a cheery shout.)* So long, Shakespeare! Thanks again, ladies — Good night!

> *He grins and ducks jauntily out.*
> Still bravely grimacing, Amanda closes the door on the gentleman caller. Then she turns back to the room with a puzzled expression. She and Laura don't dare to face each other. Laura crouches beside the victrola to wind it.

Amanda (faintly): Things have a way of turning out so badly. I don't believe that I would play the victrola. Well, well — well — Our gentleman caller was engaged to be married! Tom!

Tom (from back): Yes, Mother?

Amanda: Come in here a minute. I want to tell you something awfully funny.

Tom (enters with macaroon and a glass of the lemonade): Has the gentleman caller gotten away already?

Amanda: The gentleman caller has made an early departure. What a wonderful joke you played on us!

Tom: How do you mean?

Amanda: You didn't mention that he was engaged to be married.

Tom: Jim? Engaged?

Amanda: That's what he just informed us.

Tom: I'll be jiggered! I didn't know about that.

Amanda: That seems very peculiar.

Tom: What's peculiar about it?

Amanda: Didn't you call him your best friend down at the warehouse?

Tom: He is, but how did I know?

Amanda: It seems extremely peculiar that you wouldn't know your best friend was going to be married!

Tom: The warehouse is where I work, not where I know things about people!

Amanda: You don't know things anywhere! You live in a dream; you manufacture illusions! *(He crosses to door.)* Where are you going?

Tom: I'm going to the movies.

Amanda: That's right, now that you've had us make such fools of ourselves. The
effort, the preparations, all the expense! The new floor lamp, the rug, the
clothes for Laura! All for what? To entertain some other girl's fiancé! Go
to the movies, go! Don't think about us, a mother deserted, an unmarried
sister who's crippled and has no job! Don't let anything interfere with your
selfish pleasure! Just go, go, go — to the movies!

Tom: All right, I will! The more you shout about my selfishness to me the
quicker I'll go, and I won't go to the movies!

Amanda: Go, then! Then go to the moon — you selfish dreamer!

*Tom smashes his glass on the floor. He plunges out on the fire-escape, slamming
the door. Laura screams — cut by door.*

*Dance-hall music up. Tom goes to the rail and grips it desperately, lifting
his face in the chill white moonlight penetrating the narrow abyss of the alley.*

(Legend On Screen: "And So Good-bye . . .")

*Tom's closing speech is timed with the interior pantomime. The interior scene
is played as though viewed through sound-proof glass. Amanda appears to
be making a comforting speech to Laura who is huddled upon the sofa. Now that
we cannot hear the mother's speech, her silliness is gone and she has dignity and
tragic beauty. Laura's dark hair hides her face until at the end of the speech she
lifts it to smile at her mother. Amanda's gestures are slow and graceful, almost
dancelike, as she comforts the daughter. At the end of her speech she glances a
moment at the father's picture — then withdraws through the portieres. At
close of Tom's speech, Laura blows out the candles, ending the play.*

Tom: I didn't go to the moon, I went much further — for time is the longest distance between two places — Not long after that I was fired for writing a
poem on the lid of a shoe-box. I left Saint Louis. I descended the steps of
this fire-escape for a last time and followed, from then on, in my father's
footsteps, attempting to find in motion what was lost in space — I traveled
around a great deal. The cities swept about me like dead leaves, leaves that
were brightly colored but torn away from the branches. I would have
stopped, but I was pursued by something. It always came upon me unawares, taking me altogether by surprise. Perhaps it was a familiar bit of
music. Perhaps it was only a piece of transparent glass. Perhaps I am
walking along a street at night, in some strange city, before I have found
companions. I pass the lighted window of a shop where perfume is sold.
The window is filled with pieces of colored glass, tiny transparent bottles
in delicate colors, like bits of a shattered rainbow. Then all at once my sister
touches my shoulder. I turn around and look into her eyes . . . Oh, Laura,
Laura, I tried to leave you behind me, but I am more faithful than I intended
to be! I reach for a cigarette, I cross the street, I run into the movies or a bar,
I buy a drink, I speak to the nearest stranger — anything that can blow your

candles out! *(Laura bends over the candles.)* — for nowadays the world is lit by lightning! Blow out your candles, Laura — and so goodbye . . .

She blows the candles out.

(The Scene Dissolves.)

Edward Albee (b. 1928)
THE ZOO STORY   1959

The Players

Peter: A man in his early forties, neither fat nor gaunt, neither handsome nor homely. He wears tweeds, smokes a pipe, carries horn-rimmed glasses. Although he is moving into middle age, his dress and his manner would suggest a man younger.

Jerry: A man in his late thirties, not poorly dressed, but carelessly. What was once a trim and lightly muscled body has begun to go to fat; and while he is no longer handsome, it is evident that he once was. His fall from physical grace should not suggest debauchery; he has, to come closest to it, a great weariness.

The Scene: *It is Central Park; a Sunday afternoon in summer; the present. There are two park benches, one toward either side of the stage; they both face the audience. Behind them: foliage, trees, sky. At the beginning, Peter is seated on one of the benches.*

> *As the curtain rises, Peter is seated on the bench stage-right. He is reading a book. He stops reading, cleans his glasses, goes back to reading. Jerry enters.*

Jerry: I've been to the zoo. *(Peter doesn't notice.)* I said, I've been to the zoo. MISTER, I'VE BEEN TO THE ZOO!
Peter: Hm? . . . What? . . . I'm sorry, were you talking to me?
Jerry: I went to the zoo, and then I walked until I came here. Have I been walking north?
Peter (puzzled): North? Why . . . I . . . I think so. Let me see.
Jerry (pointing past the audience): Is that Fifth Avenue?
Peter: Why yes; yes, it is.
Jerry: And what is that cross street there; that one, to the right?
Peter: That? Oh, that's Seventy-fourth Street.
Jerry: And the zoo is around Sixty-fifth Street; so, I've been walking north.
Peter (anxious to get back to his reading): Yes, it would seem so.
Jerry: Good old north.
Peter (lightly, by reflex): Ha, ha.
Jerry (after a slight pause): But not due north.
Peter: I . . . well, no, not due north; but, we . . . call it north. It's northerly.

Jerry (watches as Peter, anxious to dismiss him, prepares his pipe): Well, boy; you're not going to get lung cancer, are you?

Peter (looks up a little annoyed, then smiles): No, sir. Not from this.

Jerry: No, sir. What you'll probably get is cancer of the mouth, and then you'll have to wear one of those things Freud wore after they took one whole side of his jaw away. What do they call those things?

Peter (uncomfortable): A prosthesis?

Jerry: The very thing! A prosthesis. You're an educated man, aren't you? Are you a doctor?

Peter: Oh, no; no. I read about it somewhere; *Time* magazine, I think. *(He turns to his book.)*

Jerry: Well, *Time* magazine isn't for blockheads.

Peter: No, I suppose not.

Jerry (after a pause): Boy, I'm glad that's Fifth Avenue there.

Peter (vaguely): Yes.

Jerry: I don't like the west side of the park much.

Peter: Oh? *(Then, slightly wary, but interested.)* Why?

Jerry (offhand): I don't know.

Peter: Oh. *(He returns to his book.)*

Jerry (he stands for a few seconds, looking at Peter, who finally looks up again, puzzled): Do you mind if we talk?

Peter (obviously minding): Why . . . no, no.

Jerry: Yes you do; you do.

Peter (puts his book down, his pipe out and away, smiling): No, really; I don't mind.

Jerry: Yes you do.

Peter (finally decided): No; I don't mind at all, really.

Jerry: It's . . . it's a nice day.

Peter (stares unnecessarily at the sky): Yes. Yes, it is; lovely.

Jerry: I've been to the zoo.

Peter: Yes, I think you said so . . . didn't you?

Jerry: You'll read about it in the papers tomorrow, if you don't see it on your TV tonight. You have TV, haven't you?

Peter: Why yes, we have two; one for the children.

Jerry: You're married!

Peter (with pleased emphasis): Why, certainly.

Jerry: It isn't a law, for God's sake.

Peter: No . . . no, of course not.

Jerry: And you have a wife.

Peter (bewildered by the seeming lack of communication): Yes!

Jerry: And you have children.

Peter: Yes; two.

Jerry: Boys?

Peter: No, girls . . . both girls.

Jerry: But you wanted boys.

Peter: Well . . . naturally, every man wants a son, but . . .

Jerry (lightly mocking): But that's the way the cookie crumbles?

Peter (annoyed): I wasn't going to say that.

Jerry: And you're not going to have any more kids, are you?

Peter (a bit distantly): No. No more. *(Then back, and irksome.)* Why did you say that? How would you know about that?

Jerry: The way you cross your legs, perhaps; something in the voice. Or maybe I'm just guessing. Is it your wife?

Peter (furious): That's none of your business! *(A silence.)* Do you understand? *(Jerry nods. Peter is quiet now.)* Well, you're right. We'll have no more children.

Jerry (softly): That *is* the way the cookie crumbles.

Peter (forgiving): Yes . . . I guess so.

Jerry: Well, now; what else?

Peter: What were you saying about the zoo . . . that I'd read about it, or see . . . ?

Jerry: I'll tell you about it, soon. Do you mind if I ask you questions?

Peter: Oh, not really.

Jerry: I'll tell you why I do it; I don't talk to many people — except to say like: give me a beer, or where's the john, or what time does the feature go on, or keep your hands to yourself, buddy. You know — things like that.

Peter: I must say I don't . . .

Jerry: But every once in a while I like to talk to somebody, really *talk;* like to get to know somebody, know all about him.

Peter (lightly laughing, still a little uncomfortable): And am I the guinea pig for today?

Jerry: On a sun-drenched Sunday afternoon like this? Who better than a nice married man with two daughters and . . . uh . . . a dog? *(Peter shakes his head.)* No? Two dogs. *(Peter shakes his head again.)* Hm. No dogs? *(Peter shakes his head, sadly.)* Oh, that's a shame. But you look like an animal man. CATS? *(Peter nods his head, ruefully.)* Cats! But, that can't be your idea. No, sir. Your wife and daughters? *(Peter nods his head.)* Is there anything else I should know?

Peter (he has to clear his throat): There are . . . there are two parakeets. One . . . uh . . . one for each of my daughters.

Jerry: Birds.

Peter: My daughters keep them in a cage in their bedroom.

Jerry: Do they carry disease? The birds.

Peter: I don't believe so.

Jerry: That's too bad. If they did you could set them loose in the house and the cats could eat them and die, maybe. *(Peter looks blank for a moment, then laughs.)* And what else? What do you do to support your enormous household?

Peter: I . . . uh . . . I have an executive position with a . . . a small publishing house. We . . . uh . . . we publish textbooks.

Jerry: That sounds nice; very nice. What do you make?

Peter (still cheerful): Now look here!

Jerry: Oh, come on.

Peter: Well, I make around eighteen thousand a year, but I don't carry more than forty dollars at any one time . . . in case you're a . . . a holdup man . . . ha, ha, ha.

Jerry (ignoring the above): Where do you live? *(Peter is reluctant.)* Oh, look; I'm not going to rob you, and I'm not going to kidnap your parakeets, your cats, or your daughters.

Peter (too loud): I live between Lexington and Third Avenue, on Seventy-fourth Street.

Jerry: That wasn't so hard, was it?

Peter: I didn't mean to seem . . . ah . . . it's that you don't really carry on a conversation; you just ask questions, and I'm . . . I'm normally . . . uh . . . reticent. Why do you just stand there?

Jerry: I'll start walking around in a little while, and eventually I'll sit down. (Recalling.) Wait until you see the expression on his face.

Peter: What? Whose face? Look here; is this something about the zoo?

Jerry (distantly): The what?

Peter: The zoo; the zoo. Something about the zoo.

Jerry: The zoo?

Peter: You've mentioned it several times.

Jerry (still distant, but returning abruptly): The zoo? Oh, yes; the zoo. I was there before I came here. I told you that. Say, what's the dividing line between upper-middle-middle-class and lower-upper-middle-class?

Peter: My dear fellow, I . . .

Jerry: Don't my dear fellow me.

Peter (unhappily): Was I patronizing? I believe I was; I'm sorry. But, you see, your question about the classes bewildered me.

Jerry: And when you're bewildered you become patronizing?

Peter: I . . . I don't express myself too well, sometimes. (He attempts a joke on himself.) I'm in publishing, not writing.

Jerry (amused, but not at the humor): So be it. The truth is: I was being patronizing.

Peter: Oh, now; you needn't say that.

> It is at this point that Jerry may begin to move about the stage with slowly increasing determination and authority, but pacing himself, so that the long speech about the dog comes at the high point of the arc.

Jerry: All right. Who are your favorite writers? Baudelaire and J. P. Marquand?

Peter (wary): Well, I like a great many writers; I have a considerable . . . catholicity of taste, if I may say so. Those two men are fine, each in his way. (Warming up.) Baudelaire, of course . . . uh . . . is by far the finer of the two, but Marquand has a place . . . in our . . . uh . . . national . . .

Jerry: Skip it.

Peter: I . . . sorry.

Jerry: Do you know what I did before I went to the zoo today? I walked all the way up Fifth Avenue from Washington Square; all the way.

Peter: Oh; you live in the Village! (This seems to enlighten Peter.)

Jerry: No, I don't. I took the subway down to the Village so I could walk all the way up Fifth Avenue to the zoo. It's one of those things a person has to do; sometimes a person has to go a very long distance out of his way to come back a short distance correctly.

Peter (almost pouting): Oh, I thought you lived in the Village.

Jerry: What were you trying to do? Make sense out of things? Bring order? The old pigeonhole bit? Well, that's easy; I'll tell you. I live in a four-story brownstone roominghouse on the upper West Side between Columbus Avenue and Central Park West. I live on the top floor; rear; west. It's a laughably small room, and one of my walls is made of beaverboard; this beaverboard separates my room from another laughably small room, so I assume that the two rooms were once one room, a small room, but not necessarily laughable. The room beyond my beaverboard wall is occupied by a colored queen who always keeps his door open; well, not always, but *always* when he's plucking his eyebrows, which he does with Buddhist concentration. This colored queen has rotten teeth, which is rare, and he has a Japanese kimono, which is also pretty rare; and he wears this kimono to and from the john in the hall, which is pretty frequent. I mean, he goes to the john a lot. He never bothers me, and he never brings anyone up to his room. All he does is pluck his eyebrows, wear his kimono and go to the john. Now, the two front rooms on my floor are a little larger, I guess; but they're pretty small, too. There's a Puerto Rican family in one of them, a husband, a wife, and some kids; I don't know how many. These people entertain a lot. And in the other front room, there's somebody living there, but I don't know who it is. I've never seen who it is. Never. Never ever.

Peter (embarrassed): Why . . . why do you live there?

Jerry (from a distance again): I don't know.

Peter: It doesn't sound like a very nice place . . . where you live.

Jerry: Well, no; it isn't an apartment in the East Seventies. But, then again, I don't have one wife, two daughters, two cats and two parakeets. What I do have, I have toilet articles, a few clothes, a hot plate that I'm not supposed to have, a can opener, one that works with a key, you know; a knife, two forks, and two spoons, one small, one large; three plates, a cup, a saucer, a drinking glass, two picture frames, both empty, eight or nine books, a pack of pornographic playing cards, regular deck, an old Western Union typewriter that prints nothing but capital letters, and a small strong-box without a lock which has in it . . . what? Rocks! Some rocks . . . sea-rounded rocks I picked up on the beach when I was a kid. Under which . . . weighed down . . . are some letters . . . please letters . . . please why don't you do this, and please when will you do that letters. And when letters, too. When will you write? When will you come? When? These letters are from more recent years.

Peter (stares glumly at his shoes, then): About those two empty picture frames . . . ?

Jerry: I don't see why they need any explanation at all. Isn't it clear? I don't have pictures of anyone to put in them.

Peter: Your parents . . . perhaps . . . a girl friend . . .

Jerry: You're a very sweet man, and you're possessed of a truly enviable innocence. But good old Mom and good old Pop are dead . . . you know? . . . I'm broken up about it, too . . . I mean really. BUT. That particular vaudeville act is playing the cloud circuit now, so I don't see how I can look at them, all neat and framed. Besides, or, rather, to be pointed about it, good old Mom walked out on good old Pop when I was ten and a half years old; she embarked on an adulterous turn of our southern states . . . a journey of a year's duration . . . and her most constant companion . . . among others, among many others . . . was a Mr. Barleycorn. At least, that's what good old Pop told me after he went down . : . came back . . . brought her body north. We'd received the news between Christmas and New Year's, you see, that good old Mom had parted with the ghost in some dump in Alabama. And, without the ghost . . . she was less welcome. I mean, what was she? A stiff . . a northern stiff. At any rate, good old Pop celebrated the New Year for an even two weeks and then slapped into the front of a somewhat moving city omnibus, which sort of cleaned things out family-wise. Well no; then there was Mom's sister, who was given neither to sin nor the consolations of the bottle. I moved in on her, and my memory of her is slight excepting I remember still that she did all things dourly: sleeping, eating, working, praying. She dropped dead on the stairs to her apartment, my apartment then, too, on the afternoon of my high school graduation. A terribly middle-European joke, if you ask me.

Peter: Oh, my; oh, my.

Jerry: Oh, your what? But that was a long time ago, and I have no feeling about any of it that I care to admit to myself. Perhaps you can see, though, why good old Mom and good old Pop are frameless. What's your name? Your first name?

Peter: I'm Peter.

Jerry: I'd forgotten to ask you. I'm Jerry.

Peter (with a slight, nervous laugh): Hello, Jerry.

Jerry (nods his hello): And let's see now; what's the point of having a girl's picture, especially in two frames? I have two picture frames, you remember. I never see the pretty little ladies more than once, and most of them wouldn't be caught in the same room with a camera. It's odd, and I wonder if it's sad.

Peter: The girls?

Jerry: No. I wonder if it's sad that I never see the little ladies more than once. I've never been able to have sex with, or, how is it put? . . . make love to anybody more than once. Once; that's it . . . Oh, wait; for a week and a half, when I was fifteen . . . and I hang my head in shame that puberty was late . . . I was a h-o-m-o-s-e-x-u-a-l. I mean, I was queer . . . *(very fast)* . . . queer, queer, queer . . . with bells ringing, banners snapping in the wind. And for those eleven days, I met at least twice a day with the park superintendent's son . . . a Greek boy, whose birthday was the same as mine, except he was a year older. I think I was very much in love . . . maybe just with sex. But that was the jazz of a very special hotel, wasn't it? And now; oh, do I love the little ladies; really, I love them. For about an hour.

Peter: Well, it seems perfectly simple to me. . . .

Jerry (angry): Look! Are you going to tell me to get married and have parakeets?

Peter (angry himself): Forget the parakeets! And stay single if you want to. It's no business of mine. I didn't start this conversation in the . . .

Jerry: All right, all right. I'm sorry. All right? You're not angry?

Peter (laughing): No, I'm not angry.

Jerry (relieved): Good. *(Now back to his previous tone.)* Interesting that you asked me about the picture frames. I would have thought that you would have asked me about the pornographic playing cards.

Peter (with a knowing smile): Oh, I've seen those cards.

Jerry: That's not the point. *(Laughs.)* I suppose when you were a kid you and your pals passed them around, or you had a pack of your own.

Peter: Well, I guess a lot of us did.

Jerry: And you threw them away just before you got married.

Peter: Oh, now; look here. I didn't *need* anything like that when I got older.

Jerry: No?

Peter (embarrassed): I'd rather not talk about these things.

Jerry: So? Don't. Besides, I wasn't trying to plumb your postadolescent sexual life and hard times; what I wanted to get at is the value difference between pornographic playing cards when you're a kid, and pornographic playing cards when you're older. It's that when you're a kid you use the cards as a substitute for a real experience, and when you're older you use real experience as a substitute for the fantasy. But I imagine you'd rather hear about what happened at the zoo.

Peter (enthusiastic): Oh, yes; the zoo. *(Then, awkward.)* That is . . . if you. . . .

Jerry: Let me tell you about why I went . . . well, let me tell you some things. I've told you about the fourth floor of the roominghouse where I live. I think the rooms are better as you go down, floor by floor. I guess they are; I don't know. I don't know any of the people on the third and second floors. Oh, wait! I do know that there's a lady living on the third floor, in the front. I know because she cries all the time. Whenever I go out or come back in, whenever I pass her door, I always hear her crying, muffled, but . . . very determined. Very determined indeed. But the one I'm getting to, and all about the dog, is the landlady. I don't like to use words that are too harsh in describing people. I don't like to. But the landlady is a fat, ugly, mean, stupid, unwashed, misanthropic, cheap, drunken bag of garbage. And you may have noticed that I very seldom use profanity, so I can't describe her as well as I might.

Peter: You describe her . . . vividly.

Jerry: Well, thanks. Anyway, she has a dog, and I will tell you about the dog, and she and her dog are the gatekeepers of my dwelling. The woman is bad enough; she leans around in the entrance hall, spying to see that I don't bring in things or people, and when she's had her midafternoon pint of lemon-flavored gin she always stops me in the hall, and grabs ahold of my coat or my arm, and she presses her disgusting body up against me to keep me in a corner so she can talk to me. The smell of her body and her breath . . . you can't imagine it . . . and somewhere, somewhere in the back of that pea-sized brain of hers, an organ developed just enough to let her eat, drink, and emit, she has some foul parody of sexual desire. And I, Peter, I am the object of her sweaty lust.

Peter: That's disgusting. That's . . . horrible.

Jerry: But I have found a way to keep her off. When she talks to me, when she presses herself to my body and mumbles about her room and how I should come there, I merely say: but, Love; wasn't yesterday enough for you, and the day before? Then she puzzles, she makes slits of her tiny eyes, she sways a little, and then, Peter . . . and it is at this moment that I think I might be doing some good in that tormented house . . . a simple-minded smile begins to form on her unthinkable face, and she giggles and groans as she thinks about yesterday and the day before; as she believes and relives what never happened. Then, she motions to that black monster of a dog she has, and she goes back to her room. And I am safe until our next meeting.

Peter: It's so . . . unthinkable. I find it hard to believe that people such as that really *are.*

Jerry (lightly mocking): It's for reading about, isn't it?

Peter (seriously): Yes.

Jerry: And fact is better left to fiction. You're right, Peter. Well, what I have been meaning to tell you about is the dog; I shall, now.

Peter (nervously): Oh, yes; the dog.

Jerry: Don't go. You're not thinking of going, are you?

Peter: Well . . . no, I don't think so.

Jerry (as if to a child): Because after I tell you about the dog, do you know what then? Then . . . then I'll tell you about what happened at the zoo.

Peter (laughing faintly): You're . . . you're full of stories, aren't you?

Jerry: You don't have to listen. Nobody is holding you here; remember that. Keep that in your mind.

Peter (irritably): I know that.

Jerry: You do? Good.

The following long speech, it seems to me, should be done with a great deal of action, to achieve a hypnotic effect on Peter, and on the audience, too. Some specific actions have been suggested, but the director and the actor playing Jerry might best work it out for themselves.

ALL RIGHT. (As if reading from a huge billboard.) THE STORY OF JERRY AND THE DOG! (Natural again.) What I am going to tell you has something to do with how sometimes it's necessary to go a long distance out of the way in order to come back a short distance correctly; or, maybe I only think that it has something to do with that. But, it's why I went to the zoo today, and why I walked north . . . northerly, rather . . . until I came here. All right. The dog, I think I told you, is a black monster of a beast: an over-sized head, tiny, tiny ears, and eyes . . . bloodshot, infected, maybe; and a body you can see the ribs through the skin. The dog is black, all black; all black except for the bloodshot eyes, and . . . yes . . . and an open sore on its . . . *right* forepaw; that is red, too. And, oh yes; the poor monster, and I do believe it's an old dog . . . it's certainly a misused one . . . almost always has an erection . . . of sorts. That's red, too. And . . . what else? . . . oh, yes; there's a gray-yellow-white color, too, when he bares his fangs. Like this: Grrrrrr! Which is what he did when he saw me for the first time . . . the day I moved in. I worried about that animal the very first minute I met him. Now, animals don't take to me like Saint Francis had birds hanging off him all the time. What I mean is: animals are indifferent to me . . . like people (he smiles slightly) . . . most of the time. But this dog wasn't indifferent. From the very beginning he'd snarl and then go for me, to get one of my legs. Not like he was rabid, you know; he was sort of a stumbly dog, but he wasn't half-assed, either. It was a good, stumbly run; but I always got away. He got a piece of my trouser leg, look, you can see right here, where it's mended; he got that the second day I lived there; but, I kicked free and got upstairs fast, so that was that. (Puzzles.) I still don't know to this day how the other roomers manage it, but you know what I *think:* I think it had to do only with me. Cozy. So. Anyway, this went on for over a week, when-ever I came in; but never when I went out. That's funny. Or, it *was* funny. I could pack up and live in the street for all the dog cared. Well, I thought about it up in my room one day, one of the times after I'd bolted upstairs, and I made up my mind. I decided: First, I'll kill the dog with kindness, and if that doesn't work . . . I'll just kill him. *(Peter winces.)* Don't react, Peter; just listen. So, the next day I went out and bought a bag of hamburgers, medium rare, no catsup, no onion; and on the way home I threw away all the rolls and kept just the meat.

Action for the following, perhaps.

When I got back to the roominghouse the dog was waiting for me. I half opened the door that led into the entrance hall, and there he was; waiting for me. It figured. I went in, very cautiously, and I had the hamburgers, you remember; I opened the bag, and I set the meat down about twelve feet from where the dog was snarling at me. Like so! He snarled; stopped snarling; sniffed; moved slowly; then faster; then faster toward the meat. Well, when he got to it he stopped, and he looked at me. I smiled; but tentatively, you understand. He turned his face back to the hamburgers, smelled, sniffed some more, and then . . . RRRAAAAGGGGGHHHH, like that . . . he tore into them. It was as if he had never eaten anything in his life before, except like garbage. Which might very well have been the truth. I don't think the landlady ever eats anything but garbage. But. He ate all the hamburgers, almost all at once, making sounds in his throat like a woman. *Then,* when he'd finished the meat, the hamburger, and tried to eat the paper, too, he sat down and smiled. I think he smiled; I know cats do. It was a very gratifying few moments. Then, BAM, he snarled and made for me again. He didn't get me this time, either. So, I got upstairs, and I lay down on my bed and started to think about the dog again. To be truthful, I was offended, and I was damn mad, too. It was six perfectly good hamburgers with not enough pork in them to make it disgusting. I was offended. But, after a while, I decided to try it for a few more days. If you think about it, this dog had what amounted to an antipathy toward me; really. And, I wondered if I mightn't overcome this antipathy. So, I tried it for five more days, but it was always the same: snarl, sniff; move; faster; stare; gobble; RAAGGGHHH; smile; snarl; BAM. Well, now; by this time Columbus Avenue was strewn with hamburger rolls and I was less offended than disgusted. So, I decided to kill the dog.

Peter raises a hand in protest.

Oh, don't be so alarmed, Peter; I didn't succeed. The day I tried to kill the dog I bought only one hamburger and what I thought was a murderous portion of rat poison. When I bought the hamburger I asked the man not to bother with the roll, all I wanted was the meat. I expected some reaction from him, like: we don't sell no hamburgers without rolls; or, wha' d'ya wanna do, eat it out'a ya han's? But no; he smiled benignly, wrapped up the hamburger in waxed paper, and said: A bite for ya pussy-cat? I wanted to say: No, not really; it's part of a plan to poison a dog I know. But, you can't say "a dog I know" without sounding funny; so I said, a little too loud, I'm afraid, and too formally: YES, A BITE FOR MY PUSSY-CAT. People looked up. It always happens when I try to simplify things; people look up. But that's neither hither nor thither. So. On my way back to the roominghouse, I kneaded the hamburger and the rat poison together between my hands, at that point feeling as much sadness as disgust. I opened the door to the entrance hall, and there the monster was, waiting to take the offering and then jump me. Poor bastard; he never learned that the moment he took to smile before he went for me gave me time enough to get out of range. BUT, there he was; malevolence with an erection, waiting. I put the poison patty down, moved toward the stairs and watched. The poor animal gobbled the food down as usual, smiled, which made me almost sick, and then BAM. But, I sprinted up the stairs, as usual, and the dog didn't get me, as usual. AND IT CAME TO PASS THAT THE BEAST WAS DEATHLY ILL. I knew this because he no longer attended me, and because the landlady sobered up. She stopped me in the hall the same evening of the attempted murder and confided the information that God had struck her puppy-dog a surely fatal blow. She had forgotten her bewildered lust, and her eyes were wide open for the first time. They looked like the dog's eyes. She sniveled and implored me to pray for the animal. I wanted to say to her: Madam, I have myself to pray for, the colored queen, the Puerto Rican family, the person in the front room whom I've never seen, the woman who cries deliberately behind her closed door, and the rest of the people in all roominghouses, everywhere; besides, Madam, I don't understand how to pray. But . . . to simplify things . . . I told her I would pray. She looked up. She said that I was a liar, and that I probably wanted the dog to die. I told her, and there was so much truth here, that I didn't want the dog to die. I didn't, and not just because I'd poisoned him. I'm afraid that I must tell you I wanted the dog to live so that I could see what our new relationship might come to.

Peter indicates his increasing displeasure and slowly growing antagonism.

Please understand, Peter; that sort of thing is important. You must believe me; it *is* important. We have to know the effect of our actions. (*Another deep sigh.*) Well, anyway; the dog recovered. I have no idea why, unless he was a descendant of the puppy that guarded the gates of hell or some such resort. I'm not up on my mythology. (*He pronounces the word myth-o-*logy.*) Are you?

Peter sets to thinking, but Jerry goes on.

At any rate, and you've missed the eight-thousand-dollar question, Peter; at any rate, the dog recovered his health and the landlady recovered her thirst, in no way altered by the bow-wow's deliverance. When I came home from a movie that was playing on Forty-second Street, a movie I'd seen, or one that was very much like one or several I'd seen, after the landlady told me puppykins was better, I was so hoping for the dog to be waiting for me. I was . . . well, how would you put it . . . enticed? . . . fascinated? . . . no, I don't think so . . . heart-shatteringly anxious, that's it; I was heart-shatteringly anxious to confront my friend again.

Peter reacts scoffingly.

Yes, Peter; friend. That's the only word for it. I was heart-shatteringly et cetera to confront my doggy friend again. I came in the door and advanced, unafraid, to the center of the entrance hall. The beast was there . . . looking at me. And, you know, he looked better for his scrape with the never-mind. I stopped; I looked at him; he looked at me. I think . . . I think we stayed a long time that way . . . still, stone-statue . . . just looking at one another. I looked more into his face than he looked into mine. I mean, I can concentrate longer at looking into a dog's face than a dog can concentrate at looking into mine, or into anybody else's face, for that matter. But during that twenty seconds or two hours that we looked into each other's face, we made contact. Now, here is what I had wanted to happen: I loved the dog now, and I wanted him to love me. I had tried to love, and I had tried to kill, and both had been unsuccessful by themselves. I hoped . . . and I don't really know why I expected the dog to understand anything, much less my motivations . . . I hoped that the dog would understand.

Peter seems to be hypnotized.

It's just . . . it's just that . . . (*Jerry is abnormally tense, now*) . . . it's just that if you can't deal with people, you have to make a start somewhere. WITH ANIMALS! (*Much faster now, and like a conspirator.*) Don't you see? A person has to have some way of dealing with SOMETHING. If not with people . . . if not with people . . . SOMETHING. With a bed, with a cock-roach, with a mirror . . . no, that's too hard, that's one of the last steps. With a cockroach, with a . . . with a carpet, a roll of toilet paper . . . no, not that, either . . . that's a mirror, too; always check bleeding. You see how hard it is to find things? With a street corner, and too many lights, all colors reflecting on the oily-wet streets . . . with a wisp of smoke, a wisp . . . of smoke . . . with . . . with pornographic playing cards, with a strong-box . . . WITHOUT A LOCK . . . with love, with vomiting, with crying, with fury because the pretty little ladies aren't pretty little ladies, with making money with your body which is an act of love and I could prove it, with howling because you're alive; with God. How about that? WITH GOD WHO IS A COLORED QUEEN WHO WEARS A KIMONO AND PLUCKS HIS EYEBROWS, WHO IS A WOMAN WHO CRIES WITH DETERMIN-ATION BEHIND HER CLOSED DOOR . . . with God who, I'm told, turned his back on the whole thing some time ago . . . with . . . some day, with people. (*Jerry sighs the next word heavily.*) People. With an idea; a concept. And where better, where ever better in this humiliating excuse for a jail, where better to communicate one single, simpleminded idea than in an entrance hall? Where? It would be A START! Where better to make a begin-ning . . . to understand and just possibly be understood . . . a beginning of an understanding, than with . . .

Here Jerry seems to fall into almost grotesque fatigue.

. . . than with A DOG. Just that; a dog.

Here there is a silence that might be prolonged for a moment or so; then Jerry wearily finishes his story.

A dog. It seemed like a perfectly sensible idea. Man is a dog's best friend, remember. So: the dog and I looked at each other. I longer than the dog. And what I saw then has been the same ever since. Whenever the dog and I see each other we both stop where we are. We regard each other with a mixture of sadness and suspicion, and then we feign indifference. We walk past each other safely; we have an understanding. It's very sad, but you'll have to admit that it is an understanding. We had made many attempts at contact, and we had failed. The dog has returned to garbage, and I to solitary but free passage. I have not returned. I mean to say, I have *gained* solitary free passage, if that much further loss can be said to be gain. I have learned that neither kindness nor cruelty by themselves, independent of each other, creates any effect beyond themselves; and I have learned that the two combined, together, at the same time, are the teaching emotion. And what is gained is loss. And what has been the result: the dog and I have attained a compromise; more of a bargain, really. We neither love nor hurt because we do not try to reach each other. And, *was* trying to feed the dog an act of love? And, perhaps, was the dog's attempt to bite me *not* an act of love? If we can so misunderstand, well then, why have we invented the word love in the first place?

There is silence. Jerry moves to Peter's bench and sits down beside him. This is first time Jerry has sat down during the play.

The Story of Jerry and the Dog: the end.

Peter is silent.

Well, Peter? *(Jerry is suddenly cheerful.)* Well, Peter? Do you think I could sell that story to the *Reader's Digest* and make a couple of hundred bucks for *The Most Unforgettable Character I've Ever Met?* Huh?

Jerry is animated, but Peter is disturbed.

Oh, come on now, Peter; tell me what you think.
Peter *(numb):* I . . . I don't understand what . . . I don't think I . . . *(Now, almost tearfully.)* Why did you tell me all of this?
Jerry: Why not?
Peter: I DON'T UNDERSTAND!
Jerry *(furious, but whispering):* That's a lie.
Peter: No. No, it's not.
Jerry *(quietly):* I tried to explain it to you as I went along. I went slowly; it all has to do with . . .
Peter: I DON'T WANT TO HEAR ANY MORE. I don't understand you, or your landlady, or her dog. . . .
Jerry: Her dog! I thought it was my . . . No. No, you're right. It *is* her dog. *(Looks at Peter intently, shaking his head.)* I don't know what I was thinking about; of course you don't understand. *(In a monotone, wearily.)* I don't live in your block; I'm not married to two parakeets, or whatever your setup is. I am a *permanent transient,* and my home is the sickening room-inghouses on the West Side of New York City, which is the greatest city in the world. Amen.
Peter: I'm . . . I'm sorry; I didn't mean to . . .
Jerry: Forget it. I suppose you don't quite know what to make of me, eh?
Peter *(a joke):* We get all kinds in publishing. *(Chuckles.)*
Jerry: You're a funny man. *(He forces a laugh.)* You know that? You're a very . . . a richly comic person.

Peter (*modestly, but amused*): Oh, now, not really. (*Still chuckling.*)

Jerry: Peter, do I annoy you, or confuse you?

Peter (*lightly*): Well, I must confess that this wasn't the kind of afternoon I'd anticipated.

Jerry: You mean, I'm not the gentleman you were expecting.

Peter: I wasn't expecting anybody.

Jerry: No, I don't imagine you were. But I'm here, and I'm not leaving.

Peter (*consulting his watch*): Well, you may not be, but I must be getting home soon.

Jerry: Oh, come on; stay a while longer.

Peter: I really should get home; you see . . .

Jerry (*tickles Peter's ribs with his fingers*): Oh, come on.

Peter (*he is very ticklish; as Jerry continues to tickle him his voice becomes falsetto*): No, I . . . OHHHHH! Don't do that. Stop, stop. Ohhh, no, no.

Jerry: Oh, come on.

Peter (*as Jerry tickles*): Oh, hee, hee, hee. I must go. I . . . hee, hee, hee. After all, stop, stop, hee, hee, hee, after all, the parakeets will be getting dinner ready soon. Hee, hee. And the cats are setting the table. Stop, stop, and, and . . . (*Peter is beside himself now*) . . . and we're having . . . hee, hee . . . uh . . . ho, ho, ho.

Jerry stops tickling Peter, but the combination of the tickling and his own mad whimsy has Peter laughing almost hysterically. As his laughter continues, then subsides, Jerry watches him, with a curious fixed smile.

Jerry: Peter?

Peter: Oh, ha, ha, ha, ha, ha. What? What?

Jerry: Listen, now.

Peter: Oh, ho, ho. What . . . what is it, Jerry? Oh, my.

Jerry (*mysteriously*): Peter, do you want to know what happened at the zoo?

Peter: Ah, ha, ha. The what? Oh, yes; the zoo. Oh, ho, ho. Well, I had my own zoo there for a moment with . . . hee, hee, the parakeets getting dinner ready, and the . . . ha, ha, whatever it was, the . . .

Jerry (*calmly*): Yes, that was very funny, Peter. I wouldn't have expected it. But do you want to hear about what happened at the zoo, or not?

Peter: Yes. Yes, by all means; tell me what happened at the zoo. Oh, my. I don't know what happened to me.

Jerry: Now I'll let you in on what happened at the zoo; but first, I should tell you why I went to the zoo. I went to the zoo to find out more about the way people exist with animals, and the way animals exist with each other, and with people too. It probably wasn't a fair test, what with everyone separated by bars from everyone else, the animals for the most part from each other, and always the people from the animals. But, if it's a zoo, that's the way it is. (*He pokes Peter on the arm.*) Move over.

Peter (*friendly*): I'm sorry, haven't you enough room? (*He shifts a little.*)

Jerry (*smiling slightly*): Well, all the animals are there, and all the people are there, and it's Sunday and all the children are there. (*He pokes Peter again.*) Move over.

Peter (*patiently, still friendly*): All right.

He moves some more, and Jerry has all the room he might need.

Jerry: And it's a hot day, so all the stench is there, too, and all the balloon sellers, and all the ice cream sellers, and all the seals are barking, and all the birds are screaming. *(Pokes Peter harder.)* Move over!

Peter (beginning to be annoyed): Look here, you have more than enough room! *(But he moves more, and is now fairly cramped at one end of the bench.)*

Jerry: And I am there, and it's feeding time at the lions' house, and the lion keeper comes into the lion cage, one of the lion cages, to feed one of the lions. *(Punches Peter on the arm, hard.)* MOVE OVER!

Peter (very annoyed): I can't move over any more, and stop hitting me. What's the matter with you?

Jerry: Do you want to hear the story? *(Punches Peter's arm again.)*

Peter (flabbergasted): I'm not so sure! I certainly don't want to be punched in the arm.

Jerry (punches Peter's arm again): Like that?

Peter: Stop it! What's the matter with you?

Jerry: I'm crazy, you bastard.

Peter: That isn't funny.

Jerry: Listen to me, Peter. I want this bench. You go sit on the bench over there, and if you're good I'll tell you the rest of the story.

Peter (flustered): But . . . whatever for? What *is* the matter with you? Besides, I see no reason why I should give up this bench. I sit on this bench almost every Sunday afternoon, in good weather. It's secluded here; there's never anyone sitting here, so I have it all to myself.

Jerry (softly): Get off this bench, Peter; I want it.

Peter (almost whining): No.

Jerry: I said I want this bench, and I'm going to have it. Now get over there.

Peter: People can't have everything they want. You should know that; it's a rule; people can have some of the things they want, but they can't have everything.

Jerry (laughs): Imbecile! You're slow-witted!

Peter: Stop that!

Jerry: You're a vegetable! Go lie down on the ground.

Peter (intense): Now *you* listen to me. I've put up with you all afternoon.

Jerry: Not really.

Peter: LONG ENOUGH. I've put up with you long enough. I've listened to you because you seemed . . . well, because I thought you wanted to talk to somebody.

Jerry: You put things well; economically, and, yet . . . oh, what is the word I want to put justice to your . . . JESUS, you make me sick . . . get off here and give me my bench.

Peter: MY BENCH!

Jerry (pushes Peter almost, but not quite, off the bench): Get out of my sight.

Peter (regaining his position): God da . . . mn you. That's enough! I've had enough of you. I will not give up this bench; you can't have it, and that's that. Now, go away.

Jerry snorts but does not move.

Go away, I said.

Jerry does not move.

Get away from here. If you don't move on . . . you're a bum . . . that's what you are. . . . If you don't move on, I'll get a policeman here and make you go.

Jerry laughs, stays.

I warn you, I'll call a policeman.

Jerry (softly): You won't find a policeman around here; they're all over on the west side of the park chasing fairies down from trees or out of the bushes. That's all they do. That's their function. So scream your head off; it won't do you any good.

Peter: POLICE! I warn you, I'll have you arrested. POLICE! *(Pause.)* I said POLICE! *(Pause.)* I feel ridiculous.

Jerry: You look ridiculous: a grown man screaming for the police on a bright Sunday afternoon in the park with nobody harming you. If a policeman *did* fill his quota and come sludging over this way he'd probably take you in as a nut.

Peter (with disgust and impotence): Great God, I just came here to read, and now you want me to give up the bench. You're mad.

Jerry: Hey, I got news for you, as they say. I'm on your precious bench, and you're never going to have it for yourself again.

Peter (furious): Look, you; get off my bench. I don't care if it makes any sense or not. I want this bench to myself; I want you OFF IT!

Jerry (mocking): Aw . . . look who's mad.

Peter: GET OUT!

Jerry: No.

Peter: I WARN YOU!

Jerry: Do you know how ridiculous you look *now*?

Peter (his fury and self-consciousness have possessed him): It doesn't matter. *(He is almost crying.)* GET AWAY FROM MY BENCH!

Jerry: Why? You have everything in the world you want; you've told me about your home, and your family, and *your own* little zoo. You have everything, and now you want this bench. Are these the things men fight for? Tell me, Peter, is this bench, this iron and this wood, is this your honor? Is this the thing in the world you'd fight for? Can you think of anything more absurd?

Peter: Absurd? Look, I'm not going to talk to you about honor, or even try to explain it to you. Besides, it isn't a question of honor; but even if it were, you wouldn't understand.

Jerry (contemptuously): You don't even know what you're saying, do you? This is probably the first time in your life you've had anything more trying to face than changing your cats' toilet box. Stupid! Don't you have any idea, not even the slightest, what other people *need*?

Peter: Oh, boy, listen to you; well, you don't need this bench. That's for sure.

Jerry: Yes; yes, I do.

Peter (quivering): I've come here for years; I have hours of great pleasure, great satisfaction, right here. And that's important to a man. I'm a responsible person, and I'm GROWNUP. This is my bench, and you have no right to take it away from me.

Jerry: Fight for it, then. Defend yourself; defend your bench.

Peter: You've *pushed* me to it. Get up and fight.

Jerry: Like a man?

Peter (still angry): Yes, like a man, if you insist on mocking me even further.

Jerry: I'll have to give you credit for one thing: you *are* a vegetable, and a slightly nearsighted one, I think . . .

Peter: THAT'S ENOUGH. . . .

Jerry: . . . but, you know, as they say on TV all the time — you know — and I mean this, Peter, you have a certain dignity; it surprises me. . . .

Peter: STOP!

Jerry (rises lazily): Very well, Peter, we'll battle for the bench, but we're not evenly matched.

He takes out and clicks open an ugly-looking knife.

Peter (suddenly awakening to the reality of the situation): You are mad! You're stark raving mad! YOU'RE GOING TO KILL ME!

But before Peter has time to think what to do, Jerry tosses the knife at Peter's feet.

Jerry: There you go. Pick it up. You have the knife and we'll be more evenly matched.

Peter (horrified): No!

Jerry (rushes over to Peter, grabs him by the collar; Peter rises; their faces almost touch): Now you pick up that knife and you fight with me. You fight for your self-respect; you fight for that goddamned bench.

Peter (struggling): No! Let . . . let go of me! He . . . Help!

Jerry (slaps Peter on each "fight"): You fight, you miserable bastard; fight for that bench; fight for your parakeets; fight for your cats, fight for your two daughters; fight for your wife; fight for your manhood, you pathetic little vegetable. *(Spits in Peter's face.)* You couldn't even get your wife with a male child.

Peter (breaks away, enraged): It's a matter of genetics, not manhood, you . . . you monster.

He darts down, picks up the knife and backs off a little; he is breathing heavily.

I'll give you one last chance; get out of here and leave me alone!

He holds the knife with a firm arm, but far in front of him, not to attack, but to defend.

Jerry (sighs heavily): So be it!

With a rush he charges Peter and impales himself on the knife. Tableau: For just a moment, complete silence, Jerry impaled on the knife at the end of Peter's still firm arm. Then Peter screams, pulls away, leaving the knife in Jerry. Jerry is motionless, on point. Then he, too, screams, and it must be the sound of an infuriated and fatally wounded animal. With the knife in him, he stumbles back to the bench that Peter had vacated. He crumbles there, sitting, facing Peter, his eyes wide in agony, his mouth open.

Edward Albee   1343

Peter (whispering): Oh my God, oh my God, oh my God. . . . (He repeats these words many times, very rapidly.)

Jerry (Jerry is dying; but now his expression seems to change. His features relax, and while his voice varies, sometimes wrenched with pain, for the most part he seems removed from his dying. He smiles): Thank you, Peter. I mean that, now; thank you very much.

Peter's mouth drops open. He cannot move; he is transfixed.

Oh, Peter, I was so afraid I'd drive you away. (He laughs as best he can.) You don't know how afraid I was you'd go away and leave me. And now I'll tell you what happened at the zoo. I think . . . I think this is what happened at the zoo . . . I think. I think that while I was at the zoo I decided that I would walk north . . . northerly, rather . . . until I found you . . . or somebody . . . and I decided that I would talk to you . . . I would tell you things . . . and things that I would tell you would . . . Well, here we are. You see? Here we *are*. But . . . I don't know . . . could I have planned all this? No . . . no, I couldn't have. But I think I did. And now I've told you what you wanted to know, haven't I? And now you know all about what happened at the zoo. And now you know what you'll see in your TV, and the face I told you about . . . you remember . . . the face I told you about . . . my face, the face you see right now. Peter . . . Peter? . . . Peter . . . thank you. I came unto you (he laughs, so faintly) and you have comforted me. Dear Peter.

Peter (almost fainting): Oh my God!

Jerry: You'd better go now. Somebody might come by, and you don't want to be here when anyone comes.

Peter (does not move, but begins to weep): Oh my God, oh my God.

Jerry (most faintly, now; he is very near death): You won't be coming back here any more, Peter; you've been dispossessed. You've lost your bench, but you've defended your honor. And Peter, I'll tell you something now; you're not really a vegetable; it's all right, you're an animal. You're an animal, too. But you'd better hurry now, Peter. Hurry, you'd better go . . . see?

Jerry takes a handkerchief and with great effort and pain wipes the knife handle clean of fingerprints.

Hurry away, Peter.

Peter begins to stagger away.

Wait . . . wait, Peter. Take your book . . . book. Right here . . . beside me . . . on your bench . . . my bench, rather. Come . . . take your book.

Peter starts for the book, but retreats.

Hurry . . . Peter.

Peter rushes to the bench, grabs the book, retreats.

Very good, Peter . . . very good. Now . . . hurry away.

Peter hesitates for a moment, then flees, stage-left.

Hurry away. . . . *(His eyes are closed now.)* Hurry away, your parakeets
are making the dinner . . . the cats . . . are setting the table . . .

Peter *(off stage; a pitiful howl):* OH MY GOD!

Jerry *(his eyes still closed, he shakes his head and speaks; a combination of scornful mimicry and supplication):* Oh . . . my . . . God.

He is dead.

CURTAIN

Tom Stoppard (b. 1937)
THE REAL INSPECTOR HOUND 1968

Characters

Moon
Birdboot
Mrs. Drudge
Simon
Felicity
Cynthia
Magnus
Inspector Hound

The first thing is that the audience appear to be confronted by their own reflection in a huge mirror. Impossible. However, back there in the gloom — not at the footlights — a bank of plush seats and pale smudges of faces. The total effect having been established, it can be progressively faded out as the play goes on, until the front row remains to remind us of the rest and then, finally, merely two seats in that row — one of which is now occupied by Moon. Between Moon and the auditorium is an acting area which represents, in as realistic an idiom as possible, the drawing-room of Muldoon Manor. French windows at one side. A telephone fairly well upstage (i.e. towards Moon). The body of a man lies sprawled face down on the floor in front of a large settee. This settee must be of a size and design to allow it to be wheeled over the body, hiding it completely. Silence. The room. The body. Moon.

    Moon stares blankly ahead. He turns his head to one side then the other, then up, then down — waiting. He picks up his program and reads the front cover. He turns over the page and reads.

    He turns over the page and reads.

    He turns over the page and reads.

    He looks at the back cover and reads.

    He puts it down, crosses his legs, and looks about. He stares front. Behind him and to one side, barely visible, a man enters and sits down: Birdboot.

    Pause. Moon picks up his program, glances at the front cover and puts it down impatiently. Pause. . . . Behind him there is the crackle of a chocolate-box, absurdly loud. Moon looks round. He and Birdboot see each other. They are clearly known to each other. They acknowledge each other with constrained waves. Moon looks straight ahead. Birdboot comes down to join him.

Note: Almost always, Moon and Birdboot converse in tones suitable for an auditorium, sometimes a whisper. However good the acoustics might be, they will have to have microphones where they are sitting. The effect must be not of sound picked up, amplified and flung out at the audience, but of sound picked up, carried and gently dispersed around the auditorium.

Anyway, Birdboot, with a box of Black Magic chocolates, makes his way down to join Moon and plumps himself down next to him, plumpish, middle-aged Birdboot and younger, taller, less-relaxed Moon.

Birdboot (sitting down; conspiratorially): Me and the lads have had a meeting in the bar and decided it's first-class family entertainment but if it goes on beyond half-past ten it's self-indulgent — pass it on . . . *(and laughs jovially.)* I'm on my own tonight, don't mind if I join you?

Moon: Hello, Birdboot.

Birdboot: Where's Higgs?

Moon: I'm standing in.

Moon and Birdboot: Where's Higgs?

Moon: Every time.

Birdboot: What?

Moon: It is as if we only existed one at a time, combining to achieve continuity. I keep space warm for Higgs. My presence defines his absence, his absence confirms my presence, his presence precludes mine. . . . When Higgs and I walk down this aisle together to claim our common seat, the oceans will fall into the sky and the trees will hang with fishes.

Birdboot (he has not been paying attention, looking around vaguely, now catches up): Where's Higgs?

Moon: The very sight of me with a complimentary ticket is enough. The streets are impassable tonight, the country is rising and the cry goes up from hill to hill — Where — is — Higgs? *(Small pause.)* Perhaps he's dead at last, or trapped in a lift somewhere, or succumbed to amnesia, wandering the land with his turn-ups stuffed with ticket-stubs.

Birdboot regards him doubtfully for a moment.

Birdboot: Yes . . . Yes, well I didn't bring Myrtle tonight — not exactly her cup of tea, I thought, tonight.

Moon: Over her head, you mean?

Birdboot: Well, no — I mean it's a sort of a *thriller*, isn't it?

Moon: Is it?

Birdboot: That's what I heard. Who-killed thing? — no-one-will-leave-the-house?

Moon: I suppose so. Underneath.

Birdboot: Underneath?!? It's a whodunnit, man! — Look at it!

They look at it. The room. The body. Silence.

Has it started yet?

Moon: Yes.

Pause. They look at it.

Birdboot: Are you sure?

Moon: It's a pause.

Birdboot: You can't start with a *pause!* If you want my opinion there's total
   panic back there. *(Laughs and subsides.)* Where's Higgs tonight, then?

Moon: It will follow me to the grave and become my epitaph — Here lies Moon
   the second string: where's Higgs? . . . Sometimes I dream of revolution, a
   bloody *coup d'état°* by the second rank — troupes of actors slaughtered by
   their understudies, magicians sawn in half by indefatigably smiling glam-
   our girls, cricket teams wiped out by marauding bands of twelfth men —
   I dream of champions chopped down by rabbit-punching sparring partners while eternal bridesmaids turn and rape the bridegrooms over the
   sausage rolls and parliamentary private secretaries plant bombs in the
   Minister's Humber° — comedians die on provincial stages, robbed of their
   feeds by mutely triumphant stooges — And march — an army of assistants
   and deputies, the seconds-in-command, the runners-up, the right-hand
   men — storming the palace gates wherein the second son has already
   mounted the throne having committed regicide with a croquet mallet —
   stand-ins of the world stand up! —

   Beat.

   Sometimes I dream of Higgs.

   *Pause. Birdboot regards him doubtfully. He is at a loss, and grasps reality in the
   form of his box of chocolates.*

Birdboot (chewing into mike): Have a chocolate!

Moon: What kind?

Birdboot (chewing into mike): Black Magic.

Moon: No thanks.

   Chewing stops dead.
      Of such tiny victories and defeats . . .

Birdboot: I'll give you a tip, then. Watch the girl.

Moon: You think she did it?

Birdboot: No, no — the *girl,* watch her.

Moon: What girl?

Birdboot: You won't know her. I'll give you a nudge.

Moon: *You* know her, do you?

Birdboot (suspiciously, bridling): What's *that* supposed to mean?

Moon: I beg your pardon?

Birdboot: I'm trying to tip you a wink — give you a nudge as good as a tip —
   for God's sake, Moon, what's the matter with you? — you could do yourself some good, spotting her first time out — she's new, from the provinces,
   going straight to the top. I don't want to put words into your mouth but a
   word from us and we could make her.

Moon: I suppose you've made dozens of them, like that.

coup d'état: (French) the sudden overthrow of a government.
Humber: a make of car.

Birdboot (instantly outraged): I'll have you know I'm a family man devoted to my
   homely but good-natured wife, and if you're suggesting —
Moon: No, no —
Birdboot: — A man of my scrupulous morality —
Moon: I'm sorry —
Birdboot: — falsely besmirched —
Moon: Is that her?

   For Mrs. Drudge has entered.

Birdboot: — don't be absurd, wouldn't be seen dead with the old — ah.

   *Mrs. Drudge is the char, middle-aged, turbanned. She heads straight for the
   radio, dusting on the trot.*

Moon (reading his program): Mrs. Drudge the Help.
Radio (without preamble, having been switched on by Mrs. Drudge): We interrupt
   our program for a special police message.

   Mrs. Drudge stops to listen.

   The search still goes on for the escaped madman who is on the run in
   Essex.
Mrs. Drudge (fear and dismay): Essex!
Radio: County police led by Inspector Hound have received a report that the
   man has been seen in the desolate marshes around Muldoon Manor.

   Fearful gasp from Mrs. Drudge.

   The man is wearing a darkish suit with a lightish shirt. He is of medium
   height and build and youngish. Anyone seeing a man answering to this
   description and acting suspiciously, is advised to phone the nearest police
   station.

   *A man answering this description has appeared behind Mrs. Drudge. He is act-
   ing suspiciously. He creeps in. He creeps out. Mrs. Drudge does not see him. He
   does not see the body.*

   That is the end of the police message.

   *Mrs. Drudge turns off the radio and resumes her cleaning. She does not see the
   body. Quite fortuitously, her view of the body is always blocked, and when it
   isn't she has her back to it. However, she is dusting and polishing her way
   towards it.*

Birdboot: So that's what they say about me, is it?
Moon: What?
Birdboot: Oh, I know what goes on behind my back — sniggers — slanders —
   hole-in-corner innuendo — What have you heard?
Moon: Nothing.
Birdboot (urbanely): Tittle tattle. Tittle, my dear fellow, tattle. I take no notice of
   it — the sly envy of scandal mongers — I can afford to ignore them, I'm
   a respectable married man —
Moon: Incidentally —
Birdboot: Water off a duck's back, I assure you.

Moon: Who was that lady I saw you with last night?

Birdboot (unexpectedly stung into fury): How dare you! *(More quietly.)* How dare you. Don't you come here with your slimy insinuations! My wife Myrtle understands perfectly well that a man of my critical standing is obliged occasionally to mingle with the world of the footlights, simply by way of keeping *au fait*° with the latest —

Moon: I'm sorry —

Birdboot: That a critic of my scrupulous integrity should be vilified and pilloried in the stocks of common gossip —

Moon: Ssssh —

Birdboot: I have nothing to hide! — why, if this should reach the ears of my beloved Myrtle —

Moon: Can I have a chocolate?

Birdboot: What? Oh — *(Mollified.)* Oh yes — my dear fellow — yes, let's have a chocolate — No point in — yes, good show. *(Pops chocolate into his mouth and chews.)* Which one do you fancy? — Cherry? Strawberry? Coffee cream? Turkish delight?

Moon: I'll have montelimar.

> *Chewing stops.*

Birdboot: Ah. Sorry. *(Just missed that one.)*

Moon: Gooseberry fondue?

Birdboot: No.

Moon: Pistacchio fudge? Nectarine cluster? Hickory nut praline? Château Neuf du Pape '55 cracknell°?

Birdboot: I'm afraid not. . . . Caramel?

Moon: Yes, all right.

Birdboot: Thanks very much. *(He gives Moon a chocolate. Pause.)* Incidentally, old chap, I'd be grateful if you didn't mention — I mean, you know how these misunderstandings get about. . . .

Moon: What?

Birdboot: The fact is, Myrtle simply doesn't *like* the theater . . . *(He trails off hopelessly.)*

> *Mrs. Drudge, whose discovery of the body has been imminent, now — by way of tidying the room — slides the couch over the corpse, hiding it completely. She resumes dusting and humming.*

Moon: By the way, congratulations, Birdboot.

Birdboot: What?

Moon: At the Theater Royal. Your entire review reproduced in neon!

Birdboot (pleased): Oh . . . that old thing.

Moon: You've seen it, of course.

Birdboot (vaguely): Well, I was passing. . . .

Moon: I definitely intend to take a second look when it has settled down.

Birdboot: As a matter of fact I have a few color transparencies — I don't know whether you'd care to . . ?

---

au fait: (French) acquainted with the facts of something; familiar with.
cracknell: chocolate with crisp texture.

Moon: Please, please — love to, love to . . .

> *Birdboot hands over a few color slides and a battery-powered viewer which Moon holds up to his eyes as he speaks.*

Yes . . . yes . . . lovely . . . awfully sound. It has scale, it has color, it is, in the best sense of the word, electric. Large as it is, it is a small masterpiece — I would go so far as to say — kinetic without being pop, and having said that, I think it must be said that here we have a review that adds a new dimension to the critical scene. I urge you to make haste to the Theater Royal, for this is the stuff of life itself. *(Handling back the slides, morosely.)* All I ever got was "Unforgettable" on the posters for . . . What was it?

Birdboot: Oh — yes — I know . . . Was that you? I thought it was Higgs.

> *The phone rings. Mrs. Drudge seems to have been waiting for it to do so and for the last few seconds has been dusting it with an intense concentration. She snatches it up.*

Mrs. Drudge (into phone): Hello, the drawing-room of Lady Muldoon's country residence one morning in early spring? . . . Hello! — the draw — Who? Whom did you wish to speak to? I'm afraid there is no one of that name here, this is all very mysterious and I'm sure it's leading up to something, I hope nothing is amiss for we, that is Lady Muldoon and her houseguests, are here cut off from the world, including Magnus, the wheelchair-ridden half-brother of her ladyship's husband Lord Albert Muldoon who ten years ago went out for a walk on the cliffs and was never seen again.

Moon: Derivative, of course.

Birdboot: But quite sound.

Mrs. Drudge: Should a stranger enter our midst, which I very much doubt, I will tell him you called. Good-bye.

> *She puts down the phone and catches sight of the previously seen suspicious character who has now entered again, more suspiciously than ever, through the french windows. He senses her stare, freezes, and straightens up.*

Simon: Ah! — hello there! I'm Simon Gascoyne, I hope you don't mind, the door was open so I wandered in. I'm a friend of Lady Muldoon, the lady of the house, having made her acquaintance through a mutual friend, Felicity Cunningham, shortly after moving into this neighborhood just the other day.

Mrs. Drudge: I'm Mrs. Drudge. I don't live in but I pop in on my bicycle when the weather allows to help in the running of charming though somewhat isolated Muldoon Manor. Judging by the time *(she glances at the clock)* you did well to get here before high water cut us off for all practical purposes from the outside world.

Simon: I took the short cut over the cliffs and followed one of the old smugglers' paths through the treacherous swamps that surround this strangely inaccessible house.

Mrs. Drudge: Yes, many visitors have remarked on the topographical quirk in the local strata whereby there are no roads leading from the Manor, though there *are* ways of getting *to* it, weather allowing.

Simon: Yes, well I must say it's a lovely day so far.

Mrs. Drudge: Ah, but now that the cuckoo-beard is in bud there'll be fog before the sun hits Foster's Ridge.

Simon: I say, it's wonderful how you country people really know weather.

Mrs. Drudge (suspiciously): Know whether what?

Simon (glancing out of the window): Yes, it does seem to be coming on a bit foggy.

Mrs. Drudge: The fog is very treacherous around here — it rolls off the sea without warning, shrouding the cliffs in a deadly mantle of blind man's buff.

Simon: Yes, I've heard it said.

Mrs. Drudge: I've known whole week-ends when Muldoon Manor, as this lovely old Queen Anne House is called, might as well have been floating on the pack ice for all the good it would have done phoning the police. It was on such a week-end as this that Lord Muldoon who had lately brought his beautiful bride back to the home of his ancestors, walked out of this house ten years ago, and his body was never found.

Simon: Yes indeed, poor Cynthia.

Mrs. Drudge: His name was Albert.

Simon: Yes indeed, poor Albert. But tell me, is Lady Muldoon about?

Mrs. Drudge: I believe she is playing tennis on the lawn with Felicity Cunningham.

Simon (startled): Felicity Cunningham?

Mrs. Drudge: A mutual friend, I believe you said. A happy chance. I will tell them you are here.

Simon: Well, I can't really stay as a matter of fact — please don't disturb them — I really should be off.

Mrs. Drudge: They would be very disappointed. It is some time since we have had a four for pontoon bridge at the Manor, and I don't play cards myself.

Simon: There is another guest, then?

Mrs. Drudge: Major Magnus, the crippled half-brother of Lord Muldoon who turned up out of the blue from Canada just the other day, completes the house-party.

> *Mrs. Drudge leaves on this. Simon is undecided.*

Moon (ruminating quietly): I think I must be waiting for Higgs to die.

Birdboot: What?

Moon: Half-afraid that I will vanish when he does.

> *The phone rings. Simon picks it up.*

Simon: Hello?

Moon: I wonder if it's the same for Puckeridge?

Birdboot and Simon (together): Who?

Moon: Third string.

Birdboot: Your stand-in?

Moon: Does he wait for Higgs and I to write each other's obituary — does he dream — ?

Simon: To whom did you wish to speak?

Birdboot: What's he like?

Moon: Bitter.

Simon: There is no one of that name here.

Birdboot: No — as a critic, what's Puckeridge like as a critic?
Moon (laughs poisonously): Nobody knows —
Simon: You must have got the wrong number!
Moon: — There's always been me and Higgs.

> *Simon replaces the phone and paces nervously. Pause. Birdboot consults his program.*

Birdboot: Simon Gascoyne. It's not him, of course.
Moon: What?
Birdboot: I said it's not him.
Moon: Who is it, then?
Birdboot: My guess is Magnus.
Moon: In disguise, you mean?
Birdboot: What?
Moon: You think he's Magnus in disguise?
Birdboot: I don't think you're concentrating, Moon.
Moon: I thought you said —
Birdboot: You keep chattering on about Higgs and Puckeridge — what's the matter with you?
Moon (thoughtfully): I wonder if they talk about me . . . ?

> *A strange impulse makes Simon turn on the radio.*

Radio: Here is another police message. Essex County police are still searching in vain for the madman who is at large in the deadly marshes of the coastal region. Inspector Hound, who is masterminding the operation, is not available for comment but it is widely believed that he has a secret plan. . . . Meanwhile police and volunteers are combing the swamps with loud-hailers, shouting, "Don't be a madman, give yourself up." That is the end of the police message.

> *Simon turns off the radio. He is clearly nervous. Moon and Birdboot are on separate tracks.*

Birdboot (knowingly): Oh yes . . .
Moon: Yes, I should think my name is seldom off Puckeridge's lips . . . sad, really. I mean, it's no life at all, a stand-in's stand-in.
Birdboot: Yes . . . yes . . .
Moon: Higgs never gives me a second thought. I can tell by the way he nods.
Birdboot: Revenge, of course.
Moon: What?
Birdboot: Jealousy.
Moon: Nonsense — there's nothing *personal* in it —
Birdboot: The paranoid grudge —
Moon (sharply first, then starting to career . . .): It is merely that it is not enough to wax at another's wane, to be held in reserve, to be on hand, on call, to step in or not at all, the substitute — the near offer — the temporary-acting — for I am Moon, continuous Moon, in my own shoes, Moon in June, April, September and no member of the human race keeps warm my bit of space — yes, I can tell by the way he nods.
Birdboot: Quite mad, of course.

Moon: What?

Birdboot: The answer lies out there in the swamps.

Moon: Oh.

Birdboot: The skeleton in the cupboard is coming home to roost.

Moon: Oh yes. (*He clears his throat . . . for both he and Birdboot have a "public" voice, a critic voice which they turn on for sustained pronouncements of opinion.*) Already in the opening stages we note the classic impact of the catalystic figure — the outsider — plunging through to the center of an ordered world and setting up the disruptions — the shock waves — which unless I am much mistaken, will strip these comfortable people — these crustaceans in the rock pool of society — strip them of their shells and leave them exposed as the trembling raw meat which, at heart, is all of us. But there is more to it than that —

Birdboot: I agree — keep your eye on Magnus.

> *A tennis ball bounces through the french windows, closely followed by Felicity, who is in her twenties. She wears a pretty tennis outfit, and carries a racket.*

Felicity (calling behind her): Out!

> *It takes her a moment to notice Simon who is standing shiftily to one side. Moon is stirred by a memory.*

Moon: I say, Birdboot . . .

Birdboot: That's the one.

Felicity (catching sight of Simon): You!

> *Felicity's manner at the moment is one of great surprise but some pleasure.*

Simon (nervously): Er, yes — hello again.

Felicity: What are you doing here?

Simon: Well, I . . .

Moon: She's —

Birdboot: Sssh . . .

Simon: No doubt you're surprised to see me.

Felicity: Honestly, darling, you really are extraordinary.

Simon: Yes, well, here I am.

Felicity: You must have been desperate to see me — I mean, I'm *flattered*, but couldn't it wait till I got back?

Simon (bravely): There is something you don't know.

Felicity: What is it?

Simon: Look, about the things I said — it may be that I got carried away a little — we both did —

Felicity (stiffly): What are you trying to say?

Simon: I love another!

Felicity: I see.

Simon: I didn't make any promises — I merely —

Felicity: You don't have to say any more —

Simon: Oh, I didn't want to hurt you —

Felicity: Of all the nerve!

Simon: Well, I —

Felicity: You philandering coward —

Simon: Let me explain —

Felicity: This is hardly the time and place — you think you can barge in anywhere, whatever I happen to be doing —

Simon: But I want you to know that my admiration for you is sincere — I don't
want you to think that I didn't mean those things I said —

Felicity: I'll kill you for this, Simon Gascoyne!

> *She leaves in tears, passing Mrs. Drudge who has entered in time to overhear her
> last remark.*

Moon: It was her.

Birdboot: I told you — straight to the top —

Moon: No, no —

Birdboot: Sssh. . . .

Simon (to Mrs. Drudge): Yes, what is it?

Mrs. Drudge: I have come to set up the card table, sir.

Simon: I don't think I can stay.

Mrs. Drudge: Oh, Lady Muldoon *will* be disappointed.

Simon: Does she know I'm here?

Mrs. Drudge: Oh yes, sir, I just told her and it put her in quite a tizzy.

Simon: Really? . . . Well, I suppose now that I've cleared the air . . . Quite a tizzy,
you say . . . really . . . really . . .

> *He and Mrs. Drudge start setting up for card game. Mrs. Drudge leaves when
> this is done.*

Moon: Felicity! — she's the one.

Birdboot: Nonsense — red herring.

Moon: I mean, it was *her!*

Birdboot (exasperated): What was?

Moon: That lady I saw you with last night!

Birdboot (inhales with fury): Are you suggesting that a man of my scrupulous
integrity would trade his pen for a mess of pottage?! Simply because in the
course of my profession I happen to have struck up an acquaintance — to
have, that is, a warm regard, if you like, for a fellow toiler in the vineyard
of greasepaint — I find it simply intolerable to be pillified and viloried —

Moon: I never implied —

Birdboot: — to find myself the object of uninformed malice, the petty slanders
of little men —

Moon: I'm sorry —

Birdboot: — to suggest that my good opinion in a journal of unimpeachable
integrity is at the disposal of the first coquette who gives me what I want —

Moon: Ssssh —

Birdboot: A ladies' man! . . . Why, Myrtle and I have been together now for —
Christ! — who's *that?*

> *Enter Lady Cynthia Muldoon through french windows. A beautiful woman in
> her thirties. She wears a cocktail dress, is formally coiffured, and carries a
> tennis racket.*
>
> *Her effect on Birdboot is also impressive. He half-rises and sinks back
> agape.*

Cynthia (entering): Simon!

> *A dramatic freeze between her and Simon.*

Moon: Lady Muldoon.
Birdboot: No, I mean — who *is* she?
Simon (coming forward): Cynthia!
Cynthia: Don't say anything for a moment — just hold me.

> *He seizes her and glues his lips to hers, as they say. While their lips are glued —*

Birdboot: She's *beautiful* — a vision of eternal grace, a poem . . .
Moon: I think she's got her mouth open.

> *Cynthia breaks away dramatically.*

Cynthia: We can't go on meeting like this!
Simon: We have nothing to be ashamed of!
Cynthia: But darling, this is madness!
Simon: Yes! — I am mad with love for you!
Cynthia: Please — remember where we are!
Simon: Cynthia, I love you!
Cynthia: Don't — I love Albert!
Simon: He's dead! *(Shaking her.)* Do you understand me — Albert's dead!
Cynthia: No — I'll never give up hope! Let me go! We are not free!
Simon: I don't care, we were meant for each other — had we but met in time.
Cynthia: You're a cad, Simon! You will use me and cast me aside as you have cast aside so many others.
Simon: No, Cynthia! — you can make me a better person!
Cynthia: You're ruthless — so strong, so cruel —

> *Ruthlessly he kisses her.*

Moon: The son she never had, now projected in this handsome stranger and transformed into lover — youth, vigor, the animal, the athlete as aesthete — breaking down the barriers at the deepest level of desire.
Birdboot: By jove, I think you're right. Her mouth *is* open.

> *Cynthia breaks away. Mrs. Drudge has entered.*

Cynthia: Stop — can't you see you're making a fool of yourself!
Simon: I'll kill anyone who comes between us!
Cynthia: Yes, what is it, Mrs. Drudge?
Mrs. Drudge: Should I close the windows, my lady? The fog is beginning to roll off the sea like a deadly —
Cynthia: Yes, you'd better. It looks as if we're in for one of those days. Are the cards ready?
Mrs. Drudge: Yes, my lady.
Cynthia: Would you tell Miss Cunningham we are waiting.
Mrs. Drudge: Yes, my lady.
Cynthia: And fetch the Major down.
Mrs. Drudge (as she leaves): I think I hear him coming downstairs now.

> *She does: the sound of a wheelchair approaching down several flights of stairs*

with landings in between. It arrives bearing Magnus at about 15 m.p.h., knocking Simon over violently.

Cynthia: Simon!
Magnus (roaring): Never had a chance! Ran under the wheels!
Cynthia: Darling, are you all right?
Magnus: I have witnesses!
Cynthia: Oh, Simon — say something!
Simon (sitting up suddenly): I'm most frightfully sorry.
Magnus (still shouting): How long have you been a pedestrian?
Simon: Ever since I could walk.
Cynthia: Can you walk now . . . ?

Simon rises and walks.

Thank God! Magnus, this is Simon Gascoyne.
Magnus: What's he doing here?
Cynthia: He just turned up.
Magnus: Really? How do you like it here?
Simon (to Cynthia): I could stay forever.

Felicity enters.

Felicity: So — you're still here.
Cynthia: Of course he's still here. We're going to play cards. There's no need to introduce you two, is there, for I recall now that you, Simon, met me through Felicity, our mutual friend.
Felicity: Yes, Simon is an old friend, though not as old as you, Cynthia dear.
Simon: Yes, I haven't seen Felicity since —
Felicity: Last night.
Cynthia: Indeed? Well, you deal, Felicity. Simon, you help me with the sofa. Will you partner Felicity, Magnus, against Simon and me?
Magnus (aside): Will Simon and you always be partnered against me, Cynthia?
Cynthia: What do you mean, Magnus?
Magnus: You are a damned attractive woman, Cynthia.
Cynthia: Please! Please! Remember Albert!
Magnus: Albert's dead, Cynthia — and you are still young. I'm sure he would have wished that you and I —
Cynthia: No, Magnus, this is not to be!
Magnus: It's Gascoyne, isn't it? I'll kill him if he comes between us.
Cynthia (calling): Simon!

The sofa is shoved towards the card table, once more revealing the corpse, though not to the players.

Birdboot: Simon's for the chop all right.
Cynthia: Right! Who starts?
Magnus: I do. No bid.

They start playing, putting down and picking up cards.

Cynthia: Did I hear you say you saw Felicity last night, Simon?
Simon: Did I? — Ah yes, yes quite — your turn, Felicity.

Felicity: I've had my turn, haven't I, Simon? — now, it seems, it's Cynthia's turn.

Cynthia: That's my trick, Felicity dear.

Felicity: Hell hath no fury like a woman scorned, Simon.

Simon: Yes, I've heard it said.

Felicity: So I hope you have not been cheating, Simon.

Simon (standing up and throwing down his cards): No, Felicity, it's just that I hold the cards!

Cynthia: Well done, Simon!

Magnus pays Simon generously in bank notes, while Cynthia deals.

Felicity: Strange how Simon appeared in the neighborhood from nowhere. We know so little about him.

Simon: It doesn't always pay to show your hand!

Cynthia: Right! Simon, it's your opening on the minor bid.

Simon plays.

Cynthia: Hm, let's see. . . . (Plays.)

Felicity: I hear there's a dangerous madman on the loose.

Cynthia: Simon?

Simon: Yes — yes — sorry. (Plays.)

Cynthia: I meld.

Felicity: Yes — personally, I think he's been hiding out in the deserted cottage on the cliffs (plays).

Simon: Flush!

Cynthia: No! Simon — your luck's in tonight!

Felicity: We shall see — the night is not over yet, Simon Gascoyne! (She exits.)

Once more Magnus pays Simon.

Simon (to Magnus): So you're the crippled half-brother of Lord Muldoon who turned up out of the blue from Canada just the other day, are you? It's taken you a long time to get here. What did you do — walk? Oh, I say, I'm most frightfully sorry!

Magnus: Care for a spin round the rose garden, Cynthia?

Cynthia: No Magnus, I must talk to Simon.

Simon: My round, I think, Major.

Magnus: You think so?

Simon: Yes, Major — I do.

Magnus: There's an Old Canadian proverb handed down from the Blackfoot Indians, which says: He who laughs last laughs longest.

Simon: Yes, I've heard it said.

Cynthia (calling): Simon!

Magnus: Well, I think I'll go and oil my gun. (He exits.)

Cynthia: I think Magnus suspects something. And Felicity . . . Simon, was there anything between you and Felicity?

Simon: No, no — it's over between her and me, Cynthia — it was a mere passing fleeting thing we had — but now that I have found you —

Cynthia: If I find that you have been untrue to me — if I find that you have falsely seduced me from my dear husband Albert — I will kill you, Simon Gascoyne!

Mrs. Drudge has entered silently to witness this. On this tableau, pregnant with significance, the act ends, the body still undiscovered. Perfunctory applause.

Moon and Birdboot seem to be completely preoccupied, becoming audible, as it were.

Moon: Camps it around the Old Vic° in his opera cloak and passes me the tat.
Birdboot: Do you believe in love at first sight?
Moon: It's not that I think I'm a better critic —
Birdboot: I feel my whole life changing —
Moon: I am but it's not that.
Birdboot: Oh, the world will laugh at me, I know . . .
Moon: It is not that they are much in the way of shoes to step into . . .
Birdboot: . . . call me an infatuated old fool . . .
Moon: . . . They are not.
Birdboot: . . . condemn me . . .
Moon: He is standing in my light, that is all.
Birdboot: . . . betrayer of my class . . .
Moon: . . . an almost continuous eclipse, interrupted by the phenomenon of moonlight.
Birdboot: I don't care, I'm a goner.
Moon: And I dream . . .
Birdboot: The Blue Angel° all over again.
Moon: . . . of the day his temperature climbs through the top of his head . . .
Birdboot: Ah, the sweet madness of love . . .
Moon: . . . of the spasm on the stairs . . .
Birdboot: Myrtle, farewell . . .
Moon: . . . dreaming of the stair he'll never reach —
Birdboot: — for I only live but once. . . .
Moon: Sometimes I dream that I've killed him.
Birdboot: What?
Moon: What?

They pull themselves together.

Birdboot: Yes . . . yes. . . . A beautiful performance, a collector's piece. I shall say so.
Moon: A very promising debut. I'll put in a good word.
Birdboot: It would be as hypocritical of me to withhold praise on grounds of personal feelings, as to withhold censure.
Moon: You're right. Courageous.
Birdboot: Oh, I know what people will say — There goes Birdboot buttering up his latest —
Moon: Ignore them —
Birdboot: But I rise above that — The fact is I genuinely believe her performance to be one of the summits in the range of contemporary theater.
Moon: Trim-buttocked, that's the word for her.
Birdboot: — the radiance, the inner sadness —
Moon: Does she actually come across with it?

Old Vic: London theater occupied by the National Theatre Company.
The Blue Angel: classic German film in which Emil Jannings plays an elderly schoolmaster infatuated with a cabaret singer played by Marlene Dietrich.

Birdboot: The part as written is a mere cypher but she manages to make Cynthia a real person —

Moon: Cynthia?

Birdboot: And should she, as a result, care to meet me over a drink, simply by way of er — thanking me, as it were —

Moon: Well, you fickle old bastard!

Bridboot (aggressively): Are you suggesting . . .? *(He shudders to a halt and clears his throat.)* Well now — shaping up quite nicely, wouldn't you say?

Moon: Oh yes, yes. A nice trichotomy of forces. One must reserve judgment of course, until the confrontation, but I think it's pretty clear where we're heading.

Birdboot: I agree. It's Magnus a mile off.

Small pause.

Moon: What's Magnus a mile off?

Birdboot: If we knew that we wouldn't be here.

Moon (clears throat): Let me at once say that it has *élan°* while at the same time avoiding *éclat°*. Having said that, and I think it must be said, I am bound to ask — does this play know where it is going?

Birdboot: Well, it seems open and shut to me, Moon — Magnus is not what he pretends to be and he's got his next victim marked down —

Moon: Does it, I repeat, declare its affiliations? There are moments, and I would not begrudge it this, when the play, if we can call it that, and I think on balance we can, aligns itself uncompromisingly on the side of life. *Je suis,* it seems to be saying, *ergo sum°.* But is that enough? I think we are entitled to ask. For what in fact is this play concerned with? It is my belief that here we are concerned with what I have referred to elsewhere as the nature of identity. I think we are entitled to ask — and here one is irresistibly reminded of Voltaire's cry, *"Voilà°"* — I think we are entitled to ask — *Where is God?*

Birdboot (stunned): Who?

Moon: Go-od.

Birdboot (peeping furtively into his program): God?

Moon: I think we are entitled to ask.

The phone rings.
    The set re-illumines to reveal Cynthia, Felicity and Magnus about to take coffee, which is being taken round by Mrs. Drudge. Simon is missing. The body lies in position.

Mrs. Drudge (into phone): The same, half an hour later? . . . No, I'm sorry — there's no one of that name here. *(She replaces phone and goes round with coffee. To Cynthia.)* Black or white, my lady?

Cynthia: White please.

élan: verve, vigor.

éclat: brilliance.

Je suis . . . ergo sum: Moon mixes French and Latin in misquoting the basic principle of the philosophy of Descartes: "I exist, therefore I am." (Descartes said, "I think. . . .")

Voilà: The French philosopher and satirist Voltaire, asked to demonstrate the existence of God, declared, *"Voilà!"* (Look, there He is!)

Mrs. Drudge pours.

Mrs. Drudge (to Felicity): Black or white, miss?
Felicity: White please.

Mrs. Drudge pours.

Mrs. Drudge (to Magnus): Black or white, Major?
Magnus: White please.

Ditto.

Mrs. Drudge (to Cynthia): Sugar, my lady?
Cynthia: Yes please.

Puts sugar in.

Mrs. Drudge (to Felicity): Sugar, miss?
Felicity: Yes please.

Ditto.

Mrs. Drudge (to Magnus): Sugar, Major?
Magnus: Yes please.

Ditto.
Mrs. Drudge leaves, and reappears with a plate of biscuits.

Mrs. Drudge (to Cynthia): Biscuit, my lady?
Cynthia: No thank you.
Birdboot (writing elaborately in his notebook): The second act, however, fails to fulfill the promise . . .
Felicity: If you ask me, there's something funny going on.

Mrs. Drudge's approach to Felicity makes Felicity jump to her feet in impatience. She goes to the radio while Magnus declines his biscuit, and Mrs. Drudge leaves.

Radio: We interrupt our program for a special police message. The search for the dangerous madman who is on the loose in Essex has now narrowed to the immediate vicinity of Muldoon Manor. Police are hampered by the deadly swamps and the fog, but believe that the madman spent last night in a deserted cottage on the cliffs. The public is advised to stick together and make sure none of their number is missing. That is the end of the police message.

Felicity turns off the radio nervously. Pause.

Cynthia: Where's Simon?
Felicity: Who?
Cynthia: Simon. Have you seen him?
Felicity: No.
Cynthia: Have you, Magnus?
Magnus: No.
Cynthia: Oh.
Felicity: Yes, there's something foreboding in the air, it is as if one of *us* —
Cynthia: Oh, Felicity, the house is locked up tight — no one can get in — and the police are practically on the doorstep.

Felicity: I don't know — it's just a feeling.
Cynthia: It's only the fog.
Magnus: Hound will never get through on a day like this —
Cynthia (shouting at him): Fog!
Felicity: He means the Inspector.
Cynthia: Is he bringing a dog?
Felicity: Not that I know of.
Magnus: — never get through the swamps. Yes, I'm afraid the madman can show his hand in safety now.

> *A mournful baying, hooting is heard in the distance, scary.*

Cynthia: What's that?!
Felicity (tensely): It sounded like the cry of a gigantic hound!
Birdboot: Rings a bell.
Magnus: Poor devil!
Cynthia: Ssssh!

> *They listen. The sound is repeated, nearer.*

Felicity: There it is again!
Cynthia: It's coming this way — it's right outside the house!

> *Mrs. Drudge enters.*

Mrs. Drudge: Inspector Hound!
Cynthia: A *police* dog?

> *Enter Inspector Hound. On his feet are his swamp boots. These are two inflatable — and inflated — pontoons with flat bottoms about two feet across. He carries a foghorn.*

Hound: Lady Muldoon?
Cynthia: Yes.
Hound: I came as soon as I could. Where shall I put my foghorn and my swamp boots?
Cynthia: Mrs. Drudge will take them out. Be prepared, as the Force's motto has it, eh, Inspector? How very resourceful!
Hound (divesting himself of boots and foghorn): It takes more than a bit of weather to keep a policeman from his duty.

> *Mrs. Drudge leaves with chattels. A pause.*

Cynthia: Oh — er, Inspector Hound — Felicity Cunningham, Major Magnus Muldoon.
Hound: Good evening.

> *He and Cynthia continue to look expectantly at each other.*

Cynthia and Hound (together): Well? — Sorry —
Cynthia: No, do go on.
Hound: Thank you. Well, tell me about it in your own words — take your time, begin at the beginning and don't leave anything out.
Cynthia: I beg your pardon?
Hound: Fear nothing. You are in safe hands now. I hope you haven't touched anything.

Cynthia: I'm afraid I don't understand.

Hound: I'm Inspector Hound.

Cynthia: Yes.

Hound: Well, what's it all about?

Cynthia: I really have no idea.

Hound: How did it begin?

Cynthia: What?

Hound: The . . . thing.

Cynthia: What thing?

Hound (rapidly losing confidence but exasperated): The trouble!

Cynthia: There hasn't *been* any trouble!

Hound: Didn't you phone the police?

Cynthia: No.

Felicity: I didn't.

Magnus: What for?

Hound: I see. *(Pause.)* This puts me in a very difficult position. *(A steady pause.)* Well, I'll be getting along, then. *(He moves towards the door.)*

Cynthia: I'm terribly sorry.

Hound (stiffly): That's perfectly all right.

Cynthia: Thank you so much for coming.

Hound: Not at all. You never know, there might have been a serious matter.

Cynthia: Drink?

Hound: More serious than that, even.

Cynthia (correcting): Drink before you go?

Hound: No thank you. *(Leaves.)*

Cynthia (through the door): I do hope you find him.

Hound (reappearing at once): Find who, Madam? — out with it!

Cynthia: I thought you were looking for the lunatic.

Hound: And what do you know about that?

Cynthia: It was on the radio.

Hound: Was it, indeed? Well, that's what I'm here about, really. I didn't want to mention it because I didn't know how much you knew. No point in causing unnecessary panic, even with a murderer in our midst.

Felicity: Murderer, did you say?

Hound: Ah — so that was not on the radio?

Cynthia: Whom has he murdered, Inspector?

Hound: Perhaps no one — yet. Let us hope we are in time.

Magnus: You believe he is in our midst, Inspector?

Hound: I do. If anyone of you have recently encountered a youngish good-looking fellow in a smart suit, white shirt, hatless, well-spoken — someone possibly claiming to have just moved into the neighborhood, someone who on the surface seems as sane as you or I, then now is the time to speak!

Felicity: . . . I . . .

Hound: Don't interrupt!

Felicity: Inspector . . .

Hound: Very well.

Cynthia: No. Felicity!

Hound: Please, Lady Cynthia, we are all in this together. I must ask you to put yourself completely in my hands.

Cynthia: Don't, Inspector. I love Albert.

Hound: I don't think you quite grasp my meaning.

Magnus: Is one of us in danger, Inspector?

Hound: Didn't it strike you as odd that on his escape the madman made a bee-line for Muldoon Manor? It is my guess that he bears a deep-seated grudge against someone in this very house! Lady Muldoon — where is your husband?

Cynthia: My husband? — you don't mean — ?

Hound: I don't know — but I have a reason to believe that one of you is the real McCoy!

Felicity: The real what?

Hound: William Herbert McCoy who as a young man, meeting the madman in the street and being solicited for sixpence for a cup of tea, replied, "Why don't you do a decent day's work, you shifty old bag of horse manure," in Canada all those many years ago and went on to make his fortune. *(He starts to pace intensely.)* The madman was a mere boy at the time but he never forgot that moment, and thenceforth carried in his heart the promise of revenge! *(At which point he finds himself standing on top of the corpse. He looks down carefully.)* Is there anything you have forgotten to tell me?

They all see the corpse for the first time.

Felicity: So the madman has struck!

Cynthia: Oh — it's horrible — horrible —

Hound: Yes, just as I feared. Now you see the sort of man you are protecting.

Cynthia: I can't believe it!

Felicity: I'll have to tell him, Cynthia — Inspector, a stranger of that description has indeed appeared in our midst — Simon Gascoyne. Oh, he had charm, I'll give you that, and he took me in completely. I'm afraid I made a fool of myself over him, and so did Cynthia.

Hound: Where is he now?

Magnus: He must be around the house — he couldn't get away in these conditions.

Hound: You're right. Fear naught, Lady Muldoon — I shall apprehend the man who killed your husband.

Cynthia: My husband? I don't understand.

Hound: Everything points to Gascoyne.

Cynthia: But who's that? *(The corpse.)*

Hound: Your husband.

Cynthia: No, it's not.

Hound: Yes, it is.

Cynthia: I tell you it's not.

Hound: Are you sure?

Cynthia: For goodness sake!

Hound: Then who is it?

Cynthia: I don't know.

Hound: Anybody?

Felicity: I've never seen him before.

Magnus: Quite unlike anybody I've ever met.

Hound: I seem to have made a dreadful mistake. Lady Muldoon, I do apologize.

Cynthia: But what are we going to do?

Hound (snatching the phone): I'll phone the police!

Cynthia: But you are the police!

Hound: Thank God I'm here — the lines have been cut!

Cynthia: You mean — ?

Hound: Yes! — we're on our own, cut off from the world and in grave danger!

Felicity: You mean — ?

Hound: Yes! — I think the killer will strike again!

Magnus: You mean — ?

Hound: Yes! One of us ordinary mortals thrown together by fate and cut off by the elements, is the murderer! He must be found — search the house!

All depart speedily in different directions leaving a momentarily empty stage. Simon strolls on.

Simon (entering, calling): Anyone about? — funny . . . *(He notices the corpse and is surprised. He approaches it and turns it over. He stands up and looks about in alarm.)*

Birdboot: This is where Simon gets the chop.

There is a shot. Simon falls dead.

   Inspector Hound runs on and crouches down by Simon's body. Cynthia appears at the french windows. She stops there and stares.

Cynthia: What happened, Inspector?!

Hound turns to face her.

Hound: He's dead . . . Simon Gascoyne, I presume. Rough justice even for a killer — unless — unless — We assumed that the body could not have been lying there before Simon Gascoyne entered the house . . . but . . . *(he slides the sofa over the body)* . . . there's your answer. And now — who killed Simon Gascoyne? And why?

"Curtain," Freeze, Applause, Exeunt.

Moon: Why not?

Birdboot: Exactly. Good riddance.

Moon: Yes, getting away with murder must be quite easy provided that one's motive is sufficiently inscrutable.

Birdboot: Fickle young pup! He was deceiving her right, left and center.

Moon (thoughtfully): Of course, I'd still have Puckeridge behind *me* . . .

Birdboot: She needs someone steadier, more mature . . .

Moon: . . . And if I could, so could he . . .

Birdboot: Yes, I know of this rather nice hotel, very discreet, run by a man of the world. . . .

Moon: Uneasy lies the head that wears the crown.

Birdboot: Breakfast served in one's room and no questions asked.

Moon: Does Puckeridge dream of me?

Birdboot (pause): Hello — what's happened?

Moon: What? Oh yes — what do you make of it, so far?

Birdboot (clears throat): It is at this point that the play, for me, comes alive. The groundwork has been well and truly laid, and the author has taken the trouble to learn from the masters of the genre. He has created a real situation, and few will doubt his ability to resolve it with a startling dénouement. Certainly that is what it so far lacks, but it has a beginning, a middle and I have no doubt it will prove to have an end. For this let us give thanks, and double thanks for a good clean show without a trace of smut. But perhaps even all this would be for nothing were it not for a performance which I consider to be one of the summits in the range of contemporary theater. In what is possibly the finest Cynthia since the war —

Moon: If we examine this more closely, and I think close examination is the least tribute that this play deserves, I think we will find that within the austere framework of what is seen to be on one level a country-house weekend, and what a useful symbol that is, the author has given us — yes, I will go so far — He has given us the human condition —

Birdboot: More talent in her little finger —

Moon: An uncanny ear that might have belonged to a Van Gogh —

Birdboot: — a public scandal that the Birthday Honors° to date have neglected —

Moon: Faced as we are with such ubiquitous obliquity, it is hard, it is hard indeed, and therefore I will not attempt, to refrain from invoking the names of Kafka, Sartre, Shakespeare, St. Paul, Beckett, Birkett, Pinero, Pirandello, Dante and Dorothy L. Sayers.

Birdboot: A rattling good evening out. I was held.

The phone starts to ring on the empty stage. Moon tries to ignore it.

Moon: Harder still — Harder still if possible — Harder still if it is possible to be — Neither do I find it easy — Dante and Dorothy L. Sayers. Harder still —

Birdboot: Others taking part included — *Moon!*

For Moon has lost patience and is bearing down on the ringing phone. He is frankly irritated.

Moon (picking up phone, barks): Hel-lo! *(Pause, turns to Birdboot, quietly.)* It's for you.

Pause.
> *Birdboot gets up. He approaches cautiously. Moon gives him the phone and moves back to his seat. Birdboot watches him go. He looks round and smiles weakly, expiating himself.*

Birdboot (into phone): Hello. . . . *(Explosion.)* Oh, for God's sake, Myrtle — I've told you never to phone me at work! *(He is naturally embarrassed, looking about with surreptitious fury.)* What? Last night? Good God, woman, this is hardly the time to — I assure you, Myrtle, there is absolutely nothing going on between me and — . I took her to dinner simply by way of keeping *au fait* with the world of the paint and the motley — yes, I promise — Yes, I do — Yes, I *said* yes — I *do* — and you are mine too, Myrtle — darling — I can't — *(whispers) I'm not alone* — *(Up.)* No, she's not! — *(He looks around furtively, licks his lips and mumbles.)* All right! I love your little pink ears and

---

Birthday Honors: titles and awards annually conferred by the Queen.

you are my own fluffy bunny-boo — Now for God's sake — Good-bye, Myrtle — *(puts down phone).*

Birdboot mops his brow with his handkerchief. As he turns, a tennis ball bounces in through the french windows, followed by Felicity, as before, in tennis outfit. The lighting is as it was. Everything is as it was. It is, let us say, the same moment of time.

Felicity (calling): Out! *(She catches sight of Birdboot and is amazed.)* You!

Birdboot: Er, yes — hello again.

Felicity: What are you doing here?!

Birdboot: Well, I . . .

Felicity: Honestly, darling, you really are extraordinary —

Birdboot: Yes, well, here I am. *(He looks round sheepishly.)*

Felicity: You must have been desperate to see me — I mean, I'm flattered, but couldn't it wait till I got back?

Birdboot: No, no, you've got it all wrong —

Felicity: What is it?

Birdboot: And about last night — perhaps I gave you the wrong impression — got carried away a bit, perhaps —

Felicity (stiffly): What are you trying to say?

Birdboot: I want to call it off.

Felicity: I see.

Birdboot: I didn't promise anything — and the fact is, I have my reputation — people do talk —

Felicity: You don't have to say any more —

Birdboot: And my wife, too — I don't know how she got to hear of it, but —

Felicity: Of all the nerve!

Birdboot: I'm sorry you had to find out like this — the fact is I didn't mean it this way —

Felicity: You philandering coward!

Birdboot: I'm sorry — but I want you to know that I meant those things I said — oh yes — shows brilliant promise — I shall say so —

Felicity: I'll kill you for this, Simon Gascoyne!

She leaves in tears, passing Mrs. Drudge who has entered in time to overhear her last remark.

Birdboot (wide-eyed): Good God . . .

Mrs. Drudge: I have come to set up the card table, sir.

Birdboot (wildly): I can't stay for a game of *cards!*

Mrs. Drudge: Oh, Lady Muldoon *will* be disappointed.

Birdboot: You mean . . . you mean, she wants to meet me . . . ?

Mrs. Drudge: Oh yes, sir, I just told her and it put her in quite a tizzy.

Birdboot: Really? Yes, well, a man of my influence is not to be sneezed at — I think I have some small name for the making of reputations — mmm, yes, quite a tizzy, you say?

Mrs. Drudge is busied with the card table. Birdboot stands marooned and bemused for a moment.

Moon (from his seat): Birdboot! — *(a tense whisper)* — Birdboot!

Birdboot looks round vaguely.

What the hell are you doing?

Birdboot: Nothing.

Moon: Stop making an ass of yourself. Come back.

Birdboot: Oh, I know what you're thinking — but the fact is I genuinely consider her performance to be one of the summits —

Cynthia enters as before. Mrs. Drudge has gone.

Cynthia: Darling!

Birdboot: Ah, good evening — may I say that I genuinely consider —

Cynthia: Don't say anything for a moment — just hold me. *(She falls into his arms.)*

Birdboot: All right! — let us throw off the hollow pretences of the gimcrack codes we live by! Dear lady, from the first moment I saw you, I felt my whole life changing —

Cynthia (breaking free): We can't go on meeting like this!

Birdboot: I am not ashamed to proclaim nightly my love for you! — but fortunately that will not be necessary — I know of a very good hotel, discreet — run by a man of the world —

Cynthia: But darling, this is madness!

Birdboot: Yes! I am mad with love.

Cynthia: Please! — remember where we are!

Birdboot: I don't care! Let them think what they like, I love you!

Cynthia: Don't — I love Albert!

Birdboot: He's dead. *(Shaking her.)* Do you understand me — Albert's dead!

Cynthia: No — I'll never give up hope! Let me go! We are not free!

Birdboot: You mean Myrtle? She means nothing to me — nothing! — she's all cocoa and blue nylon fur slippers — not a spark of creative genius in her whole slumping knee-length-knickered body —

Cynthia: You're a cad, Simon! You will use me and cast me aside as you have cast aside so many others!

Birdboot: No, Cynthia — now that I have found you —

Cynthia: You're ruthless — so strong — so cruel —

Birdboot seizes her in an embrace, during which Mrs. Drudge enters, and Moon's fevered voice is heard.

Moon: Have you taken leave of your tiny mind?

Cynthia breaks free.

Cynthia: Stop — can't you see you're making a fool of yourself!

Moon: She's right.

Birdboot (to Moon): You keep out of this.

Cynthia: Yes, what is it, Mrs. Drudge?

Mrs. Drudge: Should I close the windows, my lady? The fog —

Cynthia: Yes, you'd better.

Moon: Look, they've got your number —

Birdboot: I'll leave in my own time, thank you very much.

Moon: It's the finish of you, I suppose you know that —

Birdboot: I don't need your twopenny Grub Street° prognostications — I have found something bigger and finer —

Moon (bemused, to himself): If only it were Higgs . . .

Cynthia: . . . And fetch the Major down.

Mrs. Drudge: I think I hear him coming downstairs now.

> *She leaves. The sound of a wheelchair's approach as before. Birdboot prudently keeps out of the chair's former path but it enters from the next wing down and knocks him flying. A babble of anguish and protestation.*

Cynthia: Simon — say something!

Birdboot: That reckless bastard *(as he sits up).*

Cynthia: Thank God! —

Magnus: What's *he* doing here?

Cynthia: He just turned up.

Magnus: Really? How do you like it here?

Birdboot: I couldn't take it night after night.

> *Felicity enters.*

Felicity: So — you're still here.

Cynthia: Of course he's still here. We're going to play cards. There is no need to introduce you two, is there, for I recall now that you, Simon, met me through Felicity, our mutual friend.

Felicity: Yes, Simon is an old friend . . .

Birdboot: Ah — yes — well I like to give young up-and-comers the benefit of my — er — of course, she lacks technique as yet —

Felicity: Last night.

Birdboot: I'm not talking about last night!

Cynthia: Indeed? Well, you deal, Felicity. Simon, you help me with the sofa.

> *Cynthia and Magnus confer as in the earlier scene.*

Birdboot (to Moon): Did you see that? Tried to kill me. I told you it was Magnus — not that it *is* Magnus.

Moon: Who did it, you mean?

Birdboot: What?

Moon: You think it's not Magnus who did it?

Birdboot: Get a grip on yourself, Moon — the facts are staring you in the face. He's after Cynthia for one thing.

Magnus: It's Gascoyne, isn't it?

Birdboot: Over my dead body!

Magnus: If he comes between us . . .

Moon (angrily): For God's sake sit down!

Cynthia: Simon!

Birdboot: She needs me, Moon. I've got to make up a four.

> *Cynthia and Birdboot move the sofa as before, and they all sit at the table.*

Cynthia: Right! Who starts?

Magnus: I do. I'll dummy for a no-bid ruff and double my holding on South's queen *(while he moves cards).*

Grub Street: formerly, a London street where poorly paid hack writers had their lodgings.

Cynthia: Did I hear you say you saw Felicity last night, Simon?

Birdboot: Er — er —

Felicity: Pay twenty-ones or trump my contract. *(Discards.)* Cynthia's turn.

Cynthia: I'll trump your contract with five dummy no-trumps there *(discards)*, and I'll move West's rook for the re-bid with a banker ruff on his second trick there. *(Discards.)* Simon?

Birdboot: Would you mind doing that again?

Cynthia: And I'll ruff your dummy with five no-bid trumps there *(discards)*, and I support your re-bid with a banker for the solo ruff in the dummy trick there. *(Discards.)*

Birdboot (standing up and throwing down his cards): And I call your bluff!

Cynthia: Well done, Simon!

> *Magnus pays Birdboot while Cynthia deals.*

Felicity: Strange how Simon appeared in the neighborhood from nowhere, we know so little about him.

Cynthia: Right Simon, it's your opening on the minor bid. Hmm. Let's see. I think I'll overbid the spade convention with two no trumps and King's gambit offered there — *(discards)* and West's dummy split double to Queen's Bishop 4 there!

Magnus (as he plays cards): Faites vos jeux. Rien ne va plus. Rouge et noir. Zéro.°

Cynthia: Simon?

Birdboot (triumphant, leaping to his feet): And I call your bluff!

Cynthia (imperturbably): I meld.

Felicity: I huff.

Magnus: I ruff.

Birdboot: I bluff.

Cynthia: Twist.

Felicity: Bust.

Magnus: Check.

Birdboot: Snap.

Cynthia: How's that?

Felicity: Not out.

Magnus: Double top.

Birdboot: Bingo!

> *Climax.*

Cynthia: No! Simon — your luck's in tonight.

Felicity: We shall see — the night is not over yet, Simon Gascoyne! *(She exits quickly.)*

Birdboot (looking after Felicity): Red herring — smell it a mile off. *(To Magnus.)* Oh yes, she's as clean as a whistle, I've seen it a thousand times. And I've seen you before too, haven't I? Strange — there's something about you . . .

Magnus: Care for a spin round the rose garden, Cynthia?

Cynthia: No Magnus, I must talk to Simon.

Birdboot: There's nothing for you there, you know.

Magnus: You think so?

Faites vos jeux . . . Zéro: (French, the chant of a croupier — one in charge of a gaming table): "Place your bets. The betting is closed. Red and black. Zero."

Birdboot: Oh yes, she knows which side her bread is buttered. I am a man not without a certain influence among those who would reap the limelight — she's not going to throw me over for a heavily disguised cripple.

Magnus: There's an old Canadian proverb —

Birdboot: Don't give me that — I tumbled to you right from the start — oh yes, you chaps are not as clever as you think. . . . Sooner or later you make your mistake. . . . Incidentally, where was it I saw you? . . . I've definitely. . . .

Cynthia (calling): Simon!

Magnus (leaving): Well, I think I'll go and oil my gun. *(Exit.)*

Birdboot (after Magnus): Double bluff! — *(To Cynthia.)* I've seen it a thousand times.

Cynthia: I think Magnus suspects something. And Felicity . . . Simon, was there anything between you and Felicity?

Birdboot: No, no — that's all over now. I merely flattered her a little over a drink, told her she'd go far, that sort of thing. Dear me, the fuss that's been made over a simple flirtation —

Cynthia (as Mrs. Drudge enters behind): If I find you have falsely seduced me from my dear husband Albert, I will kill you, Simon Gascoyne!

The "Curtain" as before. Mrs. Drudge and Cynthia leave. Birdboot starts to follow them.

Moon: Birdboot!

Birdboot stops.

Moon: For God's sake pull yourself together.

Birdboot: I can't help it.

Moon: What do you think you're doing? You're turning it into a complete farce!

Birdboot: I know, I know — but I can't live without her. *(He is making erratic neurotic journeys about the stage.)* I shall resign my position, of course. I don't care I'm a goner, I tell you — *(He has arrived at the body. He looks at it in surprise, hesitates, bends and turns it over.)*

Moon: Birdboot, think of your family, your friends — your high standing in the world of letters — I say, what are you doing?

Birdboot is staring at the body's face.

Birdboot . . . leave it alone. Come and sit down — what's the matter with you?

Birdboot (dead-voiced): It's Higgs.

Moon: What?

Birdboot: It's Higgs.

Pause.

Moon: Don't be silly.

Birdboot: I tell you it's Higgs!

Moon half-rises. Bewildered.

I don't understand . . . He's dead.

Moon: Dead?

Birdboot: Who would want to . . .

Moon: He must have been lying there all the time. . . .

Birdboot: . . . kill Higgs?

Moon: But what's he doing here? I was standing in tonight. . . .

Birdboot (turning): Moon? . . .

Moon (in wonder, quietly): So it's me and Puckeridge now.

Birdboot: Moon . . . ?

Moon (faltering): But I swear I . . .

Birdboot: I've got it —

Moon: But I didn't —

Birdboot (quietly): My God . . . so that was it. . . . *(Up.)* Moon — now I see —

Moon: — I swear I didn't —

Birdboot: Now — finally — I see it all —

> *There is a shot and Birdboot falls dead.*

Moon: Birdboot! *(He runs on, to Birdboot's body.)*

> *Cynthia appears at the french windows. She stops and stares. All as before.*

Cynthia: Oh my God — what happened, Inspector?

Moon (almost to himself): He's dead. . . . *(He rises.)* That's a bit rough, isn't it? — a bit extreme! — He may have had his faults — I admit he was a fickle old . . . Who did this, and why?

> *Moon turns to face her. He stands up and makes swiftly for his seat. Before he gets there he is stopped by the sound of voices. Simon and Hound are occupying the critics' seats. Moon freezes.*

Simon: To say that it is without pace, point, focus, interest, drama, wit or originality is to say simply that it does not happen to be my cup of tea. One has only to compare this ragbag with the masters of the genre to see that here we have a trifle that is not my cup of tea at all.

Hound: I'm sorry to be blunt but there is no getting away from it. It lacks pace. A complete ragbag.

Simon: I will go further. Those of you who were fortunate enough to be at the Comédie-Française° on Wednesday last, will not need to be reminded that hysterics are no substitute for *éclat*.

Hound: It lacks *élan*.

Simon: Some of the cast seem to have given up acting altogether, apparently aghast, with every reason, at finding themselves involved in an evening that would, and indeed will, make the angels weep.

Hound: I am not a prude but I fail to see any reason for the shower of filth and sexual allusion foisted onto an unsuspected public in the guise of modernity at all costs. . . .

> *Behind Moon, Felicity, Magnus and Mrs. Drudge have made their entrances, so that he turns to face their semicircle.*

Magnus (pointing to Birdboot's body): Well, Inspector, is this your man?

Moon (warily): . . . Yes. . . . Yes. . . .

Cynthia: It's Simon . . .

Comédie-Française: A national theater in Paris, where classical plays are performed with rigorous precision.

Moon: Yes . . . yes . . . poor. . . . *(Up.)* Is this some kind of a joke?
Magnus: If it is, Inspector, it's in very poor taste.

> *Moon pulls himself together and becomes galvanic, a little wild, in grief for Birdboot.*

Moon: All right! I'm going to find out who did this! I want everyone to go to the positions they occupied when the shot was fired —

> *They move; hysterically.*

No one will leave the house!

> *They move back.*

Magnus: I think we all had the opportunity to fire the shot, Inspector —
Moon (furious): I am not —
Magnus: — but which of us would want to?
Moon: Perhaps you, Major Magnus!
Magnus: Why should I want to kill him?
Moon: Because he was on to you — yes, he tumbled to you right from the start — and you shot him just when he was about to reveal that you killed — *(Moon points, pauses and then crosses to Higgs' body and falters)* — killed — *(he turns Higgs over)* . . . this . . . chap.
Magnus: But what motive would there be for killing him? *(Pause.)* Who *is* this chap? *(Pause.)* Inspector?
Moon (rising): I don't know. Quite unlike anyone I've ever met. *(Long pause.)* Well . . . now . . .
Mrs. Drudge: Inspector?
Moon (eagerly): Yes? Yes, what is it, dear lady?
Mrs. Drudge: Happening to enter this room earlier in the day to close the windows, I chanced to overhear a remark made by the deceased Simon Gascoyne to her ladyship, viz., "I will kill anyone who comes between us."
Moon: Ah — yes — well, that's it, then. This . . . chap . . . *(pointing to the body)* was obviously killed by *(pointing to Birdboot's body)* er . . . *(the moment of Moon's betrayal, for which he is to pay with his life)* . . . by *(pause)* Simon.
Cynthia: But he didn't come between us!
Magnus: And who, then, killed Simon?
Mrs. Drudge: Subsequent to that reported remark, I also happened to be in earshot of a remark made by Lady Muldoon to the deceased, to the effect, "I will kill you, Simon Gascoyne!" I hope you don't mind my mentioning it.
Moon: Not at all. I'm glad you did. It is from these chance remarks that we in the Force build up our complete picture before moving in to make the arrest. It will not be long now, I fancy, and I must warn you, Lady Muldoon, that anything you say —
Cynthia: Yes! — I hated Simon Gascoyne, for he had me in his thrall! — But I didn't kill him!
Mrs. Drudge: Prior to that, Inspector, I also chanced to overhear a remark made by Miss Cunningham, no doubt in the heat of the moment, but it stuck in my mind as these things do, viz., "I will kill you for this, Simon Gascoyne!"

Moon: Ah! The final piece of the jigsaw! I think I am now in a position to reveal the mystery. This man *(the corpse)* was, of course, McCoy, the Canadian who, as we heard, meeting Gascoyne in the street and being solicited for sixpence for a toffee apple, smacked him across the ear, with the cry, "How's that for a grudge to harbor, you sniffling little workshy!" all those many years ago. Gascoyne bided his time, but in due course tracked McCoy down to this house, having, on the way, met, in the neighborhood, a simple ambitious girl from the provinces. He was charming, persuasive — told her, I have no doubt, that she would go straight to the top — and she, flattered by his sophistication, taken in by his promises to see her all right on the night, gave in to his simple desires. Perhaps she loved him. We shall never know. But in the very hour of her promised triumph, his eye fell on another — yes, I refer to Lady Cynthia Muldoon. From the moment he caught sight of her there was no other woman for him — he was in her spell, willing to sacrifice anything, even you, Felicity Cunningham. It was only today — unexpectedly finding him here — that you learned the truth. There was a bitter argument which ended with your promise to kill him — a promise that you carried out in this very room at your first opportunity! And I must warn you that anything you say —

Felicity: But it doesn't make sense!

Moon: Not at first glance, *perhaps.*

Magnus: Could not McCoy have been killed by the same person who killed Simon?

Felicity: But why should any of us want to kill a perfect stranger?

Magnus: Perhaps he was not a stranger to *one* of us.

Moon (faltering): But Simon was the madman, wasn't he?

Magnus: We only have your word for that, Inspector. We only have your word for a lot of things. For instance — McCoy. Who is he? Is his name McCoy? Is there any truth in that fantastic and implausible tale of the insult inflicted in the Canadian streets? Or is there something else, something quite unknown to us, behind all this? Suppose for a moment that the madman, having killed this unknown stranger for private and inscrutable reasons of his own, was disturbed before he could dispose of the body, so having cut the telephone wires he decided to return to the scene of the crime, masquerading as — Police Inspector Hound!

Moon: But . . . I'm not mad . . . I'm almost sure I'm not mad . . .

Magnus: . . . only to discover that in the house was a man, Simon Gascoyne, who recognized the corpse as a man against whom you had held a deep-seated grudge — !

Moon: But I didn't kill — I'm almost sure I —

Magnus: I put it to you! — are you the real Inspector Hound?!

Moon: You know damn well I'm not! What's it all about?

Magnus: I thought as much.

Moon: I only dreamed . . . sometimes I dreamed —

Cynthia: So it was you!

Mrs. Drudge: The madman!

Felicity: The killer!

Cynthia: Oh, it's horrible, horrible.

Mrs. Drudge: The stranger in our midst!

Magnus: Yes, we had a shrewd suspicion he would turn up here — and he walked into the trap!

Moon: What *trap?*

Magnus: I am not the real Magnus Muldoon — It was a mere subterfuge! — and *(standing up and removing his moustaches)* I now reveal myself as —

Cynthia: You mean — ?

Magnus: Yes! I am the real Inspector Hound!

Moon (pause): Puckeridge!

Magnus (with pistol): Stand where you are, or I shoot!

Moon (backing): Puckeridge! You killed Higgs — and Birdboot tried to tell me —

Magnus: Stop in the name of the law!

> *Moon turns to run. Magnus fires. Moon drops to his knees.*

I have waited a long time for this moment.

Cynthia: So you are the real Inspector Hound.

Magnus: Not only that! — I have been leading a double life — at *least!*

Cynthia: You mean — ?

Magnus: Yes! — It's been ten long years, but don't you know me?

Cynthia: You mean — ?

Magnus: Yes! — it is me, Albert! — who lost his memory and joined the Force, rising by merit to the rank of Inspector, his past blotted out — until fate cast him back into the home he left behind, back to the beautiful woman he had brought here as his girlish bride — in short, my darling, my memory has returned and your long wait is over!

Cynthia: Oh, Albert!

> *They embrace.*

Moon (with a trace of admiration): Puckeridge! . . . you cunning bastard. *(He dies.)*

THE END

Appendix

Writing about Literature

That masterful poet and critic T. S. Eliot once declared that, in approaching a work of literature to write about it, the only method he knew was to be very intelligent. Eliot wasn't boasting about his I.Q.; he was suggesting that to a critic of literature, a keen sensibility is more valuable than a carefully worked out method, any day. Although none of us may be another Eliot, all of us have some powers of reasoning and perception. And when we come to a story, a poem, or a play, we can do little other than to trust whatever powers we have, like one who enters a shadowy room, clutching a decent candle.

After all, in the study of literature, common sense (as poet Gerard Manley Hopkins said) is never out of place. For most of a class hour, a renowned English professor once rhapsodized about the arrangement of the contents of W. H. Auden's *Collected Poems.* Auden, he claimed, was a master of thematic continuity, who had brilliantly placed the poems in the best possible order, in which (to the ingenious mind) they complemented each other. Near the end of the hour, his theories were punctured — with a great inaudible pop — when a student timidly raising a hand pointed out that Auden had arranged the poems in the book not according to theme but in alphabetical order by title. The professor's jaw dropped: "Why didn't you say that sooner?" The student was apologetic: "I — I was afraid I'd sound too *ordinary.*"

Emerson makes a similar point in his essay "The American Scholar": "Meek young men grow up in libraries, believing it their duty to accept the views which Cicero, which Locke, which Bacon have given; forgetful that Cicero, Locke, and Bacon were only young men in libraries when they wrote these books." Don't be afraid to state a conviction, though it seems obvious. Does it matter that you may be repeating something that, once upon a time or even just the other day, has been said before? There are excellent old ideas as well as new.

SOME APPROACHES TO LITERATURE

Though T. S. Eliot may be right in preferring intelligence to method, there are certain familiar approaches to stories, poems, and plays which most critical essays tend to follow. Underlying each of these four approaches is a certain way of regarding the nature of a work of literature.

1. The Work by Itself. This view assumes a story, poem, or play to be an individual entity, existing on its page, that we can read and understand in its own right, without necessarily studying the life of its author, or the age in which it was written, or its possible effect on its readers. This is the approach of most papers written in response to college assignments; to study just the work (and not its backgrounds or its influence) does not require the student to spend prolonged time doing research in a library. The three common ways of writing a paper discussed earlier in this book — explication, analysis, and comparison and contrast — are concerned mainly with the work of literature in itself.

2. The Work as Imitation of Life. Aristotle called the art of writing a tragedy *mimesis:* the imitation or re-creation of an action that is serious and complete in itself. From this classic theory in the *Poetics* comes the view that a work of literature in some way imitates the world or the civilization in which it was produced. We can say, for instance, that Ibsen's play *A Doll House* places before our eyes actors whose life-like speeches and movements represent members of an upper-middle-class society in provincial Norway in the late nineteenth century and that the play reflects their beliefs and attitudes. Not only the subject and theme of a work imitate life in this view: John Ciardi has remarked that the heroic couplet, dominant stanza form in poetry read by educated people in eighteenth-century England, reflects, in its exact form and its use of antitheses, the rhythms of the minuet — another contemporary form, fashionable also among the well-to-do: "now on this hand, now on that." The writer concerned with literature as imitation usually studies the world that the literary work imitates. He or she goes into the ideas underlying the writer's society, showing how the themes, assumptions, and conventions of the writer's work arose out of that time and that place. Obviously, this takes more research than one can do for a weekly paper; it is usually the approach taken for a book or a dissertation, or perhaps an honors thesis or a term paper. (The other two approaches we will mention also take research.) Reasonably short studies of the relation between the work and its world are, however, sometimes possible: "World War II as Seen in Henry Reed's 'Naming of Parts' "; "Faulkner's 'Barn Burning': A Mirror of Mississippi?"

3. The Work as Expression. In this view, a work of literature expresses the feelings of the person who wrote it; therefore, to study it, one studies the author's life. Typical paper topics: "*A Glass Menagerie* and the Early Life of Tennessee Williams"; "Sylvia Plath's Lost Father and Her View of Him in 'Daddy.'" To write any truly deep-reaching biographical criticism takes research, clearly, but one could write a term paper on topics such as these by reading a single biography.

Biographical criticism fell into temporary disrepute around 1920, when T. S. Eliot questioned the assumption that a poem has to be a personal statement of the poet's thoughts and emotions.[1] Eliot and other critics did much to clear the air of speculation that the "Ode on a Grecian Urn" may have been shaped by what Keats had had for breakfast. Evidently, in any search for what went on in an author's mind, and for the influence of life upon work, absolute certainty is unattainable. Besides, such an approach can be grossly reductive — holding, for example, that Shakespeare was sad when he wrote his tragedies and especially happy when he wrote *A Midsummer Night's Dream*. Still, there are works that gain in meaning from even a slight knowledge of the author's biography. In reading *Moby Dick*, it helps to know that Herman Melville served aboard a whaling vessel.

4. *The Work as Influence.* From this perspective, a literary work is a force that affects people. It stirs certain responses in them, rouses their emotions, perhaps argues for ideas that change their minds. The artist, said Tolstoi in a famous pronouncement *(What Is Art?)*, "hands on to others those feelings he himself has felt, that they too may be moved, and experience them." Part of the function of art, Tolstoi continued, is to enlighten and to lead its audience into an acceptance of better moral attitudes (religious faith, or a sense of social justice). The critic who takes this approach is generally concerned with the ideas that a literary work imparts and the reception of those ideas by a particular audience: "Did *Uncle Tom's Cabin* Cause the Civil War?"; "The Early Reception of the Fiction of D. H. Lawrence." As you can see, this whole approach is closely related to viewing a literary work as an imitation of life. Still another way of discussing a work's influence is to trace its impact upon other writers: "Robert Frost's Debt to Emily Dickinson"; "*Moby Dick* and William Faulkner's *The Bear:* Two Threatened Wildernesses."

FINDING A TOPIC

Offered a choice of literary works to write about, you probably will do best if, instead of choosing what you think will impress your instructor, you choose what appeals to you. And how to find out what appeals? Whether you plan to write a short paper that requires no research beyond the story or poem or play itself, or a long term paper that will take you to the library, the first stage of your project is reading — and note

[1] See Eliot's essay "Tradition and the Individual Talent," in *Selected Essays* (New York: Harcourt Brace, 1932).

taking. To concentrate your attention, one time-honored method is to read with a pencil, marking (if the book is yours) passages that stand out in importance, jotting brief notes in a margin (*"Key symbol — this foreshadows the ending"; "Dramatic irony"; "IDIOT!!!"*; or other possibly useful remarks). In a long story or poem or play, some students asterisk certain passages that cry for comparison: for instance, all the places in which they find the same theme or symbol. Later, at a glance, they can review the highlights of a work and, when writing a paper about it, quickly refer to evidence. This method shoots holes in a book's resale value, but many find the sacrifice worthwhile. Patient souls who dislike butchering a book prefer to take notes on looseleaf notebook paper, holding one sheet beside a page in the book and giving it the book's page-number. Later, in writing a paper, they can place book page and companion note page together again. This method has the advantage of affording a lot of room for note taking; it is a good one for short poems closely packed with complexities.

But by far the most popular method of taking notes (besides writing on the pages of books) is to write on index cards — the 3 x 5 kind, for brief notes and titles; 5 x 8 cards for longer notes. Write on one side only; notes on the back of the card usually get overlooked later. Cards are easy to shuffle and, in organizing your material, to deal.

Now that coin-operated photocopy machines are to be found in many libraries, you no longer need to spend hours copying by hand whole poems and longer passages. If accuracy is essential (surely it is) and if a poem or passage is long enough to be worth the investment of a dime, you can lay photocopied material into place in your paper with transparent tape or rubber cement. The latest copyright law permits students and scholars to reproduce books and periodicals in this fashion; it does not, however, permit making a dozen or more copies for public sale.

Certain literary works, because they offer intriguing difficulties, have attracted professional critics by the score. On library shelves, great phalanxes of critical books now stand at the side of James Joyce's complex novels *Ulysses* and *Finnegans Wake,* and T. S. Eliot's allusive poem *The Waste Land.* The student who undertakes to study such works seriously is well advised to profit from the critics' labors. Chances are, too, that even in discussing a relatively uncomplicated work you will want to seek the aid of the finest critics. If you quote them, quote them exactly, in quotation marks, and give them credit. When employed in any but the most superlative student paper, a brilliant phrase (or even a not so brilliant sentence) from a renowned critic is likely to stand out like a golf ball in a gartersnake's midriff, and most English instructors are likely to recognize it. If you rip off the critic's words, then go ahead and steal the whole essay, for good critics tend to write in seamless unities. Then, when apprehended, you can exclaim — like the student whose term paper was found to be the work of a well-known scholar —

"I've been robbed! That paper cost me twenty dollars!" But of course the worst rip-off is the one the student inflicted on himself, having got nothing for his money out of a college course but a little practice in touch-typing.

Taking notes on your readings, you will want to jot down the title of every book you might refer to in your paper, and the page number of any passage you might wish to quote. Even if you summarize a critic's idea in your own words, rather than quote, you have to give credit to your source. Nothing is cheaper to give than proper credit. Certainly it's easier to take notes while you read than to have to run back to the library during the final typing.

Choose a topic appropriate to the assigned length of your paper. How do you know the probable length of your discussion until you write it? When in doubt, you are better off to define your topic narrowly. Your paper will be stronger if you go deeper into your subject than if you choose some gigantic subject and then find yourself able to touch on it only superficially. A thorough explication of a short story is hardly possible in a paper of 250 words. There are, in truth, four-line poems whose surface 250 words might only begin to scratch. A profound topic ("The Character of Shakespeare's Hamlet") might overflow a book; but a topic more narrowly defined ("Hamlet's Views of Acting"; "Hamlet's Puns") might result in a more nearly manageable term paper. You can narrow and focus a large topic while you work your way into it. A general interest in "Hemingway's Heroes," for instance, might lead you, in the process of reading, taking notes, and thinking further, to the narrower topic, "Jake Barnes: Spokesman for Hemingway."

Many student writers find it helpful, in defining a topic, to state an emerging idea for a paper in a provisional **thesis sentence:** a summing-up of the one main idea or argument that the paper will embody. (A thesis sentence is for your own use; you don't have to implant it in your paper unless your instructor asks for it.) Complete with subject and verb, a good statement of a thesis is not just a disembodied subject; it comes with both subject and verb. ("The Downfall of Oedipus Rex" is not yet a complete idea for a paper; "What Caused the Downfall of Oedipus Rex" is.) A thesis sentence helps you see for yourself what the author you are studying is *saying about* a subject. Not a full thesis, and not a sentence, "The Isolation of City-dwellers in Edward Albee's *The Zoo Story*" might be a decent title for a paper. But it isn't a useful thesis because it doesn't indicate what one might say about that isolation (nor what Albee is saying about it). While it may be obvious that isolation isn't desirable, a clear and workable thesis sentence might be, "In *The Zoo Story* Albee demonstrates that city-dwellers' isolation from one another prompts one city-dweller to action"; the paper might well go on to demonstrate just what that action is. If you wish any typical paper topics to prod your own thinking, see the lists on pages 228, 704, and 1278 for writing about fiction, poetry, and drama.

ORGANIZING YOUR THINKING

Topic in hand, perhaps in the form of a thesis sentence on paper, you now begin to sort your miscellaneous thoughts and impressions. To outline or not to outline? Unless your topic, by its very nature, suggests some obvious way to organize your paper ("An Explication of a Wordsworth Sonnet" might mean simply working through the poem line by line), then some kind of outline is practically indispensable. In high school or other prehistoric times, you perhaps learned how to construct a beautiful outline, laid out with Roman numerals, capital letters, Arabic numerals, and small letters. It was a thing of beauty and symmetry, and possibly even had something to do with paper writing. But if now you are skeptical of the value of outlining, reflect: not every outline needs to be detailed and elaborate. Some students, of course, find it helpful to outline in detail — particularly if they are planning a long term paper involving several literary works, comparing and contrasting several aspects of them. For a 500-word analysis of a short story's figures of speech, however, all you might need is a simple list of points to make, scribbled down in the order in which you will make them. This order is probably not, of course, the order in which the points first occurred to you. Thoughts, when they first come to mind, tend to be a confused rabble.

While granting the need for order in a piece of writing, the present writer confesses that he is a reluctant outliner. His tendency (or curse) is to want to keep whatever random thoughts occur to him; to polish his prose right then and there; and finally to try to juggle his disconnected paragraphs into something like logical order. The usual result is that he has large blocks of illogical thought left over. This process is wasteful, and if you can learn to live with an outline, then you belong to the legion of the blessed, and will never know the pain of scrapping pages that cost you hours. On the other hand, you will never know the joy of meandering — of bursting into words and setting them down however wildly, to see what you truly want to say. There is value in such wasteful and self-indulgent writing — but not if a deadline is imminent.

An outline is not meant to stand as an achievement in itself. It should — as Ezra Pound said literary criticism ought to do — consume itself and disappear. Here, for instance, is a once-valuable outline not worth keeping — a very informal one that enabled a student to organize the paper that appears on page 220, "The Hearer of 'The Tell-Tale Heart.'" Before he wrote, the student jotted down the ideas that had occurred to him. Looking them over, he could see that certain ones predominated. Since the aim of his paper was to analyze Poe's story for its point of view, he began with some notes about the narrator of the story. His other leading ideas had emerged as questions: is the story supposed to be a ghost story or an account of a delusion? Can we read the whole thing as a nightmare, having no reality outside the narrator's mind? Having seen that his thoughts weren't a totally disconnected jumble, he drew connections. Going down his list, he numbered with the same numbers those ideas that belonged together. His outline then looked like this:

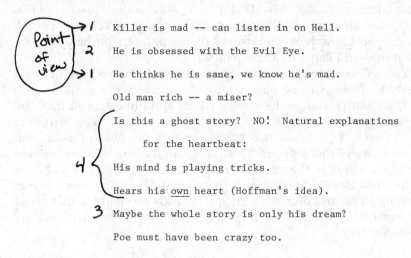

```
Point   →1   Killer is mad -- can listen in on Hell.
of      2    He is obsessed with the Evil Eye.
view    →1   He thinks he is sane, we know he's mad.
             Old man rich -- a miser?
             Is this a ghost story?  NO!  Natural explanations
                for the heartbeat:
   4    {    His mind is playing tricks.
             Hears his own heart (Hoffman's idea).
   3    Maybe the whole story is only his dream?
             Poe must have been crazy too.
```

The numbers now showed him the order in which he planned to take up each of his four chief ideas. Labeling with the number "1" his remarks about the narrator, he decided to open his paper with them, and to declare at once that they indicated the story's point of view. As you can tell from his finished paper, he discarded two notions that didn't seem to relate to his purpose: the point about the old man's wealth, and the speculation (which he realized he couldn't prove) that Poe himself was probably mad. Having completed this rough outline, he felt encouraged to return to Poe's story, and on rereading it, noticed a few additional points, which you will find in his paper. His outline didn't tell him exactly what to say at every moment, but it was clear and easy to follow; and as he wrote he discovered that each of his four leading ideas fell readily into a paragraph.

WRITING A DRAFT

Seated at last, or striking some other businesslike stance,[2] you prepare to write, only to find yourself besieged with petty distractions. All of a sudden you remember a friend you had promised to call, some dry-cleaning you were supposed to pick up, a neglected Coke (in another room) growing warmer and flatter by the minute. If your paper is to be

[2] R. H. Super of the University of Michigan wrote a definitive biography of Walter Savage Landor while standing up, typing on a machine atop a filing cabinet.

written, you have one course of action: to collar these thoughts and for the moment banish them.

Other small problems are merely mechanical: for instance, what to call the author whose work you now confront. Decide at the outset. Most critics favor the author's last name alone: "Dickinson implies . . ." ("Miss Dickinson" or "Ms. Dickinson" may sound fussily polite; "Emily," too chummy.) Will you include footnotes in your paper and, if so, do you know how they work? (Some pointers on handling the pesky things will come in a few. pages.)

You will want to give credit to any critics who helped you out, and properly to do so is to be painstaking. To paraphrase a critic, you do more than just rearrange the critic's words and phrases; you translate them into language of your own. Say you wish to refer to an insight of Randall Jarrell, who comments on the images of spider, flower, and moth in Robert Frost's poem "Design": "Notice how the *heal-all*, because of its name, is the one flower in all the world picked to be the altar for this Devil's Mass; notice how holding up the moth brings something ritual and hieratic, a ghostly, ghastly formality to this priest and its sacrificial victim. . . ." It would be incorrect to say, without any quotation marks:

```
Frost picks the heal-all as the one flower in all the world to be

the altar for this Devil's Mass.  There is a ghostly, ghastly

formality to the spider holding up the moth, like a priest holding

a sacrificial victim.
```

That rewording, although not exactly in Jarrell's language, manages to steal his memorable phrases without giving him credit. Nor is it sufficient just to list Jarrell's essay in a bibliography at the end of your paper. If you do, you are still a crook; you merely point to the scene of your crime. What is needed, clearly, is to think through Jarrell's words to the point he is making; and if you want to keep any of his striking phrases (and why not?), put them in quotation marks:

```
As Randall Jarrell points out, Frost portrays the spider as a kind

of priest in a Mass, or Black Mass, elevating the moth like an

object for sacrifice, with "a ghostly, ghastly formality."
```

To be scrupulous in your acknowledgment, you could even put a footnote after the phrase in quotation marks, citing the book and the page. But unless your instructor expects you to write such a formal, footnoted paper, the passage as it now stands would make sufficiently clear your source, and your obligation.

One more word of Dutch-uncle-ish warning. This book has offered you a vocabulary with which to discuss literature: a flurry of terms such as *irony*, *symbol*, and *theme*, printed in **bold face** when first introduced. In your writing, perhaps, you may decide to enlist a few of them. And yet, critical terminology — especially if unfamiliar — can tempt a beginning critic to sling it about. Nothing can be less sophisticated, or more misleading, than a technical term grandly misapplied: "The *myth-symbolism* of this *rime scheme* leaves one aghast." Far better to choose plain words you're already at ease with. Your instructor, no doubt, has met many a critical term and is not likely to be impressed by the mere sight of another one. Knowingly selected and placed, a critical term can help sharpen a thought and make it easier to handle. Clearly it is less cumbersome to refer to the *tone* of a story than to have to say, "the way the author makes you feel that she feels about what she is talking about." But the paper-writer who declares, "The tone of this poem is full of ironic imagery," fries words to a hash — mixed up and indigestible.

REVISING

Is it possible to write with perfect clarity on first try, to drop ideas with a single shot at them? Doubtless there are writers who can do so. Jack Kerouac, a believer in spontaneous prose, used to write entire novels on uncut ribbons of teletype paper, which custom saved him the interruption of stopping at the bottom of each page; and he declared that he rarely felt the need to change a word. His specialty, though, was fiction of ecstasy and hallucination, not essays in explication, or comparison and contrast. D. H. Lawrence also liked to let first drafts stand. If on finishing a story he felt dissatisfied, he sometimes declined to tinker with it but would write the whole thing over from scratch, hoping to do better. This habit accounts for the existence of at least three versions of his novel *Lady Chatterley's Lover*. For most of us, however, good writing is largely a matter of revising — of going back over our first thoughts word by word.

Still, to achieve good writing you have to have the courage to be wild. Aware that no reader need see your rough drafts, you can treat them mercilessly — scissor them apart, rearrange their pieces, reassemble them into a stronger order, using staples or tape or glue. The art of revising calls for a textbook in itself, but here are a few simple rules:

1. When you write your first draft, leave generous space between lines, and enormous margins. You may find later thoughts to add; make room.

2. As you reread your early draft, try to strike out any superfluous words or phrases. Eliminate whole paragraphs if they don't advance

your main argument. Watch out, though, for any gaping holes that result. Often, when you eliminate a sizeable passage, you'll need to add a transition to lead your reader on to the next idea.

3. Try reading your first draft aloud. Awkward sound effects may be detected: "An excellent excuse for exercise"; "Doom blooms in the second line . . ."

4. Short, skimpy paragraphs may indicate points that deserve more thought. Can you supply them with any more evidence, more explanation or illustration?

5. A classic method of revision is to lay your manuscript aside for a while, forget about it, and then, after a long interval (the Roman poet Horace recommended nine years), go back to it for a fresh look. If you lack that much time, take a nap, or a walk, or at least a yawn and a stretch before taking yet another look.

If you type your papers, by the way, it is a great help to be a reasonably expert typist — one who uses something other than the Christopher Columbus method (to discover a key and land on it). Then you can revise while you retype. All to what end? "Each clear sentence," according to Robert Russell, "is that much ground stripped clean of the undergrowth of one's own confusion. Sometimes it's thrilling to feel you have written even a single paragraph that makes sense."[3]

THE FORM OF YOUR FINISHED PAPER

Now that you have smoothed your rough draft as fleck-free as you can, your instructor may have specific advice for the form of your finished paper. If none is forthcoming, it is only reasonable

1. to choose standard letter-size (8½ x 11) paper;
2. to give your name at the top of your title page;
3. to leave an inch or more of margin on all four sides of each page, and a few inches of blank paper or an additional sheet after your conclusion, so that your instructor can offer comment;
4. to doublespace, or (if you handwrite) to use paper with widely spaced lines.

And what of titles of works discussed: when to put them in quotation marks, when to underline them? One rule of thumb is that titles of works shorter than book length rate quotation marks (poems, short stories, articles); while titles of books (including book-length poems: *The Odyssey*), plays, and periodicals take underlining. (In a manuscript to be set in type, an underline is a signal to the printer to use *italics*.)

A word about footnotes, if you're using them. A footnote number

[3] *To Catch an Angel* (New York: Vanguard, 1962), p. 301.

comes (following any punctuation) after the last word of a quotation or other item of information whose source you wish to credit. So that the number will stand out, roll your typewriter carriage up a click, thus lifting the number slightly above the usual level of your prose. At the bottom of your page, put the footnote itself; like this, for a book:

[8]Sylvan Barnet, A Short Guide to Writing about Literature, 4th ed. (Boston: Little, Brown, 1979), p. 102.

Or like this, for a magazine article:

[9]Paul Ramsey, "The Biding Place: Reflections on Hart Crane," Parnassus: Poetry in Review 5 (Fall/Winter 1976), 187-199.

In that last footnote, the number 5 is the volume number; *187–199* are the pages in it spanned by the article. Of course, you might wish instead to refer to a specific page. Should you return, later in your paper, for another quotation from Ramsey's article, you need not repeat all its information. Just make it

[10]Ramsey, p. 192.

(If your paper quoted two articles by Paul Ramsey, you would have to provide full information for the second article on *its* first mention; and then in further footnote references to either article, would mention its title so that the reader could tell the two apart.)

Footnotes enable your readers to go to the same place you did and read the same material. Most readers, of course, will not take the trouble to do so; but at least you give them a chance, and the process of footnoting keeps you as writer looking carefully at your sources, and so it helps you, as well.

Your readers should not have to interrupt their reading of your essay to glance down at a footnote simply to find out whom you are quoting. It is poor form to write:

Dylan Thomas's poem "Fern Hill" is a memory of the poet's

childhood: of his Aunt Ann Jones's farm, where he spent his

holidays. "Time, which has an art to throw dust on all things,

broods over the poem."[1] The farm, indeed, is a lost paradise -- a

personal garden of Eden.

---

[1]William York Tindall, A Reader's Guide to Dylan Thomas (New York: Noonday Press, 1962), p. 268.

That is annoying, because the reader has to stop reading and look at the footnote to find out who made that resonant statement about Time brooding over the poem. A better way:

"Time," as William York Tindall has observed, "which has an art to

throw dust on all things, broods over the poem."[1]

_____

[1]A Reader's Guide to Dylan Thomas (New York: Noonday Press, 1962), p. 268.

What to do now but hand in your paper? "And good riddance," you may feel, after such an expenditure of thinking, time, and energy. But a good paper is not only worth submitting, it is worth keeping. If you return to it, after a while, you may find to your surprise that it will preserve and even renew what you have learned.

Acknowledgments (continued)

Ernest Hemingway. "A Clean, Well-Lighted Place" by Ernest Hemingway is reprinted from *The Short Stories of Ernest Hemingway* with the permission of Charles Scribner's Sons. Copyright 1933 Charles Scribner's Sons.

James Joyce. "Araby" from *Dubliners* by James Joyce. Originally published by B. W. Huebsch, Inc. in 1916. Copyright © 1967 by the Estate of James Joyce. All rights reserved. Reprinted by permission of The Viking Press.

Franz Kafka. "A Hunger Artist." Reprinted by permission of Schocken Books, Inc. from *The Penal Colony* by Franz Kafka. Copyright © 1948, renewed © 1975, by Schocken Books, Inc.

D. H. Lawrence. "The Blind Man" from *The Complete Short Stories of D. H. Lawrence*, Volume II. Copyright 1922 by Thomas B. Seltzer, copyright renewed 1950 by Frieda Lawrence. Reprinted by permission of The Viking Press.

Ursula K. Le Guin. "The Ones Who Walk Away from Omelas." Copyright © 1973, 1975 by Ursula K. Le Guin; reprinted by permission of the author and the author's agent, Virginia Kidd.

Doris Lessing. "A Woman on a Roof" by Doris Lessing from *A Man and Two Women*. Copyright © 1958, 1962, 1963 by Doris Lessing. Reprinted by permission of Simon & Schuster, a Division of Gulf & Western Corporation, and McIntosh & Otis, Inc.

Bernard Malamud. "Angel Levine" from *The Magic Barrel* by Bernard Malamud. Copyright 1955 by Bernard Malamud. Reprinted with the permission of Farrar, Straus & Giroux, Inc.

Katherine Mansfield. "A Dill Pickle." Copyright 1920 by Alfred A. Knopf, Inc., and renewed 1948 by John Middleton Murry. Reprinted from *The Short Stories of Katherine Mansfield* by permission of Alfred A. Knopf, Inc.

James Alan McPherson. "Why I Like Country Music" from *Elbow Room* by James Alan McPherson. By permission of Little, Brown and Company in association with The Atlantic Monthly Press. Copyright © 1972, 1973, 1974, 1977 by James Alan McPherson. First appeared in *The Harvard Advocate*.

Joyce Carol Oates. "Where Are You Going, Where Have You Been?" Reprinted from *The Wheel of Love* by Joyce Carol Oates by permission of the publisher, Vanguard Press, Inc. Copyright © 1970, 1969, 1968, 1967, 1966, 1965 by Joyce Carol Oates.

Flannery O'Connor. "Revelation" from *Everything That Rises Must Converge* by Flannery O'Connor. Copyright © 1964 by the Estate of Mary Flannery O'Connor. Reprinted with the permission of Farrar, Straus & Giroux, Inc.

Frank O'Connor. "First Confession." Copyright 1951 by Frank O'Connor. Reprinted from *The Stories of Frank O'Connor* by permission of Alfred A. Knopf, Inc., and A. D. Peters & Co. Ltd.

Grace Paley. "The Loudest Voice" from *The Little Disturbances of Man* by Grace Paley. Copyright © 1959 by Grace Paley. Reprinted by permission of The Viking Press.

Edgar Allan Poe. Excerpt from *The French Face of Edgar Poe* by Patrick F. Quinn. Copyright 1954 by Patrick F. Quinn. Copyright © 1957 by Southern Illinois University Press. Reprinted by permission of Southern Illinois University Press.

Isaac Bashevis Singer. "Gimpel the Fool" translated by Saul Bellow from *A Treasury of Yiddish Stories*, edited by Irving Howe and Eliezer Greenberg. Copyright 1953 by Isaac Bashevis Singer. Reprinted by permission of The Viking Press.

John Steinbeck. "The Chrysanthemums" from *The Long Valley* by John Steinbeck. Copyright 1937, © 1965 by John Steinbeck. Reprinted by permission of The Viking Press.

James Thurber. "The Catbird Seat." Copyright © 1945 James Thurber. Copyright © 1963 Helen W. Thurber and Rosemary Thurber Sauers. From *The Thurber Carnival*, published by Harper & Row. Originally printed in *The New Yorker*.

Leo Tolstoi. "The Death of Ivan Ilych" from *The Death of Ivan Ilych and Other Stories* by Leo Tolstoy, trans. by Louise and Aylmer Maude and published by Oxford University Press. Reprinted by permission of Oxford University Press.

John Updike. "A & P." Copyright © 1962 by John Updike. Reprinted from *Pigeon Feathers and Other Stories* by permission of Alfred A. Knopf, Inc. Originally appeared in *The New Yorker*.

Kurt Vonnegut, Jr. "Harrison Bergeron" from *Welcome to the Monkey House*. Copyright © 1961 by Kurt Vonnegut, Jr. Originally published in *Fantasy and Science Fiction*. Reprinted by permission of Delacorte Press/Seymour Lawrence.

Eudora Welty. "Petrified Man." Copyright 1939, 1967 by Eudora Welty. Reprinted from her volume *A Curtain of Green and Other Stories* by permission of Harcourt Brace Jovanovich, Inc.

POETRY

The paintings by Pieter Breughel on page 585 (*The Kermess*, collection of Kunsthistoriches Museum, Vienna) and page 722 (*Landscape with Fall of Icarus*, collection of Museum der Schone Kunste, Brussels) are reproduced courtesy of Marburg Art Reference Bureau.

James Agee. "Sunday: Outskirts of Knoxville, Tennessee" from *The Collected Poems of James Agee*. Copyright © 1962, 1968 by the James Agee Trust. Reprinted by permission of Houghton Mifflin Company.

Edward Hathaway Allen. "The Best Line Yet," © 1972 by Edward H. Allen. First appeared in *Counter/Measures*. Reprinted by permission of the poet.

A. R. Ammons. "Auto Mobile" and "Spring Coming" from *Collected Poems, 1951–1971* by A. R. Ammons. Copyright © 1972 by A. R. Ammons. Reprinted by permission of W. W. Norton & Company, Inc.

Maya Angelou. "Harlem Hopscotch" from *Just Give Me a Cool Drink of Water 'Fore I Die* by Maya Angelou. Copyright © 1971 by Maya Angelou. Reprinted by permission of Random House, Inc.

John Ashbery. "City Afternoon" from *Self-Portrait in a Convex Mirror* by John Ashbery. Copyright © 1974 by John Ashbery. Reprinted by permission of The Viking Press.

W. H. Auden. "As I Walked Out One Evening," "Musée des Beaux Arts," and "The Unknown Citizen" from *Collected Poems* by W. H. Auden, edited by Edward Mendelson. Copyright 1940, renewed 1968 by W. H. Auden. Reprinted by permission of Random House, Inc., and Faber and Faber Ltd. "James Watt" from *Academic Graffiti* by W. H. Auden. Copyright © 1960 by W. H. Auden. Reprinted by permission of Random House, Inc.

David B. Axelrod. "Once in a While a Protest Poem" from *A Dream of Feet* by David B. Axelrod. Copyright © 1976 by David B. Axelrod. Reprinted by permission of the poet and Cross-Cultural Communications.

Max Beerbohm. "On the imprint of the first English edition of *The Works of Max Beerbohm*." Reprinted by permission of Sir Geoffrey Keynes.

Hilaire Belloc. "The Hippopotamus" from *Cautionary Verses* by Hilaire Belloc. Published in 1940 by Gerald Duckworth & Co. Ltd., 1941 by Alfred A. Knopf, Inc. Reprinted by permission of the publishers.

Edmund Clerihew Bentley. "Sir Christopher Wren" from *Clerihews Complete* by E. C. Bentley. Reprinted by permission of Nicholas Bentley.

John Berryman. "Life, friends, is boring . . ." from *77 Dream Songs* by John Berryman. Copyright © 1959, 1962, 1963, 1964 by John Berryman. Reprinted by permission of Farrar, Straus & Giroux, Inc.

John Betjeman. "In Westminster Abbey" from *Collected Poems* by John Betjeman. (Houghton Mifflin Company, 1959). Reprinted by permission of John Murray Publishers Ltd.

Elizabeth Bishop. "The Fish," "Late Air," "The Filling Station," and lines from "Little Exercise" from *The Complete Poems* by Elizabeth Bishop. Copyright 1940, 1946, 1949, © 1955 by Elizabeth Bishop, renewed © 1973 by Elizabeth Bishop. "Five Flights Up" from *Geography III* by Elizabeth Bishop. Copyright © 1974 by Elizabeth Bishop. "The Filling Station" and "Five Flights Up" appeared originally in *The New Yorker*. Reprinted by permission of Farrar, Straus & Giroux, Inc.

Robert Bly. "Driving to Town Late to Mail a Letter" from *Silence in the Snowy Field* by Robert Bly (Wesleyan University Press, 1962) and "Inward Conversation." Reprinted by permission of the poet.

Richard Brautigan. "Haiku Ambulance" excerpted from *The Pill Versus the Springhill Mine Disaster* by Richard Brautigan. Copyright © 1968 by Richard Brautigan. Reprinted by permission of Delacorte Press/Seymour Lawrence.

Gwendolyn Brooks. "The Bean Eaters" and "We Real Cool" from *The World of Gwendolyn Brooks*. Copyright © 1959 by Gwendolyn Brooks. Reprinted by permission of Harper & Row, Publishers.

Taniguchi Buson. "The Sudden Chilliness" from *An Introduction to Haiku* by Harold G. Henderson. Copyright © 1958 by Harold G. Henderson. Reprinted by permission of Doubleday & Company, Inc.

James Camp. "At the First Avenue Redemption Center" from *Carnal Refreshment*. Copyright © 1975. Reprinted by permission of the poet.

Roy Campbell. "On Some South African Novelists" from *Adamastor* by Roy Campbell. Reprinted by permission of Curtis Brown Ltd. on behalf of the Estate of Roy Campbell.

Bliss Carman. Lines from "A Vagabond Song" from *Bliss Carman's Poems*. Reprinted by permission of Dodd, Mead & Company and McClelland & Stewart Ltd.

Fred Chappell. "Skin Flick" from *The World Between the Eyes* by Fred Chappell. Copyright © 1971. Reprinted by permission of Louisiana State University Press.

Geoffrey Chaucer. Lines from Part I. "Merciles Beaute" from *The Works of Geoffrey Chaucer*. Second Edition, edited by F. N. Robinson (1957). Reprinted by permission of Houghton Mifflin Company.

G. K. Chesterton. "The Donkey" from *The Wild Knight and Other Poems* by G. K. Chesterton. Reprinted by permission of J. M. Dent & Sons Ltd.

Sarah N. Cleghorn. "The Golf Links Lie So Near the Mill" from *Portraits and Protests* by Sarah N. Cleghorn. All rights reserved. Reprinted by permission of Holt, Rinehart and Winston, Publishers.

Cid Corman. "The Tortoise" from *Words for Each Other* by Cid Corman. First appeared in *In Good Time* by Cid Corman. Reprinted by permission of Rapp and Whiting Ltd.

Frances Cornford. "The Watch" from *Collected Poems* by Frances Cornford (Cresset Press). Reprinted by permission of Barrie & Jenkins Ltd.

Hart Crane. "Black Tambourine" from *The Complete Poems and Selected Letters and Prose of Hart Crane*, edited by Brom Weber. Copyright 1933, © 1958, 1966 by Liveright Publishing Corporation. Reprinted by permission of Liveright Publishing Corporation.

Robert Creeley. "Oh No" and "A Naughty Boy" from *For Love* by Robert Creeley. Copyright © 1962 by Robert Creeley. Reprinted by permission of Charles Scribner's Sons.

Countee Cullen. "Saturday's Child" and "For a Lady I Know" from *On These I Stand* by Countee Cullen. Copyright 1925 by Harper & Row, Publishers, Inc.; renewed 1953 by Ida M. Cullen. Reprinted by permission of Harper & Row, Publishers.

E. E. Cummings. These poems from *Complete Poems 1913–1962*: "anyone lived in a pretty how town" (copyright 1940 by E. E. Cummings, copyright © 1968 by Marion Morehouse Cummings); "All in green went my love riding," "Buffalo Bill's," and "in Just-" (all copyright 1923, 1951 by E. E. Cummings); "a politician is an arse upon" (copyright 1944 by E. E. Cummings); and "r-p-o-p-h-e-s-s-a-g-r" (copyright 1935 by E. E. Cummings, copyright © 1963 by Marion Morehouse Cummings). Reprinted by permission of Harcourt Brace Jovanovich, Inc.

J. V. Cunningham. "Friend, on this scaffold . . . ," "Motto for a Sundial," "You serve the best wines . . . ," and "This Humanist whom . . ." from *The Collected Poems and Epigrams of J. V. Cunningham*. Copyright © 1971 by J. V. Cunningham. Reprinted by permission of The Swallow Press, Inc., Chicago.

Peter Davison. "The Last Word" (Part IV of "Four Love Poems") from *Pretending to Be Asleep* by Peter Davison. Copyright © 1970 by Peter Davison. Reprinted by permission of Atheneum Publishers.

Walter de la Mare. "The Listeners," reprinted by permission of the Literary Trustees of Walter de la Mare, and The Society of Authors as their representative.

James Dickey. "Cherrylog Road" from *Poems 1957–1967* by James Dickey. Copyright © 1963 by James Dickey. First appeared in *The New Yorker*. Reprinted by permission of Wesleyan University Press.

Emily Dickinson. "I taste a liquor never brewed," "Because I could not stop for Death," "I heard a Fly buzz–when I died," "I like to see it lap the Miles," "I started early–Took my Dog," "The Lightning is a yellow Fork," "The Soul selects her own Society," "Victory comes late," "It dropped so low–in my regard," and lines from "Hope is the thing with feathers" from *The Poems of Emily Dickinson*, edited by Thomas H. Johnson (Cambridge, Mass.: The Belknap Press of Harvard University Press). Copyright 1951, © 1955 by the President and Fellows of Harvard College. Reprinted by permission of the publishers and the Trustees of Amherst College.

Emanuel diPasquale. "Rain," reprinted by permission of the poet.

Reinhard Döhl. Untitled poem from *Approaches* 2 (1965). Reprinted by permission of Editions André Silvaire.

Alan Dugan. "Love Song: I and Thou" from *Poems* by Alan Dugan. Copyright © 1961 by Alan Dugan. First published by Yale University Press. Reprinted by permission.

Richard Eberhart. "The Fury of Aerial Bombardment" from *Collected Poems 1930–1976* by Richard Eberhart. Copyright © 1976 by Richard Eberhart. Reprinted by permission of Oxford University Press, Inc., and Chatto and Windus Ltd.

T. S. Eliot. "Journey of the Magi," "Rhapsody on a Windy Night," "Virginia" (from "Landscapes"), "The Love Song of J. Alfred Prufrock," and "The Boston Evening Transcript" from *Collected Poems 1909–1962* by T. S. Eliot. Copyright 1936 by Harcourt Brace Jovanovich, Inc., copyright © 1963, 1964 by T. S. Eliot. Reprinted by permission of Harcourt Brace Jovanovich, Inc., and Faber and Faber Ltd.

Abbie Huston Evans. "Wing Spread" from *Collected Poems* by Abbie Huston Evans, © 1970 by Abbie Huston Evans. Reprinted by permission of the University of Pittsburgh Press.

Donald Finkel. "Hands" from *A Joyful Noise* by Donald Finkel. Copyright © 1965, 1966 by Donald Finkel. "Gesture" from *The Garbage Wars* by Donald Finkel. Copyright © 1969, 1970 by Donald Finkel. Reprinted by permission of Atheneum Publishers.

Ian Hamilton Finlay. "The Horizon of Holland. " Reprinted by permission of the poet.

Dudley Fitts. "Elegy on Herakleitos," a translation of the poem by Kollimachos, from *Poems from the Greek Anthology* by Dudley Fitts. Copyright 1938, 1941, © 1956 by New Directions Publishing Corporation. Reprinted by permission of New Directions Publishing Corporation.

Carolyn Forché. Lines from "Dulcimer Maker" from *Gathering the Tribes* by Carolyn Forché. Copyright © 1976 by Carolyn Forché. Reprinted by permission of Yale University Press.

Robert Francis. "Catch" from *The Orb Weaver* by Robert Francis. Copyright 1950 by Robert Francis. Reprinted by permission of Wesleyan University Press.

Robert Frost. "Tree at My Window," "Never Again Would Birds' Song Be the Same," "Stopping by Woods on a Snowy Evening," "Design," "The Secret Sits," "Fire and Ice," "Mending Wall," and "The Witch of Coös" from *The Poetry of Robert Frost*, ed. Edward Connery Lathem. Copyright 1923, 1928, 1930, 1939, © 1969 by Holt, Rinehart and Winston. Copyright 1936, 1942, 1951, © 1956, 1958 by Robert Frost. Copyright © 1964, 1967, 1970 by Lesley Frost Ballantine. "In White" from *The Dimensions of Robert Frost* by Reginald L. Cook. Copyright © 1958 by Reginald L. Cook. Reprinted by permission of Holt, Rinehart and Winston, Publishers.

Frederico García Lorca. "La guitarra," translated by Keith Waldrop from *Obras Completas* by Frederico García Lorca. Copyright © Aguilar SA de Ediciones 1954. All rights reserved. Permission to publish in original Spanish and in English translation by New Directions Publishing Corporation.

Gary Gildner. "First Practice" from *First Practice* by Gary Gildner, © 1969 by the University of Pittsburgh Press. Reprinted by permission fo the University of Pittsburgh Press.

Allen Ginsberg. "Postcard to D----" from *First Blues* by Allen Ginsberg. Reprinted by permission of Full Court Press.

Paul Goodman. Lines from "Hokku" from *Collected Poems* by Paul Goodman. Copyright © 1974 by Paul Goodman. Reprinted by permission of Random House, Inc.

Robert Graves. "Down, Wanton, Down!" from *Collected Poems* by Robert Graves. Copyright 1939, © 1955, 1958, 1961, 1965 by Robert Graves. Reprinted by permission of Curtis Brown, Ltd.

Ronald Gross. "Yield" from *Pop Poems* by Ronald Gross. Copyright © 1967 by Ronald Gross. Reprinted by permission of Simon & Schuster, a Division of Gulf & Western Corporation.

Arthur Guiterman. "On the Vanity of Earthly Greatness" from *Gaily the Troubadour* by Arthur Guiterman. Copyright 1936 by E. P. Dutton & Co., Inc.; renewed 1954 by Mrs. Vida Lindo Guiterman. Reprinted by permission of Louise H. Sclove.

H. D. (Hilda Doolittle). "Heat" from *Selected Poems*. Copyright © 1957 by Norman Holmes Pearson. Reprinted by permission of New Directions Publishing Corporation.

Donald Hall. "The Town of Hill" from *The Town of Hill* by Donald Hall. Copyright © 1975 by Donald Hall. Reprinted by permission of David R. Godine, Publisher. "My Son, My Executioner" from *The Alligator Bride: Poems New and Selected*. Copyright 1954 by Donald Hall. First appeared in *The New Yorker* as "First Child." Reprinted by permission.

Thomas Hardy. "At a Hasty Wedding," "The Oxen," "The Workbox," "Channel Firing," "The Convergence of the Twain," and "Neutral Tones" from *Collected Poems* by Thomas Hardy. Copyright 1925 by Macmillan Publishing Co., Inc. Reprinted by permission of Macmillan Publishing Co., Inc., the Trustees of the Hardy Estate, Macmillan London and Basingstoke, and The Macmillan Company of Canada Limited.

Robert Hayden. "A Road in Kentucky" from *Angle of Ascent, New and Selected Poems* by Robert Hayden. Copyright © 1975, 1972, 1970, 1966 by Robert Hayden. Reprinted by permission of Liveright Publishing Corporation.

Seamus Heaney. "Digging" from *Death of a Naturalist* by Seamus Heaney. Copyright © 1966 by Seamus Heaney. Reprinted by permission of Oxford University Press, Inc., and Faber and Faber Ltd.

John Heath-Stubbs. "A Charm Against the Toothache" fron *Selected Poems* by John Heath-Stubbs (Oxford University Press). Reprinted by permission of David Higham Associates Ltd.

Anthony Hecht. "Japan" and "The Vow" from *The Hard Hours* by Anthony Hecht. Copyright 1954, © 1957, 1967 by Anthony E. Hecht. "Japan" appeared originally in *A Summoning of Stones* by Anthony Hecht. "The Vow" appeared originally in the *Hudson Review*. Reprinted by permission of Atheneum Publishers.

Geoffrey Hill. "Merlin" from *Somewhere is Such a Kingdom* by Geoffrey Hill. Copyright © 1975 by Geoffrey Hill. Reprinted by permission of Houghton Mifflin Company and Andre Deutsch Ltd.

John Hollander. "Skeleton Key" from *Types of Shape* by John Hollander. Copyright © 1969 by John Hollander. Reprinted by permission of Atheneum Publishers.

A. E. Housman. "Loveliest of trees, the cherry now," "To an Athlete Dying Young," "Terence, this is stupid stuff," "With rue my heart is laden," and "When I was one-and-twenty" from *A Shropshire Lad*, authorized edition, from *The Collected Poems of A. E. Housman*. Copyright 1939, 1940, © 1965 by Holt, Rinehart and Winston. Copyright © 1968, 1969 by Robert E. Symons. "From the wash the laundress sends" and "Eight O'Clock" from *The Collected Poems of A. E. Housman*. Copyright 1922 by Holt, Rinehart and Winston. Copyright 1936, 1950 by Barclays Bank Ltd. Copyright © 1964 by Robert E. Symons. Reprinted by permission of Holt, Rinehart and Winston, Publishers; The Society of Authors as literary representative of the Estate of A. E. Housman; and Jonathan Cape Ltd., publishers of A. E. Housman's *Collected Poems*.

Langston Hughes. "Dream Deferred" from *The Panther and the Lash: Poems of Our Times* by Langston Hughes. Copyright 1951 by Langston Hughes. Reprinted by permission of Alfred A. Knopf, Inc.

Ted Hughes. "Secretary" from *The Hawk in the Rain* by Ted Hughes. Copyright © 1957 by Ted Hughes. Reprinted by permission of Harper & Row, Publishers. "Examination at the Womb Door," "Crow's First Lesson," and "Crow and Stone" from *Crow* by Ted Hughes. Copyright © 1971 by Ted Hughes. Reprinted by permission of Harper & Row, Publishers; and Faber and Faber Ltd.

T. E. Hulme. "Image" from *The Life and Opinions of T. E. Hulme* by Alun R. Jones. Copyright © 1960 by Alun R. Jones. Reprinted by permission of Beacon Press.

David Ignatow. "Get the Gasworks" from *Figures of the Human* by David Ignatow. Copyright 1948 by David Ignatow. Reprinted by permission of Wesleyan University Press.

Randall Jarrell. From *The Complete Poems* by Randall Jarrell: "The Death of the Ball Turret Gunner" (Copyright 1945, renewed © 1973 by Mary von Schrader Jarrell) and "A Sick Child" (Copyright 1949 by Randall Jarrell, renewed © 1976 by Mary von Schrader Jarrell). Reprinted by permission of Farrar, Straus & Giroux, Inc. "The Woman at the Washington Zoo" from *The Woman at the Washington Zoo* by Randall Jarrell. Copyright © 1960 by Randall Jarrell. Reprinted by permission of Atheneum Publishers. Excerpt from *Poetry and the Age* by Randall Jarrell. Copyright 1952, 1953 by Randall Jarrell. Reprinted by permission of Alfred A. Knopf, Inc.

Robinson Jeffers. "To the Stone-Cutters" from *The Selected Poetry of Robinson Jeffers*. Copyright 1924 and renewed 1952 by Robinson Jeffers. Reprinted by permission of Random House, Inc.

Elizabeth Jennings. "Delay" from *Collected Poems* by Elizabeth Jennings, 1953, © 1967 by Elizabeth Jennings. Reprinted by permission of Macmillan London and Basingstoke.

James C. Kilgore. "The White Man Pressed the Locks" from *Poets on the Platform*. Copyright © 1970 by James C. Kilgore. Reprinted by permission of the poet.

Hugh Kingsmill. "What, still alive at twenty-two" from *The Best of Hugh Kingsmill*. Reprinted by permission of Victor Gollancz Ltd.

William Knott. "Poem" from *The Naomi Poems: Corpse and Beans* by Saint Geraud. Copyright © 1968 by William Knott. Used by permission of Follett Publishing Company.

Kenneth Koch. "Mending Sump" from *The New American Poetry*, ed. Donald M. Allen. Copyright © 1960 by Kenneth Koch. Reprinted by permission of International Creative Management and the poet.

M. Krishnamurti. "The Spirit's Odyssey" from *Cloth of Gold* by M. Krishnamurti. Reprinted by permission of the publisher, Charles E. Tuttle Co., Inc.

Maxine Kumin. "Woodchucks" from *Up Country* by Maxine Kumin. Copyright © 1971 by Maxine Kumin. Reprinted by permission of Harper & Row, Publishers.

Philip Larkin. "Wedding-Wind" from *The Less Deceived*. Copyright © 1955, 1971 by The Marvell Press. Reprinted by permission of The Marvell Press, England. "Vers de Société" from *High Windows* by Philip Larkin. Copyright © 1974 by Philip Larkin. Reprinted by permission of Farrar, Straus & Giroux, Inc., and Faber and Faber Ltd. "Days" from *The Whitsun Wedding*. Copyright © 1960 by Philip Larkin. Reprinted by permission of Faber and Faber Ltd.

D. H. Lawrence. These poems from *The Complete Poems of D. H. Lawrence*, edited by Vivian de Sola Pinto and F. Warren Roberts: "A Youth Mowing" and "Piano" (Copyright © 1964, 1971 by Angelo Ravagli and C. M. Weekley, Executors of the Estate of Frieda Lawrence Ravagli), "Bavarian Gentians" (Copyright 1933 by Frieda Lawrence. All rights reserved.) Reprinted by permission of The Viking Press.

Irving Layton. "The Bull Calf" from *A Red Carpet for the Sun*. Reprinted by permission of the Canadian publishers, McClelland and Stewart Ltd., Toronto.

Denise Levertov. "Leaving Forever" from *O Taste and See*. Copyright © 1963 by Denise Levertov Goodman. "Sunday Afternoon" and "Six Variations (part iii)" from *The Jacob's Ladder* by Denise Levertov. Copyright © 1958, 1969 by Denise Levertov Goodman. "Ways of Conquest" from *The Freeing of the Dust* by Denise Levertov. Copyright © 1975 by Denise Levertov. "Leaving Forever" and "Six Variations (part iii)" first published in *Poetry*. Reprinted by permission of New Directions Publishing Corporation.

Philip Levine. "To a Child Trapped in a Barber Shop" from *Not This Pig* by Philip Levine. Copyright © 1966 by Philip Levine. Reprinted by permission of Wesleyan University Press.

Abraham Lincoln. "My Childhood-Home I See Again" from *The Collected Works of Abraham Lincoln*. Copyright 1953 by the Abraham Lincoln Association. Reprinted by permission of the Rutgers University Press.

J. A. Lindon. "My Garden," reprinted by permission of the poet.

Vachel Lindsay. "Factory Windows Are Always Broken" from Collected Poems by Vachel Lindsay. Copyright 1914 by Macmillan Publishing Co., Inc.; renewed 1942 by Elizabeth C. Lindsay. Reprinted with permission of Macmillan Publishing Co., Inc.

Myra Cohn Livingston. "Driving" from The Malibu and Other Poems by Myra Cohn Livingston (A Margaret K. McElderry Book). Copyright © 1972 by Myra Cohn Livingston. Reprinted by permission of Atheneum Publishers.

Robert Lowell. "At the Altar" from Lord Weary's Castle by Robert Lowell. Copyright 1946 by Robert Lowell. Reprinted by permission of Harcourt Brace Jovanovich, Inc. "Meditation" from Imitations by Robert Lowell. Copyright © 1958, 1959, 1960, 1961 by Robert Lowell. Reprinted by permission of Farrar, Straus & Giroux, Inc. "Skunk Hour" from Life Studies by Robert Lowell. Copyright © 1956, 1959 by Robert Lowell. Reprinted by permission of Farrar, Straus & Giroux, Inc.

Mina Loy. "Omen of Victory" from Lunar Baedecker and Time Tables (Jargon 23, Highlands, North Carolina, 1958). Reprinted by permission of The Jargon Society, Inc.

Hugh McDiarmid. "Weesht, Weesht" from Collected Poems by Hugh McDiarmid. Copyright 1948, © 1962 by Christopher Murray Grieve. Reprinted by permission of Macmillan Publishing Co., Inc.

Archibald MacLeish. "Ars Poetica" and "The End of the World" from Collected Poems, 1917–1952 by Archibald MacLeish. Copyright 1952 by Archibald MacLeish. Reprinted by permission of Houghton Mifflin Company.

John Masefield. "Cargoes" from Poems by John Masefield. Copyright 1912 by Macmillan Publishing Co., Inc.; renewed 1940 by John Masefield. Reprinted by permission of Macmillan Publishing Co., Inc.

Rod McKuen. "Thoughts on Capital Punishment" from Stanyan Street and Other Sorrows by Rod McKuen. Copyright 1954, © 1960, 1961, 1962, 1963, 1964, 1965, 1966 by Rod McKuen. Reprinted by permission of Random House, Inc.

James Merrill. "Laboratory Poem" from The Country of a Thousand Years of Peace by James Merrill. Copyright © 1958, 1970 by James Merrill. This poem appeared originally in Poetry. Reprinted by permission of Atheneum Publishers.

W. S. Merwin. "Dead Hand" from The Moving Target by W. S. Merwin. Copyright © 1963 by W. S. Merwin. "For the Anniversary of My Death" from The Lice by W. S. Merwin. Copyright © 1967 by W. S. Merwin. Appeared originally in the Southern Review. "Song of Man Chipping an Arrowhead" from Writings to an Unfinished Accompaniment by W. S. Merwin. Copyright © 1972, 1973 by W. S. Merwin. Reprinted by permission of Atheneum Publishers.

Josephine Miles. "Reason" from Poems 1930–1960 by Josephine Miles. Reprinted by permission of Indiana University Press.

Edna St. Vincent Millay. "Counting-out Rhyme" from Collected Poems by Edna St. Vincent Millay. Copyright 1928, © 1955 by Edna St. Vincent Millay and Norma Millay Ellis. Reprinted by permission of Norma Millay Ellis.

A. A. Milne. Lines from "Disobedience" from When We Were Very Young by A. A. Milne. Reprinted by permission of E. P. Dutton & Co., Inc., and the Canadian publishers, McClelland and Stewart Ltd., Toronto.

Marianne Moore. "The Mind is an Enchanting Thing" from Collected Poems by Marianne Moore. Copyright 1944, © 1972 by Marianne Moore. Reprinted by permission of Macmillan Publishing Co., Inc.

Edwin Morgan. "Siesta of a Hungarian Snake" from The Second Life by Edwin Morgan. Copyright © 1968 by Edwin Morgan and Edinburgh University Press. Reprinted by permission of Edinburgh University Press.

Howard Moss. "Shall I Compare Thee to a Summer's Day?" from A Swim Off the Rocks by Howard Moss. Copyright © 1976. This poem appeared originally in Commentary. Reprinted by permission of Atheneum Publishers.

Ogden Nash. "Very Like a Whale" from Verses from 1929 On by Ogden Nash. Copyright 1934 by Ogden Nash. Reprinted by permission of Little, Brown and Company.

John Frederick Nims. "Perfect Rhyme" from Of Flesh and Bone by John Frederick Nims. Copyright © 1967 by Rutgers, the State University. Reprinted by permission of Rutgers University Press. "Odd Bethinkings of a Day of 'Showers Likely' at Beansey Ridge" from College English (April 1971). Copyright © 1971 by the National Council of Teachers of English. Reprinted by permission of the publisher.

Alden Nowlan. "The Loneliness of the Long Distance Runner" from Bread, Wine and Salt by Alden Nowlan. Copyright © 1967 by Clarke, Irwin & Co. Used by permission.

Charles Olson. "La Chute," copyright by Charles Olson. Reprinted from the Estate of Charles Olson.

Guy Owen. "The White Stallion" from The White Stallion by Guy Owen (John F. Blair, Publisher, 1969). Reprinted by permission of the poet.

Wilfred Owen. "Dulce et Decorum Est" from The Collected Poems of Wilfred Owen. Copyright 1946, © 1963 by Chatto and Windus Ltd. Reprinted by permission of New Directions Publishing Corporation, the Owen Estate, and Chatto and Windus Ltd.

Dorothy Parker. "Résumé" from The Portable Dorothy Parker. Copyright 1926, 1954 by Dorothy Parker. Reprinted by permission of the Viking Press.

Sylvia Plath. "Poppies in October," "Daddy," (all copyright © 1963 by Ted Hughes) and "Morning Song" (Copyright © 1961 by Ted Hughes) from Ariel by Sylvia Plath. "Metaphors" from Crossing the Water by Sylvia Plath. Copyright © 1960 by Ted Hughes. Reprinted by permission of Harper & Row, Publishers; and Olwyn Hughes, representing the estate of Sylvia Plath.

Ezra Pound. "The Seafarer," "In Station of the Metro," and "The River Merchant's Wife: a Letter" from Personae by Ezra Pound. Copyright 1926 by Ezra Pound. Reprinted by permission of New Directions Publishing Corporation. Excerpt beginning "Yaller bird, . . ." from Shih-ching: The Classic Anthology Defined by Confucius by Ezra Pound. Copyright © 1954 by the President and Fellows of Harvard College. Reprinted by permission of Harvard University Press.

Dudley Randall. "Ballad of Birmingham" from Poem Counterpoem by Margaret Danner and Dudley Randall. Copyright © 1966 by Dudley Randall. Reprinted by permission of the poet.

John Crowe Ransom. "Janet Waking" from Selected Poems. Third Edition. Revised and Enlarged by John Crowe Ransom. Copyright 1927 by Alfred A. Knopf, Inc., and renewed 1957 by John Crowe Ransom. Reprinted by permission of Alfred A. Knopf, Inc.

Henry Reed. "Naming of Parts" from A Map of Verona by Henry Reed (1946). Reprinted by permission of Jonathan Cape Ltd.

Ishmael Reed. ".05" from Chattanooga by Ishmael Reed. Copyright © 1973 by Ishmael Reed. Reprinted by permission of Random House, Inc.

Adrienne Rich. "Diving into the Wreck" from Diving into the Wreck, Poems, 1971–1972 by Adrienne Rich. Copyright © 1973 by W. W. Norton & Company. Reprinted by permission of W. W. Norton & Company, Inc.

Edwin Arlington Robinson. "Mr. Flood's Party" from Collected Poems by Edwin Arlington Robinson. Copyright 1921 by Edwin Arlington Robinson, renewed 1949 by Ruth Nivison. Reprinted with permission of Macmillan Publishing Co., Inc. "Richard Cory" from Children of the Night (1897). Reprinted by permission of Charles Scribner's Sons.

Theodore Roethke. These poems from Collected Poems of Theodore Roethke: "I Knew a Woman" (Copyright 1954 by Theodore Roethke), "The Waking" (Copyright 1953 by Theodore Roethke), "My Papa's Waltz" (Copyright 1942 by Hearst Magazines, Inc.), "Root Cellar" (Copyright 1943 by Modern Poetry Association, Inc.), "Frau Bauman, Frau Schmidt, and Frau Schwartze" (Copyright 1952 by Theodore Roethke), and "Night Crow" (Copyright 1944 by Saturday Review Association, Inc.). All poems reprinted by permission of Doubleday & Company, Inc.

Raymond Roseliep. "Clap" from Step on the Rain by Raymond Roseliep (The Rook Press; Derry, Pennsylvania). Copyright © 1977 by Raymond Roseliep. Reprinted by permission of the poet.

Carl Sandburg. "Fog" from Chicago Poems by Carl Sandburg. Copyright 1916 by Holt, Rinehart and Winston, Inc., 1944 by Carl Sandburg. Reprinted by permission of Harcourt Brace Jovanovich, Inc.

Aram Saroyan. Lines from "crickets" from Works by Aram Saroyan. Copyright © 1966 by Aram Saroyan. Reprinted by permission of the poet.

Anne Sexton. "The Kiss" from *Love Poems* by Anne Sexton. Copyright © 1967, 1968, 1969 by Anne Sexton. "The Fury of the Overshoes" from *The Death Notebooks* by Anne Sexton. Copyright © 1975 by Anne Sexton. Reprinted by permission of Houghton Mifflin Company.

Karl Shapiro. "The Dirty Word" from *Selected Poems* by Karl Shapiro. Copyright 1947 by Karl Shapiro. Reprinted by permission of Random House, Inc.

Frank Sidgwick. "The Aeronaut to His Lady" from *More Verse by "F. S."* (1921). Reprinted by permission of the publishers, Sidgwick & Jackson Ltd.

Charles Simic. "Fork" from *Dismantling the Silence* by Charles Simic. Copyright © 1971 by Charles Simic. Reprinted by permission of the publisher, George Braziller, Inc.

L. E. Sissman. Lines from "In and Out: A Home Away from Home" from *Dying: An Introduction* by L. E. Sissman. Copyright © 1966, 1967, by L. E. Sissman. Reprinted by permission of Little, Brown and Co. in association with The Atlantic Monthly Press.

Knute Skinner. "The Cold Irish Earth" from *A Close Sky over Killaspuglonae* (The Dolman Press, 1968). Reprinted by permission of the poet and the publisher.

Stevie Smith. "I Remember" from *Selected Poems* by Stevie Smith. Copyright © 1962, 1964 by Stevie Smith. Reprinted by permission of New Directions Publishing Corporation.

William Jay Smith. "American Primitive" from *New and Selected Poems* by William Jay Smith. Copyright 1953, © 1970 by William Jay Smith. Reprinted by permission of Delacorte Press/Seymour Lawrence.

W. D. Snodgrass. "The Operation" from *Heart's Needle* by W. D. Snodgrass. Copyright © 1959 by W. D. Snodgrass. Reprinted by permission of Alfred A. Knopf, Inc.

Gary Snyder. "Milton by Firelight," © 1959, 1965 by Gary Snyder. Reprinted by permission of the poet. Poems from "Hitch Haiku" from *The Back Country* by Gary Snyder. Copyright © 1968 by Gary Snyder. Reprinted by permission of New Directions Publishing Corporation.

Richard Snyder. "A Mongoloid Child Handling Shells on the Beach" from *A Keeping in Touch* by Richard Snyder (The Ashland Poetry Press, 1971). Reprinted by permission.

Sir John Squire. Lines from "It did not last," reprinted by permission of Raglan Squire, Executor.

William Stafford. "Written on the Stub of the First Paycheck" and "At the Klamath Berry Festival" from *The Rescued Year* by William Stafford. Copyright © 1960, 1961 by William E. Stafford. "Traveling Through the Dark" from *Traveling Through the Dark* by William Stafford. Copyright © by William Stafford. Reprinted by permission of Harper & Row, Publishers.

James Stephens. These poems from *The Collected Poems of James Stephens*: "The Wind" (Copyright 1915 by Macmillan Publishing Co., Inc., renewed 1943 by James Stephens) and "A Glass of Beer" (Copyright 1918 by Macmillan Publishing Co., Inc., renewed 1946 by James Stephens). Reprinted by permission of Macmillan Publishing Co., Inc., Mrs. Iris Wise, Macmillan London & Basingstoke, and The Macmillan Company of Canada Limited.

Wallace Stevens. These poems from *The Collected Poems of Wallace Stevens*: "The Emperor of Ice Cream," "Disillusionment of Ten O'Clock," "Peter Quince at the Clavier," "Thirteen Ways of Looking at a Blackbird," "Anecdote of the Jar," and lines from "Sunday Morning" and "Bantams in Pine-Woods" (Copyright 1923, renewed 1951 by Wallace Stevens); "Metamorphosis" (Copyright 1942 by Wallace Stevens); "Study of Two Pears" (Copyright 1942 by Wallace Stevens and renewed 1970 by Holly Stevens). Reprinted by permission of Alfred A. Knopf, Inc.

Mark Strand. "Eating Poetry" from *Reasons for Moving* by Mark Strand. Copyright © 1968 by Mark Strand. Reprinted by permission of Atheneum Publishers.

May Swenson. "Stone Gullets" from *Iconographs* by May Swenson. Copyright © 1970 by May Swenson. Reprinted by permission of the poet.

James Tate. "Flight" from *The Lost Pilot* by James Tate. Copyright © 1967 by Yale University. Reprinted by permission of Yale University Press.

Henry Taylor. "Riding a One-Eyed Horse" from *An Afternoon of Pocket Billiards* by Henry Taylor. Copyright © 1975 by Henry Taylor. Reprinted by permission of the poet and the University of Utah Press.

Cornelius J. Ter Maat. "Etienne de Silouette," reprinted by permission of the poet.

Dylan Thomas. "Twenty-four years," "Fern Hill," and "Do not go gentle into that good night" from *The Poems of Dylan Thomas*. Copyright 1939, 1946 by New Directions Publishing Corporation. Reprinted by permission of New Directions Publishing Corporation, J. M. Dent & Sons Ltd., and the Trustees for the Copyrights of the late Dylan Thomas.

Jean Toomer. "Reapers" from *Cane* by Jean Toomer. Copyright 1923 by Boni & Liveright, renewed 1951 by Jean Toomer. Reprinted by permission of Liveright Publishing Corporation.

John Updike. "Winter Ocean" from *Telephone Poles and Other Poems* by John Updike. Copyright © 1960 by John Updike. Reprinted by permission of Alfred A. Knopf, Inc.

David Wagoner. "Muse" from *Collected Poems 1956–1976* by David Wagoner. Reprinted by permission of the publisher, Indiana University Press.

Keith Waldrop. "On Measure" from *A Windmill Near Calvary* by Keith Waldrop. Copyright © 1968 by The University of Michigan Press. All rights reserved. Reprinted by permission of the publisher.

Rosmarie Waldrop. "Confession to Settle a Curse" from *The Aggressive Ways of the Casual Stranger* by Rosmarie Waldrop. Copyright © 1972 by Rosmarie Waldrop. Reprinted by permission of Random House, Inc.

Wang Wei. "Bird-Singing Stream," translated by Wai-lim Yip. Reprinted by permission of Wai-lim Yip.

E. B. White. "A Classic Waits for Me" from *The Second Tree From the Corner* by E. B. White. Copyright 1944 by E. B. White. Originally appeared in *The New Yorker*. Reprinted by permission of Harper & Row, Publishers, Inc.

Ruth Whitman. "Castoff Skin" from *The Passion of Lizzie Borden* by Ruth Whitman. Copyright © 1973 by Ruth Whitman. Reprinted by permission of October House.

Reed Whittemore. "The Fall of the House of Usher" from *Fifty Poems Fifty* by Reed Whittemore. Reprinted by permission of the University of Minnesota Press.

Richard Wilbur. "In the Elegy Season" and "A Simile for Her Smile" from *Ceremony and Other Poems* by Richard Wilbur. Copyright 1948, 1949, 1950 by Richard Wilbur. "In the Elegy Season" first appeared in *The New Yorker*. "Junk" from *Advice to a Prophet and Other Poems*. Copyright © 1961 by Richard Wilbur. "Sleepless at Crown Point" from *The Mind Reader* by Richard Wilbur. Copyright © 1976 by Richard Wilbur. Reprinted by permission of Harcourt Brace Jovanovich, Inc.

Miller Williams. "On the Symbolic Consideration of Hands and the Significance of Death" from *Halfway from Hoxie: New and Selected Poems* by Miller Williams. Copyright © 1964, 1968, 1971, 1973 by Miller Williams. Reprinted by permission of the publishers, E. P. Dutton.

William Carlos Williams. "The Great Figure," "Spring and All," "Poem," "This Is Just to Say," "The Red Wheelbarrow," "To Waken an Old Lady," "The Descent of Winter (section 10/30)" from *Collected Earlier Poems* by William Carlos Williams. Copyright 1938 by New Directions Publishing Corporation. "The Dance" from *Collected Later Poems* by William Carlos Williams. Copyright 1944 by William Carlos Williams. Reprinted by permission of New Directions Publishing Corporation.

Yvor Winters. "At the San Francisco Airport" from *Collected Poems* by Yvor Winters. Copyright 1952, © 1960 by Yvor Winters. Reprinted by permission of The Swallow Press, Inc., Chicago.

James Wright. "Autumn Begins in Martins Ferry, Ohio" and "A Blessing" from *Collected Poems* by James Wright. Copyright © 1961, 1962 by James Wright. "A Blessing" first appeared in *Poetry*. Reprinted by permission of Wesleyan University Press. "Saying Dante Aloud" from *Moments of the Italian Summer*. Copyright © 1976 by James Wright. Reprinted by permission.

Judith Wright. "Woman to Man" and "Woman to Child" from *Collected Poems 1942–1970* by Judith Wright. Copyright © 1971 by Judith Wright. Reprinted by permission of Angus & Robertson Publishers.

William Butler Yeats. These poems from *The Collected Poems of W. B. Yeats*: "The Lake Isle of Innisfree," "Who Goes with Fergus," "The Lamentation of an Old Pensioner" (Copyright 1906 by Macmillan Publishing Co., Inc.; renewed 1934 by William Bulter Yeats); "The Magi," (Copyright 1916 by Macmillan Publishing Co., Inc.; renewed 1944 by Bertha Georgie Yeats); "Sailing to Byzantium," "Leda and the Swan," and lines from "Among School Children" (Copyright 1928 by Macmillan Publishing Co., Inc.; renewed © 1956 by Georgie Yeats); "Crazy Jane Talks with the Bishop" (Copyright 1933 by Macmillan Publishing Co., Inc.; renewed © 1961 by Bertha Georgie Yeats); "Lapis Lazuli" (Copyright 1940 by Georgie Yeats, renewed © 1968 by Bertha Georgie Yeats, Michael Butler Yeats, and Anne Yeats); lines from "A Prayer for Old Age" (Copyright 1934 by Macmillan Publishing Co., Inc.; renewed © 1962 by Bertha Georgie Yeats); "The Second Coming" (Copyright 1924 by Macmillan Publishing Co., Inc. renewed 1952 by Bertha Georgie Yeats). From *The Variorum Edition of the Poems of W. B. Yeats*, edited by Peter Allt and Russell K. Alspach: "The Old Pensioner." Copyright © 1957 by Macmillan Publishing Co., Inc. Reprinted by permission of Macmillan Publishing Co., Inc., M. B. Yeats, Miss Anne Yeats, and Macmillan London and Basingstoke.

DRAMA

Edward Albee. *The Zoo Story*. Copyright © 1960 by Edward Albee. Reprinted by permission of Coward, McCann & Geoghegan, Inc. *The Zoo Story* is the sole property of the author and is fully protected by copyright. It may not be acted either by professionals or amateurs without written consent. Public readings, radio and television broadcasts are likewise forbidden. All enquiries concerning these rights should be addressed to the William Morris Agency, 1350 Avenue of the Americas, New York, N.Y. 10019.

Bertolt Brecht. *Mother Courage and Her Children* by Bertolt Brecht, translated by Eric Bentley. This translation copyright © 1955, 1959, 1961, 1962 by Eric Bentley; original work published under the title *Mutter Courage und Ihre Kinder*, copyright 1949 by Suhrkamp Verlag vormals S. Fischer, Frankfurt/Main. Reprinted by permission of the publishers, Grove Press, Inc. and Eyre Methuen Ltd.

Anton Chekhov. *The Marriage Proposal*, English version by Irina Prishvin and X. J. Kennedy. Printed by permission of the translators. For all amateur or professional rights, address Curtis Brown Ltd., 575 Madison Avenue, New York, N.Y. 10022.

R. C. Flickinger. Drawing "The Lycurgos Theatre of Dionysus at Athens" from *Greek Theatre and Its Drama*, p. 64. Reprinted by permission of The University of Chicago Press.

Richard Gilman. Excerpt from *The Making of Modern Drama* by Richard Gilman. Copyright © 1972, 1973, 1974 by Richard Gilman. Reprinted with the permission of Farrar, Straus & Giroux, Inc.

Lady Gregory. *The Workhouse Ward* from *The Comedies of Lady Gregory* (vol. I of the *Collected Plays*), pp. 97–105. Copyright 1970 by the Lady Gregory Estate. Reprinted by permission of Colin Smythe Ltd. (publishers of the Coole Edition of Lady Gregory's works) and the Lady Gregory Estate.

Henrik Ibsen. *A Doll House* from *Henrik Ibsen: The Complete Major Prose Plays*, translated by Rolf Fjelde. Copyright © 1965, 1970, 1978 by Rolf Fjelde. Reprinted by arrangement with The New American Library, Inc., New York, N.Y.

Harold Pinter. *The Dumb Waiter*. Copyright © 1959, 1960 by Harold Pinter. Reprinted by permission of Grove Press, Inc., and Eyre Methuen Ltd.

William Shakespeare. *The Tragedy of Othello*, edited by Alvin Kernan. Copyright © 1963 by Alvin Kernan. Copyright © 1963 by Sylvan Barnet. Reprinted by arrangement with The New American Library, New York, N.Y.

Bernard Shaw. *Pygmalion*. Copyright 1913, 1914, 1916, 1930, 1941, 1944, George Bernard Shaw. Copyright 1957 The Public Trustee as Executor of the Estate of George Bernard Shaw. Reprinted by permission of Dodd, Mead & Company, Inc., and The Society of Authors on behalf of the Bernard Shaw Estate.

Neil Simon. *Come Blow Your Horn* by Neil Simon. Copyright © 1961 by Neil Simon. Used by permission of Doubleday & Company, Inc.

Sophocles. *Oedipus Rex: An English Version* by Dudley Fitts and Robert Fitzgerald. Copyright 1949 by Harcourt Brace Jovanovich, Inc.; renewed 1977 by Cornelia Fitts and Robert Fitzgerald. Reprinted by permission of the publishers. *Caution:* All rights, including professional, amateur, motion picture, recitation, lecturing, public reading, radio broadcasting, and television are strictly reserved. Inquiries on all rights should be addressed to Harcourt Brace Jovanovich, Inc., 757 Third Avenue, New York, N.Y. 10017.

Tom Stoppard. *The Real Inspector Hound*. Copyright © 1968 by Tom Stoppard. Reprinted by permission of Grove Press, Inc., and Faber and Faber Ltd.

Tennessee Williams. *The Glass Menagerie*, by Tennessee Williams. Copyright 1945 by Edwina Williams and renewed 1973 by Tennessee Williams. Reprinted by permission of Random House, Inc.

INDEX OF FIRST LINES

The readers of the *Boston Evening Transcript*, 608
There are four men mowing down by the Isar, 775
There is a garden in her face, 665
There ought to be capital punishment for cars, 649
There's a crow flying, 527
There was a man of double deed, 493
There was an old man of Pantoum, 578
There were three ravens sat on a tree, 715
The saris go by me from the embassies, 768
The sea is calm tonight, 718
The selfsame surface that billowed once with, 729
The silver swan, who living had no note, 525
The Soul, reaching, throwing out for love, 677
The Soul selects her own Society, 739
The splendor falls on castle walls, 536
The thing could barely stand. Yet taken, 775
The time you won your town the race, 764
The trees they do grow high, and the leaves they do grow green, 519
The tusks that clashed in mighty brawls, 663
The war chief danced the old way, 811
The whiskey on your breath, 419
The wind blew all my wedding-day, 774
The wind stood up and gave a shout, 495
The world is charged with the grandeur of God, 541
The world is too much with us; late and soon, 624
They eat beans mostly, this old yellow pair, 726
They say that Richard Cory owns, 514
They sit in a row, 800
They told me, Heraclitus, they told me you were dead, 679
This *Humanist* whom no beliefs constrained, 577
This is the terminal: the light, 823
This living hand, now warm and capable, 568
This strange thing must have crept, 505
Thou ill-formed offspring of my feeble brain, 421
Thou still unravished bride of quietness, 769
Today we have naming of parts. Yesterday, 794
To freight cars in the air, 564
(*To JS/07/M/378*, 430
To see a world in a grain of sand, 492
Traveling through the dark I found a deer, 650

Treason doth never prosper; what's the reason? 576
Tree at my window, window tree, 502
True Thomas lay on Huntlie bank, 629
Turning and turning in the widening gyre, 625
'Twas brillig, and the slithy toves, 451
Twelve o'clock, 617
Twenty-four years remind the tears of my eyes, 818
Two boys uncoached are tossing a poem together, 416
Tyger! Tyger! burning bright! 725

Venerable Mother Toothache, 626
Victory comes late, 584

Watch people stop by bodies in funeral homes, 446
We dance round in a ring and suppose, 504
We real cool. We, 551
Western wind, when wilt thou blow, 717
We stood by a pond that winter day, 612
"What, are you stepping westward?" — "Yea," 825
What, still alive at twenty-two, 684
What are days for? 651
What happens to a dream deferred? 765
Wheesht, wheesht, my foolish hert, 457
When, in disgrace with Fortune and men's eyes, 802
When daisies pied and violets blue, 802
Whenever Richard Cory went down town, 514
When fishes flew and forests walked, 730
When God at first made man, 499
When he brings home a whale, 732
When icicles hang by the wall, 803
When I consider how my light is spent, 783
When I heard the learn'd astronomer, 820
When I saw that clumsy crow, 616
When I saw your head bow, I knew I had beaten you, 445
When I was one-and-twenty, 563
When my mother died I was very young, 438
While my hair was still cut straight across my forehead, 489
Who owns these scrawny little feet? *Death*, 766
Who says you're like one of the dog days? 489
Whose woods these are I think I know, 751
Who will go drive with Fergus now, 531
"Why dois your brand sae drap wi' bluid, 713
Wilt Thou forgive that sin where I begun, 500
With rue my heart is laden, 544
With serving still, 554

INDEX OF AUTHORS AND TITLES

(Each page number immediately following a poet's name indicates a line or passage from a poem quoted in text.)

Thurs. 24th

Batter my Heart p. 446
a Hymn to God the Father p. 500
a valediction: Forbidden mourning 741

Friday

804 Ode to West wind
663 Ozymandias

To the Student

Part of our job as educational publishers is to try to improve the textbooks we publish. Thus, when revising we take into account the experience of both instructors and students with the previous edition. At some time your instructor will be asked to comment extensively on *Literature: An Introduction to Fiction, Poetry, and Drama, 2nd Edition,* but right now we want to hear from you. After all, though your instructor assigned this book, you are the one who paid for it.

Please help us by completing this questionnaire and returning it to College English Developmental Group, Little, Brown and Company, 34 Beacon Street, Boston, Mass. 02106.

School _____ Course title _____

Instructor's name _____

1. Did you like *Literature*? _____

2. Was it too easy or too difficult? _____

3. Which stories did you like most? _____

_____

Which stories did you like least? _____

_____

Which of the stories were familiar to you? _____

_____

4. Which poems did you like most? _____

_____

Which poems did you like least? _____

_____

Had you read any of the poems previously? _____

_____

5. Which plays did you like best? _____

_____

Which plays did you like least? _____

_____

Which of the plays had you read before? Where? _____

_____

6. Are there any authors not included whom you would like to have

seen represented? _____

7. Did you find the chapters and appendix on writing about literature

useful? How might they be improved? _____

_____

8. General comments and suggestions: _____

_____

_____

_____

_____

May we quote you in our advertising efforts? Yes ____ No ____

Signature _____ Date _____

Mailing address _____

Saying & Suggesting pp. 476-480

Soliloquy of the Spanish Cloister 727-729

"Literal meaning" p. 446 - top 443

imagery pg. 464 - 466

my last Duchess pp. 726-727

chpt. 13

419 - 421½

423 - 425

428 - 432

INDEX OF TERMS